Treasures

A Reading/Language Arts Program

Program Authors

Dr. Donald R. Bear
University of Nevada, Reno
Reno, Nevada

Dr. Janice A. Dole
University of Utah
Salt Lake City, Utah

Dr. Jana Echevarria
California State University, Long Beach
Long Beach, California

Dr. Jan E. Hasbrouck
Educational Consultant - J.H. Consulting
Seattle, Washington

Dr. Scott G. Paris
University of Michigan
Ann Arbor, Michigan

Dr. Timothy Shanahan
University of Illinois at Chicago
Chicago, Illinois

Dr. Josefina V. Tinajero
University of Texas at El Paso
El Paso, Texas

Macmillan
McGraw-Hill

Contributors

Time Magazine, Accelerated Reader

Students with print disabilities may be eligible to obtain an accessible, audio version of the pupil edition of this textbook. Please call Recording for the Blind & Dyslexic at 1-800-221-4792 for complete information.

A

The *McGraw·Hill* Companies

Macmillan
McGraw-Hill

Published by Macmillan/McGraw-Hill, of McGraw-Hill Education, a division of The McGraw-Hill Companies, Inc., Two Penn Plaza, New York, New York 10121.

Copyright © 2009 by Macmillan/McGraw-Hill. All rights reserved. No part of this publication may be reproduced or distributed in any form or by any means, or stored in a database or retrieval system, without the prior written consent of The McGraw-Hill Companies, Inc., including, but not limited to, network storage or transmission, or broadcast for distance learning.

Printed in the United States of America

2 3 4 5 6 7 8 9 071/043 11 10 09 08

Program Authors

Dr. Donald R. Bear
University of Nevada, Reno

- Author of *Words Their Way* and *Words Their Way with English Learners*
- Director, E. L. Cord Foundation Center for Learning and Literacy

Dr. Scott G. Paris
University of Michigan, Ann Arbor

- Chair, Graduate Program in Psychology, University of Michigan
- Principal Investigator, CIERA, 1997–2004

Dr. Janice A. Dole
University of Utah

- Investigator, IES Study on Reading Interventions
- Member, National Academy of Sciences Committee: Teacher Preparation Programs, 2005–2007

Dr. Timothy Shanahan
University of Illinois at Chicago

- Member, National Reading Panel
- President, International Reading Association, 2006
- Chair, National Literacy Panel and National Early Literacy Panel

Dr. Jana Echevarria
California State University, Long Beach

- Author of *Making Content Comprehensible for English Learners: The SIOP Model*
- Principal Researcher, Center for Research on the Educational Achievement and Teaching of English Language Learners

Dr. Josefina V. Tinajero
University of Texas at El Paso

- Past President, NABE and TABE
- Co-Editor of *Teaching All the Children: Strategies for Developing Literacy in an Urban Setting* and *Literacy Assessment of Second Language Learners*

Dr. Jan E. Hasbrouck
Educational Consultant

- Developed Oral Reading Fluency Norms for Grades 1–8
- Author of *The Reading Coach: A How-to Manual for Success*

Contributing Authors

Dr. Adria F. Klein

Professor Emeritus,
California State University,
San Bernardino

- **President, California Reading Association, 1995**
- **Co-author of *Interactive Writing* and *Interactive Editing***

Dr. Doris Walker-Dalhouse

Minnesota State University,
Moorhead

- **Author of articles on multicultural literature and reading instruction in urban schools**
- **Co-chair of the Ethnicity, Race, and Multilingualism Committee, NRC**

Dolores B. Malcolm

St. Louis Public Schools
St. Louis, MO

- **Past President, International Reading Association**
- **Member, IRA Urban Diversity Initiatives Commission**
- **Member, RIF Advisory Board**

In memory of our esteemed colleague and friend, Dr. Steven A. Stahl

Program Consultants

Dr. Stephanie Al Otaiba

Assistant Professor,
College of Education
Florida State University

Dr. Susan M. Brookhart

Brookhart Enterprises LLC - Helena, MT
Coordinator of Assessment and
Evaluation
Duquesne University, Pittsburgh, PA

Kathy R. Bumgardner

Language Arts Instructional
Specialist
Gaston County Schools, NC

Dr. Douglas Fisher

Professor, Language and Literacy
Education
San Diego State University

Dr. Vicki L. Gibson

Longmire Learning Center, Inc.
College Station, TX

Dr. Connie R. Hebert

National Literacy Consultant
Lesley University
The ReadWrite Place
West Springfield, MA

Dr. Sharon F. O'Neal

Associate Professor,
College of Education
Texas State University – San Marcos

Dinah Zike

Dinah-Might Adventures, L.P.
San Antonio, TX

Program Reviewers

Mable Alfred
Reading/Language Arts
Administrator
Chicago Public Schools, IL

Suzie Bean
Teacher, Kindergarten
Mary W. French Academy
Decatur, IL

Beverly Brown
Teacher, Kindergarten
Washington Irving School
Indianapolis, IN

Linda Burch
Teacher, Kindergarten
Public School 184
Brooklyn, NY

Ann Burton
Teacher, Grade 4
Cameron Park
Elementary School
Hillsborough, NC

Debra K. Casey
Assistant Principal
Weisser Park Arts
Magnet School
Ft. Wayne, IN

Robert J. Dandorph
Principal
John F. Kennedy
Elementary School
North Bergen, NJ

Suzanne Delacruz
Principal
Washington Elementary
School
Evanston, IL

Roberta Dobrzeniecki
Teacher, Grade 2
Lafayette Elementary School
Hammond, IN

Carol Dockery
Teacher, Grade 3
Mulberry Elementary
Milford, OH

Karryl Ellis
Teacher, Grade 1
Durfee School
Decatur, IL

Christina Fong
Teacher, Grade 3
William Moore Elementary
School
Las Vegas, NV

Lenore Furman
Teacher, Kindergarten
Abington Avenue School
Newark, NJ

Beth Holland
Teacher, Kindergarten
Jeffreys Grove Elementary
School
Raleigh, NC

Renee Jones
Curriculum and Instruction
Title I Director
Indianapolis Public Schools
Indianapolis, IN

Sister Miriam Kaeser
Assistant Superintendent
Archdiocese of Cincinnati
Cincinnati, OH

Akida Kissane Lewis
Principal
54th Street Elementary School
Los Angeles, CA

Toni Kring
Principal
Forest Park Elementary School
Ft. Wayne, IN

LaVonne Lee
Principal
Rozet Elementary School
Gillette, WY

Christi Lindeman
Teacher, Grade K/1
Veterans Park Elementary
Lexington, KY

SuEllen Mackey
Teacher, Grade 5
Washington Elementary
School
Decatur, IL

Jan Mayes
Curriculum Coordinator
Kent School District
Kent, WA

Robyn Morris
Teacher, Grade 2
Druid Hills Elementary School
Charlotte, NC

Bonnie Nelson
Teacher, Grade 1
Solano School, Osborn
Elementary District
Phoenix, AZ

Cyndi Nichols
Teacher, Grade K/1
North Ridge Elementary
School
Commack, NY

Sharron Norman
Curriculum Director
Lansing School District
Lansing, MI

Renee Ottinger
Literacy Leader, Grades K–5
Coronado Hills Elementary
School
Denver, CO

Cassandra L. Perez
Bilingual/ESL Instructional
Specialist
Remynse Elementary
Grand Prairie, TX

Effie J. Phillips
Teacher, Grade 1
Vance Elementary School
Asheville, NC

Michael Pragman
Principal
Woodland Elementary School
Lee's Summit, MO

Carol Rose
Teacher, Grade 2
Churchill Elementary School
Muskegon, MI

Monica Sandoval
Principal
Wharton Elementary
Houston, TX

Laura R. Schmidt-Watson
Director of Academic Services
Parma City School District, OH

Dianne L. Skoy
Literacy Coordinator,
Grades K–5
Minneapolis Public Schools
Minneapolis, MN

Charles Staszewski
ESL Teacher, Grades 3–5
John H. William School, No. 5
Rochester, NY

Sandra Sunderland-Willis
Special Education Specialist
Fort Wayne Community
School District
Fort Wayne, IN

Patricia Synan
New York City Department
of Education

Lynne Vitkus
Teacher, Grade 3
Ernest R. Elliott Elementary
School
Munster, IN

Beth Ware
Lead Literacy Teacher
Wake County School District
Raleigh, NC

Jackie West
Principal
Sea Breeze Elementary
Bradenton, FL

Charlotte Williams
Teacher, Grade 3
Durant Elementary
Raleigh, NC

Stephanie Yearian
Teacher, Grade 2
W. J. Zahnow Elementary
Waterloo, IL

Student Reviewers: Special thanks to the students of our
program reviewers who reviewed the literature selections.

 **RESEARCH** **Why It Matters**

Phonics

Dr. Timothy Shanahan

In grades 3–6, phonics instruction helps students to think more effectively about how words are spelled and about the implications of these spelling patterns for pronunciation and meaning. Just as phonics instruction guides the young or struggling reader to use letter sounds and basic spelling patterns in order to translate printed words into pronunciations, phonics instruction for older readers emphasizes the mastery of more-complex or difficult patterns. Successful phonics instruction during these grades focuses more on multiple-syllable words, and on morphological elements such as prefixes, suffixes, and derivations. These morphological elements not only influence pronunciation and spelling, but are also closely connected to the interpretation of word meanings. Effective upper-grade phonics instruction guides students to recognize and use the spelling patterns across words for decoding and interpreting meaning.

Best Practices

Effective phonics instruction at the upper grades

- provides explicit instruction in spelling or word patterns

- emphasizes the decoding of multiple-syllable words and words with complex patterns

- focuses on spelling patterns of prefixes, suffixes, and roots

- teaches more than just pronunciation and spelling, but also links these to the interpretation of word meanings

- teaches simpler sound-symbol relations and the decoding of less-complex words to struggling readers

Professional Development

- **READING, YES! 4–6**
  Video Series: Module 4, *Decoding and Spelling*

  Online Course: Accredited college course available at **www.macmillanmh.com**

- **TREASURES FOR TEACHERS**
  Video Series: *Phonemic Awareness and Phonics*

  Online: See **www.macmillanmh.com** for best practices in phonics.

References

• Ehri, L. C., Nunes, S. R., Stahl, S. A., & Willows, D. M. (2001). Systematic phonics instruction helps students learn to read: Evidence from the National Reading Panel's meta-analysis. *Review of Educational Research*, 71, 393–447.
• Singson, M., Mahony, D., & Mann, V. (2000). The relation between reading ability and morphological skills: Evidence from derivational suffixes. *Reading and Writing: An Interdisciplinary Journal*, 12, 219–252.
• Nagy, W., Berninger, V., Abbott, R., Vaughan, K., & Vermeulen, K. (2003). Relationship of morphology and other language skills in at-risk second-grade readers and at-risk fourth-grade writers. *Journal of Educational Psychology*, 95, 730–742.

Theme: Challenges
Planning the Unit

Unit Planner **16B**

Unit Resources **16D**

Assessment Resources **16F**

Unit Opener **16H**
    Research and Inquiry Instruction and Cross-Curricular Projects

Using the Student Book

Miss Alaineus **16J**

Davy Crockett Saves the World **48A**

"Forests of the World" **78A**

Ultimate Field Trip 5 . . . . **90A**

Pipiolo and the Roof Dogs **112A**

Test Strategy: Think and Search **140**

Wrapping Up the Unit

Writing Workshop **143A**

  Personal Narrative

Computer Literacy **143I**

Unit Closer **143K**

Unit Assessment
    Diagnose and Prescribe **143M**

Glossary **143O**

Additional Lessons and Resources

Additional Lessons **T1**

Classroom Library Lessons **T13**

Theme Bibliography **T19**

Word Lists **T22**

Scope and Sequence **T28**

Index **T36**

Main Selections

Unit Assessment

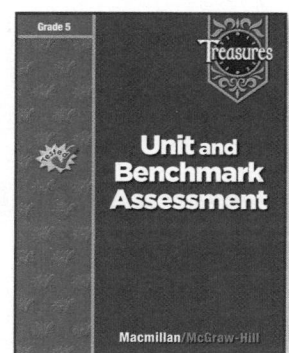

Theme: Challenges

Miss Alaineus
A VOCABULARY DISASTER
written and illustrated by
Debra Frasier

pages 16J–47V

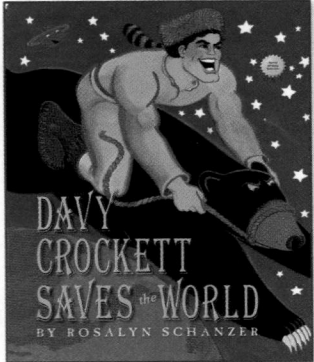

DAVY CROCKETT SAVES the WORLD
BY ROSALYN SCHANZER

pages 48A–77V

	WEEK 1	**WEEK 2**
ORAL LANGUAGE		
• Listening, Speaking, Viewing	**Theme** School Contests **Build Background**	**Theme** American Legends **Build Background**
WORD STUDY		
• Vocabulary	**Vocabulary** *capable, categories, luminous, strands, credit, soggy, slumped, gigantic* Context Clues: Synonym	**Vocabulary** *advertisement, sauntered, commenced, elected, wring, impress, original, fireball* Word Parts: Compound Words
• Phonics/Decoding	**Phonics** Short Vowels *a, e, i, o, u*	**Phonics** Long Vowels, VCe
READING		
• Comprehension	**Comprehension** **Strategy:** Analyze Story Structure **Skill:** Character and Plot	**Comprehension** **Strategy:** Analyze Story Structure **Skill:** Plot and Setting
• Fluency	**Fluency** Repeated Reading: Intonation/Pausing	**Fluency** Repeated Reading: Punctuation
• Leveled Readers/ELL Readers	**APPROACHING** *What's the Buzz About the Geography Bee?* **ON LEVEL** *Nadia Gomez Sees the Light* **BEYOND** *Car Wash Chronicles* **ENGLISH LANGUAGE LEARNERS** *Nadia and Her Science Project*	**APPROACHING** *Sluefoot Sue: An American Legend* **ON LEVEL** *Johnny Appleseed: An American Legend* **BEYOND** *Old Stormalong: An American Legend* **ENGLISH LANGUAGE LEARNERS** *Who Is Johnny Appleseed?*
LANGUAGE ARTS		
• Writing	**Writing** Personal Narrative	**Writing** Personal Narrative
• Grammar	**Grammar** Sentence Types	**Grammar** Subjects and Predicates
• Spelling	**Spelling** Words with Short Vowels	**Spelling** Words with Long Vowels

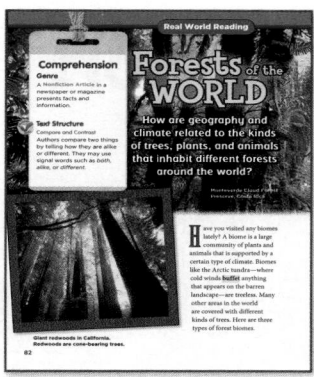

pages 78A–89V

pages 90A–111V

pages 112A–139V

Review and Assess

WEEK 3

Theme
Trees for Life

Build Background

Vocabulary
buffet, major, quest reduce, settings
Dictionary: Homographs

Phonics
Words with /ü/, /ū/, /ù/

Comprehension
Strategy: Analyze Text Structure
Skill: Compare and Contrast

Fluency

Repeated Reading: Punctuation

APPROACHING
Partners for Life

ON LEVEL
The Survival of Muir Woods

BEYOND
Wildfire!

ENGLISH LANGUAGE LEARNERS
How the Muir Woods Survived

Writing
Research Report

Grammar
Sentence Combining

Spelling
Words with /ü/, /ū/, /ù/

WEEK 4

Theme
Exploring Space

Build Background

Vocabulary
function, adjusted, disasters, environment, mission, maze, zone, gravity
Context Clues: Description or Explanation

Phonics
r-Controlled Vowels

Comprehension
Strategy: Generate Questions
Skill: Summarize

Fluency

Repeated Reading: Pronunciation

APPROACHING
On the Moon

ON LEVEL
Mission to Mars

BEYOND
Space Station

ENGLISH LANGUAGE LEARNERS
Going to Mars

Writing
Friendly Letter

Grammar
More Sentence Combining

Spelling
Words with /är/, /âr/, /ôr/

WEEK 5

Theme
Rescue Dogs

Build Background

Vocabulary
cooperation, celebration fragrance, variety, canceled, moistened, theory, transformed
Thesaurus: Synonyms

Phonics
More *r*-Controlled Vowels

Comprehension
Strategy: Generate Questions
Skill: Cause and Effect

Fluency

Repeated Reading: Pauses and Intonation

APPROACHING
It's Fun When Sam Listens

ON LEVEL
The Wag Brigade

BEYOND
Rusty to the Rescue!

ENGLISH LANGUAGE LEARNERS
Mai and Fred

Writing
Journal Entry

Grammar
Run-on Sentences

Spelling
Words with /ûr/, /îr/

WEEK 6

Test Strategy
Think and Search

Writing
Personal Narrative

Unit 1 Assessment, 7–24

Comprehension
Character, Setting, Plot; Compare and Contrast; Summarize; Cause and Effect

Vocabulary Strategies
Context Clues: Synonym; Word Parts: Compound Words; Dictionary: Homographs; Context Clues: Description or Explanation; Thesaurus: Synonyms

Text Features / Literary Elements / Study Skills
Photos and Captions; Toolbar and Link; Using the Library or Media Center; Rhyme Scheme and Rhythm; Charts

Grammar
Punctuation

Writing
Personal Narrative

Fluency Assessment

Diagnose and Prescribe
Interpret Assessment Results

Unit 1 Resources

Literature

Read-Aloud Anthology
Includes Plays for
Readers' Theater

Student Edition

Leveled Readers

ELL Leveled Readers

**Classroom Library
Tradebooks**

Teaching Support

Teacher's Edition

Transparencies

ELL Teacher's Guide

Teacher's Resource Book

**Dinah Zike
Foldables™**

Vocabulary Cards

Class Management Tools

**Small Group
How-To Guide**

**Weekly
Contracts**

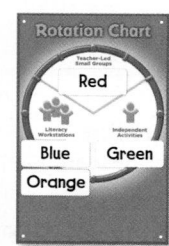

Rotation Chart

Student Practice

Approaching Level	On Level	Beyond Level	English Language Learners

Leveled Practice

Spelling Practice Book   **Grammar Practice Book**

Home-School Connection
- Take-Home Stories
- Homework Activities

Literacy Workstation Activities

Technology

 AUDIO CD
- Listening Library
- Fluency Solutions

 CD ROM
- Vocabulary PuzzleMaker
- Handwriting
- Instructional Navigator Interactive Lesson Planner
- Student Navigator
- Accelerated Reader Quizzes

LOG ON www.macmillanmh.com
- Author/Illustrator Information
- Research and Inquiry Activities
- Vocabulary and Spelling Activities
- Oral Language Activities
- Computer Literacy
- Leveled Reader Database

Professional Development

READING, YES!
- Videos
- Online Course

TREASURES FOR TEACHERS
- Videos

READING
Triumphs
AN INTERVENTION PROGRAM

Also Available

Treasure Chest
FOR ENGLISH LANGUAGE LEARNERS

Also Available

Screening, Diagnostic, and Placement Assessments

Screening

Use the Oral Reading Fluency passages on pages 40–51 in our **Screening, Diagnostic, Placement Assessment** book for screening.

Diagnostic Tools for Instructional Placement

For an individually administered Diagnostic, use the Informal Reading Inventory passages on pages 112–119 in our **Screening, Diagnostic, Placement Assessment** book.

For a group-administered Placement Test, see pages 229–238 in our **Screening, Diagnostic, Placement Assessment** book.

Use the results from these assessments to determine the instructional levels of your students for differentiated instruction grouping.

Monitoring Progress

Ongoing Informal Assessments

- Daily Quick Check Observations
- Weekly Comprehension Check
- Weekly Fluency Practice Passages

Formal Assessments

- **Weekly Assessment**
- **Fluency Assessment**
- **Running Records**
- **Unit and Benchmark Assessment**
- **ELL Practice and Assessment**
    Weekly Tests
    Unit Progress Test

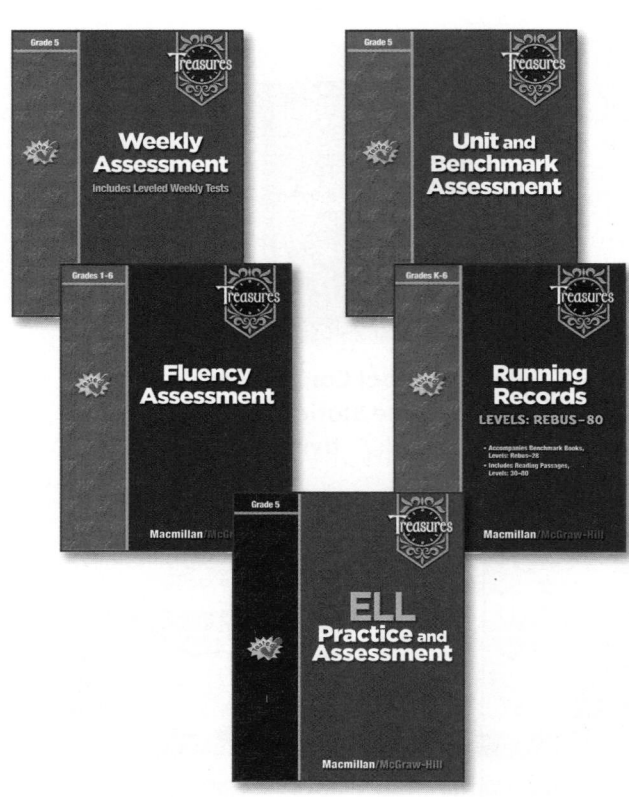

Managing and Reporting

 Assessment Online

Macmillan/McGraw-Hill

 Instructional Navigator Interactive Lesson Planner
- All Teacher Edition Pages
- Electronic Lesson Planner
- Student Blackline Masters

 Assessment Tool

National Test Alignment

GRADE 5, UNIT 1 ASSESSED SKILLS	NAEP	NAEP	ITBS	SAT10
COMPREHENSION STRATEGIES AND SKILLS				
• Strategies: Analyze Story and Text Structure, Generate Questions	◆	◆	◆	◆
• Skills: Analyze Character, Setting, and Plot, Summarize, Cause and Effect, Compare and Contrast	◆	◆	◆	◆
VOCABULARY STRATEGIES				
• Context clues	◆	◆	◆	◆
• Word parts	◆		◆	◆
• Dictionary	◆		◆	◆
• Thesaurus	◆		◆	◆
TEXT FEATURES AND STUDY SKILLS				
• Captions	◆	◆	◆	◆
• Toolbars and links	◆	◆	◆	◆
• Library/media center	◆		◆	◆
• Charts	◆	◆	◆	◆
GRAMMAR, MECHANICS, USAGE				◆
• Sentence types	◆		◆	◆
• Subjects and predicates	◆		◆	
• Sentence combining, conjunctions and compound/complex sentences	◆		◆	◆
• Run-on sentences and fragments	◆		◆	◆
• End punctuation	◆		◆	◆
• Commas	◆		◆	◆
• Letter punctuation	◆		◆	◆
WRITING				
• Personal Narrative	◆	◆		

KEY

NAEP	National Assessment of Educational Progress	**ITBS**	Iowa Tests of Basic Skills
TerraNova/ CAT6	TerraNova, the Second Edition	**SAT10**	Stanford Achievement Test

Unit 1 Opener

Theme Project

Build Background Write this theme statement on the board: *It takes imagination to overcome challenges.* Ask: What kinds of challenges do you enjoy most? What challenges are hardest for you to meet?

Research and Inquiry
Self-Selected Theme Project

 **State the Problem and Identify Needed Information** Have students generate topics by listing different kinds of challenges (physical, intellectual, artistic, personal). Have them choose one kind of challenge from their list and write a research question about it. For example: How do fiction writers like Madeleine L'Engle invent characters? How did Helen Keller learn to read, write, and speak in public?

 Identify Resources for Finding Information Have students list multiple sources of information that might help them answer their question. Possibilities include letters and diaries, biographies and autobiographies, newspapers and magazines, films and television, the Internet and databases.

 Find the Information Have students find and examine at least three kinds of print and non-print sources. Students should make a plan for evaluating the sources that they actually use. To share tips on verifying sources, see the Research Strategies box.

Organize the Information Tell students to view or read their sources and take notes. Students should evaluate the usefulness and quality of information based on purpose, accuracy, reliability, and relevance. Encourage them to explain how they rated potential sources and chose the most reliable.

See the Unit Closer on pages 143K–143L for **Step 5: Create the Presentation** and **Step 6: Review and Evaluate.**

RESEARCH STRATEGIES

Evaluate Sources

Students should make sure that their sources are accurate, timely, and reliable. To verify sources students can check:
- Date of publication
- Author background
- Facts vs. opinions
- Language and usage
- Degree of coverage (sketchy, thorough, or in-between)

Cross-Curricular Projects

SCIENCE ACTIVITY: INVESTIGATE

Challenge students to find out what foods decompose most quickly.

- Have students create a research plan to answer the question. Plans might include reading about the topic and doing their own investigation using different fruits, vegetables, and bread.

- Have students make posters to explain their procedure and results.

- Discuss what students learned about scientific processes used to solve problems.

- Hold a question-and-answer period, allowing students to ask questions that seek information not aleady discussed.

Media Activity: Critical Viewing

Point out that different media present different challenges, both to the creator and to the reader (or viewer). Print media, broadcast media, and the Internet express ideas in different ways.

- Have students research to find how different media treat the same topic. You may wish to assign a topic, such as a newly elected candidate or an award-winning design for an important building.

- Have students compare how the topic is treated in two of the following: videos, Web sites, artwork, cartoons, photographs, newspaper or magazine articles, and television programs. They should identify cause-effect relationships, distinguishing facts from opinions and probability.

- For their final presentation, have students and partners write and perform a talk radio show in which the host and guests give different perspectives on the topic.

CHARACTER BUILDING–CARING

- Have students identify positive and negative values reflected in the media that they examine. Then discuss with students the importance of caring; for example, by being compassionate, forgiving others, and expressing gratitude.
- Ask students to give specific examples of caring, either from the media or from their lives.

 For Technology research and presentation strategies see the Computer Literacy Lessons on pages 143I–143J.

Weekly Literature

Week At A Glance

Whole Group

**VOCABULARY**
slumped, soggy, capable, categories, strands, gigantic, credit, luminous

Context Clues/Synonyms

COMPREHENSION
Strategy: Story Structure
Skill: Character and Plot

WRITING
Personal Narrative

Social Studies Link

Culture

Small Group Options

Differentiated Instruction for Tested Skills

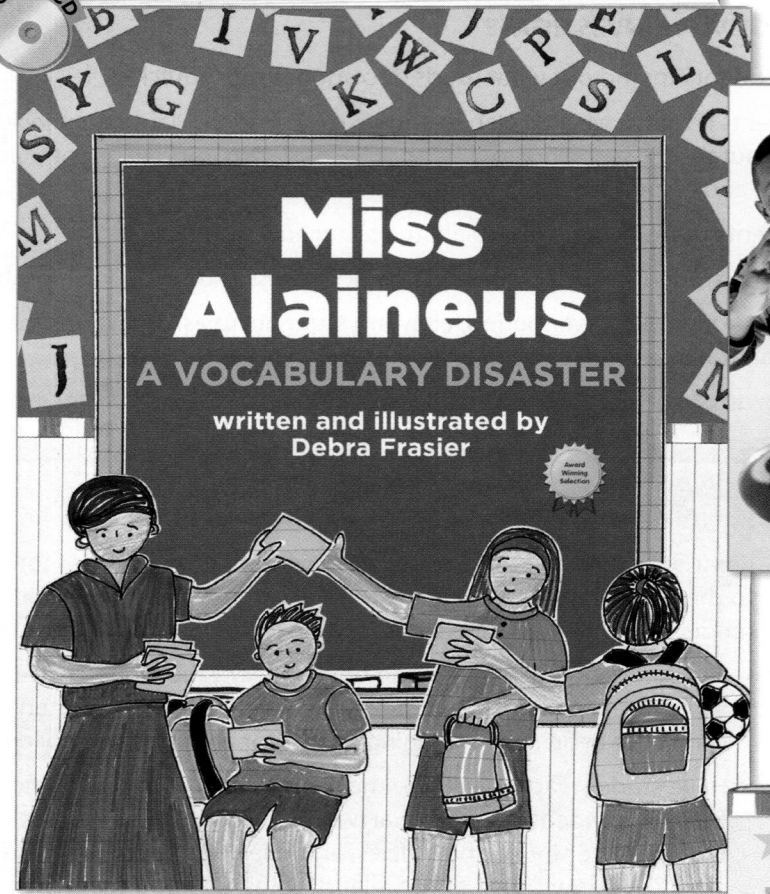

Main Selection
Genre Realistic Fiction

The Talent Contest
by Howard Gabe

Vocabulary/Comprehension

The National SPELLING BEE
by Nicole Lee

Social Studies Link
Genre Nonfiction Article

Read-Aloud Anthology
• Listening Comprehension
• Readers' Theater

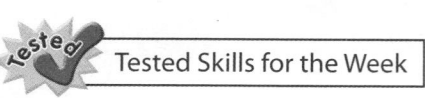Tested Skills for the Week

16J

Resources for Differentiated Instruction

Leveled Readers

GR Levels Q–V

Genre Realistic Fiction

- Same Theme
- Same Vocabulary
- Same Comprehension Skills

Approaching Level

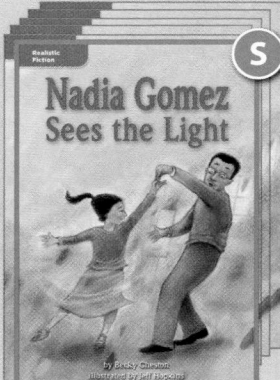

On Level

Beyond Level

English Language Leveled Reader

On Level Reader sheltered for English Language Learner

ELL Teacher's Guide also available

Also Available LEVELED READER PROGRAM

CLASSROOM LIBRARY

Genre Expository Nonficton

Approaching

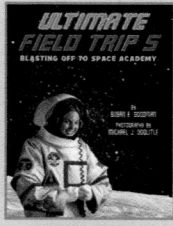

On Level

Beyond

Trade books to apply Comprehension Skills

INTERVENTION ANTHOLOGY

- Phonics and Decoding
- Comprehension
- Vocabulary

Also available, *Reading Triumphs*, Intervention Program

LEVELED PRACTICE

Approaching

On Level

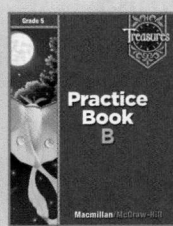

Beyond

ELL

 HOME-SCHOOL CONNECTION

- Family letters in English and Spanish
- Take-Home Stories

Technology

 ONLINE INSTRUCTION www.macmillanmh.com

 AUDIO CD
- Listening Library
- Fluency Solutions

CD ROM
- Vocabulary PuzzleMaker

Suggested Lesson Plan

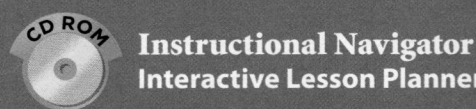

Instructional Navigator
Interactive Lesson Planner

Integrated **ELL** Support Every Day

Miss Alaineus, 20–39

Leveled Readers

Whole Group

ORAL LANGUAGE
- **Listening**
- **Speaking**
- **Viewing**

WORD STUDY
- **Vocabulary**
- **Phonics/Decoding**

READING
- **Develop Comprehension**
- **Fluency**

LANGUAGE ARTS
- **Writing**
- **Grammar**
- **Spelling**

ASSESSMENT
- **Informal/Formal**

Turn the Page for
Small Group Lesson Plan

Day 1

Listening/Speaking/Viewing
❓Focus Question What challenges, responsibilities, and emotions are involved in contests?
Build Background, 16
Read Aloud: "La Bamba," 17

Vocabulary
slumped, soggy, capable, categories, strands, gigantic, credit, luminous, 18
Practice Book A-O-B, 1
Strategy: Context Clues/Synonyms, 19

Read "The Talent Contest," 18–19
Student Book

Comprehension, 19A–19B
Strategy: Story Structure
Skill: Character and Plot
Practice Book A-O-B, 2

Fluency Partner Reading, 16R
Model Fluency, 17

Writing
Daily Writing Prompt: Write a personal narrative describing several reasons why you would enter a contest.
Personal Narrative, 46–47B

Grammar
Daily Language Activities, 47I
Sentences, 47I
Grammar Practice Book, 1

Spelling
Pretest: Short Vowels, 47G
Spelling Practice Book, 1–2

Quick Check Vocabulary, 18
Comprehension, 19B

Differentiated Instruction 47M–47V

Day 2

Listening/Speaking
❓Focus Question How does the kind of person Sage is affect the plot?

Vocabulary
Review Vocabulary Words, 20

Phonics/Decoding
Words with Short Vowels, 47E
Practice Book A-O-B, 7

Read *Miss Alaineus,* 20–39
Student Book

Comprehension, 20–41
Strategy: Story Structure
Skill: Character and Plot
Practice Book A-O-B, 3

Fluency Partner Reading, 16R

Writing
Daily Writing Prompt: Write a letter to your principal in which you propose a school contest.
Personal Narrative, 46–47B

Grammar
Daily Language Activities, 47I
Sentences, 47I
Grammar Practice Book, 2

Spelling
Short Vowels, 47G
Spelling Practice Book, 3

Quick Check Comprehension: 31, 39
Phonics, 47E

Differentiated Instruction 47M–47V

16L

Skills/Strategies

Vocabulary	Comprehension	Writing
Vocabulary Words	**Strategy:** Analyze Story Structure	Personal Narrative
Context Clues/ Synonyms	**Skill:** Character and Plot	

Turn the Page for Small Group Options

Day 3

Listening/Speaking
- **Focus Question** Describe the different contest experiences that Denny and Sage had.
- Summarize, 41

Vocabulary
- Review Words in Context, 47C
- **Strategy:** Content Clues/Synonyms, 47D
- Practice Book A-O-B, 6
- **Phonics** Decode Multisyllabic Words, 47E

Read *Miss Alaineus*, 20–39

Student Book

Comprehension
- Comprehension Check, 41
- **Maintain Skill:** Setting, 41B

Fluency Partner Reading, 16R
- Repeated Reading, 41A
- Practice Book A-O-B, 4

Writing
- Daily Writing Prompt: Write a paragraph describing talents you have that would help you win a contest.
- **Writer's Craft:** A Good Paragraph, 47A
- Personal Narrative, 46–47B

Grammar
- Daily Language Activities, 47I
- Mechanics and Usage: Punctuate Sentences, 47J
- Grammar Practice Book, 3

Spelling
- Short Vowels, 47H
- Spelling Practice Book, 4

Quick Check Fluency, 41A

Differentiated Instruction 47M–47V

Day 4

Listening/Speaking/Viewing
- **Focus Question** Write a paragraph about how to enter a local spelling bee.
- Media Literacy: Recording an Event, 38
- Expand Vocabulary: School Contests, 47F

Vocabulary
- **Content Vocabulary:** *competition, orally, eliminates,* 42
- Compound Words, 47F
- Apply Vocabulary to Writing, 47F

Read "The National Spelling Bee," 42–45

Student Book

Comprehension
- **Informational Text:** Social Studies
- **Text Features:** Photographs and Captions, 42
- Practice Book A-O-B, 5

Fluency Partner Reading, 16R

Writing
- Daily Writing Prompt: Write a journal entry about the class spelling bee from the point of view of Sage's classmate.
- **Writing Trait:** Ideas and Content, 47B
- Personal Narrative, 46–47B

Grammar
- Daily Language Activities, 47I
- Sentences, 47J
- Grammar Practice Book, 4

Spelling
- Short Vowels, 47H
- Spelling Practice Book, 5

Quick Check Vocabulary, 47D

Differentiated Instruction 47M–47V

Day 5
Review and Assess

Listening/Speaking/Viewing
- **Focus Question** What kind of new words would you add to a spelling bee list?
- Speaking and Listening Strategies, 47A

Vocabulary
- Spiral Review of Vocabulary Words, 47F

Read Self-Selected Reading 16R

Student Book

Comprehension
- Connect and Compare, 45

Fluency Partner Reading, 16R

Writing
- Daily Writing Prompt: List possible interview questions for the new spelling bee champion.
- Personal Narrative, 46–47B

Grammar
- Daily Language Activities, 47I
- Sentences, 47J
- Grammar Practice Book, 5–6

Spelling
- Posttest: Short Vowels, 47H
- Spelling Practice Book, 6

Weekly Assessment, 5–12

Differentiated Instruction 47M–47V

Differentiated Instruction

What do I do in small groups?

Teacher-Led Small Groups

Literacy Workstations

Independent Activities

 **Skills Focus** Use your **Quick Check** observations to guide additional instruction and practice.

Phonics
Words with Short Vowels

 Vocabulary Words
luminous, gigantic, categories, strands, credit, slumped, capable, soggy

 Strategy: Context Clues/Look for a Synonym

Comprehension
 Strategy: Story Structure
Skill: Character and Plot

 Fluency

Suggested Lesson Plan

 CD ROM **Instructional Navigator**
Interactive Lesson Planner

	Day 1	Day 2
Approaching Level • **Additional Instruction/Practice** • **Tier 2 Instruction**	Fluency, 47N Vocabulary, 47N Comprehension, 47O 	Phonics, 47M Vocabulary, 47O Leveled Reader Lesson, 47P • Vocabulary • Comprehension 
On Level • **Practice**	Vocabulary, 47Q Leveled Reader Lesson, 47R • Comprehension **ELL** Leveled Reader, 47U–47V 	Leveled Reader Lesson, 47R • Comprehension • Vocabulary 
Beyond Level • **Extend**	Vocabulary, 47S Leveled Reader Lesson, 47T • Comprehension 	Leveled Reader Lesson, 47T • Comprehension • Vocabulary 

For intensive intervention see **READING Triumphs**

Focus on Leveled Readers

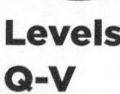

Leveled Reader Library

Levels Q-V

Apply *tested* skills and strategies while reading appropriate leveled books.

(Q) What's the Buzz About the Geography Bee?

Approaching

(S) Nadia Gomez Sees the Light

On Level

(V) The Car Wash Chronicles

Beyond

Nadia's Project

ELL

Additional Leveled Reader Resources

LOG ON

Leveled Reader Database
Go to www.macmillanmh.com

Search by

- Comprehension Skill
- Content Area
- Genre
- Text Feature

- Guided Reading Level
- Reading Recovery Level
- Lexile Score
- Benchmark Level

Subscription also available

Day 3

Phonics, 47M
Fluency, 47N
Vocabulary, 47O
Leveled Reader Lesson, 47P
- Comprehension

Fluency, 47Q
Vocabulary, 47Q
Leveled Reader Lesson, 47R
- Comprehension

Fluency, 47S
Vocabulary, 47S
Leveled Reader Lesson, 47T
- Comprehension

Day 4

Phonics, 47M
Leveled Reader Lesson, 47P
- Comprehension
- **ELL** Geography Words, 47P

Text Feature, 47Q
Leveled Reader Lesson, 47R
- Comprehension

Text Feature, 47S
Leveled Reader Lesson, 47T
- Comprehension
ELL Word Study, 47T

Day 5

Fluency, 47N
Leveled Reader Lesson, 47P
- Make Connections Across Texts

Fluency, 47Q
Leveled Reader Lesson, 47R
- Make Connections Across Texts

Fluency, 47S
Self-Selected Reading, 47T

What do I do with the rest of my class?

Teacher-Led Small Groups

Literacy Workstations

Independent Activities

Class Management Tools

My To-Do List

✓ Put a check next to the activities you complete.

Reading
- Practice fluency
- Read about school contests

Word Study
- Write with synonyms
- Use short vowels and variants

Writing
- Write a personal narrative
- Write a diary or journal entry

Science
- Research and write about contests
- Create a scientific contest

Social Studies
- Research and write about world record holders
- Read and discuss your article

Leveled Readers
- Write About It!
- Content Connection

Technology
- Vocabulary Puzzlemaker
- Fluency Solutions
- Listening Library
- www.macmillanmh.com

Independent Practice
- Practice Book, 1–7
- Grammar Practice Book, 1–6
- Spelling Practice Book, 1–6

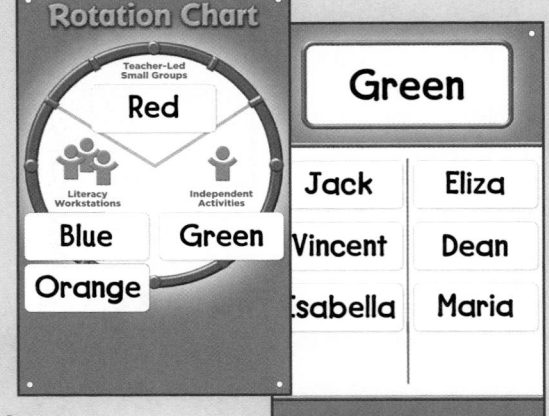

Rotation Chart

Teacher-Led Small Groups

Red

Literacy Workstations

Independent Activities

Blue   Green   Orange

Green

Jack	Eliza
Vincent	Dean
Isabella	Maria

Includes:
- How-To Guides   • Rotation Chart   • Weekly Contracts

FOLDABLES™

Hands-on activities for reinforcing weekly skills.

Fish	Frogs
habitat	habitat
food	insects
prey	prey
enemies	enemies

Eight-Tab Foldable

Word	Synonym	Antonym	Prefix or Suffix
normal	typical	unusual	normally

Folded Foldable

Independent Activities

Leveled Readers

For Repeated Readings and Literacy Activities

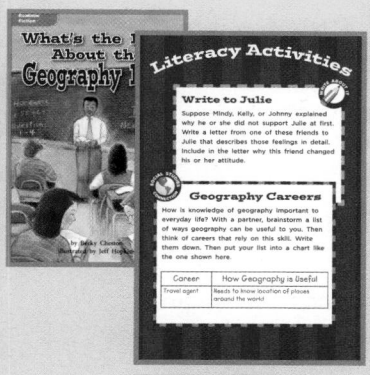
Approaching

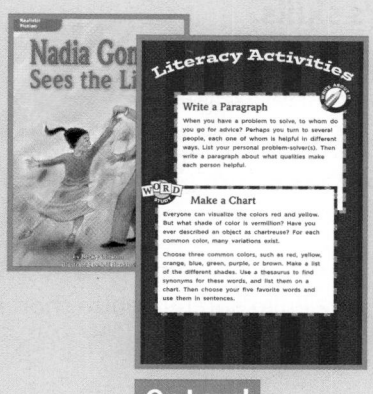
On Level

ELL

Beyond

LEVELED PRACTICE

Skills: Vocabulary (p. 1), Comprehension: Character and Plot (p. 2), Graphic Organizer (p. 3), Fluency (p. 4), Text Features: Photos and Captions (p. 5), Vocabulary Strategy: Synonyms (p. 6), Phonics (p. 7)

Approaching

On Level

Beyond

ELL

Technology

 ONLINE INSTRUCTION www.macmillanmh.com

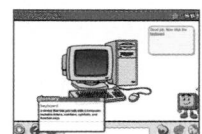

- Meet the Author/Illustrator
- Computer Literacy Lessons
- Research and Inquiry Activities

- Oral Language Activities
- Vocabulary and Spelling Activities
- Leveled Reader Database

 **LISTENING LIBRARY**
Recordings of selections
- Main Selections
- Leveled Readers
- ELL Readers
- Intervention Anthology

 **FLUENCY SOLUTIONS**
Recorded passages for modeling and practicing fluency

 **VOCABULARY PUZZLEMAKER**
Activities providing multiple exposures to vocabulary, spelling, and high-frequency words including crossword puzzles, word searches, and word jumbles

Turn the page for Literacy Workstations.

Managing the Class

Cross-Curricular Activities

All activities reinforce this week's skills.

 **Reading**

Objectives
- Time reading to practice fluency.
- Select literature for reading enjoyment.
- Read independently about school contests.
- Be enthusiastic about reading and learning to read.

 **Word Study**

Objectives
- Find and use synonyms of words.
- Build and recognize short vowel sounds and variants.

Reading — Fluency — **20 Minutes**

- Select a paragraph from the fluency passage on page 4 of your Practice Book.
- Read the selection aloud to a partner until you can read it smoothly, without stumbling over any words.
- Look up any words you don't know.

Extension
- Listen as your partner reads.
- Give corrective feedback to help your partner read more smoothly and with understanding.
- Readers Theatre: Practice fluency with the play *It Couldn't Be Done.*

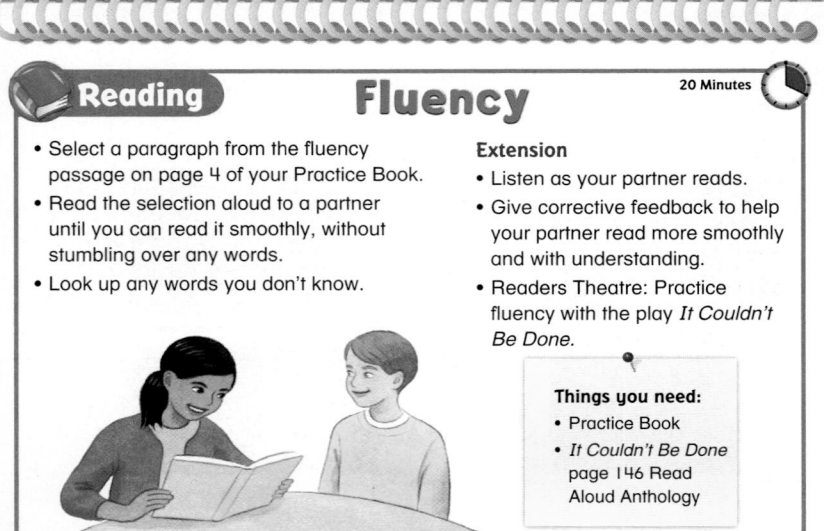

Things you need:
- Practice Book
- *It Couldn't Be Done* page 146 Read Aloud Anthology

Fluency Solutions Listening Library

(1)

Word Study — Synonyms — **20 Minutes**

- Write a list of six words having to do with contests of any kind, such as *regulations, outcome,* or *participants.*
- Using a thesaurus find one synonym for each word.
- With a partner write a newspaper article about a school contest, using as many of your synonyms as you can.

Extension
- Exchange articles with another pair of students.
- Circle all the synonyms you can find, using a different color or mark for each different set you locate.

Things you need:
- paper and pen or pencil
- markers

LOG ON For additional vocabulary and spelling games, go to www.macmillanmh.com

Vocabulary PuzzleMaker

(1)

Reading — Independent Reading — **20 Minutes**

- Find a book in the library or an article on the Internet about school contests and competitive events.
- Choose one type of contest to research and find out which schools in the United States compete in that contest.
- Write a paragraph summary of the contest, its rules, and records of winning participants.

Extension
- In your response journal, discuss other reading you might like to do about school contests.

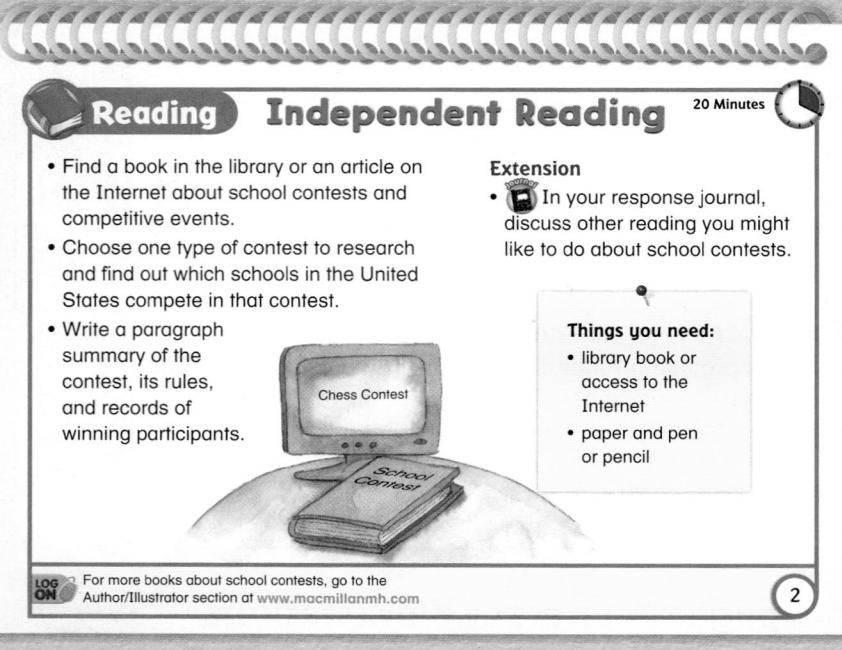

Chess Contest

School Contest

Things you need:
- library book or access to the Internet
- paper and pen or pencil

LOG ON For more books about school contests, go to the Author/Illustrator section at www.macmillanmh.com

(2)

Word Study — Short Vowels *a, e, i, o, u* and Variants — **20 Minutes**

- Make a list of words with short vowel sounds, two words for each vowel. Add to this list one word with a long vowel sound for each vowel.
- Then add to the list one variant spelling for each kind of short vowel sound. Put the words on cards.
- With a partner flash the cards quickly to see if he or she pronounces the vowels correctly.

Extension
- With your partner make sentences using as many words as possible in each sentence. Read the sentences aloud as fast as you can, being careful to pronounce all sounds correctly.

Things you need:
- note cards
- pen or pencil

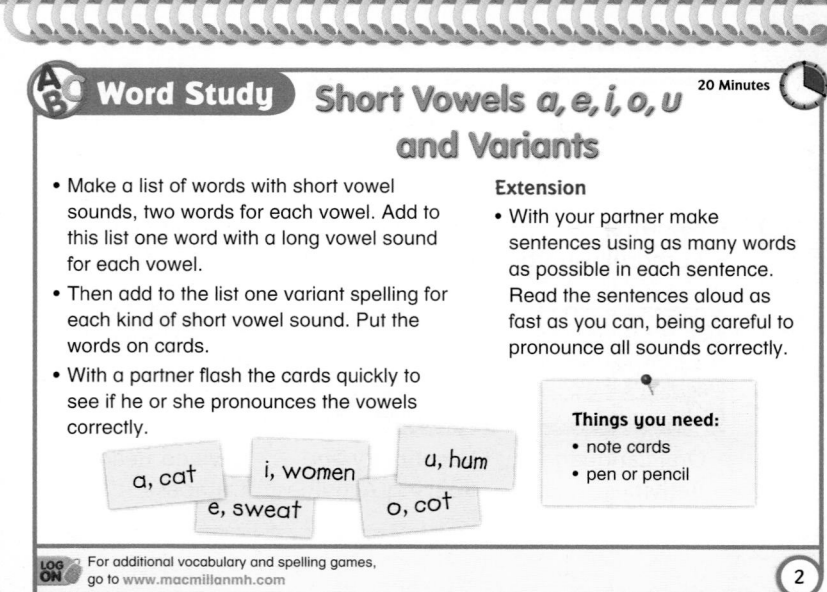

a, cat   i, women   u, hum
e, sweat   o, cot

LOG ON For additional vocabulary and spelling games, go to www.macmillanmh.com

(2)

Literacy Workstations

Writing

Objectives

- Write a personal narrative.
- Write a diary or journal entry and illustrate it.
- Be enthusiastic about writing and learning to write.
- Write voluntarily for different purposes.

Content Literacy

Objectives

- Research scientific contests and competitions.
- Write a short article based on research.
- Use discussion and conversation guidelines

Writing — Personal Narrative
20 Minutes

- Write a personal narrative about a time you entered a contest, played a game, or competed against someone. Describe how you felt before and during the contest and what the results were.
- Use supporting details as you write.

Extension

- Read your narrative aloud to a partner.
- Have a contest to see which of you can read the other's narrative aloud faster.

Things you need:
- paper and pen or pencil

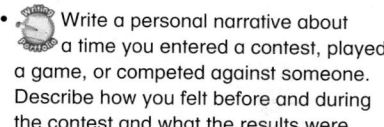

1

Science — Science Competitions
20 Minutes

- Using a library book or the Internet, research scientific contests and competitions.
- Make a list of three, and choose one to write about.
- Write a newspaper ad to announce the contest, its rules, and its goals.

Extension

- Create a contest to encourage a scientific discovery.
- Write a letter announcing this year's winner, explaining how his or her discovery will change science.

Things you need:
- library or access to the Internet
- paper and pen or pencil

1

Writing — Journal Entry
20 Minutes

- Write a diary or journal entry that describes your feelings on the day of a big contest. Use details to explain why you feel the way you do.

Extension

- Draw a picture to go with your journal entry. Include details in your picture that show what kind of contest it is.

Things you need:
- paper and pen or pencil
- markers

LOG ON Internet Research and Inquiry Activity
Students can find more facts at www.macmillanmh.com

2

Social Studies — World Records
20 Minutes

- Using an online encyclopedia or search engine, research two world record holders. One can be an athlete, the second should be in another field.
- Write a short article about each person's achievements, including a story about his or her record-breaking performances.

Extension

- Read your articles to a small group and discuss how these record-breakers have changed society.

Things you need:
- access to the Internet
- paper and pen or pencil

2

ORAL LANGUAGE
- Build Background
- Read Aloud
- Expand Vocabulary

VOCABULARY
- Teach Words in Context
- **Context Clues:** Synonyms

COMPREHENSION
- **Strategy:** Story Structure
- **Skill:** Character and Plot

SMALL GROUP OPTIONS
- Differentiated Instruction, pp. 47M–47V

Oral Language

Build Background

ACCESS PRIOR KNOWLEDGE

Share the following information:

Essay contests, sports tournaments, art competitions, spelling bees, and science fairs are popular among students.

TALK ABOUT SCHOOL CONTESTS

Discuss the weekly theme.

- Tell about school contests you know of or have participated in.

- What are the benefits and drawbacks of participating in a school contest?

 **FOCUS QUESTION** Ask a volunteer to read aloud "Talk About It" on **Student Book** page 17 and describe the photo.

- What kind of contest is taking place?

- What adjectives would you use to describe the photograph?

School Contests

16

ENGLISH LANGUAGE LEARNERS

Beginning Model Ask the following questions about the photo and model the answers if necessary: *What do the children have? They have eggs. What are they doing? They are running. It's a race. Who is the winner?* Point to the winner. Draw a picture of what will happen if the students drop the eggs.

Intermediate Share Information Discuss the photo. Ask, *Have you ever been in a contest? Tell us about it. What did you win?* Rephrase what students say in complete sentences.

Advanced Extend Language Complete the Intermediate task. Encourage students to answer using more complex structures. *Do you like to participate in contests? Yes, because I have a chance to win a trophy, and I like winning!*

Talk About It

What challenges and responsibilities come with entering a contest? What emotions can affect the contestants?

Find out more about school contests at **www.macmillanmh.com**

17

Picture Prompt

Look at the picture and respond in writing. You can write a poem, a story, or a description, or use any other type of writing you like.

Technology

For an extended lesson plan and Web site activities for **oral language development**, go to **www.macmillanmh.com**

Read Aloud
Read "La Bamba"

GENRE: Realistic Fiction Review features of realistic fiction:

Read Aloud
pages 9–16

- an invented story that could have happened in real life

- has realistic settings, characters, and problems and solutions

LISTENING FOR A PURPOSE

Ask students to listen carefully for the way the author describes the main character, Manuel, as you read "La Bamba" in the **Read-Aloud Anthology**. Choose from among the teaching suggestions.

FLUENCY Ask students to listen carefully as you read aloud, paying attention to your phrasing, expression, and tone of voice.

RESPOND TO THE STORY

Have students describe any experiences they've had performing in front of others. Discuss whether their feelings about performing were similar to Manuel's or different.

Expand Vocabulary

Ask students to find words in the story that relate to this week's theme of school contests. Write the words on the board and review their definitions as a class. Have students create word scrambles for five of the words and provide a one-word hint for each word, then trade with a partner and solve each other's scrambles.

Vocabulary

TEACH WORDS IN CONTEXT

Use the following routine:

Routine

Define: A person is **slumped** in his chair if he slides down.
Example: Jake slumped so far in his chair we couldn't see him.
Ask: How is being slumped different from sitting up straight? COMPARE AND CONTRAST

- **Soggy** is how something feels when it is full of water. Your clothes may feel soggy in the rain. What is a synonym for *soggy*? SYNONYM

- **Strands** are threads, or similar items that can be twisted together. Strands of hair can fall into your face. What other items might have strands? EXAMPLE

- **Capable** means you have the skill or power to do something well. A capable chef can cook well. What are you capable of doing? EXAMPLE

- **Categories** are groups or classes of things. These books are divided into two categories, history and geography. What are some categories of books in a bookstore? EXPLANATION

- Something **gigantic** is larger than other things. Whale sharks are gigantic compared with other fish. Name an antonym for *gigantic*. ANTONYM

- **Credit** is something given by teachers for extra work. Marie's teacher gave her extra credit for leading the debate team. What is a synonym for *credit*? SYNONYM

- Something **luminous** is very bright and shiny. Last night I saw the luminous glow of the full moon. Name something you have seen that is luminous. EXAMPLE

18

Vocabulary

slumped	strands
soggy	gigantic
capable	credit
categories	luminous

Context Clues

Synonyms are words that mean the same or almost the same thing as other words. For example, *huge* is a synonym for *gigantic*. When you read an unfamiliar word, check to see if there is a synonym nearby to use as a context clue.

The Talent Contest

by Howard Gabe

As Danny put his lunch tray onto the cafeteria table, milk spilled all over his sandwich. He sat down, hung his head forward, and **slumped** over the food in front of him. Frowning, he began peeling the **soggy** milk-soaked bread from his sandwich. "This is the most ridiculous thing I've ever done!" he said.

"It's not that bad," said his friend Elena, who was sitting across from him. "Just get another sandwich."

"Sandwich? What sandwich? I am talking about the talent contest. It's only two weeks away and I don't know what I'm doing! Everybody will laugh at me. It's inevitable. There's no way to avoid it!"

"Don't be so negative, Danny," said Elena as she rolled her eyes. "You're going to be great. You're very **capable**. You have the skills to do just about anything."

Danny moved his lunch tray to the side and rested his head on the table.

Quick Check

Do students understand word meanings?

During **Small Group Instruction**

If No → Approaching Level Vocabulary, p. 47N

If Yes → On Level Options, pp. 47Q–47R

Beyond Level Options, pp. 47S–47T

ELL — Access for All

Practice Vocabulary For *capable,* say, *If you practice dancing, you can become a capable dancer.* Use the sentence frame, *If you practice _____, you can become a capable _____.* For *gigantic,* ask students for words that describe size, for example, *small, large, tiny.* List the words in size order on the board. Add *gigantic.* Discuss objects that are gigantic.

"Sit up Danny," ordered Elena. "I have an idea. Let's brainstorm a list of things you could do. We'll divide the list into **categories** or groups. Let's start with music. You play the piano, right?"

"I stopped taking lessons in third grade," said Danny.

"What about singing a song?" suggested Elena.

Danny shook his head no. "Let's move on to another category."

"What about juggling?" asked Elena, as she twisted thin **strands** of hair around her finger.

"I don't know how to juggle!" Danny almost shouted. "Elena, how did I get myself into this huge, **gigantic** mess?"

"Stop being so…" Elena paused. "That's it, DRAMATIC!" Elena shouted excitedly. "You could do a dramatic

reading. You definitely have the talent for it. Mrs. Pace always calls on you to read aloud in class. You could read a play aloud. Maybe you could even get extra **credit** from Mrs. Pace. She rewards students with points for doing extra reading work."

Danny thought for a minute. Then he smiled. "Elena," Danny said, "you are a great friend!"

Elena smiled back. "I just want to make sure you are a bright, shiny, **luminous** star when you step out onstage."

Reread for **Comprehension**

Story Structure
Character and Plot

A Character and Plot Chart helps you figure out a character's personality and events of the plot. These traits and events are part of story structure. Use your Character and Plot Chart as you reread "The Talent Contest" to figure out Elena's traits and how her actions affect the plot of the story.

Character	Plot

19

On Level Practice Book O, page 1

A. Select the best word from the choices in parentheses. Then write the correct word on the line provided.

1. Have you seen the (categories, corners) of talents that will be allowed at the talent contest? _categories_

2. Did you see the size of the stage? It's (slow, gigantic)! _gigantic_

3. We walked to the contest in the rain, and now our clothes are (soggy, dry). _soggy_

4. The man was tired, so he (slumped, sat up) in his chair and went to sleep. _slumped_

5. Cynthia twisted (blocks, strands) of hair around her finger. _strands_

6. If we write a paper, will Mr. Price give us extra (credit, time)? _credit_

7. Our school has lights in front of the stage, so all of the performers have a (luminous, dark) glow on their faces. _luminous_

8. All of the performers were quite (splendid, capable) of putting on a good show. _capable_

B. Write new sentences for two of the vocabulary words used above. Then underline the vocabulary word.

9. _I could not use my props because they were soggy from leaving them outside in the rain._

10. _Steven was awarded a gigantic trophy for winning first place in the talent contest._

Possible responses provided above.

Approaching Practice Book A, page 1
Beyond Practice Book B, page 1

Vocabulary

STRATEGY
CONTEXT CLUES

Tested

Synonyms Explain three strategies that can help students understand a word they do not know.

- First, they can look up the word in a dictionary, if one is handy.

- Second, they can look for familiar parts within the word, such as a prefix, a suffix, or a smaller word within a compound word.

- Third, they can look for context clues, or hints, to the meaning in the surrounding text. For example, they can check for a synonym, or a word with a similar meaning, in the same sentence or paragraph.

Remind students that relating new vocabulary to prior knowledge is key to developing their vocabularies. Relating familiar synonyms to unknown words will help them understand the salient, or important, features of the new word.

Point to *gigantic* on **Student Book** page 19. Ask what other word in the sentence has nearly the same meaning. (huge)

Read "The Talent Contest"

As you read "The Talent Contest," ask students to identify clues that reveal the meanings of the highlighted words. Tell students they will read these words again in *Miss Alaineus*.

Objectives

- Analyze story structure
- Use academic language: *plot, character, flashback, foreshadowing*
- Identify character as an element of plot

Materials

- Comprehension Transparencies 1a, 1b
- Transparency 1, Graphic Organizer
- Leveled Practice Books, p. 2

Skills Trace

Character, Plot, Setting

Introduce	19A–B
Practice/ Apply	20–39; Leveled Practice, 2–3
Reteach/ Review	47M–T; 51A–B, 52–69, 77M–T; Leveled Practice, 9–10
Assess	Weekly Tests; Units 1, 4 Tests; Benchmarks Tests A, B
Maintain	41B, 71B, 133B; 395A–B; 396–411, 419M–T, 661B; Leveled Practice, 113–114

ELL
Access for All

Academic Vocabulary
To explain foreshadowing, use a concrete example. Write the numbers 1 to 4. Say, *The numbers represent story events. An author sometimes hints* (point to #2) *here that something will happen in the future* (point to #3, 4). *That's called foreshadowing.*

19A

Reread for
Comprehension

STRATEGY
ANALYZE STORY STRUCTURE

Access for All

Story structure refers to the way the author has organized the events of the plot using story elements such as character and setting, as well as literary devices such as flashback and foreshadowing. Understanding how the events of a story are organized can help readers better understand what they read.

Tested

SKILL
CHARACTER AND PLOT

Explain to students:

- The **plot** is the series of events that give a story a beginning, a middle, and an end. The parts of a plot include the beginning or exposition; the middle, which includes rising action, conflict, and the climax; and the end, which includes the falling action and resolution.

- A **character** is who the story is about. Tell students that a major character is the character that the story is mostly about. This character usually has a problem that has to be solved. Minor characters are other characters who appear in a story.

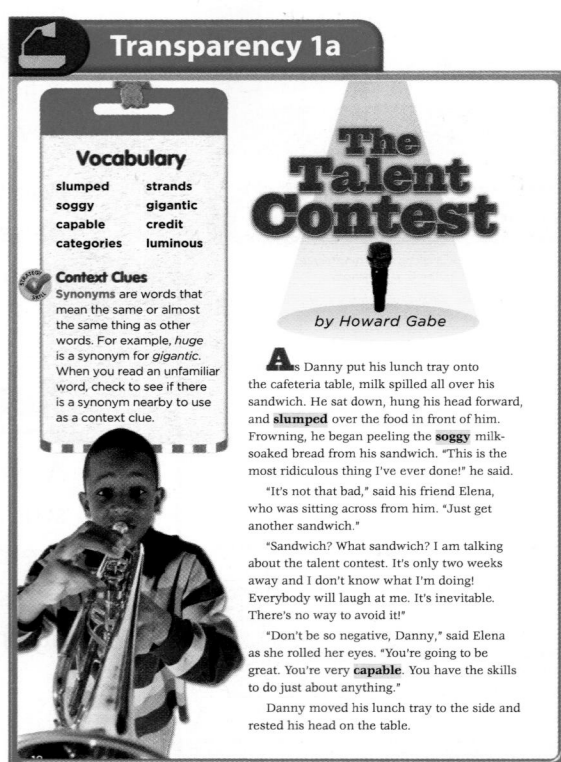
Transparency 1a

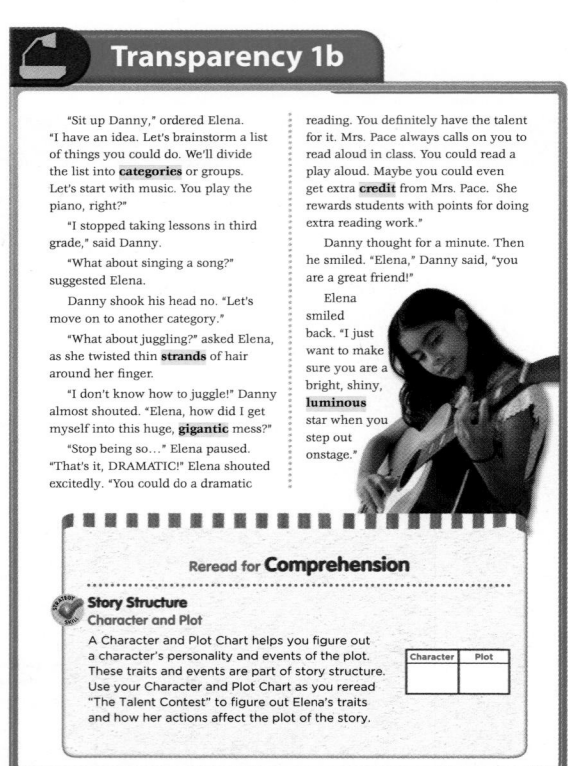
Transparency 1b

Student pages 18–19 available on Comprehension Transparencies 1a, 1b

- To find the plot, good readers identify the problem the main character faces and how he or she tries to solve it. They also look for examples of foreshadowing, or hints about what may happen, as well as flashbacks, or a return to events that took place before the story events.

MODEL

Reread the first few paragraphs of "The Talent Contest" from **Student Book** page 18.

Think Aloud Although Danny doesn't come out and say it, I can infer that he volunteered for the talent contest before thinking about what he would do. He seems upset and gets easily excited. When I get upset, I have trouble thinking clearly, and I think Danny is the same way. I think this will affect how Danny tries to solve his problem. He'll probably need help from his friend Elena.

GUIDED PRACTICE

Display **Transparency 1.**

- Begin by asking students to identify the major and minor characters. (Danny is a major character, and Elena is a minor character.)

- Help students begin to identify how each character's feelings and reactions affect the plot. Help students fill in the first two sections of the Character and Plot Chart.

APPLY

Have students complete the chart and explain why Danny would probably do a good job if he gave a dramatic reading at the school talent contest.

Transparency 1

Character and Plot Chart	
Characters	**Plot**
Danny is scared.	Danny can't decide what to do for the talent show.
Elena is a thoughtful person.	Elena tries to calm Danny down.
Danny is worried. He thinks people will laugh at him.	Elena offers to help Danny come up with ideas for the talent show.
Danny is overly dramatic and starts shouting.	Elena suggests that Danny do a dramatic reading for the talent show.

Graphic Organizer 1

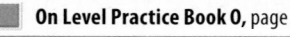

On Level Practice Book O, page 2

The **characters** are the people or animals in a story. The **plot** is a series of events that take the characters through an experience or change. In some stories the plot includes a problem that a character faces and solves.

Read the passage and answer the questions below.

    Tuesday I caught a bad cold and had to stay home from school. The next day was Wednesday, and Mrs. Mandle always assigned an essay that day. That afternoon I called my best friend, Roberto. He is a great writer and listens perfectly to Mrs. Mandle's essay questions. However, when I called Roberto, his voice was muffled and what he said wasn't very clear.
    "Mike," Roberto said, "the essay is on 'what makes blueberry pies'?"
    "What?" I said. "The essay is on 'what makes blueberry pies'?"
    "Yes," he said. "I hope you feel butter. I have to go to digger now."
    That night I wrote about blueberry pies and how to make them. The next day I felt better and went to school. I saw Roberto and talked about my blueberry pie essay.
    "Blueberry pies?" Roberto asked. "We didn't have to write about blueberry pies. Our essay was about 'what makes blue skies.' "

Possible response provided.
1. Who are the characters in this passage? Roberto, Mike, and Mrs. Mandle

2. What is Mike's main problem? Mike is sick and did not get the essay question from Mrs. Mandle in class.

3. Why does Mike call Roberto for the essay question? Mike calls Roberto because he is his best friend, is a good writer, and listens perfectly to essay questions.

4. What could Mike have done differently to solve his essay problem? Mike could have called Roberto back to make sure he got the essay question correct.

 ★ **Approaching Practice Book A,** page 2

◆ **Beyond Practice Book B,** page 2

Quick Check | **Can students analyze the characters and plot?**

During **Small Group Instruction**

If No → Approaching Level Comprehension, p. 47O

If Yes → On Level Options, p. 47Q

Beyond Level Options, p. 47S

Read

MAIN SELECTION
- *Miss Alaineus*

- **Skill:** Character and Plot

PAIRED SELECTION
- "The National Spelling Bee"
- **Text Feature:** Photos and Captions

SMALL GROUP OPTIONS
- Differentiated Instruction, pp. 47M–47V

Comprehension

GENRE: REALISTIC FICTION

Have a student read the definition of Realistic Fiction on **Student Book** page 20. As they read students should look for events that could really happen.

STRATEGY
ANALYZE STORY STRUCTURE

Analyzing story structure involves looking at how the author has organized the events of the plot using story elements such as character and setting, as well as literary devices, such as foreshadowing and flashback.

SKILL
PLOT AND CHARACTER

Plot is the series of events that take place in a story. These events give the story a beginning, a middle, and an end. The characters in a story are who the story is about. The plot usually features a problem the characters have to solve.

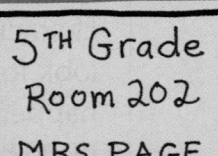

5TH Grade
Room 202
MRS. PAGE

Comprehension

Genre
Realistic Fiction uses settings, characters, and events that could actually exist.

Story Structure
Character and Plot
As you read, use your Character and Plot Chart.

Character	Plot

Read to Find Out
How does the kind of person Sage is affect the plot?

20

Vocabulary

Vocabulary Words Review the tested vocabulary words: **capable, categories, credit, gigantic, luminous, slumped, soggy, and strands.**

Story Words Students may find these words difficult. Pronounce the words and present the meanings as necessary.

archaeology (p. 34): the scientific study of the human past

chalkboard (p. 29): a hard, smooth board meant to be written or drawn on with chalk

vocabulary (p. 22): a list of words, usually arranged in alphabetical order and defined

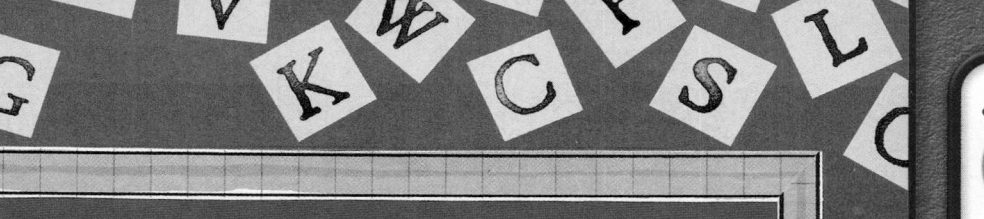

Miss Alaineus

A VOCABULARY DISASTER

written and illustrated by
Debra Frasier

21

Preview and Predict

Ask students to read the title, preview the illustrations, and note questions and predictions about the story. What makes this story seem realistic? Have them develop hypotheses based on their prior knowledge.

Set Purposes

FOCUS QUESTION Discuss the "Read to Find Out" question on **Student Book** page 20. Remind students to look for the answer as they read.

Point out the Character and Plot chart in the Student Book and on **Practice Book** page 3. Explain that students will fill it in as they read.

Read *Miss Alaineus*

Use the questions and Think Alouds for additional instruction to support the comprehension strategy and skill.

On Level Practice Book O, page 3

As you read *Miss Alaineus*, fill in the Character and Plot Chart.

Character	Plot

How does the information you wrote in this Character and Plot Chart help you analyze the story structure of *Miss Alaineus*?

⭐ **Approaching Practice Book A,** page 3

◆ **Beyond Practice Book B,** page 3

Read Together

If your students need support to read the Main Selection, use the prompts to guide comprehension and model how to complete the graphic organizer.

Read Independently

If your students can read the Main Selection independently, have them read and complete the graphic organizer. Remind students to set and modify their purposes and select appropriate strategies.

If your students need an alternate selection, choose the **Leveled Readers** that match their instructional level.

Technology

Story available on **Listening Library Audio CD**

Develop Comprehension

1 STRATEGY
ANALYZE STORY STRUCTURE

Teacher Think Aloud From the first line of the story, I'm pretty sure that the main character, Sage, is going to have a problem because she gives advice about not being sick on Vocabulary Day. I can tell that Sage is upset about missing school. Something will probably happen because of the hurried way that Sage's friend Starr gives her the vocabulary words. As I read I will pay attention to how the characters react and how that affects what happens next in the story.

2 CHARACTER

Who is the major character in *Miss Alaineus*? What words would you use to describe her? Add this information to your Character and Plot Chart. (Sage is the major character in the story. She seems to be hard-working and responsible. She is concerned about missing assignments when she is sick, and she calls a friend to get them.)

Make sure students understand that Sage is also the narrator.

None of this would have happened if it wasn't for Forest. Forest is not a *thicket of trees*. Forest is a boy. A sick boy. A boy sneezing and coughing all over my desk and pencils.

1   I caught Forest's cold and had to stay home from school on Tuesday. Tuesday is Vocabulary Day at Webster School. Follow my advice: Never get sick on Vocabulary Day.

2   On Tuesday afternoon I called my best friend, Starr, who is not *a luminous celestial object seen as a point of light in the sky*, but a very smart girl who listens perfectly on Vocabulary Day. She was late for baseball practice, so she spelled the first fourteen vocabulary words as fast as she could.

3   I had to scribble them quickly because her mom was calling her to the car. "This last one's 'Miss Alaineus'!" Starr yelled. "I gotta go. I hope you feel better tomorrow, Sage." And she hung up the phone with a crash.

22

ELL   Access for All

STRATEGIES FOR EXTRA SUPPORT

Question 2 CHARACTER

Ask, *Who is the main character?* Help students describe Sage: *Is she lazy or hardworking? Why? Is she smart? How do we know?* Write the following sentence frame on the board to help students talk about Sage: I think Sage is _____ because she . . .

I didn't feel much better on Wednesday, so my mom called Mrs. Page, who is not *a single side of a printed sheet of paper usually found bound in a book*. She's my teacher, and actually Mrs. Page is a good name for her because she reads to us every day. My mom told her yes, I had my math problems and vocabulary words, and yes, I would get better soon.

Plot
How do you think Starr's rush to give Sage the vocabulary words will affect what happens next?

VOCABULARY WORDS

1. dinosaur
2. snake
3. museum
4. reptile
5. constrictor
6. herpetologist
7. fossil
8. carnivore
9. herbivore
10. nest
11. species
12. theory
13. hypothesis
14. category
15. Miss Alaineus

23

Develop Comprehension

3 PLOT

What happens when Sage calls Starr to get the vocabulary words? (Starr was late for baseball practice, so she spelled the vocabulary words as fast as she could.) How do you think Starr's rush to give Sage the vocabulary words will affect what happens next? Add this information to your Character and Plot Chart. (Answers may vary but students should suggest that Sage may have misspelled or misunderstood some words.)

Character	Plot
Sage is hardworking and responsible. She is concerned about missing assignments when she is sick.	Starr gives Sage the words she missed in a rush, so Sage may have misunderstood some of them.

Vocabulary

Context Clues: *Multiple-Meaning Words*

Explain/Model To tell what a multiple-meaning word means in a sentence, students should check how the word is used in context.

Think Aloud Sage reveals that the word *page* is a multiple-meaning word because she says that this is her teacher's name and not a printed piece of paper. I know that *page* can also have other meanings. For example, it can be a verb, as in the sentence, *I decided to page through the book to see if I should buy it.*

Practice/Apply Have students locate the multiple-meaning word *cold* on page 22. Have them identify the meaning of *cold* as used in the first sentence of the second paragraph. (a common illness marked by sneezing and coughing) Then tell students to think of other meanings for *cold* and to use each meaning in a sentence, such as *After studying the chapter closely, I knew the lesson* cold.

Develop Comprehension

4 CONTEXT CLUES

What does the word *theme* in the first sentence mean? What clues to its meaning can you find? (The word *theme* means a subject or topic. In this sentence it is followed by the word *like* and a number of examples.) What is another meaning for the word *theme* that can be used when discussing realistic fiction such as *Miss Alaineus?* (Answers should include the overall idea or message about life the author wants to communicate.)

5 MAKE PREDICTIONS

How do the words of Sage's mother help you predict that Sage will probably make a mistake as she continues to define her words? (Sage thinks she is good at defining words. She then remembers her mother saying "Pride goeth before the fall" so although she is proud of herself now, she may make a mistake.)

4 Every week Mrs. Page gives us a list of words with a theme, like Story Writing or Musical Performance or Electricity. We're supposed to look up each word in the dictionary, but sometimes I already know the words, so I try to make the definitions sound like I looked them up.

tree: a large leafy plant with a tall wooden trunk that pushes roots into the ground and branches into the sky

automobile: a vehicle, used to transport humans, usually consisting of four wheels, a steering wheel, and a radio

I thought I was pretty good at definitions until this week.

5 My mom says, "Pride goeth before a fall."

Pride: *an unduly high opinion of oneself.*

Goeth: *Old English for "to go."*

Fall: *what happened on Monday, Vocabulary Test Day.*

24

ELL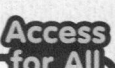

STRATEGIES FOR EXTRA SUPPORT

Question 5 MAKE PREDICTIONS

Say, *As Sage works to learn words, she makes mistakes. As a reader, you can predict what Sage will do next by carefully reading the words her mother says about Sage.* Reread the words Sage's mother said and discuss them. Ask, *So how does reading what Sage's mother said about Sage help you predict what Sage will do?*

By Thursday afternoon my head felt like it was stuffed with cotton and my throat felt swollen shut. I finished defining my vocabulary words while propped up in bed with a box of tissues on one side and a **gigantic** red dictionary on the other. It's hard to look up words in a huge book while you're in bed blowing your nose, so I made my own dictionary language for as many of them as I could. **6**

13. hypothesis : what you guess will happen in your science experiment

14. category : a bunch of things that are alike

15. Miss Alaineus :

25

Develop Comprehension

6 SUMMARIZE

What events have taken place to give you a clue that things might not go so well for Sage when she finally returns to school? (Sage has missed school because she is sick, her friend Starr copied down her assignment words in a hurry, and she is writing definitions on her own without looking them up in the dictionary. She will probably end up making mistakes.)

Comprehension

Literary Device: *Foreshadowing*

Explain Sometimes authors use a technique called **foreshadowing** to provide readers with clues about what might happen next in a story.

Discuss What clues does the author give about what may happen when Sage returns to school? (Sage doesn't feel well, has difficulty using a dictionary in bed, and makes up her own definitions for some of the vocabulary words. This might be a clue that Sage will make a mistake when she goes back to school with her definitions.)

Apply Have students use the foreshadowing clues to help them modify their story predictions. As students continue to read, have them look for additional clues in the story that provide hints about what may happen.

Vocabulary

Read the sentence that contains the word **gigantic**. Why do you think the author uses the word *gigantic* here instead of *big*? (*Gigantic* has a stronger connotation than *big*, and helps readers understand why Sage had a difficult time lifting the book while she was sick.)

Develop Comprehension

7 MAINTAIN
SETTING

Where and when does this story take place? Are the settings realistic? Explain. (The story takes place in Sage's home and at her school. Both settings are realistic. From the clothes the characters wear and the way they talk, it most likely takes place in the present.)

7 The last word seemed a little odd to me because I couldn't figure out what she had to do with snakes or **categories** or theories. Mrs. Page rarely gives us people's names on our vocabulary lists, but we have had a few that turned into words, like Louis Pasteur for **pasteurization** and George Washington for **Washington, D.C.**, so I decided she must have been included for a reason.

You should know that for years I had wondered who Miss Alaineus was. When I was little I figured out that she had something to do with the kitchen, because the Miss Alaineus drawer held the spoons too big to fit anywhere else, the sharp corn holders shaped like tiny cobs, and the spaghetti spork, that weird cross between a spoon and a fork that perfectly lifts slippery spaghetti out of the bowl. I thought maybe she was an **ancestor:** *an ancient relative long dead*, who left us all these odd things in the drawer.

Then just last year my mom and I were at the grocery store and it all fell into place. We were in one of those Very Big Hurries when she said, "You go get some of that long Italian bread and two sticks of butter. I'll get Miss Alaineus' things and meet you here at the cash register."

26

Ways to Confirm Meaning

Semantic/Meaning Cues

Explain Good readers make sure that what they read makes sense. One way they do this is by using context clues and their own background knowledge to predict and confirm meaning or to help them correct their understanding of what they have read.

Model Point out the word *ancient* on page 26. Say, *I'm not sure I know this word in Sage's definition of* ancestor. *Sage says that an ancestor is "long dead."* Ancient *must have to do with long ago or very old. If I substitute* very old *for* ancient, *it makes sense.*

Apply Encourage students to explain when to use context clues and background knowledge to predict and confirm meaning, or as a way to recognize when their understanding is breaking down. Have them apply their knowledge to words such as *devastated* on page 33 as they continue to read the selection.

I found the bread and butter, and my mom came back with spaghetti sauce, a can of Parmesan cheese, a can of corn, and a big green box of spaghetti with a beautiful woman on the front. She was drawn so that her hair tumbled perfectly across the box and ended in a little plastic window, making the spaghetti look just like the ends of the **strands** of her hair.

There she was—Miss Alaineus.

8

So, propped up on pillows in my bed, with a tissue in one hand and a pencil in the other, I wrote:

> 15. Miss Alaineus: the woman on green spaghetti boxes whose hair is the color of uncooked pasta
>
> and turns into spaghetti at the ends

And then I fell asleep.

27

Develop Comprehension

8 STRATEGY

ANALYZE STORY STRUCTURE

Teacher Think Aloud I know that Sage's flashback explains why she thought that Miss Alaineus was a person and not a word. It also shows that Sage is proud of the way she can come up with word meanings. Do you think this flashback will be important to the plot? Why or why not? Add your answer to your Character and Plot Chart.

(Encourage students to apply the strategy in a Think Aloud.)

Student Think Aloud In the flashback, Sage says that she had wondered about who Miss Alaineus was for years. She thought it had something to do with the kitchen because the miscellaneous drawer held the spoons that were too big to fit anywhere else. I think this flashback will be an important event in the story. I already know that Sage is proud that she can make up her own definitions, so she probably won't look this word up.

Character	Plot
Sage is hardworking and responsible. She is concerned about missing assignments when she is sick.	Starr gives Sage the words she missed in a rush, so Sage may have misunderstood some of them.
Sage is proud that she can make up definitions.	Miss Alaineus is a woman pictured on a spaghetti box. She is not a real person.

Comprehension

Literary Device: *Flashback*

Explain Sometimes authors do not present events in the order that they take place in the story. Authors might take the reader back in time to a past event that influences a current situation. This technique is called a **flashback.** Flashbacks are usually signaled with clue words and phrases, such as *When I was younger, a few years ago, I remember,* and so on.

Discuss What event does Sage remember in the flashback on pages 26–27 in the story? (Sage recalls the time she found out who she thought "Miss Alaineus" was when she saw her pictured on a box of spaghetti.)

Apply Have students find the clue words or phrase that signals the flashback on page 26.

Develop Comprehension

 **9**   **CHARACTER**

Why is Sage happy to be back at school on Monday? (Sage missed her friends. She is also serious about her schoolwork, so she probably didn't want to miss any more school.)

 **10**   **MONITOR AND CLARIFY: READ AHEAD**

What do you think the Tenth Annual Vocabulary Parade might be? How might the strategy "Read Ahead" help you to answer this question? (Students may not be sure if there was a reference to the Vocabulary Parade earlier in the story, but this is the first time it has been mentioned. Answers should include that reading ahead will help them clarify what the Vocabulary Parade might be.)

Remind students to monitor, or check, their understanding as they read and then use appropriate strategies to help them correct any misunderstandings.

9   I finally got better over the weekend and felt great on Monday. I turned in my homework to Mrs. Page and sat down at my desk, glad to be back at school with my friends. I was even glad to see Forest at our morning circle meeting.

10   "First, I want to remind you of the Tenth Annual Vocabulary Parade on Friday," said Mrs. Page. "I hope you are all working on your word costumes. Second, please remember to bring your bus money and permission slips for our science museum field trip tomorrow. And third, instead of our usual Monday test, we are going to have a Vocabulary Bee today.

28

Comprehension

Monitor and Clarify: Read Ahead

Explain   Tell students that if they don't understand a character's actions or an event in a story, they should keep reading to find out more information. They might understand something better when they know more about it.

Discuss   What does Sage think the word *miscellaneous* means? (She thinks it refers to a woman.) What does *miscellaneous* really mean? (It means varied, of different kinds.) Why might Sage be confused? (Answers will vary, but she's probably confused because she hears the syllable *Miss* in the word.)

Apply   Have students reread page 27 of the Student Book. Discuss how reading about the picture of the woman clarifies the plot and the reasons for Sage's confusion.

Develop Comprehension

11 MAKE PREDICTIONS

Based on what you know so far, what word do you think Mrs. Page will give Sage to define? (Mrs. Page will probably give Sage the word *miscellaneous* to define, because it was the only word that Sage seemed to wonder about.)

TODAY

Circle Time: 8:40
Vocabulary Bee: 8:55
Math : 9:30
: 10:05
R : 11:00
LU : 11:45
: 12:15

Homeworl

"Everyone line up here by the chalkboard, and I'll choose a word from our list. After I pronounce the word, please spell and define it. If you are correct, go to the end of the line. If you miss the word, please sit down at your desk and look it up in the dictionary. Write the word five times and define it once."

Starr was first with **museum**: "M-U-S-E-U-M: *a building for exhibiting objects about art or history or science,*" she said, and went to the back of the line.

Cliff, not *a high, steep face of rock,* but one very tall boy, answered to the word **dinosaur**: "D-I-N-O-S-A-U-R: *a prehistoric, extinct reptile, often huge,*" and he went to the **11** back of the line.

29

Develop Comprehension

12 CHARACTER

Why does Sage become embarrassed over misspelling a vocabulary word? (Sage prides herself in being good at defining words. Even her father thinks she's good at it; he calls her "wise-girl-with-words." Sage's name also means "someone of great wisdom." That's why she gets so embarrassed when she misses the word.)

13 PLOT

Why is Sage's embarrassment in front of her classmates an important event in the plot? (Answers may vary but should include that the way Sage reacts to being embarrassed, and what she does about it, will determine what happens in the rest of the story.) **Add your answers to the questions on this page to the Character and Plot Chart.**

Character	Plot
Sage is hardworking and responsible. She is concerned about missing assignments when she is sick.	Starr gives Sage the words she missed in a rush, so Sage may have misunderstood some of them.
Sage is proud that she can make up definitions.	Miss Alaineus is a woman pictured on a spaghetti box. She is not a real person.
Sage is embarrassed.	Sage defines and spells "miscellaneous" incorrectly.

I was tenth, and when Mrs. Page called out my word, I spelled: "Capital **M-I-S-S**, capital **A-L-A-I-N-E-U-S**," and added, *"the woman on green spaghetti boxes whose hair is the color of uncooked pasta and turns into spaghetti at the ends."*

There was a moment of silence in the room. I smiled at Mrs. Page. She waited to see if I would add anything else, and when I didn't, she grinned. Not smiled—**grinned:** *to draw back the lips and bare the teeth, as in a very wide smile*—and the entire class burst into one huge giggling, laughing, falling-down mass of kids. Forest was doubled over. Starr, my best friend, was laughing so hard tears came to her eyes. By now, even Mrs. Page was laughing.

Pride goeth before a fall. I was **Sage:** *one who shows* **12** *wisdom, experience, judgment.* Why were they laughing? "Wise-girl-with-words" my dad always called me. What had I said? I was beginning to turn red. **Red:** *the color of* **13** *embarrassment.*

30

ELL

Access for All

STRATEGIES FOR EXTRA SUPPORT

Question 12 CHARACTER
Say, *Sage is embarrassed. Here's an example of what* embarrassed *means: A very good student gets a* D *on a test. He is embarrassed. Why? He didn't get a good grade. He usually gets* As! *Why is Sage embarrassed?* You may need to give students the language for this: *She doesn't spell a word correctly. She's upset. She thinks that she is smart* and *therefore she shouldn't misspell words. Sage is embarrassed. Why do people get embarrassed?* Help students tell why Sage becomes embarrassed using this sentence prompt: *I think Sage becomes embarrassed when she misspells a word because…*

14

31

Extra Support

Character and Plot

If students have difficulty, have them reread the last paragraph on page 22 and help them paraphrase the problem Sage faces. Then have them reread page 25. Ask students how Sage was feeling and why she decided to write some of her own definitions rather than look them up in the dictionary. Finally, have students reread the last paragraph on page 30. Discuss with students how each of the events on pages 22, 25, and 30 are related and why they are important events in the development of the plot.

Read

Main Selection   Student page 31

Develop Comprehension

14 GENRE: REALISTIC FICTION

Is what happened to Sage during the Vocabulary Bee something that might happen in real life? Explain. (Yes. Sage's experience and how she reacts to it could happen in real life. Almost everyone has had the experience of making a mistake in front of other people and knows how it feels when that happens.)

Have students respond to the selection by confirming or revising their predictions and purposes for reading. Encourage students to revise or write any additional questions they may have about the selection. Remind them that asking questions will help them understand the story better.

Quick Check Can students identify the main character's thoughts, feelings, and actions, as well as the motivations for them? Are they able to recognize the important developments in the plot? If not, see the Extra Support on this page.

Stop here if you wish to read this selection over two days.

Miss Alaineus **31**

Develop Comprehension

15 **SUMMARIZE**

What problems has Sage faced in the story so far? (Sage caught a bad cold and had to stay home from school. She worried about keeping up with her assignments, so she called her friend Starr. But Sage made a mistake writing down the vocabulary words for the week, and now she's being teased by her classmates.)

16 **CHARACTER**

What does Sage's reaction to her mistake tell you about her character? Add your answer to the Character and Plot Chart. (Answers will vary but should include that Sage takes her schoolwork very seriously. She feels that she is "finished" and "ruined" because she made a mistake and is unable to laugh at herself.)

Character	Plot
Sage is hardworking and responsible. She is concerned about missing assignments when she is sick.	Starr gives Sage the words she missed in a rush, so Sage may have misunderstood some of them.
Sage is proud that she can make up definitions.	Miss Alaineus is a woman pictured on a spaghetti box. She is not a real person.
Sage is embarrassed.	Sage defines and spells "miscellaneous" incorrectly.
Sage is frightened.	Sage thinks her reputation at school will be ruined.

15 Finally the room quieted. Mrs. Page opened her dictionary and wrote on the chalkboard:

Miscellaneous: *adj. 1. consisting of various kinds or qualities 2. a collection of unrelated objects*

My jaw dropped as I looked at the spelling. My eyes bulged as I read the definition. I didn't bother to tell anyone about my mom and the spaghetti spork and the grocery store. **Humbled:** *aware of my shortcomings, modest, meek,* I dragged back to my seat and wrote **miscellaneous** five times and defined it once. And that's when I remembered I had even drawn a picture of the spaghetti box for extra credit. I was **devastated:** *wasted, ravaged.* **Ruined:** *destroyed.*

16 **Finished:** *brought to an end.*

Character
What does Sage's reaction to her mistake tell you about her character?

32

32

They called me Miss Alaineus for the rest of the day. Sometimes a person couldn't even get the words out before bending over with laughter. The day took a week to end. When I got off the bus I **slumped** home—devastated, ruined, finished.

I told my mom the whole story, from the kitchen drawer to the grocery store to the Vocabulary Bee. Even my own mother laughed a little at the part about the drawing for extra credit, but at least she stopped fast and said, "You know what I always say . . . There's gold in every mistake." **17**

Gold? *A bright yellow precious metal of great value?*

Mistake? *Something done, said, or thought in the wrong way?*

"Impossible," I told her. **Impossible:** *not capable of happening.*

33

Develop Comprehension

17 CLARIFY

Using the definitions for the words *gold* and *mistake,* what do you think Sage's mother meant by her words "There's gold in every mistake"? (A mistake is something that is not done or said correctly, and gold is something of value. Sage's mother is trying to tell her that even when you do something wrong you can sometimes find something of value in your mistake.)

Vocabulary

Read the sentence that contains the word **slumped**. Why does the author use this word to describe the way Sage walked home from the bus? (Sage says she felt devastated, ruined, finished after her first day back at school. *Slumped* has a stronger negative connotation than a phrase such as walked slowly home, and also describes how Sage looked as she walked.)

Develop Comprehension

18 **CHARACTER**

How do you think Sage feels when her classmates laugh at the museum guide's words? (She feels bad that her mistake is still on the minds of her classmates. She is having a difficult time finding something valuable in her mistake.)

19 **SYNTHESIZE**

If you were Sage, how would you try to solve her latest problem? (Answers may include: If Sage laughed at herself, her classmates might stop teasing her.)

I couldn't believe I *ever* had to go back to school. But the next day we went to the science museum, and everyone forgot all about Miss Alaineus at the snake exhibit and the dinosaur bone lab. Then the guide said, "The field of bone archaeology has been influenced by a wide and unusual array of miscellaneous discoveries around the world."

18 The class burst out laughing, and the guide was pleased with herself for entertaining us so easily. And I knew: *to apprehend with certainty*, that my mistake was still alive and well, and nothing like gold.

After school I lay on my bed and stared at the wall.

19 How could I have been so stupid?

34

My mom came in and said it was time to work on my costume for the Vocabulary Parade. We had finished the cape for **Capable**, but I still needed to make the lettering down the back.

"Mom," I said, "I could only be a mistake this year. **Miss Stake.**"

Suddenly I sat up.

I looked at my mom. She looked at me.

I smiled.

She smiled.

"Sweetheart," she said, "let's take another look at **20** that cape."

35

Develop Comprehension

20 MAKE PREDICTIONS

What do you think Sage and her mother will do? (They may make a "Miss Alaineus" costume. When Sage says "Miss Stake," it gives them the idea to dress her as "Miss Alaineus" for the parade.)

Cultural Perspectives

SCHOOL CONTESTS AROUND THE WORLD

Share the following information about different types of school contests that are held around the world with students:

- Since 1990 a Japanese company has sponsored a Japanese speech contest for students in China and Japan. The contest was started to promote cultural understanding between the countries.

- The International Mathematical Olympiad (IMO) is an annual contest for high school students all over the world. The first IMO was held in Romania in 1959.

Discuss with students what kinds of contests American students might participate in with students abroad in order to increase understanding between our countries.

Develop Comprehension

21 **CHARACTER**

Why did it take courage for Sage to walk out on the stage as Miss Alaineus, and what does that say about her character? Add the answer to your Character and Plot Chart. (Sage wasn't sure if her classmates and the audience would laugh at her or with her. It says that rather than feeling sorry for herself, Sage did something to try and solve her problem.)

22 **STRATEGY**
ANALYZE STORY STRUCTURE

How does Sage find a solution to her problem? Explain how you reached your answer and add it to your Character and Plot Chart.

Student Think Aloud I think Sage solves her problem by deciding to poke fun at herself. By dressing as "Miss Alaineus," Sage shows she is clever and has a good sense of humor.

Character	Plot
Sage is hardworking and responsible. She is concerned about missing assignments when she is sick.	Starr gives Sage the words she missed in a rush, so Sage may have misunderstood some of them.
Sage is proud that she can make up definitions.	Miss Alaineus is a woman pictured on a spaghetti box. She is not a real person.
Sage is embarrassed.	Sage defines and spells "miscellaneous" incorrectly.
Sage is frightened.	Sage thinks her reputation at school will be ruined.
Sage learns to laugh at herself.	Sage solves her problem by dressing as "Miss Alaineus."

21   It took the most courage I've ever had to walk out on that stage as **Miss Alaineus,** *Queen of All Miscellaneous Things*. But when Mr. Bell read my word and definition, **22** everyone applauded and laughed **wildly:** *in a manner lacking all restraint,* and I grinned at **23** my mom across the auditorium.

36

Forest came right after me. When he bowed, his **Precipitation** watering-can hat rained on Mr. Bell's new suit, and the entire audience gasped, then cheered when Mr. Bell smiled at his **soggy** clothes.

Develop Comprehension

23 **COMPARE AND CONTRAST**

Compare how Sage handled her problem by dressing as Miss Alaineus in the vocabulary parade to the way she handled her problem immediately after she made her mistake. How did Sage change, and what effect did this change have on the plot? (At first Sage handled her problem by feeling bad and hoping that her classmates would forget her mistake. By dressing up as Miss Alaineus she decides to turn the situation around by showing others that she can laugh at herself.)

Develop Comprehension

24 **POINT OF VIEW**

From what point of view was this story told? How do you know? How did this point of view affect your enjoyment of the story? (First person point of view; the character telling the story is "I." Students may say this point of view made the story more enjoyable because they got to know Sage well. The main character is the narrator.)

25 **IMAGERY**

What are some other "Miss" names you can think of? Describe how some of the costumes for these "Miss" names might look in a vocabulary parade. (Answers will vary. Examples: misinformation, mistake, misstep, miscommunication, mischief.)

24 To my **astonishment**: *great shock and amazement*, I won a gold trophy for The Most Original Use of a Word in the Tenth Annual Vocabulary Parade.

So this time Mom was right. There was gold in this mistake.

And next year I think I'm going to be . . .

38

Media Literacy

Recording an Event

Explain At the end of *Miss Alaineus,* Sage solved her problem in a way that she and her classmates will not soon forget.

Discuss Talk about the different ways students use media to record their important events. Possible answers may include photographs, letters, journals, and video. Ask students to describe the strengths and weaknesses of each medium when used to document an event. Discuss how facts and opinions can be presented in different media.

Apply Have students apply what they know to come up with a plan to document an upcoming school event. Encourage them to explain and justify the media choices they have made. Discuss whether students will present opinions along with facts. Also make sure students can distinguish facts from probabilities, or events that are likely to happen.

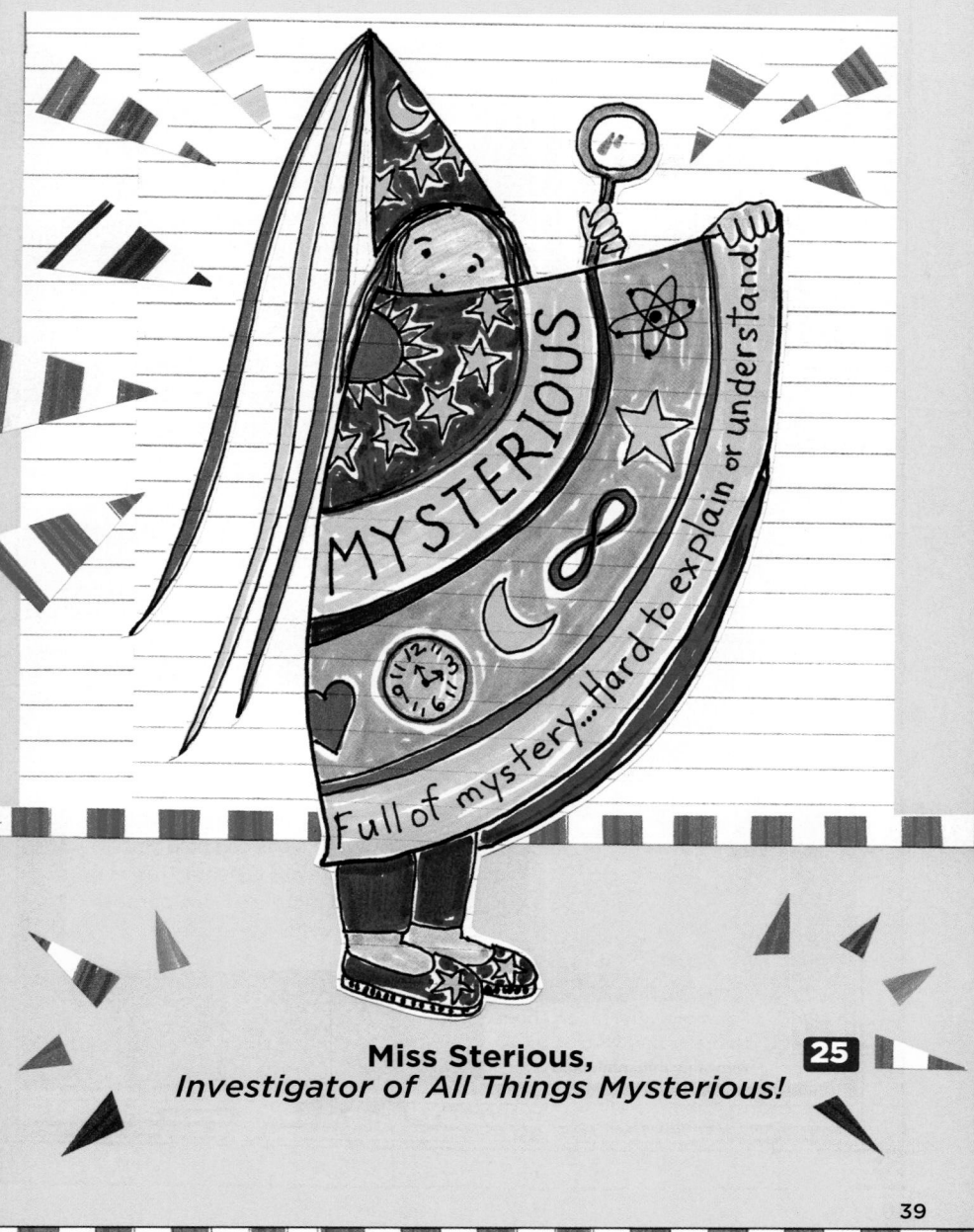

Miss Sterious,
Investigator of All Things Mysterious!

25

Develop Comprehension

RETURN TO PREDICTIONS AND PURPOSES

Review students' predictions and purposes. Were they correct? Did they find out how Sage solves her problem?

REVIEW READING STRATEGIES

How did analyzing the plot and the feelings and actions of the main character help you to enjoy this story?

PERSONAL RESPONSE

Ask students to write about a time they were able to turn a difficult or uncomfortable situation into an experience they learned from.

As an alternative, have students write an interpretative essay that summarizes the plot and describes the main character and how she changes.

> **Quick Check** Can students identify the main character's thoughts, feelings, and actions, as well as motivations? Are they able to recognize important developments in the plot?

During **Small Group Instruction**

If No → **Approaching Level** Leveled Reader Lesson, p. 47P

If Yes → **On Level** Options, p. 47Q

Beyond Level Options, p. 47S

Author-Illustrator

A FEW WORDS ABOUT DEBRA FRASIER

Have students read the biography of the author-illustrator and discuss the following questions. Remind them to use discussion and conversation guidelines.

DISCUSS

- How does Debra Frasier get ideas for writing stories?

- Why does it take Debra a long time to write and illustrate her stories?

WRITE ABOUT IT

Remind students that Sage turned her spelling mistake in class into the inspiration for an award-winning costume. Have students write a description of a mistake they made and a valuable lesson they learned.

Author's Purpose

Point out to students that authors who write fiction to entertain may have a secondary reason for writing. Encourage students to think about the way Sage solved her problem at school and what the author may want to persuade readers to try if they ever have a similar problem.

Technology

Students can find more information about Debra Frasier at www.macmillanmh.com

---

A Few Words About Debra Frasier

Debra Frasier's fifth-grade daughter said to her one day, "Mom, today I figured out that *miscellaneous* is not a person." Her daughter's new wisdom gave Debra two gifts: a good laugh and the idea to write *Miss Alaineus*. Debra says her books take a long time because she loves the creative process. Being creative is nothing new for Debra. As a child in Florida, she used to make collages with old wood she found on the beach and miles of tape.

For the illustrations, Debra again turned to her daughter for inspiration. Papers, glue, scissors, and pencils that were crammed in her daughter's desk gave her the idea for the story's school setting. At last Debra had completed a fun adventure about the usually tame world of vocabulary.

Another book by Debra Frasier:
Out of the Ocean

Author's Purpose
Authors of fiction usually write to entertain, but they may have another purpose. What clues can help you figure out if Debra Frasier had more than one purpose for writing *Miss Alaineus*?

LOG ON For more information about Debra Frasier visit www.macmillanmh.com

40

Author's Craft

Humor

Debra Frasier added **humor** to her story by showing how Sage uses words and their definitions while thinking to herself. For example:

> I called my best friend, Starr, who is not *a luminous celestial object seen as a point of light in the sky*, but a very smart girl who listens perfectly on Vocabulary Day. (p. 22)

Discuss what makes Sage's thinking humorous. Ask students if the use of humor makes Sage's character more appealing. Then talk about what makes Sage's way of thinking unusual.

When students reread *Miss Alaineus,* have them identify other examples of Sage's use of words and how they add humor to the story.

Comprehension Check

Summarize

Use your Character and Plot Chart to help you summarize *Miss Alaineus*. Include only the most important events that lead to Sage's creative solution to her problem.

Character	Plot

Think and Compare

1. *Miss Alaineus* is written from Sage's point of view. How does this help you know what she is like? What words or phrases would you use to describe her? Use story details in your answer. **Story Structure: Character and Plot**

2. Reread page 38. What does Sage mean when she says, "there was gold in this mistake"? Use details from the story to support your answer. **Analyze**

3. Even the most **capable** people make mistakes. How do you feel when you make a mistake? Compare your feelings to Sage's feelings. **Analyze**

4. Why might it be helpful to have a sense of humor when you are trying to solve a problem? **Evaluate**

5. Look back at "The Talent Contest" on pages 18–19. How is Danny's experience similar to Sage's? Use details from each selection. **Reading/Writing Across Texts**

MISS ALAINEUS
QUEEN OF ALL MISCELLANEOUS THINGS

A COLLECTION OF UNRELATED OBJECTS   A CO

41

Strategies for Answering Questions

Author and Me

Model the Author and Me strategy with questions 1 and 2.

The answer is not stated in the selection, but there may be clues. Connect the clues with what you know to answer the question.

Question 1: Think Aloud On page 30 Sage says to herself, "I was Sage: one who shows wisdom, experience, judgment. Why were they laughing?" So I think Sage is a person who takes her schoolwork seriously, and does not often make mistakes. She is also sensitive. When the class laughs at her mistake, she turns red.

Question 2: Think Aloud I know that Sage won a gold trophy, so that is one reason why she feels there was "gold in this mistake." I think Sage also feels it taught her to poke fun at herself and to not take her mistakes so seriously.

Comprehension Check

SUMMARIZE

Have partners summarize the story by paraphrasing the most important plot events in *Miss Alaineus*. Remind students to use their Character and Plot Charts to help them organize their summaries.

THINK AND COMPARE

Sample answers are given.

1. **Character and Plot:** Sage explains her feelings and reactions to events, especially her feelings of embarrassment. She takes her schoolwork seriously and is sensitive about being teased. Her definitions show that she is smart and creative, as does the clever way she manages to win a trophy for originality at the Vocabulary Parade. **USE AUTHOR AND ME**

2. **Analyze:** Sage overcame her embarrassment and turned her mistake into a learning opportunity by coming up with a winning idea for the Vocabulary Parade. **USE AUTHOR AND ME**

3. **Text to Self:** Students may say they feel embarrassed, sad, or upset when they make mistakes. Sage shared these feelings. Students may also say they try to learn from their mistakes, like Sage.

4. **Text to World:** Answers will vary. Answers may include that when a person is upset, it is difficult for him or her to think clearly and logically.

FOCUS QUESTION

5. **Text to Text:** Both Danny and Sage were nervous about a school contest.

Objectives
- Read accurately with good prosody
- Rate: 100–120 WCPM

Materials
- Fluency Transparency 1
- Fluency Solutions
- Leveled Practice Books, p. 4

RESEARCH
Why It Matters

Fluency A good preparation activity for fluency practice is to listen to the text. Model reading shows students what the reading should sound like–and this can contribute to faster progress during the students' own oral reading practice.

Timothy Shanahan

LOG ON Go to
www.macmillanmh.com

On Level Practice Book O, page 4

read, I will pay attention to pauses and breaks in the text.

	Freddy slapped the table as he snorted. "Check this out,
10	Eva!" he said between chuckles.
15	Freddy grabbed my sketchbook and held it up next to my
26	startled face. Eva frowned, looked confused, and then finally
35	a gigantic smile crossed her face.
41	"You're good, Nadia," she said. "But, I don't get it."
51	What I'd drawn was a cartoon of *me*, with an oversized
62	head and tiny body. I'd added my trademark features.
71	A banner at the top read, "Science UN-Fair." Question marks
81	spun around my head and I had a very confused look—a
93	perfect caricature, I might add.
98	Freddy turned to me and said, "Eva was in the nurse's
109	office during fifth period. Remember? She got hurt playing
118	soccer during lunch."
121	"Oh, yeah," I said. And then I told Eva what she had
133	missed. 134

Comprehension Check

1. Who is the main character of this story? **Character** Nadia.
2. What did Nadia draw in her sketchbook? **Plot**
   a caricature of herself

	Words Read	–	Number of Errors	=	Words Correct Score
First Read		–		=	
Second Read		–		=	

 Approaching Practice Book A, page 4

 Beyond Practice Book B, page 4

Fluency
Repeated Reading: Intonation/Pausing

EXPLAIN/MODEL Tell students that part of reading with good prosody, or good expression, is grouping words together in meaningful phrases. Note that pausing and stopping when reading helps to distinguish meaningful phrases. Explain that the text on **Fluency Transparency 1** has been marked with slashes that indicate pauses and stops. A single slash indicates a pause, usually between phrases or dashes. A double slash indicates a stop, usually between sentences. Have the class listen carefully to your pauses and intonation as you read.

Transparency 1

I was tenth,/ and when Mrs. Page called out my word,/ I spelled:/ "Capital M-I-S-S,/ capital A-L-A-I-N-E-U-S,"/ and added,/ *"the woman on green spaghetti boxes whose hair is the color of uncooked pasta and turns into spaghetti at the ends."*//

There was a moment of silence in the room.// I smiled at Mrs. Page.// She waited to see if I would add anything else,/ and when I didn't,/ she grinned.// Not smiled/ —grinned://
to draw back the lips and bare the teeth, as in a very wide smile// —and the entire class burst into one huge giggling,/ laughing,/ falling-down mass of kids.// Forest was doubled over.// Starr,/ my best friend,/ was laughing so hard tears came to her eyes.// By now,/ even Mrs. Page was laughing.//

Fluency Transparency 1 from *Miss Alaineus,* page 30

Cooperative Learning

Access for All

PRACTICE/APPLY Reread the first paragraph with students. Then divide them into two groups and have the groups alternate reading sentences. Students will practice fluency using **Practice Book** page 4 or Fluency Solutions Audio CD.

Quick Check
Can students read accurately with good prosody?

During **Small Group Instruction**

If No → **Approaching Level** Fluency, p. 47N

If Yes → **On Level** Options, pp. 47Q–47R

Beyond Level Options, pp. 47S–47T

Comprehension

MAINTAIN SKILL
SETTING

EXPLAIN/MODEL

- The **setting** of a story is when and where the story takes place. Stories may take place in the present, past, or future.

- The setting can have an important effect on the characters and the events in the plot.

- If a flashback occurs in a story, pay attention to the setting. The events being described took place earlier and may have occurred in a different place.

- The setting of a story is usually revealed early in the plot. As you read pay attention to where the action is set.

PRACTICE/APPLY

Have students form three groups to discuss the setting of *Miss Alaineus* and analyze how it influences the problem and resolution of the story. Each group should share its answers with the class.

- Compare Sage's school to a school in another story. How important is the setting in each story?

- Suppose *Miss Alaineus* was set in a school in the past. How might the characters and the plot be different?

- If the events of *Miss Alaineus* occurred a hundred years in the future, how might the characters and the plot be different?

For comprehension practice use Graphic Organizers on **Teacher's Resource Book** pages 40–64.

Objective

- Analyze setting

Skills Trace

Character, Plot, Setting	
Introduce	19A–B
Practice / Apply	20–39; Leveled Practice, 2–3
Reteach / Review	47M–T, 51A–B, 52–69, 77M–T; Leveled Practice, 9–10
Assess	Weekly Tests; Units 1, 4 Tests; Benchmarks Tests A, B
Maintain	41B, 71B, 133B; 395A–B; 396–411, 419M–T, 661B; Leveled Practice, 113–114

Informational Text: Social Studies

GENRE: NONFICTION ARTICLE

Have students read the bookmark on **Student Book** page 42. Explain that a nonfiction article

- provides a short description of events, discoveries, or ideas;

- contains headings and/or questions that organize the information in the text;

- may include photos and captions, diagrams, charts, graphs, or tables.

Text Features: Photographs and Captions

EXPLAIN Photographs and captions help students understand content in an informational article. Photographs and captions give the reader additional information about the subject of the article.

PRACTICE/APPLY Point out the photographs and captions on pages 43–44. Have students discuss what these elements add to this article.

Language Arts

Genre

Nonfiction Articles provide information about real people, places, or events.

Text Feature

Photographs and Captions give visual examples that help explain what the text states.

Content Vocabulary

competition

orally

eliminates

The National SPELLING BEE

by Nicole Lee

Does the word *autochthonous* sound familiar? Luckily, to David Tidmarsh, it did. David correctly spelled *autochthonous* to win the 77th National Spelling Bee. David, from South Bend, Indiana, won the spelling championship at age 14. In the final round of **competition**, David beat Akshay Buddiga, a 13-year-old boy from Colorado.

42

Content Vocabulary

Discuss the three content vocabulary words listed for "The National Spelling Bee" on Student Book page 42: *competition, orally, eliminates.*

- A **competition** is a game or a contest. What kind of competition do you enjoy?

- When you tell something **orally**, you say it out loud. When do you answer questions orally?

- When someone **eliminates** something, he or she takes it away. Who eliminates people in a contest?

Welcome to the exciting and intense world of spelling bees. The National Spelling Bee takes place each June in Washington, D.C. The competition has been around for a long time. It began in 1925 with only nine contestants. In 2004 there were 265 contestants ranging in age from 8 to 15. Contestants for the National Spelling Bee come from English-speaking countries all over the world. Students from Jamaica, Puerto Rico, and even Saudi Arabia have competed in the National Spelling Bee.

It takes a lot of hard work and dedication to advance to the National Spelling Bee finals. Students spend a lot of time preparing for competition. The words chosen for the competition are chosen from the dictionary by a panel of word experts. There are more than 470,000 words in the dictionary, and any one of these words could be chosen for the competition. David spent several months preparing for the finals. He spent many hours studying a dictionary, and a list of 10,000 words that he created. Fortunately for David, *autochthonous* was one of the words on his list. After David won he said, "I was just hoping I got a word I studied."

Spelling contestants spend months poring over the dictionary. **3**

43

Paired Selection   Student page 43

Informational Text

Read "School Contests"

As you read, remind students to apply what they have learned about photos and captions. Also have them identify clues to the meanings of the highlighted words.

1 COMPARE AND CONTRAST

How has the National Spelling Bee changed? (It has grown. Initially, there were nine contestants. In 2004 there were 265.)

2 WRITER'S CRAFT: A GOOD PARAGRAPH

Reread this paragraph. Which sentence is a topic sentence that lets the reader know what the subject of the paragraph will be? (the first sentence) What are some interesting supporting details that add information about the subject? (Answers might include that any of the 470,000 words in the dictionary might be used in the competition.)

3 TEXT FEATURES: PHOTOGRAPHS AND CAPTIONS

What does the caption tell you about the photo on this page? (The caption explains that the contestants study for months.)

ELL

Make Questions/Comparisons Summarize the selection first for students and help them generate questions about the topic.

Give other examples of the content words or demonstrate their meanings. For example, demonstrate the meaning of *eliminate* by writing "sanderwiche" on the board. Tell students to eliminate letters to guess the hidden word.

Have students point to a caption and a photo to make sure they understand the words. To help students compare Sage and David, write this sentence frame on the board: They both _____. David_____, but Sage _____.

Informational Text

4 **DRAW CONCLUSIONS**

Based on the text you have read so far, what can you conclude about the contestants who compete in spelling bees? (They are dedicated students who are willing to spend months preparing for the contest.)

5 **TEXT FEATURES: PHOTOGRAPHS AND CAPTIONS**

Tested

How do the photos and captions add to the information presented in the article? (The photos show the emotions of the contestants and other details about the events described in the text.)

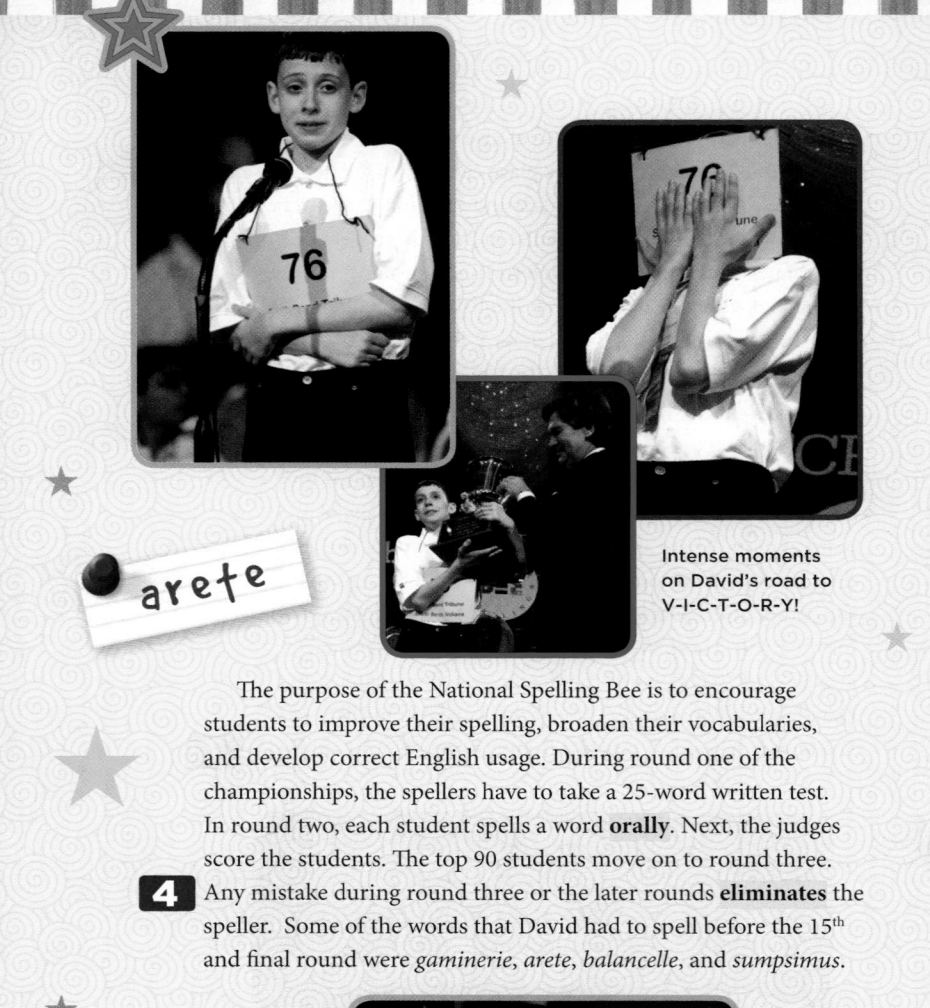

Intense moments on David's road to V-I-C-T-O-R-Y!

The purpose of the National Spelling Bee is to encourage students to improve their spelling, broaden their vocabularies, and develop correct English usage. During round one of the championships, the spellers have to take a 25-word written test. In round two, each student spells a word **orally**. Next, the judges score the students. The top 90 students move on to round three. **4** Any mistake during round three or the later rounds **eliminates** the speller. Some of the words that David had to spell before the 15th and final round were *gaminerie*, *arete*, *balancelle*, and *sumpsimus*.

5 Akshay (left) and David anxiously await their turns.

44

▪ **On Level Practice Book O,** page 5

Photographs or drawings provide a visual image of what is happening in the story. **Captions** help explain what the photographs or drawings are about.

Look at the drawing and read the caption. Then answer the questions.

Kids' Mile Finish Line

Fifth graders learn about fitness and health by running a one mile race.

1. What does the drawing show? It shows the finish line of a foot race with two students getting medals from adults.

2. What other information do you learn from the caption? The racers are fifth graders. They are running a one-mile race to learn about health and fitness.

★ **Approaching Practice Book A,** page 5
◆ **Beyond Practice Book B,** page 5

Spellers qualify for the finals by winning locally sponsored spelling bees in their home communities. Qualifying for the national competition is a significant accomplishment. Every student who advances to the national competition is awarded a prize. The champion gets $17,000, a set of encyclopedias, an engraved trophy, and several other prizes. When asked what he would do with the prize money, David said, "I might put it in a savings account," and "I'll probably take a little and spend it at the mall."

Connect and Compare

1. Look at the photo of the spellers sitting on the stage. What feelings do you think the contestants experienced during the competition? **Photographs and Captions**

2. What advice do you think David would give to someone who wanted to enter a spelling bee? **Evaluate**

3. Think about this article and *Miss Alaineus*. Compare how Sage prepared for the vocabulary bee and David prepared for the spelling bee. **Reading and Writing Across Texts**

Language Arts Activity

Does your state have spelling bees? Research spelling bees in your state and write a paragraph about what you need to do to enter a local spelling bee.

LOG ON Find out more about the National Spelling Bee at **www.macmillanmh.com**

45

Informational Text

Connect and Compare

SUGGESTED ANSWERS

1. Spellers may be nervous before their turn; upset if they misspelled a word; happy if they spell a word correctly. **PHOTOGRAPHS AND CAPTIONS**

2. David would probably suggest studying the dictionary, making flashcards, and practicing in front of other people. **EVALUATE**

FOCUS QUESTION

3. David studied the dictionary and created a list of words to study. Sage also had a list of words to study, but she made up the definitions for the vocabulary words. **READING/WRITING ACROSS TEXTS**

Language Arts Activity

Call on a volunteer to read his or her paragraph. Ask the student to share what resources he or she used.

LOG ON **Technology**

Internet Research and Inquiry Activity
Students can find more facts at
www.macmillanmh.com

Research and Inquiry

School Contests and Competitions Tell students there are contests and competitions for almost every area of interest. Have students brainstorm contests and competitions they know about.

Divide students into groups, giving each an area of interest to research, such as science, art, poetry, photography, and creative writing. Have groups research different contests and competitions. Have groups use discussion techniques to arrive at a consensus on questions that will direct the investigation, resources, and research strategies to use.

When their research is complete, have each group create an informational presentation that includes supportive, concrete details and explanations about contests, rules, and awards. Encourage students to follow up on a competition that might interest them. Allow students time to ask questions that seek information not already discussed.

Connect
Language Arts

WRITING
- Personal Narrative
- **Writer's Craft:** A Good Paragraph

WORD STUDY
- Words in Context
- Context Clues: Synonyms
- **Phonics:** Words with Short Vowels
- Vocabulary Building

SPELLING
- Words with Short Vowels

GRAMMAR
- Sentences

SMALL GROUP OPTIONS
- Differentiated Instruction, pp. 47M–47V

Writing

A Good Paragraph

READ THE STUDENT MODEL

Read the bookmark about writing a good paragraph. Explain that a well-structured paragraph helps readers understand a writer's ideas and shows that the writer has important information about the topic.

Have students turn to the first paragraph on page 46. Point out the topic sentence and supporting details.

Then have the class read Christina M.'s **personal narrative** and the callouts. Tell students they will write their own narratives, organizing their thoughts effectively by writing good paragraphs.

46

▼ Writer's Craft

A Good Paragraph

A **good paragraph** has a topic sentence that lets a reader know what the subject of the paragraph will be. Supporting details add information about the subject.

WRITE ABOUT A SCHOOL CONTEST

Always One Hundred Percent
by Christina M.

My topic sentence is a clue that practicing spelling words is the main idea of the paragraph.

I use supporting details to add information about my topic sentence.

Every Friday morning my friends and I sit on the rug in class and practice our spelling words before the weekly test. We have a contest to see who can spell the words the fastest. One of us sits in our teacher's chair and reads the spelling words. Whoever slaps the floor first gets a two-second head start spelling the word.

A few weeks ago, Miguel had been reading the words, and Kevin and I were spelling them. For one of the words, I lifted my hand in such a hurry that it flew back and hit my nose. We all laughed hysterically. Miguel laughed so hard he fell out of the teacher's chair, and that started us laughing all over again.

Our weekly contest works out well even when nothing funny happens. We get one hundred percent on our spelling tests! You should try it. It's a fun way to study spelling words.

46

Features of a Personal Narrative

In a personal narrative, the writer shares a real experience. The writer tells what happened and how he or she feels.

- A personal narrative usually tells what happened in chronological order.
- It is written from a first-person point of view and uses the words *I, me, my*, and *mine*.
- Paragraphs have clear topic sentences and appropriate supporting details.
- It includes interesting word choices and descriptive language.

Your Turn

Write two or three paragraphs about a school contest that you have entered or that you would like to enter. Tell about what happened to you and how you felt. Be sure to use a topic sentence and supporting details in each paragraph. Use the writer's checklist to check your writing.

Writer's Checklist

✓ **Ideas and Content:** Are my ideas clear?

✓ **Organization:** Did I use a topic sentence to create a strong beginning for my paragraph?

✓ **Voice:** Do the details tell how I feel? Do they make my writing sound like something I would have written?

✓ **Word Choice:** Did I choose strong words to tell what is happening?

✓ **Sentence Fluency:** Did I join related sentences to make compound sentences?

✓ **Conventions:** Did I capitalize proper nouns? Did I check my spelling?

47

 Transparency 1: **Main Idea and Details Chart**
Transparency 2: **Draft**
Transparency 3: **Revision**

 **Transparency 1**

Main Idea and Details Chart

Main Idea	Details
My friends and I practice our spelling words before the weekly test.	We try to see who can spell the words the fastest.
	One of us reads the spelling words.
	Whoever slaps the floor first gets a head start spelling the word.

Writing Transparency 1

PREWRITE

Discuss the writing prompt on page 47. Have students work in pairs or independently to brainstorm ideas. Ask them to choose topics about school contests or self-select another topic they would like to share with readers. Make sure students set a purpose for writing and identify their audience.

Display **Transparency 1.** Point out that the main idea of the second paragraph is in the first column and supporting details are in the second. Have students use main idea and details charts to plan their narratives. See page 47B for a minilesson on **Using a Graphic Organizer.**

DRAFT

Display **Transparency 2.** Discuss strategies for improving the draft by moving or adding topic sentences. Before students begin writing, present the lesson on **A Good Paragraph** on page 47A. Then have students use their charts to write their narratives. Remind them to include topic sentences and sufficient supporting details.

REVISE

Display **Transparency 3.** Discuss the revisions. Students may choose to revise their drafts or place them in portfolios to work on later. If students revise, have partners use the Writer's Checklist on page 47. Have them **proofread** their writing. Review proofreading marks on **Teacher's Resource Book** page 52. For **Publishing Options** see page 47A.

For lessons on **Sentences, Spelling,** and **Ideas and Content,** see page 47B and **5 Day Spelling** and **Grammar,** pages 47G–47J.

Publishing Options

Students can tell their stories orally to the class. See the Speaking and Listening tips below. They can also use their best cursive to write their narratives. (See **Teacher's Resource Book** pages 168–173 for cursive models and practice.) Students can then create illustrations for their narratives and compile them into a class booklet with a catchy title.

Speaking and Listening

SPEAKING STRATEGIES

- Practice reading your narrative before presenting it to the class.
- Speak clearly and with expression.
- Look up from time to time. Make eye contact with the audience.

LISTENING STRATEGIES

- Focus your attention on the speaker.
- Sit quietly and listen carefully.
- Be prepared to ask questions or express your opinion.

4- and 6-Point Scoring Rubrics

Use the rubrics on pages 143G–143H to score published writing.

Writing Process

For a complete writing process lesson, see Unit Writing pages 143A–143H.

A Good Paragraph

EXPLAIN/MODEL

Good writers organize their paragraphs in a particular way. They begin by stating the main ideas in topic sentences. Then in the following sentences writers add supporting details that explain or elaborate on the stated main ideas. Those sentences flow in a logical order. Display **Transparency 4.**

Think Aloud The first sentence tells me about the writer. These traits explain why the writer decides to run for student council historian. I can tell that the second sentence is the topic sentence because it states the main idea of the paragraph. The other sentences will give me details about the election.

Transparency 4

The Vote Is In!
by Sheldon E.

I like to write, and I like history. I decided to enter the student council election for the office of historian.

_____ I told the students why I was the best person for the job.

_____ I also made campaign buttons for students to wear.

_____ I wrote a speech to deliver to the students on Election Day.

_____ I asked my sister and a friend to act in my skit.

_____ When all the votes were counted, I learned that the school's history was in my hands—at least for this year!

_____ First, I made campaign posters to hang in the classrooms.

_____ Before the election, I spent time talking with the voters about my ideas.

_____ I included a skit with my speech.

4; 2; 5; 7; 8; 1; 3; 6

Writing Transparency 4

PRACTICE/APPLY

Work with students to place the first two or three supporting sentences in an order that makes sense for readers. Then have students continue this work in pairs. Next, have students work independently to label topic sentences and supporting details in nonfiction texts that they have read recently.

As students write their own narratives, make sure that their paragraphs follow good paragraph form, with clear topic sentences and supporting details. Encourage partners to check each other's work.

Writer's Toolbox

Writing Trait: Ideas and Content

Explain/Model As writers express different ideas in their writing, they need to make sure that their ideas are clear and that one idea leads naturally to the next. Have students review Christina's story on page 46. Point out that Christina begins by telling readers that she and her friends have found a way to study spelling, goes on to explain their process, and ends with the results of the process. All of the ideas in her paragraphs connect.

Practice/Apply As students draft their narratives, have them think about the most logical sequence for presenting their ideas. Point out that sentences that do not flow logically may need to be moved or deleted.

Using a Graphic Organizer

Explain/Model Graphic organizers help writers plan their writing before they actually start putting words on paper. Creating graphic organizers helps writers brainstorm ideas, sequence information, and solve potential problems. By taking these steps before drafting, writers often find that the entire writing process proceeds smoothly and quickly. Discuss some common graphic organizers for writing, such as story maps and idea webs.

Practice/Apply Before students begin writing, have them use main idea and details charts to organize the information they plan to present in their narratives.

Sentences

Explain/Model A sentence is a series of words that expresses a complete thought: *I ran to the mailbox.* A sentence can be a statement or a question. Some statements can be exclamations.

Practice/Apply Have students look at the article that begins on page 42. Have them identify each kind of sentence and explain their reasoning. For a complete lesson on sentences, see pages 47I–47J.

Mechanics Point out that periods, question marks, and exclamation points end sentences. Have students correct end punctuation as they proofread. Remind students to vary the types of sentences they use.

Spelling Words with Short Vowels

Point out the word *practice* in the first sentence in the narrative on page 46. The short vowel sound in the second syllable has an unexpected spelling. Other short vowel words such as *tough, rough,* and *live* have unexpected spellings. Remind students to pay attention when they spell words with short vowel sounds. They can use a print or an online dictionary to check spelling in their drafts. For a complete lesson on spelling words with short vowels, see pages 47G–47H.

Technology

Suggest that students print their work and proofread it. Have them also proof it on the screen. They may want to use the spell-check function. Then have them tell which way works best. Discuss the limits of spell-check.

Objectives

- Apply knowledge of word meaning and context clues
- Use synonyms to determine word meanings

Materials

- Vocabulary Transparencies 1, 2
- Leveled Practice Books, p. 6

Vocabulary

capable (p. 33) having skill or power

categories (p. 26) groups or classes of things

luminous (p. 22) bright; shining

strands (p. 27) things similar to threads

credit (p. 32) something owed to a person for extra work

soggy (p. 37) very wet or damp

slumped (p. 33) fell or sunk heavily

gigantic (p. 25) like a giant; huge

ELL | Access for All

Restate For each word, say, for example, *I can win. I am _____ of winning.* Students repeat the sentence with the correct vocabulary word.

Review
Vocabulary

 ## Words in Context

EXPLAIN/MODEL

Review the meanings of the vocabulary words. Display **Transparency 1.** Model how to use synonyms and context clues to fill in the first missing word.

Think Aloud In the first sentence, the word needed to describe towels must have to do with making something wet. A synonym for *wet* is *soggy*. When I try using *soggy* in the sentence it makes sense.

 Transparency 1

capable   categories   luminous   strands   credit   soggy slumped   gigantic

The (1) <u>soggy</u> towels made the seat wet.
I am able to paint, but Archie is more (2) <u>capable</u>.
I did more work, and the teacher gave me extra (3) <u>credit</u>.
The (4) <u>gigantic</u> reflection made me look huge.
The thread had to be pulled in individual (5) <u>strands</u>.
Her face looked (6) <u>luminous</u> in the pale golden light.
Dan was too tired to sit up and (7) <u>slumped</u> in his seat.
We needed ten sections, one for each of the (8) <u>categories</u>.

Vocabulary Transparency 1

PRACTICE/APPLY

 Help students complete item 2. Then instruct students to complete the remaining sentences on their own. Review students' answers as a class, or instruct them to check their answers with partners. Discuss the context clues they used to figure out the missing words.

 **Diamante Poems** Assign a word to student pairs, and have them write diamante poems. A diamante poem is written in the shape of a diamond. It does not have to rhyme but each line uses specific types of words like adjectives and *-ing* words. For example, students might write a poem using words associated with *luminous*: *light, bright, clear, brilliant*. Have pairs share poems with the class.

STRATEGY
CONTEXT CLUES: SYNONYMS

EXPLAIN/MODEL

- Locating synonyms can help readers understand the meanings of other words in a sentence. When students cannot figure out the meaning of a word with context clues or synonyms, they should consult a dictionary.

 Display **Transparency 2.** Model how to figure out the meaning of the word *luminous*. *Glowing* also describes the couple, so it might be a synonym of *luminous*.

 Transparency 2

CONTEXT CLUES/SYNONYMS
The royal couple looked simply *luminous*. Everywhere they went a glowing light seemed to wrap itself around them. Their kingdom was *gigantic*, and their presence was just as large.

Vocabulary Strategy Transparency 2

PRACTICE/APPLY

Have students use the transparency to find the context clue for *gigantic*. Then have students write a sentence including a synonym as a context clue. Then partners can trade sentences.

Quick Check
Can students determine word meanings?
Can students decode meanings with synonyms?

During **Small Group Instruction**

If No → **Approaching Level** Vocabulary, pp. 47N–47O

If Yes → **On Level** Options, pp. 47Q–47R

Beyond Level Options, pp. 47S–47T

ELL
Access for All

Synonyms Make sure students understand the text in the transparency. Have them work in pairs to create synonym word cards. Then have partners take turns showing a card and naming the word and its synonym.

On Level Practice Book O, page 6

You can learn the meaning of an unfamiliar word by using the words around it as clues. Look at the words that appear near the word that you don't know, and try to find a **synonym** of that word to help you figure out its meaning. Remember that a synonym is a word with a similar meaning.

Circle the synonym of the underlined word in each sentence.

1. The size of the hot-air balloon <u>decreased</u> and (diminished) as air was let out of it.

2. The (awful) sound was <u>unbearable</u> and it woke me up.

3. The roses <u>flourished</u> and (thrived) more than any other plant in Mrs. Lyon's garden.

4. It can be <u>hazardous</u> to play near a downed power line because electric currents are (dangerous.)

5. Chris was (modest) about winning his national award because he is <u>humble</u>.

6. The <u>extravagant</u> party <u>had circus</u> performers, an orchestra, and chefs. Bob thought it was too (expensive) for only a few guests.

7. The letter was <u>anonymous</u> so the sender is (unknown.)

8. The basketball team returned <u>victorious</u> because they had (won) the state championship.

9. The teachers said soda is <u>prohibited</u> because bottles are (forbidden) in the gym.

10. The paper towel will (soak up) the spilled milk because it will <u>absorb</u> all the moisture.

 Approaching Practice Book A, page 6

 **Beyond Practice Book B,** page 6

Objective
- Decode words with short vowels

Materials
- Leveled Practice Books, p. 7
- Teacher's Resource Book, p. 5

ELL | Access for All

Pronunciation The short vowel sound may be difficult for some speakers. Spend additional time having students pronounce the words and use them in sentences. Provide additional practice in writing and spelling the words.

On Level Practice Book O, page 7

The letters *a, e, i, o,* and *u* usually stand for the short vowel sounds /a/ in *damp,* /e/ in *ten,* /i/ in *sit,* /o/ in *hop,* and /u/ in *fun.* Some words with short vowel sounds do not follow this pattern. For example, *ea,* as in *head,* can have the /e/ sound and *ou* followed by *gh,* as in *rough,* can have the /u/ sound.

Place each word in the column that describes the short vowel sound found in the word.

batch	rough	stump	jut	tenth
dove	myth	nick	sense	cot
lead	notch	scan	tough	damp
lot	stamp	sick	fence	rhythm

short **a**	short **e**	short **i**	short **o**	short **u**
batch	tenth	myth	cot	rough
scan	sense	nick	notch	stump
damp	lead	sick	lot	jut
stamp	fence	rhythm		dove
				tough

⭐ **Approaching Practice Book A,** page 7
◆ **Beyond Practice Book B,** page 7

Phonics
Words with Short Vowels

 **EXPLAIN/MODEL** When a one-syllable word has a CVC (consonant-vowel-consonant) or CVCC (consonant-vowel-consonant-consonant) pattern, as in *can* or *back,* the vowel sound is usually short. The letters *a, e, i, o,* and *u* usually stand respectively for the sounds /a/, /e/, /i/, /o/, and /u/ when they appear in a word with one of these patterns. Share examples: *tent, wing, sock,* and *must.* Write *lamp.*

Think Aloud This one-syllable word has a CVCC pattern. A word with this pattern usually has a short vowel sound. In this case, the vowel sound is probably /a/. I know how to pronounce the consonant blends at the beginning and end. When I put them all together, I get /lamp/. That is a word I know. If I can't figure out how to say a word, I can check a dictionary.

PRACTICE/APPLY Write *luck, lock, sack, bend, tick, sung, rent, bath, ramp, rust.* Ask volunteers to read each word and identify the short vowel sound and the letter that stands for it. Help students practice using a dictionary's pronunciation key to check pronunciations of unfamiliar words.

Decode Multisyllabic Words Write *dumptruck, sandbox, thumbtack, handbag, bedrock.* Explain that these are compound words, made up of two smaller words. Model decoding *dumptruck.* Point to and read the word *dump.* Then read *truck.* Draw a line between the two words that make up this compound word. Students should repeat *dumptruck* after you. Have students decode the other compound words on their own. Students should syllabicate the compound words and sort them by short vowel sound. For more practice, see the Decodable Passages on **Teacher's Resource Book** page 5.

 **Short Vowel Combo** Have partners use the dictionary to find three unfamiliar short vowel words containing the CVCC pattern. Pairs can trade to see if they can say the new words correctly. Have them discuss the words' meanings.

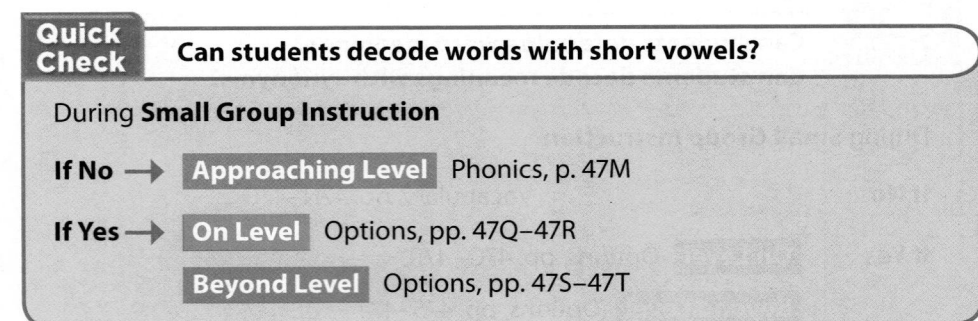

Quick Check	Can students decode words with short vowels?

During **Small Group Instruction**

If No → Approaching Level Phonics, p. 47M

If Yes → On Level Options, pp. 47Q–47R

Beyond Level Options, pp. 47S–47T

Vocabulary Building

Oral Language

Expand Vocabulary Have students make word webs using the following prompt:

Write *School Contests* on the center of a word web. Have students use the selection, as well as dictionaries, thesauruses, and encyclopedias, to find words that relate to this week's theme. You may include words such as *competitor, skillful,* or *strategy*. Write these words and as many synonyms as possible in circles that radiate from the center of the web. Have students discuss contests using the words.

Apply Vocabulary

Write a Paragraph Have students use the vocabulary words *capable, categories, credit, strands,* and *gigantic* in a paragraph about a school contest. They should include synonyms as context clues where possible. Students can read their paragraphs aloud to a partner.

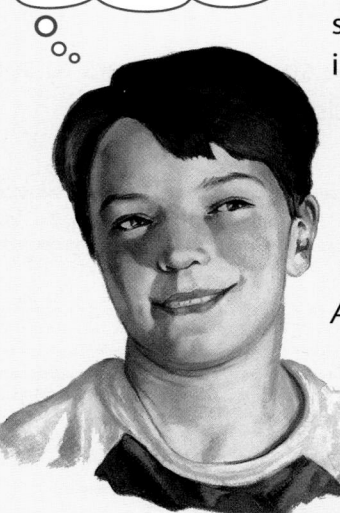

FIRST PLACE

BEST CLASS ART SHOW

Vocabulary Building

IS THIS A GRIN OR A SMILE?

Synonyms There are many synonyms placed in sentences as context clues in *Miss Alaineus,* such as "giggling, laughing, falling-down," to describe the students' reactions to Sage. Challenge students to select words from *Miss Alaineus* and to brainstorm as many synonyms for each word as they can.

Vocabulary Review

Have a Vocabulary Contest Working in pairs, have students write a short paragraph using all eight vocabulary words: *capable, categories, luminous, strands, credit, soggy, slumped, gigantic.* Students can read their paragraphs aloud. The pair who can use the most words correctly in the fewest sentences wins.

Challenge: If a student challenges any pair's word usage and is right, that pair is out, but only if the challenger can correct the mistake.

Technology

CD ROM

Vocabulary PuzzleMaker

LOG ON

For additional vocabulary and spelling games go to www.macmillanmh.com

Short Vowels

Spelling Words

jut	cot	stump
nick	fling	tough
tenth	notch	laugh
shrug	gush	guess
stuff	scan	lead
sense	batch	dove
damp	rough	

Review past, dock, plum

Challenge cinch, blond

Dictation Sentences

1. The desk <u>jut</u> out unevenly.
2. The <u>nick</u> on her leg hurt.
3. The <u>tenth</u> word was the hardest.
4. I <u>shrug</u> when I don't know.
5. <u>Stuff</u> the papers into your bag.
6. It makes no <u>sense</u> to wear a hat.
7. The <u>damp</u> air made my hair frizzy.
8. He slept in the <u>cot</u> for a few hours.
9. Don't <u>fling</u> items across the room.
10. The <u>notch</u> is at the edge.
11. I saw water <u>gush</u> from the pipe.
12. <u>Scan</u> your homework for errors.
13. She graded a <u>batch</u> of papers.
14. It was a <u>rough</u> day at school.
15. He was sitting on a tree <u>stump</u>.
16. That was a <u>tough</u> word to spell.
17. My brother loves to <u>laugh</u> loudly.
18. He took a <u>guess</u> at the answer.
19. I prefer <u>lead</u> pencils to pens.
20. A <u>dove</u> is a symbol of peace.

Review/Challenge Words

1. She won the <u>past</u> two years.
2. The ship stood at the <u>dock</u>.
3. The <u>plum</u> was juicy and sweet.
4. We agreed the test was a <u>cinch</u>.
5. The <u>blond</u> girl is new.

Words in **bold** are from the main selection.

Day 1 Pretest

ASSESS PRIOR KNOWLEDGE

Use the Dictation Sentences. Say the underlined word, read the sentence, and repeat the word. Have students write the words on **Spelling Practice Book** page 1. For a modified list, use the first 12 Spelling Words and the Review Words. For a more challenging list, use Spelling Words 3–20 and the Challenge Words. Students may correct their own tests.

Have students cut apart the Spelling Word Cards BLM on **Teacher's Resource Book** page 66 and figure out a way to sort them. They can save the cards for use throughout the week.

For additional practice, use Spelling Practice Book page 2.

For **Leveled Word Lists**, go to **www.macmillanmh.com**

Day 2 Word Sorts

TEACHER AND STUDENT SORTS

- Write *damp*, *tenth*, *fling*, *cot*, and *jut* on the board. Point out that each of these words has a short vowel sound. Underline the vowels as you pronounce the words.

- Make a chart on the board, using the short vowel sounds /a/, /e/, /i/, /o/, and /u/ as column headings. Have students copy the chart in their word study notebooks and sort the Spelling Words, Review Words, and Challenge Words by vowel sounds.

- Discuss words that have unexpected vowel spellings (*rough, tough, laugh, guess, lead, dove*). See if students can think of other words that are spelled the same way.

- Invite student partners to sort the words any other way.

Spelling Practice Book, page 1–2

Fold back the paper along the dotted line. Write the words in the blanks as they are read aloud. When you finish the test, unfold the paper. Use the list at the right to correct any spelling mistakes.

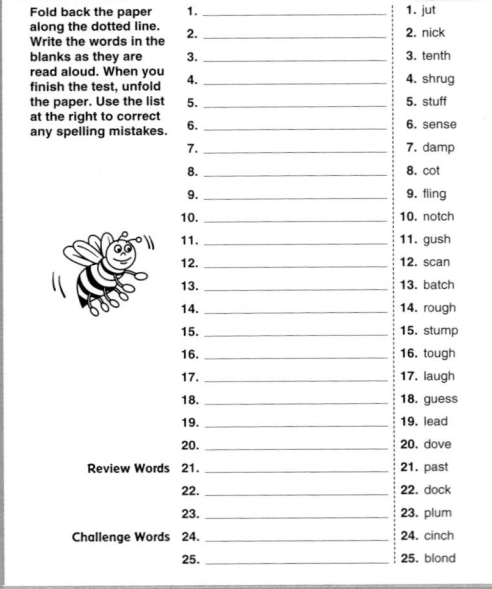

1.	1. jut
2.	2. nick
3.	3. tenth
4.	4. shrug
5.	5. stuff
6.	6. sense
7.	7. damp
8.	8. cot
9.	9. fling
10.	10. notch
11.	11. gush
12.	12. scan
13.	13. batch
14.	14. rough
15.	15. stump
16.	16. tough
17.	17. laugh
18.	18. guess
19.	19. lead
20.	20. dove
Review Words 21.	21. past
22.	22. dock
23.	23. plum
Challenge Words 24.	24. cinch
25.	25. blond

Spelling Practice Book, page 3

batch	dove	stuff	tenth	tough
nick	fling	notch	scan	stump
rough	shrug	jut	guess	laugh
lead	gush	damp	cot	sense

Sort each spelling word by finding the sound and spelling pattern to which it belongs.

Short a spelled a
1. batch
2. damp
3. scan

Short a spelled au
1. laugh

Short e spelled e
1. tenth
2. sense

Short e spelled ue
1. guess

Short e spelled ea
1. lead

Short i spelled i
1. nick
2. fling

Short o spelled o
1. cot
2. notch

Short u spelled u
1. stump
2. jut
3. shrug
4. stuff
5. gush

Short u spelled o
1. dove

Short u spelled ou
1. rough
2. tough

Word Meanings

CATEGORIES

Read each group of words below. Ask students to copy the words into their word study notebooks, completing the group by adding a Spelling Word.

1. bed, crib, _____ (cot)
2. smile, giggle, _____ (laugh)
3. robin, wren, _____ (dove)
4. wet, moist, _____ (damp)
5. toss, throw, _____ (fling)

Challenge students to come up with other word groups to which they can add Spelling Words, Review Words, or Challenge Words.

Students may write fill-in-the-blank sentences for five of the words, then exchange papers with a partner to complete each other's sentences.

Review and Proofread

SPELLING REVIEW

Continue reviewing words with short vowels. Write *past*, *dock*, and *plum* on the board. Have students identify the short vowel sounds in each word.

PROOFREAD AND WRITE

Write the following sentences on the board, including the misspelled words. Ask students to proofread, circling the misspelled words and writing them correctly.

1. I gess I need a new led pencil. (guess, lead)
2. Don't laff at the bach of cookies I made. (laugh, batch)
3. The gosh of water made their clothes demp. (gush, damp)
4. The cut needs to jot out from the wall a little more. (cot, jut)

Assess and Reteach

POSTTEST

Use the Dictation Sentences on page 47G for the Posttest.

If students have difficulty with any words in the lesson, have them place the words in a list entitled "Spelling Words I Want to Remember" in their word study notebooks.

Challenge student partners to look for other words that have the same short-vowel sounds they studied this week, either in their reading or in other materials. Partners should work together to sort the words by vowel sounds.

Spelling Practice Book, page 4

batch	dove	stuff	tenth	tough
nick	fling	notch	scan	stump
rough	shrug	jut	guess	laugh
lead	gush	damp	cot	sense

Definitions

Write the spelling word that matches each definition below.

1. throw _____ fling
2. wet _____ damp
3. small bed _____ cot
4. pour out _____ gush
5. mark _____ notch
6. stick out _____ jut
7. bird _____ dove
8. small cut _____ nick
9. confuse _____ stump
10. not smooth _____ rough
11. group _____ batch
12. read quickly _____ scan

Finish the Sentences

Write the spelling word that best completes each sentence.

13. It was a _____ tough word to spell.
14. The _____ tenth question was the hardest of all.
15. His answer did not make _____ sense.
16. She was happy and started to _____ laugh.
17. She took a _____ guess because she did not know the answer.
18. He was unsure and answered the question with a _____ shrug.
19. He had too much _____ stuff in his desk.
20. She gave him a _____ lead pencil for the test.

Spelling Practice Book, page 5

Circle the misspelled words in the set of instructions. Write the words correctly on the lines below.

You will receive a list of ten words for the spelling bee. Before the contest begins, (skain) the list of words. The (tinth) word on the list is a bonus word. Its spelling is unusual and may (stumpe) you. You will get an extra point if you spell the bonus word correctly.

Here are some tips for the contest. If a word does not make (cents) to you, ask to hear it again. If you are not sure how to spell a word, take a (gess). Last but not least, don't worry if your hands feel (dap). That just means you are feeling a little nervous.

1. _____ scan
2. _____ tenth
3. _____ stump
4. _____ sense
5. _____ guess
6. _____ damp

Writing Activity

Have you ever watched or taken part in a contest? Write a description of what happened or what you think might happen at a contest, using four spelling words.

_____
_____
_____
_____
_____
_____
_____
_____
_____
_____
_____

Spelling Practice Book, page 6

Look at the words in each set below. One word in each set is spelled correctly. Use a pencil to fill in the circle next to the correct word. Before you begin, look at the sample set of words. Sample A has been done for you. Do Sample B by yourself. When you are sure you know what to do, you may go on with the rest of the page.

Sample A:
- Ⓐ lump
- Ⓑ lumpe ●
- Ⓒ lumpp
- Ⓓ luump

Sample B:
- Ⓔ tacke
- Ⓕ taak
- Ⓖ tack
- Ⓗ takk

1.
- Ⓐ batch
- Ⓑ bach
- Ⓒ baatch
- Ⓓ bache

2.
- Ⓔ rugh
- Ⓕ rughe
- Ⓖ rough
- Ⓗ rogh

3.
- Ⓐ stumpe
- Ⓑ stuump
- Ⓒ stumpp
- Ⓓ stump

4.
- Ⓔ joot
- Ⓕ jut
- Ⓖ jat
- Ⓗ gat

5.
- Ⓐ tough
- Ⓑ touff
- Ⓒ tuf
- Ⓓ tugh

6.
- Ⓔ nik
- Ⓕ nikke
- Ⓖ nicke
- Ⓗ nick

7.
- Ⓐ shrugg
- Ⓑ shrug
- Ⓒ shruge
- Ⓓ shruug

8.
- Ⓔ tenth
- Ⓕ teenth
- Ⓖ tenthe
- Ⓗ teenthe

9.
- Ⓐ stouff
- Ⓑ stuff
- Ⓒ stufe
- Ⓓ stuffe

10.
- Ⓔ lafe
- Ⓕ laagh
- Ⓖ lagh
- Ⓗ laugh

11.
- Ⓐ gess
- Ⓑ gues
- Ⓒ guess
- Ⓓ guss

12.
- Ⓔ sense
- Ⓕ senss
- Ⓖ sens
- Ⓗ seens

13.
- Ⓐ dampe
- Ⓑ dammp
- Ⓒ daamp
- Ⓓ damp

14.
- Ⓔ kot
- Ⓕ koot
- Ⓖ cot
- Ⓗ cott

15.
- Ⓐ fling
- Ⓑ flinge
- Ⓒ fliing
- Ⓓ faling

16.
- Ⓔ guush
- Ⓕ gushe
- Ⓖ gush
- Ⓗ gussh

17.
- Ⓐ dove
- Ⓑ duv
- Ⓒ duve
- Ⓓ dov

18.
- Ⓔ lead
- Ⓕ lede
- Ⓖ leade
- Ⓗ ledd

19.
- Ⓐ nootch
- Ⓑ noch
- Ⓒ notch
- Ⓓ noutch

20.
- Ⓔ scane
- Ⓕ scan
- Ⓖ scaan
- Ⓗ schan

5 Day Grammar

Daily Language Activities

Use these activities to introduce each day's lesson. Write the day's activity on the board, or use **Daily Language Transparency 1**.

DAY 1
i caught a cold. I had to stay home from school on Tuesday I missed Vocabulary Day at school (1: I,; 2: Tuesday.; 3: school.)

DAY 2
Tomorrow we are going on our tinth field trip Bring your permission slips and bus money to school? don't forget. (1: tenth; 2: trip.; 3: school. Don't)

DAY 3
We are going to have a Vocabulary Bee today? I'll choose some tuff words. Who would like to go first (1: today.; 2: tough; 3: first?)

DAY 4
Why is everyone laffing! Mrs Page wrote the definition on the chalkboard. I was embarrassed? (1: laughing? Mrs.; 2: embarrassed.)

DAY 5
I sat on my kot and stared at the floor. i thought about the Vocabulary Parade. What kind of costume could I make (1: cot; 2: I; 3: make?)

ELL   **Access for All**

Analyze Language Write on the board: *I am reading a book. Going to the store.* Use the examples to explain a complete sentence and sentence fragment. Write other examples. Have students identify each one as a sentence or as a fragment.

Sentences

Day 1 Introduce the Concept

INTRODUCE SENTENCES

Present the following:

- A sentence is a group of words that expresses a complete thought: *Joanna showed bad behavior by walking off the field.*

- A sentence fragment is a group of words that does not express a complete thought: *leaving her team at a time when we needed her*

- Every sentence begins with a capital letter and ends with a punctuation mark.

- A statement is a sentence that tells something. It ends with a period: *We had a spelling bee at school yesterday.*

- A question is a sentence that asks something. It ends with a question mark: *Do you know the meaning of* miscellaneous?

See Grammar Transparency 1 for modeling and guided practice.

Grammar Practice Book, page 1

- A **sentence** is a group of words that express a complete thought.
- A **sentence fragment** is a group of words that does not express a complete thought.
- Every sentence begins with a **capital letter** and ends with a **punctuation mark.**
- A **statement** is a sentence that tells something. It ends with a period.
- A **question** is a sentence that asks something. It ends with a question mark.

Read each group of words. Place a period on the line at the end if it is a sentence. If it is a sentence fragment, write an *F* on the line.
1. Sage missed vocabulary day because she had a cold ____.
2. Finished defining the vocabulary words ___F___
3. Sage liked to make up her own definitions ___.
Place a period on the line at the end of the sentence if it is a *statement.* Place a question mark at the end of the sentence if it is a *question.*
4. Is "Musical Performance" the theme for this week ___?
5. She was looking forward to the Tenth Annual Vocabulary Parade ___.
6. Starr went to the end of the line after she spelled the word correctly ___.
Rewrite these sentences. Be sure to use the correct end mark.
7. Sage turned red when she heard everyone laughing
   Sage turned red when she heard everyone laughing.
8. do you have a collection of unrelated objects
   Do you have a collection of unrelated objects?
9. Mrs. Page asked the students to spell and define the words **Mrs. Page asked the students to spell and define the words.**
10. why were they laughing
   Why were they laughing?

Day 2 Teach the Concept

REVIEW SENTENCES

Discuss with students how to recognize a complete sentence. Ask them how a question differs from a statement.

INTRODUCE COMMANDS AND EXCLAMATIONS

Some sentences tell someone to do something, and some express strong feelings. Present the following:

- A command tells or asks someone to do something. It ends with a period or an exclamation point: *Sit down, please. Don't go near the rocks!*

- An exclamation expresses strong feeling. It ends with an exclamation point: *I won first prize at the Vocabulary Day Parade!*

See Grammar Transparency 2 for modeling and guided practice.

Grammar Practice Book, page 2

- A **command** tells someone to do something. It ends with a period.
- An **exclamation** expresses strong feeling. It ends with an exclamation mark.

Read each sentence. Decide if each sentence is a command or an exclamation, and write your choice on the line. Then rewrite the sentences with the correct end marks.
1. Please tell me what the vocabulary words are for this week
   command; Please tell me what the vocabulary words are for this week.
2. Write each word five times
   command; Write each word five times.
3. Be sure to include each word's definition
   command; Be sure to include each word's definition.
4. Oh my, she hung up the phone with a crash
   exclamation; Oh my, she hung up the phone with a crash!
5. Line up by the board for the Vocabulary Parade
   command; Line up by the board for the Vocabulary Parade.
6. How sad for Sage to feel so devastated
   exclamation; How sad for Sage to feel so devastated!
7. Wow, that's an amazing gold trophy that Sage won
   exclamation; Wow, that's an amazing gold trophy that Sage won!
8. Oh no, Mr. Bell's suit is all soggy
   exclamation; Oh no, Mr. Bell's suit is all soggy!

Day 3 Review and Practice

REVIEW COMMANDS AND EXCLAMATIONS

Review the difference between commands and exclamations. A command tells or asks someone to do something, and an exclamation expresses strong feeling.

MECHANICS AND USAGE: PUNCTUATE SENTENCES

- Every sentence begins with a capital letter.
- A statement ends with a period.
- A question ends with a question mark.
- A command ends with a period or an exclamation point.
- An exclamation ends with an exclamation point.

 See Grammar Transparency 3 for modeling and guided practice.

Grammar Practice Book, page 3

- Every **sentence** begins with a capital letter.
- A **statement** ends with a period.
- A **question** ends with a question mark.
- A **command** ends with a period.
- An **exclamation** ends with an exclamation mark.

Read each sentence. On the line, place a period if the sentence is a statement or command, an exclamation mark if it is an exclamation, or a question mark if it is a question. Circle any letters that should be capitals.

1. Write the vocabulary words on a sheet of paper ___.___
2. Forest is a boy in Sage's class ___.___
3. Oh no, Starr, you're late for baseball practice ___!___
4. her head felt as though it were stuffed with cotton ___.___
5. Have you seen her gigantic red dictionary ___?___
6. what does Miss Alaineus have to do with categories ___?___
7. Go get some of that long Italian bread and two sticks of butter ___.___
8. She was so excited to see Miss Alaineus ___.___
9. miss alaineus is not on the spaghetti box ___.___
10. Sage's mother had a great idea ___.___

Rewrite each statement or command below as a question.

11. We have many vocabulary words this week. **Possible answers.**
    How many vocabulary words do we have this week?
12. Please pass me that eraser.
    Would you pass me that eraser, please?
13. We will see Miss Alaineus tomorrow.
    Will we see Miss Alaineus tomorrow?

Day 4 Review and Proofread

REVIEW SENTENCES

Ask students to explain the differences among statements, questions, commands, and exclamations. Ask what punctuation mark goes at the end of each kind of sentence.

PROOFREAD

Have students identify and correct punctuation-mark errors in the following sentences.

1. Line up at the door? (.)
2. Someone has lost this lunch box? (.)
3. Who will turn off the lights! (?)
4. Wow. There are so many volunteers. (Wow!)
5. Please close the door? (.)

 See Grammar Transparency 4 for modeling and guided practice.

Grammar Practice Book, page 4

- Begin every **sentence** with a capital letter.
- Place a period at the end of a **statement**.
- Place a question mark at the end of a **question**.
- Place a period at the end of a **command**.
- Place an exclamation point at the end of an **exclamation**.

Rewrite the paragraph below. Use the correct capitalization and punctuation marks.

I like spelling? it's my favorite subject! Each week, our teacher gives us twenty spelling words? I always write the words in my notebook! the boy who sits next to me sneezed? How sick I became. I could not be at school the day our teacher gave us the spelling words? I called my friend to get the words for the week? I feel confident that I will get all the words right on the test! this is going to be easy? i hope i'm not sick the day of the spelling test!

I like spelling. It's my favorite subject! Each week, our teacher gives us twenty spelling words. I always write the words in my notebook. The boy who sits next to me sneezed. How sick I became! I could not be at school the day our teacher gave us the spelling words. I called my friend to get the words for the week. I feel confident that I will get all the words right on the test. This is going to be easy! I hope I'm not sick the day of the spelling test.

Day 5 Assess and Reteach

ASSESS

Use the Daily Language Activity and page 5 of the **Grammar Practice Book** for assessment.

RETEACH

Write the corrected sentences from the Daily Language Activities on index cards. Have students form two teams. One team draws a card and reads the sentence. The other team calls out the correct punctuation for the end of the sentence. If the team calls out the wrong punctuation, the other team has a chance to correct them. Whichever team calls out the correct answer then draws the next card.

Use page 6 of the Grammar Practice Book for additional reteaching.

 See Grammar Transparency 5 for modeling and guided practice.

Grammar Practice Book, pages 5–6

Read each sentence. Write whether it is a statement, a question, a command, or an exclamation. Then rewrite the sentence so that its end mark and capitalization are correct.

1. __question__ Why did Sage miss Vocabulary Day
   Why did Sage miss Vocabulary Day?
2. __command__ call Starr and ask her for the words
   Call Starr and ask her for the words.
3. __statement__ Sage was propped up in bed with a box of tissues
   Sage was propped up in bed with a box of tissues.
4. __exclamation__ How hard it is to study while you're blowing your nose
   How hard it is to study while you're blowing your nose!
5. __question__ do you have a spork in your miscellaneous drawer
   Do you have a spork in your miscellaneous drawer?
6. __question__ have you ever seen a fossil
   Have you ever seen a fossil?
7. __exclamation__ Oh, I love your Vocabulary Parade costume
   Oh, I love your Vocabulary Parade costume!
8. __question__ did you see the look on Mr. Bell's face
   Did you see the look on Mr. Bell's face?
9. __command__ Ask Mrs. Page when the next parade is scheduled
   Ask Mrs. Page when the next parade is scheduled.
10. __question__ what will your costume be
    What will your costume be?

Monitoring Progress

Administer the Test

 **Weekly Reading Assessment**

Passage and questions, pages 5–12

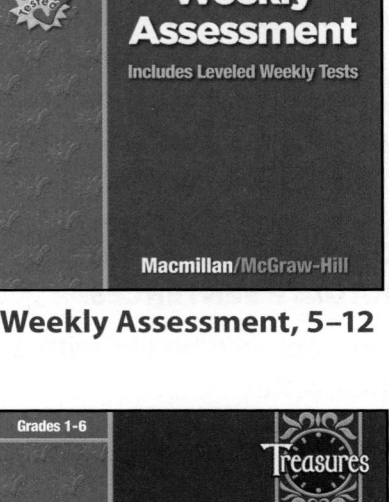

Weekly Assessment, 5–12

ASSESSED SKILLS

- Character and Plot
- Vocabulary Words
- Synonyms
- Short Vowels *a, e, i, o, u*
- Sentence Types

 **Assessment Tool**

Administer the **Weekly Assessment** online or on CD-ROM.

 **Fluency**

Assess fluency for one group of students per week. Use the Oral Fluency Record Sheet to track the number of words read correctly. Fluency goal for all students: **100–120 words correct per minute (WCPM).**

Approaching Level	Weeks 1, 3, 5
On Level	Weeks 2, 4
Beyond Level	Week 6

Fluency Assessment

 **Alternative Assessments**

- **Leveled Weekly Assessment** for Approaching Level, pages 13–20
- **ELL Assessment,** pages 32–33

ELL Practice and Assessment, 32–33

Diagnose		Prescribe
	IF...	**THEN...**
VOCABULARY WORDS **VOCABULARY STRATEGY** Synonyms Items 1, 2, 3, 4	0–2 items correct...	Reteach skills using the **Additional Lessons**, page T6.  Reteach skills: Go to **www.macmillanmh.com**  Vocabulary PuzzleMaker Evaluate for Intervention.
COMPREHENSION Skill: Character and Plot Items 5, 6, 7, 8	0–2 items correct...	Reteach skills using the **Additional Lessons**, page T1. Evaluate for Intervention.
GRAMMAR Sentence Types Items 9, 10, 11	0–1 items correct...	Reteach skills: **Grammar Practice Book** page 6.
SPELLING Short Vowels *a, e, i, o, u* Items 12, 13, 14	0–1 items correct...	Reteach skills: Go to **www.macmillanmh.com**
FLUENCY	96–99 WCPM	Fluency Solutions
	0–95 WCPM	Evaluate for Intervention.

READING
Triumphs
AN INTERVENTION PROGRAM

Also Available

To place students in the Intervention Program, use the **Diagnostic Assessment** in the Intervention Teacher's Edition.

Skills Focus ▶ Phonics

Objective   Decode one-syllable and multisyllabic words that include short vowels in both familiar and unfamiliar texts

Materials
- **Student Book** "The Talent Contest"
- **Decodable Passages, Teacher's Resource Book**, p 5

WORDS WITH SHORT VOWELS

Model/Guided Practice

■ Write the letters *d, o, c, k* on the board. Say the sound that stands for each letter. Then blend the sounds: /dok/. *Say the word with me:* dock.

■ Write CVCC under the corresponding letters *d, o, c,* and *k. This word follows a consonant-vowel-consonant-consonant pattern. Generally the vowel sound is short in such cases. It is also short in words with a CVC pattern, as in* cut.

■ *Let's check the rule. Start with the word* got. *Say the word with me. Is the vowel sound long or short? Now mark the consonant-vowel pattern:* CVC.

■ Next, use these words to recheck the rule: *best, big, can, did,* and *fast.* Have students generate five other single-syllable words with this rule. Provide constructive feedback.

■ Extend the review to include words that form short vowel sounds with vowel combinations such as *dead* and *enough.*

MULTISYLLABIC WORDS WITH SHORT VOWELS

■ Have pairs of students practice decoding longer words with short vowels. List the words below. *With your partner, choose a word. Say the word, counting the syllables. Draw lines within the word to show the syllables. Notice that each syllable contains only one vowel sound. Circle the syllables with short vowel sounds and mark the consonant-vowel patterns.*

abandon	bacteria	challenging	frantic
accommodate	bandit	checkup	district

■ Check each pair for their accuracy. Provide support as needed.

WORD HUNT: WORDS WITH SHORT VOWELS IN CONTEXT

■ Review CVC and CVCC patterns and their effects on vowel sounds. Then have students search "The Talent Contest" for words with three or more syllables that contain short vowel sounds. Have them decode the words, divide them into syllables, and label consonant-vowel patterns.

■ Check whether students have found the following words: caf/e/ter/i/a; gi/gan/tic; ri/dic/u/lous; dra/ma/tic; in/ev/i/ta/ble; neg/a/tive; ex/cit/ed/ly; def/i/nite/ly; cat/e/gor/ies; lu/mi/nous; sug/gest/ed.

■ Have students repeat the activity with the decodable passages on **Teacher's Resource Book** page 5.

Constructive Feedback

Isolate the error sound and repeat it with the group. If students say long vowel sounds rather than short vowel sounds, point out the CVC or CVCC pattern and say, for example:

Identify the CVC or CVCC pattern in the word. The vowel sound is short within these patterns. Say the short sounds with me: /a/, /e/, /i/, /o/, and /u/. Let's sound out the word *got.* The pattern is CVC. The pronunciation is /got/, not /gōt/.

Repeat as needed with other words with CVC or CVCC patterns.

Additional Resources

For each skill below, additional lessons are provided. You can use these lessons on consecutive days after teaching the lessons presented in the week.
- Character and Plot, T2
- Context Clues: Synonyms, T5
- Text Feature: Photographs and Captions, T9

Decodable Text

To help students build speed and accuracy with phonics patterns, see the additional decodable text on page 5 of the **Teacher's Resource Book**.

Fluency

Objective Read with increasing prosody and accuracy at a rate of 100–110 WCPM
Materials • **Approaching Practice Book A,** p. 4

MODEL EXPRESSIVE READING

Model reading the Fluency passage in **Practice Book A**, page 4. Tell students to pay close attention to your pauses and intonation. Then read aloud one sentence at a time and have students repeat the sentence, first as a class and then one by one. Listen carefully for accuracy.

REPEATED READING

Have students practice reading the passage as you circulate and provide constructive feedback. During independent time, partners can take turns reading the passage. One student should read each sentence aloud, and the other should repeat it. Remind students to wait until the ends of sentences before correcting partners' mistakes.

TIMED READING

At the end of the week, tell students they will do a timed reading of the passage that they have been practicing. Have each student

- place the passage from Practice Book A, page 4, face down.
- begin reading the passage aloud when you say "Go."
- stop reading the passage when you say "Stop."

As students read, note any miscues. Stop them after one minute. Help students record and graph the number of words they read correctly.

Constructive Feedback

Help students insert short pauses after each comma and longer pauses after each period or other end punctuation. Model this strategy for students by reading aloud. At each comma, stop reading, tap your finger once on a desk or table, and resume reading. For each period or other end punctuation, tap your finger twice. Then ask students to practice this strategy in pairs.

Vocabulary

Objective Apply vocabulary word meanings
Materials • **Vocabulary Cards** • **Transparencies 1a and 1b**

VOCABULARY WORDS

Display the **Vocabulary Cards** for *slumped, soggy, strands, capable, categories, gigantic, credit, luminous.* Help students identify clues for these words in "The Talent Contest" on **Transparencies 1a** and **1b.** Review each word's meaning. Ask students to think of a synonym for each word. Then have students share their synonyms with partners.

slumped
strands
soggy
capable
categories
gigantic
credit
luminous

★ **Approaching Practice Book A,** page 4

As I read, I will pay attention to pauses and breaks in the text.

	Julie took a sip of water. Then she scanned the long
11	table, looking at the 16 other contestants. Seven were out of
21	the contest. If Julie didn't get her focus back soon, she knew
33	she'd be the next to go.
39	What was the moderator asking? The questioning had
47	moved along the row until it was just three seats away. Paul
59	from Baker Junior High was asked. "What Southeast Asian
68	country was formerly named Siam?"
73	That's easy, thought Julie. Thailand. But she could see a
83	red flush spread from Paul's neck onto his cheeks.
92	"Cambodia?" he said, then slumped in his chair. Bye,
101	Paul. 102

Comprehension Check

1. How do you think Julie feels about the contest? **Character and Plot** nervous
2. How does Julie feel when Paul gives the wrong answer? **Character and Plot** She feels happy.

	Words Read	−	Number of Errors	=	Words Correct Score
First Read		−		=	
Second Read		−		=	

Vocabulary

Review this week's words (*downstairs, nervous, chuckled, nonsense, fumbled,* and *trudged*). Have students write a sentence for each word.

Student Book, or Transparencies 1a and 1b

Popular Culture Explain to students that a talent contest is a competition where participants perform skills they are good at. For example, a performer might sing, play an instrument, or do a magic trick. Have students share what talents they might perform in a talent contest.

470

Skills Focus ▶ Vocabulary

Objective	Use synonyms as context clues for unfamiliar words
Materials	• **Student Book** *Miss Alaineus*

CONTEXT CLUES: SYNONYMS

- Remind students that synonyms are words that have the same or almost the same meaning, such as *big, huge,* and *gigantic.*

- Find *luminous* on page 22 of *Miss Alaineus*. Have students suggest a synonym, such as *bright* or *brilliant.*

- Give students the following pairs of synonyms, and have them write context sentences using the words: *close/shut, begin/start, soggy/wet.*

Skills Focus ▶ Comprehension

Objective	Analyze character and plot
Materials	• **Student Book** "The Talent Contest" • **Transparencies 1a and 1b**

STRATEGY
ANALYZE STORY STRUCTURE

Explain: Story structure is the way the author has organized the events of the plot, using elements such as character and setting.

SKILL
CHARACTER AND PLOT

Explain/Model

- A character is who the story is about.

- The plot is the chain of events in a story that give it a beginning, a middle, and an end. Usually the characters have to solve a problem. The turning point occurs when the characters discover a solution building toward a climax. Following the climax, the plot events lead toward a resolution.

Display **Transparencies 1a** and **1b.** Reread the first paragraph of "The Talent Contest." Model identifying the main character and the first plot event.

Think Aloud This paragraph tells about a boy named Danny. He is probably the main character. Danny accidentally spills milk as he sits down. He seems upset. He must have a problem.

Practice/Apply

Reread the rest of "The Talent Contest." Have students circle clues about character and number plot events on the transparencies. Ask:

- What is Danny like? How does he change during the story?

- What is Elena like? How do her actions affect the plot?

- What is the main problem in the story, and how is it resolved?

Leveled Reader Lesson

Objective Read to apply strategies and skills

Materials
- **Leveled Reader** *What's the Buzz About the Geography Bee?*
- **Student Book** *Miss Alaineus*

PREVIEW AND PREDICT

Have students look at the cover and preview the first three chapters. They can review illustrations and chapter titles to predict what the story will be about. Ask students to set purposes for reading by writing any questions they have about the story.

VOCABULARY WORDS

Before reading, review the vocabulary words as needed. As you read together, discuss any context clues and possible synonyms for each word.

STRATEGY
ANALYZE STORY STRUCTURE

Remind students that analyzing story structure means looking at how the author has organized the events of the plot using story elements such as character and setting. Understanding how the events of a story are organized can help readers comprehend and remember what they read.

SKILL
CHARACTER AND PLOT

Remind students to pay attention to the characters and how their actions affect the events of the plot.

Think Aloud Julie is torn because she loves geography, but her friends think her interest is nerdy. She wants her friends to like her. I think this problem will shape the rest of the story. For example, it could determine how she will do at the Geography Bee. I'll remember this information for my Character and Plot Chart.

READ AND RESPOND

Tell students to read the first three chapters of the story. Discuss the characters and how their actions affect the plot. You may wish to help students create a Character and Plot Chart. After they finish the book, ask students what questions they have about the story.

MAKE CONNECTIONS ACROSS TEXTS

Invite students to compare *Miss Alaineus* and *What's the Buzz About the Geography Bee?* Discuss how both relate to this week's theme, School Contests.

- How do Sage and Julie handle competition?
- Are their challenges similar or different? Explain.

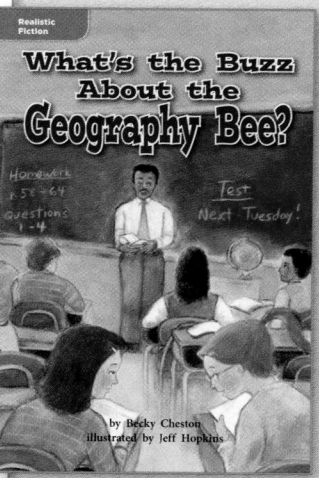

Leveled Reader

ELL Access for All

Play on Words Explain that the title of this book is a play on the words *buzz* and *bee*. The expression "What's the buzz?" means "What is everyone talking about?" A geography bee is similar to a spelling bee. English speakers also say that bumble bees buzz. Have students begin keeping track of puns they encounter as they read.

On Level Options

The Talent Contest
by Howard Gabe

Student Book

The National SPELLING BEE
by Nicole Lee

Student Book

Skills Focus ▶ Vocabulary

Objective	Use vocabulary words
Materials	• **Student Book** "The Talent Contest," *Miss Alaineus* • **Vocabulary Cards**

VOCABULARY WORDS

Use the **Vocabulary Cards** to review this week's words. Have students find three vocabulary words in "The Talent Contest" that relate to the theme of School Contests. Then have students find a synonym for each of these words in a dictionary, thesaurus, or synonym finder.

CONTEXT CLUES: SYNONYMS

Review that context clues are nearby words that help readers determine the meaning of an unfamiliar word or phrase. Authors sometimes include synonyms to help define new terms. Have students find the words *devastated* (p. 33), *precipitation* (p. 37), and *amazement* (p. 38) in *Miss Alaineus* and identify the context clues, including any synonyms, that surround each word. Have students provide additional synonyms that can be substituted for each word without changing the meaning.

Skills Focus ▶ Text Features

Objective	Analyze how photographs and captions enhance text
Materials	• **Student Book** "The National Spelling Bee" • Science textbook

PHOTOGRAPHS AND CAPTIONS

Reread "The National Spelling Bee." Discuss the purpose and importance of photographs and captions in a nonfiction passage. Have student pairs skim and scan a science textbook to locate and discuss photos and captions. Have students rewrite some captions using synonyms.

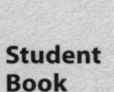
On Level Practice Book O, page 4

As I read, I will pay attention to pauses and breaks in the text.

	Freddy slapped the table as he snorted. "Check this out,
10	Eva!" he said between chuckles.
15	Freddy grabbed my sketchbook and held it up next to my
26	startled face. Eva frowned, looked confused, and then finally
35	a gigantic smile crossed her face.
41	"You're good, Nadia," she said. "But, I don't get it."
51	What I'd drawn was a cartoon of *me*, with an oversized
62	head and tiny body. I'd added my trademark features.
71	A banner at the top read, "Science UN-Fair." Question marks
81	spun around my head and I had a very confused look—a
93	perfect caricature, I might add.
98	Freddy turned to me and said, "Eva was in the nurse's
109	office during fifth period. Remember? She got hurt playing
118	soccer during lunch."
121	"Oh, yeah," I said. And then I told Eva what she had
133	missed. 134

Comprehension Check

1. Who is the main character of this story? **Character** Nadia.
2. What did Nadia draw in her sketchbook? **Plot** a caricature of herself

	Words Read	−	Number of Errors	=	Words Correct Score
First Read		−		=	
Second Read		−		=	

Skills Focus ▶ Fluency

Objective	Read fluently with appropriate prosody at a rate of 100–120 WCPM
Materials	• **On Level Practice Book O,** p. 4

REPEATED READING

Model reading the Fluency passage on page 4 of **Practice Book O.** Then work with students to begin marking phrasing cues. Remind them that one slash means "pause" and should come after commas, dashes, semicolons, and other places where they would naturally pause when speaking. Two slashes mean "stop" and should come after end marks. Partners should practice reading the passage to each other. Circulate and give feedback.

Timed Reading At the end of the week, have students read the passage for one minute and record their words correct per minute (WCPM).

Leveled Reader Lesson

Objective   Read to apply strategies and skills
Materials   • **Leveled Reader** *Nadia Gomez Sees the Light*

PREVIEW AND PREDICT

Have students preview *Nadia Gomez Sees the Light*.

- What does the title suggest about the story?

- Who is Nadia? Describe what you know about her.

- What questions do you have about the story?

Leveled Reader

STRATEGY
ANALYZE STORY STRUCTURE

Remind students that paying attention to the way the author
organizes the characters, setting, and plot of a story can increase their
understanding and enjoyment.

SKILL
CHARACTER AND PLOT

Review: A character is who a story is about. His or her actions make up
the plot, which is the series of events that take place in the story. These
events give the story a beginning, a middle, and an end. Explain that
students will add information about characters and important events to
Character and Plot Charts as they read.

VOCABULARY WORDS

As students read *Nadia Gomez Sees the Light*, ask them to point out the
vocabulary words as they appear. Discuss how each word is used. Have
students pose questions to each other using the words in both the
questions and answers.

READ AND RESPOND

Read Chapter 1 of *Nadia Gomez Sees the Light*. Pause to discuss Nadia's
personality and the decisions she makes. At the end of Chapter 1, have
students add information to their Character and Plot Charts. After students
finish reading the book, have them discuss and record how Nadia's actions
and reactions changed the events in the story. Ask students whether they
have remaining questions about the story.

MAKE CONNECTIONS ACROSS TEXTS

Invite students to summarize the plots and draw connections among the
characters and plots of *Miss Alaineus* and *Nadia Gomez Sees the Light*.

- Are Sage and Nadia challenged in the same way? How?

- How does each of them handle competition?

Invite students to form literature circles to discuss the two texts in
addition to any other similar stories they might know. Encourage
groups to deliver formal oral presentations on plot and character.

ELL
Leveled Reader
Go to pages
47U–47V.

Student Book

Skills Focus ➤ Vocabulary

Objective	Use vocabulary words to compose stories
Materials	• **Vocabulary Cards**

EXTEND VOCABULARY

Use the **Vocabulary Cards** to review this week's words. Ask students to write short stories about competitive school contests. They should use this week's vocabulary words in their stories. Have them edit their stories or partners' stories. Invite volunteers to read their stories aloud. Remind them to modulate the volume of their voices while reading.

Skills Focus ➤ Text Features

Objective	Use photos to create captions
Materials	• **Student Book** "The National Spelling Bee" • magazines

PHOTOGRAPHS AND CAPTIONS

Point out that photographs and captions are examples of visual information in a nonfiction text. Discuss with students how the photos and captions in "The National Spelling Bee" add additional information or describe what is happening in the text.

Have students use photos from magazines to create two photo-and-caption pairings.

Skills Focus ➤ Fluency

Objective	Read fluently with appropriate prosody at a rate of 110–120 WCPM
Materials	• **Beyond Practice Book B,** page 4

REPEATED READING

Model reading the Fluency passage on page 4 of **Practice Book B.** Then work with students to begin marking phrasing cues. Remind students that one slash means "pause" and should come after commas and dashes and in places where they would naturally pause when speaking. Two slashes mean "stop" and should come after end marks or semicolons and in places where a speaker makes a point. Partners can finish marking their passages together. Then they should practice reading to each other.

During independent time, partners can continue to take turns reading the passages they have marked. Remind students to wait until their partners get to the next punctuation marks before correcting mistakes.

Timed Reading At the end of the week, have students read the passage and record their reading rate. Offer constructive feedback as needed.

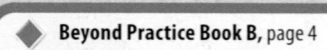

◆ **Beyond Practice Book B,** page 4

As I read, I will pay attention to pauses and breaks in the text.

	The first thing readers should understand is this: I don't normally do
12	journals. My friend Lucy Matsuko, on the other hand, is capable of filling
25	up a book each month. It can be puffy and pink, or fitted with a heart-
41	shaped lock, or one of those old marbled notebooks you buy at the
54	drugstore. And everything goes on those pages—every boring thought or
65	mundane occurrence. No offense, Luce, if you're reading this.
74	But sometimes, an event comes along that changes everything. When
84	that happened to me, I had to write it all down. There had to be some kind
101	of official record.
104	Technically, I suppose, what you're about to read isn't just a journal.
116	It's really more like a scrapbook—which makes it more than just my
129	story. Anything that anyone had to say about it got thrown in here
142	(accompanied, of course, by my running commentary).
148	It all happened last spring, and I put this book together this summer,
161	while the whole thing was fresh in my mind. 170

Comprehension Check

1. How does the narrator feel about most journals? **Character** She thinks they are filled with boring details.

2. Why did the narrator change his mind about writing a journal? **Plot and Character** The events of last spring were so important that they had to be written.

	Words Read	–	Number of Errors	=	Words Correct Score
First Read		–		=	
Second Read		–		=	

Leveled Reader Lesson

Objective   Read to apply strategies and skills
Materials   • **Leveled Reader** *The Car Wash Chronicles*

PREVIEW AND PREDICT

Have students preview *The Car Wash Chronicles*, predict what it will be about, and set purposes for reading. Ask them to record any questions they have about the story. Review vocabulary words as necessary.

STRATEGY
ANALYZE STORY STRUCTURE

Explain that recognizing how a story is organized, or structured, can help a reader understand the plot. As students read they should look for elements—character, setting, and flashbacks—that advance the plot.

SKILL
CHARACTER AND PLOT

Ask a volunteer to explain what the terms *character* and *plot* mean and why they are important to understanding the plot development of a story. Explain that students will read *The Car Wash Chronicles* together and that they will look for information about the story's characters and events.

READ AND RESPOND

As they read, have students identify the characters and central plot events and complete their Character and Plot Charts. Have students note any questions they have about the story.

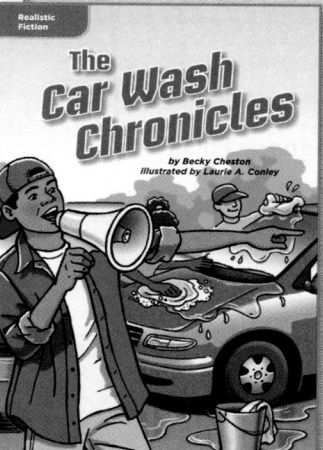

Leveled Reader

Skills Focus

Self-Selected Reading

Objective   Read independently to analyze character and plot and to make connections across texts
Materials   • Leveled Readers or trade books at students' reading levels

READ TO IDENTIFY CHARACTER AND PLOT

Invite students to choose books for independent reading. Ask them to think about what criteria they use to choose a book and whether they like certain authors or genres and why. Remind students that characters' actions affect the plot. As students read, have them take notes on how characters react to events in the stories.

After students have finished reading, have them deliver formal oral responses about the stories they read. They should emphasize plot events so that the audience can follow important information. Then ask partners to brainstorm alternate endings of the stories they read.

ELL   **Access for All**

What's In a Name? Search an online book list or card catalog for other children's books with the word *chronicles* in the titles. Read the brief summary of each book. What do these books have in common with *The Car Wash Chronicles?* Complete a Venn diagram to show similarities and differences.

Academic Language

Technology

Oral Language For oral vocabulary development, go to www.macmillanmh.com

Throughout the week, the English language learners in your class will need help in building their understanding of the academic language used in daily instruction and assessment instruments. The following strategies will help to increase their language proficiency and comprehension of content and instructional words.

Strategies to Reinforce Academic Language

- **Use Context** Academic language used by the teacher (see chart below) should be explained in the context of the task during Whole Group. You may use gestures, expressions, and visuals to support meaning.

- **Use Visuals** Use charts, transparencies, and graphic organizers to explain key labels to help students understand classroom language.

- **Model** Demonstrate the task using academic language in order for students to understand instruction.

Academic Language Used in Whole Group Instruction

Content/Theme Words	Skill/Strategy Words	Writing/Grammar Words
essay contests (p. 16)	context clues (p. 19)	personal narrative (p. 46)
spelling bees (p. 16)	synonym (p. 19)	organization (p. 47)
science fairs (p. 16)	character (p. 20)	graphic organizer (p. 47B)
competition (p. 42)	plot (p. 20)	sentence fragment (p. 47I)
orally (p. 44)		statement (p. 47I)
eliminates (p. 44)		question (p. 47I)
		command (p. 47I)
		exclamation (47I)

Leveled Reader Library

ELL Leveled Reader Lesson

Realistic Fiction

Nadia's Project

by Becky Cheston
Illustrated by Jeff Hopkins

Before Reading

DEVELOP ORAL LANGUAGE

LOG ON

Build Background Elicit students' opinions of science: *What do you like about science? What don't you like? Why is science important?* Prompt volunteers to describe personal experiences doing projects for a science fair. Elicit positive and negative responses.

Tested
Review Vocabulary Write the vocabulary and story support words on the board and discuss their meanings. Model using them. *Nadia didn't think she could do it. She didn't feel* capable.

PREVIEW AND PREDICT

Point to the cover illustration and read the title aloud. *What kind of project do you think Nadia will do? Will she work alone?*

Tested
Set a Purpose for Reading Show the Character and Plot Chart and remind students they have used this chart before. Ask them to do a similar chart to record details of the characters and plot.

 During Reading

Choose from among the differentiated strategies to support students' reading at all levels of language acquisition.

Beginning	Intermediate	Advanced
Shared Reading As you read, model how to analyze plot and characters by focusing on what they say, think, and do. Check students' comprehension. *What does Nadia want? Who is Freddy? Who is Marco?*	**Read Together** Read Chapter 1. Help students analyze characters and plot. Resume reading, taking turns. Have them continue to add to their charts. Help them analyze how Nadia changes her attitude and how her brother helps her.	**Independent Reading** Have students read the story. As they do, ask them to analyze the characters and plot, noting events and attitudes of the characters. Challenge them to write a paragraph to help Nadia with her science project about the *color spectrum*.

 After Reading

Remind students to use the vocabulary and story words in their whole group activities.

Objective

- **To apply vocabulary and comprehension skills**

Materials

- **ELL Leveled Reader**

5-Day Planner

DAY 1	• Academic Language • Oral Language and Vocabulary Review
DAY 2	• Academic Language • ELL Leveled Reader
DAY 3	• Academic Language • ELL Leveled Reader
DAY 4	• Academic Language • ELL Leveled Reader
DAY 5	• Academic Language • ELL Leveled Reader Comprehension Check and Literacy Activities

Grade 5 • ELL TEACHER'S GUIDE

Treasures

English Language Learners

Macmillan/McGraw-Hill

ELL Teacher's Guide
for students who need additional instruction

Weekly Literature

Week At A Glance

Whole Group

VOCABULARY
original, wring, advertisement, commenced, fireball, impress, elected, sauntereds

Use Word Parts/Compound Words

COMPREHENSION
Strategy: Story Structure
Skill: Plot and Setting

WRITING
Personal Narrative

Social Studies Link

History

Small Group Options

Differentiated Instruction for Tested Skills

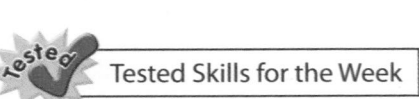
Tested Skills for the Week

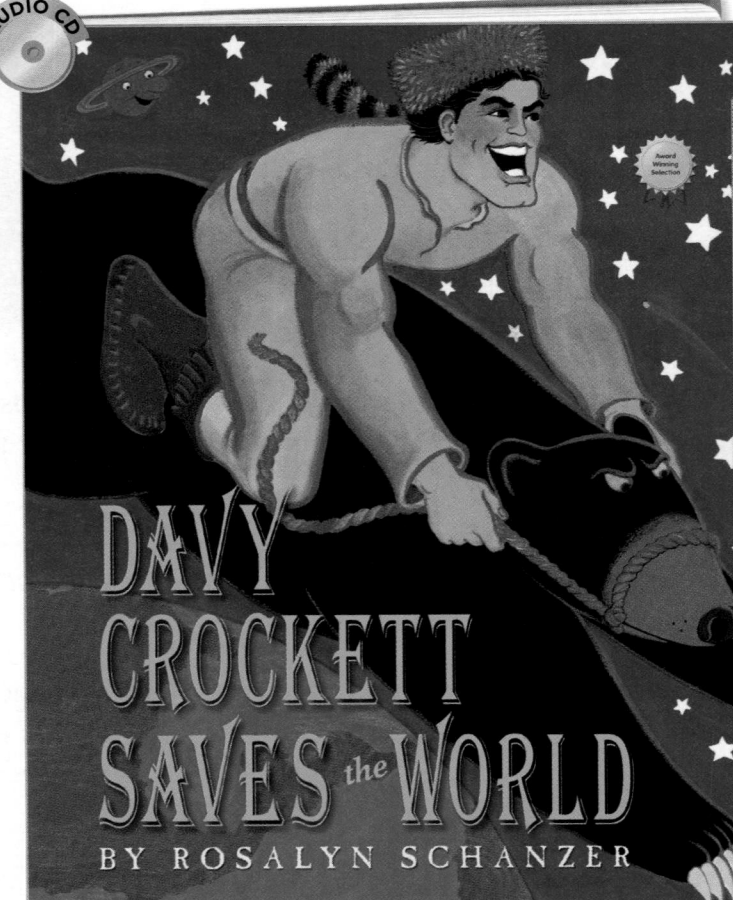

Main Selection
Genre Tall Tale

Grandma's Tales
by Daniel Fritz

Vocabulary/ Comprehension

THE TALES ARE GETTING TALLER
by Kyle Seulen

Social Studies Link
Genre Online Article

Read-Aloud Anthology
• Listening Comprehension
• Readers' Theater

Resources for Differentiated Instruction

Leveled Readers

GR Levels Q–V

Genre Tall Tale

- Same Theme
- Same Vocabulary
- Same Comprehension Skills

Approaching Level

On Level

Beyond Level

English Language Leveled Reader

On Level Reader sheltered for English Language Learner

ELL Teacher's Guide also available

Also Available LEVELED READER PROGRAM

CLASSROOM LIBRARY

Genre Expository Nonficton

Approaching

On Level

Beyond

Trade books to apply Comprehension Skills

INTERVENTION ANTHOLOGY

- Phonics and Decoding
- Comprehension
- Vocabulary

Also available, *Reading Triumphs*, Intervention Program

LEVELED PRACTICE

Approaching

On Level

Beyond

ELL

HOME-SCHOOL CONNECTION

- Family letters in English and Spanish
- Take-Home Stories

Technology

ONLINE INSTRUCTION
www.macmillanmh.com

AUDIO CD
- Listening Library
- Fluency Solutions

CD ROM
- Vocabulary PuzzleMaker

Suggested Lesson Plan

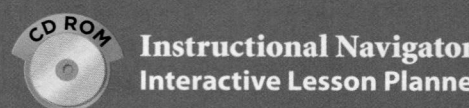

Instructional Navigator
Interactive Lesson Planner

Integrated **ELL** Support Every Day

Davy Crockett Saves the World, 52–69

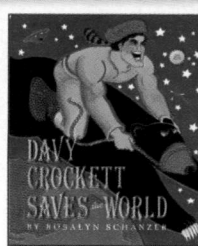

Leveled Readers

Whole Group

ORAL LANGUAGE
- **Listening**
- **Speaking**
- **Viewing**

WORD STUDY
- **Vocabulary**
- **Phonics/Decoding**

READING
- **Develop Comprehension**
- **Fluency**

LANGUAGE ARTS
- **Writing**
- **Grammar**
- **Spelling**

ASSESSMENT
- **Informal/Formal**

Turn the Page for
Small Group Lesson Plan

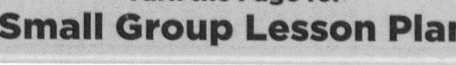

Day 1

Listening/Speaking/Viewing
❓ **Focus Question** Who are some of the legendary figures of American history? What qualities did they have?
Build Background, 48
Read Aloud: "Sally Ann Thunder Ann Whirlwind," 49

Vocabulary
 original, wring, advertisement, commenced, fireball, impress, elected, sauntered, 50
Practice Book A-O-B, 8

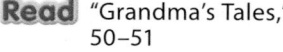 **Strategy:** Use Word Parts/Compound Words, 51

Read "Grandma's Tales," 50–51

Comprehension, 51A–51B
Strategy: Analyze Story Structure
 Skill: Plot and Setting
Practice Book A-O-B, 9

Student Book

Fluency Partner Reading, 48I
Model Fluency, 49

Writing
Daily Writing Prompt: Not everyone becomes a hero. Write a paragraph about the qualities heroes display.
Personal Narrative, 76–77B

Grammar Daily Language Activities, 77I
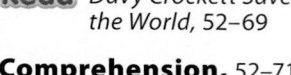 Subjects and Predicates, 77I
Grammar Practice Book, 7

Spelling Pretest: Long Vowels, 77G
Spelling Practice Book, 7–8

Quick Check Vocabulary, 50
Comprehension, 51B

Differentiated Instruction 77M–77V

Day 2

Listening/Speaking
❓ **Focus Question** What problem does Davy Crockett try to solve?

Vocabulary
Review Vocabulary Words, 52

Phonics/Decoding
Decode Words with Long Vowels, 77E
Practice Book A-O-B, 14

Read *Davy Crockett Saves the World,* 52–69

Comprehension, 52–71
Strategy: Analyze Story Structure
Skill: Plot and Setting
Practice Book A-O-B, 10

Student Book

Fluency Partner Reading, 48I
Tempo and Expression, 65

Writing
Daily Writing Prompt: Write a journal entry from the point of view of a hero you admire.
Personal Narrative, 76–77B

Grammar Daily Language Activities, 77I
Subjects and Predicates, 77I
Grammar Practice Book, 8

Spelling Long Vowels, 77G
Spelling Practice Book, 9

Quick Check Comprehension: 61, 69
Phonics, 77E

Differentiated Instruction 77M–77V

 **Skills/Strategies**

Vocabulary	Comprehension	Writing
Vocabulary Words	**Strategy: Analyze**	**Personal Narrative**
Use Word Parts/ Com-	**Story Structure**	
pound Words	**Skill: Plot and Setting**	

Turn the Page for
Small Group Options

Day 3

Listening/Speaking

❓ Focus Question Describe how Grandma would react to *Davy Crockett Saves the World*. Use details to explain your answer.

Summarize, 71

Vocabulary

Review Words in Context, 77C

Strategy: Use Word Parts/Compound Words, 77D

Practice Book A-O-B, 13

Phonics Decode Multisyllabic Words, 77E

Read *Davy Crockett Saves the World*, 52–69

Comprehension

Comprehension Check, 71

Maintain Skill: Character, 71B

Student Book

Fluency Repeated Reading, 71A

Partner Reading, 48I

Practice Book A-O-B, 11

Writing

Daily Writing Prompt: Write a letter from the hero you selected yesterday. Describe the pros and cons of being a hero.

Writer's Craft: Topic Sentence, 77A

Personal Narrative, 76–77B

Grammar Daily Language Activities, 77I

Mechanics and Usage: Commas in a Series and Appositives, 77J

Grammar Practice Book, 9

Spelling Long Vowels, 77H

Spelling Practice Book, 10

Quick Check Fluency, 71A

Differentiated Instruction 77M–77V

Day 4

Listening/Speaking/Viewing

❓ Focus Question How do you know that *Davy Crockett Saves the World* is a tall tale?

Media Literacy: Advertisements, 59

Expand Vocabulary: American Legends, 77F

Vocabulary

Content Vocabulary: *exaggerating, features, superhuman,* 72

Compound Words, 77F

Apply Vocabulary to Writing, 77F

Read "The Tales Are Getting Taller," 72–75

Comprehension

Informational Text: Social Studies

Text Features: Toolbar and Link, 72

Practice Book A-O-B, 12

Student Book

Fluency Partner Reading, 48I

Writing

Daily Writing Prompt: Write about another real-life hero. Draw one line under facts and two lines under opinions.

Writing Trait: Organization, 77B

Personal Narrative, 76–77B

Grammar Daily Language Activities, 77I

Subjects and Predicates, 77J

Grammar Practice Book, 10

Spelling Long Vowels, 77H

Spelling Practice Book, 11

Quick Check Vocabulary, 77D

Differentiated Instruction 77M–77V

Day 5
Review and Assess

Listening/Speaking/Viewing

❓ Focus Question What have you learned from this week's selections about the plot and setting of tall tales?

Speaking and Listening Strategies, 77A

Vocabulary

Spiral Review: Vocabulary Game, 77F

Read Self-Selected Reading 48I

Comprehension

Connect and Compare, 75

Student Book

Fluency Partner Reading, 48I

Practice, 71A

Writing

Daily Writing Prompt: Imagine that you are interviewing the person you wrote about yesterday. Write questions you would ask.

Personal Narrative, 76–77B

Grammar Daily Language Activities, 77I

Subjects and Predicates, 77J

Grammar Practice Book, 11–12

Spelling Posttest, 77H

Spelling Practice Book, 12

Weekly Assessment, 21–27

Differentiated Instruction 77M–77V

Differentiated Instruction

What do I do in small groups?

Teacher-Led Small Groups

Literacy Workstations

Independent Activities

 Skills Focus ▶ Use your **Quick Check** observations to guide additional instruction and practice.

Phonics
Decode Words with Long Vowels

 Vocabulary Words
advertisement, impress, sauntered, wring, commenced, original, elected, fireball
 Strategy: Word Parts/Compound Words

Comprehension
Strategy: Story Structure
 Skill: Plot and Setting

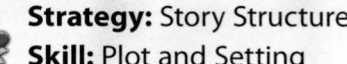 **Fluency**

Suggested Lesson Plan

 **Instructional Navigator**
Interactive Lesson Planner

	Day 1	Day 2
Approaching Level • **Additional Instruction/Practice** • **Tier 2 Instruction**	Fluency, 77N Vocabulary, 77N Comprehension, 77O 	Phonics, 77M Vocabulary, 77O Leveled Reader Lesson, 77P • Vocabulary • Comprehension 
On Level • **Practice**	Vocabulary, 77Q Leveled Reader Lesson, 77R • Comprehension **ELL** Leveled Reader, 77U–77V 	Leveled Reader Lesson, 77R • Comprehension • Vocabulary 
Beyond Level • **Extend**	Vocabulary, 77S Leveled Reader Lesson, 77T • Comprehension 	Leveled Reader Lesson, 77T • Comprehension • Vocabulary 

For intensive intervention see **READING Triumphs**

Small Group Options

Focus on Leveled Readers

Leveled Reader Library

Apply *Tested* skills and strategies while reading appropriate leveled books.

Levels Q-V

Approaching — Q

On Level — S

Beyond — V

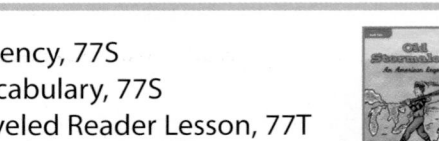

ELL

Additional Leveled Reader Resources

LOG ON

Leveled Reader Database
Go to www.macmillanmh.com

Search by

- Comprehension Skill
- Content Area
- Genre
- Text Feature
- Guided Reading Level
- Reading Recovery Level
- Lexile Score
- Benchmark Level

Subscription also available

Day 3

Phonics, 77M
Fluency, 77N
Vocabulary, 77O
Leveled Reader Lesson, 77P
- Comprehension

Fluency, 77Q
Vocabulary, 77Q
Leveled Reader Lesson, 77R
- Comprehension

Fluency, 77S
Vocabulary, 77S
Leveled Reader Lesson, 77T
- Comprehension

Day 4

Phonics, 77M
Leveled Reader Lesson, 77P
- Comprehension
- **ELL** Fact or Fiction, 77P

Text Feature, 77Q
Leveled Reader Lesson, 77R
- Comprehension

Text Feature, 77S
Leveled Reader Lesson, 77T
- Comprehension
ELL Use Rhymes and Songs, 77S

Day 5

Fluency, 77N
Leveled Reader Lesson, 77P
- Make Connections Across Texts

Fluency, 77Q
Leveled Reader Lesson, 77R
- Make Connections Across Texts

Fluency, 77S
Self-Selected Reading, 77T

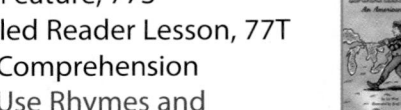

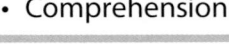
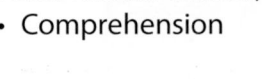

Managing the Class

What do I do with the rest of my class?

Teacher-Led Small Groups

Literacy Workstations

Independent Activities

Class Management Tools

Managing Small Groups
A How-to Guide

Dr. Vicki Gibson   Dr. Douglas Fisher

Macmillan/McGraw-Hill

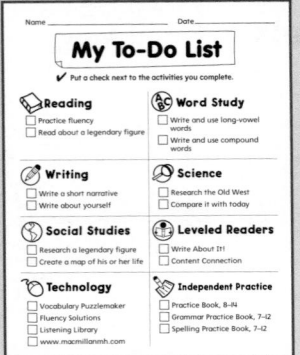

My To-Do List

✔ Put a check next to the activities you complete.

Reading
- Practice fluency
- Read about a legendary figure

Word Study
- Write and use long-vowel words
- Write and use compound words

Writing
- Write a short narrative
- Write about yourself

Science
- Research the Old West
- Compare it with today

Social Studies
- Research a legendary figure
- Create a map of his or her life

Leveled Readers
- Write About It!
- Content Connection

Technology
- Vocabulary Puzzlemaker
- Fluency Solutions
- Listening Library
- www.macmillanmh.com

Independent Practice
- Practice Book, 8–14
- Grammar Practice Book, 7–12
- Spelling Practice Book, 7–12

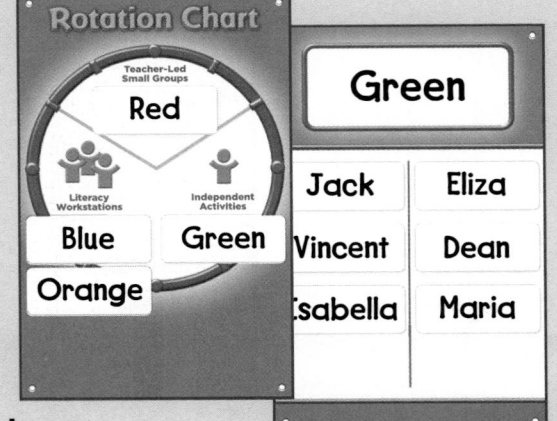

Rotation Chart

Teacher-Led Small Groups

Red

Literacy Workstations

Independent Activities

Blue   Green

Orange

Green

Jack	Eliza
Vincent	Dean
Isabella	Maria

Includes:
- How-To Guides • Rotation Chart • Weekly Contracts

FOLDABLES™

Hands-on activities for reinforcing weekly skills.

Treasures

Dinah Zike's
Foldables

3-Dimensional
Interactive
Graphic
Organizers!

Macmillan/McGraw-Hill

Fish	Frogs
habitat	habitat
food	insects
prey	prey
enemies	enemies

Eight-Tab Foldable

Word	Synonym	Antonym	Prefix or Suffix
normal	typical	unusual	normally

Folded Foldable

Independent Activities

Leveled Readers

For Repeated Readings and Literacy Activities

Approaching

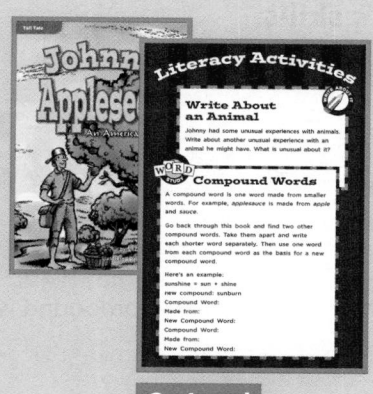

On Level

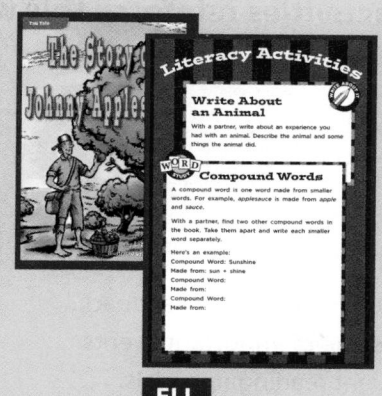

ELL

Beyond

LEVELED PRACTICE

Skills: Vocabulary (p. 8), Comprehension: Plot and Setting (p. 9), Graphic Organizer (p. 10), Fluency (p. 11), Text Features: Toolbar and Link (p. 12), Vocabulary Strategy: Compound Words (p. 13), Phonics (p. 14)

Approaching

On Level

Beyond

ELL

Technology

ONLINE INSTRUCTION www.macmillanmh.com

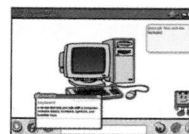

- Meet the Author/Illustrator
- Computer Literacy Lessons
- Research and Inquiry Activities

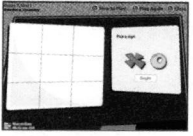

- Oral Language Activities
- Vocabulary and Spelling Activities
- Leveled Reader Database

LISTENING LIBRARY
Recordings of selections
- Main Selections
- Leveled Readers
- ELL Readers
- Intervention Anthology

FLUENCY SOLUTIONS
Recorded passages for modeling and practicing fluency

VOCABULARY PUZZLEMAKER
Activities providing multiple exposures to vocabulary, spelling, and high-frequency words including crossword puzzles, word searches, and word jumbles

Turn the page for Literacy Workstations.

Managing the Class

Cross-Curricular Activities

All activities reinforce this week's skills.

 **Reading**

 **Word Study**

Reading

Objectives

- Read passage fluently and with expression.
- Time reading to practice fluency. Offer corrective feedback.
- Read an article and make a time line of important events.
- Use criteria to choose independent reading materials.

Word Study

Objectives

- List and classify words with long vowels.
- Make compound words.

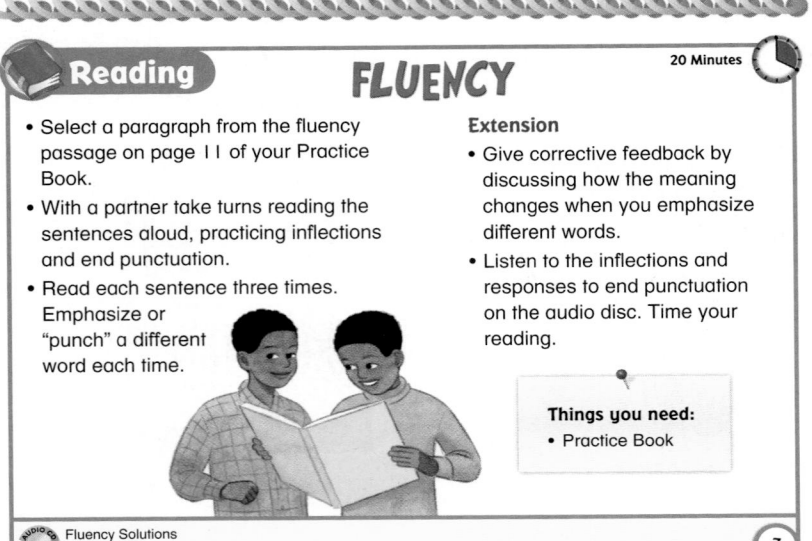

Reading FLUENCY **20 Minutes**

- Select a paragraph from the fluency passage on page 11 of your Practice Book.
- With a partner take turns reading the sentences aloud, practicing inflections and end punctuation.
- Read each sentence three times. Emphasize or "punch" a different word each time.

Extension

- Give corrective feedback by discussing how the meaning changes when you emphasize different words.
- Listen to the inflections and responses to end punctuation on the audio disc. Time your reading.

Things you need:
- Practice Book

Fluency Solutions Listening Library

3

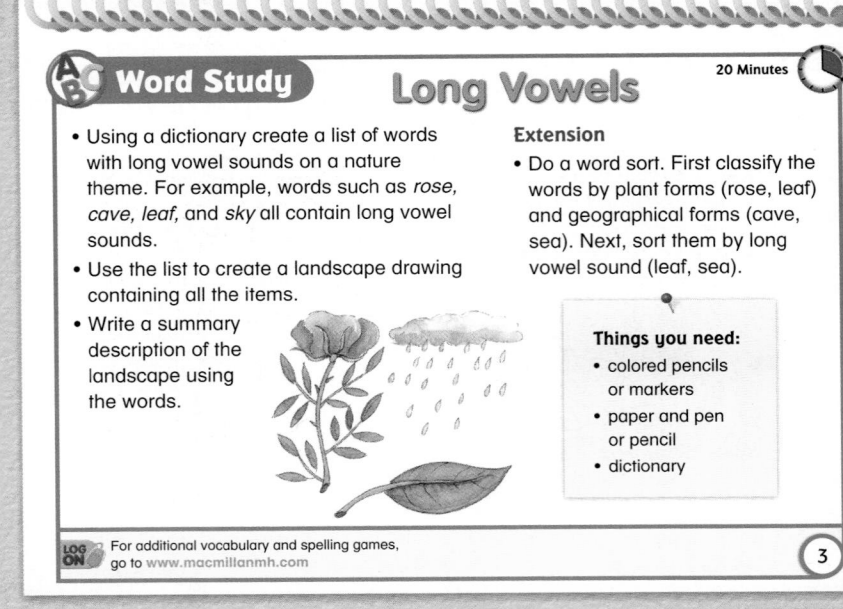

Word Study Long Vowels **20 Minutes**

- Using a dictionary create a list of words with long vowel sounds on a nature theme. For example, words such as *rose, cave, leaf,* and *sky* all contain long vowel sounds.
- Use the list to create a landscape drawing containing all the items.
- Write a summary description of the landscape using the words.

Extension

- Do a word sort. First classify the words by plant forms (rose, leaf) and geographical forms (cave, sea). Next, sort them by long vowel sound (leaf, sea).

Things you need:
- colored pencils or markers
- paper and pen or pencil
- dictionary

For additional vocabulary and spelling games, go to www.macmillanmh.com

3

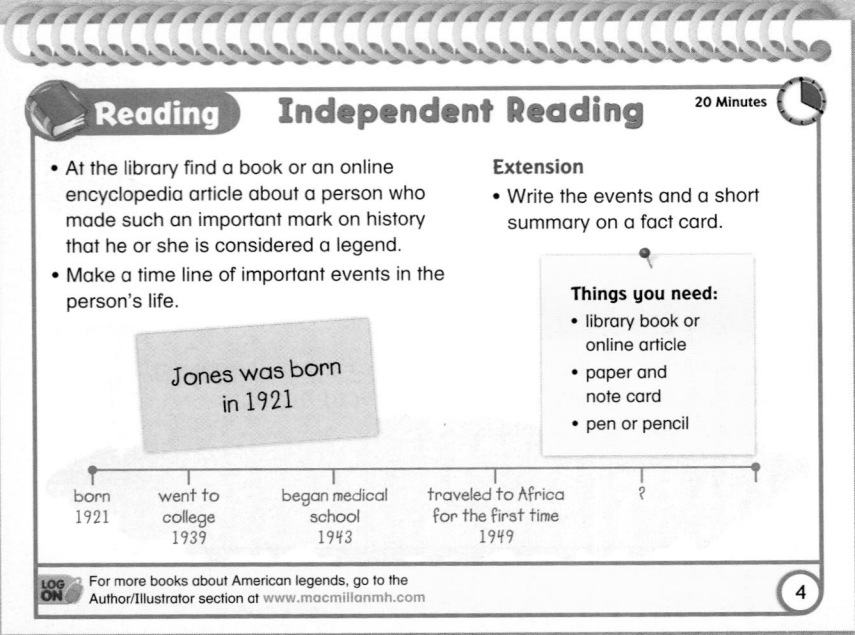

Reading Independent Reading **20 Minutes**

- At the library find a book or an online encyclopedia article about a person who made such an important mark on history that he or she is considered a legend.
- Make a time line of important events in the person's life.

Jones was born in 1921

| born 1921 | went to college 1939 | began medical school 1943 | traveled to Africa for the first time 1949 | ? |

Extension

- Write the events and a short summary on a fact card.

Things you need:
- library book or online article
- paper and note card
- pen or pencil

For more books about American legends, go to the Author/Illustrator section at www.macmillanmh.com

4

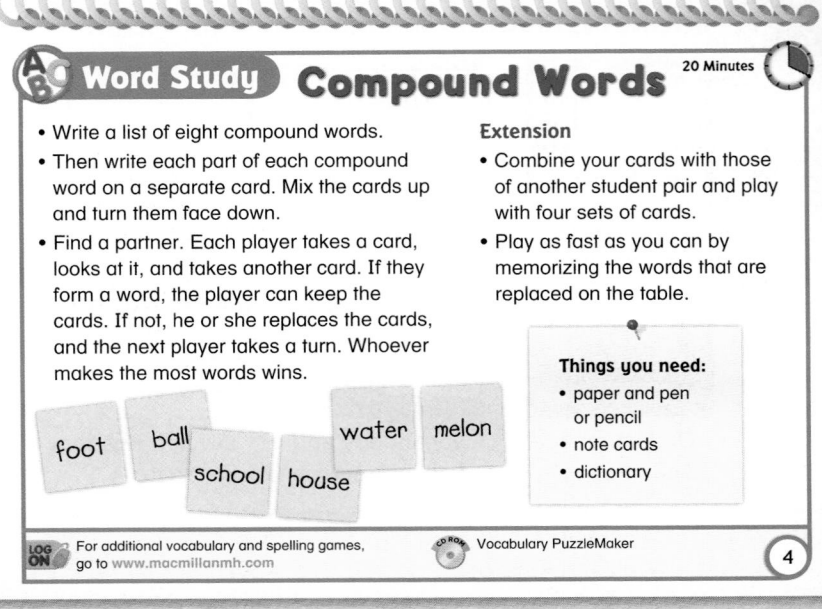

Word Study Compound Words **20 Minutes**

- Write a list of eight compound words.
- Then write each part of each compound word on a separate card. Mix the cards up and turn them face down.
- Find a partner. Each player takes a card, looks at it, and takes another card. If they form a word, the player can keep the cards. If not, he or she replaces the cards, and the next player takes a turn. Whoever makes the most words wins.

Extension

- Combine your cards with those of another student pair and play with four sets of cards.
- Play as fast as you can by memorizing the words that are replaced on the table.

Things you need:
- paper and pen or pencil
- note cards
- dictionary

For additional vocabulary and spelling games, go to www.macmillanmh.com

Vocabulary PuzzleMaker

4

Literacy Workstations

Writing

Objectives

- Write a narrative about a skilled person.
- Write a brief article about accomplishing a dream.
- Write voluntarily for different purposes.

Content Literacy

Objectives

- Use research to compare life in the American West and today.
- Map a famous person's travels and summarize the events in his or her life.

Writing — Narrative
20 Minutes

- Write a short narrative about someone you know who is known for doing or having done something well. It could be anything from drawing or telling jokes to running fast.
- Include details about the person and why he or she is known for this skill.

Extension

- Turn this narrative into a tall tale by exaggerating the details to make the subject seem like a legend.
- Make an illustration of your subject.
- Share both versions with a partner and talk about the exaggerations.

Things you need:
- paper and pen or pencil
- colored pencils or markers

3

Science — Changes in the American West
20 Minutes

- Using books or an online encyclopedia, research what life was like for a student your age living in the American West of the middle 1800s.
- Make a chart to draw comparisons to life today, with the headings *Science and Medicine*, *Daily Life*, *Sports and Games*, and *Transportation*.

Extension

- Compare the science and technology of today with that of the Old West. Make a chart showing five important changes.

Things you need:
- access to the Internet or the library
- paper and pen or pencil

3

Writing — Narrative Report
20 Minutes

- Suppose that you are known for doing something well. What is your talent or skill? As though you were a reporter writing about someone else, write a short narrative about yourself, describing how you accomplished your dream and became a legend.

Extension

- Write a letter thanking the person who inspired you to accomplish the dream that made you into a legend.

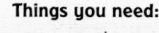
Things you need:
- paper and pen or pencil

4

Social Studies — Legendary Lives
20 Minutes

- Using an online encyclopedia or search engine, research a legendary figure such as Daniel Boone or Annie Oakley.
- Find out where this person was born, lived as a child, and went to school. Then find these places on a map.
- Draw or trace the map and create a key for it, indicating the phases of the person's life.

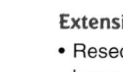

Extension

- Research any places your legendary figure has traveled and find them on a map.
- Write a brief summary of the person's travels.

Things you need:
- maps from your text
- access to the Internet or the library
- paper and pen or pencil

LOG ON Internet Research and Inquiry Activity
Students can find more facts at www.macmillanmh.com

4

48

ORAL LANGUAGE
- Build Background
- Read Aloud
- Expand Vocabulary

VOCABULARY
- **Teach Words in Context**
- **Word Parts:** Compound Words

COMPREHENSION
- **Strategy:** Story Structure
- **Skill:** Plot and Setting

SMALL GROUP OPTIONS
- Differentiated Instruction, pp. 77M–77V

Oral Language

Build Background

ACCESS PRIOR KNOWLEDGE

Share the following information:

A legend is a story handed down from the past, often based in part on historical facts. Legends usually revolve around a legendary figure, such as Paul Bunyan, the giant lumberjack.

TALK ABOUT AMERICAN LEGENDS

Discuss the weekly theme.

What do you like about legends?

**FOCUS QUESTION** Ask a volunteer to read "Talk About It" on **Student Book** page 49 and describe the photo.

- What do you see in the photo? (Paul Bunyan and Babe the Blue Ox)

- What adjectives would you use to describe the figures in the photo?

ENGLISH LANGUAGE LEARNERS

Beginning Develop Vocabulary Point to the photo and say, *This is a statue of Paul Bunyan. He is very strong. He is famous. He is an American legend.* (Relate the word to the Spanish word "leyenda.") Then ask, *Who is he? Is he famous? Is he weak or strong?*

Intermediate Character Web Discuss the photo. Ask students to name legendary figures. Discuss the special abilities each one has and write them on the board in a Character Web. Build on what they say and introduce vocabulary as needed.

Advanced Elaborate Complete the Intermediate task. Help students use more complex language to talk about the exaggerations in legends.

American Legends

Talk About It

Who are some of the legendary figures of American history? What qualities must a person have to become a legend?

 Find out more about American legends at **www.macmillanmh.com**

49

Picture Prompt

Look at the picture and respond in writing. You can write a poem, a story, or a description, or use any other type of writing you like.

LOG ON Technology

For an extended lesson plan and Web site activities for **oral language development**, go to **www.macmillanmh.com**

Read Aloud
Read "Sally Ann Thunder Ann Whirlwind"

GENRE: Tall Tale
Review features of a tall tale:

- stories with larger-than-life characters

- may involve humorous exaggerations

Read Aloud
pages 17–22

LISTENING FOR A PURPOSE

Ask students to listen carefully for the events the author describes in "Sally Ann Thunder Ann Whirlwind" in the **Read-Aloud Anthology.** They should be prepared to discuss what could actually happen in real life and what is probably exaggerated. Choose from among the teaching suggestions.

Fluency Ask students to listen carefully as you read aloud, paying attention to your phrasing, expression, and tone of voice.

RESPOND TO THE STORY

Discuss with students the qualities that Davy Crockett admires in Sally. Ask them to describe what qualities they admire in other people. Have students compare their responses.

Expand Vocabulary

Ask students to review all the things Sally Ann Thunder Ann Whirlwind can do, and make a list of words that describe her. Do any of these words relate to the theme of American legends? In what way?

Vocabulary

TEACH WORDS IN CONTEXT

Use the following routine:

Routine

Define: When you **impress** someone, you have a strong effect on that person.
Example: The actor wanted to impress the audience with his strong performance.
Ask: Tell about something you did to impress a friend. DESCRIPTION

- When you **wring** something you hold onto it tightly and twist it. Wring the dead limb from that tree. What is a synonym for the word *wring*? SYNONYM

- A **fireball** is a very bright sphere made of hot dust, gas, and vapor particles. The sun is a giant fireball. What other images come to mind when you hear the word *fireball*? EXAMPLE

- When something is **original**, it has to do with the origin, or beginning, of something. They inflated the ball to three times its original size. What is a synonym for the word *original*? SYNONYM

- **Commenced** means "started or began." When the conductor raised her hands, the orchestra commenced playing. What is an antonym for the word *commenced*? ANTONYM

- An **advertisement** is a public notice that recommends a product or service. A pet advertisement appeared in the paper. How is an advertisement different from an article? COMPARE AND CONTRAST

- When officials are **elected**, they are chosen by voters. The President of the United States is elected every four years. Which people in your school or community are elected leaders?
PRIOR KNOWLEDGE

Vocabulary

original	fireball
wring	impress
advertisement	elected
commenced	sauntered

Word Parts
Compound Words are words made by combining two smaller words. Sometimes you can figure out the meaning of a compound word by breaking it down into its word parts. For example, *fireball* is made up of *fire* and *ball* and means "a ball of fire."

by Daniel Fritz

 y grandma lives in a town in Tennessee near the place Davy Crockett was born. She is a distant relative of his and thinks people should get all the **original** facts about this American legend straight. She is determined to **wring** the truth from all those wild stories about him. She feels those stories are like the words in an **advertisement**: they exaggerate and try to convince readers that Davy Crockett could accomplish impossible feats! My grandma agrees he was a man full of

energy and enthusiasm. But she wants people to remember he was a talented human being—not a superhero.

It was a cold, snowy night the last time Grandma told me Davy Crockett's life story. We were sitting on the couch, sipping hot chocolate when she **commenced** telling me facts about Davy's early life. "Davy Crockett was born in 1786," she began. "The woods around here were beautiful then, but life wasn't easy. His family moved around a lot."

50

- A person who **sauntered** into a room walked slowly or leisurely. The family sauntered along the beach. What is an antonym for the word *sauntered*? ANTONYM

Quick Check

Do students understand word meanings?

During **Small Group Instruction**

If No → **Approaching Level** Vocabulary, p. 77N

If Yes → **On Level** Options, pp. 77Q–77R

Beyond Level Options, pp. 77S–77T

ELL   Access for All

Sentence Frames For the word *impress,* say, *When you do your school-work well, you impress the teacher.* Have students talk about ways they impress others, using this sentence frame: *When I _____ , I impress (my mom).*

For the word *original,* relate it to the Spanish word *original.* Discuss movies or music that is very original and explain why.

"Was Davy a boy when he caught a flaming **fireball** with his bare hands?" I asked. "Is that when he picked up a rattlesnake and used it for a lasso?" I continued, trying to **impress** Grandma with my knowledge. She didn't smile or laugh.

"Davy got married and had children. He farmed, hunted, and joined the army. He got interested in politics and was **elected** to Congress. He lived by the rule: 'Be sure you are right. Then go ahead,'" Grandma said.

"When he left politics, Davy decided to explore Texas," she continued. "That was where he had his last great adventure."

"Yes!" I said. "That's where he died a hero in the famous battle at the Alamo."

That statement of fact brought a huge smile to Grandma's face. "You got THAT right," she said, happily. Then she **sauntered** slowly over to the coonskin cap sitting on her mantel and plopped it on my head.

Reread for **Comprehension**

Story Structure
Plot and Setting
A Plot and Setting Chart helps you identify why the setting is important to the plot of the story. Use your Plot and Setting Chart as you reread "Grandma's Tales" to find out how the setting is an important part of the story's structure.

Plot	Setting

51

Vocabulary

STRATEGY
USE WORD PARTS

Compound Words Remind students that a compound word is made up of two or more words joined together. Students can break a compound word into its parts to figure out its meaning.

Point out the word *fireball* on **Student Book** page 51. Ask a student to identify the two words that make up the compound word and then define the word.

Read *"Grandma's Tales"*

As you read "Grandma's Tales" with students, ask them to identify clues that reveal the meanings of the highlighted words. Tell students they will read these words again in *Davy Crockett Saves the World.*

On Level Practice Book O, page 8

A. Choose a word from the box to complete each sentence.

impress	wring	fireball	original
commenced	advertisement	elected	sauntered

1. I just saw an __advertisement__ for a new book about Davy Crockett.
2. Davy Crockett packed his bag and __commenced__ his trip.
3. Davy Crockett could easily __impress__ people because he could do so many things.
4. Davy Crockett had to __wring__ a dead limb off a big oak tree.
5. Davy Crockett rode a flaming-hot __fireball__ into space.
6. He was __elected__ to Congress when he received more votes than anyone else.
7. I __sauntered__ back to the library, thinking about Davy Crockett as I strolled along.
8. The __original__ tall tale about Davy Crockett was told in the 1800s.

B. Write new sentences for two of the vocabulary words used above. Then underline the vocabulary word.

9. People elected Davy Crockett to office because they knew he could do the best job.
10. If the President needed to send an advertisement to a hero today, he could place one on the Internet.
Possible responses provided above.

 Approaching Practice Book A, page 8
 **Beyond Practice Book B,** page 8

Objectives

- Analyze story structure
- Use academic language: *plot, setting*
- Identify the plot and setting of the story

Materials

- Comprehension Transparencies 2a, 2b
- Transparency 2 Graphic Organizer
- Leveled Practice Books, p. 9

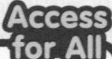

Skills Trace

Character, Plot, Setting

Introduce	19A–B
Practice / Apply	20–39; Leveled Practice 2–3
Reteach / Review	47M–T, 51A–B, 52–69, 77M–T; Leveled Practice 9–10
Assess	Weekly Tests, Units 1, 4 Tests; Benchmarks Tests A, B
Maintain	41B, 71B, 133B; 395A–B; 396–411, 419M–T, 661B; Leveled Practice 113–114

ELL | **Access for All**

Monitor Comprehension
After students read each paragraph, have them tell you what they learned about grandma and the plot. Model thinking through the paragraph to understand the important ideas. Check students' understanding of key words.

Reread for
Comprehension

STRATEGY
ANALYZE STORY STRUCTURE

Access for All

Understanding how the events of a story are organized can help readers better understand and remember what they are reading. **Story structure** looks at how the author has organized the events of the plot using story elements, such as setting.

SKILL
PLOT AND SETTING

- **Plot** is the action of the story. It presents the events that make up a story. The parts of a story include the beginning or exposition; the middle, which includes rising action, conflict, and the climax; and the end, which includes the falling action and resolution. To recognize the plot identify the problem, or conflict, the main character faces. Find the turning point, or climax, of the story, or the point at which the main character begins to find a way to solve the problem. Then identify events in the story that lead to a solution and resolution.

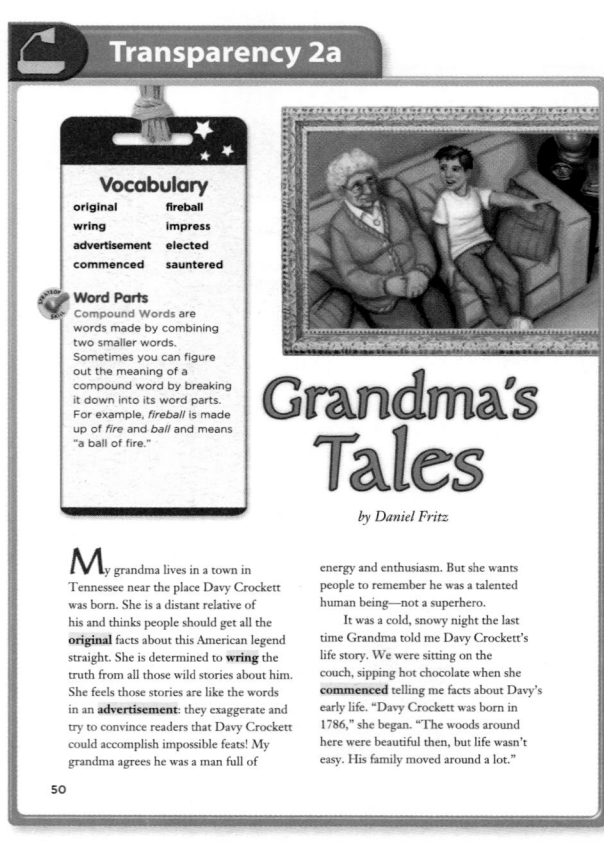

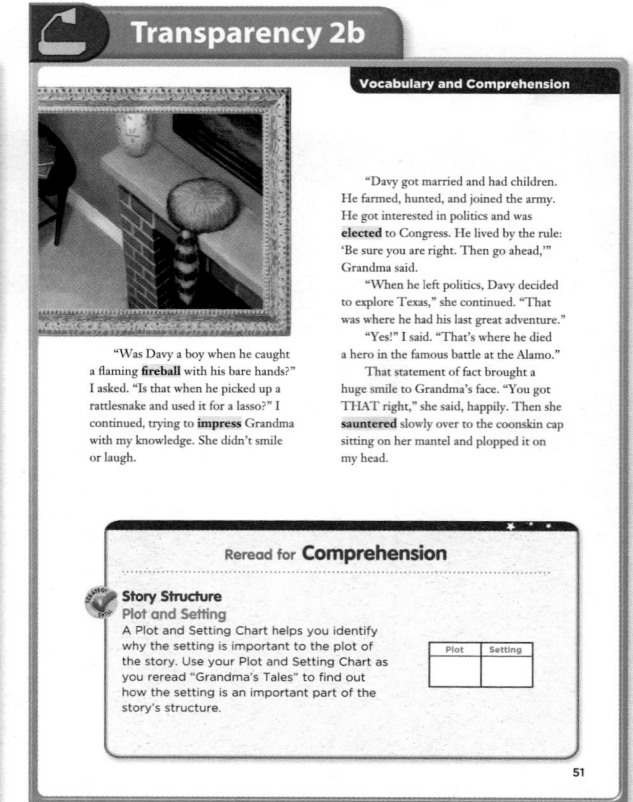

Comprehension Transparencies 2a, 2b

- The **setting** of a story tells where and when it takes place. Sometimes the date and location are stated outright; sometimes they are implied. Settings can change from one location to another within one story. Good readers try to analyze how the setting can have an impact on the characters and the events of the plot.

- Making a Plot and Setting Chart can help you see the connection between the events of a story and its setting.

MODEL

Reread the first two paragraphs of "Grandma's Tales" from **Student Book** page 50.

Think Aloud The narrator's grandmother has a problem. A distant relative of Davy Crockett, she wants her grandson and other people to stop telling tall tales about him and to focus on the facts about his life. I think the setting may help explain why the grandmother feels this way. She is only a distant relative of Davy Crockett, but they were both born and raised in Tennessee.

GUIDED PRACTICE

- Begin the Plot and Setting Chart on **Transparency 2** with the setting (Grandma's living room in Tennessee on a cold, snowy night) and the first event in the plot. (Grandma begins to tell the narrator the story of Davy Crockett.)

APPLY

Have students reread the rest of "Grandma's Tales" and complete the graphic organizer. Ask students why Grandma wants the truth about Davy Crockett to be told instead of tall tales. Have them analyze the influence of the setting on the story's problem and resolution.

Quick Check — **Can students analyze plot and setting?**

During **Small Group Instruction**

If No → **Approaching Level** Comprehension, p. 77O

If Yes → **On Level** Options, p. 77Q

Beyond Level Options, p. 77S

Transparency 2

Plot	Setting
Grandma begins to tell the story of Davy Crockett. Narrator tries to add exaggerated details to Grandma's story, but she objects. Grandma is pleased when the narrator offers correct information about Crockett's death at the Alamo.	Grandma's living room in Tennessee on a cold, snowy night

Graphic Organizer Transparency 2

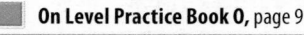

On Level Practice Book O, page 9

The **plot** is a series of events that take the characters through an experience or change. In some stories, the plot includes a problem that a character faces. The **setting** is where and when the story takes place.

Read the tall tale below. Tell the setting and the events in the plot.
Possible response provided.

When a speeding comet threatened to crash into Earth, everyone turned to Davy Crockett for help. Davy Crockett was the biggest, strongest, most courageous man alive. If anyone could save Earth, Davy Crockett could!

Everyone gathered around Davy as he prepared to climb the tallest mountain in Texas. "I'll hop right up to the top of this mountain," he exclaimed, "and grab that comet by the tail. I'll toss it away quicker than you can say 'howdy-do.'"

The people held their breath as Davy took long strides up the mountain. His legs were a blur because they moved so quickly. The crowd gasped when Davy disappeared into the clouds. Would Davy stop the comet?

Just then, the crowd jumped back with a loud roar. Davy had grabbed the comet's tail. He twirled the comet around like a lasso and then sent it flying into outer space.

Davy hadn't even begun to sweat! Davy Crockett proved once again that there was nothing he couldn't do.

Summary: Davy Crockett had to save Earth from a comet. He climbed the highest mountain in Texas so quickly that his legs were blurry. People below were amazed how quickly he moved. When the comet came by, Davy reached for its tail and twirled it like a lasso. He had sent it flying into outer space. Davy had saved Earth without breaking a sweat and proved again he could do anything.

 Approaching Practice Book A, page 9

Beyond Practice Book B, page 9

Read

MAIN SELECTION
- *Davy Crockett Saves the World*
- **Skill:** Plot and Setting

PAIRED SELECTION
- "The Tales Are Getting Taller"
- **Text Feature:** Online Encyclopedia

SMALL GROUP OPTIONS
- Differentiated Instruction, pp. 77M–77V

Comprehension

GENRE: TALL TALE

Have students read the definition of tall tale on **Student Book** page 52. As they read tell students to look for characters and events that are so exaggerated they are completely unbelievable.

STRATEGY
ANALYZE STORY STRUCTURE

Explain to students that analyzing story structure involves looking at how the author has organized the events of the plot using story elements, such as setting.

SKILL
PLOT AND SETTING

Remind students that the plot is the series of events that take place in a story. These events give the story a beginning, a middle, and an end. The setting is where and when a story takes place, and can often influence the events of the plot.

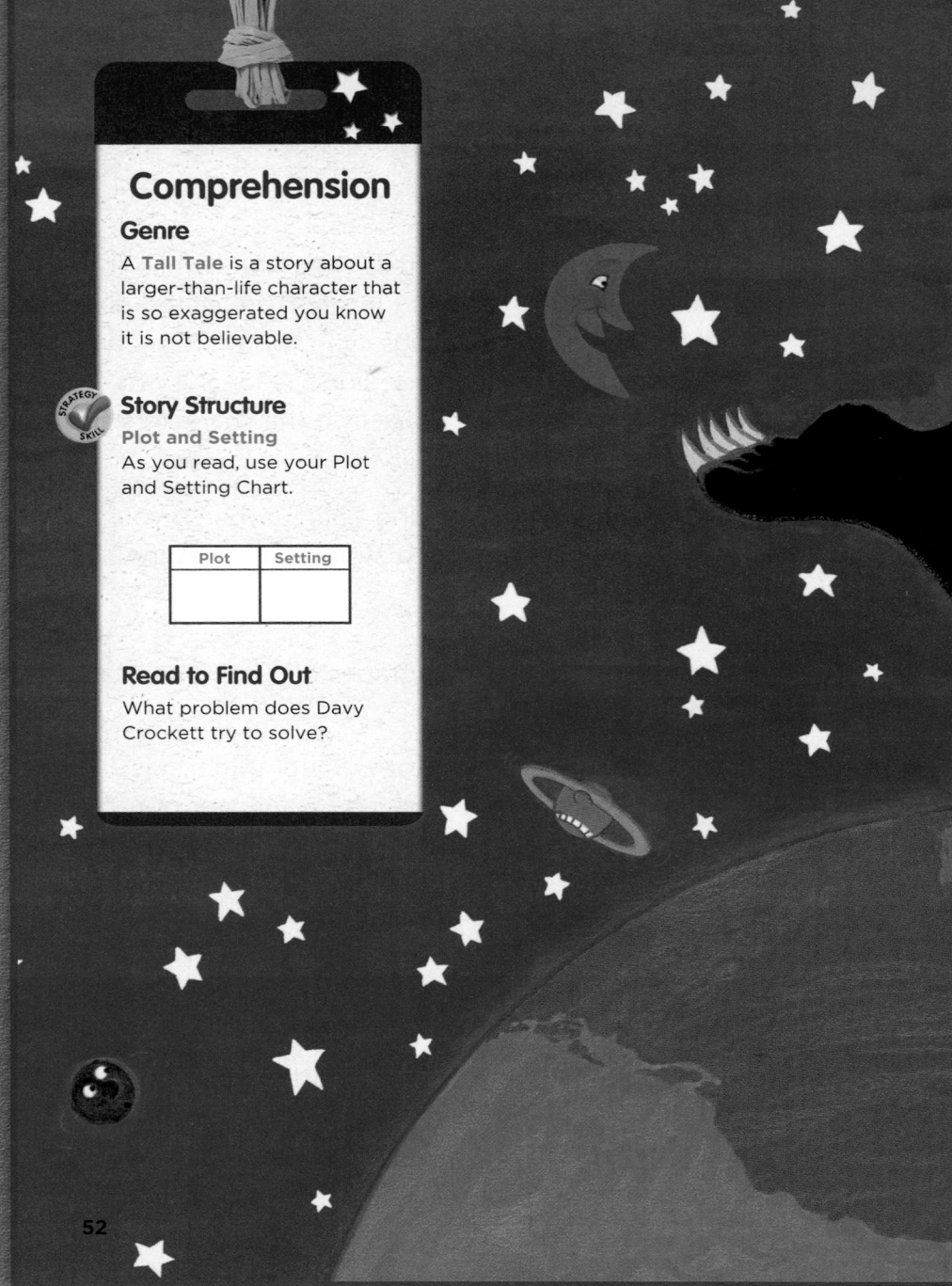

Comprehension

Genre

A **Tall Tale** is a story about a larger-than-life character that is so exaggerated you know it is not believable.

Story Structure

Plot and Setting
As you read, use your Plot and Setting Chart.

Plot	Setting

Read to Find Out

What problem does Davy Crockett try to solve?

52

Vocabulary

Vocabulary Words Review the tested vocabulary words: **advertisement, commenced, elected, fireball, impress, original, sauntered,** and **wring.**

Story Words Students may find these words difficult. Pronounce the words and present the meanings as necessary.

woodsman (p. 54): a man who lives or works in the woods

Halley's comet (p. 57): a comet that can be seen from Earth approximately every 76 years

tornadoes (p. 67): violent storms, usually over land, that produce dark funnel-shaped columns of air

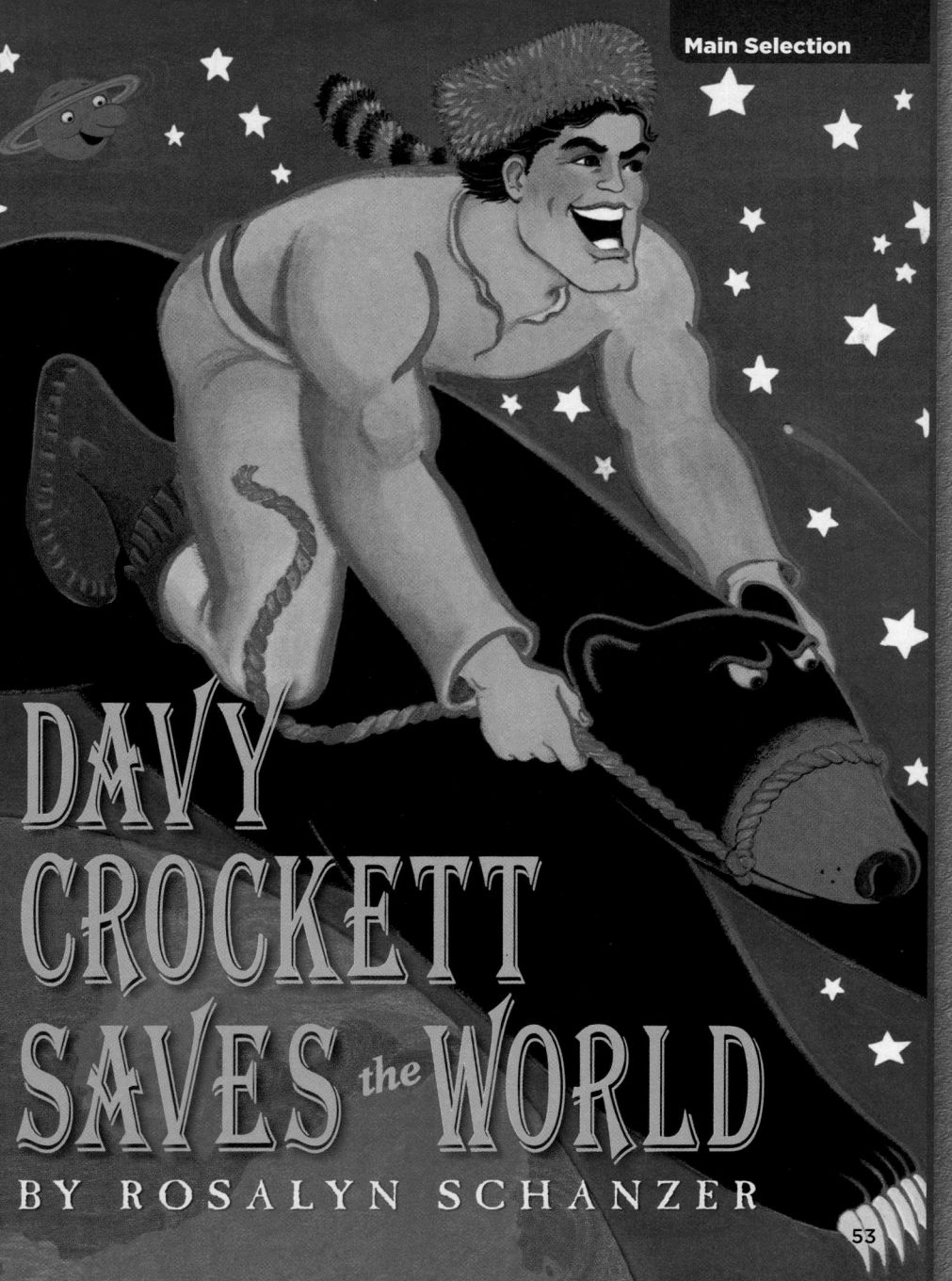

DAVY CROCKETT SAVES the WORLD

BY ROSALYN SCHANZER

53

Preview and Predict

Ask students to read the title, preview the illustrations, and note questions and predictions about the story. Have students write about their predictions and anything else they want to know about the story.

Set Purposes

FOCUS QUESTION Discuss the "Read to Find Out" question and how to look for the answer.

Point out the Setting and Plot Chart in the Student Book and in **Practice Book** page 10. Tell students they will fill it in as they read.

Read *Davy Crockett Saves the World*

Use the questions and Think Alouds for additional instruction to support the comprehension strategy and skill.

Read Together	Read Independently
If your students need support to read the Main Selection, use the prompts to guide comprehension and model how to complete the graphic organizer.	If your students can read the Main Selection independently, have them read and complete the graphic organizer. Remind students to set and modify their purposes when reading, and to use them to adjust their reading strategies.

If your students need an alternate selection, choose the **Leveled Readers** that match their instructional level.

Technology

Story available on **Listening Library Audio CD**

On Level Practice Book O, page 10

As you read *Davy Crockett Saves the World*, fill in the Plot and Setting Chart.

Plot	Setting
Halley's comet is hurling toward America.	Near the Mississippi River almost 200 years ago.
Davy's decision to go to Washington means he will try and stop Halley's comet from hitting Earth.	Eagle Eye peak. So high you can see every state, river, and mountain in a geography book.
The ocean puts out the comet's fire and melts its ice. Davy gets rid of it before it can grow back to its original size.	The Atlantic Ocean and an island.

How does the information you wrote in this Plot and Setting Chart help you analyze the story structure of *Davy Crockett Saves the World*?

 Approaching Practice Book A, page 10

 **Beyond Practice Book B,** page 10

Develop Comprehension

1 **STRATEGY**
ANALYZE STORY STRUCTURE

Teacher Think Aloud In the very first paragraph, I can recognize that the author is using the story element of setting, as well as character, to structure a tall tale. She describes Davy Crockett as someone who can whip ten times his weight in wildcats and drink the Mississippi River dry. I know that Davy Crockett was a historical figure, but no one can drink the entire Mississippi River! The author is using this well-known character and the area where he lived to write a tall tale. As I continue to read, I will look for events in the plot that could not really happen.

I reckon by now you've heard of Davy Crockett, the greatest woodsman who ever lived. Why, Davy could whip ten times his weight in wildcats and drink the Mississippi River dry. He combed his hair with a rake, shaved his beard with an ax, and could run so fast that, whenever he went out, the trees had to step **1** aside to keep from getting knocked down.

54

Folks always crow about the deeds of Davy Crockett, but the biggest thing he ever did was to save the world. This here story tells exactly how he did it, and every single word is true, unless it is false. **2**

Setting
Where and when does the story take place? What clues help you to identify the setting?

55

Develop Comprehension

2 SETTING

Where and when does the story take place? What clues helped you to identify the setting? Fill in the part of the chart labeled "Setting" with your answer. (Answers may vary but should include that although the author doesn't tell when and where the story takes place, she does mention that the land around the Mississippi was still covered with forests. She also mentions wildcats, and a wildcat's face is shown in the illustration. Many years ago the area around the Mississippi was covered with forests, and Davy Crockett was a real person who lived almost 200 years ago. These are all clues that reveal the setting of the story.)

Plot	Setting
	Near the Mississippi River almost 200 years ago.

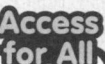

ELL   Access for All

STRATEGIES FOR EXTRA SUPPORT

Question 2 SETTING
Model looking through the text for words that describe where and when the story takes place, such as *woodsman, wildcats, Mississippi River,* and *scientists discovered a ball of fire,* and write them on the board. Encourage students to help you. Explain words as needed. Add what you know about Davy Crockett.

Develop Comprehension

3 **GENRE: TALL TALE**

What elements of a tall tale can you find in *Davy Crockett Saves the World?* (Answers will vary but should include details that are beyond the realm of belief, such as Davy Crockett combing his hair with a rake and shaving his beard with an ax, as well as a comet's tail two million miles long.)

Have students analyze the characteristics and style of the folk tale genre.

About the time our tale begins, the world was in a heap of trouble. A way past the clouds and far beyond all the stars and planets in outer space, scientists with telescopes had discovered **3** the biggest, baddest ball of fire and ice and brimstone ever to light up the heavens.

56

Ways to Confirm Meaning

Syntactic/Structural Cues

Explain Good readers use the meaning of the sentence and selection, the structure of language, and illustrations to predict the meaning of unknown words.

Model Look at the word *telescopes* on p. 56. What part of speech is *telescopes*? The sentence says scientists use them to find things in outer space. The word must be a noun. The people in the illustration are looking up. One has an object at his eye. It must be a telescope.

Apply Have students explain when to use context clues, the structure of language, and illustrations to confirm meaning or realize when meaning is breaking down. Remind them to use a dictionary to confirm predicted meanings. Then have them apply these strategies to unfamiliar words, such as *discombobulated* on page 67.

Its name was Halley's Comet, and it was hurling itself **4**
lickety-split straight toward America. Why, its tail alone was
two million miles long. If it were to hit the earth, everyone would **5**
be blown to smithereens!

57

Develop Comprehension

4 PLOT

What is taking place in America when the story opens? (Halley's comet is hurling through space toward the United States.) **Fill in the box marked "Plot" on your chart with the answer.**

5 MAKE PREDICTIONS

Making, revising, and confirming predictions makes readers more active by helping them to set a purpose for reading. Rereading and looking for text clues in order to make logical guesses about what might happen can also help you clarify your understanding of the text. What problem do you think Davy Crockett will have to solve in the story? (Answers may vary but should include that he will probably have to save America and Earth from the comet.)

Plot	Setting
Halley's comet is hurling toward the United States.	Near the Mississippi River almost 200 years ago.

Comprehension

Literary Devices: *Dialect*

Explain Point out that dialect is a form of informal language that is spoken in a particular area by a specific group of people.

Discuss Have students describe how the author's language in this story is similar to or different from what they hear in their daily lives. Ask them to discuss why they think the author is writing this way, as well as the effectiveness of the technique and what the story would be like without it.

Apply Ask students to list examples of dialect in the story so far. *(Students might suggest, for example, hurling itself lickety-split or biggest, baddest ball of fire.)*

Develop Comprehension

6 **PLOT**

Why did people write to the President of the United States about Halley's comet? (They thought he might have the power to stop it.) Why did the president decide to look for Davy Crockett? (There was nothing the president could do to stop Halley's comet, but since Crockett was a brave man, the president thought he might be able to help.)

7 **MONITOR AND CLARIFY: SELF-CORRECT**

Suppose you are reading the story and think that Davy Crockett is a realistic character. Then you see him dancing with a bear and combing his hair with a rake. How can you use the self-correct strategy to help you understand this part of the story? (I can ask myself open-ended questions such as: *Who is Davy Crockett* and *Why is he dancing with a bear?* If I look back at the beginning of the story, I find that Davy's other actions are not really realistic either, and I am reminded that this is a tall tale. So I have used questioning to correct my misunderstanding and understand what kind of character Davy is.)

The President of the United States started getting big piles of letters telling him to stop Halley's Comet before it was too late. He made a law telling the comet it couldn't crash into the earth, but the comet paid no attention. It just kept speeding toward America and growing bigger every day.

Finally the President had an idea. He had heard of a brave man named Davy Crockett, who lived somewhere in the mountains far away. **6** He put an **advertisement** in all the newspapers in America that said:

> **WANTED**
> BY THE PRESIDENT
> OF THE UNITED STATES
> **DAVY CROCKETT**
> TO PULL THE TAIL OFF OF
> *HALLEY'S COMET*

Meanwhile, Davy Crockett didn't know a thing about any comet. He had no idea that the earth was even in danger. Davy was off in the forest with his pet bear, Death Hug. He was teaching himself to dance so that he could **impress** a real purty gal named Sally Sugartree, who **7** could dance a hole through a double oak floor. He was not reading any newspapers.

It took two whole weeks, but once Davy had learned all the latest dances, he combed his hair nice and slow with his rake, shaved his face real careful-like with his ax, and **sauntered** off toward Sally Sugartree's cabin just as easy as you please.

All this time, of course, Halley's Comet was getting closer and closer to the earth and moving faster by the minute.

58

Comprehension

Monitor and Clarify: *Self-Correct*

Explain/Discuss Students can self-correct misunderstandings while they are reading. They can stop and ask open-ended questions, such as *Why?* and *What If?* and *How?* to make sense of difficult material and correct any inaccurate inferences they may have made. Tell students, *It is confusing when the president makes a law telling the comet it can't crash into Earth. To figure out how this can happen, ask:* How can the president tell a comet what to do? Look at the first part of the story to self-correct. This is a tall tale. Not every action will be realistic. That's how the president can do this.

Apply Have students practice the self-correct strategy. As they read, have them identify something they believe about the characters or plot that doesn't make sense and then ask questions to correct the misunderstanding.

8

59

Develop Comprehension

8 CHARACTER

Look at the illustration on page 59. What does it reveal about Davy Crockett's character? (Answers may vary but should include that Davy seems light-hearted and full of fun in the illustration. He does not seem to take life seriously, and spends two weeks learning all the latest dances so he can impress Sally Sugartree.)

Media Literacy

Advertisements

Explain/Discuss People use the media to fill jobs. In this story the President puts an ad in the newspaper to get Davy Crockett to fight off the comet. Talk about the different ways people use media to fill jobs and advertise vacancies. Possible answers can include written ads in periodicals, ads on the Internet, and voice-over ads on the radio. Ask students how each of these media forms contribute to communication and whether the target audience for each may differ.

Apply Have students consider the ad in the text. Ask them to write their own ad enlisting Davy Crockett's help, and remind them to use persuasive vocabulary and techniques in the appeal. Then have students evaluate several real media ads, or messages, for credibility.

Vocabulary

Read the sentence that contains the word **sauntered** on page 58. Ask students to describe the difference between *sauntered* and other forms of moving, such as *walked, ran, rambled, plodded*. Have them describe someone who sauntered and then use the word in a sentence.

Develop Comprehension

9 LITERARY DEVICE

What words does the author use on page 60 that are a kind of dialect? How do you know? (Words that are not spelled correctly, such as *purty* and *hurrycane*, are examples of dialect. They are spelled the way the characters might pronounce these words in the story.)

10 STRATEGY
ANALYZE STORY STRUCTURE

Teacher Think Aloud I know that Davy Crockett's reaction to the president's advertisement reveals more information about his character. Tell me what else this tells you about Davy, and why his reaction to the ad may be important to the story.

(Encourage students to apply the strategy in a Think Aloud.)

Student Think Aloud The fact that Davy Crockett wasn't reading newspapers and was spending all his time learning to dance made him seem to be a carefree person. After seeing the president's ad, he quickly decided that he could dance with Sally later, and he hurried off to Washington. I think this is a turning point in the story because when Davy tries to stop Halley's comet, he will start doing some of the extraordinary things that heroes do in tall tales. The author mentioned some of them at the beginning of the story, such as drinking the entire Mississippi River dry.

9 Now, Sally Sugartree was not just purty, but she was right smart too. Sally read the newspaper front to back every day, and she knew all about Halley's Comet. She had also seen the advertisement from the President.

Sally climbed up a fifty-foot hickory tree and commenced to look for Davy Crockett. Before long, she spotted him a way far off in the forest. Sally grabbed up her newspaper and waved it around just as hard as she could. When Davy saw her, he grinned and started to walk a mite faster.

As soon as Davy got close enough, Sally jumped right out of that tree. Davy caught her in his arms and gave her such a hug that her tongue stuck out half a foot and her eyes popped out like a lobster's. Then she showed Davy the want ad from the President.

Davy still didn't know what Halley's Comet was, but if the **10** President of the United States wanted to see him, he would waste no time getting to Washington. He bridled up Death Hug and set out like a high-powered hurrycane. He could dance with Sally later.

Death Hug was so fast that rocks and trees and cows and snakes and other varmints all flew out behind him.

11 **Plot**
Why is Davy's decision to go to Washington an important event in the plot?

60

Develop Comprehension

11 PLOT

 Why is Davy's decision to go to Washington an important event in the plot? Add your answer to the part of the chart labeled "Plot." (Answers should include that Davy's decision means he has decided to help the President and will try to stop Halley's comet.)

 Have students respond to the selection by confirming or revising their predictions. Encourage students to revise their questions about the selection.

Plot	Setting
Halley's comet is hurling toward America.	Near the Mississippi River almost 200 years ago.
Davy's decision to go to Washington means he will try and stop Halley's comet from hitting Earth.	

Quick Check Can students identify how the setting influences the events of the plot? If not, see the **Extra Support** on this page.

61

Extra Support

Plot and Setting

If students have difficulty, have them reread the third paragraph on page 58. Then ask, *Why didn't Davy Crockett know about Halley's comet?* (He was off in the forest with his pet bear, Death Hug) Then have students read the first two paragraphs on page 60. Ask them how Sally Sugartree was able to locate Davy Crockett. (She climbed up a fifty-foot hickory tree.) Discuss with students how the forest setting of the story has an effect on the events of the plot.

Stop here if you wish to read this selection over two days.  STOP

Develop Comprehension

12 SUMMARIZE

What has happened in the story so far? (Scientists discovered that Halley's comet was headed toward Earth. People wrote to the President of the United States, asking him to try and stop the comet. The president put an ad in all the newspapers in the United States, asking Davy Crockett to pull the tail of the comet. When Davy found out, he headed to Washington.)

13 MAKE PREDICTIONS

Do you think Davy Crockett will pull the tail off Halley's comet? Explain your answer. (Possible answer: Yes. He is stronger and braver than most people and can do all kinds of amazing things, such as drink the Mississippi River dry.)

62

Cross-Curricular Connection

HALLEY'S COMET

Share some facts about Halley's comet.

- Halley's comet has been known since at least 240 B.C. and possibly since 1059 B.C.

- The comet was named after Edmund Halley, who calculated its orbit. He determined that the comets seen in 1531 and 1607 were the same object, and followed a 76-year orbit.

- The comet's appearance in 1834 corresponds to the time period of the story *Davy Crockett Saves the World*. Andrew Jackson was President of the United States from 1829 to 1837.

Have students research some aspects of comets, such as their composition and flight paths. Instruct them to present their findings in a written report, using at least three sources of information.

By the time they reached the White House, Halley's Comet was getting so close that there wasn't a minute to lose.

The President told Davy to climb the highest mountain he could find right away, and to **wring** that comet's tail off before it could destroy the earth. Then the President posed with Davy for pictures and pretended to look calm.

Davy combed his hair with his rake, rolled up his sleeves, and ate a big plateful of pickled rattlesnake brains fried by lightning to give him energy. Then he **commenced** to climb all the way to the top of Eagle Eye Peak in the Great Smoky Mountains.

Eagle Eye Peak was so high you could see every state and river and mountain in a whole geography book.

You could also look a way far off into outer space. By the time Davy reached the top, it was night.

63

Develop Comprehension

14 SETTING

Tested

What details about the setting does the author provide on this page? How do these details add to the elements of exaggeration in this tall tale? Add them to the chart. (Answers should include that Davy climbs to the top of Eagle Eye Peak in the Great Smoky Mountains. The author says it is so high that you can see every state, river, and mountain in a geography book, but that would be impossible.)

Plot	Setting
Halley's comet is hurling toward the United States.	Near the Mississippi River almost 200 years ago.
Davy's decision to go to Washington means he will try and stop Halley's comet from hitting Earth.	Eagle Eye peak. So high you can see every state, river, and mountain in a geography book.

ELL

Access for All

STRATEGIES FOR EXTRA SUPPORT

Question 14 SETTING
Point to the illustration on page 63 and ask, *Where is Davy? Why is Davy there? What does the author tell us about Eagle Eye Peak? What details make her description an exaggeration?* Make sure students understand that the illustration shows Davy Crockett at the top of Eagle Eye Peak. Check that students understand the exaggerated details, such as being able to see every state and river from the top of the mountain.

Vocabulary

Read the sentence that contains the word **commenced** on page 63. Ask students to use a synonym for *commenced* in the sentence. (Synonyms: began, started, set off)

Develop Comprehension

15 **LITERARY ELEMENT: TONE**

What words and phrases does the author use to describe Halley's comet? (Lightning and thunder shot out of its eyes. It laughs when it sees Davy and heads toward him like a red-hot cannonball.) What can you tell about the author's tone from her description? (Answers will vary but should include the fact that the comet seems scary, but the exaggerated details the author provides are also funny.) Do you think the author's tone is effective? Why or why not? What does it contribute to the story? (Answers will vary but should include that the author's tone is effective because it adds so many exaggerated details, such as roosters crowing because Halley's comet's tail is so bright.) The narrator's tone helps convey the subject of the selection. Is the narrator a character in the tale? (No, the author or narrator is just the background voice.)

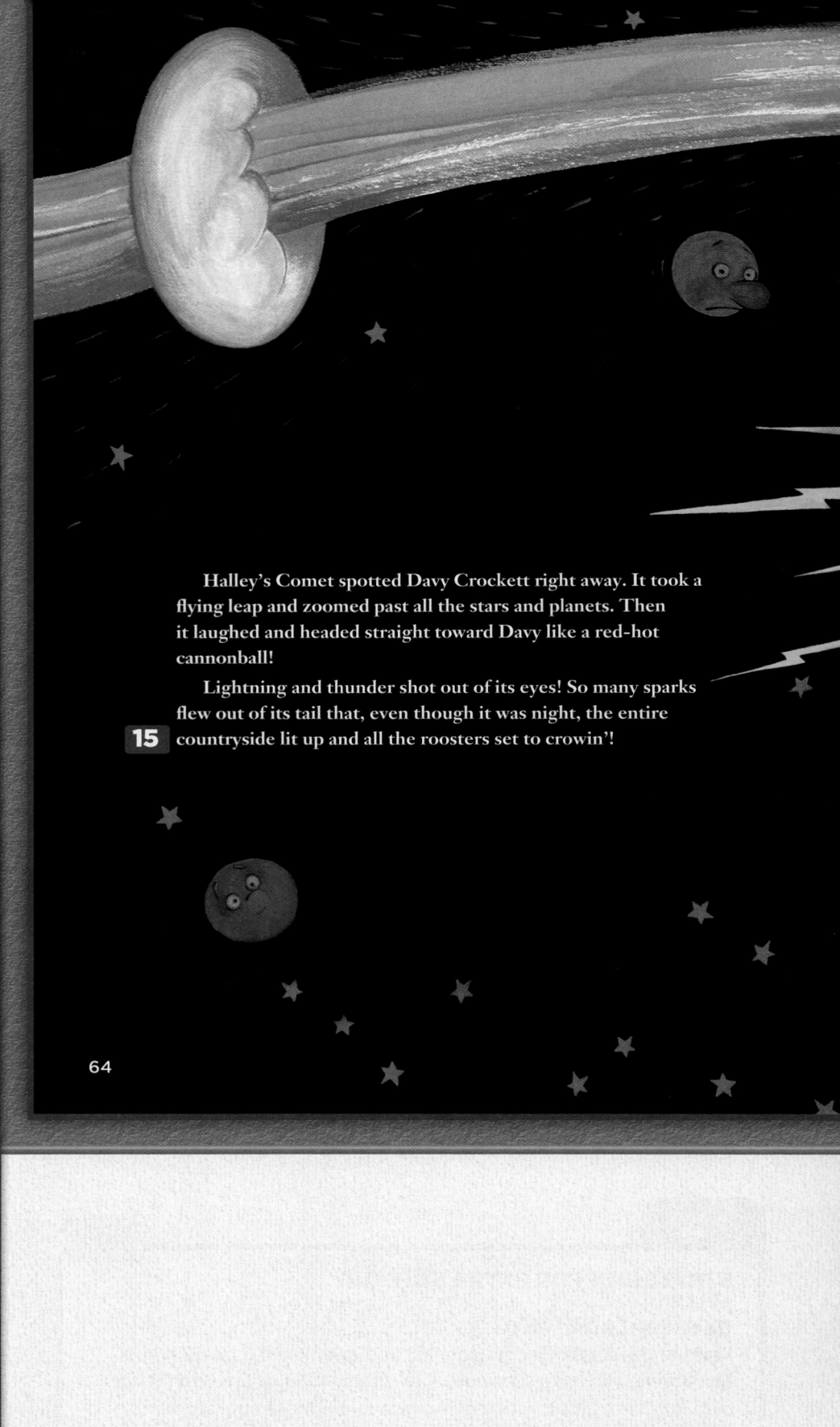

Halley's Comet spotted Davy Crockett right away. It took a flying leap and zoomed past all the stars and planets. Then it laughed and headed straight toward Davy like a red-hot cannonball!

Lightning and thunder shot out of its eyes! So many sparks flew out of its tail that, even though it was night, the entire **15** countryside lit up and all the roosters set to crowin'!

64

16

65

Develop Comprehension

16 USE ILLUSTRATION CLUES

How does the picture of Halley's comet on this page differ from the kind of picture you would find in an encyclopedia entry about the comet? (Answers should include that the illustration on page 65 shows Halley's comet with two eyes, a nose, and a mouth, in keeping with the elements of a tall tale.)

Fluency

Tempo and Expression

Explain Tempo refers to how quickly or slowly someone reads. Being able to vary the tempo and expression of your reading is the mark of a good reader. Varying tempo and expression helps you to express more accurately what is being conveyed in a passage.

Model Read aloud the first two paragraphs on **Student Book** page 64 by first reading them at a moderate pace with little or no expression. Then repeat with highly exaggerated expression.

Apply Tell the class that they will be reading the first two paragraphs chorally, or all together. Divide the class into two groups. Have one group read the paragraphs at a moderate pace with little or no expression. The other group reads the paragraphs in a highly exaggerated way. Groups should then switch roles.

Develop Comprehension

17 **USE ILLUSTRATION CLUES**

How does the illustrator of this tall tale use details from the story to make the events of the plot entertaining? (Answers will vary but students may note that the illustrations show Halley's comet with eyes and other anthropomorphic features that are mentioned in the text.) How do the illustrations compare with other media, such as animated cartoons? Do you think *Davy Crockett Saves the World* would make a good cartoon? Explain your answer. (Answers may vary but students should note that the exaggerated features on many of the principal and minor characters, as well as the depiction of Halley's comet, are the kinds of representations usually found in animated cartoons. The action in the story would probably lend itself to a cartoon adaptation.)

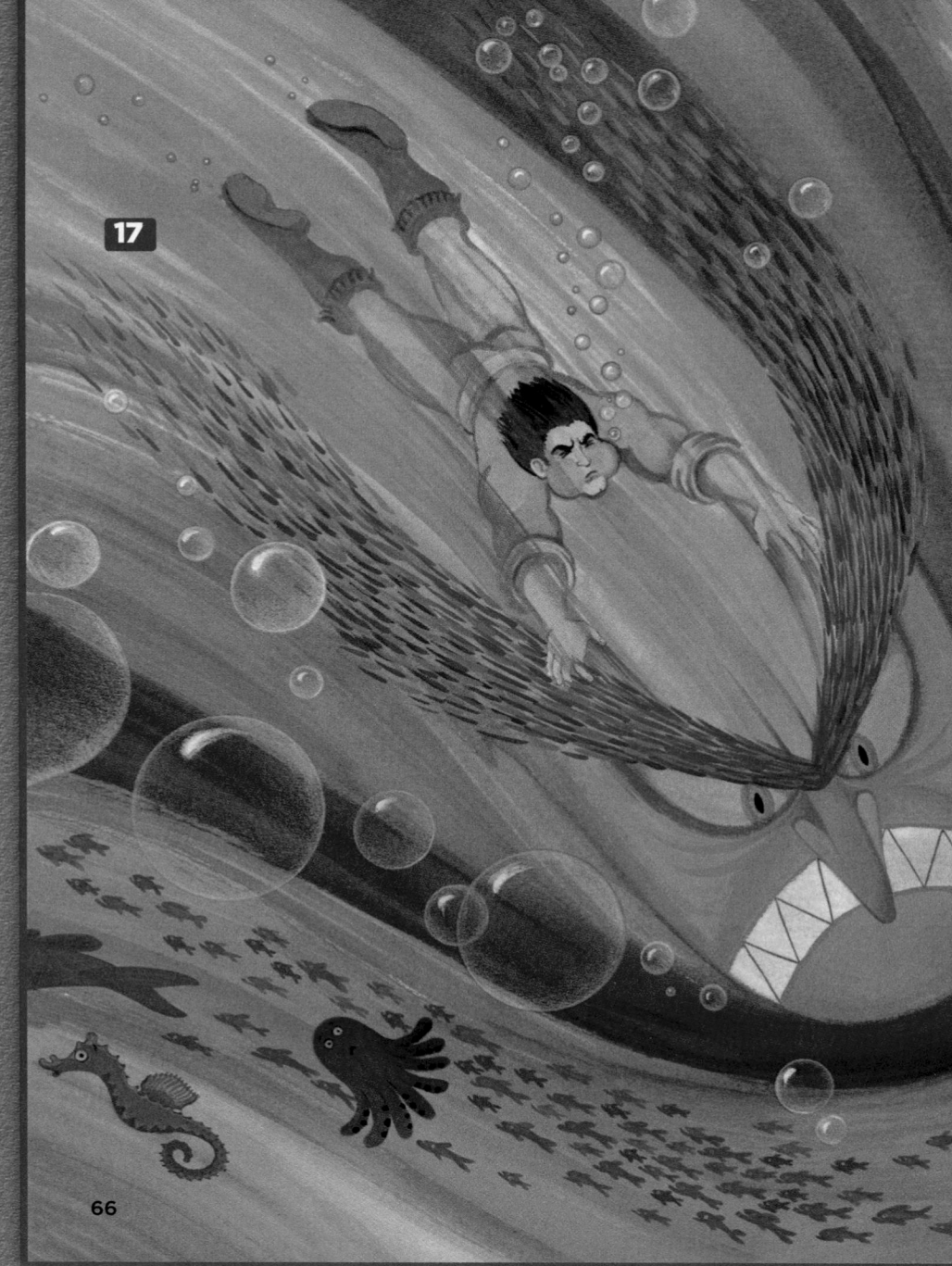

66

Cross–Curricular Connection

TALL-TALE HEROES

Tall tales are unique to North America. The tall tale originated in the 1820s with the frontiersmen and women who crossed the United States and Canada in search of new land to settle. It has remained popular well into the twentieth century. Other notable tall-tale characters include Mike Fink, "King of the Mississippi Keelboatmen." From Canada came Paul Bunyan, the lumberjack. African Americans told tales of John Henry, the railroad worker.

Have students use several sources of information to research one of these heroes. Students can illustrate their research and present their findings orally to the class. Remind students to adjust their presentation based on the audience, purpose, and situation. Allow students time to ask questions seeking information not already discussed.

That comet must have thought Davy looked mighty tender, for it licked its chops, howled louder than a hundred tornadoes, and roared toward him with its mouth wide open!

This made Davy so mad that he jumped right over its shoulders and onto its back. Then he planted his teeth around the comet's neck and hung on. Halley's Comet spun around and around like a whirlwind trying to throw Davy off, but it couldn't.

Next off, that comet tried to drown Davy by diving into the Atlantic Ocean. The water got so all-fired hot that it boiled! The whole world was covered with steam, and the sun didn't shine as bright as usual for a month.

Just in time, the ocean put out that comet's fire and melted all its ice. It washed up on an island, and before it could grow back to its **original** size, Davy grabbed what was left of Halley's tail, spun around seventeen times, and hurled the comet back into outer space. It was so discombobulated that the **18** next time it ever came in this direction, it missed the earth by 39 million miles.

67

Develop Comprehension

18 **ANALYZE STORY STRUCTURE**

Explain how the comet's attempt to drown him helps Davy to solve his problem. How does the setting contribute to the solution? Add your explanations to the chart.

Student Think Aloud Let's see. Dragging Davy into the ocean and trying to drown him was not a good idea. The ocean part of the setting puts out the comet's fire and melts its ice. Then, later, when the comet washes up on an island, Davy is able to get rid of it before it can grow back to its original size. He grabs what's left of Halley's tail and hurls it back into outer space. None of this would have happened if the comet hadn't tried to drown Davy.

Plot	Setting
Halley's comet is hurling toward America.	Near the Mississippi River almost 200 years ago.
Davy's decision to go to Washington means he will try and stop Halley's comet from hitting Earth.	Eagle Eye peak. So high you can see every state, river, and mountain in a geography book.
The ocean puts out the comet's fire and melts its ice. Davy gets rid of it before it can grow back to its original size.	The Atlantic Ocean and an island.

Develop Comprehension

19 STRATEGY
USE WORD PARTS

A compound word is a word made from two or more words joined together. Sometimes when you break a compound word into its parts, you can figure out its meaning. What is a *fireball?* (Answers will vary but should include a sphere or ball made up of hot gases that resemble a flame or fire.)

20 EXAGGERATION

How does the author describe what happened to Davy's hair after the comet burned it off? How do you know that her description is an exaggeration? (The author says that Davy's hair grew back in tufts like grass and was in such a snarl that he had to comb it with a rake. This is an exaggeration because Davy couldn't possibly comb his hair with a real rake.)

21 CAUSE AND EFFECT

What reason does the author give for Davy's wearing a coonskin cap? (Halley's comet singed the hair off of his head, so he is unable to even comb it.) Do you think this is the real reason Davy Crockett always wore a coonskin cap? Why or why not? (Possible answer: No. This is a tall tale, so the author is stretching the truth.)

That's how Davy Crockett saved the world. In fact, he did such a good job that there was a huge parade in his honor, he got to marry Sally Sugartree, and he was even **elected** to Congress.

68

Cultural Perspectives

Heroes in Literature around the World

Many famous heroes and villains can be found in literature around the world. For example: Wong Fei-Hung is one of the most treasured folk heroes in Southern Chinese culture. Don Quixote was a Spanish man who thought he was a medieval knight destined to fight against injustice by going on quests.

Have students form a book club to find different tales featuring these and other heroes and villains from world literature. They can use bookstores, libraries, and media centers for research; take notes about what they have read; and present the information in a panel discussion for the class. Encourage students to discuss how the authors used literary devices to clarify the functions and roles of heroes and villains. Students might also present dramatizations of stories for the class to demonstrate comprehension.

Of course, that infernal **fireball** singed the hair right off Davy's head. **19**
A whole new crop grew back in tufts like grass and kept in such a snarl **20**
that he couldn't even comb it without breaking his rake.

That's why these days Davy Crockett always wears a coonskin cap. **21**

69

RETURN TO PREDICTIONS AND PURPOSES

Review the predictions students made and their purposes for reading. Were they correct? Discuss with students whether they had to modify their predictions or purposes for reading as they read the story. Did they find out how the setting of *Davy Crockett Saves the World* had an impact on the events of the plot?

REVIEW READING STRATEGIES

How did thinking about ways the setting influenced the plot of this tall tale help you analyze and understand the story? What other comprehension strategies did you use to help you understand the text?

PERSONAL RESPONSE

Ask students to write down some ideas for another tall tale adventure that features Davy Crockett or Sally Sugartree as main characters. Have students think of an exciting title that will catch the reader's interest.

As an alternative, have students write an explanation of the tall tale by briefly retelling it and including examples and text-based evidence.

Quick Check   **Can students identify the setting and its effect on the events of the plot?**

During **Small Group Instruction**

If No → **Approaching Level** Leveled Reader Lesson, p. 77P

If Yes → **On Level** Options, pp. 77Q–77R

Beyond Level Options, pp. 77S–77T

Author-Illustrator

GO EXPLORING WITH ROSALYN SCHANZER

Have students read the biography of the author-illustrator.

DISCUSS

- What inspires Rosalyn Schanzer to write stories?

- Why do you think Rosalyn Schanzer illustrates her stories before she writes?

WRITE ABOUT IT

Review the historical information about Davy Crockett in this selection. Discuss the experience of reading the same facts in a history book. Now have students write a paragraph explaining their preference: learning facts from tall tales or from a history book.

Author's Purpose

Discuss with students why Rosalyn Schanzer wrote *Davy Crockett Saves the World.* Then explain that authors who write tall tales usually want to entertain readers. Ask if students found this tale entertaining. Have them explain their answers using examples from the story.

 **Technology**

Students can find more information about Rosalyn Schanzer at **www.macmillanmh.com**

GO EXPLORING WITH ROSALYN SCHANZER

Rosalyn Schanzer loves adventure just as much as Davy Crockett. She swam with sharks in Belize; kayaked with whales in Alaska; fished for piranhas in South America; and even sailed a boat through the Bermuda Triangle. When Rosalyn wants to create a new story, she treks to a different part of the globe to seek an unusual adventure.

Before words ever hit the page, Rosalyn illustrates her books. While traveling she asks questions, snaps pictures, and researches facts that can be used for artistic inspiration. After Rosalyn illustrates her new ideas and adventures, she brings the story to life with words. It seems only fitting that Rosalyn, who has gone on such unique adventures, takes such an unusual and adventurous approach to creating books.

Other books by Rosalyn Schanzer: *Gold Fever: Tales of the California Gold Rush* and *How Ben Franklin Stole the Lightning*

Author's Purpose

Tall tale heroes and heroines do amazing things. Why might Rosalyn Schanzer have written this story besides wanting to explain Halley's Comet to readers?

LOG ON Find out more about Rosalyn Schanzer at **www.macmillanmh.com**

70

Author's Craft

Informal Language

Rosalyn Schanzer made her tall tale entertaining by using **informal language** that reminds readers of the way a storyteller from Davy Crockett's time might have sounded. For example:

I reckon by now you've heard of Davy Crockett. (p. 54)

Explain to students that by using this phrase, the author sounds as if she's having a conversation with the reader. Ask students how the story's informal language reminds readers of old-fashioned storytelling, and have them find other examples of its use. Then discuss what makes the language in this story informal.

Have students continue to look for other examples of informal language when they reread the story.

Comprehension Check

Summarize

Use your Plot and Setting Chart to help you summarize *Davy Crockett Saves the World*. When preparing your summary, be sure to include only important events and characters.

Plot	Setting

Think and Compare

1. How does the setting of the Atlantic Ocean add to the excitement of the story? **Story Structure: Plot and Setting**

2. Reread page 54. Should you believe everything that is said about Davy Crockett? Why or why not? **Analyze**

3. If you were President, whom would you ask to save the world? Explain your answer. **Evaluate**

4. How would the President's **advertisement** to Davy Crockett be different if the story took place now? Explain. **Analyze**

5. Reread "Grandma's Tales" on pages 50–51. Describe how Grandma would react to *Davy Crockett Saves the World*. Use details from both stories to explain your answer. **Reading/Writing Across Texts**

71

Strategies for Answering Questions

On My Own

Model the On My Own strategy with questions 3 and 4.

The answer is not in the selection. The student has to use critical thinking skills to go beyond the text.

Question 3: Think Aloud This question seems easy on the surface, but if you start to think about it, most of our superheroes today are in the movies and comic books. They're not real people. So if I were President, I might choose someone who was very smart instead of very strong. Maybe I'd choose a famous scientist.

Question 4: Think Aloud Today the President could place an advertisement in more than one kind of media. This would improve the President's chances of reaching Davy Crockett.

Comprehension Check

SUMMARIZE

Have students summarize the tall tale by paraphrasing the events in written form. Remind students to use their Plot and Setting Chart to help them organize their summaries.

THINK AND COMPARE

Sample answers are given.

1. **Plot and Setting:** Answers will vary but should include that the comet's decision to dive into the Atlantic creates a situation that is exciting to visualize.

2. **Analyze:** No. Many of the things that Davy is said to have done are not possible. Even the writer says that "every single word is true, unless it is false."

3. **Text to Self:** Answers will vary but should include people with "heroic qualities" similar to Davy Crockett's. USE ON MY OWN

4. **Text to World:** Answers will vary. Students may suggest that the President's advertisement might include a music video or a flashy ad campaign on the Internet. USE ON MY OWN

FOCUS QUESTION

5. **Text to Text:** Possible answer: Grandma would not like the story. She was not impressed when her grandson mentioned that Davy captured a cougar with his bare hands. She probably would not be happy about the claim that Davy "could whip ten times his weight in wildcats" either.

Objectives

- Read accurately with good prosody
- Rate: 100–120 WCPM

Materials

- Fluency Transparency 2
- Fluency Solutions
- Leveled Practice Books, p. 11

ELL | Access for All

Practice Intonation
Choose a few sentences to fully explain so that students understand the imagery. Demonstrate actions and use your voice to help add meaning. Echo-read the sentences with students. Encourage students to mimic your intonation and expressiveness.

On Level Practice Book O, page 11

As I read, I will pay attention to punctuation.

	Back then it wasn't easy to feed a large family. Luckily
11	Johnny possessed a green thumb. From the time that he was
22	two years old, it seemed as if Johnny could just look at
34	a seed and a plant commenced to grow. So Johnny and his
46	green thumb fed his large family.
52	There was plenty of food, but dinnertime was extremely
61	noisy in Johnny's house. Why, it was as if a volcano was
73	exploding at dinnertime! As soon as the food hit the table,
84	the children shouted and complained.
89	"Tommy's apple pie is bigger than mine!"
96	"Why are we having apple juice again?"
103	All that noise gave Johnny a headache, so he would take
114	his dinner outside and escape to his favorite spot, the apple
125	orchard. There, Johnny felt at home. 131

Comprehension Check

1. What kind of person is Johnny? **Character**
   He liked peace and quiet and liked growing plants.
2. How did Johnny's family benefit from his green thumb? **Plot**
   Johnny provided food for his large family.

	Words Read	−	Number of Errors	=	Words Correct Score
First Read		−		=	
Second Read		−		=	

★ **Approaching Practice Book A,** page 11
◆ **Beyond Practice Book B,** page 11

Fluency
Repeated Reading: Punctuation

EXPLAIN/MODEL Remind students that echo-reading is reading aloud phrase by phrase after a live or taped model. Model reading aloud **Fluency Transparency 2**, emphasizing the punctuation in each sentence. Then read one or two sentences at a time while students echo-read. Point out that commas break longer sentences into parts and make them easier to understand. Note that an exclamation point can show surprise or excitement.

Think Aloud The last paragraph has commas that help break it up. They help me read this sentence more easily. I also do not want to forget there are exclamation points throughout.

Transparency 2

Halley's Comet spotted Davy Crockett right away. It took a flying leap and zoomed past all the stars and planets. Then It laughed and headed straight toward Davy like a red-hot cannonball!

Lightning and thunder shot out of its eyes! So many sparks flew out of its tail that, even though it was night, the entire countryside lit up and all the roosters set to crowin'!

That comet must have thought Davy looked mighty tender, for it licked its chops, howled louder than a hundred tornadoes, and roared toward him with its mouth wide open!

Fluency Transparency 2 from *Davy Crockett Saves the World,* pages 64, 67

PRACTICE/APPLY Divide students into two groups. The first group reads the passage a sentence at a time. The second group echo-reads. Then groups switch roles. Students can practice fluency using **Leveled Practice Book** page 11 or the Fluency Solutions Audio CD.

Quick Check | Can students read accurately with good prosody?

During **Small Group Instruction**

If No → **Approaching Level** Fluency, p. 77N

If Yes → **On Level** Options, pp. 77Q–77R

Beyond Level Options, pp. 77S–77T

Comprehension

MAINTAIN SKILL
CHARACTER

EXPLAIN/MODEL Discuss the function of character with students.

- A **major character** is the person a story is about. **Minor characters** appear in the story, but are not as important to the plot. Understanding a **character** in a story helps readers relate to the character, appreciate his or her feelings, and make predictions about what the character will do.

- To recognize character traits, look for the author's description of the character. Think about the character's thoughts, feelings, words, actions, and motivations. For example, the first paragraph of this selection tells a lot about Davy Crockett's character.

PRACTICE/APPLY Discuss the character of Davy Crockett.

- How does Davy feel about Sally Sugartree? How does he feel about the comet? How do his feelings affect the way he acts toward both? Use evidence from the text to support your answer.

- Davy Crockett was a real person. In what ways is tall-tale hero Davy like a real person? How is he different?

- Suppose Davy were asked to save the country from a hurricane. What might he do? What do you know about his character that helps you predict this?

Group students in pairs. Have them read the dialogue with a partner to make the characters come alive.

For comprehension practice use Graphic Organizers on **Teacher's Resource Book** pages 40–64.

Objective
- Analyze character

Skills Trace

Character, Plot, Setting

Introduce	19A–B
Practice / Apply	20–39; Leveled Practice, 2–3
Reteach / Review	47M–T, 51A–B, 52–69, 77M–T; Leveled Practice, 9–10
Assess	Weekly Tests; Units 1, 4 Tests; Benchmarks Tests A, B
Maintain	41B, 71B, 133B, 395A–B; 396–411, 419M–T, 661B; Leveled Practice, 113–114

Informational Text: Social Studies

GENRE: ONLINE ARTICLE

Have students read the bookmark on **Student Book** page 72. Explain that an online article:

- presents facts about real people, things, places, situations, or events via the Internet;

- may contain information that can be found in reference sources, such as an online encyclopedia.

Text Features:
Toolbar and Link

EXPLAIN Point out the link on page 72 and the toolbar on page 73. Explain:

- A **toolbar** is a strip of icons or symbols on a computer that allows you to visit different features on the Web page.

- A **link** is an electronic connection on a Web page that provides direct access to other documents or information.

PRACTICE/APPLY Have students discuss how they can use links and toolbars to locate information on a Web page. Students should use organizational features to locate relevant information.

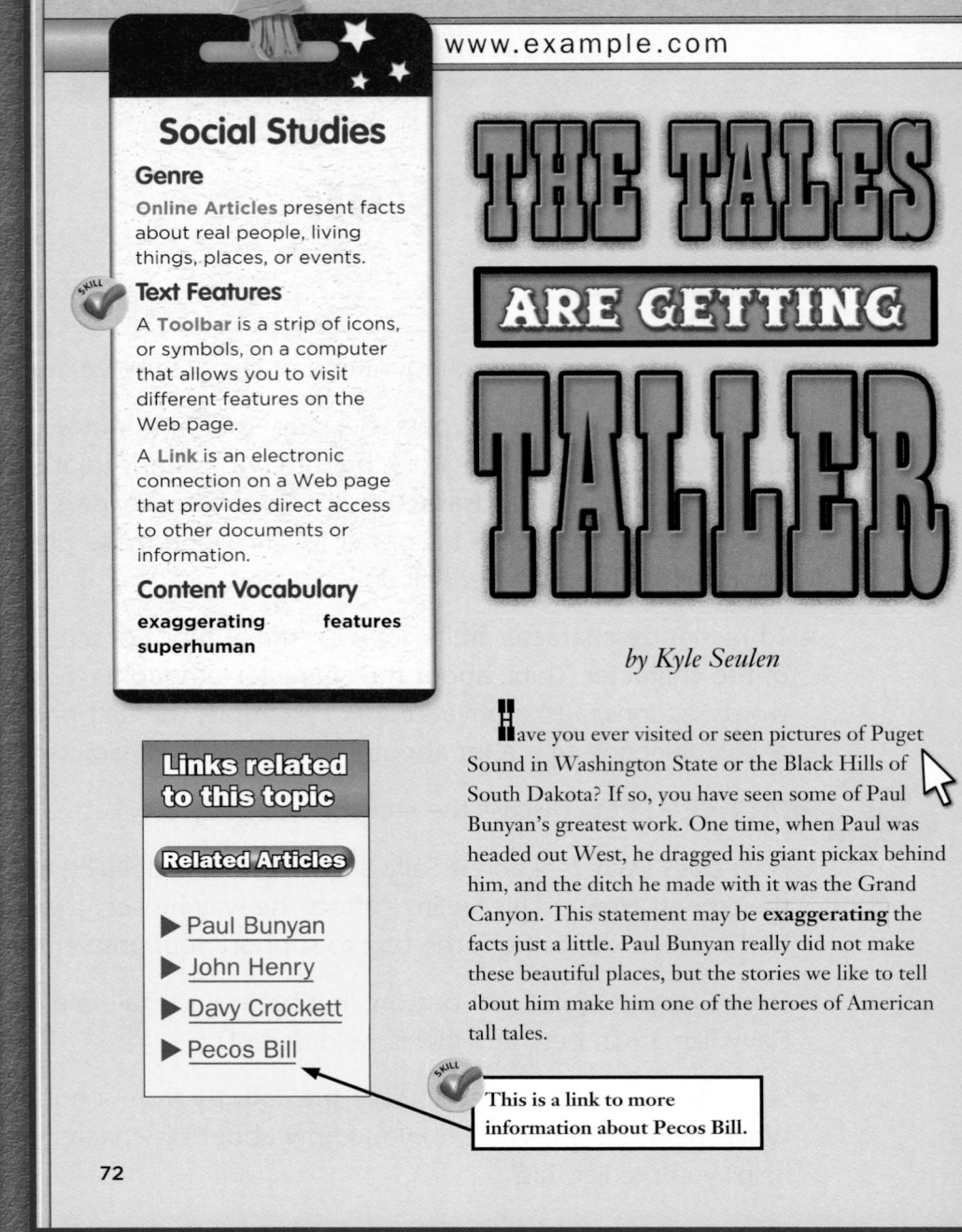

www.example.com

Social Studies

Genre

Online Articles present facts about real people, living things, places, or events.

Text Features

A **Toolbar** is a strip of icons, or symbols, on a computer that allows you to visit different features on the Web page.

A **Link** is an electronic connection on a Web page that provides direct access to other documents or information.

Content Vocabulary

exaggerating   features
superhuman

THE TALES ARE GETTING TALLER

by Kyle Seulen

Have you ever visited or seen pictures of Puget Sound in Washington State or the Black Hills of South Dakota? If so, you have seen some of Paul Bunyan's greatest work. One time, when Paul was headed out West, he dragged his giant pickax behind him, and the ditch he made with it was the Grand Canyon. This statement may be **exaggerating** the facts just a little. Paul Bunyan really did not make these beautiful places, but the stories we like to tell about him make him one of the heroes of American tall tales.

This is a link to more information about Pecos Bill.

Links related to this topic

Related Articles

▶ Paul Bunyan
▶ John Henry
▶ Davy Crockett
▶ Pecos Bill

72

Content Vocabulary

Discuss the three content vocabulary words listed for "The Tales Are Getting Taller" on Student Book page 72: *exaggerating, features, superhuman*.

- If you are **exaggerating**, you are overstating the truth. In what situations might you find yourself exaggerating?

- **Features** are qualities or characteristics. What are some features of your school?

- If someone is **superhuman**, that person can go beyond normal human limits. Name a fictional character who is superhuman.

Home   Browse   Search Tall Tales

2

This strip of icons is called a toolbar.

Paul Bunyan and Babe

John Henry

Old Stormalong

Pecos Bill

David Crockett

Tall tale heroes and the regions where they were born

What is a tall tale? Four **features** **1** make a story a tall tale. First, the hero must seem larger than life and have **superhuman** skills. Second, the hero usually has a certain job that he does better than anyone else. The hero might be a lumberjack or a cowhand, for example. Third, the hero must solve a problem in a way that surprises the reader or makes the audience laugh. Fourth, the details of the tale are exaggerated

to be made greater than they really are. Often, the hero is bursting with courage and ready to conquer any difficulty. As a rule, the heroes would be a little rough on the outside. Still, they had tender hearts and souls and possessed the most admirable qualities. They were helpful, always available to solve problems and determined to create a better world for their neighbors and friends.

73

Informational Text

Read
"The Tales Are Getting Taller"

Access for All
As you read, remind students to apply what they have learned about toolbars and links. Also have them identify clues to the meanings of the highlighted words.

1 VOCABULARY

What are the features of a tall tale? (Tall tales contain exaggeration and heroes who seem larger than life. They often have superhuman skills and solve problems in surprising ways.)

2 TEXT FEATURE: TOOLBAR

Tested
What other functions could you perform using this toolbar? (You could visit the home page or browse related subjects.)

Students should locate age-and-content-appropriate information only.

ELL

Access for All

Use Academic Vocabulary Explain the Content Vocabulary through examples. For example, for the word *exaggerating*, say *My grandfather can cook really well. This is a fact. He is the best cook in the world! This is not a fact. I am exaggerating.* Have students give examples of exaggeration: *(My dad) is _____. (He) is so (strong) that he _____.* For *features*, compare the features of Davy Crocket to those of a superhero. For the word *superhuman*, discuss popular superheroes and their superpowers using this sentence frame: *(Superhero) is superhuman because (he/she) can _____.*

Informational Text

3 **VOCABULARY**

Why do you think settlers kept exaggerating the characters in their tall tales? (Exaggeration made the characters more interesting. Exaggeration also made the pioneers feel as if they could face any kind of danger on the frontier, just like the characters in a tall tale.)

4 **TEXT FEATURE: LINK**

What kind of additional background information about Paul Bunyan might be found on the link on page 72? Do you think this link would be a reliable source of information? How would you decide? (This link might describe the people who first told Paul Bunyan stories and reveal when and where the tales first appeared. It might also give information about different versions of the tale. I think it would be reliable because the original site is a reliable source.)

5 **WRITER'S CRAFT: TOPIC SENTENCE**

Look back at this paragraph. Which sentence is the topic sentence? How can you tell? (The first sentence in the paragraph is the topic sentence. It states the main idea, and the other sentences in the paragraph provide more information about it by describing an example.)

---

http://www.example.com

4

How did the tradition of inventing tales starring characters that were larger-than-life begin? Tall tales probably started as settlers moved into America's wilderness areas. Life on the American frontier was difficult, exhausting, dangerous and uncertain. For the most part, the future was unknown and scary. When the day was done, pioneers gathered around the fire in search of relaxation and entertainment. Telling stories became a favorite pastime. It was a handy art form that could not only entertain but inspire as well. The tales that were told helped the people feel they could overcome danger, just as their favorite heroes had.

3 As the tales were repeated, they somehow took on a life of their own and grew bigger and better. For example, if someone roped a fierce bear and swung it across town, then in the retelling he

roped the same bear and swung it across country. In the next telling of the story the hero would have swung the bear so far it landed on the moon. Even though no one believed a bear landed on the moon, people certainly enjoyed listening to the story as much as the storyteller enjoyed **5** telling it.

A brand-new tall tale often had the fellow who told it or somebody from the "neighborhood" as its hero. But as the tale became more famous, people began to feel it wasn't "right" that such a wonderful story be told about an ordinary man. The pioneers decided that larger-than-life stories needed to feature larger-than-life heroes. So, they began putting famous characters in the leading roles of the stories they would tell. Some were real heroes of the day such as Davy Crockett or Jim Bridger. Others, like Paul Bunyan and Pecos Bill, were products of the imaginations of good storytellers.

A particular tall tale might also be influenced by events in the region where it was born. People who made their living from the sea liked to hear stories about the adventures of Old Stormalong and his ship. Railroad workers liked to hear stories about John Henry, who could hammer railroad spikes faster than anyone else. Ranchers and cowboys enjoyed hearing about Pecos Bill who roped a mountain

74

On Level Practice Book O, page 12

A **toolbar** is a strip of symbols that allows you to visit different features on a Web site. A **link** is an electronic connection on a Web site that provides direct access to other information.

Use the Web site page to answer the questions.
Possible responses provided.

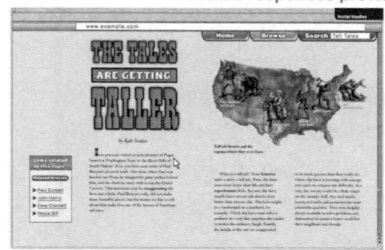

1. Why is the toolbar important? The toolbar is important because it has the Home, Browse, and Search buttons.

2. What do links do? Links are electronic connections on a Web site that will link you to more information or another Web site.

3. On this Web site, how else would you get information on tall tales? To get more information you can use the Search button on the toolbar.

 Approaching Practice Book A, page 12

◆ **Beyond Practice Book B, page 12**

lion and rode it a hundred feet at a step. They also enjoyed hearing about Slue-foot Sue who rode a catfish down the Rio Grande.

Speaking of roping, if you feel up to it, you might try to catch a ride to the lumber camp on Paul Bunyan's blue ox, Babe. It shouldn't be too hard to catch him. The distance between Babe's horns is just a little over seven ax handles. Once you rope him and he takes you to the camp, relax by the campfire. The lumberjacks there will probably have another tale or two to share with you!

Connect and Compare

1. If you were on this Web page what feature would you select to help you find out more information about Babe, Paul Bunyan's ox? **Using Toolbars and Links**

2. If you were to write a tall tale, who would be the hero? Explain your answer. **Synthesize**

3. Think about "The Tales Are Getting Taller" and *Davy Crockett Saves the World.* How do you know that *Davy Crockett Saves the World* is a tall tale? **Reading/Writing Across Texts**

 Social Studies Activity

Use an online encyclopedia to learn more about one hero on the map on page 73. Write a tall tale about the person you choose. Remember to exaggerate the tale.

 Find out more about tall tales at **www.macmillanmh.com**

75

Informational Text

Connect and Compare

SUGGESTED ANSWERS

1. I would type *Babe* in the search box. USING TOOLBARS AND LINKS

2. Answers will vary but students should select a hero and explain their selection in full. SYNTHESIZE

FOCUS QUESTION

3. Davy Crockett in this story is an exaggerated hero with outlandish dimensions. He does things that would not be possible in real life.

READING/WRITING ACROSS TEXTS

Social Studies Activity

After the students choose a tall tale hero, direct them to search by trying multiple key words. Tell them to list some different key words they will use, and offer an example list based on Davy Crockett. The sample list could include the following key words and search phrases: *Davy Crockett, tall tale, legends, frontier, folktale.*

 Technology

Internet Research and Inquiry Activity
Students can find more facts at
www.macmillanmh.com

WRITING
- Personal Narrative
- **Writer's Craft:** Topic Sentence

WORD STUDY
- Words in Context
- Word Parts: Compound Words
- **Phonics:** Words with Long Vowels
- Vocabulary Building

SPELLING
- Words with Long Vowels

GRAMMAR
- Subjects and Predicates

SMALL GROUP OPTIONS
- Differentiated Instruction, pp. 77M–77V

Writing

Topic Sentence

READ THE STUDENT MODEL

Read the bookmark about writing a topic sentence. Explain that a topic sentence tells readers what a paragraph is about. The topic sentence is often the first sentence in a paragraph and is supported by the details in the paragraph.

Have students turn to the first paragraph on page 54. Point out the topic sentence. Then have the class read Carla M.'s **personal narrative** and the callouts. Tell students that topic sentences will alert readers to the subject of a paragraph.

Write About a Hero

▼ Writer's Craft

Topic Sentence
The first sentence in a paragraph is usually the **topic sentence**. It tells what the paragraph will be about.

> My topic sentence tells about my own hero.

> I wasn't afraid to tell how I really feel about Aliyah.

Aliyah, My Hero
by Carla M.

My hero, my neighbor Aliyah, is only seven years old, but she is the bravest person I know. Aliyah has cerebral palsy. Her muscles don't work properly, so she uses a wheelchair. I'd probably be mad at the world if I were Aliyah, but you never even know when Aliyah is having a tough day. She is always smiling.

Doing many everyday tasks is a challenge for Aliyah. Picking up a dropped pencil or getting into a car are complicated tasks. Aliyah gets everything done, but she needs to move slowly and carefully. It's amazing how much patience she has. She almost never gets frustrated.

Aliyah loves jokes, riddles, and games like "Twenty Questions" and "I Spy." Aliyah is so smart that she usually wins.

I know I am lucky to be friends with Aliyah. She has taught me what it really means to be special.

76

Features of a Personal Narrative

In a personal narrative, the writer tells a true story about his or her own experiences. It may focus on the development of a single event.

- A personal narrative is written in the first-person, using words such as *I, me, my,* and *mine*.

- It describes how the author felt about the experience.

- It may chronicle a sequence of events.

- Like a fictional narrative, it tells a story and usually includes details about character and setting.

Your Turn

Write a few paragraphs about your own personal hero. Why is he or she your hero? Tell how you feel about this person. Use the writer's checklist to check your writing.

Writer's Checklist

✓ **Ideas and Content:** Does my writing say what I mean?

☐ **Organization:** Does my topic sentence let the reader know what I am writing about?

✓ **Voice:** Did I express my feelings about my hero?

✓ **Word Choice:** Did I use words that are fresh and new?

✓ **Sentence Fluency:** Did I use different sentence types?

✓ **Conventions:** Did I use commas in a series correctly? Did I check my spelling?

77

PREWRITE

Discuss the writing prompt on page 77. Have students think of heroes they would most like to introduce to readers or self-select a topic. Students should set a purpose for writing and identify their audience.

Display **Transparency 5.** Point out that Carla wrote the main focus of the narrative in the center and supporting details in the outer circles. Have students use idea webs to plan their narratives. See page 77B for **Outlining and Organizing Related Ideas** for another way students can plan their writing.

DRAFT

Display **Transparency 6.** Discuss how Carla used her web to help her draft.

Before students draft, present the **Topic Sentence** lesson on page 77A. Then have students use their webs to draft. Remind them to include clear and engaging topic sentences and to choose a good title.

REVISE

Display **Transparency 7.** Discuss the revisions. Carla combines sentences, reorders details, and adds a topic sentence. Students can revise their drafts or place them in writing portfolios to work on later. If students choose to revise, have them work with a partner and use the Writer's Checklist on page 77. Have them **proofread** their writing. For **Publishing Options** see page 77A.

For lessons on **Subjects and Predicates, Spelling,** and **Organization,** see page 77B and **5 Day Spelling** and **Grammar,** pages 77G–77J.

Transparency 5: **Idea Web**
Transparency 6: **Draft**
Transparency 7: **Revision**

Transparency 5

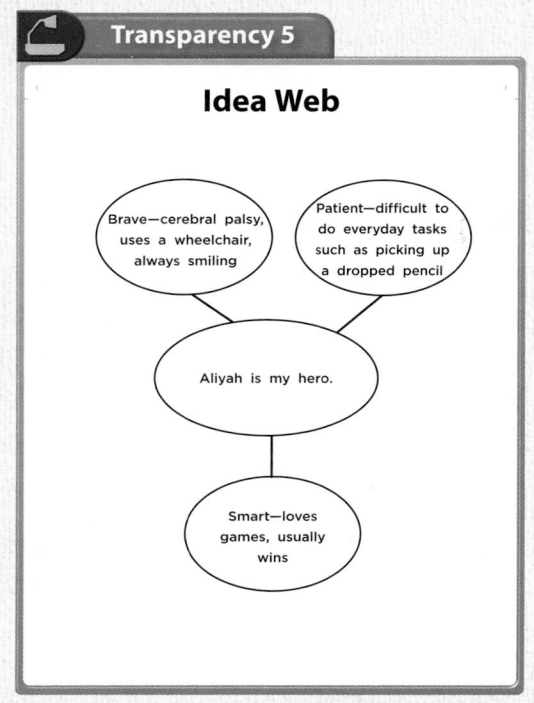

Idea Web

Brave—cerebral palsy, uses a wheelchair, always smiling

Patient—difficult to do everyday tasks such as picking up a dropped pencil

Aliyah is my hero.

Smart—loves games, usually wins

Writing Transparency 5

Topic Sentence

Publishing Options

Students can tell their stories orally to the class. See the Speaking and Listening tips below. They can also use their best cursive to write their narratives. (See **Teacher's Resource Book** pages 168–173 for cursive models and practice.) Students can then create hero collages to illustrate their work, including photographs or drawings of their heroes along with symbols that illustrate their traits. Create a classroom hero Hall of Fame.

Speaking and Listening

SPEAKING STRATEGIES

- Practice reading your narrative before presenting it to the class.

- Speak loudly enough to reach all of your listeners.

- Use an even tempo but stress important points.

LISTENING STRATEGIES

- Focus on the speaker's main points.

- Show you are interested by making eye contact.

- Be prepared to ask questions or express your opinions.

4- and 6-Point Scoring Rubrics

Use the rubrics on page 143G–143H to score published writing.

Writing Process

For a complete lesson, see Unit Writing pages 143A–143H.

77A

EXPLAIN/MODEL

Writers organize paragraphs by stating main ideas in clear and engaging topic sentences. Writers want to inform readers regarding the subject of the paragraph and invite them to keep reading. Display **Transparency 8**.

Think Aloud I can see that the focus of the essay is Josh. The writer clearly admires him. However, I didn't learn about Josh until the middle of the paragraph. I think a topic sentence at the beginning of the paragraph would help me and others know the focus right from the beginning.

Transparency 8

Superman on the Bus
by Melvin W.

During the bus ride home yesterday, a young boy dropped his backpack in the aisle. The zipper wasn't shut, so the books and papers spilled. Some of the students began laughing and kicking the papers. The student's face turned red, and tears brimmed in his eyes. Luckily for the boy, Superman was near. Josh, who was sitting near the back of the bus, heard the noise and looked up. In a flash, Josh came to the boy's rescue. He told the kids to leave the boy alone and began picking up the books and papers. Instead of stuffing them back into the backpack, Josh straightened the items and placed them neatly inside. He smiled warmly when he handed the backpack to boy, inviting him to sit with Josh for the rest of the ride. Josh doesn't know it, but he became my friend that day, too.

Possible topic sentence: My friend Josh did a great deed the other day.

Writing Transparency 8

PRACTICE/APPLY

Work with students to create a possible topic sentence for the paragraph. Then have students work in pairs to create several more possible topic sentences. Have students select the best topic sentence for the paragraph and explain their choice. Finally, have students identify topic sentences in narrative nonfiction they have read recently.

As students write their personal narratives, encourage them to write an effective topic sentence for each paragraph.

Writer's Toolbox

Writing Trait: Organization

Explain/Model Using topic sentences can help students organize their writing. They should try to begin each paragraph with a topic sentence stating the main idea and then follow it with sentences that provide supporting details. Have students review Carla's essay on page 76. Point out that Carla begins each paragraph with a clear topic sentence. Have students identify some supporting details.

Practice/Apply As students draft their narratives, have them write topic sentences that are both clear and interesting for readers. Suggest that students write compound or complex topic sentences.

Subjects and Predicates

Explain/Model Explain that a sentence contains a subject and a predicate. The subject is who or what the sentence is about. The predicate is what the subject does or is. Write: *Aliyah has cerebral palsy.* Tell them that the subject is *Aliyah* and that the predicate is *has cerebral palsy.*

Practice/Apply Have students reread the essay on page 76 and identify the subject and predicate of each sentence. For a complete lesson, see pages 77I–77J.

Mechanics In the model point out commas in a series and in appositives. Have students correct their own comma placement as they proofread.

Outlining and Organizing Related Ideas

Explain/Model Good paragraphs contain a topic sentence and supporting details. All of the sentences in a paragraph should relate to the topic sentence. To organize related ideas, writers can use outlines before they begin writing.

Practice/Apply Before students begin writing, have them decide whether to use idea webs or outlines to list main ideas and supporting details. Suggest that students write topic sentences that cite the reasons their subjects are heroes. Then tell students to include details that illustrate or elaborate on these traits.

Spelling Words with Long Vowels

Point out *bravest* in the second sentence of the essay on page 76. The long vowel sound is spelled *a.* However, some words with long vowel sounds have unexpected spellings, as in *prey* and *type.* Remind students to pay attention when they spell words with long vowels. They can use a print or online dictionary to check spelling in their drafts. For a complete lesson on spelling words with long vowels, see pages 77G–77H.

Technology

Suggest that students print their work and proofread it. Have them also proof it on the screen. They may want to use the spell-check function. Then have them tell which way works best.

Objectives

- Apply knowledge of word meaning and context clues
- Use word parts to create and decode compound words

Materials

- Vocabulary Transparencies 3, 4
- Leveled Practice Books, p. 13

Vocabulary

advertisement (p. 58) public notice or announcement recommending some product or service

sauntered (p. 58) walked along slowly or happily

commenced (p. 63) began

elected (p. 68) chosen for public office by a majority vote

wring (p. 63) to twist with force; squeeze hard

impress (p. 58) to have a strong effect on the mind or feelings

original (p. 67) of or from the beginning; first

fireball (p. 69) anything that looks like a mass of bright heat

ELL

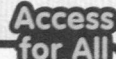

Word Web Create a word web with *original*. Brainstorm items that can be original and discuss things students have made or seen that were original. Do a similar activity for *impress*.

Review
Vocabulary
Words in Context

EXPLAIN/MODEL

Review the meanings of the vocabulary words. Display **Vocabulary Transparency 3.** Model how to use word meanings and context clues to fill in the first missing word.

Think Aloud In the first sentence, something suggests that the soap was a good product because it was powerful. I know that advertisements recommend products by claiming how good they are. So the word that will complete this sentence must be *advertisement.*

Transparency 3

| advertisement | commenced | elected | impress |
| original | sauntered | wring | fireball |

The (1) <u>advertisement</u> stated that the soap was powerful.

The man (2) <u>sauntered</u> through the park, stopping now and then.

The graduation ceremony (3) <u>commenced</u> with the class march.

The senator was (4) <u>elected</u> to office for a second term.

He tried to (5) <u>wring</u> the dead limb from the tree.

The boy tried to (6) <u>impress</u> the girl by bringing her flowers.

The (7) <u>original</u> library, rebuilt after the fire, was made of wood.

The sun hung in the sky all day, a great (8) <u>fireball</u> baking the dry earth.

Vocabulary Transparency 3

PRACTICE/APPLY

Instruct students to complete the remaining sentences on their own. Review the students' answers as a class, or instruct students to check their answers with partners. Have students add these words to a word wall.

Answer This Have student partners generate written questions for each other using the vocabulary words. For example: *How can you tell if someone* sauntered? Students should answer the questions in writing, restating the vocabulary word.

STRATEGY
USE WORD PARTS: COMPOUND WORDS

EXPLAIN/MODEL

- A long word made up of two smaller words is called a *compound word*.

- The combined meanings of the two smaller words can often help readers understand the meaning of the larger compound word.

Model determining the meaning of the compound word *cannonball* on **Transparency 4**.

> ### Transparency 4
>
> **Compound Words**
>
> 1. Then it laughed and headed straight toward Davy like a red-hot cannonball.
>   *cannon* means _____ *ball* means _____
>   cannonball means _____
> 2. That's why these days Davy Crockett always wears a *coonskin* cap.
> 3. The *cowgirl* threw the *saddlebag* over the horse's back.
> 4. Toby got a new *cookbook* and is eager to try some new recipes.
> 5. The *fisherman* caught 20 pounds of salmon today.

Vocabulary Strategy Transparency 4

PRACTICE/APPLY

Have students tell the meanings of the compound words in items 2–5. Have students write a sentence using another compound word. Then partners can trade sentences and use a dictionary to figure out the meaning of the compound word.

> **Quick Check**
> **Can students determine word meanings?**
> **Can students decode compound words?**
>
> During **Small Group Instruction**
>
> If No → **Approaching Level** Vocabulary, pp. 77N–77O
>
> If Yes → **On Level** Options, pp. 77Q–77R
>
> **Beyond Level** Options, pp. 77S–77T

> **ELL** Access for All
>
> **Compound Words**
> Discuss the meaning of the individual words that make up each compound word and compare them to the meaning of the compound word. You may need to explain the word *saddlebag* in the transparency.

> ■ **On Level Practice Book O,** page 13
>
> Sometimes two smaller words are put together to form a **compound word**. Recognizing the smaller words can help you figure out the compound word's meaning. For example, **newspaper** is a compound word made from the words **news** and **paper**. The word **newspaper** means "paper on which news is published."
>
> **Underline the compound word in each sentence. Then write the compound word's meaning using the meaning of smaller words to help you.**
>
> 1. The storyteller told an exciting tale about Davy Crockett. A storyteller is a person who tells stories.
> 2. One story is about how Pecos Bill tames a whirlwind. A whirlwind is a kind of wind that whirls or twists around.
> 3. I wrote a story about Sluefoot Sue in my notebook. A notebook is a special book in which one writes something such as notes.
> 4. The townspeople decided to ask Davy Crockett for help. Townspeople are the people who live in a town.
> 5. We could see for miles from the top of the skyscraper. A skyscraper is a building that is so tall it "scrapes the sky."
> 6. For dinner, Davy Crockett ate homegrown tomatoes in his salad. Homegrown means something like a vegetable that is grown in a person's own garden at home.
> 7. Today we will cut the grass with our electric lawnmower. A lawnmower is a machine that mows a lawn.
> 8. I bought some groceries and a magazine from the shopkeeper. A shopkeeper is a person who keeps, or works in, a shop or a small store.

 Approaching Practice Book A, page 13

◆ **Beyond Practice Book B,** page 13

Objective

- Decode words with long vowels

Materials

- Leveled Practice Books, p. 14
- Teacher's Resource Book, p. 6

ELL **Access for All**

Long Vowels In Spanish there is only one vowel sound for each vowel. The different sounds and spellings of English vowel sounds are challenging for many students. Provide opportunities for students to see, hear, and use words in the context of meaningful sentences.

On Level Practice Book O, page 14

Words that have the VCe pattern usually have a long vowel sound, as in *fame, mine,* and *bone.* The vowel digraphs *ai* and *ay* usually stand for the long a sound, as in *pail* and *play.* The digraphs *ee* and *ea* stand for the long e sound, as in *see* and *heap.* The digraphs *oa* and *ow* can stand for the long o sound, as in *boat* and *flow.* The vowel *i* can stand for the long i sound in words such as *wind, wild.* The letters *igh* in *high* can also stand for the long i sound.

A. Write the words from the box that have the same long vowel sound as the first word in each row. Underline the letters that make the long vowel sound. Possible responses provided.

| coach | bike | wheat | pain | may | deep |
| steam | flight | slate | towing | mind | float |

1. rake   pain   slate   may
2. feet   wheat   steam   deep
3. kite   bike   flight   mind
4. flow   coach   towing   float

B. Write a sentence using as many long vowel sound words as possible.

Answers will vary.

⭐ **Approaching Practice Book A**, page 14

◆ **Beyond Practice Book B**, page 14

Phonics

Decode Words with Long Vowels

 **Access for All**   **EXPLAIN/MODEL**

- In words that have the VCe (vowel-consonant-*e*) pattern, the vowel sound is usually long, as in *fame* and *mine*. The final *e* is silent.

- Sometimes a vowel digraph stands for a long vowel sound. For example, the digraphs *ai* and *ay* can stand for /ā/, as in *pail* and *play*; the digraphs *ee* and *ea* can stand for /ē/, as in *see* and *heap*; the digraphs *oa* and *ow* can stand for /ō/, as in *boat* and *flow*.

- An *i* may stand for the /ī/ sound when it is followed by two consonants, as in *mind* or *wild*. The letters *igh* also stand for /ī/.

Write *squeak* on the board.

Think Aloud The digraph *ea* can have the /e/ sound in *feather* or the /ē/ sound in *team*. When I try the /e/ sound, I get /skwek/. That doesn't make sense. When I try /ē/, I get /skwēk/. That makes sense.

PRACTICE/APPLY

Write *fine, clean,* and *plight*. Model how to decode *fine*, pointing out the silent *e*. Then help students decode the other words.

Decode Multisyllabic Words Write *un-* and *non-* on the board. Remind students that these prefixes mean "not." Write *unlikely*. Point to and read the prefix *un-* and the root word *likely*. Draw a line between them. Read them together. Tell students that *unlikely* means "not likely." Display *nonstop, nonsense, uneasy, nonfiction*. Work with students to decode the words. For more practice, see decodable passages on **Teacher's Resource Book** page 6.

 **Cooperative Learning**

Long Vowel Tic-Tac-Toe Each partner chooses a long vowel pattern, such as VCe. Partners take turns writing words on a tic-tac-toe grid until one gets three words with the same pattern in a row.

Quick Check   **Can students decode words with long vowels?**

During **Small Group Instruction**

If No → **Approaching Level** Phonics, p. 77M

If Yes → **On Level** Options, pp. 77Q–77R

        Beyond Level Options, pp. 77S–77T

Vocabulary Building

Oral Language

Expand Vocabulary Use the following prompt to have students make a class word web.

Write "American Legends" in the center of a word web. Using the main selection as well as dictionaries, thesauruses, and encyclopedias as resources, have students find and brainstorm words that relate to this week's theme. They will receive bonus points for compound words. You may include words such as *hero, extraordinary*, or *values* on the initial word web. Write these words and their definitions in circles that radiate from the center circle of your web.

Apply Vocabulary

Write a Description The word *fireball* can also mean "person having great energy." Think of a person you would describe as a fireball. Using several vocabulary words, describe this person. Make sure you describe what the person looks like as well as activities the person enjoys and what makes him or her a "fireball."

Vocabulary Building

Compound Words Suggest that each student choose a compound word. Students should first define each word that forms the compound word. (notebook: note = a piece of written information to aid memory; book = found in libraries, has covers, and written pages) Tell students to use these definitions to write riddles. Invite volunteers to pose their riddles to the class.

note + book = notebook

Vocabulary Review

Vocabulary Game Using persuasive words and language, as well as vocabulary words, have students create an advertisement for a made-up product. They should choose a target audience for their product. Post the advertisements in the classroom. Then have students write a radio ad for the product, again using vocabulary words. Instruct students not to state the name of the product in their ad, and have them take turns reading the ad to the class. Invite students to guess what the product is. Ask students if they would buy the product and what about the ad did or didn't sell them.

Technology

Vocabulary PuzzleMaker

LOG ON

For additional vocabulary and spelling games go to www.macmillanmh.com

Long Vowels

Spelling Words

paste	heap	yolk
bride	paid	folks
shave	coach	aim
spice	theme	prey
greed	type	tow
plead	oak	grind
greet	growth	

Review tenth, damp, stuff

Challenge decay, lifetime

Dictation Sentences

1. I need glue to <u>paste</u> it down.
2. Sally became Davy's <u>bride</u>.
3. He used an ax to **shave**.
4. It was full of flavor and <u>spice</u>.
5. He had no <u>greed</u> for money.
6. We had to <u>plead</u> for his help.
7. She ran to <u>greet</u> me with a hug.
8. I raked leaves into a **heap**.
9. A stranger had **paid** the bill.
10. The basketball <u>coach</u> quit.
11. I like the <u>theme</u> of the story.
12. Tulips are a <u>type</u> of flower.
13. He is as strong as an **oak** tree.
14. He had a sudden <u>growth</u> spurt.
15. She likes the egg <u>yolk</u>.
16. The <u>folks</u> in town are nice.
17. Try to <u>aim</u> for the target.
18. Coyotes hunt for <u>prey</u>.
19. The <u>tow</u> truck moved the car.
20. <u>Grind</u> wheat to make flour.

Review/Challenge Words

1. He tried for the <u>tenth</u> time.
2. The rain made her hair <u>damp</u>.
3. My job is to <u>stuff</u> envelopes.
4. Your teeth will not <u>decay</u>.
5. She finished it during her <u>lifetime</u>.

Words in **bold** are from the main selection.

Day 1 Pretest

ASSESS PRIOR KNOWLEDGE

Use the Dictation Sentences. Say the underlined word, read the sentence, and repeat the word. Have students write the words on **Spelling Practice Book** page 7. For a modified list, use the first 12 Spelling Words and the Review Words. For a more challenging list, use Spelling Words 3–20 and the Challenge Words. Students may correct their own tests.

Have students cut apart the Spelling Word Cards BLM on **Teacher's Resource Book** page 67 and figure out a way to sort them. They can save the cards for use throughout the week.

Day 2 Word Sorts

TEACHER AND STUDENT SORTS

- Write *paid, heap, grind,* and *coach* on the board and pronounce them. Point out that each of these words has a long vowel sound. Underline the letters that make the long vowel sound.

- Make a chart on the board, using the long vowel sounds /ā/, /ē/, /ī/, and /ō/ as headings. Have students copy the chart in their word study notebooks and sort the Spelling Words by vowel sounds.

- Discuss words that have unexpected spellings (*prey, type, yolk,* and *folks*). Ask students for other words with long vowels to add to the chart.

- Invite partners to sort the words any way they wish; for example, by vowel-consonant combinations (*yolk, folks; growth, tow*).

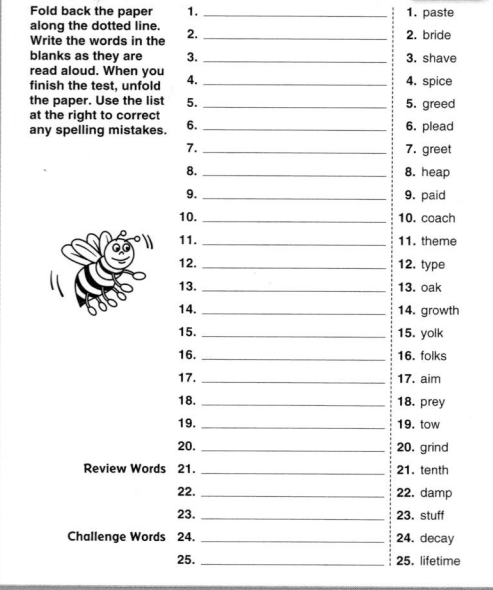

Spelling Practice Book, pages 7–8

Fold back the paper along the dotted line. Write the words in the blanks as they are read aloud. When you finish the test, unfold the paper. Use the list at the right to correct any spelling mistakes.

1.	1. paste
2.	2. bride
3.	3. shave
4.	4. spice
5.	5. greed
6.	6. plead
7.	7. greet
8.	8. heap
9.	9. paid
10.	10. coach
11.	11. theme
12.	12. type
13.	13. oak
14.	14. growth
15.	15. yolk
16.	16. folks
17.	17. aim
18.	18. prey
19.	19. tow
20.	20. grind
Review Words 21.	21. tenth
22.	22. damp
23.	23. stuff
Challenge Words 24.	24. decay
25.	25. lifetime

Spelling Practice Book, page 9

folks	aim	prey	yolk	greed
greet	grind	growth	heap	coach
oak	paid	paste	plead	shave
theme	bride	tow	spice	type

Sort each spelling word by finding the sound and spelling pattern to which it belongs.

Write the words that have long *a* spelled:

ai		*a-e*		*ey*
1. aim	1.	paste	1.	prey
2. paid	2.	shave		

Write the words that have long *e* spelled:

ee		*ea*		*e-e*
1. greed	1.	heap	1.	theme
2. greet	2.	plead		

Write the words that have long *i* spelled:

i		*y*		*i-e*
1. grind	1.	type	1.	bride
			2.	spice

Write the words that have long *o* spelled:

o		*oa*		*ow*
1. folks	1.	coach	1.	tow
2. yolk	2.	oak	2.	growth

Day 3 — Word Meanings

CONTEXT CLUES

Ask students to copy the sentences below into their word study notebooks. Say the sentences out loud and ask them to fill in the missing blanks with a Spelling Word.

1. They had an _____ tree in their backyard. *(oak)*

2. He left a large _____ of clothes on the floor. *(heap)*

3. He decided to _____ the photos in an album. *(paste)*

Challenge students to come up with other sentences for Spelling, Review, or Challenge Words.

Have students do a word hunt for the words in the weekly reading or other materials. They should identify the definition of the Spelling Word as it is used in context.

Day 4 — Review and Proofread

SPIRAL REVIEW

Review words with short vowels. Write *tenth, damp,* and *stuff* on the board. Have students identify the short vowel sound in each word.

PROOFREAD AND WRITE

Make sentence strips for these sentences:

1. Davy left the wood from the old olk tree in a heep. *(oak, heap)*

2. His new bryde was there to grete him. *(bride, greet)*

3. Some fokes like their eggs without the yoke. *(folks, yolk)*

Cut the sentences into parts and have small groups reassemble the sentences in the right order. They should proofread each sentence and correct misspelled words.

Day 5 — Assess and Reteach

POSTTEST

Use the Dictation Sentences on page 77G for the Posttest. If students have difficulty with any words in the lesson, have them place the words in a list entitled "Spelling Words I Want to Remember" in their word study notebooks.

Challenge student partners to look for other words with long vowel sounds like the ones they studied this week, either in their reading or other materials. Partners should work together to sort the words by vowel sounds.

Spelling Practice Book, page 10

folks	aim	prey	yolk	greed
greet	grind	growth	heap	coach
oak	paid	paste	plead	shave
theme	bride	tow	spice	type

Replacements

Write the spelling word that can replace the underlined word or words in each sentence below.

1. Davy wasn't like any kind of person she had ever met. ___type___
2. He pulled up the trees and threw them in a pile. ___heap___
3. Davy's new wife was as strong as he was. ___bride___
4. He used to say hello to people with a wave of his coonskin cap. ___greet___
5. His goal was to pull the tail off Halley's Comet. ___aim___
6. Davy did not want to be given money for anything he did. ___paid___
7. The message of the story is that there is a way to solve every problem. ___theme___
8. People everywhere had heard about Davy Crockett. ___Folks___

Definitions

Write the spelling word that matches each definition below.

9. part of an egg ___yolk___
10. glue ___paste___
11. pull ___tow___
12. beg ___plead___
13. kind of tree ___oak___
14. crush ___grind___
15. hunted animal ___prey___
16. desire for a lot of something ___greed___
17. development ___growth___
18. cut off hair ___shave___
19. wagon pulled by horses ___coach___
20. something added to food ___spice___

Spelling Practice Book, page 11

Circle the misspelled words in the passage. Write the words correctly on the lines below.

America is in a (hep) of trouble. Halley's Comet has made our country its (pray) The comet is speeding toward the earth. It is getting bigger every day. If it crashes into the planet, it will (grynde) everything into small pieces.

Only a special (tip) of man can stop the comet. That man is Davy Crockett. He lives far away in the mountains. We don't have to (pled) with him for help. As soon as news of the comet reaches him, he will be on his way. Pulling the tail off the comet won't be a problem for Davy Crockett. He won't even want to be (pade) for saving the world!

1. ___heap___ 3. ___grind___ 5. ___plead___
2. ___prey___ 4. ___type___ 6. ___paid___

Writing Activity

Suppose that you were bigger than life, like Davy Crockett. What do you imagine you could do? Write a tall tale about yourself, using four spelling words.

Spelling Practice Book, page 12

Look at the words in each set below. One word in each set is spelled correctly. Use a pencil to fill in the circle next to the correct word. Before you begin, look at the sample set of words. Sample A has been done for you. Do Sample B by yourself. When you are sure you know what to do, you may go on with the rest of the page.

Sample A:
- Ⓐ doom
- Ⓑ dume
- Ⓒ duum
- Ⓓ doome

Sample B:
- Ⓔ taik
- Ⓕ taak
- Ⓖ take
- Ⓗ tehk

1.
- Ⓐ fokes
- Ⓑ folks
- Ⓒ fokse
- Ⓓ fohks

2.
- Ⓔ ame
- Ⓕ aame
- Ⓖ aime
- Ⓗ aim

3.
- Ⓐ prey
- Ⓑ preye
- Ⓒ praiy
- Ⓓ prai

4.
- Ⓔ yok
- Ⓕ yolke
- Ⓖ yolk
- Ⓗ yohk

5.
- Ⓐ greed
- Ⓑ grede
- Ⓒ greid
- Ⓓ gried

6.
- Ⓔ grete
- Ⓕ greet
- Ⓖ greit
- Ⓗ griet

7.
- Ⓐ grinde
- Ⓑ grind
- Ⓒ gihnd
- Ⓓ griind

8.
- Ⓔ growth
- Ⓕ groth
- Ⓖ garoth
- Ⓗ grought

9.
- Ⓐ heep
- Ⓑ hepe
- Ⓒ heap
- Ⓓ heape

10.
- Ⓔ coche
- Ⓕ coach
- Ⓖ coch
- Ⓗ coache

11.
- Ⓐ ohk
- Ⓑ oke
- Ⓒ oak
- Ⓓ ock

12.
- Ⓔ paid
- Ⓕ pade
- Ⓖ payed
- Ⓗ paad

13.
- Ⓐ paste
- Ⓑ paist
- Ⓒ paast
- Ⓓ paiste

14.
- Ⓔ pleed
- Ⓕ plede
- Ⓖ pleid
- Ⓗ plead

15.
- Ⓐ shaiv
- Ⓑ shave
- Ⓒ shav
- Ⓓ shaive

16.
- Ⓔ heem
- Ⓕ theim
- Ⓖ theeme
- Ⓗ theme

17.
- Ⓐ brid
- Ⓑ bride
- Ⓒ briid
- Ⓓ briide

18.
- Ⓔ toh
- Ⓕ towe
- Ⓖ tow
- Ⓗ tohe

19.
- Ⓐ spyce
- Ⓑ spihc
- Ⓒ spihce
- Ⓓ spice

20.
- Ⓔ tipe
- Ⓕ type
- Ⓖ tighp
- Ⓗ typ

5 Day Grammar

Subjects and Predicates

Daily Language Activities

Use these activities to reinforce each day's lesson. Write the day's activity on the board or use **Daily Language Transparency 2.**

DAY 1
You know of Davy Crockett He was a legendary mountain man! people said he could drink the Mississippi dry (1: Crockett?; 2: man. People; 3: dry.)

DAY 2
Davy Crockett once saved the world from a terrible comet the comet was called Halley's Comet (1: comet. The; 2: Comet.)

DAY 3
The President of the United States Sally Sugartree and the American people, needed Davy Crockett's help (1: States,; 2: Sugartree,; 3: people needed; 4: help.)

DAY 4
Davy met with the President decided on a plan and went looking for the comet (1: President,; 2: plan,; 3: comet.)

DAY 5
the comet spotted Davy took a giant leap and aimed right at him Lightning fire and thunder shot out of the comet's eyes. (1: The; 2: Davy,; 3: leap,; 4: him.; 5: Lightning,; 6: fire,)

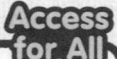

ELL — Access for All

Use Colors On chart paper write in red marker: *Subject = Whom or what the sentence is about.* Underneath, in green marker, write: *Predicate = What the subject does or is.* Write sentences using the two colors to indicate the subject and the predicate.

Day 1 — Introduce the Concept

INTRODUCE SUBJECTS AND PREDICATES

Present the following:

- The simple subject of a sentence is the main noun or pronoun that names the subject and tells whom or what the sentence is about: *The comet flew close to Earth.*

- The complete subject includes all of the words that tell whom or what the sentence is about: *The giant red comet tore through space.*

- The simple predicate is the verb that tells exactly what the subject does or is: *The comet flew close to Earth.*

- The complete predicate is the verb and all of the words that tell what the subject does or is: *The giant red comet tore through space.*

Access for All

See Grammar Transparency 6 for modeling and guided practice.

Grammar Practice Book, page 7

The **subject** of a sentence tells who or what the sentence is about. The **predicate** of a sentence tells what the subject does or is.

- The **complete subject** includes all of the words in the subject. It tells exactly who or what the sentence is about.
- The **simple subject** is the main word in the complete subject.
- The **complete predicate** includes all of the words in the predicate.
- The **simple predicate** is the main word in the complete predicate.

Read each sentence. Circle the simple subject, and underline the complete subject.

1. A brave (man) lived in the mountains.
2. Davy's pet (bear) danced in the forest.
3. The big, bad (comet) hurtled toward America.
4. Davy Crockett's red-hot (enemy) was discombobulated.
5. The beautiful (Sally Sugartree) married Davy.

Read each sentence. Circle the simple predicate, and underline the complete predicate.

6. The President (received) piles of letters.
7. Davy (learned) all the latest dances.
8. Sally (climbed) a 50-foot hickory tree.
9. Halley's Comet (howled) when it saw Davy.
10. The people (elected) Davy to Congress when he returned home.

Day 2 — Teach the Concept

REVIEW SUBJECTS AND PREDICATES

Ask students to identify the differences between simple and complete subjects and between simple and complete predicates.

INTRODUCE COMPOUND SUBJECTS AND PREDICATES

Present the following:

- A compound subject is two or more subjects in the same sentence, usually joined by a connecting word such as *and* or *or*: *Meteors and comets are space rocks.*

- A compound predicate contains two or more predicates that have the same subject: *The comet flew close and nearly hit.*

See Grammar Transparency 7 for modeling and guided practice.

Grammar Practice Book, page 8

- A **compound subject** contains two or more simple subjects that have the same predicate.
- A **compound predicate** contains two or more simple predicates that have the same subject.
- You can combine two sentences by joining two subjects or two predicates with *and* or *or*.

Read each sentence. Write *S* on the line if the sentence has a compound subject. Write *P* on the line if the sentence has a compound predicate.

1. Davy and Death Hug danced in the forest. ____S____
2. Davy combed his hair with a rake and shaved his beard with an ax. ____P____
3. The President and Davy posed for pictures. ____S____
4. Davy climbed to the top of Eagle Eye Peak and waited for the comet. ____P____

Rewrite each set of sentences as one sentence. Combine the compound subject or compound predicate in each pair with *and* or *or*.

5. Davy jumped over the comet's shoulder. Davy planted his teeth around its neck.
   Davy jumped over the comet's shoulder and planted his teeth around its neck.

6. Sally Sugartree was happy to see Davy return. The community was happy to see Davy return.
   Sally Sugartree and the community were happy to see Davy return.

Day 3 Draft

REVIEW COMPOUND SUBJECTS AND PREDICATES

Review what compound subjects and compound predicates are.

MECHANICS AND USAGE: COMMAS IN A SERIES AND IN APPOSITIVES

- Use commas to separate three or more words or phrases in a series. Do not use a comma after the last word in a series.

- Commas can separate nouns, subjects, predicates, and adjectives in a series. *My pets are a cat, dog, and bird.*

- Appositives are set off by commas. *June, my best friend, is lots of fun.*

 See Grammar Transparency 8 for modeling and guided practice.

Grammar Practice Book, page 9

> - Use commas to separate three or more words in a series.
> - Commas separate subjects, predicates, and adjectives in a series.
> - Do not use a comma after the last word in a series.

Correct each sentence. Add commas where they are needed.

1. Davy needed a comb a rake and an ax.
   Davy needed a comb, a rake, and an ax.
2. The biggest scariest meanest ball of fire was called Halley's Comet.
   The biggest, scariest, meanest ball of fire was called Halley's Comet.
3. Davy grabbed Halley's Comet spun it around and hurled it back into space.
   Davy grabbed Halley's Comet, spun it around, and hurled it back into space.
4. He could drink the water from lakes rivers and oceans.
   He could drink the water from lakes, rivers, and oceans.
5. Sally Sugartree was friendly pretty and smart.
   Sally Sugartree was friendly, pretty, and smart.
6. Davy's pet bear was so fast that rocks trees cows and snakes flew out from beneath its feet.
   Davy's pet bear was so fast that rocks, trees, cows, and snakes flew out from beneath its feet.
7. Every river tree and lake could be seen from the top of Eagle Eye Peak.
   Every river, tree, and lake could be seen from the top of Eagle Eye Peak.
8. Halley's Comet shot out sparks lightning and thunder.
   Halley's Comet shot out sparks, lightning, and thunder.

Day 4 Review and Proofread

REVIEW SUBJECTS AND PREDICATES

Ask students to explain the differences between simple, complete, and compound subjects and predicates. Ask students how to use commas in a series.

PROOFREAD

Have students identify and correct the punctuation below.

1. Davy Crockett had many adventures in his day (day.)

2. He was the strongest fastest and luckiest, man in the world. (strongest, fastest, and luckiest man)

3. His favorite pet was a bear named Death Hug? (Hug.)

4. Davy Sally and Hug saved the day. (Davy, Sally,)

 See Grammar Transparency 9 for modeling and guided practice.

Grammar Practice Book, page 10

> - Be sure that every sentence begins with a **capital letter** and ends with the correct **punctuation mark.**
> - Use commas to separate three or more words or phrases in a series.
> - When combining subjects and predicates, use the words *and* or *or.*

Rewrite the passage, combining sentences and adding commas where needed. Use correct capitalization and punctuation.

davy Crockett was a frontiersman. He chopped wood hunted wild animals and ran a powder mill. Every morning he got up early to see the sunrise. He got up early to eat breakfast.

one day, Sally Sugartree asked Davy to dance. Davy wouldn't dance because his boots were too big. He wouldn't dance because he would step on her toes. sally then asked Davy to sing. His voice was so strong that it made the trees sway the clouds move and the animals scatter. Sally liked Davy's voice so much that she decided to marry him.

    Davy Crockett was a frontiersman. He chopped wood, hunted wild animals, and ran a powder mill. Every morning he got up early to see the sunrise and eat breakfast.

    One day Sally Sugartree asked Davy to dance. Davy wouldn't dance because his boots were too big, and he would step on her toes. Sally then asked Davy to sing. His voice was so strong that it made the trees sway, the clouds move, and the animals scatter. Sally liked Davy's voice so much that she decided to marry him.

Day 5 Publish

ASSESS

Use the Daily Language Activity and page 11 of the **Grammar Practice Book** for assessment.

RETEACH

Reproduce the corrected Daily Language Activities on sheets of paper. Have students work in pairs or small groups to identify the subjects and kinds of subjects (simple, complete, compound) in each sentence. Then have students repeat the process, analyzing the predicates. Review students' answers as a class. Ask volunteers to share their answers. If students do not identify a subject or predicate correctly, review how to.

Use page 12 of the Grammar Practice Book for additional reteaching.

 See Grammar Transparency 10 for modeling and guided practice.

Grammar Practice Book, pages 11–12

Circle the letter for each correct answer.

1. Which of the following groups of words is a complete sentence?
   a. Davy's ax and rake.
   b. Was elected to Congress after saving the world.
   c. Davy could drink the Mississippi River dry.
   d. Very strong and brave.
2. Which of the following groups of words is a sentence fragment?
   a. The pretty girl was Sally Sugartree.
   b. The President's law that Halley's Comet couldn't crash into Earth.
   c. Death Hug liked to dance.
   d. Davy was fast.
3. In which sentence is the simple subject underlined?
   a. Davy enjoyed spending time in the forest.
   b. Sally danced better than anyone.
   c. Davy hurled Halley's Comet back into space.
   d. The President thanked him for his help.

Follow each direction below.

4. Underline the simple subject of this sentence.
   Davy saved the United States from trouble.
5. Underline the complete subject of this sentence.
   Sally Sugartree and Davy Crockett got married after the parade.
6. Underline the complete predicate in this sentence. Circle the simple predicate.
   Davy wears a coonskin cap on his head.

End-of-Week Assessment

Administer the Test

Weekly Reading Assessment,
Passage and questions, pages 21–28

ASSESSED SKILLS

- Plot and Setting
- Vocabulary Words
- Compound Words
- Long Vowels
- Subjects and Predicates

Administer the **Weekly Assessment** online or on CD-ROM.

Weekly Assessment, 21–28

Fluency

Assess fluency for one group of students per week. Use the Oral Fluency Record Sheet to track the number of words read correctly. Fluency goal for all students:
100–120 words correct per minute (WCPM).

Approaching Level	Weeks 1, 3, 5
On Level	Weeks 2, 4
Beyond Level	Week 6

Fluency Assessment

Alternative Assessments

- **ELL Assessment**, pages 36–37

ELL Practice and Assessment, 36–37

Diagnose		Prescribe
	IF...	**THEN...**
VOCABULARY WORDS **VOCABULARY STRATEGY** Compound Words Items 1, 2, 3, 4	0–2 items correct...	Reteach skills using the **Additional Lessons** page T7. **LOG ON** Reteach skills: Go to www.macmillanmh.com **CD ROM** Vocabulary PuzzleMaker Evaluate for Intervention.
COMPREHENSION Skill: Plot and Setting Items 5, 6, 7, 8	0–2 items correct...	Reteach skills using the **Additional Lessons** page T2. Evaluate for Intervention.
GRAMMAR Subjects and Predicates Items 9, 10, 11	0–1 items correct...	Reteach skills: **Grammar Practice Book** page 12.
SPELLING Long Vowels Items 12, 13, 14	0–1 items correct...	**LOG ON** Reteach skills: Go to www.macmillanmh.com
FLUENCY	96–99 WCPM 0–95 WCPM	**AUDIO CD** Fluency Solutions Evaluate for Intervention.

READING
Triumphs
AN INTERVENTION PROGRAM

Also Available

To place students in the Intervention Program, use the **Diagnostic Assessment** in the Intervention Teacher's Edition.

Davy Crockett Saves the World

77L

Approaching Level Options

Skills Focus ▸ Phonics

Objective Decode one-syllable and multisyllabic words that include long vowels in both familiar and unfamiliar texts

Materials
- **Student Book** "Grandma's Tales"
- **Decodable Passages, Teacher's Resource Book** p. 6

WORDS WITH LONG VOWELS

Model/Guided Practice

- Write the letters *b, a, l, e* on the board. Say the sound that each letter stands for. Then blend the sounds: /bāl/. *Say the word with me:* bale.
- Write VCe under the corresponding letters *a, l,* and *e. This word follows a vowel-consonant-silent* e *pattern. Generally, the vowel sound is long here.*
- *Let's check the rule. Start with the word* mile. *Say the word with me. Is the vowel sound long or short? Mark the vowel-consonant-silent* e *pattern: VCe.*
- Next use these words to check the rule: *flake, froze, gale, gape,* and *male.*
- Have students generate five other single-syllable words with long vowels.
- Extend the review to include words that form long vowel sounds with vowel digraphs, such as the *ai* in *fail* and the *ee* in *deep.*

MULTISYLLABIC WORDS WITH LONG VOWELS

- Write the word *parakeet* on the board. Mark the syllables: *par/a/keet.* Blend the syllables to pronounce the word: /par ə kēt/. Point out the vowel digraph that produces the long vowel sound.
- Have partners work together to practice decoding longer words with long vowels. Write the words below. *With your partner, choose a word. Say the word aloud, counting the syllables. Notice that each syllable contains only one vowel sound. Sort the words into two groups, those that follow the VCe rule and those that use vowel digraphs.*

| decrease | demonstrate | sneezing | exhale |
| otherwise | nickname | exceed | failure |

- Check each pair for accuracy. Provide constructive feedback.

WORD SORT: WORDS WITH LONG VOWELS IN CONTEXT

- Review the VCe pattern/vowel digraphs and their effects on long vowels.
- Have students identify and sort words from "Grandma's Tales" that contain long vowel sounds. Using two-column charts with the headings VCe and Vowel Digraphs, have students place words from the story in the appropriate columns.
- Have students repeat the activity with the decodable passages on **Teacher's Resource Book** page 6.

Constructive Feedback

Isolate the error sound and repeat it with the group. If students say short vowel sounds instead of long vowel sounds, point out the VCe pattern and say:

If you can identify the VCe pattern in a word, the vowel sound usually is long. Say the long vowel sounds with me: /ā/, /ē/, /ī/, /ō/, and /ū/. Let's sound out the word *file*. The pattern is VCe. The pronunciation is /fīl/ not /fil/.

Repeat as needed with other words with the VCe pattern.

Additional Resources

For each skill below, additional lessons are provided. You can use these lessons on consecutive days after teaching the lessons presented within the week.
- Plot and Setting, T2
- Compound Words, T7
- Toolbars and Links, T11

Decodable Text

To help students build speed and accuracy with phonics patterns, see the additional decodable text on page 6 of the **Teacher's Resource Book.**

Skills Focus ▶ Fluency

Objective   Read with increasing prosody and accuracy at a rate of 100–110 WCPM

Materials   • **Approaching Practice Book A,** p. 11

MODEL EXPRESSIVE READING

Model reading the passage on page 11 in **Practice Book A.** Tell students to pay close attention to how punctuation marks affect expression. Then read aloud one sentence at a time and have students repeat the sentence, first as a class and then one by one. Listen for accuracy.

REPEATED READING

Have students practice reading the passage aloud as you circulate and provide constructive feedback. Student partners can take turns reading the passage. One student should read each sentence aloud, and the other should repeat the sentence. Remind students to wait until their partners reach the ends of sentences before correcting mistakes.

TIMED READING

Tell students at the end of the week that they will do a timed reading of the passage that they have been practicing. Have each student

- place the passage from Practice Book A, page 11, face down.
- begin reading the passage aloud when you say "Go," and finish reading when you say "Stop."

As students read, note any miscues. Stop them after one minute. Help students record and graph the number of words they read correctly.

Skills Focus ▶ Vocabulary

Objective   Apply vocabulary word meanings

Materials   • **Vocabulary Cards**   • **Transparencies 2a and 2b**

Tested

VOCABULARY WORDS

Display the **Vocabulary Cards:** *commenced, fireball, sauntered, elected, impress, advertisement, original, wring.* Have students sort the cards by part of speech. Locate these words on **Transparencies 2a** and **2b.** Review the sentence where the word is used in the vocabulary passage, and have students underline context clues. Have students choose a card and write a sentence with the word.

commenced   sauntered   advertisement

elected

fireball   impress   original   wring

Constructive Feedback

Tell students to pause briefly after commas and semicolons. Students should insert longer pauses after end marks such as periods, question marks, and exclamation points. Colons also take longer pauses. Model this practice for students. Tap out one beat for a short pause and two beats for a longer pause.

⭐ **Approaching Practice Book A,** page 11

As I read, I will pay attention to punctuation.

	Sluefoot Sue was born on a ranch somewhere around
9	El Paso. She was a pretty little thing with shiny blue eyes.
21	But her parents knew right away that their daughter was
31	different.
32	First of all, as a newborn baby, she had long red curls and
45	a full set of teeth! Sue didn't act like other babies, either.
57	When she was two weeks old, she pried open the bars of her
70	crib and hopped out.
74	Then, one morning, she climbed up on the family dog,
84	Chester. He yawned and started to walk outside. As Sue
94	rode across the floor on Chester's back, a huge smile spread
105	across her face. "Yippee!" she yelled. Sue had taken her first
116	ride. 117

Comprehension Check

1. How was Sue different from other babies? **Character** Sue was different from other babies because she was born with long hair and a full set of teeth. She was also strong enough to pry open the bars on her crib and able to ride the family dog.
2. Where does this story take place? **Setting** on a ranch around El Paso

	Words Read	–	Number of Errors	=	Words Correct Score
First Read		–		=	
Second Read		–		=	

Vocabulary

Review last week's words (*slumped, soggy, strands, capable, categories, gigantic, credit, luminous*) and this week's words (*impress, wring, fireball, original, commenced, advertisement, elected, sauntered*). Have students sort the words by parts of speech and brainstorm synonyms and antonyms.

Grandma's Tales
by Daniel Fritz

**Student Book, or
Transparencies 2a and 2b**

ELL
Access for All

Connect to Personal Experience A legend or tale tells readers a lot about the culture that is identified with the legend or tale. Share with a small group a tale or legend that your family tells. Draw a series of illustrations to show the beginning, middle, and end of the tale.

Skills Focus ▶ Vocabulary

Objective	Review compound words
Materials	• **Student Book** "Grandma's Tales"

WORD PARTS: COMPOUND WORDS

Ask students to review the vocabulary passage and to identify the compound word among the vocabulary words. (fireball) Review how to use the word parts to decipher its meaning. Challenge students to find compound words that are related to any of the vocabulary words (for example: *groundbreaking* for *original*). They may use thesauruses.

Skills Focus ▶ Comprehension

Objective	Analyze plot and setting
Materials	• **Student Book** "Grandma's Tales" • **Transparencies 2a and 2b**

STRATEGY
ANALYZE STORY STRUCTURE

Remind students that story structure is how the author has organized the events of the plot using story elements such as character and setting.

SKILL
PLOT AND SETTING

Explain/Model

- Plot is the series of events that happen in a story. They give the story a beginning, a middle, and an end.
- The setting is where and when a story takes place and can influence the events of the plot. Note that a story may have more than one setting.

Display **Transparencies 2a** and **2b.** Reread the first paragraph.

Think Aloud Right from the first sentence I can tell the setting. As I read on, I can tell this story will be about how the narrator's grandmother tries to change the way people remember Davy Crockett. I will pay attention to how the plot develops from this beginning.

Ask a volunteer to circle the setting. Then ask students why this setting might be important to the plot.

Practice/Apply

Reread "Grandma's Tales" with students. Discuss the following questions:

- What happens at the beginning, middle, and end of the story?
- Where and when does the story take place? How does the author weave in and out of different time periods?

Leveled Reader Lesson

Objective Read to apply strategies and skills
Materials
- **Leveled Reader** *Sluefoot Sue: An American Legend*
- **Student Book** *Davy Crockett Saves the World*

Leveled Reader

PREVIEW AND PREDICT

Have students talk about the cover and preview the first two chapters. They can review all illustrations and chapter titles to predict what the story will be about. Have students set purposes before reading by writing questions about the story.

VOCABULARY WORDS

Before reading, review the vocabulary words as necessary. As you read together, discuss how each word is used in context.

STRATEGY
ANALYZE STORY STRUCTURE

Remind students that analyzing story structure involves looking at how the author has developed the events of the plot using story elements such as setting, as well as literary devices such as foreshadowing and flashback.

SKILL
PLOT AND SETTING

Remind students to notice how the author uses story elements, such as setting, to develop the plot.

Think Aloud I can tell the author is using the places and events in the story to develop the plot for a tall tale about a legendary figure from the West. Sluefoot Sue lives on a ranch in Texas. She can cross a stream with a horse on her shoulders and ride a catfish down the Rio Grande. I'll add this information to my Plot and Setting Chart.

READ AND RESPOND

Tell students to finish reading the first two chapters of the story. Discuss significant events and places in the story, such as Sluefoot Sue's meeting with Pecos Bill at the Rio Grande. Then read the rest of the story with the group. Have students complete their Plot and Setting Charts.

MAKE CONNECTIONS ACROSS TEXTS

Invite students to compare *Sluefoot Sue: An American Legend* with *Davy Crockett Saves the World*. Ask if they enjoy the tall-tale genre.

- What similarities exist between the plots of *Sluefoot Sue: An American Legend* and *Davy Crockett Saves the World*?

- How does the setting contribute to the plot of each story?

ELL Access for All

Fiction or Nonfiction As you preview and predict using the illustrations, point to each picture. If it shows something that could happen, say "nonfiction." If it shows something that could not happen, say "fiction."

Student Book

Skills Focus ▶ Vocabulary

Objective	Apply vocabulary words and identify compound words
Materials	• **Vocabulary Cards**

VOCABULARY WORDS

Have students use the Glossary to create a definition card for each vocabulary word. Place cards with vocabulary words face up and cards with definitions face down. Have students play a memory-matching game by taking turns selecting one word card and one definition card. If a student identifies a word and a definition as a match, he or she keeps both cards. If a student thinks that the cards do not match, he or she replaces them and the next student takes a turn.

WORD PARTS: COMPOUND WORDS

Review that compound words are words made by combining two smaller words, as in *fireball*. Have student pairs think of or search for five compound words and write a definition for each. Discuss compound words related to computers, such as *Web site* and *home page*.

Skills Focus ▶ Text Features

Objective	Use a computer's toolbar and an online link
Materials	• **Student Book** "The Tales Are Getting Taller"

TOOLBAR AND LINK

Review "The Tales Are Getting Taller." Help partners use the Internet toolbar and a search engine to gather information about comets, astronomy, and the night sky. Then have them write a summary of their findings.

On Level Practice Book O, page 11

As I read, I will pay attention to punctuation.

	Back then it wasn't easy to feed a large family. Luckily
11	Johnny possessed a green thumb. From the time that he was
22	two years old, it seemed as if Johnny could just look at
34	a seed and a plant commenced to grow. So Johnny and his
46	green thumb fed his large family.
52	There was plenty of food, but dinnertime was extremely
61	noisy in Johnny's house. Why, it was as if a volcano was
73	exploding at dinnertime! As soon as the food hit the table,
84	the children shouted and complained.
89	"Tommy's apple pie is bigger than mine!"
96	"Why are we having apple juice again?"
103	All that noise gave Johnny a headache, so he would take
114	his dinner outside and escape to his favorite spot, the apple
125	orchard. There, Johnny felt at home. 131

Comprehension Check

1. What kind of person is Johnny? **Character**
   He liked peace and quiet and liked growing plants.
2. How did Johnny's family benefit from his green thumb? **Plot**
   Johnny provided food for his large family.

	Words Read	–	Number of Errors	=	Words Correct Score
First Read		–		=	
Second Read		–		=	

Skills Focus ▶ Fluency

Objective	Read fluently with appropriate pauses and prosody at a rate of 100-120 WCPM
Materials	• **On Level Practice Book O,** p. 11

REPEATED READING

Model reading the passage on **Practice Book O** page 11. Remind students that commas let longer sentences be read more easily and that exclamation points indicate surprise or excitement. Then read one sentence at a time, and have students echo-read. Listen for accuracy. During independent time, partners can take turns modeling and echo-reading the passage.

Timed Reading At the end of the week, have students read the passage for one minute and record their number of words correct per minute.

Leveled Reader Library

Leveled Reader Lesson

Objective	Read to apply strategies and skills
Materials	• **Leveled Reader** *Johnny Appleseed: An American Legend*

Leveled Reader

PREVIEW AND PREDICT

Have students preview *Johnny Appleseed: An American Legend.*

- What does the title suggest about the story?

- What attitude will the author take toward the main character?

- What questions do you have about the story?

STRATEGY

ANALYZE STORY STRUCTURE

Have a volunteer explain how examining the structure of a story and analyzing story elements can enhance readers' understanding.

SKILL

PLOT AND SETTING

Review with students that the plot is the series of events that make up a story. These events give the story a beginning, a middle, and an end. The setting of a story is where and when it takes place and may influence the events of the plot. Explain that students will record information about the setting and important plot events in Plot and Setting Charts as they read.

ELL Leveled Reader
Go to pages 77U–77V.

READ AND RESPOND

Read the Introduction and Chapter 1. Pause to discuss how the author introduces the setting and the main characters and sets the plot in motion. At the end of Chapter 1, have students fill in their Plot and Setting Charts. Have students explain how the characters and their actions help change the events of the story. Students should complete the charts as they continue reading.

VOCABULARY WORDS

As they finish reading *Johnny Appleseed: An American Legend*, ask students to point out the vocabulary words as they appear. Discuss how each is used. Then have students pair up and ask each other questions about the story, using vocabulary words in both their questions and answers.

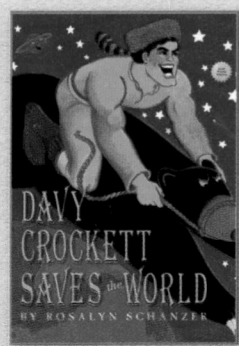

Student Book

MAKE CONNECTIONS ACROSS TEXTS

Invite students to compare the plots and settings of *Johnny Appleseed: An American Legend* and *Davy Crockett Saves the World.*

- How are the setting and plot of these stories similar and different? How does the narration provide details about settings and plot events?

- Which tall-tale hero accomplishes more amazing feats? Give evidence from the stories to support your answer.

Small Group

Student Book

Why It Matters

Comprehension Studies of effective teachers show that they are more likely to use a mix of whole class and small group insturction.

Timothy Shanahan

 For more information, go to Teacher Resources at **www.macmillanmh.com**

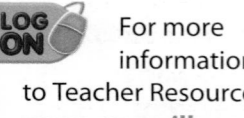

♦ **Beyond Practice Book B,** page 11

As I read, I will pay attention to punctuation.

	Little Stormy sure loved the sea. Lots of folks figured
10	that he was born at sea—no one knew—but he certainly
22	made it his second home. Some days he'd dive into the water
34	and swim clear over to Boston and back, just for fun. Other
46	days, he'd hitch a ride on a passing whale. If he was lucky,
59	the whale would dive for the bottom, taking Stormy along
69	for the ride.
72	Stormy never meant to cause anyone trouble, but
80	accidents did happen. One day he dove into the sea but
91	didn't go headfirst. He tucked up his knees and did a sort
103	of cannonball. Well, wouldn't you know it, he caused giant
113	tidal waves in Rhode Island! Folks there got pretty flustered
123	until they discovered the cause. Then they just chuckled,
132	because even in Rhode Island they had heard about little
142	Stormy.
143	As Stormy grew older and bigger, he started to feel a
154	little cramped on Cape Cod. Stormy felt hemmed in by all
165	the cute little houses and villages. 171

Comprehension Check

1. What types of accidents did Stormy cause? **Plot** tidal waves

2. Where do Stormy's adventures take place? **Setting** around Cape Cod and Boston

	Words Read	–	Number of Errors	=	Words Correct Score
First Read		–		=	
Second Read		–		=	

Skills Focus ► Vocabulary

Objective Create an advertisement using vocabulary words

 EXTEND VOCABULARY

Discuss with students how famous people often appear in advertisements for products. Advertisers hope that consumers will associate the products with the qualities people admire in the famous spokespeople. Invite students to suggest some examples of this kind of advertising and to discuss the effectiveness of these advertisements. Then challenge students to use the vocabulary words to write advertisements that feature famous people endorsing appropriate products.

Skills Focus ► Text Features

Objective Use a computer toolbar and an Internet link
Materials • **Student Book** "The Tales Are Getting Taller"

TOOLBAR AND LINK

Remind students that a toolbar is a strip of icons on a computer that allows a user to perform different functions. A link is a direct computer connection to documents or information on a Web page. Ask students to use the Internet toolbar to find more information about some of the issues or places mentioned in "The Tales Are Getting Taller." Have students compare their findings and discuss Web sites they find helpful for research.

Skills Focus ► Fluency

Objective Read fluently with appropriate prosody at a rate of 110–120 WCPM
Materials • **Beyond Practice Book B,** page 11

REPEATED READING

Model reading aloud the entire passage on page 11 of **Practice Book B**. Remind students that commas break longer sentences and that exclamation points indicate surprise or excitement. Then read one sentence at a time, and have students echo-read each sentence back to you. Provide feedback and positive reinforcement.

During independent reading, partners can take turns modeling and echo-reading. Have teams switch readers each time they encounter an exclamation point. As individual students read, listen for appropriate pausing and tone. You may wish to have students do a timed reading at the end of the week and record their reading rate.

Leveled Reader Library

Leveled Reader Lesson

Objective   Read to apply strategies and skills
Materials   • **Leveled Reader** *Old Stormalong: An American Legend*

PREVIEW AND PREDICT

Have students preview *Old Stormalong: An American Legend*, predict what it is about, and set a purpose for reading. Review vocabulary words as needed before or during reading.

STRATEGY
ANALYZE STORY STRUCTURE

Explain that analyzing story structure can help a reader understand how an author has organized the events of the plot. As students read, have them pay attention to how the author uses story elements such as setting, as well as literary elements such as foreshadowing, to structure the plot.

SKILL
PLOT AND SETTING

Ask a volunteer to explain what the terms *plot* and *setting* mean and why they are important to understanding a story. Ask another student to explain what the climax of a story is. Explain that students will read *Old Stormalong: An American Legend* together and that they will look for information about the story's plot and setting.

READ AND RESPOND

As they read, have students fill in their Plot and Setting Charts. Discuss students' questions and responses.

Folk Tale
Old Stormalong
An American Legend

by Liz West
illustrated by Brad Teare

Leveled Reader

ELL   Access for All

Use Rhymes and Songs
The author of *Old Stormalong* uses exaggeration to create humor. Listen to a rhyme or song with examples of exaggeration. Explain the humor.

Skills Focus ▶ ## Self-Selected Reading

Objective   Read independently to analyze plot and setting and to make connections across texts
Materials   • Leveled Readers or trade books at students' reading levels

READ TO ANALYZE PLOT AND SETTING

Invite students to summarize *Old Stormalong: An American Legend* and *Davy Crockett Saves the World*. Ask students to point out similarities between the plots and settings. Discuss ways in which the plot of a tall tale differs from that of other types of fiction.

Have students choose stories for independent reading. Remind them to be prepared to answer questions about plot and setting after reading. After students have finished reading, have them deliver formal oral presentations about the stories that summarize important events, setting details, and show an understanding of the ideas communicated in the works.

English Language Learners

Academic Language

Throughout the week the English language learners in your class will need help in building their understanding of the academic language used in daily instruction and assessment instruments. The following strategies will help to increase their language proficiency and comprehension of content and instructional words.

Oral Language For oral vocabulary development, go to **www.macmillanmh**

Strategies to Reinforce Academic Language

- **Use Context** Academic language used by the teacher (see chart below) should be explained in the context of the task during Whole Group. You may use gestures, expressions, and visuals to support meaning.

- **Use Visuals** Use charts, transparencies, and graphic organizers to explain key labels to help students understand classroom language.

- **Model** Demonstrate the task using academic language in order for students to understand instruction.

Academic Language Used in Whole Group Instruction

Content/Theme Words	Skill/Strategy Words	Writing/Grammar Words
exaggerating (p. 72)	setting (p. 52)	topic sentence (p. 76)
tall tales (p. 72)	summarize (p. 71)	simple subject (p. 77I)
superhuman (p. 73)	character (p. 71B)	complete subject (p. 77I)
features (p. 73)		simple predicate (p. 77I)
exaggerated (p. 73)		complete predicate (p. 77I)
larger than life (p. 74)		compound subject (p. 77I)
pastime (p. 74)		compound predicate (p. 77I)
		series (p. 77J)

Leveled Reader Library

ELL Leveled Reader Lesson

The Story of Johnny Appleseed

by Liz West
illustrated by Brad Teare

Before Reading

DEVELOP ORAL LANGUAGE

LOG ON

Build Background *Who are some superheroes you know about?* Elicit examples of other superheroes and list them on the board. Explain that a superhero has *superhuman* abilities. Point out how characters in legends can be superheroes.

Tested

Review Vocabulary Write the vocabulary and story support words on the board and discuss their meanings. Model using them. Commenced *means the same as* started. *People who have a* green thumb *can make plants grow very well.*

PREVIEW AND PREDICT

Point to the cover illustration and read the title aloud. *Do you think Johnny Appleseed was a superhero or a real person? Why? Do you think he had a green thumb? What do you think this story is about? Where does it happen?*

Tested

Set a Purpose for Reading Show the Plot and Setting Chart and remind students they have used this chart before. Ask them to do a similar chart to record details of the plot and the setting.

During Reading

Choose from among the differentiated strategies to support students' reading at all levels of language acquisition.

Beginning	**Intermediate**	**Advanced**
Shared Reading Model using the strategy to identify the plot and setting as you read. *What is the story about? Where does it happen?* Check students' comprehension and use vocabulary and support words.	**Read Together** Read through page 5. Encourage students to retell the story, focusing on plot and setting. Ask students to write responses on their chart. Continue reading as you ask for details to add to the chart.	**Independent Reading** Have students read the story. After reading each day, ask them to fill in their charts focusing on plot and setting. Encourage them to write a paragraph that summarizes the abilities of the character as a superhero.

After Reading

Remind students to use the vocabulary and story words in their whole group activities.

Objective

- **To apply vocabulary and comprehension skills**

Materials

- **ELL Leveled Reader**

5-Day Planner

DAY 1	• Academic Language
	• Oral Language and Vocabulary Review
DAY 2	• Academic Language
	• ELL Leveled Reader
DAY 3	• Academic Language
	• ELL Leveled Reader
DAY 4	• Academic Language
	• ELL Leveled Reader
DAY 5	• Academic Language
	• ELL Leveled Reader Comprehension Check and Literacy Activities

Grade 5 • ELL TEACHER'S GUIDE

English Language Learners

Treasures

Macmillan/McGraw-Hill

ELL Teacher's Guide
For students who need additional instructions

Weekly Literature

Weekly Theme: Trees for Life

Week At A Glance

Whole Group

VOCABULARY
quest, settings, reduce, buffet, major

Use a Dictionary/ Homographs

COMPREHENSION
Strategy: Text Structure
Skill: Compare and Contrast

TEST STRATEGY
Right There

WRITING
Expository Writing

Science Link

Life Science
Ecosystems

Small Group Options

Differentiated Instruction for Tested Skills

Tested Skills for the Week

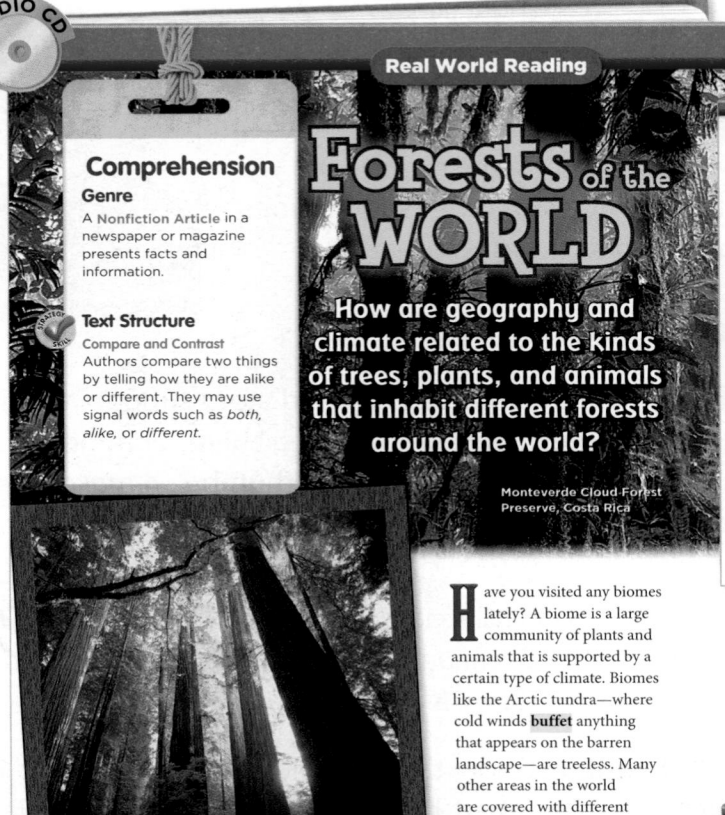

Real World Reading

Comprehension

Genre
A Nonfiction Article in a newspaper or magazine presents facts and information.

Text Structure
Compare and Contrast Authors compare two things by telling how they are alike or different. They may use signal words such as *both, alike,* or *different.*

Forests of the WORLD

How are geography and climate related to the kinds of trees, plants, and animals that inhabit different forests around the world?

Monteverde Cloud Forest Preserve, Costa Rica

Have you visited any biomes lately? A biome is a large community of plants and animals that is supported by a certain type of climate. Biomes like the Arctic tundra—where cold winds **buffet** anything that appears on the barren landscape—are treeless. Many other areas in the world are covered with different kinds of trees. Here are three types of forest biomes.

Giant redwoods in California. Redwoods are cone-bearing trees.

Real World Reading

TREE-RIFIC!

Vocabulary
quest
settings
reduce
buffet
major

The hollow trunk of this Australian baob tree was once used as a prison.

Thomas Pakenham set out on a **quest**. Armed with 30 pounds of camera equipment, the British historian went searching for fascinating trees. As Pakenham says, he was in search of trees with "noble brows and strong personalities." He wrote a book about his experiences, with photographs of the many different "personalities" he found. His portraits show the wide range in tree sizes and shapes. Some of the tiny bonsai trees of Japan are less than a foot tall, even though they are full-grown and many years old. On the other hand, in

Thomas Pakenham stands at the foot of a Montezuma cypress in Mexico.

California, Pakenham found "General Sherman"—the name given to a giant sequoia tree that is considered to be the largest single living thing on Earth.

Pakenham's search brought him face to leaf with many remarkable trees in beautiful **settings** all around the world. A tree in Mexico, the Montezuma cypress, has a trunk that is 190 feet around. Similarly, a tree called a "dancing lime" in Germany once held an orchestra on its bottom branches! Pakenham hopes these and other trees will help his message grow: "We shouldn't take them for granted."

80

Vocabulary/ Comprehension

Science Link
Main Selection

Genre Nonfiction Article

Answer Questions

Test Strategy
Right There
You can put your finger on the answer. Look for key words in the question. Then find those key words in the selection.

The aftermath of a wildfire

THE SCIENCE of WILDFIRES

Wildfires result from a combination of fuel, dryness, and a trigger. Each factor determines how strong the blaze will be. Fuel means flammable solids that, with oxygen, feed the fire. Dryness can be caused by short-term periods with little rain or by lengthy drought. Triggers can be as natural as a lightning strike, as innocent as a campfire, or as careless as a stray match.

Weather is the primary force that creates or ends wildfires. Once wildfires start burning, they create their own weather. First, smoke and heat from fires can rise thousands of feet in the air, creating an empty space below them. Cooler air rushes in to fill the space, but

the fresh air brings oxygen that fuels the flames. This convection system creates powerful, hot winds that dry out and preheat fuel ahead of the fire. This helps the fire move forward and even jump natural barriers, such as rivers.

A fire dies when it cannot get fuel, heat, or oxygen. The main strategy for fighting wildfires is containment: surround the fire and starve it. Helicopters and tanker airplanes can drop water or chemicals to slow the spread of flames. Firefighters can also set up fire lines—areas cleared of any fuel that would allow the fire to spread. Controlled fires are sometimes set to deny fuel to an approaching blaze.

86

Go On ▶

Test Strategy
Right There

Read-Aloud Anthology
• Listening Comprehension
• Readers' Theater

INTERACTIVE Read-Aloud ANTHOLOGY with PLAYS

Macmillan McGraw-Hill

Leveled Readers

GR Levels Q–V

Genre **Informational Nonfiction**

- Same Theme
- Same Vocabulary
- Same Comprehension Skills

Approaching Level

On Level

Beyond Level

English Language Leveled Reader

On Level Reader sheltered for English Language Learner

ELL Teacher's Guide also available

Also Available
LEVELED READER PROGRAM

CLASSROOM LIBRARY

Genre **Expository Nonficton**

Approaching

On Level

Beyond

Trade books to apply Comprehension Skills

INTERVENTION ANTHOLOGY

- Phonics and Decoding
- Comprehension
- Vocabulary

Also available, *Reading Triumphs*, Intervention Program

LEVELED PRACTICE

Approaching

On Level

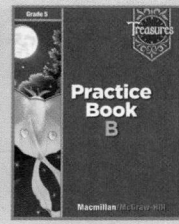

Beyond

ELL

HOME-SCHOOL CONNECTION

- Family letters in English and Spanish
- Take-Home Stories

Technology

ONLINE INSTRUCTION
www.macmillanmh.com

AUDIO CD
- Listening Library
- Fluency Solutions

CD ROM
- Vocabulary PuzzleMaker

Suggested Lesson Plan

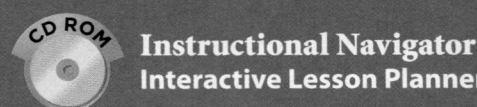

Forests of the World, 82–85

Leveled Readers

Whole Group

Integrated ELL Support Every Day

ORAL LANGUAGE
- **Listening**
- **Speaking**
- **Viewing**

WORD STUDY
- **Vocabulary**
- **Phonics/Decoding**

READING
- **Develop Comprehension**
- **Fluency**

LANGUAGE ARTS
- **Writing**
- **Grammar**
- **Spelling**

ASSESSMENT
- **Informal/Formal**

Turn the Page for
Small Group Lesson Plan

Day 1

Listening/Speaking/Viewing
❓ Focus Question What would happen if trees disappeared from the world?
Build Background, 78
Read Aloud: "A Symphony of Trees," 79

Vocabulary
Tested *quest, settings, reduce, buffet, major,* 80
Practice Book A-O-B, 15
Tested **Strategy:** Use a Dictionary/Homographs, 81

Read "Tree-Rific!" 80–81

Comprehension, 81A–81B
Strategy: Text Structure
Tested **Skill:** Compare and Contrast
Practice Book A-O-B, 16

Student Book

Fluency Model Fluency, 79
Partner Reading, 78I

✏ Writing
Daily Writing Prompt: Write a letter to a friend about some of the trees in your neighborhood. Describe the different types and their characteristics.
Brochure, 89A–89B

Grammar Daily Language Activities, 89I
Sentence Combining, 89I
Grammar Practice Book, 13

Tested **Spelling** Pretest, 89G
Spelling Practice Book, 13–14

Quick Check Vocabulary, 80
Comprehension, 81B

Differentiated Instruction 89M–89V

Day 2

Listening/Speaking
❓ Focus Question How are geography and climate related to the kinds of trees, plants, and animals that inhabit different forests around the world?

Vocabulary
Tested Review Vocabulary Words, 82

Phonics
Decode Words with /ü/, /ū/, and /u̇/, 89E
Practice Book A-O-B, 21

Read *Forests of the World,* 82–85

Comprehension, 82–85
Strategy: Text Structure
Tested **Skill:** Compare and Contrast
Practice Book A-O-B, 17

Student Book

Fluency Partner Reading, 78I

✏ Writing
Daily Writing Prompt: What if you discovered a new species of trees? Write a journal article in which you classify it.
Brochure, 89A–89B

Grammar Daily Language Activities, 89I
Sentence Combining, 89I
Grammar Practice Book, 14

Spelling Words with /ü/, /ū/, and /u̇/, 89G
Spelling Practice Book, 15

Quick Check Comprehension, 85
Phonics, 89E

Differentiated Instruction 89M–89V

Vocabulary	Comprehension	Writing
Vocabulary Words Dictionary/ Homographs	Strategy: Analyze Text Structure Skill: Compare and Contrast	Expository Writing

Turn the Page for
**Small Group
Options**

Day 3

Listening/Speaking

❓ **Focus Question** Based on "Forests of the World," what category do you think the top 5 most common trees in the United States are in?
Summarize, 85

Vocabulary

Review Words in Context, 89C
Strategy: Dictionary/Homographs, 89D
Practice Book A-O-B, 20
Phonics Decode Multisyllabic Words, 89E

Read *Forests of the World,* 82–85

Student Book

Comprehension

Comprehension Check, 85
Maintain Skill: Compare and Contrast, 85A

Fluency Partner Reading, 78I
Repeated Reading, 85A
Practice Book A-O-B, 18

✏ Writing

Daily Writing Prompt: Why do some trees only grow in certain parts of the world? Write a paragraph about the various forest biomes.
Brochure, 89A–89B

Grammar Daily Language Activities, 89I
Mechanics and Usage: Punctuate Compound Sentences, 89J
Grammar Practice Book, 15

Spelling Words with /ü/, /ū/, and /u̇/, 89H
Spelling Practice Book, 16

Differentiated Instruction 89M–89V

Day 4

Listening/Speaking/Viewing

❓ **Focus Question** Describe the role weather can play in both creating and ending wildfires. Use details from the article to support your answer.
Expand Vocabulary: Trees for Life, 89F

Vocabulary

Homographs, 89F
Apply Vocabulary to Writing, 89F

Read "The Science of Wildfires," 96–99

Test Strategy: Right There

Research and Study Skills

Using the Library and Media Center, 85B
Practice Book A-O-B, 19

Student Book

Fluency Partner Reading, 78I

✏ Writing

Daily Writing Prompt: Write a letter from the perspective of a forest firefighter. Give details about your duties.
Brochure, 89A–89B

Grammar Daily Language Activities, 89I
Sentence Combining, 89J
Grammar Practice Book, 16

Spelling Words with /ü/, /ū/, and /u̇/, 89H
Spelling Practice Book, 17

Quick Check Vocabulary, 89D

Differentiated Instruction 89M–89V

Day 5
Review and Assess

Listening/Speaking/Viewing

❓ **Focus Question** Compare and contrast how changes in an ecosystem can affect the lives of trees.
Speaking and Listening Strategies, 89A

Vocabulary

Spiral Review: Vocabulary Game, 89F

Read Self-Selected Reading, 78I

Student Book

Comprehension

**Strategy: Text Structure
Skill: Compare and Contrast**

Fluency Partner Reading, 78I

✏ Writing

Daily Writing Prompt: Why are trees important to animal life? Write an article about the consequence of deforestation.
Brochure, 89A–89B

Grammar Daily Language Activities, 89I
Sentence Combining, 89J
Grammar Practice Book, 17–18

Spelling Posttest, 89H
Spelling Practice Book, 18

Weekly Assessment, 29–43

Differentiated Instruction 89M–89V

Differentiated Instruction

What do I do in small groups?

Teacher-Led Small Groups

Literacy Workstations

Independent Activities

Skills Focus → Use your Quick Check observations to guide additional instruction and practice.

Phonics
Words with /ü/, /ū/, and /ù/

 **Vocabulary Words**
quest, settings, reduce, buffet, major
Strategy: Dictionary/Homographs

Comprehension
Strategy: Text Structure
 **Skill:** Compare and Contrast

Fluency

Suggested Lesson Plan

 **CD ROM**

Instructional Navigator
Interactive Lesson Planner

	Day 1	**Day 2**
Approaching Level • **Additional Instruction/Practice** • **Tier 2 Instruction**	Fluency, 89N Vocabulary, 89N Comprehension, 89O **ELL** Label a Diagram, 89O 	Phonics, 89M Vocabulary, 89O Leveled Reader Lesson, 89P • Vocabulary • Comprehension 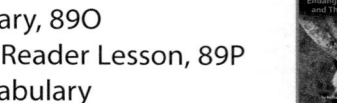
On Level • **Practice**	Vocabulary, 89Q Leveled Reader Lesson, 89R • Comprehension **ELL** Leveled Reader, 89U–89V 	Leveled Reader Lesson, 89R • Comprehension • Vocabulary 
Beyond Level • **Extend**	Vocabulary, 89S Leveled Reader Lesson, 89T • Comprehension 	Leveled Reader Lesson, 89T • Comprehension • Vocabulary 

For intensive intervention see **READING Triumphs**

Focus on Leveled Readers

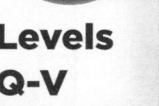

Levels Q-V

Apply **Tested** skills and strategies while reading appropriate leveled books.

Approaching

On Level

Beyond

The Muir Woods

ELL

Additional Leveled Reader Resources

Leveled Reader Database
Go to www.macmillanmh.com

Search by

- Comprehension Skill
- Content Area
- Genre
- Text Feature
- Guided Reading Level
- Reading Recovery Level
- Lexile Score
- Benchmark Level

Subscription also available

Day 3

Phonics, 89M
Fluency, 89N
Vocabulary, 89O
Leveled Reader Lesson, 89P
- Comprehension

Fluency, 89Q
Vocabulary, 89Q
Leveled Reader Lesson, 89R
- Comprehension

Fluency, 89S
Vocabulary, 89S
Leveled Reader Lesson, 89T
- Comprehension

Day 4

Phonics, 89M
Leveled Reader Lesson, 89P
- Comprehension

Study Skill, 89Q
Leveled Reader Lesson, 89R
- Comprehension

Study Skill, 89S
Leveled Reader Lesson, 89T
- Comprehension
ELL Building Background, 89S

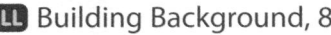

Day 5

Fluency, 89N
Leveled Reader Lesson, 89P
- Make Connections Across Texts

Fluency, 89Q
Leveled Reader Lesson, 89R
- Make Connections Across Texts

Fluency, 89S
Self-Selected Reading, 89T

Managing the Class

What do I do with the rest of my class?

Teacher-Led Small Groups

Literacy Workstations

Independent Activities

Class Management Tools

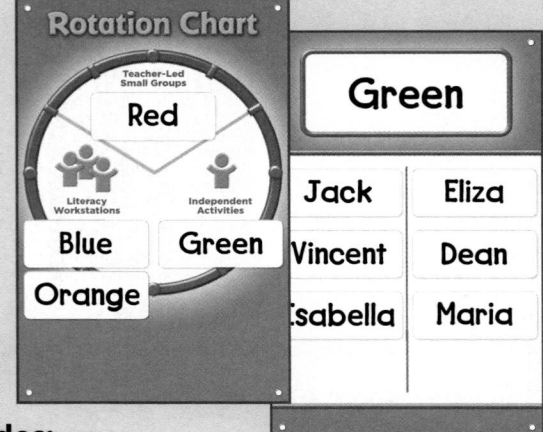

Includes:
• How-To Guides • Rotation Chart • Weekly Contracts

FOLDABLES™

Hands-on activities for reinforcing weekly skills.

Fish	Frogs
habitat	habitat
food	insects
prey	prey
enemies	enemies

Eight-Tab Foldable

Word	Synonym	Antonym	Prefix or Suffix
normal	typical	unusual	normally

Folded Foldable

Independent Activities

Leveled Readers

For Repeated Readings and Literacy Activities

Approaching

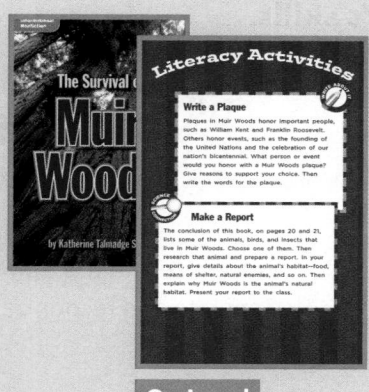

On Level

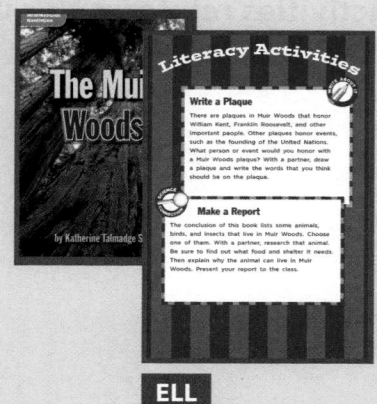

ELL

Beyond

LEVELED PRACTICE

Skills: Vocabulary (p. 15), Comprehension: Compare and Contrast (p. 16), Graphic Organizer (p. 17), Fluency (p. 18), Study Skill: Using the Library (p. 19), Vocabulary Strategy: Homographs (p. 20), Phonics (p. 21)

Approaching

On Level

Beyond

ELL

Technology

ONLINE INSTRUCTION www.macmillanmh.com

• Meet the Author/Illustrator

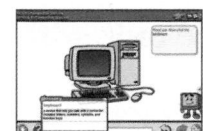

• Computer Literacy Lessons

• Research and Inquiry Activities

• Oral Language Activities

• Vocabulary and Spelling Activities

• Leveled Reader Database

LISTENING LIBRARY

Recordings of selections
• Main Selections
• Leveled Readers
• ELL Readers
• Intervention Anthology

FLUENCY SOLUTIONS

Recorded passages for modeling and practicing fluency

VOCABULARY PUZZLEMAKER

Activities providing multiple exposures to vocabulary, spelling, and high-frequency words including crossword puzzles, word searches, and word jumbles

Turn the page for Literacy Workstations.

Managing the Class

Cross-Curricular Activities

All activities reinforce this week's skills.

 **Reading**

Objectives
- Time reading to practice fluency.
- Select literature for reading enjoyment.
- Draw a picture based on a description in the text.
- Read daily for enjoyment.

 **Word Study**

Objectives
- Recognize and use homographs correctly.
- Generate and recognize words with /ü/, /ū/, and /ù/

 **Reading** — Fluency — 20 Minutes

- Read aloud the selection on page 18 in your Practice Book.
- If you stumble or pause with unfamiliar words, write them on a card. Look them up in a dictionary and then pronounce the words aloud three times each. When you have finished, read the passage again.

buffet
deciduous
conifer
frond

Extension
- With a partner repeat the process with another selection from your Practice Book.
- Time Your Reading: Listen to the Audio CD.

> **Things you need:**
> - Practice Book
> - index cards or paper
> - pen or pencil

Fluency Solutions
Listening Library

5

 Word Study — Homographs — 20 Minutes

- Using the dictionary make cards for five homographs, which are words that are spelled the same but are pronounced differently and have different meanings. Include the definition on each card. You should have a total of 10 cards.
- Then write a sentence for each word on a separate sheet of paper, leaving a blank for the homograph. Trade cards and sentences with a partner. Take turns completing each sentence aloud.

tear: liquid from the eye   tear: rip

A _____ fell from his eye.

Extension
- Play the game again with another pair. Whoever uses the most homographs correctly wins.

> **Things you need:**
> - index card and paper
> - pen or pencil
> - dictionary

For additional vocabulary and spelling games, go to www.macmillanmh.com — Vocabulary PuzzleMaker

5

Reading — Independent Reading — 20 Minutes

- Find a book at the library about trees or forests and read a chapter.
- When you finish reading, draw a picture of a tree or other plant you have read about based on description in the text.

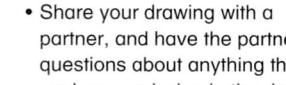

cedar
robins

Extension
- Share your drawing with a partner, and have the partner ask questions about anything that is unclear or missing in the drawing.
- If you cannot answer the questions, return to the book and reread or continue to look for the answers.

> **Things you need:**
> - library book
> - paper and colored pencils or markers

For more books about trees, go to the Author/Illustrator section at www.macmillanmh.com

6

Word Study — Words with /ü/, /ū/, /ù/ — 20 Minutes

- Create a vowel chart. Across the top write words with five different vowel sounds, including /ü/ ("oo") as in *loon,* /ū/ ("yoo") as in *mule,* and /ù/ ("oo") as in *book.* For the remaining two words, add words with two other vowel sounds that you studied previously in the unit.
- Under each vowel write four words to match each sound.
- Write each word on a card and shuffle the cards. Work with a partner. As you read each word, your partner should write the word on a blank chart under the correct vowel sound. Play until every space is filled correctly. Then play again using your partner's cards.

Extension
- Combine the two decks of cards, and play with another team.

> **Things you need:**
> - index cards
> - paper and ruler
> - pen or pencil
> - dictionary

m/ū/l

For additional vocabulary and spelling games, go to www.macmillanmh.com

6

Literacy Workstations

Writing

Objectives

- Write a descriptive and explanatory passage.
- Write an essay using sensory details.
- Write voluntarily to communicate ideas and emotions for a variety of audiences from self to unknown.

Content Literacy

Objectives

- Use research to compare and contrast trees.
- Write the history of a state tree, flower, bird, or insect.

Writing — Expository Writing
20 Minutes

- Write a description of a tree that you might want to give as a present. The tree is to celebrate an important milestone in a friend or family member's life, such as a birthday, an anniversary, or an important success or triumph.
- Explain which occasion inspired you to choose the tree as a gift. Include the tree's name, a description of what it looks like, how it will grow, and so forth. End by describing the reasons why this tree suits the friend and occasion.
- Review your explanation and combine any short sentences that could be written as one compound sentence.

Extension
- Suppose that you received a tree as a gift. Write a thank-you note for the tree.

Things you need:
- pen and paper

5

Science — Types of Trees
20 Minutes

- Research some types of trees that grow where you live.
- Draw their trunks, branches, and the shapes of their leaves.
- Make a chart of the trees. Leave a space on which you can paste a leaf for each variety of tree or make a color drawing of it.

Extension
- Research any two trees from your state that you would like to study.
- Make a chart that compares and contrasts characteristics of each tree.

Things you need:
- poster board or paper
- colored pencils or markers

maple

elm   birch   oak

LOG ON Internet Research and Inquiry Activity
Students can find more facts at www.macmillanmh.com

5

Writing — Sensory Writing
20 Minutes

- Suppose you are sitting in a tree house in an environment far from where you live, such as a rain forest.
- Write an essay for *Up in the Air* magazine, describing the tree, the environment, and what you see, hear, feel, smell, and think during a 24-hour period.
- Divide the essay into three paragraphs for morning, afternoon, and night.
- Use at least three compound sentences in your article.

Extension
- Suppose that you can climb a tree that is near where you live. Write a short description of what you see, hear, feel, smell, and think while up in this tree.

Things you need:
- paper and pen or pencil

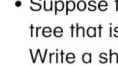

6

Social Studies — Nature in Your State
20 Minutes

- Research the official state tree, flower, bird, and insect from the state in which you live.
- Write a short history about each one that was chosen.

Extension
- Suppose you had a chance to plant trees to beautify a setting in your area. Draw a picture of a garden or a park to include your state tree, flower, bird, and insect.

Things you need:
- paper and pen
- colored pencils
- library or access to the Internet

Virginia	
Tree:	Bird:
Dogwood	Cardinal

6

Prepare

ORAL LANGUAGE
- Build Background
- Read Aloud
- Expand Vocabulary

VOCABULARY
- Teach Words in Context
- **Dictionary:** Homographs

COMPREHENSION
- **Strategy:** Text Structure
- **Skill:** Compare and Contrast

SMALL GROUP OPTIONS
- Differentiated Instruction, pp. 89M–89V

Oral Language

Build Background

ACCESS PRIOR KNOWLEDGE

Share the following information:

The world's tallest tree is the coast redwood in California, which can grow as tall as 367 feet.

TALK ABOUT TREES FOR LIFE

Discuss the weekly theme.

- Describe your visit to a forest, a wooded area, or a park.

- How can we protect trees? Why is it important to do so?

 **FOCUS QUESTION** Ask a volunteer to read aloud "Talk About It" on **Student Book** page 78 and describe the photograph.

- What do trees have to do with life?

- How would you describe the mood of the photograph?

Talk About It

What would happen if trees disappeared from the world?

 Find out more about trees at **www.macmillanmh.com**

78

ENGLISH LANGUAGE LEARNERS
Access for All

Beginning **Build Language** Point to and name items to describe the photo: *These are trees. The trees are tall.* Have students point and repeat. Ask questions: *What color are the leaves? Are the trees young or old?* Help students answer.

Intermediate **Build Background** Create a word web with the word *trees*, including parts of trees and types of trees. Draw pictures to help with meaning. Discuss and list the reasons trees are important. Help students explain their ideas in complete sentences.

Advanced **Elaborate** Complete the Intermediate task. As students talk, help them use more complex sentence structures: *Trees are important because they clean the air and provide homes for animals.*

TREES for LIFE

79

Picture Prompt

Look at the picture and respond in writing. You can write a poem, a story, or a description, or any other type of writing you like.

 **Technology**

For an extended lesson plan and Web site activities for **oral language development**, go to **www.macmillanmh.com**

Read Aloud
Read "A Symphony of Trees"

GENRE: Poetry
Review features of poetry:

- an arrangement of words in verse, sometimes according to a particular rhythm or pattern that does not always follow the rules of grammar

Read Aloud
pages 23–25

LISTENING FOR A PURPOSE

Ask students to listen carefully for descriptive and figurative language and the rhyme scheme as you read "A Symphony of Trees" in the **Read-Aloud Anthology**. They should be prepared to identify the special language in the rhyme scheme and to explain its effect on the poem. Choose from among the teaching suggestions.

Fluency Ask students to listen carefully as you read aloud, paying attention to your phrasing, expression, and tone of voice.

RESPOND TO THE POEM

Ask students to think about what tree bark might say if it could speak, and write an imaginary monologue or dialogue. Then have them recite and discuss the monologue or dialogue.

Expand Vocabulary

Have students choose three or more words from "A Symphony of Trees" that relate to this week's theme. They should use these words in a poem about trees modeled on "A Symphony of Trees."

Vocabulary

TEACH WORDS IN CONTEXT

Use the following routine:

Routine

Define: A **quest** is a search for something.

Example: James went on a quest for unusual butterflies.

Ask: Describe a quest you have read about.

DESCRIPTION

- **Settings** are backgrounds or surroundings. Maria sent me postcards with various mountain settings. Describe the most interesting settings you have seen. DESCRIPTION

- To **reduce** is to make less or lower. The gardener will reduce the number of weeds by digging them up. What is an antonym for *reduce?* ANTONYM

- **Buffet** means "to hit or strike repeatedly." When the winds buffet our apartment building, the windows shake. What is a synonym for the word *buffet?* SYNONYM

- **Major** means "greater or more important." A major reason we need trees is to produce oxygen. What are the major subjects that you study in school? SYNONYM

Vocabulary

- quest
- settings
- reduce
- buffet
- major

TREE-RIFIC!

The hollow trunk of this Australian boab tree was once used as a prison.

Thomas Pakenham stands at the foot of a Montezuma cypress in Mexico.

Thomas Pakenham set out on a **quest**. Armed with 30 pounds of camera equipment, the British historian went searching for fascinating trees. As Pakenham says, he was in search of trees with "noble brows and strong personalities." He wrote a book about his experiences, with photographs of the many different "personalities" he found. His portraits show the wide range in tree sizes and shapes. Some of the tiny bonsai trees of Japan are less than a foot tall, even though they are full-grown and many years old. On the other hand, in California, Pakenham found "General Sherman"—the name given to a giant sequoia tree that is considered to be the largest single living thing on Earth.

Pakenham's search brought him face to leaf with many remarkable trees in beautiful **settings** all around the world. A tree in Mexico, the Montezuma cypress, has a trunk that is 190 feet around. Similarly, a tree called a "dancing lime" in Germany once held an orchestra on its bottom branches! Pakenham hopes these and other trees will help his message grow: "We shouldn't take them for granted."

80

Quick Check

Do students understand word meanings?

During **Small Group Instruction**

If No → **Approaching Level** Vocabulary, p. 89N

If Yes → **On Level** Options, pp. 89Q–89R

Beyond Level Options, pp. 89S–89T

ELL — Access for All

Demonstrate Vocabulary For the word *reduce,* make a pile of pencils. Take a few away and say, *I reduced the number of pencils.* Make a pile of books and say, *If I reduce the number of books, am I adding or subtracting books?* For the word *quest,* discuss characters in stories who went on quests to search for a place or an object.

TREES AT WORK

TIME FOR KIDS

From steamy rain forests to snowy mountainsides, trees are among nature's hardest workers in any climate!

KEEP IT DOWN!

In noisy areas such as near airports and freeways, trees can absorb sound. They **reduce**, or cut down, the noise almost as effectively as stone walls.

EARTH FRIENDLY

Trees reduce the effects of carbon dioxide, a cause of global warming. Trees absorb and "lock up" carbon dioxide, keeping it from harming the environment.

TAKE A BREATHER

In just one season, a mature tree can produce as much oxygen as ten people inhale in one year.

STAY COOL

Trees can reduce heating costs by breaking the force of winter winds that **buffet** and batter homes. In summer, trees can keep areas of cities as much as 12 degrees Fahrenheit cooler than areas without trees.

STRONG ROOTS

Top layers of soil can be carried away by wind and water. This can cause **major** environmental problems, such as floods and clogged waterways. Trees hold soil in place.

TOP 5 MOST COMMON TREES IN THE U.S.

In the United States, the last Friday in April is Arbor Day. More than 1 million trees were planted on the first Arbor Day in 1872. In 2002, 130 years later, Americans celebrated by planting 18 million trees during the year. Here are the most common trees in this country. Are any of them in your neighborhood?

 **1. Silver Maple**

 2. Black Cherry

 3. Box Elder

 4. Eastern Cottonwood

 5. Black Willow

 **LOG ON** Find out more about identifying trees at www.macmillanmh.com

81

Vocabulary

Tested

STRATEGY
USE A DICTIONARY

Homographs Explain to students that homographs are words that are spelled the same way but are often pronounced differently and have different meanings. For example, the word *bow* can refer to the front of a ship or a curved weapon that uses an arrow. *Bow* can also be a gesture of respect. When a word that you know does not make sense in a sentence, check the dictionary to see what part of speech it is and whether there is another meaning for that word.

Tell students that homonyms are words that are spelled and pronounced the same, but have different meanings, such as *lean* meaning "to bend" and *lean* meaning "thin."

Point to the word *buffet* on **Student Book** page 81. Ask students to use a dictionary to find another meaning and pronunciation for *buffet*. Ask them to also say what part of speech it is. (a meal at which guests serve themselves, noun)

Remind students that they can use the pronunciation in a dictionary entry and the pronunciation key to help them decode unfamiliar words.

Read "TREE-RIFIC!"

As you read "Tree-Rific!" with students, ask them to identify clues that reveal the meanings of the highlighted words. Tell students they will read these words again in *Forests of the World*.

On Level Practice Book O, page 15

A. Choose the word from the box that best completes each sentence.

| quest | settings | reduce | buffet | major |

1. Air pollution is a _____ **major** _____ environmental problem.
2. During storms, winds _____ **buffet** _____ trees causing several of them to fall.
3. Our _____ **quest** _____ in the unexplored forest was to find new plants and animals that live there.
4. Rain forests are located in many different kinds of _____ **settings** _____, and can be found all over the world.
5. Firefighters try to _____ **reduce** _____ the number of wildfires by reminding people to watch their campfires closely.

B. Use the sentences in part A to help define these vocabulary words.

6. **settings:** the surroundings of something; background

7. **quest:** a search or pursuit

8. **major:** greater in size, amount, value, importance, or rank

9. **reduce:** to make less or become smaller in size, number, or degree

10. **buffet:** to knock about

★ **Approaching Practice Book A,** page 15

◆ **Beyond Practice Book B,** page 15

Objectives

- Analyze text structure
- Use academic language: *compare, contrast*
- Identify compare-and-contrast text structure

Materials

- Comprehension Transparency 3
- Leveled Practice Books, p. 16

Skills Trace

Compare and Contrast

Introduce	81A–B
Practice / Apply	82–85, Leveled Practice 16–17
Reteach / Review	89M–T, 329A–B, 330–349, 355M–T, Leveled Practice 97–98
Assess	Weekly tests, Unit 1, 3 Tests; Benchmark Tests A, B
Maintain	85A, 383B

ELL **Access for All**

Academic Vocabulary
Display the Problem and Solution chart for "Davy Crockett," the main selection from last week, and the Compare and Contrast chart for this week. Discuss how they differ in terms of what to look for in each text. Then write sentences comparing a pen and pencil. Use the words and phrases that signal compare and contrast in your sentences.

Reread for
Comprehension

Access for All

STRATEGY
ANALYZE TEXT STRUCTURE

Text structure is an organizational pattern chosen by an author to meet his or her purpose for presenting information. Different kinds of text structures include sequence, description, cause and effect, problem and solution, and compare and contrast. Evaluating text structure helps a reader understand the author's purpose and how effectively a text is organized.

Tested ✓

SKILL
COMPARE AND CONTRAST

Explain to students:

- To identify a compare-and-contrast text structure, think about how the people, objects, or events in the text are alike and different.

- As you read, pay attention to words that signal likenesses, such as *similarly* and *also.* Look for words and phrases that signal differences, such as *but, different,* and *on the other hand.*

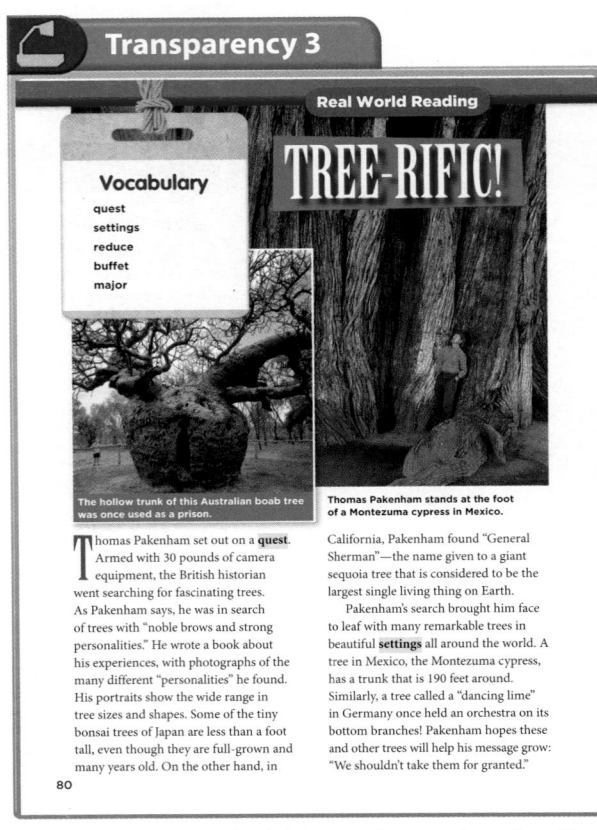

Transparency 3

Real World Reading

TREE-RIFIC!

Vocabulary
quest
settings
reduce
buffet
major

The hollow trunk of this Australian boab tree was once used as a prison.

Thomas Pakenham stands at the foot of a Montezuma cypress in Mexico.

Thomas Pakenham set out on a **quest**. Armed with 30 pounds of camera equipment, the British historian went searching for fascinating trees. As Pakenham says, he was in search of trees with "noble brows and strong personalities." He wrote a book about his experiences, with photographs of the many different "personalities" he found. His portraits show the wide range in tree sizes and shapes. Some of the tiny bonsai trees of Japan are less than a foot tall, even though they are full-grown and many years old. On the other hand, in

California, Pakenham found "General Sherman"—the name given to a giant sequoia tree that is considered to be the largest single living thing on Earth.

Pakenham's search brought him face to leaf with many remarkable trees in beautiful **settings** all around the world. A tree in Mexico, the Montezuma cypress, has a trunk that is 190 feet around. Similarly, a tree called a "dancing lime" in Germany once held an orchestra on its bottom branches! Pakenham hopes these and other trees will help his message grow: "We shouldn't take them for granted."

80

Student page 80, available on Comprehension Transparency 3

MODEL

Reread the first few paragraphs of "Tree-Rific!" from **Student Book** page 80.

Think Aloud Thomas Pakenham wanted to photograph trees of different sizes and shapes. I see the word *different*, and I know that's a signal word that suggests the author may be comparing and contrasting something. Pakenham photographed bonsai trees that were less than a foot tall. This detail contrasts with the information about "General Sherman," the largest living thing on Earth.

GUIDED PRACTICE

- Begin by asking students to identify the elements that the story compares and contrasts. ("General Sherman," Montezuma cypress, "dancing lime," and bonsai trees)

- Help students begin to identify how recognizing a compare-and-contrast text structure helps them understand and remember the information the author presents.

APPLY

Ask students to explain what other elements the author might go on to compare and contrast. (how much oxygen is produced by plants; how many trees were cut down in 2002; similarities and differences among the five most common trees)

On Level Practice Book O, page 16

One way to organize information in a nonfiction text is to **compare** and **contrast.** When you compare two things, you show how they are similar. When you contrast two things, you show how they are different.

Read the passage below. Then complete the Venn diagram with information about the two kinds of forests.

Two important biomes, or communities of plants and animals in a particular climate, are the coniferous forest biome and the deciduous forest biome. Coniferous forests are made up primarily of trees that bear cones, such as spruce and fir. Because no leaves fall to the ground and decompose, the soil in coniferous forests is not very rich. Coniferous forests are often found in colder climates in parts of North America, Europe, and Asia.

Deciduous forests have trees with leaves. Oak and maple trees are found in deciduous forests. When leaves fall to the ground and decay, they make the soil very rich. The climate of a deciduous forest is mild. These forests are also found in North America, Europe, and Asia.

Coniferous Forests
trees have cones
spruce and fir trees
soil not rich
cold climate

Alike
forests are found in North America, Europe, and Asia

Deciduous Forests
trees have leaves
oak and maple
soil very rich
mild climate

★ **Approaching Practice Book A,** page 16
◆ **Beyond Practice Book B,** page 16

Quick Check | **Can students compare and contrast?**

During **Small Group Instruction**

If No → Approaching Level Comprehension, p. 89O

If Yes → On Level Options, pp. 89Q–89R

Beyond Level Options, pp. 89S–89T

MAIN SELECTION
- *Forests of the World*
- **Skill:** Compare and Contrast

TEST PREP
- *The Science of Wildfires*
- **Test Strategy:** Right There

SMALL GROUP OPTIONS
- Differentiated Instruction, pp. 89M–89V

Comprehension

GENRE: NONFICTION ARTICLE

Have students read the definition of a Nonfiction Article on **Student Book** page 82. Students should look for facts as they read and be able to explain the difference between fiction and nonfiction.

STRATEGY
ANALYZE TEXT STRUCTURE

Remind students that a text structure is the organizational pattern a writer uses to present information.

SKILL
COMPARE AND CONTRAST

Remind students that when you compare, you recognize how things are alike. When you contrast, you identify how things are different.

Comprehension

Genre

A Nonfiction Article in a newspaper or magazine presents facts and information.

Text Structure

Compare and Contrast
Authors compare two things by telling how they are alike or different. They may use signal words such as *both*, *alike*, or *different*.

Forests of the WORLD

How are geography and climate related to the kinds of trees, plants, and animals that inhabit different forests around the world?

Monteverde Cloud Forest Preserve, Costa Rica

Giant redwoods in California. Redwoods are cone-bearing trees.

82

H ave you visited any biomes lately? A biome is a large community of plants and animals that is supported by a certain type of climate. Biomes like the Arctic tundra—where cold winds **buffet** anything that appears on the barren landscape—are treeless. Many other areas in the world are covered with different kinds of trees. Here are three types of forest biomes.

Vocabulary

Vocabulary Words Review the tested vocabulary words: **quest, settings, reduce, buffet,** and **major**.

Selection Words Students might find these words difficult.

barren (p. 82): producing no fruit or growth

ermine (p. 83): a weasel with fur that changes color with the seasons

vegetation (p. 84): plants in a specific region or area

Deciduous forest in autumn

Coniferous Forest

If you are on a **quest** to find a coniferous forest biome, you will want to head south of the Arctic tundra. This type of forest stretches from Alaska southward across North America as well as across Europe and Asia.

Coniferous forests consist mainly of cone-bearing trees such as spruce, hemlock, and fir. The soil is not very rich, because there are no leaves to decompose and make the ground suitable for growth. This will **reduce** the growth of other kinds of plant life.

Some animals that thrive in this biome are ermine, moose, red fox, snowshoe rabbits, and great horned owls.

Deciduous Forest **1**

Do you want to visit a deciduous forest in person? This biome is in the mild-temperate zone of the Northern Hemisphere. **Major** deciduous forests are found in eastern North America, Europe, and eastern Asia.

Deciduous trees lose their leaves in the fall. The natural decaying of the fallen leaves enriches the soil and allows all kinds of plant life to grow.

83

Read Together

If your students need support to read the Main Selection, use the prompts to guide comprehension and model how to complete the graphic organizer.

Read Independently

If your students can read the Main Selection independently, have them set a purpose for reading and complete the graphic organizer. Remind students to adjust their reading rate when reading informational nonfiction.

If your students need an alternate selection, choose the **Leveled Readers** that match their instructional level.

Technology

Story available on **Listening Library Audio CD**

Preview and Predict

Ask students to read the title, preview the photographs, and make predictions about the article. Then have students write about their predictions and any questions they have about the article.

Set Purposes

FOCUS QUESTION Discuss the question under the article title. Point out the Venn diagram on **Leveled Practice Book** page 17. Explain that students will use this diagram to compare and contrast information in the article.

Read *Forests of the World*

1 **STRATEGY**
ANALYZE TEXT STRUCTURE

Teacher Think Aloud I know from what I have read so far that forests can be very different from one another. This article describes different kinds of forest biomes and how they vary. What clues help you know how the author has organized the information in this article?

(Encourage students to apply the strategy in a Think Aloud.)

Student Think Aloud The text of the article is divided up into sections with the headings *Coniferous Forest*, *Deciduous Forest*, and *Rain Forest*. The author will probably describe the similarities and differences between these types of forests. I will read through the information under these headings and look for traits shared by all three kinds of forests. I will also look for how these forests are different from one another.

Develop Comprehension

2 **COMPARE AND CONTRAST**

How are coniferous and deciduous forests different? How are they the same? Place the similarities in the center of the Venn diagram. (Deciduous forests have trees that lose their leaves in the fall. Coniferous forests have evergreen trees that keep their leaves all year long. The soil in coniferous forests is not rich, whereas the soil in deciduous forests makes all kinds of plants grow. Both of these forests, though, are found on the same three continents and are homes to a variety of animals.)

3 **STRATEGY**
ANALYZE TEXT STRUCTURE

How does the structure of the article help you compare and contrast the different forests? (The article is divided into three sections that discuss three different kinds of forests: coniferous, deciduous, and rain. In each section, the author first explains where the forests are located. Then the article discusses soil and vegetation, and finally it gives information about what animals live there. This text structure makes it easy to compare and contrast the different forests.)

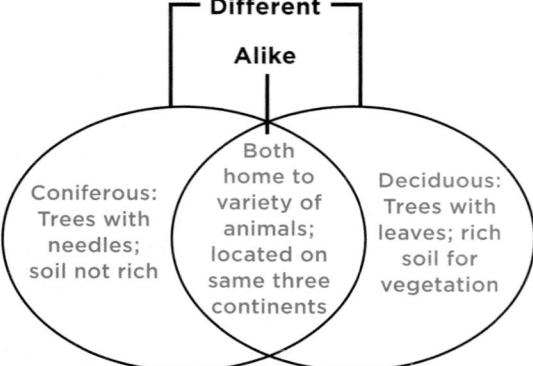

Different

Alike

Coniferous: Trees with needles; soil not rich

Both home to variety of animals; located on same three continents

Deciduous: Trees with leaves; rich soil for vegetation

This Costa Rican rain forest has many layers of plant life.

Oak, beech, ash, and maple trees are typical of deciduous forests, and many types of insect and animal life abound. In the U.S., these forests are home to many animals, including deer, American gray squirrels, rabbits, raccoons, and woodpeckers.

3 **Rain Forest**

Tropical rain forests are found in Asia, Africa, South America, Central America, and on many of the Pacific islands. Almost half the total area of the world's rain forests is in Brazil.

Tropical rain forests receive at least 70 inches of rain each year and have more species of plants and animals than any other biome. The thick vegetation absorbs moisture, which then evaporates and falls as rain.

A rain forest grows in three layers, like the levels in a stadium. The canopy, or tallest level, has trees between 100 and 200 feet tall. The second level, or understory, contains a mix of small trees,

84

Biomes of the World

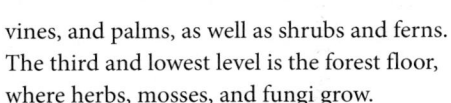

- ■ Tundra
- ■ Coniferous forest
- ■ Grasslands
- ■ Deciduous forest
- ■ Chaparral
- ■ Desert
- ■ Desert-scrub
- ■ Savanna
- ■ Rain Forest
- ■ Alpine

Orangutan

vines, and palms, as well as shrubs and ferns. The third and lowest level is the forest floor, where herbs, mosses, and fungi grow.

The combination of heat and moisture makes tropical rain forests the perfect **settings** for more than 15 million types of plants and animals. Some of the animals of the tropical rain forest are the anteater, jaguar, lemur, orangutan, macaw, sloth, and toucan. Among the many plant species are bamboo, banana trees, and rubber trees.

The floor of this rain forest is covered with ferns and mosses.

Think and Compare

1. What three types of forest biomes does this article describe?

STRATEGY SKILL

2. How is the soil in a coniferous forest different from the soil in a deciduous forest?

3. Think of a forest you have visited or that grows near where you live. Describe the plants and animals that live there.

4. The trees listed in the "Top 5 Most Common Trees in the U.S." on page 81 can be classified into a single category. Based on "Forests of the World," what category do you think that is?

85

Quick Check Can students identify compare-and-contrast text structure?

During **Small Group Instruction**

If No → **Approaching Level** Leveled Reader Lesson, p. 89P

If Yes → **On Level** Options, pp. 89Q–89R

Beyond Level Options, pp. 89S–89T

Personal Response

Have students respond to the selection by confirming or revising their predictions.

Comprehension Check

SUMMARIZE

Have students summarize "Forests of the World" by paraphrasing the main ideas and important details. Remind students to use their Venn diagrams to help them organize their summaries.

THINK AND COMPARE

Sample answers are given.

1. **Comprehension:** The three types of forest biomes that this article describes are the coniferous forest, the deciduous forest, and the rain forest.

2. **Compare and Contrast:** The soil in a coniferous forest allows for less plant growth than the soil in a deciduous forest. A deciduous forest contains leaves, which fall off the trees, decay, and help plant life grow. A coniferous forest has no leaves, only needles, and so does not give nutrients to the soil.

3. **Text to World:** Answers will vary but should be detailed, giving descriptive qualities about the forest and the types of plants and animals that live there.

4. **Text to Text:** Based on "Forests of the World," the top 5 most common trees are all in the deciduous forest category. These common trees all have leaves, which is a trait of the trees found in a deciduous forest.

Objectives

- Read accurately with good prosody
- Rate: 100–120 WCPM
- Identify compare-and-contrast text structure

Materials

- Fluency Transparency 3
- Fluency Solutions
- Leveled Practice Books, p. 18

Transparency 3

Thomas Pakenham set out on a quest. Armed with 30 pounds of camera equipment, the British historian went searching for fascinating trees. As Pakenham says, he was in search of trees with "noble brows and strong personalities." He wrote a book about his experiences, with photographs of the many "personalities" he found. His portraits show the wide range in tree sizes and shapes. Some of the tiny bonsai trees of Japan are less than a foot tall, even though they are full-grown and many years old. On the other hand, in California, Pakenham found "General Sherman"—the name given to a giant sequoia tree that is considered to be the largest single living thing on Earth.

Fluency Transparency 3

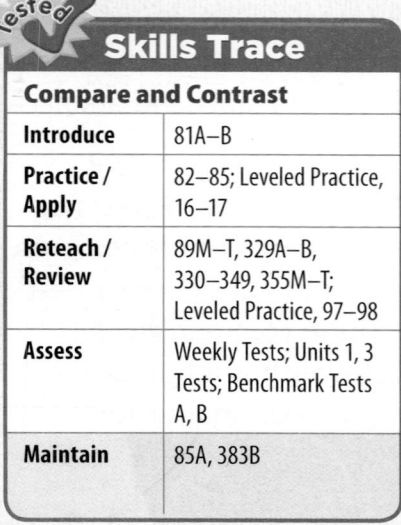

Skills Trace

Compare and Contrast	
Introduce	81A–B
Practice / Apply	82–85; Leveled Practice, 16–17
Reteach / Review	89M–T, 329A–B, 330–349, 355M–T; Leveled Practice, 97–98
Assess	Weekly Tests; Units 1, 3 Tests; Benchmark Tests A, B
Maintain	85A, 383B

Fluency
Repeated Reading: Punctuation

EXPLAIN/MODEL Model reading **Fluency Transparency 3** aloud. Have students echo-read after you. Before reading, point out the **punctuation** used in the paragraph: periods, commas, and quotation marks. Discuss the function of each: periods indicate a stop, commas indicate a pause, and quotation marks indicate a person speaking or the special use of a word.

PRACTICE/APPLY Divide students into two groups. The first group reads the passage a sentence at a time. The second group echo-reads. Then have groups switch roles. For additional practice, have students use **Practice Book** page 18 or the Fluency Solutions Audio CD. Do a Quick Check to see which students need small-group instruction.

Comprehension

MAINTAIN SKILL
COMPARE AND CONTRAST

EXPLAIN/MODEL

- When you compare, you analyze how things are alike. When you contrast, you analyze how things are different. Authors of nonfiction often use a compare-and-contrast text structure because they find it is an effective way to meet their purpose of informing the reader.

- Look for things that are being compared and contrasted to each other as you read. Think about how they are alike and different. Some writers use words and phrases to signal likenesses and differences, such as *like, just as, also, but, different,* and *on the other hand.*

- Recognizing that an author has used a compare-and-contrast text structure can help readers better understand and remember the most important information in the text.

PRACTICE/APPLY

- Identify any words the author uses to signal readers when a contrast or comparison is being made.

- Divide students into groups to discuss another selection in terms of compare and contrast.

Research
Study Skills

Using the Library and Media Center

EXPLAIN/MODEL

Tell students that if they are researching the life spans of trees, they can find materials on that topic in the library media center. Discuss how to use card catalogs.

A card catalog lists all the books, tapes, DVDs, CD-ROMs, and other materials that can be found in a library. Each book has three cards in the card catalog: the author card, the title card, and the subject card.

Use the author card when you know the author of the book but not the title. Use the title card when you know the title but not the author. Use the subject card when you need a book on a particular topic and do not know any specific titles. The call number tells where the book can be found in the library.

Discuss how to use electronic catalogs. In an electronic catalog you can search for a book by its author, title, and subject. To search by subject, enter key words about the topic.

A search result will show you a numbered list of titles. Type in the number of the book and press enter. The screen for a particular book will give the same information found in a card catalog. The screen will also tell you whether the book is available.

Display **Transparency 1.**

Think Aloud To find a book about the life spans of trees, I typed the key word *trees* in the electronic card catalog. The catalog showed me four titles. I selected *Fascinating Facts About Trees*. The card catalog gave me all the information I needed to find the book.

PRACTICE/APPLY

Have students use a library catalog to check out a book on different types of trees or plants that live in their area. Have them identify other materials in the media center they can use to research the topic, such as electronic storage devices (including CD-ROMs) or grade-appropriate reference materials. For example, they may wish to locate and use DVDs or technical manuals that give instructions on planting and caring for trees that thrive in the area.

Objective
- Use library catalogs and media resources to research a topic

Materials
- Study Skill Transparency 1
- Leveled Practice Books, p. 19

 Transparency 1

USING THE LIBRARY AND MEDIA CENTER SUBJECT SEARCH
Item Information   3. *Fascinating Facts About Trees*
by Brackman, Joseph Frank 1944-
Nature Press, c 2002
Call # 582.17B
Subjects: • Trees - worldwide - facts and identification
Series: • Nature field guide series
Responsibility: by Joseph Frank Brackman; illustrated by Frances Kurtz; edited by Harold Frim
Place of publication: New York, NY
Language: English
Description: 325 p.: 279 ill., 20 maps
Notes: Bibliography, pp. 321-322
Library Holdings: 6 copies   5 checked in

Study Skill Transparency 1

On Level Practice Book O, page 19

A **library** often holds more than collections of books and magazines. Due to advances in technology, information can be stored and presented in many different forms. To use a library or **media center** successfully, choose the correct resources.

Choose the resource from the chart that would provide useful information for each item below. Write the name of the resource on the line provided.

Sample of Media Center Resources
Thomas Pakenham's book of photographs about trees around the world
online encyclopedia, key words "wildfire" and "containment"
CD entitled *The Music of the Brazilian Rain Forest*
video documentary called *Three Forest Biomes and the Animals that Live in Them*
print encyclopedia, volume B, article about common trees
CD-ROM entitled *Maps, Geography, and the Environment*

1. Which resource would you use to read articles about these common trees in the United States: black cherry, box elder, black willow? print encyclopedia, volume B

2. Which resource would you use to hear what a typical day in a rain forest sounds like? CD titled *The Music of the Brazilian Rain Forest*

3. Which resource would you use to find pictures of a tree named "General Sherman" in California and a tree called a "dancing lime" in Germany? Thomas Pakenham's book of photographs about trees around the world

4. Which resource would you use to learn about techniques used to control wildfires? Online encyclopedia, key words "wildfire," "containment"

 Approaching Practice Book A, page 19

Beyond Practice Book B, page 19

Answer Questions

Test Strategy: Right There

EXPLAIN

Tell students that good test takers know that sometimes the answer to a question can be found right in the selection.

- Identify key words in the question that tell you what you need to know.
- Skim the passage for clues and locate the key words that you identified in the question

MODEL

Remind students not to write in their books but to record their answers on a separate sheet of paper.

Question 1 Read the question and all of the answer choices.

Think Aloud I know that I need to find key words. In this question some key words are *strategy*, *fight*, *wildfire*, and *fuel*. The first part of the selection defines wildfires, and the second part addresses fighting wildfires. Therefore, I need to skim the second part of the selection, looking for the key words strategy, fight, wildfire, and fuel. I find them at the beginning of the last paragraph. The second sentence of this paragraph says that containment means "surrounded" and "starve." Therefore, the best answer choice is C.

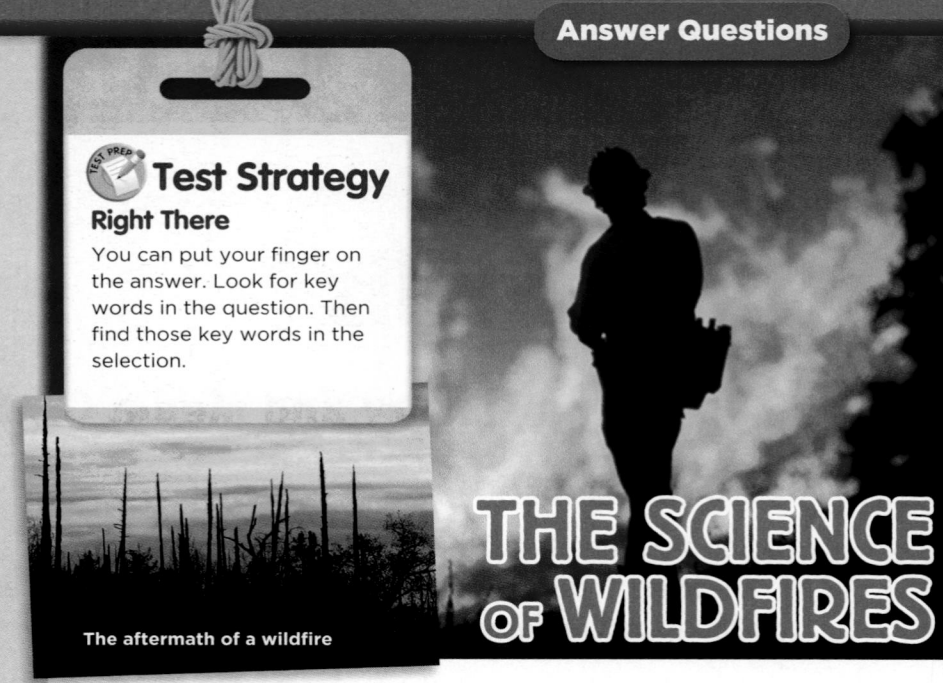

Test Strategy

Right There
You can put your finger on the answer. Look for key words in the question. Then find those key words in the selection.

The aftermath of a wildfire

THE SCIENCE OF WILDFIRES

Wildfires result from a combination of fuel, dryness, and a trigger. Each factor determines how strong the blaze will be. Fuel means flammable solids that, with oxygen, feed the fire. Dryness can be caused by short-term periods with little rain or by lengthy drought. Triggers can be as natural as a lightning strike, as innocent as a campfire, or as careless as a stray match.

Weather is the primary force that creates or ends wildfires. Once wildfires start burning, they create their own weather. First, smoke and heat from fires can rise thousands of feet in the air, creating an empty space below them. Cooler air rushes in to fill the space, but the fresh air brings oxygen that fuels the flames. This convection system creates powerful, hot winds that dry out and preheat fuel ahead of the fire. This helps the fire move forward and even jump natural barriers, such as rivers.

A fire dies when it cannot get fuel, heat, or oxygen. The main strategy for fighting wildfires is containment: surround the fire and starve it. Helicopters and tanker airplanes can drop water or chemicals to slow the spread of flames. Firefighters can also set up fire lines—areas cleared of any fuel that would allow the fire to spread. Controlled fires are sometimes set to deny fuel to an approaching blaze.

86

Go On ▶

Directions: Answer the questions.

1. **Which term means a strategy to fight a wildfire by depriving it of fuel?**
   A   triggering
   B   flame retardant
   C   containment
   D   convection system

2. **What triggers wildfires?**
   A   Matches, campfires, or lightning can trigger a wildfire.
   B   Controlled fires provide fuel for the blaze.
   C   Hot, dry winds preheat fuel to create a convection system.
   D   Tanker airplanes spread the flames.

3. **Why do firefighters set up fire lines?**
   A   to create a fuel-free area
   B   to create a fire-resistant forest
   C   to restore grassland
   D   to create safe zones for forest homes

4. **How might dropping chemicals and creating fire lines be more effective together than if used separately?**

5. **Describe the role weather can play in both creating and ending wildfires. Use details from the article to support your answer.**

Tip
Look for key words.

 87

GUIDED PRACTICE

Question 2 Read the question and all of the answer choices. Ask students: *Which word in the question can be considered a key word?* (triggers)

Where should I look for the information? (in the first part of the selection) *Is the key word here part of the selection?* (The key word is in the first paragraph.) *The first paragraph says that wildfires are triggered by campfires or matches combined with fuel and dryness, so the best answer is A.*

APPLY

Question 3 Read the question and all of the answer choices.

Have students use the Right There strategy to choose an answer.

Which words in the question are key words? (*firefighters* and *fire lines*)

Where did you search for the answer? (in the second part of the selection)

Where are the key words? (in the last paragraph)

What is the best answer? (The best answer is A.)

Have students think critically and write clearly when answering questions 4 and open-ended essay question 5.

Question 4 Answer: Dropping chemicals starves the fire; creating fire lines contains it. Together these methods control wild fires. Separately, they would not be as thorough.

Question 5 Answer: Weather creates wildfires through drought. A lightning strike can also be a trigger for wildfires. Weather can also play a role in ending wildfires when it rains.

Connect
Language Arts

WRITING
- **Tested Writing:** Extended Response to Literature
- **Expository:** Brochure
- Research and Inquiry

WORD STUDY
- Words in Context
- **Dictionary:** Homographs
- Phonics
- Vocabulary Building

SPELLING
- Words with /ü/, /ū/, /ù/

GRAMMAR
- Sentence Combining

SMALL GROUP OPTIONS
- Differentiated Instruction, pp. 89M–89V

Writing Prompt

EXPLAIN/MODEL

Help students analyze the writing prompt on **Student Book** page 88.

Determine the Mode and Form What type of writing is the prompt asking the student to write? (essay) How can you tell? (the heading *extended response to literature;* the phrases *use examples, specific details*)

Determine the Purpose What clue tells what the writing should be about? (*Explain what strategies you would use to fight a wildfire*)

Determine the Audience Does the prompt tell the student to whom she is writing? (no) To whom should she write? (the teacher)

Write to a Prompt

In the selection "The Science of Wildfires," you read about forest fires. Explain what strategies you would use to fight a wildfire that was moving rapidly toward your community. Use examples from the selection to support your answer. Include specific details to support your main idea.

Let's Fight Fires!

The fire in our community is spreading too quickly for firefighters to put out. Our tanker planes have not improved the situation at all.

If we want to save our homes, we must fight fire with fire. We need to cut all the trees and brush on the edge of our community. This will steal the fire's fuel and, we hope, stop the fire before it reaches our town.

I used details to make my point and support my ideas.

There are no guarantees. The wind can carry embers half a mile. We will have to do more. We will need to set a backfire. This means setting fire to the forest between the wildfire and the fire line we create. The prevailing wind will spread the fire toward us. I know it sounds crazy, but we really won't be helping the wildfire. By setting this smaller, more controllable fire, we hope to stop the wildfire more easily at the fire line. The backfire will burn away all the fuel between us and the wildfire. When the wildfire reaches the burned out area, it will go out.

88

SCORING RUBRIC

4 Points	**3** Points	**2** Points	**1** Point
Writing is on topic and interesting. There is a beginning, a middle, and an end. Writing shows accuracy in punctuation and capitalization.	Writing is on topic. There is an attempt to sequence or develop thought. The writing holds the reader's attention. Errors occur but do not interfere with understanding.	Writing is generally on topic. There is an attempt to form good sentences, but sentences may be simple or incomplete with limited vocabulary. Errors may make understanding difficult.	Writing may show little or no development of topic, but may contain meaningful vocabulary. There is an attempt to form sentences. Written vocabulary is limited. Writing shows no use of writing conventions.

Writing Prompt

In the selection "The Science of Wildfires," you read different ideas about the best way to deal with forest fires. Explain which two of the approaches described in the article you think will work the best. Write your response in two paragraphs, and include specific details that support your main ideas.

Writer's Checklist

☑ Ask yourself, who is my audience?

☑ Think about your purpose for writing.

☑ Use details to support your main idea.

☑ Plan your writing before beginning.

☑ Be sure your ideas are clear and organized.

☑ Use your best spelling, grammar, and punctuation.

89

Picture Prompt

For further timed writing practice use the picture prompt on page 162 of the **Teacher's Resource Book.**

Teacher's Resource Book, page 162

Write to a picture prompt. Why are trees important? Look at the photograph below. Write a story about what might happen if trees disappeared from your community.

✎ **Writing Tips**

• Use a graphic organizer to organize your thoughts.
• Write your story on lined paper.
• Proofread your story.

PRACTICE

Have students use the writer's checklist to determine how well the essay on page 88 addresses the prompt.

Then have students read the writing prompt on page 89 and find the clues that determine the mode, form, purpose, and audience. Explain that the writing mode is the overall category of writing (such as narrative or expository) and the writing form is the specific type of writing (such as short story or essay).

Mode and Form: clues—in the selection, described in the article, response in two paragraphs, and specific details that support

Purpose: clues—best way to deal with forest fires

Audience: no clues, so write the essay to your teacher

APPLY

Ask students to summarize the information in the prompt.

TIMED WRITING PRACTICE

You may wish to have students practice writing to the prompt by simulating a test-taking situation. Tell students that after they have analyzed the prompt, they will have 45 minutes to write their responses.

You may use scrap paper to organize your thoughts before you begin drafting your response. I will tell you when to begin, and I will tell you when you have 15 minutes left to finish the response. Use the writer's checklist to make sure that you have included all of the information.

Publishing Options

To publish their brochures, students should make neat final copies and include clearly labeled drawings or photographs of the trees. Additionally, ask students to assume the role of a park ranger or nature program host. In these roles, invite students to read aloud their brochures to small groups of younger students. Students might also post their brochures on a bulletin board.

Speaking and Listening

SPEAKING STRATEGIES

- Speak loudly and clearly so that everyone can hear you.
- Use words that fit your purpose and your audience.
- Point to any drawings or illustrations.

LISTENING STRATEGIES

- Listen carefully for the speaker's main idea.
- Keep your eyes on the speaker.

4-Point Scoring Rubric

Use the four-point scoring rubric on **Teacher's Resource Book** page 156 to score published writing.

Writing Process

For a complete writing process lesson, see Unit Writing pages 143A–143H.

Expository: Brochure

GENERATE QUESTIONS

Direct students to "Tree-Rific!" on **Student Book** page 80. Explain that they will research tree identification and write explanatory brochures. Review that brochures contain descriptive details and drawings or photos. Show a sample, if possible. Explain that brochures often have short paragraphs with headings. Point out that the Internet link on page 81 will help students with their research.

Have students choose trees they would like to describe in their brochures. Encourage students to generate research questions: *What type of leaves does the tree have? What color are the leaves? Where does the tree grow? How tall does the tree grow to be?* Draw a web on the board and work with students to fill in a sample organizer.

FIND INFORMATION

Explain that a library or media center has a variety of materials and resources. The reference section includes books for research, such as encyclopedias, atlases, and almanacs. A media center may also include videotapes, audiotapes, DVDs, and software. Discuss how to use an online card catalog, including what a call number means. Use the **Taking Notes** lesson on page 89B and **Transparency 9** before students begin their research.

ORGANIZE INFORMATION

Once students decide to use a resource, they should take notes and make outlines. Use the **Outlining lessons** on page 89B and **Transparency 10** to help students learn how to organize ideas.

SYNTHESIZE AND WRITE

Have students use their outlines to write drafts of their brochures. Discuss the draft on **Transparency 11** and then the revisions on **Transparency 12**. Have students revise their work and then review it with a partner.

Writer's Toolbox

Outlining

Tell students they will use the notes they take during research to create outlines. Display **Transparency 10.** Discuss with students how to create an outline. Main ideas are listed under Roman numerals and supporting details are listed under capital letters. Show students how to cut and paste their outlines to reorder the progression of ideas, if necessary.

Transparency 10

I. Ginkgo bilobas are trees with a long history.
  A. Are relatives of a million-year-old plant
  B. Dinosaurs ate this plant in the Mezozoic Era.
II. Properties of a Ginkgo
  A. Green, fan-shaped leaves
  B. Bad smell
  C. Brown bark
  D. Usually reach 80 ft.
III. Where they grow
  A. Anywhere with a lot of sun and deep, dryish soil

Writing Transparency 10

Taking Notes

Remind students that they will have to evaluate the usefulness of reference materials quickly. Explain that skimming and scanning a passage means reading it quickly. Skimming can help students get an overview of what a passage is about. Scanning can help students locate key words and main ideas. While they skim and scan, remind students to take notes in their own words, citing the author, title, publication date and location, and page numbers. Show **Transparency 9**. Explain that this is an example of a note card one student created during research. Discuss how the student summarized information and kept track of one source.

Transparency 9: **Notetaking**

Research Tips

Evaluating Sources Remind students to ask themselves questions about their sources: *Is this information accurate and current? What are the author's credentials? Will this information help me write my brochure? Is this material too difficult for me to read?* Have students compare and contrast the information from different sources. Point out that information they find in multiple sources usually is more reliable than information they find in only one source.

Objectives

- Apply knowledge of word meaning and context clues
- Choose the correct meaning of a homograph when using a dictionary

Materials

- Vocabulary Transparencies 5, 6
- Leveled Practice Books, p. 20

Vocabulary

quest (p. 64) search or hunt

settings (p. 64) surroundings or background

reduce (p.65) make less; make smaller; decrease

buffet (p. 65) knock about, strike, or hurt

major (p. 65) important; large; great

ELL   Access for All

Identify Synonyms After reviewing vocabulary, say a sentence using a synonym of a word and help students repeat the sentence with the correct word.

Review
Vocabulary
 **Words in Context**

EXPLAIN/MODEL

Review the meanings of the vocabulary words. Display **Transparency 5.** Model how to use word meanings and context clues to fill in the first missing word.

Think Aloud In the first sentence, the knight wants to find the dragon. Synonyms for *find* include *discovery* or *search*. *Quest* also means "search or hunt." The correct answer is *quest*.

 Transparency 5

quest major settings buffet reduce

The knight went on a (1) <u>quest</u> to find the dragon.

The trees and flowers provided lovely (2) <u>settings</u> for the picnic.

(3) <u>Reduce</u> waste by recycling.

The high winds tend to (4) <u>buffet</u> buildings, causing damage.

Going to college is a (5) <u>major</u> opportunity for me.

Vocabulary Transparency 5

PRACTICE/APPLY

Instruct students to complete the remaining sentences on their own.

 Review students' answers as a class, or instruct students to exchange papers with a partner, check answers, and discuss the context clues they used to figure out the missing words.

Word Collecting Have students look back at this week's selections to collect interesting words they would like to remember and use in their own writing. Have them list the words in a word study notebook and add definitions paraphrased from a dictionary. Have partners share and discuss the words they collected.

STRATEGY
DICTIONARY: HOMOGRAPHS

EXPLAIN/MODEL

Homographs are words that are spelled the same but have different meanings and sometimes different pronunciations. They are often different parts of speech as well. When students cannot figure out the meaning of a homograph using context clues, they should consult a dictionary.

Display **Transparency 6.** Model using the dictionary entries to figure out the meaning of the underlined homograph in the example sentence.

Transparency 6

VOCABULARY IN CONTEXT: HOMOGRAPHS

Trees can reduce heating costs by breaking the force of winter winds that <u>buffet</u> and batter homes.

¹**buffet** (bə fā, bủ fā) *noun* **1.** cabinet or counter where food is served. **2.** a meal spread out on accessible tables.

²**buffet** (buf′ it) *verb* knock about, strike

1. We put the snacks on the buffet so everyone could help themselves.

2. The force of a storm's waves can buffet a large boat.

Vocabulary Strategy Transparency 6

PRACTICE

Have students identify which homograph is used in items 1 and 2. Then have them find the homographs *wind, lead,* and *entrance* in a dictionary and write sentences using them.

Quick Check

Can students determine word meanings?
Can students figure out which homograph to use?

During **Small Group Instruction**

If No → **Approaching Level** Vocabulary, pp. 89N–89O

If Yes → **On Level** Options, pp. 89Q–89R

Beyond Level Options, pp. 89S–89T

ELL / Access for All

Dictionary Use Model how to use the dictionary to find the homographs for the words in the Practice activity. Point out where to find the word's part of speech. Help students pronounce the word. Give additional examples of each word in sentences.

On Level Practice Book O, page 20

Sometimes words have one spelling but two distinct pronunciations and two different meanings. These words are called **homographs.** You can use a dictionary to learn the different definitions and pronunciations of a homograph. For example, if you look up the word **bass** in a dictionary, you will find that it is a kind of fish (pronounced with a short *a* vowel sound). You will also find that **bass** pronounced with a long *a* vowel sound) refers to a deep sound or tone.

Use a dictionary to write the meanings and pronunciations of these homographs.

Word		Pronunciation	Definition
1. buffet	a.	buf´it	to pound repeatedly
	b.	bə fē´, bủ fē´	a meal people serve themselves
2. bow	a.	bō	a weapon for shooting arrows
	b.	bou	the front part of a ship
3. tear	a.	târ	to pull apart by force
	b.	tîr	a liquid that moistens the eye
4. wind	a.	wind	a movement of the air
	b.	wīnd	to wrap or coil
5. object	a.	ob´jikt	a thing that is seen or felt
	b.	əb jekt´	to protest

 Approaching Practice Book A, page 20

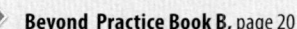 **Beyond Practice Book B,** page 20

Word Study

Objective

- Decode words with /ü/, /ū/, and /ù/

Materials

- Leveled Practice Books, p. 21
- Teacher's Resource Book, p. 7

ELL | Access for All

Pronunciation On the board write the words in categories by their sound. Say each word and have students repeat. Explain its meaning. Use it in sentences. Then co-construct a sentence with students using the word.

On Level Practice Book O, page 21

- The vowel *u* in *tuna*, the vowels *oo* in *soon*, and the letters *ew* in *grew* can stand for the /ü/ sound. The VCe pattern in *plume* can also stand for the /ü/ sound.
- The vowel *u* in *music*, the vowels *ue* in *cue*, the letters *ew* in *few*, and the VCe pattern in *cute* can also stand for the /ū/ sound.
- The vowels *oo* can also stand for the /ù/ sound in *book*.

Read each sentence. Circle the word that has the vowel sounds in *loon*, *mule*, or *book*. Then write the word in the column for that vowel sound.

1. It is important to (prune) a tree's branches.
2. Don't fasten those (hooks) to the tree branches!
3. The wildfire has a deep yellow (hue.)
4. My (handbook) about trees has great pictures.
5. We plant a (few) trees in the park each year.
6. Some (flutes) are made from trees.
7. This tree will provide (wood) for the people.
8. There are many ways to (use) that timber.
9. The horse carried the (food) up the hill.

l**oo**n /ü/	m**u**le /ū/	b**oo**k /ù/
prune	hue	hooks
flutes	few	handbook
food	use	wood

★ **Approaching Practice Book A,** page 21
◆ **Beyond Practice Book B,** page 21

Phonics

Decode Words with /ü/, /ū/, and /ù/

 **EXPLAIN/MODEL**

- The *u* in *tuna*, the digraph *oo* in *soon*, and the *ew* in *grew* can stand for the /ü/ sound. The VCe pattern in *plume* can also stand for the /ü/ sound.

- The *u* in *music*, the digraph *ue* in *cue*, the *ew* in *few*, and the VCe pattern in *cute* can also stand for the /ū/ sound.

- The digraph *oo* can also stand for the /ù/ sound in *book*.

Write the word *bamboo* on the board.

Think Aloud The second syllable of this word has *oo*, and *oo* can have the /ü/ sound in *too* or the /ù/ sound in *book*. When I try the /ù/ sound, I get /bam bù/. That doesn't make sense. Now, I'll try the /ü/ sound. /bam bü/. That sounds like a word I know. Bamboo is a kind of plant.

PRACTICE/APPLY Write *amuse, handbook, union, crooks, bruise, hue, lose.* Ask students to identify the letters that stand for /ü/, /ū/, or /ù/ in each word. Point out that in some parts of the country, people may use the /ū/ sound instead of the /ü/ sound in words such as *duty* or *due.*

Decode Multisyllabic Words Explain that *-ing*, and *-ed* are endings added to a word; *-ing* shows an action that is happening in the present; *-ed* shows an action that happened in the past. Write *blooming* on the board. Point to and say the base *bloom* and then the ending. Read the word. Write *consumed, hooking,* and *shampooing.* Help students decode the words. For more practice, see the decodable passages on **Teacher's Resource Book** page 7.

 **Tic-Tac-Toe** Have partners play tic-tac-toe with /ü/, /ū/, and /ù/ words. Each player is assigned one sound. They take turns writing words on the tic-tac-toe grid until one gets three words in a row.

Quick Check | Can students decode words with /ü/, /ū/, and /ù/?

During **Small Group Instruction**

If No → **Approaching Level** Phonics, p. 89M

If Yes → **On Level** Options, pp. 89Q–89R

Beyond Level Options, pp. 89S–89T

Vocabulary Building

Oral Language

Expand Vocabulary Write *Trees for Life* in the center of a word web. Using the *Time for Kids* articles as well as dictionaries, thesauruses, and encyclopedias, have students find and brainstorm words that relate to this week's theme. You may include words such as *oxygen*, *shade*, or *lumber*. Write these words and their definitions in circles that radiate from the center circle of your web.

Vocabulary Building

Homographs and Homonyms Display the following list of words and challenge students to define as many as possible. Then have them come up with their own homographs or homonyms. Have students display the homographs on a word wall. They should use a dictionary to check their word meanings and parts of speech and then use them in sentences. Then have students write context sentences for the homographs and homonyms, trade with a partner, and figure out their meanings.

wound	flounder
content	hamper
object	pupil

Apply Vocabulary

Write a Menu Give students the following writing prompt:

Today, many people are on a quest to find foods that taste good and are nutritious. Using books and encyclopedias about food and nutrition, write a menu for a healthy buffet meal. Use homographs in your descriptions where possible.

Spiral Review

Vocabulary Game Using construction paper, make a large tree to post on the board. On each of the tree's leaves, write this week's vocabulary words as well as words from previous weeks. Invite each student to remove a vocabulary leaf from the tree. On the back of the leaves, have students write clue words to and phrases for the vocabulary words. Students should replace the tree's leaves with the clue words and phrases showing. Divide the class into several teams. Choose leaves from the tree, and read the clues aloud to students. Have groups take turns identifying the vocabulary words. If a group correctly identifies a word, they get to keep the leaf. The team with the most leaves at the end wins.

quest   settings   reduce   buffet   major

Technology

Vocabulary PuzzleMaker CD–ROM

For additional vocabulary and spelling games go to
www.macmillanmh.com

Words with /ü/, /ū/, and /u̇/

Spelling Words

tuna	crooks	amuse
duty	hoof	plume
lose	hooks	hue
few	booth	view
doom	handbook	bruise
bamboo	prove	union
brood	mute	

Review theme, coach, bride

Challenge strewn, accuse

Dictation Sentences

1. We ate <u>tuna</u> sandwiches.
2. It's their <u>duty</u> to protect people.
3. She refuses to <u>lose</u> the game.
4. My dad is a man of <u>few</u> words.
5. Laziness will <u>doom</u> this project.
6. Panda bears eat **bamboo.**
7. She will often <u>brood</u> in silence.
8. The <u>crooks</u> were not honest.
9. He didn't recognize the <u>hoof</u> mark.
10. Hang your coats on the <u>hooks</u>.
11. Pay at the <u>booth</u> to enter.
12. The <u>handbook</u> explains it.
13. Steve will <u>prove</u> he is right.
14. She was <u>mute</u> and said nothing.
15. Your jokes <u>amuse</u> me.
16. We saw a <u>plume</u> of smoke.
17. The sky was a deep blue <u>hue</u>.
18. The best <u>view</u> is from the top.
19. Mimi had a <u>bruise</u> on her leg.
20. We formed a <u>union</u>.

Review/Challenge Words

1. We discussed the <u>theme</u> of the book.
2. The <u>coach</u> blew his whistle.
3. We stood when the <u>bride</u> entered.
4. The yard was <u>strewn</u> with leaves.
5. There's no proof to <u>accuse</u> him.

Word in **bold** is from the main selection.

Day 1 Pretest

ASSESS PRIOR KNOWLEDGE

Use the Dictation Sentences. Say the underlined word, read the sentence aloud, and repeat the word. Have students write the words on **Spelling Practice Book** page 13. For a modified list, use the first 12 Spelling Words and the Review Words. For a more challenging list, use Spelling Words 3–20 and the Challenge Words. Students may correct their own tests.

Have students cut apart the Spelling Word Cards BLM on **Teacher's Resource Book** page 68 and figure out a way to sort them. They can save the cards for use throughout the week.

For **Leveled Word Lists** lists go to **www.macmillanmh.com**

Day 2 Word Sorts

TEACHER AND STUDENT SORTS

- Write *amuse, bamboo, crooks, tuna,* and *few* on the board. Pronounce each word and sort them by vowel sound: *crooks; bamboo, tuna; amuse, few.*

- Tell students they will sort the Spelling Words and Challenge Words by vowel sounds. Use the words above to identify categories for the sort. Say the words again, and underline the relevant vowels. Discuss words that have unexpected spellings: *prove, lose.*

- Write and pronounce the column headings /ü/, /ū/, /u̇/ on the board. Repeat each example word above, and list it under the correct heading. Students may copy the chart in their word study notebooks and continue sorting.

- Have students complete the sort.

Spelling Practice Book, pages 13–14

Fold back the paper along the dotted line. Write the words in the blanks as they are read aloud. When you finish the test, unfold the paper. Use the list at the right to correct any spelling mistakes.

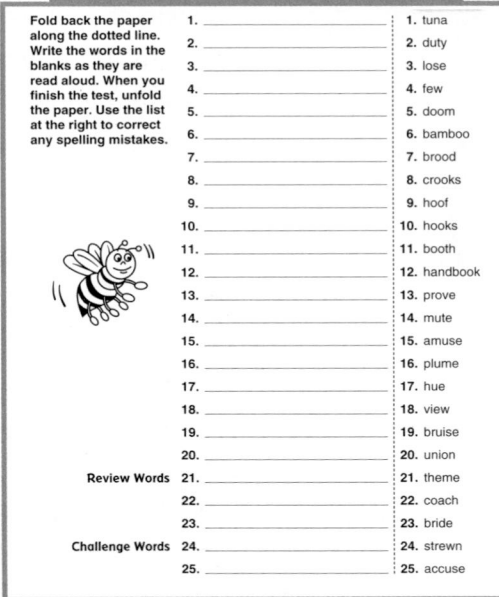

1. _____		1. tuna
2. _____		2. duty
3. _____		3. lose
4. _____		4. few
5. _____		5. doom
6. _____		6. bamboo
7. _____		7. brood
8. _____		8. crooks
9. _____		9. hoof
10. _____		10. hooks
11. _____		11. booth
12. _____		12. handbook
13. _____		13. prove
14. _____		14. mute
15. _____		15. amuse
16. _____		16. plume
17. _____		17. hue
18. _____		18. view
19. _____		19. bruise
20. _____		20. union
Review Words 21. _____		21. theme
22. _____		22. coach
23. _____		23. bride
Challenge Words 24. _____		24. strewn
25. _____		25. accuse

Spelling Practice Book, page 15

amuse	bamboo	brood	crooks	tuna
doom	few	view	hoof	hooks
hue	bruise	booth	lose	duty
handbook	prove	mute	plume	union

Sort each spelling word by finding the sound and spelling pattern to which it belongs.

Write the words that have the /ü/ sound in *boot* spelled:

u
1. tuna
2. duty

o-e
1. prove
2. lose

u-e
1. plume

oo
1. bamboo
2. brood
3. doom
4. booth

ui
1. bruise

Write the words that have the /ū/ sound in *cute* spelled:

u-e
1. amuse
2. hue
3. mute

ew
1. few
2. view

u
1. union

Write the words that have the /u̇/ sound in *book* spelled:

oo
1. crooks
2. hoof
3. hooks
4. handbook

Day 3 — Word Meanings

DEFINITIONS

- With students' help, compose a short poem using four Spelling Words and four words that rhyme with them. Enlist students' help in brainstorming appropriate rhyming words.

- Have student pairs select several other Spelling Words. Tell students to use each word in a sentence to demonstrate understanding of its meaning.

- Challenge students to write their own poems using the Spelling Words they have selected and other words that rhyme with them. Students may brainstorm rhyming words or consult an elementary rhyming dictionary.

- Invite students to illustrate their poems and share them with others in a class poetry reading.

Day 4 — Review and Proofread

SPIRAL REVIEW

Review words with long vowels. Write *coach*, *theme*, and *bride* on the board. Have students identify the long vowel sound in each word.

PROOFREAD AND WRITE

Write these sentences on the board, including the misspelled words. Ask students to proofread, circling the misspelled words and writing them correctly.

1. He didn't want to brewd, because that only led to feelings of dume. (brood, doom)

2. To amuese himself, he made a flute out of bambu. (amuse, bamboo)

3. The handbuck said that it was their dooty to plant trees on Arbor Day. (handbook, duty)

Day 5 — Assess and Reteach

POSTTEST

Use the Dictation Sentences on page 89G for the Posttest.

If students have difficulty with any words in the lesson, have them copy the words in a list entitled "Spelling Words I Want to Remember" in their word study notebooks.

Challenge student partners to look for words that have the same /ü/, /ū/, and /u̇/ vowel sounds that they studied this week, either in their reading or in other materials. Partners should work together to sort the words by vowel sounds.

Spelling Practice Book, page 16

amuse	bamboo	brood	crooks	tuna
doom	few	view	hoof	hooks
hue	bruise	booth	lose	duty
handbook	prove	mute	plume	union

Fill in the Blank

Write the spelling word that best completes each sentence.

1. Banana trees, rubber trees, and __bamboo__ grow in tropical rain forests.
2. The canopy of trees in a rain forest blocks the __view__ of the sky.
3. A __plume__ of smoke rose over the forest.
4. __Few__ plants can grow in the soil of coniferous forests.
5. Deciduous trees __lose__ their leaves in the fall.
6. It is everyone's __duty__ to protect forests.
7. The leaves have a beautiful __hue__ in autumn.
8. He found its name in a __handbook__ to trees in North America.

Similar Meanings

Write the spelling word that has the same, or almost the same, meaning.

9. silent __mute__
10. bump __bruise__
11. worry __brood__
12. animal foot __hoof__
13. entertain __amuse__
14. bent pieces of metal __hooks__
15. box-like space __booth__
16. coming together __union__
17. show __prove__
18. large fish __tuna__
19. disaster __doom__
20. dishonest people __crooks__

Spelling Practice Book, page 17

Circle the misspelled words in the paragraph. Write the words correctly on the lines below.

Our backyard has only a (fue) trees. The big maple tree is my favorite. I have a good (vyoo) of it from my room. All the trees in the yard are deciduous. They all (loos) their leaves in the fall. Before that happens, though, their leaves change color. The maple's leaves turn a red (hiew) I (amewz) myself by collecting maple leaves each fall. Once I found a (ploom) from a bird on the ground by the maple. I saved it along with the leaves I had collected.

1. __few__   3. __lose__   5. __amuse__
2. __view__   4. __hue__   6. __plume__

Writing Activity

Write about something in nature that interests you. Use four spelling words in your description.

_____

_____

_____

_____

_____

_____

_____

Spelling Practice Book, page 18

Look at the words in each set below. One word in each set is spelled correctly. Use a pencil to fill in the circle next to the correct word. Before you begin, look at the sample set of words. Sample A has been done for you. Do Sample B by yourself. When you are sure you know what to do, you may go on with the rest of the page.

Sample A:
- Ⓐ loot
- Ⓑ lut
- Ⓒ loote
- Ⓓ lote

Sample B:
- Ⓔ tock
- Ⓕ tuk
- Ⓖ took
- Ⓗ tuke

1.
- Ⓐ amuse
- Ⓑ amyuse
- Ⓒ amyoos
- Ⓓ amoose

2.
- Ⓔ bambu
- Ⓕ bamboo
- Ⓖ bambuu
- Ⓗ bambo

3.
- Ⓐ broode
- Ⓑ brood
- Ⓒ brode
- Ⓓ brod

4.
- Ⓔ croks
- Ⓕ crokes
- Ⓖ crooks
- Ⓗ crookes

5.
- Ⓐ toona
- Ⓑ tuna
- Ⓒ tuuna
- Ⓓ tona

6.
- Ⓔ dume
- Ⓕ doom
- Ⓖ dum
- Ⓗ doome

7.
- Ⓐ fyoo
- Ⓑ few
- Ⓒ foo
- Ⓓ fu

8.
- Ⓔ vu
- Ⓕ vyoo
- Ⓖ view
- Ⓗ voo

9.
- Ⓐ huf
- Ⓑ hof
- Ⓒ hoof
- Ⓓ huuf

10.
- Ⓔ hucks
- Ⓕ hookes
- Ⓖ hukes
- Ⓗ hooks

11.
- Ⓐ hue
- Ⓑ hoo
- Ⓒ hyoo
- Ⓓ hu

12.
- Ⓔ bruise
- Ⓕ broose
- Ⓖ broos
- Ⓗ bruse

13.
- Ⓐ buthe
- Ⓑ boothe
- Ⓒ booth
- Ⓓ buth

14.
- Ⓔ lose
- Ⓕ loos
- Ⓖ luse
- Ⓗ lus

15.
- Ⓐ dootee
- Ⓑ duty
- Ⓒ dooty
- Ⓓ dutey

16.
- Ⓔ handbook
- Ⓕ handbuk
- Ⓖ handbooke
- Ⓗ handbuke

17.
- Ⓐ proove
- Ⓑ proov
- Ⓒ prove
- Ⓓ pruve

18.
- Ⓔ myoot
- Ⓕ moote
- Ⓖ mute
- Ⓗ miut

19.
- Ⓐ ploom
- Ⓑ plume
- Ⓒ ploome
- Ⓓ pluhm

20.
- Ⓔ oonon
- Ⓕ unon
- Ⓖ unun
- Ⓗ union

5 Day Grammar

Sentence Combining

Grammar

Daily Language Activities

Use these activities to reinforce each day's lesson. Write the day's activity on the board, or use **Daily Language Transparency 3.**

DAY 1

Please open you're books to page 25 did the war begin in 1775. the colonies declared independence in 1776. (1: your; 2: 25. Did; 3: 1775? The)

DAY 2

Americans have holidays and they honor important people? some people celebrate the Fourth of July with parades? Others go on picnics! (1: holidays,; 2: people. Some; 3: parades. picnics.)

DAY 3

The Fourth of July is a special day? we have a family party and play games and go to the carnival. (1.; day. 2. We have a family party, play games, and)

DAY 4

Mandy looked in the handbock she found bambo Everyone wanted to vieu the pictures. (1: handbook, and; 2: bamboo.; 3: view)

DAY 5

Selena found one flower Marcus found three. Tricia found poison ivy she didn't touch it. James found a pluem (1: flower, and; 2: ivy, but she didn't; 3: plume.)

ELL   **Access for All**

Use Students' Experiences

Ask students to make simple statements about what they did over the weekend. Write the statements on the board. Point out that these are examples of simple sentences. Combine ideas in sentences to show examples of the other kinds of sentences.

INTRODUCE COMPOUND SENTENCES AND CONJUNCTIONS

Present the following:

- A simple sentence expresses one complete thought.

- A compound sentence contains two simple sentences joined by a comma and the word *and*, *but*, or *or*.

- A conjunction joins words or groups of words; *and, but,* and *or* are conjunctions.

- A semicolon can also join two simple sentences that are related: *Ed painted trees; he also drew portraits.*

 See Grammar Transparency 11 for modeling and guided practice.

Grammar Practice Book, page 13

- Two related sentences can be joined with a comma and *and*, *but*, or *or*.
- A sentence that contains two sentences joined by *and, but,* or *or* is called a **compound sentence**.

Read each pair of sentences. Rewrite them as a single sentence, using *and*, *but*, or *or* along with a comma.

1. Pakenham went searching for trees. He wrote a book about them.
   Pakenham went searching for trees, and he wrote a book about them.

2. General Sherman is the name of a person. It is also the name of a giant sequoia.
   General Sherman is the name of a person, but it is also the name of a giant sequoia.

3. Would you like to visit a coniferous forest biome? Would you like to see a deciduous forest?
   Would you like to visit coniferous forest biome, or would you like to see a deciduous forest?

4. The fallen leaves enrich the soil. They allow all kinds of plant life to grow.
   The fallen leaves enrich the soil, and they allow all kinds of plant life to grow.

5. Oak, beech, ash, and maple trees are typical of a deciduous forest. Many types of insects and animals live in that habitat.
   Oak, beech, ash, and maple trees are typical of a deciduous forest, and many types of insects and animals live in that habitat.

REVIEW COMPOUND SENTENCES AND CONJUNCTIONS

Discuss with students how to form a compound sentence. Ask how a compound sentence differs from a simple sentence, what conjunctions you use to make a compound sentence, and what punctuation you use before the conjunction. Review how to use semicolons.

INTRODUCE RUN-ON SENTENCES

- A run-on sentence joins together two or more sentences that should be written separately: *She felt bad she went home.*

- You can correct a run-on sentence by rewriting it as a compound sentence: *She felt bad, and she went home.*

 See Grammar Transparency 12 for modeling and guided practice.

Grammar Practice Book, page 14

- A **conjunction** joins words or groups of words. *And, but,* and *or* are conjunctions.
- A sentence that contains two sentences joined by *and, but,* or *or* is called a **compound sentence**.
- In a **compound sentence**, a comma is placed before the conjunction.

Read each sentence below. Underline the conjunction, and put a comma in the correct place.

1. Limited rainfall or lengthy drought can cause wildfires, but these fires can also be caused by campfires or a stray match.

2. Helicopters can drop chemicals to slow flames, and firefighters can set up fire lines.

3. Tiny bonsai trees may look like young plants, but they are full grown.

4. Many areas in the world are covered with trees, but the Arctic tundra is treeless.

5. Moisture is absorbed, and then it evaporates and falls as rain.

Read each sentence below. If it is a compound sentence, write C on the line. If it is not a compound sentence, leave the line blank.

6. There are no leaves to decompose and make the ground suitable for growth. ___blank___

7. Some plants will not thrive in a coniferous forest, but some animals do well in this biome. ___C___

8. North America, Europe, and eastern Asia all have deciduous forests. ___blank___

Day 3 | Review and Practice

REVIEW RUN-ON SENTENCES

Review with students that a run-on sentence joins together two or more sentences that should be written separately.

MECHANICS AND USAGE: PUNCTUATE COMPOUND SENTENCES

- When you write a compound sentence, use a comma before *and, but*, or *or*.

- When you correct a run-on sentence, use a comma before *and, but*, or *or*.

- To coordinate two closely related sentences without using a conjunction, use a semicolon (;): *I went back home; I thought it was important.*

 See Grammar Transparency 13 for modeling and guided practice.

Grammar Practice Book, page 15

- Use a comma before *and, but,* or *or* when you join two sentences to form a compound sentence.
- Begin every sentence with a capital letter.
- When you form a compound sentence, do not begin the second part with a capital letter.

Read each group of words. Then write them as correct sentences on the lines. Be sure to use capital letters and commas in the correct places.

1. trees produce oxygen and they reduce the effects of carbon dioxide.
   Trees produce oxygen, and they reduce the effects of carbon dioxide.

2. Trees should be planted in certain areas or the soil could be carried away by wind and water.
   Trees should be planted in certain areas, or the soil could be carried away by wind and water.

3. a stone wall might be an effective way to cut down noise but a row of trees is usually more attractive
   A stone wall might be an effective way to cut down noise, but a row of trees is usually more attractive.

4. arbor Day was successful in 1872 but it was even more successful in 2002.
   Arbor Day was successful in 1872, but it was even more successful in 2002.

5. trees are considered to be among nature's hardest workers and this is true in any climate. **Trees are considered to be among nature's hardest workers, and this is true in any climate.**

6. Could you identify the trees in your neighborhood by yourself or would you need some help?
   Could you identify the trees in your neighborhood by yourself, or would you need some help?

Day 4 | Review and Proofread

REVIEW COMPOUND SENTENCES AND CONJUNCTIONS

Ask students to explain the differences between simple, compound, and run-on sentences. Ask what conjunctions and punctuation should be used in compound sentences.

PROOFREAD

Have students correct the following sentences.

1. We watched the fireworks and we played many games. (fireworks,)

2. We saw their brightness we heard how loud they were! (brightness, and)

3. Should we buy candy? Should we buy popcorn? (candy, or should)

 See Grammar Transparency 14 for modeling and guided practice.

Grammar Practice Book, page 16

- Use commas to separate three or more words in a series.
- Two related sentences can be joined with a comma and *and, but,* or *or.*

Read the passage below. Circle mistakes in capitalization and punctuation. Then rewrite the passage.

Almost half of the world's rain forests are in Brazil but many are found in Asia Africa South america Central America and on many Pacific Islands. the vegetation in a rain forest is thick and this means that a great deal of moisture is absorbed into the atmosphere. The moisture eventually evaporates. The moisture falls back to Earth as rain. Amazingly, tropical rain forests receive 70 inches of rain a year.

A rain forest has three layers. the canopy is the tallest. The understory is in the middle. The forest floor is on the bottom. The forest floor is very dense. It is covered with ferns and mosses.

Almost half of the world's rain forests are in Brazil, but many are found in Asia, Africa, South America, Central America, and on many Pacific Islands. The vegetation in a rain forest is thick, and this means that a great deal of moisture is absorbed into the atmosphere. The moisture eventually evaporates and falls back to Earth as rain. Amazingly, tropical rain forests receive 70 inches of rain a year!

A rain forest has three layers. The canopy is the tallest, the understory is in the middle, and the forest floor is on the bottom. The forest floor is very dense, and it is covered with ferns and mosses.

Day 5 | Assess and Reteach

ASSESS

Use the Daily Language Activity and page 17 of the **Grammar Practice Book** for assessment.

RETEACH

Play "Stand-Up Sentences." Think of some simple and compound sentences. Students stand up when they hear a compound sentence and remain seated when they hear simple sentences. Remind students that simple sentences can also contain *and, but*, and *or*. Players are "out" if they stand up for simple sentences or sit down for compound sentences. Invite students to make their own sentences.

Use page 18 of the Grammar Practice Book for additional reteaching.

 See Grammar Transparency 15 for modeling and guided practice.

Grammar Practice Book, pages 17–18

Circle the letter for each correct answer.

1. Which of the following sentences has a conjunction?
   a. What are the five most common trees in the United States?
   b. I like black cherry trees.
   c. We planted a black cherry tree, and it is doing very well.

2. Which of the following sentences uses a comma correctly?
   a. Tiny bonsai trees are from Japan and they can be less than a foot tall.
   b. Tiny bonsai trees are from Japan, and they can be less than a foot tall.
   c. Tiny bonsai trees are from Japan and they, can be, less than a foot tall.

3. Which of the following sentences is a compound sentence?
   a. Trees absorb carbon dioxide and keep it from harming the environment.
   b. Trees absorb carbon dioxide, and keep it from harming the environment.
   c. Trees absorb carbon dioxide, and this absorption keeps the carbon dioxide from harming the environment.

4. Which of the following compound sentences uses a conjunction correctly?
   a. Deciduous trees lose their leaves, in the natural decaying enriches the soil.
   b. Deciduous trees lose their leaves, or the natural decaying enriches the soil.
   c. Deciduous trees lose their leaves, and the natural decaying enriches the soil.

5. In the space below, draw a picture of the type of forest you like best. Under the picture, write a compound sentence that explains why you like this type of forest.

End-of-Week Assessment

Administer the Test

Weekly Reading Assessment

Passage and questions, pages 29–36

ASSESSED SKILLS

- Compare and Contrast
- Vocabulary Words
- Use a Dictionary: Homographs
- Words with /ü/, /ū/, /ů/
- Sentence Combining

Administer the **Weekly Assessment** online or on CD-ROM.

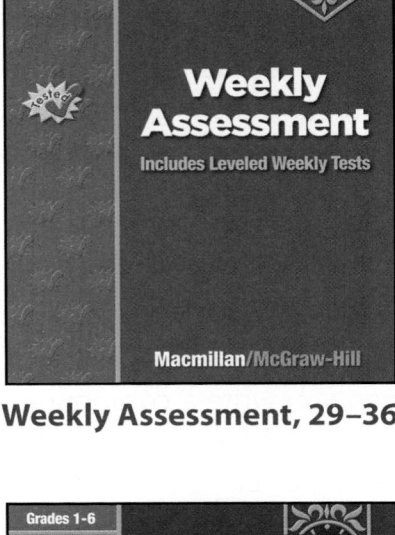

Weekly Assessment, 29–36

Fluency

Assess fluency for one group of students per week. Use the Oral Fluency Record Sheet to track the number of words read correctly. Fluency goal for all students:
100–120 words correct per minute (WCPM).

Approaching Level	Weeks 1, 3, 5
On Level	Weeks 2, 4
Beyond Level	Week 6

Fluency Assessment

Alternative Assessments

- **Leveled Weekly Assessment** for Approaching Level, pages 37–44
- **ELL Assessment,** pages 40–41

ELL Practice and Assessment, 40–41

Diagnose		Prescribe
	IF...	**THEN...**
VOCABULARY WORDS **VOCABULARY STRATEGY** Use a Dictionary: Homographs Items 1, 2, 3, 4	0–2 items correct...	Reteach skills using the **Additional Lessons** page T8. **LOG ON** Reteach skills: Go to www.macmillanmh.com **CD ROM** Vocabulary PuzzleMaker Evaluate for Intervention.
COMPREHENSION Skill: Compare and Contrast Items 5, 6, 7, 8	0–2 items correct...	Reteach skills using the **Additional Lessons** page T3. Evaluate for Intervention.
GRAMMAR Sentence Combining Items 9, 10, 11	0–1 items correct...	Reteach skills: **Grammar Practice Book** page 18.
SPELLING Words with /ü/ /ū/ /ù/ Items 12, 13, 14	0–1 items correct...	**LOG ON** Reteach skills: Go to www.macmillanmh.com
FLUENCY	96–99 WCPM	**AUDIO CD** Fluency Solutions
	0–95 WCPM	Evaluate for Intervention.

READING
Triumphs
AN INTERVENTION PROGRAM

Also Available

To place students
in the Intervention
Program, use
the **Diagnostic
Assessment** in the
Intervention Teacher's
Edition.

Skills Focus ▶ Phonics

Objective	Decode one-syllable and multisyllabic words with /ü/, /ū/, and /ů/ sounds in both familiar and unfamiliar texts
Materials	• **Student Book** "Tree-rific!" and "Trees at Work" • **Decodable Passages, Teacher's Resource Book** p. 7

WORDS WITH /ü/, /ū/, AND /ů/ SOUNDS

Model/Guided Practice

■ Write the letters *g, l, u, e* on the board. Say the sound that each letter or digraph stands for. Point out that the *e* is silent. Then blend the sounds: */glü/. Say the word with me:* glue.

■ *The sound /ü/ is spelled* u. *This same sound can also be spelled* oo, *as in* moon, *and* ew, *as in* blew. *The sound can also be produced through the VCe pattern, as in* rude.

■ Write the word *dune* on the board. *Say the word with me. How is the /ü/ sound formed?*

■ Next use these words to check the rules: *troupe, loom, include, produce, flew,* and *confuse.*

■ Extend the review to include the sounds /ū/, spelled *ue, ew,* and with the VCe pattern (examples: *continue, few,* and *huge*) and /ů/, spelled *oo* (examples: *boot, food*). Listen as each student sounds out the words and provide constructive feedback.

MULTISYLLABIC WORDS WITH /ü/, /ū/, AND /ů/ SOUNDS

■ Write the word *altitude* on the board. Break the word into syllables: *al/ti/tude.* Then blend the syllables: /al´ tə tood/. Point out the /ü/ sound.

■ Have pairs of students work together to practice decoding longer words. Write the following words on the board. *With your partner, choose a word. Say the word aloud. Locate the /ü/, /ū/, or /ů/ sound. Note its spelling. Group the words according to sounds and spellings.*

aluminum	musical	revolution	educate
peculiar	souvenir	furious	perfume
vacuum	fabulous	resolution	valuable

■ Check each pair for accuracy. Provide support as needed.

WORD TREE: WORDS WITH /ü/, /ū/, AND /ů/ SOUNDS IN CONTEXT

■ Review words with /ü/, /ū/, and /ů/ sounds and their spellings.

■ Have students search "Tree-rific!" and "Trees at Work" for words with /ü/, /ū/, and /ů/ sounds. Then have students make construction paper leaves for a vocabulary tree. Tell students to circle the /ü/, /ū/, or /ů/ sounds.

■ Have students repeat the activity with the Decodable Passages on page 7 in the **Teacher's Resource Book**.

Constructive Feedback

Isolate the error sound and repeat it with the group. If students pronounce the short vowel sound instead of /ü/, point out the spelling *u* produces more than one sound and say:

The words *dune* and *sun* both have *u* spellings. However, the sounds are different. In *dune, u* makes the /ü/ sound as in *tune.* Note the VCe pattern that produces this sound. In *sun,* the *u* makes the short *u* sound as in *fun.*

Repeat as needed with other spellings that have more than one sound.

Additional Resources

For each skill below, additional lessons are provided. You can use these lessons on consecutive days after teaching the lessons presented within the week.
• Compare and Contrast, T2
• Homographs, T8
• Library/Media Center, T12

Decodable Text

To help students build speed and accuracy with reading multisyllabic words, use the additional decodable text on **Teacher's Resource Book** page 7.

 **Skills Focus** ▶ Fluency

Objective	Read with increasing prosody and accuracy at a rate of 100–110 WCPM
Materials	• **Approaching Practice Book A,** page 18

MODEL EXPRESSIVE READING

Model reading the passage on **Practice Book A** page 18. Tell students to pay close attention to your pronunciation of difficult or unfamiliar words and how you express punctuation. Then read one sentence at a time, and have students repeat the sentence. Listen for accuracy.

REPEATED READING

Have students continue practicing reading the passage aloud as you circulate and provide constructive feedback. During independent reading time, student partners can take turns reading the passage. One partner reads each sentence aloud, and the other partner repeats. Remind students to wait until their partners reach the ends of sentences before correcting mistakes.

TIMED READING

At the end of the week, tell students that they will do a timed reading of the passage that they have been practicing. Instruct each student:

■ Place the passage from **Practice Book A**, page 18, face down.

■ When I say "Go," begin reading the passage aloud.

■ When I say "Stop," stop reading the passage.

As students read, note any miscues. Stop each after one minute. Help students record and graph the number of words they read correctly.

Constructive Feedback

Pay attention to students' miscues and offer decoding support. Suggest that students break difficult or unfamiliar words into syllables to aid pronunciation. Model this practice for students.

⭐ **Approaching Practice Book A,** page 18

As I read, I will pay attention to pronunciation.

	The panda's habitat is shrinking. People have cleared
8	forests for new homes and farms.
14	Clearing the land **reduces** their bamboo supply, but the
23	pandas face another problem. Every few years, bamboo dies.
32	These are natural events. At these times, the stalks flower,
42	wither, and die. Scientists haven't yet learned why.
50	In the 1970s, there was a huge die-off. The pandas had
61	little food. More than 100 pandas starved to death. Another
71	die-off came in 1983. But this time people stepped in to help.
83	First, the Chinese government asked for helpers.
90	Volunteers found hungry pandas and took them to health
99	stations. There the pandas were fed and cared for. Next, the
100	government created reserves.103

Comprehension Check

1. Why is the panda's habitat shrinking? **Main Idea and Details** People are clearing forests to make new homes and to make farms.

2. How have people helped pandas? **Summarize** Volunteers gather hungry pandas and take them to health stations.

	Words Read	–	Number of Errors	=	Words Correct Score
First Read		–		=	
Second Read		–		=	

 **Skills Focus** ▶ Vocabulary

Objective	Apply vocabulary word meanings
Materials	• **Vocabulary Cards** • **Student Book** "Tree-rific!" and "Trees at Work"

VOCABULARY WORDS

Display the **Vocabulary Cards**: *buffet, major, quest, reduce,* and *settings.* Help students locate these words in "Tree-rific!" and "Trees at Work" and identify any context clues. Review each word's meaning. Challenge students to write short stories using all the words. They may work alone or in pairs. Then invite volunteers to read their stories aloud.

buffet   major   quest   reduce   settings

Vocabulary

Review last week's words (*impress, wring, fireball, original, commenced, advertisement, elected, sauntered*) and this week's words (*quest, settings, reduce, buffet, major*). Have students write a sentence for each word.

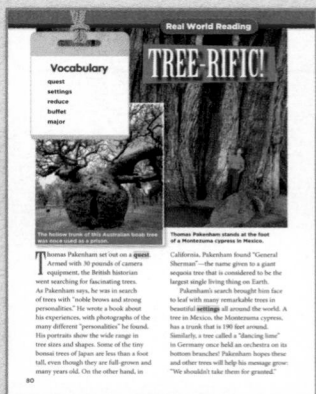

Student Book, or Transparency 3

ELL

Access for All

Label a Diagram Draw and label a diagram of a tree including external and internal parts. Use a two-column chart to list each label and its plural such as *root/roots* and *leaf/leaves*. Notice any words that have irregular plurals. Keep in mind that not all languages add *s* to the end of nouns to make them plural.

Skills Focus ▶ Vocabulary

Objective Define and use homographs

Materials • **Student Book** "Tree-rific!" and "Trees at Work"

DICTIONARY: HOMOGRAPHS

- Review that homographs are words that are spelled alike but are different in meaning and sometimes different in pronunciation. Discuss the homographs *lead* (verb) and *lead* (noun) and *dove* (verb) and *dove* (noun) as examples.

- Ask students to review the vocabulary passages to identify which vocabulary word is a homograph. (*buffet*) Discuss its meanings, parts of speech, and pronunciations. Students may consult dictionaries.

Skills Focus ▶ Comprehension

Objective Identify compare-and-contrast text structure

Materials • **Student Book** "Tree-rific!" and "Trees at Work" • **Transparency 3**

STRATEGY
ANALYZE TEXT STRUCTURE

Remind students that text structure is an organizational pattern chosen by an author to meet his or her purpose for presenting information. Different kinds of text structures include sequence, description, cause and effect, and compare and contrast. Evaluating a text structure helps a reader understand the author's purpose and how effectively a text is organized.

SKILL

COMPARE AND CONTRAST

Explain/Model

- Authors can compare and contrast two or more ideas, facts, people, objects, events, or stories.

- Signal words such as *both, too, similarly, but, rather,* and *however* can indicate likenesses and differences.

Display **Transparency 3**. Reread the first paragraph of "Tree-rific!" Model how to identify one difference between bonsai trees and giant sequoias.

Practice/Apply

Reread "Tree-rific!" and "Trees at Work." Have students continue identifying similarities and differences among topics. After reading, discuss the following questions:

- How are the two articles alike? How are they different?

- What signal words for comparison and contrast did you identify?

Leveled Reader Lesson

Objective   Read to apply strategies and skills
Materials   • **Leveled Reader** *Partners*

PREVIEW AND PREDICT

Discuss the cover and have students skim the introduction and first two chapters. They can review the illustrations, sidebars, and chapter titles to predict what subjects will be compared and contrasted. Have students note any questions they have about the story prior to reading.

VOCABULARY WORDS

Before reading, review the vocabulary words as necessary. As you read together, discuss how each word is used in context.

Leveled Reader

STRATEGY
ANALYZE TEXT STRUCTURE

Remind students that text structure is an organizational pattern chosen by an author to meet his or her purpose for presenting information. Different kinds of text structures include sequence, description, cause and effect, and compare and contrast. Evaluating a text structure helps a reader understand the author's purpose and how effectively a text is organized.

SKILL
COMPARE AND CONTRAST

Remind students that when readers compare, they tell how things are alike. When they contrast, they tell how things are different.

Think Aloud In the first chapter, the author explains the difference between the two types of pandas. I will read the section carefully and look at the pictures to see how they are similar and different. Then I'll enter that information in my Venn diagram.

READ AND RESPOND

Tell students to finish reading the introduction and first two chapters of the story. Discuss interesting or surprising facts they've learned. Ask students to finish reading the book and discuss what they can do to help endangered animals.

MAKE CONNECTIONS ACROSS TEXTS

Have students compare and contrast *Partners* and *Forests of the World*.

- What two kinds of living things are being compared and contrasted in these selections? Name two ways in which they are different.

- How does each reading communicate the importance of respecting nature? Which do you think is more effective? Explain.

On Level Options

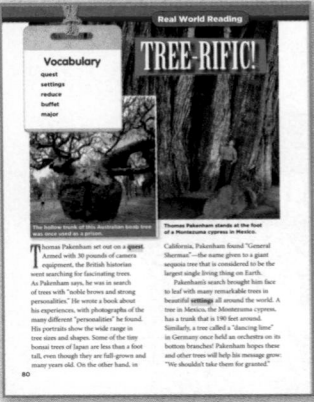

Student Book

Skills Focus ▸ Vocabulary

Objective Apply vocabulary words

Materials
• magazines and newspapers, dictionaries
• **Student Book** "Tree-rific!," "Trees at Work"

VOCABULARY WORDS

Provide students with magazines and newspapers. Send teams of four students on "quests" for the following vocabulary words: *quest, settings, major, buffet, reduce.* Students should clip the articles or advertisements that feature the words. Team members should then highlight or underline the vocabulary words and write short definitions based on context.

DICTIONARY: HOMOGRAPHS

Review with students that homographs are words with the same spelling but different meanings, origins and sometimes pronunciations. Have student pairs search "Tree-rific!" and "Trees at Work" for homographs. (range, season, winds, batter, top, soil, major, last, box) Students should use dictionaries to list the meanings and parts of speech of the homographs.

Skills Focus ▸ Study Skill

Objective Use card and electronic catalogs

USING THE LIBRARY MEDIA CENTER

Review the following:

■ How many cards are there for a title in a card catalog? How do you use a card catalog?

■ How are electronic catalogs similar to card catalogs? Different?

Have students use the catalog systems at a local library.

On Level Practice Book O, page 18

As I read, I will pay attention to pronunciation.

	Two thousand years ago, redwood forests stretched along
8	the Pacific Coast of North America. Today only about
17	four percent of them remain. These survivors live in a narrow
28	band along the foggy coasts of Oregon and northern
37	California. Part of that forest stands just north of San
47	Francisco. This is Muir Woods.
52	The **secluded**, or hidden, setting of Muir Woods is a deep
63	canyon. In this narrow valley, strong winds cannot **buffet**
72	the redwoods.
74	Visitors compare Muir Woods to a cathedral—a silent,
83	dark church with a very high ceiling. The silence of Muir
94	Woods comes from its green carpet of moss that hushes
104	footsteps. It is dark because the trees grow closely together,
114	shutting out most sunlight. The "high ceiling" comes from
123	the tall redwoods. These are the tallest trees in the world.
134	Most grow to be about 200 to 275 feet (61 to 84 m) tall. 143

Comprehension Check

1. How has the population of redwoods changed over the years? **Compare and Contrast** The population of redwoods has decreased significantly.
2. Why can the wind not buffet the redwoods? **Main Idea and Details** Redwoods grow close together.

	Words Read	–	Number of Errors	=	Words Correct Score
First Read		–		=	
Second Read		–		=	

Skills Focus ▸ Fluency

Objective Read fluently with accuracy at a rate of 100–120 WCPM

Materials • **On Level Practice Book O,** p. 18

REPEATED READING

Model reading aloud the entire passage on page 18 of **Practice Book O.** Tell students to pay close attention to your pronunciation of difficult or unfamiliar words and how you express puncutation. Then read one sentence at a time, and have students repeat the sentence. During independent reading time, partners can take turns reading the passage.

Timed Reading At the end of the week, have students read the passage for one minute and record their reading rate.

Leveled Reader Lesson

Objective   Read to apply strategies and skills

Materials   • **Leveled Reader** *The Survival of Muir Woods*

PREVIEW AND PREDICT

Have students preview *The Survival of Muir Woods*. Have them generate questions to set purposes.

■ What does the title suggest about the story?

■ What things are likely to be compared and contrasted in this story?

STRATEGY

ANALYZE TEXT STRUCTURE

Remind students that different kinds of text structures include sequence, description, cause and effect, and compare and contrast. Readers can evaluate text structure to help them understand an author's purpose.

SKILL

COMPARE AND CONTRAST

Review: When writers compare, they tell how things are alike. When they contrast, they tell how things are different. Signal words such as *similarly, also, in addition,* and *but, different, on the other hand* can help readers recognize compare-and-contrast structures. Recognizing compare-and-contrast text structure helps readers absorb important information.

READ AND RESPOND

Read the Introduction and Chapter 1. Discuss similarities and differences. Point out that in the first chapter, the author reports facts about Muir Woods as it was 2,000 years ago. What comparisons or contrasts do students think the author will introduce later? Have them continue reading and looking for comparisons and contrasts.

VOCABULARY WORDS

As they finish the book, ask students to point out the vocabulary words. Discuss how each is used in context. Have students use the vocabulary words in questions and answers related to *The Survival of Muir Woods*.

MAKE CONNECTIONS ACROSS TEXTS

Invite students to compare and contrast *The Survival of Muir Woods* and *Forests of the World*.

■ What kinds of forests are compared and contrasted in *The Survival of Muir Woods* and *Forests of the World*?

■ How are people trying to use and protect forests?

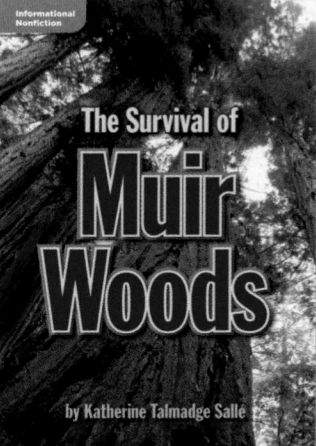

Leveled Reader

ELL
Leveled Reader
Go to pages
89U–89V.

Vocabulary

Skills Focus

Objective Generate questions and answers to practice using vocabulary words

EXTEND VOCABULARY

Challenge student groups to develop quizzes to test recognition of vocabulary words and their definitions. Suggest formats such as matching, multiple choice, fill-in-the-blank, "Who Am I?" questions, and definitions with missing words. Have the members of different groups practice completing each other's quizzes.

Study Skill

Skills Focus

Objective Become more familiar with a library and media center

USING THE LIBRARY AND MEDIA CENTER

Review with students the differences between the print sections of a library and the media center. Then ask volunteers to describe how they would use the resources of a library or media center to find information about famous people in their state's history.

Have students visit the school library and explore the range of text and electronic resources that can be found there. Tell students to make lists of the resources (for example: books, magazines, CDs, card catalog) and the media in which they are available (for example: paper, electronic, microfilm). Back in the classroom, invite students to brainstorm uses for such resources. Discuss what kinds of information they would look for in a book or a magazine, why they would use a card catalog or an online database, and so on.

Fluency

Skills Focus

Objective Read fluently with accuracy at a rate of 110–120 WCPM
Materials • **Beyond Practice Book B,** page 18

REPEATED READING

Model reading aloud the entire passage on page 18 of **Practice Book B**. Tell students to pay close attention to your pronunciation of difficult or unfamiliar words and your expression of punctuation. Then read one sentence at a time and listen for accuracy as individual students read each sentence back.

During independent reading time, partners can take turns reading the passage. At the end of the week, tape students doing timed readings of the passage and then let them critique each other's tapes.

◆ **Beyond Practice Book B,** page 18

As I read, I will pay attention to pronunciation.

Not all fires are started by people. Lightning is also a
11 **major** cause of wildfires. Most lightning occurs during
19 thunderstorms. However, lightning can happen when it's not
27 raining. This is called dry lightning and it is the most
38 dangerous type because the ground is dry and can burn faster.
49 Sometimes weather patterns make it easier for small fires
58 to spread and grow out of control. Each region of our nation
70 has an annual fire season when most wildfires happen. In the
81 West it is June through October. In the Southeast it is March
93 through May. In the Northeast it is late fall. During these
104 months the weather tends to be hot and dry. Droughts,
114 or periods without rain, often occur. Hot, dry winds provide
124 further danger. For example, the Chinook and Santa Ana
133 winds bring fire hazards to western forests. They act like
143 hair dryers, blowing through the forests at high speeds,
152 drying everything out.
155 The shape of the land helps fires to grow. Rising smoke
166 and heat cause fires to burn faster uphill than downhill. For
177 the same reason, fires can jump from short trees to tall trees. 189

Comprehension Check

1. Why is dry lightning the most dangerous type of lightning? **Main Idea and Details** The ground is dry and can catch fire quickly.

2. What is the weather normally like during the fire season? **Main Idea and Details** hot, dry

	Words Read	–	Number of Errors	=	Words Correct Score
First Read		–		=	
Second Read		–		=	

Leveled Reader Lesson

Objective	Read to apply strategies and skills
Materials	• **Leveled Reader** *Wildfire!*

Leveled Reader

PREVIEW AND PREDICT

Have students preview *Wildfire!* Then have them predict what they will learn in the book and set purposes for reading.

STRATEGY

ANALYZE TEXT STRUCTURE

Remind students that readers can evaluate text structure to help them understand an author's purpose.

SKILL

COMPARE AND CONTRAST

Ask a volunteer to describe a compare-and-contrast text structure and explain why identifying text structure is important for remembering and understanding what one reads. Explain that students will read *Wildfire!* together and that they will discuss similarities and differences within the text.

READ AND RESPOND

As they read, have students look for items that are being compared and contrasted. Ask students to pay attention to and make lists of words that signal likenesses and differences.

VOCABULARY WORDS

Discuss the meanings of the vocabulary words, and have students brainstorm some synonyms for them. Then have students discuss *Wildfire!* with a partner, using both the synonyms and the vocabulary words.

Self-Selected Reading

Objective	Read independently to compare and contrast and make connections across texts
Materials	• Leveled Readers or trade books at students' reading levels

READ TO COMPARE AND CONTRAST

Have students choose books for independent reading. After reading, have students compare and contrast details among the subjects the three authors address, as well as the text structures the authors chose to organize their writing. Have them synthesize key points and supporting details among the three books to form conclusions about the effectiveness of the text structures in conveying information. Then have them make formal presentations of their findings.

Academic Language

Throughout the week, the English language learners in your class will need help in building their understanding of the academic language used in daily instruction and assessment instruments. The following strategies will help to increase their language proficiency and comprehension of content and instructional words.

LOG ON Technology

Oral Language For oral vocabulary development, go to **www.macmillanmh.com**

Strategies to Reinforce Academic Language

- **Use Context** Academic language used by the teacher (see chart below) should be explained in the context of the task during Whole Group. You may use gestures, expressions, and visuals to support meaning.

- **Use Visuals** Use charts, transparencies, and graphic organizers to explain key labels to help students understand classroom language.

- **Model** Demonstrate the task using academic language in order for students to understand instruction.

Academic Language Used in Whole Group Instruction

Content/Theme Words	Skill/Strategy Words	Writing/Grammar Words
forest (p. 78)	analyze text structure (p. 78)	expository (p. 89A)
redwood (p. 78)	homographs (p. 78)	audience (p. 89A)
poetry (p. 79)	compare (p. 81A)	combining (p. 89I)
biomes (p. 82)	contrast (p. 81A)	compound sentence (p. 89I)
coniferous forest (p. 83)	differences (p. 81A)	conjunction (p. 89I)
deciduous forest (p. 83)		comma (p. 89I)
rain forest (p. 84)		run-on sentence (p. 89I)

ELL Reader Lesson

Informational Nonfiction

The Muir Woods

by Katherine Talmadge Sallé

Before Reading

DEVELOP ORAL LANGUAGE

Build Background *Why are trees cut down every day?* Brainstorm answers. Explain how forests have disappeared as the human population has increased. Discuss why it is important to protect the few forests left in the world.

Review Vocabulary Write the vocabulary and story support words on the board and discuss their meanings. Model using them. *In my* quest *for a perfect report card, I have to study more. I have to* reduce *the number of hours I watch television.*

PREVIEW AND PREDICT

Point to the cover illustration and read the title aloud. *Why do you think Muir Woods has not disappeared?* Ask students to make further predictions using the Table of Contents.

Set a Purpose for Reading Show a Venn diagram and remind students they have used it before. Ask them to use a similar diagram to compare and contrast Muir Woods in the past and today.

During Reading

Choose from among the differentiated strategies to support students' reading at all levels of language acquisition.

Beginning	**Intermediate**	**Advanced**
Shared Reading As you read, pause to compare and contrast the past and present of Muir Woods. Model filling in the diagram. Check students' comprehension. *What was* the quest *of William Kent?*	**Read Together** Read through Chapter 1. Have students recall features of Muir Woods in ancient times and record them in the diagram. Have them read with a partner to identify and record recent features.	**Independent Reading** Have students read the book. Ask them to fill in a diagram that compares and contrasts Muir Woods in the past and today. Challenge students to create a time line of its main events.

After Reading

Remind students to use the vocabulary and story words in their whole-group activities.

Objective

- To apply vocabulary and comprehension skills

Materials

- ELL Leveled Reader

5-Day Planner

DAY 1	• Academic Language
	• Oral Language and Vocabulary Review
DAY 2	• Academic Language
	• ELL Leveled Reader
DAY 3	• Academic Language
	• ELL Leveled Reader
DAY 4	• Academic Language
	• ELL Leveled Reader
DAY 5	• Academic Language
	• ELL Leveled Reader Comprehension Check and Literacy Activities

Grade 5 • ELL TEACHER'S GUIDE

Treasures

English Language Learners

Macmillan/McGraw-Hill

ELL Teacher's Guide for students who need additional instruction

Weekly Literature

Weekly Theme: Exploring Space

Week At A Glance

Whole Group

VOCABULARY
mission, disasters, environment, zone, gravity, maze, adjusted, function

Context Clues/Description or Explanation

COMPREHENSION
Strategy: Generate Questions
Skill: Summarize

WRITING
Personal Narrative

Science Link

Earth Science
Astronomy

Small Group Options

Differentiated Instruction for Tested Skills

Tested Skills for the Week

ULTIMATE FIELD TRIP 5
BLASTING OFF TO SPACE ACADEMY
BY SUSAN E. GOODMAN
PHOTOGRAPHS BY MICHAEL J. DOOLITLE

Science Link
Main Selection
Genre Nonfiction

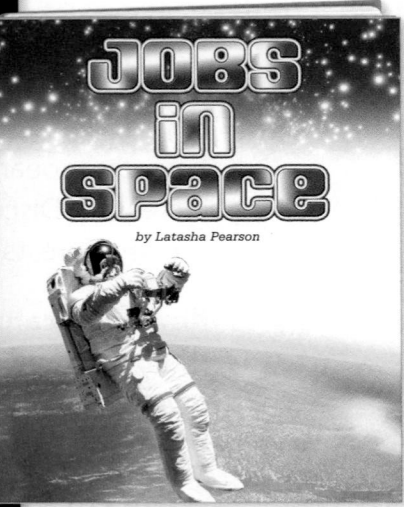

JOBS in SPACE
by Latasha Pearson

Vocabulary/ Comprehension

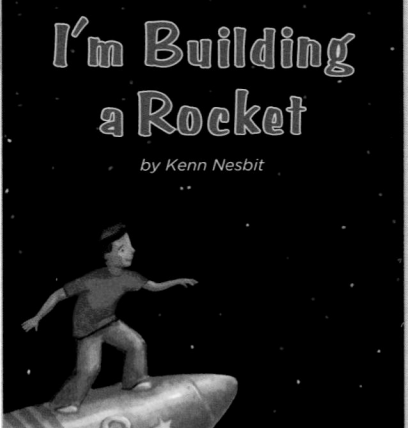

I'm Building a Rocket
by Kenn Nesbit

Genre Poetry

INTERACTIVE Read-Aloud ANTHOLOGY with PLAYS
Macmillan McGraw-Hill

Read-Aloud Anthology
• Listening Comprehension
• Readers' Theater

Resources for **Differentiated Instruction**

Leveled Readers

GR Levels Q–V

Genre Informational Nonfiction

- Same Theme
- Same Vocabulary
- Same Comprehension Skills

Q ON THE MOON
by Emily Wortman-Wunder

Approaching Level

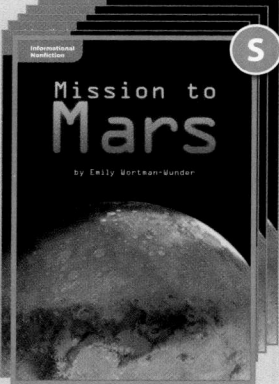
S Mission to Mars
by Emily Wortman-Wunder

On Level

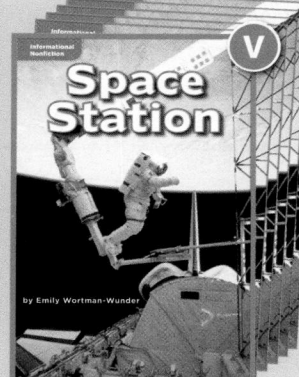
V Space Station
by Emily Wortman-Wunder

Beyond Level

Going to Mars
by Emily Wortman-Wunder

English Language Leveled Reader

On Level Reader sheltered for English Language Learner

ELL Teacher's Guide also available

Also Available LEVELED READER PROGRAM

CLASSROOM LIBRARY

Genre Expository Nonficton

The Snake Scientist

Approaching

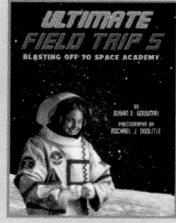
ULTIMATE FIELD TRIP 5
BLASTING OFF TO SPACE ACADEMY

On Level

Jennifer Owings Dewey
Antarctic Journal
Four Months at the Bottom of the World

Beyond

Trade books to apply Comprehension Skills

INTERVENTION ANTHOLOGY

- Phonics and Decoding
- Comprehension
- Vocabulary

Also available, *Reading Triumphs*, Intervention Program

READING Triumphs

LEVELED PRACTICE

Grade 5
Practice Book A
Macmillan/McGraw-Hill

Approaching

Grade 5
Practice Book O
Macmillan/McGraw-Hill

On Level

Grade 5
Practice Book B
Macmillan/McGraw-Hill

Beyond

Grade 5
ELL Practice and Assessment
Macmillan/McGraw-Hill

ELL

Grade 5
Treasures
Home-School Connection
Macmillan/McGraw-Hill

HOME-SCHOOL CONNECTION

- Family letters in English and Spanish
- Take-Home Stories

Technology

LOG ON
ONLINE INSTRUCTION
www.macmillanmh.com

AUDIO CD
- Listening Library
- Fluency Solutions

CD ROM
- Vocabulary PuzzleMaker

Suggested Lesson Plan

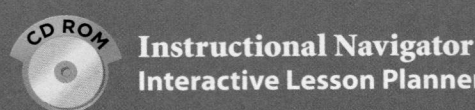

Instructional Navigator
Interactive Lesson Planner

Ultimate Field Trip 5, 94–105

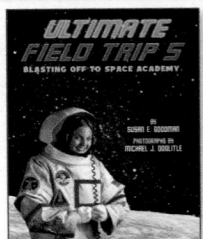    

Leveled Readers

Integrated ELL Support Every Day

Whole Group

ORAL LANGUAGE
- **Listening**
- **Speaking**
- **Viewing**

WORD STUDY
- **Vocabulary**
- **Phonics/Decoding**

READING
- **Develop Comprehension**
- **Fluency**

LANGUAGE ARTS
- **Writing**
- **Grammar**
- **Spelling**

ASSESSMENT
- **Informal/Formal**

Turn the Page for
Small Group Lesson Plan

Day 1

Listening/Speaking/Viewing
❓ Focus Question What is important about exploring space?
Build Background, 90
Read Aloud: "Who's There?" 91

Vocabulary
mission, disaster, environment, zone, gravity, maze, adjusted, function, 92
Practice Book A-O-B, 22

Strategy: Context Clues/Description or Explanation, 93

Read "Jobs in Space," 92–93
Student Book

Comprehension, 93A–93B
Strategy: Generate Questions
Skill: Summarize
Practice Book A-O-B, 23

Fluency Model Fluency, 91
Partner Reading, 90I

Writing
Daily Writing Prompt: Write an e-mail to a friend about a job you might like to have in the future in outer space.
Personal Narrative, 110–111B

Grammar Daily Language Activities, 111I
More Sentence Combining and Complex Sentences, 111I
Grammar Practice Book, 19

Spelling Pretest, 111G
Spelling Practice Book, 19–20

Quick Check Vocabulary, 92
Comprehension, 93B

Differentiated Instruction 111M–111V

Day 2

Listening/Speaking
❓ Focus Question How do astronauts prepare for space travel?

Vocabulary
Review Vocabulary Words, 94

Phonics
Decode Words with /är/, /âr/, or /ôr/, 111E
Practice Book A-O-B, 28

Read *Ultimate Field Trip 5: Blasting Off to Space Academy,* 94–105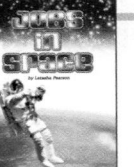
Student Book

Comprehension, 94–107
Strategy: Generate Questions
Skill: Summarize
Practice Book A-O-B, 24

Fluency Partner Reading, 90I

Writing
Daily Writing Prompt: Write a letter to the editor and give your opinion on government funding for space exploration.
Personal Narrative, 110–111B

Grammar Daily Language Activities, 111I
More Sentence Combining and Complex Sentences, 111I
Grammar Practice Book, 20

Spelling Words with /är/, /âr/, and /ôr/, 111G
Spelling Practice Book, 21

Quick Check Comprehension: 100, 105
Phonics, 111E

Differentiated Instruction 111M–111V

Skills/Strategies

Vocabulary	Comprehension	Writing
Vocabulary Words	**Strategy:** Generate Questions	Personal Narrative
Context Clues/ Description or Explanation	**Skill:** Summarize	

Turn the Page for
Small Group Options

Day 3

Listing/Speaking

? Focus Question What aspects of the jobs described aboard a space shuttle would Team Europa be prepared to do?
Summarize, 107

Vocabulary
Review Words in Context, 111C
Strategy: Context Clues/Description or Explanation, 111D
Practice Book A-O-B, 27
Phonics Decode Multisyllabic Words, 111E

Read *Ultimate Field Trip 5: Blasting Off to Space Academy,* 94–105

Student Book

Comprehension
Comprehension Check, 107
Maintain Skill: Summarize, 107B

Fluency Partner Reading, 90I
Repeated Reading, 107A
Practice Book A-O-B, 25

Writing
Daily Writing Prompt: Identify your favorite planet, and write a paragraph about what you like about it.
Writer's Craft: Important Details, 111A
Personal Narrative, 110–111B

Grammar Daily Language Activities, 111I
Mechanics and Usage: Use Commas and Capital Letters in a Letter, 111J
Grammar Practice Book, 21

Spelling Words with /är/, /âr/, and /ôr/, 111H
Spelling Practice Book, 22

 Quick Check Fluency, 107A

Differentiated Instruction 111M–111V

Day 4

Listening/Speaking/Viewing

? Focus Question What is the difference between the children in *Ultimate Field Trip 5* and the speaker in the poem?
Expand Vocabulary: Exploring Space, 111F

Vocabulary
Words in Context, 111F
Apply Vocabulary to Writing, 111F

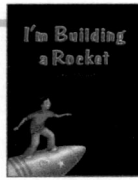

Read "I'm Building a Rocket,"108–109

Student Book

Comprehension
Literary Elements: Rhyme Scheme and Rhythm
Practice Book A-O-B, 26

Fluency Partner Reading, 90I

Writing
Daily Writing Prompt: Design a postcard from another planet. Write a note on the back and include an address.
Writing Trait: Voice, 111B
Personal Narrative, 110–111B

Grammar Daily Language Activities, 111I
More Sentence Combining and Complex Sentences, 111J
Grammar Practice Book, 22

Spelling Words with /är/, /âr/, and /ôr/, 111H
Spelling Practice Book, 23

 Quick Check Vocabulary, 111D

Differentiated Instruction 111M–111V

Day 5
Review and Assess

Listening/Speaking/Viewing

? Focus Question Summarize what you have learned about becoming an astronaut.
Speaking and Listening Strategies, 111A

Vocabulary
Spiral Review: Vocabulary Game, 111F

Read Self-Selected Reading 90I

Student Book

Comprehension
Connect and Compare, 109

Fluency Partner Reading, 90I
Practice, 107A

Writing
Daily Writing Prompt: Prepare interview questions for an astronaut who has just returned from outer space.
Personal Narrative, 110–111B

Grammar Daily Language Activities, 111I
More Sentence Combining and Complex Sentences, 111J
Grammar Practice Book, 23–24

Spelling Posttest, 111H
Spelling Practice Book, 24

Weekly Assessment, 45–52

Differentiated Instruction 111M–111V

Differentiated Instruction

What do I do in small groups?

Teacher-Led Small Groups

Literacy Workstations

Independent Activities

Skills Focus → Use your **Quick Check** observations to guide additional instruction and practice.

Phonics
Decode Words with /är/, /âr/, or /ôr/

 Vocabulary Words
gravity, zone, disasters, maze, function, environment, adjusted

 Strategy: Context Clues/Look for a Description or Explanation

Comprehension
Strategy: Generate Questions
 Skill: Summarize

 Fluency

Suggested Lesson Plan

 CD ROM
Instructional Navigator
Interactive Lesson Planner

	Day 1	**Day 2**
Approaching Level • **Additional Instruction/Practice** • **Tier 2 Instruction**	Fluency, 111N Vocabulary, 111N Comprehension, 111O **ELL** Technology, 111O 	Phonics, 111M Vocabulary, 111O Leveled Reader Lesson, 111P • Vocabulary • Comprehension 
On Level • **Practice**	Vocabulary, 111Q Leveled Reader Lesson, 111R • Comprehension **ELL** Leveled Reader, 111U–111V 	Leveled Reader Lesson, 111R • Comprehension • Vocabulary 
Beyond Level • **Extend**	Vocabulary, 111S Leveled Reader Lesson, 111T • Comprehension 	Leveled Reader Lesson, 111T • Comprehension • Vocabulary 

For intensive intervention see **READING Triumphs**

Small Group Options

Apply **Tested** skills and strategies while reading appropriate leveled books.

Levels Q-V

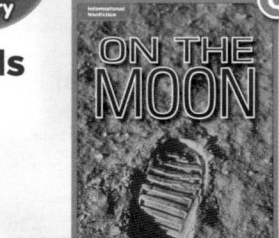

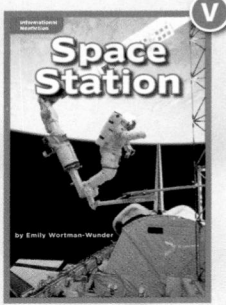

Approaching — **On Level** — **Beyond**

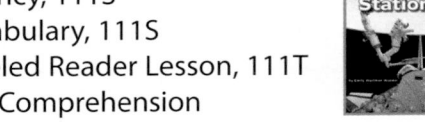

ELL

Additional Leveled Reader Resources

Leveled Reader Database

Go to **www.macmillanmh.com**

Search by
- Comprehension Skill
- Content Area
- Genre
- Text Feature
- Guided Reading Level
- Reading Recovery Level
- Lexile Score
- Benchmark Level

Subscription also available

Day 3

Phonics, 111M
Fluency, 111N
Vocabulary, 111O
Leveled Reader Lesson, 111P
• Comprehension

Fluency, 111Q
Vocabulary, 111Q
Leveled Reader Lesson, 111R
• Comprehension

Fluency, 111S
Vocabulary, 111S
Leveled Reader Lesson, 111T
• Comprehension

Day 4

Phonics, 111M
Leveled Reader Lesson, 111P
• Comprehension

Literary Elements, 111Q
Leveled Reader Lesson, 111R
• Comprehension

Literary Elements, 111S
Leveled Reader Lesson, 111T
• Comprehension
ELL Picture Clues, 111T

Day 5

Fluency, 111N
Leveled Reader Lesson, 111P
• Make Connections Across Texts

Fluency, 111Q
Leveled Reader Lesson, 111R
• Make Connections Across Texts

Fluency, 111S
Self-Selected Reading, 111T

Managing the Class

What do I do with the rest of my class?

Teacher-Led Small Groups

Literacy Workstations

Independent Activities

Class Management Tools

Managing Small Groups
A How-to Guide
Dr. Vicki Gibson   Dr. Douglas Fisher
Macmillan/McGraw-Hill

Name _____ Date _____

My To-Do List
✔ Put a check next to the activities you complete.

Reading
☐ Practice fluency
☐ Read a book about space

Word Study
☐ Write with /ār/, /ôr/, /är/ words
☐ Create a context-clues word puzzle

Writing
☐ Write a narrative text
☐ Write an informational text

Science
☐ Research Earth and Mars
☐ Draw a Venn diagram of differences and similarities

Social Studies
☐ Research astronaut qualities
☐ Write a job description

Leveled Readers
☐ Write About It!
☐ Content Connection

Technology
☐ Vocabulary Puzzlemaker
☐ Fluency Solutions
☐ Listening Library
☐ www.macmillanmh.com

Independent Practice
☐ Practice Book, 22–28
☐ Grammar Practice Book, 19–24
☐ Spelling Practice Book, 19–24

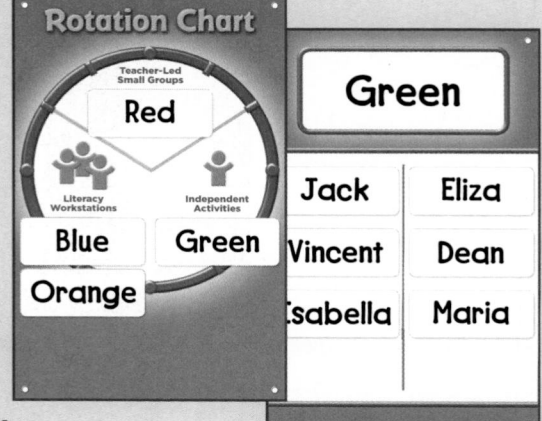

Rotation Chart

Teacher-Led Small Groups

Red

Literacy Workstations   Independent Activities

Blue   Green

Orange

Green

Jack   Eliza

Vincent   Dean

Isabella Maria

Includes:
• How-To Guides   • Rotation Chart   • Weekly Contracts

FOLDABLES™

Hands-on activities for reinforcing weekly skills.

Treasures

Dinah Zike's
Foldables

3-Dimensional
Interactive
Graphic organizers!

Macmillan/McGraw-Hill

Fish	Frogs
habitat	habitat
food	insects
prey	prey
enemies	enemies

Eight-Tab Foldable

Word	Synonym	Antonym	Prefix or Suffix
normal	typical	unusual	normally

Folded Foldable

Independent Activities

Leveled Readers

For Repeated Readings and Literacy Activities

Approaching

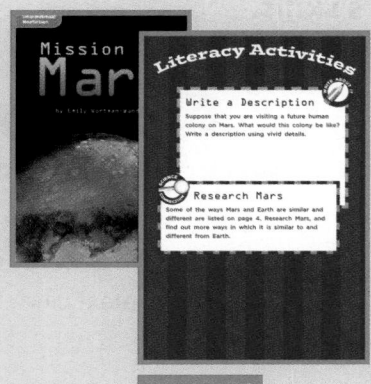

On Level

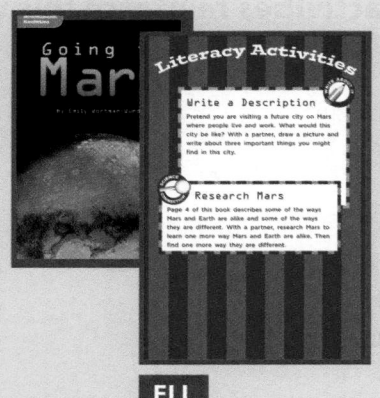

ELL

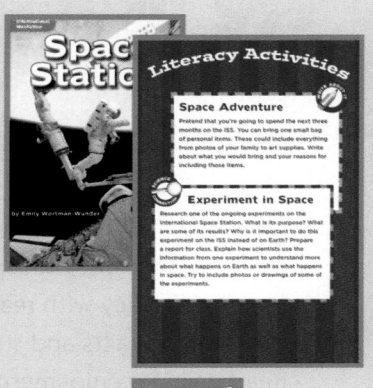

Beyond

LEVELED PRACTICE

Skills: Vocabulary (p. 22), Comprehension: Summarize (p. 23), Graphic Organizer (p. 24), Fluency (p. 25), Literary Elements: Rhyme Scheme and Rhythm (p. 26), Vocabulary Strategy: Context Clues (p. 27), Phonics (p. 28)

Approaching

On Level

Beyond

ELL

Technology

ONLINE INSTRUCTION www.macmillanmh.com

- Meet the Author/Illustrator

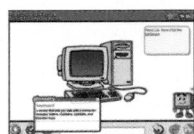

- Computer Literacy Lessons

- Research and Inquiry Activities

- Oral Language Activities
- Vocabulary and Spelling Activities
- Leveled Reader Database

LISTENING LIBRARY

Recordings of selections
- Main Selections
- Leveled Readers
- ELL Readers
- Intervention Anthology

FLUENCY SOLUTIONS

Recorded passages for modeling and practicing fluency

VOCABULARY PUZZLEMAKER

Activities providing multiple exposures to vocabulary, spelling, and high-frequency words including crossword puzzles, word searches, and word jumbles

Turn the page for Literacy Workstations.

Cross-Curricular Activities

All activities reinforce this week's skills.

 ## Reading

Objectives

- Read fluently and with speed. Offer corrective feedback.
- Practice fluency with readers' theater.
- Read to find facts and summarize.
- Read daily for enjoyment.

 ## Word Study

Objectives

- Identify and use words with /är/, /âr/, and /ôr/ sounds.
- Generate context clues for vocabulary words.

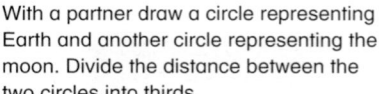 ### Reading — Fluency

20 Minutes

- With a partner draw a circle representing Earth and another circle representing the moon. Divide the distance between the two circles into thirds.
- Alternate timing how long it takes for each partner to read aloud a passage from page 25 of your Practice Book.
- Every time you improve, draw a stick figure of yourself moving one-third closer to the moon. When you both reach the moon, plant a flag that shows the fastest time.

Extension

- Time Your Reading: Listen to the Audio CD.

Things you need:
- paper and pen or pencil
- timer and Practice Book

Fluency Solutions Listening Library

7

Word Study — Words with /är/, /âr/, /ôr/

20 Minutes

- Before space exploration there was travel on the high seas. Your task is to tell the story of "R Matey, the Pirate Who Stole the R," using such words as *stars, torch, arm, oar, are, yard, stare, rare, foghorn,* and other words with the sounds /är/, /âr/, /ôr/.
- Write the title and the first paragraph of your adventure story, using as many /är/, /âr/, /ôr/ words as you can.

Extension

- Trade your story with a partner. Write the next paragraph of your partner's story with as many /är/, /âr/, /ôr/ words as you can. Trade back after three minutes.
- Write a conclusion to your story, and read it aloud to your partner, emphasizing the /är/, /âr/, /ôr/ sounds in the words.

Arrr

Things you need:
- paper and pen
- dictionary

For additional vocabulary and spelling games, go to www.macmillanmh.com

7

Reading — Independent Reading

20 Minutes

- Find a book at the library about space travel, the science of speed, or gravity.
- Open the book anywhere, and read aloud the first paragraph you find. Write down one fact you learned on a strip of paper and make a bookmark there.
- Locate four more paragraphs in the chapter and place a bookmark for each fact.

Extension

- Reread your bookmarks and write a one- or two-sentence summary of what you read. In your response journal, explain whether or not you like this genre. Tell why.

Things you need:
- library book
- scissors
- paper and pen

For more books about exploring space, go to the Author/Illustrator section at www.macmillanmh.com

8

Word Study — Context Clues

20 Minutes

- With a partner write a short passage about space that needs four of the eight vocabulary words. Leave blanks for those words.
- Make a key to your vocabulary puzzle.
- Trade puzzles with another pair and see how fast you can complete the puzzle correctly. If the context clues aren't clear, ask the writers to give you another clue.

Extension

- Write another passage using the remaining four vocabulary words.
- Trade puzzles again.

The crazy paths looked like a <u>maze</u>.

Things you need:
- paper and pen or pencil
- vocabulary list

For additional vocabulary and spelling games, go to www.macmillanmh.com/voc-spelling

Vocabulary PuzzleMaker

8

Literacy Workstations

Writing

Objectives
- Write a personal narrative using precise language.
- Research and write an informational paragraph.
- Be enthusiastic about writing and learning to write.

Content Literacy

Objectives
- Use a Venn diagram to make comparisons between planets.
- Research skills an astronaut must have.

Writing — Personal Narrative
20 Minutes

- Suppose that you are talking to a friend on a cell phone that is capable of receiving and sending pictures. You suddenly pick up a transmission of pictures from space.
- Write a narrative to describe the series of pictures that appear on your phone. Use precise words to describe to your friend what you see, as well as the differences between pictures as they change.
- Use at least two complex sentences in your narrative.

Extension
- Exchange narratives with a partner. Each of you should illustrate what the other has described and ask questions about details that you do not understand.
- Then write descriptions that answer the questions for your partner.

Things you need:
- paper and pen
- colored pencils

(7)

Science — Comparing Planets
20 Minutes

- Research the composition, size, atmosphere, distance from sun, and other facts about Earth and about Mars.
- Create a Venn diagram that shows the similarities and differences between the two planets.

Earth — Earth and Mars — Mars

Extension
- Based on what you have read, draw the two planets side by side and illustrate major differences and similarities.

Things you need:
- access to the Internet or reference books
- paper and pen or pencil
- colored pencils or markers

(7)

Writing — Writing to Give Information
20 Minutes

- Using the Internet or the library, research the surfaces of other planets.
- Write a paragraph to summarize the information you find. Be factual and precise, and include in a logical order the information you think is important.

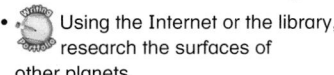 

Extension
- Compare the information about another planet's surface to that of Earth. Make a list of similarities and differences.
- Write a travel brochure to the other planet, including what a human would need to survive on the surface.

Things you need:
- paper and pen or pencil

LOG ON Internet Research and Inquiry Activity
Students can find more facts at www.macmillanmh.com

(8)

Social Studies — SPACE CAREERS
20 Minutes

- Research the talents and skills that an astronaut must have. What age range is acceptable? In what subjects should an astronaut excel? What education and skills must the person have to work as a pilot or scientist? What physical tests must he or she pass?
- Make a list of these qualities and skills.

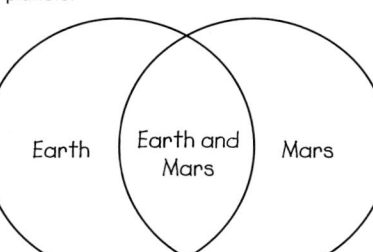

Extension
- Write a job description for an astronaut that includes the necessary training that astronauts must have.
- Then turn this description into a short want ad for a newspaper.

Things you need:
- access to the Internet or the library
- paper and pen or pencil

(8)

Prepare

ORAL LANGUAGE
- Build Background
- Read Aloud
- Expand Vocabulary

VOCABULARY
- Words in Context
- **Context Clues:** Description/Explanation

COMPREHENSION
- **Strategy:** Generate Questions
- **Skill:** Summarize

SMALL GROUP OPTIONS
- Differentiated Instruction, pp. 111M–111V

Oral Language

Build Background

ACCESS PRIOR KNOWLEDGE

Share the following information:

To be selected as an astronaut by NASA, candidates must have a background in math and science, be in good health, and have clear vision.

TALK ABOUT EXPLORING SPACE

Discuss the weekly theme.

What have we learned from sending people and satellites into space?

 FOCUS QUESTION Ask a volunteer to read aloud "Talk About It" on **Student Book** page 91 and describe the photograph.

- How would you describe the astronaut's clothes and equipment?

EXPLORING SPACE

90

ENGLISH LANGUAGE LEARNERS

Access for All

Beginning **Model** Point to items and name them: *This is an astronaut. This is space.* Have students point and repeat. Ask questions and model answers: *Where is he? He's in space.* Help students answer.

Intermediate **Develop Vocabulary** Ask students to describe the photo. Help them use complete sentences. Provide vocabulary as needed. Brainstorm words students know about space and space travel, write them on the board, and discuss them. Make sure students understand words such as *orbit, NASA,* and *satellite.*

Advanced **Elaborate** Complete the Intermediate task. As students discuss the words, ask questions to help them clarify their ideas. Help students use more complex sentence structures in their speech.

90

Talk About It

What draws people to want to explore space? Why should we continue to explore space?

 Find out more about exploring space at **www.macmillanmh.com**

91

Picture Prompt

Look at the picture and respond in writing. You can write a poem, a story, or a description, or use any other type of writing you like.

LOG ON Technology

For an extended lesson plan and Web site activities for **oral language development**, go to **www.macmillanmh.com**

Read Aloud
Read "Who's There?"

GENRE: Science Fiction Review features of science fiction:

- a story that tells about imaginary events based on science or technology

Read Aloud
pages 26–32

LISTENING FOR A PURPOSE

Ask students to listen carefully for important events and details as you read "Who's There?" in the **Read-Aloud Anthology.** They should be prepared to retell the story in their own words. Choose from among the teaching suggestions.

Fluency Ask students to listen carefully as you read aloud, paying attention to your phrasing, expression, and tone of voice.

RESPOND TO THE STORY

Discuss a time when students were surprised by a noise that could not be identified. Ask students to describe how they felt and what they did. Have them compare responses with those of their peers.

Expand Vocabulary

Invite students to find words from "Who's There?" that identify it as a science-fiction story. For example, *orbit, spaceships, satellite.* Have students look up the definitions and write True-or-False statements for each word. Students can share these with the class so others can guess the correct answer.

Vocabulary

TEACH WORDS IN CONTEXT

Use the following routine.

Routine

Define: A **mission** is a special assignment or task.
Example: The Coast Guard was sent on a rescue mission to find the lost boat.
Ask: Can you name another type of mission? EXAMPLE

- **Disasters** cause destruction. Natural disasters, such as hurricanes, are caused by events in nature. What are some other types of natural disasters? EXAMPLE

- To **function** is to work or act. The television will function when you plug it into an outlet. How does a bicycle function? EXPLANATION

- **Gravity** is a force that pulls objects on Earth's surface toward Earth's center. When you throw a stone, gravity causes it to fall. How does gravity make throwing a stone different on the moon? COMPARE AND CONTRAST

- A **maze** is a confusing network of paths or passageways. The farmer built a maze in his cornfields. If you got lost in a maze, what would you do to try and get out? PRIOR KNOWLEDGE

- When something is **adjusted** it is changed or arranged differently. Dan adjusted the painting so that it would hang straight. What is a synonym for the word *adjusted*? SYNONYM

- The **environment** includes the air, water, and land that surround living things. I like a natural environment. Compare your environment with a lion's environment. COMPARE AND CONTRAST

Vocabulary

mission	gravity
disasters	maze
environment	adjusted
zone	function

Context Clues

Descriptions or explanations can be **Context Clues** that will help you figure out the meaning of unfamiliar words. Sometimes you can find these clues if you keep reading until the end of a sentence or paragraph.

JOBS in SPACE

by Latasha Pearson

In the early years of space travel, an astronaut's job was to pilot a spacecraft. Astronauts of today do many other types of jobs. These jobs change depending on the goal of the **mission** that needs to be accomplished.

Astronaut Pilots control and direct the space shuttle. One astronaut pilot is the captain. Captains must make sure the mission is a success. Their job is to keep the crew safe. Captains know that working as a team can prevent **disasters** in space.

Mission Specialists run tests and take care of the equipment on board. The equipment may need to be **adjusted** to fit the task. Sometimes they walk in space or handle the shuttle's robot arm. Astronaut pilots and mission specialists

92

- A **zone** is an area or space that has a special rule or use. This sidewalk is a no-parking zone. What is another example of a zone? EXAMPLE

Quick Check

Do students understand word meanings?

During **Small Group Instruction**

If No → **Approaching Level**
Vocabulary, p. 111N

If Yes → **On Level** Options, pp. 111Q–111R

Beyond Level Options, pp. 111S–111T

ELL   Access for All

Demonstrate Vocabulary
Drop an object. Say, *It falls because of gravity. Space doesn't have gravity.* Demonstrate how the ball would "float" in space. Ask, *What would happen if I* (mime the action) *poured milk in space?* Explain. For *function*, say, *When something works well, we say it functions well. Skateboards function well in nice weather but not in rainy weather.* Discuss other examples.

work for the National Aeronautics and Space Administration (NASA). They learn to live and work in an unusual **environment**. They learn to move in a special **zone** where there is zero **gravity**, the force that pulls things back to Earth. They also figure out how to operate the confusing **maze** of equipment that fills the space shuttle.

Payload Specialists do not work for NASA. These crew members have specific skills and are usually in charge of special projects. They train with the astronauts. Like everyone else getting settled on the shuttle, these specialists have to get used to life in space.

Educator Astronauts are teachers who travel into space. Their job is to encourage students to study science and math. This will help the next generation of astronauts **function** well in space and carry out their jobs successfully.

Reread for **Comprehension**

Generate Questions
Summarize
A Summary Chart helps you ask questions about the main ideas in a selection. Use your Summary Chart as you reread "Jobs in Space" to summarize the main ideas.

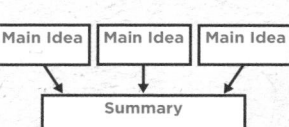

93

Vocabulary

STRATEGY
CONTEXT CLUES

Look for a Description or Explanation Tell students that writers often provide clues to help readers figure out the meanings of unfamiliar words. Some writers use commas to signal the definition for a difficult word (gravity, the force that pulls things back to Earth). Sometimes helping words, such as *or*, signal a synonym for a difficult word (mission or assignment).

Ask students: What other examples of vocabulary context clues can you find in the selection? (special setting or environment; zone or area; function or work well)

Read *"Jobs in Space"*

As you read "Jobs in Space" with students, ask them to identify context clues that reveal the meanings of the highlighted words. Tell students they will read these words again in *Ultimate Field Trip 5: Blasting Off to Space Academy*.

On Level Practice Book O, page 22

A. Match each vocabulary word with its definition. Write the vocabulary word on the line provided.

| mission | function | maze | environment |
| disasters | gravity | adjusted | zone |

1. the air, water, soil, and all the other things surrounding a person, animal or plant __environment__
2. special assignment or job __mission__
3. changed or rearranged __adjusted__
4. terrible and unexpected events __disasters__
5. a confusing system of paths or passageways __maze__
6. to work properly __function__
7. the force that attracts objects to Earth __gravity__
8. an area set off from other areas __zone__

B. Answer each question. Possible responses below.
9. Why is **gravity** important? Gravity is important because it keeps us on the ground so people, animals, and things can't float away.
10. How might a **maze** slow you down? A maze could slow you down because it is a confusing system of paths that is difficult to get out of.

 Approaching Practice Book A, page 22

◆ **Beyond Practice Book B,** page 22

Objectives

- Generate questions while reading
- Use academic language: *summarize*
- Summarize by identifying the most important ideas in the text

Materials

- Comprehension Transparencies 4A, 4B
- Transparency 4, Graphic Organizer
- Leveled Practice Books, p. 23

Skills Trace

Summarize	
Introduce	93A–B
Practice / Apply	94–107; Leveled Practice, 23–24
Reteach / Review	111M–T, 607A–B, 608–627, 633M–T; Leveled Practice, 178–179
Assess	Weekly Tests; Unit 1, 5 Tests; Benchmark Tests A, B
Maintain	107B, 199A, 691B

ELL

Access for All

Model Self-Monitoring

Begin reading "Jobs in Space" and model self-questioning: *In the first paragraph the word* jobs *is mentioned three times. Maybe I'll find out more about that. I wonder what kind of work they do.* As you continue modeling, invite students to share their questions and thinking.

Reread for Comprehension

STRATEGY

GENERATE QUESTIONS

Explain that good readers always try to **generate questions** as they read: *Do I understand what is happening here? What does this word or phrase mean? Why has the author included this information?* Looking for clues in the text that will answer these and other questions can help the reader summarize important ideas and information and improve comprehension.

Access for All

Tested

SKILL

SUMMARIZE

A **summary** is a short statement of the most important ideas or information in a selection. To summarize, readers identify the topic and main idea, select the most important subtopics with supporting details, and then restate them in their own words.

Transparency 4a

Vocabulary

mission	gravity
disasters	maze
environment	adjusted
zone	function

Context Clues

Descriptions or explanations can be Context Clues that will help you figure out the meaning of unfamiliar words. Sometimes you can find these clues if you keep reading until the end of a sentence or paragraph.

JOBS in SPACE

by Latasha Pearson

In the early years of space travel, an astronaut's job was to pilot a spacecraft. Astronauts of today do many other types of jobs. These jobs change depending on the goal of the **mission** that needs to be accomplished.

Astronaut Pilots control and direct the space shuttle. One astronaut pilot is the captain. Captains must make sure the mission is a success. Their job is to keep the crew safe. Captains know that working as a team can prevent **disasters** in space.

Mission Specialists run tests and take care of the equipment on board. The equipment may need to be **adjusted** to fit the task. Sometimes they walk in space or handle the shuttle's robot arm. Astronaut pilots and mission specialists

92

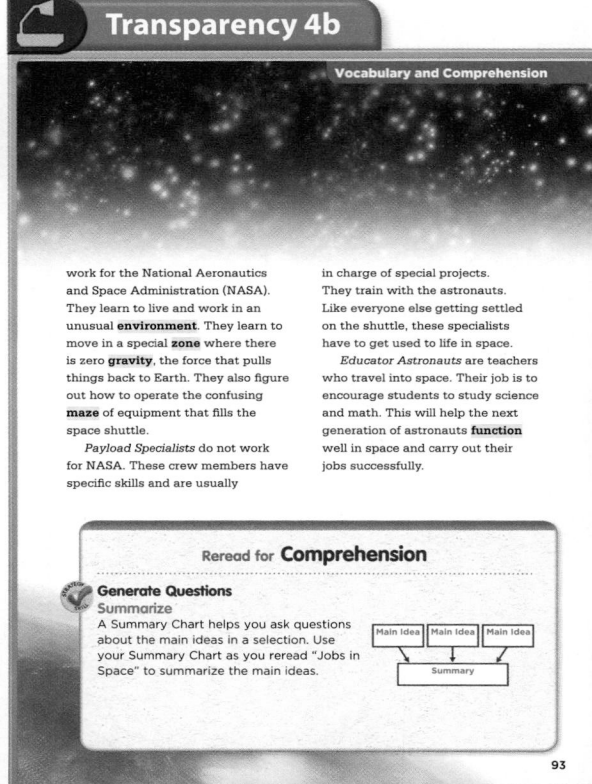

Transparency 4b

Vocabulary and Comprehension

work for the National Aeronautics and Space Administration (NASA). They learn to live and work in an unusual **environment**. They learn to move in a special **zone** where there is zero **gravity**, the force that pulls things back to Earth. They also figure out how to operate the confusing **maze** of equipment that fills the space shuttle.

Payload Specialists do not work for NASA. These crew members have specific skills and are usually

in charge of special projects. They train with the astronauts. Like everyone else getting settled on the shuttle, these specialists have to get used to life in space.

Educator Astronauts are teachers who travel into space. Their job is to encourage students to study science and math. This will help the next generation of astronauts **function** well in space and carry out their jobs successfully.

Reread for Comprehension

Generate Questions

Summarize

A Summary Chart helps you ask questions about the main ideas in a selection. Use your Summary Chart as you reread "Jobs in Space" to summarize the main ideas.

93

Student pages 92–93 available on Comprehension Transparencies 4a, 4b

MODEL

Read the first two paragraphs of "Jobs in Space" from **Student Book** page 92.

Think Aloud I can put the main idea into my own words: Astronauts today do many kinds of jobs. This would be my topic sentence in a summary. The following detail in the second paragraph provides information that supports the main idea: Astronaut pilots control the space shuttle. I would include this detail in my summary.

GUIDED PRACTICE

Display Transparency 4.

- Begin the Summary Chart with the main ideas at the beginning of the article. (Astronaut pilots control and direct the space shuttle).

- Fill in the next item together. Tell students to identify the responsibilities of each kind of astronaut, helping them distinguish between major and minor details. Minor details do not belong on a Summary Chart.

APPLY

Have students reread the rest of "Jobs in Space" and complete the Summary Chart. Ask students why there are so many different kinds of astronauts today.

 Transparency 4

Main Ideas	Main Ideas	Main Ideas
Astronaut pilots control and direct the space shuttle. Mission specialists run tests and take care of equipment.	Astronaut pilots and mission specialists work for NASA and train in special settings. Payload specialists are in charge of special projects.	Educator astronauts are teachers who travel in space.

Summary
Astronauts do many kinds of jobs.

Graphic Organizer 4

On Level Practice Book O, page 23

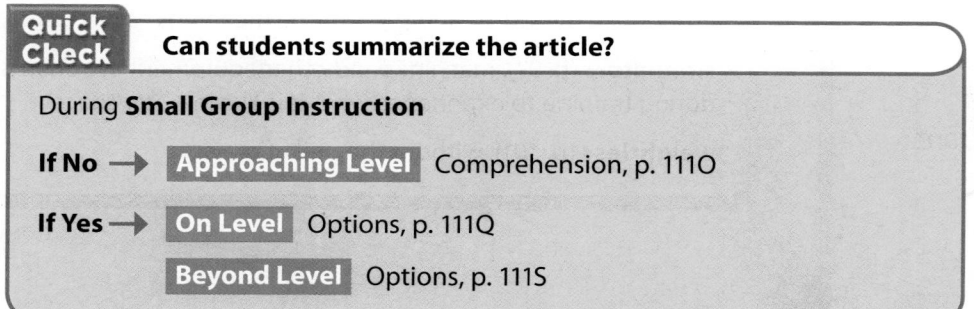

When you **summarize** nonfiction, you retell it briefly in your own words. In the retelling you focus on the most important ideas or events in the passage. The main idea of a paragraph is often found in the first sentence. Supporting details tell you more about a paragraph's main idea. A summary should include important details that describe or explain the main ideas.

Read the two paragraphs below, and then write a summary of the passage on the lines provided. Be sure to include the most important ideas and supporting details in your summary.

Becoming an Astronaut
Astronauts must go through difficult training because just about everything is done differently in space. Astronauts must learn how to walk and work without gravity. They must practice wearing spacesuits. They must even learn how to eat and sleep while weightless.

Many different machines help the astronauts prepare for space travel. Some machines are simulators, or machines that recreate some of the conditions of outer space here on Earth. The 1/6 Gravity Chair simulates the moon's weaker gravity. On the moon a person weighs one-sixth of what he or she weighs on Earth. In the Multi-Axis Trainer (MAT), astronauts experience what it is like to be in a tumbling spacecraft. The Five Degrees of Freedom (5DF) Chair simulates the challenges of floating weightlessly.

Summary: Possible response provided: Astronauts must train hard because everything is done differently in space. They practice wearing spacesuits. They learn to walk, work, eat, and sleep without gravity. Machines also help astronauts train. In simulators astronauts practice walking and floating without gravity.

 Approaching Practice Book A, page 23
Beyond Practice Book B, page 23

Quick Check **Can students summarize the article?**

During **Small Group Instruction**

If No → **Approaching Level** Comprehension, p. 111O

If Yes → **On Level** Options, p. 111Q

Beyond Level Options, p. 111S

Read

MAIN SELECTION
- *Ultimate Field Trip 5: Blasting Off to Space Academy*
-  **Skill:** Summarize

PAIRED SELECTION
- "I'm Building a Rocket"
- **Literary Elements:** Rhyme Scheme and Rhythm

SMALL GROUP OPTIONS
- Differentiated Instruction, pp. 111M–111V

Comprehension

GENRE: NONFICTION

Have students read the definition of Nonfiction on **Student Book** page 94. As they read, students should look for subheadings and boldfaced words that can help them organize the information in their summaries.

STRATEGY
GENERATE QUESTIONS

Remind students that generating questions as they read can help them clarify meaning, understand the author's purpose for writing, or locate a specific answer in the text.

SKILL
SUMMARIZE

When good readers summarize all or part of a text they look for the main ideas and then find the most important details in the text to support them.

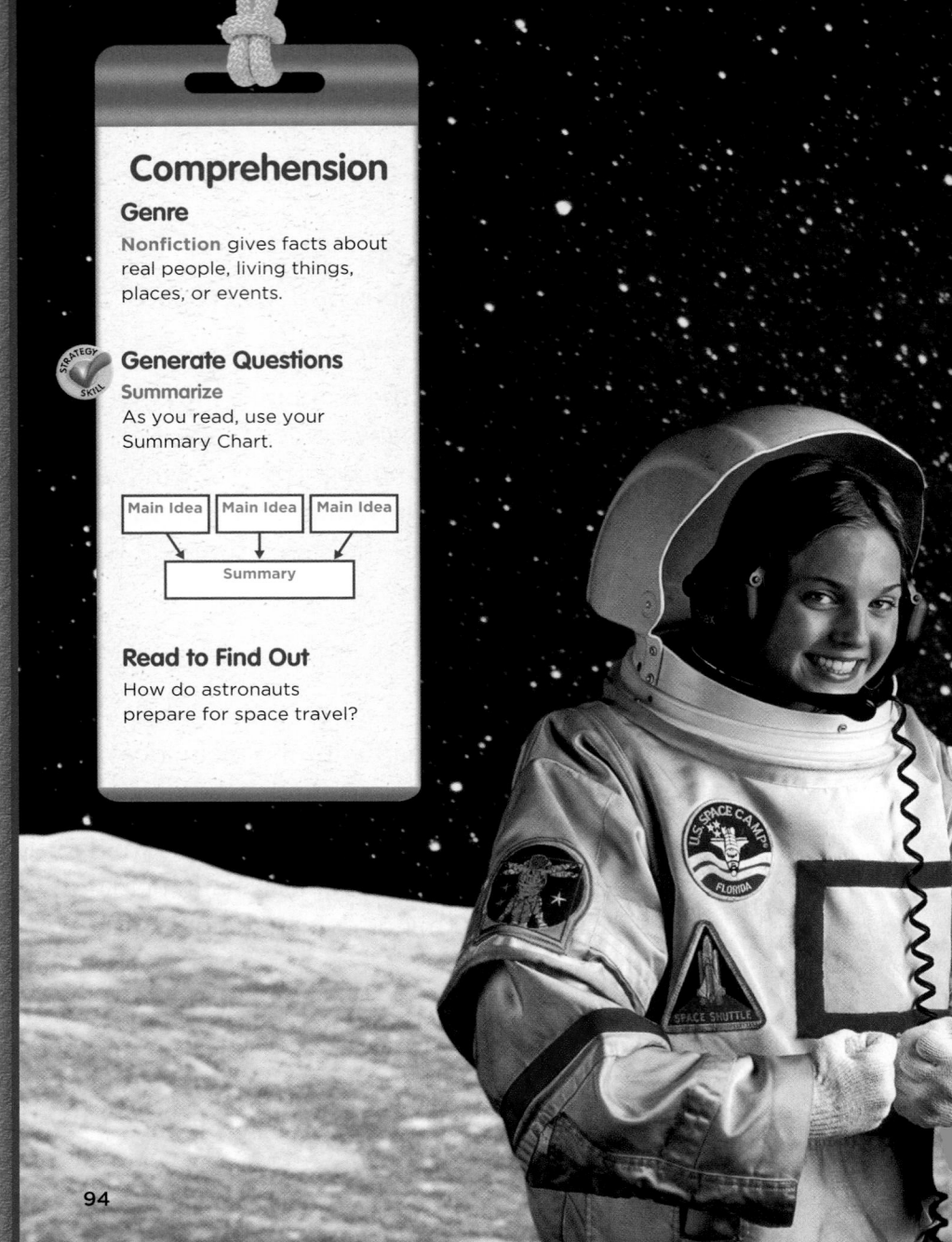

Comprehension

Genre

Nonfiction gives facts about real people, living things, places, or events.

Generate Questions

Summarize
As you read, use your Summary Chart.

Main Idea	Main Idea	Main Idea

Summary

Read to Find Out

How do astronauts prepare for space travel?

94

Vocabulary

Vocabulary Words Review the tested vocabulary words: **adjusted, disasters, environment, function, gravity, maze, mission,** and **zone**.

Selection Words Students may find these words difficult. Pronounce the words and present the meanings as necessary.

simulators (p. 97): machines and other equipment astronauts use during training to experience what it is like in outer space

weightless (p. 101): without the pull of gravity

ULTIMATE FIELD TRIP 5

BLASTING OFF TO SPACE ACADEMY

BY
SUSAN E. GOODMAN

PHOTOGRAPHS BY
MICHAEL J. DOOLITLE

95

Preview and Predict

Ask students to read the title, preview the illustrations, and make predictions about what kind of information they might find in this selection. Have students write about their predictions and any questions they have about the selection.

Set Purposes

FOCUS QUESTION Discuss the "Read to Find Out" question and how to look for the answer as students read.

Point out the Summary Chart in the **Student Book** and on **Practice Book** page 24. Tell students they will use the chart as they read.

Read *Ultimate Field Trip 5: Blasting Off to Space Academy*

Use the questions and Think Alouds for additional instruction to support the comprehension strategy and skill.

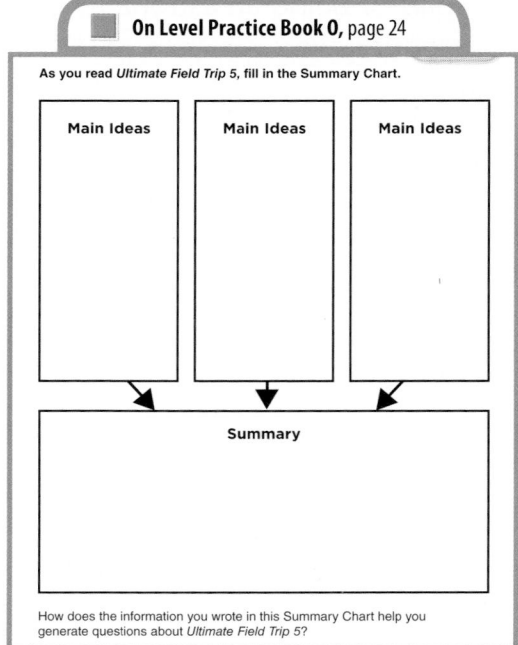

On Level Practice Book O, page 24

As you read *Ultimate Field Trip 5*, fill in the Summary Chart.

Main Ideas	Main Ideas	Main Ideas

Summary

How does the information you wrote in this Summary Chart help you generate questions about *Ultimate Field Trip 5*?

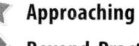 **Approaching** Practice Book A, page 24

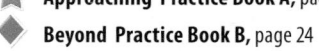 **Beyond** Practice Book B, page 24

Read Together	Read Independently
If your students need support to read the Main Selection, use the prompts to guide comprehension and model how to complete the graphic organizer.	If your students can read the Main Selection independently, have them read and complete the graphic organizer. Suggest they set and modify both purposes for reading and their reading rate.

If your students need an alternate selection, choose the **Leveled Readers** that match their instructional level.

Technology

Story available on **Listening Library Audio CD**

Develop Comprehension

1 STRATEGY
GENERATE QUESTIONS

Teacher Think Aloud I see that this selection opens with a series of questions about the best part of being an astronaut. Reading further I can generate my own questions about the selection, and then read to see if they are answered. This will give me a purpose for reading. For example, what do kids who go to the U.S. Space Academy get to experience? Why do half of all astronauts experience space sickness at the beginning of a space voyage? These questions will help me locate specific answers in the text. I can then use the answers to help me summarize important information.

2 SYNTHESIZE

What do you think would be the best part of being an astronaut? Explain your answer. (Answers will vary.)

Countdown to Adventure

What's the best part of being an astronaut? Is it the thrill of rocketing out of Earth's atmosphere at 25,000 miles per hour? Is it the chance to make new scientific discoveries? Or is it the adventure of leaving the familiar behind and going, as someone once put it, "where no man has gone before?"

Few people actually get to answer these questions by traveling into space. But some kids took the first step by going to U.S. Space Academy at the United States Space and Rocket Center in Huntsville, Alabama.

1

AMAZING SPACE FACTS

At least half the astronauts experience space sickness at the beginning of their voyage. That's why John Young didn't do Gus Grissom any favor when he smuggled him a corned beef sandwich on the Gemini 3 mission. The story is Grissom threw up; in weightless conditions, that's a difficult cleanup job.

"I can't tell whether this fits or not," said Shane. "Do I look like an astronaut?" Another kid's comment: "If you have to go to the bathroom quick, these flight suits are a bummer."

2

96

Vocabulary

Word Parts: *Roots*

Explain/Model Explain that roots are word parts to which other word parts, such as prefixes and suffixes, have been added. Many roots in English come from Greek and Latin words. The Greek root *astro*, for example, means "star."

Think Aloud I know that an astronaut is a person who flies in or helps to fly a spacecraft. When I see the Greek root *astro* in a word such as *astronaut*, I know the word has something to do with outer space. In this case, the word literally means "someone who travels among the stars." Knowing what this root means can help me learn and remember words.

Practice/Apply Have students think of other words that contain the root *astro*, and that are related to space or the study of space. (*astronomy*, the science that deals with planets, stars, and other heavenly bodies; *astronomer*, a person who is an expert in astronomy; *astronautics*, the science that deals with the design and construction of spacecraft)

For almost a week they used the same simulators that real astronauts use and learned how to walk on the Moon and work without **gravity**. They built their own rockets and visited the ones scientists used to launch the Apollo astronauts to the Moon. They tried tasting space food and wearing space suits. They learned how to eat in space, sleep in space, even how to go to the bathroom without any gravity. **3**

During their training they became a team, Team Europa, named after one of Jupiter's seven moons. Then, Europa blasted off on a mission of its own **4** **5**

> The Habitat, where kids sleep at Space Academy, was designed as an earthbound space station with stairs and handrails to get from floor to floor. In space, you'd float where you need to go.

97

Develop Comprehension

3 SUMMARIZE

Summarize what the students at Space Academy did to learn what it is like to travel into space. (Answers may vary but should include that the campers learned what it was like to travel into space by participating in many activities that simulated a real astronaut's experience.)

4 DRAW CONCLUSIONS

Think back to a time when you were part of a team. How did your team achieve its goals? Why do you think the campers at Space Academy were grouped together as a team? (Answers will vary. The students were probably put on a team because astronauts travel into space with other astronauts. Each astronaut has a different role (physician, scientist, pilot, technician) and has to fulfill his or her job in order for the mission to be successful.)

5 MAKE PREDICTIONS

What kind of mission do you think Team Europa will attempt? (Answers will vary.)

ELL

Access for All

STRATEGIES FOR EXTRA SUPPORT

Question 3 SUMMARIZE
Reread the first paragraph on page 97 with students. Have students retell what they have understood. You may need to explain words such as *simulator* and *launch*. As students retell, explain that they are telling you details. Model how to create a summary from the details.

Vocabulary

Read the sentence that contains the word **mission**. Have students think of some synonyms for *mission* and use them in the sentence. *(trip, voyage, expedition)*

Develop Comprehension

6 SUMMARIZE

Summarize what the campers saw as they toured the training floor. Then fill in the first box in the Summary Chart. (Answers may vary but should include that the campers saw different kinds of machines that real astronauts use to train for space travel. The machines were being used by other teams.)

7 DRAW CONCLUSIONS

Why does it take astronauts many years to train for a space mission? (Answers may vary but should include that astronauts have to learn to work in an environment that is very different from ours here on Earth. They must practice using machines that simulate weightlessness so they can move and make repairs effectively in an environment without gravity.)

Main Ideas	Main Ideas	Main Ideas
The campers saw different kinds of machines that real astronauts use to train for space travel. They were being used by other teams.		

Summary

On the Training Floor

"**E**uropa, the training center is a dirt-free **zone**," said Paul. "Gum and drinks can create **disasters** here."

Paul, one of Europa's team leaders, led the kids through a **maze** of strange-looking machines. As they walked, the kids peeked at other teams jumping high enough to dunk a basketball and spinning in what looked like a giant gyroscope. Paul explained

6 that astronauts trained for years before going into space. It takes a lot of practice to learn how to **function** in such a different **environment**. On space walks, for example, they must make delicate repairs while floating upside down. In their ships they

7 must learn how to drift rather than walk through the air.

How do they learn these things while anchored by Earth's gravity? To find out, Europa tried some of the simulators that astronauts have used.

The training center is equipped with many simulators.

98

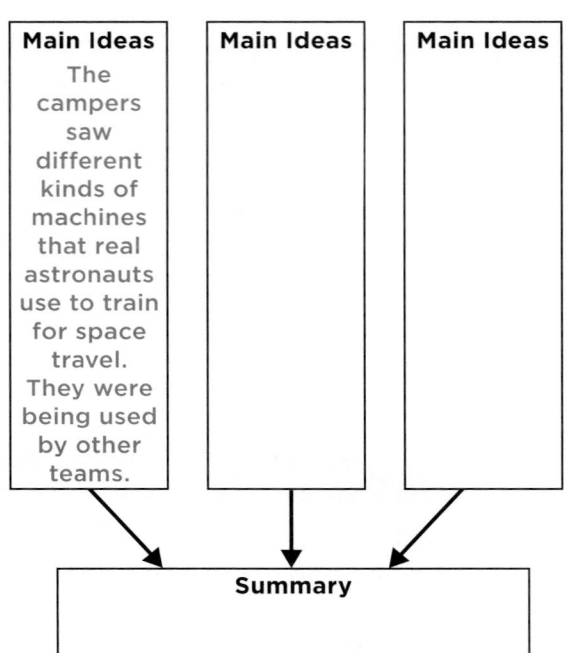

Comprehension

Monitor and Clarify: *Paraphrase*

Explain Tell students that paraphrasing means restating in their own words something they've read. Unlike a summary, a paraphrase includes all the details in the text, not just the important ones.

Discuss How can paraphrasing help you make sense of something you don't understand? (By substituting words they know, students can make the meaning more clear.)

Apply Have students paraphrase aloud the first two paragraphs on page 99 of the Student Book. (Paraphrases might include: If you weigh 120 pounds on Earth, you would weigh only 20 pounds on the moon. This is because the moon has only 1/6 of our gravity. The kids used a 1/6 gravity chair to practice walking under these conditions. A slow jog and a bunny hop are the best ways to get around in this chair.)

The 1/6 Gravity Chair 8

"The Moon has only one-sixth of our gravity," explained Paul. "If you weigh one hundred twenty pounds here, you'd only weigh twenty pounds on the Moon. And you'd have to learn to walk differently because there isn't as much traction."

To practice this movement, the kids used a 1/6 Gravity Chair similar to the Apollo astronauts'. In fact, Europa learned from the astronauts' experiences. The best ways to get around were a slow jog and the bunny hop.

John waited impatiently while Paul **adjusted** the chair to offset five-sixths of his weight.

"Bunny hop for me," said Paul.

"You've got to be kidding," answered John. "I can barely reach the ground."

Soon, however, he was leaping across the training floor.

"This looks like good practice for the high jump," said Stephanie.

"It shouldn't be; you want to jump for distance, not height," said Paul. "Astronaut Charlie Duke of *Apollo 16* tried to set a height record. But his life-support pack changed his center of gravity. He landed on his back and couldn't get up, just like a beetle. If John Young hadn't been around to help him, he could have been stuck there until *Apollo 17!*"

"I felt like I was on a trampoline," said Lindsay, "but I didn't go down—just up!"

 Summarize
What did the kids of Team Europa do to help them prepare for a possible trip into space?

9

99

Develop Comprehension

8 **USE TEXT FEATURES: SUBHEADS**

The author uses various text features, including captions, sidebars, and subheads, to help her present information. How do the subheads that organize the information help you to identify the main idea in each part? (Each subhead gives readers a clue to what the text that follows will be about.)

9 **SUMMARIZE**

 What did the kids of Team Europa do to help them prepare for a possible trip into space? (They used the 1/6 Gravity Chair to help them learn how to function in an environment that has less gravity. They watched as other teams used machines that spun around like a giant gyroscope.)

Have students respond to the selection by confirming or revising their predictions. Encourage them to revise their questions about the selection based on what they have read so far.

Extra Support

Summarize

If students have difficulty identifying important details in the text to include in a summary, have them reread the subheading at the top of page 99. Then ask them what the information on this page will be about. (the 1/6 Gravity Chair) Have them reread the text and look for details that describe the 1/6 Gravity Chair and how it works. Discuss with students what main ideas they would include in a summary of the information on this page. (The 1/6 Gravity Chair offsets five-sixths of a person's weight. It helps people learn how to walk on the moon, which has only 1/6 of Earth's gravity. The best ways to get around in the chair are with a slow jog or the bunny hop.) After the discussion, have students write a summary that contains the main ideas.

Vocabulary

Read the sentence that contains the word **zone**. Ask students to replace *zone* with a synonym. (area, space)

 **Quick Check**   **Can students identify important details to include in their summaries? If not, see the Extra Support on this page.**

Stop here if you wish to read this selection over two days.

Develop Comprehension

10 **MAINTAIN**
COMPARE AND CONTRAST

How is the MAT like an atom? (The person sitting in the center of the MAT is like the nucleus in the center of an atom. The circles surrounding the nucleus are like the electrons that orbit about the nucleus of an atom.)

11 **WRITER'S CRAFT: IMPORTANT DETAILS**

What are two important details in this paragraph? How do these details help readers better understand the children's experience? (Students may say that the details about some kids taking off their jewelry and the separately spinning outer circles of the MAT are important. The details help readers understand what the children saw and felt.)

12 **SYNTHESIZE**

Why is it important to experience being out of control before going into space? (Answers may vary but should include the fact that there are many opportunities for things to go wrong on a space mission. If astronauts have prepared for these possibilities they will be better prepared for an emergency, such as their spacecraft going out of control.)

The Multi-Axis Trainer (MAT)

"Remove everything from your pockets," said Bethany, Europa's other team leader. "Take off your necklaces, too, so you don't get whacked in the face."

To get ready for the MAT, some kids took off jewelry; others just took a few deep breaths. The MAT looks like an atom gone wild, with each of its three outer circles spinning separately and you as its whirling nucleus. The Mercury astronauts used it to learn how to regain control of a tumbling spacecraft.

The MAT never turns more than twice in the same direction, which is supposed to keep you from feeling sick. That didn't keep a lot of kids from getting nervous. But once they tried it, the glint of silver braces flashed through their smiles.

"It was terrific," said Stacy, "but next time, I'll tie my hair back so it doesn't keep hitting my face."

"It's awesome," Stephanie agreed.

When asked how she'd feel doing it for a ten-minute stretch in a spaceship, Stephanie added, "Your head spins like crazy, but it doesn't feel bad."

"I couldn't help smiling all the time because it was so much fun," said Lindsay.

100

Cross–Curricular Connection

CALCULATING TRAVEL TIME IN SPACE

Astronauts rocket away from the launch pad at speeds of 25,000 miles per hour. Tell students to consider a part of the solar system they would like to visit and then calculate how long it would take them to reach it if they could travel that fast.

Have students assume the role of an astronaut plotting a space voyage to the destination of their choice. Explain that their first step will be to research the distance from Earth to their destination. Then have them calculate their travel time if their rocket speed is 25,000 miles per hour by using the following formula: speed ÷ distance = time.

The Five Degrees of Freedom (5DF) Chair

On Earth, when you jump up, gravity pulls you back down. In space, you just keep going up. If you push away from a wall, you keep going backward. Bending quickly to grab something could make you do somersaults. To get used to the weightless tumble of space, the Gemini and Apollo astronauts—and the kids at Space Academy—used the 5DF Chair. This chair glided over the floor on a cushion of air like the puck in an air hockey game.

"This is what an EVA, an extravehicular activity, or space walk, feels like," Bethany said, tipping and rolling the chair in all direction to give the kids a taste of the different movements.

Bethany held on to the 5DF Chair to keep it safe. In space, astronauts are tethered to their ship. It's a good thing, too. When astronaut Pete Conrad went on his space walk, he lost hold of *Skylab*. That tether was the only thing that kept him from floating away.

In the 5DF Chair, kids practiced inching their way along a wall. Once Lindsay pushed herself away by accident, she had a hard time getting back.

"Swim, Lindsay, swim!" Courtney called out.

Lindsay tried to breaststroke her way back to the wall—it was hopeless.

"Oh, well," said Charles, "she's *Lost in Space!*"

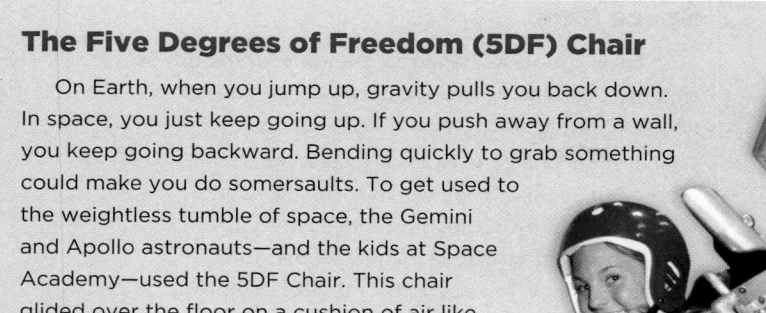

101

Comprehension

Literary Devices: *Tone*

Explain Tell students that tone is a writer's attitude toward his or her subject. For example, a writer's tone might be humorous, sad, angry, or informative, among many other possibilities.

Discuss Ask students to brainstorm words that accurately describe Susan E. Goodman's tone. (Students might use words such as *informative* or *factual*.) Why is her tone a good choice for nonfiction? (Students might note that nonfiction is often filled with facts.)

Apply Ask students to write the first paragraph of a story about someone who has become lost in space. Have them use either a humorous or serious tone. Encourage them to notice the importance of tone in expressing their ideas.

Develop Comprehension

13 CONTEXT CLUES: DESCRIPTION/EXPLANATION

Tested

Context clues are words or phrases around an unfamiliar word that give clues to its meaning. What context clues help explain the meaning of the word *tether*? (The text says Pete Conrad lost hold of Skylab, and the tether kept him from floating away. The text also states that in space, astronauts are tethered to their ship. Students should suggest that a tether is something that ties something down.)

14 GENERATE QUESTIONS

Teacher Think Aloud I know that Lindsay isn't in a pool. She's using the 5DF Chair. So I am a bit puzzled why Courtney calls out to her "Swim, Lindsay, swim!" What kind of question could you generate that might explain what Courtney says?

(Encourage students to apply the strategy in a Think Aloud.)

Student Think Aloud Here's a question I could ask: In what way is using the chair similar to being in a pool of water? I know that when you're floating in a pool, and your feet can't touch the bottom, it's almost like a form of weightlessness. Lindsay can't walk when she's in the chair, so she had to move her arms and feet the way she might if she were in a pool. That's probably why Courtney called out for her to "swim."

Develop Comprehension

15 **SYNTHESIZE**

Some people call the Space Shot an "elevator with an attitude." Do you think that's a good way to describe it? Why or why not? (Answers will vary but should include the fact that since the Space Shot rockets skyward much faster than a normal elevator, saying it has an "attitude" distinguishes it from the elevators you might find in a tall building.)

16 **GENRE: EXPOSITORY NONFICTION**

Ultimate Field Trip 5 gives information about the Space Academy. What are some features of **informational nonfiction** that the author used in the text? (Answers will vary but should include special boldfaced vocabulary words, subheadings, and sidebars to help further explain some information in the selection.) Students should use such organizational features to locate relevant information.

17 **LITERARY DEVICE: TONE**

List some facts that the author gives on this page that contribute to the informative tone of the selection. (Students may list facts such as "astronauts last walked on the moon in 1972" and "the moon does not have an atmosphere.")

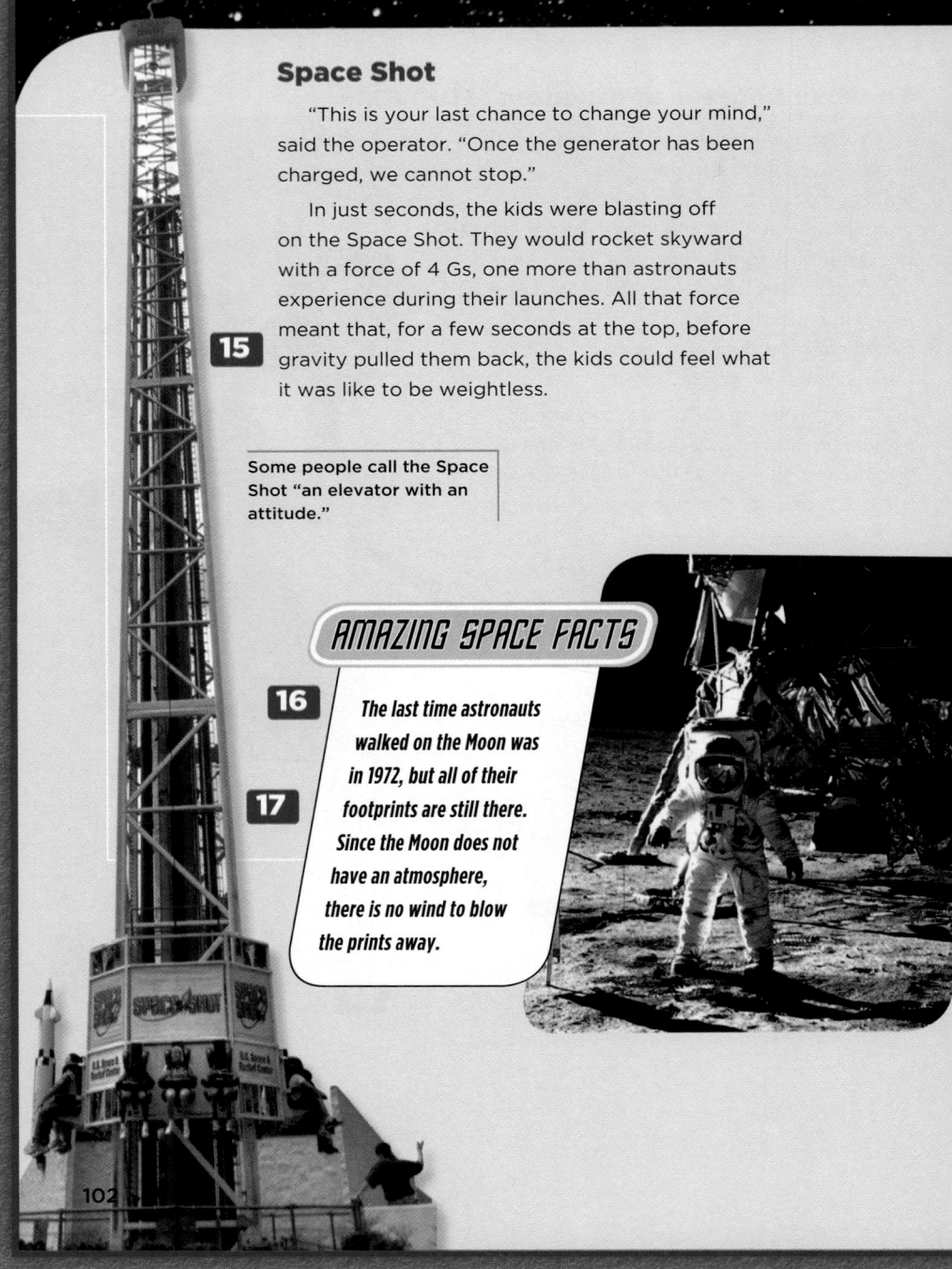

Space Shot

"This is your last chance to change your mind," said the operator. "Once the generator has been charged, we cannot stop."

In just seconds, the kids were blasting off on the Space Shot. They would rocket skyward with a force of 4 Gs, one more than astronauts experience during their launches. All that force meant that, for a few seconds at the top, before **15** gravity pulled them back, the kids could feel what it was like to be weightless.

Some people call the Space Shot "an elevator with an attitude."

AMAZING SPACE FACTS

16

17
The last time astronauts walked on the Moon was in 1972, but all of their footprints are still there. Since the Moon does not have an atmosphere, there is no wind to blow the prints away.

102

NASA doesn't use the Space Shot to simulate weightlessness; it trains astronauts aboard its KC-135 airplane. The plane climbs sharply and then free-falls straight toward the ground, up again, then down again, and again. For twenty-five seconds, at the top of each roller-coaster ride, the plane's passengers are weightless. But many astronauts have paid a price for this amazing experience. The KC-135 is nicknamed the "Vomit Comet" for good reason.

"I wish I hadn't eaten so much breakfast," said Erin as she waited for her turn on the Space Shot. "I'm going to scream. It helps you not throw up."

Before her second ride, Erin was too excited to feel sick. "I love that feeling of just shooting up there," she said.

"Then you rise up out of your chair and float there for a second," said Stacy. "Weightlessness, I wish it lasted a lot longer."

Summarize
How did each machine Team Europa used help them to experience what it's like to travel in space?

This is the way Frank and most kids feel going up on the Space Shot . . .

. . . and they feel this way coming down. Devin was amazed that one kid in line thought the experience would cure his fear of heights.

Develop Comprehension

18 MAKE INFERENCES

Why do you think the campers simulate weightlessness using the Space Shot rather than the KC-135 airplane? (Answers may vary but may include that using airplanes to train for space is expensive and risky.)

19 SUMMARIZE

How did each machine Team Europa used help them to experience what it's like to travel in space? Explain your answer, and add it to your Summary Chart. (The 1/6 Gravity Chair gave the campers experience walking on the moon, while the 5DF Chair helped them to find out what it's like to walk in space. The Multi-Axis Trainer gave students experience with a spaceship tumbling in space. The Space Shot offered them the opportunity to experience weightlessness.)

Main Ideas	**Main Ideas**	**Main Ideas**
The campers saw different kinds of machines that real astronauts use to train for space travel. They were being used by other teams.	The 1/6 Gravity Chair, the 5DF Chair, the Multi-Axis Trainer, and the Space Shot gave students the opportunity to experience what it's like to walk and travel in space.	

Summary

ELL

Access for All

STRATEGIES FOR EXTRA SUPPORT

Question 19 SUMMARIZE
Help students talk about how each machine helped the team using the following sentence frame: The *(1/6 Gravity Chair)* helped the team experience *(walking on the moon)*.

Develop Comprehension

20 SUMMARIZE

What methods have the campers used to imitate the feeling of weightlessness? Fill in the third box in your Summary Chart with the answer. (Working underwater to build a cube, as well as using the 1/6 Gravity Chair, the 5DF Chair, and the Space Shot have all helped the campers experience the feeling of weightlessness.)

21 GENERATE QUESTIONS

Why would astronauts not need the ability to hold their breath? Think of another question to help you answer this one.

Student Think Aloud Maybe I can think of another question to help me understand this one. Is there air in outer space? No, there isn't. I know that astronauts wear helmets in space that are hooked up to a supply of air. So now I understand what Bethany means when she says that an ability to hold your breath is something she hopes astronauts don't need.

Main Ideas	Main Ideas	Main Ideas
The campers saw different kinds of machines that real astronauts use to train for space travel. They were being used by other teams.	The 1/6 Gravity Chair, the 5DF Chair, the Multi-Axis Trainer, and the Space Shot gave students the opportunity to experience what it's like to walk and travel in space.	Working underwater to build a cube, as well as using the 1/6 Gravity Chair, the 5DF Chair, and the Space Shot have all helped the campers experience the feeling of weightlessness.

Summary

The Pool

20 Another way the earthbound astronauts simulate working in weightlessness is by going underwater. At Houston's Lyndon B. Johnson Space Center, astronauts practice in a huge water tank holding a full-scale model of the Shuttle's payload bay. At Space Academy, the kids went to a swimming pool.

"Your job is to build a cube underwater as fast as possible," said Bethany. "It takes teamwork, an ability to **21** work in weightlessness, and—something astronauts don't need, I hope—an ability to hold your breath."

Each strut, or tube, belonged in a specific place.

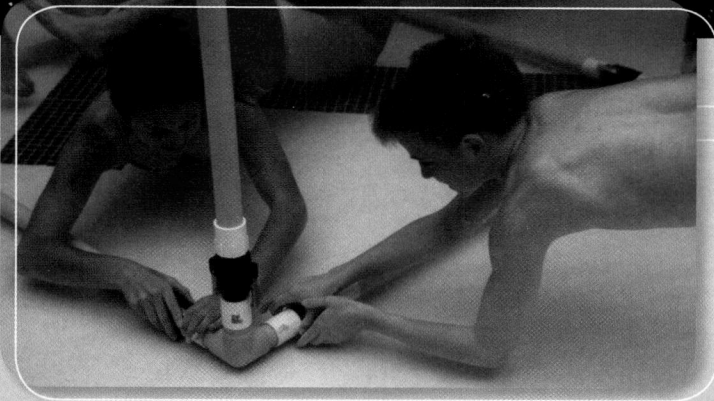

The water started boiling as kids grabbed struts and dove underwater. It kept boiling as they came up for air again and again, slowly realizing they needed a better plan. . . .

"Ten minutes and fifty-six seconds," Bethany said when they finally finished. "Well, every astronaut has to start somewhere. How could you have gone faster?"

"Talk more to each other?" said Isabelle.

"That's right," Bethany agreed. "Communication, letting your leaders lead, and teamwork. It's true in the pool, and it will be even more important when you work to make your own space mission a real success."

> Once the kids started working together, the cube was built quickly.

22

AMAZING SPACE FACTS

Flawed when it went into orbit in 1990, the Hubble Space Telescope was repaired in 1993 during a spectacular mission that required five space walks. Located above our hazy atmosphere, the Hubble sees deep into the universe to reveal black holes, new galaxies, the birth of some stars and the death of others. Its "eagle-eyed vision" is so acute that if the Hubble were on Earth, it could spot a firefly ten thousand miles away!

105

Quick Check
Are students able to generate questions in order to help them summarize important points in the text?

During **Small Group Instruction**

If No → **Approaching Level** Leveled Reader Lesson, p. 111P

If Yes → **On Level** Options, pp. 111Q–111R

Beyond Level Options, pp. 111S–111T

Develop Comprehension

22 SUMMARIZE

 Use information in the three boxes labeled "Main Idea" to write a summary of *Ultimate Field Trip 5.* Add your summary to the Summary Chart. (Answers should include details listed on students' Summary Charts.)

REVIEW READING STRATEGIES

How did summarizing help you remember the most important information in the selection?

 **PERSONAL RESPONSE**

Ask students to write about whether they would like to attend Space Camp. Have students support their decision with evidence from the text.

Main Ideas	Main Ideas	Main Ideas
The campers saw different kinds of machines that real astronauts use to train for space travel. They were being used by other teams.	The 1/6 Gravity Chair, the 5DF Chair, the Multi-Axis Trainer, and the Space Shot gave students the opportunity to experience what it's like to walk and travel in space.	Working underwater to build a cube, as well as using the 1/6 Gravity Chair, the 5DF Chair, and the Space Shot have all helped the campers experience the feeling of weightlessness.

Summary

At Space Camp the members of Team Europa saw different kinds of machines that real astronauts use to train for space travel. The 1/6 Gravity Chair, the 5DF Chair, the Multi-Axis Trainer, the Space Shot, and building a cube underwater gave students the experience of working in a weightless environment.

Author

BLAST OFF WITH SUSAN E. GOODMAN

Have students read the biography of the author.

DISCUSS

- Why did Susan E. Goodman attend space camp?

- How do Susan E. Goodman's experiences help her to write better stories?

WRITE ABOUT IT

Remind students that participants in the U.S. Space Academy have experiences similar to those of real astronauts. Using specifics, have students write about whether or not they would like to attend the academy.

Author's Purpose

Remind students that authors who write to inform present facts about a topic. Help students see that Susan E. Goodman probably wrote mainly for this purpose. Suggest that students review the text and captions and use their Summary Charts to find details that support that idea.

LOG ON   Technology

Students can find more information about Susan E. Goodman at www.macmillanmh.com

---

BLAST OFF WITH SUSAN E. GOODMAN

Susan E. Goodman writes her stories by trying them out first. For this story she actually went to Space Camp at the U.S. Space Academy. There she learned how to do everyday things at zero gravity, like brushing her teeth and "walking." Experiencing different ways of living helps Susan find the right words when it comes to writing about them. For other stories Susan has stayed in an underwater hotel and even balanced on a girder fifty stories above the ground.

Another book by Susan E. Goodman:
On This Spot: An Expedition Back Through Time

LOG ON Find out more about Susan E. Goodman at www.macmillanmh.com

Author's Purpose

Authors of nonfiction often write to inform readers about something. Do you think that is why Susan E. Goodman wrote *Ultimate Field Trip 5*? Explain what clues in the text and captions make you think so.

Author's Craft

Third-Person Point of View

Susan E. Goodman wrote this text from the **third-person point of view.** It allowed her to record what the campers in the story thought, felt, and did. For example:

> In just seconds the kids were blasting off on the Space Shot. They would rocket skyward with a force of 4 Gs, one more than astronauts experience during their launches. (p. 102)

Discuss how the text would change if Susan E. Goodman described events from the first-person point of view. Ask students to rewrite the sentences above from the first-person point of view. Then ask students to retell part of the story from a first-person point of view.

Comprehension Check

Summarize

Use your Summary Chart to summarize *Ultimate Field Trip 5: Blasting Off to Space Academy*. Your summary should include the main ideas from the selection. These will usually appear at the beginning of each paragraph.

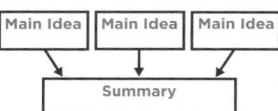

Main Idea	Main Idea	Main Idea

Summary

Think and Compare

1. Summarize one section of *Ultimate Field Trip 5: Blasting Off to Space Academy*. Be sure to only include important events and information. **Generate Questions: Summarize**

2. Reread page 99. Why do Team Europa and actual astronauts use a gravity chair? Give reasons for your answer. **Analyze**

3. Which activity from space camp would you enjoy most? Explain your answer. **Evaluate**

4. Do you think a future **mission** into space will improve our lives on Earth? **Analyze**

5. Reread "Jobs in Space" on pages 92–93. What aspects of the jobs described aboard a space shuttle would Team Europa be prepared to do? Use details from both stories to explain your answer. **Reading/Writing Across Texts**

107

Strategies for Answering Questions

On My Own

Model the On My Own strategy with question 4

The answer is not in the selection. You have to use critical thinking skills that go beyond the text, using what you already know to answer the question.

Question 4: Think Aloud I know the answer to this question cannot be found in the text. I have to use my own prior knowledge to go beyond the text and answer the question. I think a future mission to space may very well improve our lives here on Earth. Astronauts may discover rare minerals on other planets in our solar system that could be used as alternative fuel sources. The discovery of primitive forms of life on other planets or moons in the solar system may give us clues about how life began on Earth.

Comprehension Check

SUMMARIZE

Have partners summarize the selection by paraphrasing the main ideas. Remind students to use their Summary Charts to help them organize their summaries.

THINK AND COMPARE

Sample answers are given.

1. **Summarize:** Students may discuss the exciting experience of using simulators to learn to walk on the Moon, as well as learning to live and work without gravity. They may mention building their own rockets, tasting space food, wearing space suits, and the experience of eating and sleeping in space.

2. **Analyze:** Team Europa and the actual astronauts use a gravity chair so that they can learn to move around in nearly weightless conditions. The moon has only 1/6 of Earth's gravity.

3. **Text to Self:** Students should support the activity they choose with valid reasons.

4. **Text to World:** Answers will vary. Students may suggest that future space missions will expand our understanding and knowledge of the universe. USE ON MY OWN

FOCUS QUESTION

5. **Text to Text:** The mission specialists have to be able to work in zero gravity. Team Europa's training in the 5DF Chair and underwater helped them learn how to control their movements in zero gravity.

Objectives

- Read fluently with correct pronunciation
- Rate: 100–120 WCPM

Materials

- Fluency Transparency 4
- Fluency Solutions
- Leveled Practice Books, p. 25

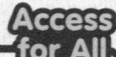

ELL / Access for All

Fluency Summarize the paragraph for students so that they understand the content. Echo-read the passage with students. Write difficult words from the passage on the board and practice pronouncing them, first in isolation and then in their sentences.

On Level Practice Book O, page 25

As I read, I will pay attention to pronunciation.

	People on Earth have long looked at Mars with excitement
10	and fear. Mars is Earth's nearest neighbor and has an
20	environment similar to Earth's in many ways. The surface
29	of Mars is much like the surface of parts of Earth, dry and
42	hard. Temperatures on Mars range from –225° to 60°
49	Fahrenheit (-140° to 25° Celsius). There are important
55	differences, too. The atmosphere of Mars is almost all carbon
65	dioxide and doesn't have enough oxygen to support humans.
74	On Mars, **gravity,** the force that pulls us toward the ground,
85	is not as strong as gravity on Earth.
93	However, of all the planets in the solar system, Mars
103	is the one that seems most possible for humans to visit and
115	even colonize. It is close to us, and it has a surface and
128	surface temperature most similar to that of Earth. 136

Comprehension Check

1. Why does Mars seem like the most likely planet for humans to visit? **Main Idea and Details** Mars is the closest planet to Earth, and it has temperatures similar to Earth's temperatures.
2. What are some differences between Earth and Mars? **Compare and Contrast** Mars has less gravity and less oxygen than Earth.

	Words Read	–	Number of Errors	=	Words Correct Score
First Read		–		=	
Second Read		–		=	

⭐ **Approaching Practice Book A,** page 25

◆ **Beyond Practice Book B,** page 25

Fluency
Repeated Reading: *Pronunciation*

EXPLAIN/MODEL Tell students they will be doing a choral reading. Model reading aloud the text on **Fluency Transparency 4.** Ask students to pay attention to your pronunciation of possibly unfamiliar vocabulary words.

Transparency 4

On Earth, when you jump up, gravity pulls you back down. In space you just keep going up. If you push away from a wall, you keep going backward. Bending quickly to grab something could make you do somersaults. To get used to the weightless tumble of space, the Gemini and Apollo astronauts—and the kids at Space Academy—used the 5DF Chair. This chair glided over the floor on a cushion of air like the puck in an air hockey game.

"This is what an EVA, an extravehicular activity, or space walk, feels like," Bethany said, tipping and rolling the chair in all directions to give the kids a taste of the different movements.

Fluency Transparency 4
from *Ultimate Field Trip 5: Blasting Off to Space Academy*, page 101

PRACTICE/APPLY Have the class do a choral reading as follows: One student reads a sentence. The next student joins in, and then a third. Repeat until all students are reading together. When students reach the end of the passage, have them go back to the beginning until everyone has been included in the reading. Students will practice fluency using **Practice Book** page 25 or Fluency Solutions Audio CD. Have partners practice together.

Quick Check Can students read fluently with correct pronunciation?

During **Small Group Instruction**

If No → **Approaching Level** Fluency, p. 111N

If Yes → **On Level** Options, pp. 111Q–111R

Beyond Level Options, pp. 111S–111T

Comprehension

 **MAINTAIN SKILL**
SUMMARIZE

EXPLAIN/MODEL

- To **summarize,** good readers look for the main idea by locating a topic sentence in the text or passage, or by creating their own topic sentence based on information in the text.

- To find the most important details to include in a summary, good readers ask themselves: Would I understand the main idea without this detail? If not, the detail should be included.

- A summary should be in the reader's own words, but should not include personal opinions about the text or passage.

 **PRACTICE/APPLY** Summarize the main ideas and supporting details under each of the headings in *Ultimate Field Trip 5.*

- What is the most important point Susan E. Goodman wanted readers to understand about the Space Academy?

- Why does the writer relate Space Academy activities to what NASA and real astronauts do? Why does she use quotations from the students at Space Academy?

Have students write a summary that contains the main idea and the most significant details of the selection. Remind them to use formal paragraph structure, including paragraph indents. Students may also form a literature circle to brainstorm responses.

For comprehension practice use Graphic Organizers on **Teacher's Resource Book** pages 40–64.

Objective
- Summarize a selection or passage

Skills Trace

Summarize	
Introduce	93A–B
Practice/Apply	94–107; Leveled Practice, 23–24
Reteach/Review	111M–T, 607A–B, 608-627, 633M–T; Leveled Practice, 178–179
Assess	Weekly Tests; Unit 1, 5 Tests; Benchmark Tests A, B
Maintain	107B, 199A, 691B

Poetry

GENRE: SIMPLE POEMS

Have students read the bookmark on **Student Book** page 108. Explain that simple poems

- have a regular rhyming pattern and rhythm;

- are often focused on one image, emotion, or idea;

- may have one, two, or several stanzas, or groups of lines.

Literary Elements:
Rhyme Scheme and Rhythm

EXPLAIN Tell students that literary elements enhance poetry. Rhyme schemes and rhythm are examples of sound techniques.

- Rhyme scheme, a pattern of words that ends in the same sound, is usually determined by the last words in the lines of a poem.

- Rhythm is the regular repetition of accented and unaccented syllables within each line.

PRACTICE/APPLY Have students identify the rhyming words in each stanza of the poem. Discuss whether the rhyme scheme for the first stanza, a b c d, is used in the remaining two stanzas on this page.

After students have finished reading, have them interpret the poem and discuss its style and type. Then have them write an interpretive essay discussing the impact of rhythm and rhyme on their understanding of the poem.

Poetry

Simple Poems have a regular rhyme scheme and rhythm.

Literary Elements

Rhyme Schemes are the patterns of rhyming words in poems. Rhyme schemes are written with small letters, beginning with *a*.

Rhythm is the regular repetition of syllables.

I'm Building a Rocket

by Kenn Nesbit

I'm building a rocket.
As soon as I'm done
I'm taking my friends
On a trip to the sun.

> The rhyme scheme for this stanza would be *a, b, c, b.*

But what do you mean
That the sun is too hot?
Oh, well, I suppose
I'll just pick a new spot.

1 I'm building a rocket.
I'm finishing soon
And taking my friends
On a trip to the moon!

108

1 LITERARY ELEMENT: RHYTHM

How many accented syllables are there in each line of the first stanza? (There are two accented syllables in each line. For example, in line 1, "build" from "building" and "rock" from "rocket" are accented.)

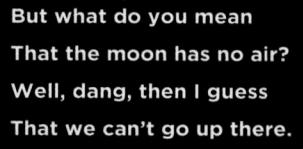

Poetry

But what do you mean
That the moon has no air?
Well, dang, then I guess
That we can't go up there.

I'm building a rocket.
It's going to fly.
I'm taking my friends
Way up high in the sky.

But what do you mean
When you ask how we'll land?
This rocket is harder
To build than I planned.

To heck with the rocket.
It's out in the shed.
I'm taking my friends
Out for pizza instead. **2**

> There are six syllables in lines 1 and 4 and five syllables in lines 2 and 3. This is an example of *rhythm.*

Connect and Compare

1. What are some other examples of rhyme schemes and rhythm that make this a simple poem? **Rhyme Schemes and Rhythm**

2. Read the poem aloud. How does the rhythm help you read the poem with expression? **Evaluate**

3. Compare this poem with *Ultimate Field Trip 5: Blasting Off to Space Academy.* What is the difference between the children in the book and the speaker in this poem? **Reading/Writing Across Texts**

LOG ON Find out more about poetry at **www.macmillanmh.com**

109

Read

Paired Selection Student pages 108–109

Poetry

2 RHYME SCHEME

How can you determine a poem's rhyme scheme? (You can assign a letter to the last word of each line to figure out a poem's rhyme scheme. For instance, in stanza 7, "rocket" would be A; "shed" would be B; "friends" would be C; "instead," since it rhymes with "shed," would also be B. That's why the rhyme scheme for this stanza is ABCB.)

Connect and Compare

SUGGESTED ANSWERS

1. Answers will vary but should include the fact that lines 2 and 4 in each stanza rhyme and that lines in a stanza have the same number of syllables, which results in the same beat. RHYME SCHEMES AND RHYTHMS

2. Answers will vary but should include that the established syllable pattern gives the poem a predictable quality. EVALUATE

3. In *Ultimate Field Trip 5*, the kids at space camp learn about real space travel, but the speaker in the poem knows very little about space and space travel. READING/WRITING ACROSS TEXTS

LOG ON Technology

Internet Research and Inquiry Activity
Students can find more facts at
www.macmillanmh.com

On Level Practice Book O, page 26

When you read poetry, pay attention to the poem's **rhyme scheme** and **rhythm**. The rhyme scheme is a pattern of words that have the same ending sound, such as *light* and *tight*. Rhythm is the regular repetition of accented or stressed syllables in the lines of a poem. Rhythm gives the poem a steady beat, almost like that of music.

A. In the poem below, fill in the blanks by choosing a word from the list that completes the rhyme scheme. Write the word on the lines provided.

right	round	glow	roar

1. We're in the rocket, set to go.
   The lift-off lights begin to ___glow___.
2. The engines rumble, then they ___roar___
   Can we still run right out the door?
3. The spacecraft rolls from left to ___right___
   And soon we rocket out of sight.
4. But wait! It's over. We're all safe and sound.
   Oh, it was just the simulator spinning ___round___.

B. Identify the rhythm in these lines of the poem. Underline the accented syllables.

The spacecraft rolls from left to right.
And soon we rocket out of sight.
But wait! It's over. We're all safe and sound.
Oh, it was just the simulator spinning round.

⭐ **Approaching Practice Book A,** page 26

◆ **Beyond Practice Book B,** page 26

WRITING
- Personal Narrative
- **Writer's Craft:** Important Details

WORD STUDY
- Words in Context
- **Context Clues:** Descriptions/ Explanations
- **Phonics:** Words with /är/, /âr/, /ôr/
- Vocabulary Building

SPELLING
- Words with /är/, /âr/, and /ôr/

GRAMMAR
- Sentence Combining/ Complex Sentences

SMALL GROUP OPTIONS
- Differentiated Instruction, pp. 111M–111V

Writing

Important Details

READ THE STUDENT MODEL

Read the bookmark about including important details. Explain that details, such as descriptions, explanations, and examples, help readers understand the ideas presented in topic sentences.

Have students turn to the first paragraph on page 110 and identify important details. Then have the class read Marcella W.'s letter and the callouts.

Tell students they will write letters about an exciting experience. They will also learn to include important details to clarify their subjects for readers.

Writer's Craft

Important Details

Important details that describe or explain make writing interesting. Readers need detailed descriptions, explanations, and examples to better understand your experience.

Write About an Experience

I included important details to tell my teacher about a great experience.

I used descriptive details to describe the costumes.

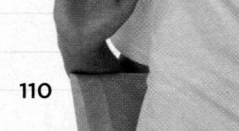

September 19

Dear Mrs. Hansen,

I miss my old school and friends. I know you said I would have some great experiences in my new town. Now I know you were right! I'm writing to tell you about last weekend.

We went to an international parade called Folkmoot. People in costumes from all over the world came to sing, dance, and perform their music.

The colorful costumes were decorated with red, blue and green beads and some even had feathers. The beads were so sparkly they nearly blinded me. Who would have thought I'd have this incredible experience in a small North Carolina town?

Sincerely,
Marcella W.

110

Features of a Friendly Letter

In a friendly letter, the writer may state a purpose, make a request, give a compliment, or just share news and say hello to a friend.

- It is usually written in the first person, using words such as *I, me,* and *my.*

- It is usually addressed to one person and always includes the date.

- All proper nouns—including the names of people, places, and events—are capitalized.

- Its tone is usually informal, and the writer may use interesting adjectives to create strong descriptions.

Your Turn

Write a letter about an exciting experience you have had. Choose descriptive details that help the person you are writing to share the experience with you. Use the writer's checklist to check your letter.

Greetings from TEXAS

Writer's Checklist

☑ **Ideas and Content:** Does my letter include important details?

☑ **Organization:** Did I separate my letter into paragraphs so it is easy to read?

☑ **Voice:** Will the person who reads my letter know I wrote it before he or she sees my signature?

☑ **Word Choice:** Did I use precise words related to sight, sound, smell, taste, and touch?

☑ **Sentence Fluency:** Did I sometimes use long sentences instead of short, choppy sentences?

☑ **Conventions:** Did I use the correct punctuation? Did I check my spelling?

111

PREWRITE

Discuss the writing prompt on page 111. Have students brainstorm exciting experiences they have had that they would most like to share in a letter. Have students set a purpose for writing and identify their audience.

Display **Transparency 13.** Discuss how Marcella used a Details/Precise Words Chart to plan her letter. Have students use similar charts to plan their letters.

DRAFT

Display **Transparency 14.** Point out that a word other than *bright* might better convey the writer's voice. Tell students that appropriate descriptive words paint a picture of the event.

Before students begin writing, present the lesson on **Important Details** on page 111A. Then have students use their charts to write their letters. Remind them to supply important details to support each main idea. Tell students to think about how they can convey their own personalities in their writing. See page 111B for a minilesson on **Voice**.

REVISE

Display **Transparency 15.** Discuss the revisions. Students can revise their drafts or place them in writing portfolios to work on later. If students choose to revise, have them work with a partner and use the Writer's Checklist on page 111. Have them **proofread** their writing. For **Publishing Options** see page 111A.

For lessons on **Complex Sentences, Spelling,** and **Voice** see page 111B and **5 Day Spelling** and **Grammar,** pages 111G–111J.

Transparency 13: **Details/ Precise Words Chart**
Transparency 14: **Draft**
Transparency 15: **Revision**

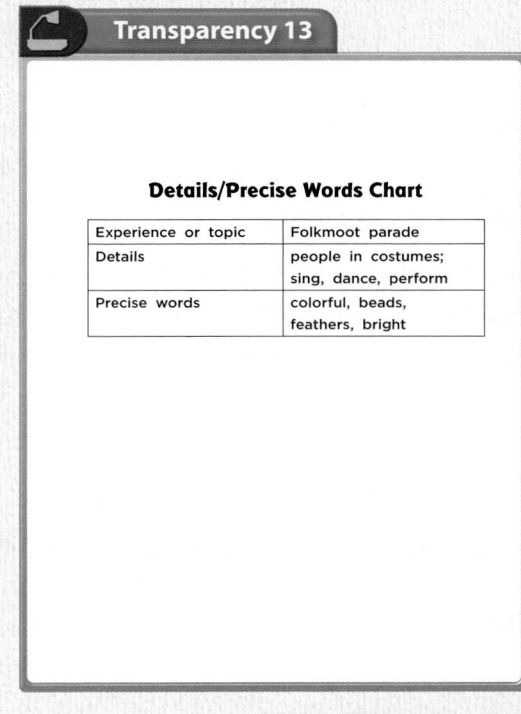

Transparency 13

Details/Precise Words Chart

Experience or topic	Folkmoot parade
Details	people in costumes; sing, dance, perform
Precise words	colorful, beads, feathers, bright

Writing Transparency 13

Writer's Craft

Publishing Options

Students can read their letters orally to the class. See the Speaking and Listening tips below. They can also use their best cursive to write their letters. (See **Teacher's Resource Book** pages 168–173 for cursive models and practice.) Then they can learn to correctly address envelopes and mail their letters. Offer an incentive for students to share any responses they receive orally with the class.

Speaking and Listening

SPEAKING STRATEGIES

- Practice reading your letter in front of others.
- Speak with expression.

LISTENING STRATEGIES

- Listen to the letter and discuss the content and how a letter helps readers get to know the writer better. Ask open-ended questions.
- Respect the age, culture, and interests of the listeners and of the speaker.

4- and 6-Point Scoring Rubrics

Use the rubrics on pages 143G–143H to score published writing.

Writing Process

For a complete lesson, see Unit Writing pages 143A–143H.

Important Details

EXPLAIN/MODEL

Writers organize paragraphs by stating main ideas in topic sentences. Although a topic sentence tells readers what to expect in a paragraph, it doesn't help readers connect with the topic or know fully what really happens. To provide this connection, writers include important details that elaborate on the topic. Display **Transparency 16.** Discuss how detailed descriptions, explanations, and examples help writers better convey their ideas.

Think Aloud The part that has the most details seems the most enjoyable to read. Joaquin probably enjoyed that part of the reunion best of all. However, I think he could add even more descriptive words and comparisons to make the narrative better.

Transparency 16

Roses Are Bigger and Better in Texas
by Joaquin P.

My father's family in Texas invited us to a family reunion over the Thanksgiving holiday. The five of us, including my mom, dad, and two sisters, packed our things into the van. We headed south for some turkey and some fun.

During one afternoon, the adults took all the kids on a field trip to a local rose garden. There were roses of all colors and sizes. I saw _____ roses. I saw _____ roses and roses the size of _____. They all had such _____ names. I remember that one _____ rose was called a _____. The rose bushes were planted in mazes. I crossed a _____ bridge that spanned a _____ stream. There were also many _____ trees that grabbed the sky with their _____. My cousins and I played hide-and-seek among the rose bushes, laughing and teasing each other as the sun set in Texas.

Descriptive words and phrases will vary.

Writing Transparency 16

PRACTICE/APPLY

Work with students to add comparisons or adjectives to the first few blanks. Then have students work in pairs to finish the description. Have students experiment with how different word choices affect the voice of the narrative. Next, have students work independently to underline important details in narrative nonfiction texts that they have read recently.

As students write their letters, have them include important details for each main idea. Tell students to think about how their word choices convey their personalities as narrators.

Writer's Toolbox

Writing Trait: Voice

Explain/Model Writers reveal their personalities to readers through word choice and the details they include. Ask students to think about how they perceive a writer who uses the word *sparkly* instead of the word *shiny*. Ask students to use details in Marcella's letter on page 110 to describe what kind of person Marcella seems to be. Draw attention to words and phrases such as *sparkly* and *nearly blinded me*.

Practice/Apply As students draft their letters, have them think about which words, phrases, and details will best convey their personalities to readers.

Denotation and Connotation

Explain/Model All words have dictionary meanings; many words also have meanings that people associate with them. For example, the word *sparkly* means "shiny," which is its denotative meaning. However, the word *sparkly* also has the connotation of a glittering, dazzling brightness.

Practice/Apply Before students begin their letters, have them write both the denotative and the connotative meanings for words in their Details/ Precise Words Charts. Have partners discuss what these words suggest about the writers' personalities and attitudes toward their subjects. Students should revise their word choices to accurately convey voice and tone.

Sentence Combining/ Complex Sentences

Explain/Model Writers can use the conjunctions *and, but*, and *or* to combine sentences, making compound sentences. When conjunctions such as *because, however,* and *while* are used to combine sentences, the result is a complex sentence.

Practice/Apply Have students look at the letter on page 110. Have them identify compound sentences. For a complete lesson on sentence combining, complex sentences, and mechanics, see pages 111I–111J.

Mechanics Point out commas, colons, and capital letters in the student model. Explain how to place them. Have students correct their use of commas, colons, and capital letters as they proofread.

Spelling Words with /är/, /âr/, /ôr/

Write the words *starch, heart,* and *course* on the board. The sounds /är/, /âr/, and /ôr/ are spelled *ar, ear,* and *our.* These sounds also have other spellings, such as those found in *square* or *aboard.* Remind students to pay attention when they spell words with these sounds. They can use a print or online dictionary to check spelling in their drafts. For a complete lesson on spelling words with /är/, /âr/, and /ôr/ sounds, see pages 111G–111H.

Technology

Advise students that many word-processing programs have letter writing formats that they can use.

Objectives
- Apply knowledge of word meaning and context clues
- Use context clues to find a description or explanation

Materials
- Vocabulary Transparencies 7, 8
- Leveled Practice Books, p. 27

Vocabulary

function (p. 98) to work or act

adjusted (p. 99) changed to make fit

disasters (p. 98) events that cause much suffering, damage, or loss

environment (p. 98) surrounding conditions

mission (p. 96) operation or expedition

maze (p. 98) network of paths through which it is hard to find one's way

zone (p. 98) region or area

gravity (p. 97) natural force that causes objects to fall toward the center of Earth

ELL   Access for All

Think Aloud Continue modeling the strategy through a Think Aloud but bring students into your thinking: *What word do you think would fit? Let's try it.*

Review
Vocabulary

Words in Context

EXPLAIN/MODEL
Review the meanings of the vocabulary words. Display **Transparency 7**. Model how to use word meanings and context clues to fill in the missing word.

Think Aloud I know that people use cars to travel from one place to another. That is the purpose of a car. The word *purpose* would work in this sentence. I know another word for *purpose* is *function*. That word makes sense, too. The answer is *function*.

Transparency 7

adjusted disasters environment function gravity maze mission zone

The (1) <u>function</u> of a car is to get people to various places.

The father (2) <u>adjusted</u> the seat belt for the small child.

The earthquakes were natural (3) <u>disasters</u> that ruined the city.

The (4) <u>environment</u> at the park is peaceful and shady.

The astronaut's (5) <u>mission</u> is to discover life on other planets.

The (6) <u>maze</u> was confusing but a lot of fun.

Without (7) <u>gravity</u>, we would all float in space.

The no cell-phone (8) <u>zone</u> in the train was quiet.

Vocabulary Transparency 7

PRACTICE/APPLY
Instruct students to complete the remaining sentences on their own. Review the students' answers as a class.

Homographs and Homonyms Have students search for homographs, such as *buffet*, and homonyms, such as *lean*, in their reading. Then direct students to write context sentences, leaving a blank for the homograph or homonym. Have them write the missing words at the top of the paper out of order, trade papers with a partner, and fill in the missing homonym or homograph.

STRATEGY
CONTEXT CLUES: DESCRIPTION OR EXPLANATION

EXPLAIN/MODEL

Tell students that the words and phrases in a sentence and in surrounding sentences are called context clues, which are descriptions or explanations of difficult words.

Display **Transparency 8.** Use the example to model how to find the context clue that is a description or explanation for *gravity.*

 Transparency 8

CONTEXT CLUES

The astronauts were trying to learn how to move in an atmosphere without *gravity.* Gravity is the force that causes objects to have weight.

1. The simulators, special machines used for training astronauts by letting them feel what real conditions are like in space, helped students learn how to walk without gravity.
2. The Milky Way is the galaxy in which we live. This large group of stars includes our sun and the planets that revolve around it.

Vocabulary Strategy Transparency 8

PRACTICE/APPLY

 Have students identify the context clues in items 1 and 2. Then have them use a social studies or science text book to find more examples of context clues that are descriptions or explanations.

Quick Check
Can students determine word meanings?
Can students use descriptions and explanations?

During **Small Group Instruction**

If No → **Approaching Level** Vocabulary, pp. 111N–111O

If Yes → **On Level** Options, pp. 111Q–111R

Beyond Level Options, pp. 111S–111T

ELL  Access for All

Context Clues Draw students' attention to page 102. Read aloud the last paragraph. Use a Think Aloud to model how to figure out the meaning of the words *force* and *weightless.*

On Level Practice Book O, page 27

If you are reading and come to an unfamiliar word, look at the other words in the sentence. These words might give you hints as to the meaning of the unfamiliar word. We call these hints **context clues.** For example, context clues might explain or describe an unfamiliar word.

Use context clues to help define the underlined words in the passage. Circle the letter of the response that best completes each sentence.

1. At the U.S. Space Academy, we felt what it was like to be weightless and float through the air.

   If you are weightless, you are not affected by _____.

   a. air   **b.** gravity   c. space

2. Astronauts use simulators in order to feel like what it will be like in space.

   What are simulators _____?

   a. machines   b. portals   c. missions

3. Since space has no atmosphere, special suits need to be worn to supply astronauts with air and protect them from the sun.

   The special suits provide _____.

   a. sunlight and gravity   b. gas and bubbles   **c.** protection from the sun and air

4. The mission crew was asked to deploy the robot that was being stored to work on a broken satellite.

   The robot was deployed to complete an _____.

   a. operation   b. orbit   c. astronaut

5. Someday it might be possible to colonize the moon so people could live there.

   You cannot colonize a place without _____.

   a. sidewalks   **b.** people   c. bikes

 Approaching Practice Book A, page 27

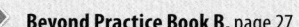 **Beyond Practice Book B,** page 27

Word Study

Objective
- Decode words with *r*-controlled vowels

Materials
- Leveled Practice Books, p. 28
- Teacher's Resource Book, p. 8
- index cards

ELL   Access for All

Pronunciation
Pronouncing *r*-controlled vowels may be difficult for students. Spend additional time pronouncing the words and using them in sentences. Make sure students understand the word meanings. Provide additional examples: *far, fair, for.*

On Level Practice Book O, page 28

- The letters *ar* usually stand for the /är/ sound in *car* and *carve*.
- The letters *ear* and *are* can stand for the /âr/ sound in *bear* and *care*.
- The letters *or, ore, oar, our* can stand for the /ôr/ sound in *for, core, roar,* and *your.*

A. Underline the words in the paragraph that have the /är/ sound in *car*, /âr/ sound in *bear*, or the /ôr/ sound in *for*. Then sort them on the chart below.

The astronauts climbed aboard their space ship. They wore space suits made from special fabric. Their goal was to travel far into space and explore a nearby star. During the flight, they had many chores to do. They also had to take care not to tear holes in their suits.

B. Sort the underlined words in the paragraph according to the vowel + r sound.

/är/ sound in *car*	/âr/ sound in *bear*	/ôr/ sound in *for*
far	care	aboard
star	tear	wore
		explore
		chores

★ **Approaching Practice Book A,** page 28
◆ **Beyond Practice Book B,** page 28

Phonics
Decode Words with /är/, /âr/, or /ôr/

Access for All
- The letters *ar* can stand for the /är/ sound in *car* and *carve*.

- The letters *ear* can stand for the /âr/ sound in *bear* and *stare*.

- The letters *or, ore, oar, our* can stand for the /ôr/ sound in *for, core, roar,* and *your.*

Write the word *course* on the board.

Think Aloud I see the letters *our* in the middle of this word. I know that the letters *our* can stand for the /our/ sound in the word *flour* or the /ôr/ sound in *your*. When I try the /our/ sound in *flour*, I get /kours/ That doesn't make sense, so I will try the /ôr/ sound in *your*—/kôrs/. *Course* is a word I know. In the word *course,* the letters *our* stand for the /ôr/ sound.

PRACTICE/APPLY List the vocabulary words below on the board. Have students identify the letters that stand for /är/, /âr/, or /ôr/.

1. force	**3.** scorn	**5.** smart
2. harsh	**4.** care	**6.** wear

Decode Multisyllabic Words Have students add word endings to the vocabulary words to see if another syllable changes pronunciation (not usually): *forceful, harshly, carefully,* and so on. Remind students that understanding and recognizing word families and spelling patterns for words with the /är/, âr/, or /ôr/ sounds can help them decode unfamiliar words. For more practice with multisyllabic words, use the decodable passages on **Teacher's Resource Book** page 8.

Cooperative Learning

Vowel Match Have partners write six words each with the sound /är/, /âr/, or /ôr/ on separate index cards for a total of eighteen words. Then have them arrange the cards face down and take turns trying to match two words with the same vowel sound. If a player does not make a match, both cards are turned face down and the partner takes a turn. The person with the most pairs wins.

Quick Check   **Can students decode words with /är/, /âr/, or /ôr/?**

During **Small Group Instruction**

If No → **Approaching Level** Phonics, p. 111M

If Yes → **On Level** Options, pp. 111Q–111R

Beyond Level Options, pp. 111S–111T

Vocabulary Building

Oral Language

Expand Vocabulary Use the following prompt to have students make word webs.

Write *Space* in the center of a word web. Using the main selection, dictionaries, thesauruses, and encyclopedias, have students find and brainstorm words that relate to this week's theme. You may include words such as *astronaut, rocket,* or *exploration*. Then have students discuss space exploration using these words.

Apply Vocabulary

Write a Letter Give students the following writing prompt:

Suppose you received a letter from NASA inviting you to travel to another planet. Would you go? Why or why not? Using your vocabulary words, reply to the letter.

Vocabulary Building

Words in Context Display the following lists and challenge two groups to make as many context clue sentences as possible, leaving a blank for the word from the list. Note that some words have more than one meaning. Then have groups switch papers and guess the main words.

Group A	Group B
credit	impress
maze	commencement
elect	original

Vocabulary Review

Vocabulary Game Turn your classroom into an antigravity simulator by suspending note cards with each of the vocabulary words from the ceiling. Challenge pairs of student astronauts to retrieve the words by offering a sentence for each word that includes a description or explanation. To win the word, one student must offer the sentence and another must explain the meaning of the vocabulary word based on the sentence. Allow students pairs to take turns retrieving the words.

Technology

Vocabulary PuzzleMaker CD–ROM

For additional vocabulary and spelling games go to
www.macmillanmh.com

Spelling Words

heart	starch	harsh
swear	source	scarce
aboard	fare	coarse
squares	barge	flare
swore	thorn	course
chart	marsh	sword
scorn	force	

Review brood, prove, hoof

Challenge uproar, gorge

Dictation Sentences

1. Jerry's <u>heart</u> skipped a beat.
2. They had to <u>swear</u> to tell the truth.
3. She is **aboard** the spacecraft.
4. I cut the brownies into <u>squares</u>.
5. She <u>swore</u> not to do it again.
6. The teacher made a seating <u>chart</u>.
7. I'm afraid they'll <u>scorn</u> my ideas.
8. The <u>starch</u> made the shirt crisp.
9. Food is a <u>source</u> of energy.
10. I need money for the bus <u>fare</u>.
11. She hates when I <u>barge</u> in.
12. The <u>thorn</u> cut her finger.
13. Jay passed the muddy <u>marsh</u>.
14. The **force** of gravity pulls down.
15. This was a very <u>harsh</u> winter.
16. Water is <u>scarce</u> in the desert.
17. The fabric's surface was <u>coarse</u>.
18. I see the red <u>flare</u> of the rocket.
19. Track the <u>course</u> of the flight.
20. The <u>sword</u> had a metal blade.

Review/Challenge Words

1. It doesn't help to <u>brood</u> about it.
2. It's hard to <u>prove</u> there is life on the planet.
3. We watched the blacksmith file the horse's <u>hoof</u>.
4. The angry crowd caused an <u>uproar</u>.
5. Water flows through the <u>gorge</u>.

Words in **bold** are from the main selection.

Words with /är/, /âr/, and /ôr/

Day 1 Pretest

ASSESS PRIOR KNOWLEDGE

Using the Dictation Sentences, say the underlined word, read the sentence, and repeat the word. Have students write the words on **Spelling Practice Book** page 19. For a modified list, use the first 12 Spelling Words and the Review Words. For a more challenging list, use Spelling Words 3–20 and the Challenge Words. Students may correct their own tests.

Have students cut apart the Spelling Word Cards BLM on **Teacher's Resource Book** page 69 and figure out a way to sort them. They can save the cards for use throughout the week.

For **Leveled Word Lists**, go to **www.macmillanmh.com**

Day 2 Word Sorts

TEACHER AND STUDENT SORTS

- Write *chart*, *fare*, and *scorn* on the board. Point out that all three words have vowel sounds controlled by the letter *r*. Pronounce each word aloud.

- Use /är/, /âr/, and /ôr/ as column headings and help students sort the words on the board in their word study notebooks. Pronounce each Spelling and Challenge Word, and have students complete the sort.

- Ask students to identify any words that have unexpected vowel spellings, such as *course*, *coarse*, and *heart*. Help them think of other words with these spellings.

- Challenge students to sort the words any way they wish, for example, by homographs or homophones.

Spelling Practice Book, pages 19–20

Fold back the paper along the dotted line. Write the words in the blanks as they are read aloud. When you finish the test, unfold the paper. Use the list at the right to correct any spelling mistakes.

1.	1. heart
2.	2. swear
3.	3. aboard
4.	4. squares
5.	5. swore
6.	6. chart
7.	7. scorn
8.	8. starch
9.	9. source
10.	10. fare
11.	11. barge
12.	12. thorn
13.	13. marsh
14.	14. force
15.	15. harsh
16.	16. scarce
17.	17. coarse
18.	18. flare
19.	19. course
20.	20. sword
Review Words 21.	21. brood
22.	22. prove
23.	23. hoof
Challenge Words 24.	24. uproar
25.	25. gorge

Spelling Practice Book, page 21

force	scorn	sword	swore	source
aboard	course	coarse	chart	barge
harsh	marsh	starch	heart	scarce
squares	swear	flare	fare	thorn

Sort each spelling word by finding the sound and spelling pattern to which it belongs.

Write the words that have /är/ spelled:

ar
1. chart   4. marsh
2. barge   5. starch
3. harsh

ear
1. heart

Write the words that have /âr/ spelled:

are
1. squares
2. flare
3. fare

ar_e
1. scarce

ear
1. swear

Write the words that have /ôr/ spelled:

our
1. source
2. course

ore
1. swore

or
1. force
2. scorn
3. sword
4. thorn

oar
1. aboard
2. coarse

Day 3 — Word Meanings

CATEGORIES

Ask students to copy the words below in their word study notebooks, completing the group by adding a Spelling Word.

1. swamp, bog, _____ (marsh)
2. circles, rectangles, _____ (squares)
3. canoe, rowboat, _____ (barge)
4. brain, kidney, _____ (heart)
5. price, cost, _____ (fare)

Challenge students to come up with other word groups to which they can add Spelling Words, Review Words, or Challenge Words.

Have students write a sentence for each Spelling Word, leaving a blank space for the word. They can exchange papers with others and fill in the blanks.

Day 4 — Review and Proofread

SPIRAL REVIEW

Review words with /ü/, /ū/, and /ù/. Write *brood*, *prove*, and *hoof* on the board. Have students identify the vowel sound in each word.

PROOFREAD AND WRITE

Write these sentences on the board, including the misspelled words. Ask students to proofread, circling the misspelled words and correcting them.

1. When she saw the flaire of the comet, her hart beat faster. (flare, heart)

2. Without a charte, he knew they would soon go off coarse. (chart, course)

3. He was hurt because her words were harshe and full of scorne. (harsh, scorn)

Day 5 — Assess and Reteach

POSTTEST

Use the Dictation Sentences on page 111G for the Posttest. If students have difficulty with any words in the lesson, have them place the words in a list entitled "Spelling Words I Want to Remember" in their word study notebooks.

Challenge student partners to look for other words that have the *r*-controlled /är/, /âr/, and /ôr/ sounds they studied this week, either in their reading or in other materials. Partners should work together to sort the words by vowel sounds.

Spelling Practice Book, page 22

force	scorn	sword	swore	source
aboard	course	coarse	chart	barge
harsh	marsh	starch	heart	scarce
squares	swear	flare	fare	thorn

Fill in the Blanks

Write the spelling word that best completes each sentence.

1. Only the astronauts were allowed ___aboard___ the spacecraft.
2. Her ___heart___ beat quickly as she listened to the countdown.
3. Scientists tracked the ___course___ of the spacecraft.
4. The ___force___ of gravity is weaker on the Moon than on Earth.
5. The astronauts' jobs for each day were listed on a ___chart___.
6. The ___flare___ of the rockets could be seen for miles.
7. Their landing was ___harsh___, but nothing was damaged.
8. He ___swore___ that he would return to the Moon one day.

Related Words

Write the spelling word that is related to the sets of words below.

9. circles, triangles, ___squares___
10. rough, stiff ___coarse___
11. swamp, bog, ___marsh___
12. needle, spike, ___thorn___
13. soap, water, ___starch___
14. promise, pledge, ___swear___
15. blade, weapon, ___sword___
16. boat, ship, ___barge___
17. price, charge, ___fare___
18. rare, limited, ___scarce___
19. hatred, dislike, ___scorn___
20. beginning, cause, ___source___

Spelling Practice Book, page 23

Circle the misspelled words in the message. Write the words correctly on the lines below.

Dear Tyra,

We have been abored the spacecraft for two days now. Everything is going smoothly. We are right on corce to reach the space station. You can see where we are if you look at the cheart I gave you.

It's hard to describe what it felt like to blast off from Earth. The fours of the rockets was incredible. We couldn't see the flare of the rockets when we took off. I bet you had a good view, though. I sware my hart skipped a beat. I wonder how you felt as you watched the spacecraft lift off.

I'll be home sooner than you think. Take care of your little brother!

Love, Dad

1. ___aboard___
2. ___course___
3. ___chart___
4. ___force___
5. ___swear___
6. ___heart___

Writing Activity

Imagine that you are on a space trip. Write an e-mail message home to a friend or your family. Use four spelling words in your message.

Spelling Practice Book, page 24

Look at the words in each set below. One word in each set is spelled correctly. Use a pencil to fill in the circle next to the correct word. Before you begin, look at the sample set of words. Sample A has been done for you. Do Sample B by yourself. When you are sure you know what to do, you may go on with the rest of the page.

Sample A:
- Ⓐ spot
- Ⓑ spott
- Ⓒ spote
- Ⓓ spoht

Sample B:
- Ⓔ taak
- Ⓕ taik
- Ⓖ take
- Ⓗ tak

1. Ⓐ force Ⓑ fohrce Ⓒ fors Ⓓ fource
2. Ⓔ skohrn Ⓕ scorne Ⓖ scorn Ⓗ skorn
3. Ⓐ sorde Ⓑ sword Ⓒ sord Ⓓ soord
4. Ⓔ swor Ⓕ sooor Ⓖ suore Ⓗ swore
5. Ⓐ sorce Ⓑ source Ⓒ sors Ⓓ sohrce
6. Ⓔ aboard Ⓕ abourd Ⓖ aborde Ⓗ abord
7. Ⓐ corse Ⓑ cohrs Ⓒ coarse Ⓓ coors
8. Ⓔ corse Ⓕ cohrs Ⓖ course Ⓗ coors
9. Ⓐ chort Ⓑ charte Ⓒ chart Ⓓ chorte
10. Ⓔ borje Ⓕ barg Ⓖ barge Ⓗ bahrge
11. Ⓐ horsh Ⓑ harshe Ⓒ haarsh Ⓓ harsh
12. Ⓔ marsh Ⓕ maarsh Ⓖ morsh Ⓗ marshe
13. Ⓐ staarch Ⓑ starche Ⓒ starch Ⓓ storch
14. Ⓔ haart Ⓕ hahrt Ⓖ heart Ⓗ harte
15. Ⓐ scarce Ⓑ scaerce Ⓒ scearce Ⓓ scarc
16. Ⓔ skwaers Ⓕ squares Ⓖ squeres Ⓗ squarez
17. Ⓐ sware Ⓑ swar Ⓒ swear Ⓓ swere
18. Ⓔ flaere Ⓕ flar Ⓖ flare Ⓗ flaer
19. Ⓐ faer Ⓑ faar Ⓒ fare Ⓓ fer
20. Ⓔ thorne Ⓕ thorn Ⓖ thohrn Ⓗ thourn

Sentence Combining/Complex Sentences

Daily Language Activities

Use these activities to reinforce each day's lesson. Write the day's activity on the board, or use **Daily Language Transparency 4.**

DAY 1
Astronauts pilots and kids can experience the world without gravity. They can find out what it's like. If they go to the Space Academy. (1: Astronauts, pilots,; 2: like if they go)

DAY 2
They practice without gravity for a long time. Because they need to know how to move in space. (1: time because)

DAY 3
dear Grandma:
I dreamed about traveling in space, while I was in school today. I have always wanted to be an astronaut. sincerely Amber (1: Dear Grandma,; 2: space while; 3: Sincerely,)

DAY 4
Astronauts learn about teamwork. When they train. They practice in a swimming pool. Because it's like being in space. (1: teamwork when; 2: pool because)

DAY 5
April 18 2005
Dear Diary,
I don't think I want to be an astronaut. I think I could be a reporter, because I like to write. Yours truly, Zack (1: April 18,; 2: reporter because)

ELL Access for All

Conjunctions
Write two clauses and model how to combine them using a conjunction. Discuss its meaning.

Day 1 — Introduce the Concept

INTRODUCE MORE WAYS TO COMBINE SENTENCES

Present the following:

- You can use conjunctions to combine sentences.

- The conjunctions *and, but,* and *or* are used to turn two simple sentences into a compound sentence.

- Some conjunctions tell where, when, why, how, or under what conditions. They function as transitions. These conjunctions include *after, although, as, because, before, if, since, so that, until, when, whether,* and *while.*

Point out that writers use conjunctions and transitional conjunctions to improve the flow of their writing.

See Grammar Transparency 16 for modeling and guided practice.

Grammar Practice Book, page 19

- The conjunctions *and, but,* and *or* are used to form **compound sentences.**
- Some conjunctions tell *where, when, why, how,* or *under what conditions.* These conjunctions include *after, although, as, because, before, if, since, so that, until, when, whether,* and *while.*

Combine each pair of sentences, using the conjunction in parentheses.

1. Some tasted space food. Others wore spacesuits. (and)
   Some tasted space food and others wore space suits.

2. Gum and drinks are not allowed. They can create disasters in the dirt-free zone. (because)
   Gum and drinks are not allowed because they can create disasters in the dirt-free zone.

3. The students were told to remove their jewelry. They would not be injured. (so that)
   The students were told to remove their jewelry so that they would not be injured.

4. The trainer would hold onto the chair. The last student had a turn. (until)
   The trainer would hold onto the chair until the last student had a turn.

5. He volunteered to sit in the gravity chair. He realized how hard it was to move around. (before)
   He volunteered to sit in the gravity chair before he realized how hard it would be to move around.

Day 2 — Teach the Concept

REVIEW MORE WAYS TO COMBINE SENTENCES

Have students explain how conjunctions are used to combine sentences and which are used to make compound sentences.

INTRODUCE COMPLEX SENTENCES

- A sentence containing two related ideas joined by a conjunction other than *and, but,* or *or* is called a complex sentence: *I ate my sandwich because I was hungry.*

- The conjunction can appear at the beginning of the complex sentence or in the middle. If the sentence begins with the conjunction, a comma should follow the last word in that part of the sentence.

See Grammar Transparency 17 for modeling and guided practice.

Grammar Practice Book, page 20

A sentence that contains two related ideas joined by a conjunction other than *and, but,* or *or* is called a **complex sentence.** These conjunctions include *after, although, as, because, before, if, since, so that, until, when, whether,* and *while.* The conjunction can appear at the beginning of the sentence or in the middle of the sentence.

- If the **complex sentence** begins with the conjunction, then a comma should follow the last word in that part of the sentence.
- Sometimes the comma is unnecessary if the conjunction appears in the middle of the sentence.

From each pair of conjunctions in parentheses, choose the conjunction that combines the sentences into a single sentence that makes sense. Write the new sentence, using a comma if necessary.

1. The Hubble Telescope must be powerful. It can spot a firefly ten thousand miles away. (because/although)
   The Hubble Telescope must be powerful because it can spot a firefly ten thousand miles away.

2. I was feeling brave. I saw how fast the multi-axis trainer was spinning. (so that/before)
   I was feeling brave before I saw how fast the multi-axis trainer was spinning.

3. Bethany held on to the 5DF Chair. The kids practiced moving along the wall. (while/because)
   Bethany held onto the 5DF Chair while the kids practiced moving along the wall.

4. The moon does not have an atmosphere. There is no wind to blow the prints away. (until/since)
   Since the moon does not have an atmosphere, there is no wind to blow the prints away.

Day 3 | Review and Practice

REVIEW COMPLEX SENTENCES

Review the rules for writing complex sentences.

MECHANICS AND USAGE: COMMAS, COLONS, AND CAPITAL LETTERS

- Begin the greeting and the closing of a letter with a capital letter.

- Use a colon to introduce a list. *We visited the following states: Ohio, Iowa, and Kansas.*

- Use a comma between the names of a city and a state or district, and between the day and the year in a date.

- Use a colon after the greeting of a business letter, a comma in a friendly letter.

 See Grammar Transparency 18 for modeling and guided practice.

Grammar Practice Book, page 21

- Begin the greeting and the closing of a letter with capital letters.
- Use a comma after the greeting in a friendly letter and the closing in all letters.
- Use a comma between the names of a city and a state.
- Use a comma to separate the day and year in a date.

Correct the following letter.

July 1 2007
dear mom and dad

Thank you for letting me go to the Space Academy. I'm having so much fun. We've eaten space food and tried on spacesuits. Today we used a special chair that helped us move around. Tomorrow we're going to get into a machine that will spin us around. Please write back to the address below.

your son
Kyle
P.O. Box 345
Huntsville Alabama

July 1, 2007
Dear Mom and Dad,

Thank you for letting me go to the Space Academy. I'm having so much fun. We've eaten space food and tried on space suits. Today we used a special chair that helped us move around. Tomorrow we're going to get into a machine that will spin us around. Please write back to the address below.

Your son,
Kyle
P.O. Box 345
Huntsville, Alabama

Day 4 | Review and Proofread

REVIEW MORE WAYS TO COMBINE SENTENCES

Ask students to explain what a complex sentence is and the role of a conjunction in a complex sentence. Ask how the conjunctions in complex sentences are different from those in compound sentences.

PROOFREAD

Have students correct the punctuation in the sentences below.

1. Dear Mr. Girardi, (Girardi:)

2. I'm writing, because I want to apply to space camp. (writing because)

3. Although I am not old enough this year I would like to go next year. (year,)

4. thank you Jess Davies (Thank you,)

 See Grammar Transparency 19 for modeling and guided practice.

Grammar Practice Book, page 22

- If a **complex sentence** begins with a conjunction, then a comma should follow the last word in that part of the sentence.
- Sometimes a comma is necessary if the conjunction appears in the middle of the sentence.

- Begin the greeting and the closing of a letter with capital letters.
- Use a comma after the greeting in a friendly letter and the closing in all letters.
- Use a comma between the names of a city and a state.
- Use a comma to separate the day and the year in a date.

Read the diary entry below. Correct errors in capitalization and punctuation. Use commas where needed.

February 18 2008
dear diary:

you'll never believe what I did today. I got to use a gravity chair. Before I sat down I made sure to watch the person in front of me so I would know what to do. I was scared at first but the team leaders made me relax and have fun. I can't wait to try it again tomorrow.

your friend
Lindsay

February 18, 2008
Dear Diary,

You'll never believe what I did today. I got to use a gravity chair! Before I sat down, I made sure to watch the person in front of me so I would know what to do. I was scared at first, but the team leaders made me relax and have fun. I can't wait to try it again tomorrow.

Your friend,
Lindsay

Day 5 | Assess and Reteach

ASSESS

Use the Daily Language Activity and page 23 of the **Grammar Practice Book** for assessment.

RETEACH

Write the corrected sentences from the Daily Language Activities on a transparency and display them. Go over each activity, asking students to explain how to tell whether a sentence is complex and what the conjunctions mean. If students cannot answer or answer incorrectly, call on another to explain. Make sure all students have a chance to participate.

Use page 24 of the Grammar Practice Book for additional reteaching.

 See Grammar Transparency 20 for modeling and guided practice.

Grammar Practice Book, pages 23–24

A. Circle the letters of the sentences that best combine the sentence pairs below.

1. Pay attention to the leader. You do not hurt yourself while training.
   a. Pay attention to the leader so that you do not hurt yourself while training.
   b. Pay attention to the leader unless you do not hurt yourself while training.
   c. Pay attention to the leader while you do not hurt yourself while training.

2. They practiced for a long time. The environment was so different from that of Earth.
   a. They practiced for a long time before the environment was so different from that of Earth.
   b. They practiced for a long time because the environment was so different from that of Earth.
   c. They practiced for a long time, while the environment was so different from that of Earth.

3. They got ready for the MAT. The students removed everything from their pockets.
   a. Until they got ready for the MAT, the students removed everything from their pockets.
   b. They got ready for the MAT since the students removed everything from their pockets.
   c. Before they got ready for the MAT, the students removed everything from their pockets.

4. Their time wasn't very good. The students did build the cube.
   a. Because their time wasn't very good, the students did build the cube.
   b. Their time wasn't very good if the students did build the cube.
   c. Although their time wasn't very good, the students did build the cube.

B. Circle the letter of the conjunction that best completes each complex sentence.

5. _____ the students arrived at the camp, they tried on spacesuits.
   a. When
   b. Although
   c. Whether

6. He did do the bunny hop, _____ it was difficult at first.
   a. when
   b. although
   c. whether

Administer the Test

 ### Weekly Reading Assessment,
Passage and questions, pages 45–52

ASSESSED SKILLS

- Summarize
- Vocabulary Words
- Use Context Clues: Description or Explanation
- Sentence Combining and Complex Sentences
- Words with /är/, /âr/, /ôr/

 **Assessment Tool**

Administer the **Weekly Assessment** online or on CD-ROM.

Weekly Assessment, 45–52

 ### Fluency

Assess fluency for one group of students per week. Use the Oral Fluency Record Sheet to track the number of words read correctly. Fluency goal for all students:
100–120 words correct per minute (WCPM).

Approaching Level	Weeks 1, 3, 5
On Level	Weeks 2, 4
Beyond Level	Week 6

Fluency Assessment

 ### Alternative Assessments

- **ELL Assessment,** pages 44–45

ELL Practice and Assessment, 44–45

Diagnose	IF...	THEN...
VOCABULARY WORDS **VOCABULARY STRATEGY** Use Context Clues: Description or Explanation Items 1, 2, 3, 4	0–2 items correct...	Reteach skills using the **Additional Lessons** page T9. Reteach skills: Go to www.macmillanmh.com Vocabulary PuzzleMaker Evaluate for Intervention.
COMPREHENSION Skill: Summarize Items 5, 6, 7, 8	0–2 items correct...	Reteach skills using the **Additional Lessons** page T4. Evaluate for Intervention.
GRAMMAR Sentence Combining and Complex Sentences Items 9, 10, 11	0–1 items correct...	Reteach skills: **Grammar Practice Book** page 24
SPELLING Words with /är/, /âr/, and /ôr/ Items 12, 13, 14	0–1 items correct...	Reteach skills: Go to www.macmillanmh.com
FLUENCY	96–99 WCPM	Fluency Solutions
	0–95 WCPM	Evaluate for Intervention.

READING
Triumphs
AN INTERVENTION PROGRAM

Also
Available

To place students
in the Intervention
Program, use
the **Diagnostic
Assessment** in the
Intervention Teacher's
Edition.

Ultimate Field Trip 5   **111L**

Constructive Feedback

Isolate the error sound and repeat it with the group. If students say /our/ instead of /ôr/, point out that the spelling of *our* has more than one sound and say:

*The word *sour* and the word *four* both have *our* spellings. However, the letters are pronounced differently. In many cases you will recognize only one word. Say /four/ and /fôr/. In other examples this trick will not work. Say /sour/ and /sôr/. In such cases use context clues to determine which pronunciation is correct.*

Repeat as needed with other words with /âr/, /är/, or /or/ sounds.

Additional Resources

For each skill below, additional lessons are provided. You can use these lessons on consecutive days after teaching the lessons provided within the week.
• Summarize, T4
• Context Clues: Description and Explanation, T5

Decodable Text

To help students build speed and accuracy with reading multisyllabic words, use additional decodable text on page 8 of the **Teacher's Resource Book.**

Skills Focus ▶ Phonics

Objective   Decode words with /är/, /âr/, or /ôr/ sounds
Materials   • **Student Book** "Jobs in Space"

WORDS WITH /är/, /âr/, or /ôr/

Model/Guided Practice

■ Write the letters *f, o, r, g, e* on the board. First segment the sounds: /f/ /ôr/ /j/. Then blend the sounds: /fôrj/. *Say the word with me:* forge.

■ Point out that the sound /ôr/ is spelled *or*. The /ôr/ sound can also be spelled *ore, oar,* or *our*.

■ Start with *four. Say the word with me. How is the /ôr/ sound spelled?*

■ Next, identify how the /ôr/ sound is spelled in each of these words: *more, pour, score, pore,* and *board*. Then have students name five other single-syllable words with the /ôr/ sound. Provide constructive feedback.

■ Extend the review to include words that have the sounds /är/ and /âr/, such as *harp, spark, large, stare, wear,* and *care*.

MULTISYLLABIC WORDS WITH /är/, /âr/, or /ôr/

■ Write the word *absorbent* on the board. Mark the syllables: *ab/sor/bent*. Blend the syllables: /ab sôr bənt/. Note the /ôr/ sound and its spelling.

■ Have pairs of students work together to practice decoding longer words with /är/, /âr/, or /ôr/ sounds. Write the words below on the board. *With your partner, choose a word. Say the word aloud. Circle the /är/, /âr/, or /ôr/ sound and note the spelling. List other ways that the same sound might be spelled if there are any alternate spellings. For example,* more *might be spelled* m-o-r-e, m-o-a-r, *or* m-o-u-r.

award	hardship	pardon	hairy
border	harpoon	remarkable	marvelous
export	import	scarlet	wearable

■ Check each pair for progress and accuracy. Provide support and feedback.

JOB DESCRIPTION: WORDS WITH /är/, /âr/, or /ôr/

■ Review the /är/, /âr/, or /ôr/ sounds and their possible spellings. You may wish to point out that /âr/ can be spelled *ere*, as in *there*, or *air*, as in *pair*.

■ Have students identify words from "Jobs in Space" that have /är/, /âr/, or /ôr/ sounds: *their, there, care, force, board, are, arm, charge, where, carry*.

■ Then have students use words with /är/, /âr/, or /ôr/ sounds to write descriptions of jobs with which they are familiar. They should share the descriptions aloud.

Skills Focus ▶ Fluency

Objective Read with increasing prosody and accuracy at a rate of 100–110 WCPM
Materials • **Approaching Practice Book A,** page 25

MODEL EXPRESSIVE READING

Model reading the passage on **Practice Book A** page 25. Tell students to pay close attention to your pronunciation, especially of unfamiliar or difficult words. Then read aloud one sentence at a time, and have students repeat it. Listen carefully for accuracy. You may also wish to do a cloze reading in which students chime in on difficult words.

REPEATED READING

Have students practice reading the passage aloud as you circulate and provide constructive feedback. During independent time, partners can take turns reading the passage. One partner reads each sentence aloud, and the other repeats the sentence. Remind students to wait until the end of a sentence before they correct a mistake.

TIMED READING

At the end of the week, tell students to do a timed reading. They should

- place the passage from Practice Book A, page 25, face down.
- begin reading the passage aloud when you say "Go."
- stop reading the passage when you say "Stop."

As students read, note any miscues. Stop each after one minute. Help students record and graph the number of words they read correctly.

Constructive Feedback

Show students how to break unfamiliar or difficult words into syllables. Then model how to use phonics skills to pronounce the words. For example, *atmosphere* has three syllables: *at/mos/phere*. It's pronounced at//mōs//fîr/.

Skills Focus ▶ Vocabulary

Objective Apply vocabulary word meanings
Materials • **Vocabulary Cards** • **Transparencies 4a and 4b**

VOCABULARY WORDS

Display the **Vocabulary Cards** for this week's words: *function, adjusted, disasters, environment, mission, maze, zone, gravity*. Review the words as they are used in "Jobs in Space" on **Transparencies 4a** and **4b** and have students circle any synonyms, anyonyms, or other context clues. Invite students to create word association lists for each of these words. Turn this activity into a game by giving students thirty seconds for each vocabulary word and having them write as many related words as possible.

function
adjusted
maze
zone
environment

⭐ **Approaching Practice Book A,** page 25

As I read, I will pay attention to pronunciation.

Space is very different than Earth. There is no
9 atmosphere, so it is impossible to breathe. Earth's
17 atmosphere contains the oxygen that we need to live.
26 **Gravity** on the moon is much less than gravity on Earth.
37 By 1969 scientists knew that humans could survive in a
47 low-gravity **environment**, but they were not sure how it
57 would affect trying to walk on the moon. The moon has
68 some gravity, but it is much less than that of Earth. Would
80 the astronauts able to **function** there?
87   The astronauts were in constant communication with
94 Earth, but they were still alone. If anything went wrong, they
105 would have to fix it. 110

Comprehension Check

1. How is space different from Earth? **Compare and Contrast** Earth has an atmosphere that contains oxygen and gravity and space does not.

2. What is gravity like on the moon? **Main Ideas and Details** It is much less than that of Earth.

	Words Read	–	Number of Errors	=	Words Correct Score
First Read		–		=	
Second Read		–		=	

Vocabulary

Review last week's words **(quest, settings, reduce, buffet, major)** and this week's words **(mission, disasters, function, gravity, maze, adjusted, environment, zone)**. Have students look up each word in the Glossary.

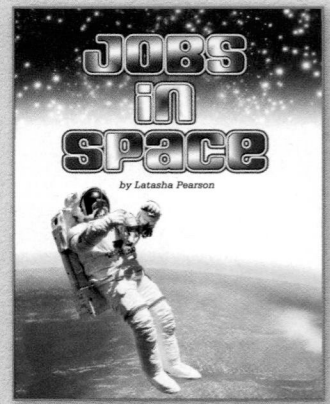

Student Book, or Transparencies 4a and 4b

ELL
Access for All

Use Technology Visit the Neil Armstrong Science Museum on the Web. Look for other links to photos of the American astronaut. Select a photograph that you like and write a list of words to describe the picture. Put two ideas together to make a sentence.

Skills Focus

Vocabulary

Objective Use context clues such as description and explanation for unfamiliar words
Materials • **Student Book** *Ultimate Field Trip 5*

CONTEXT CLUES: DESCRIPTION AND EXPLANATION

Help students locate each of the following words in *Ultimate Field Trip 5*: *simulators* (p. 97), *gyroscope* (p. 98), *nucleus*, (p. 100), and *tethered* (p. 101). Ask them to identify context clues, such as a description or explanation, that are helpful in figuring out the word meanings.

Skills Focus

Comprehension

Objective Identify main idea and details
Materials • **Student Book** "Jobs in Space" • **Transparencies 4a and 4b**

STRATEGY
GENERATE QUESTIONS

Remind students that good readers generate questions as they read: *Do I understand what happened? Why did the author share this information?* By looking for answers, readers will better understand the text.

SKILL
SUMMARIZE

Explain/Model

■ To summarize, first identify the most important ideas and supporting details in a passage or selection.

■ Then restate those main ideas and details in your own words.

Display **Transparencies 4a** and **4b.** Reread the last paragraph of "Jobs in Space" and model how to summarize the main idea. Then have a volunteer underline details that support the main idea.

Think Aloud As I read this selection, I noticed that, after the opening, each paragraph tells about a different type of astronaut. Here's how I would sum up the main idea of the last paragraph: Educator astronauts are teachers whose main job is to inspire students.

Practice/Apply

Have students reread "Jobs in Space." Discuss these questions:

■ What are the main ideas? What important details support them?

■ How would you summarize the duties of each job discussed?

Leveled Reader Lesson

Objective Read to apply strategies and skills
Materials   • **Leveled Reader** *On the Moon* • **Student Book** *Ultimate Field Trip 5*

PREVIEW AND PREDICT

Discuss the cover and have students preview the introduction and first two chapters, including the illustrations. Ask students to predict what the selection will be about and to note any questions they have.

VOCABULARY WORDS

Before reading, review the vocabulary words as needed. As you read together, discuss how each word is used in context.

STRATEGY
GENERATE QUESTIONS

Remind students to generate questions as they read *On the Moon* to help them clarify meaning, locate information and answers to their questions, and understand the author's purpose for writing.

SKILL
SUMMARIZE

Summarizing the main idea of a paragraph, section of text, or book helps readers understand the most important point an author is making. The author may state the main idea directly or leave it unstated. Model summarizing the text on pages 2 and 4.

Think Aloud The introduction tells me that in July 1969, the whole world watched as America's astronauts landed on the moon. The first paragraph of Chapter 1 tells me that the Soviet Union sent the first person into space and President Kennedy wanted the United States to put the first man on the moon. I need to keep reading, summarizing as I go, to understand how the astronauts got to the moon and made history.

READ AND RESPOND

Finish reading *On the Moon* with students. Discuss the challenges and rewards of space exploration and students' personal responses to the selection.

MAKE CONNECTIONS ACROSS TEXTS

Invite students to compare *On the Moon* and *Ultimate Field Trip 5*.

■ How are the experiences students have in *Ultimate Field Trip 5* a realistic simulation of what astronauts go through? Use what you learned in *On the Moon* to help you answer the question. Review both selections to summarize why students and astronauts enjoy their experiences.

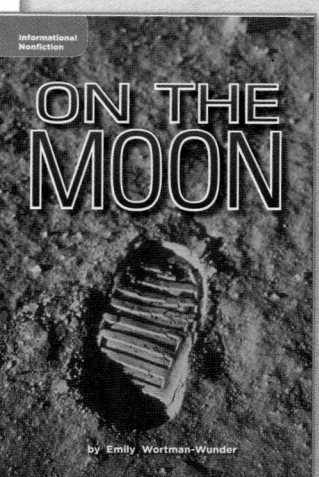

Leveled Reader

ELL Access for All

Building Background
There is a very famous quotation from Apollo 11 astronaut Neil Armstrong, the first person to walk on the moon: "That's one small step for (a) man, one giant leap for mankind." Discuss the meaning of this quotation and why it may explain the picture on the book cover.

On Level Options

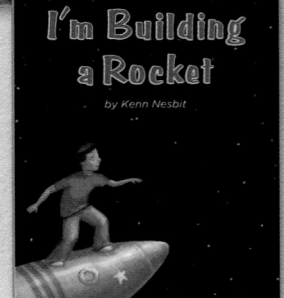

Student Book

Student Book

Skills Focus ▶ Vocabulary

Objective	Use vocabulary words and context clues
Materials	• **Student Book** *Ultimate Field Trip 5* • **Vocabulary Cards**

VOCABULARY WORDS

Review this week's words using the Vocabulary Cards. Tell students to imagine they are members of a team training to be astronauts. Have them write two paragraphs describing the experience. Instruct students to use and underline all of the vocabulary words. When students have finished, call on volunteers to read their descriptions aloud.

CONTEXT CLUES: DESCRIPTION OR EXPLANATION

Review with students that context clues can include descriptions or explanations that will help them determine the meanings of unfamiliar words. Have student pairs identify context clues for each of these words in *Ultimate Field Trip 5*: *simulators* (p. 97), *gyroscope* (p. 98), *nucleus,* (p. 100), and *tethered* (p. 101).

Skills Focus ▶ Literary Elements

Objective	Write a poem with a rhyme scheme and rhythm
Materials	• **Student Book** "I'm Building a Rocket"

RHYME SCHEME AND RHYTHM

Discuss the rhyme scheme and rhythm in "I'm Building a Rocket." Then have each student write an original poem about a time when he or she built something. Students should create a rhyme scheme for their poems.

Skills Focus ▶ Fluency

Objective	Read accurately with prosody at a rate of 100–120 WCPM
Materials	• **On Level Practice Book O,** p. 25

REPEATED READING

Model reading aloud the entire passage on page 25 of **Practice Book O.** Emphasize that slowly breaking down unfamiliar words into syllables helps students pronounce words correctly. Then read one sentence at a time, and have students read each sentence back chorally. Listen for accuracy.

During independent reading time, partners can take turns reading. Have students practice slowly breaking unfamiliar words into syllables.

Timed Reading At the end of the week, have students read the passage for one minute and record their reading rate.

On Level Practice Book O, page 25

As I read, I will pay attention to pronunciation.

	People on Earth have long looked at Mars with excitement
10	and fear. Mars is Earth's nearest neighbor and has an
20	environment similar to Earth's in many ways. The surface
29	of Mars is much like the surface of parts of Earth, dry and
42	hard. Temperatures on Mars range from −225° to 60°
49	Fahrenheit (-140° to 25° Celsius). There are important
55	differences, too. The atmosphere of Mars is almost all carbon
65	dioxide and doesn't have enough oxygen to support humans.
74	On Mars, **gravity,** the force that pulls us toward the ground,
85	is not as strong as gravity on Earth.
93	However, of all the planets in the solar system, Mars
103	is the one that seems most possible for humans to visit and
115	even colonize. It is close to us, and it has a surface and
128	surface temperature most similar to that of Earth. 136

Comprehension Check

1. Why does Mars seem like the most likely planet for humans to visit? **Main Idea and Details** Mars is the closest planet to Earth, and it has temperatures similar to Earth's temperatures.
2. What are some differences between Earth and Mars? **Compare and Contrast** Mars has less gravity and less oxygen than Earth.

	Words Read	−	Number of Errors	=	Words Correct Score
First Read		−		=	
Second Read		−		=	

Leveled Reader Lesson

Objective   Read to apply strategies and skills
Materials   • **Leveled Reader** *Mission to Mars*

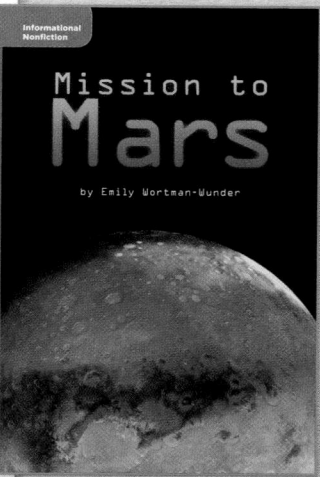

Leveled Reader

PREVIEW AND PREDICT

Have students preview *Mission to Mars* and generate questions before reading to set purposes.

- What does the title suggest about the selection?

- Look at the headings and boldfaced words. What information in the story seems important?

- Look at the information in the side columns and boxes. What additional information do these text features contain?

VOCABULARY WORDS

As they read *Mission to Mars,* ask students to point out the vocabulary words as they appear. Discuss how each word is used.

STRATEGY

GENERATE QUESTIONS

Ask a volunteer to explain why generating questions can be a helpful reading strategy.

SKILL

SUMMARIZE

- A summary is a short statement of the most significant ideas in a passage or selection.

- It includes the main ideas and the most important details.

Students should add this information to Summary Charts as they read.

READ AND RESPOND

Read the Introduction. Pause to discuss the main ideas. At the end of Chapter 1, have students fill in the Summary Charts. Have students identify which information is important in the selection and which information is less important. Repeat this process when students complete the book. Also have students share questions and personal responses.

MAKE CONNECTIONS ACROSS TEXTS

Invite students to summarize *Mission to Mars* and *Ultimate Field Trip 5.* Then have students make connections between the texts. They should give an example from each of the texts when answering the following questions.

- Why is it important that space explorers study hard and be well trained?

- What is some of the research or activities that astronauts and NASA scientists perform?

ELL
Leveled Reader
Go to pages
111U–111V.

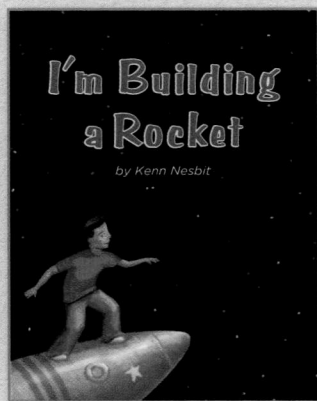

Student Book

Skills Focus ▶ Vocabulary

Objective   Generate safety rules using vocabulary words

EXTEND VOCABULARY

Invite students to write safety rules that people should follow when living on a space station. Tell them to include as many of the vocabulary words as they can in their lists of rules, leaving a blank for each word. Then have students trade lists and use context clues to fill in the missing words.

Skills Focus ▶ Literary Elements

Objective   Write a poem with a rhyme scheme and rhythm
Materials   • **Student Book** "I'm Building a Rocket"

RHYME SCHEME AND RHYTHM

Point out that rhyme scheme and rhythm create a musical quality in a poem. Ask a volunteer to read aloud "I'm Building a Rocket" on **Student Book** page 108. Ask students to be aware of the sounds of language and how the rhyme scheme and rhythm create a musical effect. Explain how these elements suggest a tempo or a melody, a verse and a chorus, or some other musical feature.

Then have each student write an original poem about a time when he or she built something. Students should create both a rhyme scheme and a rhythm for their poems. Stage a poetry reading for interested volunteers.

Skills Focus ▶ Fluency

Objective   Read fluently with accuracy at 110–120 WCPM
Materials   • **Beyond Practice Book B,** page 25

REPEATED READING

Model reading the passage on page 25 of **Practice Book B.** Emphasize that breaking unfamiliar words into syllables helps students pronounce the words correctly. Then read one sentence at a time, and listen for accuracy as students read each sentence back chorally.

During independent reading time, partners can take turns reading the passage. Circulate and provide constructive feedback. Tell students to practice breaking unfamiliar words into syllables. Remind students to wait until their partner reaches the next punctuation mark before they correct a mistake. As an extension students can audiotape themselves and then offer critiques. You may also wish to have students do a timed reading at the end of the week.

◆ **Beyond Practice Book B, page 25**

As I read, I will pay attention to pronunciation.

	When a space shuttle crew's job at the ISS is done, it undocks, fires
14	its thrusters, and heads back to Earth. Three crewmembers are left on
26	the ISS to work for the next four to six months.
37	One of the most important things the astronauts do is run
48	experiments. The ISS is running long-term studies on how human
58	bodies behave in a low **gravity environment**. This might involve
68	researching how people sleep. It might mean taking frequent blood
78	samples. These samples can show how a crewmember's body
87	chemistry is changing or how his or her immune system is responding
99	to living in a very enclosed space. The experiments also might involve
111	measuring a crewmember's bone density.
116	Another set of important experiments on the ISS studies how
126	various materials act in space. The results of these studies will help us
139	make better metals and materials to use in space.
148	While some astronauts are gathering data, others are working on
158	computers to record the results of their studies. 166

Comprehension Check

1. What are some experiments the astronauts run on the ISS? **Summarize** how people sleep, how immune system responds in a closed space, measuring bone density
2. How do the astronauts know if the experiments are successful or not? **Main Idea and Details** while some gather data, others record the results on computers

	Words Read	−	Number of Errors	=	Words Correct Score
First Read		−		=	
Second Read		−		=	

Leveled Reader Lesson

Objective   Read to apply strategies and skills
Materials   • **Leveled Reader** *Space Station*

PREVIEW AND PREDICT

Have students preview *Space Station*, predict topics the book might cover, and set a purpose for reading. Review vocabulary words as necessary.

SKILL
SUMMARIZE

Ask a volunteer to explain how identifying main ideas and important details improves both a reader's comprehension and helps them to summarize a text. Explain that students will read *Space Station* and identify main ideas and important details for summary charts.

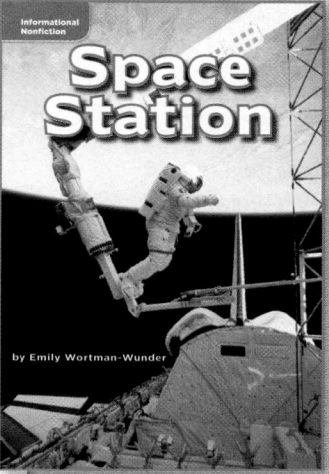

Leveled Reader

READ AND RESPOND

As they read, have students summarize major points in the book and fill in their Summary Charts. Then have partners compare charts and discuss the main idea and relevant details they would use to summarize the selection. Ask partners to explain how their charts were different.

VOCABULARY WORDS

Discuss the meanings of the vocabulary words. Ask questions such as, *What would a typical day be like on the space station?* Then have students identify the vocabulary words as used in the selection. As an extension, have them write questions about the selection using all the words.

Skills Focus

Self-Selected Reading

Objective   Read independently to summarize the main idea and identify supporting details of a text

Materials   • Leveled Readers and informational trade books at students' reading level

READ AND SUMMARIZE

Invite students to summarize *Space Station* and *Ultimate Field Trip 5*. Ask which events or details they might leave out if they needed to shorten each story. Then, in a literature circle, have students explain how they decided which ideas and details to keep and which to delete.

Next, invite students to choose nonfiction or science books for independent reading. After reading, have students summarize the main ideas of the texts and identify the details that support them. Ask them to create and share a lesson for a younger student about how to use the skill of summarizing nonfiction texts.

ELL   **Access for All**

Use Picture Clues Visit the NASA Website to review photos from and information about the International Space Station. Write about one new fact you have learned and add it to the Summary Chart.

Academic Language

Throughout the week the English language learners in your class will need help in building their understanding of the academic language used in daily instruction and assessment instruments. The following strategies will help to increase their language proficiency and comprehension of content and instructional words.

LOG ON Technology

Oral Language For oral vocabulary development, go to **www.macmillanmh.com**

Strategies to Reinforce Academic Language

■ **Use Context** Academic language used by the teacher (see chart below) should be explained in the context of the task during Whole Group. You may use gestures, expressions, and visuals to support meaning.

■ **Use Visuals** Use charts, transparencies, and graphic organizers to explain key labels to help students understand classroom language.

■ **Model** Demonstrate the task using academic language in order for students to understand instruction.

Academic Language Used in Whole Group Instruction

Content/Theme Words	Skill/Strategy Words	Writing/Grammar Words
NASA (p. 90)	summarize (p. 107B)	friendly letter (p. 110)
satellites (p. 90)	main idea (p. 107B)	important details (p. 110)
astronaut (p. 90)	supporting details (p. 107B)	compound sentence (p. 111I)
science fiction (p. 91)	rhyme scheme (p. 108)	complex sentence (p. 111I)
technology (p. 91)	rhythm (p. 108)	colon (p. 111J)
orbit (p. 91)	stanza (p. 108)	comma (p. 111J)

ELL Reader Lesson

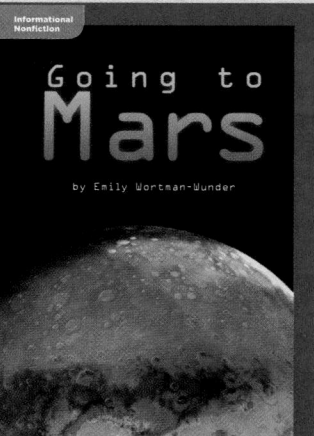

Informational Nonfiction

Going to Mars

by Emily Wortman-Wunder

Before Reading

DEVELOP ORAL LANGUAGE

Build Background *What do you know about space exploration?* Brainstorm reasons for finding out what Mars is like and visiting it in the future.

Review Vocabulary Write the vocabulary and story support words on the board and discuss their meanings. Model using them. *Scientists are working on a* mission *to send people to Mars. Land that is* barren *is dry and rocky and has no plants.*

PREVIEW AND PREDICT

Point to the cover illustration and read the title aloud. *Would you be interested in being part of a* Going to Mars *mission? Why or why not?* Preview the table of contents and elicit predictions. Have students point out details that show this is a nonfiction book.

Set a Purpose for Reading Show the Summary Chart and remind students they have used this chart before. Ask them to do a similar chart to record the most important information and then write a summary.

During Reading

Choose from among the differentiated strategies to support students' reading at all levels of language acquisition.

Beginning	**Intermediate**	**Advanced**
Shared Reading Model summarizing the main ideas as you read. *Why are people interested in Mars?* Check students' comprehension and use vocabulary and support words.	**Read Together** Read through Chapter 1. Encourage students to summarize equipment used to explore Mars. Ask them to fill in their charts as you continue reading. Add information to the chart. Have students summarize using the chart.	**Independent Reading** Have students read the story. After reading each day, ask them to fill in their charts with the most important information. Then have them write a summary of the book, using their notes and pictures.

After Reading

Remind students to use the vocabulary and story words in their whole group activities.

Objective

• To apply vocabulary and comprehension skills

Materials

• ELL Leveled Reader

5-Day Planner	
DAY 1	• Academic Language
	• Oral Language and Vocabulary Review
DAY 2	• Academic Language
	• ELL Leveled Reader
DAY 3	• Academic Language
	• ELL Leveled Reader
DAY 4	• Academic Language
	• ELL Leveled Reader
DAY 5	• Academic Language
	• ELL Leveled Reader Comprehension Check and Literacy Activities

ELL Teacher's Guide for students who need additional instruction

Weekly Literature

Weekly Theme: Rescue Dogs

Week At A Glance

Whole Group

VOCABULARY
variety, transformed, celebration, moistened, fragrance, cooperation, canceled, theory

Use a Thesaurus/Synonyms

COMPREHENSION
Strategy: Generate Questions
Skill: Cause and Effect

WRITING
Personal Narrative

Science Link

Life Science
Animal Diversity

Small Group Options

Differentiated Instruction for Tested Skills

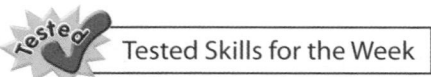
Tested Skills for the Week

Main Selection
Genre Fantasy

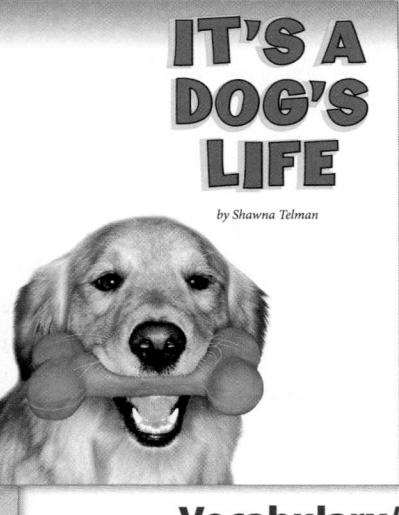

Vocabulary/ Comprehension

Science Link
Genre Nonfiction Article

Read-Aloud Anthology
• Listening Comprehension
• Readers' Theater

112A

Leveled Readers

 AUDIO CD

GR Levels Q–V

Genre Realistic Fiction

- Same Theme
- Same Vocabulary
- Same Comprehension Skills

It's Fun When Sam Listens
by Katherine Talmadge Sallé
illustrated by Chi Chung

Q

Approaching Level

THE WAG BRIGADE
by Katherine Talmadge Sallé
illustrated by Chi Chung

S

On Level

RUSTY to the Rescue!
by Katherine Talmadge Sallé
illustrated by Chi Chung

V

Beyond Level

AND FRED
by Katherine Talmadge Sallé
illustrated by Chi Chung

English Language Leveled Reader

On Level Reader sheltered for English Language Learner

ELL Teacher's Guide also available

Also Available
LEVELED READER PROGRAM

CLASSROOM LIBRARY

Genre Expository Nonficton

The Snake Scientist

Approaching

ULTIMATE FIELD TRIP 5

On Level

Antarctic Journal

Beyond

Trade books to apply Comprehension Skills

INTERVENTION ANTHOLOGY

- Phonics and Decoding
- Comprehension
- Vocabulary

Also available, *Reading Triumphs*, Intervention Program

LEVELED PRACTICE

Practice Book A

Approaching

Practice Book O

On Level

Practice Book B

Beyond

ELL Practice and Assessment

ELL

HOME-SCHOOL CONNECTION

- Family letters in English and Spanish
- Take-Home Stories

Technology

ONLINE INSTRUCTION
www.macmillanmh.com

AUDIO CD
- Listening Library
- Fluency Solutions

CD ROM
- Vocabulary PuzzleMaker

Suggested Lesson Plan

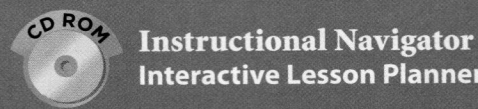

Instructional Navigator
Interactive Lesson Planner

Integrated **ELL** Support Every Day

Pipiolo and the Roof Dogs, 116–131

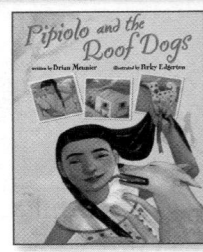

Leveled Readers

Whole Group

ORAL LANGUAGE
- **Listening**
- **Speaking**
- **Viewing**

WORD STUDY
- **Vocabulary**
- **Phonics/Decoding**

READING

- **Develop Comprehension**

- **Fluency**

LANGUAGE ARTS
- **Writing**

- **Grammar**

- **Spelling**

ASSESSMENT
- **Informal/Formal**

Turn the Page for
Small Group Lesson Plan

Day 1

Listening/Speaking/Viewing

? Focus Question What abilities do dogs have that make them useful for rescue work?
Build Background, 112
Read Aloud: "Barry: The Dog Who Saved People," 113

Vocabulary
variety, transformed, celebration, moistened, fragrance, cooperation, canceled, theory, 114
Practice Book A-O-B, 29

Strategy: Use a Thesaurus/Synonyms, 115

Read "It's a Dog's Life," 114–115

Student Book

Comprehension, 115A–115B
Strategy: Generate Questions
Skill: Cause and Effect
Practice Book A-O-B, 30

Fluency Model Fluency, 113
Partner Reading, 112I

Writing
Daily Writing Prompt: Pipiolo was an amazing dog. Write a brief tall tale about an amazing dog that rescues someone.
Personal Narrative, 138–139B

Grammar Daily Language Activities, 139I
Run-on Sentences, 139I
Grammar Practice Book, 25

Spelling
Pretest: Words with /ûr/ and /îr/, 139G
Spelling Practice Book, 25–26

Quick Check Vocabulary, 114

Comprehension, 115B

Differentiated Instruction 139M–139V

Day 2

Listening/Speaking

? Focus Question How does Pipiolo change the lives of the roof dogs?

Vocabulary
Review Vocabulary Words, 116

Phonics
Decode Words with *r*-Controlled Vowels, 139E
Practice Book A-O-B, 35

Read *Pipiolo and the Roof Dogs,* 116–131

Student Book

Comprehension, 116–133
Strategy: Generate Questions
Skill: Cause and Effect
Practice Book A-O-B, 31

Fluency Partner Reading, 112I

Writing
Daily Writing Prompt: Write a diary entry from the point of view of a roof dog. How might the dog feel and what would it see from its roof?
Personal Narrative, 138–139B

Grammar Daily Language Activities, 139I
Run-on Sentences, 139I
Grammar Practice Book, 26

Spelling
Words with /ûr/ and /îr/, 139G
Spelling Practice Book, 27

Quick Check Comprehension: 125, 131

Phonics, 139E

Differentiated Instruction 139M–139V

Skills/Strategies

Vocabulary	Comprehension	Writing
Vocabulary Words Use a Thesaurus/ Synonyms	**Strategy:** Generate Questions **Skill:** Cause and Effect	Personal Narrative

Turn the Page for
Small Group
Options

Day 3

Listening/Speaking

❓**Focus Question** Describe the similarities and differences between Sparky and Pipiolo's jobs. Use details from both stories to support your answer.

Summarize, 133

Vocabulary

Review Words in Context, 139C

**Strategy:** Use a Thesaurus/Synonyms, 139D
Practice Book A-O-B, 34

Phonics Decode Multisyllabic Words, 139E

Read *Pipiolo and the Roof Dogs*, 116–131

Comprehension

Comprehension Check, 133
Maintain Skill: Plot, 133B

Student Book

Fluency Repeated Reading, 133A
Practice Book A-O-B, 32

Writing

Daily Writing Prompt: Write a newspaper article about a dog that rescued someone. Answer the questions *who, what, when, where, why* and *how*.

Writer's Craft: Unimportant Details, 139A
Personal Narrative, 138–139B

Grammar Daily Language Activities, 139I
Correcting Fragments, 139J
Grammar Practice Book, 27

Spelling

Words with /ûr/ and /îr/, 139H
Spelling Practice Book, 28

Quick Check Fluency, 133A

Differentiated Instruction 139M–139V

Day 4

Listening/Speaking/Viewing

❓**Focus Question** What characteristics do Pipiolo and a SAR dog have in common? 135

Media Literacy: Media Events, 129
Expand Vocabulary: Dogs to the Rescue, 139F

Vocabulary

Content Vocabulary: *relays, characteristics, stamina, retrieve,* 134
Synonyms, 139F
Apply Vocabulary to Writing, 139F

Read "Doggone Work," 134–137

Comprehension

Informational Text:
Social Studies

Text Feature: Charts, 134
Practice Book A-O-B, 33

Student Book

Fluency Partner Reading, 112I

Writing

Daily Writing Prompt: Write a poem about Pipiolo or another dog, fictional or real, that acted heroically.

Writing Trait: Word Choice, 139B
Personal Narrative, 138–139B

Grammar Daily Language Activities, 139I
Run-on Sentences, 139J
Grammar Practice Book, 28

Spelling

Words with /ûr/ and /îr/, 139H
Spelling Practice Book, 29

Quick Check Vocabulary, 139D

Differentiated Instruction 139M–139V

Day 5
Review and Assess

Listening/Speaking/Viewing

❓**Focus Question** Compare how the actions of the dogs in this week's selections help others.

Speaking and Listening Strategies, 139A

Vocabulary

Spiral Review: Vocabulary Game, 139F

Read Self-Selected Reading, 112I

Comprehension

Connect and Compare, 137

Student Book

Fluency Partner Reading, 112I
Practice, 133A

Writing

Daily Writing Prompt: If you were interviewing someone who was saved from a burning building by a dog or other animal, what questions would you ask?

Personal Narrative, 138–139B

Grammar Daily Language Activities, 139I
Run-on Sentences, 139J
Grammar Practice Book, 29–30

Spelling

Posttest, 139H
Spelling Practice Book, 30

Weekly Assessment, 53–67

Differentiated Instruction 139M–139V

Pipiolo and the Roof Dogs 112D

Differentiated Instruction

What do I do in small groups?

Teacher-Led Small Groups

Literacy Workstations

Independent Activities

Skills Focus ▶ Use your **Quick Check** observations to guide additional instruction and practice.

Phonics
Decode Words with /ûr/ and /îr/

 Vocabulary Words
celebration, fragrance, variety, cooperation, transformed, moistened, canceled, theory
Strategy: Thesaurus/Synonyms

Comprehension
 Strategy: Generate Questions
Skill: Cause and Effect

 Fluency

Suggested Lesson Plan

 Instructional Navigator
Interactive Lesson Planner

	Day 1	**Day 2**
Approaching Level • **Additional Instruction/Practice** • **Tier 2 Instruction**	Fluency, 139N Vocabulary, 139N Comprehension, 139O **ELL** Graphic Organizer, 139O 	Phonics, 139M Vocabulary, 139O Leveled Reader Lesson, 139P • Vocabulary • Comprehension 
On Level • **Practice**	Vocabulary, 139Q Leveled Reader Lesson, 139R • Comprehension **ELL** Leveled Reader, 139U-139V 	Leveled Reader Lesson, 139R • Comprehension • Vocabulary 
Beyond Level • **Extend**	Vocabulary, 139S Leveled Reader Lesson, 139T • Comprehension 	Leveled Reader Lesson, 139T • Comprehension • Vocabulary 

For intensive intervention see **READING Triumphs**

112E

Small Group Options

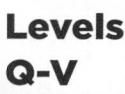

Apply skills and strategies while reading appropriate leveled books.

Levels Q-V

It's Fun When Sam Listens — Q

Approaching

THE WAG BRIGADE — S

On Level

RUSTY to the Rescue! — V

Beyond

MAI AND FRED

ELL

Additional Leveled Reader Resources

LOG ON

Leveled Reader Database
Go to **www.macmillanmh.com**

Search by

- Comprehension Skill
- Content Area
- Genre
- Text Feature

- Guided Reading Level
- Reading Recovery Level
- Lexile Score
- Benchmark Level

Subscription also available

Day 3

Phonics, 139M
Fluency, 139N
Vocabulary, 139O
Leveled Reader Lesson, 139P
- Comprehension

Fluency, 139Q
Vocabulary, 139Q
Leveled Reader Lesson, 139R
- Comprehension

Fluency, 139S
Vocabulary, 139S
Leveled Reader Lesson, 139T
- Comprehension

Day 4

Phonics, 139M
Leveled Reader Lesson, 139P
- Comprehension

Text Features, 139Q
Leveled Reader Lesson, 139R
- Comprehension

Text Features, 139S
Leveled Reader Lesson, 139T
- Comprehension
ELL Model Questions, 139S

Day 5

Fluency, 139N
Leveled Reader Lesson, 139P
- Make Connections
  Across Texts

Fluency, 139Q
Leveled Reader Lesson, 139R
- Make Connections
  Across Texts

Fluency, 139S
Self-Selected Reading, 139T

Managing the Class

What do I do with the rest of my class?

- Teacher-Led Small Groups
- Literacy Workstations
- Independent Activities

Class Management Tools

Includes:
- How-To Guides
- Rotation Chart
- Weekly Contracts

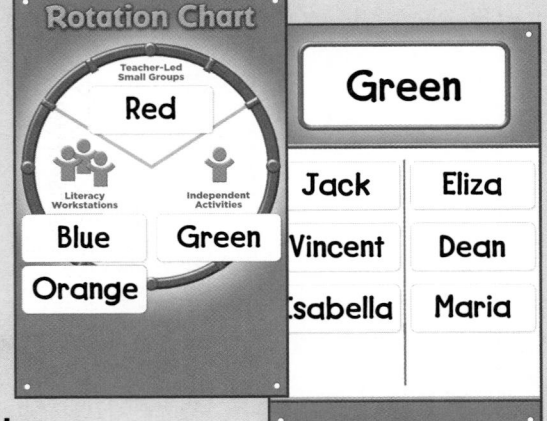

FOLDABLES™

Hands-on activities for reinforcing weekly skills.

Fish	Frogs
habitat	habitat
food	insects
prey	prey
enemies	enemies

Eight-Tab Foldable

Word	Synonym	Antonym	Prefix or Suffix
normal	typical	unusual	normally

Folded Foldable

Independent Activities

Leveled Readers

For Repeated Readings and Literacy Activities

Approaching

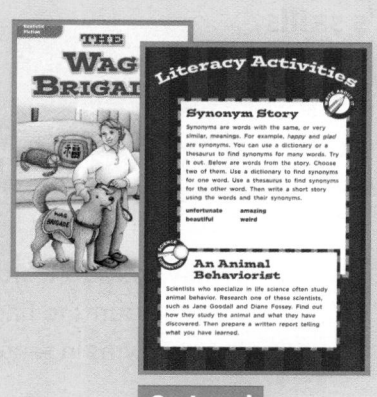

On Level

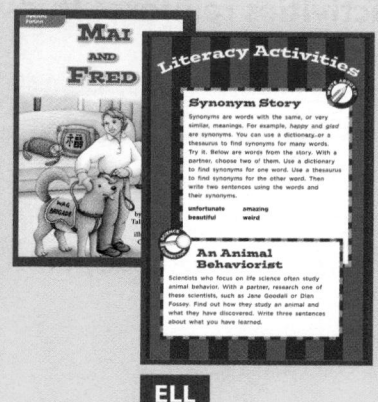

ELL

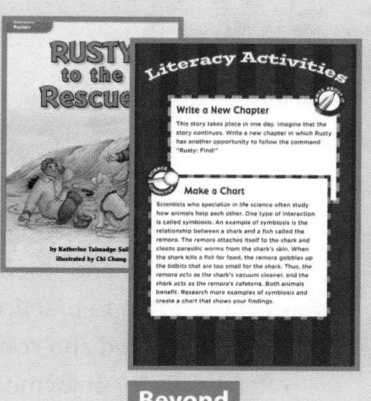

Beyond

LEVELED PRACTICE

Skills: Vocabulary (p. 29), Comprehension: Cause and Effect (p. 30), Graphic Organizer (p. 31), Fluency (p. 32), Text Features: Charts (p. 33), Vocabulary Strategy: Synonyms (p. 34), Phonics (p. 35)

Approaching

On Level

Beyond

ELL

Technology

 ONLINE INSTRUCTION www.macmillanmh.com

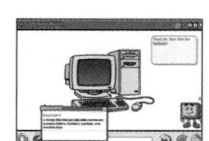

- Meet the Author/Illustrator
- Computer Literacy Lessons
- Research and Inquiry Activities

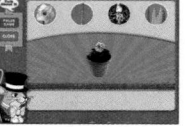

- Oral Language Activities
- Vocabulary and Spelling Activities
- Leveled Reader Database

 LISTENING LIBRARY
Recordings of selections
- Main Selections
- Leveled Readers
- ELL Readers
- Intervention Anthology

 FLUENCY SOLUTIONS
Recorded passages for modeling and practicing fluency

 **VOCABULARY PUZZLEMAKER**
Activities providing multiple exposures to vocabulary, spelling, and high-frequency words including crossword puzzles, word searches, and word jumbles

Turn the page for Literacy Workstations.

Managing the Class

Cross-Curricular Activities

All activities reinforce this week's skills.

📖 Reading

Objectives

- Read fluently and smoothly. Offer corrective feedback.
- Time reading to practice fluency.
- Read for speed and comprehension.
- Read daily for enjoyment.

🅰🅱 Word Study

Objectives

- Identify and sort words with /ûr/ and /îr/ sounds.
- Use a thesaurus to find synonyms.
- Use synonyms in sentences.

📖 Reading — Fluency
20 Minutes

- With a partner take turns reading aloud from Practice Book page 32.
- Read the selection until you both read smoothly.

Extension

- Offer each other corrective feedback. Encourage each other to read with understanding and expression.
- Time Your Reading: Listen to Audio CD.

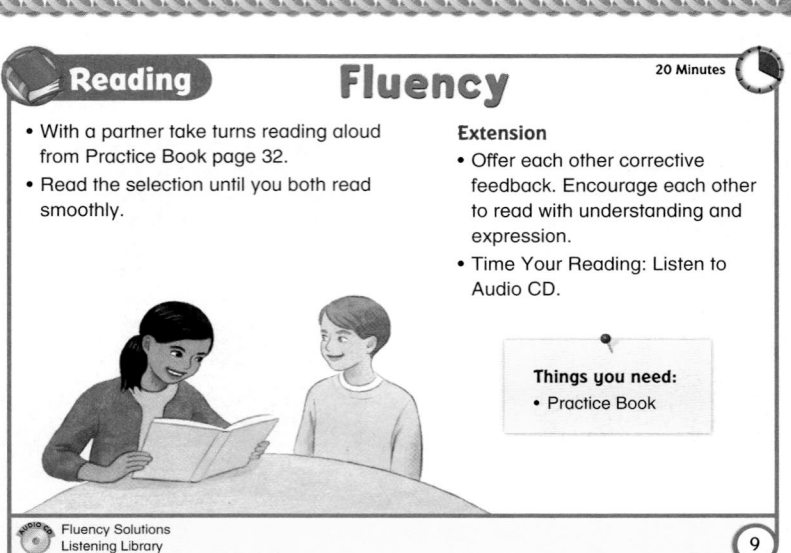

Things you need:
- Practice Book

Fluency Solutions Listening Library

9

🅰🅱 Word Study — Words with /ûr/ and /îr/
20 Minutes

- Use the dictionary to locate a variety of words that contain /ûr/ and /îr/ sounds. Some examples include *fur, word,* and *blur.* Try to find at least ten and write them in a list.

Extension

- With a partner combine your lists and write a rhyming poem, adding any other words you need for sense.
- Read the poem aloud together to another pair. See how many /ûr/ and /îr/ words each poem used.

A blur of fur

Things you need:
- index cards
- pencils or markers
- dictionary

For additional vocabulary and spelling games, go to www.macmillanmh.com

9

📖 Reading — Independent Reading
20 Minutes

- At the library find a book with information about your favorite breed of dog.
- Set a timer and see how many words you can read in five minutes.
- Reset the timer and read the same passage again. Record how many more words you read the second time.

Extension

- Continue reading for three minutes.
- Check to see how much information you can recall by writing a brief summary.

Things you need:
- library book
- paper and pen
- timer

For more books about rescue dogs, go to the Author/Illustrator section at www.macmillanmh.com

10

🅰🅱 Word Study — Thesaurus: Synonyms
20 Minutes

- Use a thesaurus to find two synonyms each for the vocabulary words *variety* and *theory.*
- Look up the pronunciations, and write the words in sentences.

Extension

- Read your synonym sentences to a partner.
- Write out a conversation using the vocabulary words and their synonyms. Read the dialogue aloud to another pair.

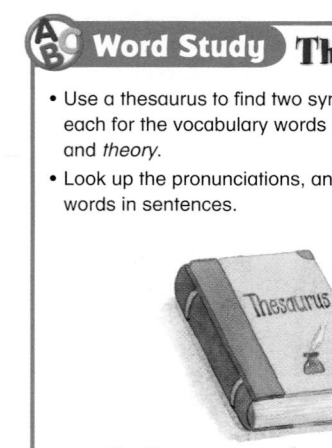

What's a synonym for *thesaurus?*

Things you need:
- paper and pen or pencil
- dictionary or thesaurus

For additional vocabulary and spelling games, go to www.macmillanmh.com/voc-spelling

Vocabulary PuzzleMaker

10

Literacy Workstations

Writing

Objectives
- Write a journal entry.
- Write a proclamation or award certificate.
- Write voluntarily for different purposes.
- Write in reading log and reflect on gains.

Writing — Journal Entry
20 Minutes

- Write a journal entry about a dog or other animal that has special skills.
- Use what you know from any experiences that you have had with dogs or other animals.

Extension
- Turn your journal entry into a personal narrative for a magazine.
- Illustrate your narrative.

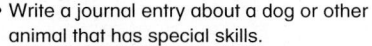

Things you need:
- paper and pen or pencil
- colored pencils or markers

9

Writing — Write a Citation
20 Minutes

- Write a proclamation or award certificate for a dog hero. Describe a situation in which humans were in danger and a dog saved them. The proclamation should include the specifics of the event, the dog's name, and what the dog did.

Extension
- Write a thank-you speech from the dog's point of view.

Things you need:
- paper and pen or pencil

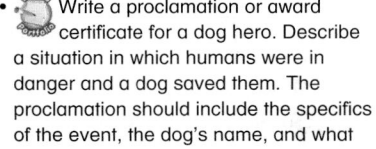

PROCLAMATION
Dog is a hero

10

Content Literacy

Objectives
- Research the needs of different types of dogs.
- Research and compare two breeds of dogs.
- Select the best source for a given purpose.

Science — Research a Dog
20 Minutes

- Research the type of dog that is best suited to the area in which you live. Base your choice on the temperature, weather, and the environment. List the special traits the dog needs to survive in your area.

Extension
- Research the type of dog that is best suited to your home. Consider whether there is a yard and its size, other pets, the other people in the home, and your family's habits or hobbies.

Retriever

German Shepherd   Terrier

Things you need:
- access to the Internet or library
- paper and pen or pencil

LOG ON — Internet Research and Inquiry Activity
Students can find more facts at www.macmillanmh.com

9

Social Studies — Compare Two Breeds
20 Minutes

- Research two breeds of dogs that you would consider owning, and make a chart of their special characteristics.
- Now list the positive and negative sides to owning each breed.

Extension
- Based on your research, write a summary paragraph about each dog, including which type of dog is best for you.

Dalmation (Yes)
Dalmation (No)

Things you need:
- access to the Internet or the library
- paper and pen or pencil

10

RESCUE DOGS

112

Prepare

ORAL LANGUAGE
- Build Background
- Read Aloud
- Expand Vocabulary

VOCABULARY

- **Teach Words in Context**
- **Thesaurus:** Synonyms

COMPREHENSION
- **Strategy:** Generate Questions
- **Skill:** Cause and Effect

SMALL GROUP OPTIONS
- Differentiated Instruction, pp. 139M–139V

Oral Language

Build Background

ACCESS PRIOR KNOWLEDGE

Share the following information:

Rescue dogs are trained to find people by tracking scents. Their excellent senses of smell and hearing make them more efficient than human searchers.

TALK ABOUT RESCUE DOGS

Discuss the weekly theme. Say:

Describe a situation where you have seen rescue dogs at work, either on TV or in real life.

 **FOCUS QUESTION** Ask a volunteer to read aloud "Talk About It" on **Student Book** page 113 and describe the photo.

- What do you think is happening?

- How does the dog in the photo seem different from a pet dog?

ENGLISH LANGUAGE LEARNERS Access for All

Beginning Develop Background Discuss the picture with students. Point to unknown items, name them, and have students repeat after you. Encourage students to say what they can about the picture.

Intermediate Develop Language Discuss what is happening in the picture, providing language as needed. Encourage students to express their ideas in complete sentences. Find out what they know about rescue dogs and their jobs. Ask, *How is a rescue dog different from a regular dog?* Help students make comparisons.

Advanced Build Language Skills Complete the Intermediate task. List the qualities rescue dogs must have and discuss why they are important. As students talk, restate what they say using more complex language structures.

112

🐾

Talk About It

In what situations do you hear about dogs coming to the rescue? What abilities do dogs have that make them useful for rescue work?

LOG ON Find out more about dogs at **www.macmillanmh.com**

113

Picture Prompt

Look at the picture and respond in writing. You can write a poem, a story, or a description, or use any other type of writing you like.

LOG ON Technology

For an extended lesson plan and Web site activities for **oral language development,** go to **www.macmillanmh.com**

Read Aloud Read "Barry: The Dog Who Saved People"

GENRE: Narrative Nonfiction
Review features of narrative nonfiction:

- a story or account about real people, things, or events

- told by a narrator   **Read Aloud** pages 33–38

LISTENING FOR A PURPOSE

Ask students to listen carefully for the way the author describes Barry as they read "Barry: The Dog Who Saved People" in the **Read-Aloud Anthology**. They should be prepared to describe Barry's actions and what he does to help people. Choose from among the teaching suggestions.

Fluency Ask students to listen carefully as you read aloud, paying attention to your phrasing, expression, and tone of voice.

RESPOND TO THE SELECTION

Discuss what a dog like Barry could do in students' communities. What are some ways he could help people?

Expand Vocabulary

Ask students to find three words in the story that describe Barry. Challenge students to think of synonyms for each of these words. Keep a list of all the words on the board.

Vocabulary

TEACH WORDS IN CONTEXT

Use the following routine:

Routine

Define: A **fragrance** is a sweet or pleasant smell.
Example: The fragrance of lilacs always makes me think of spring.
Ask: Tell about your favorite fragrance.
DESCRIPTION

- A **celebration** is a special event. Our school held a celebration when we won the national spelling bee. Tell about a celebration that you recently attended. **DESCRIPTION**

- If you have a **variety** of apples, you have different kinds of apples. Mom keeps a variety of healthful snacks. Tell what you think this famous quotation means: "Variety is the spice of life." **EXPLANATION**

- Something that is **moistened** is made slightly wet. The light rain moistened the ground. What is an antonym for the word *moistened?* **ANTONYM**

- **Cooperation** takes place when everyone works together on a task. Mr. Berman asked for the students' cooperation. How is cooperation similar to teamwork? **COMPARE AND CONTRAST**

- When something is **canceled**, it is called off. The game was canceled because many players were sick. Why might a bike race be canceled? **EXAMPLE**

- A **theory** is a possible explanation that has not been proven true. The doctor had a theory about what was making his patients sick. What is your theory about why dinosaurs became extinct? **EXPLANATION**

Vocabulary

variety	fragrance
transformed	cooperation
celebration	canceled
moistened	theory

Thesaurus

A **Thesaurus** is a tool that can help you find synonyms for a particular word. For example, the word *fragrance* may have the following synonyms listed: *aroma, perfume,* or *scent.*

114

- If something is **transformed**, it is changed. In fairy tales a frog is sometimes transformed into a handsome prince. How is a tadpole transformed into a frog? **EXPLANATION**

Quick Check

Do students understand word meanings?

During **Small Group Instruction**

If No → **Approaching Level** Vocabulary, p. 139N

If Yes → **On Level** Options, pp. 139Q–139R

Beyond Level Options, pp. 139S–139T

IT'S A DOG'S LIFE

by Shawna Telman

My name is Sparky and I work for Ms. Toni Graham. I am her in-home companion. My trainer calls what I do "work" but I think my job is fun! I especially enjoy the **variety** in my job: I do many different things for Ms. Toni every day. She says I have **transformed** her life. I have changed things so her daily routine is easier.

Ms. Toni suffers from an illness that makes her hands shake and causes her muscles to stiffen up. She has a hard time bending over. On a bad day, Ms. Toni can lose her balance and fall. Whenever she drops something, I pick it up for her. It's part of my job.

Another part of my job is to help Ms. Toni with her work. She has an office in her home. Last week she was preparing to mail invitations for some major **celebration** that will raise money for a charity. How did I help? I learned how to lick the flaps of envelopes. They needed to be **moistened**, so that they could seal shut. For once my slimy doggy tongue came in handy!

ELL

Reinforce Vocabulary
For the word *variety,* point to a poster or other object in the classroom that has a variety of colors. Discuss varieties of milk. Ask, *Do we have a variety of food in the cafeteria? Explain.* For *cooperation,* give specific examples of how students show cooperation in the classroom. Have students tell how they show cooperation.

Every afternoon I accompany Ms. Toni on a walk around town. Exercise is important for her health so we never miss a day. We often see a new sight or smell a new **fragrance** along our route. Ms. Toni rests when we get back. She needs my **cooperation** during this time. I help her by being very quiet. I stay by the front door and keep my eye on things. If Ms. Toni needs me, she rings a bell.

Every so often Ms. Toni can't sleep, so naptime is **canceled**. At these times she likes me to hang out and relax with her. The **theory** behind this is that petting me makes her feel calm. The idea makes sense. She talks to me and brushes me. This is one of the best parts of my job.

I am very lucky to be a part of Ms. Toni's life. People who have a hard time with day-to-day chores can become sad and lonely. Dogs like me help them feel happy.

Reread for **Comprehension**

Generate Questions
Cause and Effect

A Cause and Effect Chart helps you ask questions to figure out what happens in a story (an effect) and why it happens (a cause). Use your Cause and Effect Chart as you reread "It's a Dog's Life" to find several effects and their causes.

Cause → Effect
→
→
→
→

115

Vocabulary

STRATEGY
USE A THESAURUS

Synonyms Explain to students that a thesaurus is a collection of synonyms, or words that have similar meanings. For example, synonyms for *fragrance* include *odor, scent,* and *perfume.* Some synonyms make better choices than others, depending on the point the writer wants to get across.

Write: *The freshly painted store had a strange (fragrance, aroma, odor).* Ask students to choose the synonym that best suits the context of the sentence. (odor)

Read "It's a Dog's Life"

As you read "It's a Dog's Life" with students, ask them to identify clues that reveal the meanings of the highlighted words. Tell students they will read these words again in *Pipiolo and the Roof Dogs.*

On Level Practice Book O, page 29

Choose the vocabulary word that best replaces the underlined word or words. Write your choice on the line provided.

fragrance	celebration	variety	moistened
cooperation	canceled	theory	transformed

1. One possible explanation for the roof dogs' disappearance was that they flew off into the night. ____ **theory**

2. If you have a collection of different types of dogs, some will most likely be working dogs. ____ **variety**

3. When called into action, the search-and-rescue dog changed from a friendly pet into a life-saving hero. **transformed**

4. There is usually a joyful party at the animal shelter when a dog finds a new home. **celebration**

5. Most dogs can smell any odor or pleasant scent. ____ **fragrance**

6. With shared efforts, the dog and the park rangers found the lost camper. **cooperation**

7. Even when rain has dampened a scent trail, dogs with good noses will be able to follow the smell. **moistened**

8. The search was called off when a dog found the missing person in the woods. ____ **canceled**

 Approaching Practice Book A, page 29

Beyond Practice Book B, page 29

Objectives

- Generate questions
- Use academic language: *cause, effect*
- Identify cause and effect

Materials

- Comprehension Transparencies 5a, 5B
- Transparency 5, Graphic Organizer
- Leveled Practice Books, p. 30

Skills Trace

Cause and Effect

Introduce	115A-B
Practice / Apply	116–133; Leveled Practice, 30–31
Reteach / Review	139M–T, 569A–B, 570–573, 577M–T; Leveled Practice, 164–165
Assess	Weekly Tests; Unit 1, 5 Tests; Benchmark Tests A, B
Maintain	163B, 307B

ELL — Access for All

Academic Vocabulary
Write on the board *Cause and Effect*. Give examples, such as *If I drop a book, it'll make a loud noise. If you do good work, you will get good grades.* Write each cause (drop a book) and effect (make a loud noise) on the board. Have students work in pairs to provide more examples.

Reread for Comprehension

STRATEGY
GENERATE QUESTIONS

 Remind students that active readers always try to **generate questions** as they read. They ask such questions as: *What is the setting and how does it affect the events in the story? What problem does the main character have? Are the reasons for the characters' actions clear?* Looking for clues in the text that will answer these and other questions can help readers identify cause-and-effect situations in the plot and also arrive at a clear understanding of what happens in the story.

SKILL
IDENTIFY CAUSE AND EFFECT

- A **cause** is an event or action that makes something happen. An **effect** is what happens because of an event or action. Cause-and-effect relationships help make up the events in a story.

Transparency 5a

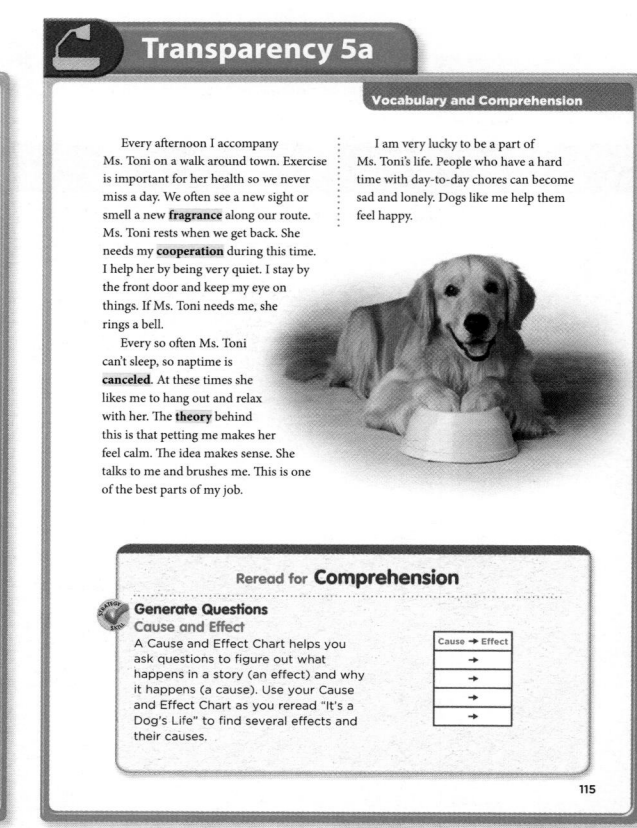

Transparency 5a

Student pages 114–115, available on Comprehension Transparencies 5a, 5b

- Ask, *"What happened?"* to find the effect. Ask, *"Why?"* to find the cause. Signal words, such as *because, so, since* and *as a result,* can help locate stated cause-and-effect relationships.

- Sometimes a cause-and-effect relationship has no signal words. Then it is implied. Making a Cause and Effect Chart can help clarify cause-and-effect situations that the author does not directly state.

MODEL

Read the second paragraph of "It's a Dog's Life" from **Student Book** page 114.

Think Aloud I understand that Sparky is a dog that works for Ms. Toni. When Ms. Toni needs help, Sparky reacts. For example, Ms. Toni might drop a pen. This causes Sparky to pick up the pen. Ms. Toni's action is the cause, and Sparky's reaction is the effect.

GUIDED PRACTICE

Display **Transparency 5.**

- Begin the Cause and Effect Chart with the cause *(Ms. Toni drops things.)* and the effect. *(Sparky picks up the things that Ms. Toni drops.)*

- Fill in the next item together. Help students identify the things that Ms. Toni does that cause Sparky to act.

APPLY

Have students reread the remainder of "It's a Dog's Life" and complete the Cause and Effect Chart. Have them tell whether the cause-and-effect relationship is stated or implied. Ask students why Sparky feels like a lucky dog.

 Transparency 5

Cause	→	Effect
Ms. Toni drops things.	→	Sparky picks up the things that Ms. Toni drops.
Ms. Toni prepares invitations.	→	Sparky licks the envelopes.
Ms. Toni goes for a walk downtown.	→	Sparky accompanies her.
Ms. Toni takes a nap.	→	Sparky is quiet.
Ms. Toni can't sleep.	→	Ms. Toni pets and brushes Sparky.

Graphic Organizer 5

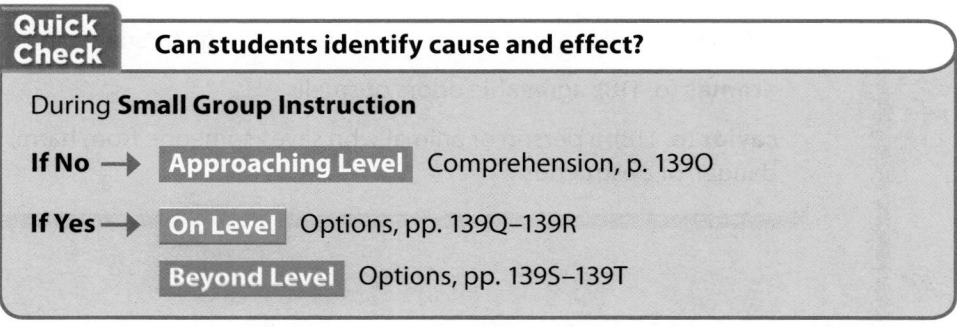

On Level Practice Book O, page 30

A **cause** is the reason why something happens. An **effect** is the result, or what happens. Many story events are connected through cause-and-effect relationships. Signal words such as *because, so, as a result* help readers identify cause-and-effect relationships.

Read the passage. On the lines below, write the most likely cause or effect. Possible responses provided.

Sherri's collie, Hap, was a talented herding dog. Hap's job was to run out to the field and gather the sheep every morning and evening. Hap nudged the sheep to get them to move.

One evening Hap ran up to Sherri, barking wildly and running in circles. Sherri grabbed her coat and ran after the dog. Hap led Sherri out to the field. None of the sheep were moving. Sherri followed Hap to the edge of a deep hole. "Now I see what's wrong," Sherri said. She slid down into the hole next to a little lamb that couldn't get out. "Good job, Hap," she said. Sherri carried the frightened creature out of the hole.

Sherri released the lamb back into the herd. The sheep started to move, and Hap urged them along. Now everyone would go home together.

1. Cause: Hap nudged the sheep.
   Effect: The sheep walked from the field to the ranch.
2. Cause: Hap barked wildly and ran in circles.
   Effect: Sherri grabbed her coat and ran.
3. Cause: Hap ran to the hole.
   Effect: Sherri found the lamb.
4. Cause: Sherri returned the lamb to the herd.
   Effect: The sheep finally started to move.

Approaching Practice Book A, page 30

Beyond Practice Book B, page 30

Quick Check | **Can students identify cause and effect?**

During **Small Group Instruction**

If No → | Approaching Level | Comprehension, p. 139O

If Yes → | On Level | Options, pp. 139Q–139R

| Beyond Level | Options, pp. 139S–139T

Read

MAIN SELECTION
- *Pipiolo and the Roof Dogs*

- **Skill:** Cause and Effect

PAIRED SELECTION
- "Doggone Work"
- **Text Feature:** Chart

SMALL GROUP OPTIONS
- Differentiated Instruction, pp. 139M–139V

Comprehension

GENRE: FANTASY

Have students read the definition of fantasy on **Student Book** page 116. As they read, students should look for events that could not really happen in real life.

STRATEGY
GENERATE QUESTIONS

Remind students that generating questions as they read can help them clarify meaning, understand the author's purpose for writing, or locate a specific answer in the text.

SKILL
CAUSE AND EFFECT

Cause-and-effect relationships help make up the events of a story. Often one event or action in the plot will lead directly to another event or action. A cause-and-effect relationship can be stated or implied.

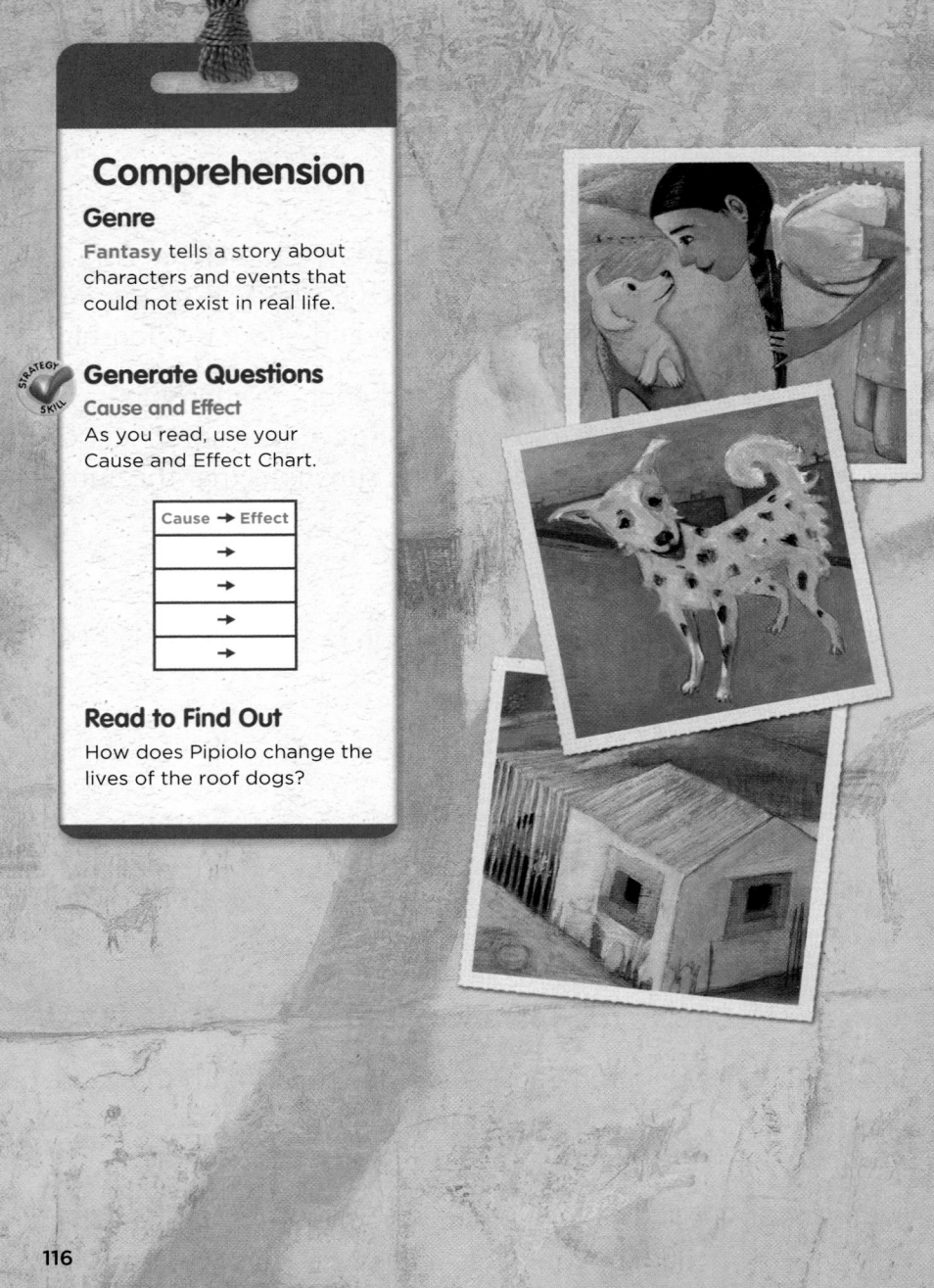

Comprehension

Genre

Fantasy tells a story about characters and events that could not exist in real life.

Generate Questions

Cause and Effect
As you read, use your Cause and Effect Chart.

Cause → Effect	
	→
	→
	→
	→

Read to Find Out

How does Pipiolo change the lives of the roof dogs?

116

Vocabulary

Vocabulary Words Review the tested vocabulary words: **canceled, celebration, cooperation, fragrance, moistened, theory, transformed** and **variety.**

Story Words Students may find these words difficult. Pronounce the words and define the meanings as necessary.

adobe (p. 118): sun-dried brick, used as a building material

aromas (p. 118): agreeable odors or smells

savior (p. 118): a person or animal who saves someone from harm, danger, or destruction

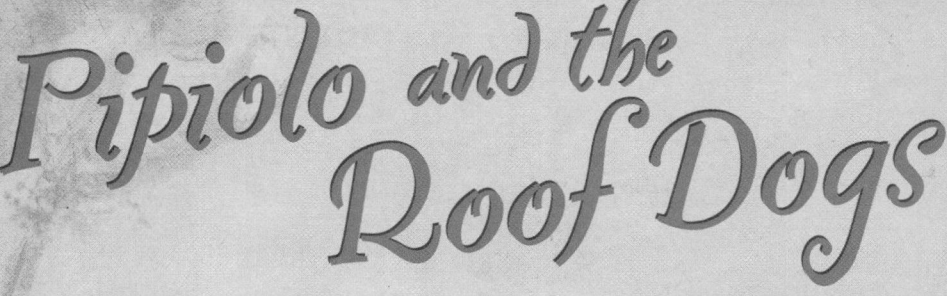

Pipiolo and the Roof Dogs

written by **Brian Meunier**   illustrated by **Perky Edgerton**

The village of San Pablo Etla is on the edge of a wide valley in southern Mexico. My father built our house on the mountainside overlooking the village. From there I can see the whole valley, the distant villages, and every house in San Pablo.

117

Read Together	Read Independently
If your students need support to read the Main Selection, use the prompts to guide comprehension and model how to complete the graphic organizer.	If your students can read the Main Selection independently, have them read and complete the graphic organizer. Remind them to set and modify purposes for reading and to use them to set and adjust their reading rate.

If your students need an alternate selection, choose the **Leveled Readers** that match their instructional level.

Technology

Story available on **Listening Library Audio CD**

Preview and Predict

Ask students to read the title, preview the illustrations, generate a theory or hypothesis based on prior knowledge, and note questions and predictions about the story. Have students write about their predictions and anything else they want to know about the selection.

Set Purposes

FOCUS QUESTION Discuss the "Read to Find Out" question on page 116. Remind students to look for the answer. Point out the Cause and Effect Chart in the Student Book and on **Practice Book** page 31. Students will use the chart to keep track of cause-and-effect situations.

Read *Pipiolo and the Roof Dogs*

Use the questions and Think Alouds for additional instruction to support the comprehension strategy and skill.

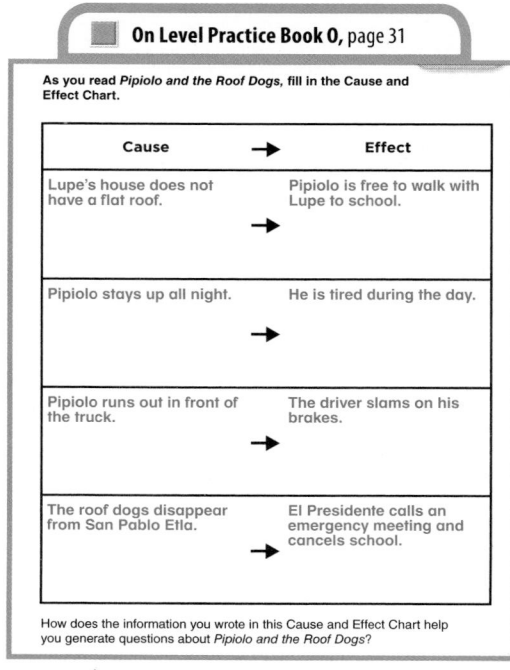

On Level Practice Book O, page 31

As you read *Pipiolo and the Roof Dogs*, fill in the Cause and Effect Chart.

Cause	→	Effect
Lupe's house does not have a flat roof.		Pipiolo is free to walk with Lupe to school.
Pipiolo stays up all night.		He is tired during the day.
Pipiolo runs out in front of the truck.		The driver slams on his brakes.
The roof dogs disappear from San Pablo Etla.		El Presidente calls an emergency meeting and cancels school.

How does the information you wrote in this Cause and Effect Chart help you generate questions about *Pipiolo and the Roof Dogs*?

⭐ **Approaching Practice Book A,** page 31

◆ **Beyond Practice Book B,** page 31

Develop Comprehension

1 STRATEGY
GENERATE QUESTIONS

Teacher Think Aloud When I read I can generate my own questions about a selection and then read on to see if they are answered. This will not only give me a purpose for reading but will also help me to identify cause-and-effect situations in the story and understand a character's thoughts, feelings, and actions. For example, what does Lupe mean when she says that her dog Pipiolo is the "savior of the roof dogs?" What is a roof dog? I've never heard that term before. I will continue reading to see if my questions are answered in the story.

2 FICTION

What does the term *fiction* mean, and what elements of fiction can you find in this story? (Students may consult a dictionary to find the meaning of *fiction*, a written work that tells a story about characters and events that are not real. They may notice details from the text such as Lupe's statement that she can smell Pipiolo's dreams as being unrealistic and something that would not appear in a work of nonfiction.)

My eyes have seen a lot of things, but my nose knows more. When evening comes and an inky darkness drapes over the great valley, I only have to close my eyes and my nose travels. I can smell the goats coming down from the mountains even before I hear the tinkling of the bells around their necks. And I can smell the truck delivering oranges before it reaches the long road to our village. I know it's coming even before the roof dogs know . . . and the roof dogs bark at everything coming up that road.

1 My name is Lupe, but this story is not about me. It is about my dog, Pipiolo, "the Savior of the Roof Dogs."

I found Pipiolo five years ago, near a path on the edge of our cornfield. He was curled up asleep inside an old shoe, and he must have been only a few days old. As I bent down to take a closer look, he raised his tiny head and looked me straight in the eye. And I saw greatness.

Pipiolo was such a perky puppy! So anxious to start the day that he would wake me even before the rooster crowed. We would spend our days sniffing in the mountains, exploring all the wonderful aromas the world had to offer.

At night Pipiolo slept outside, under my window. Through the cracks of our adobe house, I could smell him sleeping.

2 I could smell his dreams.

118

Comprehension

Figurative Language: *Metaphor*

Explain Help students understand that authors use figurative language to create vivid images in readers' minds and that metaphors are one type of figurative language. A metaphor compares one thing to another without using the words *like* or *as*. For example, *The bush was a shiny green jewel in the desert.*

Discuss Discuss with students the meaning of the phrase *inky darkness drapes over the valley.* Ask, *What things are being compared in this metaphor? How does the word* drapes *help you understand the image the author is trying to create?* (Students should recognize that the darkness is being compared both to ink and to cloth. The word *drapes* is used as a verb and means "to cover with cloth.")

Apply Have students invent their own metaphors for the darkness and look for more examples of figurative language as they read.

Develop Comprehension

3 **CHARACTER AND SETTING**

What is the setting of this story? Who is the story going to be about? (The setting of the story is San Pablo Etla, a village in southern Mexico. The story will be about a girl named Lupe and her dog, Pipiolo.)

3

119

Vocabulary

Homophones

Explain/Model Explain that homophones are words that sound alike but have different spellings and different meanings. Recognizing homophones can help readers decode unknown words.

Think Aloud When I read the first sentence on page 118, I recognize that *nose* and *knows* are homophones. The position of these words in the sentence helps me identify the word *nose* as a noun and *knows* as a verb. If I were unfamiliar with the meanings of these words, this information would help me decode them.

Practice/Apply Have students locate the words *I, days*, and *road* on page 118. Then call on volunteers to name homophones for each of these words. (*eye, daze,* and *rode*) Have students list the homophones on a sheet of paper and then write a sentence for each word that illustrates the word's definition.

Develop Comprehension

 **MAKE INFERENCES**

Why do you think the roof dogs are frightened when they see Lupe and Pipiolo pass through the village? (Answers will vary but should include the idea that dogs, like people, are sometimes frightened by things they do not understand. The roof dogs cannot figure out why Pipiolo is allowed to run free.)

 **CAUSE AND EFFECT**

Why doesn't Pipiolo share the same fate as the other dogs in San Pablo Etla? Add the answer to your Cause and Effect Chart. (The other dogs have to stay on the flat roofs to act as guard dogs. Lupe's house doesn't have a flat roof, so Pipiolo is free to walk with Lupe to school.)

6 VOCABULARY: SYNONYMS

What does the word *whiff* mean? (to inhale or smell an odor) What are some synonyms for the word *whiff*? (Answers may vary but may include *scent, smell*.)

Cause	→	Effect
Lupe's house does not have a flat roof.	→	Pipiolo is free to walk with Lupe to school.
	→	
	→	
	→	

120

Pipiolo walked with me to school each morning. As we passed through the village, the roof dogs would run to the edge of their roofs and furiously bark down at us. They never scared me much, because I knew they were the ones **4** who were frightened. Pipiolo would race around barking, flaunting his own freedom. Much too proud, I thought. "Poor roof dogs!" I said to Pipiolo. "To be put up on roofs as puppies to serve as guard dogs, imprisoned on a small patch of hot concrete their whole lives. Never to smell the wet earth and feel the delicious squish of mud between their toes."

"You're lucky, Pipiolo, that we don't have a flat roof, or Papa would have put you up there a long time ago. **5** Besides," I added, "I know you're just showing off for the cute one, Chulita."

He looked at me with his clear brown eyes, and I knew he understood.

One day, as we were traipsing through a field, Pipiolo gave out a sudden yelp. He then buried his nose in a tuft of grass. I got down and took a sniff. It had a kind of musty goat smell, with a hint of mint. Suddenly, I understood what Pipiolo was trying to tell me!

Using my school ruler as a shovel, I dug up a clump and stuffed it into my backpack. We ran to the village, where I broke the clump into many pieces. I tossed a piece to each angry roof dog, saving the piece with the flower in it for Chulita.

You should have heard the dogs as they experienced **6** their first whiff of real earth—their barks turned from anger to delight. A unified howl of surprise and discovery! And Pipiolo and I howled right along with them in their **7** symphony of **celebration**.

We had made a difference!

 Cause and Effect
Why doesn't Pipiolo share the same fate as the other dogs in San Pablo Etla?

120

ELL

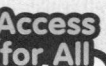
Access for All

STRATEGIES FOR EXTRA SUPPORT

Question 5 CAUSE AND EFFECT

Explain that to "share someone's fate" means to share their future in terms of what happens to them. Fate usually means something bad. Ask, *Will Pipiolo's future life—fate—be the same as the other dogs?* Reread aloud the first two paragraphs on page 120 and have students raise their hands when they hear information that answers the question.

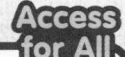

Develop Comprehension

7 **FIGURATIVE LANGUAGE: METAPHOR**

What things is the author comparing when he writes that Lupe and Pipiolo "howled right along with them in their symphony of celebration"? Explain the comparison. (The author is comparing the howling of the dogs to the sounds of musical instruments playing. They are expressing their joy by howling, just as a person might express joy by singing.)

8 **MAKE PREDICTIONS**

Now that Pipiolo has given the roof dogs their first whiff of fresh earth, what do you think he will do next? (Answers will vary but some students may say that Pipiolo will try and come up with a plan to free the roof dogs.)

121

ELL

Access for All

STRATEGIES FOR EXTRA SUPPORT

Use Illustration Clues Point to specific illustrations as you use and explain words. For example: *These buildings make up the village. This is the roof of a house in the village. This is the edge of the roof. This roof dog is barking* [act this out] *down from the edge of the roof. Here is Pipiolo racing around.* Do the same for the other illustrations in the story.

Develop Comprehension

9 SUMMARIZE

What has happened in the story so far? (Answers will vary but should include the following points: a young girl named Lupe lives in a small village in Mexico; one day she discovers a puppy in a field; she keeps him as a pet and names him Pipiolo; since her house does not have a flat roof, Lupe's father cannot put Pipiolo on the roof to act as a guard dog like the other dogs in the village; Pipiolo and Lupe feel sorry for the roof dogs; they figure out a way to help them get a whiff of real earth.)

10 CAUSE AND EFFECT

Why is Pipiolo so tired during the day? Add the answer to your Cause and Effect Chart. (He stays up all night to watch television at a store in town.)

Cause		Effect
Lupe's house does not have a flat roof.	→	Pipiolo is free to walk with Lupe to school.
Pipiolo stays up all night.	→	He is tired during the day.

Vocabulary

Read the sentence that contains the word **variety**. Ask students to name a variety of vegetables, fruits, or meats. Have them use *variety* aloud in a sentence listing the foods: *I like a variety of fruits, such as _____.*

---

9 Every day, Pipiolo and I would dig up another **fragrance** and share it with the roof dogs. We worked hard to find a good **variety**, sometimes overlooking the very pungent for the rare and unusual.

Life went on like this for some time, until it dawned on me that, on many days, Pipiolo would not even get up with me in the morning to walk to school. He was spending more and more time sleeping in the shade during the day, while I was doing all the work myself in the hot sun!

One night, as I stepped out into our yard to smell the evening air, I saw Pipiolo's shadow slip into the cornfield. I crouched down so he wouldn't see me and followed him on all fours as he sauntered down the mountainside. Wherever he sniffed, I sniffed. I followed him through several cornfields, through a drainage pipe, and under fences. Straight to the only store in town that was still open, Tienda Soliz.

Now I understood why he was so tired during the day.

10 He had a night life!

Even before I saw the flickering of blue light, I could smell the heated plastic of a television waft through the cool dark night. Tienda Soliz had the only television set in our village. We are so high up in these mountains that this television can only get one channel. And that one channel only shows old American westerns.

11 Pipiolo walked right up to the front of the television and plopped down. The mayor of our village, El Presidente, greeted him nonchalantly.

It was obvious Pipiolo was a regular.

My dog has been watching TV every night! I thought as I hid behind a corner to watch Pipiolo—and the movie, too.

122

Cross-Curricular Connection

MEXICAN FOLK ART

Small, rural villages are found in many parts of Mexico. Villagers often produce folk art that features brightly painted pictures, walls, or signs. Many Mexican folk artists, such as Saulo Moreno and the Aguilar sisters, Josefina, Guillermina, Concepcion, and Irene, are famous.

Have students research different cultural styles in Mexican folk art, as practiced by different artists in different historical time periods. Suggest that students give a short oral presentation about the illustrator they have chosen to persuade the class of the artist's importance, using visuals if possible and choosing vocabulary carefully for impact. Students can then compare and contrast the ideas and techniques used by each artist.

123

Develop Comprehension

11 STRATEGY
GENERATE QUESTIONS

Teacher Think Aloud I know that Pipiolo is a very smart dog. He gave Lupe the idea of digging up clumps of earth for the roof dogs. Now I discover that Pipiolo also likes to watch old Western movies on television. I wonder what effect this event will have on the plot of the story. Tell me what questions you could generate, or ask, about this event in the plot.

(Encourage students to apply the strategy in a Think Aloud.)

Student Think Aloud I know that Pipiolo is trying to help the roof dogs. But what does that have to do with watching old Westerns? So the first question I would ask is, why does Pipiolo like watching old Western movies? I think the answer to that question might give me clues as to what might happen next in the story. I know that in many old Western movies, outlaws escape and hide from the sheriff, or make narrow escapes from dangerous situations. Maybe the old Westerns will give Pipiolo an idea that would help the roof dogs escape from their roofs.

Comprehension

Causal, Hierarchical, and Temporal Relationships

Explain/Discuss There are different kinds of cause-and-effect relationships. In a **causal** relationship, one action causes another action and reaction. In a **hierarchical** relationship, one action is the underlying cause behind a chain of actions and reactions. In a **temporal** cause-and-effect relationship, the reader looks at a sequence of events and decides which causal relationship was the reason for the effect. Temporal cause-and-effect relationships often occur in myths or legends.

Apply As students read *Pipiolo and the Roof Dogs,* have them identify different kinds of cause-and-effect relationships. Discuss whether the cause-and-effect relationships are stated or implied.

Develop Comprehension

12 | **MAINTAIN**
PLOT AND SETTING

How does the setting effect the plot events in the story? (Answers may vary but should include that, because Lupe's village is in the mountains, it can get only one TV channel. This channel only shows American westerns, so this is the only kind of program Pipiolo can watch.)

12

124

Comprehension

Monitor and Clarify: *Reread to Clarify*

Explain Help students understand that rereading is one way to try to clarify cause-and-effect relationships in a story or to reconsider information in order to draw conclusions. Encourage students to reread material if they're unclear about why something is happening.

Discuss What events lead up to Lupe's decision to follow Pipiolo one night? (He sleeps during the day, leaving Lupe to dig up earth by herself.)

Apply Ask students to reread pages 120 and 122 of the Student Book. Have them list some of the events that lead directly to another event or action, and that help shape events in the story. Remind students to apply and use this strategy independently. (Answers might include: Lupe tosses clumps of earth up to the roof dogs, and the new scent the dogs experience causes them to want freedom.)

The actor, Juan Wayne, was trapped on the roof of a burning building. Just when it looked as though all was lost, four horses pulling a hay wagon galloped through the town, and as it passed by, Juan Wayne jumped down into the hay to safety. At that moment, Pipiolo jumped up and let out an earthshaking howl. The men in the *tienda* sprang to their feet, visibly shaken. "Get that dog out of here!" shouted El Presidente.

Pipiolo raced out into the street, and I ran after him.

He ran down the main street of San Pablo. I looked up at the roof dogs and saw that they were all quietly watching Pipiolo.

They had been waiting for him!

I had never heard Pipiolo bark so long and so eloquently. He spoke of freedom, courage, **cooperation**, and action—and of all the smells yet to be experienced. The roof dogs and I were transfixed. And when he was through barking, they were **transformed**.

At his command, they all sat down to wait.

I must have fallen asleep, because suddenly I awoke to the tang of ripe oranges, followed by the familiar sound of a truck grinding its gears as it climbed along the long, steep road to our village.

Pipiolo barked, and the roof dogs stood up and began to leap from house to house toward the last two roofs at the end of the village. All, that is, except for Chulita, who shivered, frozen with terror.

The truck stopped at Tienda Soliz to make the delivery of oranges, then drove on to the end of the village to turn around. Pipiolo barked again, and the dogs all jumped down onto the pile of oranges in the back of the truck.

Chulita was now the only dog left. She barked forlornly as the truck started to make its way back through the village—and to leave Chulita behind.

The only roof dog in San Pablo Etla. **14**

Develop Comprehension

13 CAUSE AND EFFECT

Why does Pipiolo let out an earth-shaking howl when he sees the movie actor "Juan" Wayne jump from a building onto a moving hay wagon on television? (It gives him an idea for rescuing the roof dogs of his village.)

14 MAKE PREDICTIONS

Do you think Chulita will get down from the roof? Explain your answer. (Answers will vary but should include that since Pipiolo was showing off for Chulita before, he will somehow find a way to get her down. Up to this point, he has not failed to help the roof dogs.)

Vocabulary

Vocabulary Read the sentence that contains the word **transformed**. Ask students to give a synonym for *transformed* in the sentence. (changed, converted, different)

Have students respond to the selection by confirming or revising their predictions and purposes for readings.

Quick Check Can students identify cause-and-effect relationships in the story? If not, see the Extra Support on this page.

Stop here if you wish to read this selection over two days.

Extra Support

Cause and Effect

If students are having difficulty identifying cause-and-effect relationships in the story, have them reread the last two paragraphs on page 120 and help them to paraphrase the cause-and-effect situation. Ask them why the barks of the roof dogs turned from anger to delight. (They experienced their first whiff of real earth.) Explain that the real earth is the cause that makes something happen. The joyous barking of the dogs is the effect, or what happens because of an event or action. Then have students reread page 122. Ask them why Pipiolo sleeps all day. Then have them identify both the cause and the effect.

Develop Comprehension

15 CAUSE AND EFFECT

Why does Pipiolo run out in front of the truck? Explain your answer and add it to your Cause and Effect Chart. (Answers may vary but should include that Pipiolo runs in front of the truck to make it stop. This will give Chulita one last chance to jump from the roof.)

16 STRATEGY
GENERATE QUESTIONS

Do you think the driver of the truck is aware that the roof dogs are leaping down onto the oranges he is carrying? Explain how you used the strategy to reach your answer.

Student Think Aloud I can ask myself a question to help me understand what is going on at this point in the story. After slamming on his brakes, wouldn't the driver have gotten out and looked in his truck if he thought dogs were back there? I think the answer must be yes. Since he continues on his way after Pipiolo moves out of the street, I think he has no idea that the dogs are jumping down onto his truck.

Cause	→	Effect
Lupe's house does not have a flat roof.	→	Pipiolo is free to walk with Lupe to school.
Pipiolo stays up all night.	→	He is tired during the day.
Pipiolo runs out in front of the truck.	→	The driver slams on his brakes and stops.

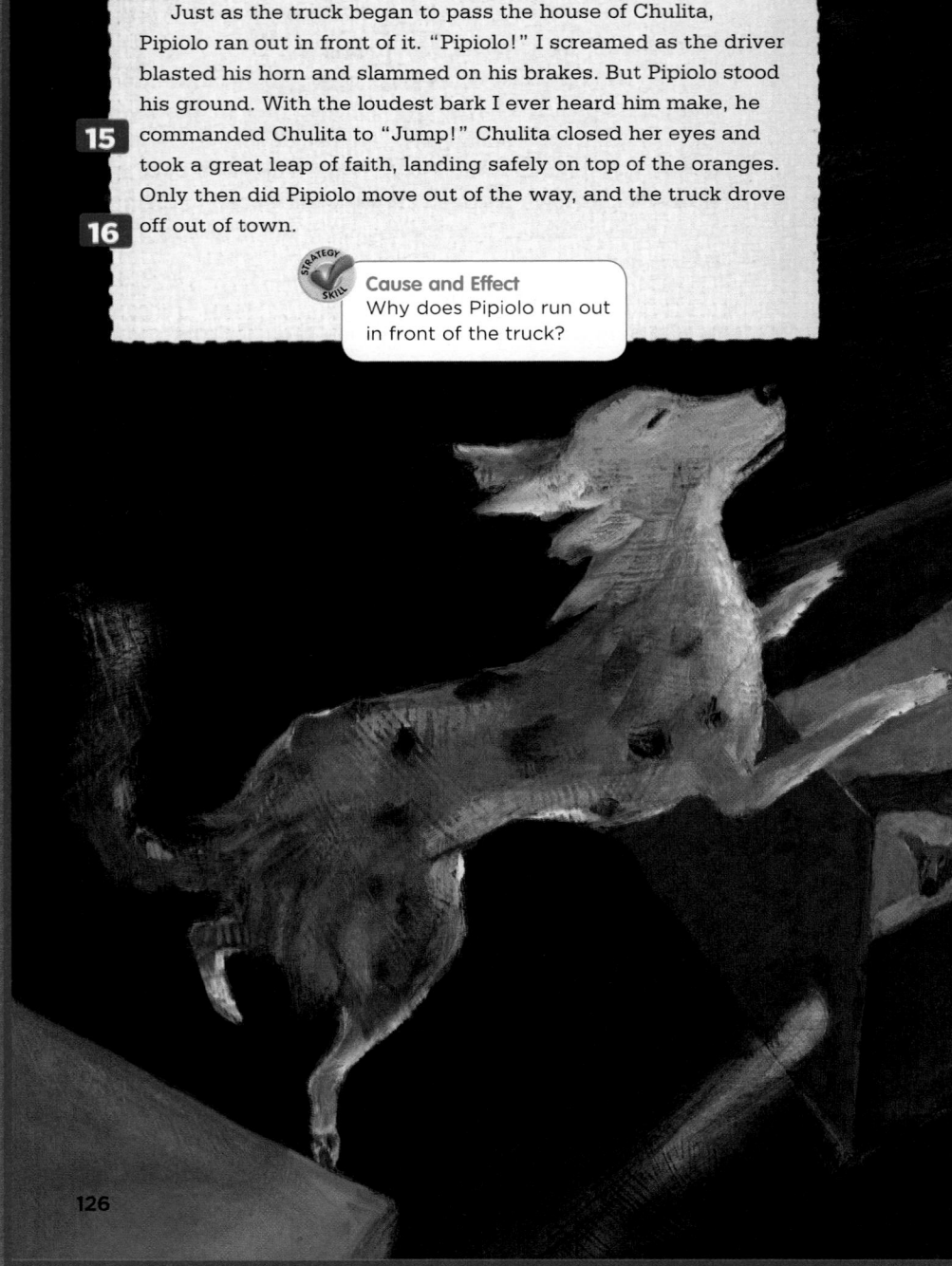

Just as the truck began to pass the house of Chulita, Pipiolo ran out in front of it. "Pipiolo!" I screamed as the driver blasted his horn and slammed on his brakes. But Pipiolo stood his ground. With the loudest bark I ever heard him make, he **15** commanded Chulita to "Jump!" Chulita closed her eyes and took a great leap of faith, landing safely on top of the oranges. Only then did Pipiolo move out of the way, and the truck drove **16** off out of town.

Cause and Effect
Why does Pipiolo run out in front of the truck?

126

17

127

Develop Comprehension

17 CHARACTER

What words would you use to describe Pipiolo? (Answers will vary but should include that Pipiolo is smart, resourceful, determined, and brave. He figures out a way to help the roof dogs, and he runs in front of the truck in order to give Chulita one last chance for freedom.)

Cross–Curricular Connection

MEXICO

Share some facts about Mexico with students.

- Few countries have as wide a variety of landscapes and climates within such short distances of one another as Mexico. Towering mountains cover more than 2/3 of the country. Mexico also has tropical forests and hot deserts.

- Mexico has a rich and diverse history. It was settled by the Olmec civilization from 800 to 400 BC. They were followed by the Maya from about AD 300 to 900, the Toltec from 900 to 1200, and then the Aztecs from 1200 to 1519.

- After the Aztecs came the Spanish conquistadores in the early 16th century. They ruled the country until 1821.

Have students pick one of these civilizations to research and then share their findings with the class.

Develop Comprehension

RESEARCH
Why It Matters

Comprehension "Student Think Alouds ask students to talk out loud about what they are thinking just after they read parts of a text. Research indicates that thinking aloud shows students how a reader makes sense of a challenging text. It also shows students how an expert reader might use different strategies as they process text. Finally, it shows students how to adjust their reading based on how well they understand."

Janice Dole

 for more information, go to
www. macmillanmh.com

128

ELL  Access for All

Simplify Look at the picture on these pages. *What are the roof dogs doing now? Who are they following? What do the dogs have now? Who gave them this? What does Lupe hear? How do you think she feels about what Pipiolo did?*

Provide Sentence Prompts Use these sentences:

Now the roof dogs have…

They have this because…

Just before the truck disappeared down the road, I saw all the dogs, one by one, leap off the back of it and follow Pipiolo into the cornfield and out of sight.

As they did, I whispered, "*Tierra y Libertad*—Land and Freedom."

I slowly walked home and crawled into bed. Closing my eyes, I could smell the roof dogs racing through the fields, exhilarated by the first touch of soft earth beneath their paws, their fur **moistened** by the tall grass. They were headed for the mountains.

As I listened, I heard the joyous barking of the newly free. And in that sound, the voice of one dog stood out among them all. My Pipiolo!

18

129

Develop Comprehension

18 **MONITOR AND CLARIFY: REREAD TO CLARIFY**

Why do you think the roof dogs disappear into the cornfield and head for the mountains instead of staying in the village? How can rereading to clarify information help you to answer this question? (If students reread they will note that earlier in the story Lupe and Pipiolo shared smells from the mountains with the roof dogs. Answers will vary but should include that not only do the fields and mountains hold the promise of different scents and aromas, but staying in the village would be dangerous for the roof dogs. If their owners caught them the next morning, they would probably put them back on the roofs.)

Media Literacy

Media Events

Explain/Discuss The media often cover unusual events such as the disappearance of the dogs in San Pablo Etla. Discuss ways the media could cover this event. What headline might appear in a local newspaper? Remind students that media creators always have a purpose and target audience. Ask students to evaluate and interpret the various ways the story would be covered in a newspaper, on the Internet, or on a television news show.

Apply Have students work individually and collaboratively to write both a television newscast and a newspaper story for the class that covers the disappearance of the San Pablo Etla roof dogs with and without technology and visual aids. Call on volunteers to present their reports to the class. Students should make inferences based on the oral presentations.

Develop Comprehension

19 **CAUSE AND EFFECT**

What effect does the disappearance of the roof dogs have on the town of San Pablo Etla? Add your answer to the Cause and Effect Chart. (Answers should include that El Presidente calls an emergency meeting and even cancels school.)

20 **DRAW CONCLUSIONS**

Why did Lupe share clumps of earth with the roof dogs of Viquera? (She gave them clumps of earth to smell, just as she had with the roof dogs of her own village. She wants to prepare them for Pipiolo's arrival.)

Cause	→	Effect
Lupe's house does not have a flat roof.	→	Pipiolo is free to walk with Lupe to school.
Pipiolo stays up all night.	→	He is tired during the day.
Pipiolo runs out in front of the truck.	→	The driver slams on his brakes and stops.
The roof dogs disappear from San Pablo Etla.	→	El Presidente calls an emergency meeting and cancels school.

130

Cultural Perspectives

ROOF DOGS IN MEXICO

Share information about the cultural traditions of keeping roof dogs in Mexico: Mexico has a large dog population. Some are strays. Many people keep dogs as companions or for protection. Few houses in small villages and towns throughout Mexico have yards, so the dogs are often kept in courtyards, or on the roof. In many communities where there are more than a few roof dogs, there is an "hour of barking" in the evening and morning.

Have students work in small groups and use the Internet with supervision to find as much information about the roof dogs of Mexico as they can. Have interested groups report back to the class, comparing and contrasting the way people in Mexico keep dogs with the way dogs are kept by most people in the United States. Have students give oral reports in standard American English.

In my small village, things remain the same from day to day. The mysterious disappearance of the roof dogs was the biggest event ever to happen in San Pablo Etla. El Presidente called an emergency meeting and even **canceled** school. Everyone had a **theory**, but most agreed that it had to have been some kind of supernatural event. My little cousin, Inocencia, stood up and pronounced it "*El Milagro de San Pablo!*"—the Miracle of San Pablo!   **19**

The next morning, I got up especially early to take the long route to school, through the neighboring village of Viquera.

When I stepped out into my yard, I saw Pipiolo curled up in his usual spot under my window! I ran over to give him a big hug, but he was so deeply asleep, I decided not to wake him. Instead, I softly whispered in his ear, "Sleep, my dear Pipiolo. You've been busy, but you have much more to do."

On my long walk to the next village, I explored several different aromas, finally settling on the very best. And this I shared with the roof dogs of Viquera.

As I did, I whispered to each dog in turn:

"Be patient. Pipiolo will be here soon."   **20**

131

RETURN TO PREDICTIONS AND PURPOSES

Review students' predictions and purposes for reading. Were their predictions correct? Did they find out what made Pipiolo a special dog in San Pablo Etla? Ask students to generate additional questions about any story events they feel need further clarification.

REVIEW READING STRATEGIES

Ask: How did generating questions about the story help you clarify meaning, as well as identify cause-and-effect situations?

PERSONAL RESPONSE

Ask students to write a poem about a pet they have had, known, or read about that did something extraordinary. Before they write, they may wish to read other grade-level-appropriate, published poetry for inspiration and style.

Students may also write a response in which they identify a literary device, such as figurative language or foreshadowing, that the author used in this story and explain why the author used it.

Quick Check   **Can students identify cause-and-effect relationships between events in the story?**

During **Small Group Instruction**

If No → **Approaching Level**   Leveled Reader Lesson, p. 139P

If Yes → **On Level**   Options, pp. 139Q–139R

Beyond Level   Options, pp. 139S–139T

Author and Illustrator

COME ALONG WITH BRIAN MEUNIER AND PERKY EDGERTON

Have students read the biographies of the author and illustrator.

DISCUSS

- Why might Brian Meunier have decided to write a story with a dog as the main character?

- How are Perky Edgerton's illustrations dreamlike?

WRITE ABOUT IT

Review with students why Pipiolo was a special dog and what was extraordinary about what he did for the roof dogs of San Pablo Etla. Then talk about how ordinary events, such as shopping, playing a sport, or walking to school, can sometimes turn out to be special. Have students write about a time when they did something or experienced something they consider to be extraordinary.

Author's Purpose

Point out to students that authors who write fiction and even fantasies to entertain readers may still have an additional purpose in mind. Students may state that, besides writing to entertain, the author may have wanted to inform readers about roof dogs in Mexico (or teach a lesson about them) since he describes them so vividly.

LOG ON **Technology**

Students can find more information about Brian Meunier and Perky Edgerton at www.macmillanmh.com

---

Come Along With
Brian Meunier and Perky Edgerton

Brian Meunier wrote this story, but he is an artist, too. His large wood and metal bird sculptures are in museums and galleries all around the country. Brian is also a professor of fine arts. When he started writing, he didn't stop with this story. It is the first in a trilogy, which means there are two more books on a similar theme coming out soon.

Perky Edgerton worked on this story with her husband, Brian. She illustrated this story with paintings that are warm, complex, and dreamlike, which makes them a great fit for Brian's story. The original paintings for this book were in an exhibition. Perky and Brian live in Pennsylvania with their two daughters and a dog named Chulita.

 LOG ON Find out more about Brian Meunier and Perky Edgerton at **www.macmillanmh.com**

Author's Purpose
Pipiolo and the Roof Dogs is a fantasy because not all of the events could take place in real life. Do you think Brian Meunier wrote just to entertain, or could he have had another purpose? Explain.

132

Author's Craft
First-Person Point of View

The narrative point of view is the author's choice of narrator or speaker. The narrative point of view can be first person, third person, or omniscient. Brian Meunier made this story more realistic by using the first-person point of view. The person telling the story is a character in it, and the character describes events that happened to him or her. The author uses pronouns such as *I, me, my,* and *we.* For example:

> Suddenly, I understood what Pipiolo was trying to tell me! (p. 120)

> We had made a difference! (p. 120)

Discuss what is different about a story told from the first-person point of view as opposed to stories told from other points of view. Ask students to think of a story that they have read recently. Have them identify the narrative point of view in it.

Comprehension Check

Summarize

Use your Cause and Effect Chart to help you summarize *Pipiolo and the Roof Dogs*. In your own words, tell how Pipiolo changed the lives of the roof dogs.

Cause → Effect
→
→
→
→

Think and Compare

1. What caused Pipiolo to want to free the roof dogs from their lives as guard animals? Use what you know about Pipiolo's character from the story. **Generate Questions: Cause and Effect**

2. Reread page 131. Predict what will happen when Pipiolo gets to the town of Viquera. **Synthesize**

3. What **fragrances** would you share with the roof dogs? Explain your choices. **Evaluate**

4. Pipiolo used creative thinking to free the roof dogs. Explain how thinking creatively can help solve a problem. **Analyze**

5. Reread "It's a Dog's Life" on pages 114–115. Both Sparky and Pipiolo help others. Describe the similarities and differences between the jobs that both dogs do. Use details from both stories to support your answer. **Reading/Writing Across Texts**

133

Strategies for Answering Questions

Author and Me

Model the Author and Me strategy with question 1.

The answer to this question is not directly stated in the text, but the author may provide clues to help you answer it. You have to think about what you already know and link it to what you know from the selection.

Question 1: Think Aloud First I will look for possible causes in the story. At first, Pipiolo would race around flaunting his freedom to the other dogs. Then Lupe tells Pipiolo how the roof dogs have to serve as guard dogs, imprisoned on their owners' roofs. She says that when Pipiolo looked at her with his clear brown eyes, she knew he understood what she was saying. He felt lucky to be free, and that's probably why he wanted to help the roof dogs.

Comprehension Check

SUMMARIZE

Have students work in groups to summarize the most important events in *Pipiolo and the Roof Dogs*. Ask a volunteer from each group to read the group's summary aloud. Then ask how their Cause-and-Effect Charts helped them prepare their summaries.

THINK AND COMPARE

Sample answers are given.

1. **Cause and Effect:** Pipiolo is aware that he has freedom; he is proud of this, and becomes determined to share it with the roof dogs when Lupe tells him they are imprisoned on their owners' roofs. Pipiolo is also interested in a female roof dog named Chulita. USE AUTHOR AND ME

2. **Synthesize:** Pipiolo will probably free the roof dogs of Viquera.

3. **Text to Self:** Answers will vary, but students should have reasonable explanations for their choices.

4. **Text to World:** Answers may vary but should include considering the opinions of other people to open up more creative ways of approaching and solving a problem.

FOCUS QUESTION

5. **Text to Text:** Answers may include that Sparky is helping a human, but Pipiolo is helping other dogs. Both dogs rely on their sense of smell, and both value freedom. Pipiolo is looking for a way to help the roof dogs escape. Sparky helps Ms. Toni Graham live more freely.

Objectives

- Read accurately with good prosody
- Rate: 100–120 WCPM

Materials

- Fluency Transparency 5
- Fluency Solutions
- Leveled Practice Books, p. 32

ELL · **Access for All**

Chunking Text
Demonstrate an example and tell students: *Good readers read groups of words together instead of one word at a time.* Read phrases and have student echo-read. Discuss the overall meaning of the passage.

On Level Practice Book O, page 32

As I read, I will pay attention to tempo.

	"It's finally here!" I said to myself as I got off the school
13	bus that Friday afternoon. "And it's going to be great!"
23	I had been patient. I'd waited and waited for the big
34	family party. It was just one day away. From all over the city
47	and even as far away as Baltimore, my family was meeting
58	at our house for a cookout supper Saturday night. My older
69	sister, Mai, was excited, too. She had promised to decorate our
80	backyard and even string little lights all over the trees and
91	bushes. We'd start today, and then finish up tomorrow
100	morning before her big soccer game. I never missed Mai's
110	soccer games. She and her team were the city champions,
120	and their games were really fun to watch.
128	But now it was time to decorate the yard. 137

Comprehension Check

1. Why is the narrator excited? **Cause and Effect**
   He is excited for the big family party.
2. What is Mai's responsibility for the party? **Plot**
   Mai is supposed to decorate the backyard.

	Words Read	−	Number of Errors	=	Words Correct Score
First Read		−		=	
Second Read		−		=	

★ **Approaching Practice Book A,** page 32
◆ **Beyond Practice Book B,** page 32

Fluency
Repeated Reading: Pauses and Intonation

EXPLAIN/MODEL Tell students that good readers learn to read groups of words together in phrases. Explain that the text on **Fluency Transparency 5** has been marked with slashes that indicate pauses and stops. A single slash indicates a pause, usually between phrases. A double slash indicates a stop, usually between sentences. Have the class listen carefully to your pauses and intonation as you read.

Transparency 5

Pipiolo walked with me to school each morning.// As we passed through the village,/ the roof dogs would run to the edge of their roofs and furiously bark down at us.// They never scared me much,/ because I knew they were the ones who were frightened.// Pipiolo would race around barking,/ flaunting his own freedom.// Much too proud,/ I thought.// "Poor roof dogs!"/ I said to Pipiolo.// "To be put up on roofs as puppies to serve as guard dogs,/ imprisoned on a small patch of concrete their whole lives.// Never to smell the wet earth and feel the delicious squish of mud between their toes."//

Fluency Transparency 5
from *Pipiolo and the Roof Dogs*, page 120

PRACTICE/APPLY Divide the class into two groups. Have the groups alternate reading the sentences. Then have groups switch roles. Students will practice fluency using **Practice Book** page 32 or Fluency Solutions Audio CD. Encourage partners to work together and to offer feedback as appropriate.

Cooperative Learning · **Access for All**

Quick Check | **Can students read accurately with good prosody?**

During **Small Group Instruction**

If No → **Approaching Level** Fluency, p. 139N

If Yes → **On Level** Options, pp. 139Q–139R

Beyond Level Options, pp. 139S–139T

Comprehension

MAINTAIN SKILL
PLOT

EXPLAIN/MODEL

Remind students that **plot** is the series of events in a story. These events give the story a beginning, a middle, and an end. Explain:

- To analyze the plot, first identify the problem the main, or major, character faces and how he or she tries to solve it. Find the turning point, or climax, at which the character begins to find a solution. Then identify the story events that lead to a solution.

- For instance, the main problem in *Pipiolo and the Roof Dogs* is that the roof dogs are prisoners on their owners' roofs.

PRACTICE/APPLY

Discuss the plot of *Pipiolo and the Roof Dogs*. Ask:

- What is the turning point in the plot when the main character thinks she has found a solution to the problem?

- How is the problem solved in *Pipiolo and the Roof Dogs*?

Have students form groups to make an idea web recording different ways the problem might be solved. Have groups present their ideas.

For comprehension practice use Graphic Organizers on **Teacher's Resource Book** pages 40–64.

Objective
- Analyze plot

Skills Trace

Character, Plot, Setting	
Introduce	19A–B
Practice / Apply	20–41; Leveled Practice 2–3
Reteach / Review	47M–T, 51A–B, 52–71, 77M–T; Leveled Practice 9–10
Assess	Weekly Tests, Units 1, 4 Tests; Benchmark Tests A, B
Maintain	41B, 71B, 133B; 661B; 395A–B; 396–413, 419M–T, Leveled Practice 113–114

Informational Text: Social Studies

GENRE: NONFICTION ARTICLE

Have students read the bookmark on **Student Book** page 134. Explain that a nonfiction article is **informational nonfiction** that:

- presents facts about real people, places, situations, or events;

- can present information on many subjects, including history, literature, and science;

- often includes special features such as charts, diagrams, tables, and graphs to present additional information.

Text Feature: Charts

Point out that charts provide a visual summary of information from the story. They provide information using numbers or words presented in columns and rows.

- Charts may show different categories to help the reader organize information.

- Sometimes charts include pictures or other graphics.

Science

Genre
Nonfiction Articles present facts about real people, living things, places, or events.

Text Feature
Charts organize information and make it easy to read.

Content Vocabulary
relays   retrieve
characteristics
stamina

DOGGONE WORK

by Lori Marquez

In January 1925 many of the children in Nome, Alaska, were very ill with a serious disease called diphtheria. Their only hope was a serum used to cure the disease.

The serum was nearly a thousand miles away in Anchorage, Alaska. It was the middle of winter and blizzards had brought heavy snows, making it impossible for planes to land. Dogsleds were the only way to get the medicine from Anchorage to Nome.

Balto at the lead of a dog team

134

Content Vocabulary

Discuss the spelling and meaning of each content vocabulary word for "Doggone Work" on Student Book page 134: *relays, characteristics, stamina, retrieve.*

- **Relays** are fresh teams or supplies that replace others. *Have you ever participated in relays? What kind of relays were they?*

- **Characteristics** are special qualities or features that belong to and help identify a person or thing. *What characteristics of your best friend do you like most?*

- If you have **stamina**, you can endure tough conditions even though you are tired. *When have you needed great stamina?*

- To **retrieve** an object, you must find it and return it. *What have you needed to retrieve recently?*

Dog teams and their drivers began a series of dangerous journeys. The teams worked in **relays**, one team handing the serum off to the next team. Balto was the lead dog of the twentieth team. Strong and smart, Balto led the team safely across icy paths. His team reached Nome with the serum and the children were saved.

Why could Balto and the other dog teams make this journey? Different dogs have changed or adapted over centuries for different functions. Sled dogs like Balto have **characteristics** that help them pull sleds. They move their feet quickly **1** and have remarkable strength for their size. Their double coat of fur protects them from cold, snow, and ice. These

Sledder Gunnar Kasson hugs his famous dog Balto

dogs have great **stamina** and keep going no matter what the conditions are. Also, they know how to find the safest way to travel. These qualities make them well adapted to pulling a sled in the worst winter weather.

Reading a Chart

This chart helps you organize information about dog breeds, their adaptations, and the work that each breed does.

DOG ADAPTATIONS

Breed	Adaptation	Job
Husky	Strong; fast; thick fur	Pulling sleds
Collie	Instinct for herding other animals; good eyesight	Tending sheep and cattle
Bloodhound	Excellent sense of smell	Searching and rescuing

2

135

Informational Text

Read "Doggone Work"

Access for All

As you read, remind students to apply what they have learned about charts. Also have them identify clues to the meanings of the highlighted words.

1 ANALYZE

What characteristics make sled dogs so successful at pulling sleds? (Sled dogs can move their feet quickly. They are strong for their size. Their thick coats protect them from the cold, and the dogs have great stamina. They can find safe routes through heavy snow.)

2 TEXT FEATURE: CHARTS

Tested

According to the chart, which breed of dog has adapted to herding other animals? (The collie is a herding dog.)

ELL

Access for All

Academic Vocabulary Prepare students to read the selection by giving them a short summary of what it is about. Use the photos to convey information. Have students ask questions about what they will read. Point out the chart and explain that as students read, they can refer to the chart to help them understand the information.

For the Content Vocabulary, give additional examples. For example, for the word *relays,* act it out using a short distance with three students. For *characteristics,* compare the difference in characteristics between two dogs.

Informational Text

3 TEXT FEATURE: CHARTS

What kinds of dogs, such as "sled dogs," would be listed in a chart like the one on page 135 summarizing the dog adaptations mentioned in this passage? (Sled dogs, SAR dogs, service dogs, agriculture dogs, herding dogs, or sheepdogs.)

4 COMPARE AND CONTRAST

How is the job that SAR dogs do different from the job a service dog does? (The job of search-and-rescue [SAR] dogs is to help find missing people. Service dogs help people live with physical challenges, such as blindness or deafness.)

SAR DOGS

Sled dogs are not the only dogs who work for a living. For example, Bronte is a search-and-rescue dog, or a SAR dog. Bronte is a rottweiler who helps find missing people. In 1995, after an explosion in a building in Oklahoma City, Oklahoma, Bronte was brought in to search through the rubble. When she began to scratch and sniff in one place, her handler knew that she had found someone. Rescuers dug quickly and found a 15-year-old girl who was alive under the debris.

What makes a good SAR dog? First, SAR dogs need an especially good sense of smell. Dogs use their whiskers to help them smell. Whiskers help dogs know the direction of the wind so they can tell where a scent is coming from. SAR dogs use scents in the air to find a person in a certain area. They can also sniff an item of human clothing and then track the scent of the person who wore it. **3**

It takes about a year to train a SAR dog. These dogs are likely to be friendly, eager to please, and happy to **retrieve** things. Trainers use different forms of the game hide-and-seek to teach SAR dogs. The trainer hides an object. When the dog finds the hidden item, it drags the object back to the trainer. This training along with the dog's natural characteristics make it perfectly suited for search-and-rescue missions.

A rescue dog named Tracer picks up the scent of a diver in ten feet of water.

136

On Level Practice Book O, page 33

Charts are useful to organize and display information. Charts allow you to list a series of things in one column and information about those things in other columns. A chart usually has headings at the top of each column to describe the information the columns contain.

Possible responses provided.
Use the chart about different dog breeds to answer the questions below.

Dogs with Jobs		
Breed	**Originally Used For . . .**	**Now Often Used To . . .**
Welsh Corgi	driving other people's cattle off protected land	gather livestock and herd animals home
Dalmatian	running beside coaches to clear a path for the horses	be companion animals
Newfoundland	dragging carts and carrying heavy loads	rescue people from water
golden retriever	picking up game for hunters	serve as guide dogs for people who are blind

1. What task did golden retrievers originally perform? They were used by hunters to pick up game.

2. How are Dalmatians put to use today? They are kept as pets.

3. How is a Welsh Corgi's job today different from its original job? A Welsh Corgi's original job was to chase away animals. Today its job is to gather animals and keep them together.

4. Which breed is now known for rescuing people in the water? Newfoundland

5. Which breed is often used to help people who are blind? Golden retriever

---

 Approaching Practice Book A, page 33

Beyond Practice Book B, page 33

SERVICE DOGS

Other dogs have other jobs. Service dogs provide people with different types of services, depending on their needs. If you visit a sheep farm, you might see dogs herding sheep. Sheep dogs help move sheep from field to field or into holding pens. Some dogs help people. These dogs are trained to cross streets, open doors, and even make beds! You might even see an agriculture dog working at an airport. These dogs smell suitcases and packages, looking for harmful insects that might be hiding in food.

This service dog helps a blind woman cross the street.

Connect and Compare

1. Look at the dog adaptations chart on page 135. What characteristics do dogs that tend sheep have? **Reading a Chart**

2. If your family decided to adopt a dog, what characteristics would you look for? **Evaluate**

3. Think about "Doggone Work" and *Pipiolo and the Roof Dogs*. What characteristics do Pipiolo and a SAR dog have in common? **Reading/Writing Across Texts**

 Science Activity

Research three other dog breeds. Make a chart listing the work the dogs do and the characteristics that help each dog do that work.

 Find out more about dogs at **www.macmillanmh.com**

137

Informational Text

Connect and Compare

SUGGESTED ANSWERS

1. Dogs that tend sheep have a keen sense of sight and an instinct for herding other animals.
   READING A CHART

2. Answers will vary but should include an analysis of family characteristics matched with dog characteristics. **EVALUATE**

FOCUS QUESTION

3. They are smart; they exhibit leadership skills; they are independent; they have great problem-solving skills; each has the ability to put himself in another's place. **READING/WRITING ACROSS TEXTS**

 ### Science Activity

Have students use the Internet to find information about dog breeds, or have them use nonfiction books from the school or public library. If they are doing Internet research, remind them to use information from sites that end in *.edu* or *.gov* as sources, and to avoid sites that end in *.com* or *.net*.

 **Technology**

Internet Research and Inquiry Activity
Students can find more facts at
www.macmillanmh.com

WRITING
- Personal Narrative
- **Writer's Craft:** Unimportant Details

WORD STUDY

- Words in Context
- **Thesaurus/Dictionary:** Synonyms
- **Phonics:** Words with /ûr/ and /îr/
- Vocabulary Building

SPELLING
- Words with /ûr/ and /îr/

GRAMMAR
- Run-On Sentences

SMALL GROUP OPTIONS
- Differentiated Instruction, pp. 139M–139V

Writing

Unimportant Details

READ THE STUDENT MODEL

Read the bookmark. Explain that some details might be interesting but do not help readers understand the topic, and they may even distract readers.

Have students turn to the first paragraph on page 125. Ask students if any details there do not seem necessary. Then have the class read Bao's journal entry and the callouts. Tell students they will write journal entries about animals, learning how to delete unimportant details to clarify their writing for readers.

▼ Writer's Craft

Unimportant Details
Delete **unimportant details** that do not tell about your topic. Also delete details that may tell something about your topic but are not really important.

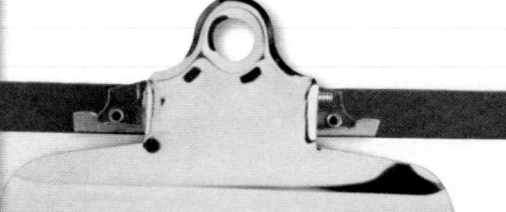

Write About an Experience with an Animal

Monday, October 3

> My teacher encourages us to keep a journal. Here are details about last night.

I've had my African gray parrot for about three years. His name is Frank. He's about a foot tall, with gray feathers all over, except for his brilliant red tail. His eyes are yellow.

> I decided I should give descriptive details about African gray parrots.

I've been talking to Frank for three years, but in all this time he's only squawked back at me.

Last night all of that changed. I was reading in bed. All of a sudden I heard, "Hi, Bao!" I glanced over, and Frank was staring at me. Then he said it again, "Hi, Bao!" I couldn't believe it! Not only was Frank talking to me, but he was using my name! I answered him: "Hi, Frank!" He was quiet. I reached over to turn off my bedside lamp. Just then I heard Frank's voice again. "Goodnight!" he said. "Goodnight, Frank!" I replied.

138

Features of a Journal Entry

A journal entry is one form of personal narrative. The writer describes a personal experience and provides important details about it. One purpose for writing a journal entry is to remember an event. The writer is the audience, although the journal entry may be shared with others.

- A journal entry is usually organized according to time or chronology.

- It is written from a first-person point of view and uses the pronouns *I, me,* and *my.*

- It often contains the writer's feelings as well as descriptions, explanations, and examples to clarify main ideas.

Your Turn

Write a journal entry about an encounter you have had with an animal. The animal could be a pet, one you saw at the zoo, or a wild animal. Use lots of details so that the reader can understand your experience. Use the writer's checklist to check your writing.

Writer's Checklist

 Ideas and Content: Did I delete unimportant details that do not help the reader to understand my ideas?

✓ **Organization:** Do my ideas flow together in a logical way?

✓ **Voice:** Does my journal entry sound like something I would say?

✓ **Word Choice:** Did I use strong and colorful words?

✓ **Sentence Fluency:** When I read my journal entry aloud, does it sound pleasing?

✓ **Conventions:** Are all of my sentences complete? Did I check my spelling?

139

Transparency 17: **Experience/ Details Chart**
Transparency 18: **Draft**
Transparency 19: **Revision**

Transparency 17

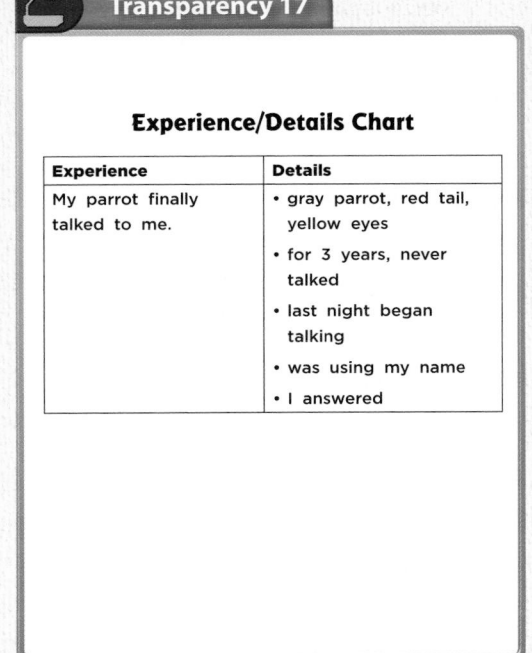

Experience/Details Chart

Experience	Details
My parrot finally talked to me.	• gray parrot, red tail, yellow eyes • for 3 years, never talked • last night began talking • was using my name • I answered

Writing Transparency 17

PREWRITE

Discuss the writing prompt on page 139. Have students talk about experiences they have had with animals. Ask them to choose the experiences they would most like to share or self-select another topic. Students should set a purpose for writing and identify their audience.

Display **Transparency 17.** Discuss how Bao used an Experience/Details Chart to plan his writing. Have students create their own Experience/Details Charts to plan their journal entries. Have them discuss their ideas with classmates. See page 139B for **Conferencing Tips.**

DRAFT

Display **Transparency 18.** Discuss how Bao used his chart to write his journal entry. Then have students use their webs to write their journal entries.

REVISE

Display **Transparency 19.** Discuss the revisions. Then present the lesson on **Unimportant Details** on page 139A. Students can revise their drafts or place them in portfolios to work on later. If students choose to revise, have them work with a partner and use the Writer's Checklist on page 139. Students may work with partners to **proofread** their writing. For **Publishing Options,** see page 139A.

For lessons on **Run-On Sentences, Spelling,** and **Word Choice,** see page 139B, and **5 Day Spelling** and **Grammar** on pages 139G–139H.

Students can present their writing orally to the class. See the Speaking and Listening tips below. They can also use their best cursive to write their entries. Tell students to be sure that their side margins are even. (See **Teacher's Resource Book** pages 168–173 for cursive models and practice.) Then they can use these entries as starting points for ongoing journal writing. Discuss the advantages of journal writing and establish a schedule for students to create and share entries.

Speaking and Listening

SPEAKING STRATEGIES

■ Read your journal entry several times to memorize the important parts.

■ Practice in front of a mirror to see if your gestures and expressions recreate the emotion you felt.

LISTENING STRATEGIES

■ Pay attention to the speaker's verbal and nonverbal clues.

■ Try to see a picture in your mind of the events.

4- and 6-Point Scoring Rubrics

Use the rubrics on pages 143G–143H to score published writing.

Writing Process

For a complete lesson, see Unit Writing pages 143A–143H.

139A

Unimportant Details

EXPLAIN/MODEL

When writers are drafting, they often include many details about a topic, writing whatever comes to mind. During the revision process, however, writers must decide which details are important for the focus of the story and which details take away from the focus. Once these decisions are made, writers can delete unimportant details. Display **Transparency 20.**

Think Aloud The writer includes many important details as she describes the experience in the woods with Baby. She tells what happened, and she uses good word choices to help readers understand the event. For example, she tells us that the creek water was green. However, there are some unimportant details that need to be deleted.

Transparency 20

Monday, October 3

    I've had my African gray parrot for about three years. His name is Frank. He's ~about a foot tall, with~ gray ~feathers all over,~ except for his ~brilliant~ red tail. His eyes are yellow.

    I've been talking to Frank for three years, but in all this time he ~'s only squawked back at me~ ~hasn't talked.~

    Last night all of that changed. I was reading in bed. All of a sudden I heard, "Hi Bao!" I glanced over, and Frank was staring at me. Then he said it again, "Hi, Bao!" ~I couldn't believe it! Not only was Frank talking to me, but he was using my name!~ I answered him: "Hi, Frank!" He was quiet. I reached over to turn off my bedside lamp. Just then I heard Frank's voice again. "Goodnight!" he said. ~"Goodnight, Frank!" I replied.~

Writing Transparency 20

PRACTICE/APPLY

Work with students to delete one or two unimportant details, and discuss why they are unnecessary. Then, have students work in pairs to finish the task. Next, have students work independently to identify unimportant details in nonfiction texts that they have read recently.

As students revise their journal entries, have them delete unimportant details. Also, tell students to think about how their word choices convey information to readers.

Writer's Toolbox

Writing Trait: Word Choice

Explain/Model The best writers choose words that *show* readers what they write rather than words that just *tell* information. Consider the difference between these two sentences: *The sun was hot. I wiped the sweat from my forehead.* Have students review Bao's journal entry on page 138. Ask students to identify words and phrases, such as "about a foot tall" and "brilliant red tail" that help them visualize what Bao describes.

Practice/Apply As students draft and revise their journal entries, have them think about words and phrases that will best convey descriptions to readers. Suggest that students add adjectives and comparisons to their journal entries.

Run-On Sentences

Explain/Model A run-on sentence combines two independent clauses as if they were one sentence: *The sun is hot I put on a hat.* Point out that each sentence has a subject and a predicate. Model strategies for fixing run-on sentences: adding a period or rewriting the sentence as a compound or complex sentence.

Practice/Apply Revise Bao's journal entry on page 138 to include several run-on sentences. Provide students with copies of this revised entry to edit. For a complete lesson on fixing run-on sentences and mechanics, see pages 139I–139J.

Mechanics Review sentence fragments. Have students correct fragments as they proofread.

Conferencing Tips

Peer Conferencing Have students review each other's Experience/Details Charts. Encourage them to point out important and unimportant details. Students can ask these questions as they conference.

- How does this detail help readers understand the story?

- If this detail were missing, would the story still make sense? Would it be as interesting?

Spelling Words with /ûr/ and /îr/

Write the words *stern* and *clear* on the board. The /ûr/ sound is spelled *er*. The /ûr/ sound can also be spelled *ur* and *uir*. The /îr/ sound is spelled *ear*. The /îr/ sound can also be spelled *eer*. Remind students to pay attention when they spell words with these sounds. They can use a print or online dictionary to check spelling in their drafts. For a complete lesson on spelling words with /ûr/ and /îr/ sounds, see pages 139G–139H.

Technology

Suggest that students use the grammar check as they proofread their writing. Tell them that on most programs, the grammar check will alert writers to errors in sentence punctuation.

Objectives

- Apply knowledge of word meaning and context clues
- Use a thesaurus or dictionary for synonyms

Materials

- Vocabulary Transparencies 9, 10
- Leveled Practice Books, p. 34

Vocabulary

cooperation (p. 125) act or process of working together with others

celebration (p. 120) special activities in honor of a person, act, time, or day

fragrance (p. 122) sweet smell; pleasing odor

variety (p. 122) difference; change; a choice of

canceled (p. 131) ended; withdrawn

moistened (p. 129) made wet

theory (p. 131) explanation based on observation or reasoning

transformed (p. 125) changed in appearance

ELL | Access for All

Make Connections For *transformed*, discuss how superheroes transform into their superhero forms. For *canceled*, ask, *If I canceled a subject tomorrow, which subject should I cancel? Explain why.*

Review
Vocabulary

Words in Context

EXPLAIN/MODEL

Review the meanings of the vocabulary words. Display **Transparency 10.** Model how to use word meanings and context clues to fill in the missing words.

Think Aloud I can tell that the word that would complete the first sentence must be a noun. It's something that the neighbors did together. Cleaning a park is a big job, so I'm sure that the neighbors had to work together. *Cooperation* is a word that means "working together." That word would make sense in the sentence.

Transparency 9

| canceled | celebration | cooperation | fragrance |
| moistened | theory | transformed | variety |

The (1) <u>cooperation</u> among neighbors was impressive.

The (2) <u>celebration</u> included a parade.

The (3) <u>fragrance</u> of the baking cake made me hungry.

There was a (4) <u>variety</u> of things to do at the amusement park.

The program was (5) <u>canceled</u> after people stopped watching it.

She (6) <u>moistened</u> the towel with water.

Jane had a (7) <u>theory</u> about why her cat had been missing.

The boy (8) <u>transformed</u> his looks by cutting his long hair.

Vocabulary Transparency 9

PRACTICE/APPLY

Instruct students to complete the remaining sentences on their own. Review the students' answers as a class.

Word Towers Using word families, have students build word towers. For example, students can write the vocabulary word *celebration* in the middle of a sheet of paper. They can then stack related words either above or below *celebration* to form a tower shape. Sample related words: *celebrate, celebrant, celebrated, celebrity.* Have partners shape and discuss their towers.

STRATEGY
THESAURUS/DICTIONARY: SYNONYMS

EXPLAIN/MODEL

- A dictionary identifies the part of speech and states the definition(s) of a word.

- A thesaurus lists other words that have almost the same meaning as a given word.

 Display **Transparency 10** and model how to use a thesaurus to find a synonym for *walked* in item 1. Remind students to look up the present tense forms of verbs.

 Transparency 10

SYNONYMS IN CONTEXT

1. Original: "No," John said as he <u>walked</u> into the room.

   Revision: "No," John said as he <u>strolled</u> into the room.

2. The day was <u>hot</u>.

3. Jane and Mary <u>argued</u>.

4. The kitchen smelled <u>good</u>.

5. The girl was <u>beautiful</u>.

Vocabulary Strategy Transparency 10

PRACTICE/APPLY

Guide students to complete items 2–5 on the transparency. Have them use a thesaurus to find synonyms for the underlined words.

Quick Check
Can students determine word meanings?
Can students use reference materials to find synonyms?

During **Small Group Instruction**

If No → **Approaching Level** Vocabulary, pp. 139N–139O

If Yes → **On Level** Options, pp. 139Q–139R

Beyond Level Options, pp. 139S–139T

ELL **Access for All**

Synonyms Point out the context clue words in each sentence on the transparency: 1) *walked*, 2) *hot*, 3) *argued*, 4) *good*, 5) *beautiful*. Help students use the thesaurus to look up the words and find a synonym. Have students work with partners.

■ **On Level Practice Book O,** page 34

Synonyms are words that have very similar meanings. A thesaurus contains lists of synonyms. A dictionary often includes synonyms for a word along with the word's definition.

aroma *n.* smell, scent, odor
brave *adj.* courageous, fearless
dog *n.* hound, mutt, pooch
village *n.* metropolis, town, city

Use the thesaurus entries in the box to find synonyms for the underlined word in each sentence. Rewrite each sentence using one of the synonyms.

1. The <u>aroma</u> of baking bread made my mouth water.
   The smell of the baking bread made my mouth water.

2. The <u>brave</u> firefighter rescued three people from the burning building.
   The courageous firefighter rescued three people from the burning building.

3. Our <u>village</u> was growing larger and larger as new people moved in.
   Our town was growing larger and larger as new people moved in.

4. We saw a spotted <u>dog</u> with long fur sitting by our door.
   We saw a spotted hound with long fur sitting by our door.

⭐ **Approaching Practice Book A,** page 34

◆ **Beyond Practice Book B,** page 34

Objective
- Decode words with /ûr/ and /îr/

Materials
- Leveled Practice Book, p. 35
- Teacher's Resource Book, p. 9

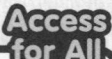

ELL / **Access for All**

Pronunciation
Pronouncing *r*-controlled vowels can be difficult for many students. Spend additional time having students say the words in isolation and in sentences. Make sure students understand the meanings of the words.

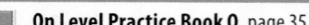

On Level Practice Book O, page 35

The letters *ur, er, ir,* or *ear* can stand for the /ûr/ sound in *fur, her, bird,* and *earn.* The letters *ear* and *eer* can stand for the /îr/ sound, as in *fear* and *deer.*

A. Place each word in the column that best represents its vowel sound.

| squirm | dreary | engineer | verse | clear |
| nerve | lurch | learn | sneer | ear |

fur /ûr/		fear /îr/	
1. squirm		6. dreary	
2. nerve		7. engineer	
3. lurch		8. clear	
4. learn		9. sneer	
5. verse		10. ear	

B. Answer the questions using the chart above.

11. How can the /ûr/ sound be spelled?
ir, er, ur, ear

12. How can the /îr/ sound be spelled?
ear, eer

★ **Approaching Practice Book A,** page 35

◆ **Beyond Practice Book B,** page 35

Phonics
Words with /ûr/ and /îr/

 **Access for All**

EXPLAIN/MODEL

- The letters *ur, er, ir,* or *ear* can stand for the /ûr/ sound, as in *fur, her, bird,* and *earn.*

- The letters *ear* and *eer* can stand for the /îr/ sound, as in *fear* and *deer.*

Write the word *yearn* on the board.

Think Aloud I know that *ear* can stand for the /âr/ sound in *bear,* the /îr/ sound in *fear,* or the /ûr/ sound in *earn.* I can try all three ways of saying *ear* in this word and see which makes sense. I find that /yîrn/ using the /îr/ sound in *near* and /yârn/ using the /âr/ sound in *bear* don't make sense. When I try the /ûr/ sound in *earn,* I get /yûrn/. *Yearn* is a word I know. *Yearn* means "to long for."

PRACTICE/APPLY List these words: *squirm, nerve, year, lurk, spur, sneer, stern, blurt, verse.* Ask students to sort the words by sound, organizing them in two columns on their papers. Remind students that recognizing word families and spelling patterns for words with /ûr/ or /îr/ can help them decode unfamiliar words.

Decode Multisyllabic Words Write *rehearse, purchase, immerse, earache, disturbance, advertisement, urgent, cheerleading.* Model syllabicating the words. Challenge students to identify the *r*-controlled vowel sound in each word. Then have them sort the words first by sound and next by spelling. For more practice, see the Decodable Passages on **Teacher's Resource Book** page 9.

 **Cooperative Learning**

Word Families Create and distribute word cards for *turn, fear, hurt, earth,* and *near.* Model adding *re-* to *turn.* Challenge teams to add on to each other word without changing the *r*-controlled vowel sound. Teams should say their new words. Give one point for each correct answer and a bonus point for any three-syllable answer. Samples: *fearlessly, hurtful, earthworm, nearby.*

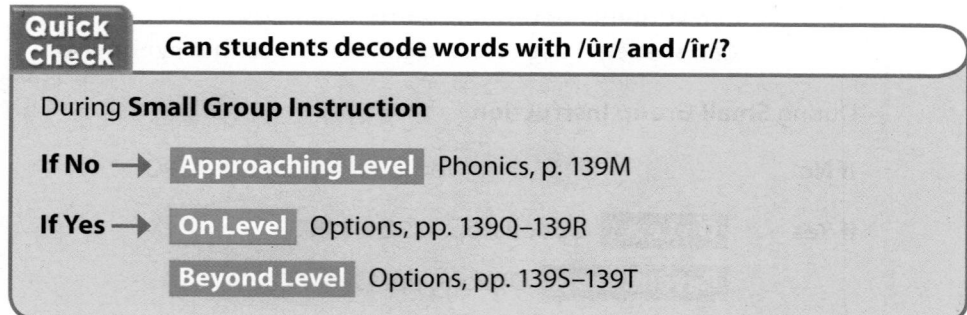

Quick Check **Can students decode words with /ûr/ and /îr/?**

During **Small Group Instruction**

If No → **Approaching Level** Phonics, p. 139M

If Yes → **On Level** Options, pp. 139Q–139R

Beyond Level Options, pp. 139S–139T

Vocabulary Building

Oral Language

Expand Vocabulary Use the following prompt to have students make word webs.

Write *Dogs to the Rescue* in the center of a word web. Using the main selection, dictionaries, thesauruses, and encyclopedias, have students find and brainstorm words that relate to this week's theme. You may include words such as *brave*, *intelligent*, or *loyal*. Discuss these words and several synonyms for each word in circles that radiate from the center circle of your web.

Vocabulary Building

Synonyms Tell student pairs to compose a dialogue of about ten lines. Give the students subjects that complement another unit of study currently going on in the classroom from which to choose. Then ask students to circle all the words in the dialogue that are not descriptive, such as *said* and *walked*. Instruct students to use thesauruses or dictionaries to replace the nondescriptive words with more descriptive synonyms. Invite volunteers to perform their revised dialogues for the class.

Apply Vocabulary

Write a Nomination Give students the following writing prompt:

Nominate your pet for an Amazing Pet award. Describe your pet and why you believe that he or she is amazing. If you do not have a pet, nominate a pet you know, or write about a pet that you would like to have.

Vocabulary Review

Vocabulary Game

- Write each vocabulary word on a note card. Punch a hole in each card and tie a string through the hole.

- Have each student hang one word around his or her neck with the card hanging toward the student's back.

- Students move around the room talking to each other and providing one another with synonym clues for the words on each of their backs.

- Tell students to identify the vocabulary words on their backs through the synonym clues.

 Technology

 Vocabulary PuzzleMaker

 For additional vocabulary and spelling games go to www.macmillanmh.com

5 Day Spelling

Words with /ûr/ and /îr/

clear	stern	jeer
nerve	spurts	sneer
squirt	lurch	dreary
verse	blurt	squirm
surf	thirst	swerve
lurk	spur	yearns
year	engineer	

Review aboard, barge, scarce

Challenge smear, rehearse

Dictation Sentences

1. It was a **clear**, cloudless day.
2. It takes nerve to get up there.
3. Squirt oil on the rusty hinge.
4. Ken read a verse from the poem.
5. Dana likes to surf at the beach.
6. The dog likes to lurk under the porch.
7. He grew two inches in a **year**.
8. She spoke in a stern voice.
9. The water came out in spurts.
10. The car will only lurch forward.
11. Try not to blurt out the answer.
12. She drank to quench her thirst.
13. It was a spur of the moment decision.
14. My mom is a chemical engineer.
15. Fans jeer at the visiting team.
16. Wipe the sneer from your face.
17. Roof dogs lead a dreary life.
18. The puppy tried to squirm free.
19. The car had to swerve suddenly.
20. Every roof dog yearns to be free.

Review/Challenge Words

1. The captain shouted "All aboard!"
2. We crossed the river on a barge.
3. Food is scarce in this poor town.
4. The chalk might smear your shirt.
5. We'll rehearse before the concert.

Words in **bold** are from the main selection.

Day 1 Pretest

ASSESS PRIOR KNOWLEDGE

Use the Dictation Sentences. Say the underlined word, read the sentence, and repeat the word. Have students write the words on **Spelling Practice Book** page 25. For a modified list, use the first 12 Spelling Words and the Review Words. For a more challenging list, use Spelling Words 3–20 and the Challenge Words. Students may correct their own tests.

Have students cut apart the Spelling Word Cards BLM on **Teacher's Resource Book** page 70 and figure out a way to sort them. They can save the cards for use throughout the week.

For additional practice, use Spelling Practice Book page 26.

For **Leveled Word Lists**, go to www.macmillanmh.com

Day 2 Word Sorts

TEACHER AND STUDENT SORTS

- Write *dreary, swerve, sneer, spur, and thirst* and read each one aloud.

- Help students notice the vowel sounds. Tell them to use /ûr/ and /îr/ as column headings for a word sort of the Spelling Words and Challenge Words in their word study notebooks.

- Students can begin with the words from the board. Then use the Word Cards to read the rest of the words aloud so students can complete the sort. Check the sort as a class.

- Ask students to describe sound and spelling patterns they notice among the listed words. Invite students to sort the words any other way.

Spelling Practice Book, pages 25–26

Fold back the paper along the dotted line. Write the words in the blanks as they are read aloud. When you finish the test, unfold the paper. Use the list at the right to correct any spelling mistakes.

1. ___	1. year
2. ___	2. nerve
3. ___	3. surf
4. ___	4. verse
5. ___	5. clear
6. ___	6. squirm
7. ___	7. dreary
8. ___	8. jeer
9. ___	9. thirst
10. ___	10. sneer
11. ___	11. squirt
12. ___	12. lurk
13. ___	13. yearns
14. ___	14. spurts
15. ___	15. swerve
16. ___	16. stern
17. ___	17. blurt
18. ___	18. lurch
19. ___	19. spur
20. ___	20. engineer
Review Words 21. ___	21. aboard
22. ___	22. barge
23. ___	23. scarce
Challenge Words 24. ___	24. smear
25. ___	25. rehearse

Spelling Practice Book, page 27

squirm	dreary	nerve	squirt	verse
surf	lurk	swerve	stern	spurts
lurch	blurt	thirst	spur	engineer
jeer	sneer	clear	year	yearns

Sort each spelling word by finding the sound and spelling pattern to which it belongs.

Write the words that have /ûr/ spelled:

er
1. nerve
2. verse
3. swerve
4. stern

ur
surf
1. lurk
2. spurts
3. lurch
4. blurt
5. spur

ir
1. squirm
2. squirt
3. thirst

ear
1. yearns

Write the words that have /îr/ spelled:

1. ___
2. ear

eer
1. engineer
2. jeer
3. sneer

Day 3 — Word Meanings

CATEGORIES

Read each group of words below. Help students notice that the words in each group rhyme. Have students copy the words into their word study notebooks, completing the group by adding a Spelling Word that rhymes with the others.

1. swerve, curve, _____ (nerve)
2. hear, fear, _____ (jeer, sneer)
3. firm, worm, _____ (squirm)
4. teary, weary, _____ (dreary)

Challenge students to use one of the word groups to write a three-line or four-line rhyming poem. Poems should be fun but also demonstrate an understanding of the words. Have students share their poems with the class.

Day 4 — Review and Proofread

SPIRAL REVIEW

Review words with /är/, /âr/, and /ôr/. Write *aboard, barge,* and *scarce* on the board. Ask students to identify the *r*-controlled vowel sounds in each word.

PROOFREAD AND WRITE

Write these sentences on the board, including the misspelled words. Ask students to proofread the sentences, circling the misspelled words and correcting them.

1. His sturn, disapproving look made me squarm in fear. (stern, squirm)
2. The skuirt of water did not satisfy my therst. (squirt, thirst)
3. She yerns to blurte out her secret. (yearns, blurt)

Day 5 — Assess and Reteach

POSTTEST

Use the Dictation Sentences on page 139G for the Posttest. If students have difficulty with any words in the lesson, have them place the words in a list entitled "Spelling Words I Want to Remember" in their word study notebooks.

Challenge student partners to look for other words that have the same /ûr/ and /îr/ sounds they studied this week, either in their reading or in other materials. Partners should work together to sort the words by vowel sounds.

Spelling Practice Book, page 28

squirm	dreary	nerve	squirt	verse
surf	lurk	swerve	stern	spurts
lurch	blurt	thirst	spur	engineer
jeer	sneer	clear	year	yearns

Opposites

Write the spelling word whose meaning is the opposite of each clue below.

1. smiling __stern__
2. applaud __jeer__
3. cheery __dreary__
4. be still __squirm__
5. cloudy __clear__
6. smile warmly __sneer__

Fill in the Blank

Write the spelling word that best completes each sentence.

7. Every roof dog __yearns__ to be free.
8. Most dogs do not have the __nerve__ to escape.
9. They __lurk__ in the shadows of the buildings.
10. A __year__ is too long to be tied up.
11. The dogs would __lurch__ at anyone who passed by.
12. They would bark in __spurts__ during the day.
13. Pipiolo would __blurt__ out a bark in reply.
14. He would __swerve__ away from the other dogs.
15. He tried to __spur__ them to escape.
16. It would take an __engineer__ to break their chains.
17. Lupe wanted to take Pipiolo for a run in the __surf__.
18. She liked to __squirt__ water in his mouth.
19. He had a great __thirst__ for water.
20. Lupe sang a __verse__ of her favorite song to him.

Spelling Practice Book, page 29

Circle the misspelled words in the diary entry below. Write the words correctly on the lines below.

Dear Diary,

The roof dogs will never (jere) at Pipiolo again. Today he was the (enginear) of their escape. Pipiolo knew the dogs finally had the (nurv) to break free. He gave them (cler) instructions about what to do. Then he told the dogs to wait. A little later, a truck came up the road to the village to deliver oranges. The dogs jumped into the back of the truck. With a (lirch) the truck headed out of the village. The roof dogs had left their (drery) lives behind!

1. __jeer__
2. __engineer__
3. __nerve__
4. __clear__
5. __lurch__
6. __dreary__

Writing Activity

Pretend that Pipiolo is your pet dog. Write a paragraph about what you and Pipiolo might do together. Use four words from the spelling list.

_____
_____
_____
_____
_____
_____
_____

Spelling Practice Book, page 30

Look at the words in each set below. One word in each set is spelled correctly. Use a pencil to fill in the circle next to the correct word. Before you begin, look at the sample set of words. Sample A has been done for you. Do Sample B by yourself. When you are sure you know what to do, you may go on with the rest of the page.

Sample A:
- Ⓐ first
- Ⓑ furst
- Ⓒ foorst
- Ⓓ fuhrst

Sample B:
- Ⓔ deir
- Ⓕ dere
- Ⓖ deer
- Ⓗ der

1.
- Ⓐ skwirm
- Ⓑ squirm
- Ⓒ sqirm
- Ⓓ sqoorm

2.
- Ⓔ dreary
- Ⓕ drery
- Ⓖ dreary
- Ⓗ drerey

3.
- Ⓐ nerve
- Ⓑ nurv
- Ⓒ nirv
- Ⓓ nirve

4.
- Ⓔ skwirt
- Ⓕ sqirt
- Ⓖ sqoort
- Ⓗ squirt

5.
- Ⓐ verss
- Ⓑ virse
- Ⓒ verse
- Ⓓ virs

6.
- Ⓔ surf
- Ⓕ sirf
- Ⓖ soorf
- Ⓗ surfe

7.
- Ⓐ lurk
- Ⓑ loork
- Ⓒ lurke
- Ⓓ lerke

8.
- Ⓔ swurve
- Ⓕ swurv
- Ⓖ swerve
- Ⓗ swirve

9.
- Ⓐ stirn
- Ⓑ sturne
- Ⓒ sturn
- Ⓓ stern

10.
- Ⓔ spurtes
- Ⓕ sperts
- Ⓖ spurts
- Ⓗ spourts

11.
- Ⓐ lirtch
- Ⓑ lirch
- Ⓒ lurche
- Ⓓ lurch

12.
- Ⓔ blurt
- Ⓕ blirt
- Ⓖ blerte
- Ⓗ blert

13.
- Ⓐ thurst
- Ⓑ therst
- Ⓒ thirst
- Ⓓ thirste

14.
- Ⓔ spir
- Ⓕ spurre
- Ⓖ spur
- Ⓗ spuhr

15.
- Ⓐ engineer
- Ⓑ enginire
- Ⓒ enginir
- Ⓓ enginere

16.
- Ⓔ jeir
- Ⓕ jere
- Ⓖ jeer
- Ⓗ jir

17.
- Ⓐ snir
- Ⓑ sneer
- Ⓒ snere
- Ⓓ snear

18.
- Ⓔ clir
- Ⓕ cleer
- Ⓖ clere
- Ⓗ clear

19.
- Ⓐ yir
- Ⓑ yeer
- Ⓒ yere
- Ⓓ year

20.
- Ⓔ yurns
- Ⓕ yearns
- Ⓖ yirns
- Ⓗ yerns

Run-On Sentences

Daily Language Activities

Use these activities to reinforce each day's lesson. Write the day's activity on the board, or use **Daily Language Transparency 5**.

DAY 1

Lupe found her dog Pipiolo, when he was just a puppy. because he was so tiny he fit inside a shoe. (1: Pipiolo when; 2: Because; 3: tiny, he)

DAY 2

Pipiolo and Lupe walked into town? all the dogs barked at them from the rooftops Pipiolo was not afraid. (1: town. All; 2: rooftops, but)

DAY 3

Walked through a field. Pipiolo started sniffing and barking and Lupe understood exactly what to do. (1: Lupe and Pipiolo walked; 2: barking, and)

DAY 4

Lupe used her ruler to dig up some grass she and Pipiolo tossed some to each angry roof dog the roof dogs barked in surprise. (1: grass. She; 2: roof dog. The)

DAY 5

Pipiolo went out at night Lupe did not know one night she followed him she found him watching television in town. (1: night, but; 2: know. One; 3: him. She)

ELL | **Access for All**

Run-On Sentences Review punctuation marks: *period, comma*. Write two sentences, ending each with a period. Read the sentences aloud. Erase the period, then read the two sentences as one sentence. Explain that this is called a run-on sentence.

Day 1 | Introduce the Concept

INTRODUCE RUN-ON SENTENCES

Present the following:

Access for All

- A run-on sentence joins two or more sentences that should be written separately: *Maria walks the dogs Tina feeds the cat.*

- You can correct run-on sentences by separating the complete ideas into separate sentences: *Maria walks the dogs. Tina feeds the cat.*

See Grammar Transparency 21 for modeling and guided practice.

Grammar Practice Book, page 25

- A **run-on sentence** joins together two or more sentences that should be written separately.
- You can correct run-on sentences by separating the complete ideas into separate sentences or by rewriting run-on sentences as compound sentences.

Correct the following run-on sentences.

1. San Pablo Etla is on the edge of a valley Lupe's father built their house on the mountainside.
   San Pablo Etla is on the edge of a valley. Lupe's father built their house on the mountainside.

2. Lupe found Pipiolo asleep inside an old shoe she saw greatness when he opened his eyes.
   Lupe found Pipiolo asleep inside an old shoe, and she saw greatness when he opened his eyes.

3. The roof dogs guarded the roofs they would bark furiously down at Lupe and Pipiolo.
   The roof dogs guarded the roofs, and they would bark furiously down at Lupe and Pipiolo.

4. Pipiolo slipped into a cornfield Lupe followed him.
   Pipiolo slipped into a cornfield, and Lupe followed him.

5. Pipiolo barked all the dogs jumped down onto the pile of oranges in the truck.
   Pipiolo barked, and all the dogs jumped down onto the pile of oranges in the truck.

6. Lupe took a walk over to the village of Viquera it was a longer route to her school.
   Lupe took a walk over to the village of Viquera. It was a longer route to her school.

Day 2 | Teach the Concept

REVIEW RUN-ON SENTENCES

Ask students what makes a sentence a "run-on." Ask how a run-on sentence differs from a complete sentence.

CORRECTING RUN-ON SENTENCES

- You can correct a run-on sentence by separating its complete thoughts into separate sentences.

- You can also correct a run-on by rewriting it as a compound sentence: *Maria walks the dogs, and Tina feeds the cat.*

- You can correct a run-on by rewriting it as a complex sentence: *Maria walks the dogs when Tina feeds the cat.*

See Grammar Transparency 22 for modeling and guided practice.

Grammar Practice Book, page 26

You can correct a run-on sentence in several ways.

- Correct a run-on sentence by separating its complete thoughts into separate sentences.
- Correct a run-on sentence by rewriting it as a compound sentence.

Correct the run-on sentences below either by separating them as two sentences or by rewriting them as a compound sentence.

1. Lupe lived in San Pablo Etla the village is in southern Mexico.
   Lupe lived in San Pablo Etla. The village is in southern Mexico.

2. The roof dogs would run to the edge of their roofs they would bark furiously at Lupe and Pipiolo.
   The roof dogs would run to the edge of their roofs, and they would bark furiously at Lupe and Pipiolo.

3. The dogs didn't frighten Lupe she knew they were the ones who were frightened.
   The dogs didn't frighten Lupe. She knew they were the ones who were frightened.

4. Pipiolo was lucky Lupe didn't have a flat roof Papa would have put him up there.
   Pipiolo was lucky Lupe didn't have a flat roof, or Papa would have put him up there.

5. Lupe gave each roof dog a tuft of grass she saved the piece with a flower for Chulita.
   Lupe gave each roof dog a tuft of grass. She saved the piece with a flower for Chulita.

6. Lupe continued to dig up grass Pipiolo slept in the shade.
   Lupe continued to dig up grass, but Pipiolo slept in the shade.

Day 3 Review and Practice

REVIEW CORRECTING RUN-ON SENTENCES

Review correcting run-on sentences by using capital letters, commas, and end marks.

MECHANICS AND USAGE: CORRECTING FRAGMENTS

- A sentence fragment is a group of words that does not tell a complete thought. A fragment may be missing a subject, a verb, or both: *The lonely boy.* (missing a verb); *Ran for the bus.* (missing a noun); *While waiting.* (missing a noun and a verb)

- Correct a fragment by adding the missing part of speech: *The lonely boy made a friend. Tony ran for the bus. While waiting, I read a book.*

See Grammar Transparency 23 for modeling and guided practice.

Grammar Practice Book, page 27

- A **run-on sentence** joins together two or more sentences that should be written separately. You can correct a run-on sentence by separating the two complete ideas into two sentences. You can also rewrite a run-on sentence as a compound sentence.
- A **sentence fragment** is a group of words that does not contain a complete thought. A fragment may be missing a subject, a verb, or both. You can correct a fragment by adding the missing part of speech.

Correct the run-on sentences below by writing separate sentences or compound sentences.

1. Pipiolo was a perky puppy he loved to run in the mountains. **Pipiolo was a perky puppy, and he loved to run in the mountains.**
2. The village of San Pablo Etla is very small it is on the edge of a wide valley in southern Mexico. **The village of San Pablo Etla is very small. It is on the edge of a wide valley in southern Mexico.**
3. The roof dogs smelled the aromas of freedom they missed the smell of freshly dug earth. **The roof dogs smelled the aromas of freedom. They missed the smell of freshly dug earth.**

Correct the sentence fragments below by adding a subject, a verb, or both. Write the new sentences on the lines provided.

4. Commanded the roof dogs to escape. **Pipiolo commanded the roof dogs to escape.**
5. Was the only dog left on the truck. **Chulita was the only dog left on the truck.**
6. The big truck. **The big truck rumbled down the mountain road.**

Day 4 Review and Proofread

REVIEW RUN-ON SENTENCES

Ask students to explain what a run-on sentence is. Then have them explain ways to correct a run-on sentence.

PROOFREAD

Have students correct the items below.

1. Every night Pipiolo would watch television then he would go bark at the rooftop dogs (television. Then; dogs.)

2. they were planning their escape Only Pipiolo. Knew when they would leave. (They; escape.; Pipiolo knew)

3. Pipiolo and Lupe loved the soil, the trees, and the flowers they. enjoyed being close to all these things. every day (flowers. They enjoyed; things every day.)

See Grammar Transparency 24 for modeling and guided practice.

Grammar Practice Book, page 28

- A **run-on sentence** joins together two or more sentences that should be written separately.
- A run-on sentence can be broken into two separate sentences or rewritten as a compound or complex sentence.
- Remember to add a comma before *and*, *but*, or *or* when changing a run-on sentence into a compound sentence. Also, use commas to separate three or more words or phrases in a series.

Proofread the following paragraph. Rewrite it correctly on the lines provided.

Pipiolo and Chulita went on many adventures together they traveled over mountains across prairies and through forests. Wherever they went, they helped more roof dogs escape to freedom they even made a few friends along the way.

one day, they came across the village of Viquera there were many dogs trapped on the flat, concrete roofs. Pipiolo came up with a plan to set them all free Chulita told the dogs about the plan. Because they were so excited they barked loudly all day long.

Pipiolo and Chulita went on many adventures together. They traveled over mountains, across prairies, and through forests. Wherever they went, they helped more roof dogs escape to freedom, and they even made a few friends along the way.

One day, they came across the village of Viquera. There were many dogs trapped on the flat, concrete roofs. Pipiolo came up with a plan to set them all free, and Chulita told the dogs about the plan. Because they were so excited, they barked loudly all day long.

Day 5 Assess and Reteach

ASSESS

Use the Daily Language Activity and page 29 of the **Grammar Practice Book** for assessment.

RETEACH

Display the uncorrected and corrected Daily Language Activities on a transparency. As a class, try solving the run-on sentences in yet another way. For example, if the first solution was to break the run-on sentence into two sentences, challenge students to rewrite the two sentences as a compound sentence. Have volunteers write their answers on the board.

Use page 30 of the Grammar Practice Book for additional reteaching.

See Grammar Transparency 25 for modeling and guided practice.

Grammar Practice Book, pages 29–30

Correct the run-on sentences below. To do so, you may write two shorter sentences, or you may add a conjunction to create a compound sentence.

1. The people of San Pablo Etla had roof dogs the dogs protected their homes from trespassers.
   The people of San Pablo Etla had roof dogs, and the dogs protected their homes from trespassers.

2. Lupe's cousin Inocencia thought that the roof dogs' escape was a miracle everyone else was upset about it.
   Lupe's cousin Inocencia thought that the roof dogs' escape was a miracle. Everyone else was upset about it.

3. Pipiolo barked loudly all of the dogs understood his message.
   Pipiolo barked loudly, and all of the dogs understood his message.

4. Lupe found Pipiolo when he was just a puppy he was so small he fit inside a shoe.
   Lupe found Pipiolo when he was just a puppy. He was so small he fit inside a shoe.

5. The Tienda Soliz had the only television in town its only channel showed old American westerns.
   The Tienda Soliz had the only television in town, and its only channel showed old American westerns.

6. John Wayne jumped onto a wagon full of hay that is what gave Pipiolo the idea to free the roof dogs.
   John Wayne jumped onto a wagon full of hay, and that is what gave Pipiolo the idea to free the roof dogs.

End-of-Week Assessment

Administer the Test

Weekly Reading Assessment,
Passage and questions, pages 53–60

ASSESSED SKILLS

- Cause and Effect
- Vocabulary Words
- Use a Thesaurus: Synonyms
- Words with /ûr/ and /îr/
- Run-on Sentences

 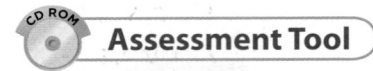

Macmillan/McGraw-Hill

Administer the **Weekly Assessment** online or on CD-ROM.

Weekly Assessment, 53–60

Fluency

Assess fluency for one group of students per week. Use the Oral Fluency Record Sheet to track the number of words read correctly. Fluency goal for all students:
100–120 words correct per minute (WCPM).

Approaching Level	Weeks 1, 3, 5
On Level	Weeks 2, 4
Beyond Level	Week 6

Fluency Assessment

Alternative Assessments

- **Leveled Weekly Assessment** for Approaching Level, pages 61–68
- **ELL Assessment,** pages 48–49

ELL Practice and Assessment, 48–49

Diagnose		Prescribe
	IF...	**THEN...**
VOCABULARY WORDS **VOCABULARY STRATEGY** Use a Thesaurus: Synonyms Items 1, 2, 3, 4	0–2 items correct...	Reteach skills using the **Additional Lessons** page T10. Reteach skills: Go to **www.macmillanmh.com** Vocabulary PuzzleMaker Evaluate for Intervention.
COMPREHENSION Skill: Cause and Effect Items 5, 6, 7, 8	0–2 items correct...	Reteach skills using the **Additional Lessons** page T5. Evaluate for Intervention.
GRAMMAR Run-on Sentences Items 9, 10, 11	0–1 items correct...	Reteach skills: **Grammar Practice Book** page 30.
SPELLING Words with /ûr/ and /îr/ Items 12, 13, 14	0–1 items correct...	Reteach skills: Go to **www.macmillanmh.com**
FLUENCY	96–99 WCPM	Fluency Solutions
	0–95 WCPM	Evaluate for Intervention.

READING
Triumphs
AN INTERVENTION PROGRAM

Also Available

To place students in the Intervention Program, use the **Diagnostic Assessment** in the Intervention Teacher's Edition.

Skills Focus ▸ Phonics

Objective	Decode one-syllable and multisyllabic words that include *r*-controlled vowels in both familiar and unfamiliar text
Materials	• **Student Book** "It's a Dog's Life"
	• **Decodable Passages, Teacher's Resource Book** p. 9

WORDS WITH *R*-CONTROLLED VOWELS

Model/Guided Practice

■ Write the letters *b, u, r, n, t* on the board. Then blend the sounds: /bûrnt/.

■ Point out that the sound /ûr/ is spelled *ur*. The /ûr/ sound can also be spelled *er, ir,* or *ear*.

■ Say: *Look at* learn. *Say the word with me. How is the /ûr/ sound spelled?*

■ Next identify how the /ûr/ sound is spelled in *berth, hurl, girl, curb,* and *lurch*. Listen as students say the words. Provide constructive feedback.

■ Have students generate five other single-syllable words with /ûr/.

■ Extend the review to include words with different spellings that have the /îr/ sound, such as *her, heard,* and *word*.

MULTISYLLABIC WORDS WITH *R*-CONTROLLED VOWELS

■ Write the word *merchandise* on the board. Mark the syllables: *mer/chan/dise*. Blend the syllables to pronounce the word: /mûr chən dīz/. Identify the /ûr/ sound and its spelling.

■ Have pairs of students work together to practice decoding longer words with *r*-controlled vowels. Write the following words on the board and say: *With your partner, choose a word. Say the word aloud, emphasizing the r-controlled vowel sound. Circle the* r-controlled *vowel and note the spelling. What do you notice about the* r-controlled *vowels in this list of words?*

burden	furrow	perfume	neighborhood
burglar	hurdle	purchase	furnish
fertilizer	merchant	serpent	survey

■ Circulate and provide support as needed to each pair.

WORD HUNT: WORDS WITH *R*-CONTROLLED VOWELS

■ Review words with *r*-controlled vowels and the possible spellings of these sounds. Have students identify words from "It's a Dog's Life" that have *r*-controlled vowels.

■ Check whether students have found the following:
work, every, learned, her, easier, afternoon, trainer, suffers, exercise variety, whenever, never, different, major, cooperation, during.

■ Report the activity with the decodable passages on page 9 in the **Teacher's Resource Book.**

Constructive Feedback

Isolate the error sound and repeat it with the group. If students say /âr/ instead of /ûr/, point out that the spelling *ear* has more than one sound and say:

The word *learn* and the word *wear* both have *ear* spellings. However, the letters are pronounced differently. Say the word with both sounds: /lârn/ and /lûrn/. You will recognize only one word. However, this strategy doesn't always work: /wâr/ and /wûr/. In these cases, use context clues to determine the correct word and the correct sound.

Repeat as needed with other words with *r*-controlled vowels.

Additional Resources

For each skill below, additional lessons are provided. You can use these lessons on consecutive days after teaching the lessons provided within the week.
• Cause and Effect, T5
• Thesaurus: Synonyms, T10
• Charts, T12

Decodable Text

To help students build speed and accuracy with phonics patterns, use additional decodable text on page 9 of the **Teacher's Resource Book.**

Skills Focus ▶ Fluency

Objective Read with increasing prosody and accuracy at a rate of 100–110 WCPM
Materials • **Approaching Practice Book A,** page 32

MODEL EXPRESSIVE READING

Model reading the Fluency passage in **Practice Book A**, page 32. Tell students to pay close attention to your pauses and intonation as you read. Then read one sentence at a time, and have students repeat the sentence, first as a class and then one by one. Increase your tempo as you go along. As students read, listen carefully for accuracy.

REPEATED READING

Have students continue practicing reading the passage aloud as you circulate and provide constructive feedback. During independent reading time, student partners can take turns reading the passage. One partner reads each sentence aloud, and the other repeats the sentence. Remind students to wait until their partner reaches the end of a sentence before correcting a mistake.

TIMED READING

Tell students that they will be doing a timed reading of the passage at the end of the week.

■ Place the passage from Practice Book A, page 32, face down.

■ When you say "Go" and "Stop," students begin and finish reading the passage aloud. Stop students after one minute.

As students read, note any miscues. Help students record and graph the number of words they read correctly.

Skills Focus ▶ Vocabulary

Objective Apply vocabulary word meanings
Materials • **Vocabulary Cards** • **Transparencies 5a and 5b**

VOCABULARY WORDS

Display the **Vocabulary Cards** for this week's words: *canceled, celebration, cooperation, fragrance, moistened, theory, transformed, variety.* Review how each word is used in "It's a Dog's Life" on **Transparencies 5a** and **5b**. Have students circle any context clues to the words on the transparencies. Ask students to write sentences that illustrate the meanings of the words.

Constructive Feedback

Have students use a stop watch to time their reading of a passage. Tell them to try to decrease their time in subsequent readings. Ask students to pinpoint the most effective speed for the reading and to explain why. Have students use this same strategy as they work with partners to develop fluency.

RESEARCH Why It Matters

Vocabulary Explicit vocabulary instruction, in which children are taught the meanings of specific words, improves reading comprehension.

Timothy Shanahan

 LOG ON

Go to
www.macmillanmh.com

 **Approaching Practice Book A,** page 32

As I read, I will pay attention to tempo.

	"It's my turn to pick a book!" Matthew yelled, drying the
11	supper dishes.
13	"You always pick books that are hard to read!" said his
24	sister, Jill.
26	"Come on, you two, stop fighting," their mother said.
35	"We have a variety of new library books. You can each pick
47	one."
48	Every night, Matthew, Jill, and Mom had a "story time"
58	just before bed. They sat on Mom's bed and took turns
69	reading. Tonight there was a problem.
75	"Can't we watch television instead? I don't want to read
85	tonight," Jill said.
88	"Why? What's wrong?" Matthew asked.
93	"I'm tired, and reading's too hard when you're tired," she
103	answered.
104	"But I thought you enjoyed reading with us," Mom said.
114	Why do we always have to do things that Matthew's good
125	at?" Jill wailed. 128

Comprehension Check

1. Why are Matthew and Jill arguing? **Cause and Effect** Matthew always picks books that are difficult to read.

2. Why doesn't Jill want to read? **Plot** Jill is tired.

	Words Read	−	Number of Errors	=	Words Correct Score
First Read		−		=	
Second Read		−		=	

Small Group

Vocabulary

Review last week's words (*mission, disasters, function, gravity, maze, adjusted, environment, zone*) and this week's words (*fragrance, celebration, variety, moistened, cooperation, canceled, theory, transformed*). Have students write sentences using at least six different vocabulary words.

Student Book, or Transparencies 5a and 5b

ELL   Access for All

Use Graphic Organizers
Use a cause-and-effect organizer to list other cause and effect relationships in "It's a Dog's Life."

Skills Focus ▶ Vocabulary

Objective	Use a thesaurus to find synonyms
Materials	• **Student Book** *Pipiolo and the Roof Dogs* • thesaurus

THESAURUS: SYNONYMS

Ask students to use a thesaurus to find synonyms for the vocabulary words as they are used in *Pipiolo and the Roof Dogs*. Remind them to make sure the synonyms are the same parts of speech as the vocabulary words. Keep a list of all the synonyms on the board.

Skills Focus ▶ Comprehension

Objective	Analyze cause and effect
Materials	• **Student Book** "It's a Dog's Life" • **Transparencies 5a and 5b**

STRATEGY
GENERATE QUESTIONS

Active readers generate questions as they read to help them understand the text: *Are the reasons for the characters' actions clear? What is the setting? What problem does the main character face?* Looking for clues in the text that will answer these and other questions can help readers identify cause-and-effect relationships in the plot.

SKILL
CAUSE AND EFFECT

Explain/Model

- A cause tells how or why something happens. An effect is the result of something that has happened.

- Explicit cause-and-effect situations are sometimes indicated by signal words and phrases including *as a result, because, but, consequently, due to, for, in order to, resulting from, since, so, therefore*, and so on.

Display **Transparencies 5a** and **5b**. Reread the first paragraph of "It's a Dog's Life." Model identifying cause and effect. Ask a volunteer to underline one cause on the transparency and then to circle its effect. Discuss how identifying and understanding cause-and-effect relationships will improve students' reading.

Practice/Apply

Reread the rest of "It's a Dog's Life," and discuss the following questions:

- What causes Ms. Toni to need Sparky's help?

- What effects does Sparky have on Ms. Toni and her life?

Leveled Reader Lesson

Objective   Read to apply strategies and skills
Materials   • **Leveled Reader** *It's Fun When Sam Listens*   • **Student Book** "It's a Dog's Life"

Leveled Reader

PREVIEW AND PREDICT

Discuss the cover and have students preview the first two chapters. Ask students to predict what the story will be about and who Sam might be. Have students write questions to set purposes for reading.

VOCABULARY WORDS

Before reading, review the vocabulary words as necessary. As you read together, discuss how each word is used in the story. Help students identify context clues. Ask: *How do these clues help you decode the word?*

STRATEGY
GENERATE QUESTIONS

Active readers generate questions as they read to help them understand the text: *Are the reasons for the characters' actions clear? What is the setting? What problem does the main character face?* Looking for clues in the text that will answer these and other questions can help readers identify cause-and-effect relationships in the plot.

SKILL
CAUSE AND EFFECT

Remind students to look for cause-and-effect relationships as they read. Help them set up Cause-and-Effect Charts.

Think Aloud In the first chapter, I learn that something is wrong with Jill. She gets mad at Matthew and wants to watch television instead of reading with him and their mom. She bursts into tears when it's her turn to read. Could the cause of Jill's problem be that she's having a hard time reading? I'll continue reading the story to check whether my question is answered. I'll also add this information to my chart.

READ AND RESPOND

Tell students to finish reading the first two chapters of the story. Discuss any questions students ask while reading. Have students complete their Cause-and-Effect Charts after they complete the book.

MAKE CONNECTIONS ACROSS TEXTS

Invite students to compare *It's Fun When Sam Listens* and "It's a Dog's Life."

■ What causes the characters in *It's Fun When Sam Listens* and "It's a Dog's Life" to need help from dogs?

ELL   Access for All

Use Contractions These titles contain the contraction *it's*. Not all languages have contractions. Explain to students that *it's* combines the words *it* and *is*. Contractions are examples of informal language. Have students scan the passages for other contractions. Encourage students to create lists of contractions and their meanings.

On Level Options

Skills Focus ▶ Vocabulary

Objective Use vocabulary words and identify synonyms
Materials • **Student Book** "It's a Dog's Life"

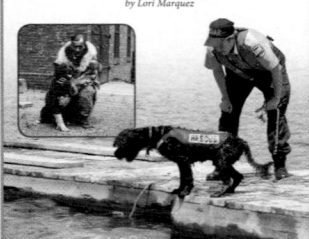

Student Book

VOCABULARY WORDS

Have students create and distribute a word-search puzzle containing the vocabulary words for classmates to solve. Have students supply a list of definitions. To solve the puzzle, the other students must determine which vocabulary word is indicated by the definition and then find that word within the grid. Have the students who created the puzzle check their classmates' work.

THESAURUS: SYNONYMS

Review with students that a thesaurus is a tool that can help them find synonyms for particular words. Have student pairs use a thesaurus to identify synonyms for each vocabulary word in "It's a Dog's Life."

Student Book

Skills Focus ▶ Text Features

Objective Create charts
Materials • **Student Book** "Doggone Work" • Internet, encyclopedia

CHARTS

Discuss the importance of charts in an article such as "Doggone Work." Have students work together to create charts that organize information about their favorite breeds of dogs. Students can use the Internet or an encyclopedia to gather information.

Skills Focus ▶ Fluency

Objective Read fluently with appropriate expression at a rate of 100–120 WCPM
Materials • **On Level Practice Book O,** p. 32

REPEATED READING

Model reading aloud the entire passage on page 32 of **Practice Book O.** Begin reading the passage, slowing for pauses and intonation, and increase the speed and fluency of your reading as the passage continues. Then read one sentence at a time, exaggerating the pauses and intonation. Have students echo-read each sentence with the same expression you used. Listen for accuracy.

Timed Reading At the end of the week, have students read the passage and record their reading rate.

On Level Practice Book O, page 32

As I read, I will pay attention to tempo.

"It's finally here!" I said to myself as I got off the school
13 bus that Friday afternoon. "And it's going to be great!"
23 I had been patient. I'd waited and waited for the big
34 family party. It was just one day away. From all over the city
47 and even as far away as Baltimore, my family was meeting
58 at our house for a cookout supper Saturday night. My older
69 sister, Mai, was excited, too. She had promised to decorate our
80 backyard and even string little lights all over the trees and
91 bushes. We'd start today, and then finish up tomorrow
100 morning before her big soccer game. I never missed Mai's
110 soccer games. She and her team were the city champions,
120 and their games were really fun to watch.
128 But now it was time to decorate the yard. 137

Comprehension Check

1. Why is the narrator excited? **Cause and Effect**
He is excited for the big family party.
2. What is Mai's responsibility for the party? **Plot**
Mai is supposed to decorate the backyard.

	Words Read	–	Number of Errors	=	Words Correct Score
First Read		–		=	
Second Read		–		=	

139Q

Leveled Reader Lesson

Objective Read to apply strategies and skills
Materials
- **Leveled Reader** *The Wag Brigade*
- **Student Book** *Pipiolo and the Roof Dogs*

Leveled Reader

PREVIEW AND PREDICT

Have students preview *The Wag Brigade*.

- What events do you think will happen in the story? What might cause these events? What might be the effects of these events?
- Do you have any questions you would like to ask about the story?

STRATEGY
GENERATE QUESTIONS

Discuss how asking questions as they read can help students become more engaged in a story.

SKILL
CAUSE AND EFFECT

Review: A cause is an event or action that makes something happen. An effect is what happens as a result of an event or action. Ask "Why?" to find the cause. Ask "What happened?" to find the effect. Signal words such as *because, so, since*, and *as a result* can indicate cause-and-effect situations. Sometimes a cause-and-effect relationship does not have any signal words. Then it is implied. Making Cause-and-Effect Charts can help clarify implied causes.

READ AND RESPOND

Read Chapter 1. Pause during reading to discuss causes and effects. At the end of Chapter 1, have students fill in the Cause-and-Effect Charts. Remind students that the effect of one action may be the cause of another action.

VOCABULARY WORDS

As they read *The Wag Brigade*, students should point out the vocabulary words. Discuss how each word is used. Then have them pose questions and answer them using the words when discussing *The Wag Brigade*.

MAKE CONNECTIONS ACROSS TEXTS

Invite students to analyze and discuss causes and effects in *The Wag Brigade* and *Pipiolo and the Roof Dogs*.

- Which events in *The Wag Brigade* have more than one cause? What are those causes? Which events in *Pipiolo and the Roof Dogs* have more than one effect? What are those effects?
- How are the two texts similar in the way they use cause and effect?

ELL
Leveled Reader
Go to pages
139U–139V.

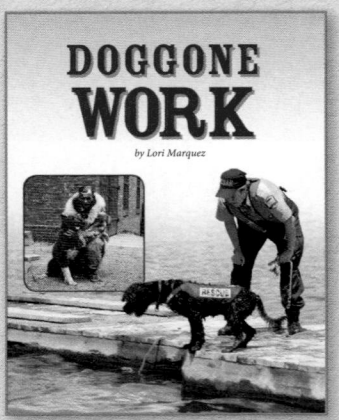

Student Book

Skills Focus ▶ Vocabulary

Tested

Objective   Apply vocabulary words using fill-in-the-blank sentences

EXTEND VOCABULARY

Provide students with a list of the vocabulary words and their definitions. Delete words from each definition. For example:

fragrance: a _____, particularly a _____ one (smell, pleasant)

cooperation: the act of _____ together (working)

theory: an _____ about what might be true; a way to _____ why an event happened (idea, explain)

Provide students with a list of the missing words, and ask them to complete the definitions. Alternatively, have students create the definitions for partners to solve. They can use the Glossary for help with definitions.

Skills Focus ▶ Text Features

Tested

Objective   Analyze how charts organize information

Materials   • **Student Book** "Doggone Work"   • Charts from magazine articles

CHARTS

Point out that charts help organize information. Discuss with students how the charts perform this function in "Doggone Work." Ask students why presenting information in a chart can be more helpful for readers than putting the information in sentences and paragraphs in the text.

Then have students write a paragraph about their favorite breeds of dogs. Students should create charts to accompany their paragraphs, highlighting key facts about the breeds.

Skills Focus ▶ Fluency

Objective   Read fluently with appropriate expression at a rate of 110–120 WCPM

Materials   • **Beyond Practice Book B,** page 32

REPEATED READING

Model reading aloud the entire passage on page 32 of **Practice Book B.** Begin reading the passage with exaggerated pauses and intonations, and increase the speed and fluency as you continue reading. Then read one sentence at a time in various tempos, listening for accuracy as individual students echo-read each sentence at the same tempo and with the same expression you use. During independent reading time, students can practice reading the passage using different levels of expression and different tempos.

◆ Beyond Practice Book B, page 32

As I read, I will pay attention to tempo.

	"Wow!" Arlene said happily, as she stood back to admire
10	the jungle scene she and Aunt Violet had painted on a piece
22	of canvas. Arlene had to admit that they had done fantastic
33	work. "It's unbelievable! I'll get the stepladder so we can
43	hang it up!"
46	"My goodness, Arlene. Let the paint dry first!" Aunt
55	Violet said. "On a rainy day like this, that paint could take
67	a while to dry. While we're waiting, let's go over the list of
80	party foods. Now where did I put my glasses? I can't seem
92	to keep track of them!"
97	Arlene and Aunt Violet were finishing up the preparations
106	for a party that night. It was a birthday celebration for Arlene's
118	little brother, Gary. He loved wild animals, so Arlene and
128	Aunt Violet had transformed Aunt Violet's living room into
137	a jungle. There was even a cardboard giraffe peeking out
147	from behind the big red chair!
153	While Aunt Violet went over her list, Arlene glanced over
163	the room. It was turning out just as she had planned. 174

Comprehension Check

1. What are Arlene and Aunt Violet preparing for? **Plot** a birthday party for Arlene's brother, Gary

2. What does the word *transformed* mean? **Context Clues** *Transformed* means *changed.*

	Words Read	–	Number of Errors	=	Words Correct Score
First Read		–		=	
Second Read		–		=	

Leveled Reader Lesson

Objective   Read to apply strategies and skills

Materials   • **Leveled Reader** *Rusty to the Rescue!*

PREVIEW AND PREDICT

Have students preview *Rusty to the Rescue!*, predict what it is about, and set a purpose for reading.

SKILL
CAUSE AND EFFECT

Ask a volunteer to define cause and effect. Then have him or her explain why identifying cause-and-effect relationships is a useful approach to understanding how the events in a plot are organized. Explain that students will read *Rusty to the Rescue!* together and that they will record cause-and-effect relationships in charts.

READ AND RESPOND

As they read, have students identify cause-and-effect relationships and fill in their Cause-and-Effect Charts. Then have students compare charts with a partner and discuss the causes and effects they would include in a summary.

VOCABULARY WORDS

Discuss the meanings of the vocabulary words. Ask cause-and-effect questions, such as *What happens when something is transformed? Why?* Then have students respond to these questions, indicating an understanding of the vocabulary words and illustrating cause and effect wherever possible.

Leveled Reader

ELL   Access for All

Model Questioning Help English learners practice the strategy of asking questions while reading by modeling some typical questions readers might pose: *What will happen next? Why did (the character) do that?*

Skills Focus ▶ Self-Selected Reading

Objective   Read independently to analyze cause and effect and to make connections across texts

Materials   • Leveled Readers or a trade book at students' reading level

READ TO IDENTIFY CAUSE AND EFFECT

Invite students to choose books for independent reading and to list cause-and-effect situations they notice while reading. Students can then hold a literature circle where they can compare and discuss what they have read. Encourage students to consider the types of selections for which identifying cause and effect is most helpful.

Academic Language

Throughout the week the English language learners in your class will need help in building their understanding of the academic language used in daily instruction and assessment instruments. The following strategies will help to increase their language proficiency and comprehension of content and instructional words.

Oral Language For oral vocabulary development, go to **www. macmillanmh.com**

Strategies to Reinforce Academic Language

- **Use Context** Academic language used by the teacher (see chart below) should be explained in the context of the task during Whole Group. You may use gestures, expressions, and visuals to support meaning.

- **Use Visuals** Use charts, transparencies, and graphic organizers to explain key labels to help students understand classroom language.

- **Model** Demonstrate the task using academic language in order for students to understand instruction.

Academic Language Used in Whole Group Instruction

Content/Theme Words	Skill/Strategy Words	Writing/Grammar Words
communities (p. 113)	generate questions (p. 112)	journal entry (p. 138)
relays (p. 134)	cause and effect (p. 112)	unimportant details (p. 138)
retrieve (p. 134)	plot (p. 133B)	run-on sentence (p. 139I)
characteristics (p. 135)	turning point (p. 133B)	compound sentence (p. 139I)
stamina (p. 135)	solution (p. 133B)	complex sentence (p. 139I)
search-and-rescue dog (p. 136)	charts (p. 134)	sentence fragment (p. 139J)

ELL Reader Lesson

Realistic Fiction

MAI
AND
FRED

by Katherine
Talmadge Sallé

illustrated by
Chi Chung

 **Before Reading**

DEVELOP ORAL LANGUAGE

 Build Background *What do you know about animals that help others?* Have students discuss animals and ways they help people.

 **Review Vocabulary** Write the vocabulary and story support words on the board and discuss their meanings. Model using them in sentences. *We were going to have a cookout celebration on Sunday. It was canceled because it rained all day.*

PREVIEW AND PREDICT

Point to the cover illustration and read the title aloud. *When have you seen a dog helping people? What happens in the story? Why is the dog on the cover?* Preview pictures in the book and encourage students to make predictions.

Set a Purpose for Reading Show the Cause and Effect Chart and remind students they have used this chart before. Ask them to do a similar chart to identify and record causes and effects in the story.

 **During Reading**

Choose from among the differentiated strategies to support students' reading at all levels of language acquisition.

Beginning	Intermediate	Advanced
Shared Reading As you read, pause to model how to identify causes and effects. Check students' comprehension. *Why was the cookout celebration canceled?*	**Read Together** Read the first chapter, prompting students to identify causes or effects. Ask students to write them on their charts. Have students read with a partner, taking turns to list events in their chart's.	**Independent Reading** Have students read the story. After reading each day, ask them to identify causes and effects and record them on their charts. Have students discuss how they would feel if something similar happened to them.

 **After Reading**

Remind students to use the vocabulary and story words in their whole group activities.

Objective

- **To apply vocabulary and comprehension skills**

Materials

- **ELL Leveled Reader**

5-Day Planner

DAY 1	• Academic Language
	• Oral Language and Vocabulary Review
DAY 2	• Academic Language
	• ELL Leveled Reader
DAY 3	• Academic Language
	• ELL Leveled Reader
DAY 4	• Academic Language
	• ELL Leveled Reader
DAY 5	• Academic Language
	• ELL Leveled Reader Comprehension Check and Literacy Activities

Grade 5 • ELL TEACHER'S GUIDE

English Language Learners

Treasures

Macmillan/McGraw-Hill

ELL Teacher's Guide for students who need additional instruction

Answer Questions

Test Strategy: Think and Search

EXPLAIN

- Good test takers think about places in the selection where they are most likely to find the best answer to a question.

- **Think** about what the question is asking.

- **Search** the selection for the part or parts that will give the correct answer.

- **Keep reading:** Often the information needed to answer a question is in more than one place. Be sure to read the entire selection to gather all of the information.

MODEL

Remind students not to write in their books, but to record their answers on a separate sheet of paper.

Question 1 *Read the question and all of the answer choices.*

THINK

Think Aloud I know this question is asking me about ways that the Elmers help save Paul Bunyan time.

Test Strategy

Think and Search
The answer is in more than one place. Keep reading to find the answer.

The Year of the Two Winters

retold by Tricia Gentle

Characters

PAUL BUNYAN, superhuman lumberjack
SIX LUMBERJACKS, each named Elmer
LUCY, the purple cow
SOURDOUGH SAM, the cook
OLÉ, the blacksmith

Job	Workers	Date Done
Sharpen Axes	Elmer	Postponed due to Snow
Cut Trees	Elmer	Postponed due to Snow
Hire Workers	Paul Bunyan	Postponed due to Snow
Shoe Babe	Olé	Postponed due to Snow
Make Griddle	Olé	Postponed due to Snow

[Setting: A lumber camp in Michigan. It is May, but snow covers the trees. Paul Bunyan is digging through the snow and finds three of the Elmers, Lucy, and Sourdough Sam frozen underneath.]

PAUL BUNYAN: If I wait for the spring thaw, we won't get any work done this year. *(Shouts back over his shoulder.)* Olé, I found Sam and some others, but they're frozen stiff! Let's get a fire going over here!

140

Go On ▶

Genre: Plays

Plays are stories that are intended to be performed.

- **Characters:** The people or animals that tell the story

- **Setting:** The place or places where the story takes place

- **Stage directions:** The text in parentheses that describes characters' actions and feelings

- **Dialogue:** The text that shows what the characters say

- **Scenes:** The different sections that make up a play

OLÉ: (*Calls from offstage.*) Okay, Paul, I'm on my way!

(*Olé arrives and builds a fire near the frozen characters. When the fire begins to roar, the characters caught in the frozen scene come to life.*)

SOURDOUGH SAM: (*Rubs warmth back into his body.*) Thank you, Olé. I was starting to think it would be summer before I'd lay eyes on you again. I know everyone must be hungry, like me. Snow doesn't make much of a meal, you know.

PAUL: I sent my ox for a load of pork and beans. Babe should be back any time now.

SOURDOUGH SAM: Great! Paul, will you lend me some Elmers to get a meal going?

PAUL: Be glad to, Sam. (*Turns and shouts over his shoulder.*) Elmer!

(*The three Elmers from the frozen scene appear along with three others who come from offstage.*)

PAUL: (*Chuckling.*) Best idea I ever had, hiring all of these Elmers. It saves me a lot of time.

SOURDOUGH SAM: Elmers, go build fires on the shore all around that icy lake over there. (*They leave.*) We'll boil the water in that lake and make a pot of pork and beans. We'll have hot food for the rest of the year.

PAUL: But what will we wash it all down with?

SOURDOUGH SAM: I'd suggest milk, but judging by the looks of Lucy over there, I guess we're out of luck. She produces only when the grass is green, and last time I saw that color on the ground was last month!

Go On ▶ 141

SEARCH

Think Aloud This question is about what the Elmers do to help Paul Bunyan. I read that Paul lends the Elmers to Sourdough Sam to help get a meal going. I will search for more information. Next I read that the Elmers will build fires around the lake to boil water to make the pork and beans. So far, answer B is the best answer. As I continue reading, I find that one of the Elmers starts to milk Lucy. So B is the best answer, because the Elmers do many jobs to help Paul Bunyan.

GUIDED PRACTICE

Question 2 *Read the question and all of the answer choices.*

THINK

Where do you think you might find the answer? (in the dialogue and stage directions)

SEARCH

Look at what the characters say about food on page 141. What does Paul Bunyan say? (Babe is bringing pork and beans that they are going to cook with lake water.) Now search for more information. What does Sourdough Sam say about something to drink? (He suggests that they drink milk from Lucy the cow.)

Using this information, which answer would you choose? (Answer C) What other information do you find? (Elmer milks the cow, so they will have milk.) The best answer is C.

APPLY

Question 3 Read question 3 and all of the answer choices.

- Have students use the **Think and Search** strategy to choose an answer.

- After the students have chosen an answer, ask: What do you think the question is asking you to do? (find the jobs that the Elmers do)

- Where did you search for the answer? (in the chart in the illustration and in the play)

- To make sure that you chose the best answer, what did you need to do? (keep reading)

- Where did you find more information about the Elmers? (in the chart, in Paul Bunyan's lines, and in the stage directions)

- The best answer is D. The Elmers could sharpen axes, cut trees, and milk Lucy.

Have students answer questions 4 and 5.

Open-Ended Question 4 Answer: During the year of two winters, Paul Bunyan finds members of his lumber camp frozen under the snow. Paul Bunyan rescues his frozen friends. Then he makes plans to feed the members of his camp and keep them warm.

Essay Question 5 Answers should demonstrate clarity and higher level thinking skills. They may include that the frontier was often a dangerous place. The stories helped pioneers believe that they could overcome dangers, just as their favorite heroes had done. Stories like this one helped them believe that they could solve their problems and survive the harsh conditions.

Answer Questions

PAUL: (*Taking green glasses from his pocket.*) If green is what she needs, then green is what we'll give her. If she wears these glasses, the snow will look like grass. (*Paul goes to Lucy and puts glasses on her. Lucy starts grazing. An Elmer arrives with a pail and begins milking her.*)

(*It starts to snow.*)

SOURDOUGH SAM: (*Disgusted.*) Snow, again! How many winters are we going to have this year?

PAUL: It's hard to say, Sam. Sure looks like we're not having much of a spring. I'm going to tell the Elmers to let their beards grow. They can wrap themselves in their beards until summer.

SOURDOUGH SAM: That's a good idea, Paul. 'Cause from the looks of things, this is going to be a Paul Bunyan–sized winter or winters. (*Laughs and claps Paul on the back.*)

142

Go On ▶

Directions: Answer the questions.

Tip

Keep reading. The answer may be in more than one place.

1. How do the Elmers help Paul save time?

   A   They like to cook pork and beans.
   B   They help with many jobs.
   C   They shoe Babe.
   D   They give Lucy glasses.

2. What foods does Sourdough Sam suggest they prepare?

   A   pork and beans and snow
   B   green grass and milk
   C   pork and beans and milk
   D   They cannot cook because of the snow.

3. Look at the chart and the play. What jobs could the Elmers do?

   A   sharpen axes, cut trees, milk the cow
   B   start the fire, shoe Babe, cook pork and beans
   C   cook pork and beans, shovel snow, light a fire
   D   make a griddle, cook pork and beans, milk the cow

4. Summarize the play. Briefly tell what happens in the beginning, middle, and end.

5. Using what you know and what you have read, explain why tall tales are fun to read. Include examples from the selection in your answer.

Writing Prompt

Have you ever had a problem due to weather? What happened? Write a letter to a friend about a time weather caused a problem for you. Write three to five paragraphs and include details to tell what happened.

 143

Writing Prompt

EXPLAIN

Find the following information in the writing prompt:

- What is the **mode** or **type** of writing?
- What is the **purpose** for my writing?
- What is the **form** for my writing?
- Who is my **audience**?

MODEL/PRACTICE

Determine the writing mode Whom does the prompt ask you to write about? (me)

What clues in the prompt tell you that you should write about a real event? (*a time when weather caused a problem for you*)

Determine the purpose What clues in the prompt tell you what your personal narrative should be about? (a time when weather caused a problem for you)

Determine the form What clues in the prompt tell you what your personal narrative should include and in what form to write a letter? (three to five paragraphs, details; a letter)

Determine the audience Does the prompt identify your audience? (a friend)

ASSESS/CLOSE

Have students summarize the information in the prompt and how the clue words helped them. Include mode, purpose, form, and audience.

Objectives

- Identify features of a personal narrative
- Plan and organize ideas for a personal narrative
- Draft and revise a personal narrative
- Proofread, publish, and present a personal narrative

Materials

- Unit Writing Transparencies 1–6

Features of a Personal Narrative

- It tells a true story about the **writer's own experiences** and is entertaining to read.
- It describes the **writer's feelings** about the experience.
- It is written in the **first person,** using words such as *I, my, our,* and *we.*
- It tells about events in a sequence, often using **time-order words.**

ELL **Access for All**

Retell Tell students that the literature model is the story of what happened to a girl after she was bitten by a snake. Reread the model, then invite students to retell the incident. Ask *who, what, why, where,* and *when* questions to prompt students to recall details as well as the order of events.

Personal Narrative

Read Like a Writer

Read aloud the following excerpt from *Snakebite,* by Jennifer Owings Dewey in the **Read-Aloud Anthology.** Explain to students that this story is a personal narrative—a true story based on the writer's own experiences . Ask students to listen for

- the **writer's experiences** and her **feelings** about them
- how the writer uses *I* and *my*
- time-order words the writer uses to tell the **sequence of events**

Snakebite

In the fraction of a second the snake took to strike, it buzzed its rattle. My horse did not hear the sound. If she had, she'd have bolted. She feared snakes as much as most horses do.

I slid like a rag doll down the slope. I swung onto my horse's back and turned for home, clamping my good hand around a swatch of her mane. I held on as if my life depended on it.

I urged my horse to run, beating her sides with my heels. She was old and lazy and hated running.

Ten minutes into the twenty-minute ride my stomach backed up and I started feeling dizzy. I was afraid of falling off the horse. The earth and sky rotated. Blue mountains in the distance reeled and rolled. My vision began to cloud over. Black shadows moved across my eyes until all I could see was a tiny pinpoint of light.

I wondered if I'd make it home before I died.

Discuss the Features

After reading, discuss the following questions with students:

- **Who tells this story?** (a first-person narrator; the writer)
- **How do you know?** (words such as *I* and *my* are used)
- **What words does the writer use to describe her feelings?** (held on as if my life depended on it; feeling dizzy; afraid)
- **What sequence of reactions to the bite does the writer describe?** (stomach backed up; felt dizzy; vision clouded)

Prewrite

Set a Purpose Remind students that one purpose or reason for writing a personal narrative is to share thoughts and feelings about an experience with readers. Another purpose is to entertain readers.

Know the Audience Explain that students need to think about who will read their narratives, such as family or classmates. Invite them to consider what they want others to learn about themselves.

Choose a Topic Have students brainstorm times when they have overcome a challenge. Use the following prompts to help generate story details:

- Think about something new that you learned to do.
- Think about an event in which you competed with others.
- Remember a time you were asked to perform.
- Remember a time you achieved something you were afraid to try.

You may also wish to allow students to self-select a different topic or to develop one of their weekly writing pieces.

Mini Lesson | Organization

Display **Transparency 1.** Explain that together you will follow Sierra G.'s progress as she develops a personal narrative. With students, point out the following elements of Sierra's cluster map:

- She writes the topic of her narrative, her **own experience** of overcoming a fear of heights, in the center, and other details in the surrounding ovals.
- She uses the word *my* in the center circle to show that her story will be written in the **first person.**
- She uses **time-order words** such as *first, next,* and *then* to show the order in which the events happened.

Organize Ideas Tell students they will create their own cluster maps to record the events of their narratives. Use the transparency to demonstrate how to organize ideas.

Peer Review

Think, Pair, Share Invite students to discuss their cluster maps with a partner. As they share their cluster maps, have them consider whether each plan lists events in the correct order. Ask partners to suggest time-order words that might help their partner's writing.

Flexible Pairing Option Encourage students to pair with a student who is writing about a similar type of challenge.

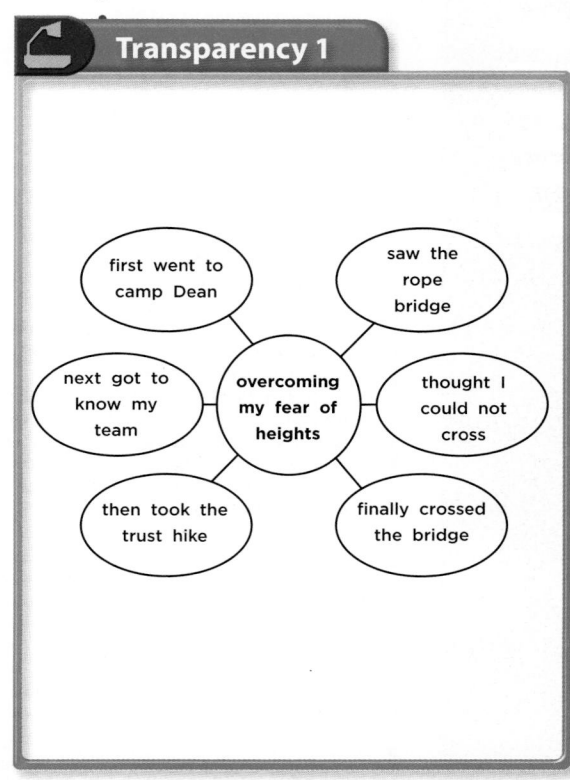

Writing Topic
Write about an interesting experience. Narrow your focus by writing about a challenge you faced. Include details about how you felt about the challenge and how you overcame it. Tell events in the correct order. Elaborate by using sensory details, vivid words, colorful descriptions, and figurative language to help readers visualize an experience.

Transparency 1

- first went to camp Dean
- saw the rope bridge
- next got to know my team
- **overcoming my fear of heights**
- thought I could not cross
- then took the trust hike
- finally crossed the bridge

Unit Writing Transparency 1

ELL | Access for All

Use Descriptive Words In some languages, adjectives usually come after the noun they describe. Point out that in English, an adjective usually comes before the noun it describes. Have students take turns pointing out a classroom object and describing it with a descriptive adjective such as *heavy book* or *black marker*.

Transparency 2

High Drama
by Sierra G.

I have always been afraid of high places. I also don't like spiders, loud noises, and I get afraid when the electricity goes out at night. That's why what happened last year at camp Dean was so good.

We spent the day getting to know each other. When I first arrived at camp, a counsler assigned us teams for the week. Next we played name games and shared our biggest fears. I told them about my fear of heights.

One activity was a trust hike. We had to go through a maze, follow a trail and then cross the river. The maze was hard. I helped untangle one girl's shirt when she got stuck under a fence. Even though we struggled, our team was the first to reach the river.

Thats where I stopped. The river crossing was a rope bridge suspended about ten feet above the water. I knew I'd never make it. My feet felt stuck to the ground. Then I saw all my teammates standing around me. They helped me. I held my breath and let them lead the way. In a flash we were on the other side.

My team helped me beat my fear. I was happy. I couldn't wait to cross the bridge again on my way back to camp.

Unit Writing Transparency 2

Draft

Mini Lesson | Personal Experience

Display **Transparency 2,** and read it with students. As you discuss Sierra's draft, point out the following details:

■ It is clear from reading this draft that this is something that happened to Sierra. She writes a true, entertaining story about her **personal experiences** at camp.

■ Sierra uses words such as *always been afraid, happy,* and *couldn't wait* to express her **feelings.**

■ The words *I, me, we,* and **us** help make it clear that this experience is something that happened to Sierra.

■ The **time-order words** such as *first, next,* and *then* help you visualize the sequence of events experienced by Sierra.

Note that Sierra will have the chance to revise and proofread her draft in later stages.

Check Your Cluster Map Have students review their cluster maps. Direct them to look back at their plan regularly.

Write the Draft Remind students that the purpose of writing a first draft is to get their ideas on paper. Share the following tips:

■ Tell an entertaining story about a personal experience and use first-person words such as *I, my,* and *we.*

■ Begin each paragraph with a topic sentence. Include only important details.

■ Include words that describe your feelings about the experience.

■ Tell events in the story in the correct sequence and use time-order words such as *first, next,* and *then.*

Writer's Resources
Use Primary Sources

Explain to students that one way to remember the feelings evoked by a particular event or experience is to look at photographs taken at the time. Point out that photographs are strong visual reminders of events and can therefore help recall feelings or reactions that might otherwise have been forgotten.

As students write their drafts, invite them to bring photographs of the event they are describing. Using the pictures, have students list words and phrases that describe how they felt about the event. Then, encourage students to include their feelings in their narratives.

Revise

| **Mini Lesson** | Ideas and Content |

Display **Transparency 3,** and point out how Sierra revises a good story to make it excellent.

■ She deletes a sentence in the first paragraph that tells about unrelated fears. (Ideas and Content)

■ She replaces the word *good* with *amazing* to give a better sense of her feelings. (Word Choice)

■ In the third and fourth paragraphs, she adds important details to clarify how her friends helped her. (Ideas and Content)

■ In the third paragraph, she adds a time-order word to clarify the sequence of events. (Word Choice)

You may want to note that Sierra will need to proofread her story to make final corrections. Guide students to think about the following writing traits as they revise their personal narratives.

Ideas and Content Did you tell a true story about an experience that happened to you? Is your topic focused on a single challenging experience? Did you delete unimportant details? Was your story entertaining to read?

Organization Have you told the events of your story in the correct sequence? Did you use topic sentences and supporting details?

Voice Did you write your story in the first person? Did you engage readers by sharing your feelings?

Word Choice Did you use words such as *I, my, our,* and *we* to personalize the story? Does your story have enough time-order words such as *first, next,* and *then* to help readers keep track of the sequence of events?

Peer Review

Think, Pair, Share Have individual students think about the kinds of feelings writers include in a strong narrative. Using this information, pair students with a partner and have them read their narratives to each other. Invite partners to comment on whether there is enough information about feelings in the writer's account of events.

Flexible Pairing Option Consider pairing stronger writers who write longer stories with those who are less proficient and write a minimal amount.

ELL Access for All

Use Sentence Strips
Give students experience building compound sentences. Write short sentences on sentence strips. Then create word cards with conjunctions such as *and, but, yet,* and *or.* Invite students to combine sentence strips by placing the conjunctions between them. Then have them read the new sentence aloud. Encourage students to use compound sentences in their narratives.

 Transparency 3

High Drama
by Sierra G.

I have always been afraid of high places. I ~~also don't like spiders, loud noises, and I get afraid when the electricity goes out at night.~~ That's why what happened last year at camp Dean was so ~~good~~. *amazing*

We spent the day getting to know each other. When I first arrived at camp, a counselor assigned us teams for the week. Next we played name games and shared our biggest fears. I told them about my fear of heights.

Our last One activity was a trust hike. We had to go through a maze, follow a trail and then cross the river. The maze was ~~hard~~. *really challenging* I helped untangle one girl's shirt when she got stuck under a fence. Even though we struggled, our team was the first to reach the river.

Thats where I ~~stopped~~. *froze* The river crossing was a rope bridge suspended about ten feet above the water. I knew I'd never make it. My feet felt stuck to the ground. Then I saw all my teammates standing around me. They ~~helped~~ me. *walked with me and they reminded me not to look down* I held my breath and let them lead the way. In a flash we were on the other side.

My team helped me beat my fear. I was *proud and excited all at once* happy. I couldn't wait to cross the bridge again on my way back to camp.

Unit Writing Transparency 3

Speaking and Listening

Have students read their personal narratives aloud and share their videotaped presentations with the class. Share these strategies.

Speaking Strategies

- Speak slowly, clearly, and in a loud voice.
- Vary your tone to make your presentation more interesting.
- Remember to look at your audience.

Listening Strategies

- Listen actively for enjoyment and respond appropriately.
- Try to visualize the speaker's experience.
- Focus on what is being said. After the presentation, ask questions.

 Transparency 4

High Drama
by Sierra G.

I have always been afraid of high places. I ~~also don't like spiders, loud noises, and I get afraid when the electricity goes out at night.~~ That's why what happened last year at camp Dean was so good. *amazing*

We spent the day getting to know each other. When I first arrived at camp, a counsler assigned us teams for the week. Next we played name games and shared our biggest fears. I told them about my fear of heights.

One activity was a trust hike. We had to go through a maze, follow a trail and then cross the river. The maze was hard. I helped untangle one girl's shirt when she got stuck under a fence. Even though we struggled, our team was the first to reach the river.

Thats where I stopped. The river crossing was a rope bridge suspended about ten feet above the water. I knew I'd never make it. My feet felt stuck to the ground. Then I saw all my teammates standing around me. They helped me. I held my breath and let them lead the way. In a flash we were on the other side.

My team helped me beat my fear. I was happy. I couldn't wait to cross the bridge again on my way back to camp.

Unit Writing Transparency 4

Proofread

Mini Lesson | Conventions

Display **Transparency 4** to point out examples of Sierra's proofreading corrections.

- She capitalizes *Camp* because it is a proper noun.
- She adds a comma after *me* in the fourth paragraph to correctly punctuate a compound sentence.
- She adds a comma after *Then* in the fourth paragraph.

Have students reread their narratives to find and correct mistakes. Review the use of proofreading marks on page 152 of the **Teacher's Resource Book.** Remind students to eliminate sentence fragments and use commas in compound sentences.

Peer Review

Think, Pair, Share Have students identify the different types of sentences in their narratives. Then invite partners to exchange papers and tally each sentence type. Have students use this information to evaluate their writing.

TEACHER CONFERENCE

Address individual students with the following questions to foster self-assessment: How did you express feelings in your story? What first-person words did you use? What other time-order words could you have included?

Publish

Ask students to write or type a final copy of their personal narratives. Remind students to use appropriate spacing between words, sentences, and paragraphs, and to use standard margins. Encourage them to select an appropriate format for publication. Also encourage students to consider publishing weekly writing from their portfolios.

PRESENTATION

Invite students to create a videotaped presentation of their narratives to show to the class or to share photographs of their experiences.

Author's Chair Allow students who have written strong narratives to share their stories from the Author's Chair.

Raising Scores

READ AND SCORE

Display **Transparency 5,** and invite a volunteer to read it aloud. Then direct students to use their student rubric on page 153 of the **Teacher's Resource Book** to assess the writing sample.

Guide students to understand that this personal narrative is only a fair writing sample, which would score only a 2, and that they will work together in groups to improve it.

RAISE THE SCORE

Point out the following shortfalls in the writing sample:

Ideas and Content The writer tried to tell a story about earning money to buy a new bike, but the events and details lack a clear focus. Some ideas would be better in a different story, and some ideas need more development.

Organization The writer does not tell the events of the story in a clear order. Time-order words would help make more sense out of the story.

Voice The writer does not sound interested in the story.

Ask small groups to revise the personal narrative to raise the score. Have them use the student rubric, and remind them to apply the writing skills they learned in this unit.

SHARE AND COMPARE

Have groups share their revised versions with the class, explaining how they improved the writing. Then display **Transparency 6** to show the same story written at an excellent level. Have groups compare this with their revised versions. Remind students that although two versions vary, they may both be considered excellent papers. Then have students review the personal narratives they wrote to raise their scores.

Objective

- Revise a personal narrative to raise the writing score from a 2 to a 4

CREATE A RUBRIC

Make copies of the blank rubric on pages 159 and 160 in the **Teacher's Resource Book** and distribute to students. Remind students that a personal narrative rubric should assess whether the story tells a personal experience, includes feelings, is written in the first person, and relates events in order. Students should include the following four levels to assess writing: Excellent, Good, Fair, and Unsatisfactory.

 Transparency 6

My New Bike
by Tyler C.

I desperately needed a new bike. My old bike had a flat tire and a broken chain. I loved my friend Allen's bike, but it was too expensive. My parents offered to pay half the cost of the bike I wanted. That meant that I had to pay for the other half.

Luckily, I already had a job. I walk my neighbor's dog. He pays me five dollars a week, but it would take me years to earn enough for the bike. So, I decided to start a dog walking business.

First, I asked my friends. One friend just got a new puppy and she was looking for someone to walk the dog after school. Next, I asked my mom to help me make some signs and we put them all around our neighborhood. People started to call a few days later.

By the end of the week, I had five new jobs! I actually had to hire my sister to help me. Two months later, I had enough money to buy the bike I wanted. I even paid my sister for her help.

My mom and dad were proud of me. I was pretty proud of myself, too. I kept my dog walking business. I love the dogs, and I'm hoping to save enough money to buy a new helmet.

Unit Writing Transparency 6

4-Point Rubric

Use this four-point rubric to assess student writing.

Portfolio

Remind students to keep a list of writing ideas in their portfolio. Encourage students to review their personal collection of writing samples, determine the progress they've made, and evaluate whether their personal narratives should be included in their portfolios. Remind students that portfolios should include more than just finished work. It should include informational, literary, interpretive, and responsive writing as well as critical analysis, evaluation, and social communication. Have students jot down ideas for future writing assignments or tell what they learned about personal narratives to include in their portfolios. Have students review their writing to determine their progress and to note strengths in order to set goals for improvement.

SCORING RUBRIC FOR PERSONAL NARRATIVE			
4 Excellent	**3 Good**	**2 Fair**	**1 Unsatisfactory**
Ideas and Content Creates a clear, entertaining story drawn from a personal experience; includes the writer's thoughts and feelings about key events	**Ideas and Content** Relates a personal experience; includes some thoughts and feelings about events	**Ideas and Content** Relates a personal experience, but lacks focus; sometimes wanders from topic	**Ideas and Content** Does not share a personal experience; writing is not focused or entertaining to read
Organization Details unfold in a logical, easy-to-follow sequence	**Organization** Tells the story in the correct order	**Organization** Some events are told out of order	**Organization** Events are told out of order and are confusing
Voice Relates events in the first person; clearly expresses the writer's feelings	**Voice** Events told mostly in the first person; expresses writer's feelings	**Voice** Strays from first person; insufficient amount of feeling about events is conveyed	**Voice** Not in first person; does not express feelings of writer
Word Choice Consistently uses first-person pronouns; uses many time-order words	**Word Choice** Uses first-person pronouns; uses time-order words	**Word Choice** Lacks sufficient number of first-person pronouns; not enough time-order words to guide readers	**Word Choice** Missing first-person pronouns and time-order words
Sentence Fluency Consistently uses a variety of types of sentences; varies sentence length to create a natural rhythm	**Sentence Fluency** Includes both simple and compound sentences; some sections have rhythm and flow	**Sentence Fluency** Uses simple sentences; reader may have to reread in order to follow the meaning	**Sentence Fluency** Sentences are fragmented or run together, or are otherwise difficult to read
Conventions Narrative is free or almost entirely free from mechanical, grammatical, and spelling errors	**Conventions** Spelling, capitalization, punctuation, and usage are mostly correct; incorrect elements do not interfere with meaning	**Conventions** Makes frequent errors that interfere with a clear understanding of the story	**Conventions** Makes significant and repeated errors in spelling, word choice, punctuation, and usage
Presentation Text is easy to read whether word-processed or handwritten; spacing and the use of white space allow the reader to focus on the message without distractions	**Presentation** Text is readable; spacing is mostly uniform; margins are standard	**Presentation** Text is readable, but variations in size, slant, or font are distracting; margins are inconsistent	**Presentation** The text is difficult to read and understand because of severe changes in slant, font, or size; spacing is random or confusing

Refer to Anchor Papers for personal narratives on pages 192–195 in the **Unit and Benchmark Assessment** for a sample of writing at different levels.

6-Point Rubric

Use this six-point rubric to assess student writing.

SCORING RUBRIC FOR PERSONAL NARRATIVE

6 Exceptional	**5** Excellent	**4** Good	**3** Fair	**2** Poor	**1** Unsatisfactory
Ideas and Content Crafts an appealing, well-detailed story drawn from a personal experience; ideas are focused and build upon each other	**Ideas and Content** Original ideas are developed with a clear focus and supported with well-chosen details	**Ideas and Content** Develops adequate ideas that move the story along in a natural way	**Ideas and Content** Shows some difficulty in developing ideas that are clear and focused	**Ideas and Content** Writing is vague; may present events without a clear focus	**Ideas and Content** Does not tell a personal story; shows no attempt to develop ideas that are clear and focused
Organization Demonstrates a thoroughly planned story sequence	**Organization** Crafts a consistent structure with events narrated in sequence	**Organization** Has a well-planned story line with good sequence of events	**Organization** Displays some organizational problems, such as presenting some events out of order	**Organization** Lacks structure; events are mostly out of order, leaving the reader with a sense of confusion	**Organization** Sequence is lacking, causing much confusion as to the flow of events; may contain no structure at all
Voice Expresses a unique personal first-person voice that effectively communicates feelings	**Voice** First-person voice that shows originality and demonstrates a consistent awareness of audience; feelings communicated well	**Voice** Makes a strong effort to share a first-person personal voice that expresses feelings and matches the purpose and audience	**Voice** Makes an effort to employ a first-person voice; writing style may not communicate feelings effectively	**Voice** Inconsistent use of first-person voice; does not communicate writer's feelings	**Voice** Not in first person; makes no attempt to communicate writer's feelings
Word Choice Consistent use of first-person pronouns; abundance of time-order words; chooses words that are accurate, distinct, and advanced to paint a clear picture of events	**Word Choice** Uses many first-person pronouns and time-order words; imaginative language reflects a sophisticated vocabulary	**Word Choice** Adequate use of first-person pronouns and time-order words; chooses words that are expressive and clear	**Word Choice** Insufficient use of first-person pronouns and time-order words; uses predictable wording	**Word Choice** Missing first-person pronouns and time-order words; chooses inaccurate words	**Word Choice** Uses no first-person pronouns and time-order words; uses words that are confusing and disrupt the text
Sentence Fluency Crafts effective simple and complex sentences that flow in a smooth rhythm	**Sentence Fluency** Crafts varied sentences that sound natural	**Sentence Fluency** Crafts easy-to-follow sentences that demonstrate an appropriate control of language	**Sentence Fluency** Crafts sentences with some variation, though sometimes lacks an easy flow	**Sentence Fluency** Some sentence fragments are present; little to no variety of sentence type apparent	**Sentence Fluency** Choppy, rambling, and awkward sentences make reading difficult
Conventions Demonstrates a strong grasp of standard writing conventions	**Conventions** Shows control of most spelling, punctuation, capitalization, and usage conventions	**Conventions** Some editing is necessary, but errors do not interfere with meaning or flow	**Conventions** Makes some errors in writing conventions that interrupt the flow of text	**Conventions** Demonstrates a difficulty in understanding standard writing conventions; much editing necessary	**Conventions** Serious and frequent errors interfere with readability
Presentation Form and presentation of text enhance the reader's ability to relate to and understand the text	**Presentation** Shows creative, clear design that makes reading the text pleasing	**Presentation** Creates an appropriate layout that makes reading and focusing on the message possible	**Presentation** Text is readable; discrepancies in form and spacing make some parts easier to read than others	**Presentation** Much of the text is difficult to read due to crowding or confusing font and sizing choices	**Presentation** Variability in handwriting, lack of proper spacing, and/or inappropriate or multiple fonts make text indecipherable

Refer to Anchor Papers for personal narratives on pages 192–195 in the **Unit and Benchmark Assessment** for a sample of writing at different levels.

Unit 1 Computer Literacy

Objectives

- Understand why and how the Internet is helpful for finding information
- Use specific search techniques to narrow searches
- Learn to cite URLs properly

Materials

- **www.macmillanmh.com**

Vocabulary

Web browser a computer program that enables a person to explore the Internet

URL (Uniform Resource Locator) the location or address of a Web page that starts with the abbreviation http://

search engine a software program that looks for word matches based on specified key words

key word search a type of search where a key word is used to help find information on a specific topic

cite to quote a passage or author

Searching on the Internet

ACCESS PRIOR KNOWLEDGE

Ask students about their experience with the Internet.

- *Why do you use the Internet?*

- *How have you used the Internet to search for information?*

EXPLAIN

Introduce the lesson vocabulary by writing each word on the board and asking for its definition.

- Tell students that when they research a topic online, they should open a **Web browser** and type in the **URL** of a **search engine.**

- Help students brainstorm topics they would like to search for with the Internet and write down possible **key word searches** for students.

- To narrow down searches, they can use "and" between key words to find Web pages that contain all of the words. Or they can use quotes to find Web pages that contain the exact words.

MODEL

- Show students how to find a **search engine** on the Internet.

- Choose a **key word** search from the list and show students how to conduct a search. Narrow down the search results for students by using quotation marks or an "and" in your search.

Using Citations

- Explain that students must be able to **cite URLs** in their writing to avoid plagiarism.

- Post an example of a correct URL citation for students: Author's name. "Title of Article or Link." <u>Name of Web Page</u>. Date of Update. Name of Organization Associated with the Site. Access Date. <Web Address>.

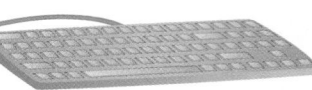

GUIDED PRACTICE

Have students connect to **www.macmillanmh.com** and go to Computer Literacy Lesson Grade 5 Unit 1.

Remind students never to give out their name, address, phone number, or e-mail address to anyone on the Internet.

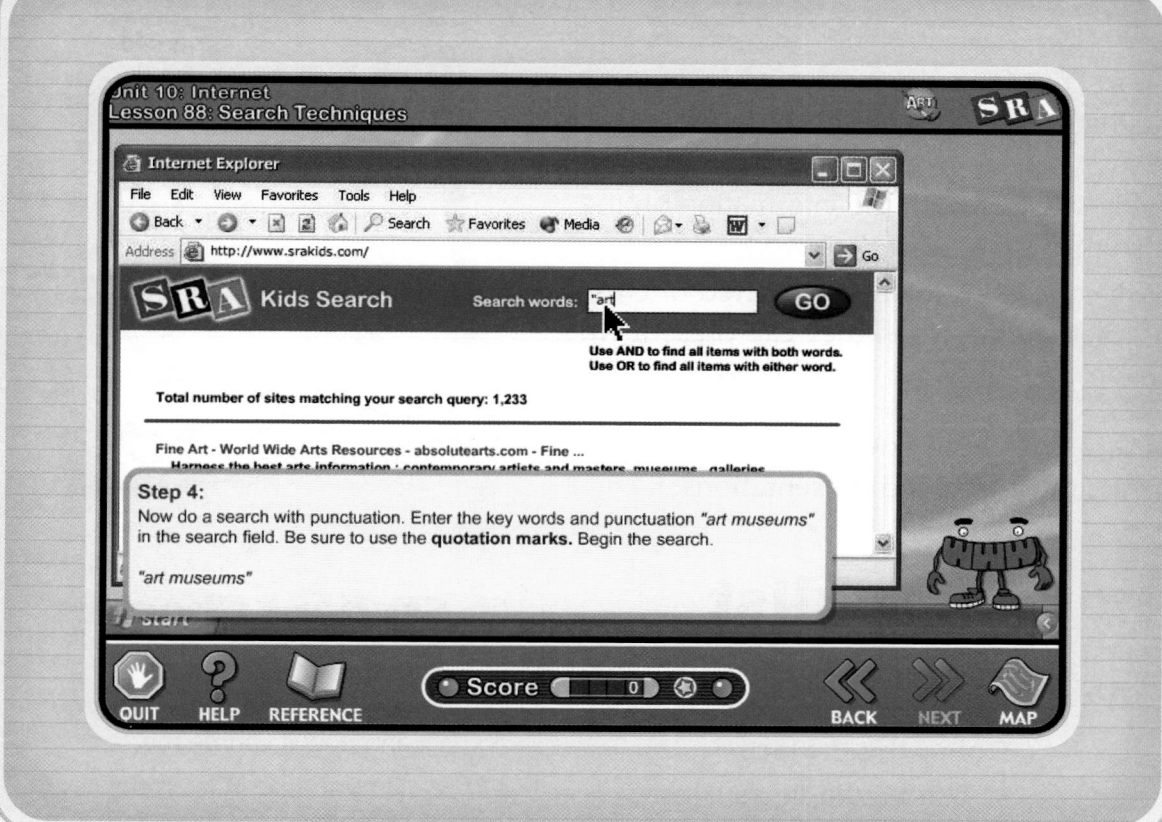

The online practice lesson is an excerpt from SRA TechKnowledge. For information about the full SRA TechKnowledge program, go to **www.sratechknowledge.com.**

Leveled Practice

Approaching	On Level	Beyond Level
Have students choose a search topic and use search techniques to find information. They can record the number of hits they get for each type of search.	Have students choose a search topic, use search techniques to find information, and record the number of hits they get. Have them write down a piece of information they found and cite the URL where they found it.	Have students choose a search topic and effectively search the Internet for information. Ask students to write a paragraph about the topic using information that is accurately cited from at least two different Web sites.

Theme Project Wrap-Up
Research and Inquiry

After students complete Step 1, Step 2, Step 3, and Step 4 of their project, have them work on the following:

 Step 5 Create the Presentation Have students present what they learned by writing a script for a short play. Students can either choose classmates to help them perform their play or work in small groups to collaborate on both writing and performance. Provide students with the information on the Student Checklist so they can review their work.

When students have completed their self-selected or cross-curricular projects, plan a time when they can present what they have learned.

 Step 6 Review and Evaluate Use these questions to help you and students evaluate their research and presentations.

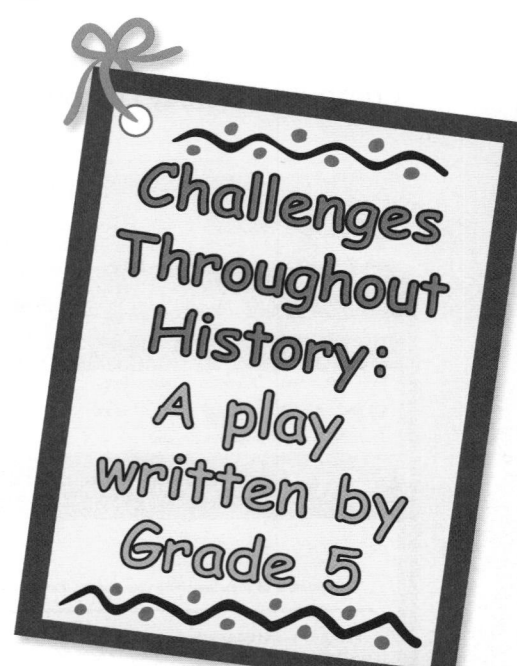

Challenges Throughout History: A play written by Grade 5

Teacher Checklist

Assess the Research Process

Planning the Project
- ✔ Participated in theme discussion
- ✔ Formulated well-focused research question
- ✔ Evaluated multiple sources

Doing the Project
- ✔ Used multiple sources
- ✔ Synthesized information
- ✔ Wrote original script

Assess the Presentation

Speaking
- ✔ Performers held audience's attention
- ✔ Audience could understand every word
- ✔ Presentation was interesting through use of expressions, gestures, and tone of voice

Representing
- ✔ Scripts treated research question about meeting a challenge
- ✔ Stage sets and costumes helped engage the audience

Assess the Listener

- ✔ Listened without interrupting
- ✔ Focused on the performers
- ✔ Used prior knowledge and experiences to analyze content

Student Checklist

Research Process
- ✔ Did you investigate a challenge and how it can be met?
- ✔ Did you use at least three reliable sources and cite them correctly?
- ✔ Did you write a script showing your information and your own ideas?

Presenting

Speaking
- ✔ Did you rehearse?
- ✔ Did you use gestures and facial expressions?

Representing
- ✔ Did the performance include a variety of images and sounds?
- ✔ Did you use props and costumes?
- ✔ Did the performance show imagination?

SCORING RUBRIC FOR THEME PROJECTS

4 Excellent	**3** Good	**2** Fair	**1** Unsatisfactory
The student • presents the information in a clear and imaginative way • uses words and visuals that effectively present important information • may offer sophisticated personal reflections	**The student** • presents the information in a fairly clear way • uses words and visuals that present relevant information • may offer thoughtful personal reflections	**The student** • struggles to present the information clearly • may use adequate words and visuals • may offer irrelevant personal reflections	**The student** • may not grasp the task • may present sketchy information in a disorganized way • may have extreme difficulty with research

 Home-School Connection

Have students work with a partner or a small group to write an invitation to family members, other students, and members of the community to attend students' presentations of their projects.

■ Introduce each guest by name and relationship to students or the community.

■ Videotape the presentations for family members to borrow or to show at the parent/teacher conferences.

■ Before the event, remind students to prepare and practice the play so that it will fit within a given time limit.

■ Remind students to adjust their communication based on the audience, purpose, and situation and to adjust diction, enunciation, volume and inflection as they speak.

■ Remind students in the audience to evaluate the situation, identify their purpose for listening, assume an appropriate listening mode, and use their prior experience to analyze the content of the plays.

■ During the presentation, remind students that as listeners and speakers, they need to respect the age, position, gender, and culture of the audience and their peers.

■ Finally, have partners or small groups thank-you notes to the people who attended the presentation.

End-of-Unit Assessment

Administer the Test

UNIT 1 READING ASSESSMENT, pp. 9–24

Tested Skills and Strategies

COMPREHENSION STRATEGIES AND SKILLS

- Strategies: Story and Text Structure, Generate Questions
- Skills: Character, Setting, and Plot, Cause and Effect, Compare and Contrast, Summarize

VOCABULARY STRATEGIES

- Context clues
- Word parts
- Dictionary
- Thesaurus

TEXT FEATURES AND STUDY SKILLS

- Photos and captions
- Toolbars and links
- Library/media center
- Charts

GRAMMAR, MECHANICS, USAGE

- Sentence types
- Subject and predicates
- Sentence combining, conjunctions, and compound/complex sentences
- Run-on sentences and fragments
- End punctuation
- Commas
- Letter punctuation

WRITING

- Personal Narrative

Use Multiple Assessments for Instructional Planning

To create instructional profiles for your students, look for patterns in the results from any of the following assessments.

Fluency Assessment

Plan appropriate fluency-building activities and practice to help all students achieve the following fluency goal: **100–120 WCPM**.

Running Records

Use the instructional reading level determined by the Running Record calculations for regrouping decisions.

Benchmark Assessments

Administer tests three times a year as an additional measure of both student progress and the effectiveness of the instructional program.

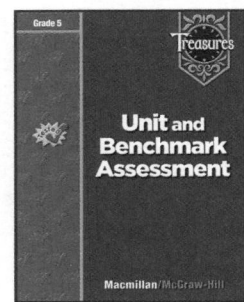

Timed Writing

For timed writing, give students 40–55 minutes to complete their work.

Technology

  Assessment Tool

- Administer the **Unit Assessment** electronically.
- Create alternative tests using the item bank.
- Score all tests electronically.
- Available online or on CD-ROM.

Analyze the Data

Use information from a variety of informal and formal assessments, as well as your own judgment, to assist in your instructional planning. Students who consistently score at the lowest end of each range should be evaluated for Intervention. Use the **Diagnostic Assessment** in the Intervention Teacher's Edition.

Diagnose		Prescribe
ASSESSMENTS	**IF...**	**THEN...**
UNIT TEST	0–23 questions correct	Reteach tested skills using the **Additional Lessons** (pp. T1–12)
FLUENCY ASSESSMENT		
Oral Reading Fluency	96–99 WCPM	Fluency Solutions
	0–95 WCPM	Evaluate for Intervention
RUNNING RECORDS	Level 40 or below	Reteach comprehension skills using the **Additional Lessons** (pp. T1–5)
		Provide additional Fluency activities

READING
Triumphs
AN INTERVENTION PROGRAM

Also Available

To place students in the Intervention Program, use the **Diagnostic Assessment** in the Intervention Teacher's Edition.

Glossary

Introduce students to the Glossary by reading through the introduction and looking over the pages with them. Encourage the class to talk about what they see.

Words in a glossary, like words in a dictionary, are listed in **alphabetical order.** Point out the **guide words** at the top of each page that tell the first and last words appearing on that page.

ENTRIES

Point out examples of **main entries,** or entry words, and entries. Read through a sample entry with the class, identifying each part. Have students note the order in which information is given: entry word(s), syllable division, pronunciation respelling, part of speech, definition(s), example sentence(s).

Note if more than one definition is given for a word, the definitions are numbered. Note the format used for a word that is more than one part of speech.

Review the **parts of speech** by identifying each in a sentence:

Inter.	article	n.	conj.	adj.	n.
Wow!	A	dictionary	and	useful	glossary

v.	adv.	pron.	prep.	n.
tell	almost	everything	about	words!

HOMOGRAPHS/HOMOPHONES/HOMONYMS

Point out that some entries are for multiple-meaning words called **homographs.** Homographs have the same spellings but have different origins and meanings, and, in some cases, different pronunciations.

Explain that students should not confuse homographs with **homophones** or **homonyms.** Homophones are words that have the same pronunciation but have different spellings and meanings. Homonyms are words that have the same pronunciation and spelling but have different meanings. Provide students with examples.

PRONUNCIATION KEY

Explain the use of the pronunciation key (either the short key, at the bottom of every other page, or the long key, at the beginning of the Glossary). Demonstrate the difference between primary stress and secondary stress by pronouncing a word with both. Pronounce the words both correctly and incorrectly to give students a clearer understanding of the proper pronunciations.

WORD HISTORY

The Word History feature explains the **etymology** of select words. Explain that *etymology* is the history of a word from its origin to its present form. A word's etymology explains which language it comes from and what changes have occurred in its spelling and/or meaning. Many English words are derivatives of words from other languages, such as Latin or Greek. Derivatives are formed from base or root words.

Glossary

What Is a Glossary?

A glossary can help you find the **meanings** of words in this book that you may not know. The words in the glossary are listed in **alphabetical order**. **Guide words** at the top of each page tell you the first and last words on the page.

Each word is divided into syllables. The way to pronounce the word is given next. You can understand the pronunciation respelling by using the **pronunciation key**. A shorter key appears at the bottom of every other page. When a word has more than one syllable, a dark accent mark (ʹ) shows which syllable is stressed. In some words a light accent mark (ʹ) shows which syllable has a less heavy stress. Sometimes an entry includes a second meaning for the word.

Guide Words
First word on the page   Last word on the page

abandon/attraction

Sample Entry

Pronunciation   Part of Speech

Main entry and
Syllable division — **a•lert** (ə lûrt´) *noun*. A signal that warns of possible danger. *The navy ships heard an alert as they traveled into rough seas.* — Definition

Example sentence

Pronunciation Key

Phonetic Spelling	Examples	Phonetic Spelling	Examples
a	at, bad, plaid, laugh	d	dear, soda, bad
ā	ape, pain, day, break	f	five, defend, leaf, off, cough, elephant
ä	father, calm	g	game, ago, fog, egg
âr	care, pair, bear, their, where	h	hat, ahead
e	end, pet, said, heaven, friend	hw	white, whether, which
ē	equal, me, feet, team, piece, key	j	joke, enjoy, gem, page, edge
i	it, big, give, hymn	k	kite, bakery, seek, tack, cat
ī	ice, fine, lie, my	l	lid, sailor, feel, ball, allow
îr	ear, deer, here, pierce	m	man, family, dream
o	odd, hot, watch	n	not, final, pan, knife, gnaw
ō	old, oat, toe, low	ng	long, singer
ô	coffee, all, taught, law, fought	p	pail, repair, soap, happy
ôr	order, fork, horse, story, pour	r	ride, parent, wear, more, marry
oi	oil, toy	s	sit, aside, pets, cent, pass
ou	out, now, bough	sh	shoe, washer, fish, mission, nation
u	up, mud, love, double	t	tag, pretend, fat, dressed
ū	use, mule, cue, feud, few	th	thin, panther, both
ü	rule, true, food, fruit	th	these, mother, smooth
ů	put, wood, should, look	v	very, favor, wave
ûr	burn, hurry, term, bird, word, courage	w	wet, weather, reward
ə	about, taken, pencil, lemon, circus	y	yes, onion
b	bat, above, job	z	zoo, lazy, jazz, rose, dogs, houses
ch	chin, such, match	zh	vision, treasure, seizure

764

765

Aa

a•ban•don (ə ban´dən) *verb*. To leave and not return. *The sailors jumped into the ocean when they were given the order to abandon the ship.*

ac•com•pa•ny (ə kum´pə nē) *verb*. To go together with. *My friend decided to accompany me to the store so that I would have someone to talk to.*

ad•ap•ta•tions (ad´əp tā´shənz) *noun, plural.* Changes in a plant or animal so that it is better suited to survive in its environment. *Fur and the shape of an animal's teeth are adaptations.*

ad•just•ed (ə jus´tid) *verb*. Changed or arranged to fit a need or demand. *We adjusted the schedule to include two more singers in the program.*

ad•ver•tise•ment (ad´vûr tīz´mənt, ad vûr´tis ment) *noun*. A public notice that tells people about a product, event, or something a person needs. *A successful advertisement will convince shoppers to buy a product.*

a•lert (ə lûrt´) *noun*. A heightened sense of watchfulness for possible danger. *The navy ship was put on alert after an ice storm was reported in the area.*

a•mend•ment (ə mend´mənt) *noun*. A change in a law caused by voting of government officials or changes to the Constitution. *Women were given the right to vote in all states by an amendment to the Constitution.*

a•nat•o•my (ə nat´ə mē) *noun*. The structure of an animal or plant or any of its parts. *Medical students study anatomy to learn how to treat illnesses in people.*

an•chored (ang´kərd) *verb*. Being held in place by a heavy metal device or object. *The crew is lucky they anchored the boat to a rock because the sudden storm would have blown them far from shore.*

ap•pre•ci•a•tion (ə prē´shē ā´shən) *noun*. A feeling of being thankful. *To show his appreciation, Javier gave the boy who found his wallet a small reward.*

ar•chae•ol•o•gists (är´kē ol´ə jists) *noun, plural.* Students of or experts in past cultures and histories. *Archaeologists dig in the earth for clues to Earth's past.*

a•rous•ing (ə rouz´ing) *verb*. Stirring up or causing excitement. *The opposing team's fans were arousing a lot of attention in the bleachers with their cheering.*

ar•roy•o (ə roi´ō) *noun*. A small river or stream. *The small arroyo had plenty of fish.*

ar•ti•facts (är´tə fakts´) *noun, plural.* Things left over from an earlier time. *Some tools are artifacts from a time when they were useful to people.*

at•mos•phere (at´məs fîr´) *noun*. **1.** The layer of gases that surrounds Earth. *We watched on television as the space shuttle entered the atmosphere after its mission to the moon was over.* **2.** A surrounding mood or environment. *Our house has a merry atmosphere during the holiday season.*

at•tor•ney (ə tûr´nē) *noun*. A lawyer; one who helps with legal matters. *Before arguing your case in court, it may be a good idea to hire an attorney.*

at•trac•tion (ə trak´shən) *noun*. A person or thing that draws attention. *The new baby elephant was an attraction that drew a lot of people at the zoo.*

au•to•graph (ô´tə graf´) *noun*. A person's signature written in that person's own handwriting. *My sister got her favorite singer's autograph.*

a•vail•a•ble (ə vāl´ə bəl) *adjective*. Possible to get. *There were seats available at the front of the theatre.*

Bb

banned (band) *verb*. Officially forbidden; prohibited. *Many school boards have banned books that contain inaccurate information.*

bed•lam (bed´lam) *noun*. A place or condition of wild uproar and confusion. *There was bedlam in the hallways when the fire alarm sounded.*

be•hav•ior (bi hāv´yər) *noun*. A way of acting. *The campers were yelled at by the counselor for their mischievous behavior.*

bi•ol•o•gy (bī ol´ə jē) *adjective*. Characterized by the study of living things. *The biology teacher enjoyed the study of plants.* *—noun*. The study of living things. *Biology is my favorite subject in school.*

blared (blârd) *verb*. Made a loud, harsh sound. *The trumpets blared as the Olympic ceremonies began.*

blurt•ed (blûr´tid) *verb*. Said suddenly or without thinking. *I blurted out the answer before the teacher finished asking the question.*

boy•cott (boi´kot) *noun*. A planned and organized refusal to have anything to do with a person, group, or nation. *The strikers called for a boycott of the company's products.*

bri•dle (brī´dəl) *noun*. The part of a horse's or donkey's harness that fits over the head and is used to guide or control the animal. *The cowboy fitted the bridle over the horse's head before going for a ride.*

brim•ming (bri´ming) *adjective*. Full to the upper edge of a container. *The brimming mugs were filled with hot cocoa and whipped cream.*

buf•fet¹ (buf´it) *verb*. To knock about. *We felt the rough water buffet the raft.*

buf•fet² (bəf´ā, bu´fā) *noun*. **1.** A piece of furniture with a flat surface for serving food. *Please put the rice on the buffet after it has been passed around the table.* **2.** A meal laid out on a table so that guests can serve themselves. *The buffet at the wedding featured foods from many countries.*

bul•le•tin board (bůl´i tin bôrd) *noun*. A board for posting notices, announcements, and pictures. *The teacher uses a bulletin board to report all class events.*

bun•dle (bun´dəl) *noun*. A group of things held together. *The deliveryman left a bundle of newspapers outside the grocery store.*

bur•dens (bûr´dənz) *noun, plural.* Things that are carried. *The mule carried the burdens down the trail into the canyon.*

Cc

cam•ou•flage (kam´ə fläzh´) *noun*. Any disguise, appearance, or behavior that serves to conceal or deceive, such as the protective coloring of an animal. *An octopus uses camouflage to change its skin color and blend into its surroundings.*

at; āpe; fär; câre; end; mē; it; īce; pîerce; hot; ōld; sông; fôrk; oil; out; up; ūse; rūle; půll; tûrn; chin; sing; shop; thin; this; hw in white; zh in treasure.

The symbol ə stands for the unstressed vowel sound in about, taken, pencil, lemon, and circus.

766

767

can•celed (kan'səld) *verb.* Did away with, stopped, or called off. *The picnic was **canceled** due to rain.*

ca•pa•ble (kā'pə bəl) *adjective.* Having skill or power; able. *The new planes are **capable** of even greater speed.*

car•ni•vores (kär'nə vôrz') *noun, plural.* Animals or plants such as sharks, eagles, dogs, and Venus's-flytraps that feed chiefly on flesh. *Lions are **carnivores** who hunt and feed on smaller animals.*

cat•e•go•ries (kat'i gôr'ēz) *noun, plural.* Groups or classes of things. *The menu was divided into three **categories**: snacks, main courses, and desserts.*

cel•e•bra•tion (sel'ə brā'shən) *noun.* The act of honoring with festivities. *My grandma's ninetieth birthday called for a big **celebration**.*

char•ac•ter•is•tics (kar'ik tə ris'tiks) *noun, plural.* Qualities or features that are typical of or serve to distinguish a person, group, or thing from others. *Courage and bravery are **characteristics** that my cousin possesses.*

chis•eled (chi'zəld) *verb.* Cut or shaped with a sharp metal tool called a chisel. *The numbers were **chiseled** into the stone next to the front doors.*

civ•i•li•za•tion (siv'ə lə zā'shən) *noun.* A society in which agriculture, trade, government, art, and science are highly developed. *The museum had a number of objects that showed how **civilization** has developed over the last 600 years.*

clenched (klencht) *verb.* Grasped or closed tightly. *The boy **clenched** his fist when he saw the bully walking angrily towards him.*

colo•nel (kûr'nəl) *noun.* One of the ranks of a military officer. *Kevin Andretti was promoted to full **colonel** last month.*

com•bined (kəm bīnd') *adjective.* Characterized by being joined together or united. *Thanks to the **combined** efforts of the voters in our city, the mayor was reelected.* —*verb.* Joined together; united. *The baker **combined** eggs, butter, sugar, and flour to make cookie dough.*

com•menced (kə menst') *verb.* Began or started. *When the audience was seated and quiet, the play **commenced**.*

com•mon•wealth (kom'ən welth') *noun.* A nation or state that is governed independently but is associated with another country. *Puerto Rico is a **commonwealth** of the United States.*

com•pan•ion (kəm pan'yən) *noun.* A person or animal who keeps somebody company. *A dog can be a good **companion** for a lonely person.*

com•pelled (kəm peld') *verb.* Urged, or caused with force. *The rain **compelled** us to postpone our picnic.*

com•pe•ti•tion (kom'pi tish'ən) *noun.* The act of trying to win or gain something from another person or other people. *We're in **competition** with two other teams for the swimming championship.*

com•plex (kəm pleks') *adjective.* Hard to understand or do. *The math problems were very **complex** because they involved many steps.*

con•sent•ed (kən sen'tid) *verb.* Gave permission or agreed to. *My mom **consented** to my sleeping over at Maria's house for her slumber party.*

con•tact (kon'takt) *noun.* A touching or meeting of persons or things. *My uncle burned his arm when it came in **contact** with the hot stove.*

con•tam•i•na•tion (kən tam'ə nā'shən) *noun.* The process of spoiling or the state of being spoiled; pollution. *Food should be kept covered to prevent **contamination**.*

con•ti•nent (kon'tə nənt) *noun.* One of the seven large land areas on Earth. *I live in the United States which is on the **continent** of North America.*

co•op•er•a•tion (kō op'ə rā'shən) *noun.* Working with another or others for a common purpose. *With **cooperation**, the friends quickly decorated the room for the surprise party.*

co•or•di•na•tion (kō ôr'də nā'shən) *noun.* The ability of parts of the body to work together well. *A gymnast needs good **coordination** when performing on the balance beam.*

cor•ri•dor (kôr'i dər, kor'i dər) *noun.* A long passageway or hallway. *The students walked down the **corridor** towards the gymnasium.*

creased (krēst) *adjective.* Characterized by lines or marked by wrinkling. *My teacher would not accept my **creased** book report because it was messy looking.*

cred•it (kred'it) *noun.* **1.** Praise or honor; something owed to a person. *The students who included a visual display with their speeches earned extra **credit**.* **2.** Trust in a person to pay a debt at a later time. *The store gave me **credit** today so I could buy the shirt and pay for it on Friday.*

cross•breed•ing (krôs'brē'ding) *verb.* Breeding different kinds of plants or animals in order to produce hybrids. *The farmer was **crossbreeding** small, sweet peppers with large, tasteless peppers to get large, sweet peppers.*

Dd

dam•ag•es (dam'ij iz) *noun, plural.* Harm that makes things less valuable or useful. ***Damages** to the city totaled in the millions of dollars after the storm.*

dan•gling (dang'ling) *verb.* Hanging loosely. *The diamonds **dangling** from Erin's ears looked pretty in the light.*

de•cen•cy (dē'sən sē) *noun.* Proper behavior, as in speech, actions, and dress. *Mary had the **decency** to admit she made a mistake.*

ded•i•cat•ed (ded'i kā'tid) *verb.* Set apart for a special purpose or use. *The mayor **dedicated** a new museum to the memory of the founders of the city.*

de•fec•tive (di fek'tiv) *adjective.* Having a flaw or weakness; not perfect. *The zipper was **defective** so the coat wouldn't close all the way up.*

at; āpe; fär; câre; end; mē; it; īce; pîerce; hot; ōld; sông; fôrk; oil; out; up; ūse; rüle; pu̇ll; tûrn; chin; sing; shop; thin; t͟his; hw in white; zh in treasure.

The symbol ə stands for the unstressed vowel sound in about, taken, pencil, lemon, and circus.

del•i•ca•cies (del'i kə sēs) *noun, plural.* Rare or excellent food. *At the food festival there were **delicacies** from around the world.*

de•liv•er•ing (di liv'ə ring) *verb.* Taking or carrying something to a particular place or person. *My job is **delivering** groceries to people's homes.*

dense (dens) *adjective.* Packed closely together. *The smoke was very **dense**, making it difficult for the firefighters to see anything.*

de•scend•ed (di sen'did) *verb.* Moved from a higher place to a lower one. *The woman **descended** down the mountain on skis.*

de•spair (di spâr') *noun.* A complete loss of hope. *The student was filled with **despair** when he couldn't complete his assignment for tomorrow's deadline.*

de•struc•tion (di struk'shən) *noun.* Great damage or ruin. *The tornadoes caused a lot of **destruction** in our neighborhood.*

di•ag•nose (dī'əg nōs') *verb.* To make a ruling as to the nature of an illness. *The doctor can **diagnose** the patient's illness based on a description of the symptoms.*

dic•ta•tors (dik'tā tərz, dik tā'tərz) *noun, plural.* Rulers who have absolute power and authority, ruling a country without sharing power or consulting anyone else. ***Dictators** can pass laws that take away people's rights, such as the right to vote.*

dis•as•ters (di zas'tərz) *noun, plural.* Events that cause much suffering, distress, or loss. *Hurricanes are examples of natural **disasters**.*

dis•cus•sions (di skush'ənz) *noun, plural.* Acts of talking about something or exchanging opinions. *There were many **discussions** among the voters about what the politician promised them.*

dis•in•te•grate (dis in'ti grāt') *verb.* To break into many small pieces or fragments. *A blow with the heavy hammer caused the stone to **disintegrate**.*

dis•man•tled (dis man'təld) *verb.* Took something apart piece by piece. *The workers dismantled the outdooor stage after the concert.*

dis•miss (dis mis') *verb.* To take away the job of, or fire. *The manager needed to **dismiss** one of his workers for doing a poor job.*

dis•re•spect•ful (dis'ri spekt'fəl) *adjective.* Having or showing disrespect; rude; impolite. *It is **disrespectful** behavior to make fun of your guests.*

di•verse (di vûrs', dī vûrs') *adjective.* Not all the same; varied. *The people in my neighborhood come from **diverse** backgrounds.*

dor•mant (dôr'mənt) *adjective.* Temporarily quiet or not active. *Many tourists visited the dormant volcano because the chance of an eruption was low.*

Ee

ease (ēz) *verb.* To move slowly or carefully. *I tried to **ease** the heavy clock off the table without dropping or scratching it.*

ed•u•cate (ej'ə kāt') *verb.* To teach or train. *It is important to **educate** the students about dangers in the science lab so that no one gets hurt.*

e•lect•ed (i lek'tid) *verb.* Chosen by voting. *The class **elected** a representative to discuss the issue of recess with the principal.*

el•e•gant (el'i gənt) *adjective.* Showing richness and good taste; showing grace and dignity. *The **elegant** dress was trimmed with gold lace.*

el•e•ment•ar•y (el'ə mən'tə rē, el'ə men'trē) *adjective.* Dealing with the simple parts or beginnings of something. *We learned **elementary** facts about life cycles by observing how things change as they grow.*

el•e•ments (el'ə mənts) *noun, plural.* Basic parts from which something is made or formed. *A story should have these basic **elements**: a beginning, a middle, and an end.*

e•lim•i•nates (i lim'ə nāts') *verb.* Gets rid of; removes. *The new detergent **eliminates** tough stains on clothing.*

e•merged (i mûrjd') *verb.* Came into view. *After the giant wave knocked over Pietro, he **emerged** from the water with a piece of seaweed in his mouth.*

en•light•ened (en lī'tənd) *verb.* Gave knowledge or wisdom to; freed from prejudice or ignorance. *The teacher **enlightened** her students to the customs of the foreign tribe.*

en•list•ed (en lis'tid) *verb.* Joined the military voluntarily. *Michael's brother **enlisted** in the army after he graduated from high school.*

en•thu•si•asm (en thü'zē az'əm) *noun.* Eager and lively interest. *The audience expressed great **enthusiasm** for the play by applauding loudly.*

en•vi•ron•ment (en vī'rən mənt, en vī'ərn mənt) *noun.* The air, water, soil, and all the other things that surround a person, animal, or plant. *Living things need time to get used to changes in their **environment**.*

e•qual•i•ty (i kwol'i tē) *noun.* The quality or condition of being equal. *The Constitution of the United States provides for the **equality** of all Americans under the law.*

e•rupt•ed (i rup'tid) *verb.* Forced out or burst forth. *The area was filled with lava after the volcano **erupted**.*

e•vap•o•rates (i vap'ə rāts') *verb.* To be changed from a liquid or solid into a vapor. *Water **evaporates** when it is boiled.*

ex•ag•ger•at•ing (eg zaj'ə rā'ting) *verb.* Making something seem greater, larger, or more than it is; overstating. *I was **exaggerating** when I described the fish I had caught.*

ex•hib•its (eg zib'its) *noun, plural.* Things shown on display. *We went to see the **exhibits** of African art at the museum.*

ex•pe•di•tion (ek'spi dish'ən) *noun.* A journey with a specific purpose. *The members of the **expedition** had to go back down the mountain because the wind was too strong.*

Ff

fare (fâr) *noun.* The cost of a ride on a bus, train, airplane, ship, or taxi. *My mother paid my **fare** on the bus.*

fea•tures (fē'chərz) *noun, plural.* Important or distinctive parts or characteristics of something. *Great speed and power steering are **features** of this car.*

fire•ball (fīr'bôl') *noun.* A bright body from space that may trail bright sparks. *The **fireball** shot across the sky and briefly lit up our backyard.*

at; āpe; fär; câre; end; mē; it; īce; pîerce; hot; ōld; sông; fôrk; oil; out; up; ūse; rüle; pu̇ll; tûrn; chin; sing; shop; thin; t͟his; hw in white; zh in treasure.

The symbol ə stands for the unstressed vowel sound in about, taken, pencil, lemon, and circus.

flick•ered (flik'ərd) *verb.* Shone or burned with an unsteady or wavering light. *The candles **flickered** in the breeze.*

flukes (flüks) *noun, plural.* Chance happenings; unexpected or accidental events, especially lucky ones. *Some discoveries were **flukes** and resulted when scientists were trying to find other things.*

fo•cused (fō'kəst) *verb.* Concentrated or directed attention on. *The basketball player was so **focused** on scoring that he didn't hear the fans roaring.*

for•bid•den (fər bid'ən, fôr bid'ən) *verb.* Ordered not to do something; not allowed. *The children were **forbidden** to play outside after dark.*

for•ma•tions (fôr mā'shənz) *noun, plural.* Things that have been formed in a certain way and place. *Geologists study rock **formations** to understand Earth's history.*

frac•tures (frak'chərz) *noun, plural.* Cracks, splits, or breaks, as in a bone. *The boy's leg had multiple **fractures** after he fell out of the tree.*

fra•grance (frā'grəns) *noun.* A sweet or pleasing smell. *Roses have a strong **fragrance**.*

frig•id (frij'id) *adjective.* Very cold. *The **frigid** water was full of ice and snow.*

frus•trat•ed (frus'trā tid) *verb.* Kept from doing something. *Lita was **frustrated** in trying to light the candle because of the wind.*

func•tion (fungk'shən) *verb.* To work or act; to serve. *Mr. Martinez will **function** as the principal while Mrs. Arnold is out of town.*

fused (fūzd) *verb.* To blend or unite. *All the crayons in the box were **fused** together because they were left in the hot sun.*

Gg

gey•sers (gī'zərz) *noun, plural.* A natural hot spring from which steam and hot water shoot into the air after being heated below the surface by surrounding masses of hot rock. *Many people visit national parks to see the **geysers** spurt water.*

gi•gan•tic (jī gan'tik) *adjective.* Like a giant; huge and powerful. *The airplane looked **gigantic** when I saw it up close.*

glimpse (glimps) *noun.* A brief look or a passing glance. *I caught a **glimpse** of the actor as he dashed into the car.*

gnarled (närld) *adjective.* Having many rough, twisted knots. *The worker's hands looked as **gnarled** as a tree trunk.*

gos•siped (gos'ipt) *verb.* Talked or spread rumors, often unfriendly, about matters related to another person. *Kayla **gossiped** to her friends about Beth because she was jealous of Beth's good grades.*

gov•er•nor (guv'ər nər) *noun.* The person elected to be the head of a state government in the United States, or of a territory. *The **governor** of my state will sign the new law.*

grav•i•ty (grav'i tē) *noun.* The force that pulls things toward the center of Earth, causing objects to have weight. *Because of **gravity**, a ball thrown in the air will fall back to the ground.*

guar•an•teed (gar'ən tēd') *verb.* Made sure or certain. *The salesman **guaranteed** this was the lowest price for a mountain bike.*

gushed (gusht) *verb.* Poured out suddenly and in large amounts. *The quiet fountain suddenly **gushed**, surprising the children.*

Hh

hem•i•sphere (hem'i sfîr') *noun.* One half of Earth. *The equator divides Earth into the Northern and Southern **Hemispheres.** Earth is also divided into the Western Hemisphere and the Eastern Hemisphere.*

her•it•age (her'i tij) *noun.* Something that is handed down from the past; tradition. *Celebrating festivals is part of the Native American **heritage**.*

hes•i•ta•tion (hez'i tā'shən) *noun.* A delay due to fear or doubt. *The talented dancers showed no **hesitation** on stage.*

ho•ri•zon (hə rī'zən) *noun.* The line where the sky and the earth or sea seem to meet. *We watched as the ship seemed to disappear into the **horizon**.*

hu•man•i•ty (hū man'i tē, ū man'i tē) *noun.* The quality or condition of being human; human character or nature. *Keeping our air and water clean will help all **humanity**.*

hur•ri•canes (hûr'i kānz', hur'i kānz') *noun, plural.* Storms with strong winds and heavy rain. ***Hurricanes** can rip trees out of the ground.*

hy•brids (hī'bridz) *noun, plural.* The offspring of two animals or plants of different varieties. *Pluots are **hybrids** that combine the qualities of plums and apricots.*

hy•dro•gen (hī'drə jən) *noun.* A gas that has no odor, color, or taste and burns easily. *Today in class we learned that **hydrogen** was used in early balloons because it was the lightest element.*

Ii

i•den•ti•ty (ī den'ti tē) *noun.* Who or what a person or place is. *The man at the bank used his driver's license as proof of his **identity**.*

im•press (im pres') *verb.* To have a strong effect on the mind or feelings. *The display of artwork will **impress** the audience.*

in•ev•i•ta•ble (in ev'i tə bəl) *adjective.* Not able to be avoided; bound to happen. *An **inevitable** result of closing your eyes is not being able to see.*

in•flate (in flāt') *verb.* To cause to swell by filling with air or gas. *My father used the air pump at the gas station to **inflate** the front tires.*

in•ju•ry (in'jə rē) *noun.* Damage or harm done to a person or thing. *Luckily, Roberto's football **injury** was not serious.*

in•quire (in kwīr') *verb.* To ask questions or seek information. *I went into the restaurant to **inquire** about getting a job as a waitress.*

in•still (in stil') *verb.* To put in or introduce little by little. *Good teachers **instill** a love of learning in their students.*

in•struct (in strukt') *verb.* To provide with knowledge, information, or skill; to teach. *The dance teacher will **instruct** the students in tap, ballet, and jazz.*

at; āpe; fär; câre; end; mē; it; īce; pîerce; hot; ōld; sông; fôrk; oil; out; up; ūse; rüle; pu̇ll; tûrn; chin; sing; shop; thin; <u>th</u>is; **hw** in white; **zh** in treasure.

The symbol ə stands for the unstressed vowel sound in about, taken, pencil, lemon, and circus.

in•ten•tions (in ten'shənz) *noun, plural.* Plans to act in a certain way; purposes. *Franklin hated baseball so his **intentions** for joining the team were unclear.*

in•ter•act (in'tə rakt') *verb.* To act upon one another. *Members of the band walked into the audience so they could **interact** with fans.*

in•ter•sec•tion (in'tər sek'shən, in'tər sek'shən) *noun.* A place where two or more things meet and cross each other, such as roads or streets. *Look both ways before crossing an **intersection**.*

in•va•sion (in vā'zhən) *noun.* The entering of an army into a region to conquer it. *When planning an **invasion**, generals pay close attention to where the enemy troops are stationed.*

ir•re•sist•i•ble (ir'i zis'tə bəl) *adjective.* Not capable of being resisted or opposed. *On a hot day, a cold drink is so tempting that it is **irresistible**.*

Ll

la•bor (lā'bər) *noun.* Hard work; toil. *The construction workers were tired from the backbreaking **labor** they were hired to do.* —*verb.* To do hard work. *Tired runners **labor** up the steep hill at the end of the race.*

land•scape (land'skāp') *noun.* The stretch of land or scenery viewed from one point or place. *The **landscape** was filled with tall trees and green pastures.*

> **Word History**
>
> The term **landscape** comes from the Dutch *landschap*, meaning "province, or painting of a land scene." The Dutch word came from the root *land* and the suffix *-schap*, which means "ship."

launched (lôncht) *verb.* Sent off or started in motion. *The science club **launched** a rocket into the air.*

leg•is•la•ture (lej'is lā'chər) *noun.* A government body having the power to make laws. *People depend on members of the **legislature** to make laws that are fair.*

lim•it•less (lim'it lis) *adjective.* Without bounds or restrictions. *There seems to be a limitless number of stars in the sky.*

lo•ca•tion (lō kā'shən) *noun.* An exact position or place. *The airplane flew by several times before spotting the **location** of the lost hikers.*

lu•mi•nous (lü'mə nəs) *adjective.* Bright; shining. *The **luminous** glow coming from the windows made the house look warm.*

lung•ing (lun'jing) *verb.* Making a sudden forward movement. *The pitcher was **lunging** for the ball when the runner tagged the base.*

Mm

ma•jor (mā'jər) *adjective.* Greater in size, amount, value, importance, or rank. *The Rockies are a **major** mountain system in America.* —*noun.* An officer in the armed forces. *My uncle is a **major** in the Army.*

mam•mals (mam'əlz) *noun, plural.* Creatures that are warm-blooded and have a backbone. *Female mammals produce milk to feed their young. Human beings, cattle, bats, and whales are **mammals**.*

maze (māz) *noun.* A confusing series of paths or passageways through which people may have a hard time finding their way. *There is a **maze** in my town where people try to find their way through tall stalks of corn.*

me•chan•i•cal (mi kan'i kəl) *adjective.* Produced or operated by a machine. *John likes to play with **mechanical** toys.*

me•di•a (mē'dē ə) *noun, plural.* Means or form of communication that reaches a large audience. A plural of **medium**. *Television and newspapers are **media** that influence our daily life.*

mer•chan•dise (mûr'chən dīz', mûr'chən dīs') *noun.* Things for sale. *A shipment of new **merchandise** was delivered to the electronics store last night.*

me•te•or (mē'tē ər) *noun.* A mass of metal or rock that enters Earth's atmosphere from space. *It is rare for a **meteor** to strike Earth, but it can happen.*

mim•ic•ry (mim'i krē) *noun.* The close outward resemblance of one kind of animal to another or to an object in its natural environment. *One type of fly uses **mimicry** to fool animals into thinking it is a wasp.*

mis•chie•vous (mis'chə vəs) *adjective.* Full of mischief, or conduct that is often playful but causes harm. *Cal likes to be **mischievous** by playing practical jokes.*

mis•sion (mish'ən) *noun.* A special job or task. *My mom sent me on a **mission** to find my sister's favorite stuffed bear.*

moist•ened (moi'sənd) *verb.* Dampened or made slightly wet. *Ellen **moistened** the flaps of the envelopes with a damp sponge.*

mourn•ful (môrn'fəl) *adjective.* Feeling, expressing, or filled with grief or sorrow. *The **mournful** song on the radio made the listeners feel sad.*

murk•y (mûr'kē) *adjective.* Dark or cloudy. *It was scary sitting in the row boat because there was **murky** water all around us.*

Nn

nat•u•ral•ist (nach'ər ə list) *noun.* A person who specializes in the study of things in nature, especially plants and animals. *The **naturalist** spent a lot of time hiking and camping in the woods.*

nav•i•ga•tion (nav'i gā'shən) *noun.* The art or science of figuring out the position and course of boats, ships, and aircraft. *For proper **navigation**, pilots rely on equipment to direct them.*

nes•tled (nes'əld) *verb.* Located in a snug and sheltered spot. *Her desk was **nestled** between piles of books in the back corner of the warehouse.*

at; āpe; fär; câre; end; mē; it; īce; pîerce; hot; ōld; sông; fôrk; oil; out; up; ūse; rüle; pu̇ll; tûrn; chin; sing; shop; thin; <u>th</u>is; **hw** in white; **zh** in treasure.

The symbol ə stands for the unstressed vowel sound in about, taken, pencil, lemon, and circus.

no•mads (nō′madz) *noun, plural.* Members of groups or tribes that have no permanent home and move from place to place in search of food or land on which to graze their animals. ***Nomads** often live in desert areas.*

Word History

The word **nomad** comes from the Latin word *nomas*, meaning "wanderer." It is related to the Greek word *nomas*, which means "wandering, as in search of pasture."

Oo

ob•ser•va•tions (ob′zər vā′shənz) *noun, plural.* The act, practice, or power of seeing and noticing. *The detective's careful **observations** helped to solve the crime.*

ob•serv•er (əb zûr′vər) *noun.* A person who watches carefully and with attention. *The nature photographer was a keen **observer** of flowers and insects.*

o•ral•ly (ôr′əl ē) *adverb.* Using speech as opposed to writing. *Each contestant was given a chance to spell the word **orally**.*

or•gan•isms (ôr′gə niz′əmz) *noun, plural.* Living things. Animals, plants, mushrooms, protozoans, and bacteria are all organisms. *The scientist studied **organisms** that live in ponds.*

o•rig•i•nal (ə rij′ə nəl) *adjective.* Made, done, thought of, or used for the first time. *All of the wood floors in the old house are **original**.*

out•cast (out′kast′) *noun.* A person rejected by and driven out of a group. *Jason felt like an **outcast** when he was thrown off the debating team.*

Pp

parched (pärcht) *adjective.* Dry or thirsty. *The **parched** land seemed to cry out for rain.*

par•ti•cles (pär′ti kəlz) *noun, plural.* Small bits or pieces of an element. *Tiny **particles** connect together to make up solid objects.*

pa•tri•ots (pā′trē əts) *noun, plural.* People who love and enthusiastically support their country. *American history views George Washington and John Adams as true **patriots**.*

per•mis•sion (pər mish′ən) *noun.* Consent or agreement from someone in authority. *I had to get **permission** from my parents before leaving on the school trip.*

phy•si•cal (fiz′i kəl) *adjective.* Having to do with the body. *Doing **physical** activities that increase your heart rate will help you stay in shape.*

poll•ing (pōl′ling) *adjective.* The casting and recording of votes in an election. *Voters go to a **polling** station to cast their votes.*

post•pone (pōst pōn′) *verb.* To put off to a later time. *The officials decided to **postpone** the baseball game until tomorrow because of rain.*

pre•cip•i•ta•tion (pri sip′i tā′shən) *noun.* Any form of water that falls to Earth, such as rain, hail, or snow. *Desert regions get very little **precipitation** each year.*

pred•a•tors (pred′ə tərz) *noun, plural.* Animals that live by preying on, or hunting and eating, other animals. *Lions and wolves are natural **predators** who hunt smaller animals for food.*

pre•oc•cu•pied (prē ok′yə pīd′) *adjective.* Absorbed in thought; engrossed. *The bride was so **preoccupied** with wedding plans that she couldn't concentrate on her work.*

pres•ence (prez′əns) *noun.* Something felt to be present in a specific place at a given time. *I could sense my mother's **presence** even before I saw her.*

pres•i•den•tial (prez′ə den′shəl) *adjective.* Of or relating to the president. *The candidates prepared for a **presidential** debate.*

pre•vail•ing (pri vā′ling) *adjective.* Most common at a particular time. *The **prevailing** winds made the day really cold.*

prey (prā) *noun.* Any animal hunted or killed by another animal for food. *Nature films often show lions hunting down their **prey**.*

prog•ress (prog′res) *noun.* A forward movement or gradual betterment. *This century has seen a lot of **progress** in computer science.*

prop•er•ty (prop′ər tē) *noun.* A piece of land. *If you're thinking of building a house, the **property** next to my house is for sale.*

Qq

qual•i•fy (kwol′ə fī′) *verb.* To make fit, as for a certain job or task. *In order to **qualify** for the Olympics, you must be one of the best athletes in the country.*

quest (kwest) *noun.* A search or pursuit. *The explorers went on a **quest** for gold.*

Word History

The word **quest** comes from the Old French word *queste*, which means "search." It goes back to Latin *quaesita*, meaning "thing sought."

Rr

ra•vine (rə vēn′) *noun.* A deep, narrow valley, especially one worn by running water. *As you walk along the edge of the road, be careful not to fall into the **ravine**.*

re•duce (ri düs′, ri dūs′) *verb.* To make less or become smaller in size, number, or degree. *The store should **reduce** its prices.*

re•flect•ed (ri flek′təd) *verb.* Light, sound, images, or heat that is turned, thrown, or bent back at an angle. *The white tents **reflected** the heat from the hot sun onto the sand.*

re•lays (*n.,* rē′lāz; *v.* rē′lāz, ri lāz′) *noun, plural.* Fresh sets or teams, as of workers or animals, prepared to replace or relieve another. *The Pony Express used **relays** to deliver mail across long distances.* —*verb.* Passes along. *When I'm not home, my mother **relays** your messages to me.*

re•luc•tant (ri luk′tənt) *adjective.* Unwilling or hesitant. *My friend wants to try the high dive, but I am **reluctant** to join him because I'm afraid.*

re•pet•i•tive (ri pet′i tiv) *adjective.* Full of, marked by, or containing repetition. *Some factories use robots to do **repetitive** tasks.*

at; āpe; fär; câre; end; mē; it; īce; pîerce; hot; ōld; sông; fôrk; oil; out; up; ūse; rüle; pull; tûrn; chin; sing; shop; thin; this; hw in white; zh in treasure.

The symbol ə stands for the unstressed vowel sound in about, taken, pencil, lemon, and circus.

rep•re•sent•a•tive (rep′ri zen′tə tiv) *noun.* A person who is chosen to represent or stand for another or others. *A **representative** from each district was sent to City Hall to vote for the law.*

re•search (ri sûrch′, rē′sûrch′) *noun.* A careful study to find and learn facts about a subject. *Fawn had to do a lot of **research** at the library before she wrote her paper.*

res•er•va•tion (rez′ər vā′shən) *noun.* **1.** Land set aside by a government for a special purpose, such as for Native American tribes to live on. *Native Americans preserved their culture and traditions on the **reservation** where they lived.* **2.** An arrangement to have something kept for another person or persons. *We asked the travel agent to make a plane **reservation** for us.* **3.** Something that causes doubt. *Her serious **reservations** about walking home after dark made sense.*

re•trieve (ri trēv′) *verb.* To get back; recover; regain. *The golfer tried to **retrieve** the golf ball from the lake.*

re•veal (ri vēl′) *verb.* To make known. *The journalist would not **reveal** the source of her story.*

re•versed (ri vûrst′) *verb.* Moved in the opposite direction from what is usual. *We **reversed** our direction when we realized we were going the wrong way.*

rig•id (rij′id) *adjective.* Not changing; fixed. *Our **rigid** schedule did not allow us to make an unplanned stop at the new park.*

riv•er•bank (riv′ər bangk′) *noun.* The raised ground bordering a river. *The **riverbank** was a very popular place for summer picnics.*

ro•bot (rō′bot) *noun.* A machine designed to perform certain human tasks. *The **robot** did a job that was too dangerous for humans to do.*

ro•tat•ed (rō tā′tid) *verb.* Turned around on an axis. *As the wheels **rotated**, the car moved forward.*

Ss

sagged (sagd) *verb.* Drooped down in the middle from weight. *The tent **sagged** from all the rainwater that had collected on top.*

sat•is•fac•to•ry (sat′is fak′tə rē) *adjective.* Good enough to meet a need or desire. *The work done on the house was **satisfactory**, so the owners could move in.*

saun•tered (sôn′tərd) *verb.* Walked in a slow or relaxed way; strolled. *The family **sauntered** through the lush grass in the park.*

scald (skôld) *verb.* To heat to a temperature just below the boiling point. *The cook taught us how to **scald** the milk by taking it off the burner before it bubbles.*

scen•er•y (sē′nə rē) *noun.* The sights of a place or region. *We admired the beautiful **scenery** while we rode through the mountain range on the train.*

sci•en•tif•ic (sī′ən tif′ik) *adjective.* Having to do with or used in science. *The **scientific** discovery of gravity changed the way people thought about Earth.*

scorch•ing (skôr′ching) *adjective.* Causing intense heat to dry or burn the surface of something. *The **scorching** sun dried up all the plants.*

scoured (skourd) *verb.* Cleaned, cleared, or worn away. *We **scoured** the pan with cleanser until it shone.*

scraw•ny (skrô′nē) *adjective.* Thin, bony, or skinny. *The cat was **scrawny** because she hadn't eaten in days.*

se•clud•ed (si klü′did) *adjective.* Shut off from view. *We found a quiet, **secluded** area in the park for our picnic.*

seg•re•ga•tion (seg′ri gā′shən) *noun.* The practice of separating one racial group, especially African Americans, from the rest of society by making them use different schools and social facilities or making them live in certain areas. ***Segregation** forced African American children to attend schools with poor facilities.*

set•tings (set′ingz) *noun, plural.* The surroundings of something; background; environment. *The gallery showed paintings of cottages in beautiful **settings**.*

shield (shēld) *noun.* A person or thing that protects against danger, injury, or distress. *I used a magazine as a **shield** against the bright sunlight because I forgot my sunglasses.*

short•age (shôr′tij) *noun.* A small amount or lack of supply. *The storm destroyed many farms, so there was a **shortage** of watermelon.*

shrieks (shrēks) *verb.* Makes loud, shrill cries or sounds. *My little sister **shrieks** when I tickle her.*

site (sīt) *noun.* The position or location of something. *Our house is at a mountain **site** with a beautiful view.*

slumped (slumpt) *verb.* Fell or sunk heavily. *The tired woman **slumped** down in the back seat.*

slurp (slûrp) *verb.* To drink or eat noisily. *It is impolite to **slurp** soup, especially in public.*

sog•gy (sog′ē) *adjective.* Very wet or damp; soaked. *The juicy tomatoes on the sandwich made the bread **soggy**.*

spe•cies (spē′shēz) *noun.* A group of animals or plants that have many characteristics in common. *German shepherds belong to one **species**, and wolves belong to another.*

spec•i•mens (spes′ə mənz) *noun, plural.* Items or parts typical of a group. *The scientist collected **specimens** of some germs that could make people sick.*

spec•tac•u•lar (spek tak′yə lər) *adjective.* Very impressive or unusual. *We watched the **spectacular** fireworks display from our backyard.*

sprawled (sprôld) *verb.* Lay or sat with the body stretched out in an awkward or careless manner. *My brother was so tired from swimming that he **sprawled** out on the blanket and left no room for anyone else.*

spunk (spungk) *noun.* An informal word for courage, spirit, or determination. *The gymnast showed her **spunk** by climbing back up on the balance beam after falling.*

stag•gered (stag′gərd) *verb.* Moved unsteadily or with a swaying motion. *The tired runners **staggered** to the finish line.*

stam•i•na (stam′ə nə) *noun.* The physical ability to withstand fatigue, disease, or hardship; endurance. *A long-distance runner must have **stamina** to finish a race.*

stark (stärk) *adjective.* Bare. *All of the trees had been cut down so the landscape appeared **stark**.*

at; āpe; fär; câre; end; mē; it; īce; pîerce; hot; ōld; sông; fôrk; oil; out; up; ūse; rüle; pull; tûrn; chin; sing; shop; thin; this; hw in white; zh in treasure.

The symbol ə stands for the unstressed vowel sound in about, taken, pencil, lemon, and circus.

Additional Lessons and Resources

CONTENTS

Additional Lessons

Comprehension: Character and Plot T1

Comprehension: Setting and Plot T2

Comprehension: Compare and Contrast T3

Comprehension: Summarize T4

Comprehension: Cause and Effect T5

Vocabulary: Context Clues (Synonyms) T6

Vocabulary: Word Parts
(Compound Words) T7

Vocabulary: Dictionary (Homographs) T8

Vocabulary: Context Clues
(Description or Explanation) T9

Vocabulary: Thesaurus (Synonyms) T10

Study Skills: Photographs/Captions
and Toolbars/Links T11

Study Skills: Using the Library/Media Center
and Charts T12

Classroom Library Lessons T13

Theme Bibliography T19

Author/Illustrator Awards T21

Word Lists T22

Scope & Sequence T28

Index T36

Glossary

strands (strandz) *noun, plural.* Things similar to threads. *Strands of spaghetti were wrapped around the fork.*

strat•e•gy (strat′i jē) *noun.* A careful plan for achieving a goal. *Our coach used a new strategy that confused the best team in the league.*

stunned (stund) *verb.* Shocked or overwhelmed. *Everyone was stunned when I won the essay contest because I usually needed help with my writing assignments.*

sub•mit (səb mit′) *verb.* **1.** To give up; to give in to someone's power. *Soldiers may submit to the enemy if they are too weak to fight.* **2.** To present. *My teacher asked us to submit our reports on Friday.*

suc•ceed (sək sēd′) *verb.* **1.** To follow in sequence, especially immediately. *The prince was able to succeed to the throne after the king stepped down.* **2.** To have a good result. *The debating team will succeed in winning the award.*

suf•frage (suf′rij) *noun.* The right or privilege of voting. *The women who marched at the rally in Washington, D.C., were fighting for suffrage.*

su•per•hu•man (sū′pər hū′mən, sū′pər ü′mən) *adjective.* Beyond ordinary human ability or power. *Folk tale heroes often have superhuman strength.*

su•per•vise (sū′pər vīz′) *verb.* To watch over and direct. *It was a huge responsibility to supervise all the children swimming in the pool.*

surge (sûrj) *noun.* A large wave or series of waves during a storm. *The storm surge caused a lot of damage along the coast.*

sur•round•ings (sə roun′dingz) *noun, plural.* The objects, influences, or conditions of a place. *The cabin had beautiful surroundings: flowers, plants, and a nearby lake.*

sur•vive (sər vīv′) *verb.* To live and be active through and after an event. *One must know how to find food and shelter to survive in the woods.*

sus•pend•ed (sə spen′dəd) *verb.* Held in place as if attached from above. *The spider was suspended from the roof by a strand of web.*

swag•ger (swag′ər) *noun.* A walk or behavior that is bold, rude, or arrogant. *The star athlete walked into the room with a swagger.*

swerved (swûrvd) *verb.* Turned aside suddenly. *The car swerved to miss the dog crossing the road.*

sym•pa•thy (sim′pə thē) *noun.* The ability to share the feelings of another or others. *I felt great sympathy for Jim because I knew what it felt like to have my feelings hurt.*

Tt

the•o•ry (thē′ə rē) *noun.* An idea that explains a group of facts or an event; something that has not been proven true. *Do you have a theory that explains why leaves turn color in the fall?*

to•kens (tō′kənz) *noun, plural.* **1.** Pieces that mark movement on a board game. *Andrea moved her tokens six spaces ahead and won the game.* **2.** Pieces of metal, like coins, used as substitutes for money. *We put tokens in the machine to play video games at the mall.*

tra•di•tion•al (trə dish′ə nəl) *adjective.* The knowledge, beliefs, or customs that one generation passes to another. *Our traditional Thanksgiving includes eating turkey and watching television.*

traits (trāts) *noun, plural.* Aspects, qualities, or characteristics that a person or thing possesses. *Bravery and honesty are traits a person can display.*

trans•formed (trans fôrmd′) *verb.* Changed in shape, form, or appearance. *The builder transformed the backyard by adding a patio.*

treach•er•ous (trech′ər əs) *adjective.* Full of danger. *The sharp curves on the treacherous road caused many traffic accidents.*

treas•ur•er (trezh′ər ər) *noun.* The person in charge of the money of a business or a group. *The treasurer became nervous when he realized money was missing from the company bank account.*

tri•umph (trī′umf) *verb.* To be successful or win. *Everyone is confident that we will triumph over the problems we are having due to the weather.*

ty•rant (tī′rənt) *noun.* A person who uses power or authority in a cruel or unjust way. *The king was a tyrant because he punished his subjects unfairly.*

Word History

The word **tyrant** comes from Old French *tiran*, which means "despot." The Old French word came from the Latin word *tyrannus*, which means "ruler or despot." Tyrant can also be traced to the Greek word *tyrannos*, which means "absolute ruler."

Uu

un•con•sti•tu•tion•al (un′kon sti tū′shə nəl) *adjective.* Not in keeping with the constitution of a country, state, or group, especially the Constitution of the United States. *The Supreme Court in this country decides if a law is unconstitutional.*

un•en•thu•si•as•ti•cal•ly (un′en thū′zē as′tik ə lē) *adverb.* Not in an enthusiastic manner; not zealous. *The crowd laughed unenthusiastically at the comedian's bad jokes.*

un•for•tu•nate (un fôr′chə nit) *adjective.* Unlucky. *It was very unfortunate that it rained on the day we had tickets to the outdoor concert.*

un•heed•ed (un hē′did) *adjective.* Not paid attention to; disregarded. *The disaster occurred because warnings were unheeded.*

at; āpe; fär; câre; end; mē; it; īce; pîerce; hot; ōld; sông; fôrk; oil; out; up; ūse; rūle; pull; tûrn; chin; sing; shop; thin; this; hw in white; zh in treasure.

The symbol ə stands for the unstressed vowel sound in about, taken, pencil, lemon, and circus.

un•in•hab•it•ed (un′in hab′i tid) *adjective.* Not lived in. *The uninhabited house had broken windows and a leaky roof.*

un•pleas•ant (un plez′ənt) *adjective.* Offensive or not pleasing. *There was a very unpleasant smell near the restaurant's garbage container.*

un•rea•son•a•ble (un rē′zə nə bəl) *adjective.* Not showing or using good sense or judgment. *The teacher was being unreasonable when he punished the whole class for the bad behavior of one student.*

Vv

va•cant (vā′kənt) *adjective.* Not having anyone or anything in it; empty. *If that seat is vacant, you can sit in it.*

va•ri•e•ty (və rī′i tē) *noun.* A number or collection of different things; things of various kinds or parts. *I enjoy eating a wide variety of fruits and vegetables.*

vast•ness (vast′nis) *noun.* Greatness in size, extent, or number. *The vastness of the desert made it seem to stretch for miles.*

ven•tured (ven′chərd) *verb.* Went despite risk or danger. *Lucy ventured out into the storm to look for her dog.*

ver•sions (vûr′zhənz) *noun, plural.* Different or changed forms of an original. *I wrote many versions of the story before I completed the final draft.*

vet•er•i•nar•i•an (vet′ər ə nâr′ē ən, vet′rə nâr ē ən) *noun.* A person trained and licensed to give medical or surgical treatment to animals. *I took my dog to the veterinarian for a checkup.*

vi•brates (vī′brāts) *verb.* Moves back and forth or up and down very fast. *The cell phone vibrates instead of making a loud ring when someone calls.*

vol•ume (vol′ūm, vol′yəm) *noun.* The amount of space occupied. *Find the volume of a building block by multiplying its height by its length by its width.*

Ww

wares (wârz) *noun, plural.* Things for sale. *My mother inspects the quality of the wares at the market before buying anything.*

wheel•chair (hwēl′châr′, wēl′châr′) *noun.* A chair on wheels that is used by someone who cannot walk to get from one place to another. *My grandmother needed to use a wheelchair after she fell and broke her hip.*

wring (ring) *verb.* To squeeze or twist; to get by force. *I had to wring out my swimsuit before hanging it in the laundry room.*

Zz

zone (zōn) *noun.* A region or area that has some special quality, condition, or use. *There is a "No Parking" zone on this street.*

Comprehension

Objective: Review character and plot using text clues

Character and Plot

Intervention/Remediation

Materials "The Talent Contest, Student Book pp. 18–19

Explain Say: *All stories have characters and a plot. Characters are the people or animals in a story. Plot is how the events unfold.*

Model Read aloud the first three paragraphs of "The Talent Contest." Say: *I think that Danny is the main character in this story. Danny faces a problem: identifying something that he can do well in the talent contest. The plot will tell how Danny solves the problem.* To help students identify the characters and plot, tell them to look for names and important events.

Guided Practice Have students skim the rest of the story. Ask: *How did Danny solve his problem? Who can tell the plot in one or two sentences?*

Constructive Feedback

Ask: *What is revealed in the first conversation between Danny and Elena? What do Danny and Elena do in their brainstorming session? How does the story end?* Have students use their responses to tell the plot.

Practice Have students construct a flowchart showing the series of events that give "The Talent Contest" a beginning, middle, and end.

Constructive Feedback

Ask: *Who can divide the story into three sections to show beginning, middle, and end? What problem is revealed in the beginning? How do Danny and Elena try to solve the problem in the middle? How is it solved at the end?*

Character and Plot

Explain Write the following on the board: *Muffin was a timid little dog. As a puppy, she was afraid to go outside. She would shiver and shake.* Read the sentences with students. Tell them they will practice identifying character and plot.

Guided Practice Lead a class discussion about the story elements described in the sentence. Ask: *What is the character's name? What is Muffin's problem?* Remind students that the character's problem will determine the plot.
Say: *We know that Muffin's problem is her fear of the outdoors. What prediction can we make about the plot, based on Muffin's problem?* Prompt students to predict that Muffin will have an experience that will help her overcome her fear.

Practice Write on the board: *One morning Muffin was whining to come indoors, when she met a friendly dog named Rufus. The two became friends and played together. Muffin learned to love taking walks with her new buddy.* Have a volunteer circle words and phrases that advance the plot by showing how Muffin's problem is solved.
Visual/Kinesthetic

Mind Pictures

Materials *Miss Alaineus,* Student Book p. 22; markers or colored pencils; drawing paper

Explain Tell students they will draw pictures of a character based on a description you will read aloud.

Guided Practice/Practice As students listen with closed eyes, read aloud the first paragraph of *Miss Alaineus* on page 22. Have students draw a picture of Forest. Auditory/Visual

Comprehension

Objective: Review characteristics of plot and setting

Plot and Setting

Intervention/Remediation

Materials "Grandma's Tales," Student Book pp. 50–51

Explain Say: *Plot is the action of a story. Setting tells where and when a story takes place.* Explain how to find the plot. Say: *Identify the problem or conflict the main character faces. Find the turning point, when the problem begins to be solved.*

Model Read aloud the first page of "Grandma's Tales" on **Student Book** page 50. Say: *The narrator's grandmother has a problem. People have made her famous distant relative, Davy Crockett, into a superhero. She wants people to understand that Davy was a real human being.*

Guided Practice Guide students to identify the setting by using the text and illustrations to tell where and when the story takes place. Ask: *What is the turning point?*

Constructive Feedback

Have students reread the first sentence and look at the pictures to identify the setting. For the turning point, explain that by giving the narrator facts about Davy, Grandma is accomplishing her goal "to wring the truth from all those wild stories."

Practice Have students write a short paragraph identifying the plot resolution in "Grandma's Tales." Tell them to include a detail showing that Grandma achieved her goal.

Constructive Feedback

If students cannot identify the resolution, ask: *When does Grandma see that the narrator is beginning to understand who Davy really was?*

Plot and Setting

Explain Write the following on the board: *The old house moaned and creaked as the wind blew through the broken windows. It was midnight. Jason had no business standing at the door, which was hanging halfway off its hinges.* Read the sentences with students. Tell them to look for clues to the plot and setting.

Guided Practice Help students identify the setting described above. Ask: *Where does this story take place? When does it take place?* Have students identify the problem that will determine the plot. Ask: *What problem is introduced? What do you think will happen next?*

Practice Have students write a paragraph developing the plot in the story above. Tell them to include words that will help readers visualize the setting. Linguistic/Kinesthetic

My Favorite Place

Materials large pieces of paper, markers

Explain Tell students that they will make a web to describe a favorite place and use the information create a setting for a story.

Guided Practice/Practice On the board draw a web with a central circle and five lines radiating outward. Label each line with one of the five senses. Have students copy the web. Ask them to choose a favorite place and write it in the central circle. On the lines, have students list sensory details about the place. Tell students to use their completed webs to write the first paragraph of a story, in which the setting is vividly described. Visual/Linguistic

Comprehension

Objective: Review comparing and contrasting using context clues

Compare and Contrast

Intervention/Remediation

Materials "Tree-Rific" Student Book pp. 80–81

Explain Remind students that comparing and contrasting is one kind of text structure. Say: *Think about how people, objects, or events in the text are alike and different. Pay attention to words that signal likenesses and differences.*

Model Read aloud the first paragraph of "Tree-Rific!" on page 80. Pause when you come to the phrase *on the other hand*. Say: *The phrase* on the other hand *tells me that now the writer will tell about a tree that is different from the bonsai. Sure enough, the next sentence contrasts the tiny bonsai with the giant sequoia, General Sherman.*

Guided Practice Continue reading page 80. Have students raise their hands when they hear a word that signals a likeness or difference.

Constructive Feedback

Draw a Venn diagram, label the left circle "Montezuma cypress" and the right circle "dancing lime." Tell students to write in the overlapping space how the trees are alike.

Practice Have students read the italicized introduction under "Trees at Work." Ask them to identify the comparison and write a sentence to explain it. (Steamy rain forests and snowy mountainsides both have "hard-working" trees.)

Constructive Feedback

Remind students that a comparison tells how things are alike. Ask: *What two things does the writer name in the phrase* From steamy rain forests to snowy mountainsides? *What do they have in common?*

Compare and Contrast

Explain Write the following on the board: *Pine and oak trees are both strong and tall. Pine trees have tiny leaves that stay green all year. Oak trees have large, flat leaves. They turn color and drop off in the fall.*

Guided Practice Read the text with students. Ask: *What text structure did the writer use in the sentences? What two things are being compared and contrasted? How are pine and oak trees alike? How are they different?*

Practice Have students make a Venn diagram to compare and contrast pine trees and oak trees. Visual

Vacation Spots

Materials paper, pencils, colored pencils

Explain Tell students that they will write and illustrate a compare-and-contrast paragraph about places to go on vacation.

Guided Practice/Practice Have students identify two vacation spots, such as the mountains and the beach or the Grand Canyon and Yellowstone National Park. Then assign students to list characteristics of each place. Have students use their lists to write a paragraph telling how the two places are alike and different, and explaining where they would rather go on vacation. Have students illustrate their paragraphs. Linguistic/Visual

Comprehension

Objective: Review summarizing

Summarize

Intervention/Remediation

Materials "Jobs in Space," Student Book pp. 92–93

Explain Say: *A summary is a short statement of the most important ideas or information in a text. To summarize, identify the main idea and supporting details.*

Model Read aloud the second paragraph of "Jobs in Space." Say: *The topic sentence gives the main idea of the paragraph. It provides a summary.* Read the paragraph's topic sentence.

Guided Practice Help students formulate a topic sentence for a summary by identifying the most important idea in "Jobs in Space" and restating it in their own words. Begin by having students silently reread the selection. Ask: *What does every paragraph address? Who can give a topic sentence for a summary of the selection?*

Constructive Feedback

Have students reread the first paragraph of page 92. Ask: *What important idea does the writer state about astronauts today? How much of the selection supports the idea that astronauts today do many jobs?* Help students formulate a topic sentence.

Practice Write on the board: *Astronauts today do many kinds of jobs.* Have students find major details in the text to support the topic sentence. Then write a summary.

Constructive Feedback

Remind students that minor details do not belong in a summary. Guide students to distinguish major and minor details in the text. Have them revise their summaries.

Summarize

Explain Write the following on the board: *Sally searched everywhere for her money. She hunted through every part of the house, including the garage. Finally she gave up and sat down to read. When she opened her book, she found the money. She'd used it as a bookmark!*

Guided Practice Read the text with students. Ask them to summarize it. (Sally searched everywhere for her lost money and finally found it in her book.) Ask: *How did you tell which details to leave out and include?* Have students give examples from the text to explain their choices.

Practice Ask students to write a paragraph about losing and finding something. Have students trade papers and orally summarize the paragraph they receive. Help resolve any disputes they have about which main ideas and important details belong in the summaries. Linguistic/Auditory

What I Heard

Materials story excerpt, paper, pencils

Explain Tell students that they will summarize a text that you read aloud.

Guided Practice/Practice Read aloud one or two paragraphs from a story. As students listen, suggest they jot down key ideas or information. When you have finished, have students write summaries of what they heard. Auditory/Linguistic

Tested **Comprehension**

Objective: Review cause and effect using story clues

Cause and Effect

Intervention/Remediation

Materials "It's a Dog's Life," Student Book pp. 114–115

Explain Say: *A cause is an event or action that makes something happen. An effect is the result of an event or action. Cause-and-effect relationships help make up the events in a story.*

Model Read the second paragraph of page 114. Say: *As I examine the cause-and-effect relationship in the paragraph, I see a cause with more than one effect. Ms. Toni's illness makes her hands shake. It also causes her muscles to stiffen up. This sometimes makes her lose balance.*

Guided Practice Write on the board: *Effect: Nap time is canceled every so often. Cause: _____.* Have students read the first sentence in the second paragraph on page 115 for the cause.

Constructive Feedback

Ask: *What signal word can you find in the sentence? What can you find after this signal word? Why is nap time sometimes canceled?*

Practice Have students imagine what makes Sparky feel happy or sad and write a sentence that contains a cause-and-effect relationship. Tell them to use Sparky's feelings as the effect. Call on students to read their sentences aloud.

Constructive Feedback

If students' sentences do not show a cause-and-effect relationship, review the definitions. Have students decide what action or event makes Sparky feel happy or sad. Have them rewrite their sentences using a signal word or phrase such as *because, so, since,* or *as a result.*

Cause and Effect

Explain Write on the board: *The man fell down because he slipped on a banana peel.*

Guided Practice Help students identify the cause-and-effect relationship presented in the sentence. Point out that the effect (man fell down) is listed before the cause (man slipped on banana peel). Draw students' attention to the signal word *because.*

Practice Tell students to construct two cause-and-effect relationships, one with and one without the signal word *because.* Linguistic

Pantomime It

Explain Tell students they will be working in groups to pantomime cause-and-effect relationships.

Guided Practice/Practice Use the example of one person giving another a present. Suggest that students act out giving each other gifts. The person who receives the gift can express joy in receiving the gift. The audience can identify the cause-and-effect relationships. Kinesthetic

Additional Lessons

Vocabulary

Objective: Recognize and use synonyms as context clues

Context Clues (Synonyms)

Intervention/Remediation

Materials "The Talent Contest," Student Book, pp. 18–19

Explain Say: *When you come across a word you do not know, you can use context clues to help you figure out what the word means. Sometimes writers give synonyms as context clues. Synonyms are words that have similar meanings.*

Model Have students look at the sentence with the word *soggy* in "The Talent Contest." Say: *As I read this sentence, I see a synonym for* soggy. *The synonym,* milk–soaked, *is a context clue. The synonym helps me figure out that* soggy *means "soaked."*

Guided Practice Read the sentence with the word *categories* on page 19. Ask: *Who can identify a synonym for* categories? (groups) *How would you divide a list of words into categories?* (Examples: by part of speech, by first letter, or by related topic.)

> ### Constructive Feedback
> If students have trouble, review the Explain section.

Practice Have students define the words *gigantic* and *luminous* on page 19 by identifying and using synonyms.

> ### Constructive Feedback
> If students have trouble identifying the synonyms that serve as context clues, slowly read aloud the sentences with *gigantic* and *luminous* as students follow along. Say: *Raise your hands when you hear synonyms for those words.* (huge; bright)

Context Clues (Synonyms)

Materials Student Book

Explain Write the following on the board: *My friend and I settled our small* <u>dispute</u> *before it grew into a big argument.*

Guided Practice Tell students they can use a synonym in the sentence to figure out the meaning of dispute. Ask students to identify a synonym of dispute. Explain, as needed: *The sentence tells me a small dispute is something that can grow into a big argument. So a small dispute must be a small argument. Argument is a synonym for dispute.*

Practice Have students choose three vocabulary words from Unit 1 and write three sentences with context clues that are synonyms for the words. Tell them to use the example on the board as a model. Visual

Create Word Clues

Materials "The National Spelling Bee," Student Book, pages 42–45; pencils

Explain Tell students that they will delete three words from the selection and have their partners use context clues to replace the words with synonyms.

Guided Practice/Practice Have students gently mark through three words in the selection and use context clues to supply three new words. Tell students to read the revised sentences aloud as partners check that they gave correct synonyms for the original words. Auditory/Visual

Vocabulary

Objective: Recognize and define compound words

Word Parts: Compound Words

Intervention/Remediation

Materials "Grandma's Tales," Student Book, pp. 50–51

Explain Say: *A compound word is made up of two or more words joined together. You can break a compound word into parts to figure out its meaning.*

Model Read the word *rattlesnake* in "Grandma's Tales." Write the word on the board, and draw a line between the two word parts. Explain: *The compound word* rattlesnake *is made up of the words* rattle *and* snake. *Combining the two words' meanings, I figure out that a rattlesnake is a kind of snake that makes a rattling sound.*

Guided Practice Direct students' attention to the noun *superhero* on page 50. Ask: *Which two words make up the compound word* superhero? *Who can tell what the compound word means?*

Constructive Feedback

If students have trouble defining *superhero*, ask: *What does* super *mean?* (great or extra) *What is a hero?* (someone looked up to)

Practice Have students identify another compound word on page 51 and write its definition.

Constructive Feedback

If students cannot complete the Practice, first draw their attention to the highlighted word *fireball*. Next restate the definition of compound word. Point out that *fireball* is a compound. Ask: *What two words make up this compound word? Who can use the meanings of* fire *and* ball *to tell what the compound means?*

Compound Words

Materials dictionaries

Explain Write the following on the board: *Susie and Drew played handball on the playground.*

Guided Practice Guide students to identify the two compound words in the sentence. Ask: *What two words are made of two smaller words?* (handball, playground) Then have students define the words based on their parts. Remind students: *To figure out what* handball *and* playground *mean, think about the meanings of* play *and* ground *and* hand *and* ball.

Practice Have students write three sentences, using at least one compound word in each. Allow students to use a dictionary to identify compound words. Visual

Compound Creations

Materials index cards, drawing paper, markers

Explain Tell students that they will make up and illustrate compound words.

Guided Practice/Practice Write familiar words on cards not usually part of a compound word. Challenge students to create a new compound word by having them select two words from a pile and putting the words together. Give students the example of *teachertime* or *mousechair*. Have students illustrate their new words and and give their pictures to a partner to guess the new word. Kinesthetic/Visual

Additional Lessons

Vocabulary

Objective: Define and use homographs

Dictionary: Homographs

Intervention/Remediation

Materials "Tree-Rific!" Student Book, pp. 80–81, dictionaries

Explain Say: *Homographs are words that are spelled the same but are often pronounced differently and have different meanings. When a word does not make sense in a sentence, check the dictionary to see if it has another entry.*

Model Have students turn to page 81. Point out the word *buffet* in the "Stay Cool" section. Say: *I know that one meaning of this word is a meal placed on a table so guests can serve themselves. But the word has a different meaning here. It means "to knock around."*

Guided Practice Draw students' attention to the word *wind*, in the "Strong Roots" section on page 81. Have students use dictionaries to find a meaning for *wind* that makes sense.

Constructive Feedback

If students have difficulty identifying the correct meaning for *wind*, review the Explain section.

Practice Direct students' attention to the sentence with the word *can*, in "Stay Cool." Have them write two definitions for *can*, circling the definition that makes sense in the selection.

Constructive Feedback

If students have difficulty, help them to substitute definitions of *can* in the sentence.

Dictionary: Homographs

Explain Write the following on the board: *The captain looked toward the bow of the ship. Robin Hood carried a bow and arrow. After the performance, the actor took a bow.*

Guided Practice Ask volunteers to read the sentences aloud. Discuss the different pronunciations of the word *bow* and the different meanings. Ask: *How are the homographs alike? How are they different?* (They are spelled the same and have different meanings.)

Practice Assign students one more homograph, such as *close* or *desert* to use in two sentences. Tell students to write sentences with context clues to the meaning and pronunciation of the homograph. Visual

Book of Misunderstandings

Materials dictionaries, markers or colored pencils, drawing paper

Explain Tell students that they will create an illustrated book of silly sentences that contain homographs.

Guided Practice/Practice Call on volunteers to identify one homograph and write it on the board. Allow students to use dictionaries as needed. Have each student choose one homograph to use in a sentence and illustrate in a silly way. Give students this example: *For the sentence* I saw a bat flying last night, *you could draw a baseball bat with wings flying through the air.* Compile students' work in a book of misunderstandings. Visual/Kinesthetic

Vocabulary

Objective: Use description or explanation to form context clues

Context Clues (Description or Explanation)

Intervention/Remediation

Materials "Jobs in Space," Student Book, pp. 92–93

Explain Say: *Writers often provide clues to help readers figure out the meanings of unfamiliar words. Some writers use commas to signal the definition for a difficult word.*

Model Have students turn to "Jobs in Space." Read aloud the sentence with the highlighted word *gravity.* Then explain: *The comma after the word gravity signals the definition, "the force that pulls things back to Earth."*

Guided Practice Read aloud the first two sentences in the last paragraph on page 93 as students follow along. Ask: *What term does the writer define?* How could the writer revise the two sentences and use a comma to signal the definition?

Constructive Feedback

If students have trouble, ask: *What term is defined in the first sentence?* Circle *Educator Astronauts.* Insert a comma after the term. Ask: *What do I need to do to create one sentence with a definition clue?* (Erase *are,* change the comma after *space* to a period, and lowercase *Their.*)

Practice Write the following on the board: *Astronaut pilots and mission specialists learn to move in a special zone.* Have students provide a definition clue to the meaning of *zone.*

Constructive Feedback

If students have trouble providing a definition clue, ask: *What does the word* zone *mean?* (area) Guide them through the revision.

Context Clues (Description or Explanation)

Explain Write the following on the board: *The leaf wafted by my window. It was carried lightly through the air.*

Guided Practice Help students to define *wafted* based on the context clue given. Ask: *The second sentence gives a definition for* wafted. *What is it?* (carried lightly)

Practice Have students write two sentences each using context clues to describe or explain the two vocabulary words *maze* and *function.* Have students exchange sentences with partners, read aloud their completed sentences, and identify each other's context clues. Visual/Auditory

Context Clue Charades

Materials index cards, markers

Explain Tell students that they will use aural and visual context clues to figure out word meanings.

Guided Practice/Practice On index cards write nouns and verbs from Unit 1 that can be acted out in a game of charades. Have students take turns drawing cards and giving aural clues or pantomiming the word's meaning until classmates identify the word. Before students begin, show them how to present the noun *gravity* by jumping up and (as you are pulled down) giving an aural context clue: a thump. Kinesthetic/Auditory

Vocabulary

Objective: Use a thesaurus to locate synonyms

Thesaurus: Synonyms

Intervention/Remediation

Materials "It's a Dog's Life," Student Book, pp. 114–115; thesauruses

Explain Say: *A thesaurus is a collection of synonyms, or words that have similar meanings.*

Model Have students turn to the selection "It's a Dog's Life." Direct their attention to the sentence with the word *theory* on page 115. Read it aloud. Explain: *The thesaurus gives me the synonyms* explanation, rationale, *and* hypothesis *for* theory. *If I replace* theory *with each synonym,* hypothesis *makes the most sense.*

Guided Practice Have a volunteer read aloud the sentence with the word *cancelled* on page 115. Ask: *Who can give me a synonym for* cancelled? List students' responses on the board. Have them find additional synonyms in the thesaurus. Ask: *Which synonym best suits the sentence?* (Possible response: called off)

Constructive Feedback

If students have trouble identifying the best synonym, substitute each synonym that students identified. Ask: *Which synonym fits best in the sentence?*

Practice Point out the sentence with the word *transformed* on page 114. Have students use a thesaurus to identify a synonym for *transformed.* Call on volunteers to share their responses.

Constructive Feedback

If students have difficulty identifying a synonym that fits the context, ask: *What does* transformed *mean in the sentence?* Which synonym best fits the context? (changed)

Thesaurus: Synonyms

Materials thesauruses

Explain Write the following on the board: *My homework was very <u>difficult</u>.* a. hard b. laborious c. strenuous

Guided Practice Read the sentence aloud three times, replacing difficult with synonyms a, b, and c. Ask: Which synonym best suits the context? (a: hard)

Practice Using a thesaurus, have students identify and two more synonyms for *difficult.* Assign them to write two sentences whose context matches the synonyms that they identified. Visual

Synonym Webs

Materials construction paper, scissors, markers, tape, thesauruses

Explain Tell students they will work in groups to make webs showing families of synonyms.

Guided Practice/Practice Organize students in small groups. Give each group a sheet of construction paper that has a word for which there are many synonyms written in the center. (Strong word choices include *huge*, *bad*, *cold*, *pretty*, and *frightened*.) Have groups use a thesaurus to find synonyms for their assigned word; cut out construction paper triangles and write on the triangles the synonyms that they identified; and assemble their webs by taping the triangles to the wall or the board. Students can use the synonym displays for reference. Visual/ Kinesthetic

Study Skill

Objective: Understand the purposes of photos, captions, toolbars, and links

Photographs and Captions, Toolbars and Links

Intervention/Remediation

Materials high school, community, or city newspapers; pencil and paper; safety scissors; tape

Explain Remind students: *Photographs and captions can help you understand an article by giving more information about the subject. Photographs visually show what the text explains or describes. Captions provide information about photographs.*

Guided Practice/Practice Group students to share newspapers. Have groups locate a captioned photograph in a news or feature article. Ask: *What does the caption tell you about the photograph you are examining?* Have students skim the article, then ask: *How do the photo and caption add to the information presented in the article?* Finally, invite groups to identify another captioned photo and read the article in which it appears. Have them cut out the article, tape it to paper, and write answers to the two questions above.

Constructive Feedback

If students have difficulty linking the captioned photograph to the content of the article, remind them to ask what the photograph shows and locate information on the same topic in the text. Students should be able to use organizational features of text to locate relevant information.

Intervention/Remediation

Materials Student Book "The Tales Are Getting Taller" pp. 72–75, computers with Internet access

Explain Have students turn to "The Tales Are Getting Taller" on page 72 of their books. Remind them: *A toolbar is a strip of icons, or symbols, on a computer that allows you to visit different features on a Web page.* Have students point to the toolbar and each of the icons in their books. Say: *A link is an electronic connection on a Web page. When you click on a link, it takes you to other documents or information on the same topic or a related topic.* Read aloud the links on page 72 as other students follow along.

Guided Practice/Practice Demonstrate how to use a toolbar and links on a computer. First connect to the home page of a student–friendly search engine. Ask: *Where is the toolbar? What icons are on the toolbar and where do they take you?* Then conduct a search on a topic that students select. Explore one or two of your "hits" by clicking on the links. Ask: *What kind of information do these links provide?* Assign students to groups. Have them take turns navigating Web pages that they find on a student–friendly search engine. Circulate around the room to observe each group. Have students demonstrate how to use a toolbar and links.

Constructive Feedback

If students have difficulty using toolbars or accessing links, show them how to move the cursor and help them click in the correct places.

 **Study Skill**

Objective: Use a Library/Media Center and organize information in a chart

Using the Library/Media Center and Charts

Intervention/Remediation

Materials access to library or online library

Explain Say: *The library organizes books using the Dewey Decimal System. This system gives each book a number, referring to where in the library the book is kept. If you use the card catalogue to find a book, you can copy down the number and then look for the book on the right shelf. Sometimes the card catalogue is on a computer.* Ask students to share their experiences at the library.

Guided Practice/Practice If possible, take a class trip to the library. Demonstrate for students how to look up a book in the card catalogue or do a search in the online catalogue. Then, have students write down the number and show them how to find the book. Point out the various sections of the library and allow students to guess where the book you have chosen will be kept based on its content. Assign students a topic, such as a historical figure. Have students locate a book in the library about the assigned topic. Ask: *Should we search by author, title, or subject? What words should we use to search?*

Constructive Feedback

If students have difficulty using the library, suggest that they walk through the library and look at the different sections. Select a book and explain how it is labeled. Show them how the books are arranged by number in ascending order.

Intervention/Remediation

Materials chart paper, markers

Explain Remind students: *A chart gives a visual summary of information. Sometimes charts include pictures. Sometimes they show different categories, such as insects, birds, and mammals.* Draw on the board a blank chart with two rows and five columns. Explain that a chart is organized in columns that run vertically and rows that run horizontally. Ask: *How many rows does the chart have? How many columns?*

Guided Practice/Practice Tell students that they will fill in the chart. Give them this information: *A penny has a picture of President Lincoln. A nickel has a picture of President Jefferson. A dime has a picture of President Roosevelt. A quarter has a picture of President Washington.* In the first row of the first column, write "Coin;" in the first row of the second column, write "President." Explain that these are labels for the categories in the chart. Have students copy and complete the chart, adding a title.

Constructive Feedback

If students have difficulty placing information on a chart, lead them through the given information. Reread each sentence and ask: *What kind of coin is named? Which President's picture is on this coin?* Demonstrate on the board how to record the information on the chart.

The Snake Scientist
by Sy Montgomery

Before Reading

BUILD BACKGROUND
Explain that the snakes in this book are red-sided garter snakes. Brainstorm a list of different kinds of snakes with students. Ask students:

- Are all snakes dangerous?
- How do snakes move about? How do they find food?
- What kind of dangers do snakes face in their habitats?

PREVIEW AND SET PURPOSES
Invite students to look at the cover photograph and read the title. Have students preview some of the photographs inside the book. They may state that this book is nonfiction, so ask them to explain how they have reached that conclusion. Then have students set a purpose for reading, such as to find out why people in the book appear to be handling snakes.

During Reading

APPLY COMPREHENSION SKILLS AND STRATEGIES
Following are suggestions for dividing the reading into manageable sections. For each section, think alouds and discussion questions are provided. Use these to review comprehension strategies and skills taught in this unit.

Pages 3–17

STRATEGY
ANALYZE TEXT STRUCTURE

Think Aloud Text structure is the way an author organizes a nonfiction text in order to meet his or her purpose in presenting information. Identifying a nonfiction text structure helps a reader figure out the author's purpose and understand the text.

Compare and Contrast How are a snake's senses the same as or different from those of other animals? (Possible responses: Snakes have no ears. They sense vibrations through the bones in their jaw. Other animals have ears that sense vibrations. Snakes taste odors instead of smelling them. Other animals have an acute sense of smell that works together with their sense of taste.)

Objectives

- Analyze text structure
- Compare and contrast
- Generate questions
- Identify cause and effect
- Summarize

Genre | Expository Nonfiction

Approaching Level

Summary

Dr. Robert Mason is the "Snake Scientist." This book explains the experiments he conducts and observations he makes as he studies thousands of harmless garter snakes emerging from hibernation every spring.

 **for your information**

As humans develop areas of wilderness and disturb animal habitats, scientists attempt to find ways to help animals in their migrations. For example, thousands of snakes are run over by cars as they try to cross Highway 17 in Canada on their way to marshes. Scientists have tried to redirect the snakes across the highway using fences and tunnels, but this has not been a complete success. The snakes prefer the road because of the warm asphalt. Researchers are further experimenting with ways to entice the snakes through the tunnels, with the hope of luring them to use an underground route instead of the pavement.

Cross-Curricular Connection

Research Biologists

Tell students they are research biologists who will spend the next year studying a life form of their choice. What will they choose? Where will they go to study it? What sort of lab will they need to set up in the field? Have students answer these questions in the form of an action plan as they prepare for their year of field study.

Cross-Curricular Connection

Snake Lengths

Have students work in small groups to make a poster that shows the comparative lengths of several snake species. Ask groups to select several species and research their average lengths. Then, on poster paper, have them draw an illustration that shows the actual length of each snake. Suggest that students quantify lengths by labeling each snake with both metric and standard measurements.

Pages 18–37

STRATEGY
GENERATE QUESTIONS

Teacher Think Aloud As I read I find I have many questions about how the researchers handle the snakes. Asking questions helps me find information and check my understanding of a topic. Why do they keep dozens of snakes in pillowcases? Wouldn't it hurt snakes to keep them in a refrigerator? I will look for answers as I continue to read.

Cause and Effect What effect does keeping a specimen in a refrigerator have on a snake? Why does this reaction occur? (By briefly placing a snake in the refrigerator, it becomes sluggish and easier to handle. This is because snakes are cold-blooded.)

Chapters 38–44

STRATEGY
GENERATE QUESTIONS

Teacher Think Aloud I have questions as I read this section. Asking questions helps me keep track of whether I understand what the author is telling me. Why are so many people afraid of snakes? Why do those people who are not afraid of them do so little to protect them? I will look for answers to these questions as I continue to read this part of the book.

Summarize How would you summarize the chapter titled "Who Needs Snakes?" (Possible responses: Snakes may one day help people. They may help scientists find cures for some human diseases. What we learn from wild animals can help us keep ourselves and our planet healthy.)

After Reading

LITERATURE CIRCLES

Use page 174 in the Teacher's Resource Book to review Listening and Speaking guidelines for a discussion. Have students discuss the book in small groups, using questions such as these.

- What part of this book did you find the most interesting?
- How do snakes find their prey, or locate other snakes?
- What is the most important part of Dr. Mason's research?
- Why do you think it is important for scientists to study snakes?

Write About It

Have students write a letter indicating whether they will accept or decline a job offer with Dr. Mason to work with snakes for the summer. Students should give reasons for their decisions. If necessary, review the format for a business letter before students begin writing. Tell students to double-check to make sure that each sentence begins with a capital letter and ends with the proper punctuation.

Ultimate Field Trip 5: Blasting Off to Space Academy

by Susan E. Goodman

Before Reading

BUILD BACKGROUND

Explain that NASA stands for the National Aeronautics and Space Administration, and this government agency is in charge of the United States' space programs. Use a word web as you brainstorm what students know about space exploration. Ask students:

- What do you know about the U.S. space program?

- What kinds of things do astronauts do? What qualifications do they need?

- What other jobs are related to space exploration?

- Why might people want to explore space?

PREVIEW AND SET PURPOSES

Have students read the title and examine the cover photograph. Then preview some of the book's photographs. Ask students what they think they will learn from reading the book and viewing the photographs. Then have students set a purpose for reading, such as to find out what kind of experiences children might enjoy at a space camp.

During Reading

APPLY COMPREHENSION SKILLS AND STRATEGIES

Following are suggestions for dividing the reading into manageable sections. For each section, think alouds and discussion questions are provided. Use these to review comprehension strategies and skills taught in this unit.

Chapters 1–2

STRATEGY
ANALYZE TEXT STRUCTURE

Think Aloud Text structure is the way an author organizes a nonfiction text in order to meet his or her purpose in presenting information. Identifying a nonfiction text structure helps a reader figure out the author's purpose and understand the text.

Compare and Contrast In what way is doing work in space different from doing work on Earth? (On Earth, gravity pulls us back down, but in space, we would feel nearly weightless. One could tumble and float away in space.)

Objectives

- Analyze text structure
- Compare and contrast
- Generate questions
- Summarize

Genre | Expository Nonfiction

On Level

Summary

This nonfiction text shares the experiences of a group of students at a special summer camp as they go through certain phases of astronaut training and a simulated shuttle launch.

 for your information

The glossary at the back of a nonfiction text helps readers clarify confusing or unfamiliar vocabulary. The space camp relies on many acronyms, such as EVA and OMS, when referring to equipment. Read through the glossary to help familiarize readers with acronyms they will encounter within the text.

Cross–Curricular Connection

Planet Posters

Have students review the comparative facts illustration on page 15. Ask students to create a similar poster for one of the other planets in our solar system. Students should research facts to include on the poster and use art materials to create realistic images of Earth and the planet of their choice. Display the posters.

Cross–Curricular Connection

Moon Colony

Ask small groups to picture a colony on the moon. Have each group list what the colony would need in order to stay happy and healthy. Tell students to consider social, psychological, economic, and political factors that would add to the well-being of the colonists. Have groups share and compare their lists. Then have students do research on colonizing the moon or other planets, using several sources. Have students identify and use text structures—sequence, question/answer, comparison/contrast, cause/effect—as well as headings, graphics, and charts to help them gather information. Have them compare the information they found and then draw conclusions about it.

Chapters 3–4

STRATEGY
GENERATE QUESTIONS

Teacher Think Aloud Asking questions is one way I can check my understanding of what I am reading. I wonder how long it takes an astronaut to get used to doing things without gravity. Is it comfortable sleeping while strapped to a wall? Do astronauts like eating and drinking foods that come in pouches? As I read, I will look for answers to these questions.

Summarize How would you summarize the students' experiences building rockets? (Students follow instructions to build rockets. These rockets demonstrate the principles at work when a space shuttle launches into space, but on a much simpler, safer level. Some students don't follow the instructions precisely enough and their rockets malfunction. One of the rockets functions properly and has a good launch and landing.)

Chapters 5–6

STRATEGY
GENERATE QUESTIONS

Teacher Think Aloud I continue to ask questions as I read to make sure I understand all the information the author presents. For example, what do the people at the controls do if there is a malfunction? I want to keep reading to see if my questions are answered.

Summarize How would you summarize Chapter 6? (Possible response: The kids graduate at the end of space academy. They reminisce about the experiences and shared what they have learned with each other. They are all glad they went to the Space Academy, and they learned that there are many more roles in a space mission than they previously thought.)

After Reading

LITERATURE CIRCLES

Use page 174 in the Teacher's Resource Book to review Listening and Speaking guidelines for a discussion. Use these questions to discuss the book in small groups.

- What part of the book did you find most interesting?
- Why do you think the Space Academy exists?
- Do you think you would like living in space? Explain.
- Which job connected with a shuttle launch most appeals to you?

Write About It

Have students write a personal narrative about a field trip that they found particularly memorable. Have them include details about where they went, what they experienced, and how the trip affected them. Remind students to organize their narratives in chronological order.

Antarctic Journal: Four Months at the Bottom of the World

by Jennifer Owings Dewey

Before Reading

BUILD BACKGROUND

Explain that the South Pole is located on the continent of Antarctica. Invite students to brainstorm a list of facts they know about this continent. Ask students:

- What animals and plant life are found in Antarctica?

- How do the weather, geography, and wildlife in Antarctica compare with conditions where you live?

- For what reasons do people travel to Antarctica?

PREVIEW AND SET PURPOSES

Have students look at the cover, read the title, and scan the illustrations. Ask students to predict what they think they will read about in this text. Point out that an artist who stayed in Antarctica for four months wrote this narrative. Then have students set a purpose for reading, such as finding out what the author experienced during her adventure.

During Reading

APPLY COMPREHENSION SKILLS AND STRATEGIES

Following are suggestions for dividing the reading into manageable sections. For each section, think alouds and discussion questions are provided. Use these to review comprehension strategies and skills taught in this unit.

Pages 6–25

STRATEGY
ANALYZE TEXT STRUCTURE

Think Aloud Text structure is the way an author organizes a nonfiction text in order to meet his or her purpose in presenting information. Identifying a nonfiction text structure helps a reader figure out the author's purpose and understand the text.

Compare and Contrast Reread the list of facts about Antarctica in the journal entry on pages 16 and 17. How is Antarctica similar to and different from the continent on which you live? (It is similar because it is a continent and it has fresh water. It is different in that it has no land-based predators and has no native human population.)

Objectives

- Analyze text structure
- Compare and contrast
- Generate questions
- Summarize

Genre Expository Nonfiction

Beyond Level

Summary

The author spent four months in Antarctica sketching the landscape and animal life that she encountered there. Through sketches, photographs, journal entries, and personal letters, she gives readers a snapshot of the last great wilderness on Earth.

FYI for your information

Jennifer Owens Dewey was able to take this trip because of a grant she received from the National Science Foundation. The book is written in journal form, with dates and labeled sketches. The author asked her family and friends to keep the letters she sent home so they could be included in the book as primary sources that would help her tell her narrative.

Classroom Library

Cross-Curricular Connection

Penguin Chart

Have students conduct further research on the two penguin species mentioned in the book, the Adélie and the Gentoo. Ask them to make a chart by drawing illustrations of each penguin and writing facts below the two drawings to compare appearance, behavior, mating and offspring, and survival techniques. Display completed charts on a bulletin board.

Cross-Curricular Connection

Temperature Line Graph

Students can use the Internet or print sources to find the average monthly temperatures for their own community and for Palmer Station. Have students plot the data from both places on a line graph, showing the change in temperature month by month over a year's time. Suggest they use different colors to differentiate each location's range of temperature.

Chapters 26–41

STRATEGY
GENERATE QUESTIONS

Teacher Think Aloud Asking myself questions helps me think about what I have read. Some questions may be answered as I continue reading. Sometimes I need to reread to be sure I did not overlook an answer.

Summarize What happened to the author on December 24? (She went outside at 3 a.m. A crevasse opened up, and she fell in, but only up to her shoulders. She struggled for an hour to get on firm ice. Then she crawled down the glacier, testing each spot before she moved forward.)

Pages 42–63

STRATEGY
ANALYZE TEXT STRUCTURE

Think Aloud Text structure is the way an author organizes a nonfiction text in order to meet his or her purpose in presenting information. Identifying a nonfiction text structure helps a reader figure out the author's purpose and understand the text.

Compare and Contrast What was unusual about the red tide that the author witnessed? How was it similar to other red tides? (This one was unusual because red tides are a rare occurrence in Antarctic waters and it was caused by organisms that were not toxic. Like other red tides, this one was caused by small organisms that give the water a bright orange-red tint and it lasted several days until currents carried the organisms away.)

After Reading

LITERATURE CIRCLES

Use page 174 in the Teacher's Resource Book to review Listening and Speaking guidelines for a discussion. Use these questions to discuss the book in small groups.

- Which was your favorite journal entry? Why?
- Would you like to journey to Antarctica? Explain.
- Why do people keep journals? Why would it be a good idea to keep a journal when you are traveling?

Write About It

Ask students to think about a fictional trip they have taken to Antarctica. Invite them to use the sights, sounds, and experiences from *Antarctic Journal* as they write an informal, friendly letter about their experiences to a friend or family member. Remind them to state their purpose at the beginning. They can "borrow" memorable events from the book or come up with their own original experiences.

Additional Readings:

	WEEK 1	WEEK 2
By the Authors and Illustrators	**Frasier, Debra.** *On the Day You Were Born.* **Harcourt, 1991.** Earth celebrates the birth of a newborn baby. `APPROACHING`	**Schanzer, Rosalyn.** *Gold Fever! Tales from the California Gold Rush.* **National Geographic Society, 1999.** Excerpts from letters, journals, and newspaper articles are used to relate the story of the California Gold rush of 1848. `ON LEVEL`

	WEEK 1	WEEK 2
Related to the Theme	**Child, Lauren.** *Utterly Me, Clarice Bean.* **Candlewick, 2003.** Someone steals the winner's trophy for the school book project, but Clarice plays detective and saves the day. `APPROACHING`	**Hopkinson, Deborah.** *Apples to Oregon* **Atheneum, 2004.** An original tall tale about a pioneer father transporting his fruit trees and his family to Oregon in the mid-nineteenth century. `APPROACHING`
	Seuling, Barbara. *Oh No, It's Robert.* **Front Street, 1999.** Robert is in the remedial reading group, but enters the classroom achievement contest to show everyone he can succeed. `APPROACHING`	**Wiley, Margaret.** *Clever Beatrice and the Best Little Pony.* **Atheneum, 2004.** Clever Beatrice seeks out Mr. LePain, the bread baker, to help her protect her pony from the little bearded man who rides him every night. `APPROACHING`
	O'Connor, Barbara. *Fame and Glory in Freedom, Georgia.* **Farrar, 2003.** Burdette Weaver persuades the new boy at school to be her partner for a spelling bee. `ON LEVEL`	**Shepard, Aaron.** *Master Man: A Tall Tale of Nigeria.* **HarperCollins, 2001.** A boastful man learns a lesson that is harder than his muscles when he encounters a very powerful Nigerian superhero. `ON LEVEL`
	McMullan, Kate. *Wheel of Misfortune.* **Grosset & Dunlap, 2003.** Erica, Angus, and Wiglaf are representing their school in the "Rain Power" tournament, but worry that they can't compete with the Knights Noble Conservatory team. `ON LEVEL`	**Wood, Audrey.** *The Bunyans.* **Blue Sky Press, 1996.** Paul Bunyan and his family do some things that result in the formation of Niagara Falls, Bryce Canyon, and other well-known national monuments. `ON LEVEL`
	Konigsburg, E. L. *The View From Saturday.* **Thorndike, 1996.** Four students become friends and are chosen to represent their class in the Academic Bowl competition. `BEYOND`	**Steig, Jeanne.** *Tales from Gizzard's Grill.* **Joanna Cotler Books, 2004.** Here is a collection of three tall tales from the Old West town of Fiasco where the sheriff, who is a woman, keeps the peace. `BEYOND`
	McDonald, Megan. *Judy Moody Saves the World.* **Candlewick, 2002.** Judy Moody manages to inspire her class to undertake an award-winning project that focuses on saving the environment. `BEYOND`	**Fleischman, Sid.** *McBroom the Rainmaker.* **Price, Stern, Sloan, 1999.** When a drought across the prairie causes cows to give powdered milk and mosquitoes to grow as large as cowsheds, McBroom comes up with an unusual idea for making rain. `BEYOND`

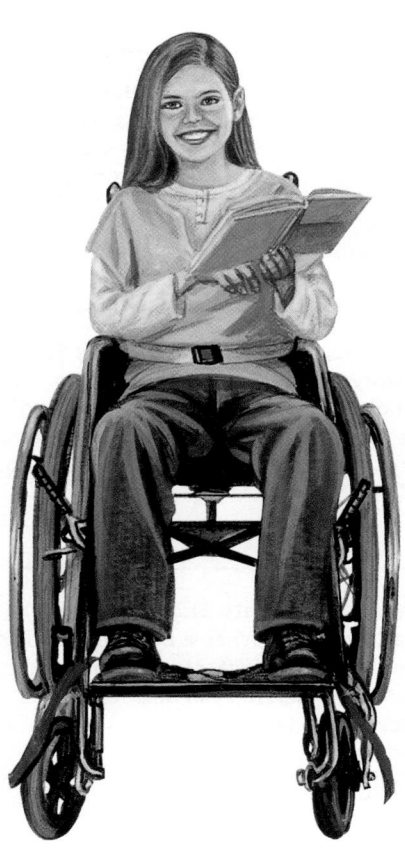

WEEK 3	WEEK 4	WEEK 5
Editors of TIME for Kids. *TIME for Kids: Bats!* **HarperTrophy, 2005.** Bats rise at night just as people are going to sleep. There are more than a thousand kinds of bats. Some are tiny. Others have a wingspan as wide as a car! Find out about these fascinating fliers. **APPROACHING**	**Goodman, Susan E.** *On This Spot: An Expedition Back Through Time.* **Greenwillow, 2004.** The drama of change is present as the author takes a look at New York City 175, 350, and 400 years ago, and then takes us back as far as the Ice Age. **APPROACHING**	**Schanzer, Rosalyn.** *Escaping to America.* **HarperCollins, 2000.** The author tells the story of her family and how they left Poland to make a better life for themselves in the United States in the early twentieth century. **APPROACHING**
Pfeffer, Wendy. *A Log's Life.* **Simon & Schuster.** Here is an introduction to the life cycle of a tree, with superb illustrations and an informative text about the life, death, and decay of an oak tree. **APPROACHING**	**Haddon, Mark.** *The Sea of Tranquility.* **Harcourt, 1996.** A man remembers his boyhood fascination with the moon and the night Neil Armstrong bounced through the dust in the Sea of Tranquility. **APPROACHING**	**Jackson, Donna.** *Hero Dogs: Courageous Canines in Action.* **Little, Brown, 2003.** A variety of stories of dogs who have helped humans in many ways, including those involved in the search and rescue at the World Trade Center in 2001. **APPROACHING**
Sanders, Scott R. *Meeting Trees.* **National Geographic. 1997.** A boy and his father walk in the woods and share what they know about the bark, leaves, and fruit of the different trees they see. **APPROACHING**	**Siy, Alexandra.** *Footprints on the Moon.* **Charlesbridge, 2001.** This is an outstanding look at our journeys to the moon during the Apollo program, with full-color photos. **APPROACHING**	**Hall, Lynn.** *Barry, The Bravest Saint Bernard.* **Random House, 1992.** This is the story of a young monk and his dog, Barry, who saved more than 40 lives during an avalanche in the Swiss Alps. **APPROACHING**
Burnie, David. *Tree.* **Dorling Kindersley, 2000.** This explores the anatomy and life cycle of trees and examines the kinds of bark, seeds, and leaves on different types of trees. **ON LEVEL**	**Sipiera, Diane M.** *Project Mercury.* **Children's Press, 1997.** Describes early space exploration and the six missions of Project Mercury that constituted the first step toward the moon. **ON LEVEL**	**George, Charles.** *Search and Rescue Dogs.* **Capstone, 1998.** Describes the history, selection, training, and accomplishments of different search and rescue operations. **ON LEVEL**
Cherry, Lynne. *The Great Kapok Tree.* **Harcourt, 1990.** The importance of rain-forest conservation is focused on in this tale of a kapok tree, the animals that live in it, and the man who wants to cut it down. **ON LEVEL**	**Tocci, Salvatore.** *NASA.* **Franklin Watts, 2003.** Describes how NASA functions and discusses its various programs and achievements. **ON LEVEL**	**Patent, Dorothy Hinshaw.** *Hugger to the Rescue.* **Cobblehill Books, 1994.** The training and work done by Newfoundland dogs is discussed in this interesting history of the breed. **ON LEVEL**
Souza, Dorothy. *Wacky Trees.* **Franklin Watts, 2004.** Strange trees, including the baobab, strangler fig, mangrove, and bristlecone pine, are represented in full-color photos with informative text to fascinate young researchers. **BEYOND**	**Stone, Tanya Lee.** *Ilan Ramon, Israel's First Astronaut.* **Millbrook, 2003.** A biography of the Israeli astronaut who died in the explosion of the space shuttle *Columbia* on February 1, 2003. **BEYOND**	**Hubbard, Coleen.** *Mountain Dog Rescue: A Story of a Bernese Mountain Dog.* **Scholastic, 2000.** This gives a history of the breed along with several stories about rescues performed by one particular dog. **BEYOND**
Lynch, L. M. *How I Wonder What You Are.* **Knopf, 2001.** As Laurel is about to enter sixth grade, her best friend doesn't want to associate with her anymore, and the best climbing tree in town has been mysteriously cut down. **BEYOND**	**Vogt, Gregory.** *John Glenn's Return to Space.* **Millbrook, 2000.** Here is the inspiring story of John Glenn's second flight into space in 1998, contrasted with his first in 1962. **BEYOND**	**Harlow, Joan Hiatt.** *Star in the Storm.* **Aladdin, 2000.** When a boat crashes along the shore, Maggie faces a difficult choice. She knows her dog can help rescue the people on board, but that puts his own life in danger. **BEYOND**

Selection Honors, Prizes, and Awards

Miss Alaineus

Unit 1, p. 20
by **Debra Frasier**

Author/Illustrator: Debra Frasier, selected for American Institute of Graphics Arts Annual Booklist (1992) for *The Animal That Drank Up Sound*; winner of the Minnesota Book Award (1998), ABA's Pick of the List (1998) for *Out of the Ocean*; Parents' Choice Gold Award for Illustration (1991), ABA List of Ten Best Books (1993) for *On the Day You Were Born*

Davy Crockett Saves the World

Unit 1, p. 52
by **Rosalyn Schanzer**

ALA Booklist Editor's Choice (2001), IRA/CBC Children's Choice Award (2002)

Author: Rosalyn Schanzer, winner of Parent's Guide Children's Media Award for Outstanding Achievement in Children's Books (2003), IRA/CBC Children's Choice and Teacher's Choice (2004) for *How Ben Franklin Stole the Lightning*; National Council of Social Studies Notable Children's Trade Book (1997) for *How We Crossed the West: The Adventures of Lewis & Clark*

Ultimate Field Trip 5: Blasting Off to Space Academy

Unit 1, p. 94
by **Susan E. Goodman**

Author: Susan E. Goodman, winner of the Chicago Public Library's Best of the Best List (1998) and Parent's Guild Children's Media Award (1998) for *Ultimate Field Trip 2: Digging Into Southwest Archaeology*; Parents' Choice Award for *Ultimate Field Trip 3: Wading Into Marine Biology*; CBC/NSTA Best Trade Science Book (2002) for *Seeds, Stems, and Stamens: The Ways Plants Fit into Their World* and *Claws, Coats, and Camouflage: The Ways Animals Fit into Their World*

Unit 1

Week		Vocabulary	Spelling			
1	**Miss Alaineus** *Leveled Books:* *What's the Buzz About* *the Geography Bee?* *Nadia Gomez Sees* *the Light* *Car Wash Chronicles*	slumped soggy capable categories strands gigantic credit luminous	batch rough stump jut tough **Review Words:** **Challenge Words:**	nick shrug **tenth** **stuff** laugh past cinch	guess sense damp cot fling dock blond	gush dove lead notch scan plum
2	**Davy Crockett Saves the World** *Leveled Books:* *Sluefoot Sue: An* *American Legend* *Johnny Appleseed: An* *American Legend* *Old Stormalong: An* *American Legend*	original wring advertisement commenced fireball impress elected sauntered	folks aim prey yolk greed **Review Words:** **Challenge Words:**	greet grind growth coach tenth decay	**oak** **paid** paste plead **shave** damp lifetime	theme bride tow spice type stuff
3	**Forests of the World** *Leveled Books:* *Partners: Endangered* *Animals and Their* *Habitats* *The Survival of Muir* *Woods* *Wildfire!*	quest settings reduce buffet major	amuse bamboo brood crooks tuna **Review Words:** **Challenge Words:**	doom few view hoof hooks coach strewn	hue bruise booth lose duty theme accuse	handbook prove mute plume union bride
4	**Ultimate Field Trip 5: Blasting Off to Space Academy** *Leveled Books:* *On the Moon* *Mission to Mars* *Space Station*	mission disasters environment zone gravity maze adjusted function	**force** scorn sword swore source **Review Words:** **Challenge Words:**	**aboard** course coarse chart barge brood uproar	harsh marsh starch heart scarce prove gorge	squares swear flare fare thorn hoof
5	**Pipiolo and the Roof Dogs** *Leveled Books:* *It's Fun When Sam* *Listens* *The Wag Brigade* *Rusty to the Rescue!*	variety transformed celebration moistened fragrance cooperation canceled theory	squirm dreary nerve squirt verse **Review Words:** **Challenge Words:**	surf lurk swerve stern spurts aboard smear	lurch blurt thirst spur engineer barge rehearse	jeer sneer **clear** **year** yearns scarce

Key Spelling words in bold appear in the selection.

LOG ON Go to **www.macmillanmh.com** for **Leveled Spelling Lists.**

Unit 2

Week		Vocabulary	Spelling			
1	**Shiloh** *Leveled Books:* *The Habits of Rabbits* *The Elephant in the Room* *Black Bear's Backyard*	injury mournful sympathy delivering slurp shrieks decency bulletin board	**afternoon** background cornfield **cornmeal** earthworm	**flagpole** **footstep** mountaintop overcome pillowcase	rooftop cardboard ice-skating ninety-one vice president	all right field trip armchair cheerleader eggshell
			Review Words: blurt	jeer	thirst	
			Challenge Words: first-class	briefcase		
2	**Rattlers!** *Leveled Books:* *Giants of the Snake World* *Sea Snakes* *Alien: The Brown Tree Snake Story*	species survive alert vibrates surroundings prey predators lunging	abilities countries batches difficulties eddies	**fangs** identities lashes liberties notches	possibilities **rattlers** **reptiles** rodeos **surroundings**	taxes losses potatoes zeroes beliefs
			Review Words: flagpole	vice president	ninety-one	
			Challenge Words: mangoes	sinews		
3	**Maya Lin, Architect of Memory** *Leveled Books:* *The Oregon Trail: Westward Ho!* *Ellis Island: The Golden Doors* *The Erie Canal: Low Bridge, Everybody Down!*	dedicated equality artifacts exhibits site	amusing applied complicated deserved dripping	easing envied fascinated forbidding gnarled	injured jogging qualified raking regretted	relied renewing skimmed threatening referred
			Review Words: difficulties	notches	rodeos	
			Challenge Words: adoring	diaries		
4	**The Night of San Juan** *Leveled Books:* *Nothing Is Impossible* *Where We Belong* *All or Nothing*	forbidden reluctant gossiped irresistible elegant blared mischievous hesitation	bawl **brought** **cautious** **counter** coil	foul **foundation** **fountain** joint **mouthful**	dawdle sprawls sprouts **turmoil** stout	hoist clause turquoise douse scrawny
			Review Words: relied	forbidding	easing	
			Challenge Words: buoyant	renown		
5	**Black Cowboy Wild Horses** *Leveled Books:* *Nat Love: A Man of the Old and New West* *Alice Greenough: A New Woman of the Old West* *William F. Cody: Showman of the Old West*	vastness enthusiasm horizon ravine presence swerved flickered suspended	absent valley pigment blizzard empire	mutter goggles fifteen **gallop** dentist	jogger kennel summon champion **mustang**	flatter fragment hollow **vulture** culture
			Review Words: sprawls	sprouts	mouthful	
			Challenge Words: clammy	hammock		

Word List

Week		Vocabulary	Spelling			
1	**Sleds on Boston Common** *Leveled Books:* *The Battle of Saratoga* *The Shot Heard Around the World* *The Battle of Bunker Hill*	navigation instruct swagger patriots tyrant stark governor spunk	**tyrant** profile smoky minus **local**	equal linen legal loser decent	humor closet comet punish vacant	recent student shiver cavern panic
			Review Words: valley		fifteen	culture
			Challenge Words: fatigue		fugitive	
2	**When Esther Morris Headed West** *Leveled Books:* *Let's Vote* *How Women Got the Vote* *The Story of African American Voting Rights*	representative colonel attorney qualify postpone submit legislature satisfactory	**ideas** poet riot video piano	diary radio fluid genuine rodeo	meteor cruel casual meander diameter	fuel patriot ruin diet trial
			Review Words: recent		closet	minus
			Challenge Words: situation		variety	
3	**Beyond the Horizon** *Leveled Books:* *Garbage: Where Does It Go?* *Animals in the Neighborhood* *Farming for the Future: How Do We Feed Ourselves?*	humanity inevitable unheeded enlightened prevailing	orphan complain hilltop concrete instant	reckless handsome fairground grassland landlord	pilgrim district address improve although	partner footprint dolphin cockpit fiddler
			Review Words: ideas		piano	fuel
			Challenge Words: mischief		laughter	
4	**My Great-Grandmother's Gourd** *Leveled Books:* *Atacama Desert: The Driest Place on Earth* *Where Two Deserts Meet* *The Gobi Desert*	brimming gushed landscape scorching parched scrawny gnarled progress	**python** **scorching** **season** dozen motion	phony active canvas expert embrace	coastal reserve govern flurry copper	appoint **beside** cocoon restore observe
			Review Words: partner		footprint	dolphin
			Challenge Words: superb		bleachers	
5	**Zathura** *Leveled Books:* *Return to Planet Weird* *Me, Robot?* *The Terrarium*	robot defective meteor rotated staggered reversed dangling tokens	director **shatter** soldier governor error	commander peddler professor pillar splendor	scissors vapor scholar sugar equator	labor founder crater **saucer** gentler
			Review Words: appoint		season	canvas
			Challenge Words: **refrigerator**		remainder	

Key Spelling words in bold appear in the selection.

Go to **www.macmillanmh.com** for **Leveled Spelling Lists.**

Unit 4

Week		Vocabulary	Spelling			
1	**Goin' Someplace Special** *Leveled Books:* *The Way It Should Be* *Gramma's Garden* *Sandy's Song*	scald permission autograph fare blurted clenched chiseled spectacular	angle heron lengthen marvel woolen	listen bushel signal nozzle practical	barrel captain frighten slogan mountain	**pretzel** fable global sandal **chuckle**
			Review Words: scissors		pillar	governor
			Challenge Words: dungeon		salmon	
2	**Carlos and the Skunk** *Leveled Books:* *Survival Instincts: Mammals* *Survival Instincts: Reptiles* *Survival Instincts: Insects*	glimpse secluded behavior arroyo arousing stunned nestled unpleasant	allow **arousing** boundary bestow grownup	coward **doubting** rowdy **encounter** power	shower trousers grouchy applause lawyer	August laundry caution flawless faucet
			Review Words: angle		mountain	sandal
			Challenge Words: southern		roughness	
3	**Getting Out the Vote** *Leveled Books:* *Coming in Third* *Political Debates: Lincoln versus Douglas* *The Constitutional Convention*	compelled presidential disrespectful unenthusias- tically succeed preoccupied	excuse contest content refuse protest	conduct subject extract permits insert	desert rebel combat conflict research	compact contract entrance present minute
			Review Words: doubting		allow	caution
			Challenge Words: effect		affect	
4	**Hurricanes** *Leveled Books:* *Blizzard* *Tornado* *Earthquake*	damages property available contact atmosphere destruction hurricanes surge	future creature searcher feature fracture	gesture legislature pressure measure mixture	**moisture** nature pasture pleasure azure	stretcher treasure rancher butcher lecture
			Review Words: contest		desert	entrance
			Challenge Words: miniature		disclosure	
5	**The Catch of the Day** *Leveled Books:* *Coyote and the Rock* *Brer Rabbit and the Gizzard Eater* *How Thor Got His Hammer*	riverbank wares treasurer merchandise educate burdens appreciation unfortunate	ambulance appearance assistance attendance brilliance	dependence substance disturbance **balance** hesitance	ignorance importance performance persistence radiance	resistance reluctance absence residence distance
			Review Words: creature		measure	rancher
			Challenge Words: vigilance		inference	

Unit 5

Week		Vocabulary	Spelling			
1	**Spirit of Endurance** *Leveled Books:* *Animals of the Poles* *The Lure of the Poles* *Science in the Snow*	frigid treacherous triumph uninhabited expedition labor dismantled abandon	agent baggage budge challenge damage	plunge **jigsaw** jolt journal judgment	jumble knowledge lodge luggage margin	legend ranger **ridge** surge dodge
			Review Words: assistance	importance	absence	
			Challenge Words: oxygen	surgeon		
2	**Weslandia** *Leveled Books:* *Food Fight* *Fruit From Space* *Land of the Peppertoes*	shortage bedlam outcast reflected strategy civilization traditional complex	suite sweet pier peer currant	current **manner** manor pole poll	stationary stationery **waist** waste peal	peel presents presence council counsel
			Review Words: journal	budge	ranger	
			Challenge Words: kernel	colonel		
3	**A Historic Journey** *Leveled Books:* *The Adamsons: Living* *with Animals* *Animal Observers* *Rachel Carson: Nature's* *Champion*	instill combined naturalist vacant diverse	disapprove discomfort dishonest dismount disobey	mistaken mistrust misunderstand incorrect preview	preheats inexpensive injustice indefinite disable	discolor disconnect misjudge prejudge prewash
			Review Words: presence	stationary	current	
			Challenge Words: prehistoric	misbehave		
4	**The Unbreakable Code** *Leveled Books:* *Braille and Beyond:* *Inventions for* *the Blind* *Secret Languages* *Lost Languages*	corridor reservation enlisted invasion shield location sagged creased	**bottomless** ceaseless **darkness** effortless emptiness	fearless fierceness fondness foolishness forgiveness	fullness hopeless gladness meaningless harmless	motionless needless **stillness** sadness weakness
			Review Words: dishonest	mistaken	preheats	
			Challenge Words: weightlessness	thoughtlessness		
5	**The Gri Gri Tree** *Leveled Books:* *Dan's Whale* *Into the Depths of the* *Sea* *The Gold at Sunset Cove*	ventured emerged unreasonable attraction inquire discussions sprawled focused	concentrate concentration confuse confusion correct	correction decorate decoration elect **election**	estimate estimation exhaust exhaustion impress	impression locate location discuss **discussion**
			Review Words: hopeless	fearless	forgiveness	
			Challenge Words: conclude	conclusion		

Key Spelling words in bold appear in the selection.

 Go to **www.macmillanmh.com** for **Leveled Spelling Lists.**

Unit 6

Week		Vocabulary	Spelling			
1	**The Golden Mare, the Firebird, and the Magic Ring** *Leveled Books:* *Graham the Kind-Hearted* *Daisies in Winter* *The Three Sisters*	dismiss intentions despair bridle descended accompany delicacies consented	astronaut autograph automatic automobile **mythical** **Review Words:** **Challenge Words:**	telegraph telephone telescope television telegram correction videophone	homophone phonics disaster astronomer photograph discussion photogenic	photography myth mechanic mechanical telephoto decoration
2	**Skunk Scout** *Leveled Books:* *A Visit to Big Bend National Park* *A Visit to Grand Canyon National Park* *A Visit to Yellowstone National Park*	guaranteed supervise frustrated coordination ease scenery bundle fused	suspect distract export **inspect** spectator **Review Words:** **Challenge Words:**	spectacle subtraction tractor import transport telescope spectacular	transportation attraction inspector missile mission astronaut protractor	committee intermission portable respect dismiss photograph
3	**A Dream Comes True** *Leveled Books:* *Everybody Is a Star: The Special Olympics Story* *Sports for Everyone!* *Uplifted from the Dark: Helen Keller and Annie Sullivan*	elementary physical rigid interact wheelchair	cereal terrace gracious echo gigantic **Review Words:** **Challenge Words:**	ocean atlas clothes territory parasol suspect jovial	mortal fury furious January Olympics inspect venerable	salute cycle cyclone lunar fortune mission
4	**Up in the Air: The Story of Balloon Flight** *Leveled Books:* *The Sky's the Limit* *Airships: Sailors of the Skies* *Up, Up, and Away: Science in the Sky*	launched particles dense inflate anchored companion hydrogen scientific	uniform bisect tricycle triplet triple **Review Words:** **Challenge Words:**	unicorn unify unison universe unicycle cereal bilingual	biweekly binoculars triangle bicycle **trio** terrace trilogy	**century** centipede centimeter tripod university atlas
5	**Hidden Worlds** *Leveled Books:* *Searching for Cures* *Life on the Deep Sea Floor* *Searching for Tomorrow's Energy*	specimens erupted murky dormant scoured biology research observer	collapsible breakable affordable usable bearable **Review Words:** **Challenge Words:**	favorable capable enjoyable honorable convertible uniform manageable	invisible reasonable respectable sensible unbelievable bicycle tangible	possible suitable laughable likable comfortable triangle

Scope and Sequence

	K	1	2	3	4	5	6
READING: FOUNDATIONS FOR LITERACY							
Concepts of Print							
Recognize own name							
Understand directionality (tracking print from left to right; return sweep)							
Understand that print provides information							
Develop print awareness (concept of letter, word, sentence)							
Understand that spoken words consist of phonemes							
Understand that written words are represented in written language by a specific sequence of letters							
Distinguish between letters, words, sentences							
Identify and distinguish paragraphs							
Match oral and written words							
Distinguish uppercase and lowercase letters							
Understand correct book handling							
Recognizes parts of a book; recognize that parts of a book contain information							
READING: ALPHABETICS							
Phonemic Awareness							
Identify spoken sounds, words, and sentences							
Recognize and produce rhyming words; distinguish between rhyming and nonrhyming		✔					
Segment word into phonemes, sentence into words	✔	✔					
Identify, segment, and combine syllables		✔					
Blend and segment onsets and rimes	✔	✔					
Add, delete, and substitute phonemes	✔	✔					
Identify and isolate initial, medial, and final consonants	✔	✔					
Blend phonemes to make a spoken word	✔	✔					
Categorize phonemes							
Understand alliteration							
Count and track sounds in syllables, syllables in words							
Decoding Phonics Analysis							
Understand the Alphabetic Principle							
Sound/letter association	✔						
Blend sounds to make syllables and words; blend word families: including CVC, CVCe, CVVC words	✔	✔	✔				
Initial consonant blends		✔	✔	✔			
Final consonant blends		✔	✔	✔			
Initial and medial short vowels	✔	✔	✔	✔	✔	✔	
Long vowels		✔	✔	✔	✔	✔	
Variant vowels		✔	✔	✔	✔	✔	✔
r–Controlled vowels		✔	✔	✔	✔	✔	✔
Hard/soft consonants			✔	✔	✔	✔	
Initial digraphs		✔	✔	✔	✔	✔	✔
Medial and final digraphs		✔	✔	✔	✔	✔	✔
Diphthongs		✔	✔	✔	✔	✔	✔

KEY ✔ = Assessed Skill
Tinted panels show skills, strategies, and other teaching opportunities.

	K	1	2	3	4	5	6
Silent letters			✔	✔	✔	✔	✔
Schwa words			✔	✔	✔	✔	✔
Inflected endings			✔	✔	✔	✔	✔
Triple-consonant clusters			✔	✔	✔	✔	✔
Decoding Structural Analysis							
Common spelling patterns (word families)							
Common syllable patterns							
Inflectional endings: including plurals		✔	✔	✔	✔	✔	✔
Contractions		✔		✔	✔		
Compound words		✔	✔	✔	✔	✔	✔
Prefixes and suffixes		✔	✔	✔	✔	✔	✔
Root or base words		✔			✔	✔	✔
Comparatives, superlatives		✔	✔	✔	✔	✔	✔
Greek and Latin roots			✔	✔	✔	✔	✔

READING: FLUENCY

Fluency

	K	1	2	3	4	5	6
Read regularly on independent and instructional levels							
Read orally with fluency from familiar texts (choral, echo, partner, Readers Theater)							
Read silently and independently							
Use appropriate pace, expression, intonation, and phrasing		✔	✔	✔	✔	✔	✔
Read with automaticity (accurately and effortlessly)		✔	✔	✔	✔	✔	✔
Use punctuation cues in reading							
Adjust reading rate to purpose							
Repeated readings							
Timed readings							

Self-Selected Reading

	K	1	2	3	4	5	6
Use personal criteria to choose own reading: including favorite authors, genres, recommendations from others							
Read a variety of literature for assigned tasks as well as for enjoyment							

READING: VOCABULARY/WORD IDENTIFICATION

Word Meaning Skills and Strategies

	K	1	2	3	4	5	6
Identify academic language							
Identify persons, places, things, actions							
Classify and categorize words	✔	✔	✔				
Synonyms, antonyms, and opposites	✔	✔	✔	✔	✔	✔	✔
High-frequency words	✔	✔					
Use context clues: word, sentence, paragraph; definition, example, restatement		✔	✔	✔	✔	✔	✔
Use word identification strategies		✔	✔	✔	✔	✔	✔
Unfamiliar words		✔		✔	✔		
Multiple-meaning words	✔	✔	✔	✔	✔	✔	✔
Use dictionary to locate meanings, pronunciation, and derivatives		✔	✔	✔	✔	✔	✔
Compound words					✔	✔	✔
Words ending in -er and -est			✔	✔	✔		
Prefixes and suffixes			✔	✔	✔	✔	✔
Greek and Latin roots			✔	✔	✔	✔	✔

KEY	✔ = Assessed Skill
	Tinted panels show skills, strategies, and other teaching opportunities.

Word Meaning Skills and Strategies (continued)	K	1	2	3	4	5	6
Denotation and connotation			✔	✔	✔	✔	✔
Word families			✔	✔	✔	✔	✔
Inflected-ending words and plurals		✔	✔	✔	✔		
Use thesaurus					✔	✔	✔
Use reference sources for word meaning		✔	✔	✔	✔	✔	✔
Homographs				✔	✔	✔	✔
Homophones				✔	✔	✔	✔
Contractions				✔			
Figurative language				✔			
Idioms				✔	✔	✔	✔
Analogies					✔	✔	✔
Word origins					✔	✔	✔
READING: COMPREHENSION							
Prereading Strategies							
Build background							
Use prior knowledge							
Preview and predict							
Set and adjust purpose for reading							
Comprehension Strategies							
Analyze		✔	✔	✔	✔	✔	✔
Evaluate		✔	✔	✔	✔	✔	✔
Generate questions							
Inferences, making	✔	✔	✔	✔	✔	✔	✔
Monitor comprehension: including reread, adjust reading rate, paraphrase, self-correct, read ahead, seek help							
Summarize		✔	✔	✔	✔	✔	✔
Story structure, analyzing		✔	✔	✔	✔	✔	✔
Text structure, analyzing		✔	✔	✔	✔	✔	✔
Visualize							
Comprehension Skills							
Author's perspective					✔	✔	✔
Author's purpose		✔	✔	✔	✔	✔	✔
Cause and effect	✔	✔	✔	✔	✔	✔	✔
Character	✔	✔	✔	✔	✔	✔	✔
Compare and contrast	✔	✔	✔	✔	✔	✔	✔
Classify and categorize	✔	✔	✔				
Conclusions, drawing	✔	✔	✔	✔	✔	✔	✔
Description as text structure			✔	✔	✔	✔	✔
Fact and opinion				✔	✔	✔	✔
Fantasy and reality; fact and fiction	✔	✔	✔	✔			
Generalizations, making				✔	✔	✔	✔
Illustrations	✔	✔	✔				
Inferences, making	✔	✔	✔	✔	✔	✔	✔
Judgments, making			✔	✔	✔	✔	✔
Main idea and supporting details	✔	✔	✔	✔	✔	✔	✔
Persuasion/persuasive techniques					✔	✔	✔

KEY	✔ = Assessed Skill Tinted panels show skills, strategies, and other teaching opportunities.

	K	1	2	3	4	5	6
Plot	✔	✔	✔	✔	✔	✔	✔
Predictions, making/confirming	✔	✔	✔				
Problem and solution			✔	✔	✔	✔	✔
Sequence	✔	✔	✔	✔	✔	✔	✔
Setting	✔	✔	✔	✔	✔	✔	✔
Summarize, retell	✔	✔	✔	✔	✔	✔	✔
Theme				✔	✔	✔	✔

LITERATURE

Genre: Fiction

	K	1	2	3	4	5	6
Drama/play							
Fantasy							
Historical fiction							
Humorous fiction							
Mystery							
Picture book							
Realistic fiction							
Rhyming story							
Science fiction							
Short story							
Traditional stories: fairy tale, fable, folk tale, tall tale, myth							

Genre: Nonfiction

	K	1	2	3	4	5	6
Biography/autobiography							
Diary/journal							
Encyclopedia							
Expository text							
Functional text							
How-to							
Informational text							
Letter							
Nonfiction							
Narrative							
Newsletter							
Newspaper							
Science article							
Personal essay							
Persuasive essay							
Photo essay							

Genre: Poetry

	K	1	2	3	4	5	6
Forms (refrain, cinquain, free verse, haiku, limerick, lyric, narrative, simple)							
Literary elements							

Literary Devices and Elements

	K	1	2	3	4	5	6
Alliteration			✔	✔	✔	✔	✔
Consonance and assonance				✔	✔	✔	✔
Dialect						✔	
Figurative language (metaphors, similes, personification)		✔	✔	✔	✔	✔	✔
Foreshadowing; flashback					✔	✔	✔

KEY	✔ = Assessed Skill Tinted panels show skills, strategies, and other teaching opportunities.

Literary Devices and Elements (continued)	K	1	2	3	4	5	6
Imagery			✔	✔	✔	✔	✔
Meter					✔	✔	✔
Onomatopoeia			✔	✔	✔	✔	✔
Repetition		✔	✔	✔	✔	✔	✔
Rhyme/rhyme schemes		✔	✔	✔	✔	✔	✔
Rhythm			✔	✔	✔	✔	✔
Sensory words and details				✔	✔	✔	✔
Symbolism					✔	✔	✔
Author and Illustrator Craft							
Analyze author and illustrator craft							
Analyze role of author and illustrator							
Analyze how illustrations enhance and interpret text							
Literary Response							
Reflect and respond to text							
Connect and compare text characters, events, ideas to self							
Connect and compare text characters, events, ideas across texts							
Connect and compare text characters, events, ideas to world							
Connect literary texts to other curriculum areas							
Identify cultural elements of text							
Identify historical elements of text							
Read to understand and perform tasks and activities							
Interpret text through creative response							
Interpret text ideas through writing, discussion, media, research							

STUDY SKILLS, RESEARCH AND INFORMATIONAL LITERACY

Study Skiills	K	1	2	3	4	5	6
Directions: read, write, give, follow		✔	✔	✔			
Evaluate directions for sequence and completeness							
Use library/media center		✔	✔	✔	✔	✔	✔
Use parts of book to locate information		✔	✔	✔	✔	✔	✔
Interpret information from graphic aids		✔	✔	✔	✔	✔	✔
Use graphic organizers to organize information and comprehend text							
Use functional, everyday documents				✔	✔	✔	✔
Apply study strategies: skimming and scanning, note-taking, outlining, K-W-L							
Apply test prep and test-taking strategies							

Text Features	K	1	2	3	4	5	6
Recognize and identify text and organizational features of nonfiction texts		✔	✔	✔	✔	✔	✔
Recognize and identify text features of poetry, fiction, drama		✔	✔	✔	✔	✔	✔
Captions and labels, headings, subheadings, footnotes, endnotes, key words, bold print		✔	✔	✔	✔	✔	✔
Graphics: including photographs, illustrations, maps, charts, diagrams, graphs, time lines				✔	✔	✔	✔

Research and Informational Literacy	K	1	2	3	4	5	6
Generate and revise questions for research							
Narrow focus of research							
Find and locate information using print and electronic resources							
Record information systematically (note-taking, outlining)							
Develop a systematic research plan							

KEY	✔ = Assessed Skill
	Tinted panels show skills, strategies, and other teaching opportunities.

	K	1	2	3	4	5	6
Evaluate reliability, credibility, usefulness of sources and information							
Use primary sources to obtain information				✔	✔	✔	✔
Synthesize, evaluate, and draw conclusions from information							
Cite and list sources of information							
Technology							
Use computer, Internet, CD-ROM, and technology resources to access information			✔	✔	✔	✔	✔
Use text and organizational features of electronic resources: including search engines, key words, e-mail, hyperlinks, URLs, Web pages, databases, graphics				✔	✔	✔	✔

WRITING

	K	1	2	3	4	5	6
Modes and Forms							
Descriptive writing			✔	✔	✔	✔	✔
Explanatory writing		✔	✔	✔	✔	✔	✔
Expository writing		✔	✔	✔	✔	✔	✔
Narrative writing: personal and fictional			✔	✔	✔	✔	✔
Persuasive writing		✔	✔	✔	✔	✔	✔
Writing that compares			✔	✔	✔	✔	✔
Prompts							
Determine the audience and purpose		✔	✔	✔	✔	✔	✔
Determine the mode		✔	✔	✔	✔	✔	✔
Timed writing		✔	✔	✔	✔	✔	✔
Writer's Craft							
Topic sentence, details							
Write a good paragraph							
Beginning, middle, end							
Strong opening, strong conclusion							
Precise words							
Informal and formal language							
Figurative language							
Dialogue							
Tone, mood							
Fact and opinion							
Transitions							
Writing Traits							
Organization, ideas and content, word choice, conventions		✔	✔	✔	✔	✔	✔
Sentence fluency, Voice		✔	✔	✔	✔	✔	✔
Processes							
Prewriting, drafting, revising, editing, publishing							
Evaluating, rubrics, assessment							
Penmanship							
Write uppercase and lowercase letters using correct formation and spacing							
Write using left-to-right and top-to-bottom directionality							
Write using appropriate spacing between words, letters, sentences							
Write using appropriate margins and indentations							
Write legibly in manuscript or cursive							

KEY	✔ = Assessed Skill Tinted panels show skills, strategies, and other teaching opportunities.

Grammar, Mechanics, and Usage

	K	1	2	3	4	5	6
Sentence concepts: statements, questions, exclamations, commands		✔	✔	✔	✔	✔	✔
Complete and incomplete sentences; sentence fragments				✔	✔	✔	✔
Nouns: including common, proper, singular, plural, irregular plural, possessive		✔	✔	✔	✔	✔	✔
Verbs: including action, helping, linking, irregular		✔	✔	✔	✔	✔	✔
Verb tenses: including past, present, future, perfect, and progressive		✔	✔	✔	✔	✔	✔
Pronouns: including possessive, subject and object, pronoun-verb agreement		✔	✔	✔	✔	✔	✔
Adjectives: including articles		✔	✔	✔	✔	✔	✔
Adverbs: including telling how, when, where; comparative; superlative; irregular			✔	✔	✔	✔	✔
Subject, predicate				✔	✔	✔	✔
Subject-verb agreement				✔	✔	✔	✔
Contractions		✔	✔	✔	✔	✔	✔
Conjunctions				✔	✔	✔	✔
Prepositions and prepositional phrases					✔	✔	✔
Negatives, correcting double negatives					✔	✔	✔
Use correct capitalization in sentences, proper nouns, titles, abbreviations		✔	✔	✔	✔	✔	✔
Use correct punctuation (periods, questions marks, exclamation marks, commas, apostrophes, quotation marks, colons, hyphens, or semicolons)		✔	✔	✔	✔	✔	✔
Antecedents					✔	✔	✔
Homophones						✔	

Spelling

	K	1	2	3	4	5	6
Spell independently by using pre-phonetic knowledge							
Use spelling approximations and some conventional spelling							
Spell own name and write high-frequency words							
Words with short vowels		✔	✔	✔	✔	✔	✔
Words with long vowels		✔	✔	✔	✔	✔	✔
Words with digraphs, blends, consonant clusters, double consonants		✔	✔	✔	✔	✔	✔
Words with variant and ambiguous vowels		✔	✔	✔	✔	✔	✔
Words with diphthongs		✔	✔	✔	✔	✔	✔
Words with r-controlled vowels		✔	✔	✔	✔	✔	✔
Schwa words			✔	✔	✔	✔	✔
Words with silent letters			✔	✔	✔		✔
Words with hard and soft letters			✔	✔	✔	✔	
Inflectional endings: including plural, past tense, drop final e and double consonant when adding -ed and -ing)		✔	✔	✔	✔	✔	✔
Compound words			✔	✔	✔	✔	✔
Homonyms/homophones					✔	✔	✔
Prefixes and suffixes					✔	✔	✔
Root and base words				✔	✔	✔	✔
Syllables: patterns, rules, accented, stressed, closed, open					✔	✔	✔
Words with Greek and Latin roots					✔	✔	✔
Words from mythology						✔	✔
Words from around the world							✔
Words with spelling patterns, word families		✔	✔	✔	✔	✔	✔

KEY ✔ = Assessed Skill
Tinted panels show skills, strategies, and other teaching opportunities.

LISTENING, SPEAKING, VIEWING, REPRESENTING

	K	1	2	3	4	5	6
Listening							
Identify musical elements of language							
Determine the purpose for listening (for information, to solve problems, for enjoyment)		✔	✔	✔	✔	✔	✔
Understand and follow directions		✔	✔	✔	✔	✔	✔
Develop oral vocabulary and concepts							
Listen responsively, attentively, and critically							
Listen to distinguish fact from fiction; fact from opinion							
Listen responsively to oral presentation: stories, poems, skits, songs, personal accounts, speeches, classic and contemporary works							
Ask and answer relevant questions (for clarification; to follow up on ideas)							
Apply comprehension strategies and skills in listening activities							
Interpret speaker's verbal and nonverbal messages, purposes, and perspectives							
Speaking							
Use repetition, rhyme, and rhythm in oral texts: including songs, poems, and stories							
Participate in classroom activities and discussions							
Ask and answer questions							
Stay on topic when speaking							
Use language appropriate to situation, purpose, and audience							
Use nonverbal communications such as eye contact, gestures, and props							
Use verbal communication in effective ways							
Retell a story or spoken message by summarizing							
Clarify and support spoken ideas with evidence and examples							
Oral presentations: focus, organizational structure, audience, purpose; types: narrative, persuasive, informational, descriptive							
Give and follow directions							
Consider audience when speaking or preparing a presentation							
Viewing							
Various media genres: including posters, pictures, videos, slide shows, technology							
Summarize the main idea or message from visuals, graphics, and media							
Use graphics, illustrations to analyze and interpret information							
Identify structural features of popular media and use the features to obtain information: including newspapers, magazines, and online information							
Distinguish between fact and opinion in visuals and media							
Analyze media source; recognize effects of media in one's mood and emotion							
Make informed judgments about print and nonprint media							
Representing							
Select, organize, or produce visuals to complement or extend meaning							
Select, organize, and create media compositions for various purposes							
Show how language, medium, and presentation contribute to the message							
Use technology, media, multimedia to present information							
Use technology/media to compare ideas information and viewpoints							

KEY ✔ = Assessed Skill
Tinted panels show skills, strategies, and other teaching opportunities.

Aa

Abbreviations, 459J, 472

Academic language, 19A–19B, 47U, 47V, 51A–51B, 77U, 77V, 81A–81B, 89U, 89V, 93A, 111U, 111V, 115A, 139U, 139V, 147A, 169U, 169V, 173A, 191U, 191V, 195A, 203U, 203V, 207A, 227U, 227V, 231A, 255U, 255V, 263A, 289U, 289V, 293A, 313U, 313V, 317A, 325U, 325V, 329A, 355U, 355V, 359A, 387U, 387V, 395A, 419U, 419V, 423A, 447U, 447V, 451A, 459U, 459V, 463A, 481U, 481V, 485A, 509U, 509V, 517A, 541U, 541V, 545A, 565U, 565V, 569A, 577U, 577V, 581A, 603U, 603V, 607A, 633U, 633V, 641A, 667U, 667V, 671A, 697U, 697V, 701A, 709U,709V, 713A, 735U, 735V, 739A, 759U, 759V

Accelerated Reader Quizzes. *See* Technology: CD-ROM.

Access for All. *See* English Language Learners.

Accessing prior knowledge, 16, 47V, 48, 77V, 78, 89V, 90, 111V, 112, 139V, 143I, 144, 169V, 170, 191V, 192, 203V, 204, 227V, 228, 255V, 259I, 260, 289V, 290, 313V, 314, 325V, 326, 355V, 356, 387V, 391I, 392, 419V, 420, 447V, 448, 459V, 460, 481V, 482, 509V, 513I, 514, 541V, 542, 565V, 566, 577V, 578, 603V, 604, 633V, 637I, 638, 667V, 668, 697V, 698, 709V, 710, 735V, 736, 763I

Acknowledgments, 5.1: T63–T64; **5.2:** T51–T52; **5.3:** T52–T53; **5.4:** T53–T54; **5.5:** T54–T55; **5.6:** T53–T54

Additional Lessons, 5.1: T1–T12; **5.2:** T1–T9; **5.3:** T1–T10; **5.4:** T1–T11; **5.5:** T1–T12; **5.6:** T1–T11

Adjectives. *See* Grammar: adjectives.

Adverbs. *See* Grammar: adverbs.

Advertisements, 59, 168–169B, 260I, 313F, 553. *See also* **Media Literacy; Writing forms and modes:** advertisements.

Affixes. *See* Phonics/Spelling; Spelling; Vocabulary: prefixes, suffixes.

Alliteration, 284–287, 289Q, 289S. *See also* **Literary devices; Poetry.**

Almanac, 222–225, 227Q, **5.2:** T10

Analogies. *See* Vocabulary: analogies.

Analyzing. *See* Comprehension strategies: analyze.

Antecedents, 419I–419J. *See also* Grammar.

Antonyms. *See* Vocabulary: antonyms.

Apostrophes, 227I–227J, 255I-255J, 259E, 325J, 509J. *See also* **Grammar:** punctuation.

Approaching Level Options

comprehension, 47O, 47P, 77O, 77P, 89O, 89P, 111O, 111P, 139O, 139P, 169O, 169P, 191O, 191P, 203O, 203P, 227O, 227P, 255O, 255P, 289O, 289P, 313O, 313P, 325O, 325P, 355O, 355P, 387O, 387P, 419O, 419P, 447O, 447P, 459O, 459P, 481O, 481P, 509O, 509P, 541O, 541P, 565O, 565P, 577O, 577P, 603O, 603P, 633O, 633P, 667O, 667P, 697O, 697P, 709O, 709P, 735O, 735P, 759O, 759P

   strategies, 47O, 77O, 89O, 111O, 139O, 169O, 191O, 203O, 227O, 255O, 289O, 313O, 325O, 355O, 387O, 419O, 447O, 459O, 481O, 509O, 541O, 565O, 577O, 603O, 633O, 667O, 697O, 709O, 735O, 759O

fluency, 47N, 77N, 89N, 111N, 139N, 169N, 191N, 203N, 227N, 255N, 289N, 313N 325N, 355M, 355N, 387N, 419N, 447N, 459N, 481N, 509N, 541N, 565M, 565N, 577N, 603N, 633N, 667N, 697N, 709N, 735N, 759N

phonics, 47M, 77M, 89M, 111M, 139M, 169M, 191M, 203M, 227M, 255M, 289M, 313M 325M, 355M, 387M, 419M, 447M, 459M, 481M, 509M, 541M, 565M, 577M, 603M, 633M, 667M, 697M, 709M, 735M, 759M

vocabulary, 47N, 47O, 77N, 77O, 89N, 89O, 111N, 111O, 139N, 139O, 169N, 169O, 191N, 191O, 203N, 203O, 227N, 227O, 255N, 255O, 289N, 289O, 313N, 313O, 325N, 325O, 355N, 355O, 387N, 387O, 419N, 419O, 447N, 447O, 459N, 459O, 481N, 481O, 509N, 509O, 541N, 541O, 565N, 565O, 577N, 577O, 603N, 603O, 633N, 633O, 667N, 667O, 697N, 697O, 709N, 709O, 735N, 735O, 759N, 759O

Assessment, 47K–47L, 77K–77L, 89K–89L, 111K–111L, 139K–139L, 143M-143N, 169K–169L, 191K–191L, 203K–203L, 227K–227L, 255K–255L, 259M-259N, 289K–289L, 313K–313L, 325K–325L, 355K–355L, 387K–387L, 391M-391N, 419K–419L, 447K–447L, 459K–459L, 481K–481L, 509K–509L, 513M-513N, 541K–541L, 565K–565L, 577K–577L, 603K–603L, 633K–633L, 637M-637N, 667K–667L, 697K–697L, 709K–709L, 735K–735L, 759K–759L, 763M-763N

alternative, 47K, 77K, 89K, 111K, 139K, 169K, 191K, 203K, 227K, 255K, 289K, 313K, 325K, 355K, 387K, 419K, 447K–447L, 459K, 481K, 509K, 541K, 565K, 577K, 603K, 633K, 667K, 697K, 709K, 735K, 759K

fluency, 47K, 77K, 89K, 111K, 139K, 169K, 191K, 203K, 227K, 255K, 289K, 313K, 325K, 355K, 387K, 419K, 447K, 459K, 481K, 509K, 541K, 565K, 577K, 603K, 633K, 667K, 697K, 709K, 735K, 759K

formal/informal, 16F, 144F, 260F, 392F, 514F, 638F

National Test Alignment chart, 16G, 144G, 260G, 392G, 514G, 638G

Quick Check and observational assessments. *See individual skills listings for* **Comprehension skills, Comprehension strategies, Fluency, Grammar, Phonics/Spelling; Spelling; Vocabulary, Writing.**

scoring rubrics, 47A, 77A, 88, 89A, 111A, 139A, 143G, 143H, 169A, 191A, 202, 203A, 227A, 255A, 259G, 259H, 289A, 313A, 324, 325A, 355A, 387A, 391G, 391H, 419A, 447A, 458, 459A, 481A, 509A, 513G, 513H, 541A, 565A, 576, 577A, 603A, 633A, 637G, 637H, 667A, 697A, 708, 709A, 735A, 759A, 763G, 763H

Test Prep, 86–89, 140–143, 200–203, 256–259, 322–325, 456–459, 574–577, 706–709

Test Strategy

  Author and Me, 41, 133, 200–201, 256–258, 383, 388–390, 441, 505, 561, 627, 634–636, 691, 731, 760–761

  On My Own, 71, 107, 187, 251, 307, 413, 456–457, 574–575, 599

  Right There, 86–87, 163, 510–512, 574, 661

  Think and Search, 140–142, 221, 283, 322–323, 349, 456, 477, 535, 574, 706–707, 753

  writing prompts, 88–89, 202–203, 324–325, 458–459, 576–577, 708–709

Theme Project, 16H–16I, 147K–147L, 148H–148I, 275K–275L, 276H–276I, 409K–409L, 410H–410I, 539K–539L, 540H–540I, 661K–661L, 662H–662I, 787K–787L

Timed-reading, 43N, 43Q, 69N, 69Q, 81N, 81Q, 107N, 107Q, 143N, 143Q, 175N, 175Q, 207N, 207Q, 219N, 219Q, 247N, 247Q, 271N, 271Q, 303N, 303Q, 329N, 329Q, 341N, 341Q, 373N, 373Q, 405N, 405Q, 443N, 443Q, 469N, 469Q, 481N, 481Q, 507N, 507Q, 535N, 535Q, 561N, 561Q, 591N, 591Q, 603N, 603Q, 631N, 631Q, 657N, 657Q, 687N, 687Q, 717N, 717Q, 729N, 729Q, 757N, 757Q, 783N, 783Q

Timed-writing, 81, 219, 341, 481, 603, 729

unit, 16F–16G, 148F–148G, 276F–276G, 410F–410G, 540F–540G, 662F–662G

weekly reading, 47K–47L, 77K–77L, 89K–89L, 111K–111L, 139K–139L, 169K–169L, 191K–191L, 203K–203L, 227K–227L, 255K–255L, 289K–289L, 313K–313L, 325K–325L, 355K–355L, 387K–387L, 419K–419L, 447K–447L, 459K–459L, 481K–481L, 509K–509L, 541K–541L, 565K–565L, 577K–577L, 603K–603L, 633K–633L, 667K–667L, 697K–697L, 709K–709L, 735K–735L, 759K–759L,

writing, 88–89, 202–203, 324–325, 458–459, 576–577, 708–709

Assonance, 252–253, 255Q, 255S. *See also* **Literary devices; Poetry.**

Author/illustrator biographies, 40, 70, 106, 132, 162, 186, 220, 250, 282, 306, 348, 382, 412, 440, 476, 504, 534, 560, 598, 626, 660, 690, 730, 752

Author's Craft, 40, 70, 106, 132, 162, 186, 220, 250, 282, 306, 348, 382, 412, 440, 476, 504, 534, 560, 598, 626, 660, 690, 730, 752

  action verbs, 440

  character development, 282, 626, 660

  classification, 476

  dialect, 162, 220, 404

  dialogue, 382, 412

  figurative language, 250, 598

  first–person point of view, 106, 132

  headings, 186

  humor, 40

  informal language, 70, 162, 220, 306

  mood, 534

  photographs and captions, 752

  point of view, 297, 690

  repetition, 504

  sensory details and images, 348, 560, 730

  third–person point of view, 106

  word choice, 303, 306

Authors, main selection

  Armstrong, Jennifer, 518–533, 534

  Borden, Louise, 264–281, 282

  Delacre, Lula, 208–219, 220

  Fleischman, Paul, 546–559, 560

  Frasier, Debra, 20–39, 40

  Goodman, Susan E, 94–105, 106

  Hunter, Sara Hoagland, 582–597, 598

  Joseph, Lynn, 608–625, 626

  Kessler, Cristina, 330–347, 348

  Kramer, Stephen, 740–751, 752

  Lambeth, Ellen, 174–185, 186

  Lauber, Patricia, 714–729, 730

  Lester, Julius, 232–249, 250

  Lomax, John A., 252

  Longfellow, Henry Wadsworth, 284–287

  McKissack, Patricia C, 396–411, 412

  Medearis, Angela Shelf, 486–503, 504

  Meunier, Brian, 116–131, 132

  Naylor, Phyllis Reynolds, 148–161, 162

  Sanderson, Ruth, 642–659, 660

  Schanzer, Rosalyn, 52–69, 70

  Simon, Seymour, 464–475, 476

  Stevens, Jan Romero, 424–439, 440

  Van Allsburg, Chris, 360–381, 382

  Woolridge, Connie Nordhielm, 294–305, 306

  Yep, Laurence, 672–689, 690

Author's perspective. *See* **Comprehension skills: author's perspective.**

Author's purpose. *See* **Comprehension skills: author's purpose.**

Autobiographies. *See* **Genre: reading nonfiction.**

Bb

Base words. *See* **Vocabulary: base words.**

Beyond Level Options

  comprehension, 47T, 77T, 89T, 111T, 139T, 169T, 191T, 203T, 227T, 255T, 289T, 313T, 325T, 355T, 387T, 419T, 447T, 459T, 481T, 509T, 541T, 565T, 577T, 603T, 633T, 667T, 697T, 709T, 735T, 759T

fluency, 47S, 77S, 89S, 111S, 139S, 169S, 191S, 203S, 227S, 255S, 289S, 313S, 325S, 355S, 387S, 419S, 447S, 459S, 481S, 509S, 541S, 565S, 577S, 603S, 633S, 667S, 697S, 709S, 735S, 759S

vocabulary, 47S, 47T, 77S, 77T, 89S, 89T, 111S, 111T, 139S, 139T, 169S, 169T, 191S, 191T, 203S, 203T, 227S, 227T, 255S, 255T, 289S, 289T, 313S, 313T, 325S, 325T, 355S, 355T, 387S, 387T, 419S, 419T, 447S, 447T, 459S, 459T, 481S, 481T, 509S, 509T, 541S, 541T, 565S, 565T, 577S, 577T, 603S, 603T, 633S, 633T, 667S, 667T, 697S, 697T, 709S, 709T, 735S, 735T, 759S, 759T

Bibliographies, 455B, 459Q, 459S, 513C, 514H

Biographies. See **Genre: reading nonfiction.**

Book, parts of, 455B, 459Q, 459S. See also **Study Skills; Text Features.**

Build Background, 16H, 16, 47V, 48, 77V, 78, 89V, 90, 111V, 112, 139V, 144H, 144, 169V, 170, 191V, 192, 204, 227V, 228, 255V, 260H, 260, 289V, 290, 313V, 314, 325V, 326, 329H, 355V, 356, 387V, 392, 419V, 420, 447V, 448, 459V, 460, 481V, 482, 509V, 514H, 514, 541V, 542, 565V, 566, 577V, 578, 603V, 604, 633V, 638H, 638, 667V, 668, 697V, 698, 709V, 710, 735V, 736, 759V

Byline, 384–387, 387Q. 387S, **5.3::** T10

Cc

Capitalization. See **Grammar: capitalization.**

Captions, 42–45, 47Q, 47S, 164–167, 169Q, 169S, 638H, 752, **5.2:** T9

Causal, hierarchical, temporal relationships, 123

Cause and effect. See **Comprehension skills: cause and effect.**

Character. See **Comprehension skills: character.**

Character Building, 16I, 144I, 260I, 392I, 514I, 638I

Charts. See **Graphic organizers: charts; Text features: charts.**

Chronology. See **Comprehension skills: sequence; Writing traits: organization.**

Cinquain poetry, 600–601

Citations. See **Computer literacy; Research and Inquiry; Study skills.**

Classroom Library Lessons, 5.1: T13–T18; **5.2:** T11–T16; **5.3:** T11–T16; **5.4:** T12–T17; **5.5:** T13–T18; **5.6:** T13–T17

Colon. See **Grammar: punctuation.**

Commas. See **Grammar: punctuation.**

Compare and contrast. See **Comprehension skills: compare/contrast.**

Compound words. See **Phonics/Spelling; Spelling; Vocabulary.**

Comprehension skills

author's perspective, 454, 581A–581B, 582–597, 599, 603O, 603P, 603R, 603T, 621, 627B, **5.5:** T4

author's purpose, 40, 70, 106, 132, 162, 186, 220, 250, 282, 306, 348, 382, 412, 423A–423B, 424–439, 440, 447O, 447P, 447R, 447T, 472, 476, 477B, 485A–485B, 486–503, 504, 509O, 509P, 509R, 509T, 524, 534, 535B, 550, 557, 560, 561B, 598, 626, 660, 690, 730, 752, **5.4:** T2

cause/effect, 68, 115A–115B, 116–131, 133, 139O, 139P, 139R, 139T, 159, 163B, 183, 223, 269, 303, 307B, 309, 346, 528, 569A–569B, 570–573, 577O, 577P, 577R, 577T, 721, 727, 748, **5.1:** T5, **5.3:** T3

character, 19A–19B, 20–39, 41, 47O, 47P, 47R, 47T, 59, 71B, 119, 127, 158, 266, 279, 298, 338, 364, 395A–395B, 396–411, 419O–419P, 419R, 419T, 529, 587, 646, 653, 658, 661B, 685, **5:1:** T1; **5.4:** T1

compare/contrast, 37, 43, 81A–81B, 82–85, 85A, 89O, 89P, 89R, 89T, 100, 136, 157, 215, 309, 329A–329B, 330–347, 355O, 355P, 355R, 355T, 380, 383B, 409, 416, 417, 444, 549, 587, 629, 662–665, 674, 726, **5.1:** T3; **5.3:** T3

description as text structure, 432, 463A–463B, 464–475, 477, 481O, 481P, 481R, 481T, **5.4:** T4

drawing conclusions, 44, 97, 98, 99, 130, 166, 198, 237, 245, 246, 248, 263A–263B, 264–281, 286, 289O, 289P, 289R, 289T, 300, 310, 333, 337, 338, 342, 345, 346, 349B, 359A–359B, 360–381, 383, 385, 387O, 387P, 387R, 387T, 399, 402, 407, 413B, 416, 436, 441B, 466, 470, 472, 488, 493, 494, 497, 498, 531, 586, 587, 589, 591, 595, 613, 619, 622, 624, 646, 647, 688, 717, 722, 724, 733, 742, 745, **5.3:** T1

fact and opinion, 293A–293B, 294–305, 307, 313O, 313P, 313R, 313T, 317A–317B, 318–321, 325O, 325P, 325R, 325T, 455A, **5.3:** T2

generalizations, making, 451A–451B, 452–455, 459O, 459P, 459R, 459T, 490, 505B, 573A, 713A–713B, 714–729, 735O, 735P, 735R, 735T, 746, 753B, **5.4:** T3; **5.6:** T4

inferences, making, 103, 120, 147A–147B, 148–161, 163, , 169O, 169P, 169R, 169T, 181, 187B, 210, 221B, 231A–231B, 232–249, 255O, 255P, 255R, 255T, 270, 283B, 285, 298, 333, 340, 360, 407, 431, 435, 467, 500, 501, 521, 525, 531, 588, 589, 590, 592, 594, 621, 623, 630, 652, 722, 745, 746, 749, 750, **5.2:** T1

judgments, making, 494, 671A–671B, 672–689, 697O, 697P, 697R, 697T, **5.6:** T2 main idea and details, 173A–173B, 174–185, 191O, 191P, 191R, 191T, 195A–195B, 196–199, 199A, 203O, 203P, 203R, 203T, 321A, 705A, **5.2**: T2

persuasion, techniques of, 701A–701B, 702–705, 709O, 709P, 709R, 709T, **5.6**: T3

plot, 19A–19B, 20–39, 41B, 47O, 47P, 47R, 47T, 51A–51B, 52–69, 71, 77O, 77P, 77R, 77T, 124, 133B, 154, 239, 266, 410, 431, 554, 659, 661B, **5.1**: T1, T2

  conflict, climax, and resolution, 301, 410, 659

predictions, making. *See* Predictions, making.

problem and solution, 207A–207B, 208–219, 227O, 227P, 227R, 227T, 251B, 517A–517B, 518–533, 535, 541O, 541P, 541R, 541T, **5.2**: T3; **5.5**: T1

sequence of events, 180, 434, 641A–641B, 642–659, 667O, 667P, 667R, 667T, 719, 731B, 739A–739B, 740–751, 759O, 759P, 759R, 759T, **5.6**: T1

setting, 26, 41B, 51A–51B, 52–69, 71, 77O, 77P, 77R, 77T, 119, 124, 239, 266, 395A–395B, 396–411, 419O, 419P, 419R, 419T, 531, 584, 623, 661B, **5.1**: T2, **5.4**: T1

summarize, 25, 32, 41, 62, 71, 85, 93A–93B, 94–105, 107, 107B, 111O, 111P, 111R, 111T, 122, 133, 155, 163, 165, 176, 178, 184, 187, 196, 199A, 199, 217, 221, 251, 272, 283, 300, 307, 321, 341, 349, 351, 370, 407, 413, 430, 441, 455, 469, 477, 496, 505, 529, 535, 558, 561, 573, 592, 599, 607A–607B, 608–625, 627, 633O, 633P, 633R, 633T, 691B, **5.1**: T4; **5.5**: T5

theme, 274, 277, 346, 545A–545B, 546–559, 561, 565O, 565P, 565R, 565T, 599B, **5.5**: T2

Comprehension strategies

analyze, 19A–19B, 20–39, 47O, 47R, 51A–51B, 52–69, 77O, 77R, 81A–81B, 82–85, 89O, 128, 135, 221, 239, 251, 263A–263B, 264–281, 283, 289O, 289R,

330–347, 359A–359B, 360–381, 389O, 389R, 395A–395B, 396–411, 419O, 419R, 441, 443, 463A–463B, 464–475, 481O, 481R, 535, 537, 545A–545B, 546, 561, 565O, 565R, 569A–569B, 570–573, 577O, 599, 627

story structure, 19A–19B, 20–39, 47O, 47R, 51A–51B, 52–69, 77O, 128, 280, 332, 334, 359A–359B, 362, 366, 378, 395A–395B, 396–411, 419O, 419R, 443

text structure, 81A–81B, 82–85, 89O, 463A–463B, 464–475, 481O, 481R, 501, 537, 570–573

evaluate, 293A–293B, 294–305, 313O, 313R, 317A–317B, 318–321, 325O, 325R, 423A–423B, 424–439, 447O, 447R, 451A–451B, 452–455, 459O, 459R, 485A–485B, 486–503, 509O, 509R, 535B, 554, 621

generate questions, 93A–93B, 94–105, 111O, 110R, 115A–115B, 116–131, 139O, 139R, 517A–517B, 518–533, 541O, 541R, 581A–581B, 582–597, 603O, 603R, 607A–607B, 608–625, 633O, 633R,

inferences, making, 263A–263B, 264–281, 289O, 289R, 329A–329B, 330–347, 355O, 355R, 359A–359B, 360–381, 387O, 387R, 545A–545B, 546–559, 565O, 565R, 569A–569B, 570–573, 577O, 577R

monitor comprehension, 28, 33, 58, 98, 124, 129, 147A–147B, 148–161, 169O, 169R, 231A–231B, 232–249, 255O, 255R, 267, 268, 301, 400, 433, 470, 491, 525, 595, 671A–671B, 672–689, 697O, 697R, 701A–701B, 702–705, 709O, 709R, 713A–713B, 714–729, 735O, 735R. *See also* **Monitor and Clarify.**

summarize, 173A–173B, 174–185, 191O, 191R, 195A–195B, 196–199, 203O, 203R, 207A–207B, 208–219, 227O, 227R, 641A–641B, 642–659, 667O, 667R, 739A–739B, 740–751, 759O, 759R,

synthesize, 34, 96, 100, 102, 133, 151, 160, 181, 217, 239, 275, 379, 471, 558, 590, 615, 704, 743

Computer Literacy, 143I–143J, 259I–259J, 391I–391J, 513I–513J, 637I–637J, 763I–763J. *See also* Internet; Technology.

citations, URL, 143I–143J, 514H, 637I–637J

databases, 199B, 203T, 513I, 513J

drawing and graphics, 637I–637J

  clip art, 637I–637J, 763I–763J

  multimedia files, 637I–637J, 763I–763J

  text box, 637I–637J

e-mail and e-mail attachments, 391I–391J

evaluating online resources, 199B, 203A, 203P, 203R, 203T

guided practice for, 143J, 259J, 391J, 513J, 637J, 763J

hyperlinks and key words, 562–563, 565P, 565R, 565T

Internet, using, 16H, 75, 137, 143I–143J, 144H, 199B, 203A, 203P, 203R, 203T, 260H, 392H, 514H, 637I, 763C

key word searches, 143I–143J, 199B, 203A, 203P, 203R, 203T, 562–563

making a presentation, 763I–763J

online practice, 143J, 259J, 391J, 513J, 637J, 763J

protecting computers and networks, 391I–391J

safety alerts, 143J, 259J, 391J, 513J, 637J, 763J

search engines, 143I–143J, 199B, 203A, 203P, 203R, 203T

search techniques, 199B, 203A, 203P, 203R, 203T

slide/layout, 763I

spreadsheets, using and formatting, 513I–513J

technology and the world, 259I–259J, 513I–513J

tool bar and link, 72, 391I–391J

URLs, 143I–143J

viruses, 391I–391J

Web browser, 143I–143J

Web sites and addresses, 199B, 203A, 203P, 203R, 203T

word processing, 259I–259J

changing font and type, 259I

cutting and pasting, 259I

writing process and, 259C, 259I–259J

Conclusions, drawing. *See* Comprehension skills: drawing conclusions.

Conflict/climax/resolution, 301, 410, 659

Conjunctions. *See* Grammar: conjunctions.

Connect and Compare, 45, 75, 109, 137, 167, 189, 225, 253, 287, 311, 353, 385, 417, 445, 479, 507, 539, 563, 601, 631, 665, 695, 733, 757. *See also* **Informational text; Text connections.**

Connections, making. *See* **Text connections.**

Connotations, 168–169, 169A–169B, 329, 341, 355D, 355F, 355Q, 355S, 667B

Consonance, 600–601, 603Q, 603S

Constructive Feedback. *See individual skiill listings for* **Additional Lessons; Fluency; Phonics/spelling; Spelling.**

Content Area Reading, 42–45, 72–75, 82–85, 134–137, 164–167, 196–199, 222–225, 308–311, 318–321, 350–353, 384–385, 414–417, 442–445, 452–455, 536–539, 562–563, 628–631, 662–665, 692–695, 702–705, 760–762

Content vocabulary, 42–45, 72–75, 82–85, 134–137, 164–167, 196–199, 222–225, 308–311, 318–321, 350–353, 384–385, 414–417, 442–445, 452–455, 536–539, 562–563, 628–631, 662–665, 692–695, 702–705, 760–762.

Context clues. *See* **Vocabulary: context clues.**

Context, teaching words in. *See* Vocabulary: teaching words in context.

Contractions. *See* Grammar: contractions.

Cooperative Learning, 47C, 47E, 77C, 77E, 89C, 89E, 111C, 111E, 139C, 139E, 169C, 169E, 191C, 191E, 203C, 203E, 227C, 227E, 255C, 255E, 289C, 289E, 313C, 313E, 325C, 325E, 355C, 355E, 387C, 387E, 419C, 419E, 447C, 447E, 459C, 459E, 481C, 481E, 509C, 509E, 541C, 541E, 565C, 565E, 577C, 577E, 603C, 603E, 667C, 667E, 709C, 709E, 735C, 735E

Cross-Curricular connections. *See also* **Theme Projects.**

art, 122, 392I, 494, 532, 551

geography, 539

health, 341, 531

language arts, 45, 66, 376, 392I, 405, 522, 528, 557, 592, 638I, 650, 651

math, 150, 303, 438, 533, 682

music, 144I, 243, 268, 400, 718

science, 16I, 16S, 48J, 62, 78J, 90J, 100, 112J, 137, 144S, 170J, 182, 192J, 204J, 228J, 260S, 290J, 314J, 326J, 353, 356J, 379, 385, 392S, 420J, 430, 445, 448J, 460J, 467, 474, 482J, 514I, 514S, 542J, 559, 566J, 578J, 604J, 631, 638S, 668J, 695, 698J, 710J, 725, 736J, 744, 747

social studies, 16S, 48J, 75, 78J, 90J, 112J, 127, 144I, 144S, 167, 170J, 192J, 204J, 217, 225, 228J, 244, 260I, 260S, 270, 290J, 311, 314J, 326J, 356J, 392S, 417, 420J, 448J, 460J, 482J, 514S, 520, 525, 542J, 558, 566J, 578J, 590, 604J, 623, 638I, 638S, 668J, 698J, 710J, 736J

workstations, 16R–16S, 48I–48J, 78I–78J, 90I–90J, 112I–112J, 144R–144S, 170I–170J, 192I–192J, 204I–204J, 228I–228J, 260R–260S, 290I–290J, 314I–314J, 326I–326J, 356I–356J, 392R–392S, 420I–420J, 448I–448J,

460I–460J, 482I–482J, 514R–514S, 542I–542J, 566I–566J, 578I–578J, 604I–604J, 638R–638S, 668I–668J, 698I–698J, 710I–710J, 736I–736J

Cultural Perspectives, 35, 68, 130, 183, 218, 248, 297, 335, 402, 431, 438, 489, 491, 498, 520, 530, 590, 595, 618, 685

Dd

Daily Language Activities, 47I, 77I, 89I, 111I, 139I, 169I, 191I, 203I, 227I, 255I, 289I, 313I, 325I, 355I, 387I, 419I, 447I, 459I, 481I, 509I, 541I, 565I, 577I, 603I, 633I, 667I, 697I, 709I, 735I, 759I. *See also* **Grammar.**

Decodable Passages, 47E, 47M 77E, 77M, 89E, 89M, 111E, 111M, 139E, 139M, 169E, 169M, 191E, 191M, 203E, 203M, 227E, 227M, 255E, 255M, 289E, 289M, 313E, 313M, 325E, 325M, 355E, 355M, 387E, 387M, 419E, 419M, 447E, 447M, 459E, 459M, 481E, 481M, 509E, 509M, 541E, 541M, 565E, 565M, 577E, 577M, 603E, 633M, 667E, 697M, 709E, 709M, 735E, 759M

Denotation, 111B, 329, 341, 355B, 355D, 355F, 355Q, 355S, 667B

Description. *See* Comprehension skills: description as text structure.

Details. *See* Comprehension skills: main ideas and details; Writer's Craft.

Diagrams, 144H, 638H, 662–665, 667Q, 667S, 726, **5.3:** T10. *See also* **Graphic organizers: diagrams.**

Dialogue, 139F, 192J, 326J, 354-355B, 355J, 382, 412, 448J, 542J

Dictionary, using, 47D, 47F, 77D, 78I, 81, 89D, 89F, 89O, 111F, 118, 139D, 139F, 147, 156, 169D, 169Q, 170I, 263, 290I, 293, 313D, 313F, 313O, 313Q, 329, 447F, 463, 468, 481D, 481F, 481O, 481Q, 541D,

552, 565D, 565F, 565O, 565Q, 569,
573B, 577D, 577O, 577Q, 577S, 641,
671, 697D, **5.1:** T8; **5.2:** T4; **5.3:** T5;
5.5: T7, T12. *See also* **Study skills;
Vocabulary: dictionary, using.**

Differentiated Instruction, 16K,
16N–16O, 48B, 48E–48F, 78B, 78E–
78F, 90B, 90E–90F, 112B, 112E–112F,
144K, 144B, 144N–144O, 170B,
170E–170F, 192B, 192E–192F, 204B,
204E–204F, 228B, 228E–228F, 260K,
260N–260O, 290B, 290E–290F,
314B, 314E–314F, 326B, 326E–326F,
356B, 356E–356F, 392K, 392N–392O,
420B, 420E–420F, 448B, 448E–448F,
460B, 460E–460F, 482B, 482E–482F,
514K, 514N–514O, 542B, 542E–542F,
566B, 566E–566F, 578B, 578E–578F,
604B, 604E–604F, 638K, 638N–
638O, 668B, 668E–668F, 698B,
698E–698F, 710B, 710E–710F, 736B,
736E–736F. *See also* **Approaching
Level Options; Beyond Level
Options; ELL; Leveled Reader
Lessons; On Level Options; Small
Group Options.**

Directions, following and writing,
430, 696–697B, 751

Ee

Encyclopedia, 562–563, 709G

English Language Learners. *See
also* **Academic language.**

beginning/intermediate/advanced,
18, 19A, 41A, 47C, 47D, 47E, 47I,
50, 51A, 71A, 77C, 77D, 77E, 77I,
80, 81A, 89C, 89D, 89E, 89I, 92,
93A, 107A, 111C, 111D, 111E, 111I,
114, 115A, 133A, 139C, 139D, 139E,
139I, 146, 147A, 163A, 169C, 169D,
169E, 169I, 172, 173A, 187A, 191C,
191D, 191E, 191I, 194, 195A, 203C,
203D, 203E, 203I, 206, 207A, 221A,
227C, 227D, 227E, 227I, 230, 231A,
251A, 255C, 255D, 255E, 255I, 262,
263A, 283A, 289C, 289D, 289E,
289I, 292, 293A, 307A, 313C, 313D,
313E, 313I, 316, 317A, 325C,
325D, 325E, 325I, 328, 329A,

349A, 355C, 355D, 355E, 355I, 358,
359A, 383A, 387C, 387D, 387E,
387I, 394, 395A, 413A, 419C, 419D,
419E, 419I, 422, 423A, 441A, 447C,
447D, 447E, 447I, 450, 451A, 459C,
459D, 459E, 459I, 462, 463A,
477A, 481C, 481D, 481E, 481I, 484,
485A, 505A, 509C, 509D, 509E,
509I, 516, 517A, 535A, 541C, 541D,
541E, 541I, 544, 545A, 561A, 565C,
565D, 565E, 565I, 568, 569A,
577C, 577D, 577E, 577I, 580, 581A,
599A, 603C, 603D, 603E, 603I,
606, 607A, 627A, 633C, 633D,
633E, 633I, 640, 641A, 661A, 667C,
667D, 667E, 667I, 670, 671A, 691A,
697C, 697D, 697E, 697I, 700, 701A,
709C, 709D, 709E, 709I, 712, 713A,
731A, 735C, 735D, 735E, 735I, 738,
739A, 753A, 759C, 759D, 759E,
759I

comprehension, 19A, 51A, 81A, 93A,
115A, 147A, 173A, 195A, 207A, 231A,
263A, 293A, 317A, 329A, 359A,
395A, 423A, 451A, 463A, 485A,
517A, 545A, 569A, 581A, 607A,
641A, 671A, 701A, 713A, 739A

fluency, 41A, 71A, 107A, 133A,
163A, 187A, 221A, 251A, 283A,
307A, 349A, 383A, 413A, 441A,
477A, 505A, 535A, 561A, 599A,
627A, 661A, 691A, 731A, 753A

grammar, 47I, 77I, 89I, 111I, 139I,
169I, 191I, 203I, 227I, 255I, 289I,
313I, 325I, 355I, 387I, 419I, 447I,
459I, 481I, 509I, 541I, 565I, 577I,
603I, 633I, 667I, 697I, 709I, 735I,
759I

oral language, 16, 47V, 48, 77V,
78, 89V, 90, 111V, 112, 139V, 144,
169V, 191V, 192, 203V, 204, 227V,
228, 255V, 260, 289V, 290, 313V,
314, 325V, 326, 355V, 356, 387V,
392, 419V, 420, 447V, 448, 459V,
460, 481V, 482, 509V, 514, 541V,
542, 565V, 566, 577V, 578, 603V,
604, 633V, 638, 667V, 668, 697V,
698, 709V, 710, 735V, 736, 759V

phonics, 47E, 77E, 89E, 111E, 139E,
169E, 191E, 203E, 227E, 255E,
289E, 313E, 325E, 355E, 387E,
419E, 447E, 459E, 481E, 509E,
541E, 565E, 577E, 603E, 633E,
667E, 697E, 709E, 735E, 759E

vocabulary, 18, 47C, 47D, 47V, 50,
77C, 77D, 77V, 80, 89C, 89D, 89V,
92, 111C, 111D, 111V, 114, 139C,
139D, 139V, 146, 169C, 169D,
169V, 172, 191C, 191D, 191V, 194,
203C, 203D, 203V, 206, 227C,
227D, 227V, 230, 255C, 255D,
255V, 262, 289C, 289D, 289V,
292, 313C, 313D, 313V, 316, 325C,
325D, 325V, 328, 355C, 355D,
355V, 358, 387C, 387D, 387V,
394, 419C, 419D, 419V, 422, 447C,
447D, 447V, 450, 459C, 459D,
459V, 462, 481C, 481D, 481V,
484, 509C, 509D, 509V, 516,
541C, 541D, 541V, 544, 565C,
565D, 565V, 568, 577C, 577D,
577V, 580, 603C, 603D, 603V,
606, 633C, 633D, 633V, 640,
667C, 667D, 667V, 670, 697C,
697D, 697V, 700, 709C, 709D,
709V, 712, 735C, 735D, 735V, 738,
759C, 759D, 759V

Evaluating. *See* **Comprehension
strategies: evaluate.**

Everyday communications, 705B,
709A, 709Q, 709S, **5.6:** T11

Expository nonfiction. *See* **Genre:
reading nonfiction.**

Extra Support, 22, 24, 30, 31, 55, 61,
63, 97, 99, 103, 120, 121, 125, 151,
154, 155, 156, 158, 178, 179, 181,
210, 212, 215, 240, 241, 247, 266,
272, 273, 296, 298, 299, 332, 339,
340, 363, 369, 375, 398, 403, 404,
428, 433, 434, 435, 454, 466, 468,
471, 490, 495, 496, 527,529, 549,
554, 555, 588, 589, 591, 596, 646,
647, 649, 657, 716, 717, 721, 723,
729, 742, 745, 749

Ff

Fable, 483, 506–507

Fact and opinion. *See*
**Comprehension skills: fact and
opinion.**

Fairy tale, 639, 642–659

Fantasy, 116–131, 546–559

Figurative language. *See* Literary devices: figurative language; Poetry: figurative language.

First person point–of–view, 46, 76, 110, 132, 138, 288, 386, 690

Fix-up strategies. *See* Monitor and Clarify; Predictions, making.

Fluency, 16R, 17, 41A, 47K, 47L, 47N, 47Q, 47S, 48I, 65, 71A, 77K, 77L, 77N, 77Q, 77S, 78I, 85A, 89K, 89L, 89N, 89Q, 89S, 90I, 107A, 111K, 111L, 111N, 111Q, 111S, 112I, 133A, 139K, 139L, 139N, 139Q, 139S, 144R, 163A, 169K, 169L, 169N, 169Q, 169S, 170I, 187A, 191I, 191K, 191L, 191N, 191Q, 191S, 192I, 199A, 203K, 203L, 203N, 203Q, 203S, 204I, 221A, 227K, 227L, 227N, 227Q, 227S, 228I, 242, 251A, 255K, 255L, 255N, 255Q, 255S, 260R, 276, 283A, 283B, 289K, 289L, 289N, 289Q, 289S, 290I, 307A, 313K, 313L, 313N, 313Q, 313S, 314I, 315, 321A, 325K, 325L, 325N, 325Q, 325S, 326I, 349A, 355K, 355L, 355N, 355Q, 355S, 356I, 383A, 387K, 387L, 387N, 387Q, 387S, 392R, 413A, 419K, 419L, 419N, 419Q, 419S, 420, 420I, 421, 441A, 447K, 447L, 447N, 447Q, 447S, 448I, 455A, 459K, 459L, 459N, 459Q, 459S, 460I, 477A, 481K, 481L, 481N, 481Q, 481S, 482I, 483, 501, 505A, 509K, 509L, 509N, 509Q, 509S, 514R, 515, 535A, 541K, 541L, 541N, 541Q, 541S, 542I, 561A, 561B, 565K, 565L, 565N, 565Q, 565S, 566I, 573A, 577K, 577L, 577N, 577Q, 577S, 578I, 587, 599A, 603K, 603L, 603N, 603Q, 603S, 604I, 627A, 633K, 633L, 633N, 633Q, 633S, 638R, 661A, 667K, 667L, 667N, 667Q, 667S, 668I, 691A, 697K, 697L, 697N, 697Q, 697S, 698I, 709K, 709L, 709N, 709Q, 709S, 710I, 731A, 735K, 735L, 735N, 735Q, 735S, 736I, 746, 753A, 759K, 759L, 759N

accuracy, speed, prosody, 41A, 71A, 85A, 107A, 133A, 163A, 187A, 199A, 221A, 251A, 283A, 307A, 321A, 349A, 383A, 413A, 441A, 455A, 477A, 505A, 535A, 561A, 573A, 599A, 627A, 661A, 691A, 705A, 731A, 753A

Approaching Level Options for. *See* Approaching Level Options: fluency.

Beyond Level Options for. *See* Beyond Level Options: fluency.

choral reading, 65, 107A, 111Q, 111S, 135Q, 163A, 169Q, 169S, 203Q, 203S, 289S, 355Q, 355S, 383A, 441A, 447Q, 447S, 501, 535A, 541Q, 541S, 561A, 599A, 603Q, 661A, 667S, 709Q, 709S, 735A, 735S, 746, 759Q

cooperative learning, 41A, 71A, 85A, 107A, 133A, 163A, 187A, 199A, 221A, 251A, 283A, 307A, 321A, 349A, 383A, 413A, 441A, 455A, 477A, 505A, 535A, 561A, 573A, 599A, 627A, 661A, 691A, 705A, 731A, 753A

echo reading, 71A, 77Q, 77S, 85A, 133A, 139S, 191Q, 199A, 251A, 255Q, 255S, 276, 307A, 313Q, 321A, 325Q, 387Q, 413A, 455A, 481Q, 481S, 565Q, 565S, 573A, 587, 627A, 661A, 691A, 697Q, 697S, 731A

ELL, 41A, 71A, 107A, 133A, 163A, 187A, 221A, 251A, 283A, 307A, 349A, 383A, 413A, 441A, 477A, 505A, 535A, 561A, 599A, 627A, 661A, 691A, 731A, 753A

explain/model/practice, 41A, 71A, 85A, 107A, 133A, 163A, 187A, 199A, 221A, 251A, 283A, 307A, 321A, 349A, 383A, 413A, 441A, 455A, 477A, 505A, 535A, 561A, 573A, 599A, 627A, 661A, 691A, 705A, 731A, 753A

Fluency Solutions Audio CD, 41A, 71A, 85A, 107A, 133A, 163A, 187A, 199A, 221A, 251A, 283A, 307A, 321A, 349A, 383A, 413A, 441A, 455A, 477A, 505A, 535A, 561A, 573A, 599A, 627A, 661A, 691A, 705A, 731A, 753A

group reading, 41A, 71A, 85A, 133A, 163A, 187A, 199A, 221A, 251A, 283A, 307A, 321A, 349A, 383A, 413A, 441A, 455A, 477A, 501, 505A, 535A, 561A, 573A, 599A, 627A, 661A, 691A, 705A

modeling fluent expressive reading, 17, 47N, 49, 77N, 79, 89N, 91, 111N, 113, 139N, 145, 169N, 171, 191N, 193, 203N, 205, 227N, 229, 255N, 261, 289N, 291, 313N, 315, 325N, 327, 355N, 357, 387N, 393, 419N, 421, 447N, 449, 459N, 461, 481N, 483, 509N, 515, 541N, 543, 565N, 567, 577N, 579, 603N, 605, 633N, 639, 667N, 669, 697N, 699, 709N, 711, 735N, 737, 759N

On Level Options for. *See* On Level Options: fluency.

partner reading, 47N, 77N, 77Q, 89N, 111N, 139N, 169N, 175N, 191N, 203N, 203Q, 203S, 227N, 227S, 255N, 255Q, 289N, 289S, 313N, 325N, 355N, 387N, 392, 419Q, 447N, 459N, 481S, 509S, 541N, 565N, 577N, 587, 633N, 633Q, 667N, 697S, 709N, 735N, 735S, 759N. *See also*

pauses, stops, and intonation, 41A, 47N, 47Q, 47S, 133A, 139Q, 175N, 187A, 191Q, 221A, 227Q, 227S, 283A, 289Q, 321A, 325N, 325S, 383A, 441A, 477A, 447Q, 459Q, 549S, 561A, 599A, 603N, 661A, 667N, 697Q, 753A, 759Q

phrase-cued text, 133A, 187A, 227Q, 227S, 283A, 315, 421, 447Q, 477A, 483, 515, 561A, , 599A, 603Q, 603S, 669, 753A, 759Q

practice, 41A, 47N, 47Q, 47S, 71A, 77N, 77Q, 77S, 85A, 89N, 89Q, 89S, 107A, 111N, 111Q, 111S, 133A, 139N, 139Q, 139S, 163A, 169N, 169Q, 169S, 187A, 191N, 191Q, 191S, 199A, 203N, 203Q, 203S, 221A, 227N, 227Q, 227S, 251A, 255N, 255Q, 255S, 283A, 289N, 289Q, 289S, 307A, 313N, 313Q, 313S, 321A, 325N, 325Q, 325S, 349A, 355N, 355Q, 355S, 383A, 387N, 387Q, 387S, 413A, 419N, 419Q, 419S, 441A, 447N, 447Q, 447S, 455A, 459N, 459Q, 459S, 477A, 481N, 481Q, 481S, 505A, 509N, 509Q, 509S, 535A, 541N, 541Q, 541S, 561A, 565N, 565Q, 565S, 573A, 577N, 577Q, 577S, 599A, 603N, 603Q, 603S,

Key 5.1 = Grade 5, Book 1

627A, 633N, 633Q, 633S, 661A, 667N, 667Q, 667S, 691A, 697N, 697Q, 697S, 705A, 709N, 709Q, 709S, 731A, 735N, 735Q, 735S, 753A, 759N, 759Q, 759S

pronunciation, 77N, 77S, 89N, 89Q, 89S, 107A, 111N, 111Q, 111S, 191S, 209N, 203Q, 203S, 307A, 313N, 313S, 481S, 514R, 535A, 535R, 541N, 541Q, 709N, 709Q, 731A, 735Q, 759S

punctuation, 48I, 71A, 77N, 77Q, 77S, 85A, 89Q, 89S, 163A, 169Q, 169S, 191Q, 191S, 199A, 203Q, 242, 289S, 321A, 349A, 387Q, 387S, 413A, 419Q, 419S, 455A, 501, 573A, 577Q, 577S, 603S, 633S, 667S, 691A, 705A, 709S, 746

reading with expression and intonation, 48I, 65, 71A, 77N, 77Q, 77S, 79, 112I, 113, 133A, 139Q, 139S, 163A, 169N, 169Q, 169S, 171, 187A, 191Q, 191S, 205, 291, 315, 327, 357, 387S, 393, 421, 441A, 444A, 447Q, 447S, 449, 461, 477A, 483, 515, 541Q, 543, 577Q, 577S, 561A, 603N, 603Q, 633S, 661A, 667N, 669, 711, 753A, 759Q

repeated reading, 41A, 47N, 47Q, 47S, 71A, 77N, 77Q, 77S, 85A, 89N, 89Q, 89S, 107A, 111N, 111Q, 111S, 133A, 139N, 139Q, 139S, 163A, 169N, 169Q, 169S, 187A, 191N, 191Q, 191S, 199A, 203N, 203Q, 203S, 221A, 227N, 227Q, 227S, 251A, 255N, 255Q, 255S, 283A, 289N, 289Q, 289S, 307A, 313N, 313Q, 313S, 321A, 325N, 325Q, 325S, 349A, 355N, 355Q, 355S, 383A, 387N, 387Q, 387S, 413A, 419N, 419Q, 419S, 441A, 447N, 447Q, 447S, 455A, 459N, 459Q, 459S, 477A, 481N, 481Q, 481S, 505A, 509N, 509Q, 509S, 535A, 541N, 541Q, 541S, 561A, 565N, 565Q, 565S, 573A, 577N, 577Q, 577S, 587, 599A, 603N, 603Q, 603S, 627A, 633N, 633Q, 633S, 661A, 667N, 667Q, 667S, 691A, 697N, 697Q, 697S, 705A, 709N, 709Q, 709S, 731A, 735N, 735Q, 735S, 753A, 759N, 759Q, 759S

tempo and pace, 65, 139N, 139Q, 139S, 203Q, 225Q, 251A, 255Q, 255S, 349A, 355N, 355Q, 355S, 477A, 505A, 509Q, 509S, 633Q, 731A, 735N, 735S

timed reading, 47N, 47Q, 77N, 77Q, 89N, 89Q, 111N, 111Q, 139N, 139Q, 169N, 169Q, 191N, 191Q, 203N, 203Q, 227N, 227Q, 255N, 255Q, 289N, 289Q, 313N, 325Q, 325N, 355N, 355Q, 387N, 387Q, 419N, 419Q, 447N, 447Q, 459N, 459Q, 481N, 481Q, 509N, 509Q, 541N, 541Q, 565N, 565Q, 577N, 577Q, 603N, 603Q, 633N, 633Q, 667N, 667Q, 697N, 697Q, 709N, 709Q, 735N, 735Q, 759N, 759Q

workstations, 16R, 48I, 78I, 90I, 112I, 144R, 170I, 192I, 204I, 228I, 260R, 290I, 314I, 326I, 356I, 392R, 420I, 448I, 460I, 482I, 514R, 542I, 566I, 578I, 604I, 638R, 668I, 698I, 710I, 736I

Focus question, 16, 21, 41, 45, 48, 53, 71, 75, 78, 83, 90, 107, 109, 112, 133, 137, 144, 163, 167, 170, 187, 189, 192, 204, 221, 225, 228, 251, 253, 260, 283, 287, 290, 307, 311, 314, 319, 326, 349, 353, 356, 383, 385, 392, 413, 417, 420, 441, 445, 448, 460, 477, 479, 482, 505, 507, 514, 535, 539, 542, 561, 563, 566, 578, 599, 601, 604, 627, 631, 638, 661, 665, 668, 691, 695, 698, 710, 731, 733, 736, 753, 757

Folk tale, 699

Footnotes and end notes, 144H, 455B, 459Q, 459S

Free verse, 478–479, 205

Functional documents, 388–389. See also Everyday communications.

Gg

Generalizations, making. See Comprehension skills: generalizations, making.

Genre. See also Informational text; Poetry.

features of, 17, 20, 49, 66, 79, 91, 102, 113, 118, 140, 145, 171, 179, 193, 204, 205, 229, 245, 248, 256, 261, 279, 291, 297, 315, 327, 357, 369, 388, 393, 421, 429, 449, 461, 470, 483, 493, 498, 510, 515, 529, 543, 567, 579, 605, 634, 639, 644, 669, 676, 699, 711, 716, 737, 748

reading fiction
fable, 483, 506–507
fairy tale, 639, 642–659
fantasy, 116–131, 546–559
folk tale, 699
historical fiction, 264–281, 396–411, 582–597
legend, 188–189
myth, 754–757
play, 140–142, 486–503
Pourquoi tale, 605
realistic fiction, 17, 20–39, 148–161, 208–219, 330–347, 424–439, 608–625, 672–689
science fiction, 91, 360–381
song lyrics, 252–253
tall tale, 49, 52–69
trickster tale, 498

reading nonfiction. See also Informational text.
almanac entry, 222–225, 227R
autobiography, 171, 245, 414–417
biography, 229, 232–249, 261, 294–305, 510–511, 567, 669, 711
encyclopedia online entries, 562–563
expository nonfiction, 179, 464–475, 529
functional article, 388–389
informational nonfiction, 42–45, 72–75, 82–85, 94–105, 113, 134–137, 145, 164–167, 171, 174–185, 193, 196–198, 222–225, 227R, 229, 245, 256, 261, 291, 294–305, 308–311, 315, 318–320, 350–353, 357, 384–387, 388–389, 414–417,

421, 442–445, 449, 452–455, 461, 464–475, 510–511, 518–533, 536–539, 541P, 541R, 541T, 543, 562–563, 567, 570–573, 579, 628–631, 669, 711

journals, 536–539, 541P, 541R, 541T

letters, 315–317, 536–539, 541P, 541R, 541T

narrative nonfiction, 113, 711, 716

newspaper article, 384–387

online article, 72–75, 562–563

primary sources, 536–539, 541P, 541R, 541T

speech, 449

textbook article, 308–311

reading poetry, 79, 108–109, 205, 284–287, 327, 393, 478–479, 515, 600–601, 737. *See also* **Poetry.**

Glossary, 455B, 459P–459Q, 459S

Grammar, 47I–47J, 77I–77J, 89I–89J, 111I–111J, 139I–139J, 169I–169J, 191I–191J, 203I–203J, 227I–227J, 255I–255J, 289I–289J, 313I–313J, 325I–325J, 355I–355J, 387I–387J, 419I–419J, 447I–447J, 459I–459J, 481I–481J, 509I–509J, 541I–541J, 565I–565J, 577I–577J, 603I–603J, 633I–633J, 667I–667J, 697I–697J, 709I–709J, 735I–735J, 759I–759J

abbreviations, 459J, 472

adjectives

articles, 565B, 565I–565J

comparative, 577I–577J, 603B, 603I–603J, 633B, 633I–633J, 637E

demonstrative, 541B, 541I–541J

proper, 541I–541J

superlative, 577I–577J, 603I–603J, 633I–633J

usage, 565I, 603I–603J, 633J

adverbs

that compare, 667I–667J, 697B, 697I–697J

usage, 667J, 697J

antecedents, 419I–419J

capitalization, 47I–47J, 111J, 227B, 313J, 541J, 577J

first word in sentence, 47I–47J, 577J, 759J, **5.1:** T14

in letters, 111J

in poetry, 313J

proper adjectives, 541J

proper nouns, 169J, 577J

titles, 255J, 577J

conjunctions, 89I–89J, 111I–111J

contractions, 325J, 509B, 509I–509J, 709I–709J

negative, 709I–709J

homophones, 509I–509J, 565B. *See also* **Phonics; Spelling; Vocabulary.**

interjections, 509F

mechanics and usage, 47J, 77J, 89J, 111J, 139J, 169J, 191J, 203J, 227J, 255J, 289J, 313J, 325J, 355J, 387J, 419J, 447J, 459J, 481J, 509J, 541J, 565J, 577J, 603J, 633J, 667J, 697J, 709J, 735J, 759J

negatives, 325J, 709I–709J, 759I–759J

nouns

common, 169I

plural, 191B, 191I–191J, 203I–203J, 227I–227J, 255B, 255I–255J

possessive, 227I–227J, 255I–255J, 259E

proper, 169I, 169J

singular, 191B, 191I–191J

usage, 203J

possessives, 227B, 227I–227J, 255B, 255I–255J, 481I–481J, 509I–509J

prepositions, 735B, 735I–735J, 759I–759J

prepositional phrases, 735I–735J, 759I–759J

pronouns

antecedents, 419D, 419I–419J

possessive, 481B, 481I–481J, 509I–509J

pronoun-antecedent agreement, 419J

pronoun-verb agreement, 459I–459J

subject and object, 447B, 447I–447J

usage of, 419J, 447J, 477J

punctuation

apostrophes, 227I–227J, 255I–255J, 259E, 325J, 509J

colon, 111J, 565J

commas, 77J, 89I–89J, 111I–111J, 143E, 391D, 513E, 541B, 763E

between city and state, 111J

between day and year, 111J

in a series, 77J

in complex sentences, 111I–111J

in compound sentences, 89I–89J, 143E

in dialogue, 355J

to separate introductory words and phrases, prepositional phrases, 391E, 513E, 541B, 735J, 759J

dialogue, 355J

hyphens, 481J

letter, 111J, 191J

plays, 565J

poetry, 313J

quotation marks, 355J

sentence, 47I–47J, 89I–89J, 111I–111J, 169B, 259E, 513E, 759J

titles, 577J

underlining, 255B

sentences, 47B, 47I–47J, 77I–77J, 89I–89J, 111I–111J, 139I–139J

combining, 89I–89J, 111B, 111I–111J, 759B, 759I–759J

combining with adjectives, adverbs, prepositional phrases, 759I–759J

correcting run-ons and sentence fragments, 47I, 89I–89J, 139B, 139I–139J

sentence structure

complex, 111B, 111I–111J

compound, 77I–77J, 111I–111J, 139I–139J

subjects and predicates, 77B, 77I–77J

types, 47I–47J

subject-verb agreement, 289I–289J, 763E

plurals and, 289I–289J

verbs

action, 289B, 289I–289J

contractions with, 325J

helping, 325I–325J

irregular, 387B, 387I–387J

linking, 355B, 355I–355J

main, 325I–325J

past and present participles, 325I–325J

tenses, 313B, 313I–313J, 391E, 763E

usage, 387J

Graphic aids. *See* Graphic organizers; Text features.

Graphic organizers

charts

author's perspective, 454, 583, 585, 586, 588, 596

author's purpose, 425, 427, 428, 437, 487, 490, 498, 502, 581, 581B, 585, 586, 588, 596

cause and effect, 117, 120, 122, 126, 130, 572

character/plot, 21, 23, 27, 30, 32, 36

character/setting, 397, 398, 401, 406, 408

conclusion, 265, 267, 273, 276, 278, 280

description, 465, 466, 468, 473, 474

fact and opinion, 295, 296, 299, 302, 320

generalization, 454

inferences, 149, 150, 152, 156, 160, 233, 236, 238, 240, 245, 247

judgments, 675, 680, 684, 686

K–W–L, 203A, 459A, 481A, 513B, 577A, 638H

plot and setting, 53, 55, 57, 61, 63, 67

problem and solution, 209, 211, 212, 214, 218

sequence chart, 643, 647, 648, 653, 657, 741, 744, 749

summary, 95, 98, 103, 104, 105, 609, 612, 614, 620, 624

theme, 547, 549, 551, 553, 556

diagrams

compare and contrast, 331, 332, 336

draw conclusions, 361, 363, 375, 380

Venn diagram, 84, 329B, 331, 332, 336, 662, 667Q, 667S, 667T, **5.6:** T10. *See also* **Venn diagram.**

maps

problems and solutions, 519, 523, 526, 528, 532

webs

main idea and supporting details, 175, 176, 177, 182, 184, 198

Graphs, 144H, 628–631, 633Q, 633S

Greek roots. *See* Phonics/Spelling; Spelling; Vocabulary.

Guided Practice. *See* Comprehension skills; Fluency: practice; Phonics/Spelling; Spelling; Vocabulary.

Hh

Haiku, 732–733. *See also* **Poetry**

Handwriting. *See* Penmanship.

Headings, 186, 442–443, 447Q, 447S, 638H, 752

Headline, 384–387, 387Q, 387S

Hero, 188–189, 191Q, 191S

Higher level thinking, 41, 45, 71, 75, 85, 107, 109, 133, 137, 163, 167, 187, 189, 199, 221, 225, 251, 253, 283, 287, 307, 311, 321, 349, 353, 383, 385, 413, 417, 441, 445, 455, 477, 479, 505, 507, 535, 539, 561, 563, 573, 599, 601, 627, 631, 661, 665, 691, 695, 705, 731, 733, 753, 757. *See also* **Comprehension skills; Comprehension strategies; Text connections.**

Historical fiction, 264–281, 396–411, 582–597

Home School Connection, 143L, 259L, 391L, 513L, 637L, 763L

Homographs, 78I, 81, 89D, 89F, 89O, 89Q, 448I, 459E, 459G–459H, **5.4:** T5. *See also* **Phonics/Spelling; Spelling; Vocabulary.**

Homophones, 392R, 395, 401, 419D, 419F, 419O, 419Q, 509I–509J, 542I, 565E, 565G–565H, 638Q, 641, 644, 667D, 667F, 667O, 667Q, **5.6:** T5. *See also* **Grammar; Phonics/ Spelling; Spelling; Vocabulary.**

Hyperlinks, 562–563, 565Q, 565S, **5.5:** T11

Ii

Idioms, 144R, 147, 156, 169D, 169F, 169Q, 169S

Illustrations/photographs, using, 65, 66, 121, 157, 181, 234, 269, 368, 377, 426, 445, 522, 548, 557, 618, 638H, 654, 726, 740. *See also* **Picture prompt.**

Illustrators and photographers

Arnold, Jeanne, 440

Baggetta, Marla, 626

Edgerton, Perky, 132

Frasier, Debra, 40

Hawkes, Kevin, 560

Krudop, Walter Lyon, 348

Kunkel, Dennis, 752

Maughan, William, 534

Miner, Julia, 598

Parker, Robert Andrew, 282

Pinkney, Jerry, 250, 412

Rogers, Jacqueline, 306

Sanderson, Ruth, 660

Schanzer, Rosalyn, 70

Spector, Joel, 149

Trang Winson, 690

Van Allsburg, Chris, 382

Imagery, 48, 478–479, 481Q, 481S

Independent Practice for Managing the Class, 16P–16Q, 48G–48H, 78G–78H, 90G–90H,

112G–112H, 144P–144Q, 170G–170H, 192G–192H, 204G–204H, 228G–228H, 260P–260Q, 290G–290H, 314G–314H, 326G–326H, 356G–356H, 392P–392Q, 420G–420H, 448G–448H, 460G–460H, 482G–482H, 514P–514Q, 542G–542H, 566G–566H, 578G–578H, 604G–604H, 638N–638O, 668G–668H, 698G–698H, 710G–710H, 736G–736H

Independent Workstations. *See* Cross-Curricular: workstations.

Index, 455B, 459Q, 459S

Inferences, making. *See* Comprehension skills: inferences making; Comprehension strategies: inferences, making.

Information and Media literacy. *See* Computer literacy; Informational text; Media literacy; Research and Inquiry; Technology.

Informational text
   connect and compare, 45, 75, 109, 137, 167, 189, 225, 253, 287, 311, 353, 385, 417, 445, 479, 507, 539, 563, 601, 631, 665, 695, 733, 757
   content vocabulary, 42–45, 72–75, 134–137, 164–167, 222–225, 308–311, 350–353, 384–385, 414–417, 442–445, 536–539, 562–563, 628–631, 662–665, 692–695
   features of, 42–45, 72–75, 134–137, 164–167, 222–225, 308–311, 350–353, 384–385, 414–417, 442–445, 536–539, 562–563, 628–631, 662–665, 692–695
   types
      almanac entry, 222–225, 227R
      autobiography, 171–173, 245, 414–417
      biography, 232–249, 294–305, 510–511, 567, 669, 711
      encyclopedia article (online), 562–563
      expository nonfiction, 179, 464–475, 529
      functional article, 388–389

      journals, 536–539, 541Q, 541S
      letters, 315–317, 536–539, 541Q, 541S
      narrative nonfiction, 113–115
      newspaper article, 384–387
      nonfiction articles, 42–45, 72–75, 82–85, 94–105, 134–137, 145–147, 164–167, 174–185, 196–198, 222–225, 261–263, 291–293, 318–320, 350–353, 357–359, 384–387, 421–423, 442–445, 452–455, 518–533, 536–539, 543–545, 562–563, 570–573, 579, 628–631, 692–695
      online article, 72–75, 562–563
      primary sources, 536–539, 541Q, 541S
      science articles, 350–353, 384–387, 442–445, 536–539, 562–563, 628–631, 692–695
      social studies articles, 42–45, 72–75, 134–137, 164–167, 222–225, 308–311, 414–417, 536–539
      speech, 449
      textbook article, 308–311

Instructional Navigator Interactive CD-ROM. *See* Technology: CD-ROM; Lesson Plan, suggested weekly.

Internet. *See* Computer literacy; Study skills; Technology.

Intervention Program, 47L, 77L, 89L, 111L, 139L, 169L, 191L, 203L, 227L, 255L, 289L, 313L, 325L, 355L, 387L, 419L, 447L, 459L, 481L, 509L, 541L, 565L, 577L, 603L, 633L, 667L, 697L, 709L, 735L, 759L

Interview, 508–509, 509A–509B, 692–695, 697Q, 697S, **5.6:** T10

Journal writing, 21, 31, 39, 53, 61, 69, 83, 85, 95, 99, 105, 117, 125, 131, 139A–139B, 149, 155, 161, 175, 181,

185, 197, 199, 209, 219, 233, 241, 249, 265, 273, 281, 295, 305, 319, 321, 331, 339, 347, 361, 371, 381, 397, 403, 411, 425, 433, 439, 453, 455, 465, 471, 475, 487, 495, 503, 519, 527, 533, 541F, 547, 555, 559, 571, 573, 583, 591, 597, 609, 617, 625, 643, 659, 673, 689, 703, 705, 715, 729, 741, 751, 759F

Judgments, making. *See* Comprehension skills: judgments making.

Language, variations, 57, 70, 153, 162, 220, 306, 404, 431, 590, 638I, 735F

Latin roots. *See* Phonics/spelling; Spelling; Vocabulary.

Legend, 188–189

Lesson Plans, suggested weekly, 16L–16O, 48C–48F, 78C–78F, 90C–90F, 112C–112F, 144L–144O, 170C–170F, 192C–192F, 204C–204F, 228C–228F, 260L–260O, 290C–290F, 314C–314F, 326C–326F, 356C–356F, 392L–392O, 420C–420F, 448C–448F, 460C–460F, 482C–482F, 514L–514O, 542C–542F, 566C–566F, 578C–578O, 604C–604F, 638L–638O, 668C–668F, 698C–698F, 710C–710F, 736C–736F

Letters, 110-111B, 111J, 191A–191B. *See also* **Grammar; Writing forms.**

Leveled Reader Lessons
   Approaching Level Options, 47P, 77P, 89P, 111P, 139P, 169P, 191P, 203P, 227P, 255P, 289P, 313P, 325P, 355P, 387P, 419P, 447P, 459P, 481P, 509P, 541P, 565P, 577P, 603P, 633P, 667P, 697P, 709P, 735P, 759P
   Beyond Level Options, 47T, 77T, 89T, 111T, 139T, 169T, 191T, 203T, 227T, 255T, 289T, 313T, 325T, 355T, 387T, 419T, 447T, 459T, 481T, 509T, 541T, 565T, 577T, 603T, 633T, 667T, 697T, 709T, 735T, 759T

ELL, 47V, 77V, 89V, 111V, 139V, 169V, 191V, 203V, 227V, 255V, 289V, 313V, 325V, 355V, 387V, 419V, 447V, 459V, 481V, 509V, 541V, 565V, 577V, 603V, 633V, 667V, 697V, 709V, 735V, 759V

On Level Options, 47R, 77R, 89R, 111R, 139R, 169R, 191R, 203R, 227R, 255R, 289R, 313R, 325R, 355R, 387R, 419R, 447R, 459R, 481R, 509R, 541R, 565R, 577R, 603R, 633R, 667R, 697R, 709R, 735R, 759R

Library or media center, using, 85B, 89A, 89Q, 89S, 144H, 144I, 392H, 392I, 514H, 514I, 638H, 638I *See also* **Study skills.**

Links, 72–75, 77Q, 77S, 5.5: T11

Listening. *See also* **Speaking.**

active and attentive listening, 16H, 16I, 17, 47A, 49, 77A, 70, 89A, 91, 111A, 113, 139A, 143E, 143K–143L, 144H, 144I, 145, 169A, 171, 191A, 193, 203A, 205, 227A, 229, 255A, 259E, 259K–259L, 260H, 260I, 261, 289A, 291, 313A, 315, 325A, 327, 355A, 357, 387A, 391E, 391K–391L, 392H, 392I, 393, 419A, 421, 447A, 449, 459A, 461, 481A, 483, 509A, 513E, 513K–513L, 514H, 514I, 515, 541A, 543, 565A, 567, 577A, 579, 603A, 605, 633A, 637E, 637K–637L, 638H, 638I, 639, 667A, 669, 697A, 699, 709A, 711, 735A, 759A, 763E, 763K–763L

comprehension. *See* **Listening comprehension.**

discussion and conversation guidelines, 16I, 144I, 260I, 392I, 514I, 638I

for a purpose, 17, 47A, 49, 77A, 79, 89A, 91, 111A, 113, 139A, 143K–143L, 145, 169A, 171, 191A, 193, 203A, 205, 227A, 229, 255A, 259K–259L, 261, 289A, 291, 313A, 315, 325A, 327, 355A, 357, 387A, 391K–391L, 393, 419A, 421, 447A, 449, 459A, 461, 481A, 483, 509A, 513K–513L, 515, 541A, 543, 565A, 567, 577A, 579, 603A, 605, 633A, 637K–637L, 639, 667A, 669, 697A, 699, 709A, 711, 735A, 737, 759A, 763K–763L

formulate questions, 47A, 77A, 227A, 325A, 419A, 447A, 481A, 509A, 541A, 667A, 759A

Listening comprehension, 17, 49, 79, 91, 113, 145, 171, 193, 205, 229, 261, 291, 315, 327, 357, 393, 421, 449, 461, 483, 515, 543, 567, 579, 605, 639, 669, 699, 711, 737

Listening Library, 21, 53, 83, 95, 117, 149, 175, 197, 209, 233, 265, 295, 319, 331, 361, 397, 425, 453, 465, 487, 519, 547, 571, 583, 609, 643, 673, 703, 715, 741

strategies for, 47A, 77A, 89A, 111A, 139A, 143E, 143K–143L, 169A, 191A, 203A, 227A, 255A, 259E, 259K–259L, 289A, 313A, 325A, 355A, 387A, 391E, 391K–391L, 419A, 447A, 459A, 481A, 509A, 513E, 513K–513L, 541A, 565A, 577A, 603A, 633A, 637E, 637K–637L, 667A, 697A, 709A, 735A, 759A, 763E, 763K–763L

to develop oral language, 16, 17, 48, 49, 78, 79, 90, 91, 112, 113, 144, 144, 145, 170, 171, 192, 193, 204, 205, 228, 229, 260, 261, 290, 291, 314, 315, 326, 327, 356, 357, 392, 393, 420, 421, 448, 449, 460, 461, 482, 483, 514, 515, 542, 543, 566, 567, 578, 579, 604, 605, 638, 639, 668, 669, 698, 699, 710, 711, 736, 737

to interpret verbal and nonverbal messages, 16I, 17, 47A, 49, 77A, 79, 89A, 91, 111A, 113, 139A, 143E, 144I, 145, 169A, 171, 191A, 193, 203A, 205, 227A, 229, 255A, 259E, 260I, 261, 289A, 291, 313A, 315, 325A, 327, 355A, 357, 387A, 391E, 392I, 393, 419A, 421, 447A, 449, 459A, 461, 481A, 483, 509A, 513E, 514I, 515, 541A, 543, 565A, 567, 577A, 579, 603A, 605, 633A, 637E, 638I, 639, 667A, 669, 697A, 699, 709A, 711, 735A, 737, 759A, 763E

to presentations, 16I, 47A, 77A, 89A, 111A, 139A, 143E, 144I, 169A, 191A, 203A, 227A, 255A, 259E, 260I, 261, 289A, 313A, 325A, 355A, 387A, 391E, 392I, 419A, 447A, 459A, 481A, 509A, 513E, 514I, 541A, 565A, 577A, 603A, 633A, 637E, 638I, 667A, 697A, 709A, 735A, 759A, 763E

Literary devices

alliteration, 284–287, 289Q, 289S

assonance, 252–253, 255Q, 255S

consonance, 600–601, 603Q, 603S

dialect, 57, 60, 162, 220

dialogue, 355J, 382, 412

exaggeration, 52, 63, 64, 68

figurative language, 38, 118, 121, 152, 155, 188–189, 191Q, 191S, 238, 336, 338, 340, 343, 366, 391C, 404, 410, 478–479, 481Q, 481S, 481, 506–507, 509Q 509S, 598, 611, 615, 716, 732–733, 735Q, 735S, 754, 755, 756, 759Q, 759S

imagery, 38, 478–479, 481Q, 481S

metaphor, 118, 121, 238, 404, 410, 506–507, 509Q, 509S, 732–733, 735Q, 735S

personification, 188–189, 191Q, 191S, 238, 338, 340, 478–479, 481Q, 481S, 615, 716

simile, 152, 155, 238, 250, 343, 404, 598, 615, 732–733, 755, 735Q, 735S

flashback, 27

foreshadowing, 25

hero, 188–189, 191Q, 191S

humor, 40, 373

meter, 284–287, 289Q, 289S

mood, 534, 616, 678

moral, 506–507, 509Q, 509S

onomatopoeia, 478–479, 481Q, 481S

repetition, 252–253, 255PQ, 255S, 279, 504

rhyme/rhyme scheme, 108–109, 111Q, 111S

rhythm, 108–109, 111Q, 111S

sensory words and images, 348, 560

sounds of language, 284–287, 289Q, 289S, 349A, 478–479, 481Q, 481S suspense, 366, 371

symbolism, 600–601, 603Q, 603S, 754–757, 759Q 759S

tone, 64, 101, 102, 678

word choice, 213, 216, 303, 306

Literary response. *See also* **Text connections.**

personal, 39, 69, 105, 131, 161, 185, 199, 219, 249, 281, 305, 321, 347, 381, 411, 439, 455, 475, 503, 533, 559, 573, 597, 625, 659, 689, 705, 729, 751

reading and responding, 47P, 47R, 47T: 47P, 47R, 47T, 77P, 77R, 77T, 89P, 89R, 89T, 111P, 111R, 111T, 139P, 139R, 139T, 169P, 169R, 169T, 191P, 191R, 191T, 203P, 203R, 203T, 227P, 227R, 227T, 255P, 255R, 255T, 289P, 289R, 289T, 313P, 313R, 313T, 325P, 325R, 325T, 355P, 355R, 355T, 387P, 387R, 387T, 419P, 419R, 419T, 447P, 447R, 447T, 459P, 459R, 459T, 481P, 481R, 481T, 509P, 509R, 509T, 541P, 541R, 541T, 565P, 565R, 565T, 577P, 577R, 577T, 603P, 603R, 603T, 633P, 633R, 633T, 667P, 667R, 667T, 697P, 697R, 697T, 709P, 709R, 709T, 735P, 735R, 735T, 759P, 759R, 759T

respond to read alouds, 17, 49, 79, 91, 113, 145, 171, 193, 205, 229, 261, 291, 315, 327, 357, 393, 421, 449, 461, 483, 515, 543, 567, 579, 605, 639, 669, 699, 711, 737

response journal, 16R, 39, 69, 85, 105, 131, 161, 185, 199, 219, 249, 281, 305, 321, 347, 381, 411, 439, 455, 475, 503, 533, 559, 573, 597, 625, 659, 689, 705, 729, 751

Literature selections, main

"Beyond the Horizon," 318–321

Black Cowboy Wild Horses (Lester), 232–249

Carlos and the Skunk (Stevens), 424–439

Catch of the Day! (Medearis), 486–503

Davy Crockett Saves the World (Schanzer), 52–69

A Dream Comes True, 702–705

"Forests of the World," 82–85

"Getting Out the Vote," 452–455

Goin' Someplace Special (McKissack) 396–411

The Golden Mare, the Firebird, and the Magic Ring (Sanderson), 642–659

The Gri Gri Tree (Joseph), 608–625

Hidden Worlds (Kramer), 740–751

"A Historic Journey," 570–573

Hurricanes (Simon), 464–475

"Maya Lin: Architect of Memory," 196–199

Miss Alaineus (Frasier), 20–39

My Great–Grandmother's Gourd (Kessler), 330–347

"The Night of San Juan" from *Salsa Stories (Delacre),* 208–219

Pipiolo and the Roof Dogs (Meunier), 116–131

Rattlers! (Lambeth), 174–185

Shiloh (Naylor), 148–161

Skunk Scout (Yep), 672–689

Sleds on Boston Common (Borden), 264–281

Spirit of Endurance (Armstrong), 518–533

Ultimate Field Trip 5 (Goodman), 94–105

The Unbreakable Code (Hunter), 582–597

Up in the Air: The Story of Balloon Flight (Lauber), 714–729

Weslandia (Fleischman) 546–559

When Esther Morris Headed West (Wooldridge), 294–305

Zathura (Van Allsburg), 360–381

Literature selections, paired

"Animal Self–Defense" (Wainwright), 442–445

"Blue Potatoes and Square Watermelons" (Naid), 562–563

"The Bottom of the World" (Williams), 536–539

"Doggone Work" (Marquez), 134–137

"The Fox and the Crow" (Kirimoto), 506–507

"Home on the Range" (Lomax), 252–253

"Hot–Air Balloon Haiku" (Bristol), 732–733

"How Poison Came Into the World" (Sirls), 188–189

"I'm Building a Rocket" (Nesbit), 108–109

"Islands of the Caribbean" (Smith), 222–225

"The Largest Creature on Earth" (Robertson) 628–631

"Love at First Sight" (Yin), 164–167

"More than Sand" (Gupta), 350–353

"Mountain of Fire: A Native American Myth" (Armstrong), 754–757

"The National Spelling Bee" (Lee), 42–45

"Our National Parks" (Sumanga), 692–695

"Navajo Code Talkers: Five Cinquains" (Willie), 600–601

"Paul Revere's Ride" (Longfellow), 284–287

"Robots Today and Tomorrow" (Brackman), 384–385

"Suffrage for Women" (Chan), 308–311

"Suspense" (Mora), 478–479

"A Tale Told Around the World" (Gray), 662–665

"The Tales are Getting Taller" (Seulen), 72–75

"Through My Eyes" (Bridges), 414–417

Literature selections, vocabulary, 18–19, 50–51, 80–81, 92–93, 114–115, 146–147, 172–173, 194–195, 206–207, 230–231, 262–263, 292–293, 316–317, 328–329, 358–359, 394–395, 422–423, 450–451, 462–463, 484–485, 516–517, 544–545, 568–569, 580–581, 606–607, 640–641, 670–671, 700–701, 712–713, 738–739

Lyric, song, 252–253

Mm

Magazine articles, 420J, 460J, 480–481B

Main ideas. *See* **Comprehension skills: main ideas and details.**

Mechanics and usage. *See* **Grammar: mechanics and usage.**

Media Literacy, 16I, 38, 59, 129,

144H, 157, 168–169, 260I, 378, 392I, 469, 514I, 553, 727

advertising, 38, 59, 168–169, 260I, 553, 727

analyzing and evaluating media and media forms, 16I, 38, 59, 129, 144H, 157, 260I, 378, 392I, 469, 514I, 553

creating multimedia presentations, 259K, 695

impact of media on daily life, 469

persuasive techniques in media, 59, 157, 260I, 705

target audiences for media, 59, 260I, 553

Metacognitive strategies. *See* **Monitor and Clarify.**

Metaphor, 118, 121, 238, 404, 410, 506–507, 509Q, 509S, 732–733, 735Q, 735S. *See* **Literary devices; Poetry.**

Meter, 284, 285, 286, 289Q, 289S. *See also* **Poetry.**

Modeling. *See* **Comprehension; Fluency; Phonics/spelling; Spelling; Vocabulary.**

Monitor and Clarify. *See also* **Predictions, making; Ways to Confirm Meaning.**

generate questions, 21, 47O, 47R, 53, 77O, 77R, 83, 89O, 89R, 93A–93B, 94–105, 111O, 111R, 115A–115B, 116–131, 139O, 139R, 149, 169O, 169R, 175, 191O, 191R, 191T, 197, 203O, 203R, 209, 227O, 227R, 233, 255O, 255R, 265, 289O, 289R, 295, 313O, 313R, 319, 325O, 325R, 331, 355O, 355R, 361, 387O, 387R, 397, 419O, 419R, 425, 447O, 447R, 453, 459O, 459R, 465, 481O, 481R, 487, 509O, 509R, 517A–517B, 518–533, 541O, 541R, 547, 565O, 565R, 571, 577O, 577R, 581A–581B, 582–597, 603O, 603R, 607A–607B, 608–625, 633O, 633R, 643, 667O, 667R, 673, 697O, 697R, 703, 709O, 709R, 715, 729, 735O, 735R, 741, 759O, 759R

monitor comprehension, 28, 33, 58, 98, 124, 129, 147A–147B, 148–161, 169O, 169R, 231A–231B, 232–249, 255O, 255R, 267, 268, 301, 400, 433, 470, 491, 525, 595, 671A–671B, 672–689, 697O, 697R, 701A–701B, 702–705, 709O, 709R, 713A–713B, 714–729, 735O, 735R

paraphrase, 98, 321B, 651, 756

read ahead, 28, 154, 213, 433, 720

reading rate, 21, 53, 83, 95, 117, 149, 175, 177, 197, 209, 233, 265, 295, 319, 331, 361, 397, 409, 425, 453, 465, 487, 519, 547, 571, 583, 609, 643, 673, 703, 715, 741

reread, 124, 129, 301, 525, 679

seek help, 267, 268, 470, 749

self-correct, 58, 147A–147B, 148, 169M, 255S, 331, 344, 361, 425, 491, 595, 709S, 713A

visualize, 234, 235, 376, 378, 553

Moral, 506–507, 509PQ, 509S

Multiple-meaning words, 23, 460I, 463, 468, 481D, 481F, 481O, 668I, 671, 697D, 697F, 697O, 697Q, **5.4:** T8; **5.6:** T6

Myth, 754–757

Nn

Narrator, 38, 132, 690

Negatives. *See* **Grammar: negatives.**

Newspaper article, 384–387

Nonfiction. *See* **Genre; Informational text.**

Note taking, 16H, 68, 89A, 144H, 203A, 260H, 321B, 325A, 325P, 325T, 392H, 459A, 472, 513B, 513D, 514H, 577A, 637K, 709A

Nouns. *See* **Grammar: nouns.**

Oo

On Level Options, 47Q–47R, 77Q–77R, 89Q–89R, 111Q–111R, 139Q–139R, 169Q–169R, 191Q–191R, 203Q–203R, 227Q–227R, 255Q–255R, 289Q–289R, 313Q–313R, 325Q–325R, 355Q–355R, 387Q–387R, 419Q–419R, 447Q–447R, 459Q–459R, 481Q–481R, 509Q–509R, 541Q–541R, 565Q–565R, 577Q–577R, 603Q–603R, 633Q–633R, 667Q–667R, 697Q–697R, 709Q–709R, 735Q–735R, 759Q–759R

comprehension skill, 47R, 77R, 89R, 111R, 139R, 169R, 191R, 203R, 227R, 255R, 289R, 313R, 325R, 355R, 387R, 419R, 447R, 459R, 481R, 509R, 541R, 565R, 577R, 603R, 633R, 667R, 697R, 709R, 735R, 759R

fluency, 47Q, 77Q, 89Q, 111Q, 139Q, 169Q, 191Q, 203Q, 227Q, 255Q, 289Q, 313Q, 325Q, 355Q, 387Q, 419Q, 447Q, 459Q, 481Q, 509Q, 541Q, 565Q, 577Q, 603Q, 633Q, 667Q, 697Q, 709Q, 735Q, 759Q

vocabulary, 47Q, 47R, 77Q, 77R, 89Q, 89R, 111Q, 111R, 139Q, 139R, 169Q, 169R, 191Q, 191R, 203Q, 203R, 227Q, 227R, 255Q, 255R, 289Q, 289R, 313Q, 313R, 325Q, 325R, 355Q, 355R, 387Q, 387R, 419Q, 419R, 447Q, 447R, 459Q, 459R, 481Q, 481R, 509Q, 509R, 541Q, 541R, 565Q, 565R, 577Q, 577R, 603Q, 603R, 633Q, 633R, 667Q, 667R, 697Q, 697R, 709Q, 709R, 735Q, 735R, 759Q, 759R

Online article, 72–75, 562–563

Onomatopoeia, 478–479, 481Q, 481S

Oral Language, 16–17, 47V, 48–49, 77V, 78–79, 89V, 90–91, 111V, 112–113, 139V, 144–145, 169V, 170–171, 191V, 192–193, 203V, 204–205, 227V, 228–229, 255V, 260–261, 289V, 290–291, 313V, 314–315, 325V, 326–327,

355V, 356–357, 387V, 392–393, 419V, 420–421, 447V, 448–449, 459V, 460–461, 481V, 482–483, 509V, 514–515, 541V, 542–543, 565V, 566–567, 577V, 578–579, 603V, 604–605, 633V, 638–639, 667V, 668–669, 697V, 698–699, 709V, 710–711, 735V, 736–737, 759V

Outlining, 89B, 203B, 321B, 325B, 325T, 459B, 513B, 513C, 577B, 709B

Pp

Paraphrasing. *See* Monitor and Clarify; Research and Inquiry.

Parts of a book, 455B, 459Q, 459S, **5.4:** T11. *See* Study skills; Text features.

Penmanship, 47B, 77B, 89B, 111B, 139B, 143E, 169B, 191B, 203B, 227B, 255B, 259E, 289B, 313B, 325B, 355B, 387B, 391E, 419B, 447B, 459B, 481B, 509B, 513E, 541B, 565B, 577B, 603B, 633B, 637E, 667B, 697B, 709B, 735B, 759B, 763E

Personification, 238, 338, 340, 478–479, 481Q, 481S, 716

Persuasion, techniques of. *See* Comprehension skills: persuasion, techniques of; Media literacy; Writing: persuasive.

Phonics/Spelling, 16R, 47E, 47G–47H, 47M, 48I, 77E, 77G-77H, 77M, 78I, 89E, 89G-89H, 89M, 90I, 111E, 111G-111H, 111M, 112I, 139E, 139G-139H, 139M, 144R, 169E, 169G-169H, 169M, 170I, 191E, 191G-191H, 191M, 192I, 203E, 203G-203H, 203M, 204I, 227E, 227G-227H, 227M, 228I, 255E, 255G-255H, 255M, 260I, 289E, 289G-289H, 289M, 313E, 313G-313H, 313M, 314I, 325E, 325G-325H, 325M, 326I, 355E, 355G-355H, 355M, 356I, 387E, 387G-387H, 387M, 419E, 419G-419H, 419M, 420I, 447E, 447G-447H, 447M, 448I, 459E, 459G-459H, 459M, 460I, 481E, 481G-481H, 481M, 482I, 509E, 509G-509H, 509M, 514R, 541E, 541G-541H, 541M, 542I, 565E,

565G-565H, 565M, 566I, 577E, 577G-577H, 577M, 578I, 603E, 603G-603H, 603M, 604I, 633E, 633G-633H, 633M, 638I, 667E, 667G-667H, 667M, 668I, 697E, 697G-697H, 697M, 709E, 709G-709H, 709M, 710I, 735E, 735G-735H, 735M, 736I, 759E, 759G-759H, 759M. *See also* Spelling.

decodable passages, 47E, 47M, 77E, 77M, 89E, 89M, 111E, 11M, 139E, 139M, 169E, 169M, 191E, 191M, 203E, 203M, 227E, 227M, 255E, 255M, 289E, 289M, 313E, 313M, 325E, 325M, 355E, 355M, 387E, 387M, 419E, 419M, 447E, 447M, 459E, 459M, 481E, 481M, 509E, 509M, 541E, 541M, 565E, 565M, 577E, 577M, 603E, 633M, 667E, 697M, 709E, 709M, 735E, 759M

decode multisyllabic words, 47E, 47M 77E, 77M, 89E, 89M, 111E, 11M, 139E, 139M, 169E, 169M, 191E, 191M, 203E, 203M, 227E, 227M, 255E, 255M, 289E, 289M, 313E, 313M, 325E, 325M, 355E, 355M, 387E, 387M, 419E, 419M, 447E, 447M, 459E, 459M, 481E, 481M, 509E, 509M, 541E, 541M, 565E, 565M, 577E, 577M, 603E, 633M, 667E, 697M, 709E, 709M, 735E, 759M

explain/model/practice/apply, 47E, 77E, 89E, 111E, 139E, 169E, 191E, 203E, 227E, 255E, 289E, 313E, 325E, 355E, 387E, 419E, 447E, 459E, 481E, 509E, 541E, 565E, 577E, 603E, 633E, 667E, 697E, 709E, 735E, 759E

words from mythology, 709E, 709G-709H, 709M

words with *able, ible,* 736I, 759E, 759G-759H, 759M

words with added *ion,* 604I, 633E, 633G-633H, 633M

words with *ance, ence,* 482I, 509E, 509G-509H, 509M

words with /är/, /âr/, /ôr/, 90I, 111E, 111G-111H, 111M

words with /chər/ and /zhər/, 460I, 481E, 481G-481H, 481M

words with compound words, 144R, 169E, 169G-169H, 169M

words with /ər/, 356I, 387E, 387G-387H, 387M

words with final /əl/ən, 392R, 419E, 419G-419H, 419M

words with Greek roots, 667E, 667G-667H, 667M

words with homographs, 459E, 459G-459H, 459M

words with homophones, 565E, 565G-565H, 565M

words with inflected endings, 192I, 203E, 203G-203H, 203M

words with Latin roots, 668I, 697E, 697G-697H, 697M

words with long vowels, 48I, 77E, 77G-77H, 77M

words with number prefixes *uni-, bi-, tri-, cen-t,* 710I, 735E, 735G-735H, 735M

words with /ô/, /ou/, /oi/, 204I, 227E, 227G-227H, 227M

words with plurals, 191E, 191G-191H, 191M

words with prefixes *dis-, in-, mis–, pre-,* 566I, 577E, 577G-577H, 577M

words with r-controlled vowels, 139E, 139G-139H, 139M

words with schwa, 419E, 419G-419H, 419M, 481E, 481G-481H, 481M

words with short vowels, 16R, 47E, 47G–47H, 47M

words with soft *g,* 514R, 541E, 541G-541H, 541M

words with suffixes *-less and -ness,* 578I, 603E, 603G-603H, 603M

words with syllables

accented syllables,326I, 447E, 447G-447H, 447M, 459E, 459G-459H, 459M

unaccented syllables, 387E, 387G-387H, 387M

words with /ü/ /ū/ /ù/, 78I, 89E, 89G-89H, 89M

Key 5.1 = Grade 5, Book 1

words with v/cv and vc/v pattern, 260R, 289E, 289G-289H, 289M

words with v/v, 290I, 313E, 313G-313H, 313M

words with vcccv, 314I, 325E, 325G-325H, 325M

words with vccv, 255E, 255G-255H, 255M

words with vowel patterns in accented syllables, 355E, 355G-355H, 355M

Phonics/structural analysis. *See* Phonics/spelling; Spelling.

Picture prompt, 17, 49, 79, 91, 113, 145, 171, 193, 205, 229, 261, 291, 315, 327, 357, 393, 421, 449, 461, 483, 515, 543, 567, 579, 605, 639, 669, 699, 711, 737

Plays. *See* Genre: play; Writing forms and modes; Play.

Plot. *See* Comprehension skills: plot.

Plurals. *See* Grammar: plurals; Vocabulary: plurals.

Poetry

features of, 108, 284, 478, 600, 732

forms of

cinquain, 600–601

free verse, 478–479, 205

haiku, 732–733

lyric/song, 252–253

narrative, 284–287

simple, 108–109, 737

literary elements in

alliteration, 284–287, 289Q, 289S

assonance, 252–253, 255Q, 255S

consonance, 600–601, 603Q, 603S

figurative language in, 478, 479, 732–733

imagery, 38, 478, 479

metaphor, 732–733, 735Q, 735S

meter, 284–287

onomatopoeia, 478–479, 481Q 481S

personification, 478–479

punctuation in, 313J

repetition, 252–253, 255Q, 255S

rhyme/rhyme schemes, 79, 108–109, 515

rhythm, 108–109, 205, 515

simile, 732–733, 735Q, 735S

symbolism, 600–601, 603Q, 603S

structures of

lines, 732–733

stanzas, 108–109, 312–313, 313A–313B

writing, 255F, 312–313B, 459F, 632–633B

Point of view

first, 38, 46, 76, 106, 110, 132, 288, 690

narrator, 132, 690

omniscient, 132, 690

third, 106, 132, 288, 690

Possessives, 227I–227J, 255I–255J, 481I–481J, 509I–509J. *See also* Grammar: possessives.

Predictions and purposes, return to, 39, 47, 69, 77, 85, 89, 111, 131, 139, 161, 169, 185, 191, 199, 203, 219, 227, 249, 255, 281, 289, 305, 313, 325, 347, 355, 381, 387, 411, 419, 439, 447, 455, 459, 475, 481, 503, 509, 533, 541, 559, 565, 573, 577, 597, 603, 625, 633, 659, 667, 689, 697, 705, 709, 729, 735, 751, 759

Predictions, making, 21, 24, 29, 35, 47P, 47R, 47T, 47V, 53, 57, 62, 77P, 77R, 77T, 77V, 83, 89P, 89R, 89T, 89V, 95, 97, 111P, 111R, 111T, 111V, 117, 121, 125, 139P, 139R, 139T, 139V, 149, 169P, 169R, 169T, 175, 191P, 191R, 191T, 191V, 197, 203P, 203R, 203T, 203V, 209, 213, 227P, 227R, 227T, 227V, 233, 243, 248, 255P, 255R, 255T, 255V, 265, 289P, 289R, 289T, 289V, 295, 313P, 313R, 313T, 313V, 319, 325P, 325R, 325T, 325V, 331, 340, 343, 355P, 355R, 355T, 355V, 361, 367, 375, 387P, 387R, 387T, 387V, 397, 399, 419P, 419R, 419T, 419V, 425, 429, 447P, 447R, 447T, 447V, 453, 459P, 459R, 459T, 459V, 465, 481P, 481R, 481T, 481V, 487, 492, 495, 499, 500, 509P, 509R, 509T, 509V, 519, 541P, 541R, 541T, 541V, 547, 557, 565P, 565R, 565T, 565V, 571, 577P, 577R, 577T, 577V, 583, 603P, 603R, 603T, 603V, 609, 633P, 633R, 633T, 633V, 643, 645, 667P, 667R, 667T, 667V, 673, 697P, 697R, 697T, 697V, 703, 709P, 709R, 709T, 709V, 715, 735P, 735R, 735T, 735V, 741, 748, 759P, 759R, 759T, 759V

Prefixes. *See* Phonics/spelling; Spelling; Vocabulary: prefixes.

Prepositions and prepositional phrases, 735I–735J, 759I–759J. *See also* Grammar.

Prereading strategies. *See* Predictions, making; Previewing literature; Setting purposes for reading.

Previewing literature, 21, 24, 29, 35, 47P, 47R, 47T, 47V, 53, 57, 62, 77P, 77R, 77T, 77V, 83, 89P, 89R, 89T, 89V, 95, 97, 111P, 111R, 111T, 111V, 117, 121, 125, 139P, 139R, 139T, 139V, 149, 169P, 169R, 169T, 175, 191P, 191R, 191T, 191V, 197, 203P, 203R, 203T, 203V, 209, 213, 227P, 227R, 227T, 227V, 233, 243, 248, 255P, 255R, 255T, 255V, 265, 289P, 289R, 289T, 289V, 295, 313P, 313R, 313T, 313V, 319, 325P, 325R, 325T, 325V, 331, 340, 343, 355P, 355R, 355T, 355V, 361, 367, 375, 387P, 387R, 387T, 387V, 397, 399, 419P, 419R, 419T, 419V, 425, 429, 447P, 447R, 447T, 447V, 453, 459P, 459R, 459T, 459V, 465, 481P, 481R, 481T, 481V, 487, 492, 495, 499, 500, 509P, 509R, 509T, 509V, 519, 541P, 541R, 541T, 541V, 547, 557, 565P, 565R, 565T, 565V, 571, 577P, 577R, 577T, 577V, 583, 603P, 603R, 603T, 603V, 609, 633P, 633R, 633T, 633V, 643, 645, 667P, 667R, 667T, 667V, 673, 697P, 697R, 697T, 697V, 703, 709P, 709R, 709T, 709V, 715, 735P, 735R, 735T, 735V, 741, 748, 759P, 759R, 759T, 759V

Primary sources, 143C, 536–539, 541Q, 541S

Problem and solution. *See* Comprehension skills: problem and solution.

Pronouns, 419I–419J, 447I–447J, 459I–459J, 481I–481J, 509I–509J. *See also* Grammar: pronouns.

Pronunciation. *See* Fluency: pronunciation.

Pronunciation key, 290I, 293, 302, 313D, 313F, 313O

Punctuation. *See* Fluency: punctuation; Grammar: punctuation.

Purposes, setting for reading. *See* Setting purposes for reading.

Qq

Questions. *See* Listening: formulate questions; Monitor and Clarify: generate questions; Research and Inquiry: generating questions for.

Quotations, 321B, 355J

Rr

Read Alouds, 17, 49, 79, 91, 113, 145, 171, 193, 205, 229, 261, 291, 315, 327, 357, 393, 421, 449, 461, 483, 515, 543, 567, 579, 605, 639, 669, 699, 711, 737

Readers' Theater, 460I, 501, 604I

Reading and responding. *See* Literary Response: reading and responding.

Reading independently, 16R, 21, 47M, 47N, 47Q, 47S, 48I, 53, 77M, 77N, 77Q, 77S, 78I, 83, 89M, 89N, 89Q, 89S, 91, 95, 111M, 111N, 111Q, 111S, 112I, 117, 139M, 139N, 139Q, 139S, 144R, 149, 169M, 169N, 169Q,

169S, 170I, 175, 191M, 191N, 191Q, 191S, 192I, 197, 203M, 203N, 203Q, 203S, 204I, 209, 227M, 228N, 227Q, 227S, 228I, 233, 255M, 255Q, 255S, 260R, 265, 289M, 289N, 289Q, 289S, 290I, 295, 313M, 313N, 313Q, 313S, 314I, 319, 325M, 325Q, 325S, 326I, 331, 355M, 355N, 355Q, 355S, 356I, 361, 387M, 387N, 387Q, 387S, 392R, 397, 419M, 419N, 419Q, 419S, 420I, 425, 447M, 447N, 447Q, 447S, 448I, 453, 459M, 459N, 459Q, 459S, 460I, 465, 481M, 481N, 481Q, 481S, 482I, 487, 509M, 509N, 509Q, 509S, 514R, 519, 541M, 541N, 541Q, 541S, 542I, 547, 565M, 565N, 565Q, 565S, 566I, 571, 577M, 577N, 577Q, 577S, 578I, 583, 603M, 603N, 603Q, 603S, 604I, 609, 633M, 633N, 633Q, 633S, 638R, 643, 667M, 667N, 667Q, 667S, 668I, 673, 697M, 697N, 697Q, 697S, 698I, 703, 709M, 709Q, 709S, 710I, 715, 735M, 735N, 735Q, 735S, 736I, 741, 759M, 759N, 759Q, 759S

Reading rate. *See* Monitor and Clarify: reading rate.

Reading together, 21, 53, 83, 95, 117, 149, 175, 197, 209, 233, 265, 295, 319, 331, 361, 397, 425, 453, 465, 487, 519, 547, 571, 583, 609, 643, 673, 703, 715, 741

Realistic fiction. *See* Genre: reading fiction.

Reference sources and resources, using. *See* Research and Inquiry; Study Skills; Vocabulary.

Repetition, 252, 253, 279, 504

Reread for comprehension, 19A–19B, 51A–51B, 81A–81B, 93A–93B, 115A–115B, 147A–147B, 173A–173B, 195A–195B, 207A–207B, 231A–231B, 263A–263B, 293A–293B, 317A–317B, 329A–329B, 359A–359B, 395A–395B, 423A–423B, 451A–451B, 463A–463B, 485A–485B, 517A–517B, 545A–545B, 569A–569B, 581A–581B, 607A–607B, 641A–641B, 671A–671B, 701A–701B, 713A–713B, 739A–739B

Research and Inquiry, 16H, 16I, 16S, 45, 48J, 62, 66, 68, 78J,

89A–89B, 90J, 137, 144H, 144I, 144S, 167, 170J, 192J, 203A–203B, 204J, 225, 228J, 260H, 260I, 290J, 311, 314J, 325A–325B, 326J, 353, 356J, 392H, 392I, 392S, 417, 420J, 445, 448J, 459A–459B, 460J, 473, 514H, 514I, 514S, 539, 542J, 566J, 573B, 577A–577B, 578J, 595, 631, 638H, 638I, 695, 709A–709B. *See also* Cultural Perspectives; Cross-Curricular connections.

 bibliographies, 513C, 514H

 citing and evaluating sources, 16H, 89B, 203B, 321B, 325B, 459B, 513E, 577B, 709B

 drawing conclusions, 144H

 finding information, 16H, 16I, 16S, 45, 48J, 62, 66, 68, 78J, 89A, 90J, 137, 144H, 144I, 144S, 167, 170J, 192J, 203A, 203B, 204J, 225, 228J, 260H, 260I, 290J, 311, 314J, 325A, 325B, 326J, 353, 356J, 392H, 392I, 392S, 417, 420J, 445, 448J, 459A, 459B, 460J, 473, 514H, 514I, 514S, 539, 542J, 566J, 573B, 577A, 577B, 578J, 595, 631, 638H, 638I, 695, 709A, 709B

 formulating questions, 16H, 16I, 45, 89A, 137, 144H, 144I, 203A, 225, 260H, 260I, 325A, 392H, 392I, 417, 445, 459A, 514H, 514I, 539, 573B, 577A, 638H, 638I, 709A

 identifying resources, 16H, 89A, 144H, 203A, 260H, 325A, 392H, 459A, 514H, 577A, 638H, 709A

 narrowing focus of research, 16H, 16I, 45, 89A, 137, 144H, 144I, 203A, 225, 260H, 260I, 325A, 392H, 392I, 417, 445, 459A, 514H, 514I, 539, 573B, 577A, 638H, 638I, 709A

 note taking and outlining, 89A, 89B, 203A, 203B, 325A, 325B, 459A, 459B, 577A< 577B, 709A, 709B

 organizing information, 16H, 89A, 89B, 144H, 203A, 203B, 260H, 321A, 321B, 325A, 325B, 325P, 392H, 417, 459A, 459B, 514H, 539, 577A, 577B, 638H, 709A, 709B

 paraphrasing, 89B, 203B, 577B

Key 5.1 = Grade 5, Book 1

plagiarism, 514H

quoting material, 321B

self-selected theme projects, 16H, 143K–143L, 144H, 259K–259L, 260H, 391K–391L, 392H, 513K–513L, 514H, 637K–637L, 638H, 763K–763L

skimming and scanning, 89B, 321B, 325A, 325Q, 325S, 459A, 577B, 638H

strategies, 16H, 144H, 260H, 392H, 514H, 638H

using key words and questions, 16H, 75, 144H, 260H, 321A, 392H, 514H, 573A, 638H

using print and electronic primary and secondary resources, 16H, 16I, 45, 62, 66, 68, 85B, 89A, 137, 144H, 144I, 167, 199A, 203A, 225, 260H, 260I, 311, 321A, 325A, 353, 392H, 392I, 417, 445, 455B, 459A, 514H, 514I, 539, 573A, 573B, 577A, 595, 631, 638H, 638I, 695, 705B, 709A

Research process. See Research and Inquiry, Theme Project.

Research: Why It Matters, 41A, 77T, 81, 128, 139O, 147, 178, 203D, 255N, 263, 313N, 325D, 419O, 451, 481T, 491, 535B, 541N, 667E, 682, 701B

Response to Literature. See Literary response.

Rhyme and rhyme schemes, 79, 108–109, 111Q, 111S

Rhythm, 108–109, 111Q, 111

Root words. See Phonics/spelling; Spelling; Vocabulary: root words.

Rubrics. See Scoring rubrics.

Ss

Science fiction, 91, 356J, 360–381

Scoring rubrics
creating, 143F, 259F, 391F, 513F, 637F, 763F

theme projects, 143L, 259L, 391L, 513L, 637L, 763L

writing, 47A, 77A, 88, 89A, 111A, 139A, 143G, 143H, 169A, 191A, 202, 203A, 227A, 255A, 259G, 259H, 289A, 313A, 324, 325A, 355A, 387A, 391G, 391H, 419A, 447A, 458, 459A, 481A, 509A, 513G, 513H, 541A, 565A, 576, 577A, 603A, 633A, 637G, 637H, 667A, 697A, 708, 709A, 735A, 759A, 763G, 763H

Self-correction strategies. See Monitor and Clarify.

Self-monitoring strategies. See Monitor and Clarify.

Self-selected reading, 16R, 47T, 48I, 77T, 78I, 89T, 90I, 111T, 112I, 139T, 144R, 169T, 170I, 191T, 192I, 203T, 204I, 227T, 228I, 255T, 259B, 260R, 289T, 290I, 313T, 314I, 325T, 326I, 355T, 356I, 387T, 391B, 392R, 419T, 420I, 447T, 448I, 459T, 460I, 481T, 482I, 509T, 514R, 541T, 542I, 565T, 566I, 577T, 578I, 603T, 604I, 633T, 638R, 667T, 668I, 697T, 698I, 709T, 710I, 735T, 736I, 759T

Sentences. See Grammar: sentences; Writing traits: sentences.

Sequence. See Comprehension skills: sequence of events; Writing traits: organization.

Setting. See Comprehension skills: setting.

Setting purposes for reading, 21, 47P, 47R, 47T, 47V, 53, 77P, 77R, 77T, 77V, 83, 89P, 89R, 89T, 89V, 95, 111P, 111R, 111T, 111V, 117, 139P, 139R, 139T, 139V, 149, 169P, 169R, 169T, 175, 191P, 191R, 191T, 191V, 197, 203P, 203R, 203T, 203V, 209, 227P, 227R, 227T, 227V, 233, 255P, 255R, 255T, 255V, 265, 289P, 289R, 289T, 289V, 295, 313P, 313R, 313T, 313V, 319, 325P, 325R, 325T, 325V, 331, 355P, 355R, 355T, 355V, 361, 387P, 387R, 387T, 387V, 397, 419P, 419R, 419T, 419V, 425, 447P, 447R, 447T, 447V, 453, 459P, 459R, 459T, 459V, 465, 481P, 481R, 481T, 481V,

487, 509P, 509R, 509T, 509V, 519, 541P, 541R, 541T, 541V, 547, 565P, 565R, 565T, 565V, 571, 577P, 577R, 577T, 577V, 583, 603P, 603R, 603T, 603V, 609, 633P, 633R, 633T, 633V, 643, 667P, 667R, 667T, 667V, 673, 697P, 697R, 697T, 697V, 703, 709P, 709R, 709T, 709V, 715, 735P, 735R, 735T, 735V, 741, 759P, 759R, 759T, 759V

Similes. See Literary devices: figurative language; Poetry: figurative language.

Skimming and scanning, 321B, 325Q, 325S. See also Study Skills.

Small Group Options, 47M–47V, 77M–77V, 89M–89V, 111M–111V, 139M–139V, 169M–169V, 191M–191V, 203M–203V, 227M–227V, 255M–255V, 289M–289V, 313M–313V, 325M–325V, 355M–355V, 387M–387V, 419M–419V, 447M–447V, 459M–459V, 481M–481V, 509M–509V, 541M–541V, 565M–565V, 577M–577V, 603M–603V, 633M–633V, 667M–667V, 697M–697V, 709M–709V, 735M–735V, 759M–759V. See also Approaching Level Options; Beyond Level Options; Differentiated Instruction; English Language Learners; Leveled Reader Lessons; On Level Options.

Speaking. See also Listening.

checklists and rubrics, 143K–143L, 259K–259L, 391K–391L, 513K–513L, 637K–637L, 763K–763L

discussions,16, 17, 19, 47P, 47R, 47T, 48, 49, 51, 77P, 77R, 77T, 78, 79, 81, 89P, 89R, 89T, 90, 91, 93, 111P, 111R, 111T, 112, 113, 115, 139P, 139R, 139T, 144, 145, 147, 169P, 169R, 169T, 170, 171, 173, 191P, 191R, 191T, 192, 193, 195, 203P, 203R, 203T, 204, 205, 207, 227P, 227R, 227T, 228, 229, 231, 255P, 255R, 255T, 260, 261, 263, 289P, 289R, 289T, 290, 291, 293, 313P, 313R, 313T, 314, 315, 317, 325P, 325R, 325T, 326, 327, 329, 355P, 355R, 355T, 356, 357, 359, 387P, 387R, 387T, 392, 393, 395, 419P,

419R, 419T, 420, 421, 423, 447P, 447R, 447T, 448, 449, 451, 459P, 459R, 459T, 460, 461, 463, 481P, 481R, 481T, 482, 483, 485, 509P, 509R, 509T, 514, 515, 517, 541P, 541R, 541T, 542, 543, 545, 565P, 565R, 565T, 566, 567, 569, 577P, 577R, 577T, 578, 579, 581, 603P, 603R, 603T, 604, 605, 607, 633P, 633R, 633T, 638, 639, 641, 667P, 667R, 667T, 668, 669, 671, 697P, 697R, 697T, 698, 699, 701, 709P, 709R, 709T, 710, 711, 713, 735P, 735R, 735T, 736, 737, 739, 759P, 759R, 759T

oral presentations, 16I, 47A, 77A, 89A, 111A, 139A, 143E, 143K, 144I, 169A, 191A, 203A, 227A, 255A, 259E, 259K, 260I, 261, 289A, 313A, 325A, 355A, 387A, 391E, 391K, 392I, 419A, 447A, 459A, 481A, 509A, 513E, 513K, 514I, 541A, 565A, 577A, 603A, 633A, 637E, 637K, 638I, 667A, 697A, 709A, 735A, 759A, 763E, 763K

performances, 16I, 139F, 143K-143L, 5.3: T16

strategies, 16H–16I, 47A, 77A, 89A, 111A, 139A, 143B, 143E, 143K–143L, 144H–144I, 169A, 191A, 203A, 227A, 255A, 259B, 259E, 259K–259L, 260H–260I, 289A, 313A, 325A, 355A, 387A, 391B, 391E, 391K–391L, 392H–392I, 419A, 447A, 459A, 481A, 509A, 513B, 513E, 513K–513L, 514H–514I, 541A, 565A, 577A, 603A, 633A, 637B, 637E, 637K–637L, 638H–638I, 667A, 697A, 709A, 735A, 759A, 763B, 763E, 763K–763L

using nonverbal and verbal techniques, 16I, 47A, 77A, 89A, 111A, 139A, 143E, 143K, 144I, 169A, 191A, 203A, 227A, 255A, 259E, 259K, 260I, 261, 289A, 313A, 325A, 355A, 387A, 391E, 391K, 392I, 419A, 447A, 459A, 481A, 509A, 513E, 513K, 514I, 541A, 565A, 577A, 603A, 633A, 637E, 637K, 638I, 667A, 697A, 709A, 735A, 759A, 763E, 763K

using props and visuals, 143K–143L, 259K–259L, 391K–391L, 513K–513L, 637K–637L, 763K–763L

Spelling, 47B, 47G–47H, 77B, 77G–77H, 89G–89H, 111B, 111G–111H, 139B, 139G–139H, 169B, 169G–169H, 191B, 191G–191H, 203G–203H, 227B, 227G–227H, 255B, 255G–255H, 289B, 289G–289H, 313B, 313G–313H, 325G–325H, 355B, 355G–355H, 387B, 387G–387H, 419B, 419G–419H, 447B, 447G–447H, 459G–459H, 481B, 481G–481H, 509B, 509G–509H, 541B, 541G–541H, 565B, 565G–565H, 577G–577H, 603B, 603G–603H, 633B, 633G–633H, 667B, 667G–667H, 697B, 697G–697H, 709G–709H, 735B, 735G–735H, 759B, 759G–759H. See also Phonics/spelling; Spelling.

challenge words, 47G, 77G, 89G, 111G, 139G, 169G, 191G, 203G, 227G, 255G, 289G, 313G, 325G, 355G, 387G, 419G, 447G, 459G, 481G, 509G, 541G, 565G, 577G, 603G, 633G, 667G, 697G, 709G, 735G, 759G

dictation sentences, 47G, 77G, 89G, 111G, 139G, 169G, 191G, 203G, 227G, 255G, 289G, 313G, 325G, 355G, 387G, 419G, 447G, 459G, 481G, 509G, 541G, 565G, 577G, 603G, 633G, 667G, 697G, 709G, 735G, 759G

posttest, 47H, 77H, 89H, 111H, 139H, 169H, 191H, 203H, 227H, 255H, 289H, 313H, 325H, 355H, 387H, 419H, 447H, 459H, 481H, 509H, 541H, 565H, 577H, 603H, 633H, 667H, 697H, 709H, 735H, 759H

pretest, 47G, 77G, 89G, 111G, 139G, 169G, 191G, 203G, 227G, 255G, 289G, 313G, 325G, 355G, 387G, 419G, 447G, 459G, 481G, 509G, 541G, 565G, 577G, 603G, 633G, 667G, 697G, 709G, 735G, 759G

spiral review, 89H, 111H, 139H, 169H, 191H, 203H, 227H, 255H, 289H, 313H, 325H, 355H, 387H, 419H, 447H, 459H, 481H, 509H, 541H, 565H, 577H, 603H, 633H, 667H, 697H, 709H, 735H, 759H

teacher and student word sorts, 47G, 77G, 89G, 111G, 139G, 169G, 191G, 203G, 227G, 255G, 289G, 313G, 325G, 355G, 387G, 419G, 447G, 459G, 481G, 509G, 541G, 565G, 577G, 603G, 633G, 667G, 697G, 709G, 735G, 759G

words from mythology, 709G–709H

words that are compound words, 169B, 169G–169H

words with able, ible, 759B, 759G–759H

words with added ion, 633B, 633G–633H

words with ance, ence, 509B, 509G–509H

words with /är/, /âr/, /ôr/, 111B, 111G–111H

words with /chər/ and /zhər/, 481B, 481G–481H

words with /ər/, 387B, 387G–387H

words with final /əl/ ən, 419B, 419G–419H

words with Greek roots, 667B, 667G–667H

words with homographs, 459B, 459G–459H

words with homophones, 565B, 565G–565H

words with inflected endings, 203G–203H

words with Latin roots, 697B, 697G-697H

words with long vowels, 77B, 77G–77H

words with number prefixes uni–, bi–, tri–, cent–, 735B, 735G–735H

words with /ô/, /ou/, /oi/, 227B, 227G–227H

words with plurals, 191B, 191G–191H

words with prefixes dis–, in–, mis–, pre–, 577G–577H

words with r-controlled vowels, 139B, 139G–139H

words with short vowels, 47B, 47G–47H

words with soft g, 541B, 541G–541H

Key 5.1 = Grade 5, Book 1

words with suffixes *–less and
–ness,* 603B, 603G–603H

words with syllables

accented syllables, 447B, 447G–
447H, 459B, 459G–459H

unaccented syllables, 387B,
387G–387H

words with /ü/ /ū/ /ù/, 89G–89H

words with v/cv and vc/v pattern,
289B, 289G–289H

words with v/v, 313B, 313G–313H

words with vcccv, 325G–325H

words with vccv, 255B, 255G–255H

words with vowel patterns in
accented syllables, 355B,
355G–355H

Spiral Review, 47F, 47O, 77F, 77H,
77O, 89F, 89H, 89O, 111F, 111H,
111O, 139F, 139H, 139O, 169F, 169H,
169O, 191F, 191H, 191O, 203F, 203H,
203O, 227F, 227H, 227O, 255F, 255H,
255O, 289F, 289H, 289O, 313F, 313H,
313O, 325F, 325H, 325O, 355F, 355H,
355O, 387F, 387H, 387O, 419F, 419H,
419O, 447F, 447H, 447O, 459F, 459H,
459O, 481F, 481H, 481O, 509F, 509H,
509O, 541F, 541H, 541O, 565F, 565H,
565O, 577F, 577H, 577O, 603F, 603H,
603O, 633F, 633H, 633O, 667F, 667H,
667O, 697F, 697H, 697O, 709F, 709H,
709O, 735F, 735H, 735O, 759F, 759H,
759O

Story structure. *See*
Comprehension strategies.

Structural analysis. *See* Phonics/
Stuctural analysis; Vocabulary.

Study skills, 85B, 89Q, 89S, 199B,
203Q, 203S, 321B, 325Q, 325S,
455B, 459Q, 459S, 573B, 577Q,
577S, 705B, 709Q, 709S, , **5.1:** T11,
T12; **5.2:** T9, T10; **5.3:** T9, T10; **5.4:**
T10, T11; **5.5:** T11; **5.6:** T10, T11. *See
also* Computer literacy; Research
and Inquiry; Text features.

dictionary and thesaurus, using,
573B, 577D, 577Q, 577S. *See also*
Vocabulary: dictionary, using.

alphabetical order, 573B, 577Q,
577S

entry words, 577Q, 577**S**

guide words, 573B, 577Q, 577S

pronunciation, 573B, 577Q,
577S

everyday communications, 705B,
709A, 709Q, 709S

library and media center, using,
85B, 89A, 89Q, 89S, 144H, 144I,
392H, 392I, 514H, 514I, 638H,
638I

author and title searches, 85B,
89A, 89Q, 89S, 392H

call number, 85B, 89A, 89Q, 89S,
392H

card catalogs, print and
electronic, 85B, 89A, 89Q,
89S, 392H

evaluating sources, 199B, 203A,
203Q, 203S

Internet, using, 199B, 203A,
203Q, 203S, 763C

key word searches, 85B, 89A,
89Q, 89S, 199B, 203A, 203Q,
203S, , **5.5:** T11

search engines, 199B, 203A,
203Q, 203ST

Web addresses and sites, 199B,
203A, 203Q, 203S

parts of a book, 455B, 459Q, 459S,
5.4: T11

bibliography, 455B, 459Q, 459S

end notes and foot notes,
455B, 459Q, 459S

glossary, 455B, 459Q, 459S

index, 455B, 459Q, 459S

table of contents, 455B, 459Q,
459S

title page, 455B, 459Q, 459ST

study strategies, 321B, 325Q, 325S

citing sources, 321B, 325B,
325Q, 325S, 513CC

note-taking, 321B, 325Q, 325S

organizing notes, 321B, 325Q,
325S

outlining, 321B

quoting material, 321B

skimming and scanning, 321B,
325Q, 325S

Suffixes. *See* Phonics/spelling;
Spelling: words with sufixes;
Vocabulary: suffixes.

Summarizing, *See* Comprehension
skills: summarize;
Comprehension strategies:
summarize.

Symbolism, 600–601, 603Q, 603S,
754–757, 759Q, 759S

Synonym. *See* Vocabulary:
synonyms.

Synthesize. *See* Comprehension
strategies: synthesize.

Tt

Table of contents, 144H, 455B,
459Q, 459S

Talk About It. *See* Oral Language.

Tall tale, 49, 52–69

Technology, 16K, 48B, 78B, 90B,
112B, 143I–143J, 144K, 170B, 192B,
204B, 228B, 259I–259J, 260K,
290B, 314B, 326B, 356B, 391I–391J,
392K, 420B, 448B, 460B, 482B,
513I–513J, 514K, 542B, 566B, 578B,
604B, 637I–637J, 638K, 668B, 698B,
710B, 736B, 763I–763J. *See also*
Computer Literacy.

audio CDs, 16K, 48B, 78B, 90B,
112B, 144K, 170B, 192B, 204B,
228B, 260K, 290B, 314B, 326B,
356B, 392K, 420B, 448B, 460B,
482B, 514K, 542B, 566B, 578B,
604B, 638K, 668B, 698B, 710B,
736B. *See also* Fluency: Fluency
Solutions audio CD; Listening
Library.

CD-ROMs, 16K, 48B, 78B, 90B, 112B,
144K, 170B, 192B, 204B, 228B,
260K, 290B, 314B, 326B, 356B,
392K, 420B, 448B, 460B, 482B,
514K, 542B, 566B, 578B, 604B,
638K, 668B, 698B, 710B, 736B

online instruction

author/illustrator information,
40, 70, 106, 132, 162, 186, 220,

250, 282, 306, 348, 382, 412, 440, 476, 504, 534, 560, 598, 626, 660, 690, 730, 752

computer literacy, 143I–143J, 259I–259J, 391I–391J, 513I–513J, 637I–637J, 763I–763J

lesson plans, 17, 49, 79, 91, 113, 145, 171, 193, 205, 229, 261, 291, 315, 327, 357, 393, 421, 449, 461, 483, 515, 543, 567, 579, 605, 639, 669, 699, 711, 737

oral language development, 17, 49, 79, 91, 113, 145, 171, 193, 205, 229, 261, 291, 315, 327, 357, 393, 421, 449, 461, 483, 515, 543, 567, 579, 605, 639, 669, 699, 711, 737

vocabulary and spelling, 16K, 48B, 78B, 90B, 112B, 144K, 170B, 192B, 204B, 228B, 260K, 290B, 314B, 326B, 356B, 392K, 420B, 448B, 460B, 482B, 514K, 542B, 566B, 578B, 604B, 638K, 668B, 698B, 710B, 736B

Test Strategy. *See* **Assessment: test strategy.**

Text connections

    connect and compare, 45, 75, 109, 137, 167, 189, 225, 253, 287, 311, 353, 385, 417, 445, 479, 507, 539, 563, 601, 631, 665, 695, 733, 757

    making connections across texts, 47P, 47R, 47T, 77P, 77R, 77T, 89P, 89R, 89T, 111P, 111R, 111T, 139P, 139R, 139T, 169P, 169R, 169T, 191P, 191R, 191T, 203P, 203R, 203T, 227P, 227R, 227T, 255P, 255R, 255T, 289P, 289R, 289T, 313P, 313R, 313T, 325P, 325R, 325T, 355P, 355R, 355T, 387P, 387R, 387T, 419P, 419R, 419T, 447P, 447R, 447T, 459P, 459R, 459T, 481P, 481R, 481T, 509P, 509R, 509T, 541P, 541R, 541T, 565P, 565R, 565T, 577P, 577R, 577T, 603P, 603R, 603T, 633P, 633R, 633T, 667P, 667R, 667T, 697P, 697R, 697T, 709P, 709R, 709T, 735P, 735R, 735T, 759P, 759R, 759T

reading/writing across texts, 45, 75, 109, 137, 167, 189, 225, 253, 287, 311, 353, 385, 417, 445, 479, 507, 539, 563, 601, 631, 665, 695, 733, 757

    text to self, 41, 71, 107, 133, 163, 187, 199, 221, 251, 283, 307, 349, 383, 413, 441, 455, 477, 505, 535, 561, 573, 599, 627, 661, 691, 731, 753

    text to text, 41, 71, 85, 107, 133, 163, 187, 199, 221, 251, 283, 307, 321, 349, 383, 413, 441, 477, 505, 535, 561, 599, 627, 661, 691, 705, 731, 753

    text to world, 41, 71, 85, 107, 133, 163, 187, 221, 251, 283, 307, 349, 383, 413, 441, 455, 477, 505, 535, 561, 599, 627, 661, 691, 705, 731, 753

Text features

    almanac entries, 222–225, 227Q, **5.2:** T10

    bibliography, 455B, 459Q, 459S

    byline, 384–387, 387Q, 387S, **5.3:** T10

    captions, 42–45, 47Q, 47S 164–167, 169Q 169S, 638H, 752, **5.2:** T9

    charts, 134–137, 139Q, 139S, 144H, 227Q, 227S, 638H

    deck, 442–445, 447Q, 447S, **5.4:** T10

    definitional sidebars, 752

    diagrams, 144H, 638H, 662–665, 667Q, 667S, 726, **5.3:** T10

      process diagrams, 350-353, 355Q, 355S, **5.3:** T10

    footnotes and end notes, 144H, 455B, 459Q, 459S

    glossary, 455B, 459PQ, 459S

    graphs, 144H, 628–631, 633Q, 633S

    headings, 186, 442–443, 447Q, 447S, 638H, 752

    headlines, 384–385, 387Q, 387S, 444-445, **5.3:** T10; **5.4:** T10

    hyperlinks, 562–563, 565Q, 565S, **5.5:** T11

    illustrations, 65, 66, 157, 181, 234, 269, 368, 377, 426, 445, 522, 548, 557, 618, 638H, 654, 726

index, 455B, 459Q, 459S

interview, 692–695, 697Q, 697ST

key words, 562–563, 565Q, 565S, **5.5:** T11

links, 72–75, 77PQ 77S, **5.5:** T11

map labels and legends, 144H

photos, 42–45, 47Q, 47S, 164–167, 169Q 169S, 704, 752, **5.2:** T9

plays, 493, 564–565, 565A–565B, 565J

primary sources, 536-539, 541PQ 541S, **5.5:** T11

    journals and letters, 536-539, 541S, **5.5:** T11

print, bold, color, type, 638H, 740, 752

quotations, 704

subheadings, 726

table of contents, 144H, 455B, 459Q, 459S

time lines, 308–311, 313P, 313R, 313T, 414–417, 419Q, 419S 726, **5.3:** T9; **5.4:** T10

toolbar, 72–75, 77Q, 77S

Venn diagram, 662–665, 667Q, 667S

Text structure. *See* **Comprehension strategies: text structure.**

Theme. *See also* **Comprehension skills: theme; Theme projects.**

    introduction to, 16, 48, 78, 90, 112, 144, 170, 192, 204, 228, 260, 290, 314, 326, 356, 392, 420, 448, 460, 482, 514, 542, 566, 578, 604, 638, 668, 698, 710, 736

Theme projects, 16H–16I, 143K–143L, 144H–144I, 259K–259L, 260H–260I, 391K–391L, 392H–392I, 513K–513L, 514H–514I, 637K–637L, 638H–638I, 763K–763L

Thesaurus, 15, 139D, 139F, 139Q, 139S, 169B, 329, 355D, 569, 573B, 577D, 577F, 577Q, 577S, 735B

Think and Compare, 41, 71, 85, 107, 133, 163, 187, 199, 221, 251, 283, 307, 321, 349, 383, 413, 441, 455, 477, 505, 535, 561, 573, 599, 627, 661, 691, 705, 731, 753

Key 5.1 = Grade 5, Book 1

Timed reading, 47N, 47Q, 77N, 77Q, 89N, 89Q, 111N, 111Q, 139N, 139Q, 169N, 169Q, 191N, 191Q, 203N, 203Q, 227N, 227Q, 255N, 255Q, 289N, 289Q, 313N, 313Q, 325N, 325Q, 326I, 355N, 355Q, 356I, 387N, 387Q, 392R, 419N, 419Q, 420I, 447N, 447Q, 448I, 459N, 459Q, 481N, 481Q, 482I, 509N, 509Q, 514R, 541N, 541Q, 542I, 565N, 565Q, 566I, 577N, 577Q, 578I, 603N, 603Q, 633N, 633Q, 667N, 667Q, 668I, 697N, 697Q, 709N, 709Q, 710I, 735N, 735Q, 736I, 759N, 759Q

Timed writing, 89, 203, 325, 459, 577, 709

Time for Kids

"Beyond the Horizon," 318–321
"A Dream Comes True," 702–705
"Forests of the World," 82–85
"Getting Out the Vote," 452–455
"A Historic Journey," 570–573
"Maya Lin: Architect of Memory," 196–199

Time lines. *See* **Text features.**

Toolbar, 72–75, 77Q, 77S

Uu

Unit projects. *See* **Theme projects.**

Unit writing. *See* **Writing Workshop.**

Vv

Venn diagram, 84, 329B, 330, 331, 332, 336, 349, 662–665, 667Q, 667S, **5.6:** T10

Verbs. *See* **Grammar: verbs.**

Vocabulary. *See also* **Word Study.**

affixes, 517, 541D, 541F, 541O

analogies, 228I, 231, 244, 255D, 255F, 255O, 356I, 359, 374, 387D, 387F, 387O, 387Q, 482I, 485, 509D, 509F, 509O, **5.2:** T8; **5.3:** T8; **5.4:** T9

antonyms, 228I, 231, 244, 255D, 255F, 255O, 255R, 566I, 569, 577D, 577F, 577O, 577Q, **5.2:** T8; **5.5:** T8

Approaching Level Options for. *See* **Approaching Level Options: vocabulary.**

base words/root words, 96, 216, 260Q, 517, 541D, 541F, 541O, 541Q

Beyond Level Options for. *See* **Beyond Level Options: vocabulary.**

compound words, 48I, 51, 68, 77D, 77F, 77O, 77Q, 144Q, 169E, **5.1:** T7

connotation, 326I 329, 341, 355D, 355F, 355O, 355Q, **5.3:** T7

content, 42–45, 72–75, 82–85, 134–137, 164–167, 196–199, 222–225, 308–311, 318–321, 350–353, 384–385, 414–417, 442–445, 452–455, 536–539, 562–563, 628–631, 662–665, 692–695, 702–705, 760–762

context clues, 19, 23, 24, 26, 47D, 47O, 47P, 47R, 90I, 93, 101, 111D, 111F, 111Q, 170I, 173, 179, 191D, 191F, 191O, 191Q, 420I, 423, 431, 447D, 447F, 578I, 581, 591, 603D, 603F, 603O, 603Q, 698I, 701, 709D, 709F, 709O, 709Q, **5.1:** T6, T9; **5.2:** T5; **5.4:** T6; **5.5:** T9; **5.6:** T7

look for description/ explanation, 19, 24, 47D, 51, 93, 101, 111D, 111Q, 431, 581, 591, **5.1:** T9

look for restatement, 173, 179, 191D, 191F, 191O, 191Q

sentence and paragraph, 423, 447D, 447F, 447O, 447Q, 790Q

denotation, 329, 341, 355D, 355F, 355O, 355Q, **5.3:** T7

dictionary, using 47D, 47F, 77D, 78I, 81, 89D, 89F, 89O, 111F, 118, 139D, 139F, 147, 156, 169D, 169Q, 170I, 263, 290I, 293, 313D, 313F, 313O, 313R, 329, 447F, 463, 468, 481D, 481F, 481O, 481Q, 541D, 552, 565D, 565F, 565O, 565Q, 569, 573B, 577D, 577O,

577O, 577Q, 641, 671, 697D, **5.1:** T8; **5.2:** T4; **5.3:** T5; **5.5:** T7, T12

English Language Learners. *See* **English Language Learners: Vocabulary.**

expand, 17, 47F, 47O, 49, 77F, 77O, 79, 89F, 89O, 91, 111F, 111O, 113, 139F, 139O, 145, 169F, 169O, 171, 191F, 191O, 193, 203F, 203O, 205, 227F, 227O, 229, 255F, 255O, 289F, 289O, 291, 313F, 313O, 315, 325F, 325O, 327, 355F, 355O, 357, 387F, 387O, 419F, 419O, 421, 447F, 447O, 459F, 459O, 461, 481F, 481O, 483, 509F, 509O, 515, 541F, 541O, 565F, 565O, 577F, 577O, 579, 603F, 603O, 633F, 633O, 639, 667F, 667O, 697F, 697O, 699, 709F, 709O, 711, 735F, 735O, 737, 759F, 759O

extend, 47T, 77T, 89T, 111T, 139T, 169T, 191T, 203T, 227T, 255T, 289T, 313T, 325T, 355T, 387T, 419T, 447T, 459T, 481T, 509T, 541T, 565T, 577T, 603T, 633T, 667T, 697T, 709T, 735T, 759T

games, 47F, 77F, 89F, 111F, 139F, 169F, 191F, 203F, 227F, 255F, 289F, 313F, 325F, 355F, 387F, 419F, 447F, 459F, 481F, 509F, 541F, 565F, 577F, 603F, 633F, 667F, 697F, 709F, 735F, 759F

Greek roots, 96, 638Q, 667E, 667G–667H, 710I, 713, 728, 735D, 735F, 735O, 735Q, 736I, 739, 743, **5.6:** T8, T9

homographs, 78I, 81, 89D, 89F, 89O, 89Q, 448I, 687F, **5.1:** T8 **5.4:** T5

homophones, 392Q, 395, 401, 419D, 419F, 419O, 419Q, 509I– 509J, 542I, 565E, 565G–565H, 638Q, 641, 644, 667D, 667F, 667O, 667Q, **5.6:** T5

idioms, 144Q, 147, 156, 169D, 169F, 169O, 169Q

inflectional endings, 192I, 195, 203D, 203E, 203G–203H, 203O, **5.2:** T6

Latin roots, 607, 612, 633D, 633F, 633O, 633Q, 668I, 736I, 739, 743, 759D, 759F, 759O, 759Q, **5.5:** T10

multiple-meaning words, 23, 460I, 463, 468, 481D, 481F, 481Q, 668I, 671, 697D, 697F, 697O, 697Q, **5.4:** T8; **5.6:** T6

On Level Options for. *See* **On Level Options: vocabulary.**

prefixes, 317, 325D, 325F, 325O, 325Q, 451, 459D, 459O, 459Q, 514R, 517, 541F, 566I, 577E, 577G–577H, 710I, **5.3:** T6

  absorbed, 314I

pronunciation key, 290I, 293, 302, 313D, 313F, 313O,

semantic meaning cues, 26, 185, 336, 470

spiral review, 47F, 47O, 77F, 77O, 89F, 89O, 111F, 111O, 139F, 139O, 169F, 169O, 191F, 191O, 203F, 203O, 227F, 227O, 255F, 255O, 289F, 289O, 313F, 313O, 325F, 325O, 355F, 355O, 387F, 387O, 419F, 419O, 447F, 447O, 459F, 459O, 481F, 481O, 509F, 509O, 541F, 541O, 565F, 565O, 577F, 577O, 603F, 603O, 633F, 633O, 667F, 667O, 697F, 697O, 709F, 709O, 735F, 735O, 759F, 759O

strategies, 19, 47D, 77D, 81, 89D, 93, 111D, 115, 139D, 147, 169D, 173, 191D, 195, 203D, 207, 227D, 231, 255D, 262, 263, 289D, 293, 313D, 317, 329, 359, 387D, 395, 419D, 423, 447D, 451, 459D, 463, 481D, 509D, 517, 541D, 545, 565D, 569, 577D, 581, 591, 603D, 607, 633D, 641, 650, 739

suffixes, 204I, 207, 227D, 227F, 227O, 277Q, 451, 459D, 459O, 459Q, 514Q, 541F, 578I, 603E, **5.2:** T7

synonyms, 19, 47D, 47F, 47O, 47Q, 112I, 115, 120, 139D, 139F, 139O, 139Q, 326I, 356I, 359, 374, 387D, 387F, 387O, 387Q, 545, 573B, 577F **5.1:** T10

syntactic cues, 56, 159, 271, 524, 550, 748

teach words in context, 18, 47C, 50, 77C, 80, 89C, 92, 111C, 114, 139C, 146, 169C, 172, 191C, 194, 203C, 206, 227C, 230, 255C, 262, 289C, 292, 313C, 316, 325C, 328,

355C, 358, 387C, 394, 419C, 422, 447C, 450, 459C, 462, 481C, 484, 509C, 516, 541C, 544, 565C, 568, 577C, 580, 603C, 606, 633C, 640, 667C, 670, 697C, 700, 709C, 712, 735C, 738, 759C

thesaurus, 47F, 111F, 112I, 115, 139D, 139F, 139O, 139Q, 170I, 329, 355D, 355O, 387Q, 387S, 569, 573B, 577D, 577F, 57O, 577Q ,**5.3** T7

using resources to acquire, 89F, 111F, 139F, 169F, 227F, 255F, 289F, 313F, 325F, 355FG, 387F, 387Q, 387S, 419F, 447F, 459F, 481F, 509F, 541F, 565F, 577F, 603F, 633F, 667F, 697F, 709F, 739F.

word families, 260Q, 263, 274, 289D, 289F, 289O, 759F

word origins, 542I, 545, 552, 565D, 565O, 565Q, 709G, 713, 728, 735D, 735F, 735O, 735Q, 739, 743, 759D, 759F, 759O, 759Q, **5.5:** T7

word parts, 51, 68, 77O, 77Q, 96, 195, 203D, 203O, 207, 216, 227D, 263, 289D, 314I, 325D, 317, 448I, 451, 459D, 459O, 459Q, 514Q, 517, 527, 541D, 541Q, 604I, 607, 612, 633D, 633F, 633O, 633Q, 713, 728, 735D, 735F, 735O, 735Q, 739, 759D, 759F, 759Q, **5.3:** T6; **5.4:** T7; **5.5:** T6; **5.6:** T8

word web, 47F, 77F, 89F, 111F, 139F, 169F, 191F, 227F, 255F, 289F, 313F, 325F, 355F, 387F, 419F, 447F, 459F, 481F, 565F, 577F, 603F, 633F, 667F, 697F, 709F, 735

Vocabulary PuzzleMaker, 47F, 77F, 89F, 111F, 139F, 169F, 191F, 203F, 227F, 255F, 289F, 313F, 325F, 355F, 387F, 419F, 447F, 459F, 481F, 509F, 541F, 565F, 577F, 603F, 633F, 667F, 697F, 709F, 735F, 759F

Ww

Ways to confirm meaning, 26, 159, 185, 271, 336, 429, 470, 499, 524, 527, 550, 655, 685, 748

Weekly contract, 16N, 48E, 78E, 90E, 112E, 144N, 170E, 192E, 204E, 228E, 260N, 290E, 314E, 326E, 356E, 392N, 420E, 448E, 460E, 482E, 514N, 542E, 566E, 578E, 604E, 638N, 668E, 698E, 710E, 736E

Word Study, 16R, 47C–47F, 48I, 77C–77F, 78I, 89C–89F, 90I, 111C–111F, 112I, 139C–139F, 144R, 169C–169F, 170I, 191C–191F, 192I, 203C–203F, 204I, 227C–227F, 228I, 255C–255F, 260R, 289C–289F, 290I, 313C–313F, 325C–325F, 326I, 355C–355F, 356I, 387C–387F, 392R, 419C–419F, 447C–447F, 448I, 459C–459F, 460I, 481C–481F, 482I, 509C–509F, 541C–541F, 542I, 565C–565F, 566I, 577C–577F, 578I, 603C–603F, 604I, 633C–633F, 667C–667F, 697C–697F, 709C–709F, 735C–735F, 759C–759F. *See also* **Vocabulary.**

Write About It, 40, 70, 106, 132, 162, 186, 220, 250, 282, 306, 348, 382, 412, 440, 476, 504, 534, 560, 598, 626, 660, 690, 730, 752, **5.1:** T14, T16, T18, **5.2:** T12, T14, T16, **5.3:** T12, T14, T16, **5.4:** T13, T15, T17; **5.5:** T14, T16, T18, **5.6:** T14, T16, T18

Write and respond, 46–47, 76–77, 88–89, 110–111, 138–139, 168–169, 190–191, 202–203, 226–227, 254–255, 288–289, 312–313, 324–325, 354–355, 386–387, 418–419, 446–447, 458–459, 480–481, 508–509, 540–541, 564–565, 576–577, 602–603, 632–633, 666–667, 696–697, 708–709, 734–735, 758–759

Writer's checklist, 47, 77, 89, 111, 139, 169, 191, 203, 227, 255, 289, 313, 325, 355, 387, 419, 447, 459, 481, 509, 541, 565, 577, 603, 633, 667, 697, 709, 735, 759

Writer's Craft. *See also* **Writing traits.**

  beginning, middle, end, 540, 541A, 747, 758, 759A

  dialogue, 344, 354, 355A

  facts and opinions, 418, 419A

  figurative language, 632, 633A

  formal and informal language, 446, 447B

Key 5.1 = Grade 5, Book 1

good paragraph, a, 43, 46, 47A

good topic, a, 288, 289A

important details, 100, 110, 111A

mood, 564, 565A

multiple paragraphs, 226, 227A

precise words, 507, 508, 509A

rearrange ideas, 719, 734, 735A

strong conclusion, a, 190, 191A

strong opening, a, 168. 169A

time-order words, 679, 696, 697A

tone, 470, 480, 481A

topic sentence, 76, 77A

transitions, 386, 387A, 602, 603A

transition words, 386, 387A

unimportant details, 138, 139A

vary sentences, 254, 255A

voice, 564, 565B, 666, 667A, 667B

word choice, 312, 313A, 438

Writer's resources, 143C, 259C, 391C, 513B, 513C, 637C, 763C

Writer's Toolbox, 47B, 77B, 89B, 111B, 139B, 169B, 191B, 203B, 227B, 255B, 289B, 313B, 325B, 355B, 387B, 419B, 447B, 459B, 481B, 509B, 541B, 565B, 577B, 603B, 633B, 667B, 697B, 709B, 735B

Writing. *See also* Scoring rubrics, writing; Timed writing practice; Write About It; Write and respond; Writer's checklist; Writer's resources; Writing forms and modes; Writing prompt; Writing process; Writing traits; Writing Workshop.

audience and purpose, 143B, 259B, 391B, 513B, 637B, 763B

Author's Chair, 143E, 259E, 391E, 513E, 637E, 763E

daily, 16L–16O, 48C–48F, 78C–78F, 90C–90F, 112C–112F, 144L–144O, 170C–170F 192C–192F, 204C–204F, 228C–228F, 260L–260O, 290C–290F, 314C–314F, 326C–326F, 356C–356F, 392L–392O, 420C–420F, 448C–448F, 460C–460F, 482C–482F, 514L–514O, 542C–542F, 566C–566F, 578C–578F, 604C–604F, 638L–638O, 668C–668F, 698C–698F, 710C–710F, 736C–736F

features of, 46, 76, 110, 138, 143A, 168, 190, 226, 254, 259A, 288, 312, 324, 386, 391A, 418, 446, 480, 508, 513A, 540, 564, 602, 632, 637A, 666, 696, 734, 758, 763A

independent. *See* Picture prompt.

options for student writing. *See* Independent writing; Write About It; Writing: daily; Writing forms and modes.

peer review and conferencing, 139B, 143B, 143D, 143E, 259B, 259D, 259E, 391B, 391D, 391E, 513D, 513E, 637B, 637D, 637E, 763B, 763D, 763E

outlining in, 77B. *See also* Research and inquiry.

student models for, 46, 76, 110, 138, 168, 190, 226, 254, 288, 312, 324, 386, 418, 446, 480, 508, 540, 564, 602, 632, 666, 696, 734, 758

teacher conference, 143E, 259E, 391E, 513E, 637E, 763E

types of leads in, 255B

using technology in, 47B, 77B, 89B, 111B, 139B, 169B, 191B, 203B, 227B, 255B, 289B, 313B, 325B, 355B, 387B, 419B, 447B, 459B, 481B, 509B, 541B, 565B, 577B, 603B, 633B, 667B, 697B, 709B, 735B

Writing forms and modes

advertisement, 16S, 77F, 144S, 168-169B, 313F

article, 203A–203B, 325A–325B, 420J, 459A–459B, 577A–577B

biography, 709A–709B

brochure, 89A–89B, 203B, 225, 355F

character sketch, 288–289B

coded message, 603F

compare/contrast, 602–603B

descriptive writing, 77F, 78J, 112J, 144S, 204J, 514S, 540–541B, 542J, 564–565B, 578J, 602–603B, 604J, 632–633B, 673A–673H, 697F, 710J

dialogue, 139F, 192J, 326J, 354–355B, 448J, 542J, 564–565B

diary entry, 16S, 386–387B

directions, 696–697B

editorial, 698J

e-mail, 709F

essays, 78J, 192J, 226–227B, 228J, 259A–259F, 392J, 392S, 448J, 602–603B, 668J, 698J, 734–735B, **5.4:** T17; **5.6:** T17

everyday, 89A–89B, 203B, 225, 355F, 734–735B

explanatory writing, 514S, 542J, 666–667B, 667F, 696–697B, 708–709B, 710J, 734–735B, 758–759B, 763G–763H

expository writing, 78J, 89A–89B, 192J, 203A–203B, 325A–325B, 418–419B, 446–447B, 448J, 459A–459B, 480–481B, 508–509B, 513A–513H, 566I, 577–578, 666–667B, 696–697B, 709A–709B, 734–735B, 758–759B

eyewitness account, 638S, 666–667B

fable, 509F

fact cards, 228J, 604J, 710J, 736J

fairy tale, 638S

fictional narrative, 48J, 260S, 288–289B, 290J, 326J, 354–355B, 386–387B, 391A–391H, 578J, 604J

functional, 89A–89B, 203B, 225, 355F, 696–697B

how-to writing, 667F, 668J, 696–697B

humorous story, 387F

interview, 482J, 508–509B

journal entry, 16S, 112J, 139A–139B, 203F, 289F, 541F, 604J, 759F. *See also* Journal.

letters

business or formal letters, 111F, 144S, 170J, 191A–191B, 204J, 314J, 356J, 577F, 709F, 735F

friendly letters, 48J, 111A–111B, 204J, 260S, 356J, 419F

letter to the editor, 190–191B, 325F

lists, 90J, 112J, 228J, 326J, 460J, 482J, 578J, 668J, **5.1:** T16 magazine article, 420J, 460J, 480–481B

message, 603F

myth, 759T

news article, 392S, 418–419B, **5.4:** T15

news release, 759F

nomination, 139F

paragraphs, 45, 47F, 90J, 111F, 169F, 220, 447F, 638S, 668J, 697F

personal narrative, 16S, 46–47B, 48J, 76–77B, 90J, 110–111B, 138–139B, 143A–143E, 170J, 386–387B, 668J, **5.1:** T16

persuasive, 168–169B, 190–,191B, 204J, 226–227B, 228J, 254–255B, 259A–259H

plan, 326J

play, 542J, 564–565B

poem, 111F, 255F, 290J, 312–313B, 459F, 460J, 632–633B, **5.2:** T16

poster, 260I, **5.1:** T14, T16

presentation, 481F

problem and solution essay, 758–759B

proclamation, 112J, **5.4:** T15

research reports, 89A–89B, 170J, 203A–203B, 297, 314J, 325A–325B, 392J, 420I, 448J, 459A–459B, 539, 566J, 577A–577B, 709A–709B, **5.3:** T15, **5.5:** T18

review, 254–255, 255A–255B

science fiction, 356J

scientific observation, 446–447B, **5.4:** T17

short story, 420J

speech, 112J, 514S, 540–541, 541A–541B

story, 227F, 387F, 578J, 633F, 638S

summaries, 48J, 90J, 228J, 307, 417, 578J

tall tale, 75

travel brochure, 355F

Writing portfolio, 143G, 259G, 391G, 513G, 637G, 763G

Writing process

drafting, 47, 77, 89, 111, 139, 143C, 169, 191, 203, 227, 255, 259C, 289, 313, 325, 355, 387, 391C, 419, 447, 459, 481, 509, 513C, 541, 565, 577, 603, 633, 637C, 667, 697, 709, 735, 759, 763C

presenting, 47A, 77A, 89A, 111A, 139A, 143B, 143E, 169A, 191A, 203A, 227A, 255A, 259B, 259E, 289A, 313A, 325A, 355A, 387A, 391B, 391E, 419A, 447A, 459A, 481A, 509A, 513B, 513E, 541A, 565A, 577A, 603A, 633A, 637B, 637E, 667A, 697A, 709A, 735A, 759A, 763B, 763E

prewriting, 47, 77, 89, 111, 139, 169A, 191, 203, 227, 255, 289, 313A, 325, 355, 387, 419, 447, 459A, 481, 509, 513, 541, 565, 577A, 603, 633, 637, 667, 697, 709A, 735, 759A

proofreading and editing, 47, 77, 89, 111, 139, 143E, 169, 191, 203, 227, 255, 259E, 289, 313, 325, 355, 387, 391E, 419, 447, 459, 481, 509, 513E, 541, 565, 577, 603, 633, 637E, 667, 697, 709, 735, 759, 763E

publishing, 47, 77, 89, 111, 139, 143E, 169, 191, 203, 227, 255, 259E, 289, 313, 325, 355, 387, 391E, 419, 447, 459, 481, 509, 513E, 541, 565, 577, 603, 633, 637E, 667, 697, 709, 735, 759, 763E3

revising, 47, 77, 89, 111, 139, 143D, 169, 191, 203, 227, 255, 259D, 289, 313, 325, 355, 387, 391D, 419, 447, 459, 481, 509, 513D, 541, 565, 577, 603, 633, 637D, 667, 697, 709, 735, 759, 763D

Writing prompts, 88–89, 143, 202–203, 259, 324–325, 391, 458–459, 513, 576–577, 637, 708–709, 763

determine audience, 88, 202, 324, 458, 576, 708

determine mode and form, 88, 202, 324, 458, 576, 708

determine purpose 88, 202, 324, 458, 576, 708

practice, 89, 203, 325, 459, 577, 709

Writing traits. *See also* Writer's Checklist; Writer's Craft.

conventions, 47B, 77B, 89B, 111B, 139B, 143E, 169B, 191B, 203B, 227B, 255B, 259E, 289B, 313B, 325B, 355B, 387B, 391E, 419B, 447B, 459B, 481B, 509B, 513E, 541B, 565B, 577B, 603B, 633B, 637E, 667B, 697B, 709B, 735B, 763E

ideas and content, 47B, 143D, 227B, 259D, 387B, 391D, 513D, 541B, 697B, 763C

organization, 77B, 143B, 143D, 191B, 259B, 313B, 391B, 391D, 419B, 513D, 603B, 637B, 735B, 763B, 763C

sentence fluency, 191B, 255B, 259D, 391D, 481B, 513D, 763C

voice, 111B, 143D, 259D, 289B, 391D, 481B, 509B, 513D, 565B, 763C

word choice, 139B, 143D, 169B, 169B, 259D, 313B, 391D, 447B, 513D, 633B, 637D, 697B, 763C

Writing Workshop, 47, 77, 89, 111, 139, 143A–143H, 169, 191, 20, 227, 255, 259A–259H, 289, 313, 325, 355, 387, 391A–391H, 419, 447, 459, 481, 509, 513A–513H, 541, 565, 577, 603, 633, 637A–637H, 667, 697, 709, 735, 759, 763A–763H

Key 5.1 = Grade 5, Book 1

Acknowledgments

The publisher gratefully acknowledges permission to reprint the following copyrighted material:

"Snakebite" from RATTLESNAKE DANCE: TRUE TALES, MYSTERIES, AND RATTLESNAKE CEREMONIES by Jennifer Owings Dewey. Copyright © 1997 by Jennifer Owings Dewey. Used by permission of Caroline House.

Photography Credits

All photographs are by Macmillan/McGraw Hill (MMH) and Ken Karp for MMH except as noted below:

16I: Anton Vengo/Superstock. 41B: Charles Shoffner/Index Stock Imagery/PictureQuest. 71B: Elise Amendola/AP. 107B: Frank Whitney/Getty Images. 143C: Ryan McVay/Getty Images. 143F: Comstock/PictureQuest. 143G: Royalty-Free/CORBIS.

Illustration Credits

47F: (bl) David Erikson; (tr) Lance Lekander. 47U: Stacy Schuett. 77F: Hector Bolassca. 77U: Stacy Schuett. 89U: Stacy Schuett. 111F: Matt Straub. 111U: Stacy Schuett. 133B: Peter Thornton. 139F: (bl) Robert Casilla; (tr) Sam Ward. 139U: Stacy Schuett.

Acknowledgments

(Continued from Copyright page.)

"Miss Alaineus" by Debra Frasier. Copyright © 2000 by Debra Frasier. Reprinted by permission of Harcourt, Inc.

"My Great-Grandmother's Gourd" by Christina Kessler, illustrations by Walter Lyon Krudop. Text copyright © 2000 by Christina Kessler. Illustrations copyright © 2000 by Walter Lyon Krudop. Reprinted by permission of Orchard Books, A Grolier Company.

"The Night of San Juan" is from SALSA STORIES by Lulu Delacre. Copyright © 2000 by Lulu Delacre. Reprinted by permission of Scholastic Press, a division of Scholastic Inc.

"Paul Revere's Ride" by Henry Wadsworth Longfellow is from OUR NATION. Copyright © 2003 by Macmillan/McGraw-Hill.

"Pipiolo and the Roof Dogs" by Brian Meunier, illustrations by Perky Edgerton. Text copyright © 2003 by Brian Meunier. Illustrations copyright © 2003 by Perky Edgerton. Reprinted by permission of Dutton Children's Books, a division of Penguin Young Readers Group.

"Rattlers!" by Ellen Lambeth (sidebar by John Cancalosi) is from RANGER RICK. Copyright © 1998 by the National Wildlife Federation. Reprinted by permission of the National Wildlife Federation.

"Shiloh" is from SHILOH by Phyllis Reynolds Naylor. Copyright © 2000 by Phyllis Reynolds Naylor. Reprinted by permission of Aladdin Paperbacks, an imprint of Simon & Schuster Children's Publishing Division.

"Skunk Scout" is from SKUNK SCOUT by Laurence Yep. Copyright © 2003 by Laurence Yep. Reprinted by permission of Hyperion Books for Children.

"Sleds on Boston Common" by Louise Borden, illustrations by Robert Andrew Parker. Text copyright © 2000 by Louise Borden. Illustrations copyright © 2000 by Robert Andrew Parker. Reprinted by permission of Margaret K. McElderry Books, an imprint of Simon & Schuster Children's Publishing Division.

"Spirit of Endurance" by Jennifer Armstrong, illustrations by William Maughan. Text copyright © 2000 by Jennifer Armstrong. Illustrations copyright © 2000 by William Maughan. Reprinted by Crown Publishing, a division of Random House Inc.

"Suffrage for Women" is from OUR NATION. Copyright © 2003 by Macmillan/McGraw-Hill.

"Suspense" is from THE BIG SKY by Pat Mora. Copyright © 1998 by Pat Mora. Reprinted by permission of Scholastic Press, a division of Scholastic, Inc.

"Through My Eyes" is from THROUGH MY EYES by Ruby Bridges. Copyright © 1999 by Ruby Bridges. Reprinted by permission of Scholastic Press, a division of Scholastic, Inc.

"Ultimate Field Trip 5: Blasting Off to Space Academy" is from ULTIMATE FIELD TRIP 5: BLASTING OFF TO SPACE ACADEMY by Susan E. Goodman. Text copyright © 2001 by Susan E. Goodman. Illustrations copyright © 2001 by Michael J. Doolittle. U.S. Space Camp and U.S. Space Academy are registered trademarks of the U.S. Space Rocket Center. Reprinted by permission of Atheneum Books for Young Readers, an imprint of Simon & Schuster Children's Publishing Division.

"The Unbreakable Code" by Sara Hoagland Hunter, illustrations by Julia Miner. Text copyright © 1996 by Sara Hoagland Hunter. Illustrations copyright © 1996 by Julia Miner. Reprinted by permission of Rising Moon Books for Young Readers from Northland Publishing.

"Weslandia" by Paul Fleischman, illustrations by Kevin Hawkes. Text copyright © 1999 by Paul Fleischman. Illustrations copyright © 1999 by Kevin Hawkes. Reprinted by permission of Candlewick Press.

"When Esther Morris Headed West" by Connie Nordhielm Wooldridge, illustrations by Jacqueline Rogers. Text copyright © 2001 by Connie Nordhielm Wooldridge. Illustrations copyright © 2001 by Jacqueline Rogers. Reprinted by permission of Holiday House.

"Zathura" by Chris Van Allsburg. Copyright © 2002 by Chris Van Allsburg. Reprinted by permission of Houghton Mifflin Company.

ILLUSTRATIONS

Cover Illustration: Leland Klanderman

20-41:Debra Frasier 50-51:Jeff Crosby 52-69:Rosalyn Schanzer 72-73: Owen Smith 75: Owen Smith 95:Susan E. Goodman 108-109:David Gordon III:John Hovell 116-133:Perky Edgerton 140,142:Erika LeBarre 148-163:Joel Spector 169:Erika LeBarre 178:Richard Orr 186-187: Siede Preis/Getty Images 188-189:Mercedes McDonald 208-221:Edel Rodriguez 222:Joe LeMonnier 232-251:Jerry Pinkney 252-253:Jeff Slemons 263:John Hovell 265-283:Robert Andrew Parker 284-286: Greg Newbold 287:John Burgoyne 289:Neal Armstrong 294-307: Jacqueline Rogers 330-349:Walter Lyon Krudop 351:Argosy 358: Tyson Mangelsdorf 360-383:Chris Van Allsburg 394:Rick Powell 396-413:Jerry Pinkney 419:John Hovell 422-423:Loretta Krupinski 424-441:Jeanne Arnold 478-479:Susan Swan 484-485:Mark Weber 486-505:Wendy Born Hollander 506-507:Daniel Powers 518-519, 526,528-532: William Maughan 533:Kailey LeFaiver 534-535: William Maughan 539:Joe LeMonnier 541:Erika LeBarre 544-545: John Parra 546-561:Kevin Hawkes 562-563 Argosy 565:Erika LeBarre 571:Rick Nease for TFK 582-599:Julia Miner 603:(bg)Julia Miner (tr)Kevin Hawkes 606:Donna Perrone 608-627:Marla Baggetta 634-635:Cezanne Studios 640-641:Rebecca Walsh 642-661:Ruth Sanderson 662-665:Maryana Beletskaya 672-690:Winson Trang 693:Joe LeMonnier 695:John Hovell 702-705:Courtesy of Boundless Playgrounds 727:Sharon and Joel Harris 732-733:Tom Foty 735:Erika LeBarre 764-765:Wendy Born Hollander

PHOTOGRAPHY

All photographs are by Macmillan/McGraw-Hill except where noted below:

16-17:(bg)Zelick Nagel/Getty 17:(i)Glenn Mitsui/Getty 18:(tcr)Royalty-free/CORBIS;(bl) SW Productions/Photodisc/Getty 19:Tony Freeman/PhotoEdit 40: Courtesy James Henkel 42:(tr)Steve Cole/Getty;(i)Linda Spillers/AP 43:Royalty-Free/CORBIS 44:(tl) Matthew Cavanaugh/Stringer/ Getty;(tr)Linda Spillers/Stringer/AP;(c)Linda Spillers/Stringer/AP 46:Thinkstock/Getty 47:SW Productions/Getty 48-49(bg) Joe Sohm/ Alamy 49:(i)Arthur Tilley/PictureQuest 50-51:C Squared Studios/Getty 54:Courtesy Rosalyn Schanzer 76:Scott T. Baxter/Photodisc/Getty 77:Tom Carter/ PhotoEdit 78-79:Photo 24/Brand X/Getty 80:Thomas Pakenham 81:(tl)Goodshot/Punchstock;(l)Courtesy Ohio Department of Natural Resources;(2)John Serrao/Photo Researchers;(3)Dan Tenaglia;(4)Courtesy Time for Kids;(5) Courtesy Time for Kids 82:(bl)CORBIS/Punchstock 82-83:(t)Stuart Franklin/Magnum Photos 83:(c)David Lorenz Winston/Brand X Pictures 84:Stuart Franklin/Magnum Photos 85:(t)Rick Nease for TFK;(tr)Ryan McVay/Photodisc/Getty;(bl)CORBIS/Punchstock 86: David McNew/Getty 88:SW Productions/Getty 89:(tr)C Squared Studios/Getty;(bl)Photodisc/Getty;(b)Dian Lofton for TFK;(br)Dian Lofton for TFK 90-91:(bg)James McDivitt/ NASA/AP 91:(i)Stock Trek/Getty 92:(bc) Photodisc/Getty 92-93:(t)Ian McKinnell/Getty 94:(cl)Michael J. Doolittle/Image Works 94-95:(bg) Stock Trek/Getty 95:(tr) Bettman/CORBIS 96:(r)Michael J. Doolittle/Image Works 96-97:(t) Stock Trek/Getty 97-98:(b)Michael J. Doolittle/Image Works 98-99:(t)StockTrek/Getty 99-100:(t) Michael J. Doolittle/Image Works 100-101:(t)StockTrek /Getty 101:(t)Michael J. Doolittle/Image Works 102:(c)CORBIS SYGMA/CORBIS;(l)Michael J. Doolittle/Image Works 102-103:(t)StockTrek/Getty 103:(l) Michael J. Doolittle/Image Works (r)Michael J. Doolittle /Image Works 104:(c)Michael J. Doolittle/Image Works 104-105:(t) StockTrek/Getty 105:(t)Michael J. Doolittle/Image Works;(b) NASA/AP 106:(t)Michael J. Doolittle/Image Works;(i)Courtesy Susan E. Goodman 106-107:(bg) StockTrek/Getty 110:MedioImages/Getty 112-113: (bg)Tom Kidd/Alamy 113:(i)Photodisc/Getty 114: Alley Cat Productions/Brand X Pictures/Getty 115: American Images/Getty 132:Courtesy Brian Meunier 134:(c)2005 Carrie McLean Museum/Alaska Stock Images 135:(tr)Bettmann/CORBIS;(l)Tracy Morgan/Getty;(2)Yann Arthus-Bertrand/CORBIS;(3)David Ward/DK Images 136:(b)Jack Sauer /AP 137: Peter Skinner/Photo Researchers 138:Royalty-free/CORBIS 139:GK Hart/Vikki Hart/Photodisc/Getty 144-145:(bg)Paul Wayne Wilson/PhotoStockFile/Alamy 145:(i)Edmond Van Hoorick/Photodisc/Getty 146-147:(b)Chas & Elizabeth Schwartz Trust/Animals Animals/Earth Scenes 147:(cr)Eric and David Hosking/CORBIS 162:Courtesy Simon & Schuster 164:(bl)zefa/Masterfile 164-165:(bg)Jack Hollingsworth/Photos.com 165:(bl)RaeAnn Meyer/Struve Labs 166: (b)Joe Munroe/Getty 166-167:(bg) Jack Hollingsworth/ Photos.com 168:Tom L. Geoff/Digital Vision/Getty 170-171:(bg)David A. Northcott/CORBIS 171:(i)Photodisc/Getty 172:Joe McDonald/CORBIS 173:OSF/Fogden, M./Animals Animals/Earth Scenes 174-175:(bg)Tom McHugh/Photo Researchers 176:Paul Chesley/Getty 177:(tl) Will Crocker/Getty; (br)© Lee Kline 178: Breck P. Kent/Animals Animals/Earth Scenes 179: (t) Joe McDonald/Animals Animals/Earth Scenes;(br)John Cancalosi/DRK 180: John Cancalosi 181:David Boag/ Alamy 182:(t)David A.

783

Northcott/DRK;(br)Deborah Allen 183:(tr)Stephen Cooper/Getty; (bl)Zigmund Leszczynski/Animals Animals/Earth Scenes 184-185: (bg)Gary McVicker/Index Stock 185:John Cancalosi 186:(tl)Courtesy Ellen Lambeth;(c)Breck P. Kent/Animals Animals/Earth Scenes 190: Paul Edmondson/ Getty 191:Tanya Guerrero 192-193:(bg)Izzy Schwartz /Photodisc/Getty 194:AP 195:(tl)UPI/NewsCom;(l) McDaniel Woolf/Photodisc/Getty;(2)Royalty-Free/CORBIS,(3)Royalty-Free/ CORBIS,(4) Creatas/ Punchstock;(5)Adalberto Rios Szalay/Sexto Sol/ Photodisc/Punchstock 196:AP 197:(tl) AP;(br) J. Scott Applewhite/AP 198-200:AP 202:Comstock Images 203:Dian Lofton for TFK 204-205: (bg)Bob Krist /CORBIS 205:(i)Jeremy Hoare/Life File/Getty 206-207: Theo Allofs /CORBIS 220:Courtesy Scholastic, Inc. 222-223:(bg)J. Lightfoot/Getty 223:(tcr)Bruce Adams; Eye Ubiquitous/CORBIS 224:(br)Robert Harding World Imagery/Alamy;(tl)Richard Bickel/ CORBIS 224-225: (bg)J. Lightfoot/Getty 225:(tcr)Royalty-Free/ Masterfile 226:Richard Hutchings/PhotoEdit 227:Buddy Mays/ CORBIS 228-229:(bg)Jeff Vanuga/CORBIS 229:(i)C Squared Studios/ Getty 230-231:(b)Lake County Museum/CORBIS 231:(tr)Dallas Historical Society, Texas, USA/Bridgeman 250:(tl)Courtesy Julius Lester;(tcr)Courtesy Simon & Schuster 254:Richard Hutchings/ PhotoEdit 255:Guy Grenier Masterfile 256:Hot Ideas/Index Stock 257:William Gottlieb/CORBIS 258:Bluestone Productions/ SuperStock 260-261:(bg)Art Resource, NY 261:(i) Photolink/Getty 262:(tr)C Squared Studios/ Getty;(i) Courtesy the Rhode Island Historical Society 264-265:Kevin Fleming/CORBIS 282:Courtesy Simon & Schuster 283:Kevin Fleming/CORBIS 288:Dynamic Graphic Group/IT Stock Free/Alamy 290-291: (bg) Underwood & Underwood/ CORBIS 291:(i)Photolink/Getty 292-293:(b) WorldTravelPhoto.com/ Alamy 293:(cr)Jeff Greenberg/Image Works 306:(tl)Terri Jepson; (tcr)Courtesy Holiday House 308:(cr) Museum of London/Topham-HIP/Image Works;(tcr)Wisconsin Historical Society, Image ID: 9320;(bl) Museum of London/Topham-HIP/Image Works 309: Hulton-Deutsch Collection/CORBIS 310:Bettmann/CORBIS 311:(tl) Museum of London/Topham-HIP/Image Works;(tc)Bettmann/ CORBIS 312:BananaStock/PictureQuest 313:(tr)Photodisc/Getty;(i) Library of Congress 314-315:Digital Vision 316:Digital Vision/Getty 317:(tl)The Jackson Citizen Patriot;(l)Photodisc/Getty;(2)Creatas; (3-5) Digital Vision 318-319: (bg)Jeff Hunter/Getty 319:(tl)Paul McErlane/Reuters/NewsCom 320-321:Joseph Van Os/Getty 322-323: John Coutlakis/Asheville Citizen Times 324:Photodisc/Getty 325: (bl)Burke/Triolo Productions/ Brand X/Alamy;(b)Dian Lofton for TFK;(br)Tracy Montana/PhotoLink/Getty 326-327:(bg)Joel Sartore/ National Geographic 327:(i)Robert Glusic/Getty 328:(bl)Yva Momatiuk/John Eastcott/Minden 328-329:(bg)Craig C. Sheumaker/ Panoramic Images 348:(tcl) Courtesy Cristina Kessler;(cr) Courtesy Walter Lyon Krudop 350:(bl)Ludovic Maisant/CORBIS 350-351:(bg) Kaz Chiba/Getty 351:(tr)Galen Rowell/CORBIS 352:(tr)Charles Bowman/Getty; (bcl) Walter Bibikaw/Index Stock 353:Photowood/ CORBIS 354:Bob Daemmrich/Image Works 355:Ross Anania/Getty 356-357:(bg)Rick Fischer/Masterfile 357:(i) Photodisc/Getty 382: Courtesy Constance Brown 384:LJW/PB Korea Teajon/HO/Reuters 385:Toshiyuki Aizawa/Reuters 386:SW Productions/Brand X Pictures/Getty 387:Photos.com 389:Getty 390:Tony Freeman/ PhotoEdit 392-393:(bg)Jorge Silva/Reuters 393:(i)CORBIS 412:(tcl)Courtesy Simon & Schuster; (cr)Alan S. Orling 414:(bc)C Squared Studios/Getty;(i)Reproduced by permission of the Norman Rockwell Family Agency, Inc.; Collection of the Norman Rockwell Museum at Stockbridge, Massachusetts 415-416:AP 417:(tr)Steven Senne/AP 418:Amos Morgan/Photodisc/Getty 420-421:(bg)J. Sneesby/B. Wilkins/Getty 421:(i)Getty 440:Courtesy Northland Publishing 442-443:(bg)Leszczynski, Zigmund/Animals Animals/ Earth Scenes 443:(br)Gloria H. Chomica/Masterfile 444:(bl)Frans Lanting/ Minden 444-445:(b)Steve Bloom/Alamy 445: (tc)Dwight Kuhn;(tcr)zefa/Masterfile 446:Getty 447:Martin Ruegner/ ImageState/Alamy 448-449:AP 450:Granger 451:(bl)AP;(tr)Granger 452-453:(br)AP 453:(t) Erich Hartmann/Magnum Photos 454-455:AP 456:(t)Chris Mello/Lonely Planet;(bcl)Digital Vision/ Punchstock 458:Amos Morgan/Photodisc/Getty 459:(r)Dian Lofton for TFK;(bl)Tracy Montana/ PhotoLink/Getty;(b)Dian Lofton for TFK 460-461:(bg)Larry L. Miller/Photo Researchers 461:(i)Don Farrall/ Getty 462-463:(bg) Reuters America LLC 463:(tr)James Leynse/ CORBIS 464-465: Weatherstock/Omni-Photo Communications 466-467:Kjell B. Sandved/Visuals Unlimited 468-469:Greg Lovett/ Palm Beach Post (Image digitally altered by MMH) 470-471:Science VU/NOAA/NASA/Visuals Unlimited 472-473:David Lane/Palm Beach Post 474: Nancy P. Alexander 476:(tcl)Courtesy Seymour Simon 476-477: (bg)StockTrek/Getty 480:Tom & Dee Ann McCarthy/CORBIS 481:Getty 482-483:(bg) Tim Davis/CORBIS 483:(i)Greg Kuchik/Getty

504:Courtesy Angela Shelf Medearis 508:Medioimages/Alamy 509: Ellen Senisi/Image Works 510:Stock Montage/Getty 511:Schenectady Museum; Hall of Electrical History Foundation/CORBIS 512:(t to b)Charles H. Phillips/Time Life Pictures/Getty; Michael Freeman/ CORBIS; Bettmann/CORBIS; Schenectady Museum; Hall of Electrical History Foundation/CORBIS; Bettmann/CORBIS; Schenectady Museum; Hall of Electrical History Foundation/CORBIS; Yevgeny Khaldei/CORBIS 514-515:(bg)Hinrich Baesemann/UNEP/ Peter Arnold 515:(i)Photolink/Getty 516-517:(b)Royalty-Free/CORBIS 517:(cr) Digital Vision/ PictureQuest 520-533: Licensed with permission of the Scott Polar Research Institute, University of Cambridge 534:(tcr) Emma Dodge Hanson;(bcl)Courtesy William Maughan 536-539:(bg) Digital Vision/Punchstock 540:Ariel Skelley/CORBIS 542-543: (bg) © Viesti Associates 543:(i)C Squared Studios/Getty 562:(br)USDA 562-563: (bg)Kyodo News 564:Image Source/Getty 566-567:Flip Nicklin/ Minden 568: Mark A. Philbrick/Brigham Young University 569:(tl) Joe Andrews;(bcr)AP 570:David Bowers 571:Courtesy Independence National Historical Park 572:(tr)Jeremy Woodhouse/Masterfile; (bl)Missouri Historical Society 573:Jose Azel/Aurora 574: (t) Royalty-Free/CORBIS;(tcl) NASA/Science Photo Library/Photo Researchers; (bcr)CORBIS 576:Ryan McVay/ Photodisc/Punchstock 577:(tr)Dian Lofton for TFK;(b)Dian Lofton for TFK;(bc)Dian Lofton for TFK;(br) Tracy Montana/PhotoLink/Getty 578-579:(bg) © CORBIS 579:(i) CMCD/Getty 580-581: J. Speer/ Tama News-Herald 598:Courtesy Northland Publishing 600-601:(bl)Official US Marine Corps Photo USMC/National Archives;(l to r)Christie's Images/CORBIS 601: (tr)Saunder, Defense Dept Photo (Marine Corps)/National Archives; 602:Ryan McVay/Photodisc/Getty 604-605:(bg)James Watt/Animals Animals/Earth Scenes 605:(i)Creatas/PictureQuest 626:(tcr)Ed Scott; (cl)Courtesy Marla Baggeta 628-629:Kelvin Aitken/AGE Fotostock 630:(tl)Paul Sutherland Photography 630-631:(bc)Stuart Westmorland/CORBIS 631:(cr)Flip Nicklin/Minden 632:Jim Arbogast/ Getty 633:Georgette Douwma/Getty 636: W.A. Sharman; Milepost 92 1/2/CORBIS 638-639:(bg)David Sanger/Alamy 639:(i)Andrew Ward/ LifeFile/Getty 660:Courtesy Morgan Robinson 666:Digital Vision/Getty 667:Pete Saloutos/CORBIS 668-669:(bg)George and Monserrate Schwartz/Alamy 669:(i)PhotoLink/Getty 670:Martin Fox/Index Stock 670:(tcl)Joanne Ryder;(br)Courtesy Winson Trang 692-693:Masterfile /Masterfile 694:(b)Sharon Collyer 694-695:(bg) Scott T. Smith/CORBIS 696:(bl)Ryan McVay/Photodisc/Getty 697: Hein Heuvel/ Zefa/Masterfile 698-699:Petrus Karagjias 700:(tr)Elena Dorfman; (bl) Andrew Kaufman/Contact 701:AP 702:Courtesy Boundless Playgrounds 703:(t)James Keyser/Time-Life Pictures/ Getty;(b) Courtesy Boundless Playgrounds 704:AP 705:Dwight Carter 706:Jeaneen Lund 708:Photodisc/Getty 709:(l)Dian Lofton for TFK; (b) Dian Lofton for TFK;(br)Tracy Montana/PhotoLink/ Getty 710-711: (bg) Andrea Booher/Getty 711:(i)PhotoLink/Getty 712: Fast Track/Getty 713: (cr)Myrleen Ferguson Cate/PhotoEdit 714-715: K. Oster/Zefa/Masterfile 716:George D. Lepp/CORBIS 718:Granger 719:San Diego Aerospace Museum 720:Bettmann/CORBIS 721: © CORBIS 722:French School,(18th century) / Musee d'Art et d'Histoire, Meudon, France, Lauros/Giraudon/Bridgeman 723:De Frene (18th century)/Bibliotheque Nationale, Paris, France, Lauros/Giraudon/ Bridgeman 724-725:Bettmann/CORBIS 726:Jay Syverson/ CORBIS 728:(tcl) Bettmann/CORBIS;(tr)Hulton-Deutsch Collection/ CORBIS;(bl) Getty; (bcl) Bettmann/ CORBIS 728-729:(bg)Getty 729:(tl)AP;(tr)Tony Ruta /Index Stock;(bl)Fabrice Coffrini/ Keystone/ AP;(bcr)David Parker/Photo Researchers 730:(bg)K. Oster/Zefa/ Masterfile;(tcr)Russell Frost;(br) Kevin R. Morris/CORBIS 730-731:(bg) Photodisc/Getty 731:K. Oster/Zefa/Masterfile 734:Bob Daemmrich/ PhotoEdit 736-737: (bg) Douglas Faulkner/Photo Researchers 737:(i)Jules Frazier/Getty 738-739: (b)Royalty-Free/CORBIS 739:(cr) Hasselbalch Imaging 740-750: Dennis Kunkel Microscopy 751: Stephen Kramer 752:(tcr) Joshua Kramer;(bcl) Courtesy Dennis Kunkel;(bl)Dennis Kunkel Microscopy 752-753: (bg)Photodisc/Getty 753:(br)Dennis Kunkel Microscopy 754-755:(bg) David Muench/ CORBIS;(t)Christie's Images/CORBIS 756: (bg)Gary Braasch/CORBIS 756-757:(bg)Christie's Images/ CORBIS 758:Amos Morgan/ Photodisc/Getty 759:Steve Skjold/Alamy 761:(cl)C Squared Studios/ Getty;(i) Grand Canyon of the Yellowstone Park (oil on canvas), Moran, Thomas (1837-1926)/Private Collection/www.bridgeman. co.uk 762:Digital Vision 766:ASAP Ltd/Index Stock 768:Rolf Bruderer/ CORBIS 769:Geostock/Getty 771:BananaStock/Alamy 772: Sarkis Images/Alamy 774:PhotoLink/Getty 775: Royalty-free/CORBIS 777:Digital Vision 778:(tr)photolibrary.com.pty.ltd /Index Stock;(bl) Image Source/CORBIS 780:Foodcollection.com/Alamy 781:Royalty-Free/CORBIS 782:PhotoLink/Getty

Teacher's Notes

PEARSON
realize™
www.PearsonRealize.com

Go online to access additional resources including:
Primary Sources • Biographies • Supreme Court cases •
21st Century Skill Tutorials • Maps • Graphic Organizers.

Objectives

Objective 1: Explain the multiple reasons why a plan was needed for Reconstruction of the South.

Objective 2: Compare the strengths and weaknesses of the Reconstruction plans of Lincoln, Johnson, and Congress.

Objective 3: Discuss Johnson's political difficulties and impeachment.

LESSON 1 ORGANIZER		PACING: APPROX. 1 PERIOD, .5 BLOCKS			
				RESOURCES	
		OBJECTIVES	**PACING**	**Online**	**Print**
Connect					
DIGITAL START UP ACTIVITY **Setting Goals for Reconstruction**			5 min.	●	
Investigate					
DIGITAL TEXT 1 **The Challenges of Reconstruction**		Objective 1	10 min.	●	●
DIGITAL TEXT 2 **Competing Reconstruction Plans**			10 min.	●	●
DIGITAL TEXT 3 **The Johnson Presidency and Reconstruction**		Objective 2	10 min.	●	●
INTERACTIVE CHART **Comparing Viewpoints on Reconstruction**			10 min.	●	
DIGITAL TEXT 4 **Congress Passes a Plan for Reconstruction**		Objective 3	10 min.	●	●
Synthesize					
DIGITAL ACTIVITY **Plans for Reconstruction**			5 min.	●	
Demonstrate					
DIGITAL QUIZ **Lesson Quiz and Class Discussion Board**			10 min.	●	

Plans for Reconstruction Clash

▮ CONNECT

DIGITAL START UP ACTIVITY
Setting Goals for Reconstruction

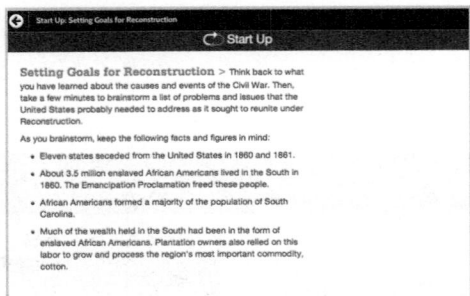

Project the Start Up Activity Ask students to brainstorm their lists as they come in and get settled. Have students share their ideas with a partner, either in class or through a chat or blog space.

Discuss Ask students to reflect on the most significant challenges facing the nation after the Civil War. *(how will states return to union, how will formerly enslaved African Americans join society, how will the southern economy recover)*

Tell students that in this lesson they will be learning about the challenges of political reunification after the Civil War.

Aa Vocabulary Development: Use the Interactive Reading Notepad to preview the Key Terms and Academic Vocabulary in this lesson with students.

⇧ FLIP IT!
Assign the Flipped Video for this lesson.

▮ STUDENT EDITION PRINT
PAGES: 284–290

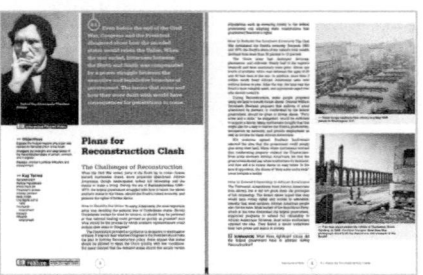

▮ INVESTIGATE

DIGITAL TEXT 1
The Challenges of Reconstruction

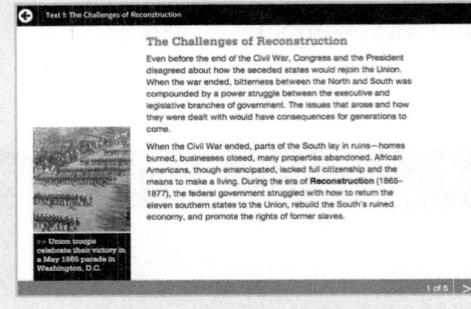

Objective 1: Explain the multiple reasons why a plan was needed for Reconstruction of the South.

Quick Instruction
Direct students' focus to the photograph of two people meeting amid the rubble of Charleston, South Carolina. Begin a discussion by asking students to describe the photograph and the effects of war on the country or region that lost the conflict. Ask: What economic challenges did many southern states face following the war? *(The Union Army had destroyed factories, railroads, and plantations. Nearly half of the region's livestock and farm machinery were gone. Approximately one fourth of southern white men between the ages of the 20 and 40 had died during the war, leaving the region with a limited workforce.)*

Summarize General William Tecumseh Sherman's plan to help emancipated African Americans. *(Sherman proposed that land abandoned or confiscated by the federal government during the war should be given to formerly enslaved peoples. He thought that this might be an efficient way to restore the South's economic productivity and provide employment as well as income for many formerly enslaved African Americans.)*

Infer Why did some disagree with Sherman's plan to give abandoned or confiscated land to formerly enslaved people? Did the plan ever come to pass? *(Some questioned the legality and appropriateness of giving away land taken in time of war without financially compensating the original owners; the plan never gained wide support and didn't come to pass.)*

Further Instruction
Draw Conclusions How might the end of the war affect the more than 3 million newly freed African Americans? *(Many would be homeless and unemployed because the plantations on which they lived and worked were destroyed.)*

Express Problems Clearly What major political obstacles made a plan for reconstruction especially challenging? *(Political leaders could not agree on a plan. The Constitution provided no guidance on secession or readmission of states. It was not clear whether Congress or the President should take the lead in forming Reconstruction policy, consequently, a power struggle between the executive and legislative branches of government developed.)*

  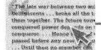

DIGITAL TEXT 2
Competing Reconstruction Plans

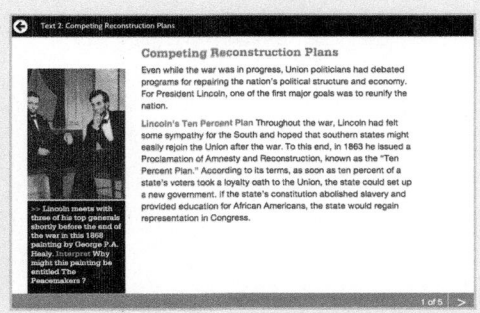

DIGITAL TEXT 3
The Johnson Presidency and Reconstruction

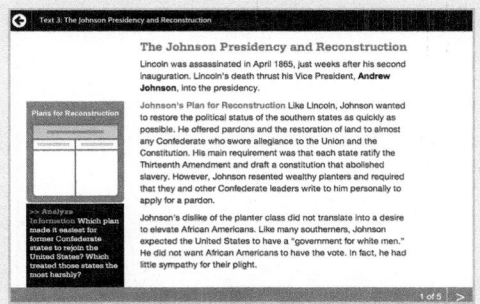

INTERACTIVE CHART
Comparing Viewpoints on Reconstruction

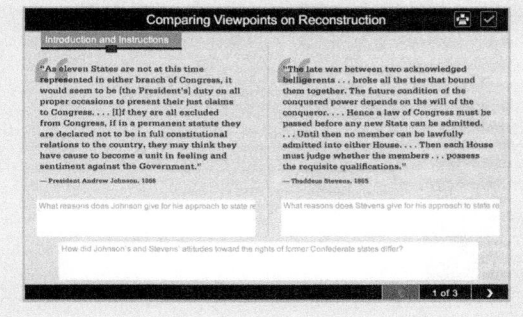

Objective 2: Compare the strengths and weaknesses of the Reconstruction plans of Lincoln, Johnson, and Congress.

Quick Instruction

Interactive Chart: Comparing Viewpoints on Reconstruction Project the Interactive Chart. Prompt students to set the chart's primary source quotes into the larger context of Reconstruction. Ask: What were the key issues in the Reconstruction debate? *(the severity of punishment for former Confederate states, terms of readmission to the Union, and how to handle emancipated African Americans)* Prompt students to identify the key arguments made by President Johnson and Senator Stevens as they answer the questions.

Cite Evidence Aside from basic relief efforts, what other services did the Freedmen's Bureau provide? *(The Freedmen's Bureau helped reunite families that had been separated by slavery and war. It worked to provide education to African American and white refugees. It negotiated fair labor contracts between former slaves and white landowners. By representing African Americans in the courts, the Bureau also established a precedent that African American citizens had legal rights.)*

ACTIVE CLASSROOM

Conduct a Take a Stand activity. Ask students to take a stand on the following question: With which point of view do you agree most: President Johnson's or Senator Stevens's? Ask students to divide into two groups based on their answer and move to separate areas of the classroom. Ask students to talk with each other to compare their reasons for their position.

D Differentiate: Extra Support Clarify that President Johnson did not want African Americans to have the vote. Johnson supported the idea of the former Confederate states maintaining a degree of political autonomy relative to the federal government. States should therefore individually determine the political rights of *formerly* enslaved African Americans.

ELL Use the ELL activity described in the ELL chart.

Further Instruction

Determine Point of View How did President Lincoln try to strike a balance between the views of the Radical Republicans and more moderate groups? *(Lincoln wanted to make it relatively easy for southern states to rejoin the Union after the war. He was willing to grant pardons to former Confederates, and he considered compensating them for lost property. He recognized pro-Union governments in Arkansas, Louisiana, and Tennessee even though they denied African Americans the right to vote. Lincoln, however,*

supported the Radical Republican plan of the Freedmen's Bureau to help African Americans (as well as white refugees) after the war.)

Determine Points of View How did the clash between President Johnson and Congress reflect differences over the political relationship between the federal and state governments? *(Many in Congress believed that the federal government had the constitutional authority to guarantee political rights for formerly enslaved peoples. Johnson and many southerners thought that the states, and not the federal government, should play that role.)*

Compare the three plans for Reconstruction, referring to the chart in Text 3 if necessary. In your opinion, which would have been the most effective at meeting the goals of reintegrating the southern states into the union, while protecting the rights of African Americans? *(Possible response: In my opinion, Lincoln's plan would have gotten the states back into the union with less ill will than the Radical Republican plan but did not have enough safeguards to protect the rights of African Americans. Johnson's plan had the same flaw. If the Radical Republican plan could have been less focused on punishing the South, it might have been a smoother and less rancorous reintegration while still establishing rights for African Americans.)*

Plans for Reconstruction Clash

DIGITAL TEXT 4
Congress Passes a Plan for Reconstruction

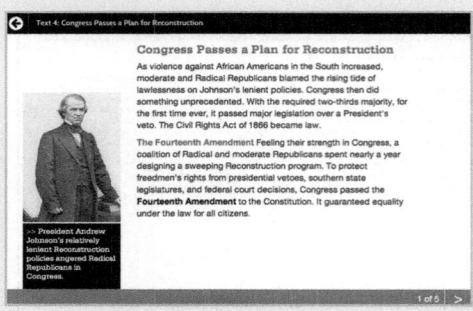

Objective 3: Discuss Johnson's political difficulties and impeachment.

Quick Instruction

Display the map showing the military districts in the South. Explain that the Military Reconstruction Act of 1867 divided the ten southern states that had yet to be readmitted into the Union into five military districts governed by former Union generals. Point out that Congress passed this legislation over Johnson's veto. In what other instances did Congressional action contradict President Johnson's views? *(the Civil Rights Act of 1866, proposing the Fourteenth Amendment, impeachment)*

Generate Explanations How did the Tenure of Office Act reflect the tension between Congress and President Johnson? *(The President has the constitutional authority to select candidates for positions in the cabinet, who in turn require Senate approval to serve. The Tenure of Office Act however was unprecedented legislation passed to limit the President's ability to remove a cabinet official.)*

ELL Use the ELL activity described in the ELL chart.

Further Instruction

Go through the Interactive Reading Notepad questions and use the discussion to ensure students' understanding of the causes and effects of Reconstruction.

Express Problems Clearly What weaknesses in the Fourteenth and Fifteenth Amendments could states potentially exploit if they disagreed with either? *(Both amendments contained loopholes that allowed states to impose voting restrictions based on literacy or property qualifications, which in effect would exclude most African Americans, most of whom were not functionally literate and did not own property.)*

Infer Why was the election of Ulysses S. Grant a sign that the problems of Reconstruction were not yet resolved? *(Although Grant won the electoral vote by a huge margin and had a significant lead in the popular vote, his opponent, Horatio Seymour, a Democrat from New York, received a majority of the white vote. This highlights the fact that many white Americans did not agree with the course of Reconstruction.)*

SYNTHESIZE

DIGITAL ACTIVITY

Plans for Reconstruction

DEMONSTRATE

DIGITAL QUIZ

Lesson Quiz and Class Discussion Board

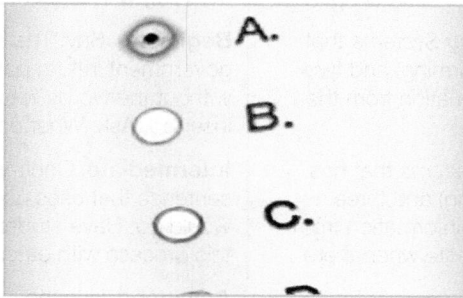

Before students begin their graphic organizers, have students work with a partner to review and discuss the reasons a Reconstruction plan was necessary and the major points of each Reconstruction plan.

Discuss When students have completed the activity, ask them to reflect on the Topic Essential Question: How can we ensure equality for all? Invite volunteers to decide which Reconstruction plan they learned about offered the best course for ensuring equality for all Americans. Direct students to support their positions with information from the lesson.

Assign the online Lesson Quiz for this lesson if you haven't already done so. Students will be offered automatic remediation or enrichment based on their score.

Pose these questions to the class on the Discussion Board:

In *Plans for Reconstruction Clash*, you read about how American lawmakers scrambled to come up with plans to reunite and "reconstruct" the country following the Civil War. Political reunion and assimilating millions of formerly enslaved African Americans proved challenging.

Draw Conclusions How did Reconstruction reignite debate about the federal government's power relative to the states in the Constitution?

Assess Credibility Do you think the Radical Republican Congress abused its power by impeaching President Johnson? Support your answer with reasons.

Make Predictions Will Reconstruction prove to be a success in reuniting the country? Why or why not?

Topic Inquiry

Have students continue their investigations for the Topic Discussion.

Reconstruction Changes the South

Supporting English Language Learners

Use with the reading, **Land Distribution in the South**.

Learning
Explain that like taking notes, recording a text's key information in a chart can help students learn that information and see how it is interconnected.

Beginning Display a partially filled-in chart titled *Farming Systems* that has three rows (sharecropping, share-tenancy, tenant-farming) and two columns (crops, home). Invite students to suggest information from the text to complete the rest of the chart.

Intermediate Display an empty chart titled *Farming Systems* that has three rows (sharecropping, share-tenancy, tenant-farming) and three columns (crops, home, supplies). Invite students to use information from the text to complete the rest of the chart, as well as to note when there might not be information available for a given cell.

Advanced Invite pairs of students to create a chart titled *Farming Systems* that has three rows (sharecropping, share-tenancy, tenant-farming) and three columns (crops, home, supplies). Have pairs complete the chart using information from the text.

Advanced High Invite pairs of students to create a chart that organizes information about the farming systems described in the text. Encourage them to consider the chart's rows and columns carefully so that they can record the most important information in the most logical way.

Use with the reading, **Changes in the South Spark Violence**.

Listening
Point out the expression *in turn* in the text's first paragraph and discuss its meaning with students.

Beginning Say: The Ku Klux Klan was violent and out of control. The government in turn passed Enforcement Acts. Then display the sentences without the words *in turn*, and have students identify where they should be inserted. Ask: What does *in turn* mean in this context?

Intermediate Contrast the meanings of *in turn* and *turn in*. Then say a sentence that uses one of these two expressions, leaving a pause where it would go. Have students identify which expression is appropriate. Repeat this process with other sentences (about the text and in other contexts).

Advanced Use the expressions *in turn*, *turn in*, and *turn into* in sentences about the text. After each sentence, pause so that pairs of students can determine the expression's meaning. Then invite pairs to practice using all three expressions as they discuss the text.

Advanced High Display these expressions: *in turn*, *turn in*, *turn into*, *out of turn*, and *turn out*. Invite pairs of students to discuss their meanings, referring to a dictionary if necessary. Then have them use each expression as they discuss the text.

▣ Differentiate Instruction

Use the Differentiated Instruction notes throughout the lesson plan to support the varied skill sets, levels of readiness, and interests in the mixed-ability classroom.

Challenge These notes include suggestions for expanding the activity for advanced students.

On-Level These notes include suggestions for modifying the activity to address different interests or learning styles.

Extra Support These notes include ideas for providing more scaffolding or reading spuport.

Special Needs These notes provide ideas for adapting instruction to support the needs of various special needs students.

■ NOTES

PEARSON
realize™
www.PearsonRealize.com

Go online to access additional resources including:
Primary Sources • Biographies • Supreme Court cases •
21st Century Skill Tutorials • Maps • Graphic Organizers.

Objectives

Objective 1: Explain how Republicans gained control of southern state governments.

Objective 2: Analyze how freedmen adjusted to freedom and the role of the Freedmen's Bureau.

Objective 3: Evaluate the South's new economic system and its impact on poor farmers.

Objective 4: Summarize efforts to limit African Americans' rights and the federal government's response.

LESSON 2 ORGANIZER	PACING: APPROX. 1 PERIOD, .5 BLOCKS				
				RESOURCES	
		OBJECTIVES	PACING	Online	Print
Connect					
	DIGITAL START UP ACTIVITY **An African American in the Senate**		5 min.	●	
Investigate					
	DIGITAL TEXT 1 **Republicans Dominate Government**	Objective 1	10 min.	●	●
	INTERACTIVE GALLERY **Reconstruction-Era Political Groups**		10 min.	●	
	BEFORE AND AFTER **Atlanta Reconstructed**		10 min.	●	
	DIGITAL TEXT 2 **Freed People Rebuild Their Lives**	Objective 2	10 min.	●	●
	DIGITAL TEXT 3 **Land Distribution in the South**	Objective 3	10 min.	●	●
	INTERACTIVE CHART **The Cycle of Poverty**		10 min.	●	
	DIGITAL TEXT 4 **Changes in the South Spark Violence**	Objective 4	10 min.	●	●
Synthesize					
	DIGITAL ACTIVITY **Challenges After Emancipation**		5 min.	●	
Demonstrate					
	DIGITAL QUIZ **Lesson Quiz and Class Discussion Board**		10 min.	●	

Topic  8 Lesson 2

Reconstruction Changes the South

■ CONNECT

DIGITAL START UP ACTIVITY
An African American in the Senate

Project the Start Up Activity As students enter and get settled, direct their attention to the quote from Hiram Revels. Encourage students to spend several minutes discussing the quote with a partner before they begin responding to the questions.

Discuss Reflect on additional responsibilities Revels might have carried with him to Washington. *(Possible response: Revels probably felt a sense of pressure as one of the first African American Congressmen.)*

Tell students that in this lesson they will be learning about how the Republican party took control of Southern state governments, the role of the Freedman's Bureau, and the political conflict over African American rights.

Aa Vocabulary Development: Use the Interactive Reading Notepad to preview the Key Terms and Academic Vocabulary in this lesson with students.

⇅ FLIP IT!
Assign the Flipped Video for this lesson.

■ STUDENT EDITION PRINT PAGES: 291–298

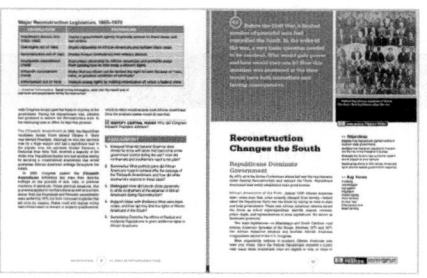

■ INVESTIGATE

DIGITAL TEXT 1
Republicans Dominate Government

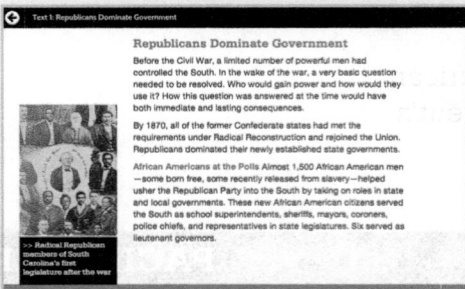

Objective 1: **Explain how Republicans gained control of southern state governments.**

Quick Instruction
Interactive Gallery: Reconstruction-Era Political Groups Project the Interactive Gallery and navigate through the images about influential political groups in the South during Reconstruction with students. Introduce the activity by reviewing how Americans were divided over terms of readmission to the Union, rebuilding the South's ruined economy, and promoting the rights of former slaves.

Before and After: Atlanta Reconstructed Project the Before and After and use the slider to navigate between the contrasting images of Atlanta. Prompt students to evaluate the extent of the destruction and rebuilding process in the South after the Civil War. How did rebuilding Atlanta's railroads contribute to the reconstruction effort in Atlanta and elsewhere? *(Railroads would have been necessary to bring in supplies and people to help rebuild the city. Also, as Atlanta's economy picked up and agricultural products were produced, railroads would have been used to transport goods to other markets.)*

INTERACTIVE GALLERY
Reconstruction-Era Political Groups

📷 ACTIVE CLASSROOM
Conduct a Wallpaper activity. Have students review information about the Reconstruction-era political groups by designing a piece of "wallpaper" with text and images that encapsulates a key aspect of each political group. Post the wallpaper and have students take a gallery/"wisdom" walk and note what others have written/illustrated.

📷 ACTIVE CLASSROOM
Conduct a Circle Write. Break students into groups and provide this question as a writing prompt: How did Reconstruction improve life in Atlanta after the Civil War? Have students write as much as they can for one minute then switch with the person on their right. The next person tries to improve or elaborate the response where the other person left off. Continue to switch until the paper comes back to the first person. The group then decides which is the best composition (or response) and shares that with the larger group.

BEFORE AND AFTER
Atlanta Reconstructed

D Differentiate: **Challenge/Gifted** Ask students to do additional research on the rebuilding of Atlanta or another major southern city after the war and present their findings. Suggest that students enhance their reports with visuals that are similar to the interactivity.

Further Instruction
Go through the Interactive Reading Notepad questions and use appropriate questions to launch a discussion about how Americans viewed the influential political groups during Reconstruction. Direct students' attention to the carpetbagger cartoon and the 1870 political cartoon depicting two leading railroad investors. Invite students to discuss the cartoons and answer the caption questions. To add depth to the discussion, assign 21st Century Skill Tutorials: Analyze Political Cartoons.

Summarize how Republicans gained control in the South. *(Millions of southern African American men voted to support Reconstruction efforts. Since the Radical Republicans required a loyalty oath, many white southerners were either not eligible to vote or chose to stay away from the constitutional conventions and subsequent elections. This gave a great advantage to Republicans.)*

Analyze Information How did Republican governments provide new opportunities in the South? *(Republican governments welcomed those who had been previously disenfranchised by providing political opportunities, including positions such as school superintendents, sheriffs, mayors, coroners, police chiefs, and representatives in state legislatures. Republican governments also aggressively promoted economic development, which provided jobs for many people and helped boost economies across the South.)*

DIGITAL TEXT 2
Freed People Rebuild Their Lives

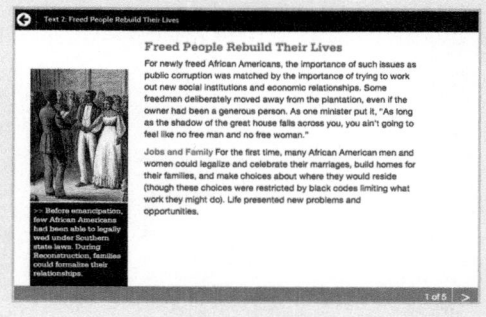

Objective 2: **Analyze how freedmen adjusted to freedom and the role of the Freedmen's Bureau.**

Quick Instruction
Direct students' attention to the illustration of the African American wedding ceremony. Remind students that before emancipation, few African Americans had been able to legally wed under Southern state laws. Point out that families were often torn apart under the slavery system. Why would formal recognition of marriage be important? *(Formal recognition would make the marriage legal and legitimize a couple's children. It would underscore the fact that, as free people, families could depend on being able to stay together, rather than fearing that they would be torn apart at any time, as they did under slavery.)*

Identify Central Issues How did religion and churches help African Americans during Reconstruction? *(African American churches often served as school sites, community centers, employment agencies, and political rallying points. By providing an arena for organizing, public speaking, and group planning, churches helped develop African American leaders.)*

Determine Relevance How would access to schools benefit newly emancipated slaves? *(Schools would teach freed people to learn reading and math skills as well as new occupational skills. The ability to read could lead to new jobs and would be important when negotiating labor agreements to guarantee fair treatment and wages.)*

Reconstruction Changes the South

DIGITAL TEXT 3
Land Distribution in the South

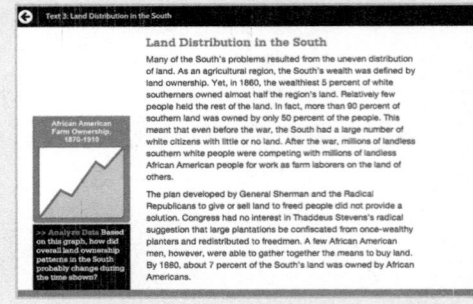

INTERACTIVE CHART
The Cycle of Poverty

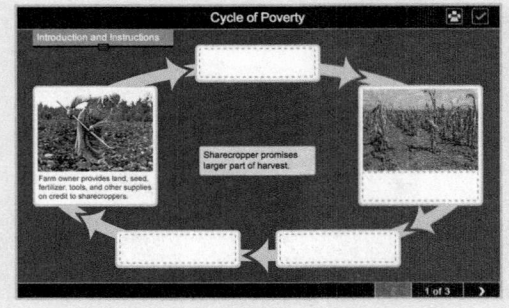

Further Instruction

Support Ideas with Examples What examples in the text show some of the challenges facing recently freed African Americans during Reconstruction? *(Black codes limited and restricted what work they might do; lacking an education, many had to remain in rural areas and settle for what they had under slavery—substandard housing and poor food in return for hard labor.)*

Generate Explanations In your opinion, what was the most beneficial service provided by the Freedmen's Bureau immediately after the war? *(Possible response: In my opinion, although education became a extremely important service provided by the Freedmen's Bureau later in Reconstruction, its initial goal of providing food, clothing, health care for both African American and white refugees in the South was most beneficial.)*

Objective 3: Evaluate the South's new economic system and its impact on poor farmers.

Quick Instruction

Project the Interactive Chart and prompt students to sort the tiles into the appropriate boxes to demonstrate difficulties facing many sharecroppers. How did the Civil War affect agriculture in the South? *(The Union army had destroyed many plantations, and nearly half of the region's livestock and farm machinery were gone. Land had become the South's most valuable asset, but few landowners had cash to pay workers, and few workers had cash to buy land.)*

Infer How might the state of southern agriculture affect freed African Americans as they tried to start new lives? *(Freed African Americans, like poorer southern whites, did not own land and did not have the resources to buy valuable land; more than likely they would have to work on land owned by others.)*

📷 ACTIVE CLASSROOM

Conduct a Conversation with History activity. Have students imagine that they are having a conversation with the sharecropper in the Interactive Chart's photo. Ask them to write down a question they would like to ask, then what that person would say to them, and what they would say in response.

ELL Use the ELL activity described in the ELL chart.

Further Instruction

Draw Conclusions Why was the sharecropping system considered an endless cycle for southern farmers? *(Sharecroppers had to pay landowners on credit for everything—food, shelter, supplies for farming. The sale of their share of the crop often didn't cover these expenses. Hence, sharecroppers were perpetually in debt to the landowner.)*

Generate Explanations Although tenant farming offered greater independence, what risks were involved? *(The tenant farmer had to rely on an adequate harvest yield and good crop prices in order to pay for all the necessities of living. A poor harvest or low price would leave a tenant farmer unable to pay for anything.)*

SYNTHESIZE

DEMONSTRATE

DIGITAL TEXT 4
Changes in the South Spark Violence

DIGITAL ACTIVITY
Challenges After Emancipation

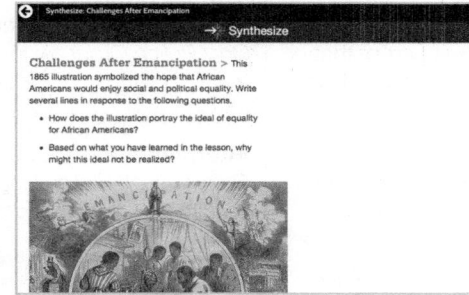

DIGITAL QUIZ
Lesson Quiz and Class Discussion Board

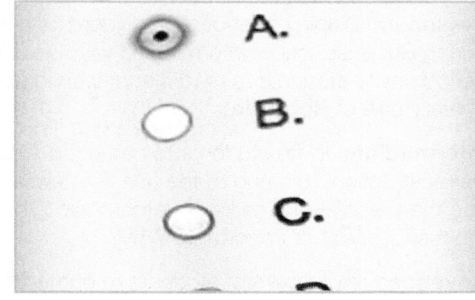

Objective 4: Summarize efforts to limit African Americans' rights and the federal government's response.

Quick Instruction
Summarize Why did racial violence increase after 1870? How did the federal government respond? *(The Fifteenth Amendment was ratified in 1870, guaranteeing voting rights regardless of race or previous condition of servitude. This angered many white Americans and led them to resist government actions. The federal government responded by passing the Enforcement Acts in 1870 and 1871, also known as the Ku Klux Klan Acts, making it a federal offense to interfere with another citizen's right to vote.)*

ELL Use the ELL activity described in the ELL chart.

Further Instruction
Identify Central Issues What factors motivated many white southerners in their insistence that African Americans not have full citizenship? *(Fierce economic competition and economic uncertainty in the devastated southern states motivated many southern whites to resist full citizenship for African Americans.)*

Infer What was one African American from Philadelphia implying when he stated, "The Ku Klux of the South are not by any means the lower classes of society"? *(He was implying that many wealthy and perhaps politically powerful people were members of the Ku Klux Klan.)*

Have students spend several minutes examining and discussing the image with a partner. Have students share their ideas with the class before answering the questions.

Discuss Focus on the second question from the activity: Based on what you have learned in the lesson, why might this ideal (equality for African Americans) not be realized? Invite students to share their responses with the class. Then direct students to elaborate on their responses by writing a paragraph in which they describe the greatest challenges African Americans will face as Reconstruction continues in the South.

Assign the online Lesson Quiz for this lesson if you haven't already done so. Students will be offered automatic remediation or enrichment based on their score.

Pose these questions to the class on the Discussion Board:

In *Reconstruction Changes the South*, you read about the challenges and struggles freed African Americans faced during Reconstruction—in the South and North—while trying to build lives as free and equal citizens.

Draw Conclusions How did African American's commitment to the Republicans affect their political status in the South?

Make Predictions How do you think the passage of the Fifteenth Amendment would affect the future women's suffrage movement?

Topic Inquiry
Have students continue their investigations for the Topic Inquiry.

Reconstruction's Impact

Supporting English Language Learners

Use with the reading, **Reconstruction Leaves a Mixed Legacy**.

Speaking
Review techniques for expressing ideas clearly, whether they be someone else's or one's own.

Beginning Display a list of several ideas that were successfully carried out during Reconstruction, intermingled with ideas that were not part of that period. Invite students to read aloud each idea and identify those that were actually part of Reconstruction.

Intermediate Invite students to name the successful ideas of Reconstruction, referring to the text if necessary. Record their responses and then read aloud the list together. Ask: Which idea do you think was most successful or important? Why?

Advanced Invite pairs of students to name and discuss the successful ideas of Reconstruction. Then have them answer these questions: What ideas do you think might have healed the bitterness between the North and South? Why do you think ideas like yours were not tried?

Advanced High Invite students to suppose they are politicians living in the time of Reconstruction. Have them create a short speech that explains in a persuasive way the ideas of Reconstruction. Invite partners to read aloud their speeches to each other.

Use with the reading, **The South Restricts African American Rights**.

Reading
Display the photograph from the text that depicts an establishment serving only African Americans.

Beginning Point out the leftmost sign on the building that reads *Colored Only Police Order*. Ask: What did the police order: (a) food and drinks (b) that only African Americans enter the building, or (c) that African Americans have to wait outside?

Intermediate Together, read the leftmost sign on the building that reads *Colored Only Police Order*. Invite students to restate each two-word phrase in their own words. Ask: What is the purpose of the sign?

Advanced Invite pairs of students to discuss the leftmost sign on the building that reads *Colored Only Police Order*. Have them answer these questions: What does the sign mean? Who do you think put up the sign, and why?

Advanced High Invite students to read the signs on the building's left that reads *Colored Only Police Order* and top that reads *ICE COLD Jax . . . .* Ask them to write out answers to these questions: What does each sign mean? What was each sign's purpose? How do you think the African Americans in the photograph felt about each sign? Have partners discuss their ideas.

▣ Differentiate Instruction

Use the Differentiated Instruction notes throughout the lesson plan to support the varied skill sets, levels of readiness, and interests in the mixed-ability classroom.

Challenge These notes include suggestions for expanding the activity for advanced students.

On-Level These notes include suggestions for modifying the activity to address different interests or learning styles.

Extra Support These notes include ideas for providing more scaffolding or reading spuport.

Special Needs These notes provide ideas for adapting instruction to support the needs of various special needs students.

■ NOTES

PEARSON ● ● ●
realize™
www.PearsonRealize.com

Go online to access additional resources including:
Primary Sources • Biographies • Supreme Court cases •
21st Century Skill Tutorials • Maps • Graphic Organizers.

Objectives

Objective 1: Explain why Reconstruction ended.

Objective 2: Evaluate the successes and failures of Reconstruction.

Objective 3: Describe the experience of African Americans in the changing South.

Objective 4: Assess how whites created a segregated society in the South and how African Americans responded.

LESSON 3 ORGANIZER		OBJECTIVES	PACING	Online	Print
Connect					
DIGITAL START UP ACTIVITY **President Grant's Inaugural Address**			5 min.	●	
Investigate					
DIGITAL TEXT 1 **Reconstruction Comes to an End**		Objective 1	10 min.	●	●
INTERACTIVE CARTOON **Worse than Slavery**			10 min.	●	
DIGITAL TEXT 2 **Reconstruction Leaves a Mixed Legacy**		Objective 2	10 min.	●	●
DIGITAL TEXT 3 **The South Restricts African American Rights**		Objectives 3, 4	10 min.	●	●
DIGITAL TEXT 4 **African American Leaders Seek Reform**			10 min.	●	●
Synthesize					
INTERACTIVE CHART **Effects of Reconstruction**			5 min.	●	
Demonstrate					
DIGITAL QUIZ **Lesson Quiz and Class Discussion Board**			10 min.	●	

PACING: APPROX. 1 PERIOD, .5 BLOCKS (header: RESOURCES spans Online/Print)

Reconstruction's Impact

▪ CONNECT

DIGITAL START UP ACTIVITY
President Grant's Inaugural Address

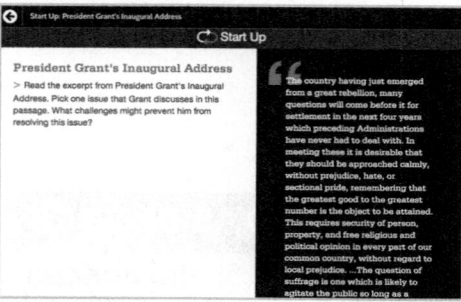

Project the Start Up Activity Ask students to read the quote as they enter and get settled. Then have them write a paragraph reflecting on the quote. Have students share their ideas with a partner, either in class or through a chat or blog space.

Discuss Pair students and have them respond to the following question: Do you agree with President Grant's opinion that the goal of Reconstruction should be attaining "the greatest good to the greatest number"? Why or why not? Meet as a class and have student pairs share their thinking.

Tell students that in this lesson they will be learning about the end of Reconstruction and the continuing challenges of African Americans in the South.

Aa Vocabulary Development: Use the Interactive Reading Notepad to preview the Key Terms and Academic Vocabulary in this lesson with students.

↗ FLIP IT!

Assign the Flipped Video for this lesson.

▪ STUDENT EDITION PRINT PAGES: 299–307

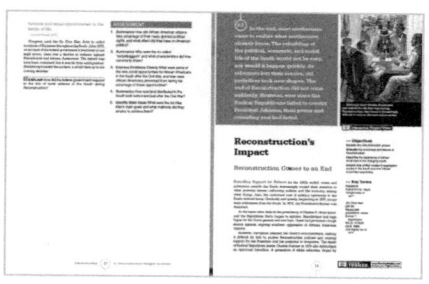

▪ INVESTIGATE

DIGITAL TEXT 1
Reconstruction Comes to an End

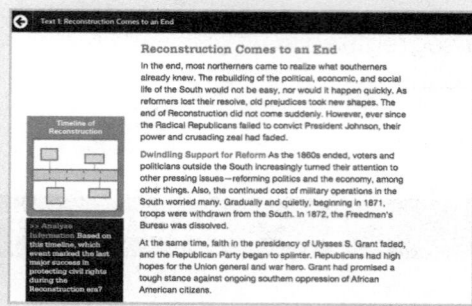

INTERACTIVE CARTOON
Worse than Slavery

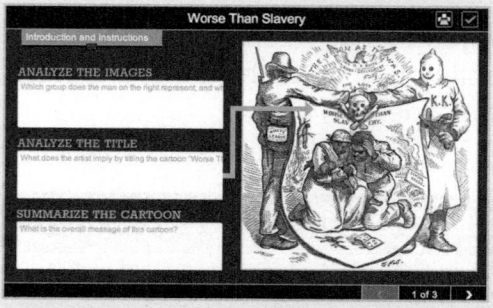

Objective 1: Explain why Reconstruction ended.

Quick Instruction

Interactive Cartoon: Worse than Slavery
Project the Interactive Cartoon and prompt students to explain what each part of the cartoon symbolizes as well as its overall message and tone. Remind students that though institutional slavery had been abolished, the struggles of African Americans continued. Invite students to discuss the challenges African Americans faced. *(Discrimination, intimidation, and violence; state and local governments made laws designed to circumvent the Thirteenth, Fourteenth, and Fifteenth Amendments to the Constitution, setting up poll taxes, literacy tests, and segregation laws.)*

Determine Author's Purpose In your opinion, what does Thomas Nast's cartoon suggest about the success of Reconstruction? *(Nast is expressing the idea that Reconstruction has not been successful because the environment created by racist groups has made the condition of African Americans during Reconstruction worse than slavery.)*

🗣 ACTIVE CLASSROOM

Conduct a Make Headlines activity. Ask: If you were to write a headline that captured what you thought was the most significant challenge formally enslaved people faced after Reconstruction, what would that headline be? Allow students to use subheadings to communicate more information. Have students pass their headlines to a partner for them to review.

D Differentiate: Challenge Invite interested students to conduct research on additional political cartoons that present various views on Reconstruction. Ask students to share what they learn with the rest of the class and display the cartoons they explored.

Further Instruction

Identify Central Issues What factors turned the nation's focus away from the problems in the South? *(Many citizens were more concerned with political corruption and viewed political reform as a more pressing issue. The country's struggling economy and the continued cost of military operations in the South worried many.)*

Summarize How did southern Redeemers gain power? *(Redeemers gained power by compromising with southern Republicans. They found common issues that united white southerners around the goal of regaining power in Congress.)*

Support a Point of View with Evidence Based on what you learned, what was the primary factor that ended Reconstruction? *(A revitalized Democratic Party was able to unite many southerners opposed to Reconstruction. These southern Democrats regained political power and derailed Reconstruction policies.)*

DIGITAL TEXT 2

Reconstruction Leaves a Mixed Legacy

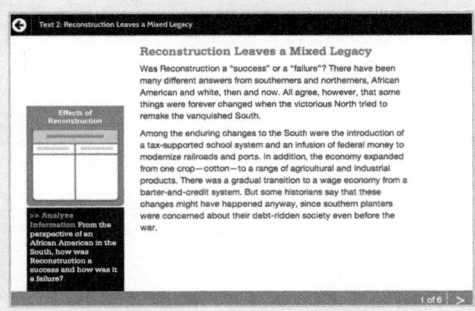

DIGITAL TEXT 3

The South Restricts African American Rights

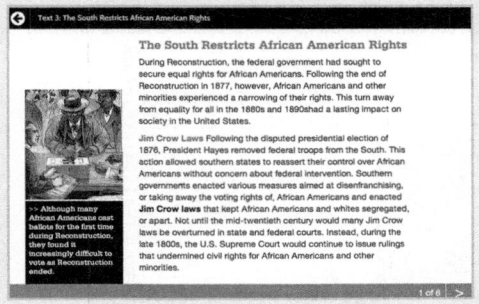

Objective 2: Evaluate the successes and failures of Reconstruction.

Quick Instruction

Direct students' attention to the Effects of Reconstruction chart on the whiteboard. Review the descriptions to ensure students' understanding and challenge them to explain how each was either a positive or negative consequence. Encourage students to reflect on other effects of Reconstruction on different groups of people that they have learned about.

Identify Point of View Explain how Reconstruction was both a success and a failure from the perspective of an African American in the South. *(Positive effects include raised expectations of the right to citizenship under the Thirteenth, Fourteenth, and Fifteenth Amendments and an increase in previously denied opportunities. The Freedmen's Bureau helped reunite freed slaves with their families and promoted literacy within African American communities. However, some groups like the Ku Klux Klan emerged as a backlash against expanded political rights, and economic and social mobility was still significantly limited.)*

ELL Use the ELL activity described in the ELL chart.

Further Instruction

Infer Why might some people consider Reconstruction a temporary setback for the women's suffrage movement? *(Amendments that granted voting rights to African American men did not apply to women. In addition, the debate of the issues created divisions within the movement that weakened the suffrage cause.)*

Draw Conclusions How did the end of Reconstruction affect the scope and power of the federal government? *(The expanded power of the federal government to implement many of the goals of Reconstruction created a backlash that motivated many to support stronger states' rights and a limited federal government. In the end, American voters and their representatives in government opted for a balance of power at the expense of protecting freed people in the South.)*

Objectives 3: Describe the experience of African Americans in the changing South; 4: Assess how whites created a segregated society in the South and how African Americans responded.

Quick Instruction

Present the illustration showing the segregated train car. Invite volunteers to describe what they see and the image's overall message and tone. Review the definitions of segregation *(forced separation, oftentimes by race)*, de facto segregation *(segregation by unwritten custom or tradition)*, and Jim Crow laws *(segregation laws enacted in the South after Reconstruction)*.

Summarize the ways in which the rights of African Americans were restricted following the end of Reconstruction. *(Southern governments enacted various measures aimed at disenfranchising, or taking away the voting rights of, African Americans. State and local governments also enacted Jim Crow laws that kept African Americans and whites segregated, or apart. In addition to Jim Crow railroad cars and waiting stations, southern states established Jim Crow jury boxes and Bibles, as well as cemeteries, restaurants, parks, beaches, and hospitals. Even in northern states African American migrants found many examples of de facto segregation—or segregation in act if not in law, such as restrictions on where they were allowed to live and work.)*

Reconstruction's Impact

DIGITAL TEXT 4

African American Leaders Seek Reform

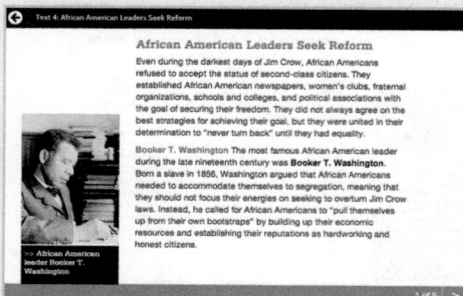

Contrast How did Booker T. Washington and W.E.B. Du Bois differ on their views of education for African Americans? *(Washington and his Tuskegee Institute placed a heavy emphasis on "industrial education," or vocational education. Du Bois stressed that African Americans should not limit themselves to vocational education.)*

ELL Use the ELL activity described in the ELL chart.

Further Instruction

Infer Why did poll taxes have a particularly negative effect on African Americans? *(Many African Americans were less likely to be able to afford such a fee, leaving them unable to vote in elections because they were too poor to do so.)*

Draw Conclusions How did the decision in *Plessy* v. *Ferguson* support the existence of Jim Crow laws? *(The decision concluded that it was constitutional for many southern states to continue segregating public facilities based on race, so long as the separate facilities were considered "equal.")*

Evaluate Arguments Based on what you learned about the post-Reconstruction atmosphere in the country, do you agree with Ida B. Wells' assertion that "If Southern white men are not careful, they will over-reach themselves and public sentiment will have a reaction"? Explain. *(No. At the time the majority of Americans were not focused on African American equality. The "reaction" she predicts would take many years to materialize.)*

SYNTHESIZE

INTERACTIVE CHART

Effects of Reconstruction

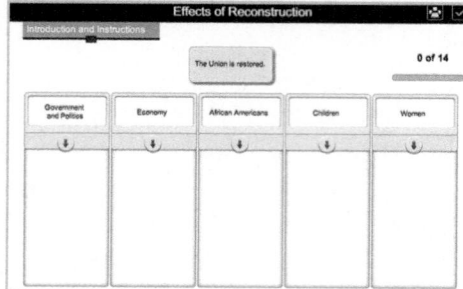

Interactive Chart: Effects of Reconstruction Project the Interactive Chart and provide time for students to view the information, place the tiles in the correct categories, and answer the questions. Discuss the information on each tile and clarify any vocabulary and terms with which students might have trouble.

DEMONSTRATE

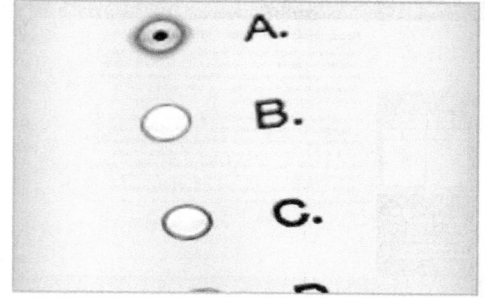

DIGITAL QUIZ

Lesson Quiz and Class Discussion Board

Assign the online Lesson Quiz for this lesson if you haven't already done so. Students will be offered automatic remediation or enrichment based on their score.

Pose these questions to the class on the Discussion Board:

In *Reconstruction's Impact*, you read about how southern Democrats managed to block, weaken, and overturn key efforts to secure civil rights for African Americans and other minorities. As focus on Reconstruction shifted to other issues in the country, old prejudices took on new forms, which would define race relations in the South and throughout the country for decades to come.

Interpret How did key Supreme Court decisions impact the original goals of Reconstruction?

Support a Point of View with Examples Has the United States fully reunited since Reconstruction?

Topic Inquiry

Have students continue their investigations for the Topic Inquiry.

Reconstruction

○ A.
○ B.
○ C.

▮ SYNTHESIZE

DIGITAL ACTIVITY
Reflect on the Essential Question and Topic

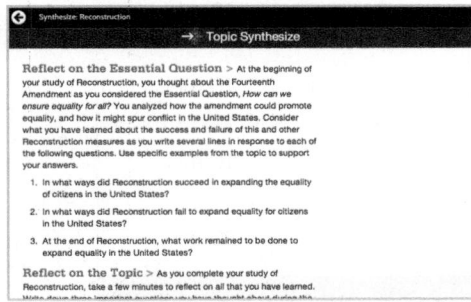

First ask students to reconsider the Essential Question for this topic: How can we ensure equality for all? Have students consider their responses in the Start Up Activity regarding passage of the Fourteenth Amendment. Then ask students to answer the questions using specific examples from the topic to support their answers.

Ask: What were the conflicts centered on equal rights that arose during Reconstruction? What actions did citizens and governments take to resolve the conflicts and work toward equal rights for all citizens? Have students give examples from the topic. Discuss their responses as a class or ask students to post their answers on the Class Discussion Board.

Next ask students to reflect on the topic as a whole and write down 1–3 questions they have thought about during the topic. Share these examples if students need help getting started:

- Would Reconstruction have been more effective had President Lincoln served a complete second term? Why or why not?
- What motivated many Americans to oppose Reconstruction?
- Are constitutional amendments the most effective method with which to guarantee equal rights? Explain.

You may ask students to share their questions and answers on the Class Discussion Board.

Topic Inquiry
Have students complete Step 3 of the Topic Inquiry.

▮ DEMONSTRATE

DIGITAL TOPIC REVIEW AND ASSESSMENT
Reconstruction

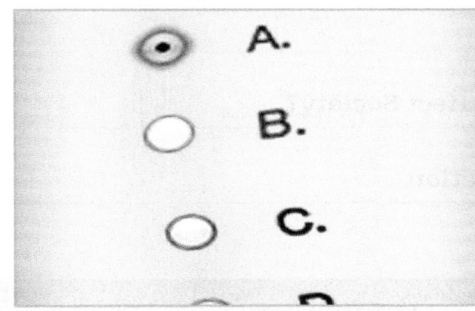

Students can prepare for the Topic Test by answering the questions in the Topic Review and Assessment online or the Assessment questions in the Print Student text. They can also prepare by reviewing their answers to the Interactive Reading Notepad questions or reviewing their notes in the Reading and Notetaking Study Guide.

DIGITAL TOPIC TEST
Reconstruction

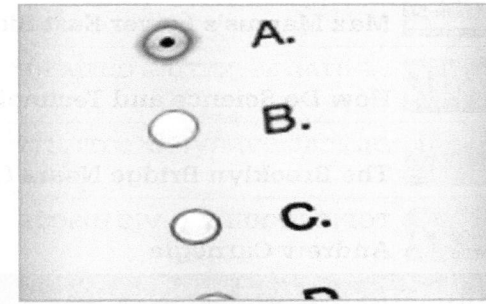

TOPIC TEST
Assign the Topic Test to assess students' understanding of topic content.

BENCHMARK TESTS
Assign these benchmark tests as you complete the relevant topics to monitor student progress toward mastering the course content and as preparation for the End-of-Course Test.

Benchmark Test 1: Topics 1–3
Benchmark Test 2: Topics 4–6
Benchmark Test 3: Topics 7–9
Benchmark Test 4: Topics 10–12
Benchmark Test 5: Topics 13–15
Benchmark Test 6: Topics 16–18
Benchmark Test 7: Topics 19–20

Industry and Immigration

TOPIC 9 ORGANIZER	PACING: APPROX. 9 PERIODS, 4.5 BLOCKS

	PACING
Connect	1 period
MY STORY VIDEO **Max Marcus's Lower East Side**	10 min.
DIGITAL ESSENTIAL QUESTION ACTIVITY **How Do Science and Technology Affect Society?**	10 min.
DIGITAL OVERVIEW ACTIVITY **The Brooklyn Bridge Nears Completion**	10 min.
TOPIC INQUIRY: CIVIC DISCUSSION **Andrew Carnegie**	20 min.
Investigate	3–6 periods
TOPIC INQUIRY: CIVIC DISCUSSION **Andrew Carnegie**	Ongoing
LESSON 1 Innovation Boosts Growth	30–40 min.
LESSON 2 Big Business Rises	30–40 min.
LESSON 3 The Organized Labor Movement	30–40 min.
LESSON 4 The New Immigrants	30–40 min.
LESSON 5 A Nation of Cities	30–40 min.
LESSON 6 New Ways of Life	30–40 min.
Synthesize	1 period
DIGITAL ACTIVITY **Reflect on the Essential Question and Topic**	10 min.
TOPIC INQUIRY: CIVIC DISCUSSION **Andrew Carnegie**	20 min.
Demonstrate	1–2 periods
DIGITAL TOPIC REVIEW AND ASSESSMENT **Industry and Immigration**	10 min.
TOPIC INQUIRY: CIVIC DISCUSSION **Andrew Carnegie**	20 min.

Andrew Carnegie

In this Topic Inquiry, students work in teams to examine different perspectives on this issue by analyzing several sources, arguing both sides of a Yes/No question, then developing and discussing their own point of view on the question: **Overall, did Andrew Carnegie have a positive influence on America?**

STEP 1: CONNECT
Develop Questions and Plan the Investigation

Launch the Civic Discussion

Divide the class into groups of four students. Students can access the materials they'll need in the online course or you can distribute copies to each student. Read the main question and introduction with the students.

Have students complete Step 1 by reading the Discussion Launch and filling in Step 1 of the Information Organizer. The Discussion Launch provides YES and NO arguments on the main question. Students should extract and paraphrase the arguments from the reading in Step 1 of their Information Organizers.

Next, students share within their groups the arguments and evidence they found to support the YES and NO positions. The group needs to agree on the major YES and NO points and each student should note those points in their Information Organizer.

Resources
- Student Instructions
- Discussion Launch
- Information Organizer

⏻ PROFESSIONAL DEVELOPMENT

Civic Discussion

Be sure to view the Civic Discussion Professional Development resources in the online course.

STEP 2: INVESTIGATE
Apply Disciplinary Concepts and Tools

Examine Sources and Perspectives

Students will examine sources with the goal of extracting information and perspectives on the main question. They analyze each source and describe the author's perspective on the main question and key evidence the author provides to support that viewpoint in Information Organizer Step 2.

Ask students to keep in mind:

- **Author/Creator:** Who created the source? An individual? Group? Government agency?
- **Audience:** For whom was the source created?
- **Date/Place:** Is there any information that reveals where and when the source was created?
- **Purpose:** Why was the source created? Discuss with students the importance of this question in identifying bias.
- **Relevance:** How does the source support one argument or another?

Suggestion: Reading the source documents and filling in Step 2 of the Information Organizer could be assigned as homework.

Resources
- Student Instructions
- Source documents
- Information Organizer

Andrew Carnegie *(continued)*

STEP 3: SYNTHESIZE
Use Evidence to Formulate Conclusions

Formulate Compelling Arguments with Evidence

Now students will apply perspectives and evidence they extracted from the sources to think more deeply about the main question by first arguing one side of the issue, then the other. In this way students become more prepared to formulate an evidence-based conclusion on their own.

Within each student group, assign half of the students to take the position of YES on the main question and the others to take the position of NO. Students will work with their partners to identify the strongest arguments and evidence to support their assigned YES or NO position.

Present Yes/No Positions

Within each group, those assigned the YES position share arguments and evidence first. As the YES students speak, those assigned NO should listen carefully, take notes to fill in the rest of the Compelling Arguments Chart (Step 3 in Information Organizer) and ask clarifying questions.

When the YES side is finished, students assigned the NO position present while those assigned YES should listen, take notes, and ask clarifying questions. Examples of clarifyin questions are:

- I think you just said [x]. Am I understanding you correctly?
- Can you tell me more about [x]?
- Can you repeat [x]? I am not sure I understand, yet.

Suggestion: You may want to set a 5 minute time limit for each side to present. Provide a two-minute warning so that students make their most compelling arguments within the time frame.

Switch Sides

The students will switch sides to argue the opposite point of view. To prepare to present the other position, partners who first argued YES will use the notes they took during the NO side's presentation, plus add any additional arguments and evidence from the reading and sources. The same for students who first argued the NO position.

STEP 4: DEMONSTRATE
Communicate Conclusions and Take Informed Action

Individual Points of View

Now the students will have the opportunity to discuss the main question from their own points of view. To help students prepare for this discussion, have them reflect on the YES/NO discussions they have participated in thus far and fill in Step 4 of their Information Organizers.

After all of the students have shared their points of view, each group should list points of agreement, filling the last portion of Step 4 on their Information Organizers.

Reflect on the Discussion

Ask students to reflect on the civic discussion thinking about:

- The value of having to argue both the YES and NO positions.
- If their individual views changed over the course of the discussion and why.
- What they learned from participating in the discussion.

Resources
- Student Instructions
- Information Organizer

Industry and Immigration

The last decades of the 1800s was a period of almost unbelievable change in the United States. Healed from the Civil War, the country expanded in every way possible: physically, economically, socially, demographically, and technologically. Two of the main drivers of these change were industry and immigration. The complex web of emerging networks started to shape the United States in ways that are still apparent today.

◼ CONNECT

| MY STORY VIDEO | DIGITAL ESSENTIAL QUESTION ACTIVITY | DIGITAL OVERVIEW ACTIVITY |

MY STORY VIDEO
Max Marcus's Lower East Side

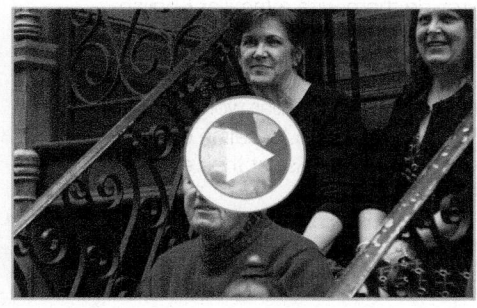

Watch a video about the experiences of the son of immigrants trying to succeed in business in New York City.

Check Understanding What lesson in business did Max Marcus learn? *(the need to change with the times)*

Hypothesize What were some of the qualities that may have pushed Max Marcus to achieve success in business? *(Students may mention the work ethic of immigrants to succeed and make a better life for their families, as well as Max Marcus's ability to understand the fundamentals of meeting customer needs and changing with the times.)*

DIGITAL ESSENTIAL QUESTION ACTIVITY
How Do Science and Technology Affect Society?

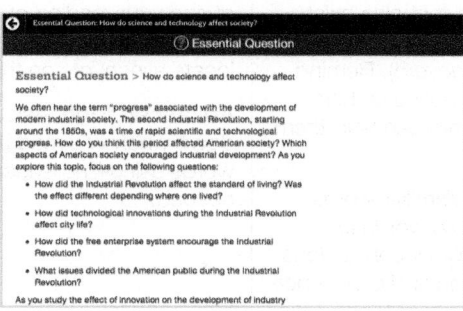

The topic essential question centers on the relationship between the technological innovation of the second Industrial Revolution and American society.

Generate Explanations What effect did the Industrial Revolution have on urbanization in the United States during the late 1800s? *(Possible answers may include the influx of immigrants and migration from rural areas of people in search of employment, as well as the effects of population growth on urban infrastructure.)*

Make Generalizations How might technological development have increased standards of living for many people in the United States during the late 1800s? *(Possible answers may include the ability of mass production techniques to manufacture goods more cheaply, and innovations such as the electric light, elevator, etc., that made daily living more comfortable for many people.)*

DIGITAL OVERVIEW ACTIVITY
The Brooklyn Bridge Nears Completion

Technological innovations during the late 1800s also had a significant impact on transportation infrastructure. The Brooklyn Bridge, for example, could not have been built without refined methods that produced steel cables.

Hypothesize What effect do you think the Brooklyn Bridge had on urbanization in New York City? *(Possible answers include the increased ease with which people can move about the city. The city could support a larger population with increased job opportunities.)*

Topic Inquiry
Launch the Topic Inquiry with students after introducing the topic.

Innovation Boosts Growth

Supporting English Language Learners

Use with Digital Text 1, **American Industry Grows.**

Learning
Read aloud the last section, titled *Laissez-Faire Policies Encourage Growth*. Explain to students that even though some words are unfamiliar, using their prior knowledge will help them to define these words.

Beginning Select several challenging key words in the text (e.g., *government*, *private*, *coast*). Provide students with images that will be familiar to them from their prior knowledge and experiences that will help them to understand the meaning of each word.

Intermediate Ask students to identify unfamiliar words in the text. Illustrate one or more of these words by creating simple sentences using examples from your life. Then have students do the same using examples from their lives. Point out that they are drawing from their prior knowledge and experiences to understand the meaning of these English words.

Advanced Create a list of unknown words from the text that also exist in other forms. Help students to define each word by identifying other members of its word family (e.g., *government/governor/govern*). Remind them to look for similarities between words as they read because their prior knowledge or experience of one word in a word family can help them understand unfamiliar words in the same family.

Advanced High Have students contribute to a list of unfamiliar words from the text. Ask where else they have encountered these words (or suggest possible situations to them). Guide students to draw conclusions about the words' meanings based on this prior knowledge and experience gathered from the whole class.

Use with Digital Text 4, **The Effects of Industrialization.**

Reading
Read linguistically accommodated content area material aloud slowly such as the section titled *Concerns About the Environment*. Encourage students to write down unfamiliar words as they hear them (explaining that spelling does not count).

Beginning Select challenging words from the text and teach each word separately using images, dramatization, and other visual methods. Then reread the text slowly, encouraging students to picture the words' meanings as they hear them.

Intermediate Invite students to read the text with a partner. Provide students with a print or online bilingual dictionary in which they can look up unfamiliar words. Pair students with the same first language if possible.

Advanced Ask students to share the unfamiliar words they wrote down during your reading of the text. Provide them with a familiar English-language synonym for each word or have them search a thesaurus to locate synonyms on their own.

Advanced High Ask students to share the unfamiliar words they wrote down when you read the text. If students are able to define one another's words using English, encourage them to do so. Assist their efforts as needed.

D Differentiate Instruction

Use the Differentiated Instruction notes throughout the lesson plan to support the varied skill sets, levels of readiness, and interests in the mixed-ability classroom.

Challenge These notes include suggestions for expanding the activity for advanced students.

On-Level These notes include suggestions for modifying the activity to address different interests or learning styles.

Extra Support These notes include ideas for providing more scaffolding or reading spuport.

Special Needs These notes provide ideas for adapting instruction to support the needs of various special needs students.

■ NOTES

PEARSON
realize™
www.PearsonRealize.com

Go online to access additional resources including:
Primary Sources • Biographies • Supreme Court cases •
21st Century Skill Tutorials • Maps • Graphic Organizers.

Objectives

Objective 1: Analyze the factors that encouraged industrialization in the United States in the late 1800s.

Objective 2: Explain how new inventions, scientific discoveries, and technological innovations fueled growth and improved the standard of living.

Objective 3: Explain the challenges faced by the South in industry and agriculture in the late 1800s.

Objective 4: Describe the impact of industrialization in the late 1800s.

LESSON 1 ORGANIZER		PACING: APPROX. 1 PERIOD, .5 BLOCKS			
				RESOURCES	
		OBJECTIVES	**PACING**	**Online**	**Print**
Connect					
DIGITAL START UP ACTIVITY **The 1876 Centennial**			5 min.	●	
Investigate					
DIGITAL TEXT 1 **American Industry Grows**		Objective 1	10 min.	●	●
INTERACTIVE MAP **Railroads Spur Economic Development in Cities**			10 min.	●	
DIGITAL TEXT 2 **Innovation Drives Economic Development**		Objective 2	10 min.	●	●
INTERACTIVE GALLERY **Major Inventions of the Late 1800s**			10 min.	●	
DIGITAL TEXT 3 **Industrialization and the New South**		Objective 3	10 min.	●	●
DIGITAL TEXT 4 **The Effects of Industrialization**		Objective 4	10 min.	●	●
Synthesize					
DIGITAL SYNTHESIZE ACTIVITY **The Impact of Railroads**			5 min.	●	
Demonstrate					
DIGITAL QUIZ **Lesson Quiz and Class Discussion Board**			10 min.	●	

Innovation Boosts Growth

■ CONNECT

DIGITAL START UP ACTIVITY
The 1876 Centennial

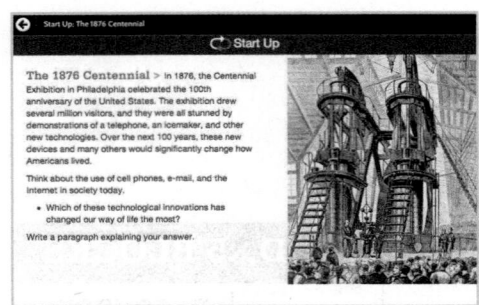

Project the Start Up Activity Ask students to answer the questions as they enter and get settled. Then have them share their ideas with another student, either in class or through a chat or blog space.

Discuss Ask students to think about the use of cell phones, mail, and the Internet today. What technologies have you already used today? Which of these technologies have changed your way of life the most? Why?

Tell students that in this lesson they will be learning about the second Industrial Revolution and how it affected Americans. It was a time of rapid change and new innovations, in some ways not that different from the last twenty years.

Aa Vocabulary Development: Use the Interactive Reading Notepad to preview the Key Terms and Academic Vocabulary in the lesson with students.

⇅ FLIP IT!

Assign the Flipped Video for this lesson.

■ STUDENT EDITION PRINT
PAGES: 312–320

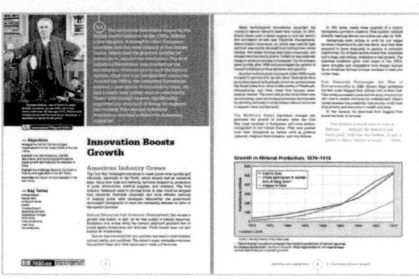

■ INVESTIGATE

DIGITAL TEXT 1
American Industry Grows

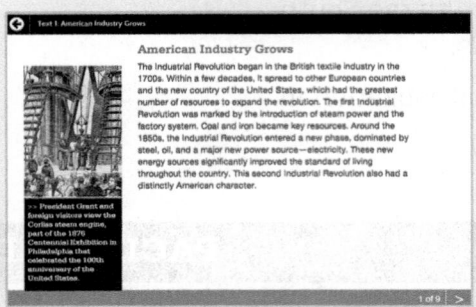

INTERACTIVE MAP
Railroads Spur Economic Development in Cities

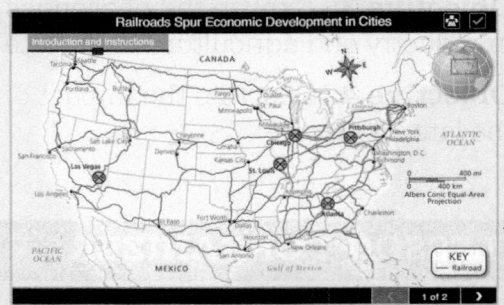

Objective 1: Analyze the factors that encouraged industrialization in the United States in the late 1800s.

Quick Instruction

Interactive Map: Railroads Spur Economic Development in Cities Project the map on the whiteboard and click the railroad sign icons to reveal information about the impact of railroads. Introduce the activity by asking students how the growth of railroads went hand-in-hand with the growth of industry. Explain that the railroads were an industry unto itself, that they were supplied by other industries (steel, wood), and that they encouraged a spiral of growth in other industries that relied on the shipment of raw materials and finished goods.

💬 ACTIVE CLASSROOM

Conduct a Graffiti Concepts exercise. Ask students to reflect on the economic impact that the growth of railroads had on other industries. Have them create a visual image and/or phrases that represents this relationship between the railroads and other industries. Allow approximately 3–5 minutes.

Ask students to post their "graffiti" on the board or on chart paper. Ask students to look at all the various responses then discuss the similarities and differences in the responses as a group.

D Differentiate: Extra Support Provide students with an example of the relationship between the railroads and other industries, such as farmers who needed to ship their grain to markets in different cities.

ELL Use the ELL activity described in the ELL chart.

Further Instruction

Go through the Interactive Reading Notepad questions and discuss the answers with the class.

Project the Interactive Graphic Organizer. Explain that history can be thought of as long chains of causes and effects, with effects becoming new causes.

Identify Cause and Effect Invite students to identify both the causes and effects of the growth of industrialization in the late 1800s. *(Possible causes: the increased demand for goods as a result of the Civil War; the large supply of natural resources; improved methods of transportation, such as waterways and a growing railway system; technological innovations, such as a steam-powered drill and a steel-making process; a large, mobile workforce; and the government's support of the free enterprise system. Possible effects: an increase in the number and types of goods available; an increase in the number and types of jobs open to workers; increased mobility; enhanced opportunities for financial success; a higher standard of living.)*

Analyze Interactions Among Events What relationship existed between the free enterprise system and entrepreneurship? *(Entrepreneurs were people willing to invest their own time and money into growing a successful business. The free enterprise system allowed these individuals to freely own and manage businesses in order to make a profit. It also encouraged businesses to run more efficiently so they could lower prices. This would in turn benefit consumers and help businesses remain competitive with others in the same industry.)*

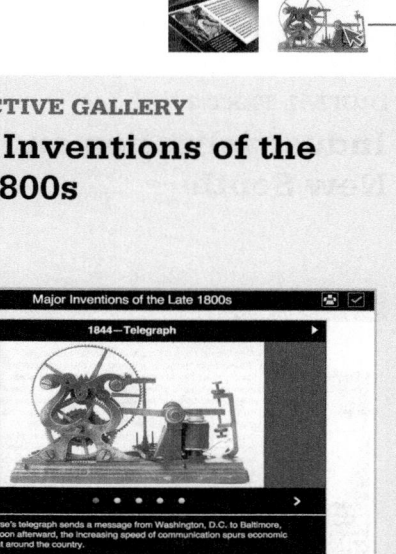

DIGITAL TEXT 2
Innovation Drives Economic Development

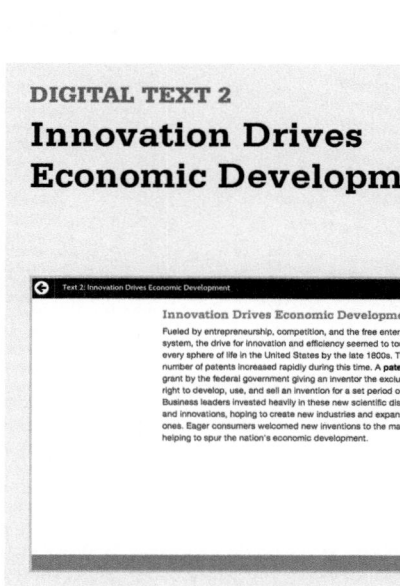

Text 2: Innovation Drives Economic Development

Innovation Drives Economic Development

Fueled by entrepreneurship, competition, and the free enterprise system, the drive for innovation and efficiency seemed to touch every sphere of life in the United States by the late 1800s. The number of patents increased rapidly during this time. **A patent** is a grant by the federal government giving an inventor the exclusive right to develop, use, and sell an invention for a set period of time. Business leaders invested heavily in these new scientific discoveries and innovations, hoping to create new industries and expand old ones. Eager consumers welcomed new inventions to the market, helping to spur the nation's economic development.

1 of 8 >

INTERACTIVE GALLERY
Major Inventions of the Late 1800s

Major Inventions of the Late 1800s

1844—Telegraph

Samuel Morse's telegraph sends a message from Washington, D.C. to Baltimore, Maryland. Soon afterward, the increasing speed of communication spurs economic development around the country.

1 of 3 >

Generate Explanations Upon what assumption are laissez-faire policies based, and how do they encourage economic growth? *(Laissez-faire policies are based on the idea that minimal government interference and regulations will allow businesses to thrive on their own in the free market. Many businesses were relatively free from governmental interference and regulations that would inhibit economic growth because of these policies and were so able to efficiently offer goods and services that in turn strengthened the economy.)*

Objective 2: Explain how new inventions, scientific discoveries, and technological innovations fueled growth and improved the standard of living.

Quick Instruction
Interactive Gallery: Major Inventions of the Late 1800s Project the gallery and look at each image individually. For each, ask students how it might have affected average Americans of the time. Then challenge students into classifying the technological innovation and scientific discoveries into categories, like communication and transportation, that improved the standard of living in the United States.

Ask students to explain the effects of electric power, petroleum-based products, and steel production on the economic development of the United States. Prompt them to discuss the relationship between an improved standard of living and economic development.

👥 ACTIVE CLASSROOM

Have students *Make Headlines* for each invention depicted in the Interactive Gallery. Ask: If you were to write a headline for each invention that captured the most important aspect that should be remembered, what would that headline be? Emphasize to students that their headlines should not just state the technological innovation or scientific discovery but also capture why it is significant, how it will improve the standard of living, and its impact on the economic development of the United States. Allow them to use subheadings if they would like. Have students pass their headlines to a partner for him or her to review.

Further Instruction
Go through the Interactive Reading Notepad questions and discuss the answers with the class.

The exciting technological innovations and scientific discoveries of this period both spurred and were spurred by the free enterprise system. Inventors, like Edison, knew that a useful and unique invention could be sold for a profit. Business leaders looked for such inventions to start new companies or to help them make or transport the products they already made faster and more efficiently.

Identify Cause and Effect Ask students to analyze how the free enterprise system encouraged the development of technological innovations and scientific discoveries and vice versa. *(Entrepreneurs helped fund the experiments of inventors like Edison. Also, many inventors became entrepreneurs to bring their new inventions to the masses. In term, new innovations and discoveries helped entrepreneurs make, sell, or distribute their products faster and easier.)*

Identify Central Issues Ask students to explain how technological innovations that encouraged industrialization in the United States in the late 1800s also improved the standard of living, especially in terms of transportation and communication. *(Sample answer: The growth of industry increased people's economic well-being and contributed to the availability of a wide variety of products. Railroads allowed people to travel around the country more quickly, safely, and cheaply than before. Telegraphs and telephones eased communication between individuals and sped the spread of news.)*

Innovation Boosts Growth

DIGITAL TEXT 3

Industrialization and the New South

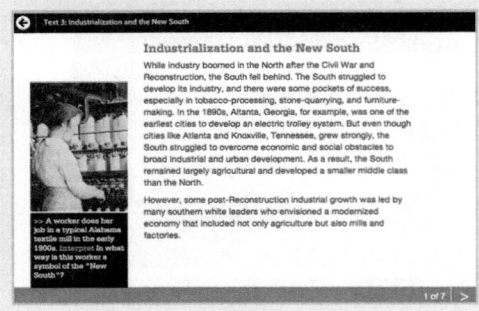

DIGITAL TEXT 4

The Effects of Industrialization

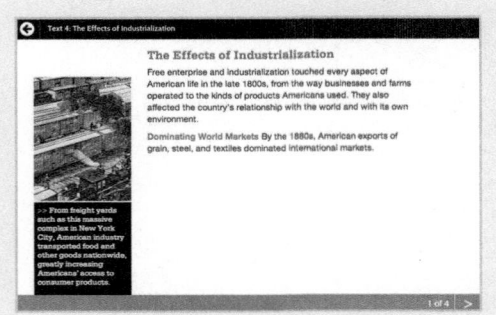

Objective 3: **Explain the challenges faced by the South in industry and agriculture in the late 1800s.**

Quick Instruction

Identify Central Issues Project the graph of Per Capita income in the South. Ensure understanding of the graph itself by reviewing the title, the term *per capita*, and the circle graphs. Ask: What is the main idea of these graphs? *(the relative poverty of the South after Reconstruction)* Challenge students to explain how the graphs reflect standards of living and led to people to call for a "New South."

Further Instruction

After the Civil War, industry did grow in the South, but the southern industrial economy faced some serious obstacles, including lack of capital and a trained workforce.

Project the Interactive Graphic Organizer. Guide students in completing it to compare and contrast industrialization and agriculture in the old and new South.

Identify Central Issues What effect did innovations in transportation have on Southern cities and industry? *(As railroad networks expanded throughout the South, many cities were increasingly connected with rural areas. Businesses were also able to transport raw and manufactured goods more efficiently to markets in both southern rural areas and northern cities.)*

Summarize What economic issues did the South struggle with while trying to industrialize? *(The South lacked adequate capital to fund new industries and the infrastructure to teach workers new skills.)*

Distinguish What economic issues affected farms and the price of cotton? *(Southern farms had been shipping their cotton to European markets, but after the Civil War, many European textile factories found cotton supplies elsewhere. This reduced demand for southern cotton, even as southern farms continued to produce increasing quantities, depressed cotton prices, which left many farms struggling to survive.)*

Objective 4: **Describe the impact of industrialization in the late 1800s.**

Quick Instruction

Categorize Direct students' attention to the illustration of the factory. As they view it, call on them one by one to each identify a way the factory in the illustration affected the people and the land near it. Effects should be both positive and negative. *(provides jobs, improves standard of living, pollutes air, etc.)* Emphasize to students the fundamental, widespread, and dramatic changes—both positive and negative—that industrialization brought to the United States.

ELL Use the ELL activity described in the ELL chart.

Further Instruction

Go through the Interactive Reading Notepad questions and discuss the answers with the class.

Draw Inferences Have students analyze the economic benefits and problems of industrialization. Ask: What were some benefits of industrialization to the United States? What were some problems that it caused? Have students use details from the lesson as well as their own ideas and experience to list and explain at least two significant "pluses" and two possible "minuses" of industrialization. *(Possible answer: Benefits might include more opportunities to earn a living or succeed financially, a higher overall standard of living, a stronger and more diversified economy, and the ability to become a world leader. Possible problems might include poor working conditions, damage to the land caused by the consumption of natural resources and the loss of family farms and autonomy as people who had once been farmers moved to cities to work in factories.)*

■ SYNTHESIZE

DIGITAL SYNTHESIZE ACTIVITY
The Impact of Railroads

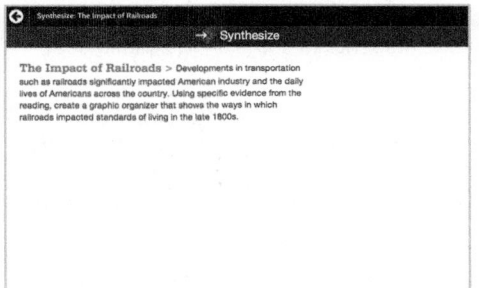

Discuss Ask students to define the concept "standards of living." Help them to better qualify this idea in the lesson context. Prompt students to think of the connections between an expanding network of railroads, the way in which businesses took advantage of those networks to ship products and how those products in turn affected the lives of many Americans.

Ask students to take five minutes to create a graphic organizer and then share their answers with a talking partner. Have pairs share their graphic organizers with the class.

■ DEMONSTRATE

DIGITAL QUIZ
Lesson Quiz and Class Discussion Board

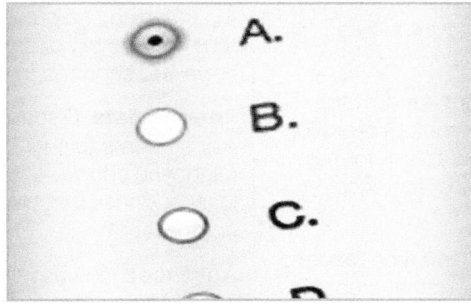

Assign the online Lesson Quiz for this lesson if you haven't already done so. Students will be offered automatic remediation or enrichment based on their score.

Pose these questions to the class on the Discussion Board:

In the text *Innovation Boosts Growth*, you read about a "second Industrial Revolution" that fundamentally transformed life in the United States. Some historians also speak of a communications revolution that took place in the 1800s, as well as a transportation revolution.

Categorize What developments that you read about might be considered part of a communications revolution? What developments might be part of a transportation revolution?

Identify Patterns What historical developments that you read about in this lesson are evident in American life today?

Topic Inquiry
Have students continue their investigations for the Topic Inquiry.

Big Business Rises

Supporting English Language Learners

Use with Digital Text 1, **Corporations Find New Ways of Doing Business.**

Reading
Ask students to look at the infographic *Big Business: Vertical vs. Horizontal Integration* as both a visual and contextual support to help students understand grade-appropriate content area concepts of horizontal and vertical integration. Then, read aloud the section titled, *Business Management Innovations*, or ask volunteers to do so.

Beginning Guide students through the infographic. Point out how the symbols and their arrangement illustrate vertical and horizontal integration. Ask students to read aloud the text in the infographic and to ask for help with challenging vocabulary. If necessary, give the following sentence starter: "Will you explain what _____ means?"

Intermediate Ask students to first look at the graphics and then read the text of the infographic. Ask questions about the infographic that students can answer in simple sentences, such as: What kinds of businesses are combined in vertical integration? What happens to businesses in horizontal integration?

Advanced Ask pairs of students to look at the graphics and read the text of the infographic. Ask each pair of students to write a description of the infographic that explains either horizontal or vertical integration.

Advanced High Ask students to look at the graphics and read the text of the infographic. Challenge students to explain the concepts of horizontal and vertical integration using the infographic as a visual aid.

Use with Digital Text 2, **The Pros and Cons of Big Business.**

Learning
Explain that students will be using prior experiences to understand word meanings in English.

Beginning Have students make a list of five stores or companies. Discuss the meaning of *big business*. Ask students whether the businesses on their lists are big or small. Encourage students to share their experiences: Have you shopped in a big business?

Intermediate Discuss the meanings of *big business* and *competition*. Ask students to share their prior experiences by asking questions like: Why might you choose one store rather than a similar one? Can you name a local business that closed? Can you name two local businesses that are in competition?

Advanced Discuss the meanings of *squeezed out* and *bought up*, including how the verbs' meanings change when not joined to these prepositions. Ask pairs of students to use prior experiences to discuss businesses that they saw squeezed out or bought up businesses.

Advanced High Discuss the meaning of *squeezed out*, as well as any vocabulary needed to describe the business environment of the 1880s. Have pairs of students discuss their prior experiences with big businesses with which they might associate modern-day robber barons (e.g., as customer, employee, or observer).

▷ Differentiate Instruction

Use the Differentiated Instruction notes throughout the lesson plan to support the varied skill sets, levels of readiness, and interests in the mixed-ability classroom.

Challenge These notes include suggestions for expanding the activity for advanced students.

On-Level These notes include suggestions for modifying the activity to address different interests or learning styles.

Extra Support These notes include ideas for providing more scaffolding or reading spuport.

Special Needs These notes provide ideas for adapting instruction to support the needs of various special needs students.

■ NOTES

PEARSON realize.™
www.PearsonRealize.com

Go online to access additional resources including:
Primary Sources • Biographies • Supreme Court cases •
21st Century Skill Tutorials • Maps • Graphic Organizers.

Objectives

Objective 1: Analyze different management innovations that businesses used to increase their profits.

Objective 2: Describe the public debate over the pros and cons of big business.

Objective 3: Explain how the government took steps to block abuses of corporate power.

LESSON 2 ORGANIZER		PACING: APPROX. 1 PERIOD, .5 BLOCKS			
				RESOURCES	
		OBJECTIVES	**PACING**	**Online**	**Print**
Connect					
	DIGITAL START UP ACTIVITY **Different Perspectives on Big Business**		5 min.	●	
Investigate					
	DIGITAL TEXT 1 **Corporations Find New Ways of Doing Business**	Objective 1	10 min.	●	●
	DIGITAL TEXT 2 **The Pros and Cons of Big Business**	Objective 2	10 min.	●	●
	INTERACTIVE GALLERY **Captains of Industry**		10 min.	●	
	DIGITAL TEXT 3 **The Changing Relationship Between Government and Business**	Objective 3	10 min.	●	●
	INTERACTIVE CHART **The Courts, Business, and Labor Regulation**		10 min.	●	
Synthesize					
	DIGITAL SYNTHESIZE ACTIVITY **Your Opinion**		5 min.	●	
Demonstrate					
	DIGITAL QUIZ **Lesson Quiz and Class Discussion Board**		10 min.	●	

Big Business Rises

■ CONNECT

DIGITAL START UP ACTIVITY
Different Perspectives on Big Business

Project the Start Up Activity As students enter and get settled, ask them what a tycoon is. Explain that the word *tycoon* comes from a Japanese term that means "great lord." Remind students that John D. Rockefeller was a tycoon who created Standard Oil. Focus their attention on the questions they need to answer.

Discuss What is the essential difference between Folsom's and Josephson's view of big business leaders? *(Folsom takes a positive view of big business, while Josephson focuses on the negative aspects of big business.)* Which view do you think is more accurate for big companies today?

Tell students that in this lesson they will be learning about the growth of big business and business innovations and the evolving relationship between big business and the federal government.

Aa Vocabulary Development: Use the Interactive Reading Notepad to preview the Key Terms and Academic Vocabulary in the lesson with students.

⇗ FLIP IT!
Assign the Flipped Video for this lesson.

■ STUDENT EDITION PRINT
PAGES: 321–326

■ INVESTIGATE

DIGITAL TEXT 1
Corporations Find New Ways of Doing Business

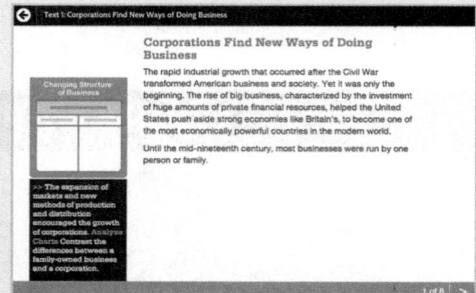

Objective 1: Analyze different management innovations that businesses used to increase their profits.

Quick Instruction
Infographic: Horizontal vs. Vertical Integration Project the infographic. Explain that both types of integration were management innovations in the work place. Break students into two groups and assign one kind of integration to each group. Ask the groups to explain how the integration worked and describe its impact on business and labor.

ELL Use the ELL activity described in the ELL chart.

Further Instruction
Go through the Interactive Reading Notepad questions and discuss the answers with the class.

Summarize How did management innovations applied in the workplace help businesses thrive? *(Some businesses utilized an innovation known as horizontal integration, in which they were able to either buy up or merge with their competitors. The new, larger company could then lower its production costs and pass those savings onto consumers. Another management innovation is vertical integration, in which one business gains control of the entire manufacturing process of its product. This allowed businesses to produce their products more efficiently.)*

Support a Point of View with Evidence What evidence from the text can you use to support the point of view that Andrew Carnegie applied management innovations in his businesses? *(Carnegie owned steel mills, but he also owned the mines that provided his raw materials and the ships and railroads that transported his raw materials to the mills. Carnegie was utilizing vertical integration, because he controlled much of his product's manufacturing process.)*

DIGITAL TEXT 2

The Pros and Cons of Big Business

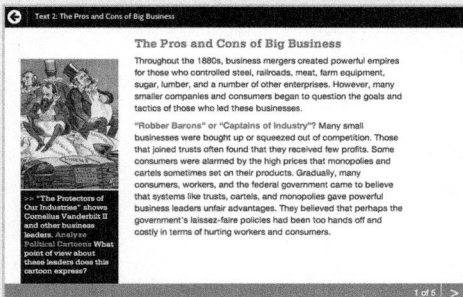

INTERACTIVE GALLERY

Captains of Industry

DIGITAL TEXT 3

The Changing Relationship Between Government and Business

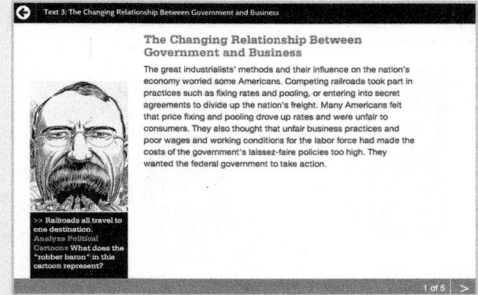

Objective 2: Describe the public debate over the pros and cons of big business.

Quick Instruction

Interactive Gallery: Captains of Industry Project the gallery and select the images to learn more about these significant political and social leaders and the impact of their philanthropic contributions, both in the late nineteenth century and today.

📹 ACTIVE CLASSROOM

Conduct a *Take a Stand* activity: Ask students to take a stand on the following question: Did captains of industry benefit or harm society?

Ask students to divide into two groups based on their answer and move to separate areas of the classroom.

Ask students to talk with each other to compare their reasons for answering yes or no. Then have a representative from each side present and defend the group's point of view.

ELL Use the ELL activity described in the ELL chart.

Further Instruction

Go through the Interactive Reading Notepad questions and discuss the answers with the class.

Support Ideas with Examples How would you support the idea that business leaders like Andrew Carnegie made significant social contributions to their communities? *(Many business leaders gave some of the money they earned to public institutions that promoted education, establishing libraries, museums, and even universities.)*

Apply Concepts What is Social Darwinism, and how was it used to rationalize social inequality? *(According to Social Darwinism, financial success is a measure of human "fitness." Those who believed in this idea equated high income with a high level of ability. This idea was used to justify prejudice by asserting that the poverty from which many minorities suffered was evidence of their lack of "fitness" or ability rather than the result of racism.)*

Summarize Ask students to describe the biggest pros and biggest cons of big business, supporting their categorizations with evidence from the text. *(Possible answer: Pros—big business helped to create a thriving, growing industrial economy, providing jobs and bringing new products to consumers; Cons— some people felt that big business sometimes drove smaller businesses out, reducing competition, and paid workers too little to work in poor conditions)*

Objective 3: Explain how the government took steps to block abuses of corporate power.

Quick Instruction

Interactive Chart: The Courts, Business, and Labor Regulation Project the chart. Invite a volunteer to remind the class of why Supreme Court rulings are so important. *(The Supreme Court is the highest court in the land; its decisions cannot be appealed.)* Then have students guide you in identifying whether each case was for or against big business. Ask students whether they agree with each decision and why. Discuss each case within the broader context of the changing relationship between the federal government and private business.

📹 ACTIVE CLASSROOM

Conduct a *Circle Write* activity. Break into groups and provide the objective as a writing prompt. Have students write as much as they can for one minute before they switch with the person on their right. The next person tries to improve or elaborate the response where the other person left off. Continue to switch until the paper comes back to the first person. Each group then shares their composition with the class.

Big Business Rises

INTERACTIVE CHART
The Courts, Business, and Labor Regulation

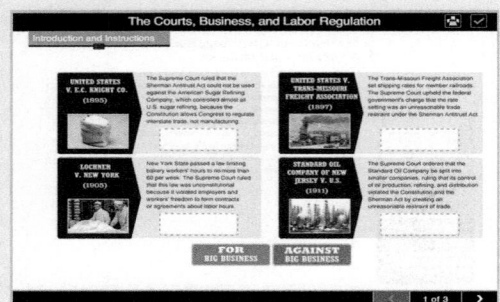

■ SYNTHESIZE

DIGITAL SYNTHESIZE ACTIVITY
Your Opinion

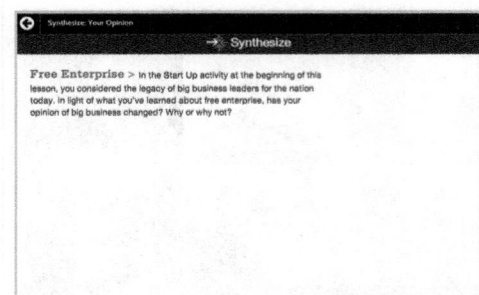

■ DEMONSTRATE

DIGITAL QUIZ
Lesson Quiz and Class Discussion Board

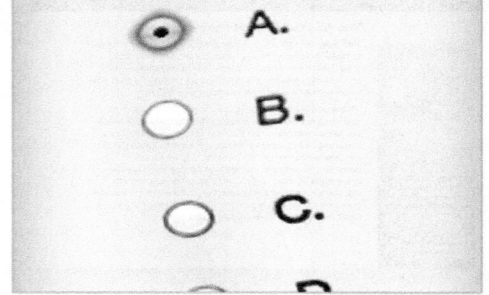

Further Instruction

In the late 1800s, the federal government, spurred by Americans who thought that the costs of laissez-faire were outweighing its benefits, took some initial steps towards regulating perceived abuses by large corporations. The government's actions, particularly establishing the Interstate Commerce Commission and passing the Sherman Antitrust Act, were meant to benefit consumers and business by ensuring fair competition but did not always have the intended effect.

Interpret What was the purpose of the Sherman Antitrust Act, and what impact did it initially have on private business? *(The purpose of the Sherman Antitrust Act was to increase the regulatory power of the federal government over trusts that were perceived to be unfairly controlling commerce between states. Although many of the early court rulings related to the Act fell in favor of business owners, the federal encroachment on private business practices would continue to grow.)*

Make Generalizations Based on the creation of the Interstate Commerce Commission and legislation like the Sherman Antitrust Act, how was the federal government's relationship to private business changing? *(The federal government was becoming increasingly involved in regulating private business to encourage a competitive marketplace that would benefit consumers.)*

Discuss Before students begin writing, review the essentials of the lesson content including what motivated business leaders and the role of the free enterprise system relative to the economic development of the United States.

Assign the online Lesson Quiz for this lesson if you haven't already done so. Students will be offered automatic remediation or enrichment based on their score.

Pose these questions to the class on the Discussion Board:

In Big Business Rises, you read about innovations in managing and organizing businesses that big business leaders used to increase the efficiency of their business empires. You also read about debates about this kind of business practice had a positive or negative impact, and the role of the government in regulating business in general.

Interpret James Madison, the fourth President of the United States, stated, "If men were angels, no government would be necessary." How does this quotation relate to what you learned about in this lesson?

Identify Cause and Effect Do you think the costs of the federal government's laissez-faire policy outweighed the benefits? Why or why not?

Topic Inquiry
Have students continue their investigations for the Topic Inquiry.

PEARSON
realize™
www.PearsonRealize.com
Access your Digital Lesson

The Organized Labor Movement

Supporting English Language Learners

Use with Digital Text 1, **Workers Endure Difficulties.**

Learning
Help students monitor their oral language production, employing self-corrective techniques as necessary, using the activities that follow. Read aloud the section *Children in the Workplace*. Point out some of the language used to describe child labor and its effects.

Beginning Display sentences with a blank for one word found in the text (e.g. *Children worked so their _____ could have more money.*) Ask students to determine each missing word. Then read aloud the sentence and have students repeat after you.

Intermediate Ask students questions about children in the workplace that they can answer with a complete sentence. Repeat each student's answer, modeling correct grammar and pronunciation. Invite students to adjust their speech as they repeat after you.

Advanced Invite pairs of students to take turns reading the text. Provide them with a print or online dictionary with which they can check the pronunciation of difficult words. Ask them to monitor their own and their partner's pronunciation and correct it (respectfully) as needed.

Advanced High Pair students, and ask them to take turns summarizing what they know about children in the workplace. Encourage partners to offer each other suggestions for improving their delivery of the information.

Use with Digital Text 3, **Labor Unions Lead Protests.**

Reading
Help students use visual and contextual support to aid in understanding using the following activities. Read aloud the entire reading or invite volunteers to do so. Point out the individual section headings and discuss how reviewing headings can enhance and confirm understanding.

Beginning Ask students to divide a sheet of paper into three sections labeled as follows: Workers Protest in Chicago, Steelworkers Clash with the Pinkertons, A Union Addresses Social Issues in a Pullman Town. Prompt students to use words and pictures to summarize these sections of the text.

Intermediate Display a chart of the section headings along with a list of key words and phrases from the text, as visual and contextual support for students. Ask students to match each word or phrase to its corresponding section as well as to add words and phrases of their own.

Advanced Ask student pairs to utilize the section headings and key words in bold in the text to write the main idea of each section in one or two sentences. Tell them to use each section's heading as the basis for the main ideas.

Advanced High Ask students to utilize the section headings and key words and phrases in the text to create an outline summary of the reading. Encourage them to integrate the text's section headings into their outline.

▣ Differentiate Instruction

Use the Differentiated Instruction notes throughout the lesson plan to support the varied skill sets, levels of readiness, and interests in the mixed-ability classroom.

Challenge These notes include suggestions for expanding the activity for advanced students.

On-Level These notes include suggestions for modifying the activity to address different interests or learning styles.

Extra Support These notes include ideas for providing more scaffolding or reading spuport.

Special Needs These notes provide ideas for adapting instruction to support the needs of various special needs students.

■ NOTES

_____

_____

_____

_____

_____

The Organized Labor Movement

Objectives

Objective 1: Assess the impact of business practices on workers in the late 1800s.

Objective 2: Compare the goals and strategies of the first labor unions.

Objective 3: Analyze the causes and effects of strikes in the late 1800s.

LESSON 3 ORGANIZER		PACING: APPROX. 1 PERIOD, .5 BLOCKS			
				RESOURCES	
		OBJECTIVES	PACING	Online	Print
Connect					
DIGITAL START UP ACTIVITY **Job Security**			5 min.	●	
Investigate					
DIGITAL TEXT 1 **Workers Endure Difficulties**		Objective 1	10 min.	●	●
DIGITAL TEXT 2 **The Growth of Labor Unions**		Objective 2	10 min.	●	●
INTERACTIVE CARTOON **A Different Kind of Knight**			10 min.	●	
DIGITAL TEXT 3 **Labor Unions Lead Protests**		Objective 3	10 min.	●	●
INTERACTIVE CHART **Major Strikes of the 1800s**			10 min.	●	
Synthesize					
DIGITAL SYNTHESIZE ACTIVITY **Labor Unions**			5 min.	●	
Demonstrate					
DIGITAL QUIZ **Lesson Quiz and Class Discussion Board**			10 min.	●	

PEARSON **realize**™
www.PearsonRealize.com

Go online to access additional resources including:
Primary Sources • Biographies • Supreme Court cases •
21st Century Skill Tutorials • Maps • Graphic Organizers.

▮ CONNECT

DIGITAL START UP ACTIVITY
Job Security

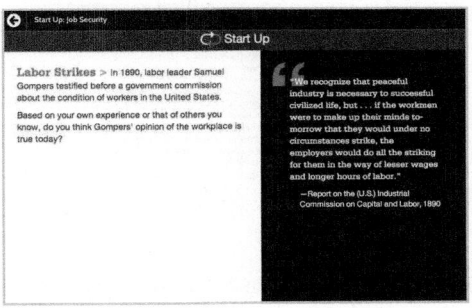

Project the Start Up Activity Ask students to answer the questions as they enter and get settled.

Discuss Ask students to consider if business owners and workers naturally at odds or naturally on the same side. Challenge students to think about instances when it would benefit business owners to pay workers less and when it would benefit to pay them more. Guide them into thinking about how the labor market changes over time.

Aa Vocabulary Development: Use the Interactive Reading Notepad to preview the Key Terms and Academic Vocabulary in the Lesson with students.

Tell students that in this lesson they will be learning about the relationship between business and labor unions.

↕ FLIP IT!
Assign the Flipped Video for this lesson.

▮ STUDENT EDITION PRINT
PAGES: 327–333

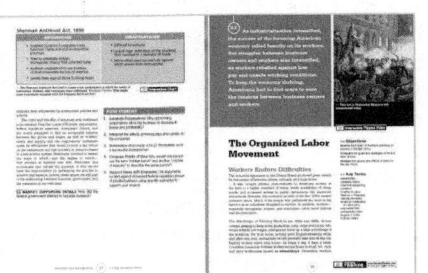

▮ INVESTIGATE

DIGITAL TEXT 1
Workers Endure Difficulties

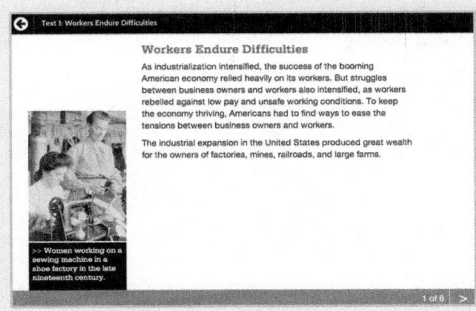

Objective 1: Assess the impact of big business practices on workers in the late 1800s.

Quick Instruction

Analyze Images Direct students attention to the illustration of the sweatshop. Explain that there were thousands of such dirty and dangerous workplaces. Invite volunteers to identify details of the image that depict unsafe or at least unpleasant working conditions. Ask: Would you work there? What if you had no other option to feed your family? Encourage students to empathize with what the workers went through.

Draw Conclusions What social issues would have in turn affected the number of children in workplaces such as sweatshops? *(Many employers paid workers poorly. Low wages forced many families to ask children to work in order to bring in more money for the family.)*

ELL Use the ELL activity described in the ELL chart.

Further Instruction
Go through the Interactive Reading Notepad questions and discuss the answers with the class.

Identify Cause and Effect Why did public pressure to reform child labor laws grow by the end of the nineteenth century? *(Social workers and the general public increasingly noticed that child laborers were frequently denied access to education because their families needed them to work. Conditions in the workplace were also inhibiting the physical and mental development of many children.)*

Draw Conclusions How were many businesses associated with company towns able to hold on to unwilling workers? *(The high costs of living in the company towns would force many workers to borrow money at high interest from their employers. Many workers in turn would incur more debt to their employers than they were able to pay with the money they earned, leaving the workers vulnerable to arrest if they left the company town.)*

Topic 9   291   Industry and Immigration

The Organized Labor Movement

DIGITAL TEXT 2
The Growth of Labor Unions

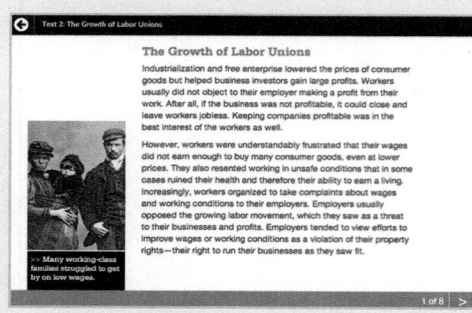

INTERACTIVE CARTOON
A Different Kind of Knight

DIGITAL TEXT 3
Labor Unions Lead Protests

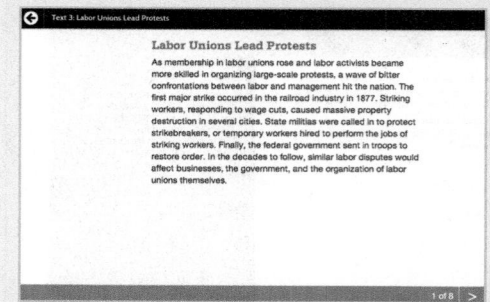

Objective 2: Compare the goals and strategies of the first labor unions.

Quick Instruction
Interactive Cartoon: A Different Kind of Knight Project the cartoon on the board. Invite volunteers to explain what each part of the cartoon symbolizes and its message and tone. Remind students that the Knights of Labor was formed in 1869 by Uriah Smith Stephens. Review the accomplishments of Terence V. Powderly, who helped the organization grow to some 700,000 men and women nationwide. Challenge students to counter all of the negative messages by analyzing some issues born of industrialization that encouraged the growth of labor unions. What are the arguments on the other side? *(Many felt that unions were a necessary counterweight to the power of business owners. Many workers were frustrated with low wages and poor working conditions, and they felt that unionizing offered the best opportunity for change.)*

D Differentiate: Extra Support Directing students' attention to one character at a time in the cartoon may help them focus on the cartoon's overall message.

🎦 ACTIVE CLASSROOM
Have students *Cartoon It* by creating political cartoons of their own. They should create a quick copy of one compelling image from this lesson on a piece of paper. Ask them to turn it into a political cartoon that supports labor unions.

Further Instruction
Go through the Interactive Reading Notepad questions and discuss the answers with the class.

Apply Concepts Summarize the essential ideas of socialism and explain the impact it had on the growth of labor unions in the United States. *(Socialism generally advocates public control and ownership of property and income with the goal of more equitable distribution of wealth across society. The idea of more equitable income was attractive to many workers who saw the discrepancies in living standards between workers and owners. Labor unions like The Knights of Labor advocated worker's cooperatives in place of privately owned businesses as a more equitable way to share profits.)*

Cite Evidence In what ways did labor unions such as the American Federation of Laborers (AFL) turn away from the ideals of socialism? *(Rather than advocating for broad societal change, the AFL chose to work within the existing capitalist system, focusing on specific issues such as increasing wages and improving working conditions.)*

Analyze Information Ask students to describe the growth of labor unions. *(As industry grew, workers noticed problems with pay and working conditions. Early labor unions formed but were mostly local and short-lived. In 1869, the Knights of Labor was founded by a tailor and included skilled and unskilled workers, focusing on broad social reform. In 1886, the American Federation of Labor was formed by joining together many smaller skilled trade unions into one large organization. It focused on specific problems, rather than broad reform.)*

Objective 3: Analyze the causes and effects of strikes in the late 1800s.

Quick Instruction
Interactive Chart: Major Strikes of the Late 1800s Project the chart onto the board. Invite a volunteer to set the scene by providing context for the chart. What was happening in the American economy during the nineteenth century? *(expansion and industrialization)* How would this set the stage for conflicts between businesses and workers? *(both wanted their share of wealth; businesses wanted to minimize expenses; it was a time of rapid and unsettling changes in general)* Guide the class into identifying the correct causes and effects of each of the major strikes of the late 1800s.

🎦 ACTIVE CLASSROOM
Conduct a *Take a Stand* activity for each of the major strikes: Railroad Strikes, 1877; Homestead Strike, 1892; Pullman Strike, 1894; Haymarket Square, 1886.
Ask students to take a stand on the following question: Which side was right during the strike?
- Ask students to divide into two groups based on their answer and move to separate areas of the classroom.
- Ask students to talk with each other to compare their reasons for choosing one side or the other.
- Ask a representative from each side to present and defend the group's point of view.
- Ask students to consider how each strike affected the overall growth of labor unions. Did each help or hurt the movement as a whole?

INTERACTIVE CHART

Major Strikes of the 1800s

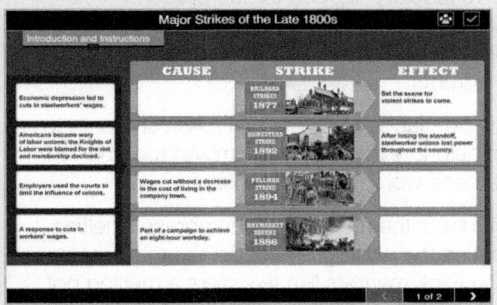

 SYNTHESIZE

DIGITAL SYNTHESIZE ACTIVITY

Labor Unions

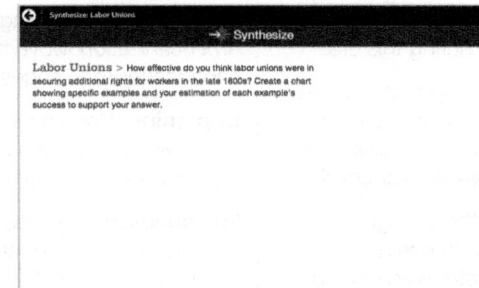

 DEMONSTRATE

DIGITAL QUIZ

Lesson Quiz and Class Discussion Board

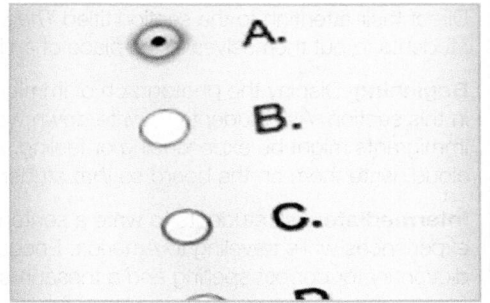

ELL Use the ELL activity described in the ELL chart.

Further Instruction

Go through the Interactive Reading Notepad questions and discuss the answers with the class.

Hypothesize How did the Supreme Court rule in the decision about Eugene Debs and his role in the Pullman Strike? What subsequent effect might that ruling have had on the influence of labor unions? *(The Supreme Court upheld the legality of Debs's conviction. Its ruling established judicial precedent that protected the private property rights of businesses and interstate commerce of business, which would make it more difficult for labor unions to win legal victories.)*

Discuss Ask students to evaluate three examples from the lesson that can help them judge the effectiveness of labor unions in the late 1800s. Prompt students by summarizing the effects of the Pullman Strike before they complete a chart with two other examples on their own.

Assign the online Lesson Quiz for this lesson if you haven't already done so. Students will be offered automatic remediation or enrichment based on their score.

Pose these questions to the class on the Discussion Board:

In this lesson, you learned about practices common to many big businesses in the late nineteenth century, the conditions under which many children were forced to work, and the efforts of labor unions to improve wages and conditions for workers.

Predict Consequences How might the lives of many children change as wages gradually rose?

Topic Inquiry

Have students continue their investigations for the Topic Inquiry.

The New Immigrants

Supporting English Language Learners

Use with Digital Text 1, **Optimism and the Immigrant Experience.**

Learning
To help students monitor their written language production, employing self-corrective or other improvement techniques, do the following activity. Direct their attention to the section titled *The Long Journey to America*. Ask students to put themselves in the place of an immigrant during this era.

Beginning Display the photograph of immigrants on a ship that appears in this section. Ask students to write down words that describe what the immigrants might be experiencing or feeling. As students share their words aloud, write them on the board so that students can correct their spelling.

Intermediate Ask students to write a sentence about the immigrants' experiences while traveling to America. Encourage them to use a dictionary for correct spelling and a thesaurus for accurate word choice.

Advanced Have students write a paragraph in first person that describes an immigrant's possible thoughts and feelings. Provide time for them to read their paragraph to a partner in order to check for consistent tone and point of view.

Advanced High Ask pairs of students to write a short dialogue between two immigrants on a ship. Record them reading their dialogue, and then play the recording so students can revise content, tone, and other aspects of their writing.

Use with Digital Text 3, **Social Issues Affecting Immigrants.**

Reading
Do the following activity to help students learn how to use visual and contextual support to develop vocabulary needed to comprehend increasingly challenging language. Read aloud the section titled *Americanization Movement*, or invite volunteers to do so. Then read the captions for the images of immigrants.

Beginning Draw a picture of a pot; label it "melting pot." Ask students to select words from the text that help to explain what is "mixed together" in the American melting pot. List these words inside the picture.

Intermediate Discuss with students the meaning of the phrase "melting pot". Then, have students examine the photograph of immigrants buying and selling goods. Ask: "Do you think markets like this were a melting pot for different cultures?" Provide the following sentence frames: "Yes, I think cultures mixed together in markets like this because..." or "No, I don't think cultures mixed together in markets like this because...."

Advanced Ask students to find the bold word "Americanized" and read the description that follows of Americanization programs. Discuss what it means to be Americanized. Have students examine the photograph of immigrants buying and selling goods. Ask: Do you think the people in this image being Americanized, maintaining their old customs, or a mix of both? Why do you think so?

Advanced High Have students examine the photograph of immigrants buying and selling goods. Ask them to write a paragraph explaining how the photo illustrates the terms *Americanization* and *melting pot*.

Ⓓ Differentiate Instruction

Use the Differentiated Instruction notes throughout the lesson plan to support the varied skill sets, levels of readiness, and interests in the mixed-ability classroom.

Challenge These notes include suggestions for expanding the activity for advanced students.

On-Level These notes include suggestions for modifying the activity to address different interests or learning styles.

Extra Support These notes include ideas for providing more scaffolding or reading spuport.

Special Needs These notes provide ideas for adapting instruction to support the needs of various special needs students.

■ NOTES

PEARSON
realize™
www.PearsonRealize.com

Go online to access additional resources including:
Primary Sources • Biographies • Supreme Court cases •
21st Century Skill Tutorials • Maps • Graphic Organizers.

Objectives

Objective 1: Compare the "new immigrants" of the late 1800s to earlier immigrants.

Objective 2: Explain the push and pull factors leading immigrants to America.

Objective 3: Describe the challenges that immigrants faced establishing new lives in America.

Objective 4: Analyze how immigrants adapted to American life while contributingto American culture.

LESSON 4 ORGANIZER		PACING: APPROX. 1 PERIOD, .5 BLOCKS			
				RESOURCES	
		OBJECTIVES	**PACING**	**Online**	**Print**
Connect					
DIGITAL START UP ACTIVITY **Starting Over**			5 min.	●	
Investigate					
DIGITAL TEXT 1 **New Immigrants Seek Better Lives**		Objectives 1, 2	10 min.	●	●
INTERACTIVE CHART **Immigration, 1870–1910**			10 min.	●	
DIGITAL TEXT 2 **Optimism and the Immigrant Experience**		Objective 3	10 min.	●	●
DIGITAL TEXT 3 **Social Issues Affecting Immigrants**			10 min.	●	●
DIGITAL TEXT 4 **Immigrants Affect American Society**		Objective 4	10 min.	●	●
INTERACTIVE GALLERY **Selected Contributions of Immigrants to American Culture**			10 min.	●	
Synthesize					
DIGITAL ACTIVITY **Pros and Cons of Immigration**			5 min.	●	
Demonstrate					
DIGITAL QUIZ **Lesson Quiz and Class Discussion Board**			10 min.	●	

The New Immigrants

■ CONNECT

DIGITAL START UP ACTIVITY
Starting Over

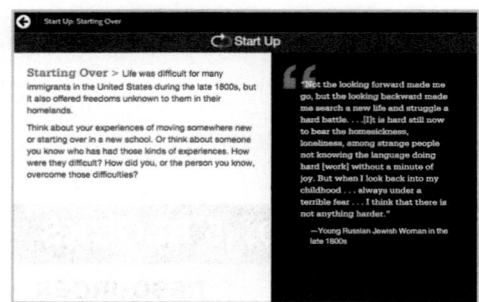

Project the Start Up Activity Ask students to answer the questions as they enter and get settled.

Discuss Encourage students to empathize with immigrants who traveled such a far distance to a country they had never seen. What challenges and fears would they have had to overcome? *(Sample answer: Challenges for immigrants include needing to quickly learn a new language to find a job, adapting to a new culture, and making new friends.)*

Aa Vocabulary Development: Use the Interactive Reading Notepad to preview the Key Terms and Academic Vocabulary in the lesson with students.

Tell students that this lesson will be about the challenges of immigration and the effects of immigration on the United States in the late 1800s.

⚡ FLIP IT!
Assign the Flipped Video for this lesson.

■ STUDENT EDITION PRINT
PAGES: 334–340

■ INVESTIGATE

DIGITAL TEXT 1
New Immigrants Seek Better Lives

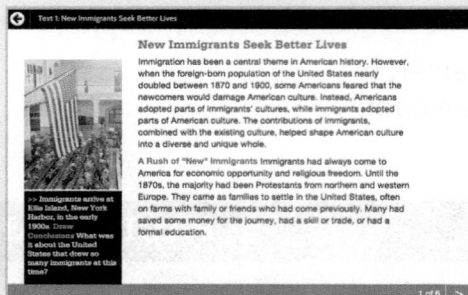

Objectives 1: Compare the "new immigrants" of the late 1800s to earlier immigrants; 2: Explain the push and pull factors leading immigrants to America.

Quick Instruction
Interactive Chart: Immigration, 1870–1910 Project the chart. Ask students to describe it. *(It is a bar graph showing the number of people who immigrated to the United States in years ranging from 1870 to 1910 from various regions.)* If students are struggling to read the chart, have them look at the 21st Century Skill Tutorial: Read Charts and Graphs. Discuss the push and pull factors associated with the increasing or decreasing number of immigrants from each region, including actions taken by people to expand economic opportunities.

👥 ACTIVE CLASSROOM
Conduct a *See-Think-Wonder* activity with the class. Students work in pairs posing and answering questions about geographic distributions and patterns in order to analyze and interpret the social studies information on the graph. Have student pairs share insights with the class.

INTERACTIVE CHART
Immigration, 1870–1910

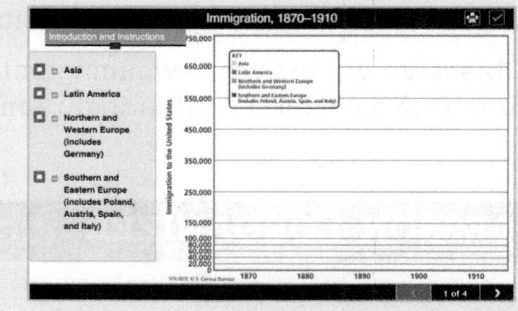

Further Instruction
Go through the Interactive Reading Notepad questions and discuss the answers with the class.

Analyze Images Direct students attention to the image of the immigrants entering Ellis Island. Discuss some of the differences between the "old" immigrants of the first part of the 1800s and the "new" immigrants of the last part of the century in regards to region of origin, religion, etc. Discuss the causes of this change to the demographic patterns of legal immigration to the United States.

Draw Conclusions Why might many of the "new" immigrants who came to the United States between 1870 and 1910 have struggled to adapt to the United States more than their predecessors? *(In contrast to their predecessors, many of the "new" immigrants had little education or skills with which they could find work. They also had difficulty learning English and adapting to American culture.)*

DIGITAL TEXT 2

Optimism and the Immigrant Experience

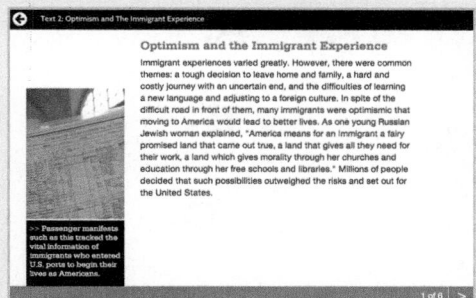

Optimism and the Immigrant Experience

Immigrant experiences varied greatly. However, there were common themes: a tough decision to leave home and family, a hard and costly journey with an uncertain end, and the difficulties of learning a new language and adjusting to a foreign culture. In spite of the difficult road in front of them, many immigrants were optimistic that moving to America would lead to better lives. As one young Russian Jewish woman explained, "America means for an immigrant a fairy promised land that came out true, a land that gives all they need for their work, a land which gives morality through her churches and education through her free schools and libraries." Millions of people decided that such possibilities outweighed the risks and set out for the United States.

>> Passenger manifests such as this tracked the vital information of immigrants who entered U.S. ports to begin their lives as Americans.

1 of 6 >

DIGITAL TEXT 3

Social Issues Affecting Immigrants

Social Issues Affecting Immigrants

Passing immigration inspections was just the first step. Once in America, immigrants immediately faced tough decisions such as where to settle and how to find work. On top of that, most had to learn a new language and new customs. Sometimes immigrants worked with an agent who spoke their language for help finding work and housing, but many agents took advantage of the newcomers to make money. Lucky immigrants had contacts through family and friends who could help them navigate a new and strange world.

>> Many immigrants lived together in tenement housing after they first arrived in the United States

1 of 6 >

DIGITAL TEXT 4

Immigrants Affect American Society

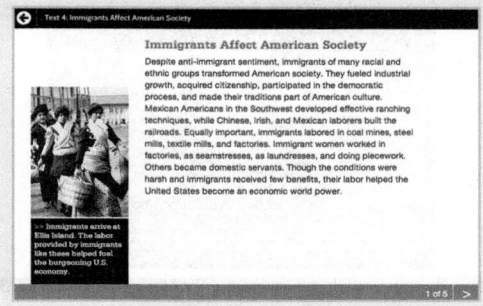

Immigrants Affect American Society

Despite anti-immigrant sentiment, immigrants of many racial and ethnic groups transformed American society. They fueled industrial growth, acquired citizenship, participated in the democratic process, and made their traditions part of American culture. Mexican Americans in the Southwest developed effective ranching techniques, while Chinese, Irish, and Mexican laborers built the railroads. Equally important, immigrants labored in coal mines, steel mills, textile mills, and factories. Immigrant women worked in factories, as seamstresses, as laundresses, and doing piecework. Others became domestic servants. Though the conditions were harsh and immigrants received few benefits, their labor helped the United States become an economic world power.

>> Immigrants arrive at Ellis Island. The labor provided by immigrants like these helped fuel the burgeoning U.S. economy.

1 of 5 >

Objective 3: Describe the challenges that immigrants faced while establishing new lives in America.

Quick Instruction

Analyze Images Direct students attention to the image of the Statue of Liberty. Use the ideals that the Statue represented as a springboard for a class discussion about the optimism of the many immigrants who sought a better life. Ask students to describe the reasons immigrants were optimistic. *(Possible answers: the hope of political and religious freedom, opportunities for education and work).* Then, discuss the challenges immigrants faced. Have students list the basic steps that most immigrants had to go through. *(hard decision to leave, long and costly voyage, learning a new language, finding employment, adjusting to American culture.)*

D Differentiate: **Extra Support** Further discuss the phrase *melting pot* with students. Provide some examples of this ideal of assimilation and prompt students to think about the positive and negative effects of the pressure to assimilate on immigrants.

ELL Use the ELL activity described in the ELL chart.

Further Instruction

Go through the Interactive Reading Notepad questions and discuss the answers with the class.

Interpret Ask students to analyze the social issue of discrimination that immigrants faced. What were some areas where immigrants faced discrimination? *(Many immigrants faced discrimination in housing, employment, and other areas because of they came from different racial or religious backgrounds and were not native-born citizens.)*

Identify Cause and Effect What led to the passage of the Chinese Exclusion Act of 1882? *(Extreme hostility toward Chinese laborers led Congress to pass act.)* What were the provisions of this act? *(The act prohibited immigration by Chinese laborers, limited the civil rights of Chinese immigrants already in the United States, and forbade the naturalization of Chinese residents.)* Explain the economic issues caused by this act. *(The act had unintended negative consequences on the economy, especially in states such as California that relied on cheap Chinese labor. Restricting the immigration of Chinese laborers made it difficult for large single-crop ranches to be profitable.)*

Generate Explanations What connection do you see between the Americanization movement and the metaphor of a melting pot associated with immigration? *(The Americanization movement encouraged immigrants to assimilate quickly into American culture by learning the language and customs related to food and dress. The metaphor of a melting pot is similar in that the many cultures represented by new immigrants would blend together into a single, shared culture.)*

Objective 4: Analyze how immigrants adapted to American life while trying to maintain familiar cultural practices.

Quick Instruction

Interactive Gallery: Selected Contributions of Immigrants to American Culture Project the interactive gallery. Show each image and have student volunteers read the captions aloud to the class. Explain how the contributions of people of various ethnic and religious groups shape American culture. Have the class determine each person's approximate age when he or she immigrated to the United States. Ask: What would be the advantage of immigrating earlier in life? *(Easier to adjust to a new culture and language)* Then segue into a discussion about how older immigrants adapted to American life while trying to maintain familiar cultural practices. Review the concepts of assimilation, Americanization, the idea of the "melting pot," and nativism.

> **📷 ACTIVE CLASSROOM**
>
> Direct students to have a *Conversation with History* with an immigrant from American history. The immigrant can be a prominent individual or representative of a certain group. Have students suppose that they are having a conversation with their selected individual about how that person's contributions have shaped American culture. Students should write down a question they would like to ask, what that person would say to them, and what they would say in response.

The New Immigrants

 **SYNTHESIZE**

 DEMONSTRATE

INTERACTIVE GALLERY

Selected Contributions of Immigrants to American Culture

DIGITAL ACTIVITY

Pros and Cons of Immigration

DIGITAL QUIZ

Lesson Quiz and Class Discussion Board

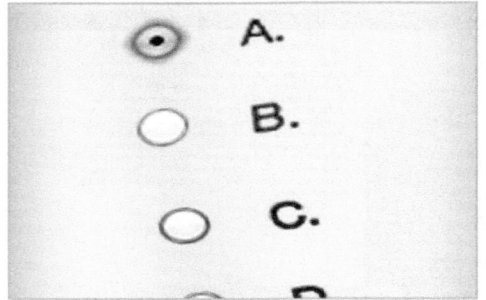

Further Instruction

Go through the Interactive Reading Notepad questions and discuss the answers with the class.

Support Ideas with Evidence What evidence can you find from the text to support the idea that many immigrants had a significant impact on political and social movements in the United States? *(Possible answers include: immigrants like Samuel Gompers and Mary Harris Jones impacted the American labor movement and fought for worker's rights. Andrew Carnegie donated much of his money to social and educational causes.)*

Have partners work together to think about the pros and cons of immigration and complete a two-column chart outlining the positive and negative effects of immigration at the end of the nineteenth century.

Discuss Ask students if they agree or disagree with the idea that the immigration to the United States in the late 1800s was good for the country. Students should support their answers with specific evidence from the lesson.

Assign the online Lesson Quiz for this lesson if you haven't already done so. Students will be offered automatic remediation or enrichment based on their score.

Pose this question to the class on the Discussion Board:

Identify Cause and Effect How did American society change immigrants in the late 1800s? How did immigrants change American society in the late 1800s?

Topic Inquiry

Have students continue their investigations for the Topic Inquiry.

A Nation of Cities

Supporting English Language Learners

Use with Digital Text 1, **Technology Improves City Life.**

Learning

Use strategic learning techniques to help students acquire basic and grade-level vocabulary with one of the following activities. Have students read the section titled, *Electricity Drives New Industries and Economic Development*, either alone or in pairs. Explain that they will use concept mapping to assimilate and organize terms and ideas from the text.

Beginning Display a partially completed concept map (with *mass transit* as the center phrase), as well as a word bank containing vocabulary to complete the map. Include words such as commuter rail, subway, trolley, and cable car in the bank. Discuss the meaning of these words, and then ask students to move words from the bank into the map.

Intermediate Provide students with a concept map that contains a few key words (use *mass transit* as the center phrase). Have students fill out the map using appropriate vocabulary from the text.

Advanced Ask students to create a concept map based on the text. Encourage them to select their center word first, then the next tier of key words, and finally details that support the key words.

Advanced High Have students create a concept map based on the text. Then challenge them to summarize the content of their map by writing a descriptive paragraph that utilizes the map's vocabulary.

Use with Digital Text 3, **Urban Living Creates Social Issues.**

Reading

Display the photograph of a tenement's exterior, and use it to provide visual support as you help students grasp the language structure of prefixes.

Beginning Display the words *healthy* and *unhealthy*. Define the words and the prefix *un-*. Ask students to use the visual support of the photograph to complete and read this sentence: Living in a crowded tenement was _____ for people.

Intermediate Display and discuss these words: *healthy*, *able*, and *paved*. Then define the prefix *un-* and ask what *unhealthy*, *unable*, and *unpaved* mean. Have students use the visual support of the photograph to create sentences about tenements with *unhealthy*, *unable*, and *unpaved*.

Advanced Display these words from the text: *unhealthy*, *unpaved*, *multifamily*. Define the prefixes *un-* and *multi-*, and ask students to define each word. Have pairs of students use the visual support of the photograph to write sentences with these words. Ask pairs to read one another's sentences.

Advanced High Display these words from the text: *overcrowding*, *overflowing*, *overcome*. Point out the prefix *over-* in each word, and ask students to guess the words' meanings based on this and prior knowledge. Have students use the visual support of the photograph to write sentences with these words. Ask partners to read each other's sentences.

▣ Differentiate Instruction

Use the Differentiated Instruction notes throughout the lesson plan to support the varied skill sets, levels of readiness, and interests in the mixed-ability classroom.

Challenge These notes include suggestions for expanding the activity for advanced students.

On-Level These notes include suggestions for modifying the activity to address different interests or learning styles.

Extra Support These notes include ideas for providing more scaffolding or reading spuport.

Special Needs These notes provide ideas for adapting instruction to support the needs of various special needs students.

■ NOTES

A Nation of Cities

Objectives

Objective 1: Analyze urban growth in the late 1800s.

Objective 2: Explain how technology improved city life.

Objective 3: Evaluate the problems caused by rapid urban growth and ways that city dwellers tried to solve them.

LESSON 5 ORGANIZER		PACING: APPROX. 1 PERIOD, .5 BLOCKS			
				RESOURCES	
		OBJECTIVES	**PACING**	**Online**	**Print**
Connect					
	DIGITAL START UP ACTIVITY **The Rich and the Poor in American Cities**		5 min.	●	
Investigate					
	DIGITAL TEXT 1 **Americans Migrate to Cities**	Objective 1	10 min.	●	●
	INTERACTIVE GALLERY **Immigration, 1870–1910**		10 min.	●	
	DIGITAL TEXT 2 **Technology Improves City Life**	Objective 2	10 min.	●	●
	INTERACTIVE ILLUSTRATION **The Flatiron Building**		10 min.	●	
	DIGITAL TEXT 3 **Urban Living Creates Social Issues**	Objective 3	10 min.	●	●
	3-D MODEL **Living in a Tenement**		10 min.	●	
Synthesize					
	DIGITAL ACTIVITY **Reflecting Back**		5 min.	●	
Demonstrate					
	DIGITAL QUIZ **Lesson Quiz and Class Discussion Board**		10 min.	●	

PEARSON realize.™
www.PearsonRealize.com

Go online to access additional resources including:
Primary Sources • Biographies • Supreme Court cases •
21st Century Skill Tutorials • Maps • Graphic Organizers.

▣ CONNECT

DIGITAL START UP ACTIVITY
The Rich and the Poor in American Cities

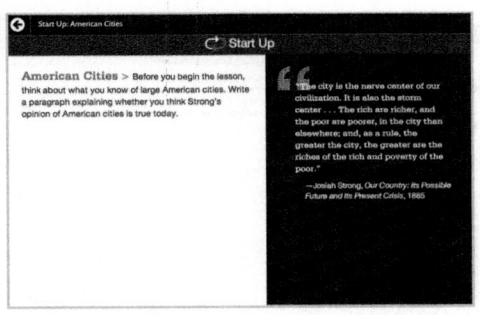

Project the Start Up Activity Ask students to answer the questions as they enter and get settled.

Discuss Ask students to share their thoughts with specific examples on Josiah Strong's quote about cities. Ask students if this observation about cities from 1885 is still true today and why they think that is the case.

Tell students that in this lesson they will be learning about the relationship between urban growth, technological innovation, and problems specifically related to urban areas.

Aa Vocabulary Development: Use the Interactive Reading Notepad to preview the Key Terms and Academic Vocabulary in the lesson with students.

⇅ FLIP IT!
Assign the Flipped Video for this lesson.

▣ STUDENT EDITION PRINT PAGES: 341–346

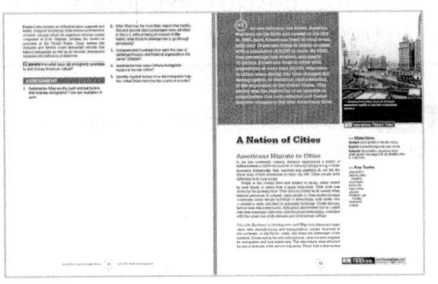

▣ INVESTIGATE

DIGITAL TEXT 1
Americans Migrate to Cities

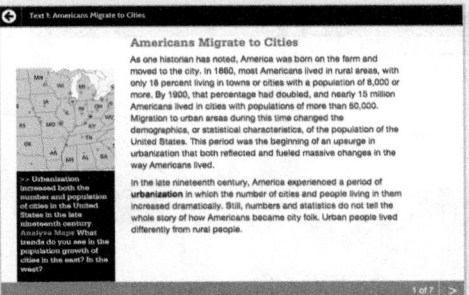

Objective 1: Analyze urban growth in the late 1800s.

Quick Instruction
Interactive Gallery: Growth of the Cities, 1870–1900 Project the gallery and click on the images to reveal information about urban growth in the late 1800s. After you have worked your way through the entire gallery, challenge students to use the question words (who, what, where, when, why, and how) to generate six separate questions about urban growth in the late 1800s and answer them.

▣ ACTIVE CLASSROOM

Conduct a *Graffiti Concepts* activity. Ask students to reflect on the different aspects of urban growth in the late 1800s and create a visual image and/or phrase that represents each aspect. (Allow approximately 3–5 minutes.) Then ask students to post their graffiti on the board or on chart paper. Ask them to look at all the various aspects and then discuss them as a group.

Further Instruction
Go through the Interactive Reading Notepad questions and discuss the answers with the class.

Project this graphic organizer as you work with students through the lesson to help them note the central ideas. (*Urbanization, technological innovation, city-specific problems*)

INTERACTIVE GALLERY
Growth of the Cities, 1870–1900

Support Ideas with Evidence What details can you find to explain the causes of rural-to-urban migration in the late nineteenth century? *(Economic opportunity in rural areas was becoming increasingly scarce. Many farmers moved to cities looking for work as prices for many crops were too low to be profitable. Manufacturing and transportation networks in many cities afforded increasing opportunities to jobs that paid better wages than what was available in rural areas.)*

Identify Patterns What were some of the effects of rural-to-urban migration within the United States during this time? *(Rural to urban migration changed the demographics of the population as the percentage of people living in cities increased rapidly. In addition, people in cities live differently from people in rural areas. People in urban areas often had more structured, scheduled work but had opportunities for education and entertainment that were not available in rural areas.)*

Draw Conclusions What relationship do you see between urbanization and economic opportunities for women? *(Possible answer: Urbanization created more opportunities for women. For example, service sector jobs increased as many people had increasing amounts of disposable income. Women with some education were also able to take positions in offices or as teachers.)*

A Nation of Cities

DIGITAL TEXT 2

Technology Improves City Life

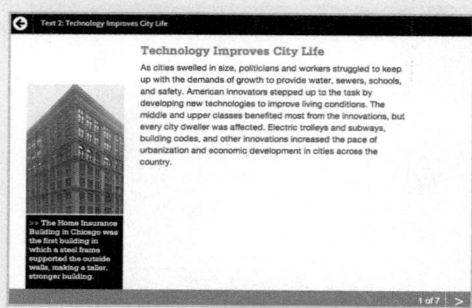

INTERACTIVE ILLUSTRATION

The Flatiron Building

DIGITAL TEXT 3

Urban Living Creates Social Issues

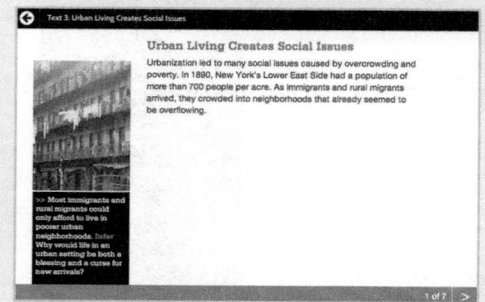

Objective 2: Explain how technology improved city life.

Quick Instruction

Interactive Illustration: The Flatiron Building Project the image of the area around the Flatiron Building. Explain that the building, located in New York City, has a triangular shape like that of an old-fashioned flatiron (metal clothes iron that was heated externally), hence its name. It is 23 stories tall and was completed in 1903. Manipulate the images to show how the area around the building changed. Then, invite the class to consider the impact of energy on the American way of life in the late nineteenth century. Explain how each of the following technological innovations improved urban standards of living during this period: water systems, sewer systems, electricity, steel framing, elevators, central heating, and mass transit.

📹 ACTIVE CLASSROOM

Organize students to create a *Circle Write*. Break students into groups of two or three and provide this question as a writing prompt: How did technological innovations make construction of the Flatiron Building possible? Have students write as much as they can for one minute then switch with the person on their right. The next person tries to improve or elaborate the response where the other person left off. Continue to switch until the paper comes back to the first person. The group then decides which is the best composition (or response) and shares that with the larger group.

D Differentiate: Extra Support As the class discusses technological innovations that impacted urban life, it may be helpful to explicitly point out the difference between closed and open sewer systems as well as water filtration systems that allow tap water to be consumed.

ELL Use the ELL activity described in the ELL chart.

Further Instruction

Go through the Interactive Reading Notepad questions and discuss the answers with the class.

Analyze Interactions What effects did the technological innovation of electric power have on the economic development of the United States? *(Urban transit increasingly relied on electric power, which was cleaner and more efficient than horse-drawn trolleys or coal-driven engines. Electric cable cars and subways allowed urban economies to expand even faster. Elevators also ran on electricity, enabling the construction of taller buildings which in turn increased apartment space and office space. The growing population density led to economic growth as consumer demand increased. and further stimulated economic development in urban areas.)*

Draw Conclusions How did the application of technological innovations to transportation improve the standard of living in cities throughout the United States? *(Technological innovations in transportation made urban travel less dirty and allowed more people to move easily throughout the city. Improved transportation also allowed some people to live in the cleaner, quieter suburbs and travel to work.)*

Objective 3: Evaluate the problems caused by rapid urban growth and ways that city dwellers tried to solve them.

Quick Instruction

3-D Model: Living in a Tenement Direct students attention to the image of the tenement. Click at the various locations to reveal what life in a tenement was truly like. For each, ask students to declare whether it shows a positive or a negative aspect of tenement life. Then challenge students to connect that aspect of tenement life to larger social issues affecting women, children, and immigrants caused by rapid urban growth (e.g., sanitation, fire, conflict, etc.) Finally, ask students how city dwellers tried to solve each problem.

📹 ACTIVE CLASSROOM

Tell students that they can learn more about life in a tenement if they *Act it Out*. Review the images and information about tenements and tenement living. Then challenge students to create a short sketch that brings the picture to life by depicting appropriate challenges faced by tenement dwellers (e.g., overcrowding, conflict, fetching water, etc.).

ELL Use the ELL activity described in the ELL chart.

3-D MODEL
Living in a Tenement

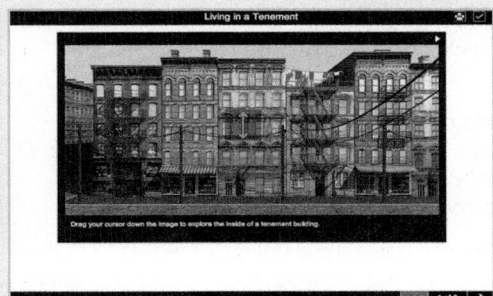

Further Instruction
Go through the Interactive Reading Notepad questions and discuss the answers with the class.

Summarize What sort of social issues were directly related to urbanization? *(More people moving to cities meant the problem of overcrowding became worse. Public health concerns also affected many people in cities as disease spreads rapidly in dirty, cramped conditions. Fire and crime were also social issues relating to urbanization, leading many cities to establish professional firefighting teams and police forces.)*

Identify Cause and Effect How were the changing demographic patterns resulting from immigration a cause of tension in cities during this time? *(Many different ethnic and racial groups immigrated to American cities, and these groups sometimes came into conflict with each other.)* What was one effect? *(New, professional urban police forces had to try to find ways to deal with these conflicts.)*

Identify Central Issues How did urban planners respond to cholera outbreaks and improve urban standards of living? *(In response to cholera outbreaks in the late 1800s, planners and other officials took steps to improve the quality of drinking water and to ensure closed sewage systems functioned properly.)*

■ SYNTHESIZE

DIGITAL ACTIVITY
Reflecting Back

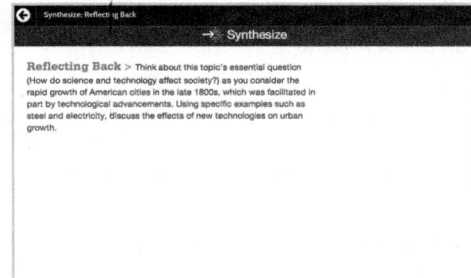

Ask students to recall the Topic Essential Question, "How do science and technology affect society?" Have them use the Think-Pair-Share strategy to answer the question in the *Reflecting Back* activity.

Discuss Given the wave of technological innovation in the late 1800s, ask students to speculate whether or not Josiah Strong would have changed his opinion of cities in the early 1900s.

DEMONSTRATE

DIGITAL QUIZ
Lesson Quiz and Class Discussion Board

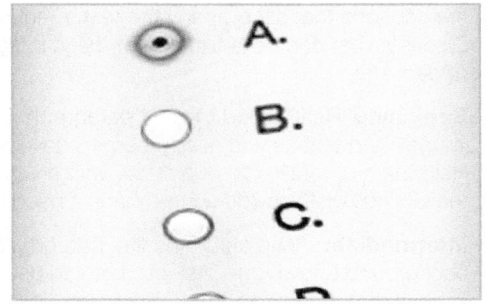

Assign the online Lesson Quiz for this lesson if you haven't already done so. Students will be offered automatic remediation or enrichment based on their score.

Pose these questions to the class on the Discussion Board:

Identify Central Issues What social and economic factors caused urbanization in the late 1800s?

Express Problems Clearly Why was life for tenement dwellers challenging?

Topic Inquiry
Have students continue their investigations for the Topic Inquiry.

New Ways of Life

Supporting English Language Learners

Use with Digital Text 1, **Free Enterprise Improves Life.**

Reading
To develop background knowledge on this subject by using contextual and visual support, have students examine the photographs and read the captions that accompany the text, *Free Enterprise Improves Life*. Discuss what can be learned from these images about an era called the Gilded Age.

Beginning Read aloud the first paragraph. Invite students to refer to the images and text as you assist them to develop background knowledge. Help them complete this sentence with a word or phrase: People _____ in the Gilded Age. Provide a word bank if needed.

Intermediate Read aloud the first paragraph as a prompt to develop background knowledge. Ask students to use what they learned from the images and the text to write a list of predictions about how life changed in the *Gilded Age*. Ask students to review their predictions after they finish reading the text.

Advanced Have students work in small groups and ask a volunteer from each to read aloud the first paragraph in order to assist the group to develop background knowledge. Ask: How did looking at the photographs beforehand help you understand the term *Gilded Age* when you encountered it? Did any of your ideas change after reading first paragraph?

Advanced High Have students work in small groups and take turns reading aloud the first three paragraphs in order to assist the group to develop background knowledge. Ask students to write new captions for the reading's photographs, using the term *conspicuous consumerism* in each.

Use with Digital Text 2, **A Mass Culture Develops.**

Learning
Read aloud the first paragraph under the heading, *The Growth of Public Schools*. As you read, select challenging words and model how to use learning strategies such as asking for assistance, employing nonverbal cues, and using synonyms and circumlocution if the English words are not known.

Beginning Have students write down three words they do not understand. Then, have students practice asking for assistance. Provide the following sentence frames: "Will you explain what _____ means?" and "Does _____ mean the same as _____?"

Intermediate Ask students to write down three unfamiliar words from the text. Have students work in pairs to practice asking for help and explaining meaning using similar words. Encourage students to use various speaking strategies define the words in their own words. If necessary, provide the following sentence frames: "So you are saying this word means_____?" and "The meaning of _____ is the same as_____."

Advanced Have pairs of students take turns reading the paragraph aloud. Encourage them to pause when they encounter an unfamiliar word and ask their partner for assistance. The partner should then employ strategies such as nonverbal cues and circumlocution to explain the word.

Advanced High Invite students to give a short impromptu speech that summarizes the paragraph's main ideas. Encourage them to use strategies such as nonverbal cues and circumlocution to communicate their ideas more effectively.

▣ Differentiate Instruction

Use the Differentiated Instruction notes throughout the lesson plan to support the varied skill sets, levels of readiness, and interests in the mixed-ability classroom.

Challenge These notes include suggestions for expanding the activity for advanced students.

On-Level These notes include suggestions for modifying the activity to address different interests or learning styles.

Extra Support These notes include ideas for providing more scaffolding or reading spuport.

Special Needs These notes provide ideas for adapting instruction to support the needs of various special needs students.

■ NOTES

PEARSON
realize™
www.PearsonRealize.com

Go online to access additional resources including:
Primary Sources • Biographies • Supreme Court cases •
21st Century Skill Tutorials • Maps • Graphic Organizers.

Objectives

Objective 1: Explain how technology, new types of stores, and marketing changed Americans' standard of living.

Objective 2: Analyze mass culture and education in the late 1800s.

Objective 3: Describe new popular cultural movements in the late 1800s.

LESSON 6 ORGANIZER		PACING: APPROX. 1 PERIOD, .5 BLOCKS			
		OBJECTIVES	**PACING**	**RESOURCES**	
				Online	**Print**
Connect					
	DIGITAL START UP ACTIVITY **Advertising**		5 min.	●	
Investigate					
	DIGITAL TEXT 1 **Free Enterprise Improves Life**	Objective 1	10 min.	●	●
	INTERACTIVE ILLUSTRATION **Turn-of-the-Century Department Store**		10 min.	●	
	DIGITAL TEXT 2 **A Mass Culture Develops**	Objective 2	10 min.	●	●
	DIGITAL TEXT 3 **A Boom in Popular Entertainment**	Objective 3	10 min.	●	●
	INTERACTIVE GALLERY **Leisure Activities at the Turn of the Century**		10 min.	●	
Synthesize					
	DIGITAL ACTIVITY **Mass Culture Then and Now**		5 min.	●	
Demonstrate					
	DIGITAL QUIZ **Lesson Quiz and Class Discussion Board**		10 min.	●	

New Ways of Life

■ CONNECT

DIGITAL START UP ACTIVITY
Advertising

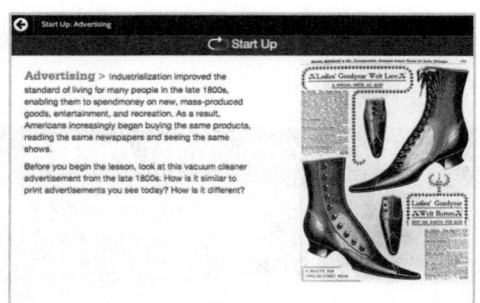

Project the Start Up Activity Ask students to answer the question as they enter and get settled.

Discuss Ask students to share their thoughts on the mass culture produced by industrialization. What are the positive and negative effects of many Americans reading the same newspaper, seeing the same shows, or in this case, buying the same type of footwear?

Tell students that in this lesson they will be learning how industrialization and mass culture affected standards of living, as well as the growth of public education.

Aa Vocabulary Development: Use the Interactive Reading Notepad to preview the Key Terms and Academic Vocabulary in the lesson with students.

⇅ FLIP IT!
Assign the Flipped Video for this lesson.

■ STUDENT EDITION PRINT
PAGES: 347–352

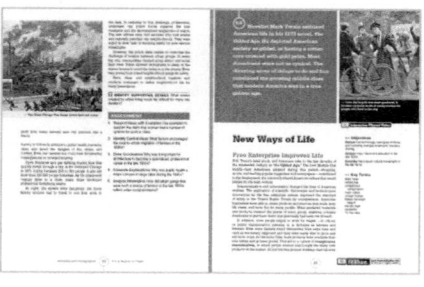

■ INVESTIGATE

DIGITAL TEXT 1
Free Enterprise Improves Life

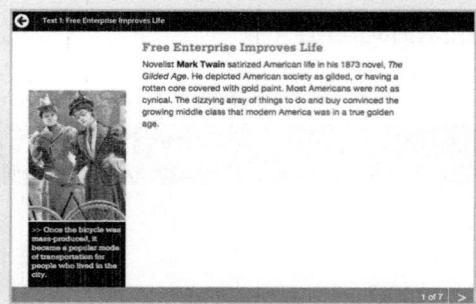

INTERACTIVE ILLUSTRATION
Turn-of-the-Century Department Store

Objective 1: Explain how technology, new types of stores, and marketing changed Americans' standard of living.

Quick Instruction
Interactive Illustration: Turn-of-the-Century Department Store Project the gallery and click on the images to reveal information about the department store, the items in it, its employees, and its customers. Discuss each aspect of the store. Challenge students to explain how the production and distribution of the store's goods were made possible by the application of technological innovation and scientific discoveries by the free enterprise system. *(Mass production made goods available and lowered prices, transportation networks (railroads and subways) delivered the goods and workers to the store, and mass communication enabled effective advertising.)*

💬 ACTIVE CLASSROOM
Invite students to *Connect Two Terms* from their learning. List the following terms on the board for students to copy on small pieces of paper: Mark Twain, Gilded Age, industrialization, urbanization, transportation, free enterprise, standard of living, products and services, department store, and technology. Read the list of words with students. Ask students to "connect two" or choose two words they think might belong together, and state the reason, e.g. "I would connect _____ and _____ because _____ ." Invite the other students to comment on the connections.

ELL Use the ELL activity described in the ELL chart.

Further Instruction
Go through the Interactive Reading Notepad questions and discuss the answers with the class.

Compare and Contrast Invite students to compare and contrast the standards of living they see reflected in the turn-of-the-century department store with a contemporary department store today. *(Possible answers will vary but should draw comparisons between turn-of-the-century goods and comparable goods today.)*

Generate Explanations Explain the relationship between technological innovations and scientific discoveries such as mass production and the corresponding improvement in the standard of living in the United States. *(Innovation in mass production methods allowed many American businesses to produce their goods more cheaply. The lower production costs in turn led to lower prices, affording more American consumers the opportunity to purchase these goods and improve their standard of living. Also, scientific discoveries and innovations around sanitation, including indoor plumbing, as well as better health care also improved life expectancy and improved the standard of living.)*

DIGITAL TEXT 2

A Mass Culture Develops

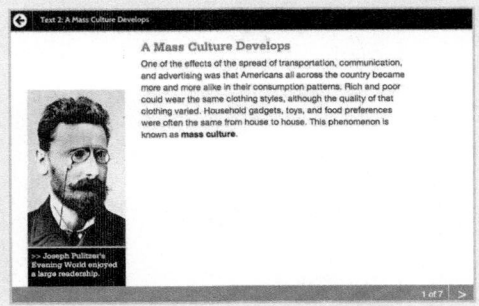

Text 2: A Mass Culture Develops

A Mass Culture Develops

One of the effects of the spread of transportation, communication, and advertising was that Americans all across the country became more and more alike in their consumption patterns. Rich and poor could wear the same clothing styles, although the quality of that clothing varied. Household gadgets, toys, and food preferences were often the same from house to house. This phenomenon is known as **mass culture**.

>> Joseph Pulitzer's Evening World enjoyed a large readership.

1 of 7   >

Objective 2: Analyze mass culture and education in the late 1800s.

Quick Instruction

Summarize Direct students' attention to the image of the crowded neighborhood. Invite a volunteer to explain how this art work might reflect many characteristics and issues of this time in U.S. history. *(increasing population, urbanization, mass culture)* What is mass culture? *(widespread similarity of consumption patterns)* Why did mass culture develop in the late 1800s? *(the spread of transportation, communication, and advertising)* How was this related to education? *(Literacy rates climbed dramatically as an increasing number of people attended public schools.)*

Describe What was the impact of Tin Pan Alley on American culture? *Tin Pan Alley was a section of New York City that became the center of the music publishing industry and the name of the style of popular music developed there. These music publishers influenced American culture by selling sheet music that Americans throughout the country could enjoy in their homes, encouraging the growth of a mass culture for music.*

ELL Use the ELL activity described in the ELL chart.

Further Instruction

Go through the Interactive Reading Notepad questions and discuss the answers with the class.

Identify Supporting Details The turn of the century brought many "firsts," including advances in entertainment, education, and the arts. Keep track of those innovations by using a graphic organizer as you read *Mass Culture* and *New Kinds of Popular Entertainment*. *(Possible answers: Entertainment—vaudeville, ragtime music, baseball and other sports, amusement parks. Education—compulsory grade-school education, development of the liberal arts education in the United States, new educational opportunities for African Americans and women. Art—novels that described realistic problems, paintings that depicted city life in real and honest ways.)*

Hypothesize Issues in U.S. history are often reflected in various genres of literature, and the works of novelist Edith Wharton were no exception. She often questioned society's rigid rules of conduct in her stories. How might this same theme reflect social issues affecting women at the end of the nineteenth century? *(Many women were afforded new economic opportunities, but many did not enjoy the same degree of social and political autonomy as men.)*

DIGITAL TEXT 3

A Boom in Popular Entertainment

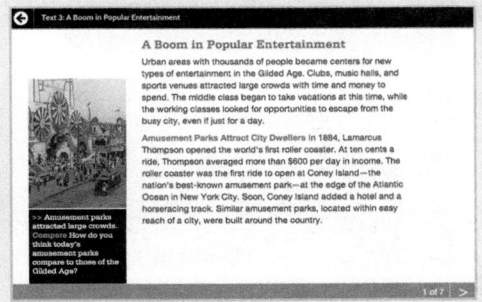

Text 3: A Boom in Popular Entertainment

A Boom in Popular Entertainment

Urban areas with thousands of people became centers for new types of entertainment in the Gilded Age. Clubs, music halls, and dance venues attracted large crowds with time and money to spend. The middle class began to take vacations at this time, while the working classes looked for opportunities to escape from the busy city, even if just for a day.

Amusement Parks Attract City Dwellers In 1884, Lamarcus Thompson opened the world's first roller coaster. At ten cents a ride, Thompson averaged more than $600 per day in income. The roller coaster was the first ride to open at Coney Island—the nation's best-known amusement park—at the edge of the Atlantic Ocean in New York City. Soon, Coney Island added a hotel and a horseracing track. Similar amusement parks, located within easy reach of a city, were built around the country.

>> Amusement parks attracted large crowds. Compare How do you think today's amusement parks compare to those of the Gilded Age?

1 of 7   >

Objective 3: Describe new popular cultural movements in the late 1800s.

Quick Instruction

Interactive Gallery: Leisure Activities at the Turn of the Century Project the gallery. Click each image to display information about popular entertainment at the turn of the century. As you guide students through the gallery, have them compare and contrast the examples of each form of entertainment they see with a parallel form that is popular today.

ACTIVE CLASSROOM

Invite students learning about popular leisure activities to *Act It Out*. Have small groups of students pantomime various leisure activities they have learned about and challenge the rest of the class to correctly identify what the group is portraying.

D Differentiate: Extra Support Prompt students to explicitly connect the images they see with main ideas in the text about the development of popular cultural movements.

New Ways of Life

INTERACTIVE GALLERY
Leisure Activities at the Turn of the Century

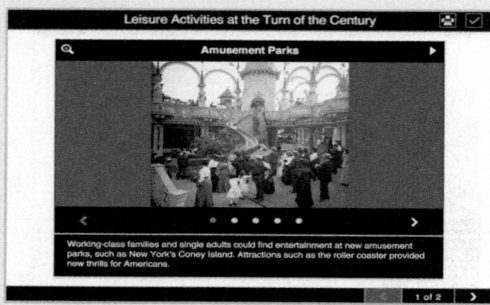

Further Instruction
Go through the Interactive Reading Notepad questions and discuss the answers with the class.

Hypothesize How might a film with a title like *The Great Train Robbery* reflect characteristics or issues in U.S. history? *(Possible answers: The film reflects American's fascination with the technological innovations associated with the development of the railroads.)*

■ SYNTHESIZE

DIGITAL ACTIVITY
Mass Culture Then and Now

Ask students to use the Think-Pair-Share strategy to answer the question in the *Mass Culture Then and Now* activity.

Discuss Ask students to share their answers with the class. Encourage them to draw parallels between the relationship of the Internet with contemporary mass culture and the growth of mass media in the late nineteenth century.

■ DEMONSTRATE

DIGITAL QUIZ
Lesson Quiz and Class Discussion Board

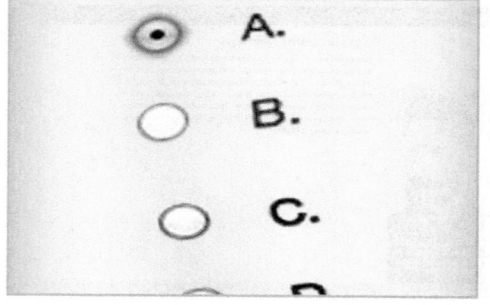

Assign the online Lesson Quiz for this lesson if you haven't already done so. Students will be offered automatic remediation or enrichment based on their score.

Pose this question to the class on the Discussion Board:

Compare and Contrast How was American life in the late 1800s most similar to life today? How was it most different?

Topic Inquiry
Have students continue their investigations for the Topic Inquiry.

Industry and Immigration

▇ SYNTHESIZE

DIGITAL ACTIVITY
Reflect on the Essential Question and Topic

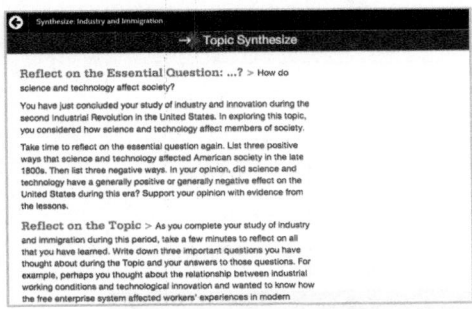

First ask students to reconsider the Essential Question for the topic: How do science and technology affect society? Students should focus on the positive and negative effects of technological innovation in the late 1800s on American society.

Ask students which five technological innovations they thought had the greatest impact on American society in the 1800s. Ensure they provide specific examples from the lesson to support their answers. Ask students to revisit the push and pull factors that facilitated an increase in immigration to the United States during the latter half of the nineteenth century, as well as the challenges they faced when they arrived.

Next, ask students to reflect on the topic as a whole and jot down 1–3 questions they've thought about during the topic. Share an examples like this to prompt their thinking.

- How were the changes in American society in the late 1800s due to technological change similar to changes in American society today? How were they different?

- What impact did increased immigration have on American society and the nation's economy in the late nineteenth century?

- What parallels can you draw between the consumer culture of the late nineteenth century and that which you see today?

- You may ask students to share their questions and answers on the Class Discussion Board.

Topic Inquiry
Have students continue the Topic Inquiry.

▇ DEMONSTRATE

DIGITAL TOPIC REVIEW AND ASSESSMENT
Industry and Immigration

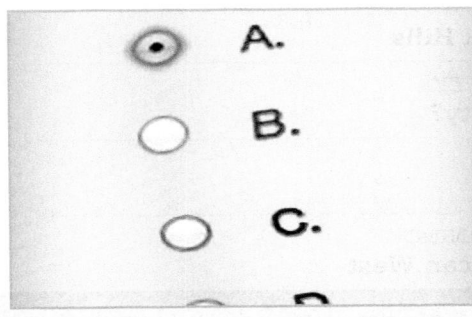

Students can prepare for the Topic Test by answering the questions in the Topic Review and Assessment online or the Assessment questions in the Print Student text. They can also prepare by reviewing their answers to the Interactive Reading Notepad questions or reviewing their notes in the Reading and Notetaking Study Guide.

DIGITAL TOPIC TEST
Industry and Immigration

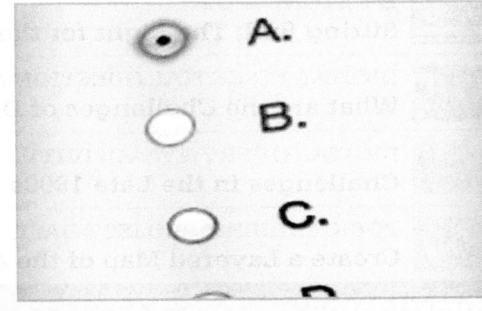

TOPIC TEST
Assign the Topic Test to assess students' understanding of topic content.

BENCHMARK TESTS
Assign these benchmark tests as you complete the relevant topics to monitor student progress toward mastering the course content and as preparation for the End-of-Course Test.

Benchmark Test 1: Topics 1–3

Benchmark Test 2: Topics 4–6

Benchmark Test 3: Topics 7–9

Benchmark Test 4: Topics 10–12

Benchmark Test 5: Topics 13–15

Benchmark Test 6: Topics 16–18

Benchmark Test 7: Topics 19–20

Challenges in the Late 1800s

TOPIC 10 ORGANIZER	PACING: APPROX. 7 PERIODS, 3.5 BLOCKS	
		PACING
Connect		1 period
MY STORY VIDEO **Sitting Bull, The Fight for the Black Hills**		10 min.
DIGITAL ESSENTIAL QUESTION ACTIVITY **What are the Challenges of Diversity?**		10 min.
DIGITAL OVERVIEW ACTIVITY **Challenges in the Late 1800s**		10 min.
TOPIC INQUIRY: PROJECT-BASED LEARNING **Create a Layered Map of the American West**		20 min.
Investigate		2–4 periods
TOPIC INQUIRY: PROJECT-BASED LEARNING **Create a Layered Map of the American West**		Ongoing
LESSON 1 American Indians Under Pressure		30–40 min.
LESSON 2 The West Is Transformed		30–40 min.
LESSON 3 Corruption Plagues the Nation		30–40 min.
LESSON 4 Farm Issues and Populism		30–40 min.
Synthesize		1 period
DIGITAL ACTIVITY **Reflect on the Essential Question and Topic**		10 min.
TOPIC INQUIRY: PROJECT-BASED LEARNING **Create a Layered Map of the American West**		20 min.
Demonstrate		1–2 periods
DIGITAL TOPIC REVIEW AND ASSESSMENT **Challenges in the Late 1800s**		10 min.
TOPIC INQUIRY: PROJECT-BASED LEARNING **Create a Layered Map of the American West**		20 min.

TOPIC INQUIRY: PROJECT-BASED LEARNING

Create a Layered Map of the American West

In this Topic Inquiry, students work in teams to create a multi-layered map showing six different distributions of various human characteristics of the American West during the 1800s. Learning how conflict impacts the lives of people will contribute to students' understanding of the Topic Essential Question: What are the challenges of diversity?

STEP 1: CONNECT
Develop Questions and Plan the Investigation

Launch the Project and Generate Questions
Display the call to service letter from George C. Washburn of the Western Association of States and Territories. Tell students that for their project, each team will need to research information for only three of the layers. The information for the first three layers is listed in the *Information Organizer*. Briefly take time to discuss possible types of patterns and distributions and ask students to think about which they want to research.

Suggestion: If you'd like to ensure that a variety of human characteristics are chosen, assign the layer topics rather than letting the teams choose them.

Plan the Investigation
Form students into teams. Have them learn about working as a team by taking a tutorial, signing the *Project Contract*, and beginning the *Need-to-Know Questions*.

Suggestion: If you prefer that each student research and create a map layer, either form groups of three or tell larger groups to do more than three layers.

Resources
- Project Launch
- Need-to-Know Questions
- Rubric for a Layered Map of the American West
- Project Contract
- Student Instructions

STEP 2: INVESTIGATE
Apply Disciplinary Concepts and Tools

Explore Human Characteristics, Types of Data, and Choose a Medium
Teams will work together to decide the human characteristics they want to map. Help students by asking them to review the possible types of human patterns and distributions listed in the student instructions.

To prepare for and guide their research, teams will create a list of *Need-to-Know Questions* about the themes they are researching and mapping. Refer students to helpful resources within the core content of the Topic to help answer their questions. For example, if they are researching Native Americans and significant conflicts with settlers, refer them to Lesson One's readings and activities. Help students begin to fill out the *Information Organizer*.

The teams should plan how to present the information they will gather. If your class has limited access to the Internet, supply and review procedures for using layers of transparency paper. If students will be using online software, briefly guide students in the registering process for sites such as http://www.buildamap.com. Students can review the *Getting Started with Build-A-Map Guide*.

Conduct Research and Pose and Answer Questions
The teams should conduct research and document the information about the map layer themes. Encourage students to use the *Need-to-Know Questions* to help guide their research. Students should be adding to and answering questions on the resource.

Suggestion: If your class has limited access to the Internet, you could make books available to students, such as *Bury My Heart at Wounded Knee* by Dee Brown. A good online source for maps that students can use to create their layers can be found at http://www.lib.utexas.edu/maps/.

Resources
- Project Tracker
- Information Organizer
- Sample Layered Map
- Need-to-Know Questions
- Getting Started with Build-A-Map Guide

⏻ PROFESSIONAL DEVELOPMENT

Project-Based Learning
Be sure to view the Project-Based Learning Professional Development resources in the online course.

Create a Layered Map of the American West *(continued)*

STEP 3: SYNTHESIZE
Evaluate Sources and Use Evidence to Formulate Conclusions

Create Your Map Layers

Now have students get together to create their map layers. If students are having trouble using the online map-making software, remind them to review *Getting Started* with *Build-A-Map Guide*. Review each team's layered maps to make sure they are on track. For students who are having trouble, walk them through the *Sample Layered Map* to get ideas. Remind students to review skills tutorials describing using and creating maps if necessary.

Suggestion: Take a few minutes to review each team's initial progress. If more than one team is having difficulties transferring information to the maps, briefly hold a class discussion in which you and students provide ideas and suggestions to help create the maps. For instance, for the population totals in layer three, students could shade states in the same range the same color.

Pose and Answer Questions

Review the posing and answering criteria for the project. Ask teams to review their layered maps and generate two questions and two answers for each map layer using the project *Information Organizer*.

Suggestion: Remind students to use the questions listed in the *Student Instructions* to help them evaluate the relevance and appropriateness of their questions and answers.

Resources
- Sample Layered Map
- Getting Started with Build-A-Map Guide
- Information Organizer
- Student Instructions

STEP 4: DEMONSTRATE
Communicate Conclusions and Take Informed Action

Present Your Layered Map of the American West

Have students prepare their layered map presentations, then watch the team presentations. To help the teams structure their time, set up a clock in the back of the room, and alert them when they have only a few minutes left.

Suggestion: For a less technology-dependent end product, have students create a museum exhibit or gallery with their layered maps. To take the technology a step further, have students set up a mock web site or slide show that displays their work. Ask each group to present one of their map layers and to discuss their conclusions.

Reflect on the Project

After students have finished their *Self Assessments*, help them go over what they thought went well and what did not so they can be more effective in the future.

Suggestion: As an extension activity, have students research and map the geographic distributions and patterns in your state or community.

Resources
- Rubric for a Layered Map of the American West
- Self Assessment

Challenges in the Late 1800s

The dynamic economic growth and its rapid changes of the late 1800s excited many Americans, but others found the rapid change hard to take. Disillusioned with the corruption, poverty, and dishonesty around them, Mark Twain and Charles Dudley Warner published *The Gilded Age* in 1873 to present their views. Eventually, the term *Gilded Age* came to define the era because excessive extravagance and wealth concealed mounting social problems, government corruption, and poverty.

Among the problems were those faced by farmers. In desperation, dissatisfied farmers joined the Populist Party. Although racial and other differences continued to divide Americans, some people saw the need for diverse groups to work together to meet shared goals. How would Americans respond to these challenges and what impact would it have on the country?

■ CONNECT

MY STORY VIDEO
Sitting Bull, The Fight for the Black Hills

Watch a video showing the story of the Lakota Sioux in the late 1800s.

Check Understanding By the 1860s, what was a concern of the Lakota Sioux? *(the incursion of white settlers and troops on their land)*

Determine Point of View The Lakota Sioux have long refused compensation for their land. Is this refusal justified? Explain your answer. *(The students may admire the moral grounds behind the decision to refuse money. Others may point out the poverty in which the Sioux live today and the benefits that compensation may bring.)*

DIGITAL ESSENTIAL QUESTION ACTIVITY
What are the Challenges of Diversity?

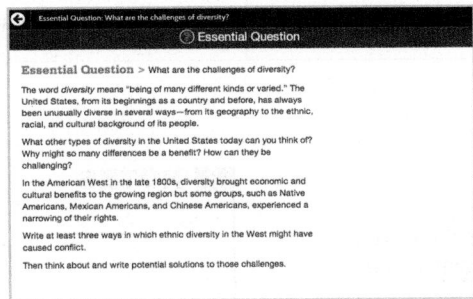

Ask students about the Essential Question for this Topic: What are the challenges of diversity? Forging a diverse nation is difficult. How should a country make sure all have equal opportunities and rights?

Support a Point of View with Evidence Do the benefits of diversity outweigh the costs? Explain. *(Yes, the benefits of diversity are greater. When cultures and races mix, everyone benefits from new ideas and ways of life, creating a more exciting environment with more opportunities for everyone.)*

Identify Central Issues Write at least three ways in which ethnic diversity in the emerging frontier might cause conflict. How might these conflicts be resolved? *(Causes of conflict may include racial prejudice, cultural fights, and wars with Native Americans. Governments can minimize these conflicts by educating people about different cultures and races.)*

DIGITAL OVERVIEW ACTIVITY
Challenges in the Late 1800s

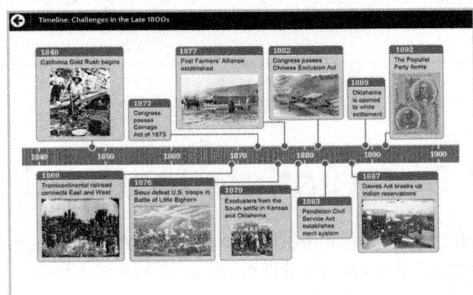

Display the timeline showing the major events and acts of legislation related to the social and political issues in the late 1800s in the United States. During this Topic, students will learn about these events and many more, but this timeline will provide a framework into which they can place the events they learn about.

Analyze Timelines In which decades of the 1800s do most of the timeline events occur? *(1870s and 1880s—four events each)*

Generate Explanations Why might the timeline begin in 1848 with the California Gold Rush? *(The California Gold Rush was a key event that opened the West to large numbers of Americans and immigrants.)*

Topic Inquiry
Launch the Topic Inquiry with students after introducing the topic.

American Indians Under Pressure

Supporting English Language Learners

Use with Digital Text 1, **Cultures Forced to Adapt.**

Reading
Help students read the content area text using support from peers and their teacher. Read aloud the text under the heading *American Settlers Move West*. Ask students to follow along in preparation for their own reading.

Beginning In small groups, invite students to take turns reading sentences from the section. Move from group to group and support students by asking them to raise a hand each time they encounter a word they cannot pronounce. Say the word for them and have them repeat it as they continue reading.

Intermediate In small groups, have a student read aloud the first paragraph while other group members follow along. Then answer students' questions about any reading challenges. Repeat this process for the remaining paragraphs.

Advanced Ask pairs of students to take turns reading aloud the section. Encourage them to ask each other questions about pronunciation and other reading challenges, both during and after the reading.

Advanced High As students read the section silently, have them write down any questions they have about pronunciation or other reading challenges. Invite pairs of students to help each other to answer the questions (using their own knowledge or additional resources).

Use with Digital Text 2, **Settlers and Native Americans Collide.**

Learning
Help students to internalize new vocabulary by using and reusing it in meaningful ways. Direct students' attention to the first two paragraphs of the section titled *Efforts to Promote Peace Fail*. Explain that they will practice using vocabulary from the paragraphs in order to better understand the text.

Beginning Display three sentences using a basic, yet challenging word from the text in three different contexts (including how it is used in the original text). Have students select the word that fits all of the sentences and then read the sentences aloud.

Intermediate With students, create a list of challenging basic vocabulary from the paragraphs. Read the sentence in which each word is found and discuss its meaning. Then ask students to say two sentences: one that uses the word in the same context, and one that uses it in a different context.

Advanced Ask pairs of students to select four challenging words from the paragraphs. Have them dialogue about any social studies topic in which they can integrate the words at least once.

Advanced High Present a volunteer with four challenging words from the paragraphs. Invite the volunteer to speak briefly on any social studies topic in which he or she can integrate the list of words. Repeat with other volunteers and word sets.

D Differentiate Instruction

Use the Differentiated Instruction notes throughout the lesson plan to support the varied skill sets, levels of readiness, and interests in the mixed-ability classroom.

Challenge These notes include suggestions for expanding the activity for advanced students.

On-Level These notes include suggestions for modifying the activity to address different interests or learning styles.

Extra Support These notes include ideas for providing more scaffolding or reading spuport.

Special Needs These notes provide ideas for adapting instruction to support the needs of various special needs students.

■ NOTES

PEARSON realize.™
www.PearsonRealize.com

Go online to access additional resources including:
Primary Sources • Biographies • Supreme Court cases •
21st Century Skill Tutorials • Maps • Graphic Organizers.

Objectives

Objective 1: Compare the ways Native Americans and white settlers viewed and used the land.

Objective 2: Describe the conflicts between white settlers and Indians.

Objective 3: Analyze the impact of the Indian Wars.

Objective 4: Evaluate the effectiveness of the government's Americanization and reservation policies towards American Indians.

LESSON 1 ORGANIZER		PACING: APPROX. 1 PERIOD, .5 BLOCKS			
				RESOURCES	
		OBJECTIVES	**PACING**	**Online**	**Print**
Connect					
	DIGITAL START UP ACTIVITY **Justifying Resistance**		5 min.	●	
Investigate					
	DIGITAL TEXT 1 **Cultures Forced to Adapt**	Objective 1	10 min.	●	●
	DIGITAL TEXT 2 **Settlers and Native Americans Collide**	Objective 2	10 min.	●	●
	INTERACTIVE MAP **Major Indian Wars, 1861–1886**		10 min.	●	
	DIGITAL TEXT 3 **The Indian Wars Conclude**	Objective 3	10 min.	●	●
	DIGITAL TEXT 4 **The Government Encourages Assimilation**	Objective 4	10 min.	●	●
	INTERACTIVE TIMELINE **Legislative Acts Affecting Native Americans**		10 min.	●	
Synthesize					
	DIGITAL ACTIVITY **Native Americans and Reservations**		5 min.	●	
Demonstrate					
	DIGITAL QUIZ **Lesson Quiz and Class Discussion Board**		10 min.	●	

American Indians Under Pressure

▮ CONNECT

DIGITAL START UP ACTIVITY
Justifying Resistance

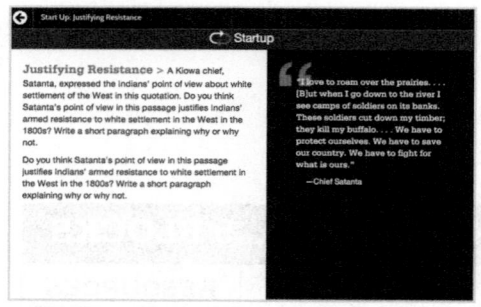

Project the Start Up Activity Ask students to answer the questions as they enter and get settled. Then have them share their ideas with another student, either in class or through a chat or blog space.

Discuss Do you think Satanta's point of view in this passage justifies Native Americans' armed resistance to white settlement in the West in the 1800s? *(Yes—Satanta witnessed the destruction of his people's resources and believed the only way to protect his way of life was to fight for it. No—Satanta should have pursued peaceful solutions. Loss of land does not justify violence.)*

Aa **Vocabulary Development:** Use the Interactive Reading Notepad to preview the Key Terms and Academic Vocabulary in the lesson with students.

▮ FLIP IT!

Assign the Flipped Video for this lesson.

▮ STUDENT EDITION PRINT
PAGES: 358–365

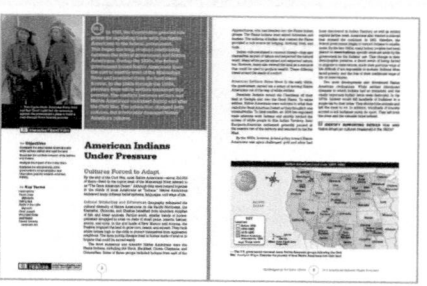

▮ INVESTIGATE

DIGITAL TEXT 1
Cultures Forced to Adapt

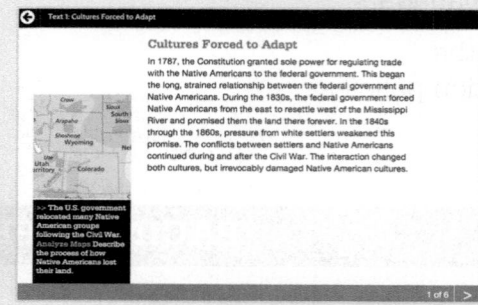

Objective 1: Compare the ways Native Americans and white settlers viewed and used the land.

Quick Instruction

Be sure students understand that Native Americans in the past—and today—embraced many different belief systems, languages, and ways of life. Point out, however, that Indian cultures throughout North America shared a belief in which they saw themselves as part of nature and had great respect for their place in the natural world.

Analyze Maps Project the map showing Native American land loss and discuss how geography influenced the ways Native Americans lived and how they used natural resources. Point out that differences in the use of natural resources and the westward movement of white Americans led to conflicts between Native Americans and settlers. Discuss the resulting resettlement and gradual shrinking of lands controlled by Native Americans on the map.

ELL Use the ELL activity described in the ELL chart.

Further Instruction

Project and discuss the Interactive Reading Notepad questions, including the graphic organizer asking students to identify and explain events in the struggle between the Native Americans and white settlers.

Review the events with the class and fill in the graphic organizer on the whiteboard as you go. Westward expansion by American settlers impacted Native American demographic patterns. Indians were forced to migrate to reservations, which made their previous ways of life impossible to sustain. Ask students to find examples of political issues and federal Indian policies that created conflict about natural resources and that altered the way Native Americans used the land. *(Government policies such as relocating the Cherokees, opening of Indian Territory to mine gold and silver, and the signing and breaking of treaties forced Indians into different ways of life. Political issues like whites' desire for land to build a Transcontinental Railroad also affected Native Americans.)*

Make Generalizations How would you describe life for Native Americans on reservations? What social issues did reservation life create? *(Life on reservations was very different from what most Native Americans were accustomed. They must have felt trapped. Reservation life created poverty and led to more contact with white settlers who introduced diseases for which the Native Americans had no immunity.)*

Predict Consequences Ask students to predict what the impact of western expansion into lands once used by nomadic Native Americans will be. *(The Plains Indians will fight back to protect their lands and preserve their ways of life.)*

DIGITAL TEXT 2

Settlers and Native Americans Collide

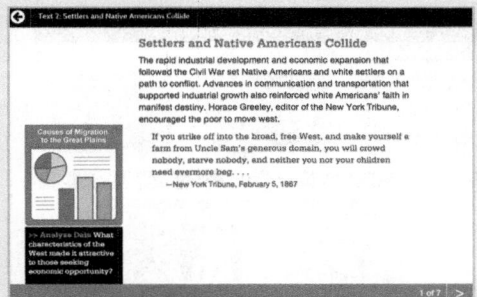

INTERACTIVE MAP

Major Indian Wars, 1861–1886

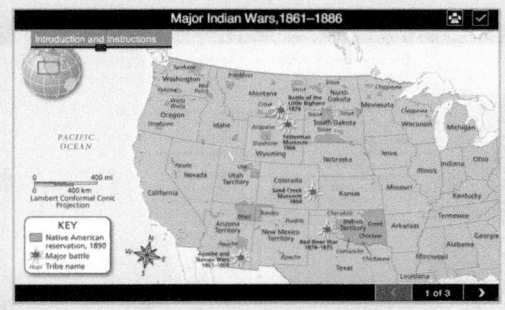

DIGITAL TEXT 3

The Indian Wars Conclude

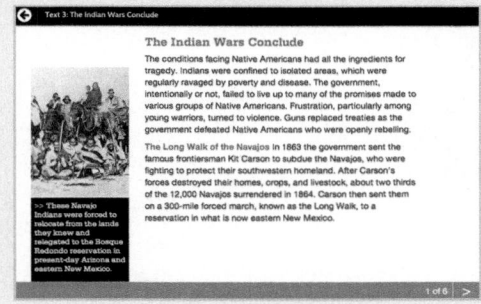

Objective 2: Describe the conflicts between white settlers and Native Americans.

Quick Instruction

Interactive Map: Major Indian Wars, 1861–1886 Project the map and click through the hot spots on the map. Prompt students to think about the effects of westward expansion on relationships between white settlers and Native Americans. Introduce the map activity by telling students that as white settlers populated the West, Native American peoples were pressured to give up the land on which they lived. Remind students that not all Native Americans were willing to relocate. Some fought to protect their land and way of life.

Discuss Prompt students to analyze political issues such as Native American policies. Remind students that in an effort to contain the conflicts on the Plains, the federal government offered the Fort Laramie Treaty of 1868 to the Sioux and other Plains Indian groups. Discuss the key provisions of the treaty with students.

ACTIVE CLASSROOM

Ask the following question using the If Photos Could Talk Strategy: What do you think the Native Americans in the photographs would say if they could talk? What's your evidence? *(They would say that they are trying to protect their way of life using whatever means they can, including violence.)*

D Differentiate: **Challenge** Ask students to do additional research on the Fort Laramie Treaty and present their findings.

ELL Use the ELL activity described in the ELL chart.

Further Instruction

Project and discuss the Interactive Reading Notepad questions, as well as the graphic organizer. Continue reviewing the events with the class and filling in the graphic organizer as you go.

Review the debate that Americans had about how to manage westward expansion. Be sure that students understand that the government-appointed United States Indian Peace Commission concluded that lasting peace would come only if Native Americans settled on farms and reservations and adapted to the white way of life.

Predict Consequences Ask students to predict the impact of using recruitment posters that promised soldiers could claim any "horses or other plunder" taken from Native Americans? *(U.S. cavalry troops will try to take as much as possible from Native Americans, creating even more conflict.)*

Support a Point of View with Evidence Was the Fort Laramie Treaty beneficial to the Sioux? Why or why not? *(In the long run, the treaty was not beneficial. The treaty was good for the Sioux at first because it stopped the fighting. It also prevented the road from being built. However, the Sioux had to live on reservations and be supported by the government. This was completely different from their previous way of life. Also, many reservations were not fully supplied by the government, so the Sioux suffered.)*

Objective 3: Analyze the impact of the Indian Wars.

Quick Instruction

Review with students how the federal government failed to live up to many of the promises it made to various groups of Native Americans. Guide students to understand that the broken promises and Indian policies led to frustration among many Native Americans, who then turned to violence. Settlers and soldiers then responded with violence. The violence often escalated into attacks on civilians on both sides, leading to even more bitter feelings between the groups.

Discuss Project the image of Sitting Bull and discuss the causes and effects of his actions with students. Point out that with the loss of many of their leaders and the destruction of their economy, Native Americans could not adequately resist the U.S. forces or the encroaching settlers.

Hypothesize In response to their situations, many Native Americans welcomed a religious revival based on the Ghost Dance. Why do you think many Native Americans turned to a spiritual solution to their plight? *(They probably thought they had no other course of action other than turning to their religious beliefs to help them survive.)*

Further Instruction

Work through the Interactive Reading Notepad questions. Update the timeline as you go. Discuss the impact of Native American leaders such as Sitting Bull, Crazy Horse, and Chief Joseph.

American Indians Under Pressure

DIGITAL TEXT 4

The Government Encourages Assimilation

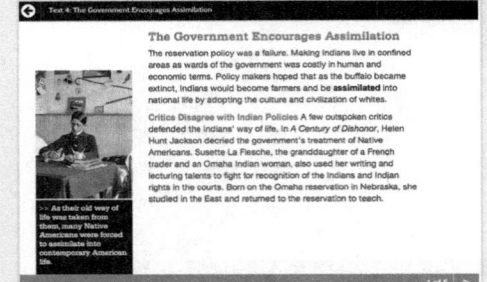

INTERACTIVE TIMELINE

Legislative Acts Affecting Native Americans

Identify Central Issues Based on Chief Joseph's speech, what are his key concerns? *(His key concerns are the welfare of his people and taking care of them.)*

Make Predictions Ask students to predict what will happen to Native Americans once they are all relocated to reservations. *(Living on the reservations will slowly erode the cultures of Native Americans. Because the government had done such a poor job of providing supplies, the Native Americans on reservations will probably suffer as well.)*

Objective 4: Evaluate the effectiveness of the government's Americanization and reservation policies towards American Indians.

Quick Instruction

Because the government policy of relocating Native Americans to reservations was failing, government leaders turned to a new goal of assimilating Indians into the dominant American culture. They called this policy Americanization. Policy-makers tried to weaken Native Americans' tribal cultures. Reformers believed that Indians had to give up tribal loyalties and behaviors before they could adopt mainstream American values and assimilate into American culture.

Interactive Timeline: Legislative Acts Affecting Native Americans Project the interactive timeline and click through the dates when key legislation that impacted Native Americans was introduced. Point out that the legislation reflects the shifting views on how to resolve the conflicts with Native Americans.

👥 ACTIVE CLASSROOM

Use the Ranking Strategy to have students go through the acts of legislation displayed in the activity, and rank which ones had the greatest positive impact on Native Americans and which had the greatest harmful impact.

Further Instruction

Go through the Interactive Reading Notepad questions and discuss the answers with the class.

Discuss Be sure that students understand that there were Americans who disagreed with the government's Indian policies. Discuss the ways in which these critics expressed their disagreements. Although government Indian policies shifted over time as conditions and viewpoints changed, the complex social issues affecting relations with Native Americans remained a problem.

Synthesize Why is forced assimilation destined to fail? What social issues does forced assimilation create? *(Culture is very important to groups of people. Forcing a group to lose its cultural heritage is morally wrong and counterproductive. People will eventually fight back to protect their heritage, creating more problems. Forced assimilation often creates warfare and often forces those who must assimilate in dire situations, such as poverty.)*

Infer Why did the federal government encourage Native Americans to assimilate? Why did government leaders think that Americanization would solve the problems with the reservations? *(Government leaders wanted to end hostilities with Native Americans. They believed that if Native Americans embraced living within the dominant American culture, conflicts would end. Many government leaders also believed that their white American culture was superior to that of Native American groups, and that Indians would be better off if they did assimilate.)*

▮ SYNTHESIZE

DIGITAL ACTIVITY

Native Americans and Reservations

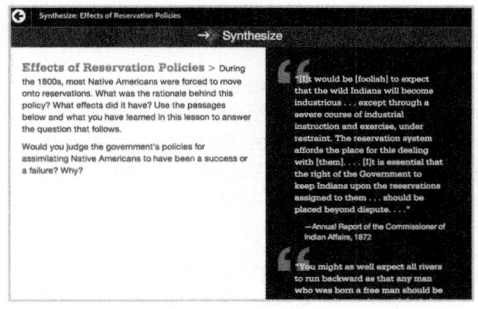

Ask students to recall the rationale behind the federal government's relocation of Native Americans to reservations. Have student partners read the quotes in the Native Americans and Reservations activity. Ask them to take 5 minutes to write down their thoughts and feelings about the quotes, including identifying possible biases of the sources of the quotes.

Have partners think about the following question: Would you judge the government's policies for assimilating Native Americans to have been a success or a failure? Why? Have pairs share their answers with the class.

Discuss Ask students to think about their responses to the Start Up Activity Settlement in the West. Discuss if they think that the Native Americans' armed resistance to the loss of their lands and relocation to reservations was inevitable.

▮ DEMONSTRATE

DIGITAL QUIZ

Lesson Quiz and Class Discussion Board

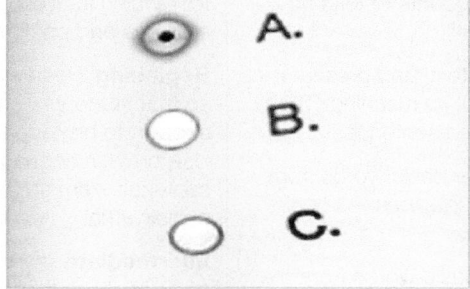

Assign the online Lesson Quiz for this lesson if you haven't already done so. Students will be offered automatic remediation or enrichment based on their score.

Pose this question to the class on the Discussion Board:

In *American Indians Under Pressure*, you read about how Native Americans had lived in North America and used its natural resources for thousands of years before white settlers spread across the land seeking to use the vast resources in different ways. The increased competition for land and resources led to conflict. Unable to match the U.S. government in power, Native Americans fought to protect their ways of life but ultimately were defeated. Native Americans were forced to live on reservations and encouraged to assimilate into white American culture.

Predict Consequences What will be the lingering effects of the forced assimilation of Native Americans and their relocation to reservations? *(Native Americans will feel resentment towards the government and possibly white Americans for many years. They will continue to fight to reclaim their lands and their cultures.)*

Topic Inquiry

Have students continue their investigations for the Topic Inquiry.

The West Is Transformed

Supporting English Language Learners

Use with Digital Text 1, Mining and the Growth of Railroads.

Learning

Help students internalize new basic language by using it and reusing it in writing activities. Read aloud the section titled *Mining Towns Expand Across the West*, or invite volunteers to do so. Ask students to take note of unfamiliar words as they follow along.

Beginning Select an unfamiliar basic word from the text, and present it in a new written sentence about the same topic. Discuss its meaning. Then work with students to reuse the word in another written sentence.

Intermediate With students, create a list of unfamiliar basic words from the text. Discuss their meanings within their original sentences. Ask pairs of students to write new sentences that use the words.

Advanced With students, create a list of unfamiliar basic words from the text. Ask pairs of students to look up and discuss the words' meanings. Then have the pairs write new sentences that use the words.

Advanced High Ask students to work independently to select five unfamiliar words from the reading. Have them use the five words to write an original paragraph about mining towns. Encourage students to use a dictionary if needed.

Use with Digital Text 3, Farmers Settle the Plains.

Reading

Introduce the section titled *Homesteading the Plains* by summarizing the information it contains. Explain that previewing a text is good preparation for reading it. Prompt students to use support from peers and teachers to enhance and confirm understanding.

Beginning Read aloud the first paragraph, pausing at frequent intervals so that students can repeat after you. Encourage students to ask for support to help identify words and phrases that they do not understand. Use simpler language to clarify their meaning. Have students use this sentence stem as they ask for help with unfamiliar language: "Will you explain what ____ means?"

Intermediate Invite volunteers to take turns reading the section. Pause periodically so that students can ask content-related questions to enhance their understanding of the text. If students are having difficulty asking questions about the content, provide them with the following sentence stem: "Would you please explain_____?"

Advanced Have pairs of students take turns reading aloud the section. Encourage them to pause as needed in order to summarize and clarify what was read.

Advanced High Have students read the section independently. Prompt them to record any questions they have about content as they do so. Then encourage students to support each other. Pair students and provide time for them to discuss each other's questions. Ensure the questions enhance and confirm understanding.

▣ Differentiate Instruction

Use the Differentiated Instruction notes throughout the lesson plan to support the varied skill sets, levels of readiness, and interests in the mixed-ability classroom.

Challenge These notes include suggestions for expanding the activity for advanced students.

On-Level These notes include suggestions for modifying the activity to address different interests or learning styles.

Extra Support These notes include ideas for providing more scaffolding or reading spuport.

Special Needs These notes provide ideas for adapting instruction to support the needs of various special needs students.

■ NOTES

PEARSON
realize.™
www.PearsonRealize.com

Go online to access additional resources including:
Primary Sources • Biographies • Supreme Court cases •
21st Century Skill Tutorials • Maps • Graphic Organizers.

Objectives

Objective 1: Analyze the impact of mining and railroads on the settlement of the West.

Objective 2: Explain the impact of physical and human geographic factors on the settlement of the Great Plains.

Objective 3: Analyze treatment of Chinese immigrants and Mexican Americans in the West.

Objective 4: Discuss the ways various groups used land in the West and conflicts among them.

LESSON 2 ORGANIZER		OBJECTIVES	PACING	RESOURCES	
				Online	Print
Connect					
DIGITAL START UP ACTIVITY **Technology and Population Growth**			5 min.	●	
Investigate					
DIGITAL TEXT 1 **Mining and the Growth of Railroads**		Objective 1	10 min.	●	●
INTERACTIVE CHART **Gold and Silver Rushes**			10 min.	●	
DIGITAL TEXT 2 **The Cattle Industry Boom**		Objective 2	10 min.	●	●
DIGITAL TEXT 3 **Farmers Settle on the Plains**		Objective 2	10 min.	●	●
3-D MODEL **Nineteenth-Century Sod House**		Objective 2	10 min.	●	
DIGITAL TEXT 4 **Minorities Encounter Difficulties**		Objective 3	10 min.	●	●
INTERACTIVE GALLERY **Mexican and Chinese American Contributions to the American West**			10 min.	●	
DIGITAL TEXT 5 **Struggles and Change Across the West**		Objective 4	10 min.	●	●
Synthesize					
DIGITAL ACTIVITY **Technology and Free Enterprise**			5 min.	●	
Demonstrate					
DIGITAL QUIZ **Lesson Quiz and Class Discussion Board**			10 min.	●	

The West Is Transformed

■ CONNECT

DIGITAL START UP ACTIVITY
Technology and Population Growth

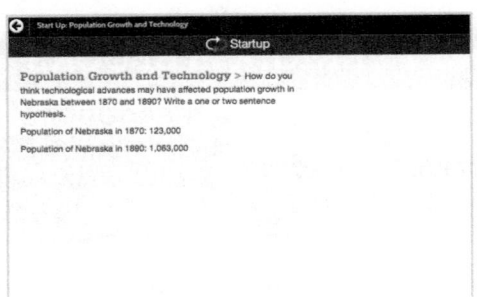

Project the Start Up Activity Ask students to answer the question as they enter and get settled. Then have them share their ideas with another student, either in class or through a chat or blog space.

Discuss How do you think technological advances may have affected population growth in Nebraska between 1870 and 1890? *(Railroad advancements probably played a large role in providing the means for people to settle in Nebraska. Farming innovations would have helped farmers grow more successful crops.)*

Tell students that in this lesson they will be learning about the various factors that played a role in the settling of the West by white settlers.

Aa Vocabulary Development: Use the Interactive Reading Notepad to preview the Key Terms and Academic Vocabulary in the lesson with students.

⇅ FLIP IT!

Assign the Flipped Video for this lesson.

■ STUDENT EDITION PRINT PAGES: 366–374

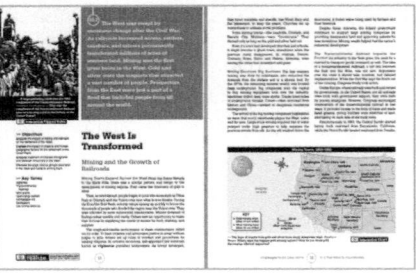

■ INVESTIGATE

DIGITAL TEXT 1
Mining and the Growth of Railroads

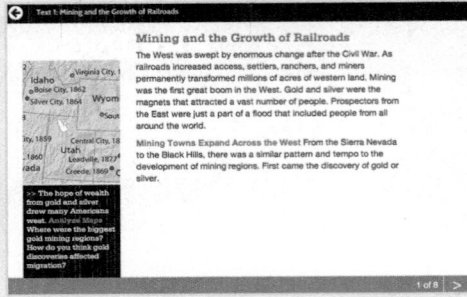

INTERACTIVE CHART
Gold and Silver Rushes

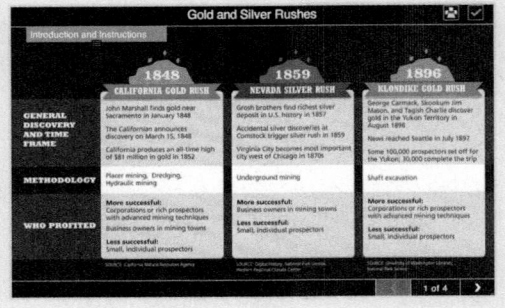

Objective 1: Analyze the impact of mining and railroads on the settlement of the West.

Quick Instruction

The American West was a vast land filled with natural resources. As railroads increased access, settlers, ranchers, and miners permanently transformed millions of acres of western land.

Interactive Chart: Gold and Silver Rushes Introduce the activity by telling students that mining and the wealth it produced helped fuel the nation's industrial development. Communities emerged around mining areas as thousands of Americans moved west to try to strike it rich. Step through the Gold and Silver interactive chart with students, focusing on the impact of physical and human geographic factors on the California and Klondike gold rushes well as the Nevada Silver Rush.

Evaluate Impact How did the business people who opened stores and provided services to prospectors affect the settlement of the west? *(These business people helped establish communities near mining centers. Unlike miners who often left once mining operations were finished, the business people stayed in the new communities.)*

📷 ACTIVE CLASSROOM

Ask the following question using the Sticky Note Strategy: Viewed together, what do these images tell you about the work and effort required to mine for gold and silver? *(Mining for most prospectors was very difficult work. All the photographs show miners using hand tools, so it must have been extremely demanding and inefficient.)*

ELL Use the ELL activity described in the ELL chart.

Further Instruction

Project and discuss the Interactive Reading Notepad questions and the graphic organizer, asking students to identify the sequence by which mining helped created new communities. Point out that by the 1870s, mining operations required new technological innovations developed through the free-enterprise system to access the prized metals and minerals. Mention that as industry and populations in the West grew, the need for a railroad to transport goods increased as well.

Identify Cause and Effect How did the building of the railroad networks throughout the United States change the country's demographic patterns? *(Railroad companies brought recruits from China and Irish immigrants to work building the railroads. Many of the workers stayed in the West.)* For what reasons did political boundaries of the United States change in the late 1800s? *(As more people were drawn West by mining, farming, and business opportunities, ten territories gained enough population to become new states.)*

Evaluate Impact What was the economic impact of the growing network of railroads? *(The impact was significant. Railroads tied the nation together, moving products and people from all regions of the country. The railroads spurred industrial development.)*

DIGITAL TEXT 2
The Cattle Industry Boom

DIGITAL TEXT 3
Farmers Settle on the Plains

3-D MODEL
Nineteenth-Century Sod House

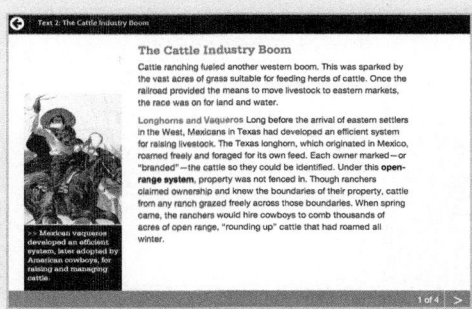

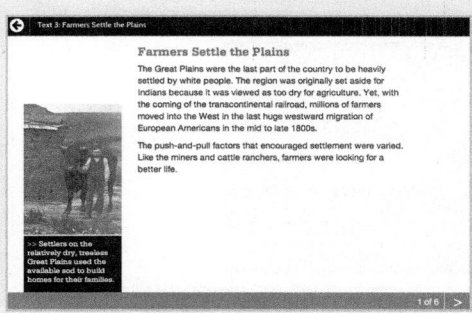

Objective 2: Explain the impact of physical and human geographic factors on the settlement of the Great Plains.

Quick Instruction
Without rich mineral deposits, the Great Plains were one of the last regions to be settled. Remind students that settlers who moved to the relatively dry, treeless Great Plains used whatever resources they could to survive. Most new arrivals could not afford to buy lumber to build a home. Instead they used the available sod to build homes for their families.

3-D Model: Nineteenth-Century Sod House
Explore the 3-D Model of the sod house with students. The resulting home was dark and dingy, but many settlers worked with the resources available to them to build new lives on the Plains.

Generate Explanations How was the cattle industry boom related to the growth of railroads in the West? *(As the railroad system expanded westward, ranchers used the railroads to transport their cattle to large markets back east. As demand for beef in the eastern United States grew, so did the cattle industry.)*

ACTIVE CLASSROOM
Engage students in using the Conversation With History Strategy to explore life in a sod house. Ask students to imagine they are having a conversation with a person who lives in a sod house. Have students write down several questions they would like to ask that person and what the response might be. Ask them to include one question on how geographical factors affected the person they are interviewing. Encourage students to write several conversational exchanges.

ELL Use the ELL activity described in the ELL chart.

Further Instruction
Discuss the Interactive Reading Notepad questions and the graphic organizer. Continue reviewing the events with the class and filling in the graphic organizer on the whiteboard as you go. Discuss the federal laws that encouraged further settlement and ranching and farming in the West.

Point out to students that people from various ethnic and minority groups moved to the Great Plains. Remind students that Mexican vaqueros developed an efficient system for raising and managing cattle that was later adopted by American cowboys. Discuss how the system of the vaqueros helped develop the cattle industry. Exodusters were African Americans who were looking to expand their economic opportunities.

Predict Consequences Ask students to predict the economic impact of the Homestead Act. *(More people will move to the Great Plains, establishing farms and communities. In addition, farmland will be put into use. What few trees there were will probably be used to construct buildings.)*

Apply Concepts Ask students to analyze how physical and human geographic factors in the West and the Great Plains helped provide for an economic boom. *(Physical: The large open ranges in the West and on the Plains provided the ideal resources needed to raise cattle. Human: Railroads were built to handle the shipping of cattle. This further created growth in cattle towns.)*

Draw Conclusions Based on your viewing of the 3-D sod house, how would you characterize the economic situation of the families that lived in such structures? *(Most farmers living in sod houses would have struggled economically. Those with more money would have been able to build homes using standard building materials brought from the eastern United States.)*

The West Is Transformed

DIGITAL TEXT 4

Minorities Encounter Difficulties

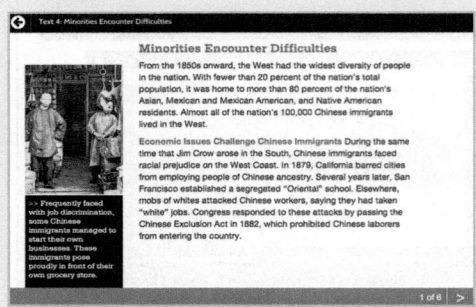

INTERACTIVE GALLERY

Mexican and Chinese American Contributions to the American West

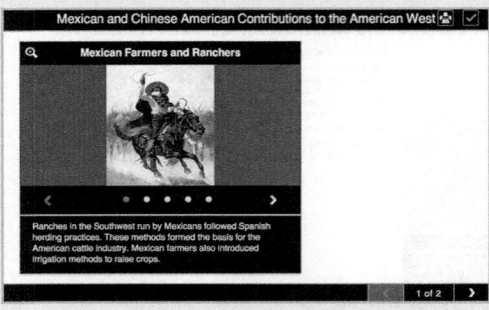

DIGITAL TEXT 5

Struggles and Change Across the West

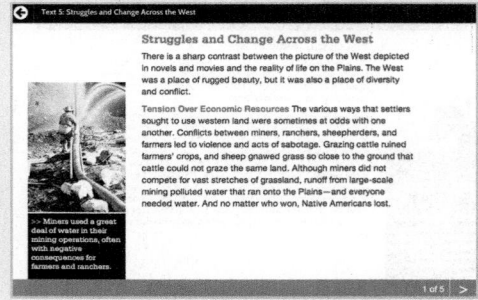

Objective 3: Analyze the treatment of Chinese immigrants and Mexican Americans in the West.

Quick Instruction

The migration to settle the West created great diversity of people. Although the West had less than 20 percent of America's population, it was home to more than 80 percent of the nation's Asian, Mexican and Mexican American, and Native American residents.

Interactive Gallery: Mexican and Chinese American Contributions to the American West Project the gallery and look at each image individually and then the collection of images as a whole.

Analyze Images What does the sixth image in the gallery (San Francisco Chinatown) reveal about Chinese Americans' economic contributions? *(It shows how busy and crowded the area is, reflecting a vibrant, business-friendly environment.)*

Cite Evidence Why might some Mexican American people and groups have found it especially frustrating that they were discriminated against in the Southwest and had to fight for economic and political opportunities? *(Mexicans and Mexican Americans had been living in*

ACTIVE CLASSROOM

Use the Make Headlines Strategy to encourage students to reflect on the images in the interactive gallery. Have students write a headline that captures the action in one image of their choosing. Ask them to focus on the most important aspect that should be remembered. Have students pass their headline to a partner for review. Ask for volunteers to share their reasoning about the headlines they wrote with the class.

the Southwest for a long time. They were guaranteed property rights but many still lost their land. The court system made it difficult for Mexican Americans, and they had no political power.)

D Differentiate: Extra Support After finishing the Active Classroom activity, allow students 5 minutes to think about the activity individually. Tell them to write down information from the activity as a whole with which they are familiar, such as Mexican and Chinese foods. Encourage students to think about the other contributions and personal knowledge they might have. Then continue with the group activity.

Further Instruction

Go through the Interactive Reading Notepad questions and discuss the answers with the class. Be sure students understand that various individuals and groups worked to expand economic and political opportunities for Mexican and Chinese Americans. Ask students to identify people who worked to help ethnic and racial groups in the West. *(Some Chinese Americans, such as Saum Song Bo, expressed their opinions in writing while others took legal action. The Mexican American groups Las Gorras Blancas and Alianza Hispano-Americana used various means to protect the rights and interests of Mexican Americans and other Americans.)*

Compare and Contrast How did the U.S. Supreme Court help and hurt Chinese Americans with its rulings? *(The Court helped Chinese Americans by ruling that individuals of Chinese descent, born in the United States, could not be stripped of their citizenship. However, it ruled that the Chinese Exclusion Act and several other discriminatory measures were constitutional, hurting Chinese trying to immigrate to the United States.)*

Objective 4: Discuss the ways various groups used land in the West and conflicts among them.

Quick Instruction

The various ways that settlers sought to use western land were sometimes at odds with one another. Conflicts between miners, ranchers, sheepherders, and farmers led to violence and acts of sabotage. Ask students to identify examples how different uses of land impacted others who relied on land and its natural resources. *(Miners used large quantities of land that were often polluted, and then pollution often spilled onto farm fields. Cattle grazing destroyed farm fields as well. Sheep ranchers needed land that cattle ranchers needed.)*

Identify Cause and Effect How did the economic impact of technological innovation such as the Transcontinental Railroad and legislative acts like the Homestead Act contribute to the closing of the American frontier? *(Both created great demand for land that was eventually populated. The Transcontinental Railroad allowed large numbers of setters to move west.)*

SYNTHESIZE

DIGITAL ACTIVITY

Technology and Free Enterprise

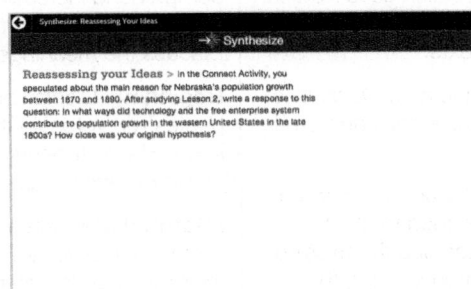

DEMONSTRATE

DIGITAL QUIZ

Lesson Quiz and Class Discussion Board

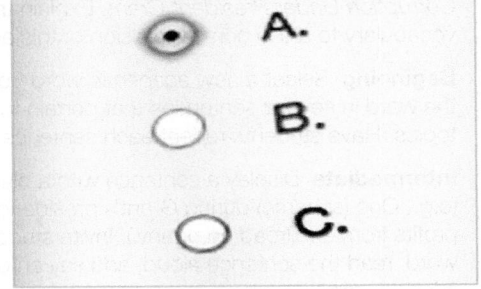

Further Instruction

Discuss the various ethnic and minority groups that either had lived in or migrated to the West and Great Plains regions and how they interacted with each other. Differences in food, religion, and cultural practices reinforced each group's fear and distrust of the others. But discrimination was openly displayed more often in larger cities or towns.

Express Problems Clearly How did economic and cultural diversity cause conflicts in the West? *(Different ethnic groups had contrasting views on who owned natural resources. For example, Mexican and American clashed over the El Paso salt beds. Ranchers and farmers, who were of different economic classes, often had conflicts.)*

Ask students to recall their responses to the Connect activity about technology and population growth: In what ways did technology and the free-enterprise system contribute to population growth in the western United States in the late 1800s?

Ask students to write a response to this question: How close was your original hypothesis? Ask students to share their answers with the class.

Apply Concepts Have partners take 5 minutes to list the technologies that helped spur growth in Nebraska. Ask students to rank their lists according to impact on population growth. Have pairs share their ranked lists with the class.

Assign the online Lesson Quiz for this lesson if you haven't already done so. Students will be offered automatic remediation or enrichment based on their score.

Pose this question to the class on the Discussion Board:

In *The West Is Transformed*, you read about the forces that drove the settlement and development of the American West. Mining and farming the rich land fueled great economic growth and the large numbers of Americans and immigrants moving to the West transformed the country.

Make Predictions How might the settling of the West impact the rest of the country? *(The country's population will increase dramatically with many new immigrants arriving to live in the West. The country will become wealthier because of mining, agriculture, and the emergence of many new businesses.)*

Topic Inquiry

Have students continue their investigations for the Topic Inquiry.

Corruption Plagues the Nation

Supporting English Language Learners

Use with Digital Text 1, **Political Power Proves Difficult to Keep.**

Learning
Help students internalize new academic language by using and reusing it in speaking activities. Draw students' attention to the section titled *Political Corruption Under President Grant*. Explain that students will focus on key vocabulary to aid in comprehension of this and other texts.

Beginning Select a new academic word from the text (e.g., *radical*). Use the word in several sentences that pertain to Grant's presidency and other topics. Have students repeat each sentence after you.

Intermediate Display a sentence with a blank for a new academic word (e.g., One (scheme) during Grant's presidency was designed to steal profits from a railroad company.). Invite students to determine the missing word, read the sentence aloud, and say an original sentence using the missing word.

Advanced Display a list of new academic words from the text (e.g., *radical, investigated, implicated, scheme, financier, advocated*). Have one volunteer ask a question using one of the words, while another answers using the word. Repeat for all the words on the list.

Advanced High Provide a list of new academic words to pairs of students. Ask them to look up the word and its word family in a dictionary, then to practice using at least two of the variants in a brief dialogue.

Use with Digital Text 2, **Growth of Political Machines and Corruption.**

Reading
Help students learn how to use support from peers and teachers to comprehend increasingly challenging vocabulary. Read aloud the section titled *Political Supporters Are Given Jobs* while students follow along. Discuss the meanings of the boldface terms.

Beginning Display or write out these sentences: _____ helped political parties win votes. In the _____, people got jobs because of whom they knew. Have students complete the sentences with *spoils system* and *political machines* and read them aloud. Assist as needed.

Intermediate Reread the sentences with the boldface terms *spoils system* and *political machines*. Ask students to define the two terms in their own words. Offer support as they search for adequate vocabulary to do so.

Advanced Have pairs of students reread the paragraphs with the boldface terms *spoils system* and *political machines*. Ask them to write down other words that they do not understand and then work together to determine the meaning of these words. Then, ask each pair write a definition and one important idea for each of the boldface terms.

Advanced High Ask students to reread the section, noting every instance of the terms *spoils system* and *political machines*. With a partner, have them discuss how each instance of a term adds to their understanding of it.

▣ Differentiate Instruction

Use the Differentiated Instruction notes throughout the lesson plan to support the varied skill sets, levels of readiness, and interests in the mixed-ability classroom.

Challenge These notes include suggestions for expanding the activity for advanced students.

On-Level These notes include suggestions for modifying the activity to address different interests or learning styles.

Extra Support These notes include ideas for providing more scaffolding or reading spuport.

Special Needs These notes provide ideas for adapting instruction to support the needs of various special needs students.

▮ NOTES

PEARSON
realize™
www.PearsonRealize.com

Go online to access additional resources including:
Primary Sources • Biographies • Supreme Court cases •
21st Century Skill Tutorials • Maps • Graphic Organizers.

Objectives

Objective 1: Analyze the issues of weak leadership and corruption in national politics in the 1870s through 1890s.

Objective 2: Discuss civil service reform in the late 1800s.

Objective 3: Assess the importance of economic issues in the late 1800s.

LESSON 3 ORGANIZER		OBJECTIVES	PACING	RESOURCES Online	Print
Connect					
DIGITAL START UP ACTIVITY **The Spoils System**			5 min.	●	
Investigate					
DIGITAL TEXT 1 **Political Power Proves Difficult to Keep**		Objective 1	10 min.	●	●
INTERACTIVE CHART **Gridlock in Congress in the Late 1800s**			10 min.	●	
DIGITAL TEXT 2 **Growth of Political Machines and Corruption**		Objective 2	10 min.	●	●
INTERACTIVE GALLERY **Thomas Nast**			10 min.	●	
DIGITAL TEXT 3 **Economic Policy Challenges Continue**		Objective 3	10 min.	●	●
Synthesize					
DIGITAL ACTIVITY **Addressing Corruption**			5 min.	●	
Demonstrate					
DIGITAL QUIZ **Lesson Quiz and Class Discussion Board**			10 min.	●	

PACING: APPROX. 1 PERIOD, .5 BLOCKS

Corruption Plagues the Nation

■ CONNECT

DIGITAL START UP ACTIVITY
The Spoils System

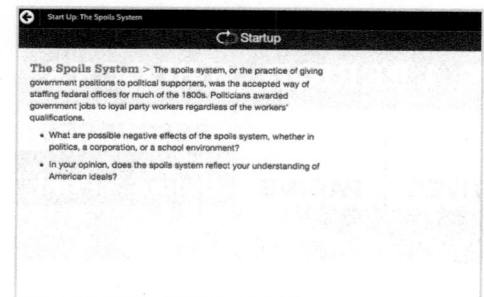

Project the Start Up Activity Ask students to answer the questions as they enter and get settled. Then have them share their ideas with another student, either in class or through a chat or blog space.

Discuss What are possible negative effects of the spoils system, whether in politics, a corporation, or a school environment? *(It leads to corruption by either a single person or a group of people who are awarded jobs or privileges based on loyalty or other factors rather than qualifications or experience.)*

Tell students that in this lesson they will learn about causes and effects of the rise of political machines that created a spoils system and political corruption.

Aa Vocabulary Development: Use the Interactive Reading Notepad to preview the Key Terms and Academic Vocabulary in the lesson with students.

↻ FLIP IT!
Assign the Flipped Video for this lesson.

■ STUDENT EDITION PRINT
PAGES: 375–379

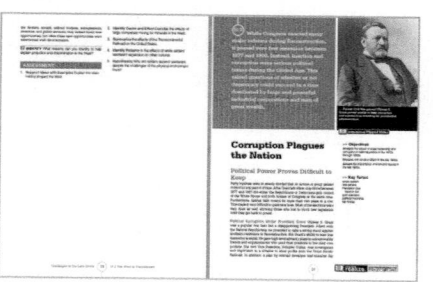

■ INVESTIGATE

DIGITAL TEXT 1
Political Power Proves Difficult to Keep

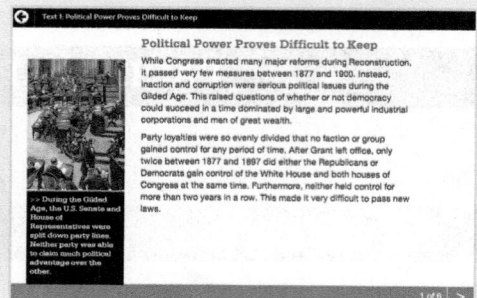

INTERACTIVE CHART
Gridlock in Congress in the Late 1800s

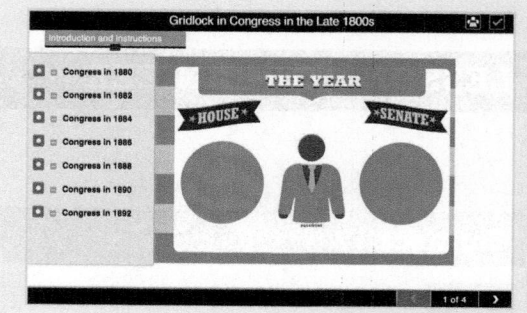

Objective 1: Analyze the issues of weak leadership and corruption in national politics in the 1870s through 1890s.

Quick Instruction
As Americans were accomplishing momentous and historic achievements while settling parts of the American West, American politicians in the East were not faring as well. Inaction and political corruption characterized the political scene in the late 1800s. This raised questions of whether or not democracy could succeed in a time dominated by large and powerful industrial corporations and men of great wealth.

Interactive Chart: Gridlock in Congress in the Late 1800s Project the interactive chart. Look at the chart for each year. Point out that the charts show that during the Gilded Age, no political party gained power for any length of time.

💬 ACTIVE CLASSROOM
Break students groups and use the Circle Write Strategy to explore the following question: Even though a balanced Congress often results in gridlock, why would American voters continue to vote in ways that undermine clear party majorities?

Identify Cause and Effect How does the balance of power between political parties affect Congress's productivity? *(When the make-up of Congress is balanced, parties have difficulty passing legislation because they do not have the majority needed to pass laws. This leads to gridlock and inaction.)*

ELL Use the ELL activity described in the ELL chart.

Further Instruction
Go through the Interactive Reading Notepad questions and discuss the answers with the class. Scandals in the Grant administration and throughout the country left Americans sensing an aura of greed surrounding American politics. Consequently, confidence in public officials plummeted. Discuss the role that newspapers, and in particular, political cartoonists might have played in contributing to the political feelings of the era.

Make Generalizations How would you characterize the American political landscape during the Gilded Age? *(I would consider the political landscape as basically ineffective and broken. Politics during the Gilded Age was filled with corrupt politicians who worked against the benefit of all Americans.)*

DIGITAL TEXT 2
Growth of Political Machines and Corruption

INTERACTIVE GALLERY
Thomas Nast

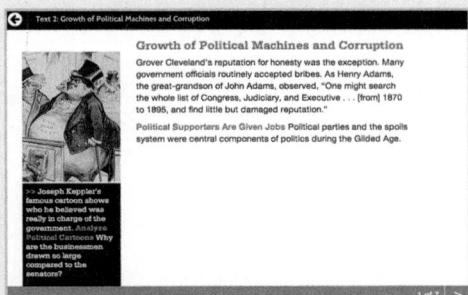

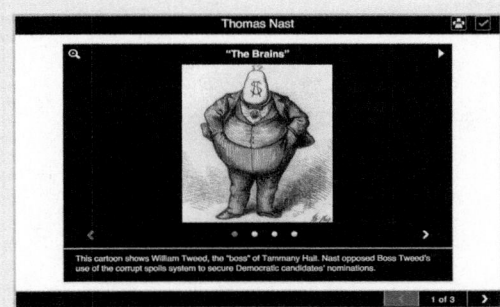

Objective 2: Discuss civil service reform in the late 1800s.

Quick Instruction

Corruption not only permeated politics at the federal level during the Gilded Age, it also infected local politics as well. Political parties developed sophisticated political machines that reached virtually into every ward, every precinct, and many cities in the nation. Political cartoonists, such as Thomas Nast, expressed their concern about the damaging effects of the spoils system and corruption, prompting public support for civil service reform.

Interactive Gallery: Thomas Nast Project the slideshow. Look at each cartoon individually and then the collection of cartoons as a whole. Based on the textual descriptions in the first cartoon, what implication is Nast making by using a bag with a dollar sign on it to symbolize Tweed's head? *(Nast is implying that Tweed is motivated by greed and has used money to get what he wants.)*

Identify Central Issues How were political machines able to maintain political power in cities? *(The strength of political machines was their ability to improve the standard of living in neighborhoods of specific immigrant groups, such as improving public sanitation. These immigrant groups would in turn vote en masse for the candidates the political machines supported.)*

🎦 ACTIVE CLASSROOM

Use the Cartoon It Strategy and have students choose one compelling image or event described in this lesson and turn it into a political cartoon. Point out that the cartoon should illustrate a key concept or main idea in a satirizing or thought-provoking way.

D Differentiate: Extra Support After explaining the Cartoon It activity, allow students 5 minutes to think about the activity individually. Point out that students might think about the following for possible cartoon ideas: the spoils system; the Pendleton Civil Service Act; President Rutherford B. Hayes; Tammany Hall; U.S. Postal Service. Then continue with the group activity.

ELL Use the ELL activity described in the ELL chart.

Further Instruction

Go through the Interactive Reading Notepad questions and discuss the answers with the class. Review the negative and positive aspects of the spoils system. Be sure that students understand that need for civil service reform and that the Pendleton Civil Service Act in 1883 reduced the power of the spoils system.

Hypothesize In your opinion, why might political cartoons have been effective in exposing corruption and scandals? *(Cartoons are usually funny, which draws interest and helps people remember them. Cartoons can caricaturize politicians and situations, emphasizing or drawing attention to a person's bad behavior or deeds. This makes them very powerful.)*

Analyze Issues Why were the growth of political machines and lack of civil service reform major political issues during the Gilded Age? *(Both the use of political machines and the spoils system influenced voters in an unfair and often unethical way, leading to a small group of people having power that they abused.)*

Predict Consequences Ask students to predict what the impact of civil service reform will be. *(There will be less corruption because politicians will not be able to use their power to get votes. On the other hand, because politicians have less ability to take care of their electorates, there will be less interest in voting and in supporting the political machines.)*

Corruption Plagues the Nation

DIGITAL TEXT 3
Economic Policy Challenges Continue

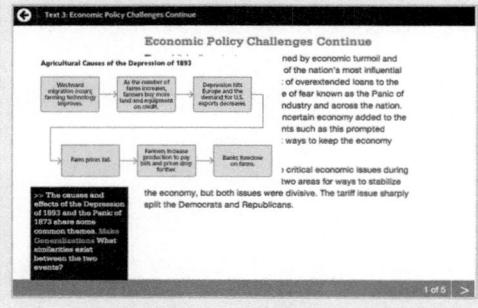

Objective 3: Assess the importance of economic issues in the late 1800s.

Quick Instruction

Point out to students that the tariff and monetary policy were critical economic issues during the Gilded Age. Review the gold and silver standards with students, and then address the issue of fiat money, which is money not pegged to any precious substance. Ask students to identify arguments from those who supported using the gold and silver standards. *(Those who supported the gold standard claimed that it increased the value of U.S. money. Those who wanted to use the silver standard wanted to increase inflation to prop up prices and help them increase their incomes.)*

Express Problems Clearly What are some possible implications of basing the value of money on the gold and silver standards at the same time? *(The value of gold and silver are different and fluctuating, making it impossible to determine the true value of U.S. currency.)*

Draw Conclusions What advantages does using fiat money offer? *(Using fiat money increases the amount of the money supply, making it easier for people to acquire it.)*

Further Instruction

Go through the Interactive Reading Notepad questions and discuss the answers with the class. Point out that American politicians had debated the tariff issue for a long time. Ask students to compare and contrast the major differences between Republicans and Democrats on the issue of tariffs during the Gilded Age. *(Republicans argued that a high tariff would help American industries and lead to more jobs. Democrats thought that high tariffs increased prices for Americans and made it harder for American farmers to sell their goods to foreign countries.)*

Generate Explanations In your opinion, why was the tariff issue so controversial and why couldn't the issue be resolved? *(Republicans and Democrats had completely different views on tariffs and seemed to represent different interests, making compromise impossible. Because neither party could win a solid majority in Congress, a resolution could not be found.)*

SYNTHESIZE

DIGITAL ACTIVITY
Addressing Corruption

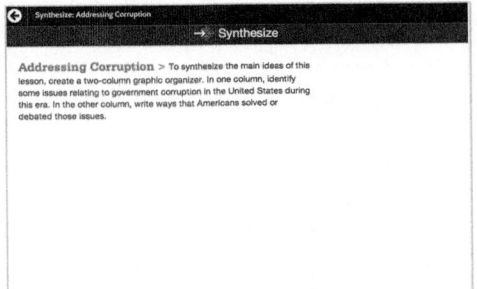

Have partners think about the following questions: What were the most significant corruption issues in the Gilded Age? How did Americans and their leaders solve these issues? Are there corruption issues from the Gilded Age that, in your opinion, are not possible to solve? Explain.

Have pairs share their answers with the class.

DEMONSTRATE

DIGITAL QUIZ
Lesson Quiz and Class Discussion Board

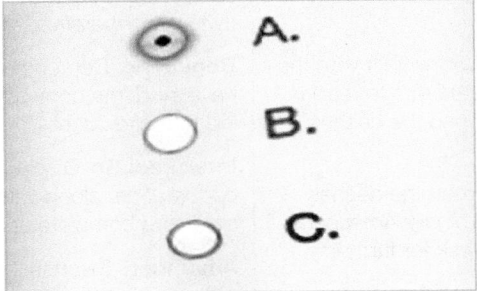

Assign the online Lesson Quiz for this lesson if you haven't already done so. Students will be offered automatic remediation or enrichment based on their score.

Pose these questions to the class on the Discussion Board:

In *Corruption Plagues the Nation*, you read examples of how politicians sometimes misuse the power given to them by voters. Political parties and the spoils system were central components of politics during the Gilded Age.

Apply Concepts What, if anything, do you think voters and politicians learned from the political corruption issues that plagued the Gilded Age? *(Voters probably learned that not all politicians could be trusted and were not always looking out for the best interests of voters. Politicians learned that voters can make a difference at the ballot box by voting out corrupt elected officials.)*

Make Predictions Do you think America's leaders will solve the tariff issue once and for all as the country nears the end of the 1800s? *(No. The issue is too complex and it is constantly changing due to many unpredictable and uncontrollable factors.)*

Topic Inquiry
Have students continue their investigations for the Topic Inquiry.

Farm Issues and Populism

Supporting English Language Learners

Use with Digital Text 1, **Farmers Face Economic Difficulty.**

Reading
Help students use support from peers and their teacher to develop a grasp of language structures that will help them comprehend increasingly challenging language. Start by reading aloud the introduction or asking a volunteer to do so. Point out the use of dashes in the last sentence of the first paragraph.

Beginning Write out the sentence that uses dashes. Also write it with the dashes (and the phrase between them) removed. Ask students to read both sentences and determine to what the phrase between the dashes refers (*ordinary Americans*).

Intermediate Ask students to replace the phrase between the dashes with an original phrase that also expands on the term *ordinary Americans*. Have pairs of students read each other's sentence and ask for further explanation of the new phrase if needed.

Advanced Ask pairs of students to reword the sentence with dashes so that the meaning remains intact but the dashes are not used. Ask pairs to read their new sentence and explain the changes they made to structure and language.

Advanced High Have students read the last sentence of the first paragraph and the last sentence of the paragraph before the section *Big Business Practices Affect Farmers*. Ask pairs of students to compare and contrast the use of the dash in these sentences.

Use with Digital Text 2, **Farmers Seek Change Through Alliances.**

Learning
Have students use writing activities to build concept and language attainment while internalizing new academic language by using and reusing it in meaningful ways. Direct students' attention to the section titled *Alliances Encourage Reform*. Point out the occurrences of *cooperatives* (twice), *cooperative*, and *cooperation*.

Beginning Demonstrate the meaning of cooperation through a skit. Then have students copy and complete this sentence: The _____ of everyone led to their success.

Intermediate Display the words *cooperatives*, *cooperative*, and *cooperation*, along with three fill-in-the-blank sentences. Have students copy and complete each sentence with one of the words.

Advanced Discuss the differences in meaning and part of speech among *cooperatives*, *cooperative*, and *cooperation*. Have pairs of students write an original sentence for each word.

Advanced High Ask students to use a dictionary to look up the various meanings of *cooperatives*, *cooperative*, and *cooperation*. Have them write a cohesive paragraph that includes all three of these words at least once.

▣ Differentiate Instruction

Use the Differentiated Instruction notes throughout the lesson plan to support the varied skill sets, levels of readiness, and interests in the mixed-ability classroom.

Challenge These notes include suggestions for expanding the activity for advanced students.

On-Level These notes include suggestions for modifying the activity to address different interests or learning styles.

Extra Support These notes include ideas for providing more scaffolding or reading spuport.

Special Needs These notes provide ideas for adapting instruction to support the needs of various special needs students.

■ NOTES

PEARSON
realize™
www.PearsonRealize.com

Go online to access additional resources including:
Primary Sources • Biographies • Supreme Court cases •
21st Century Skill Tutorials • Maps • Graphic Organizers.

Objectives

Objective 1: Analyze the economic issues farmers faced in the late 1800s.

Objective 2: Describe the groups farmers formed to address their problems and what they accomplished.

Objective 3: Evaluate the impact of the Populist Party, and explain why the party did not last.

LESSON 4 ORGANIZER		PACING: APPROX. 1 PERIOD, .5 BLOCKS			
		OBJECTIVES	**PACING**	**RESOURCES**	
				Online	**Print**
Connect					
	DIGITAL START UP ACTIVITY **Farmers and Populism**		5 min.	●	
Investigate					
	DIGITAL TEXT 1 **Farmers Face Economic Difficulty**	Objective 1	10 min.	●	●
	DIGITAL TEXT 2 **Farmers Seek Change Through Alliances**	Objective 2	10 min.	●	●
	DIGITAL TEXT 3 **The Beginnings of Populism**		10 min.	●	●
	DIGITAL TEXT 4 **Populism's Declining Influence**	Objective 3	10 min.	●	●
	INTERACTIVE GALLERY **Legacy of Populism**		10 min.	●	
	INTERACTIVE CHART **The Populist Party**		10 min.	●	
Synthesize					
	DIGITAL ACTIVITY **American Rights and Populism**		5 min.	●	
Demonstrate					
	DIGITAL QUIZ **Lesson Quiz and Class Discussion Board**		10 min.	●	

Farm Issues and Populism

■ CONNECT

DIGITAL START UP ACTIVITY
Farmers and Populism

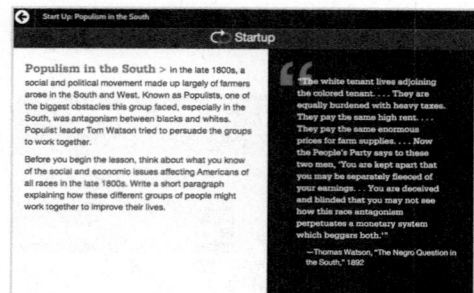

Start Up: Populism in the South

Startup

Populism in the South > In the late 1800s, a social and political movement made up largely of farmers arose in the South and West. Known as Populists, one of the biggest obstacles this group faced, especially in the South, was antagonism between blacks and whites. Populist leader Tom Watson tried to persuade the groups to work together.

Before you begin the lesson, think about what you know of the social and economic issues affecting Americans of all races in the late 1800s. Write a short paragraph explaining how these different groups of people might work together to improve their lives.

"The white tenant lives adjoining the colored tenant.... They are equally burdened with heavy taxes. They pay the same high rent.... They pay the same enormous prices for farm supplies.... Now the People's Party says to these two men, 'You are kept apart that you may be separately fleeced of your earnings.... You are deceived and blinded that you may not see how this race antagonism perpetuates a monetary system which beggars both.'"

—Thomas Watson, "The Negro Question in the South," 1892

Project the Start Up Activity Ask students to answer the questions as they enter and get settled. Then have them share their ideas with another student, either in class or through a chat or blog space.

Discuss Before you begin the lesson, ask students to think about social and economic issues affecting Americans of all races in the late 1800s, and how people might work together to improve their lives. After students have finished writing their paragraphs, have them share their work.

Tell students that in this lesson they will learn about the Populist Party, which was formed by different groups of Americans in the 1890s.

Aa Vocabulary Development: Use the Interactive Reading Notepad to preview the Key Terms and Academic Vocabulary in the lesson with students.

⚡ FLIP IT!

Assign the Flipped Video for this lesson.

■ STUDENT EDITION PRINT
PAGES: 380–386

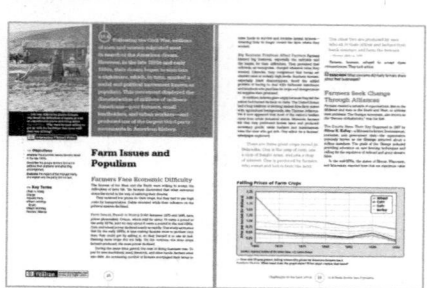

■ INVESTIGATE

DIGITAL TEXT 1
Farmers Face Economic Difficulty

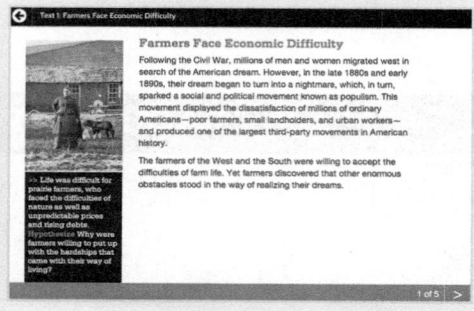

Text 1: Farmers Face Economic Difficulty

Farmers Face Economic Difficulty

Following the Civil War, millions of men and women migrated west in search of the American dream. However, in the late 1880s and early 1890s, their dream began to turn into a nightmare, which, in turn, sparked a social and political movement known as populism. This movement displayed the dissatisfaction of millions of ordinary Americans—poor farmers, small landholders, and urban workers— and produced one of the largest third-party movements in American history.

The farmers of the West and the South were willing to accept the difficulties of farm life. Yet farmers discovered that other enormous obstacles stood in the way of realizing their dreams.

>> Life was difficult for prairie farmers, who faced the difficulties of nature as well as unpredictable prices and rising debts. Hypothesize Why were farmers willing to put up with the hardships that came with their way of living?

1 of 5 >

Objective 1: Analyze the economic issues farmers faced in the late 1800s.

Quick Instruction
Following the Civil War, millions of men and women migrated west in search of the American dream. Economic factors, however, posed enormous obstacles that hindered the way toward realizing their dreams.

Project the food production chart and ask students to study it for a few minutes. What does the chart suggest about the amount of food produced between 1866 and 1896? *(Possible answer: The supply of crops may have been increasing even though demand did not, resulting in lower prices.)*

Analyze Data Based on the information about economic farm issuesin the chart, what would you expect farmers' incomes to do? Why? *(I would expect farmers' incomes to decrease because the price of the crops they produced was falling.)* What did farmers' incomes actually do, even though they were producing more crops? *(Farmers' incomes dropped because the price of crops dropped across the board.)*

Make sure that students understand that even as crop prices dropped, the cost of supplies and to borrow money increased. This created a situation where farmers found it increasingly difficult to continue farming.

ELL Use the ELL activity described in the ELL chart.

Further Instruction
Project and discuss the Interactive Reading Notepad questions, including the graphic organizer, asking students to explain the causes and effects of farmers' economic problems and the actions they took. Review the causes, effects, and actions with the class and fill in the graphic organizer as you go.

Be sure that students understand that falling crop prices and rising supply costs were just two immediate reasons many farmers were struggling and felt mistreated. Discuss the relationship of farmers with big business and farmers' perception that they possessed less political power than the railroads and banks.

Predict Consequences Faced with such economic burdens, what do you think farmers will do? *(Possible answer: I would expect them to try to force changes by pressuring lawmakers.)*

Draw Conclusions In your opinion, how might the inability of Congress to clarify monetary policy affect farmers? *(Uncertain monetary values would have hurt farmers since they depended on loans to buy the supplies needed to farm. A limited supply of money that was tied to the gold standard would have made it more difficult and much more expensive for farmers to get loans.)*

DIGITAL TEXT 2

Farmers Seek Change Through Alliances

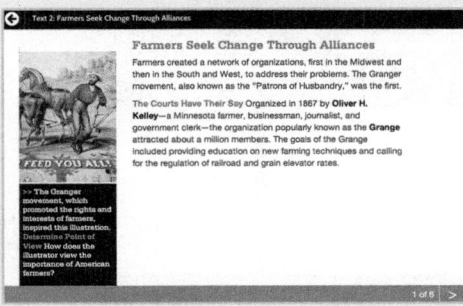

DIGITAL TEXT 3

The Beginnings of Populism

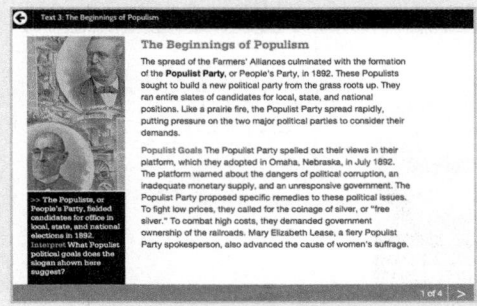

Objective 2: Describe the groups farmers formed to address their problems and what they accomplished.

Quick Instruction

Display the different illustrations of farmers. Ask students to discuss the perception of farmers. How might a farmer from the era respond to viewing this illustration? *(I think the farmer would agree that the work is as difficult as it looks.)*

Display the illustration from the text that shows the African American farmer. Farmers created a network of organizations to address farm issues. Groups like the Grange, the Farmers' Alliance, the Southern Farmers' Alliance, and the Colored Farmers' Alliance worked to protect and promote farmers' rights and economic opportunities.

Summarize Ask students to find examples of economic issues that these groups worked to solve. *(The Grange provided agricultural education and pushed for the regulation of railroad and grain elevator rates. The Southern Farmers' Alliance pushed the federal government to create banks to provide farmers with low-interest loans. The Colored Farmers' Alliance worked on similar issues but also dealt with the racial tensions African American farmers faced.)*

ELL Use the ELL activity described in the ELL chart.

Further Instruction

Go through the Interactive Reading Notepad questions and discuss the answers with the class. Review the most significant economic issues facing farmers.

Make Predictions Ask students to predict the success of the farmers' organizations in addressing their economic issues and to explain why they think as they do. *(I think the farmers' groups will have very little success in fighting the big businesses. The farmers' groups are too unorganized and too widely spread around the country to have a significant impact.)*

Objective 3: Evaluate the impact of the Populist Party, and explain why the party did not last.

Quick Instruction

The spread of the Farmers' Alliances culminated with the formation of an alternative to the Democratic and Republican parties. This third party was the Populist Party, or People's Party, in 1892. The impact of the Populist Party was significant. The ideas of populism—defending the interests of and giving voice to ordinary citizens—have remained influential in American politics even if the Populist party itself has not. Make sure that students understand the Populist Party's platform warned about the dangers of political corruption, an inadequate monetary supply, and an unresponsive government. Point out that all these issues have remained controversial since the 1890s.

Farm Issues and Populism

DIGITAL TEXT 4
Populism's Declining Influence

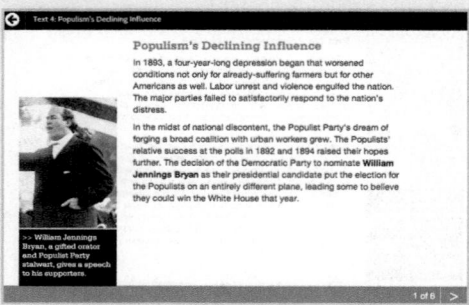

INTERACTIVE GALLERY
Legacy of Populism

INTERACTIVE CHART
The Populist Party

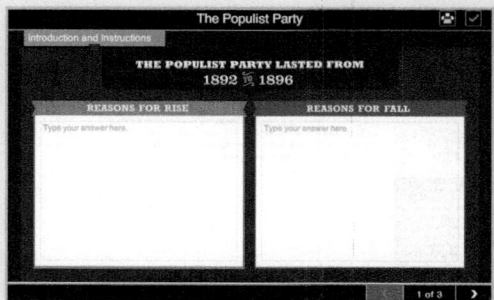

Interactive Gallery: Legacy of Populism Project the interactive gallery. Look at each image individually and then the collection of images and text as a whole.

Interactive Chart: The Populist Party Project the interactive chart. Prompt students to discuss the reasons for the rise and fall of the Populist Party as you complete the chart.

Make Inferences In your opinion, why did many Americans cast ballots for leaders who promoted political issues associated with populist ideas? *(The leaders reflected some people's strongly-held beliefs. For many followers, the leaders represented or sought to help the "common" American, those who were being ignored by the main political parties and the government.)*

ACTIVE CLASSROOM

Using the Graffiti Concept, ask students to reflect on the Populist Party and its legacy. Engage students in creating a visual image and accompanying phrase that represents the Populist Party and what it stood for. Have students post their "graffiti" in the class and ask students to look at all the various works and discuss similarities and differences as a group.

ACTIVE CLASSROOM

Conduct a Circle Write activity. Break students into groups and project the interactive chart. Ask half the groups to write on the reasons for the rise of the Populist Party and the other half to write on the Populist Party's fall. Have students write as much as they can for one minute then switch with the person on their right. The next person tries to improve or elaborate the response where the other person left off. Continue to switch until the paper comes back to the first person. The group then decides which is the best response and shares that with the larger group.

D Differentiate: Challenge Ask students to do additional research on William Jennings Bryan and present their findings.

Further Instruction

Go through the Interactive Reading Notepad questions and discuss the answers with the class. Point out to students that the Populist Party lost influence in part because of William Jennings Bryan's emphasis on monetary reform. This issue, which was popular with rural Americans, did not appeal to urban workers. Moreover, the decision for the Democratic Party to endorse Bryan weakened the Populists at the local and state levels, and the party declined after the 1896 election.

Make Generalizations In what way(s) might the Tea Party of the twenty-first century reflect elements of the Populist Party? *(The Tea Party focused on economic issues that they felt were being ignored by the federal government, which is somewhat similar to Ross Perot and earlier populist ideas.)*

Generate Explanations What role might shifting demographics in the United States at the turn of the twentieth century have played in the decline of the Populist Party? *(The country was becoming more urban at the close of the nineteenth century. The Populist Party supported policies that were very popular in rural areas but not so much in urban areas. Consequently the party was less influential.)*

■ SYNTHESIZE

DIGITAL ACTIVITY
American Rights and Populism

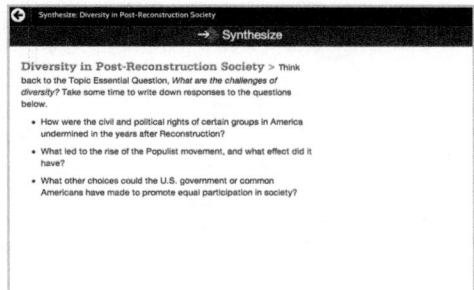

Ask students to recall the Topic Essential Question: What are the challenges of diversity? Have them use the Think Pair Share Strategy to answer the questions in the American Rights and Populism Activity. Ask them to take 5 minutes to write down some brief answers to the questions below, then share their answers with a talking partner.

Have partners think about the following question: What led to the rise of the Populist movement, and what impact did it have? *(The Populist movement grew out of the farming alliances that were created in rural areas. The Populist Party won several Congressional seats and the governorships in several states. Many ideas of the populist movement eventually became laws in the twentieth century.)*

Discuss Ask students to describe populist ideas or policies that they see in American politics or legislation today. *(Focus on sound economic policy; a graduated income tax; an appeal to average Americans' concerns; a more efficient and responsive federal government)*

■ DEMONSTRATE

DIGITAL QUIZ
Lesson Quiz and Class Discussion Board

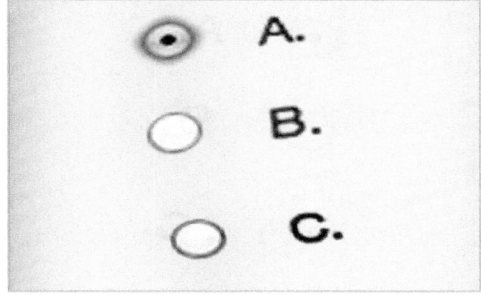

Assign the online Lesson Quiz for this lesson if you haven't already done so. Students will be offered automatic remediation or enrichment based on their score.

Pose these questions to the class on the Discussion Board:

In *Farm Issues and Populism*, you read about how various farm alliances worked together to eventually form the Populist Party. Although short-lived, the Populist fervor swept the country in the 1890s, winning millions of votes in elections and influencing political discussions and policy decisions.

Make Generalizations Why was the Populist Party short-lived? *(Key issues in the Populist Party platform were not supported by citizens in the large urban areas of the Northeast and Midwest. These areas were gaining more influence while Populist strongholds were losing influence.)*

Apply Concepts What, if anything, could the Populist Party have done to remain a viable and influential political party? *(The party could have reached out to urban voters on other issues to form alliances. The party needed to expand its base by working with different groups of voters. It also could have adjusted its position on monetary policy to bring in more people.)*

Topic Inquiry
Have students continue their investigations for the Topic Inquiry.

PEARSON realize™   www.PearsonRealize.com
Access your Digital Lesson

Challenges in the Late 1800s

■ SYNTHESIZE

DIGITAL ACTIVITY
Reflect on the Essential Question and Topic

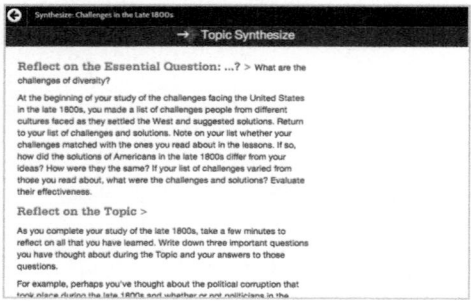

First ask students to reconsider the Essential Question for the topic: What are the challenges of diversity? Remind students of the challenges they listed at the start of the topic and the solutions to those challenges.

Ask students if their challenges matched those that they read about in the lessons. How did the solutions of Americans in the late 1800s differ from your ideas? How were they the same? Evaluate the effectiveness of the solutions as a class. Post students' response on the Class Discussion Board.

Next ask students to reflect on the topic as a whole and jot down one to three questions they've thought about during the topic. Share these examples if students need help getting started:

- What role should the government play in protecting and expanding the economic and civil rights of citizens?
- How can technology lead to settlement and economic growth in new regions?
- What factors can lead to political corruption?
- How can groups of people best address and seek resolution to economic and social issues that affect them?

You may ask students to share their questions and answers on the Class Discussion Board.

Topic Inquiry
Have students complete Step 3 of the Topic Inquiry.

■ DEMONSTRATE

DIGITAL TOPIC REVIEW AND ASSESSMENT
An Era of Change

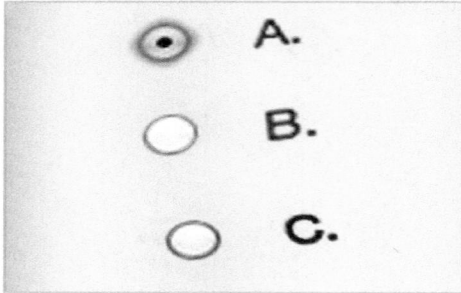

Students can prepare for the Topic Test by answering the questions in the Topic Review and Assessment online or the Assessment questions in the Print Student text. They can also prepare by reviewing their answers to the Interactive Reading Notepad questions or reviewing their notes in the Reading and Notetaking Study Guide.

DIGITAL TOPIC TEST
An Era of Change

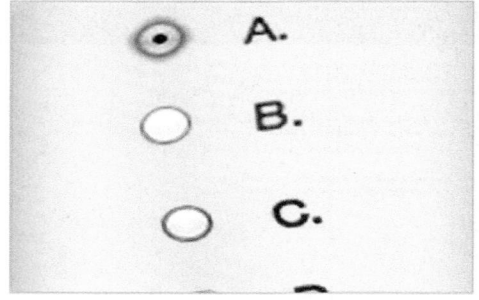

TOPIC TEST
Assign the Topic Test to assess students' understanding of topic content.

BENCHMARK TESTS
Assign these benchmark tests as you complete the relevant topics to monitor student progress toward mastering the course content and as preparation for the End-of-Course Test.

Benchmark Test 1: Topics 1–3

Benchmark Test 2: Topics 4–6

Benchmark Test 3: Topics 7–9

Benchmark Test 4: Topics 10–12

Benchmark Test 5: Topics 13–15

Benchmark Test 6: Topics 16–18

Benchmark Test 7: Topics 19–20

America Comes of Age

TOPIC 11 ORGANIZER	PACING: APPROX. 10 PERIODS, 5 BLOCKS	
		PACING
Connect		1 period
MY STORY VIDEO **Jane Addams, Neighboring With the Poor**		10 min.
DIGITAL ESSENTIAL QUESTION ACTIVITY **What can individuals do to affect society?**		10 min.
DIGITAL TIMELINE ACTIVITY **Timeline 1890–1920**		10 min.
TOPIC INQUIRY: DOCUMENT-BASED QUESTION **Historians' Viewpoints on the Spanish-American War**		20 min.
Investigate		3–7 periods
TOPIC INQUIRY: DOCUMENT-BASED QUESTION **Historians' Viewpoints on the Spanish-American War**		Ongoing
LESSON 1 Progressives Drive Reform		30–40 min.
LESSON 2 Women Gain Rights		30–40 min.
LESSON 3 Striving for Equality		30–40 min.
LESSON 4 Reformers in the White House		30–40 min.
LESSON 5 American Influence Grows		30–40 min.
LESSON 6 The Spanish-American War		30–40 min.
LESSON 7 The United States Emerges as a World Power		30–40 min.
Synthesize		1 period
DIGITAL ACTIVITY **Reflect on the Essential Question and Topic**		10 min.
TOPIC INQUIRY: DOCUMENT-BASED QUESTION **Historians' Viewpoints on the Spanish-American War**		20 min.
Demonstrate		1–2 periods
DIGITAL TOPIC REVIEW AND ASSESSMENT **America Comes of Age**		10 min.
TOPIC INQUIRY: DOCUMENT-BASED QUESTION **Historians' Viewpoints on the Spanish-American War**		20 min.

TOPIC INQUIRY: DOCUMENT-BASED QUESTION

Historians' Viewpoints on the Spanish-American War

In this Topic Inquiry, students work independently to explore the writings of American historians from several eras who have researched and studied the Spanish-American War. Students will reflect on this information and then write an essay in which they answer the question: **How have historians' viewpoints about the factors that led to the Spanish-American War changed over time?**

STEP 1: CONNECT
Develop Questions and Plan the Investigation

Launch the DBQ Writing Activity
Write the term "historiography" on the board and explain that it is the study of why and how historians write the way they do. In short, historiography is the history of history. Tell students that for their projects, they will explore and come to understand how and why historians interpret the past the way they do. Present the video "The Spanish-American War" and provide opportunities to discuss and answer questions students may have about the information in the video.

Suggestion: Provide opportunities for multiple viewings to help students gather as much background information as necessary.

Generate Questions
Students may benefit from working with a partner to discuss and explore the causes of the Spanish-American War. Encourage partners to answer the discussion questions and take notes that capture information from the video and the lessons. Suggest that students note any conflicting information and to briefly describe why the information might be different.

Suggestion: Remind students that their essays will focus on the historiography of the Spanish-American War, or how historians' viewpoints of the war have changed over time. Prompt students to look for similarities and differences in the writings they will be reading.

Resources
- Video
- Student Instructions

STEP 2: INVESTIGATE
Apply Disciplinary Concepts and Tools

Analyze the Documents
Students will work individually to read and analyze the six sources that relate to the American intervention in Cuba. Remind students that documents reflect the changing viewpoints historians have held since the Spanish-American War. Refer students to helpful resources within the core content of the Topic or back to the introduction video to help answer any lingering questions or to confirm changing views and information.

Suggestion: Consider briefly previewing the documents or viewing them as a class to clarify any vocabulary or content issues.

Check Your Understanding
When students have completed reading the documents and answering the multiple choice and short answer questions, meet as a class to review students' responses. Point out to students that they might disagree with the viewpoints of the historians based on their own knowledge of the subject.

Resources
- Documents A through F

⏻ PROFESSIONAL DEVELOPMENT

Document-Based Question
Be sure to view the Document-Based Question Professional Development resources in the online course.

STEP 3: SYNTHESIZE	STEP 4: DEMONSTRATE
Evaluate Sources and Use Evidence to Formulate Conclusions	Communicate Conclusions and Take Informed Action

Synthesize the Information in the Documents

Now have students think about and record notes that describe how these historians' viewpoints are similar and different and why these differences may exist. For students who are having trouble, encourage them to think about the factors that might influence a person's perspective, such as the era in which he or she lived, gender, ethnicity, life, and work experience.

Suggest students think about the following questions:

- How might information about the author, including background, language, point of view, frames of reference, and historical context, affect the validity of the source?
- What information in the writings and cartoon can you identify as biased?
- How might you evaluate the validity of a source based on corroboration with other sources you have read?

Write Your Essay

Students should now write their essays. Review the essay criteria and clarify any questions students may have. Students may benefit from peer reviews of one another's writing. Remind students to offer detailed, constructive criticism of each other's work. Be sure that students use social studies terminology correctly and use standard grammar, sentence structure, and punctuation.

Suggestion: Consider displaying the Rubric for Document-Based Assessment Essay so students can better understand what is expected.

Reflect on the Project

After students have written and submitted their essays, help them go over what they thought went well and what did not, so they can be even more effective in the future.

Suggestion: As an extension activity, have students research the causes of another war in which the United States was involved. Tell students to focus on sources from two different eras and to identify the differences in viewpoints.

Resources

- Rubric for Document-Based Assessment Essay

America Comes of Age

The industrialization that swept America in the 1800s led to greater wealth, urbanization, and a wave of immigration. These changes were often beneficial. But they also created challenging social problems. Reformers worked to change government to solve the nation's problems. At the same time, American political and business leaders searched for new world markets and increased trade opportunities. The United States built a powerful navy that pushed the nation deeper into international affairs. How did America's new role change the world?

■ CONNECT

MY STORY VIDEO

Jane Addams, Neighboring With the Poor

Watch a video highlighting the life of Jane Addams.

Check Understanding What did Jane Addams found settlement houses? *(to help the poor, who often were immigrants, in urban areas)*

Identify Patterns How did Jane Addams embody the spirit of her age? *(Jane Addams came to prominence during the Progressive Era, a time of sweeping national reform.)*

DIGITAL ESSENTIAL QUESTION ACTIVITY

What can individuals do to affect society?

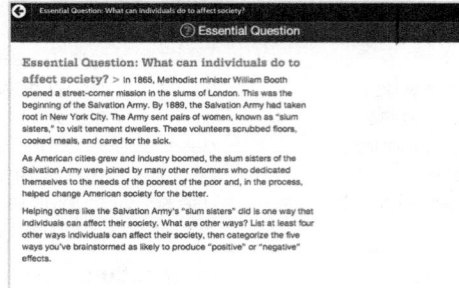

Ask students to think about the Essential Question for this Topic: What can individuals do to affect society? If students have not already done so, ask them to complete their lists and categorize each one. Then discuss students' lists as a class.

Identify Patterns Did you and your classmates list many of the same ways individuals can affect their society? If so, why?

Identify Central Issues What motivates a person to try to affect society? *(compassion, religious beliefs, empathy, kindness, greed, search for reward, fame)*

DIGITAL TIMELINE ACTIVITY

Timeline 1890–1920

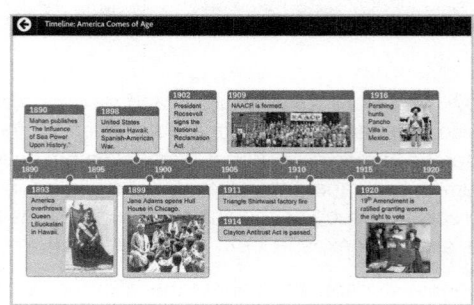

Display the timeline showing significant events in the years 1890–1920. Students will learn about all of these events and many more, but this timeline will provide a framework into which they can place significant events.

Identify Central Issues Why might some consider 1898 to be a turning point in American history? *(The United States gained control of Hawaii and defeated Spain in the Spanish-American War.)*

Topic Inquiry

Launch the Topic Inquiry with students after introducing the Topic.

Progressives Drive Reform

Supporting English Language Learners

Use with Digital Text 1, **The Progressive Era Begins.**

Learning
Display this sentence: "I made progress on my homework." Define or discuss the meaning of *progress* to ensure the word is accessible to students. Then read aloud the first paragraph of the text, asking students to listen and look for new and essential language related to *progress*.

Beginning Display this sentence: The _____ movement wanted progress in the area of social justice. Have students complete the sentence. Point out similarities between the words *progressive* and *progress*.

Intermediate Have students point to the word *progressivism* in the text. Ask: How does your knowledge of the word *progress* help you to understand the word *progressivism*?

Advanced Ask students to find instances of the words *progressivism* and *progressive* in the text. Help students to define these words based on their understanding of the word *progress*.

Advanced High Ask pairs of students to list words related to *progress* from the paragraph, and then to make a chart that lists a definition and an original sentence for each word. Remind them that the word *progressive* can be a noun or an adjective.

Use with Digital Text 2, **The Impact of Muckrakers.**

Reading
Read aloud the first paragraph of the text. Point out the words *muckrakers* and *muckrake*. Support students' understanding with the background knowledge needed to comprehend increasingly challenging language.

Beginning Show pictures of a muckrake and a stable, and act out how a muckrake is used in a stable. Then reread the sentence in parentheses and have students repeat after you.

Intermediate Show pictures of a muckrake and a stable. Then display these sentences: A _____ gathers a mess in a stable. A _____ gathers information on a mess in society. Have students complete and read aloud the sentences.

Advanced Show pictures of a muckrake and a stable. Then have them reread the paragraph. Ask them to compare and contrast how a muckrake and a muckraker work.

Advanced High Ask students to describe their knowledge about stables, farm work, and how a muckrake would be used. (Show pictures and share your own knowledge as needed.) Then have students explain why they think the term muckraker is appropriate in the context of the lesson.

▣ Differentiate Instruction

Use the Differentiated Instruction notes throughout the lesson plan to support the varied skill sets, levels of readiness, and interests in the mixed-ability classroom.

Challenge These notes include suggestions for expanding the activity for advanced students.

On-Level These notes include suggestions for modifying the activity to address different interests or learning styles.

Extra Support These notes include ideas for providing more scaffolding or reading spuport.

Special Needs These notes provide ideas for adapting instruction to support the needs of various special needs students.

◼ NOTES

Progressives Drive Reform

Objectives

Objective 1: Identify the causes of Progressivism and compare it to Populism.

Objective 2: Analyze the role that journalists and novelists played in the Progressive Movement.

Objective 3: Evaluate some of the social reforms that Progressives tackled.

Objective 4: Explain what Progressives hoped to achieve through political reforms.

LESSON 1 ORGANIZER		PACING: APPROX. 1 PERIOD, .5 BLOCKS		
	OBJECTIVES	PACING	Online	Print
Connect				
DIGITAL START UP ACTIVITY **The Need for Reform**		5 min.	●	
Investigate				
DIGITAL TEXT 1 **The Progressive Era Begins**	Objective 1	10 min.	●	●
DIGITAL TEXT 2 **The Impact of Muckrakers**	Objective 2	10 min.	●	●
DIGITAL TEXT 3 **Reformers Impact Society**	Objective 3	10 min.	●	●
INTERACTIVE GALLERY **The Triangle Shirtwaist Factory Fire**		10 min.	●	
DIGITAL TEXT 4 **Progressive Reforms Impact Government**	Objective 4	10 min.	●	●
INTERACTIVE ILLUSTRATION **Goals of Social Progressivism**		10 min.	●	
Synthesize				
DIGITAL ACTIVITY **Effects of Reforms on Children**		5 min.	●	
Demonstrate				
LESSON QUIZ **Lesson Quiz and Class Discussion Board**		10 min.	●	

PEARSON
realize™
www.PearsonRealize.com

Go online to access additional resources including:
Primary Sources • Biographies • Supreme Court cases •
21st Century Skill Tutorials • Maps • Graphic Organizers.

■ CONNECT

DIGITAL START UP ACTIVITY
The Need for Reform

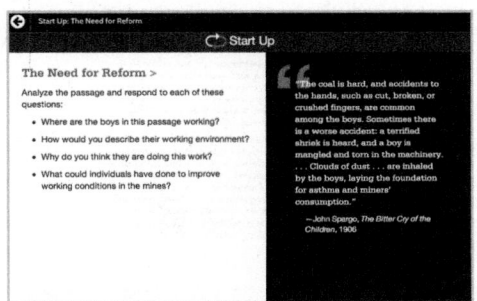

Project the Start Up Activity Ask students to answer the questions as they enter and get settled. Then have them share their ideas with another student, either in class or through a chat or blog space. Prompt students to think about the title of the book from which the quotation is taken (*The Bitter Cry of the Children*) as they answer the questions.

Determine Author's Purpose Point out the title of the book being quoted. Ask students what they might infer about the author's purpose from the title of the book. (*Probably the author wanted to prompt people to pay more attention to social issues affecting children and to advocate reform; the title appeals to the reader's emotions.*)

Aa Vocabulary Development: Use the Interactive Reading Notepad to preview the Key Terms and Academic Vocabulary in the lesson with students.

⇅ FLIP IT!
Assign the Flipped Video for this lesson.

■ STUDENT EDITION PRINT
PAGES: 392–399

■ INVESTIGATE

DIGITAL TEXT 1
The Progressive Era Begins

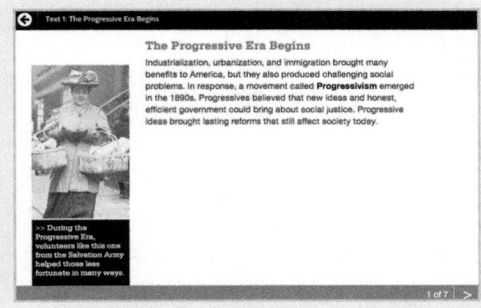

Objective 1: Identify the causes of Progressivism and compare it to populism.

Quick Instruction

Analyze Graphs Project the graphic organizer that shows similarities and differences between Progressives and populists. Ask: How were these reform movements alike? (*Both wanted to get rid of corrupt government officials and make government more responsive to people's needs. Both were concerned about social issues affecting children.*) How were these reform movements different? (*Middle-class, educated people who reasoned that science and other modern techniques could be used to improve society were at the forefront of the Progressive Movement. Leaders of the Populist movement consisted mostly of farmers and workers.*)

D Differentiate: Extra Support Prompt students to create their own graphic organizer that shows the differences and similarities between Progressives and populists.

ELL Use the ELL activity described in the ELL chart.

Further Instruction

Identify Cause and Effect Remind students that the Progressive Era emerged in the 1890s. Ask them to identify some of the factors that encouraged the growth of Progressive Era reforms. (*Some factors included the social issues associated with urbanization and industrialization, including social issues affecting children. Rapid urbanization left many people in cities without access to clean drinking water and living in substandard, overcrowded housing. Industrialization resulted in unsafe working conditions in factories and mines for many adults and children, which in turn inspired reform movements.*)

Identify Central Issues On what institutions did Progressives focus their reform efforts? *Progressives focused on reform of government, which many saw as corrupt and not acting in the interest of social welfare, and big business, which many thought responsible for poor working conditions and low pay.*

Progressives Drive Reform

DIGITAL TEXT 2

The Impact of Muckrakers

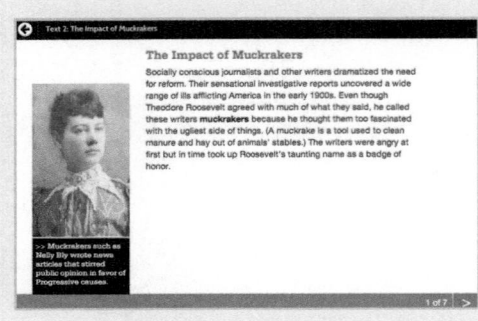

The Impact of Muckrakers

Socially conscious journalists and other writers dramatized the need for reform. Their sensational investigative reports uncovered a wide range of ills affecting America in the early 1900s. Even though Theodore Roosevelt agreed with much of what they said, he called these writers **muckrakers** because he thought them too fascinated with the ugliest side of things. (A muckrake is a tool used to clean manure and hay out of animals' stables.) The writers were angry at first but in time took up Roosevelt's taunting name as a badge of honor.

>> Muckrakers such as Nelly Bly wrote news articles that stirred public opinion in favor of Progressive causes.

1 of 7 >

Objective 2: Analyze the role that journalists and novelists played in the Progressive Movement.

Quick Instruction

Analyze Images Project the cover of *The Jungle*. Ask: What was *The Jungle*? *(A novel about the despair of immigrants working in Chicago's stockyards and about the unsanitary meat industry.)* Explain to students that this book was written by Upton Sinclair, a reform leader who they can identify as a muckraker. Who were the muckrakers? *(Muckrakers were socially conscious journalists and other writers who exposed societal ills during the Progressive Era.)*

Categorize Challenge students to name at least two other muckrakers and to describe their work. *(Lincoln Steffens, managing editor at McClure's Magazine, who wrote The Shame of the Cities; Jacob Riis, who wrote How the Other Half Lives; Ida Tarbell, who wrote The History of Standard Oil; John Spargo, who wrote about social issues affecting children; Theodore Dreiser, who wrote about social issues affecting women in Sister Carrie; Frank Norris, who wrote about the Southern Pacific Railroad's exploitation of California farmers; and; Frances Ellen Watkins, who wrote Iola Leroy.)*

ELL Use the ELL activity described in the ELL chart.

Further Instruction

Identify Central Issues How did the work of many muckrakers impact public opinion about social issues in U.S. society? *(As muckrakers wrote about the difficult conditions in which many Americans lived and worked, public opinion grew increasingly in favor of social reform, and laws were passed to address ills identified by muckrakers.)*

DIGITAL TEXT 3

Reformers Impact Society

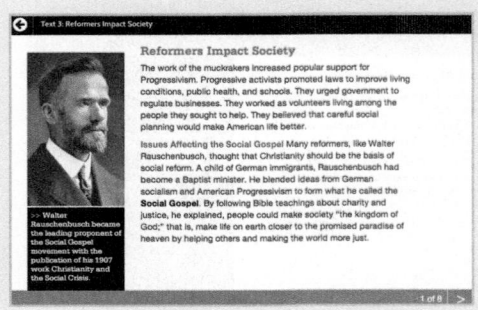

Reformers Impact Society

The work of the muckrakers increased popular support for Progressivism. Progressive activists promoted laws to improve living conditions, public health, and schools. They urged government to regulate businesses. They worked as volunteers living among the people they sought to help. They believed that careful social planning would make American life better.

Issues Affecting the Social Gospel Many reformers, like Walter Rauschenbusch, thought that Christianity should be the basis of social reform. A child of German immigrants, Rauschenbusch had become a Baptist minister. He blended ideas from German socialism and American Progressivism to form what he called the **Social Gospel**. By following Bible teachings about charity and justice, he explained, people could make society "the kingdom of God;" that is, make life on earth closer to the promised paradise of heaven by helping others and making the world more just.

>> Walter Rauschenbusch became the leading proponent of the Social Gospel movement with the publication of his 1907 work Christianity and the Social Crisis.

1 of 8 >

Objective 3: Evaluate some of the social reforms that Progressives tackled.

Quick Instruction

Interactive Gallery: The Triangle Shirtwaist Factory Fire Project the interactive gallery. Tell students that this event took place in 1911 in New York City. Work your way through the gallery so students get a sense of what caused the fire, what made the fire so deadly, and what the reaction to the fire was. Point out that the event created support for new business regulations. Ask: What social issues, including those affecting children and immigrants, did the fire help expose? *Unsafe working conditions in sweatshops, lack of safety regulations, exploitation of women, children, and immigrants, and so on.)* How was the fire an important turning point for women and immigrants? *(Women and immigrants were the majority of workers and victims of the fire. They organized to push for many new government regulations.)*

Make Generalizations How might the Triangle Shirtwaist Factory Fire be considered symbolic of the Progressive Era in general? *(The factory existed as a result of the urbanization and industrialization of the previous decades, the victims were poor workers, and the disaster led to further government regulation.)*

INTERACTIVE GALLERY

The Triangle Shirtwaist Factory Fire

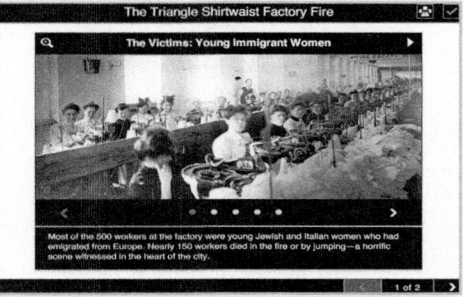

The Triangle Shirtwaist Factory Fire

The Victims: Young Immigrant Women

Most of the 500 workers at the factory were young Jewish and Italian women who had emigrated from Europe. Nearly 150 workers died in the fire or by jumping—a horrific scene witnessed in the heart of the city.

1 of 2

⬛ ACTIVE CLASSROOM

Play a game of Connect Two about the impact of the Triangle Shirtwaist Factory Fire on society. List the following terms on the board: *Progressive Era reforms, children, Industrialization, Triangle Shirtwaist Factory Fire.* Direct students to copy the terms down on note cards or small slips of paper, one term to a card or piece of paper. Review the list of terms with students. Ask students to "connect two" or choose two terms they think belong together, and state the reason for their connection. Challenge students to connect as many pairs of terms as possible. Conduct this activity before, during, and/or after student reading.

Further Instruction

Summarize Prompt students to define the Social Gospel reform movement. *(It was a reform movement that emerged in the late nineteenth century that sought to improve society by applying Christian principles like charity and justice to social policy.)* Ask the class what social issues drew the attention of reformers influenced by the Social Gospel. *(child labor and long working hours; Social Gospel adherents urged the end of child labor, a shorter workweek, and federal government limitations on the power of corporations and trusts.)*

Identify Central Issues Prompt students to think about Jane Addams, Hull House, and the settlement house movement. Then challenge them to identify the political, social, and economic contributions of Jane Addams to U.S. society. *(General contribution: building the settlment house movement in the United States; political: worked with Florence Kelley and others to lobby for legislation regulating living and working conditions and worked for women's suffrage and international peace; social: providing a variety of social services to the urban poor, including education and entertainment; economic: helping immigrants speak English and gain skills through further education made them more employable.)*

DIGITAL TEXT 4

Progressive Reforms Impact Government

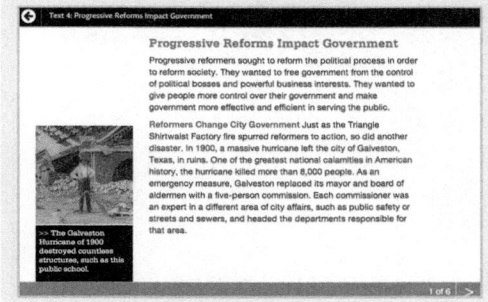

Text 4: Progressive Reforms Impact Government

Progressive Reforms Impact Government

Progressive reformers sought to reform the political process in order to reform society. They wanted to free government from the control of political bosses and powerful business interests. They wanted to give people more control over their government and make government more effective and efficient in serving the public.

Reformers Change City Government Just as the Triangle Shirtwaist Factory fire spurred reformers to action, so did another disaster. In 1900, a massive hurricane left the city of Galveston, Texas, in ruins. One of the greatest national calamities in American history, the hurricane killed more than 8,000 people. As an emergency measure, Galveston replaced its mayor and board of aldermen with a five-person commission. Each commissioner was an expert in a different area of city affairs, such as public safety or streets and sewers, and headed the departments responsible for that area.

>> The Galveston Hurricane of 1900 destroyed countless structures, such as this public school.

1 of 6

Objective 4: Explain what Progressives hoped to achieve through political reforms.

Quick Instruction

Interactive Illustration: Goals of Social Progressivism Project the interactive illustration. Remind students that the Progressive Era includes the late 1800s and early 1900s. Discuss Progressives' general beliefs: industrialization and urbanization had created social and political problems that could be solved using the power of government, reason, and religious principles of social justice. Guide the class through the illustration's interactive elements. For each, challenge students to identify an issue or a group of people that is being addressed. *(Issues include poverty, child labor, education, working conditions, health and sanitation.)*

Interpret Why do you think many Progressive Era reformers of the early twentieth century were so motivated to solve social issues like poverty and poor sanitation? *(Many Progressives were motivated by the Social Gospel's Christian ideals, as well as essential human compassion.)*

⬛ ACTIVE CLASSROOM

Ask students to use the Cartoon It Strategy to create a quick copy of one compelling image from the Interactive Illustration on a piece of paper. Turn it into a political cartoon that illustrates a key concept or main idea.

Progressives Drive Reform

SYNTHESIZE

DEMONSTRATE

INTERACTIVE ILLUSTRATION

Goals of Social Progressivism

Further Instruction

Remind students that, while we think of Progressives of social reformers, the way they achieved social reform was often through governmental action.

Identify Central Issues Ask students to identify the major political or government Progressive Era reforms. *(The Galveston plan, the direct primary, initiative, referendum, recall, and the passage of the Seventeenth Amendment)*

Apply Concepts What connection do you see between the Seventeenth Amendment and other Progressive Era political reforms such as initiative, referendum, and recall? *(The Seventeenth Amendment and other political reforms were all created with the idea of giving more political power to the voters by allowing them to directly elect Senators and to decide political issues on the ballot.)*

Evaluate Impact Direct students' attention to the infographic "Progressives and Election Reforms," as well as the text. Then ask them to evaluate the impact of the initiative, referendum, recall, and the Seventeenth Amendment on citizens. *(All of the measures listed gave more political power to voters, which they could use to possibly break up political machines and other forms of corruption. The data in the infographic shows that voters did use several of the measures frequently to direct government policy.)*

DIGITAL ACTIVITY

Effects of Reforms on Children

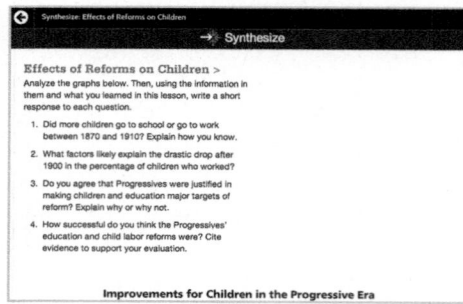

Discuss Review the questions with students. Have partners or small groups think about the reasons why Progressives encouraged education reform. Ask them to speculate how Progressives thought society as a whole would benefit from an increased focus on children's education.

Identify Central Issues Guide students into analyzing the social issues affecting children during the Progressive Era. Have them identify the two issues reflected in the graphs. *(Education and child labor)* What other social issues might affect children? *(Issues might include poverty, urbanization, health, and sanitation.)*

LESSON QUIZ

Lesson Quiz and Class Discussion Board

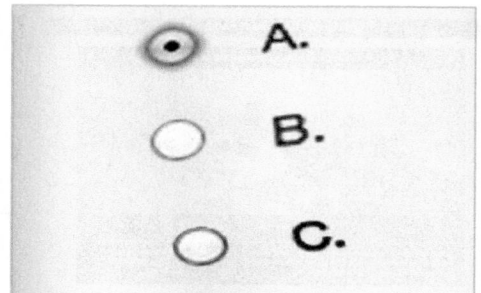

Assign the online Lesson Quiz for this lesson if you haven't already done so. Students will be offered automatic remediation or enrichment based on their score.

Pose these questions to the class on the Discussion Board:

The Progressive Era was an important one in U.S. history because it helped to shape the United States today.

Identify Cause and Effect What evidence of Progressive Era reforms do you see in the United States today?

Connect The Progressives were concerned with social issues affecting women, minorities, children, immigrants, and urbanization. Do any of these issues still concern Americans today?

Have students continue their investigations for the Topic Inquiry.

Women Gain Rights

Supporting English Language Learners

Use with Digital Text 1, **Expanding Opportunities for Women.**

Reading

Read aloud the section titled *Economic Issues for Women* in preparation for shared reading commensurate with content area and grade level needs. Point to the words as you say them so that students can follow along.

Beginning Reread the text aloud, this time letting students participate by reading known sight words in the text. Then have students complete and read aloud this sentence: Women encountered many difficulties at their _____.

Intermediate Reread the text aloud, this time letting students participate by reading key words and phrases in the text. Ask: What is one difficulty faced by women who worked?

Advanced Reread the text aloud, this time letting students participate by completing each sentence after you begin reading it. Have pairs of students discuss the main ideas of the paragraph.

Advanced High Reread the text aloud, this time letting students participate by reading every other sentence. Encourage them to match your pacing and intonation. Ask: What do you think was the most significant issue for working women and why?

Use with Digital Text 2, **Women Seek Equal Political Rights.**

Learning

Read the introductory paragraph and quotation of the text. Ensure that students understand the quotation's context as they focus on distinguishing between formal and informal English.

Beginning Read the quotation's first sentence up to the semicolon, and display the words *clean* and *free from grime*. Ask students to identify which is more formal. Then explain why *free from grime* has a more formal tone.

Intermediate Read and display the quotation's last sentence and this one: She can't even get good meat for her kids unless the government has OK'd it. Have students determine which sentence is more formal and give a reason why.

Advanced Invite a volunteer to read the quotation. Ask: Is Jane Addams' writing more formal or informal here? Have students support their conclusion with specific reasons, including how Addams might have opted to write certain phrases in an informal way.

Advanced High Have students read the quotation aloud. Using a chart to record their responses, have students evaluate the quotation's vocabulary, use of contractions, sentence structure, and emotional distance. Then have them mark the quotation's degree of formality on a continuum.

▶ Differentiate Instruction

Use the Differentiated Instruction notes throughout the lesson plan to support the varied skill sets, levels of readiness, and interests in the mixed-ability classroom.

Challenge These notes include suggestions for expanding the activity for advanced students.

On-Level These notes include suggestions for modifying the activity to address different interests or learning styles.

Extra Support These notes include ideas for providing more scaffolding or reading spuport.

Special Needs These notes provide ideas for adapting instruction to support the needs of various special needs students.

■ NOTES

Women Gain Rights

Objectives

Objective 1: Analyze actions taken by women to address social issues affecting workers and families.

Objective 2: Explain actions taken during the Progressive era to expand opportunities for women, including the right to vote.

Objective 3: Evaluate the tactics reform leaders used to win passage of the Nineteenth Amendment.

LESSON 2 ORGANIZER		PACING: APPROX. 1 PERIOD, .5 BLOCKS			
				RESOURCES	
		OBJECTIVES	PACING	Online	Print
Connect					
DIGITAL START UP ACTIVITY **Major Goals of Women in the Progressive Movement**			5 min.	●	
Investigate					
DIGITAL TEXT 1 **Expanding Opportunities for Women**		Objective 1	10 min.	●	●
INTERACTIVE GALLERY **Key Figures in the Women's Rights Movement, 1848–1920**			10 min.	●	
DIGITAL TEXT 2 **Women Seek Equal Political Rights**		Objectives 2, 3	10 min.	●	●
INTERACTIVE TIMELINE **The Women's Rights Movement, 1848 to Today**			10 min.	●	
Synthesize					
DIGITAL ACTIVITY **Reassessing Your Ideas**			5 min.	●	
Demonstrate					
DIGITAL QUIZ **Lesson Quiz and Class Discussion Board**			10 min.	●	

PEARSON
realize™
www.PearsonRealize.com

Go online to access additional resources including:
Primary Sources • Biographies • Supreme Court cases •
21st Century Skill Tutorials • Maps • Graphic Organizers.

CONNECT

DIGITAL START UP ACTIVITY
Major Goals of Women in the Progressive Movement

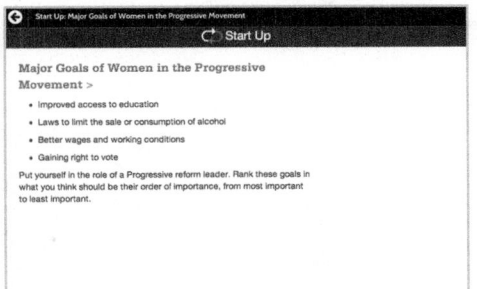

Project the Start Up Activity Review the goals with students, and challenge them to explain how each one is a social issue affecting women. *(Women were denied equal educational opportunities, wages and working conditions were poor, and the right to vote was withheld. The abuse of alcohol by husbands and fathers led to mistreatment of their wives and children, making alcohol an issue affecting women.)* Then have them share their rankings with another student, either in class or through a chat or blog space.

Tell students that in this lesson they will be learning about the ways in which women's political, social, and economic rights were expanded in the late nineteenth and early twentieth centuries.

Aa Vocabulary Development: Use the Interactive Reading Notepad to preview the Key Terms and Academic Vocabulary in this Lesson with students.

⇅ FLIP IT!

Assign the Flipped Video for this lesson.

■ STUDENT EDITION PRINT PAGES: 400–406

INVESTIGATE

DIGITAL TEXT 1
Expanding Opportunities for Women

Objective 1: Analyze actions taken by women to address social issues affecting workers and families.

Quick Instruction
Interactive Gallery: Key Figures in the Women's Rights Movement, 1848–1920 Project the gallery. Clicking on each image will give you more information about each woman to help identify her political, social, or economic contributions to U.S. society. Some of the names may be familiar to students. Begin by asking students what types of contributions the women shown made. *(Advances in women's rights, protection for workers, reduction of child labor, and temperance.)* Then ask what they know or think they know about each woman individually, as well as her specific contributions to the women's rights movement or improving conditions for women.

💻 ACTIVE CLASSROOM

Play a game of Rank It. List the following names of reform leaders on the board: *Florence Kelley, Frances Willard, Margaret Sanger, Ida B. Wells, Susan B. Anthony.*

- Ask students to rank the women according to who had the greatest impact.
- Ask students to provide a justification for the ranking decisions they made.
- Then ask students to work in pairs to share their rankings and justifications.
- Poll the class to see if there is agreement on the ranking.

INTERACTIVE GALLERY
Key Figures in the Women's Rights Movement, 1848–1920

ELL Use the ELL activity described in the ELL chart.

Further Instruction
Make Generalizations Have students think about what they have learned about women's advancement in U.S. society. Remind them it took action by individuals for women to gain economic opportunities and political rights. Point out that the issues involved in women gaining rights and opportunities were diverse. Ask them what issues affecting women were involved. *(Economic issues included a lack of economic opportunities, work hours, working conditions, and unfair prices. Social and political issues included temperance, a lack of political rights, birth control, and education.)* Given this diversity, can students make any generalizations? *(All of the issues impacted women, women themselves acted to expand their own economic opportunities and political rights, and women achieved a great deal of success from their efforts.)*

Identify Central Issues Help students focus on some key figures mentioned in this lesson. Ask: What contributions did Florence Kelley, Frances Willard, and Ida B. Well smake to improve conditions for women in American society? *(Kelley formed the Women's Trade Union League which worked to improve working conditions for women, pushed to set a minimum wage, and supported strikers. Willard founded the Women's Christian Temperance Union, which aimed to improve conditions for families by combating drinking. Wells founded the National Association of Colored Women (NACW), which helped African American women, for example by founding day-care centers to care for and educate children while their parents worked.)*

Women Gain Rights

DIGITAL TEXT 2

Women Seek Equal Political Rights

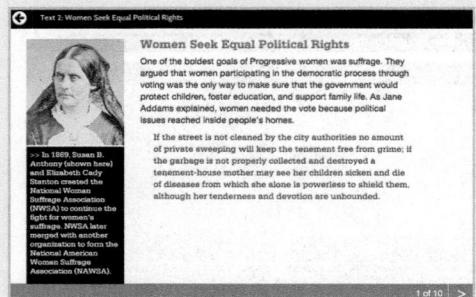

INTERACTIVE TIMELINE

The Women's Rights Movement, 1848 to Today

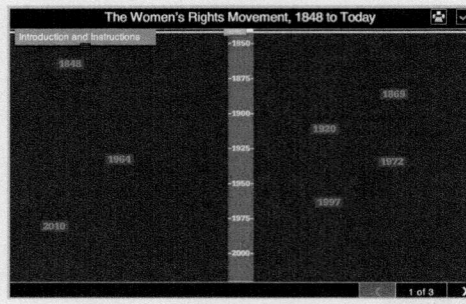

Objective 2: Explain actions taken during the Progressive Era to expand opportunities for women, including the right to vote.

Quick Instruction

Interactive Timeline: The Women's Rights Movement, 1848 to Today Project the interactive timeline. Begin by challenging students to make generalizations about how women's roles in U.S. society have changed since the late 1880s. *(Women today have greater rights, more educational opportunities, more economic opportunities, more personal freedom, and so on, than women in the late 1880s.)* Focus students on women's fight to gain rights in government and politics. Ask: What various means of achieving equality of political rights did women employ? *(To achieve equality, women built organizations to harness large numbers of women, and used conventions, public speeches, lobbying, mass parades and rallies, networking, protest marches, hunger strikes, and picketing.)* Emphasize that the timeline helps them to trace the historical development of the civil rights movement for women from the nineteenth century to present day. Invite students to explain the significance of each accomplishment in the timeline.

Objective 3: Evaluate the tactics reform leaders used to win passage of the Nineteenth Amendment.

📷 ACTIVE CLASSROOM

Direct students to each Make a Headline for one of the remarkable women they have learned about. Women to consider include Jane Addams, Susan B. Anthony, Elizabeth Cady Stanton, Florence Kelley, Frances Willard, Margaret Sanger, Ida B. Wells, Carrie Chapman Catt, and Alice Paul. Have each student select one historical figure. Ask: If you were to write a headline for your chosen individual that captured the most important impact that she had on society, what would that headline be? Encourage students to use subheadings to convey the maximum amount of information. Have students pass their headlines to a partner for them to review.

ELL Use the ELL activity described in the ELL chart.

Further Instruction

Summarize Explain to students that the impact of Nineteenth Amendment was to expand voting rights. Ask them who gained voting rights through the amendment and have them evaluate the amendment as a means of achieving political rights. *(Women gained voting rights, the amendment was a very effective means of expanding their rights.)* While reading the text, have students trace the development of the women's rights movement and the push for the Nineteenth Amendment.

Compare What political organizations led the fight to expand the right of women to participate in the democratic process in the 1900s? Explain their actions. *(The main two organizations in the twentieth century were the National American Woman Suffrage Association (NAWSA), led by Carrie Chapman Catt and the National Woman's Party (NWP), led by Alice Paul.)* What role did each of these organizations play in promoting women's rights? *(NAWSA, under Catt, had a "winning plan" that was two-pronged. Some teams lobbied for an amendment, while others worked at the state level to pass suffrage laws by referendum. NWP, under Paul, used more aggressive tactics like picketing the White House and hunger strikes, focusing mainly on the passage of the amendment.)*

Identify Cause and Effect Challenge students to discuss the historical reasons why the Constitution was amended by the Nineteenth Amendment. Remind them that the act passed in 1920, a few years after the end of World War I. *(The ratification of the Nineteenth Amendment was the result of a decades-long effort by American women (and a smaller number of male supporters) to achieve equality at the ballot box. The immediate legacy of World War I, fought to "make the world safe for democracy," provided women with a powerful moral argument for the ratification of the Nineteenth Amendment.)*

◼ SYNTHESIZE

DIGITAL ACTIVITY
Reassessing Your Ideas

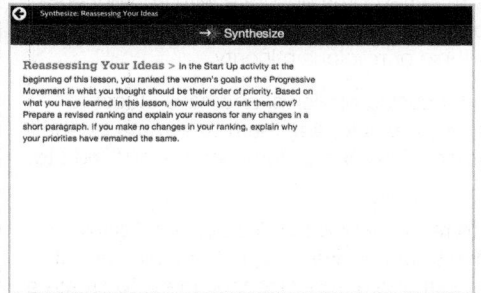

Students should revise their rankings and explain their revisions, or explain their lack of revision. To help students as they consider the issue, share this quote from the lesson:

If the street is not cleaned by the city authorities, no amount of private sweeping will keep the tenement free from grime; if the garbage is not properly collected and destroyed, a tenement-house mother may see her children sicken and die of diseases from which she alone is powerless to shield them, although her tenderness and devotion are unbounded. She cannot even secure untainted meat for her household... unless the meat has been inspected by city officials.

—*Jane Addams, Ladies Home Journal, 1910*

Discuss Ask students whether they think individual leaders such as Susan B. Anthony and Elizabeth Cady Stanton or mass movements such as parades and protests was more important in expanding the right of women to participate in the democratic process.

◼ DEMONSTRATE

DIGITAL QUIZ
Lesson Quiz and Class Discussion Board

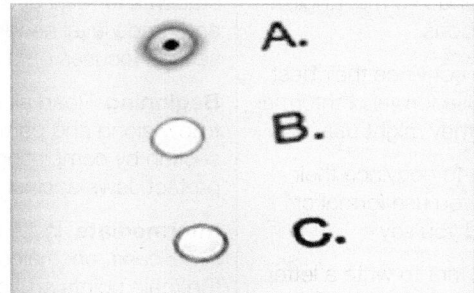

Assign the online Lesson Quiz for this lesson if you haven't already done so. Students will be offered automatic remediation or enrichment based on their score.

Pose these questions to the class on the Discussion Board:

Support Ideas with Evidence American women used many methods of expanding their right to participate in the democratic process, including lobbying, nonviolent protesting, litigation, and amendments to the U.S. Constitution. Which methods do you think were most effective? Why? Give evidence for your position.

Generate Explanations Of the various means of achieving equality of political rights that American women used, many historians consider the Nineteenth Amendment the most important. Explain why you think this is so.

Summarize Choose one important woman from the Progressive Era. Identify her political, social, and economic contributions.

Topic Inquiry
Have students continue their investigations for the Topic Inquiry.

Striving for Equality

Supporting English Language Learners

Use with Digital Text 1, **African Americans Promote Civil Rights.**

Learning
Read aloud the first two paragraphs, or invite volunteers to do so. Summarize the views of Booker T. Washington and W.E.B. Du Bois as you prompt students to demonstrate when to use formal and informal English commensurate with their grade-level learning expectations.

Beginning Have students role-play that they want to convince their best friend that Du Bois's view is correct. Ask: Would you use formal or informal English? Brainstorm a few informal words or phrases they might use.

Intermediate Have students role-play that they want to convince their best friend that Du Bois's view is correct. Ask: Would you use formal or informal English, and why? What specific things would you say?

Advanced Have pairs of students pretend that they want to write a letter to the editor about the merits of Du Bois's view. Ask them to choose a level of formality, write the letter, and then share and discuss it with another student pair.

Advanced High Have students pretend that they want to write a letter to the editor about the merits of Du Bois's view. Ask them to choose a level of formality, write the letter, and then share and discuss it with another student.

Use with Digital Text 3, **Protecting Rights for Ethnic and Religious Minorities.**

Reading
Read aloud the text or invite volunteers to do so in small groups. Prompt students to retell or summarize material commensurate with content area and grade level needs. Also point out the subheadings, noting how each section focuses on a different ethnic or religious minority.

Beginning Read aloud the part focusing on Jews, and have students follow along and participate as they are able. Ask them to summarize the section by completing this sentence: The Anti-Defamation League tried to protect Jews against _____.

Intermediate Invite students to read the part that focuses on Asian Americans, once aloud and once to themselves. Have them think about the main points and share them with the group. Use their ideas to create a summary of this part.

Advanced Assign pairs of students different parts of the text, and have them read their part at least two times. Tell them to discuss the main ideas with each other, create a summary, and then share their summary with the group.

Advanced High Assign each student a different part of the text. Have them read it silently at least two times and then think about its main ideas. Provide time for students to summarize their section aloud to a partner.

▣ Differentiate Instruction

Use the Differentiated Instruction notes throughout the lesson plan to support the varied skill sets, levels of readiness, and interests in the mixed-ability classroom.

Challenge These notes include suggestions for expanding the activity for advanced students.

On-Level These notes include suggestions for modifying the activity to address different interests or learning styles.

Extra Support These notes include ideas for providing more scaffolding or reading spuport.

Special Needs These notes provide ideas for adapting instruction to support the needs of various special needs students.

◼ NOTES

PEARSON
realize™
www.PearsonRealize.com

Go online to access additional resources including:
Primary Sources • Biographies • Supreme Court cases •
21st Century Skill Tutorials • Maps • Graphic Organizers.

Objectives

Objective 1: Analyze Progressives' attitudes toward minority rights.

Objective 2: Describe the political organizations formed by African Americans to promote civil rights.

Objective 3: Examine the actions taken by other minority groups to expand their rights.

LESSON 3 ORGANIZER		PACING: APPROX. 1 PERIOD, .5 BLOCKS		
			RESOURCES	
	OBJECTIVES	**PACING**	**Online**	**Print**
Connect				
DIGITAL START UP ACTIVITY **Progressives and Minorities**		5 min.	●	
Investigate				
DIGITAL TEXT 1 **Minorities Face Challenges in the Progressive Era**	Objective 1	10 min.	●	●
DIGITAL TEXT 2 **African Americans Promote Civil Rights**	Objective 2	10 min.	●	●
INTERACTIVE TIMELINE **African American Reform Movement, 1895–1915**		10 min.	●	
DIGITAL TEXT 3 **Protecting Rights for Ethnic and Religious Minorities**	Objective 3	10 min.	●	●
INTERACTIVE GALLERY **Reform Groups Today**		10 min.	●	
Synthesize				
DIGITAL ACTIVITY **A Progressive Failing?**		5 min.	●	
Demonstrate				
DIGITAL QUIZ **Lesson Quiz and Class Discussion Board**		10 min.	●	

Striving for Equality

■ CONNECT

DIGITAL START UP ACTIVITY
Progressives and Minorities

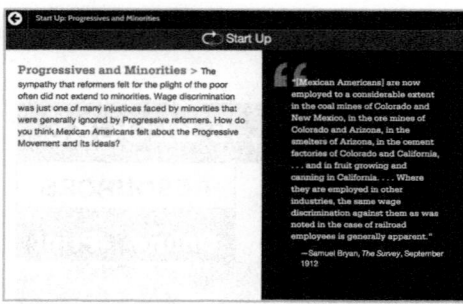

Project the Start Up Activity Ask students to answer the question as they enter and get settled. Then have them each share their ideas with another student.

Discuss Point out that the quotation from Samuel Bryan directly refers to wage discrimination, but may also indirectly refer to other types of discrimination. What might these be? *(Racial: the industries mentioned are working class and relatively dangerous; educational: may have prevented workers from obtaining better jobs.)*

Tell students that in this lesson they will be learning about the political, social, and economic challenges that minorities faced during the Progressive Era.

Aa Vocabulary Development: Use the Interactive Reading Notepad to preview the Key Terms and Academic Vocabulary in the lesson with students.

⇅ FLIP IT!
Assign the Flipped Video for this lesson.

■ STUDENT EDITION PRINT PAGES: 407–411

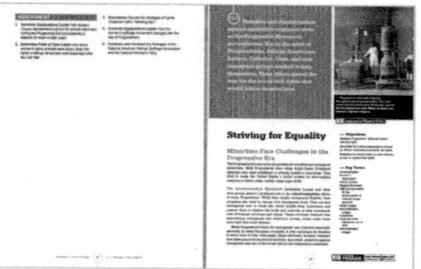

■ INVESTIGATE

DIGITAL TEXT 1
Minorities Face Challenges in the Progressive Era

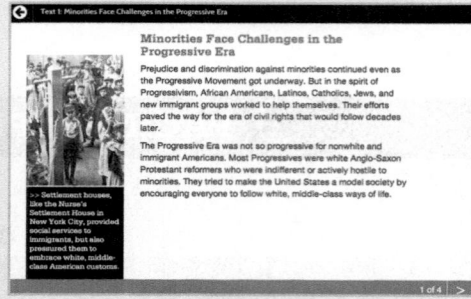

Objective 1: Analyze Progressives' attitudes toward minority rights.

Quick Instruction

Analyze Images Project the image. Ask students what aspect of life in late nineteenth- and early twentieth-century America it depicts. *(Segregation, or the separation of people by race. During the Jim Crow Era, from about the 1880s to the 1950s, segregation was legal and actively practiced.)* Go on to ask what effect of the U.S. Supreme Court decision *Plessy* v. *Ferguson* had on segregation in the United States. *(The 1896 Supreme Court decision upheld Jim Crow laws. States passed more segregation laws. By 1910, segregation was the norm across the nation.)*

Evaluate Arguments Challenge students to explain the apparent paradox between Progressives wanting better lives for women, workers, and others yet supporting segregation. *(Segregation was not viewed as unfair discrimination. Plessy stated that segregated facilities had to be equal. Moreover, Progressives shared the same prejudice against nonwhites held by other white Americans of the time.)*

Further Instruction

Generate Explanations Remind students that the Progressive Movement did not include everyone in United States, but instead was confined largely to one definable group. Ask them to identify this group. *(Most Progressives were white Anglo-Saxon Protestant reformers.)* Tell students that these reformers focused their efforts not on minorities, but on other whites. Ask students to explain this. *(They wanted to preserve a white, middle-class way of life. They also thought many nonwhites incapable of integrating into mainstream American society.)*

Evaluate Arguments Invite students to define *Americanization* and *assimilation* in context. *(Americanization is the belief that assimilating immigrants into American society would make them more loyal citizens. Assimilation is the process of immigrants absorbing and integrating into American culture.)* What was the rationale behind the Americanization movement? *(A common language and culture helps unify a country and maintains a common national identity.)* Invite students to explain if they agree or disagree with the rationale of the Americanization movement.

Identify Central Issues Have students analyze the effects of the U.S. Supreme Court decision in *Plessy* v. *Ferguson*. *(The 1896 Supreme Court decision upheld Jim Crow, or racial segregation, laws. States passed more segregation laws. By 1910, segregation was the norm across the nation.)*

DIGITAL TEXT 2
African Americans Promote Civil Rights

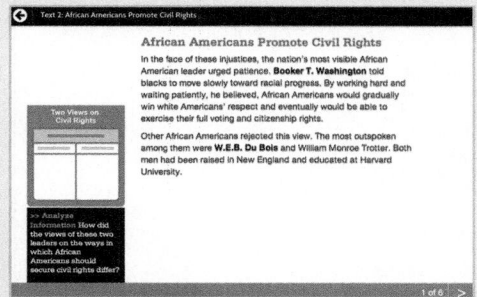

INTERACTIVE TIMELINE
African American Reform Movement, 1895–1915

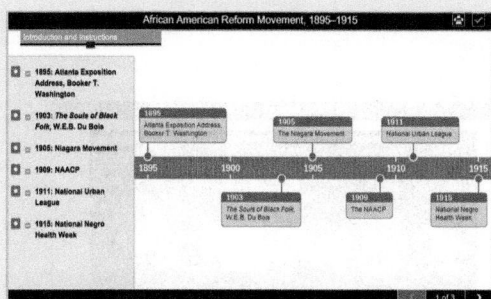

Objective 2: Describe the political organizations formed by African Americans to promote civil rights.

Quick Instruction

Interactive Timeline: African American Reform Movement, 1895–1915 Project the interactive timeline. Begin by asking students to summarize the situation of African Americans in the late 1800s and early 1900s. *(They lived in a segregated country and faced widespread, legal discrimination.)* Click on the squares for Booker T. Washington and then for W.E.B. Du Bois. Guide the class in comparing and contrasting their views and discuss the impact of these reform leaders. Then, discuss the roles of political organizations that promoted civil rights, such as the Niagara Movement, the NAACP, and the National Urban League.

Summarize How did reform leaders such as Ida B. Wells work to expand political rights for minorities? *(Wells and other reform leaders worked with the NAACP to pursue litigation in the courts in an effort to overturn unjust laws and expand political and economic rights for minorities. Wells also used her own newspaper as a means to call public attention to lynchings and other injustices.)*

🗣 ACTIVE CLASSROOM

Direct students to have a "Conversation" with one of the important figures from the African American reform movement of the late 1800s and early 1900s. Candidates include Booker T. Washington, W.E.B. Du Bois, Ida B. Wells, William Monroe Trotter, Jane Addams, Ray Stannard Baker, and Florence Kelley. Tell students to that they are going to have a fictional conversation with their chosen individual. Students should write down a question they would like to ask, what their chosen person would say, and what the student would say in response.

D Differentiate: Challenge Invite an interested student to conduct research on William Monroe Trotter and his role in the Niagara Movement. The student should share what he or she learns with the rest of the class.

ELL Use the ELL activity described in the ELL chart.

Further Instruction

Compare Points of View Tell students that Booker T. Washington and W.E.B. Du Bois were both famous and well-respected leaders who took actions to expand the economic opportunities and political rights of African Americans.Have them read the quotes from both men that appear in the chart "Two Views of Civil Rights" at the beginning of this

text reading. Ensure students understand that reform leaders did not all share the same views. Have students compare and contrast those of Washington and Du Bois. *(Washington told blacks to move slowly toward racial progress by working hard and waiting patiently. In contrast, Du Bois urged African Americans to demand their rights immediately.)*

Identify Central Issues Ask students to describe the roles of organizations formed by African Americans in the early 1900s and explain actions taken by those groups to expand political rights and economic opportunities for racial minorities. *(The NAACP sought to expand political rights by fighting in court to help African Americans gain equal access to education and job opportunities. The Urban League sought to expand economic opportunities by providing support to poor African American workers, mainly in America's cities.)*

Evaluate Arguments Ask students to identify what method the NAACP planned to use to expand the right of African Americans' to participate in the political process. *(Ida B. Wells and others planned to use litigation in the courts.)* Then ask them to analyze whether they think that method will be effective. *(Yes, because they will be arguing basics principles of freedom and democracy in front of a small but powerful audience in a court case; No, because the cases could go against the NAACP and end up harming African Americans, as Plessy v. Ferguson did.)*

Striving for Equality

DIGITAL TEXT 3

Protecting Rights for Ethnic and Religious Minorities

INTERACTIVE GALLERY

Reform Groups Today

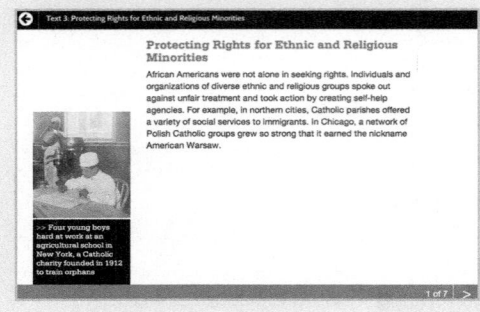

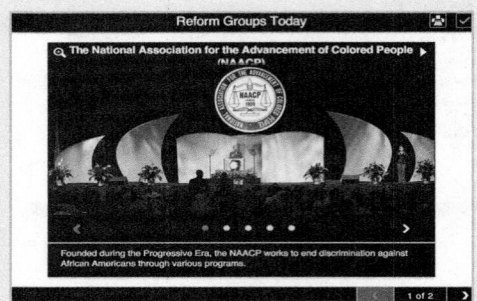

Objective 3: Examine the actions taken by members of other minority groups to expand their rights.

Quick Instruction

Interactive Gallery: Reform Groups Today Project the interactive gallery. Click on each image to reveal the origin and purpose of the group. Point out how several were formed during the Progressive Era. Point out to students that every one of these groups was formed to expand economic opportunities and political rights for racial and ethnic minorities in American society. Ask: What are some ways that the organizations work to meet this goal? *(Forming groups to help each other and litigation.)* How was the American Indian Citizenship Act of 1924 a step toward equality of political rights for Native Americans? *(It granted Native Americans citizenship and full voting rights.)* What led to its passage? *(It was passed to reward Native Americans for their service in World War I, and also to promote Americanization.)*

🗣 ACTIVE CLASSROOM

Invite students to draw Graffiti Concepts to help them remember each of the groups and organizations formed by racial and ethnic minorities to expand their economic opportunities and political rights. Assign the following to pairs or small groups of students: Anti-Defamation League, Society of American Indians, National Council of La Raza, and Native American Rights Fund. Have each group of students create a visual image and/or phrase that represents their assigned organization. Allow approximately 3–5 minutes. Direct students to post their "graffiti" on the board or on chart paper and ask students to look at all the various responses. They should then discuss similarities and differences among the organizations.

ELL Use the ELL activity described in the ELL chart.

Further Instruction

Summarize Ask students to summarize the challenges faced by each of the following racial, ethnic, and religious minorities in American society during the Progressive Era and the responses of each group to those challenges, including how members of each group fought for greater economic opportunities or expanded political rights: Jewish Americans: *(Facing growing anti-Semitism, B'nai B'rith founded the Anti-Defamation League in 1913, which fought economic and political discrimination against Jews and others.)* Mexican Americans: *(Facing discrimination, Mexican Americans organized themselves into groups like Partido Liberal Mexicano (PLM). They also formed mutual aid societies called mutualistas.)* Native Americans: *(Native Americans faced discrimination and dispossession of their land under the Dawes Act. Carlos Montezuma helped form the Society of American Indians in 1911 to promote Indian rights. The American Indian Citizenship Act of 1924 helped Native Americans achieve equality of political rights.)* Asian Americans: *(Like other minorities, Asian Americans faced discrimination. In California, Japanese immigrants were not allowed to own land. They responded by putting their land in their children's names. Immigrants from Japan, India, and China fought the law that prevented them from becoming citizens.)*

■ SYNTHESIZE

DIGITAL ACTIVITY

A Progressive Failing?

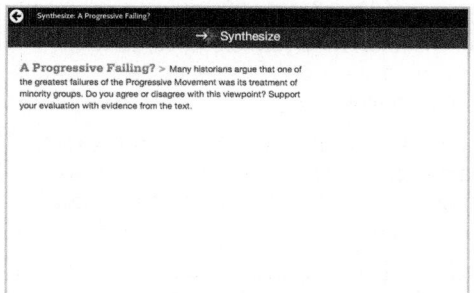

Synthesize: A Progressive Failing?

→ Synthesize

A Progressive Failing? > Many historians argue that one of the greatest failures of the Progressive Movement was its treatment of minority groups. Do you agree or disagree with this viewpoint? Support your evaluation with evidence from the text.

Emphasize that students must support their positions with reasons. Encourage students to share their responses with other students, either in class or through a chat or blog space.

Discuss Discuss the commonalities in attempts by various racial, ethnic, and religious minorities to expand economic opportunities and political rights during this period. *(The attempts were similar in that the various minorities all attempted to improve their standing in U.S. society by forming organizations and through litigation.)*

■ DEMONSTRATE

DIGITAL QUIZ

Lesson Quiz and Class Discussion Board

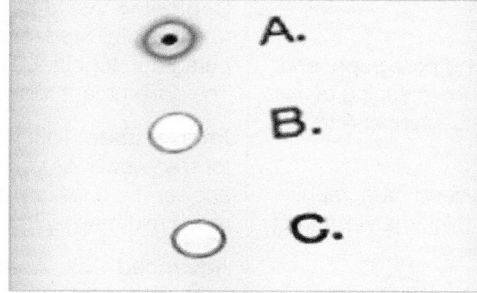

Assign the online Lesson Quiz for this lesson if you haven't already done so. Students will be offered automatic remediation or enrichment based on their score.

Pose this question to the class on the Discussion Board:

Generate Explanations Many of the organizations created during the Progressive Era to advance the political and economic status of minorities still exist. What do you make of this?

Have students continue their investigations for the Topic Inquiry.

Reformers in the White House

Supporting English Language Learners

Use with Digital Text 1, Roosevelt Changes the Relationship Between Government and Business.

Learning

Read aloud *A Trustbuster Enforces Legislation*, or invite volunteers to do so. Explain to students that they can deduce the meanings of words based on context clues. Prompt students to reason inductively or deductively while they analyze sayings and expressions commensurate with grade-level learning expectations.

Beginning Display the first two sentences of the second paragraph, and read them aloud with students. Guide them to deduce the meaning of trust used in this context by having them complete this sentence: A trust is a large _____.

Intermediate Display the first two sentences of the second paragraph, and read them aloud with students. Ask: What do you think the word trust means? What clues in the text led you to that conclusion?

Advanced Have students read thes first paragraph. Ask: What does *trustbuster* mean? What clues could lead you to that conclusion? How could breaking *trustbuster* into smaller words lead you to that conclusion?

Advanced High Have students read the second paragraph. Ask: What did people who called Roosevelt a "trust-tamer" likely think of trusts? Why did they think trusts needed taming? Who do you think these supporters were (or were not)? What led you to these conclusions?

Use with Digital Text 4, Wilson Endorses Further Regulation.

Reading

Read aloud *A New Tax on Income*, or invite volunteers to do so. Explain the importance of rereading in order to find answers to questions. Prompt students to respond to questions commensurate with content area and grade level needs.

Beginning Ask: After cutting tariffs, how did the government raise revenue? Tell students to look for the answer as you reread the second paragraph together. Then have them answer using this sentence frame: The government raised money through a(n) _____.

Intermediate Ask: What is a graduated income tax? Tell students to look for the answer as you reread the second paragraph together. After they answer the question, ask: If a poor person paid a 10% income tax, how much might a wealthy person have to pay?

Advanced Ask: What are the pros and cons of an income tax? Have pairs of students reread the section together and look for the answer. Provide time for students to share what they found and remind students to use full sentences to answer the question.

Advanced High Ask: Why did Wilson cut tariffs? What were the effects on U.S. companies, foreign companies, U.S. consumers, and the U.S. government? Have students independently reread the section and record their findings. Remind students to answer in full sentences. Provide time for students to share their answers.

▣ Differentiate Instruction

Use the Differentiated Instruction notes throughout the lesson plan to support the varied skill sets, levels of readiness, and interests in the mixed-ability classroom.

Challenge These notes include suggestions for expanding the activity for advanced students.

On-Level These notes include suggestions for modifying the activity to address different interests or learning styles.

Extra Support These notes include ideas for providing more scaffolding or reading spuport.

Special Needs These notes provide ideas for adapting instruction to support the needs of various special needs students.

◼ NOTES

PEARSON realize™
www.PearsonRealize.com

Go online to access additional resources including:
Primary Sources • Biographies • Supreme Court cases •
21st Century Skill Tutorials • Maps • Graphic Organizers.

Objectives

Objective 1: Analyze how Theodore Roosevelt influenced the changing relationship between the federal government and private business.

Objective 2: Explain the impact of Roosevelt's actions towards managing the environment.

Objective 3: Compare and contrast Roosevelt's policies with Taft's and Wilson's policies.

Objective 4: Describe Wilson's efforts to regulate the economy.

Objective 5: Assess the legacy of the Progressive Era.

LESSON 4 ORGANIZER		PACING: APPROX. 1 PERIOD, .5 BLOCKS		
	OBJECTIVES	PACING	Online	Print
Connect				
DIGITAL START UP ACTIVITY **A Progressive Reformer**		5 min.	●	
Investigate				
DIGITAL TEXT 1 **Roosevelt Changes the Relationship Between Government and Business**	Objective 1	10 min.	●	●
DIGITAL TEXT 2 **Managing the Environment**	Objective 2	10 min.	●	●
INTERACTIVE GALLERY **U.S. Public and Private Land Conservation**		10 min.	●	●
DIGITAL TEXT 3 **A New Direction In Presidential Politics**	Objective 3	10 min.	●	●
DIGITAL TEXT 4 **Wilson Endorses Further Regulation**	Objective 4	10 min.	●	●
INTERACTIVE CHART **Roosevelt and Wilson**		10 min.	●	
DIGITAL TEXT 5 **The Progressives' Legacy**	Objective 5	10 min.	●	●
Synthesize				
DIGITAL ACTIVITY **Trust-Busting**		5 min.	●	
Demonstrate				
DIGITAL QUIZ **Lesson Quiz and Class Discussion Board**		10 min.	●	

Reformers in the White House

■ **CONNECT**

A Progressive Reformer

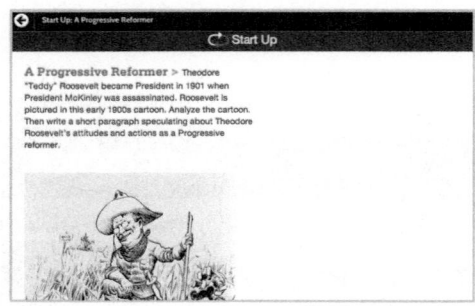

Project the Start Up Activity Ask students to study the cartoon as they enter and get settled. Then have them share their paragraphs with another student, either in class or through a chat or blog space.

Transfer Information Discuss with students the pros and cons of different media, such as political cartoons and paragraphs. Which does a better job at conveying ideas about progressivism?

Aa Vocabulary Development: Use the Interactive Reading Notepad to preview the Key Terms and Academic Vocabulary in this lesson with students.

↻ FLIP IT!

Assign the Flipped Video for this lesson.

■ STUDENT EDITION PRINT
PAGES: 412–422

■ **INVESTIGATE**

Roosevelt Changes the Relationship Between Government and Business

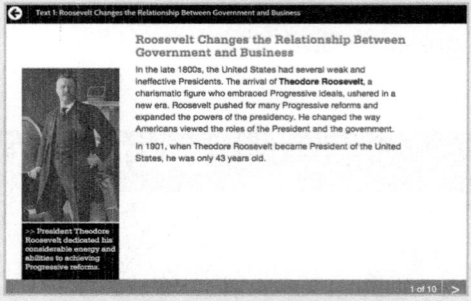

Objective 1: Analyze how Theodore Roosevelt influenced the changing relationship between the federal government and private business.

Quick Instruction

Analyze Images Project the image of Roosevelt. Invite students to suggest adjectives they associate with Teddy Roosevelt. (Adjectives may refer to him personally (e.g., vigorous, strong) or refer to his policies (e.g., progressive, anti-trust.)) Focus on Roosevelt's role as a trust-buster.

Identify Central Issues Challenge students to describe the changing relationship between the federal government and private business during Roosevelt's presidency. (Roosevelt believed what he called the Square Deal, which was a series of reforms and actions to keep the wealthy and powerful from taking advantage of small business owners and the poor. In 1902, Roosevelt had the federal government step in to help workers in a labor dispute. Roosevelt pushed Congress to pass the Elkins Act in 1903 and the Hepburn Act in 1906 to strengthen the ICC's power to regulate railroad shipping rates.)

Distinguish Identify the costs and benefits of the powers granted the Interstate Commerce Commission (ICC). (The ICC was originally charged with ensuring shippers paid similar rates for transporting goods across state lines to encourage competition. However, the ICC was granted the power to set maximum shipping rates, which some argue may have harmed the economy.)

ELL Use the ELL activity described in the ELL chart.

Further Instruction

Compare and Contrast Ask students to discuss the costs and benefits of the antitrust acts that Roosevelt enforced and consider the effects of government actions on individuals and industries, including Fifth Amendment property rights. (Costs: antitrust laws were applied unevenly and unfairly. This can be viewed as a violation of the Fifth and Fourteenth Amendments which state that the government can't take private property away from citizens without "just compensation". The effects of governmental actions on industries can be negative, making it difficult for them to do business. The effects on individuals can also be negative, costing people jobs and individual shareholders' earnings. Benefits include the protection of small businesses and individuals from unfair business practices.)

Compare and Contrast Explore the same questions about the Pure Food and Drug Act. What are the costs and benefits of the Pure Food and Drug Act? (Costs include the expenses involved in inspection and conforming to regulations. Benefits include safer food and medicine for the public.)

Summarize What effect did Upton Sinclair's The Jungle have on regulation of businesses? (The public was concerned about the unhealthy conditions of meatpacking plants that Sinclair described in his book. President Roosevelt in turn signed the Meat Inspection Act).

DIGITAL TEXT 2

Managing the Environment

INTERACTIVE GALLERY

U.S. Public and Private Land Conservation

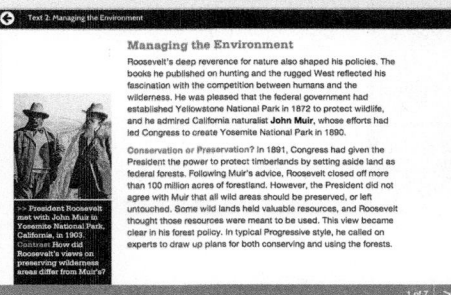

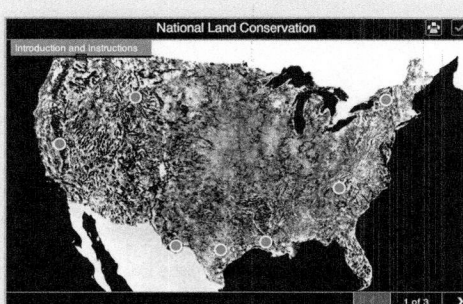

Objective 2: Explain the impact of Roosevelt's actions towards managing the environment.

Quick Instruction

National Land Conservation: Interactive Gallery Project the gallery. Clicking on each red circle will identify the various roles of governmental entities and private citizens in managing the environment, including the National Park System. Engage students in discussion about each location. Ask questions like whether they would like to visit the place, and what they would think their visit would be like. Challenge them to explain how each location is managed by governmental entities, private citizens, or both. During the discussion, give a quick overview of Roosevelt's actions towards managing the environment: He was a Progressive who drew on the "rational use" ideas of Gifford Pinchot, who recommended that forests be preserved for public use. Conservation, or the planned management of natural resources, became government policy. Roosevelt signed the National Reclamation Act, which gave the federal government the power to decide where and how water would be distributed.

Summarize Have students summarize the roles that John Muir, Gifford Pinchot, and Francis Newlands played in Roosevelt's actions towards managing the environment. *(Roosevelt admired Muir, whose efforts led to the creation of Yosemite National Park, and followed his advice to protect forestland. He also followed Pinchot's "rational use" ideas of preserving forests for public use. Newlands encouraged Roosevelt to use the federal government to help western states build huge reservoirs to hold and to conserve water.)*

💬 ACTIVE CLASSROOM

Pair students. Direct each pair to focus on the map of the conservation examples. Students should ask each other these questions:

- What do you see?
- What does that make you think?
- What are you wondering about now that you have seen this?

Pairs should then share their insights with the rest of the class.

Further Instruction

Infer Why might it make sense for the federal government, as opposed to state governments, to manage the environment, especially water resources? *(Water resources like rivers and aquifers frequently cross local community, city, and state lines. There may be conflict between local and state governments or between states themselves over allocation of scarce resources.)*

Compare Points of View President Roosevelt oftentimes supported conservation measures that seemed to contradict the property rights guaranteed in the Fifth Amendment. How did he justify those conservation measures, and what was the point of view of those who opposed conservation measures on the basis of the Fifth Amendment? *(Roosevelt believed that the needs of the community as a whole should sometimes be given consideration over the property rights of individuals. Others however argue that private property individuals who have a greater incentive to care for it.)*

Identify Central Issues What effect did increasing population growth have on the physical environment of the American southwest? *(The physical environment of the southwest is arid, and as more people moved to the southwest, there was increasing conflict over the use of water. New irrigation methods were necessary to provide water for industrial and private use, and eventually lakes and reservoirs were created to support populations with increasingly dense distributions in larger towns.)*

Reformers in the White House

DIGITAL TEXT 3

A New Direction In Presidential Politics

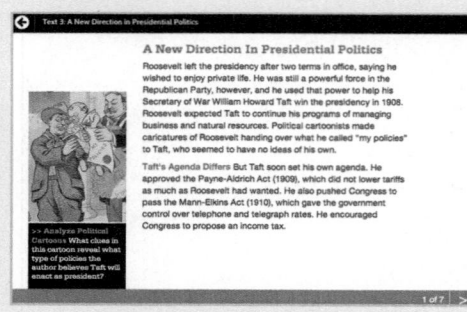

A New Direction In Presidential Politics

Roosevelt left the presidency after two terms in office, saying he wished to enjoy private life. He was still a powerful force in the Republican Party, however, and he used that power to help his Secretary of War William Howard Taft win the presidency in 1908. Roosevelt expected Taft to continue his programs of managing business and natural resources. Political cartoonists made caricatures of Roosevelt handing over what he called "my policies" to Taft, who seemed to have no ideas of his own.

Taft's Agenda Differs But Taft soon set his own agenda. He approved the Payne-Aldrich Act (1909), which did not lower tariffs as much as Roosevelt had wanted. He also pushed Congress to pass the Mann-Elkins Act (1910), which gave the government control over telephone and telegraph rates. He encouraged Congress to propose an income tax.

>> Analyze Political Cartoons What clues in this cartoon reveal what type of policies the author believes Taft will enact as president?

1 of 7 >

DIGITAL TEXT 4

Wilson Endorses Further Regulation

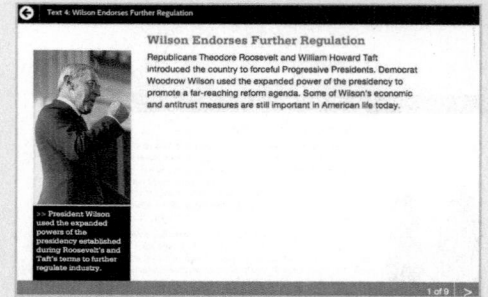

Wilson Endorses Further Regulation

Republicans Theodore Roosevelt and William Howard Taft introduced the country to forceful Progressive Presidents. Democrat Woodrow Wilson used the expanded power of the presidency to promote a far-reaching reform agenda. Some of Wilson's economic and antitrust measures are still important in American life today.

>> President Wilson used the expanded powers of the presidency established during Roosevelt's and Taft's terms to further regulate industry.

1 of 9 >

Objective 3: Compare and contrast Roosevelt's policies with Taft's and Wilson's policies.

Quick Instruction

Review with students the highlights of the American presidency following Roosevelt's departure after his second term: Roosevelt helped his Secretary of War William Howard Taft win the presidency in 1908, expecting Taft to continue his policies. Roosevelt, upset by Taft's domestic and foreign policies, spoke of his ideas for New Nationalism (restoring the government's trust-busing power). He formed the Progressive Party, which split off from the Republican Party. Roosevelt was the Progressive Party's candidate for the 1912 presidential election. This split the Republican vote, allowing Democrat Woodrow Wilson to capture the presidency.

Analyze Charts Project the chart comparing and contrasting Taft and Roosevelt. Review with students the highlights of the American presidency following Roosevelt's departure after his second term: Roosevelt helped his Secretary of War William Howard Taft win the presidency in 1908, expecting Taft to continue his policies. Taft forged his own path, however, supporting the Payne-Aldrich Act and the Mann-Elkins Act, both of which continued to change the relationship between federal government and private business.

Categorize Distinguish between Roosevelt's and Taft's views on foreign policy. Why would you categorize Taft's *dollar* diplomacy as less aggressive than Roosevelt's *dollar* diplomacy? *(While Roosevelt preferred an aggressive, "big stick" diplomacy. Taft promoted "dollar"*

diplomacy, which sought to promote American interests with trade and investment in foreign countries.)

Further Instruction

Summarize Remind students that Roosevelt left the presidency voluntarily, and fully expected his Secretary of War William Howard Taft, whom he helped win the presidency to continue his programs of managing business and natural resources. Taft did not do so, and the Taft-Roosevelt battle split the Republican Party. Roosevelt and other progressives split from the Republican party and set up the Progressive Party. Ask: What was the impact of the Progressive Party? *(The Progressive Party split the Republican vote, allowing Democrat Woodrow Wilson to capture the presidency in the next election. Thus, the differences between Roosevelt and Taft were not simply policy disagreements, but a serious divide that altered the course of American history.)*

Compare Points of View How did President Taft's view of the relationship between the federal government and private business differ from that of his predecessor, President Roosevelt? *(Taft dropped Roosevelt's distinction between good trusts and bad trusts. Taft's administration also prosecuted corporations at twice the rate that Roosevelt's had done.)*

Objective 4: Describe Wilson's efforts to regulate the economy.

Quick Instruction

Interactive Chart: Roosevelt and Wilson Project the chart. Introduce it by reminding students that both Theodore Roosevelt and Woodrow Wilson were reformers, but they had different ideas about Progressive Era reforms and how to achieve them. Guide students as they distinguish between Roosevelt's and Wilson's views on the economy, government regulation, social reform, and effective leadership.

Compare Points of View Evaluate the impact of the Sixteenth Amendment from the rationale of those for and against its passage. Why were some against and some for a federal income tax? *(Some were concerned an income tax would limit economic growth. Others thought the public investment from income tax monies would stimulate economic growth.)*

▶ ACTIVE CLASSROOM

List the following policies of the Wilson administration on the board: Underwood Tariff Bill, income tax, Federal Reserve Act, Federal Trade Commission (FTC), Clayton Antitrust Act, Workingman's Compensation Act.

- Tell students to rank the items from most to least influential.
- Direct students to provide justification for each ranking decisions they made.
- Ask students to work in pairs to share their rankings and justifications.
- Poll the class to see if there is agreement on the ranking.

INTERACTIVE CHART

Roosevelt and Wilson

DIGITAL TEXT 5

The Progressives' Legacy

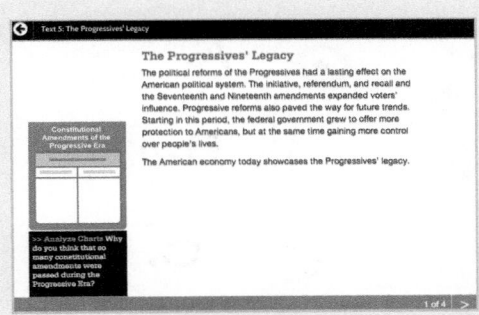

D Differentiate: **Challenge** Invite students to investigate the Federal Reserve System in more detail and create a web page about "The Fed's" role in the economy today.

ELL Use the ELL activity described in the ELL chart.

Further Instruction

Summarize Remind students that Wilson worked with Congress to establish the Federal Reserve in 1913. The Federal Reserve controls the money supply in the United States, with the goal of promoting economic stability and growth. Direct students to write brief essays that describe the emergence of monetary policy in the United States, including the Federal Reserve Act of 1913. (Students' essays should reflect an understanding of monetary policy (control of the money supply by a central authority, including influencing interest rates to promote economic growth and stability). Essays should note that, when Woodrow Wilson became president, there was no federal authority to supervise banks and establish monetary policy. Wilson pushed Congress to pass the Federal Reserve Act which placed commercial banks under the control of a Federal Reserve Board. The board established regional banks to hold the reserve funds from those commercial banks. The Federal Reserve Board also sets the interest rate that banks pay to borrow money from other banks and supervises banks.)

Objective 5: Assess the legacy of the Progressive Era.

Quick Instruction

Analyze Charts Project the chart of Progressive Era amendments. Invite students to identify the amendment they think had the most significant impact and explain the reasons for their choice. *(The Sixteenth Amendment provided for an income tax, the Seventeenth Amendment provided for the direct election of senators, and the Nineteenth Amendment extended suffrage to women.)*

Further Instruction

Summarize Ask students to summarize the major achievements of Progressive Era reformers. *(The initiative, referendum, and recall, the Seventeenth Amendment, the Nineteenth Amendment, antitrust laws, the Federal Reserve Board, consumer protections business regulation, and managing natural resources.)*

Reformers in the White House

■ SYNTHESIZE

DIGITAL ACTIVITY
Trust-Busting

Tell students to revise their paragraphs if the changes they want to make are minor. If they changes they want to make are more significant, it might be easier for them to rewrite them.

Discuss Discuss the term *trust-busting* with students. Now that they have a greater knowledge of the Progressive Era, how important of an achievement compared to other Progressive accomplishments do they think trust-busting was? Why? *(Trust-busting was probably very important, since it curbed the power of big businesses and opened the way for greater protections of small businesses and individuals.)*

■ DEMONSTRATE

DIGITAL QUIZ
Lesson Quiz and Class Discussion Board

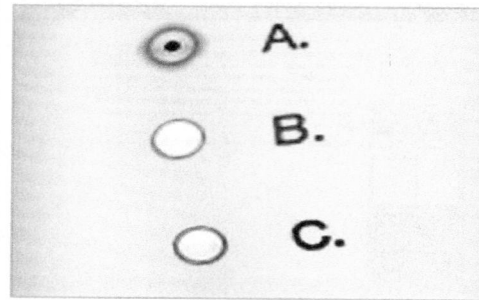

Assign the online Lesson Quiz for this lesson if you haven't already done so. Students will be offered automatic remediation or enrichment based on their score.

Pose these questions to the class on the Discussion Board:

Summarize Describe the changing relationship between the federal government and private business during the Progressive Era using specific examples from the text.

Express Ideas Clearly What is the significance of the Federal Reserve Act of 1913?

Topic Inquiry
Have students continue their investigations for the Topic Inquiry.

PEARSON
realize™
www.PearsonRealize.com
Access your Digital Lesson

American Influence Grows

Supporting English Language Learners

Use with Digital Text 1, **America on the World Stage.**

Learning
Read aloud the section titled Social Darwinism, Missionaries, and National Superiority. Articulate each syllable carefully to ensure students are able to distinguish the individual sounds of English in each sentence.

Beginning Review the letter *b* and the letter *p* sounds. Read words from the section beginning with those letters (began, best, been; picked, presence, potential). Ask students to identify the beginning sound, and then sort the words into a chart.

Intermediate Review the letter *b* and the letter *p* sounds. Read several words from the section with those letters in any position (embraced, about, ambitious; peoples, expand, spread). Ask students to identify the *p/b* sound, and sort the words into a chart.

Advanced Review the letter *f* and the letter *v* sounds. Read several words from the section with those letters in any position (justify, felt, influenced; over, survive, valve). Ask students to identify the *f/v* sound and spell out the word.

Advanced High Review the letter *f* and the letter *v* sounds. Then display several minimal pairs based on words from the text (belief/believe, life/live, safe/save, surf/serve). Read a word from each pair, and have students identify it.

Use with Digital Text 3, **The Acquisition of Hawaii.**

Reading
Read aloud the text after the heading **The Acquisition of Hawaii**, or invite volunteers to do so. Explain the purpose and general process of taking notes as you prompt students to demonstrate comprehension of increasingly complex English by taking notes commensurate with content area and grade level needs.

Beginning Display an outline with the text's title and three bullet points: rebels overthrow _____ in 1893; _____ apologizes for takeover; Hawaii becomes _____ in 1898. Guide students to complete the outline by locating the relevant information in the text.

Intermediate Have students write down the title of the reading, followed by six bullet points. Ask volunteers to read aloud. At the end of each paragraph, pause to discuss its main idea, and have students record the main idea in their own words next to a bullet point.

Advanced Tell students to write down the title of the reading, followed by six bullet points. Then have pairs of students read the text together. At the end of each paragraph, have them record its main idea next to a bullet point.

Advanced High Ask students to read the text independently, writing down important points as they go along. Give them time to reorganize or revise their notes if needed. Then have pairs of students compare the notes they took.

◨ Differentiate Instruction

Use the Differentiated Instruction notes throughout the lesson plan to support the varied skill sets, levels of readiness, and interests in the mixed-ability classroom.

Challenge These notes include suggestions for expanding the activity for advanced students.

On-Level These notes include suggestions for modifying the activity to address different interests or learning styles.

Extra Support These notes include ideas for providing more scaffolding or reading spuport.

Special Needs These notes provide ideas for adapting instruction to support the needs of various special needs students.

▪ NOTES

American Influence Grows

Objectives

Objective 1: Identify the key factors that caused Americans to want to take a greater roleoverseas.

Objective 2: Explain how the United States took its first steps toward the position of a world power.

Objective 3: Evaluate the acquisition of Hawaii by the United States.

LESSON 5 ORGANIZER		PACING: APPROX. 1 PERIOD, .5 BLOCKS			
		OBJECTIVES	PACING	RESOURCES	
				Online	Print
Connect					
	DIGITAL START UP ACTIVITY **America Eyes New Territories**		5 min.	●	
Investigate					
	DIGITAL TEXT 1 **America on the World Stage**	Objective 1	10 min.	●	●
	DIGITAL TEXT 2 **America Begins to Expand**	Objective 2	10 min.	●	●
	INTERACTIVE CHART **Reasons for American Expansionism**		10 min.	●	
	DIGITAL TEXT 3 **The Acquisition of Hawaii**	Objective 3	10 min.	●	●
	INTERACTIVE GALLERY **U.S. Economic Expansion in Hawaii**		10 min.	●	
Synthesize					
	DIGITAL ACTIVITY **Monitoring Understanding**		5 min.	●	
Demonstrate					
	DIGITAL QUIZ **Lesson Quiz and Class Discussion Board**		10 min.	●	

PEARSON •••
realize™
www.PearsonRealize.com

Go online to access additional resources including:
Primary Sources • Biographies • Supreme Court cases •
21st Century Skill Tutorials • Maps • Graphic Organizers.

■ CONNECT

DIGITAL START UP ACTIVITY
America Eyes New Territories

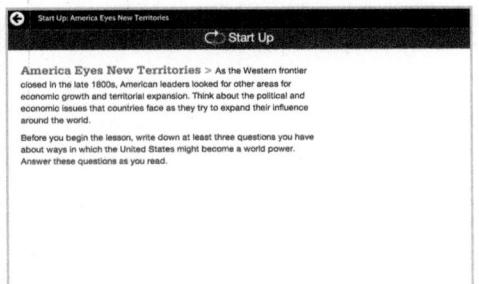

Project the Start Up Activity Encourage students to take a few minutes to think about the political and economic issues that countries face as they try to expand their influence around the world. Then have them write down at least three questions they have about ways in which the United States might become a world power. When they have completed their lists of questions, consider working together as a group to reach a consensus master list of the ten most important questions.

Tell students that in this lesson they will be learning how the United States emerged as a world power in the late nineteenth century.

Aa Vocabulary Development: Use the Interactive Reading Notepad to preview the Key Terms and Academic Vocabulary in the lesson with students.

⟳ FLIP IT!
Assign the Flipped Video for this lesson.

■ STUDENT EDITION PRINT PAGES: 423–427

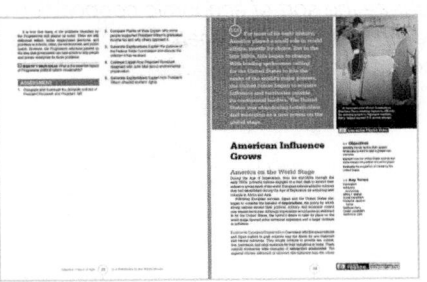

■ INVESTIGATE

DIGITAL TEXT 1
America on the World Stage

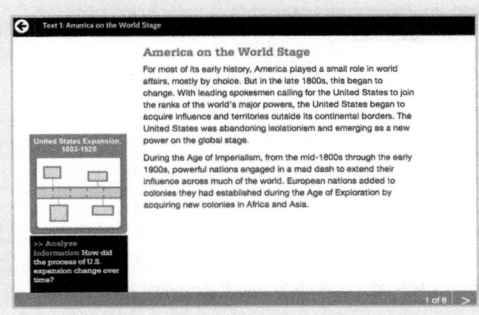

Objective 1: Identify the key factors that prodded America to expand.

Quick Instruction

Analyze Maps Project the map on the board and invite a volunteer to describe the reasons that European countries and the United States sought to expand their influence around the world. *(protect and expand economic and defense interests).* Make sure that students understand that most nations embarking on imperialism did so to acquire resources that their homelands needed. The United States had abundant resources but needed new markets in which to sell its surplus goods. Tell students that the U.S. had to increase its military strength in order to expand and protect their interests. Ask students to explain how and why significant individuals moved the United States into a position of a world power, including Alfred T. Mahan and Henry Cabot Lodge, and the actions they recommended. *(Henry Cabot Lodge and Alfred Thayer Mahan, both of whom believed a strong navy was key to expanding American interests abroad, played key roles in strengthening the naval power of the United States.)*

Apply Concepts Manifest Destiny was the nineteenth century American doctrine that held that westward expansion of the United States was not only inevitable, but a God-given right. How did U.S. expansion in the late nineteenth century extend and change the principle of Manifest Destiny? *(U.S. expansion in the late nineteenth century greatly expanded Manifest Destiny. The U.S. sought to gain greater influence throughout the world, not just within the North American continent.)*

ELL Use the ELL activity described in the ELL chart.

Further Instruction
Be sure that students understand that economic and military interests were just two of the causes of imperialism and expansionism. Remind students that nationalism and Social Darwinism were also influential in U.S. expansionism in the late nineteenth century. Review nationalism and the causes and effects of social issues such as Social Darwinism with the class.

Identify Central Issues How did missionaries move the United States into the position of a world power? *(U.S. missionaries traveled to foreign lands to convert people to Christianity. This strengthened U.S. presence in new territories.)*

Evaluate Information Which of the motives for U.S. expansionism do you think was the most important? Why? *Protecting and expanding economic interests was the most important because economic power had the greatest impact on the United States becoming a world power.)*

Identify Cause and Effect How did the idea of Social Darwinism first develop, and what effect did this idea have on U.S. expansionism? *(The idea first developed as a means to justify imperialism by asserting some races were superior to others. Some Americans in turn justified expansionism at home and overseas with the idea that doing so would help civilize and lift up native inhabitants.)*

American Influence Grows

DIGITAL TEXT 2

America Begins to Expand

INTERACTIVE CHART

Reasons for American Expansionism

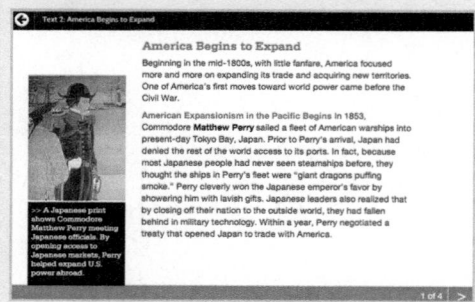

Objective 2: **Explain how the United States took its first steps toward the position of a world power.**

Quick Instruction

Interactive Chart: Reasons for American Expansionism Project the interactive chart. Review each of the actions with students by having a volunteer describe details associated with the actions. Then ask: Into which column would you place this action? Why? *(Answers will vary depending on context but should be supported.)* Discuss students' responses as a class.

Support Ideas with Evidence What impact did physical and human geographic factors have on the Klondike Gold Rush and economic development in Alaska? *(The availability of land, the discovery of natural resources, and of course, gold mines, prompted the Klondike Gold Rush. Unique climate conditions of the area, including long dark winters, complicated miners' attempts to extract gold from the land. The Gold Rush itself was short-lived, but economic growth continued as other resources were put to use, and new towns continued to develop even after the Gold Rush was over.)*

🎭 ACTIVE CLASSROOM
Have students Take a Stand.

- Ask students to take on the role of politicians in the late 1800s and take a stand on the following issue: Should the United States embark on a era of expansionism throughout the world?
- Ask students to divide into two groups based on their answer and move to separate areas of the classroom.
- Ask students to talk with each other to compare their reasons for their answers.
- Ask a representative from each side to present and defend the group's point of view.

D Differentiate: Challenge/Gifted Ask students to go online or to the library to research regions and countries in the world in which the United States has a significant military presence today. Invite students to share their findings.

Further Instruction
Remind students that U.S. expansionism outside of its borders began before the Civil War. Ask students to find examples of U.S. expansionism from the 1850s through the end of the nineteenth century and identify key figures associated with the examples.

(Matthew Perry led an American fleet into Tokyo to open Japanese ports to world markets. Secretary of State William Seward bought Alaska from Russia for $7.2 million in 1867, which provided a new source of valuable natural resources for the country and led to the Klondike Gold Rush. Secretary of State James Blaine pushed for economic cooperation between the United States and Latin American countries. This helped lead to the Pan-American Highway system, which linked the United States to Central and South America.)

Summarize Ask students to summarize Britain's reaction to the growing U.S. presence in Latin America. *(Britain was upset with the United States because it was losing power in Latin American countries in which they had once held great influence. But after some tension over a border issue in South America, Britain accepted America's growing influence in Latin America.)*

Generate Explanations What relation did foreign policy issues in Latin America have to U.S. economic growth in the region? *(The United States had an economic interest in maintaining the policies of the Monroe Doctrine in Latin America to encourage political stability. Political stability in turn would facilitate the sort of economic cooperation and growth that the Pan-American Conference encouraged.)*

PEARSON **realize**™ www.PearsonRealize.com Access your Digital Lesson

DIGITAL TEXT 3

The Acquisition of Hawaii

INTERACTIVE GALLERY

U.S. Economic Expansion in Hawaii

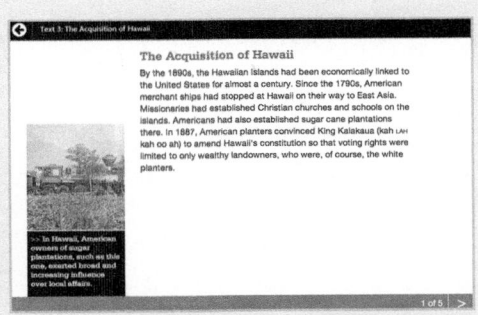

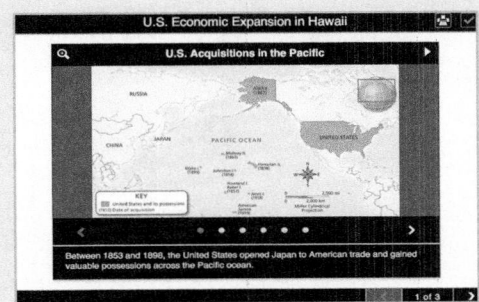

Objective 3: Evaluate the acquisition of Hawaii by the United States.

Quick Instruction

Interactive Gallery: U.S. Economic Expansion in Hawaii Project the interactive gallery on the whiteboard and view the images and charts individually. Introduce the interactivity by telling students that as trade with Asia grew in the 1800s, Americans needed adequate ports where they could refuel and resupply while crossing the Pacific Ocean. Ask: What made Hawaii such an attractive location to American businesses and shipping fleets? *(Hawaii was centrally located for ships crossing the Pacific Ocean. Also, the islands were ideally suited for growing several valuable products, such as pineapples, sugarcane, and coffee.)*

Support a Point of View with Evidence Evaluate the U.S. acquisition of Hawaii. Were the Hawaiian Islands a great enough economic interest to justify the United States pressing for annexation? Why or why not? *(Yes: Hawaii could provide great economic benefits for the United States as well as being a strategic position in the Pacific Ocean. No: Hawaii was too small to risk an armed conflict over, the United States had a foothold in other Pacific islands at the time.)*

Express Problems Clearly Based on John Stevens's quote on screen two of the interactivity, what was the biggest obstacle blocking the full economic and political development of Hawaii? *(the monarchy)*

📷 ACTIVE CLASSROOM

Have students imagine they are having a conversation with Queen Liliuokalani or Sanford B. Dole. Tell students to write down a question they'd like to ask and a probable reply from the Queen or Mr. Dole. Encourage students to write what they'd say about the issue of the annexation of Hawaii.

Further Instruction

Point out that the white American presence in Hawaii created a great deal of tension between the wealthy planters and Hawaiians. Ask students to identify examples of growing problems in Hawaii in the late 1800s. *(Wealthy planters pressured the Hawaiian King to change Hawaii's constitution, giving the minority planters more power. Queen Liliuokalani resented the increasing power of the white planters and abolished the amended constitution. Wealthy planters overthrew the queen. A majority of Hawaiians did not approve of the annexation treaty.)*

Be sure that students understand how significant individuals such as John Stevens and Sanford B. Dole and moved the United States into the position of a world power.

Identify Cause and Effect How did the missionaries who visited Hawaii contribute to the eventual annexation of Hawaii and great power for the United States? *(Missionaries were some of the first Americans to settle on the Hawaiian Islands. As more white Americans settled the islands, they established agricultural industries that would become very influential in shaping the future of Hawaii.)*

Summarize What role did Sanford B. Dole play in the acquisition of Hawaii? *(Sanford Dole led the Hawaiian government following the overthrow of the Queen. After annexation in 1898, Dole became the first governor of the new U.S. territory.)*

American Influence Grows

SYNTHESIZE

DEMONSTRATE

DIGITAL ACTIVITY
Monitoring Understanding

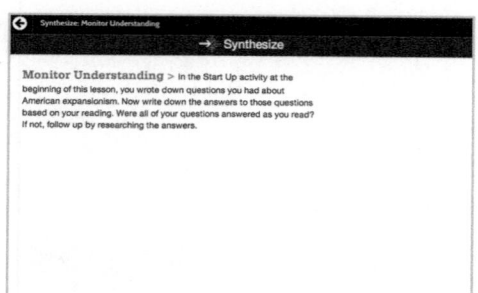

DIGITAL QUIZ
Lesson Quiz and Class Discussion Board

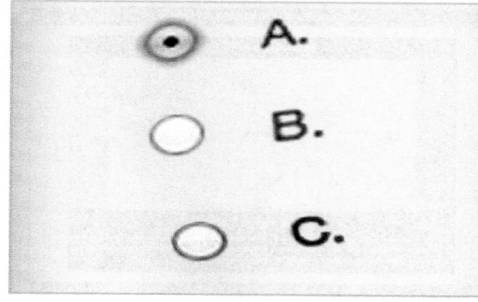

Ask students to recall the questions they had about American expansionism in the Start Up Activity at the beginning of this lesson. Provide time for students to review the answers to their questions based on reading the lesson. Discuss if all of the students' questions were answered. If not, follow up by researching the answers.

Discuss Have partners take five minutes to list the costs and benefits of American expansionism described in the Lesson. Ask students to create a new list of questions they have after reading. Have pairs share their questions with the class.

Assign the online Lesson Quiz for this lesson if you haven't already done so. Students will be offered automatic remediation or enrichment based on their score.

Pose these questions to the class on the Discussion Board:

In *American Influence Grows*, you read about the forces that drove the United States to enter a period of expansionism in the late 1800s. International economic and military competition convinced many Americans that the nation must become a world power.

Draw Conclusions What factors make a nation a world power? *(A world power must have a strong military capable of fighting multiple conflicts anywhere in the world. A strong, stable government is also needed to be a world power. In addition, I think world powers are respected by other nations, not just because of military might, but also because they symbolize opportunities and high standards and quality of life for their citizens.)*

Infer What responsibilities come with being a world power? *(World powers are often asked to resolve issues between other countries, either through economic or military means. A world power also must act responsibly toward less powerful nations.)*

Topic Inquiry
Have students continue their investigations for the Topic Inquiry.

The Spanish-American War

PEARSON realize.™

www.PearsonRealize.com
Access your Digital Lesson

Supporting English Language Learners

Use with Digital Text 1, **The Causes of the Spanish-American War.**

Listening
Read aloud the text with proper intonation. Emphasize syllables, words, and phrases as warranted so students may distinguish intonation patterns with increasing ease.

Beginning Display several multisyllabic words from the text (e.g., referred, thoroughness, dilemma). Say each word with correct intonation, and ask students to underline the stressed syllable. Then reread the words, and have students repeat after you.

Intermediate Display several phrases from the text. Say each phrase with correct intonation, and ask students to underline the stressed syllable or word. Then have students read the phrases using correct intonation.

Advanced Read aloud the introductory paragraph with correct intonation, sentence by sentence. Ask students to identify the words that you emphasized, as well as why you might have chosen to do so.

Advanced High Select various sentences from the text. Read each sentence two ways, with correct and incorrect intonation. Have students identify what you stressed in each version. Ask: Which version did I read correctly, and why do you think so?

Use with Digital Text 2, **American Forces Defeat the Spanish.**

Reading
Introduce the text by reading its title and subheadings, and by summarizing its main ideas. Explain that students will practice reading the text silently with the goal of doing so for increasingly longer periods of time.

Beginning Explain how to slow down to sound out and reread difficult words. Have students silently read the text's first sentence. Then read the sentence aloud so students can check how they did. Repeat this process for the entire paragraph.

Intermediate Explain how to minimize distractions and slow down to sound out and reread difficult words. Have students silently read the introductory paragraph. Afterward, encourage them to ask questions about difficulties they had. Then have them reread it.

Advanced Discuss the strategies of minimizing distractions and slowing down to sound out and reread difficult words. Have students read the entire text without rushing; if they finish early, have them read it again.

Advanced High Discuss the strategy of slowing down and rereading passages to increase fluent reading. Have students read the entire text without rushing; if they finish early, have them read it again.

▶ Differentiate Instruction

Use the Differentiated Instruction notes throughout the lesson plan to support the varied skill sets, levels of readiness, and interests in the mixed-ability classroom.

Challenge These notes include suggestions for expanding the activity for advanced students.

On-Level These notes include suggestions for modifying the activity to address different interests or learning styles.

Extra Support These notes include ideas for providing more scaffolding or reading spuport.

Special Needs These notes provide ideas for adapting instruction to support the needs of various special needs students.

■ NOTES

The Spanish-American War

Objectives

Objective 1: Explain the causes of the Spanish-American War.

Objective 2: Identify the major battles of the Spanish-American War.

Objective 3: Describe the consequences of the war, including the debate over imperialism.

Objective 4: Examine the causes and consequences of the Philippine insurrection.

LESSON 6 ORGANIZER		PACING: APPROX. 1 PERIOD, .5 BLOCKS			
				RESOURCES	
		OBJECTIVES	PACING	Online	Print
Connect					
DIGITAL START UP ACTIVITY **Remember the Maine**			5 min.	●	
Investigate					
DIGITAL TEXT 1 **Causes of the Spanish-American War**		Objective 1	10 min.	●	●
INTERACTIVE GALLERY **Media and the Spanish-American War**			10 min.	●	
DIGITAL TEXT 2 **American Forces Defeat the Spanish**		Objective 2	10 min.	●	●
DIGITAL TEXT 3 **The War as a Turning Point**		Objective 3	10 min.	●	●
INTERACTIVE CHART **Points of View on American Expansionism**			10 min.	●	
DIGITAL TEXT 4 **Effects of U.S. Expansionism in the Philippines**		Objective 4	10 min.	●	●
Synthesize					
DIGITAL ACTIVITY **Key Events of the Spanish-American War**			5 min.	●	
Demonstrate					
DIGITAL QUIZ **Lesson Quiz and Class Discussion Board**			10 min.	●	

PEARSON
realize.™
www.PearsonRealize.com

Go online to access additional resources including:
Primary Sources • Biographies • Supreme Court cases •
21st Century Skill Tutorials • Maps • Graphic Organizers.

CONNECT

DIGITAL START UP ACTIVITY
Remember the Maine

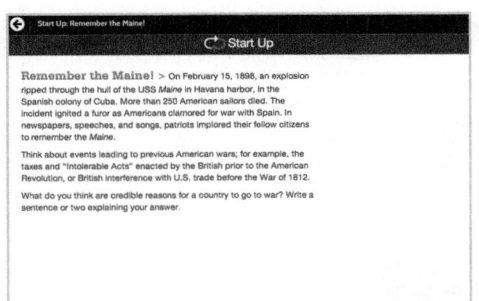

Project the Start Up Activity Ask students to think about the questions as they enter and get settled. Then have them share their ideas with another student.

Discuss What do you think are credible reasons for a country to go to war? *(A country is justified in going to war when it is attacked or when its citizens are attacked or threatened by another country.)*

Tell students that in this lesson they will be learning about the causes and effects of the war between the United States and Spain in 1898.

Aa Vocabulary Development: Use the Interactive Reading Notepad to preview the Key Terms and Academic Vocabulary in this lesson with students.

↑↓ FLIP IT!

Assign the Flipped Video for this lesson.

■ STUDENT EDITION PRINT PAGES: 428–435

INVESTIGATE

DIGITAL TEXT 1
Causes of the Spanish-American War

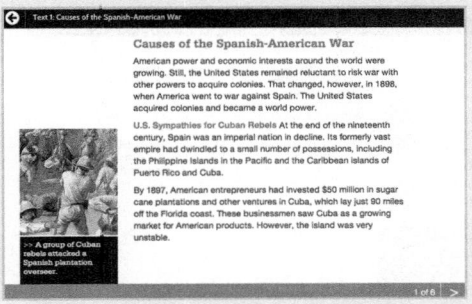

Objective 1: Explain the causes of the Spanish-American War.

Quick Instruction

Interactive Gallery: Media and the Spanish-American War Project the interactive gallery. Look at each image individually and then the collection of images as a whole.

Analyze Images Based on the images in the gallery, what significant role did the media play in the beginning of the Spanish-American War? *(The media spread knowledge of the Maine's sinking and had strong opinions about what the United States should do in retaliation.)*

ELL Use the ELL activity described in the ELL chart.

D Differentiate: Extra Support Explain that "yellow press" is another term for sensational journalism that often includes exaggerated stories. Invite students to give an example of a current form of yellow press in the media.

■■ ACTIVE CLASSROOM

Have students break into groups and use the Circle Write Strategy to address the prompt, "How did the media influence American public opinion about the war with Spain?" Have students write as much as they can for 1 minute and then switch with the person on their right. The next person tries to improve or elaborate the response where the other person left off. Continue to switch until the paper comes back to the first person. The group decides which is the best composition and shares that with the class.

INTERACTIVE GALLERY
Media and the Spanish-American War

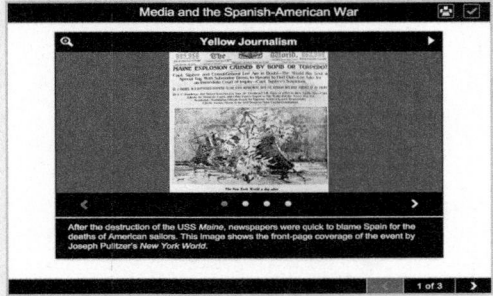

Further Instruction

Review the causes of the Spanish-American War as a class by inviting volunteers to summarize the political and economic issues that led to the outbreak of war. Be sure students understand that American leaders objected to Spain's presence in Cuba as a violation of the Monroe Doctrine and also because of Spain's treatment of the Cuban people fighting for freedom, a cause with which many Americans sympathized. Students should also describe the political instability in Cuba created economic worries for American businesses and entrepreneurs who had large investments on the island.

Identify Central Issues How did the outbreak of the Spanish-American War move the United States into a position of a world power? *(The United States had been building a larger and more powerful military in the last decades of the 1800s. The Spanish-American War was the opportunity for the United States to show the world how powerful it was. Waging the war in several locations spread across several oceans required great resources, demonstrating that power.)*

Predict Consequences Ask students to predict the significance of 1898 and the outbreak of the Spanish-American War. Encourage students to think about how the war will affect U.S. participation on the international stage. *(1898 will be a key year in U.S. history because winning the war with Spain was a turning point for the United States. It will become one of the most powerful countries in the world.)*

The Spanish-American War

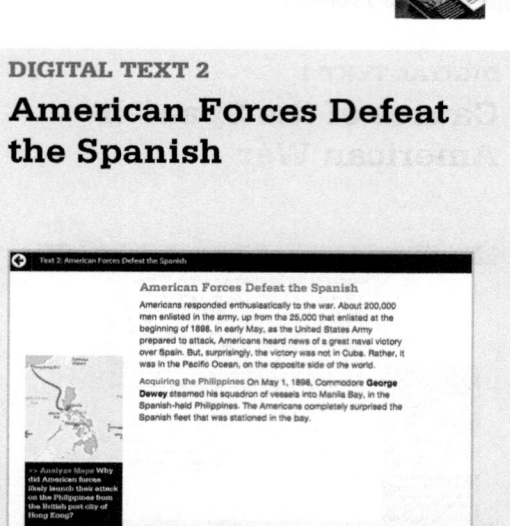

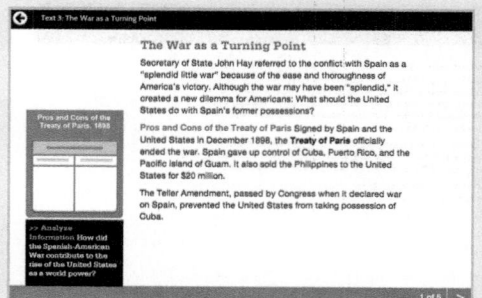

DIGITAL TEXT 2

American Forces Defeat the Spanish

American Forces Defeat the Spanish

Americans responded enthusiastically to the war. About 200,000 men enlisted in the army, up from the 25,000 that enlisted at the beginning of 1898. In early May, as the United States Army prepared to attack, Americans heard news of a great naval victory over Spain. But, surprisingly, the victory was not in Cuba. Rather, it was in the Pacific Ocean, on the opposite side of the world.

Acquiring the Philippines On May 1, 1898, Commodore **George Dewey** steamed his squadron of vessels into Manila Bay, in the Spanish-held Philippines. The Americans completely surprised the Spanish fleet that was stationed in the bay.

>> Analyze Maps Why did American forces likely launch their attack on the Philippines from the British port city of Hong Kong?

1 of 6 >

DIGITAL TEXT 3

The War as a Turning Point

The War as a Turning Point

Secretary of State John Hay referred to the conflict with Spain as a "splendid little war" because of the ease and thoroughness of America's victory. Although the war may have been "splendid," it created a new dilemma for Americans: What should the United States do with Spain's former possessions?

Pros and Cons of the Treaty of Paris Signed by Spain and the United States in December 1898, the **Treaty of Paris** officially ended the war. Spain gave up control of Cuba, Puerto Rico, and the Pacific island of Guam. It also sold the Philippines to the United States for $20 million.

The Teller Amendment, passed by Congress when it declared war on Spain, prevented the United States from taking possession of Cuba.

>> Analyze Information How did the Spanish-American War contribute to the rise of the United States as a world power?

1 of 5 >

Generate Explanations Was the media justified in stoking patriotism and feelings of revenge for the sinking of the *Maine*? Why or why not? *(Yes, the media did what was necessary at the time. The United States could not let the destruction of the Maine go without punishment, and most people assumed that Spain was connected to the sinking. No, the media should have reported the events with as little bias as possible and let public opinion evolve on its own.)*

Objective 2: Identify the major battles of the Spanish-American War.

Quick Instruction

Explain that when the United States declared war on Spain, Congress passed the Teller Amendment, which prevented the United States from taking possession of Cuba. The amendment did not, however, apply to the Philippines.

Take several minutes to discuss the key battles of the Spanish-American War. Consider focusing the discussion either chronologically or by theater of operations (Pacific Theater and Caribbean Theater). Ask students to identify key battles on each front. *(Manila Bay; surrender of Spanish forces in the Philippines; capture of Guantanamo Bay; battles of Kettle Hill and San Juan Hill; Santiago Harbor; smaller battles on Puerto Rico.)*

Summarize What role did Theodore Roosevelt play during the Spanish-American War that helped to move the United States into the position of a world power? *(Roosevelt helped lead the assaults on Kettle and San Juan hills near Santiago, Cuba. The battles essentially ended the Spanish ground war in Cuba, leading to the U.S. victory.)*

ELL Use the ELL activity described in the ELL chart.

Further Instruction

Contrast Compared to earlier wars in which U.S. forces fought, how was the Spanish-American War different? *(The Spanish-American War was one of the first foreign wars Americans fought in. Unlike the Civil War, the Spanish-American War was very quick, and American casualties were not as great.)*

Objective 3: Describe the consequences of the war, including the debate over imperialism.

Quick Instruction

Remind students that the Treaty of Paris marked the official end the war. By signing the treaty, Spain gave up control of Cuba, Puerto Rico, and the Pacific island of Guam. It also sold the Philippines to the United States for $20 million.

Interactive Chart: Points of View on American Expansionism Project the interactive chart. Ask volunteers to read each quote aloud. Then ask: With which quote do you most agree? Why? *(I think Mark Twain presents a stronger case. It was clear that the United States wanted to keep possession of the Philippines, unlike Cuba. Rather than fighting for the Filipinos freedom, the United States was fighting mostly for economic and political gains.)*

Draw Conclusions Based on your reading of the quote, what is Henry Cabot Lodge's chief argument for acquiring the Philippines? *(Lodge thinks that the Filipinos will eventually be taken over by another country or a dictator. By controlling the Philippines, the United States would help the Filipino people, promote democracy, and ensure that the United States moves into the position of a world power.)*

INTERACTIVE CHART
Points of View on American Expansionism

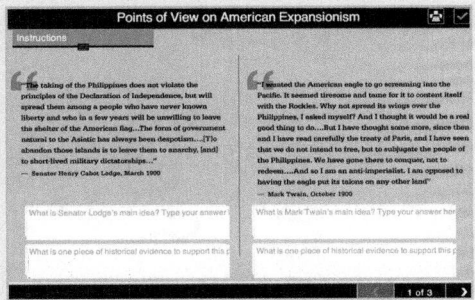

💬 ACTIVE CLASSROOM

Using the Quick Write Strategy, engage students in writing what they know about the issues surrounding the debate about the acquisition of the Philippines. Give students 30 seconds to respond and then ask them to share their writing with a partner.

Further Instruction

Point out to students that victory in the Spanish-American War and the acquisition of many new territories placed the United States in a position in which it had never been before: a global power with colonies. This position sparked debate among American politicians, writers, activists, and business leaders.

Express Ideas Clearly From the American perspective, how would you evaluate the pros of U.S. participation in international treaties such as the Treaty of Paris? What were the cons for the United States with this treaty? *(The pros in this case were that the treaty gave the United States basically everything it fought for in the war. Spain no longer had a significant presence in the Caribbean, near U.S. soil, and the United States was able to ensure acquisition of the Philippines. The treaty also mandated American acquisitions such as Guam and Puerto Rico. The cons in this case were that now the United States had to determine how to manage the Philippines, which ultimately led to an insurrection in which many more soldiers died than in the Spanish-American War.)*

Summarize Arguments What were the main arguments used by imperialists and anti-imperialists to support their positions? *(Imperialists believed that the United States would benefit economically and strategically by acquiring the former Spanish territories. Many imperialists also argued that the United States had a moral obligation to "civilize" and teach the people of the new territories and to spread U.S. culture. Anti-imperialists thought that American expansionism betrayed the principles of American democracy.)*

Evaluate Impact Who was William Jennings Bryan and what impact did he have on U.S. foreign policy? *(Bryan was a leading anti-imperialist who helped form the American Anti-Imperialist League. Bryan and others provided an opposing view to American expansionism. The anti-imperialists' fight against American expansionism stoked the debate, including tight votes in the U.S. Senate.)*

DIGITAL TEXT 4
Effects of U.S. Expansionism in the Philippines

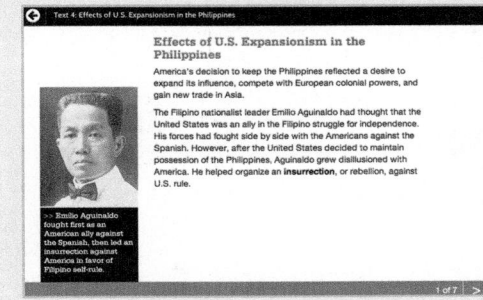

Objective 4: **Examine the causes and consequences of the Philippine insurrection**

Quick Instruction

Point out to students that to fight the Spanish-American War, the United States had to locate army and naval forces on two fronts thousands of miles apart. During the Philippine insurrection, American forces had to learn to fight against guerrilla insurgents.

Analyze Images Project the image of the Filipino school. Invite students to discuss how the Filipino students might have felt about their new school and the future of their country. Ask students: What responsibilities should a colonial power, such as the United States, assume upon taking over a nation like the Philippines? *(The United States should provide military and civil protection and assist in the formation of a stable government. Responsibilities like education and local government should be left to the citizens.)* Challenge students to summarize the American involvement in the Philippines following the Spanish-American War. Ask: What was the Filipino reaction to the continued U.S. presence in the Philippines? *(Filipino nationalists resented the U.S. presence and felt betrayed the United States)*

Support a Point of View with Evidence Evaluate U.S. expansionism in the Philippines. Do you think the United States made the right choice in ratifying the Treaty of Paris? *(No: I think the acquisition of the Philippines was a low-point in U.S. foreign policy. The Filipino insurrection led to hundreds*

The Spanish-American War

SYNTHESIZE

DEMONSTRATE

DIGITAL ACTIVITY
Key Events of the Spanish-American War

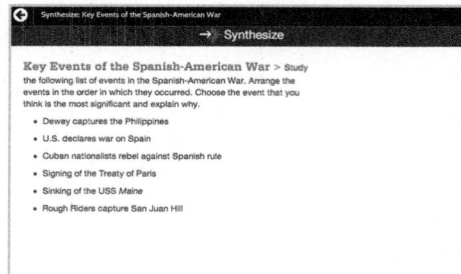

DIGITAL QUIZ
Lesson Quiz and Class Discussion Board

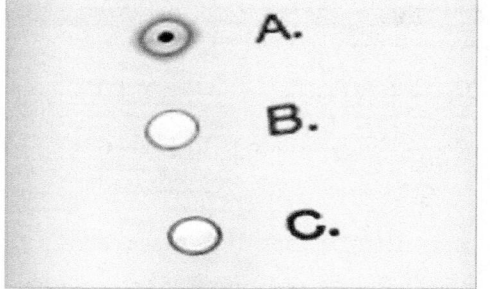

of thousands dead Filipinos and cost the United States several thousand lives. In order to gain control of the Philippines, U.S. forces had to take cruel measures similar to those that Spain used on the Cuban people. Yes: The economic benefits of acquiring the Philippines, as well as Guam and Puerto Rico, outweighed the costs of a relatively quick war. Access to additional resources and trade would raise standards of living.)

Further Instruction
Review the causes and effects of the Spanish-American War. Be sure that students understand that the war marked a turning point in the history of U.S. foreign policy. As a result of the Spanish-American War, the United States had overseas possessions and a new stature in world affairs.

Identify Central Issues Describe the economic effects of international military conflicts, such as the Spanish-American War and the Filipino Insurrection, on the United States. (The two-front Spanish-American War was incredibly expensive for the United States to fight. Army and navy forces were spread out on two fronts in two different parts of the world. The Filipino insurrection cost the U.S. government almost a half-billion dollars and the army had to supply more than 100,000 thousand soldiers. However, following the conflicts, American business interests in the Pacific and the Caribbean did expand.)

Make Predictions How will the United States be affected by its new stature in world affairs? (I think the United States will take a more active role in settling conflicts overseas. This will probably lead to more wars or small-scale conflicts. American businesses will probably have more of a presence in foreign countries.)

Discuss Before students begin the task, lead a brief discussion to ensure student understanding of the significance of 1898 and the fundamentals of the Spanish-American War. Have students work with a partner to complete the Key Events of the Spanish-American War Activity. Have pairs share their lists and their answers with the class.

Assign the online Lesson Quiz for this lesson if you haven't already done so. Students will be offered automatic remediation or enrichment based on their score.

Post these questions to the class on the Discussion Board.

In The Spanish-American War, you read about America's emergence as a world power. The United States used its growing military—including its powerful navy—to defeat Spain and to suppress the Filipino insurrection. The United States also used economic and political power to shape relations with foreign nations and its newly-won territories.

Generate Explanations How did the United States exert its power over the Philippines following the Spanish-American War?

Compare and Contrast How was the Spanish-American War similar to conflicts fought today? How was it different?

Topic Inquiry
Have students continue their investigations for the Topic Inquiry.

The United States Emerges as a World Power

Supporting English Language Learners

Use with Digital Text 1, **U.S. Trade and Intervention in China.**

Listening

Read aloud the introductory paragraphs of the text. Point out the boldface term *spheres of influence* and discuss its meaning. Prompt students to recognize the consonant cluster /f/ in order to help them recognize elements of the English sound system in newly acquired vocabulary.

Beginning Display the term *spheres of influence*. Ask students to listen for /f/ while you point to each word part and sound it out. Have students identify the letter or letters that represent /f/ in *spheres* and *influence*.

Intermediate Display the term *spheres of influence*. Ask students to listen for /f/ as you sound out each word. Have them identify the letter or letters that represent /f/ in *spheres* and *influence*. Ask: What sound does the f in of make?

Advanced Display the term *spheres of influence*. Have students read it and identify the ph and f that represent /f/ in *spheres* and *influence*. Ask: What sound does the f in of make? Then have students locate other /f/ words in the paragraphs.

Advanced High Display the term *spheres of influence*. Have students compare and contrast the sounds and spelling of *spheres* and *influence* using a Venn diagram (similarities include the presence of /f/, silent e, and consonant clusters).

Use with Digital Text 4, **"Big Stick" Diplomacy.**

Reading

Introduce the text by reading its title and subheadings. Explain that students will silently read some or all of the text for comprehension of these topics.

Beginning Discuss how to guess new words' meanings by rereading and using context clues. Have students read the first sentence of the text's first paragraph, and help them restate it in their own words. Continue this process for the entire paragraph.

Intermediate Discuss how to guess a new word's meaning by rereading and using context clues. Then have students try out both strategies while reading the section titled *Physical and Geographic Factors Impact the Panama Canal*.

Advanced Discuss the pros and cons of using a dictionary and using context clues to understand new words during silent reading. Have students try out both strategies while reading the text.

Advanced High Discuss the benefits of pausing during reading to reflect on what was just read. Have students try out this technique while silently reading the text, pausing at intervals to mentally digest and respond to it.

Ⓓ Differentiate Instruction

Use the Differentiated Instruction notes throughout the lesson plan to support the varied skill sets, levels of readiness, and interests in the mixed-ability classroom.

Challenge These notes include suggestions for expanding the activity for advanced students.

On-Level These notes include suggestions for modifying the activity to address different interests or learning styles.

Extra Support These notes include ideas for providing more scaffolding or reading spuport.

Special Needs These notes provide ideas for adapting instruction to support the needs of various special needs students.

■ NOTES

The United States Emerges as a World Power

Objectives

Objective 1: Analyze how economic concerns influenced the Open Door Policy and U.S. relations with Japan.

Objective 2: Examine what happened to Puerto Rico and Cuba after the Spanish-American War.

Objective 3: Analyze the effects of Roosevelt's "big stick" diplomacy and Taft's "dollar diplomacy."

Objective 4: Compare Wilson's "moral diplomacy" with the foreign policies of his predecessors.

LESSON 7 ORGANIZER		PACING: APPROX. 1 PERIOD, .5 BLOCKS		
	OBJECTIVES	PACING	RESOURCES	
			Online	Print
Connect				
DIGITAL START UP ACTIVITY **The Role of American Power**		5 min.	●	
Investigate				
DIGITAL TEXT 1 **U.S. Trade and Intervention in China**	Objective 1	10 min.	●	●
DIGITAL TEXT 2 **Roosevelt Works With Japan**		10 min.	●	●
DIGITAL TEXT 3 **American Foreign Policy in Latin America**	Objective 2	10 min.	●	●
DIGITAL TEXT 4 **"Big Stick" Diplomacy**	Objective 3	10 min.	●	●
INTERACTIVE GALLERY **The Panama Canal**		10 min.	●	
DIGITAL TEXT 5 **Wilson's "Moral Diplomacy"**	Objective 4	10 min.	●	●
INTERACTIVE MAP **U.S. Interventions in Latin America**		10 min.	●	
Synthesize				
DIGITAL ACTIVITY **Understanding American Expansionism**		5 min.	●	
Demonstrate				
DIGITAL QUIZ **Lesson Quiz and Class Discussion Board**		10 min.	●	

 PEARSON **realize**™
www.PearsonRealize.com

Go online to access additional resources including:
Primary Sources • Biographies • Supreme Court cases •
21st Century Skill Tutorials • Maps • Graphic Organizers.

■ CONNECT

DIGITAL START UP ACTIVITY
The Role of American Power

As students enter and get settled, ask them to think about how the United States had grown to become a world power and the responsibilities that come with it. Invite volunteers to read the quotations from Albert J. Beveridge and William Jennings Bryan.

Discuss What are Beveridge's and Bryan's visions of America's role in the twentieth century? After students write their responses, have them share their work with the class. Encourage students to work with a partner to Think-Pair-Share the thoughts on whose vision they most agree with.

Tell students that in this lesson they will be learning how the United States used its newly earned power as a new century began.

Aa Vocabulary Development Use the Interactive Reading Notepad to preview the Key Terms and Academic Vocabulary in this lesson with students.

⇅ FLIP IT!

Assign the Flipped Video for this lesson.

■ STUDENT EDITION PRINT PAGES: 436–444

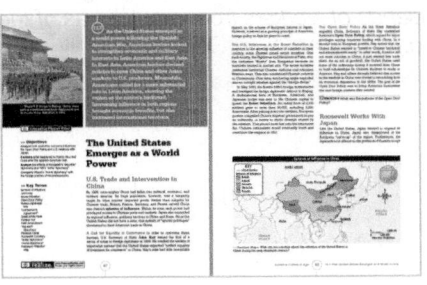

■ INVESTIGATE

DIGITAL TEXT 1
U.S. Trade and Intervention in China

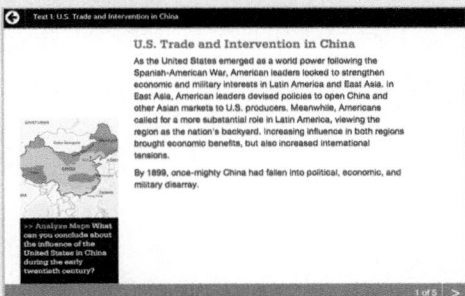

Objective 1: Analyze how economic concerns influenced the Open Door Policy and U.S. relations with Japan.

Quick Instruction

Digital Map: Spheres of Influence in China Discuss the map with students and invite them to draw conclusions about the information. Ask: Why were so many countries interested in pursuing spheres of influence in China? *(China was potentially a gigantic trade market in which countries could buy and sell goods. China was also going through turbulent political troubles at the turn of the century, so many countries wanted to protect their interests.)*

Infer Explain how foreign policies such as the Open Door Policy affected economic issues. *(As western powers consolidated their spheres of influence in China, the United States worried that its trade opportunities in China would shrink. John Hay had to resort to political, that is, foreign policy, tactics in order for the United States to gain access to Chinese markets. He issued the Open Door Policy to state U.S. intentions to trade in China.)*

ELL Use the ELL activity described in the ELL chart.

Further Instruction

President Theodore Roosevelt saw the importance of maintaining good relations with Asian countries, including Japan. Roosevelt's decision to act as a peacemaker strengthened its standing among nations in the region and helped to show that the United States had truly moved into the position of a world power.

DIGITAL TEXT 2
Roosevelt Works With Japan

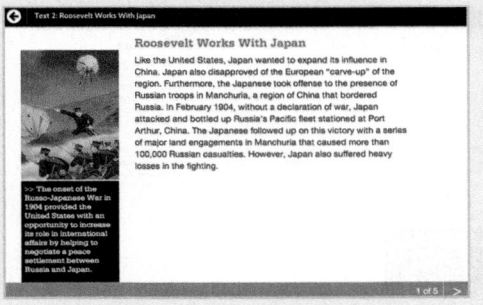

Identify Central Issues Ask students to identify the key issues related to Japan with which Roosevelt dealt. *(Negotiating peace in the Russo-Japanese War; brokering a "gentleman's agreement" that ended racial segregation in schools in San Francisco in exchange for changes to Japanese immigration policies; show of military strength to warn Japan to limit expansionary ambitions.)*

Draw Inferences In what way did American expansionism following the Spanish-American War move the United States into a position as a world power in dealing with issues in Asia? *(The new U.S. territories in the Pacific gave the United States a stronger presence in Asia and consequently more influence with other countries.)*

Evaluate Arguments In your opinion, were the members of the Righteous and Harmonious Fists (the Boxers) justified in their opposition to the growing Western influence in China? Why or why not? *(Yes. The Boxers were trying to protect China from western powers gaining more and more influence with the Chinese emperor and from controlling Chinese resources and economic activity. No. The Boxers were short sighted and couldn't see the economic benefits of opening new trade with the West.)*

The United States Emerges as a World Power

DIGITAL TEXT 3

American Foreign Policy in Latin America

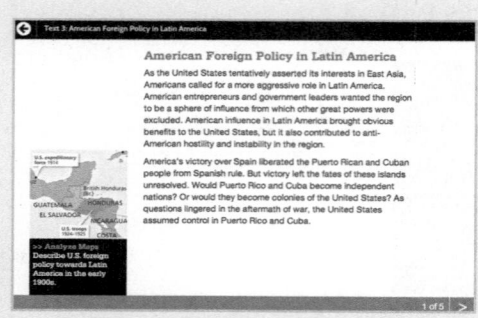

DIGITAL TEXT 4

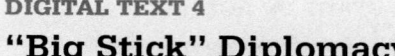

"Big Stick" Diplomacy

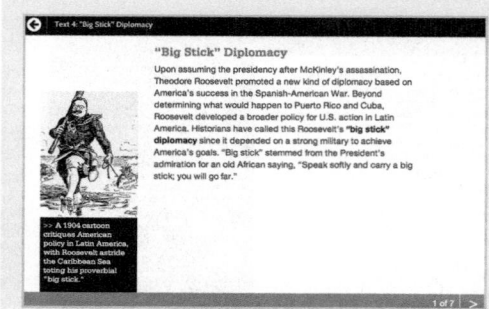

Objective 2: **Examine what happened to Puerto Rico and Cuba after the Spanish-American War.**

Quick Instruction

Analyze Maps Project the map and invite students to locate Puerto Rico and to make predictions about possible issues the United States might have with this island territory. *(Unlike the Philippines, Puerto Rico and Cuba are very close to the United States. The United States will have to exercise more control over these islands. However, doing so might cause more problems with the citizens of those countries who would rather govern themselves.)*

Summarize Summarize the Foraker Act and the significance of the Insular Cases. *(The Foraker Act established a civil government in Puerto Rico but gave the U.S. president considerable power to appoint government officials. The Insular Cases were legal decisions in which the Supreme Court determined the rights of Puerto Ricans, basically ruling that Puerto Ricans did not enjoy the same rights as U.S. citizens.)*

Support a Point of View with Evidence How would you evaluate the U.S. acquisition of Puerto Rico? *(The United States freed the Puerto Rican people from Spanish rule and replaced it with its own kind of governance. The United States retained military control of Puerto Rico, as well as considerable political power.)*

Further Instruction

Compare and Contrast How was U.S. foreign policy in Cuba similar to and different from the policies in Puerto Rico? *(Cuba, like Puerto Rico, was forced to give up power to the United States. The Platt Amendment gave the United States the "right to intervene" to preserve order in Cuba. However, the United States could not choose Cuba's leaders and Cuba was not officially a U.S. territory. The United States kept a significant military presence in both Cuba and Puerto Rico.)*

Identify Central Issues What central point does the lesson make about U.S. foreign policy in Cuba and Puerto Rico? *(The United States was unwilling to risk Cuba and Puerto Rico becoming a base for a potentially hostile great power. The United States was protecting and expanding its sphere of influence in the Caribbean.)*

Objective 3: **Analyze the effects of Roosevelt's "big stick" diplomacy and Taft's "dollar diplomacy."**

Quick Instruction

Interactive Gallery: The Panama Canal Project the slideshow. Look at each image individually and then the collection of images as a whole. Explain to students that Theodore Roosevelt and many other American leaders thought that having a canal through Central America was vital to American power in the world. A canal would save time and money for both commercial and military shipping. Construction on the canal began in 1903.

Analyze the impact of physical and human geographic factors on the Panama Canal. *(First, the United States supported the Panamanian revolution from Colombia in order to get access to the Canal Zone. Then, geographical factors such as the ifferences in the height of the Pacific and Atlantic oceans and Gatún Lake forced builders to construct locks. The rocky land required extensive blasting using explosives. In addition, mosquitoes plagued workers, resulting in disease and a high death rate among workers. A project this large required the hiring of thousands of workers from many areas of the world.)*

PEARSON realize™

www.PearsonRealize.com
Access your Digital Lesson

INTERACTIVE GALLERY
The Panama Canal

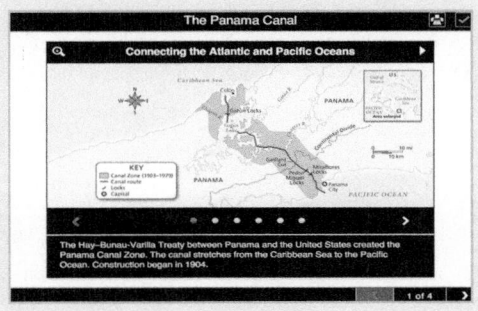

DIGITAL TEXT 5
Wilson's "Moral Diplomacy"

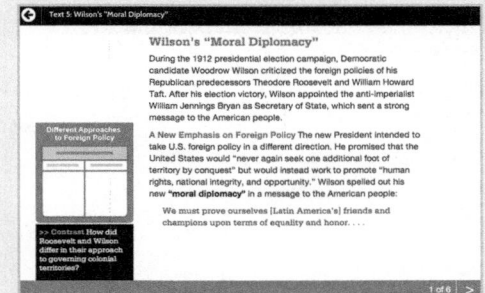

⬛ ACTIVE CLASSROOM

Use the Ranking Strategy to have students go through the images and information about the challenges of constructing the Panama Canal shown in the activity, and rank which ones were the most difficult to overcome.

ELL Use the ELL activity described in the ELL chart.

Further Instruction

As an age of expansionism and economic influence swept the world, President Roosevelt saw the need for an updated Monroe Doctrine built on diplomacy backed by a show of force. Ask students to find examples of Roosevelt's "Big stick" foreign policy. *(Great White Fleet, sending warships to Panama; Roosevelt Corollary)*

Identify Patterns How did the Roosevelt Corollary and the Platt Amendment discussed earlier reflect similar assumptions about the governments of Latin American nations? *(Both seemed to assume that Latin American countries were not capable of self-governance and needed the help of the United States.)*

Generate Explanations Explain the relationship between foreign policies such as the Roosevelt Corollary and dollar diplomacy and economic issues. *(Both Presidents wanted American investment and business in Latin American to thrive. Roosevelt saw European interference as a threat to that, so issued the Roosevelt Corollary to prevent such interference. President Taft's use of dollar diplomacy aimed to stabilize Latin American*

countries that resented the "big stick" diplomacy and the Roosevelt Corollary.)

Analyze Maps What impact would the building of the Panama Canal have on American trade and military forces? *(The canal will allow businesses and ships to move goods more efficiently much quicker throughout the world. The canal will provide the U.S. military to move troops and supplies quicker, making it a much more powerful and effective fighting force.)*

Objective 4: Compare Wilson's "moral diplomacy" with the foreign policies of his predecessors.

Quick Instruction

Interactive Map: U.S. Interventions in Latin America Project the map on the whiteboard and click through the hot spots on the map. Introduce the map activity by telling students the United States, as an emerging world power, intervened in the affairs of its Latin American neighbors often from the time of the Spanish-American War through the early 1900s.

⬛ ACTIVE CLASSROOM

Have students form an Opinion Line to agree or disagree with the following statement: As a whole, were the American interventions in Latin America successful and beneficial to the United States. *(Agree: the interventions stabilized Latin American governments and protected American influence in the region. Disagree: the interventions led to American resentment from many Latin Americans, which created more tensions and conflicts in the region.)*

D Differentiate: Extra Support After asking the students to form their opinions, allow students five minutes to think about the question individually. Tell them to write down their response (Agree or Disagree) and two reasons why they answered that way. Then continue with the group activity.

The United States Emerges as a World Power

SYNTHESIZE

DEMONSTRATE

INTERACTIVE MAP

U.S. Interventions in Latin America

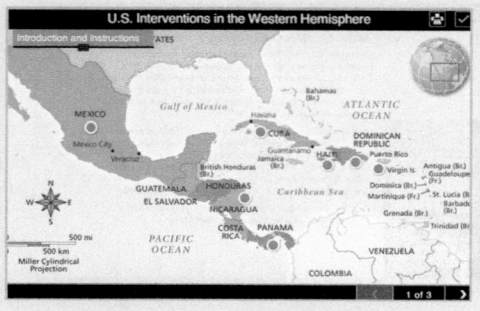

Further Instruction

Contrast How was President Wilson's "moral diplomacy" different from "big stick" and "dollar diplomacy" foreign policy? *("Moral diplomacy" was different in that it was built on the concepts of "human rights, national integrity, and opportunity" rather than the protection of American economic or strategic interests.)*

Be sure students understand that despite his stated preference for "moral diplomacy," Wilson used the military on a number of occasions to guide Latin Americans in the directions that he thought proper. Ask students to find examples of Wilson's use of the military in Latin America. *(In 1915, Wilson sent marines to Haiti; the expedition to find Pancho Villa took place in 1916-1917)*

Draw Conclusions Do you think Woodrow Wilson succeeded in carrying out the principle of "moral diplomacy" in Latin America? *(No. In the end, Wilson had to use military force several times to protect American interests rather than those of the Latin American countries.)*

DIGITAL ACTIVITY

Understanding American Expansionism

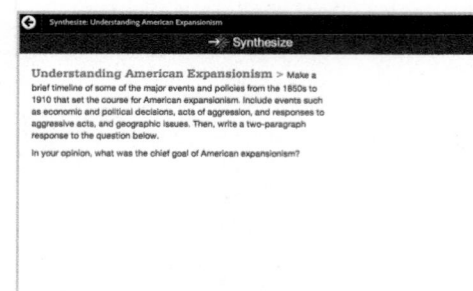

Identify Main Ideas Before students write their paragraphs, hold a quick round table discussion in which students each name an event or policy for the timelines. For each, have students identify it as economic, political, act of aggression or response to aggression, or geographic. Invite students to present their completed paragraphs to the class or in small groups.

DIGITAL QUIZ

Lesson Quiz and Class Discussion Board

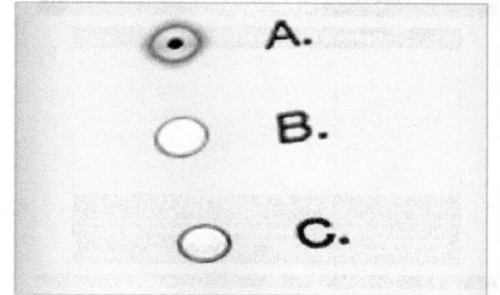

Assign the online Lesson Quiz for this lesson if you haven't already done so. Students will be offered automatic remediation or enrichment based on their score.

Pose these questions to the class on the Discussion Board:

In *The United States Emerges as a World Power*, you read about how the United States used its new power in the years following the Spanish-American War. Shifting foreign policies and a growing military provided American presidents flexibility and the strength to lead the country and exert pressures on countries around the world.

Make Predictions How will the United States use its power in the world war that will soon engulf Europe?

Express Ideas Clearly Which of the foreign policies you learned about was most effective in protecting American interests and security?

Topic Inquiry

Have students continue their investigations for the Topic Inquiry.

America Comes of Age

■ SYNTHESIZE

DIGITAL ACTIVITY
Reflect on the Essential Question and Topic

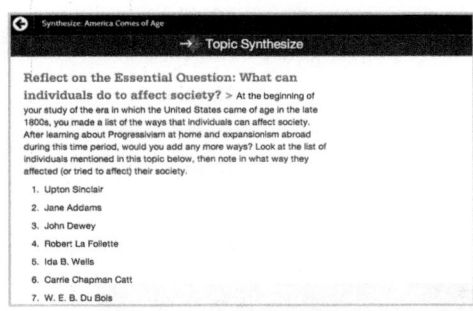

First ask students to reconsider the Essential Question for the Topic: What can individuals do to affect society? Remind students of the reasons they listed at the start of the Topic. Invite volunteers to share their lists with the class.

Then, pose this question to students: Of the people discussed in the Topic, whom do you think had the greatest positive effect on society? Who had the greatest negative effect? Discuss their answers as a class or ask students to post their answers on the Class Discussion Board.

Next ask students to reflect on the Topic as a whole and write down one to three questions they've thought about during the Topic. Share these examples if students need help getting started:

- Whom do you know or know of who is changing society today?
- What factors should the United States (or any other country) consider before using military, economic, or political pressure?
- Are journalists today as effective at identifying the need for reform as muckrakers in the early 1900s?

You may ask students to share their questions and answers on the Class Discussion Board.

Have students complete Step 3 of the Topic Inquiry.

■ DEMONSTRATE

DIGITAL TOPIC REVIEW AND ASSESSMENT
America Comes of Age

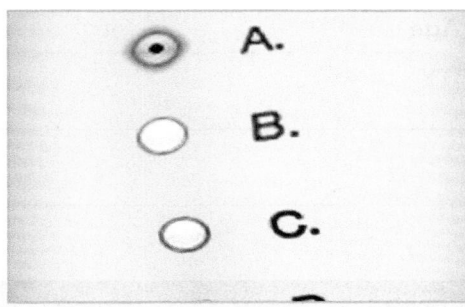

Students can prepare for the Topic Test by answering the questions in the Topic Review and Assessment online or the Assessment questions in the Print Student text. They can also prepare by reviewing their answers to the Interactive Reading Notepad questions or reviewing their notes in the Reading and Notetaking Study Guide.

DIGITAL TOPIC TEST
America Comes of Age

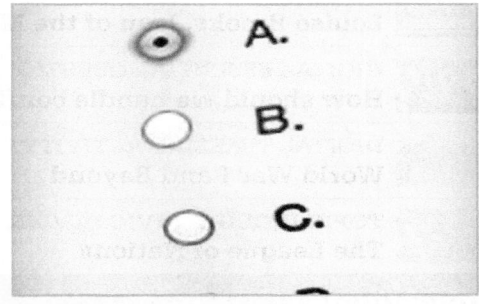

TOPIC TEST
Assign the Topic Test to assess students' understanding of topic content.

BENCHMARK TESTS
Assign these benchmark tests as you complete the relevant topics to monitor student progress toward mastering the course content and as preparation for the End-of-Course Test.

Benchmark Test 1: Topics 1–3

Benchmark Test 2: Topics 4–6

Benchmark Test 3: Topics 7–9

Benchmark Test 4: Topics 10–12

Benchmark Test 5: Topics 13–15

Benchmark Test 6: Topics 16–18

Benchmark Test 7: Topics 19–20

World War I and the 1920s

TOPIC 12 ORGANIZER	PACING: APPROX. 11 PERIODS, 5.5 BLOCKS	
		PACING
Connect		1 period
MY STORY VIDEO **Louise Brooks, Icon of the Modern Age**		10 min.
DIGITAL ESSENTIAL QUESTION ACTIVITY **How should we handle conflict?**		10 min.
DIGITAL TIMELINE ACTIVITY **World War I and Beyond**		10 min.
TOPIC INQUIRY: CIVIC DISCUSSION **The League of Nations**		20 min.
Investigate		4–8 periods
TOPIC INQUIRY: CIVIC DISCUSSION **The League of Nations**		Ongoing
LESSON 1 America Enters World War I		30–40 min.
LESSON 2 The Home Front During World War I		30–40 min.
LESSON 3 The End of World War I		30–40 min.
LESSON 4 The Postwar Economy Booms		30–40 min.
LESSON 5 Government in the 1920s		30–40 min.
LESSON 6 An Unsettled Society		30–40 min.
LESSON 7 The Roaring Twenties		30–40 min.
LESSON 8 The Harlem Renaissance		30–40 min.
Synthesize		1 period
DIGITAL ACTIVITY **Reflect on the Essential Question and Topic**		10 min.
TOPIC INQUIRY: CIVIC DISCUSSION **The League of Nations**		20 min.
Demonstrate		1–2 periods
DIGITAL TOPIC REVIEW AND ASSESSMENT **World War I and the 1920s**		10 min.
TOPIC INQUIRY: CIVIC DISCUSSION **The League of Nations**		20 min.

TOPIC INQUIRY: CIVIC DISCUSSION

The League of Nations

In this Topic Inquiry, students work in teams to examine different perspectives on this issue by analyzing several sources, arguing both sides of a Yes/No question, then developing and discussing their own point of view on the question: Should the United States have joined the League of Nations?

STEP 1: CONNECT
Develop Questions and Plan the Investigation

Launch the Civic Discussion

Divide the class into groups of four students. Students can access the materials they'll need in the online course or you can distribute copies to each student. Read the main question and introduction with the students.

Have students complete Step 1 by reading the Discussion Launch and filling in Step 1 of the Information Organizer. The Discussion Launch provides YES and NO arguments on the main question. Students should extract and paraphrase the arguments from the reading in Step 1 of their Information Organizers.

Next, students share within their groups the arguments and evidence they found to support the YES and NO positions. The group needs to agree on the major YES and NO points and each student should note those points in their Information Organizer.

Resources
- Student Instructions
- Information Organizer
- Discussion Launch

STEP 2: INVESTIGATE
Apply Disciplinary Concepts and Tools

Examine Sources and Perspectives

Students will examine sources with the goal of extracting information and perspectives on the main question. They analyze each source and describe the author's perspective on the main question and key evidence the author provides to support that viewpoint in Information Organizer Step 2.

Ask students to keep in mind:

- **Author/Creator:** Who created the source? An individual? Group? Government agency?
- **Audience:** For whom was the source created?
- **Date/Place:** Is there any information that reveals where and when the source was created?
- **Purpose:** Why was the source created? Discuss with students the importance of this question in identifying bias.
- **Relevance:** How does the source support one argument or another?

Suggestion: Reading the source documents and filling in Step 2 of the Information Organizer could be assigned as homework.

Resources
- Student Instructions
- Information Organizer
- Source documents

⏻ PROFESSIONAL DEVELOPMENT

Civic Discussion

Be sure to view the Civic Discussion Professional Development resources in the online course.

 TOPIC INQUIRY: CIVIC DISCUSSION

The League of Nations *(continued)*

STEP 3: SYNTHESIZE
Use Evidence to Formulate Conclusions

Formulate Compelling Arguments with Evidence

Now students will apply perspectives and evidence they extracted from the sources to think more deeply about the main question by first arguing one side of the issue, then the other. In this way students become more prepared to formulate an evidence-based conclusion on their own.

Within each student group, assign half of the students to take the position of YES on the main question and the others to take the position of NO. Students will work with their partners to identify the strongest arguments and evidence to support their assigned YES or NO position.

Present Yes/No Positions

Within each group, those assigned the YES position share arguments and evidence first. As the YES students speak, those assigned NO should listen carefully, take notes to fill in the rest of the Compelling Arguments Chart (Step 3 in Information Organizer) and ask clarifying questions.

When the YES side is finished, students assigned the NO position present while those assigned YES should listen, take notes, and ask clarifying questions. Examples of clarifin questions are:

- I think you just said [x]. Am I understanding you correctly?
- Can you tell me more about [x]?
- Can you repeat [x]? I am not sure I understand, yet.

Suggestion: You may want to set a 5 minute time limit for each side to present. Provide a two-minute warning so that students make their most compelling arguments within the time frame.

Switch Sides

The students will switch sides to argue the opposite point of view. To prepare to present the other position, partners who first argued YES will use the notes they took during the NO side's presentation, plus add any additional arguments and evidence from the reading and sources. The same for students who first argued the NO position.

STEP 4: DEMONSTRATE
Communicate Conclusions and Take Informed Action

Individual Points of View

Now the students will have the opportunity to discuss the main question from their own points of view. To help students prepare for this discussion, have them reflect on the YES/NO discussions they have participated in thus far and fill in Step 4 of their Information Organizers.

After all of the students have shared their points of view, each group should list points of agreement, filling the last portion of Step 4 on their Information Organizers.

Reflect on the Discussion

Ask students to reflect on the civic discussion thinking about:

- The value of having to argue both the YES and NO positions.
- If their individual views changed over the course of the discussion and why.
- What they learned from participating in the discussion.

Resources

- Student Instructions
- Information Organizer

World War I and the 1920s

Militarism, alliances, imperialism, and nationalism led to World War I in Europe. Drawn in near the end of the conflict, the United States emerged as a true world power. The end of the wartime economy, however, led to an economic downturn and social unrest. America in the 1920s rebounded and enjoyed a period of unequaled prosperity, although deep social tensions remained. Technological innovations led to a widespread shared popular culture. American women enjoyed expanded roles in society and African American influence in the arts flourished in what we call "the Roaring Twenties."

CONNECT

MY STORY VIDEO

Louise Brooks, Icon of the Modern Age

Watch a video about film star Louise Brooks.

Check Understanding Who were the "flappers" of the 1920s? *(young women who defied traditional ideas about dress and behavior)*

Make Generalizations Why has Louise Brooks been called the first female icon of the 1920s? *(Louise Brooks seemed to embody the spirit of the age through her bobbed hair, free-wheeling attitude, and short dresses. She also was one of the first movie stars of the era, serving as a role model for some young women.)*

DIGITAL ESSENTIAL QUESTION ACTIVITY

How should we handle conflict?

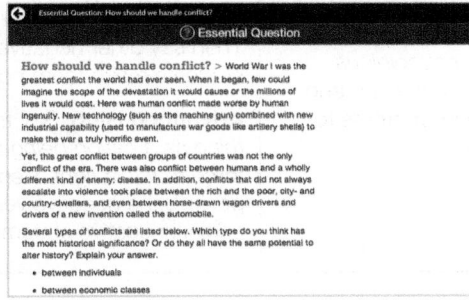

Ask students to think about the Essential Question for this topic: How should we handle conflict? Conflict is an inevitable byproduct of human interaction. What are the best ways to deal with conflict?

If students have not already done so, ask them to respond to the activity ranking list. Then go over the results as a class.

Support a Point of View with Evidence Why did you rank this conflict as most historically significant?

Identify Central Issues What types of conflicts are not solvable? *(between humans and nature; between the past and the future)*

Cause and Effect In our society today, can individuals effectively handle conflicts independently? Why or why not? *(Except for conflicts between individuals, the conflicts listed require cooperation between groups of people.)*

DIGITAL TIMELINE ACTIVITY

World War I and Beyond

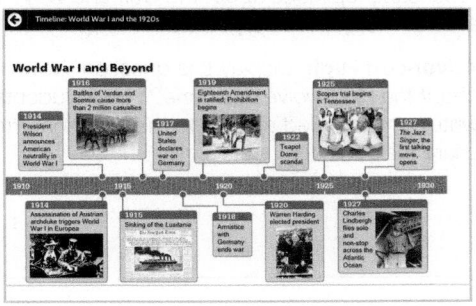

Display the timeline showing significant events. During this topic students will learn about all of these events and many more, but this timeline will provide a framework into which they can place the events they learn about.

D Differentiate: Extra Support How many years are there between the start of World War I and when the United States entered the war? *(3; war began in 1914; the United States entered in 1917)*

Infer How might World War I have led to other events listed on the timeline? *(Airplane technology refined during the war probably contributed to Lindbergh's solo non-stop flight across the Atlantic Ocean in 1927.)*

Topic Inquiry

Have students continue their investigations for the Topic Inquiry.

America Enters World War I

Supporting English Language Learners

Use with Digital Text 3, **The United States Remains Neutral.**

Reading
Explain that students are going to employ basic reading skills in order to read some or all of the text. Then they will demonstrate English comprehension by answering questions they receive in advance.

Beginning Display this question: *How many Americans were from other countries in 1914?* Have pairs of students read aloud the first paragraph of the section titled Many Americans Choose Sides and locate the answer to the question.

Intermediate Display this question: *What does it mean that Wilson wanted Americans to be impartial about the war?* Have students silently read the text's introductory paragraph. Then answer the question as a group, making sure students understand how the answer was reached.

Advanced Display this question: *What event had a major impact on Americans' opinions about the war, and why?* Have pairs read the text and answer the question together.

Advanced High Display this question: *How did Americans' opinions about the war evolve over time?* Have students silently read the text and write out a detailed answer to the question. Provide time for partners to share their answers.

Use with Digital Text 4, **Reasons for America's Entry into the War.**

Listening
Read aloud **Reasons for America's Entry into the War**, or invite volunteers to do so. Explain to students that they will practice hearing and saying the language structure of expressing negative statements in English.

Beginning Say this abridged sentence from the reading: *This promise would not last long.* Explain that the word *not* between *would* and *last* makes it negative. Then say this sentence, and ask students to make it negative: *America would stay out of the war*.

Intermediate Say sentences related to the reading using these phrases: *would not, should not, could not*. Then repeat them without the word *not*, and discuss the difference. Have students identify at least two sentences with *would (not), should (not)*, or *could (not)* from the reading.

Advanced Say this sentence from the reading: *Wilson did not have much time to enjoy his victory*. Ask students to make the sentence positive. Then say other negative/positive sentences related to the text, and have students make them positive/negative.

Advanced High Say this sentence from the reading: *There is such a thing as a nation being so right that it does not need to convince others by force that it is right*. Repeat the sentence if necessary. Have students make positive the negative verb phrase *does not need*. Then have them say original negative statements related to the text.

▣ Differentiate Instruction

Use the Differentiated Instruction notes throughout the lesson plan to support the varied skill sets, levels of readiness, and interests in the mixed-ability classroom.

Challenge These notes include suggestions for expanding the activity for advanced students.

On-Level These notes include suggestions for modifying the activity to address different interests or learning styles.

Extra Support These notes include ideas for providing more scaffolding or reading spuport.

Special Needs These notes provide ideas for adapting instruction to support the needs of various special needs students.

■ NOTES

PEARSON
realize.™
www.PearsonRealize.com

Go online to access additional resources including:
Primary Sources • Biographies • Supreme Court cases •
21st Century Skill Tutorials • Maps • Graphic Organizers.

Objectives

Objective 1: Identify the causes of World War I.

Objective 2: Analyze the impact of technological innovations in weaponry that resulted in stalemate on the Western Front.

Objective 3: Analyze reasons behind isolationism and neutrality in the United States before 1917.

Objective 4: Explain why the United States entered the conflict on the side of the Allies.

LESSON 1 ORGANIZER		PACING: APPROX. 1 PERIOD, .5 BLOCKS			
				RESOURCES	
		OBJECTIVES	PACING	Online	Print
Connect					
	DIGITAL START UP ACTIVITY **The Name of the War**		5 min.	●	
Investigate					
	DIGITAL TEXT 1 **The Causes of World War I**	Objective 1	10 min.	●	●
	DIGITAL TEXT 2 **The Great War Begins**	Objective 2	10 min.	●	●
	3-D MODEL **Trench Warfare**		10 min.	●	
	DIGITAL TEXT 3 **The United States Remains Neutral**	Objective 3	10 min.	●	●
	INTERACTIVE CHART **American Attitudes Toward Involvement in World War I**		10 min.	●	
	DIGITAL TEXT 4 **Reasons for America's Entry into the War**	Objective 4	10 min.	●	●
	INTERACTIVE TIMELINE **Buildup to War**		10 min.	●	
Synthesize					
	DIGITAL ACTIVITY **Trench Warfare**		5 min.	●	
Demonstrate					
	LESSON QUIZ **Lesson Quiz and Class Discussion Board**		10 min.	●	

Topic 12 Lesson 1

America Enters World War I

CONNECT

DIGITAL START UP ACTIVITY
The Name of the War

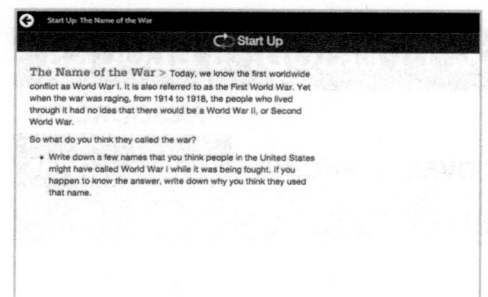

Project the Start Up Activity Ask students to read the activity introduction as they enter and get settled. Then have them share their ideas with another student.

Discuss So what do you think people in 1914 called this war that caused so much destruction and raged over so much of the world? Write down a few names that you think Americans might have called World War I while it was being fought.

Tell students that in this lesson they will be learning about the causes of World War I and how the United States remained neutral until 1917.

Aa Vocabulary Development: Use the Interactive Reading Notepad to preview the Key Terms and Academic Vocabulary in this lesson with students.

⇅ FLIP IT!
Assign the Flipped Video for this lesson.

STUDENT EDITION PRINT
PAGES: 450–458

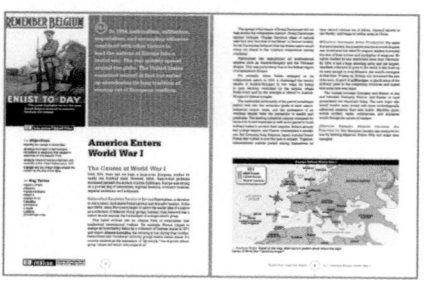

INVESTIGATE

DIGITAL TEXT 1
The Causes of World War I

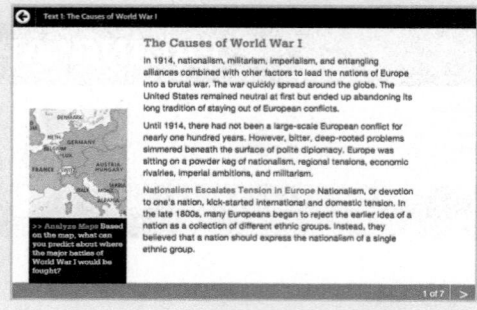

Objective 1: Identify the causes of World War I.

Quick Instruction
Remind students that 1914 was a significant year because it marked the start of World War I. Take several minutes to review and identify the causes of World War I. Invite students to analyze information about the causes of the war by sequencing key events.

Analyze Maps Direct students attention to the map of Europe before the start of World War I. Invite volunteers to identify the powerful countries/empires and describe what they know about them. Point out to students that Europe was gripped by nationalism, regional tensions, economic rivalries, imperial ambitions, and militarism. Invite students to predict the primary locations where they think where World War I would be fought. (*Central Europe, in and around the border countries.*)

Draw Conclusions What role did nationalism play in the assassination of Archduke Francis Ferdinand? (*Gavrilo Princip, the man who killed the archduke, was a Bosnian Serb who believed that Bosnia rightfully belonged to Serbia and not to Austria-Hungary. He believed that Francis Ferdinand, heir to the Austro-Hungarian throne, was a tyrant.*)

Summarize how the widespread European belief in Social Darwinism contributed to escalated tensions. (*Europeans thought that as countries competed with each other, only the strongest, or "fittest," would come out as the winner.*)

Further Instruction
Remind students economic strength and an overseas empire were the measurements of wealth and greatness. Large industrialized nations around the world competed among themselves to gain colonies in Africa, islands in the Pacific, and make inroads into China.

Generate Explanations How did imperialism in the late 1800s and early 1900s contribute to the outbreak of World War I? (*European countries, and other large industrial nations in the world, competed for lands rich in raw materials as well as for places to build military bases to protect their empires. The constant competition led to tensions between nations.*)

Compare Many European countries built up their military forces in anticipation of a war. Have students use the chart titled "Military Strength, 1914" to compare the military forces in Europe.

Apply Concepts Why did many European nations form alliances and what were the consequences of these alliances? (*Alliances protected nations from attack but they also emboldened leaders to act recklessly. National leaders knew that if they did declare war, powerful allies were obliged to fight along with them. No country wanted to be seen as an unreliable partner.*)

DIGITAL TEXT 2

The Great War Begins

3-D MODEL

Trench Warfare

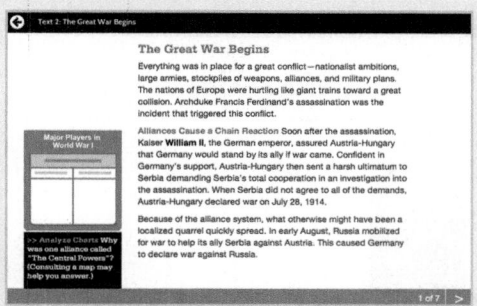

Objective 2: Analyze the impact of technological innovations in weaponry that resulted in stalemate on the Western Front.

Quick Instruction

3-D Model: Trench Warfare Project the 3-D Model and click on the red circles to reveal information about the experience of soldiers in World War I trenches. Discuss each aspect of the trench experience. Challenge students to explain how technological innovations made defenses such as trenches necessary. *(The introduction of deadly machine guns and artillery required much stronger and better defensive positions, like the trench.)* Invite students to compare and contrast World War I trench warfare with modern-day warfare. *(Modern warfare does not utilize trenches. Much of warfare today is done remotely, either by long-range missiles or drones. Airplanes and naval vessels with long-rang weapons are also important.)*

Analyze Information Have students analyze the impact of significant technological innovations in World War I such as trench warfare. How did trench warfare change the way armies engaged their enemies? *(The trench systems forced armies to change tactics and to develop new ways to attack defensive lines, such as using new weapons like tanks. Frontal assaults were extremely difficult, so moving troops to try to flank an enemy became even more crucial.)*

🔲 ACTIVE CLASSROOM

Ask students to have a "Conversation with a World War I soldier." Tell students to imagine that they are having a conversation with a soldier who has been living in a World War I trench for several months. Direct each student to write down a question he or she would like to ask, then how the soldier would respond, and then what the student would say in response.

Further Instruction

Emphasize to students that commanders on each side threw their soldiers into assaults against the enemy without fully considering new war technology. Defensive weapons of the time were better and more devastating than the offensive ones. Engage students in a discussion about the impact of significant technological innovations in warfare such as machine guns, airplanes, poison gas, and tanks and how they resulted in the stalemate on the Western Front.

Draw Conclusions What made attacking much more difficult than defending a position? *(When attacking, soldiers were in the open and moving. They became targets in the open no man's land, and it was more difficult to fire a weapon accurately when moving. Defenders were usually well protected and could aim accurately. Machine guns could quickly mow down an advancing unit.)*

Apply Concepts Why would generals continue to launch attacks knowing that their armies would sustain heavy casualties? *(At the time, the only way to end the stalemate was to send large numbers of men to overwhelm defenders and break through defensive lines. Frontal attacks were probably the only tactics that many generals were familiar with since the new weapons were relatively untried.)*

Identify Cause and Effect Ask students to explain how specific needs result in scientific discoveries and technological innovations in the military during World War I. *(Trench warfare resulted in a stalemate. Military leaders needed new weapons to defeat the trench system, such as tanks, airplanes, poison gas, and better guns and artillery.)*

Topic ⑫ Lesson 1

America Enters World War I

DIGITAL TEXT 3

The United States Remains Neutral

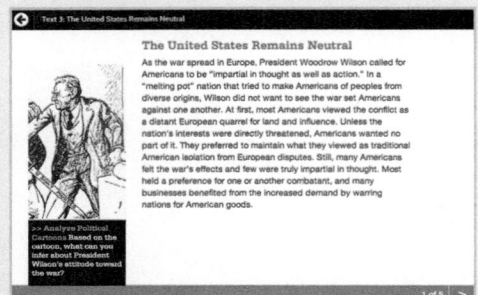

INTERACTIVE CHART

American Attitudes Toward Involvement in World War I

DIGITAL TEXT 4

Reasons for America's Entry into the War

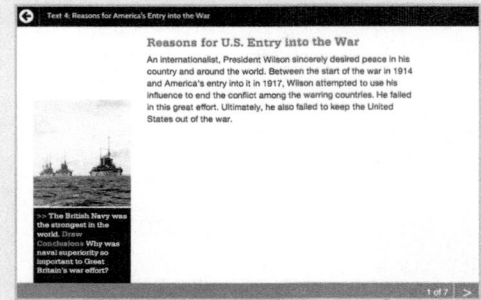

Objective 3: Analyze reasons behind isolationism and neutrality in the United States before 1917.

Quick Instruction

Interactive Chart: American Attitudes Toward Involvement in World War I Project the chart on the board. Invite a volunteer to remind the class of the traditional American policy regarding European affairs. *(The traditional policy maintained American isolation from European disputes.)* After you have worked your way through the entire gallery, challenge students to use the question words (who, what, where, when, why, and how) to generate six separate questions about the major issues raised by U.S. involvement in World War I. Encourage students to discuss the answers to these questions.

Draw Conclusions Why did President Wilson fear that the war would set Americans against one another? *(A great portion of American citizens were foreign-born and many still had strong emotional ties to their former homelands.)*

▣ ACTIVE CLASSROOM

Conduct a Graffiti Concepts Activity. Ask students to reflect on the three prevailing American positions on the war. (Allow approximately 3-5 minutes.) Then ask students to post their "graffiti" on the board or on chart paper and ask students to look at all the various positions and then discuss them as a group.

ELL Use the ELL activity described in the ELL chart.

Further Instruction

Project and discuss the Interactive Reading Notepad questions, including the graphic organizer asking students to record notes on the three distinct American attitudes toward the war in Europe. Review students' notes with the class and fill in the graphic organizer on the whiteboard as you go.

Hypothesize Why do think the German invasion of Belgium became a popular rallying cry for many Americans against the Germans and the Central Powers? *(Many Americans probably thought of the invasion as another example European imperialism, something with which Americans had a long history. The cruel way in which the Germans carried out the invasion also upset and horrified many Americans.)*

Predict Consequences Ask students to predict if the United States will remain neutral and to explain why. *(The United States will not be able to remain neutral. Citizen support for one side will eventually pressure U.S. leaders to get involved. Also, because America has so many interests around the world, sooner or later something will happen that will draw the United States into the war.)*

Objective 4: Explain why the United States entered the conflict on the side of the Allies.

Quick Instruction

Buildup to War: Interactive Timeline Project the timeline on the board and select the squares to reveal details about the reasons for U.S. entry into World War I.

Synthesize Why did the United States decide to enter the war and fight on the side of the Allies? *(American leaders grew increasingly horrified and shocked by the actions of Germany, such as the sinking of unarmed vessels and the calling on Mexico to go to war with the U.S. President Wilson and others believed that the U.S. must defeat Germany in order to protect democracy.)*

▣ ACTIVE CLASSROOM

Use the Ranking Strategy to have students go through the events described in the timeline activity, and rank which ones had the greatest impact on bringing the United States into the war.

Ⓓ Differentiate: Challenge/Gifted Ask students to do additional research on one of the events from the timeline and present their findings.

ELL Use the ELL activity described in the ELL chart.

SYNTHESIZE

DEMONSTRATE

INTERACTIVE TIMELINE
Buildup to War

DIGITAL ACTIVITY
Trench Warfare

LESSON QUIZ
Lesson Quiz and Class Discussion Board

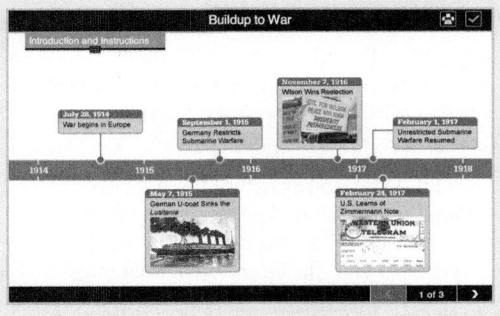

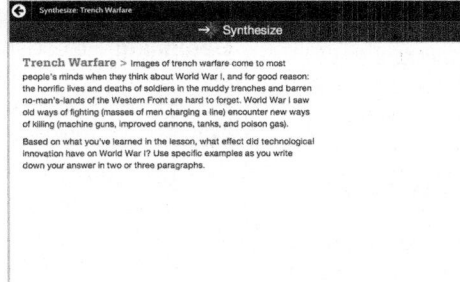

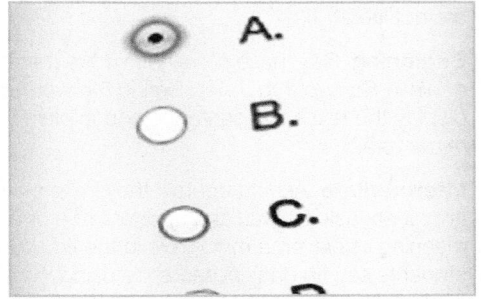

Further Instruction
Review and complete the Interactive Reading Notepad graphic organizer. Encourage students to make additional notes that add information on the positions that might have changed based on new events or information students learned.

Assess Credibility How do you know the Zimmermann note was a reliable source? *(The Germans did not deny they sent the note, and shortly after they began unrestricted submarine warfare.)*

Predict Consequences Ask students to predict and analyze what the major issues raised by U.S. involvement in World War I will be. *(The United States will add considerable power to the Allied effort. U.S. shipping may be subject to attacks from the German navy. Life within the United States will change.)*

Discuss Before students begin their paragraphs, lead the class in a brief review of previous wars students have learned about, such as the American Revolution, the Civil War, and the Spanish-American War. Ask students to contemplate the weapons and technologies use in these conflicts and how they changed from era to era based on specific needs.

Assign the online Lesson Quiz for this lesson if you haven't already done so. Students will be offered automatic remediation or enrichment based on their score.

Pose these questions to the class on the Discussion Board:

In *America Enters World War I*, you read about America's desire to remain neutral as European nations engaged in the most destructive war the world had seen to that point. The United States had previously intervened in foreign conflicts only to protect its interests around the world.

Generate Explanations Based on what you have learned about America's role in the world during the early years of World War I, did American leaders follow the right policy of trying to remain neutral? Explain.

Predict Consequences What will be the impact of the United States entering the war?

Topic Inquiry
Have students continue their investigations for the Topic Inquiry.

The Home Front During World War I

Supporting English Language Learners

Use with Digital Text 1, **Mobilizing for War.**

Listening

Read aloud the two introductory paragraphs, or invite volunteers to do so. Explain that students will learn commonly heard English expressions that are not literal.

Beginning Say these sentences: *I like to play basketball. I want to play a role in Romeo and Juliet.* Define the word *play* in these contexts. Then display the text's first sentence and explain the meaning of *played a minor role*.

Intermediate Ask students if they have played a role in a school play and, if so, ask if it was an important role or a minor one. Then discuss the meaning of *played a minor role* in the first sentence of the text, and have students say an original sentence using the expression. Have students explain the meaning of the expression by asking them to complete this sentence: "I learned the expression *play a minor role* means ____".

Advanced Ask if students have heard the expression *to take shape* in classroom instruction or interaction. Clarify its meaning, and have students use it in a classroom context. Then have pairs of students use prior knowledge to infer the meaning of *shape* in the reading's introduction.

Advanced High Ask if students have ever learned something during classroom instruction that they found touching. Discuss the phrase's meaning. Then have pairs of students practice using the expression in a classroom interaction. Have students read the last sentence of the second paragraph and discuss the meaning of *touches* by completing the following sentence: "In this sentence, the word *touches* means the same as ____".

Use with Digital Text 2, **Opposition to the War.**

Reading

Read aloud the introduction and first two sections of the text, or invite volunteers to do so. Explain that the main idea of the entire text is opposition to the war, and point out a few supporting details.

Beginning Reread the first paragraph of the section titled Women Oppose the War. Display a scrambled list of the main idea and two details. Help students to expand their reading skills by asking them to distinguish between the main idea and details.

Intermediate Ask students to read the first paragraph of the section titled Women Oppose the War. Help them expand their reading skills by determining the paragraph's main idea, as well as the details that support it. Ask: *How might a section heading help you to determine a main idea?*

Advanced Ask pairs of students to read the section titled Opposition to the Draft. Then have them expand their reading skills by writing a list of the section's main idea and three supporting details. Provide time for pairs to share their lists with one another.

Advanced High Ask students to read the section titled Opposition to the Draft. Have them expand their reading skills by recording the section's main idea and supporting details in a word web. Provide time for students to share their list with a partner.

▶ Differentiate Instruction

Use the Differentiated Instruction notes throughout the lesson plan to support the varied skill sets, levels of readiness, and interests in the mixed-ability classroom.

Challenge These notes include suggestions for expanding the activity for advanced students.

On-Level These notes include suggestions for modifying the activity to address different interests or learning styles.

Extra Support These notes include ideas for providing more scaffolding or reading spuport.

Special Needs These notes provide ideas for adapting instruction to support the needs of various special needs students.

■ NOTES

PEARSON realize www.PearsonRealize.com

Go online to access additional resources including: Primary Sources • Biographies • Supreme Court cases • 21st Century Skill Tutorials • Maps • Graphic Organizers.

Objectives

Objective 1: Analyze how the U.S. government mobilized the public to support the war effort.

Objective 2: Describe opposition to World War I and how the federal government responded to it.

Objective 3: Analyze the causes and effects of migration and social changes that occurred during World War I.

LESSON 2 ORGANIZER — PACING: APPROX. 1 PERIOD, .5 BLOCKS	OBJECTIVES	PACING	RESOURCES: Online	RESOURCES: Print
Connect				
DIGITAL START UP ACTIVITY **The Home Front**		5 min.	●	
Investigate				
DIGITAL TEXT 1 **Mobilizing for War**	Objective 1	10 min.	●	●
DIGITAL TEXT 2 **Opposition to the War**	Objective 2	10 min.	●	●
INTERACTIVE GALLERY **Constitutional Issues During World War I**	Objective 2	10 min.	●	
DIGITAL TEXT 3 **The War Changes American Society**	Objective 3	10 min.	●	●
INTERACTIVE CHART **The Great Migration**	Objective 3	10 min.	●	
Synthesize				
DIGITAL ACTIVITY **Essential Question: How do we handle conflict?**		5 min.	●	
Demonstrate				
LESSON QUIZ **Lesson Quiz and Class Discussion Board**		10 min.	●	

The Home Front During World War I

CONNECT

DIGITAL START UP ACTIVITY
The Home Front

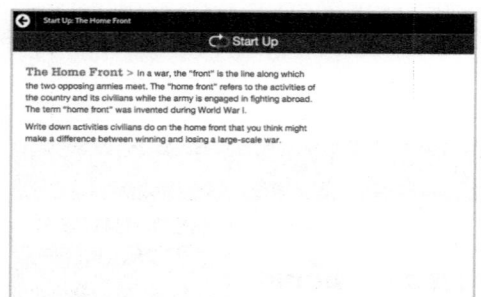

Project the Start Up Activity As students enter and get settled, draw their attention to the activity. Allow students to work in pairs to consider what is necessary for a country to win a war.

Discuss Have students write down activities civilians do on the home front that might make a difference between winning and losing a large-scale war. *(Support troops by taking care of families left behind; conserve valuable resources, such as metal, food, and other materials needed to fight a war; take over the jobs left behind by those fighting.)*

Tell students that in this lesson they will be learning how the United States mobilized its resources to fight in World War I.

Aa Vocabulary Development: Use the Interactive Reading Notepad to preview the Key Terms and Academic Vocabulary in this lesson with students.

⚡ FLIP IT!

Assign the Flipped Video for this lesson.

STUDENT EDITION PRINT PAGES: 459–465

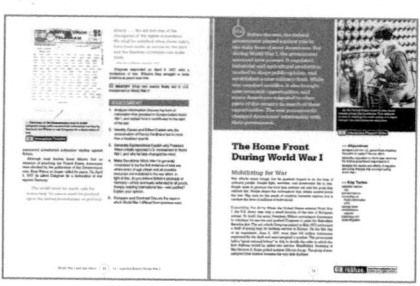

INVESTIGATE

DIGITAL TEXT 1
Mobilizing for War

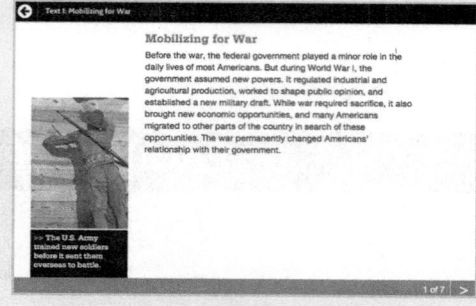

Objective 1: Analyze how the American government mobilized the public to support the war effort.

Quick Instruction

Analyze Images To fight the war, the United States had to motivate Americans to enlist in the military or help the war effort at home. Direct students attention to the photograph of the weapons factory. Point out that the huge mobilization of both people and industry in the United States required cooperation between government, private businesses, and citizens. Ask: What resources are required to fight a war? *(The greatest need is soldiers to fight the war. Armies need supplies as well, including food, clothing, weapons, vehicles for transportation.)*

Begin a discussion by asking volunteers to describe the economic effects of the international military conflict of World War I on the United States. Students should mention how food production was regulated, energy and transportation industries like coal and petroleum distribution were regulated by the government. The government determined what crops farmers grew, what products industries produced, and how supplies moved around on the nation's trains.

Summarize How did Congress ensure that the United States would have enough troops to serve in World War I? *(Congress passed the Selective Service Act to draft men into the army. President Wilson and others encouraged Americans to volunteer using techniques like posters that appealed to Americans' sense of patriotism.)*

Draw Conclusions How did Herbert Hoover's plan of conserving food on the home front help the war effort? *(If the American*

people ate less, then more food could be shipped to American and other Allied soldiers fighting the war overseas.)

ELL Use the ELL activity described in the ELL chart.

Further Instruction

Project the Interactive Reading Notepad Graphic Organizer on the whiteboard asking students to identify positive and negative aspects of the work of the Committee on Public Information. As students progress in this lesson, use the organizer to take notes about how the CPI handled its job during the war.

President Wilson and George Creel understood the importance of educating the American public about the causes and nature of the war. The CPI's most important job was convincing Americans that the war effort was a just cause. Ask students to find examples of how the CPI worked to convince Americans to support the war effort. *(The CPI used pamphlets, press releases, movies, and posters to educate the public. The CPI also hired lecturers to give speeches.)*

Evaluate Impact What was the WIB and what economic effects did it have on the war effort? *(The War Industries Board regulated all industries engaged in the war effort. The agency determined what products industries would make, where those products went, and how much they would cost to make sure the United States had enough war materials.)*

Express Problems Clearly How did the CPI create tensions on the home front? *(The CPI emphasized the cruelty and wickedness of Germany, which often led to resentment toward German Americans)*

DIGITAL TEXT 2

Opposition to the War

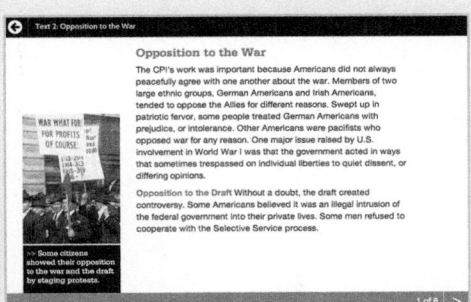

INTERACTIVE GALLERY

Constitutional Issues During World War I

Objective 2: Describe opposition to the war and how the federal government responded to it.

Quick Instruction

Interactive Gallery: Constitutional Issues During World War I Project the interactive gallery. Click on each image and have student volunteers read the information aloud to the class. Have the class explain constitutional issues raised by federal government policy changes during World War I.

Identify Point of View Why did Congress think the President should have power over the distribution of food and fuel during wartime? *(The Food and Fuel Control Act of 1917 allowed the President to stop companies from profiteering during the war. When companies profiteer, they take advantage of people and Congress probably thought that would not help the war effort.)*

Contrast How was the internment of Germans different from the other restrictions on civil liberties implemented during World War I? *(The Germans interned were arrested because of their nationality and not for any other reason. Those arrested for violating the other acts personally acted in a way that violated the laws.)*

🎥 ACTIVE CLASSROOM

Conduct a Take a Stand Activity. Ask students to take a stand on the following question: Was the American fear of German Americans a legitimate concern or an overreaction? Ask students to divide into two groups based on their answer and move to separate areas of the classroom. Ask students to talk with each other to compare their reasons for their position.

ELL Use the ELL activity described in the ELL chart.

Further Instruction

Project the Interactive Reading Notepad graphic organizer on the whiteboard and encourage students to add new information about the Committee on Public Information.

Evaluate Arguments Why did some Americans criticize the CPI? *(Some Americans thought the CPI created a mood in America that did not welcome open debate and free expression.)*

Analyze Information What major issues on the home front were raised by U.S. involvement in World War I? *(On the home front, pro-war propaganda occasionally took a negative turn by vilifying Germans to the extent that German Americans were treated unfairly. Also, several measures meant to protect the United States during the war violated right guaranteed by the Constitution.)*

Summarize the role influential women or women's organizations played in opposing the war. *(Influential American women such as Jane Addams, formed peace organizations that worked with groups in other countries to bring peace. Jeannette Rankin, a member of the U.S. House of Representatives, voted against the declaration of war.)*

Compare and Contrast the reasons some Americans did not support the war. *(Some Americans were pacifists who opposed war for any reason. Other Americans were conscientious objectors whose moral or religious beliefs forbid them to fight in wars. Some women opposed the war because of pacifist leanings.)*

The Home Front During World War I

DIGITAL TEXT 3

The War Changes American Society

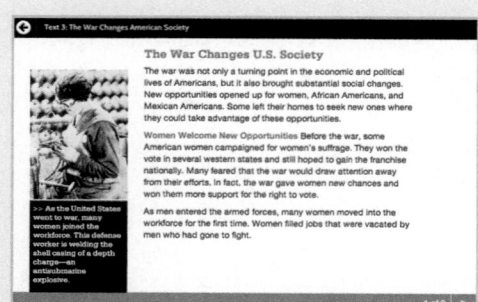

INTERACTIVE CHART

The Great Migration

Objective 3: Analyze the causes and effects of migration and social changes that occurred during the war.

Quick Instruction

Interactive Chart: The Great Migration Project the chart onto the whiteboard. Guide the class in an analysis of the causes of the Great Migration. Invite volunteers to share their charts. Push and pull factors students might list include: *(Push factors: Jim Crow segregation laws, lynching and other racial violence, and few economic opportunities, ruined crops from insects. Pull factors: economic opportunity, family and friends)*

Analyze Information Ask students to analyze the effects of changing demographic patterns resulting from the Great Migration. How did the Great Migration affect cities in the North? *(The Great Migration increased the number of African Americans in northern cities.)* What long-term impact might this have? *(African American culture will become more influential and prominent. Demographic shifts often have political consequences as large groups change voting patterns.)*

ACTIVE CLASSROOM

Emphasize the significance of World War I as a turning point in American history by inviting students to participate in a Connect Two Activity. List the following terms on the board for students to copy on small pieces of paper: Pull factor, Push Factor, women, African Americans, Mexican Americans, Nineteenth Amendment, Jim Crow segregation laws, barrios, Great Migration, Army Corps of Nurses, and, Mexican Revolution, Read the list of words with students. Ask students to "connect two" or choose two words they think might belong together, and state the reason, e.g. "I would connect _____ and _____ because." Invite the other students to comment on the connections and discuss the relationship between the terms and the changes brought about by the war.

D Differentiate: Extra Support After asking the students to connect two terms, allow students five minutes to review the list of words. Students may benefit from using the text to complete the activity. Then continue with the group activity.

Further Instruction

Go through the Interactive Reading Notepad questions and discuss the answers with the class.

Generate Explanations What effect did women's participation in the war effort have on the success of the women's suffrage movement? *(As women continued to prove themselves capable of contributing to the country's economic and political success, President Wilson equated women's efforts to support the country during WWI with the privilege to vote. Congress agreed and passed the nineteenth amendment in 1919.)*

Summarize How did World War I provide new opportunities for women, African Americans, and Mexican Americans? *(Women, African Americans, and Mexican Americans filled jobs that were vacated by men who were fighting in the war. Increased wartime demands for food and other goods created new jobs that needed filling. The war also provided opportunities to participate in military service.)*

Support Ideas with Examples What were the contributions of African Americans during the war? *(More than 360,000 African Americans served in the military during the war. Many worked in agriculture and factories in the North that helped with the war effort.)*

SYNTHESIZE

DIGITAL ACTIVITY

Essential Question: How do we handle conflict?

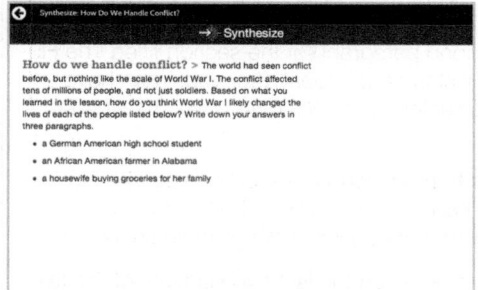

Ask students to recall the Topic Essential Question, *How do we handle conflict?* Ask them to take five minutes to write down some brief answers to the questions below, then share their answers with a talking partner.

- How would you want your government to handle a large-scale war?

- What would be the best way for civilians to handle the outbreak of a conflict?

Discuss Before students begin their descriptions, lead the class in a brief review of the home front in the United States during World War I. Engage student partners in discussing the activity assignment before they write their paragraphs.

DEMONSTRATE

LESSON QUIZ

Lesson Quiz and Class Discussion Board

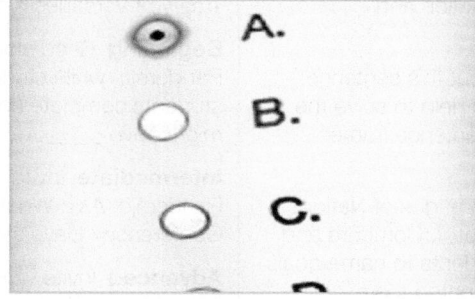

Assign the online Lesson Quiz for this lesson if you haven't already done so. Students will be offered automatic remediation or enrichment based on their score.

Pose these questions to the class on the Discussion Board:

In *The Home Front During World War I*, you read about how the efforts of the United States government to ensure public support for the war sometimes conflicted with many Americans' views about civil rights. The freedoms that were affected were ones guaranteed by the First Amendment to the Constitution.

Support Ideas with Examples Can you think of any contemporary examples of government infringing on its citizens' constitutional rights during times of war? Cite examples in your answer.

Express Ideas Clearly In your opinion, is national unity during wartime more important to a democracy than the right of free expression? Explain.

Topic Inquiry
Have students continue their investigations for the Topic Inquiry.

The End of World War I

Supporting English Language Learners

Use with Digital Text 3, **The Paris Peace Conference.**

Listening
Read aloud the text under the heading **The Paris Peace Conference,** or invite volunteers to do so. Explain that some of the reading's basic vocabulary is also commonly used in classroom instruction and interactions.

Beginning Have students listen as you say and act out this sentence: *I solve the problem.* Ask: What did Wilson think would help to solve the world's problems? Have students answer using this sentence frame: *Wilson wanted to form a _____ to solve problems.*

Intermediate Have students listen as you say: "The League of Nations was Wilson's idea. His goal was to include it in the treaty". Compare and contrast the meanings of *idea* and *goal*. Then ask students to name goals of the Paris Peace Conference and various ideas presented there.

Advanced Ask students to listen as you say (with and without the parenthesis): In addition (to free trade), the idea of a general disarmament was rejected. Ask students to say the difference between the two sentences and then discuss the meaning and usage of the phrase *in addition (to)*. Ask students: What ideas were present at the conference in addition to Wilson's?

Advanced High Read the first sentence of the reading's last paragraph. Ask students to define *randomly*. Explain that *at random* is a synonym, and *random* is the adjectival form. Split the class into pairs and have one student in each pair use one of these terms say a sentence about the text. Ask the other students to listen and then restate their partners' sentences in their own words.

Use with Digital Text 4, **America Rejects the Treaty of Versailles.**

Reading
Explain to students that they will demonstrate English comprehension and expand reading skills by predicting what might have happened with the Treaty of Versailles if certain events had gone differently.

Beginning Read aloud the second paragraph of the section titled The Flu Pandemic, while students follow along and repeat after you. Then have students complete and say this sentence: *If Wilson had been healthy, he might have _____.*

Intermediate Invite volunteers to read aloud the section titled The Flu Pandemic. Ask: What if Wilson had not been sick at the Paris Peace Conference? Have students answer the question in complete sentences.

Advanced Invite volunteers to read aloud the last two sections of the text. Ask: What might have happened if Wilson had not had a stroke, and why do you think so? Have pairs of students discuss their ideas.

Advanced High Have students silently read the text. Then discuss together what might have happened if Wilson had not fallen ill twice during the treaty process. Encourage students to support their predictions with specific details from the text.

▣ Differentiate Instruction

Use the Differentiated Instruction notes throughout the lesson plan to support the varied skill sets, levels of readiness, and interests in the mixed-ability classroom.

Challenge These notes include suggestions for expanding the activity for advanced students.

On-Level These notes include suggestions for modifying the activity to address different interests or learning styles.

Extra Support These notes include ideas for providing more scaffolding or reading spuport.

Special Needs These notes provide ideas for adapting instruction to support the needs of various special needs students.

■ NOTES

PEARSON
realize™
www.PearsonRealize.com

Go online to access additional resources including:
Primary Sources • Biographies • Supreme Court cases •
21st Century Skill Tutorials • Maps • Graphic Organizers.

Objectives

Objective 1: Understand the contributions of the American Expeditionary Force to the Allied victory in World War I.

Objective 2: Describe the issues raised by President Wilson's Fourteen Points.

Objective 3: Analyze the decisions made at the Paris Peace Conference and included in the Treaty of Versailles.

Objective 4: Evaluate the pros and cons of U.S. participation in the League of Nations.

Objective 5: Explain why the U.S. Senate did not ratify the Treaty of Versailles.

LESSON 3 ORGANIZER		PACING: APPROX. 1 PERIOD, .5 BLOCKS			
				RESOURCES	
		OBJECTIVES	**PACING**	**Online**	**Print**
Connect					
DIGITAL START UP ACTIVITY **"Over There"**			5 min.	●	
Investigate					
DIGITAL TEXT 1 **America Joins the Fighting**		Objective 1	10 min.	●	●
INTERACTIVE MAP **Key Battles Fought by Americans in World War I**			10 min.	●	
DIGITAL TEXT 2 **Wilson Wants "Peace Without Victory"**		Objective 2	10 min.	●	●
DIGITAL TEXT 3 **The Paris Peace Conference**		Objective 3	10 min.	●	●
DIGITAL TEXT 4 **America Rejects the Treaty of Versailles**		Objectives 4, 5	10 min.	●	●
INTERACTIVE CHART **Should the United States Join the League of Nations?**			10 min.	●	
Synthesize					
DIGITAL ACTIVITY **Essential Question: How do we handle conflict?**			5 min.	●	
Demonstrate					
LESSON QUIZ **Lesson Quiz and Class Discussion Board**			10 min.	●	

The End of World War I

▮ CONNECT

DIGITAL START UP ACTIVITY
"Over There"

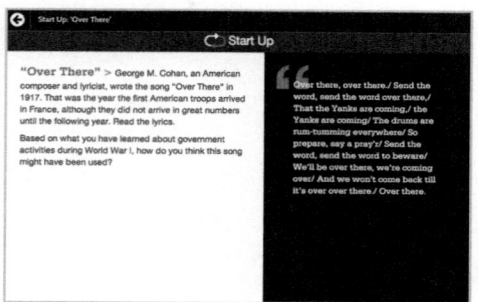

Project the Start Up Activity As students enter and get settled, draw attention to the lyrics of "Over There." Encourage them to take a few minutes to digest the lyrics and write down three thoughts or feelings the lyrics invoke. When they have completed their lists, consider working together as a group to share students' responses.

Discuss Based on what you have learned about government activities during World War I, how do you think this song might have been used? *(The song sounds like it is very patriotic. It would probably have been used as propaganda to help gather support for the war effort.)*

Tell students that in this lesson they will be learning how American "dough boys," or soldiers, contributed to winning World War I.

Aa Vocabulary Development: Use the Interactive Reading Notepad to preview the Key Terms and Academic Vocabulary in this lesson with students.

⇅ FLIP IT!

Assign the Flipped Video for this lesson.

▮ STUDENT EDITION PRINT PAGES: 466–474

▮ INVESTIGATE

DIGITAL TEXT 1
America Joins the Fighting

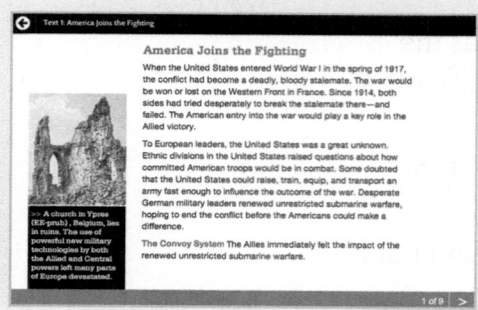

INTERACTIVE MAP
Key Battles Fought by Americans in World War I

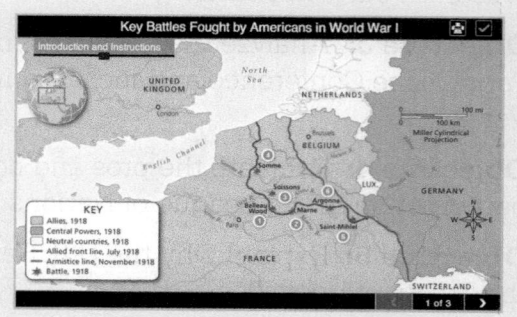

Objective 1: Understand the contributions of the American Expeditionary Force to the Allied victory in the war.

Quick Instruction

Interactive Map: Key Battles Fought by Americans in World War I Project the map on the whiteboard and click through the hot spots on the map to help students understand the contributions of the American Expeditionary Forces (AEF) led by General John J. Pershing. Introduce the map activity by reminding students that when the United States entered World War I in the spring of 1917, the conflict had become a stalemate. The appearance of the American Expeditionary Forces on the Western Front breathed new life into the Allies' cause. Ask: In what ways did General Pershing exhibit qualities of effective leadership? *(Pershing was a strong planner, making sure his troops were well-trained by the time they arrived in France. He showed determination in making sure that his American troops were independent, leading to greater American control. His troops fought successfully in significant engagements on the Western Front.)*

Identify Central Issues Ask students to describe the significance of the Battle of Argonne Forest. *(The battle resulted in a defeat for Germany and hastened the end of the war.)*

▮ ACTIVE CLASSROOM

Point out that today congressional Medal of Honor recipients include individuals of all races. Then have students Make Headlines that describes the importance of congressional Medal of Honor recipient Alvin York. Ask: If you were to write a headline for the Alvin York's actions in Meuse-Argonne region that captured the most important aspect that should be remembered, what would that headline be? Allow students to use subheadings to communicate more information. Have students pass their headlines to a partner for them to review.

D Differentiate: Challenge/Gifted Ask students to do additional research on Alvin York and his battlefield exploits and present their findings.

Further Instruction

Point out that the end of the war between Germany and Russia and new tactics in dealing with the German unrestricted submarine warfare had a great impact on World War I. Make sure students understand that as fighting ended on the Eastern Front, Germany was moving troops to the Western Front to confront arriving American troops.

Summarize Why was the convoy system such a great success? *(Ships sailing together are safer than lone ships. More ships can provide greater safety to track and destroy submarines and also rescue survivors if an attack was successful.)*

Make Predictions How might the success and valor displayed by African American units such as the 369th Infantry Regiment affect the status of African Americans in the U.S Army? *(American military leaders may consider desegregating the army.)*

DIGITAL TEXT 2

Wilson Wants "Peace Without Victory"

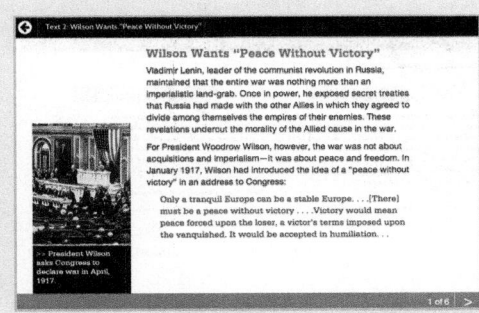

DIGITAL TEXT 3

The Paris Peace Conference

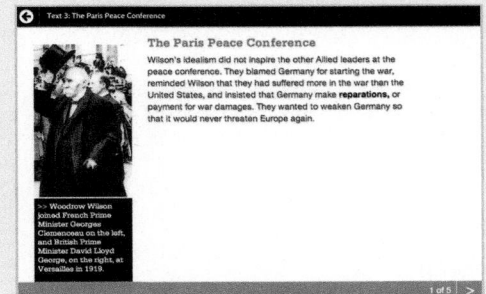

Objective 2: Describe the issues raised by President Wilson's Fourteen Points.

Quick Instruction

Analyze Charts Project the chart. Ensure understanding of Wilson's Fourteen Points by asking volunteers to read and discuss each point. Challenge students to explain why Wilson believed that a "peace without victory" would help avoid future wars. *(Wilson thought that the victorious nations would force terms and conditions on the loser. The Central Powers would be humiliated and would harbor resentment toward the Allies.)*

Infer Why did President Wilson think that the Fourteen Points were "the only possible program" for the world's peace? *(Wilson's Fourteen Points included ideas such as promoting openness, encouraging independence, and supporting freedom—ideas that would benefit every nation.)*

Further Instruction

Wilson did not invite any leading Republicans to join him at the peace conference in Versailles. This decision angered Republicans, who had won control of Congress in the 1918 elections. The animosity between Wilson and the congressional Republicans created additional conflict that highlighted differing views on America's role in the world.

Compare and Contrast How did the debate over the United States joining the League of Nations reflect disagreement over participation in international organizations and treaties? *(Wilson believed in the equality of all nations, and called for open diplomacy. All countries should be held accountable for following the same guiding principles set up by an international organization like the League of Nations. Henry Cabot Lodge and others were conscious of the disadvantages of U.S. participation in international organizations and treaties. They wanted to keep the United States moving into the role of a world power. To them, American interests came first because the United States provided "the best hopes of mankind.")*

Objective 3: Analyze the decisions made at the Paris Peace Conference and included in the Treaty of Versailles.

Quick Instruction

Analyze Images Invite a student to identify the people in the photo. *(French Prime Minister Georges Clemenceau on the left, U.S. President Woodrow Wilson, center, and David Lloyd George, Prime Minister of the United Kingdom on the right)* Challenge students to describe how Clemenceau and Lloyd George differed from Wilson on the goals of the Paris Peace Conference. *(Clemenceau and Lloyd George blamed Germany for starting the war, so they wanted to punish Germany by making it pay for war damages. They also wanted to weaken Germany so that it would never threaten Europe again.)* Ensure students understand that because Great Britain and France had suffered such great losses in the war, both countries did not agree with Wilson's "peace without victory" concept and chipped away at the Fourteen Points plan.

ELL Use the ELL activity described in the ELL chart.

Further Instruction

Encourage students to discuss and identify the new territories established by the treaties and explain reasons for changes in political boundaries resulting from the international conflict of World War I. Use that discussion as a springboard to engage students in analyzing major issues raised by the Treaty of Versailles.

The End of World War I

DIGITAL TEXT 4
America Rejects the Treaty of Versailles

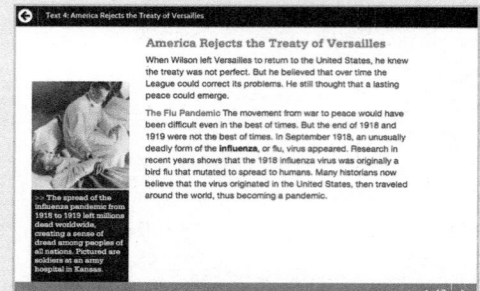

INTERACTIVE CHART
Should the United States Join the League of Nations?

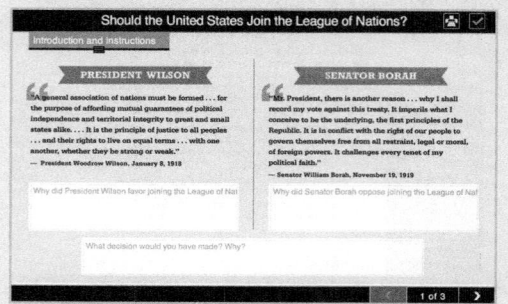

Express Problems Clearly What problems did the peace treaties solve? *(The treaties broke up the large empires that had contributed to the start of the war. Germany was punished and territory previously won was returned to former nations.)* What problems did they create? *(The treaties violated the concept of national self-determination. Many of the newly created nations, such as Iraq, had no sense of national identity. Territories were also established as mandates, overseen by another nation, which was similar to empire-building.)*

Evaluate Impact How would you evaluate Wilson's contributions to the Paris Peace Conference? *(I would say Wilson failed at getting the allied nations to adopt his key plans. Although the Treaty of Versailles included the League of Nations, many people, including those in Congress, opposed it for various reasons, making ratification questionable.)*

Objectives 4: **Evaluate the pros and cons of U.S. participation in the League of Nations; 5:** **Explain why the United States Senate did not ratify the Treaty of Versailles.**

Quick Instruction

Interactive Chart: Should the U.S. Join the League of Nations? Project the chart on the whiteboard. Engage students in evaluating the pros and cons of U.S. participation in the League of Nations by summarizing the opposing views from the interactivity. *(Wilson believed that the League of Nations was the only way to protect political independence and territories. He believed that it also would lead to greater equality and fair treatment among nations, regardless of size or power. Senator Borah thought the League of Nations took away Americans' right of self-governance. He believed the League of Nations would force the United States to follow the actions or opinions of other countries, which he considered counter to the Constitution.)*

Analyze Images Project the image of Woodrow Wilson on a speaking tour. Explain that the Treaty of Versailles needed to be submitted to the Senate Foreign Relations Committee and then ratified, or approved, by the full Senate. Challenge students to identify obstacles Wilson faced as he promoted the treaty and fought for its ratification. *(Republicans gained control of the Senate and the House of Representatives in the 1918 elections. The treaty, therefore, would have to get through the Republican-controlled Senate, which had already shown opposition to it. Also, Wilson had upset many Republicans*

by not inviting them to be a part of the Paris Peace Convention. Wilson also battled illness as the treaty debate raged.)

ACTIVE CLASSROOM

Conduct a Take a Stand Activity: Ask students to take a stand on the following question: Do the pros of joining an international organization like the League of Nation outweigh the cons? Ask students to divide into two groups based on their answer and move to separate areas of the classroom. Ask students to talk with each other to compare their reasons for answering yes or no. Ask a representative from each side to present and defend the group's point of view.

ELL Use the ELL activity described in the ELL chart.

Further Instruction
Go through the Interactive Reading Notepad questions and discuss the answers with the class.

Evaluate Arguments Based on information you have learned, how would you evaluate the arguments made by irreconcilables and reservationists? *(Some students may say the irreconcilables were right in not allowing for any flexibility in American participation in the League of Nations. Other students may say the reservationists were right because they were willing to compromise.)*

 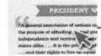

 SYNTHESIZE

DEMONSTRATE

DIGITAL ACTIVITY

Essential Question: How do we handle conflict?

LESSON QUIZ

Lesson Quiz and Class Discussion Board

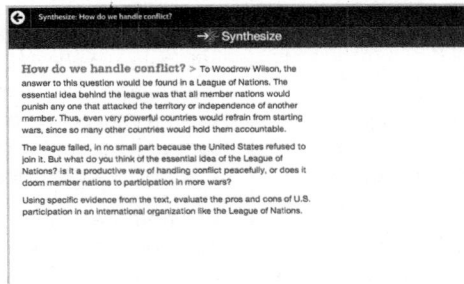

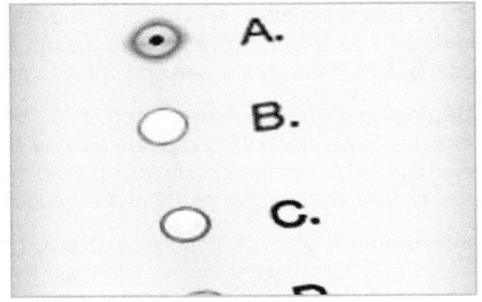

Predict Consequences Article 10 of the League covenant called for mutual defense by signers of the treaty. Why might this have raised constitutional issues if the United States had agreed to join the League of Nations? *(Under the Constitution, the United States can not declare war without the consent of Congress. Participation in the League covenant would have stripped the U.S. Congress of that authority.)*

Ask students to recall the Topic Essential Question, *How do we handle conflict?* Have them read the introduction to the Essential Question Activity: How do we handle conflict? Ask them to take five minutes to think about the reasons the League of Nations failed.

Have partners think about the following question: To what international organizations does the U.S. belong today? Have pairs share their answers with the class.

Discuss Before students begin their essays evaluating the pros and cons of U.S. participation in an international organization like the League of Nations, provide time for partners to Think-Pair-Share the questions in the activity.

Assign the online Lesson Quiz for this lesson if you haven't already done so. Students will be offered automatic remediation or enrichment based on their score.

Pose these questions to the class on the Discussion Board: In *The End of World War I*, you read about America's continued rise as a world power. Following the end of the war, American leaders wrestled with the ongoing questions of how best to participate in world affairs and handle potential conflicts.

Predict Consequences What impact will U.S. failure to approve the Treaty of Versailles have on international affairs?

Draw Inferences What factors influence a country's decision to rely on and support international organizations?

Topic Inquiry

Have students continue their investigations for the Topic Inquiry.

The Postwar Economy Booms

Supporting English Language Learners

Use with Digital Text 2, **The Impact of Henry Ford and the Automobile.**

Reading

Prepare students for the following activities by having them share what they know about life before automobiles. Prompt students to demonstrate English comprehension and expand reading skills by employing analytical skills such as evaluating written information and performing critical analyses commensurate with content area and grade level needs.

Beginning Read aloud the section titled *The Automobile Changes America*; have students participate as they are able. Ask students to evaluate written information by completing this sentence: *I (do not) agree that the automobile changed America because _____.*

Intermediate Ask volunteers to read aloud the section titled *The Automobile Changes America*. Help them to list the major changes that are described. Have them evaluate written information by asking: Is it accurate to say that America was changed by the automobile, or is it an exaggeration? Why?

Advanced Ask volunteers to read aloud the section titled *The Automobile Changes America*. Have pairs of students evaluate written information by discussing: Does the text sufficiently prove the idea (from the fourth paragraph) that automobile ownership symbolized success? Why or why not?

Advanced High Have students read the section titled *The Automobile Changes America*. Ask them to write a paragraph on whether or not they agree that the automobile significantly changed America. Encourage them to cite specific details as they employ analytical skills in evaluating the section.

Use with Digital Text 4, **Urban, Suburban, and Rural Areas.**

Listening

Explain to students that they will be learning academic vocabulary commonly heard in classroom instruction and interactions.

Beginning Use the verb *participate* in a classroom context, for example to participate in a class discussion. Help students understand its meaning. Have students listen as you read the text's last paragraph. Ask: Who participated in the consumer economy—people in the cities and suburbs, or people in the country? If necessary, give this prompt to help students answer in a complete sentence: "People in the _____ participated in the consumer economy."

Intermediate Show students familiar classroom symbols, and ask them what they symbolize. Define the academic vocabulary word *symbolize* together. Ask each student to think of an example of a symbol. Then have students pair up and listen to their partner's example. Call on students to describe his or her partner's symbol. Encourage students to use the word *symbolize* in their descriptions.

Advanced Ask: What should you do if your grades decline? What does the verb *decline* mean? Then point out this sentence from the text: *Even worse, farm incomes declined during the decade.* Ask pairs of students to discuss why they might have declined. Ask students to listen to and, if necessary, write down their partner's ideas. Call on students to repeat the points made by their partners.

Advanced High Ask: What should you do if your grades decline? What if there is a decline in your grades? Have students identify the noun and verb forms of the academic vocabulary word *decline* and define them. Then have pairs of students use both forms in a discussion about what was declining in 1920s America. Ask students to listen to their partner's ideas and then call on students to explain the points made by their partners.

▣ Differentiate Instruction

Use the Differentiated Instruction notes throughout the lesson plan to support the varied skill sets, levels of readiness, and interests in the mixed-ability classroom.

Challenge These notes include suggestions for expanding the activity for advanced students.

On-Level These notes include suggestions for modifying the activity to address different interests or learning styles.

Extra Support These notes include ideas for providing more scaffolding or reading spuport.

Special Needs These notes provide ideas for adapting instruction to support the needs of various special needs students.

■ NOTES

PEARSON realize™
www.PearsonRealize.com

Go online to access additional resources including:
Primary Sources • Biographies • Supreme Court cases •
21st Century Skill Tutorials • Maps • Graphic Organizers.

Objectives

Objective 1: Describe the economic problems America faced after World War I.

Objective 2: Explain the economic growth and prosperity of the 1920s, including how Henry Ford and the automobile industry helped spark the boom.

Objective 3: Analyze the consumer revolution and the bull market of the 1920s.

Objective 4: Compare the different effects of the economic boom on urban, suburban, and rural America.

LESSON 4 ORGANIZER		PACING: APPROX. 1 PERIOD, .5 BLOCKS			
				RESOURCES	
		OBJECTIVES	PACING	Online	Print
Connect					
	DIGITAL START UP ACTIVITY **The United States of Cars**		5 min.	●	
Investigate					
	DIGITAL TEXT 1 **Postwar Issues**	Objective 1	10 min.	●	●
	DIGITAL TEXT 2 **The Impact of Henry Ford and the Automobile**	Objective 2	10 min.	●	●
	INTERACTIVE ILLUSTRATION **Ford's Innovation: The Assembly Line**		10 min.	●	
	DIGITAL TEXT 3 **Economic Growth in the 1920s**	Objective 3	10 min.	●	●
	DIGITAL TEXT 4 **Urban, Suburban, and Rural Areas**	Objective 4	10 min.	●	●
	INTERACTIVE GALLERY **Standard of Living in the 1920s**		10 min.	●	
Synthesize					
	DIGITAL ACTIVITY **The Car as a Cause**		5 min.	●	
Demonstrate					
	LESSON QUIZ **Lesson Quiz and Class Discussion Board**		10 min.	●	

The Postwar Economy Booms

■ CONNECT

DIGITAL START UP ACTIVITY
The United States of Cars

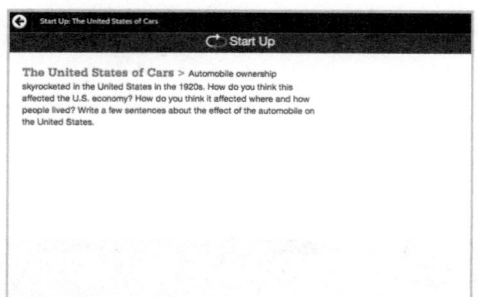

Project the Start Up Activity Ask students to think about the role of the car in American society today as they enter and get settled. Then have them share their ideas with another student.

Discuss Before students begin their lists, encourage them to think about what life would be like without automobiles. Engage students in completing the activity.

Tell students that in this lesson they will be learning how the automobile change life in the United States.

Aa Vocabulary Development: Use the Interactive Reading Notepad to preview the Key Terms and Academic Vocabulary in this lesson with students.

⬆ FLIP IT!

Assign the Flipped Video for this lesson.

■ STUDENT EDITION PRINT PAGES: 475–481

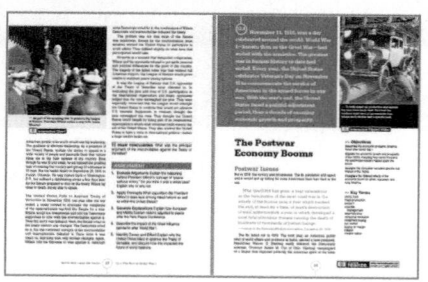

■ INVESTIGATE

DIGITAL TEXT 1
Postwar Issues

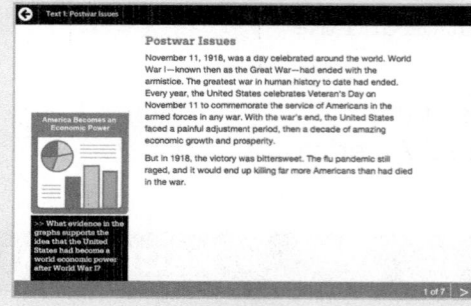

Objective 1: Describe the economic problems America faced after the war.

Quick Instruction

Analyze Graphs Project the infographic titled *America Becomes an Economic Power*. Using specific information from the infographic to support their answers, ask students to infer the economic strength of the country beginning around 1920. *(As evidenced from the rise in average earnings, GDP and stock prices, many Americans were enjoying growing prosperity.)* Ensure that students understand that immediately following World War I, a recession, or economic slowdown, created a competitive job market and negatively impacted economic growth in the United States.

Analyze Information Challenge students to analyze causes of economic growth and prosperity in the 1920s, including Warren Harding's Return to Normalcy. *(Nations that had been decimated by the war such as Britain and France had to buy American goods, which boosted the American economy. These countries had to borrow money from American bankers and obtain lines of credit with American business firms to pay for the goods. Harding's pledge to return America to normalcy helped Americans focus on economic issues that also helped lift the economy.)*

Make Generalizations Compare the economic graphs and make a generalization about farm wages versus non-farm wages in the 1920s. *(American farmers did not share in the prosperity of the 1920s.)*

Further Instruction

Express Problems Clearly What problems led to a weak postwar economy. *(Inflation, labor unrest caused by falling wages)*

Summarize the economic effects of World War I on the United States. *(By 1920, the United States was an economic giant. It was the richest, most industrialized country in the world.)*

Analyze Information How did the influenza pandemic make the transition from war to peace more difficult? *(The flu pandemic had a devastating effect on Americans, killing more Americans than had died in the war. This had a huge effect on the nation's economy as well on the spirits of most Americans trying to get back to normal life.)*

Identify Central Issues What effects did the end of the war have on race relations? *(The end of the war reduced the number of job opportunities for African Americans, wiping away all the gains they had made. The competition for jobs and housing led to race tensions, including riots.)*

PEARSON
realize™
www.PearsonRealize.com
Access your Digital Lesson

DIGITAL TEXT 2

The Impact of Henry Ford and the Automobile

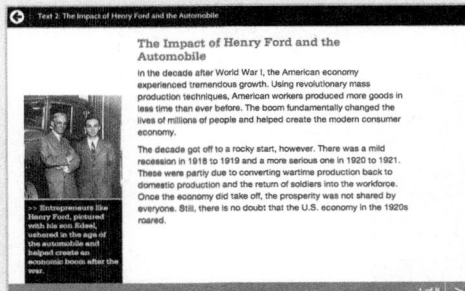

INTERACTIVE ILLUSTRATION

Ford's Innovation: The Assembly Line

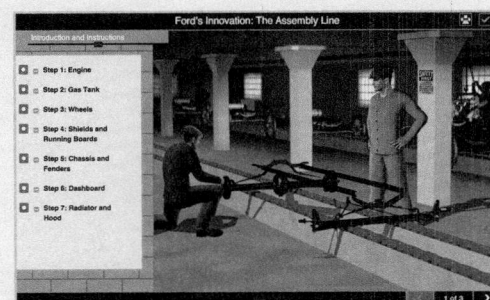

Objective 2: Explain the economic growth and prosperity of the 1920s, including how Henry Ford and the automobile industry helped spark the boom.

Quick Instruction

Interactive Illustration: Ford's Innovation: The Assembly Line Project the illustration on the board and select the squares one at a time to see how Ford's assembly line operated. Point out and discuss how Henry Ford created his assembly line by conducting time-study analyses and basing innovations to his factories' technology and management on those studies. Ask: What were the productivity enhancements that result from Ford's technological and management innovations? *(Using a moving assembly line, Ford dramatically increased production efficiency. Build time for a Model T dropped from 12 hours to 93 minutes.)*

Draw Conclusions Ask students to describe the impact of technological and management innovations in the workplace such as assembly line manufacturing on labor. *(Ford's assembly line focused workers on doing one task, making them more efficient and better at their jobs.)*

📷 **ACTIVE CLASSROOM**

Have students Make Headlines that describe the impact of Henry Ford on American industry innovations. Ask: If you were to write a headline that captured the most important aspect about Ford's role in developing new manufacturing innovations that should be remembered, what would that headline be? Emphasize to students that their headlines should not just say the innovation was, but also capture why it is significant, how it will affect the country, and so on. Allow them to use subheadings if they would like. Have students pass their headlines to a partner for them to review.

ELL Use the ELL activity described in the ELL chart.

Further Instruction

Begin a discussion about the effects of the automobile in the United States, including how petroleum-based products and increased steel output used for automobiles spurred economic development of the United States. Point out that management innovations in the workplace implemented by Henry Ford's automobile company greatly affected his labor force. Challenge students to describe several ways Ford showed that he was concerned for the well-being of his workforce. *(Ford more than doubled the wages of many workers. He also reduced their workday from 9 hours to 8 hours and gave them Saturday and Sunday off.)*

Analyze Interactions Among Events How did the production efficiencies of Ford's assembly line change and lead to the growth of industry in general? *(Ford's processes were copied by other industries in the United States. This led to American workers producing more goods in less time than ever before. Building more and more cars also created growth in other industries related to car manufacture or use, such as steel, glass, rubber, asphalt, wood, petroleum, insurance, and road-construction.)*

Draw Conclusions How did the Ford's innovations in transportation change the way Americans lived? *(The automobile changed the way spent their time. People could go where they wanted, whenever they wanted. The car also affected where people lived. They could drive to work and live farther from their places of employment. This helped create the development of suburban America.)*

Generate Explanations Starting in this ear, how did gasoline as a form of energy impact the American way of life over time? *(The oil and gas industry expanded with the automobile industry, creating new employment opportunities in all three industries that previously didn't exist. As a result, the American standard of living continued to rise.)*

The Postwar Economy Booms

DIGITAL TEXT 3

Economic Growth in the 1920s

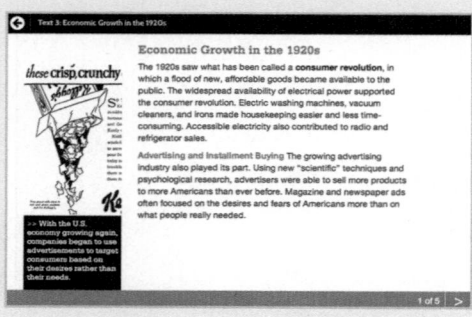

DIGITAL TEXT 4

Urban, Suburban, and Rural Areas

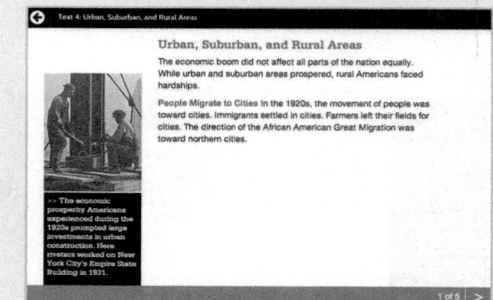

Objective 3: Analyze the consumer revolution and the bull market of the 1920s.

Quick Instruction

Analyze Images Project the image of the Kellogg's Cornflakes advertisement. Ask volunteers to describe effective advertisements they are familiar with. Discuss how advertisements affect the purchasing decisions of consumers. Point out that technologies like the widespread availability of electrical power and increased wages supported the consumer revolution in the 1920s.

Draw Conclusions Why do you think many advertisers began to focus on the benefits of their products rather than on the products themselves? *(Psychological research had shown advertisers that they could sell more products to more Americans focusing on the desires and fears of Americans.)*

Summarize What factors led to the bull market in the 1920s and what potential downsides did a bull market present? *(Confidence in the American economy and new forms of buying stocks on credit led to the bull market. More and more Americans put their money into stocks in an effort to get rich quick. However, investor over-confidence might result in purchasing stock on margins, or credit, that would put investors in debt if market values decreased.)*

D **Differentiate: Extra Support** Explain that credit is money that a bank or business will allow a person to use and then pay back in the future, usually with interest. Point out that interest is a fee that lenders charge to use the money. When buying on credit, buyers end up repaying more money than the amount they borrowed.

Further Instruction

Review with students the concept of the free enterprise system. *(a market economy in which privately owned businesses have the freedom to operate for a profit with limited government intervention.)* Remind students that during World War I, the U.S. government curtailed the free enterprise system in order to direct the nations' industries toward the war effort. Challenge students to suggest possible effects of this wartime effort. *(Some businesses might have struggled because they were forced to work for the government, which probably reduced their profits.)*

Infer How did Henry Ford and others in the transportation industry utilize the free enterprise system to improve the standard of living in the United States? *(Ford was driven to make his cars as efficiently as possible, which in turn would lead to more sales and larger profits. His innovations were developed without government interference. By developing new techniques he provided more opportunities for Americans to purchase automobiles, which raised the standard of living for large numbers of people.)*

Objective 4: Compare the different effects of the economic boom on urban and rural America.

Quick Instruction

Interactive Gallery: Standard of Living in the 1920s Project the gallery and select the images to learn more about the innovations that led to rising standards of living for many Americans. Be sure students understand that standard of living is a general term that refers to how well people live. Challenge students to discuss the factors the determine our standards of living.

Analyze Information How did innovations in the communication industry within the free enterprise system improve the standard of living in the United States? *(Radio became a major source of entertainment and news and an important advertising medium. Radios helped educate people about current events, new products, and provided a valuable source of information.)*

▶ ACTIVE CLASSROOM

Play a game of Connect Two about the rising standard of living in the 1920s. List the following terms on the board: radio, antibiotic, diet, advertising, life expectancy, consumer products, diesel engine, Clarence Birdseye, penicillin, credit, food-freezing technology, crop production. Direct students copy the terms down on notecards or small slips of paper, one term to a card or piece of paper. Review the list of terms with students. Ask students to "connect two" or choose two terms they think belong together, and state the reason for their connection. Challenge students to connect as many pairs of terms as possible. Conduct this activity before, during, and/or after student reading.

INTERACTIVE GALLERY
Standard of Living in the 1920s

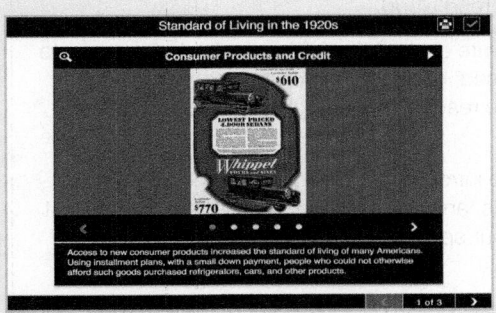

ELL Use the ELL activity described in the ELL chart.

Further Instruction

Analyze the causes and effects of the changing demographic patterns resulting from migration from rural areas to urban areas within the United States in the 1920s. *(More and more Americans left rural areas to live in urban areas to seek better economic opportunities and to experience the benefits of living in bustling, thriving consumer-driven cities. Life became harder for rural Americans left behind. They did not participate in the consumer benefits and economic gains of the decade. They were often poorer and farmers suffered from growing debt and falling farm prices.)*

Draw Conclusions What impact did the development of suburbs have on American society? Support your answer with details from the lesson. *(Suburbs drained people and resources from the cities. Suburbs were more conservative and Republican, so the shift changed the political landscape. Older urban areas eventually declined.)*

■ SYNTHESIZE

DIGITAL ACTIVITY
The Car as a Cause

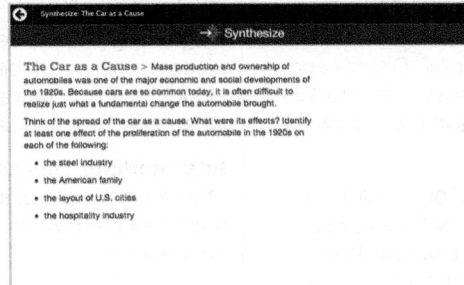

Have student partners take five minutes to discuss the following questions: Can the American economy survive without the automobile? How does the automobile impact the economy?

Discuss Before students begin their essays, review the assignment: students will write short answers describing the effect of the automobile on several aspects of American life. To help students connect these concepts, encourage to think about the readings and the interactivities they explored.

■ DEMONSTRATE

LESSON QUIZ
Lesson Quiz and Class Discussion Board

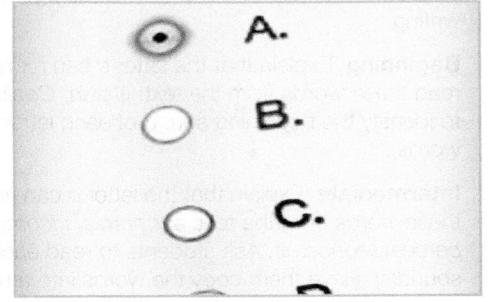

Assign the online Lesson Quiz for this lesson if you haven't already done so. Students will be offered automatic remediation or enrichment based on their score.

Pose these questions to the class on the Discussion Board:

In *The Postwar Economy Booms*, you read about how economic booms and shifting demographics affect the lives of citizens. Economic growth provides an increase in labor opportunities, consumer purchasing choices, and standard of living. Shifting demographics has a profound impact on the required resources a community can use and affects political representation.

Predict Consequences What happens when a large segment of the American public does not benefit from economic growth?

Draw Conclusions How might political representation affect the lives of minority groups in a community?

Topic Inquiry
Have students continue their investigations for the Topic Inquiry.

Government in the 1920s

Supporting English Language Learners

Use with Digital Text 2, **Economic Prosperity Under Coolidge.**

Writing
Use words from the text to help students learn relationships between sounds and letters of the English language to represent sounds when writing.

Beginning Explain that the letter *c* can represent /k/ or /s/. Display and read these words from the text: *Calvin, Coolidge, civilization*. Ask students to identify the beginning sound of each letter *c*. Then have them copy the words.

Intermediate Explain that the letter *c* can represent /k/ or /s/. Display these words from the text: *economic, income, Mexico, civilization, peace, percent, concerns*. Ask students to read each word and identify its *c* sound(s). Have them copy the words into a two-column chart.

Advanced Explain that /k/ can be represented by *c* or *k*, and /s/ by *c* or *s*. Display and read a word from the text for each category: *income, keep, percent, support*. Then have pairs of students locate additional words from the text for each category and write them in a four-column chart.

Advanced High Ask students to write the following words: *income, keep, percent, support*. Discuss the correct spellings, and review that /k/ can be represented by *c* or *k*, and /s/ by *c* or *s*. Have students locate additional words from the text for each category and write them in a four-column chart.

Use with Digital Text 3, **America's Place in a Changed World.**

Listening
Explain that students will be monitoring their understanding of spoken language as they listen to you read aloud.

Beginning Ask students to write each of the following words on separate pieces of paper: globe, collapsed, compass, victorious, confident. Read aloud the first paragraph of the reading. Tell students to hold up the word when they hear you say it.

Intermediate Read aloud the introductory paragraph of the text. Pause after every couple of sentences, and ask students to restate what you just read. Ask them what about your spoken language was easy or difficult to understand.

Advanced Read aloud the section titled Seeking Stability After World War I. Pause periodically to give students a chance to note down what they understood. Have students work in pairs to compare notes by using the following sentence frames: You said that you wrote _____. I also wrote/didn't write_____.

Advanced High Ask pairs of students to read aloud the text. Then have them monitor their understanding by trying to summarize what they read. Tell them to take turns adding sentences to the summary by listening to their partner's sentence and building on it in an appropriate way.

◨ Differentiate Instruction

Use the Differentiated Instruction notes throughout the lesson plan to support the varied skill sets, levels of readiness, and interests in the mixed-ability classroom.

Challenge These notes include suggestions for expanding the activity for advanced students.

On-Level These notes include suggestions for modifying the activity to address different interests or learning styles.

Extra Support These notes include ideas for providing more scaffolding or reading spuport.

Special Needs These notes provide ideas for adapting instruction to support the needs of various special needs students.

■ NOTES

PEARSON
realize™
www.PearsonRealize.com

Go online to access additional resources including:
Primary Sources • Biographies • Supreme Court cases •
21st Century Skill Tutorials • Maps • Graphic Organizers.

Objectives

Objective 1: Analyze how the policies of Presidents Harding and Coolidge encouraged economic growth and prosperity in the 1920s.

Objective 2: Discuss the effects of political scandals, including Teapot Dome, on Harding's presidency.

Objective 3: Explain the role that the United States played in the world during the 1920s.

LESSON 5 ORGANIZER		PACING: APPROX. 1 PERIOD, .5 BLOCKS		
			RESOURCES	
	OBJECTIVES	PACING	Online	Print
Connect				
DIGITAL START UP ACTIVITY **What is "Normal"?**		5 min.	●	
Investigate				
DIGITAL TEXT 1 **The Harding Administration**	Objective 1	10 min.	●	●
INTERACTIVE CARTOON **Teapot Dome Scandal**		10 min.	●	
DIGITAL TEXT 2 **Economic Prosperity Under Coolidge**	Objective 2	10 min.	●	●
DIGITAL TEXT 3 **America's Place in a Changed World**	Objective 3	10 min.	●	●
Synthesize				
DIGITAL ACTIVITY **Synthesize: US Domestic and Foreign Policy of the 1920s**		5 min.	●	
Demonstrate				
DIGITAL QUIZ **Lesson Quiz and Class Discussion Board**		10 min.	●	

Government in the 1920s

■ CONNECT

DIGITAL START UP ACTIVITY
What is "Normal"?

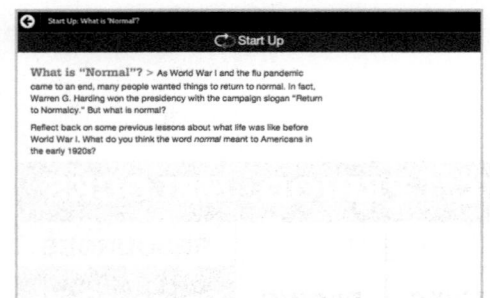

Project the Start Up Activity As students enter and get settled, ask them to think about how they would define *normal life* today. What are some features of a normal life? Focus their attention on the question, *What do you think the word* normalcy *meant to Americans in the early 1920s?* Direct students to start writing their paragraphs to answer it.

Tell students that in this lesson they will be learning how Americans recovered from World War I and faced the challenge of returning to normalcy.

Aa Vocabulary Development: Use the Interactive Reading Notepad to preview the Key Terms and Academic Vocabulary in this lesson with students.

↪ FLIP IT!

Assign the Flipped Video for this lesson.

■ STUDENT EDITION PRINT PAGES: 482–487

■ INVESTIGATE

DIGITAL TEXT 1
The Harding Administration

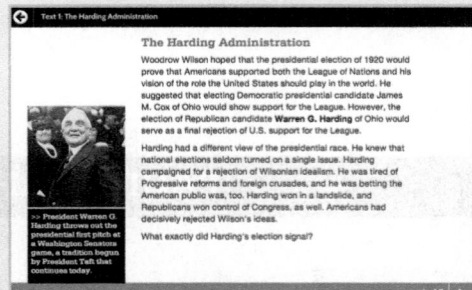

INTERACTIVE CARTOON
Teapot Dome Scandal

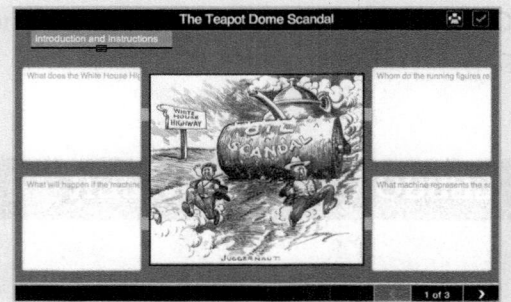

Objective 1: Analyze how the policies of Presidents Harding and Coolidge encouraged economic growth and prosperity in the 1920s.

Quick Instruction

Interactive Cartoon: Teapot Dome Scandal Direct students' attention to the political cartoon. Invite volunteers to explain the meaning of each detail in the cartoon and decipher its overall message and tone. Invite volunteers to identify the key figures in the scandal. (Secretary of the Interior Albert Fall, and President Harding by association.)

Express Problems Clearly Why might some Americans have been disappointed by scandals in Harding's administration? *(Harding was a kind, friendly, and likable man, and a very popular President.)*

Draw Conclusions Ask students to describe the effects of the Teapot Dome political scandal on the views of U.S. citizens concerning trust in the federal government and its leaders. *(The American public developed a mistrust of the executive branch.)*

🖼 ACTIVE CLASSROOM

Have students Cartoon It by creating political cartoons of their own. They should create a quick sketch of one compelling event or issue described in this lesson, such as the financial scandals of Harding's presidency. Then develop the sketch into a political cartoon.

Further Instruction

In the 1920 election, candidate Harding called for a return to "normalcy," but many Americans were not sure of what he meant by this. They soon felt the effect of Harding's Return to Normalcy, including reduced taxes and regulation, which helped to cause the economic growth and prosperity of the 1920s.

Identify Central Issues Ask students to identify Harding's "Return to Normalcy" economic policies that caused growth and prosperity in the 1920s. *(Harding and his Treasury Secretary Andrew Mellon favored more conservative policies that aided the growth of business and returned to a more laissez faire approach, which reduced government regulation of business. Harding disliked the income tax and worked to lower taxes on individuals and corporations. The administration also reduced government spending.)*

Identify Cause and Effect What economic policy of the Harding administration had an adverse effect on world trade? *(Harding raised the protective tariff rates on imported goods to help American producers to sell goods at home. However, in retaliation, European nations also hiked tariffs, making American goods harder to sell overseas. This tariff war weakened the world economy.)*

DIGITAL TEXT 2
Economic Prosperity Under Coolidge

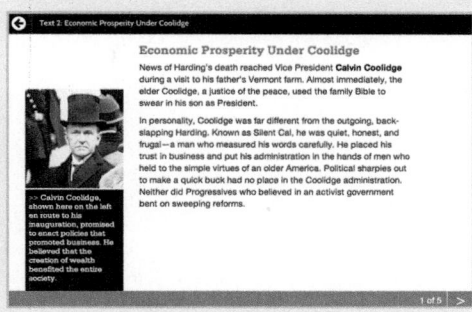

DIGITAL TEXT 3
America's Place in a Changed World

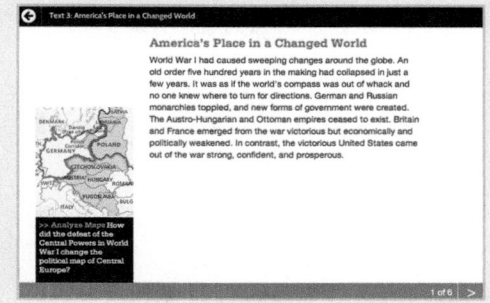

Objective 2: Analyze how the policies of Presidents Harding and Coolidge encouraged economic growth and prosperity in the 1920s.

Quick Instruction

Make sure students understand that the concept of laissez faire means a hands-off approach to managing the economy, with little government control over private business. Point out that the debate between laissez faire supporters and those who promote a more activist government continues to this day.

Make Comparisons How did the approach to government of Harding and Coolidge differ from that of the Progressives? *(Unlike the Progressives who had passed laws to break up monopolies, protect workers, and restrict the absolute freedom of business leaders, Coolidge and Harding favored a return to a more traditional laissez faire approach. Coolidge believed that the creation of wealth by businessmen and women benefited the nation as a whole. Both Harding and Coolidge mistrusted the use of legislation to achieve social change, unlike the Progressive Presidents before them.)*

Analyze Information Ask students to describe how reducing taxes led to economic growth in the 1920s. *(Lowering taxes gave incentives for businesses to expand. Overall, Americans earned more income, which resulted in higher tax revenues, higher industrial profits, growth in the stock market, and general prosperity.)*

ELL Use the ELL activity described in the ELL chart.

Further Instruction
Point out that as in other eras of economic growth, not all Americans benefited. Ask students to identify some of the groups of people who struggled economically during the prosperous 1920s. *(farmers, African Americans, Mexican Americans.)*

Infer Why do you think Calvin Coolidge remained silent on the social problems that plagued the nation in the 1920s? *(Students may say that Coolidge believed that there was little the government could do to correct these problems without becoming too powerful and too controlling of peoples' lives.)*

Objective 3: Explain the role that the United States played in the world during the 1920s.

Quick Instruction

Evaluate Arguments Many Americans in the 1920s seemed to support both isolationism and an active role in international affairs. Do you agree? *(As a growing world power, the United States could not follow these contradictory policies.)*

Make Predictions Ask students to analyze the information in the text to make a prediction about how the war reparations issue will affect the United States in the 1930s. *(Students may say that the failure to find a lasting reparations agreement will negatively affect U.S. foreign policy in the 1930s. European countries may be more wary of American involvement in international affairs.)*

ELL Use the ELL activity described in the ELL chart.

Further Instruction
Summarize how the United States supported world peace efforts in the aftermath of World War I. *(The United States was involved in and supported naval disarmament negotiations. The Kellogg-Briand Pact, negotiated in part by the U.S. Secretary of State, was a treaty to "outlaw" war "as an instrument of national policy.")*

Government in the 1920s

SYNTHESIZE

DIGITAL ACTIVITY

Synthesize: US Domestic and Foreign Policy of the 1920s

IT'S COMING!

Synthesize: US Domestic and Foreign Policy of the 1920s Project the chart. Guide the students in completing the chart. Ask: In general, do you think Presidents Harding and Coolidge showed strong leadership of the country through their policies? *(Students may say that they both followed policies that benefited the majority of Americans.)*

ACTIVE CLASSROOM

Direct students to Quick Write for 30 seconds a list of the major factors that encouraged economic growth in the United States in the 1920s.

DEMONSTRATE

DIGITAL QUIZ

Lesson Quiz and Class Discussion Board

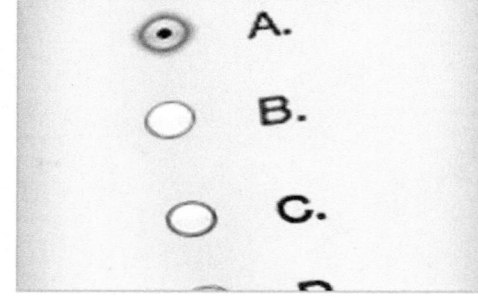

Assign the online Lesson Quiz for this lesson if you haven't already done so. Students will be offered automatic remediation or enrichment based on their score.

Pose these questions to the class on the Discussion Board:

In *Government in the 1920s,* you read about the federal government's shift towards a more "hands off" approach to economic policy. The Harding and Coolidge administrations favored economic and social policies that encouraged American businesses and citizens to tackle economic and social issues rather than relying on the intervention of government.

Make Predictions Do you think the policies of Harding and Coolidge will have a long-term positive effect in the United States? Why or why not?

Generate Explanations What role should the federal government play in addressing economic and social problems?

Topic Inquiry

Have students continue their investigations for the Topic Inquiry.

An Unsettled Society

Supporting English Language Learners

Use with Digital Text 2, **The Red Scare.**

Listening
Discuss with students what they might do when they do not understand something said by another person. Prompt students to seek clarification of spoken language as needed.

Beginning Display these questions: *Can you repeat that? What does _____ mean? So you are saying...?* Read them aloud and have students repeat after you. Then read the text's introductory paragraph, and pause after every sentence or two for students to seek clarification of spoken language by asking one of the questions.

Intermediate Brainstorm a list of possible clarifying questions that students might ask a speaker. Read aloud the section titled *A Questionable Conviction*. Pause periodically so that students can ask questions from the list, or original questions, according to their needs.

Advanced Brainstorm a list of possible clarifying questions that students might ask a speaker. Invite volunteers to read aloud the text. Ask: What is your opinion of the Red Scare, and why? As students answer this question, encourage their peers to seek clarification of the responses as needed.

Advanced High Ask pairs of students to read the text. Then have them discuss their opinions about the Red Scare. Before sharing their own thoughts, ask students to restate their partner's opinion or ask for clarification. Their partners should restate or clarify their opinions before the other students give their opinions.

Use with Digital Text 3, **Slowing the Tide of Immigration.**

Writing
Read aloud the section titled Congressional Legislation Restricts Immigration, or invite volunteers to do so. Prompt students to write using newly acquired basic vocabulary.

Beginning Display the words permit and allow, and explain their meaning. Then display these sentence frames: *The National Origins Act allowed _____. But it did not permit _____.* Have students use the newly acquired basic vocabulary to write and complete the sentences.

Intermediate Point out the word *permitted* in the first sentence of the section's last paragraph. Ask students to locate a synonym in the same paragraph (*allowed*). Discuss the words' meaning. Then have students write sentences about 1920s U.S. immigration policy using the newly acquired basic vocabulary.

Advanced Point out the word *quota* in the text. Ask students to determine its meaning based on context clues. Then have them write a paragraph about quotas in the National Origins Act that uses the newly acquired basic vocabulary word.

Advanced High Display the words *nationality* and *country*. Compare and contrast their meanings and usage with students. Then have students use the newly acquired basic vocabulary to write a paragraph explaining what nationality and country had to do with 1920s U.S. immigration policy.

D Differentiate Instruction

Use the Differentiated Instruction notes throughout the lesson plan to support the varied skill sets, levels of readiness, and interests in the mixed-ability classroom.

Challenge These notes include suggestions for expanding the activity for advanced students.

On-Level These notes include suggestions for modifying the activity to address different interests or learning styles.

Extra Support These notes include ideas for providing more scaffolding or reading spuport.

Special Needs These notes provide ideas for adapting instruction to support the needs of various special needs students.

■ NOTES

An Unsettled Society

Objectives

Objective 1: Compare economic and cultural life in rural America to that in urban America.

Objective 2: Analyze how foreign events after World War I and nativism contributed to the first Red Scare.

Objective 3: Analyze the causes and effects of changes in U.S. immigration policy in the 1920s.

Objective 4: Describe the goals and motives of the Ku Klux Klan in the 1920s.

Objective 5: Analyze the intended and unintended effects of Prohibition.

LESSON 6 ORGANIZER		PACING: APPROX. 1 PERIOD, .5 BLOCKS			
				RESOURCES	
		OBJECTIVES	PACING	Online	Print
Connect					
DIGITAL START UP ACTIVITY **Reading, Writing, and Arithmetic**			5 min.	●	
Investigate					
DIGITAL TEXT 1 **Americans Debate New Ideas and Values**		Objective 1	10 min.	●	●
DIGITAL TEXT 2 **The Red Scare**		Objective 2	10 min.	●	●
DIGITAL TEXT 3 **Slowing the Tide of Immigration**		Objective 3	10 min.	●	●
INTERACTIVE TIMELINE **Anti-Immigration Sentiment in the 1920s**			10 min.	●	
DIGITAL TEXT 4 **The Ku Klux Klan in the Early 1900s**		Objective 4	10 min.	●	●
DIGITAL TEXT 5 **Prohibition Divides Americans**		Objective 5	10 min.	●	●
INTERACTIVE GALLERY **The Prohibition Era**			10 min.	●	
Synthesize					
DIGITAL ACTIVITY **Immigration Policy Then and Now**			5 min.	●	
Demonstrate					
LESSON QUIZ **Lesson Quiz and Class Discussion Board**			10 min.	●	

PEARSON
realize™
www.PearsonRealize.com

Go online to access additional resources including:
Primary Sources • Biographies • Supreme Court cases •
21st Century Skill Tutorials • Maps • Graphic Organizers.

■ CONNECT

DIGITAL START UP ACTIVITY
Reading, Writing, and Arithmetic

Project the Start Up Activity As students enter and get settled, ask students to think about how they value their education and the role of education in society. Then focus their attention to the statistics displayed on the activity and the question, "What reasons do you think might account for this sudden surge in high school graduation rates?" Direct students to start writing their paragraphs to answer it.

Tell students that in this lesson they will be learning about significant social issues that dominated the United States in the 1920s.

Aa Vocabulary Development: Use the Interactive Reading Notepad to preview the Key Terms and Academic Vocabulary in this lesson with students.

⬆ FLIP IT!
Assign the Flipped Video for this lesson.

■ STUDENT EDITION PRINT PAGES: 488–496

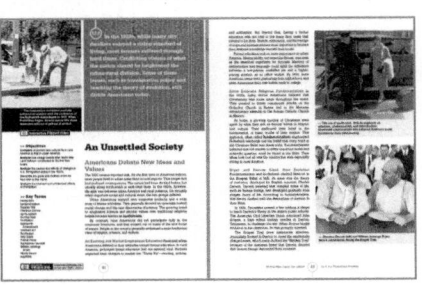

■ INVESTIGATE

DIGITAL TEXT 1
Americans Debate New Ideas and Values

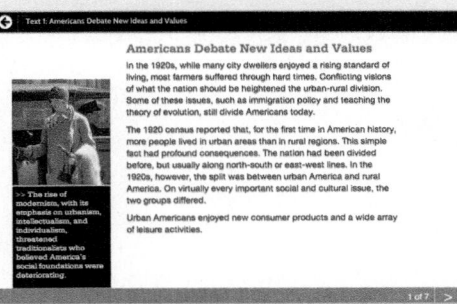

Objective 1: Compare economic and cultural life in rural America to that in urban America.

Quick Instruction

Analyze Images Direct students' attention to the image depicting modernism. Use it as a springboard for a class discussion about the differences in the way of life between urban and rural Americans. Challenge students to discuss aspects of life, including employment opportunities, religion, education, entertainment, and the availability of new technologies and products.

Make sure that students understand that the growing trend to emphasize science and secular values over traditional religious beliefs became known as Modernism.

Briefly review the basic tenets of Darwin's theory of evolution with students. *(complex forms of life, such as human beings, had developed gradually from simpler forms of life.)* Invite volunteers to summarize the issues of the Scopes trial and to describe the impact of Clarence Darrow and William Jennings Bryan on the subject.

Contrast How did the two sides in the Scopes Trial represent conflicting value systems? *(William Jennings Bryan, the prosecuting lawyer, represented the fundamentalists' viewpoint, which believed that the Bible presented the literal truth about creation. Clarence Darrow and Scopes represented the modernist value system, which depended on science to explain creation.)*

Further Instruction

Summarize How could you describe the cultural differences between rural and urban Americans in the 1920s? *(Urban Americans showed an openness toward social change and the new discoveries of science. Rural Americans followed more traditional views of religion, science, and culture. Rural life was difficult and did not provide the opportunities to participate fully in the consumer bonanzas, and rural populations missed out on many of the new forms of leisure.)*

Draw Conclusions Why did urban Americans embrace formal education? *(Higher education was needed to land a higher paying and successful job that might lead to a career.)*

Run-in How did the Scopes Trial illustrate the urban-rural split in the 1920s? *(The Scopes trial took place in rural Tennessee, where fundamentalist value systems were more widespread. Darrow was from the big city of Chicago. Darrow, the American Civil Liberties Union, and John Scopes were probably viewed as trying to bring their emphasis on science and urban secular values to Tennessee.)*

An Unsettled Society

DIGITAL TEXT 2
The Red Scare

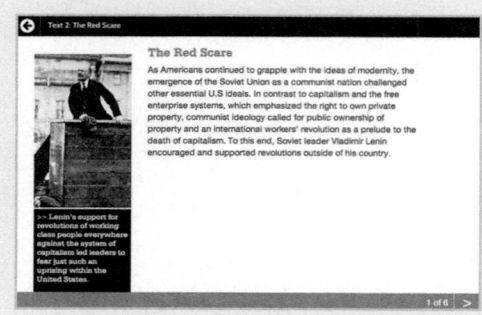

DIGITAL TEXT 3
Slowing the Tide of Immigration

Objective 2: Analyze how foreign events after World War I and nativism contributed to the first Red Scare.

Quick Instruction

Analyze Images Invite a student to identify the person in the photo. *(Soviet leader Vladimir Lenin)* Challenge students to describe Lenin's role in international affairs. *(Lenin led the communist takeover of Russia, establishing the Soviet Union.)* To help students analyze causes and effects of events and social issues such as the Red Scare, invite students to describe how they think Americans felt about Lenin. *(Many Americans were probably afraid of Lenin and what he accomplished in Russia. He represented a form of government completely at odds with American democracy.)*

Analyze Information How did the rise of communism in the Soviet Union help cause the Red Scare? *(Lenin's growing power within the Soviet Union heightened American's awareness of the threat to their form of government. Lenin called for an international workers' revolution to wipe out capitalism and he encouraged and supported revolutions outside of his country.)*

Identify Effects What were the effects of the Red Scare following World War I? *(Effects include: the Palmer Raids, deporting some immigrants who were innocent of wrongdoing, general fear and anti-immigrant, anti-union, anti-reform feelings)*

Infer Why were many Americans upset by the Palmer raids? *(Many Americans thought the Palmer raids dismantled many of the liberties that Americans believed were fundamental to American democracy. Some victims of the*

Palmer raids had done nothing wrong and were deported simply because of where they had come from.)

ELL Use the ELL activity described in the ELL chart.

Further Instruction

Briefly review the charges that were brought against Sacco and Vanzetti. Ask students to describe the evidence that was used against them. *(Very little hard evidence was presented. A key piece of evidence was that an eyewitness said they "looked Italian.")*

Determine Relevance How does the Sacco and Vanzetti case demonstrate the mindset of the Red Scare? *(During the Red Scare, people were so afraid of communism that thorough police investigations and criminal trials were weakened in order to try to protect democracy.)*

Generate Explanations What relationship do you see between the Red Scare and nativism? *(The Red Scare was based upon the threat of communism which originated outside the country. This in turn increased nativist concerns, which were demonstrated by negative feelings towards immigrants, labor unions, and other groups.)*

Objective 3: Analyze the causes and effects of changes in U.S. immigration policy in the 1920s.

Quick Instruction

Interactive Timeline: Anti-Immigration Sentiment in the 1920s Project the timeline on the whiteboard and select the squares to reveal details about the events. Point out that from our point of view today, the reactions of Americans in the 1920s might seem like overreactions to unfounded fears. However, at the time, many Americans were fearful of the changes that immigration might bring. Challenge students to summarize the causes and effects of immigration in the United States and analyze how patterns of immigration changed in the early twentieth century.

Identify Central Issues What are immigration quotas, and what effect did they have on the U.S. economy? *(Immigration quotas set a limit on the number of people who could enter the country, in effect reducing the number of people in the workforce. While many advocates of nativism probably supported immigration policies like this, in effect these policies reduced the number of people in the workforce and may have negatively affected some industries.)*

INTERACTIVE TIMELINE
Anti-Immigration Sentiment in the 1920s

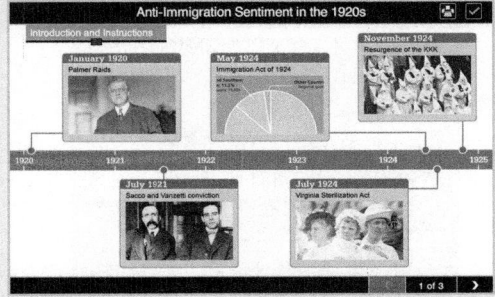

DIGITAL TEXT 4
The Ku Klux Klan in the Early 1900s

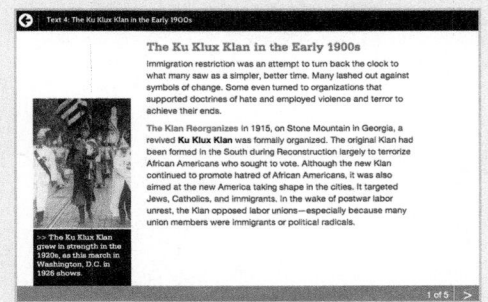

ACTIVE CLASSROOM
Conduct a Take a Stand Activity. Ask students to take a stand on the following question: Was the National Origins Act, the law that established immigration quotas, passed for legitimate concerns or was it an overreaction? Ask students to divide into two groups based on their answer and move to separate areas of the classroom. Ask students to talk with each other to compare their reasons for their position.

ELL Use the ELL activity described in the ELL chart.

Further Instruction
Review the idea of nativism with students and begin a discussion of its causes and effects in the 1920s. *(Nativists, or those who preferred native-born Americans, argued that the new arrivals took jobs away from native-born workers and threatened American religious, political, and cultural traditions. Nativism helped create policies that reduced the number of immigrants allowed into the United States)*

Analyze Information What were the causes of Social Darwinism? *(Social Darwinism, the idea that life was a competition in which only the fittest survive, was related to Charles Darwin's theory of the survival of the fittest.)* What were the causes of eugenics? *(Eugenics was developed by people who believed that human race could be improved by controlling which people had children, policies that were eventually adopted in the country.)* How were the two theories related and what effect did they both have on immigration policy? *(The*

theory of eugenics was related to Social Darwinism because its supporters sought to exclude those they thought of as weaker and undesirable, making the United States the fittest country. These theories led to legislation restricting immigration and favoring immigration from particular countries.)*

Identify Points of View Why did both supporters and opponents of immigration quotas believe they were defending American traditions and values? *(Opponents of immigration quotas believed that the immigration experience was part of what made an American an American, since almost all non-Native Americans could trace their ancestry back to people immigrating from foreign countries. Supporters of immigration quotas believed they were protecting traditional American culture from incoming immigrants, who might not fully assimilate.)*

Objective 4: Describe the goals and motives of the Ku Klux Klan in the 1920s.

Quick Instruction
Project the image of Ku Klux Klan march. Invite students to share what they know about the KKK. Begin a discussion by asking students to analyze the causes and effects of race relations and the role the Klan played. *(Race relations in the United States had always been a tense issue. Slavery, the Civil War, Reconstruction all were causes that heightened the tensions. The Klan used terror to try to stop what it perceived as the eroding of traditional American culture and values. The Klan was especially known for terrorizing African Americans, which had a great impact in further straining race relations.)*

Identify Central Issues How did the goals of the new Ku Klux Klan differ from those of the old Klan? *(The original Klan was formed in the South during Reconstruction to terrorize African Americans who sought to vote. The new Klan continued to promote hatred of African Americans but also targeted Jews, Catholics, and immigrants, all of whom they viewed as representing a changing America.)*

Further Instruction
Draw Conclusions Why do you think the new Ku Klux Klan was able to spread beyond the South and even into some urban areas? *(The goals of the new Ku Klux Klan had changed. The new Klan spread its terror to include immigrants of many different races, ethnicities, and religions, many of whom lived in urban areas where society was rapidly changing.)*

An Unsettled Society

DIGITAL TEXT 5
Prohibition Divides Americans

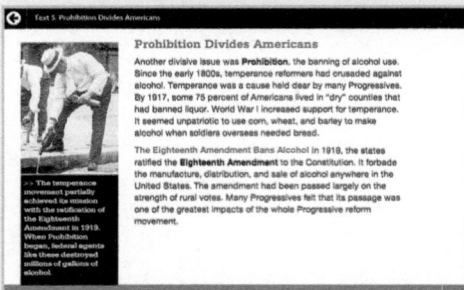

INTERACTIVE GALLERY
The Prohibition Era

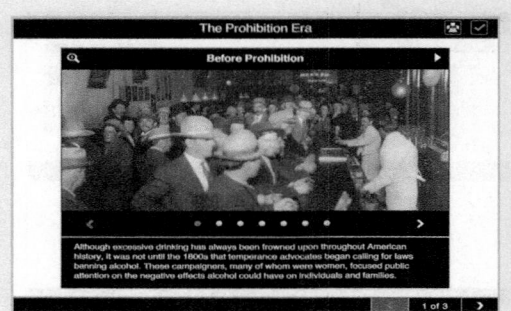

Contrast Why were political organizations that promoted civil rights and that wanted to expand rights for religious minorities opposed to the Klan? *(Organizations such as the NAACP and the Jewish Anti-Defamation League embraced the idea of racial, ethnic, religious, and cultural diversity and the expansion of religious and civil rights and therefore opposed the Klan.)*

Objective 5: **Analyze the intended and unintended effects of Prohibition.**

Quick Instruction

The movement to ban alcohol grew stronger in the early 1900s. People supported the prohibition of alcohol sales for may reasons. Point out that the causes of prohibition can be traced to Progressive Era campaigns against social ills. Many Americans believed that social problems such as poverty, unemployment, domestic violence, and liver disease were caused by alcohol consumption. Supporters of Prohibition believed that outlawing alcohol would create a better society.

Interactive Gallery: The Prohibition Era Project the interactive gallery. Look at each image and caption individually and then the collection of images as a whole.

Analyze Charts What does the second image in the gallery, Per Capita Consumption of Alcoholic Beverages,1910-1929, tell you about the effectiveness of the Eighteenth Amendment? *(It was effective in the first couple of years, but after that alcohol consumption increased.)*

📷 ACTIVE CLASSROOM

Ask the following question using the Sticky Note strategy: Viewed together, what do these images and statistics tell you about Americans' attitude toward alcohol consumption? *(Student may say that the images and statistics highlight the deep division on the topic. In general, they reveal that America's demand for alcohol was too great and that outlawing it would not work in the long run.)*

Further Instruction

Ask students to identify some of the unintended effects of prohibition. *(Prohibition contributed to many people breaking the law by making alcohol, buying it illegally, or by visiting illegal places like speakeasies. The cost for law enforcement rose and the prison population increased. Also, prohibition led to the growth of organized crime in America.)*

Draw Conclusions With the passage of the Twenty-First Amendment in 1933, the prohibition experiment came to an end. What does this tell you about the effectiveness of government to solve social problems with legislation? *(Government failed in its attempt to regulate or control this particular social problem.)*

SYNTHESIZE

DIGITAL ACTIVITY

Immigration Policy Then and Now

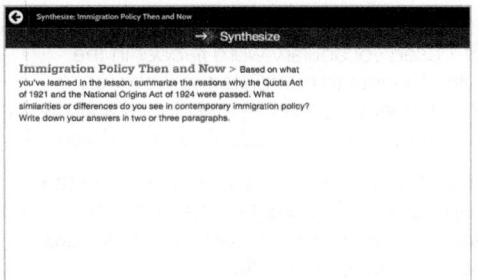

Discuss Remind students to use pre-writing techniques before they begin writing. For their paragraphs, they should create a table with three column headings: Quota Act of 1921, National Origins Act of 1924, Contemporary Immigration Policy. Have students complete the table to help them identify similarities and differences.

DEMONSTRATE

LESSON QUIZ

Lesson Quiz and Class Discussion Board

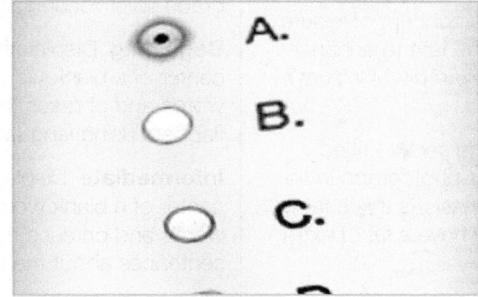

Assign the online Lesson Quiz for this lesson if you haven't already done so. Students will be offered automatic remediation or enrichment based on their score.

Pose these questions to the class on the Discussion Board:

In *An Unsettled Society*, you read about the cultural divide and clash of values that developed as America moved from a rural to urban society. Economics, culture, religion, race relations, and politics were all affected by the shift.

Make Predictions What will the role of immigration be as the United States moves into the 1930s?

Identify Central Issues What American values do you see challenged in the lesson?

Topic Inquiry
Have students continue their investigations for the Topic Inquiry.

The Roaring Twenties

Supporting English Language Learners

Use with Digital Text 1, **Popular American Culture.**

Learning Strategies Listening
Explain to students that they will be listening to you speak and using visual support to enhance and confirm their understanding of what you said.

Beginning Use basic spoken language to explain the concept of leisure and give examples. Then use the first photograph in the text to enhance and confirm students' understanding. Ask: Is this an example of leisure? What is the family doing?

Intermediate Use spoken language to paraphrase the section titled Americans Enjoy More Leisure Time. Then use the first photograph in the text to enhance and confirm students' understanding. Ask: Is this a farm or city family? What are they doing? Do you think they have a lot of extra money?

Advanced Use a somewhat complex and elaborated spoken language to talk about the leisure pursuits of farm and city inhabitants, using information from the beginning of the text. Then discuss the two leisure pursuits shown in the first two photographs.

Advanced High Use a complex and elaborated spoken language to talk about the leisure pursuits of farm and city inhabitants, using information from the beginning of the text. Then ask pairs of students to compare and contrast the two leisure pursuits shown in the first two photographs.

Use with Digital Text 3, **The Role of Women Changes.**

Learning Strategies Writing
Read aloud or review the content of the section titled Flappers Push Back Against Expectations. Prompt students to write using content-based grade-level vocabulary.

Beginning Display the content-based vocabulary word *flapper* in the center of a blank word web. Help students to complete the web with words and phrases that describe flappers. Then craft a sentence about flappers using language from the web, and have students write it down.

Intermediate Display the content-based vocabulary word *flapper* in the center of a blank word web. Help students to complete the web with words and phrases that describe flappers. Help students to write several sentences about the appearance, behavior, etc., of flappers.

Advanced Display this list of content-based vocabulary: *flapper, expectations, boundaries, role, New Woman*. Ask pairs of students to write a sentence using each word on the list. Provide time for pairs to share their sentences with one another.

Advanced High Display this list of content-based vocabulary: *flapper, expectations, boundaries, role, New Woman, Victorian Age*. Ask students to write a cohesive paragraph about the New Woman that uses at least five of these six words. Provide time for students to read their paragraph to a partner.

▣ Differentiate Instruction

Use the Differentiated Instruction notes throughout the lesson plan to support the varied skill sets, levels of readiness, and interests in the mixed-ability classroom.

Challenge These notes include suggestions for expanding the activity for advanced students.

On-Level These notes include suggestions for modifying the activity to address different interests or learning styles.

Extra Support These notes include ideas for providing more scaffolding or reading spuport.

Special Needs These notes provide ideas for adapting instruction to support the needs of various special needs students.

■ NOTES

PEARSON
realize™
www.PearsonRealize.com

Go online to access additional resources including:
Primary Sources • Biographies • Supreme Court cases •
21st Century Skill Tutorials • Maps • Graphic Organizers.

Objectives

Objective 1: Describe how increased leisure time and technological innovations led to a widespread shared popular culture in the 1920s.

Objective 2: Analyze the changing role of women in the 1920s.

Objective 3: Describe how the concept of modernism shown in art and literature reflected postwar disillusionment.

LESSON 7 ORGANIZER		PACING: APPROX. 1 PERIOD, .5 BLOCKS			
				RESOURCES	
		OBJECTIVES	**PACING**	**Online**	**Print**
Connect					
DIGITAL START UP ACTIVITY **A Right to Vote**			5 min.	●	
Investigate					
DIGITAL TEXT 1 **Popular American Culture**		Objective 1	10 min.	●	●
DIGITAL TEXT 2 **American Role Models**		Objective 1	10 min.	●	●
BEFORE AND AFTER **Technology Changes Home Life**			10 min.	●	
DIGITAL TEXT 3 **The Role of Women Changes**		Objective 2	10 min.	●	●
INTERACTIVE CHART **Rural and Urban Life**		Objective 2	10 min.	●	
DIGITAL TEXT 4 **Social Issues are Reflected in Art and Literature**		Objective 3	10 min.	●	●
Synthesize					
DIGITAL ACTIVITY **Culture and Technology**			5 min.	●	
Demonstrate					
DIGITAL QUIZ **Lesson Quiz and Discussion Board**			10 min.	●	

The Roaring Twenties

■ CONNECT

DIGITAL START UP ACTIVITY
A Right to Vote

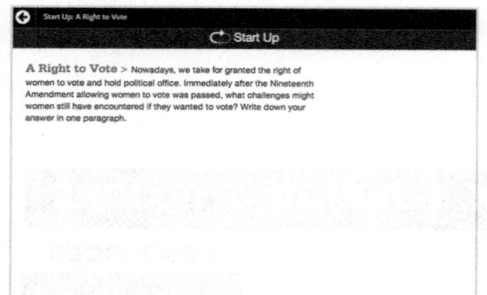

Project the Start Up Activity Ask students to consider the activity as they enter and get settled. Then have them share their paragraphs with another student.

Discuss Discuss with students the differences between what is legal and what is socially acceptable. Point out that a legal right to vote for women may have been the law, but, for many Americans, it was still not socially acceptable to them. Ask: What are some other examples of the law and society being out of synch?

Make Predictions Challenge students to predict what current aspect of American society future residents of the United States might think strange or unenlightened. Ask students to support their answers with reasons.

Aa Vocabulary Development: Use the Interactive Reading Notepad to preview the Key Terms and Academic Vocabulary in this lesson with students.

⇗ FLIP IT!

Assign the Flipped Video for this lesson.

■ STUDENT EDITION PRINT PAGES: 497–504

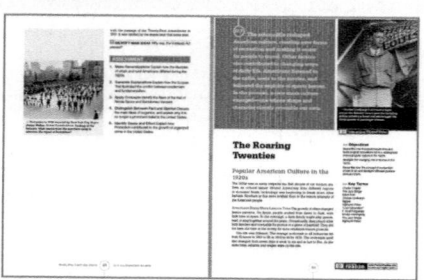

■ INVESTIGATE

DIGITAL TEXT 1
Popular American Culture

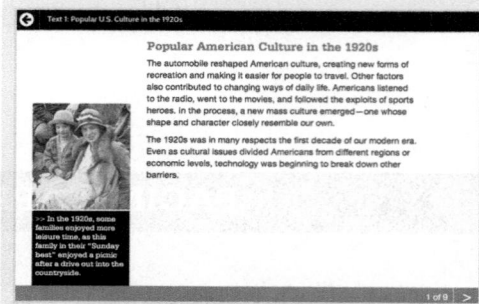

DIGITAL TEXT 2
American Role Models

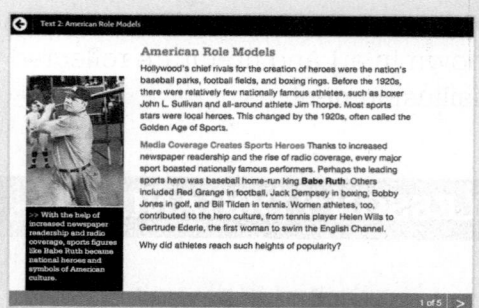

Objective 1: Describe how increased leisure time and technological innovations led to a widespread shared popular culture in the 1920s.

Quick Instruction

Before and After: Technology Changes Home Life Project the Before and After. Move the slider to see how technological innovations improved Americans' standard of living in the early 1900s. Challenge students to describe the likely effect of each technological innovation.

Summarize Which technological innovations directly led to a widespread shared popular culture in the 1920s? *(movies, the radio and the phonograph)* How did they accomplish this? *(Movies were affordable to a great majority of Americans; Americans all over the country watched the same movies, listened to the same or similar radio programs, and listened to the same or similar phonograph recordings.)*

Analyze Information Have students choose one of the significant individuals from the lesson, such as Babe Ruth, Glenn Curtiss, or Charles Lindbergh, and explain how his or her contributions shaped American culture. *(Answers will vary, but should refer to the idea that the decade needed heroes to restore Americans' faith in progress after World War I. Ensure student understanding of how Charles Lindbergh's first non-stop, solo flight across the Atlantic Ocean—using new technology to conquer distance, a feat shared worldwide on the radio—embodied key developments of the era.)*

◪◪ ACTIVE CLASSROOM

Have students choose one of the communication technologies discussed and Act It Out. Students can create their version of a radio show, movie, or phonograph record. Break the class into small groups and give students a few minutes to develop a rough outline and script. After each group performs, discuss how their medium helped create a shared popular culture in the 1920s.

ELL Use the ELL activity described in the ELL chart.

Further Instruction

Infer How do you see issues and characteristics in U.S. history reflected in various genres of music, such as Tin Pan Alley and country and western? *(Music associated with Tin Pan Alley reflected the urban experiences found in New York City, while Country and Western music reflected life in rural areas and the idea of the American frontier.)* How did country and western music, for example, have both positive and negative impacts on American society? *(Country and western music spread an admiration of cowboy culture to other parts of the country, but negative stereotypes of country-dwellers also spread. In addition, having a more universal and less local culture might not have been viewed as a positive impact by all Americans.)*

BEFORE AND AFTER
Technology Changes Home Life

DIGITAL TEXT 3
The Role of Women Changes

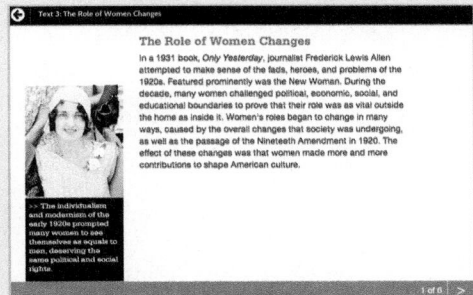

INTERACTIVE CHART
Rural and Urban Life

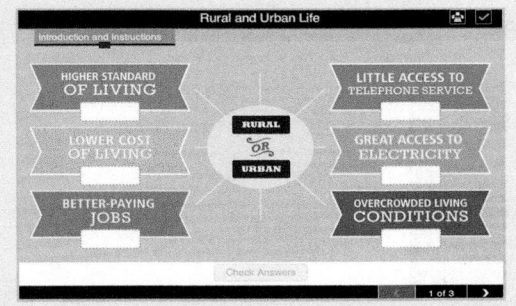

Make Generalizations What effect did innovation in the motion picture industry have on the diffusion of popular American culture on the rest of the world over time? *(Products of the American entertainment industry, such as motion pictures, reflected American cultural values. As innovation created mass-produced motion pictures with sound, these films, and American culture, became increasingly popular throughout the world.)*

Describe Have students describe how issues in U.S. history in the 1920s were reflected in various genres of film. *(Students should point out how Charlie Chaplain, for example, addressed the issue of immigration in The Immigrant.)*

Objective 2: Analyze the changing role of women in the 1920s.

Quick Instruction

Interactive Chart: Rural and Urban Life Project the chart. Point out that the 1920 census revealed that, for the first time, more than 50 percent of the population lived in urban areas. Ensure student understanding that the transformation was from rural and to urban. Guide the students in completing the chart. Ask: in general, how might whether a woman lived in the country or the city affect how her role in society might change? *(Generally, women in urban areas had more opportunities outside of the home, and were more progressive than women in urban areas.)*

Analyze Information Project the table of "Firsts" for American Women. Ask students to consider the ways in which women shaped American culture in the 1920s. *(Women's participation in politics after passage of the nineteenth amendment and athletic accomplishments such as swimming across the English Channel broke cultural barriers and redefined women's place in the political, social, and economic life of the United States.)*

📹 ACTIVE CLASSROOM

Direct students to Make Headlines that demonstrate the causes and effects of the changing role of women during the 1920s. Assign one group of students causes, and another effects. Allow students to use subheadings to communicate more information. Have students pass their headlines to a partner for them to review.

D **Differentiate: Challenge** Invite interested students to conduct online research to learn more about women's fashion of the 1920s, especially that of flappers. Have the student create a piece of art annotated with information about hair, clothing, and makeup.

ELL Use the ELL activity described in the ELL chart.

Further Instruction

Interpret Invite a student to identify the characteristics of a flapper. *(a young woman from the 1920s who defied traditional rules of conduct and dress; bobbed hair, short skirt, rouge)* What did the flapper come to symbolize? *(the changing role of women)*

Sequence Events Ask student show the Nineteenth Amendment to the Constitution impacted women's lives *(Women won the right to vote; some took on more active roles in politics, others also began moving into different kinds of careers.)* After the great battle of suffrage was won, what new roles were there for American women? *(National American Woman Suffrage Association calling on women to work in reform movements, run for office, or fight for laws to protect women and children in the workplace. The National Women's Party's primary goal was the passage of an Equal Rights Amendment. Women worked as clerks, sales people, and managers, and in journalism, aviation, banking, and the legal and medical professions. Quality of life improvements led other women to conduct charitable work, or join clubs that discussed books and ideas.)*

The Roaring Twenties

DIGITAL TEXT 4

Social Issues are Reflected in Art and Literature

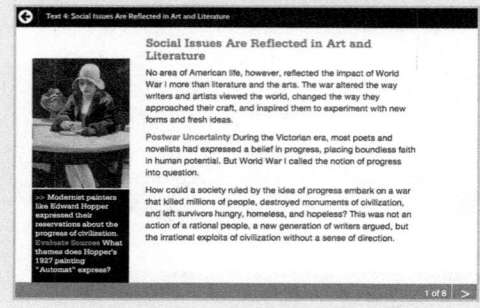

Text 4: Social Issues Are Reflected in Art and Literature

Social Issues Are Reflected in Art and Literature

No area of American life, however, reflected the impact of World War I more than literature and the arts. The war altered the way writers and artists viewed the world, changed the way they approached their craft, and inspired them to experiment with new forms and fresh ideas.

Postwar Uncertainty During the Victorian era, most poets and novelists had expressed a belief in progress, placing boundless faith in human potential. But World War I called the notion of progress into question.

How could a society ruled by the idea of progress embark on a war that killed millions of people, destroyed monuments of civilization, and left survivors hungry, homeless, and hopeless? This was not an action of a rational people, a new generation of writers argued, but the irrational exploits of civilization without a sense of direction.

>> Modernist painters like Edward Hopper expressed their reservations about the progress of civilization. Evaluate Sources What theme does Hopper's 1927 painting "Automat" express?

1 of 8 >

Objective 3: Describe how the concept of modernism shown in art and literature reflected postwar disillusionment.

Quick Instruction

Analyze Images Project the table of postwar American novelists. Remind students that the United States was victorious in World War I. Ask students what, then, was the postwar mood. Exuberance? *(The postwar mood was pessimistic and dark.)* Why? *(The war killed millions, caused vast destruction, and left survivors hungry, homeless, and hopeless.)* Explain how the war inspired modernism. Discuss how the issues and characteristics in U.S. history following World War I were reflected in various genres of literature and art. Begin by focusing on the chart, asking students why each theme came to the fore and what issue or characteristic of the time each reflected. Explain how these themes were the hallmark of the Lost Generation of writers, who were marked by disillusion with World War I and a search for a new sense of meaning. Prompt students to connect these themes to the work of specific writers in the table. Explain that, in art, the new, dark mood was reflected by modernism. Explain that modernism can roughly be described as a more abstract style as opposed to earlier representational work. Remind students that leading modernist painters included Edward Hopper, Man Ray, Joseph Stella, and Georgia O'Keeffe.

Further Instruction

Identify Patterns Discuss with students how literature and art turned darker in the post-World war I era, as the destruction and seeming pointlessness of the conflict was expressed through the creative process. Challenge students to discuss how the darker characteristics of this period in U.S. history have also have been reflected in various genres of music. *(The melodies took on darker tones and the lyrics included darker themes.)*

PEARSON realize™

www.PearsonRealize.com
Access your Digital Lesson

■ SYNTHESIZE

DIGITAL ACTIVITY
Culture and Technology

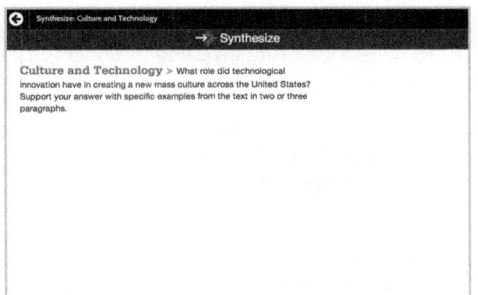

Instruct students to break the assignment into two basic parts before starting. They should make sure they understand the terms *technological innovation* and the *new mass culture* before beginning their pre-writing.

■ DEMONSTRATE

DIGITAL QUIZ
Lesson Quiz and Discussion Board

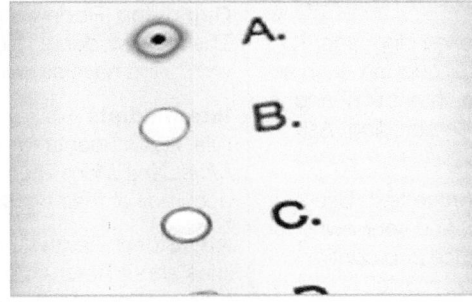

Assign the online Lesson Quiz for this lesson if you haven't already done so. Students will be offered automatic remediation or enrichment based on their score.

Pose these questions to the class on the Discussion Board:

In *The Roaring Twenties*, you learned about how the United States changed in the years after World War I. Technological innovations, like the radio and motion pictures, helped create a new mass culture in the United States. Technology also increased the standard of living in Americans' homes. Popular culture lifted significant individuals in sports, movies, and aviation to hero status. Meanwhile, women, now with the vote, expanded their role in society. The flapper symbolized this new freedom. Still, the uncertainty of the postwar era was reflected in the art and literature of the time.

Describe Describe how the characteristics and issues in the United States today are reflected in various genres of art, music, film, and literature.

Topic Inquiry
Have students continue their investigations for the Topic Inquiry.

The Harlem Renaissance

Supporting English Language Learners

Use with Digital Text 2, **The Jazz Age.**

Learning Strategies Listening

Introduce the text by asking what students know about different types of music. Prompt students to use contextual support to enhance and confirm understanding of increasingly complex and elaborated spoken language.

Beginning Explain the genre of jazz music in basic spoken language, based on information provided in the text. Use contextual support such as musical recordings, images, and your own vocal rhythm, intonation, and physical gestures to enhance and confirm students' understanding. Ask: What words do you think describe jazz music?

Intermediate Read aloud the introductory paragraph of the text. Use contextual support such as musical recordings, images, and your own vocal rhythm, intonation, and physical gestures to enhance and confirm students' understanding. Ask: How would you define jazz music?

Advanced Read aloud the text's introduction and section titled A Unique Musical Style. Play a Louis Armstrong recording for contextual support, and ask: If you were describing the jazz music of Louis Armstrong to someone who had never heard it, what would you say?

Advanced High Read aloud the text's introduction and section titled A Unique Musical Style. Play a Louis Armstrong recording to enhance students' understanding of what you say. Ask pairs to discuss: How would you describe this music to someone who had never heard it? How do you think it represents the United States in the 1920s?

Use with Digital Text 3, **The Harlem Renaissance.**

Learning Strategies Writing

Explain that students will be using book titles and quotations from the text to help them spell familiar English words with increasing accuracy.

Beginning Review the "long vowel—consonant—silent e" phonics rule. Then ask students to use that rule to write the book title *Cane*. Display the word, and have students check the accuracy of their work.

Intermediate Review the "long vowel—consonant—silent e" phonics rule. Ask students to use that rule as they write the book titles *Cane* and *Mules and Men*. Then display the titles, and have students check the accuracy of their work.

Advanced Review the homonyms *sea* and *see*. Then read the following lines about literature by Langston Hughes, reminding students to focus on their spelling as they write them down: *[It] is a big sea full of many fish. I let down my nets and pulled. I'm still pulling.* Display the quote, and have students check the accuracy of their work.

Advanced High Ask students to write down the book title *Their Eyes Were Watching God*. Display the title so students can check the accuracy of their work. Then review the homonyms *there*, *their*, and *they're*. Have students write additional sentences about the Harlem Renaissance using these homonyms.

▣ Differentiate Instruction

Use the Differentiated Instruction notes throughout the lesson plan to support the varied skill sets, levels of readiness, and interests in the mixed-ability classroom.

Challenge These notes include suggestions for expanding the activity for advanced students.

On-Level These notes include suggestions for modifying the activity to address different interests or learning styles.

Extra Support These notes include ideas for providing more scaffolding or reading spuport.

Special Needs These notes provide ideas for adapting instruction to support the needs of various special needs students.

■ NOTES

PEARSON
realize™
www.PearsonRealize.com

Go online to access additional resources including:
Primary Sources • Biographies • Supreme Court cases •
21st Century Skill Tutorials • Maps • Graphic Organizers.

Objectives

Objective 1: Analyze how the Great Migration and the philosophies of Marcus Garvey affected African Americans in the 1920s.

Objective 2: Trace the development of jazz and its impact on American society and the rest of the world.

Objective 3: Discuss the themes explored by writers and artists of the Harlem Renaissance.

LESSON 8 ORGANIZER		PACING: APPROX. 1 PERIOD, .5 BLOCKS			
				RESOURCES	
		OBJECTIVES	**PACING**	**Online**	**Print**
Connect					
	DIGITAL START UP ACTIVITY **Americans on the Move**		5 min.	●	
Investigate					
	DIGITAL TEXT 1 **Support for Black Nationalism in Urban Areas**	Objective 1	10 min.	●	●
	INTERACTIVE TIMELINE **African American Achievers of the 1920s**		10 min.	●	
	DIGITAL TEXT 2 **The Jazz Age**	Objective 2	10 min.	●	●
	DIGITAL TEXT 3 **The Harlem Renaissance**	Objective 3	10 min.	●	●
	INTERACTIVE GALLERY **Key Figures of the Harlem Renaissance**		10 min.	●	
Synthesize					
	DIGITAL ACTIVITY **The Great Migration**		5 min.	●	
Demonstrate					
	DIGITAL QUIZ **Lesson Quiz and Discussion Board**		10 min.	●	

Topic ⑫ Lesson 8

The Harlem Renaissance

CONNECT

DIGITAL START UP ACTIVITY
Americans on the Move

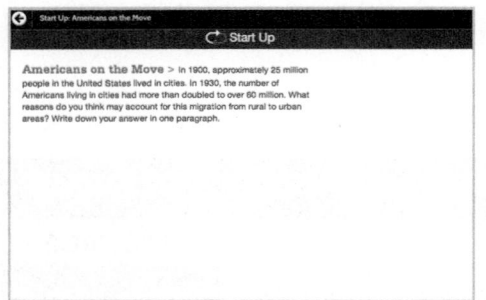

Project the Start Up Activity Ask students to consider the population figures as they enter and get settled. Then have them share their paragraphs with another student, either in class or through a chat or blog space.

Analyze Information Explain to students that people who move are often "pushed" out of their current location by certain factors while being "pulled" to a new location by other factors. Encourage them to think about what the "push" and "pull" factors might be in this instance.

Aa Vocabulary Development: Use the Interactive Reading Notepad to preview the Key Terms and Academic Vocabulary in this lesson with students.

⇅ FLIP IT!

Assign the Flipped Video for this lesson.

STUDENT EDITION PRINT PAGES: 505–510

INVESTIGATE

DIGITAL TEXT 1
Support for Black Nationalism in Urban Areas

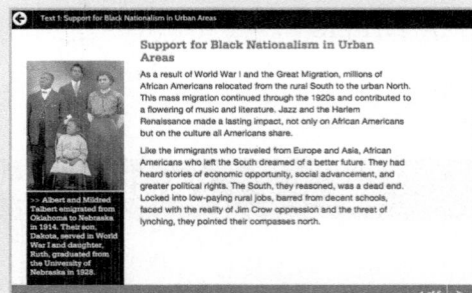

INTERACTIVE TIMELINE
African American Achievers of the 1920s

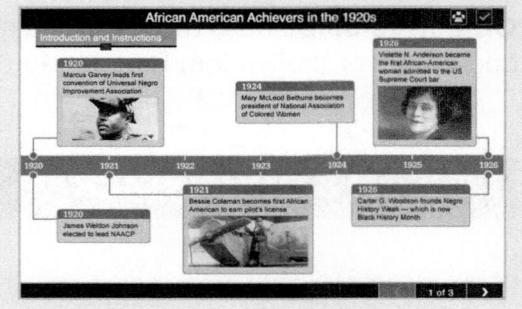

Objective 1: Analyze how the Great Migration and the philosophies of Marcus Garvey affected African Americans in the 1920s.

Quick Instruction

Interactive Timeline: African American Achievers in the 1920s Project the interactive timeline. Set the stage for instruction by reminding students about the causes of the Great Migration: in search of a better life, millions of African Americans relocated from the rural South to the urban North. Then explain one of the effects of the Great Migration: tell students that New York City's Harlem, where 200,000 blacks settled, became the focal point of African American culture. Click on 1920 on the timeline, and discuss Marcus Garvey. Tell them Marcus Garvey was a significant individual. Challenge student to analyze the impact he had. *(Garvey founded the Universal Negro Improvement Association. He was in favor of creating a homeland for African Americans in Africa. While this did not materialize, his message of racial pride, solidarity, and separateness had a lasting impact.)*

🖳 ACTIVE CLASSROOM

Have students take A Closer Look at Harlem, New York, in the 1920s. Use a whiteboard tool to divide the image into four quadrants. Direct students to look closely at each quadrant in turn. When can they learn or infer about life in Harlem in the 1920s?

Further Instruction

Draw Conclusions Tell students that Garvey's Universal Negro Improvement Association boasted almost 2.5 million members and sympathizers in the mid 1920s. Ask what they can conclude from this fact about the impact that Marcus Garvey had. *(Garvey's ideas about black separatism and a homeland were very popular or persuasive.)*

PEARSON realize™

www.PearsonRealize.com
Access your Digital Lesson

DIGITAL TEXT 2
The Jazz Age

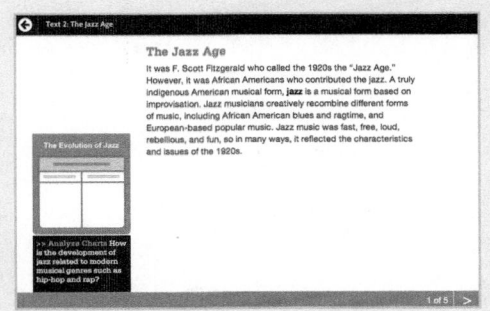

DIGITAL TEXT 3
The Harlem Renaissance

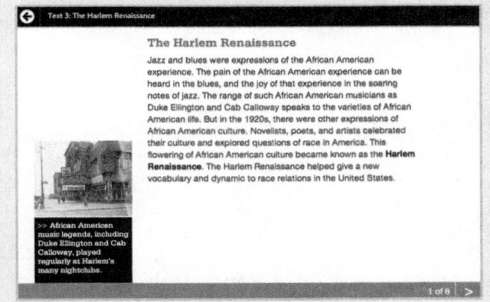

Objective 2: Trace the development of jazz and its impact on American society and the rest of the world.

Quick Instruction

Analyze Information Project the chart that shows the development of jazz. Invite comments from students. Ask: what is jazz? *(American musical form based on improvisation)* Who developed jazz? *(African American musicians)* What forms of music does jazz blend? *(blues, ragtime and European-based popular music)* Challenge students to describe how the issues and characteristics in U.S. history of the 1920s were reflected in the jazz genre of music. *(Jazz was a symbol of the Roaring Twenties, a demonstration of the richness of African American culture, and a reflection of how the contributions of people of various racial groups shape American culture.)*

Infer What aspects of American jazz music may have encouraged its popularity in the rest of the world? *(American jazz was a distinctive sound created with African rhythms and themes. Many people across the world would have identified with those themes and appreciated the blend of different cultures from which jazz was born.)*

ELL Use the ELL activity described in the ELL chart.

Further Instruction

Hypothesize Why might some have perceived cultural movements in music such as jazz as having a negative impact on American society? *(It was a new genre of music and so might have appealed to younger listeners. Jazz encouraged new styles of dance of which some may have disapproved. Jazz quickly became a symbol of modernism, standing in contrast to the cultural values associated with tradition.)*

Distinguish Between Fact and Opinion Invite some class members to provide three facts and offer three opinions about jazz, and for other class members to distinguish between the two. *(Jazz was developed by African American musicians, that it blends blues, ragtime, and European-based popular music, and that it reflected characteristics of U.S. history during the Jazz Age of the 1920s. Opinions will vary but should be appropriate.)*

Objective 3: Discuss the themes explored by writers and artists of the Harlem Renaissance.

Quick Instruction

Interactive Gallery: Key Figures of the Harlem Renaissance Project the illustration. Invite a student to identify the setting of the Harlem Renaissance in time *(the 1920s)* and in space *(based in Harlem, New York)*. Ask: what was the Harlem Renaissance? *(period during the 1920s in which African American novelists, poets, and artists celebrated their culture)* Click on the individuals in the illustration one at a time and discuss each one's contribution. Challenge students to describe both the positive and negative impacts of the cultural movement in art and literature known as the Harlem Renaissance on American society. *(The positive impacts of the art and literature produced and the pleasure it gave people, as well as an improved perception of African Americans. Negative impacts might include the movement's inability to improve the political status and economic opportunities of African Americans throughout the country.)*

📖 ACTIVE CLASSROOM

Direct students to have a "conversation" with one of the major figures from the Harlem Renaissance. Have students write down questions they would like to ask their chosen individual then what that person would say in response, and what the student would say in turn. As students formulate their questions, remind them that issues and characteristics in U.S. history are reflected in various genres of literature and art. Some students' questions might concern how the artist or writer expressed these issues and characteristics.

The Harlem Renaissance

INTERACTIVE GALLERY
Key Figures of the Harlem Renaissance

D Differentiate: Extra Support Students having difficulty grasping the concept of a cultural movement can be helped through a definition of the word *renaissance*, which means "a renewed interest." During the Harlem Renaissance, African Americans were renewing their interest in themselves and their culture.

ELL Use the ELL activity described in the ELL chart.

Further Instruction
Identify Cause and Effect Ask students why they think the Harlem Renaissance occurred. What caused it? *(The Great Migration which concentrated many African Americans in northern urban areas, including Harlem, the "New Negro" phenomenon of growing political awareness, and the human desire to express one's experience creatively.)*

Pose and Answer Questions Pair students. Direct each student to generate six questions about the Harlem Renaissance using the six questions words *(who, what, where, when, why,* and *(how)*. Student pairs should then trade questions and answer each others'.

Analyze Information Ask students what the positive impacts of the Harlem Renaissance were. *(The positive impacts of the art and literature produced and the pleasure it gave people, as well as an improved perception of African Americans.)* Might there have been some negative impacts on American society? *(The critiques of the quality of the work of the artists and writers, the cultural movement's inability to improve political and economic status of African Americans, and the separateness of the cultural movement from mainstream society.)*

DIGITAL ACTIVITY
The Great Migration

Before students write their paragraphs, hold a brief discussion the reviews how the Harlem Renaissance was an effect of the Great Migration.

DIGITAL QUIZ
Lesson Quiz and Discussion Board

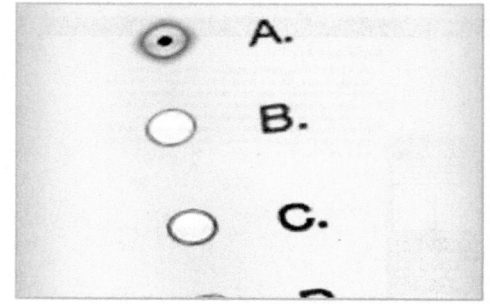

Assign the online Lesson Quiz for this lesson if you haven't already done so. Students will be offered automatic remediation or enrichment based on their score.

Pose these questions to the class on the Discussion Board:

In *The Harlem Renaissance*, you learned about the Black Nationalism that grew in urban areas in the wake of the Great Migration. Marcus Garvey embodied racial pride in his leadership of the Universal Negro Improvement Association. This period in American history also brought about the birth of jazz, a uniquely American form of music created by African Americans. The "Jazz Age" saw the spread of jazz across the country and the world. African Americans also expressed themselves in the art and literature of the Harlem Renaissance, one of the great cultural movements of the twentieth century.

Describe Describe how the spirit of the Roaring Twenties was reflected by jazz music.

Identify Main Ideas Explain how the contributions of African Americans shaped American culture during the Jazz Age.

Topic Inquiry
Have students continue their investigations for the Topic Inquiry.

World War I and the 1920s

■ SYNTHESIZE

DIGITAL ACTIVITY
Reflect on the Essential Question and Topic

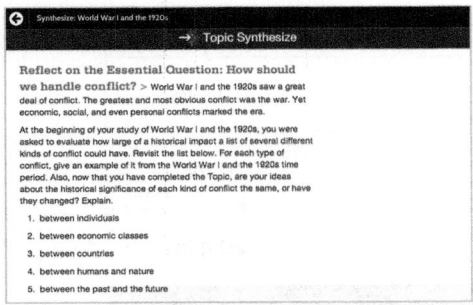

First ask students to reconsider the Essential Question for the topic: How should we handle conflict? Remind students of the kinds of conflicts they considered at the start of the topic. For example,

- between individuals
- between economic classes
- between countries
- between humans and nature
- between the past and the future

Ask students to identify the conflicts Americans dealt with during World War I and the following decade. Ask "Do you think that the United States appropriately handled these conflicts?" Ask them to give at least three reasons to support their position. Discuss their answers as a class or ask students to post their answers on the Class Discussion Board.

Next ask students to reflect on the topic as a whole and jot down one to four questions they've thought about during the topic. Share these examples if students need help getting started:

- What international organizations handle conflicts between nations today?
- How have the rights and privileges of Americans protesting against their government's actions changed since World War I?
- What new technologies and industries might spark a wave of economic growth today, like the automobile did in the early twentieth century?
- How does contemporary art and literature reflect the social issues of today?

You may ask students to share their questions and answers on the Class Discussion Board.

Have students complete Step 3 of the Topic Inquiry.

■ DEMONSTRATE

DIGITAL TOPIC REVIEW AND ASSESSMENT
World War I and the 1920s

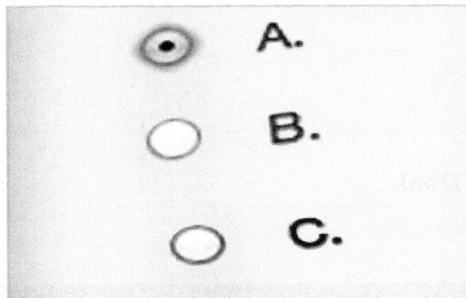

Students can prepare for the Topic Test by answering the questions in the Topic Review and Assessment online or the Assessment questions in the Print Student text. They can also prepare by reviewing their answers to the Interactive Reading Notepad questions or reviewing their notes in the Reading and Notetaking Study Guide.

DIGITAL TOPIC TEST
World War I and the 1920s

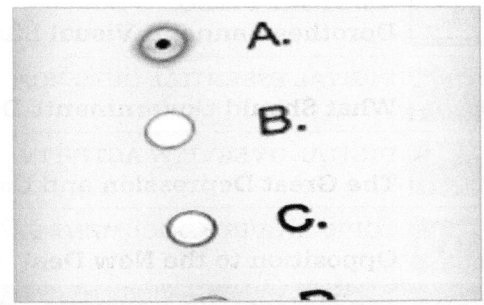

TOPIC TEST
Assign the Topic Test to assess students' understanding of topic content.

BENCHMARK TESTS
Assign these benchmark tests as you complete the relevant topics to monitor student progress toward mastering the course content and as preparation for the End-of-Course Test.

Benchmark Test 1: Topics 1-3
Benchmark Test 2: Topics 4-6
Benchmark Test 3: Topics 7-9
Benchmark Test 4: Topics 10-12
Benchmark Test 5: Topics 13-15
Benchmark Test 6: Topics 16-18
Benchmark Test 7: Topics 19-20

The Great Depression and the New Deal

TOPIC 13 ORGANIZER	PACING: APPROX. 9 PERIODS, 4.5 BLOCKS	
		PACING
Connect		1 period
MY STORY VIDEO **Dorothea Lange, A Visual Life**		10 min.
DIGITAL ESSENTIAL QUESTION ACTIVITY **What Should Governments Do?**		10 min.
DIGITAL OVERVIEW ACTIVITY **The Great Depression and the New Deal**		10 min.
TOPIC INQUIRY: DOCUMENT-BASED QUESTION **Opposition to the New Deal**		20 min.
Investigate		3–6 periods
TOPIC INQUIRY: DOCUMENT-BASED QUESTION **Opposition to the New Deal**		Ongoing
LESSON 1 Causes of the Depression		30–40 min.
LESSON 2 Americans Suffer		30–40 min.
LESSON 3 Two Presidents Respond		30–40 min.
LESSON 4 The New Deal Expands		30–40 min.
LESSON 5 Effects of the New Deal		30–40 min.
LESSON 6 Culture During the Depression		30–40 min.
Synthesize		1 period
DIGITAL ACTIVITY **The Great Depression and the New Deal**		10 min.
TOPIC INQUIRY: DOCUMENT-BASED QUESTION **Opposition to the New Deal**		20 min.
Demonstrate		1–2 periods
DIGITAL TOPIC REVIEW AND ASSESSMENT **The Great Depression and the New Deal**		10 min.
TOPIC INQUIRY: DOCUMENT-BASED QUESTION **Opposition to the New Deal**		20 min.

Opposition to the New Deal

In this Topic Inquiry, students will investigate primary source documents to evaluate the impact of New Deal legislation on the historical roles of federal government. Each student will write an essay in response to the question: Why did some Americans oppose the New Deal? Exploration of the federal New Deal programs will help students understand the Topic Essential Question: What should governments do?

STEP 1: CONNECT
Develop Questions and Plan the Investigation

Launch the Document-Based Question Activity

Tell students that the New Deal was a set of federal programs intended to alleviate the hardships of the Great Depression and provided jobs and assistance to citizens. Project the embedded video segment from *The Cradle Will Rock*.

Suggestion: Pause the video to identify key players in the hearing, such as Hallie Flanagan, Martin Dies, Jr., and Joe Starnes. Point out that *The Cradle Will Rock* is a dramatization of the hearing, but the dialogue closely follows the actual transcript. You may wish to reinforce the dialogue in the video segment by having students read aloud the exchange in the transcript from the Congressional hearing.

Generate Questions

Tell students that in this inquiry, they will examine primary source documents to evaluate the impact of New Deal legislation on the historical roles of federal government. Have students begin by working in pairs to discuss the opposition to the Federal Theater Project (FTP) expressed in the video segment. Guide them to understand that many people feared that the FTP was spreading communist propaganda. At the time, the fear of communism was a strong political and social force in the nation.

Instruct students to discuss the questions for the video in small groups. Display the Document-Based Question: Why did some Americans oppose the New Deal? Point out that the FTP employed citizens who needed jobs. Theater also provided entertainment and distraction from the hardships of the depression.

Suggestion: Encourage students to consider that people might not agree on the best ways to help people. You may also wish to remind students that federal programs cost money.

Resources
- Embedded video segment "Cherry Jones in 'Cradle Will Rock,'" Part 2
- Topic Inquiry DBQ Student Instructions

⏻ PROFESSIONAL DEVELOPMENT

Document-Based Question
Be sure to view the Document-Based Question Professional Development resources in the online course.

STEP 2: INVESTIGATE
Apply Disciplinary Concepts and Tools

Analyze the Documents

Direct student pairs to review the six primary sources, answer the questions that follow, and evaluate the validity of each source as they read and answer the questions. Instruct them to consider information about the author, language, and corrobation with other sources.

Suggestion: Remind students that President Hoover served before President Roosevelt, who campaigned on and championed the New Deal programs. Hoover and Roosevelt competed for the presidency in 1932. The first New Deal programs were enacted in 1933 and 1934, and a second round from 1935 to 1938. Ask: What bias did President Hoover have in opposing New Deal programs? *(President Hoover would have been supporting his opponent's legislative agenda had he expressed any support of the New Deal.)*

Check Your Understanding

As a class, review and discuss answers to the questions for each source. Then, revisit the ideas that students proposed at the start of the project. Ask students to consider again why people might oppose programs designed to help recovery.

Suggestion: Challenge students to categorize the reasons people might oppose the New Deal programs. For example, some reasons might be financial, or monetary, such as raising taxes. Still others might be political, such as denouncing communism or not supporting the platform of an opposing party.

Resources
- Document A: Excerpt from President Hoover's speech at Madison Square Garden on October 31, 1932
- Document B: Roosevelt's Fireside Chat, "Outlining the New Deal Program," on May 7, 1933
- Document C: Franklin D Roosevelt's address to the Seventy-third Congress on June 28, 1934
- Document D: Excerpt from Alf Landon's 1936 Speech, "I Will Not Promise the Moon"
- Document E: Article "Nothing Red but the Tape" by Paul W. Ward in *The Nation,* January 2, 1937
- Document F: News article in *The Nation* by Mordecai Ezekiel, February 26, 1938
- Topic Inquiry DBQ Student Instructions

Opposition to the New Deal *(continued)*

STEP 3: SYNTHESIZE
Evaluate Sources and Use Evidence to Formulate Conclusions

Write Your Essay

Give students instruction on how to write their essays. Recall that they need to answer the Document-Based Question: Why did some Americans oppose the New Deal? Advise students to be sure to use evidence from at least three documents, to clearly identify which documents are used, and to address at least one counter-argument to their position in the essay.

Have students work in small groups to view the 21st Century Skill Tutorials. Circulate the classroom to answer questions as students watch the tutorials.

Suggestion: Display the rubric for the project, and review expectations with students before they begin writing. Have students organize their ideas into a brief outline or into a chart according to the reasons that Americans opposed the New Deal.

Resources
- 21st Century Skill Tutorials: Organize Your Ideas
- 21st Century Skill Tutorials: Support Ideas With Evidence
- 21st Century Skill Tutorials: Consider and Counter Opposing Arguments
- 21st Century Skill Tutorials: Develop a Clear Thesis
- 21st Century Skill Tutorials: Write an Essay
- Topic Inquiry DBQ Rubric
- Topic Inquiry DBQ Student Instructions

STEP 4: DEMONSTRATE
Communicate Conclusions and Take Informed Action

Complete Your Essay

Have students revise and submit their essays. Remind students to read over their essays for any errors before turning it in.

Suggestion: When students finish drafting their essays, have them read aloud their work individually. Reading aloud will help them identify errors, problems with flow, and misconceptions. Tell students to use their Student Instructions like a checklist to ensure that have included all required elements.

Suggestion: Have students present their essays in class or post their essays on a class blog.

Assess Your Work

Tell students to reflect on the investigation and writing process. Challenge them to assess how well they did and to suggest what they might do differently on a future topic inquiry.

Evaluate New Deal Legislation

Ask students to evalute how New Deal legislation impacted the historical roles of federal government. Have them discuss their ideas in a small group. Tell groups to synthesize their ideas into one response to share with the class. Then, take a poll on the following question: Were New Deal programs more helpful or more harmful? Organize students into groups based on their responses, and have them discuss and share their reasoning.

Resources
- Topic Inquiry DBQ Rubric
- Topic Inquiry DBQ Student Instructions
- Self-Assessment

realize.™

INTRODUCTION

The Great Depression and the New Deal

Economic prosperity and cultural innovations in the 1920s masked conditions that would soon lead to economic collapse. Many people borrowed too much on credit, and others over-speculated in the stock market. While manufacturing ramped up, farms struggled. Farmers had over-produced during World War I, and could not sell enough in the post-war period. These economic factors, among others, collided in what became the Great Depression. How did the Great Depression impact the nation and its citizens? How did the government respond?

■ CONNECT

MY STORY VIDEO

Dorothea Lange, A Visual Life

Watch a video showing the impact of Dorothea Lange's photography.

Check Understanding During what era did Dorothea Lange come to prominence? *(the Great Depression)*

Determining Point of View What techniques did Dorothea Lange use to advance her point of view? *(Lange used highly realistic black-and-white images of people who—while suffering from poverty, forced relocation, or racism—were able to maintain their humanity.)*

DIGITAL ESSENTIAL QUESTION ACTIVITY

What Should Governments Do?

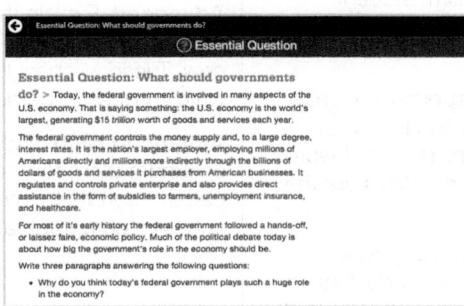

Tell students to think about the Essential Question for this Topic: What should governments do? Government can serve a variety of purposes. Some governments have more influence over people's daily lives and over economic activity than others. Challenge student groups to brainstorm a list of appropriate roles for the federal government. What do they think government should do?

Recall What powers does the federal government have over the economy today? *(The federal government can raise and collect taxes, regulate interstate and international commerce, or trade, employ people, and provide public goods and services.)*

Make Decisions In the event of economic catastrophe, should the federal government intervene to help people and businesses recover? Why or why not? Cite evidence from the Constitution to support your answer. *(Students' responses will vary. Students may argue that government should intervene because it has the power to make laws, to raise taxes, and to provide public goods and services as well as to regulate interstate commerce. These powers give federal government the authority to provide different forms of assistance.)*

DIGITAL OVERVIEW ACTIVITY

The Great Depression and the New Deal

Display the image showing the "Hooverville" outside Washington, D.C. During this Topic, students will learn what impact the Great Depression had on people in the United States as well as how individuals, businesses, and the federal government responded. This image demonstrates what a great toll the hardships of the depression had on people.

D Differentiate: Extra Support What parts of this image show that people faced hard times during the Great Depression? *(There are no houses, businesses, cars, or other signs of prosperity. The image shows only broken down shacks and lean-tos in a field, with men sitting idly in a group in front. The shacks appear to have been made from whatever materials people were able to find.)*

Analyze Images Describe what you see in the image. How does this image from the early 1930s contrast with your ideas about the Roaring Twenties? *(The Roaring Twenties were about prosperity and economic growth. This image on the other hand shows rundown shacks with a few men gathered in the foreground, looking unhappy. It does not show the prosperity inherent in the 1920s.)*

Topic Inquiry

Launch the Topic Inquiry with students after introducing the Topic.

Causes of the Depression

Supporting English Language Learners

Use with Digital Text 1, **Hidden Economic Problems in the Roaring Twenties.**

Listening

When you begin this activity, explain to students that as you speak, you will define or rephrase difficult words to enhance and confirm students' understanding. Use linguistic support as students encounter increasingly complex and elaborated spoken language.

Beginning Using basic spoken language, describe the financial situation of industrial workers during the 1920s. Provide linguistic support by defining difficult words as you proceed. Confirm student understanding by asking: Did industrial workers have a lot of disposable income?

Intermediate Using somewhat elaborated spoken language, describe the financial situation of industrial workers during the 1920s. Provide linguistic support by defining difficult words as you proceed. Confirm student understanding by asking: What was the financial position of industrial workers?

Advanced Using somewhat complex and elaborated spoken language, compare and contrast the financial positions of farmers and industrial workers in the 1920s. Provide linguistic support by defining difficult words as you proceed. Confirm student understanding by asking: What are the dangers of amassing large debts?

Advanced High Using complex and elaborated spoken language, compare and contrast the financial positions of farmers and industrial workers in the 1920s. Provide linguistic support by defining difficult words as you proceed. Ask students to confirm their understanding of the new words by using them to restate what you said.

Use with Digital Text 2, **The Stock Market Hits Bottom.**

Writing

Introduce the sound /oo/by pronouncing it and the word *Hoover*. Have students repeat after you.

Beginning Explain that *oo* is part of the spelling pattern for /oo/. Display and read these words from the text, having students repeat after you: Hoover, soothe, too, boom. Then provide students with sentences to write down and complete using these *oo* words.

Intermediate Explain that *oo*, *ew*, and *ue* are part of the spelling pattern for /oo/. Display and read these words from the text, having students repeat after you: Hoover, boom, new, Tuesday. Ask students to suggest sentences using these words. Record their suggestions, and have students write them down.

Advanced Explain that *oo*, *ew*, *ue*, and *u* can be part of the spelling pattern for /oo/. Have students read these words from the text: Hoover, new, Tuesday, speculation. Ask pairs of students to use these words to write a cohesive paragraph about the Great Crash.

Advanced High Explain that *oo*, *ew*, *ue*, *u*, and *o* can be part of the spelling pattern for /oo/. Have students find words with the /oo/ spelling pattern, sort them into a chart, and use at least five of them to write a cohesive paragraph about the Great Crash.

▣ Differentiate Instruction

Use the Differentiated Instruction notes throughout the lesson plan to support the varied skill sets, levels of readiness, and interests in the mixed-ability classroom.

Challenge These notes include suggestions for expanding the activity for advanced students.

On-Level These notes include suggestions for modifying the activity to address different interests or learning styles.

Extra Support These notes include ideas for providing more scaffolding or reading spuport.

Special Needs These notes provide ideas for adapting instruction to support the needs of various special needs students.

■ NOTES

PEARSON
realize™
www.PearsonRealize.com

Go online to access additional resources including:
Primary Sources • Biographies • Supreme Court cases •
21st Century Skill Tutorials • Maps • Graphic Organizers.

Objectives

Objective 1: Identify how weaknesses in the economy in the 1920s caused the Great Depression.

Objective 2: Explain why the stock market crashed in 1929 and the crash's effect on the economy.

Objective 3: Describe how the Great Depression deepened in the United States and spread overseas.

Objective 4: Identify the causes of the Great Depression and discuss how historians' differ about them.

LESSON 1 ORGANIZER		PACING: APPROX. 1 PERIOD, .5 BLOCKS			
				RESOURCES	
		OBJECTIVES	**PACING**	**Online**	**Print**
Connect					
DIGITAL START UP ACTIVITY **Causes of Unemployment**			5 min.	●	
Investigate					
DIGITAL TEXT 1 **Hidden Economic Problems in the Roaring Twenties**		Objective 1	10 min.	●	●
INTERACTIVE CHART **Evaluate the U.S. Economy in the 1920s**			10 min.	●	
DIGITAL TEXT 2 **The Stock Market Hits Bottom**		Objective 2	10 min.	●	●
DIGITAL TEXT 3 **The Great Depression Begins**			10 min.	●	●
DIGITAL TEXT 4 **The Causes of the Great Depression**		Objectives 3, 4	10 min.	●	●
INTERACTIVE CHART **Causes of the Great Depression**			10 min.	●	
Synthesize					
DIGITAL ACTIVITY **Causes of Unemployment Revisited**			5 min.	●	
Demonstrate					
LESSON QUIZ **Lesson Quiz and Class Discussion Board**			10 min.	●	

Causes of the Depression

CONNECT

DIGITAL START UP ACTIVITY
Causes of Unemployment

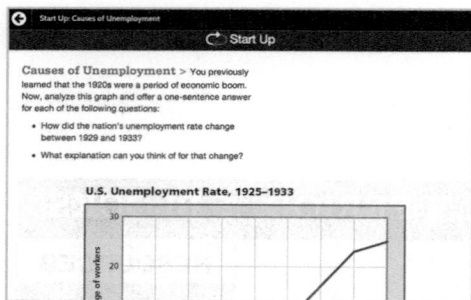

Project the Start Up Activity As students enter and get settled, challenge them to describe the relationship between unemployment and the economy. *(Student responses should reflect an understanding that unemployment negatively impacts a nation's economy.)* Focus their attention on the graph and the questions "How did the nation's unemployment rate change between 1929 and 1933?" and "What explanation can you think of for that change?" Invite students to share their answers with the class.

Tell students that in this lesson they will be learning about how rising unemployment and other critical economic factors contributed to the Great Depression.

Aa Vocabulary Development: Use the Interactive Reading Notepad to preview the Key Terms and Academic Vocabulary in this lesson with students.

⇅ FLIP IT!
Assign the Flipped Video for this lesson.

■ STUDENT EDITION PRINT PAGES: 516–523

INVESTIGATE

DIGITAL TEXT 1
Hidden Economic Problems in the Roaring Twenties

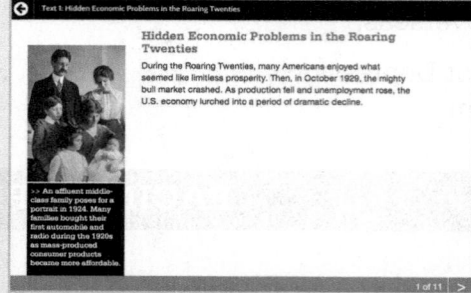

INTERACTIVE CHART
Evaluate the U.S. Economy in the 1920s

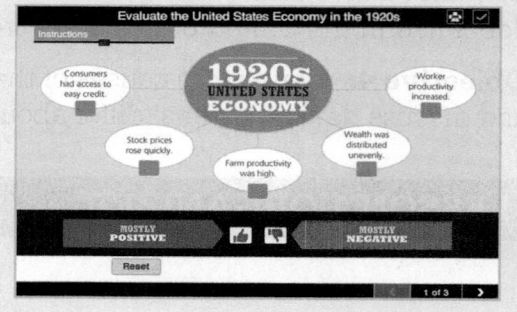

Objective 1: Identify how weaknesses in the economy of the 1920s caused the Great Depression.

Quick Instruction
Interactive Chart: Evaluate the U.S. Economy in the 1920s Project the interactive chart and guide students as they categorize factors as "mostly negative" and "most positive." Then ask them to evaluate each of the characteristics of the 1920s economy.

Make Generalizations Is it fair to suggest that the American economy was in danger of depression in 1929? Why or why not? *(Yes. There were several aspects of the economy that were warning signs, like the uneven distribution of wealth and the significant increase in consumer debt.)*

👥 ACTIVE CLASSROOM

Play a game of Connect Two about the economy of the 1920s. List the following terms on the board: easy credit, rising stock prices, high farm productivity, increased worker productivity, lowered prices, soaring corporate profits, uneven distribution of wealth, speculation, farmers, consumer debt.

Direct students to copy the terms down on notecards or small slips of paper, one term to a card or piece of paper. Review the list of terms with students. Ask students to "connect two" or choose two terms they think belong together, and state the reason for their connection. Challenge students to connect as many pairs of terms as possible.

D Differentiate: Extra Support Explain that the business cycle is an economic term describes the cycle of economic activity. The business cycle usually consists of recession, recovery, growth, and decline.

ELL Use the ELL activity described in the ELL chart.

Further Instruction
Identify Central Issues What did Herbert Hoover and the Republican party represent to the American people in 1928? *(Hoover and the Republicans represented prosperity, confidence, and the continuation of a growing economy.)*

Predict Consequences Predict what might happen if the economic problems of the 1920s are not solved. *(If the problems are not solved, they will lead to an economic recession or even depression.)*

DIGITAL TEXT 2
The Stock Market Hits Bottom

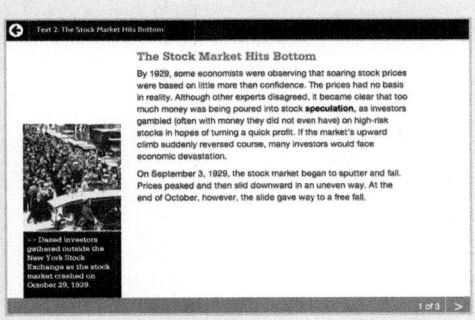

The Stock Market Hits Bottom

By 1929, some economists were observing that soaring stock prices were based on little more than confidence. The prices had no basis in reality. Although other experts disagreed, it became clear that too much money was being poured into stock speculation, as investors gambled (often with money they did not even have) on high-risk stocks in hopes of turning a quick profit. If the market's upward climb suddenly reversed course, many investors would face economic devastation.

On September 3, 1929, the stock market began to sputter and fall. Prices peaked and then slid downward in an uneven way. At the end of October, however, the slide gave way to a free fall.

>> Dazed investors gathered outside the New York Stock Exchange as the stock market crashed on October 29, 1929.

1 of 3 >

DIGITAL TEXT 3
The Great Depression Begins

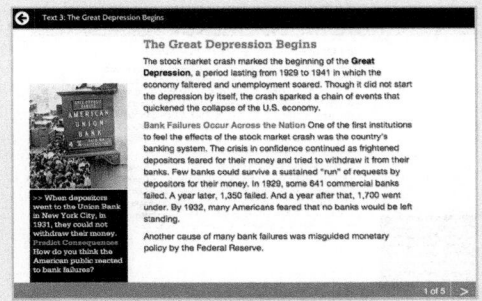

The Great Depression Begins

The stock market crash marked the beginning of the **Great Depression**, a period lasting from 1929 to 1941 in which the economy faltered and unemployment soared. Though it did not start the depression by itself, the crash sparked a chain of events that quickened the collapse of the U.S. economy.

Bank Failures Occur Across the Nation One of the first institutions to feel the effects of the stock market crash was the country's banking system. The crisis in confidence continued as frightened depositors feared for their money and tried to withdraw it from their banks. Few banks could survive a sustained "run" of requests by depositors for their money. In 1929, some 641 commercial banks failed. A year later, 1,350 failed. And a year after that, 1,700 went under. By 1932, many Americans feared that no banks would be left standing.

Another cause of many bank failures was misguided monetary policy by the Federal Reserve.

>> When depositors went to the Union Bank in New York City, in 1931, they could not withdraw their money. *Predict Consequences* How do you think the American public reacted to bank failures?

1 of 5 >

Objective 2: Explain why the stock market crashed in 1929 and the crash's effect on the economy.

Quick Instruction

Analyze Images Project the image of the man holding his head in despair on the board. Explain the significance of 1929 as a turning point during which the Great Depression began. Be sure students understand the significant impact the 1929 market crash had on many Americans. Explain that when the market's upward climb suddenly reversed course, many investors faced economic devastation. Many had to sell their belongings just to pay their bills.

Express Problems Clearly Ask students to describe stock market speculation and how it contributed to the stock market crash and helped to cause the Great Depression. *(Market speculation is the practice of making high-risk investments in hopes of obtaining large profits. Speculators often bought stock with money they did not have. When stock prices crashed, speculators owned near-worthless stocks but still had enormous debts, which many could not repay. The cycle spiraled into other economic areas, helping to lead to the depression.)*

ELL Use the ELL activity described in the ELL chart.

Further Instruction
Briefly discuss with students how Americans embraced Herbert Hoover and the general feeling of confidence in the economy in the late 1928 and early 1929.

Sequence Events Challenge students to identify and sequence key events leading up to the stock market crash. *(Student responses should identify soaring stock prices; September 3, 1929–the stock market began to sputter and fall; October 23–Dow Jones average dropped 21 points; October 24, Black Thursday–investors started to sell; October 29, Black Tuesday–the stock market collapsed in the Great Crash.)*

Generate Explanations What factors played into investors' continued practice of purchasing stocks on speculation? *(Mostly they bought stocks because they wanted to make quick profits. They also had a great deal of confidence in the economy based on the growth in the 1920s.)*

Hypothesize Remind students that President Hoover tried to soothe Americans by insisting that the "business of the country is on a sound and prosperous basis." How do you think many Americans reacted to Hoover's statement? *(I think many probably didn't believe him because of what was happening in the market and the impact it was having on Americans and the economy.)*

Objectives 3: Describe how the Great Depression deepened in the United States and spread overseas; 4: Identify the causes of the Great Depression and discuss how historians differ about them.

Quick Instruction
Guide students to understand the reasons why many banks failed during the depression: Banks profit by loaning depositors' money at interest. Unfortunately, too many loans went into default, leaving banks without enough money to repay depositors.

Interactive Chart: Causes of the Great Depression Project the chart. Invite a volunteer to set the scene by providing context for the chart. *(the Great Depression begins).* What was happening in the American economy in 1928 and 1929? *(Consumer spending was dropping, causing businesses to cut back by slowing production and firing workers. Unemployment therefore was rising. The stock market was dropping creating a lack of confidence in the economy. This pushed investors to sell stocks, creating panic in the markets.)*

Summarize Why are bank failures and the monetary policies of the Federal Reserve considered to be causes of the Great Depression? *(Bank failures quickly spread across the nation as too many people tried to withdraw their money following the stock market crash and banks did not have the cash reserves on hand. At about the same time, the Federal Reserve limited the money supply to discourage lending, which compounded the problem. Both of these issues are causes of*

Causes of the Depression

DIGITAL TEXT 4

The Causes of the Great Depression

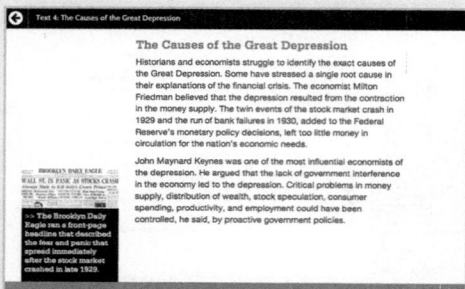

INTERACTIVE CHART

Causes of the Great Depression

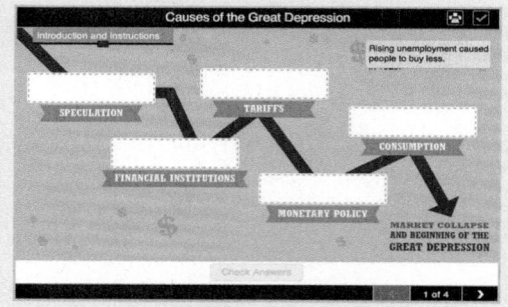

the Great Depression, because they left too little money in circulation for the economy to function properly.)

📖 ACTIVE CLASSROOM

Play a game of Rank It. Have students identify the causes of the Great Depression from the interactivity and the text. Ask students to rank the causes based on which had the greatest impact. Ask students to provide a justification for the ranking decisions they made. Then ask students to work in pairs to share their rankings and justifications. Poll the class to see if there is agreement on the ranking.

Further Instruction

Go through the Interactive Reading Notepad questions with the class. Be sure students understand and can explain the significance of 1929 as a turning point. (the Great Depression began) Use student responses to extend the discussion, focusing on the causes of the Great Depression: weaknesses in the economy, stock market speculation, bank failures, impact of tariffs on world trade, and the monetary policy of the Federal Reserve.

Draw Conclusions What impact did tariffs on world trade have on the Great Depression? (American tariff policies, such as the Hawley-Smoot tariff pushed European countries to retaliate and enact protective tariffs of their own. This was disastrous to the global economy because it seriously damaged international trade and was one of the causes of a depression spreading across the globe.)

Compare and Contrast how John Maynard Keynes' views on the Great Depression differed from some other economists. (He argued that the lack of government interference in the economy led to the depression. Keynes supported proactive government policies to tackle issues like uneven distribution of wealth, stock speculation, consumer spending, productivity, unemployment, and problems in money supply. Other influential economists like Ludwig von Mises and Friedrich von Hayek disagreed with Keynes's argument that the government should play a significant role in solving economic problems.)

SYNTHESIZE

DIGITAL ACTIVITY
Causes of Unemployment Revisited

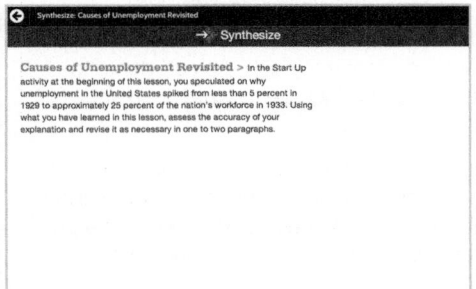

Discuss Remind students that in the Start Up Activity at the beginning of this lesson, they speculated on why unemployment in the United States spiked from less than 5 percent in 1929 to about 25 percent of the nation's workforce in 1933. Ask if they would change any of their responses now that they have learned more about the Great Depression. Direct students to assess the accuracy of their explanations and revise them.

DEMONSTRATE

LESSON QUIZ
Lesson Quiz and Class Discussion Board

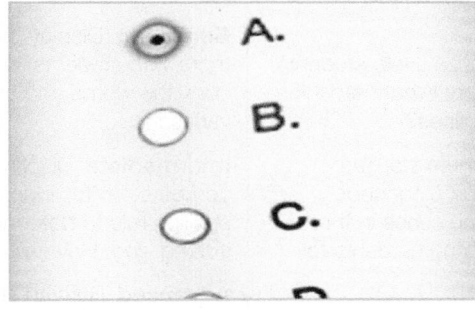

Assign the online Lesson Quiz for this lesson if you haven't already done so. Students will be offered automatic remediation or enrichment based on their score.

Pose these questions to the class on the Discussion Board:

In *Causes of the Depression*, you read about how risky speculation in the stock market, overproduction, and uneven income distribution eventually undermined the economy. Combined with poor or misinformed economic decisions by the Federal Reserve, Congress, and President Hoover, the Great Depression resulted. But economists still debate exactly why this downturn in the economy was so severe and lasted for so long.

Express Problems Clearly Why do you think economists cannot fully agree on the causes of the Great Depression?

Make Predictions How do you think that the depression will impact American's opinions of and support for the Republican and Democrat political parties?

Topic Inquiry
Have students continue their investigations for the Topic Inquiry.

Americans Suffer

Supporting English Language Learners

Use with Digital Text 1, **Economic Hardship Shakes the Cities.**

Listening
Play a recording of Woody Guthrie singing *I Ain't Got No Home*. Prompt students to listen to and derive meaning from the song to build and reinforce concept attainment.

Beginning Display and paraphrase the song's first stanza. Help students build and reinforce concept attainment with this question: What hardships from the Great Depression are brought up in these four lines?

Intermediate Display and read aloud the song's first three stanzas, paraphrasing as needed. Help students build and reinforce concept attainment with these questions: What emotions can you sense in the song's words, voice, and music? How does the song bring hardship to life?

Advanced Display the song's lyrics, and have students read along as you play the song again. Ask pairs of students to build and reinforce concept attainment with these questions: Who are the *gamblin' man* and the *workin' man* in the fifth stanza? Which does the artist represent, and how do you know?

Advanced High Display the song's lyrics, and have students read along as you play the song again. Ask pairs of students to build and reinforce concept attainment by retelling the song's story and discussing how Guthrie's specific details enhance their understanding of suffering during the Great Depression.

Use with Digital Text 3, **Hard Times Hit Most Americans.**

Writing
Prompt students to employ English spelling rules. Explain the spelling rule that verbs ending in a silent e drop that letter before adding *–ing*.

Beginning Display these words: live, lose, make, compete. Pronounce them with students, and point out the silent e in each. Ask students to copy the words and employ the above spelling rule to write their *–ing* variations.

Intermediate Display these words: live, lose, suffer, make, deny, farm, compete. Invite volunteers to read aloud the words and employ the above spelling rule to determine whether any letters need to be dropped before adding *–ing*. Have students write down both variations of each word.

Advanced Remind students that silent *e's*, not all *e's*, are dropped before adding *–ing*. Display these words: live, be, make, compete, flee, lose. Have pairs of students read aloud the words, employ the above spelling rule to determine how to add *–ing* to them, and write down the new words.

Advanced High Display these words: live, be, make, compete, flee, lose. Have students read the words, employ the above spelling rule to determine how to add *–ing* to them, and use the *–ing* words in sentences about the Great Depression.

▶ Differentiate Instruction

Use the Differentiated Instruction notes throughout the lesson plan to support the varied skill sets, levels of readiness, and interests in the mixed-ability classroom.

Challenge These notes include suggestions for expanding the activity for advanced students.

On-Level These notes include suggestions for modifying the activity to address different interests or learning styles.

Extra Support These notes include ideas for providing more scaffolding or reading spuport.

Special Needs These notes provide ideas for adapting instruction to support the needs of various special needs students.

■ NOTES

PEARSON realize ™
www.PearsonRealize.com

Go online to access additional resources including:
Primary Sources • Biographies • Supreme Court cases •
21st Century Skill Tutorials • Maps • Graphic Organizers.

Objectives

Objective 1: Examine the spread of unemployment in America's cities.

Objective 2: Analyze the effects of the Great Depression on farmers.

Objective 3: Analyze the impact of human and geographical factors that created the Dust Bowl.

Objective 4: Describe how the Great Depression affected family life and the lives of African Americans and Mexican Americans.

LESSON 2 ORGANIZER		OBJECTIVES	PACING	RESOURCES	
				Online	Print
Connect					
DIGITAL START UP ACTIVITY **Americans Suffer**			5 min.	●	
Investigate					
DIGITAL TEXT 1 **Economic Hardship Shakes the Cities**		Objective 1	10 min.	●	●
DIGITAL TEXT 2 **Rural America Struggles with Poverty**		Objectives 2, 3	10 min.	●	●
INTERACTIVE GALLERY **Effects of The Dust Bowl**			10 min.	●	
DIGITAL TEXT 3 **Hard Times Hit Most Americans**		Objective 4	10 min.	●	●
INTERACTIVE GALLERY **Life During the Great Depression**			10 min.	●	
Synthesize					
DIGITAL ACTIVITY **Your Life During the Depression**			5 min.	●	
Demonstrate					
LESSON QUIZ **Lesson Quiz and Class Discussion Board**			10 min.	●	

PACING: APPROX. 1 PERIOD, .5 BLOCKS

Americans Suffer

■ CONNECT

DIGITAL START UP ACTIVITY
Americans Suffer

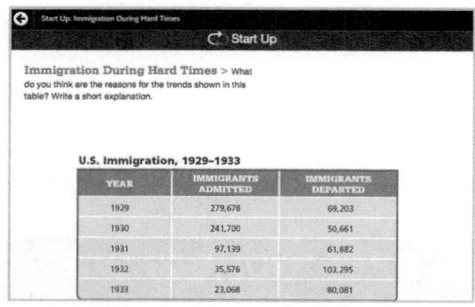

Project the Start Up Activity Provide time for students to study the data in the table. Engage student partners in discussing the role of immigration in the United States and to suggest reasons why immigration goes up and down in certain periods of time. Direct students to write down their explanations. Then have them share their ideas with the class.

Tell students that in this lesson they will be learning how Americans throughout the country were tested by extreme hardship during the depression and how they responded to the worst economic conditions in the country's history.

Aa Vocabulary Development: Use the Interactive Reading Notepad to preview the Key Terms and Academic Vocabulary in this lesson with students.

⇅ FLIP IT!

Assign the Flipped Video for this lesson.

■ STUDENT EDITION PRINT PAGES: 524–531

■ INVESTIGATE

DIGITAL TEXT 1
Economic Hardship Shakes the Cities

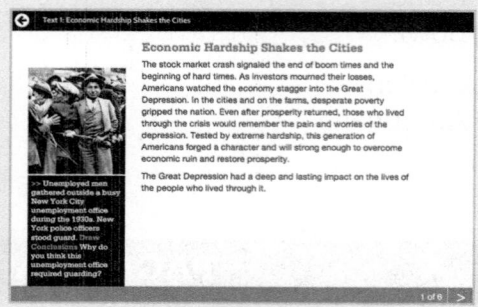

Objective 1: Examine the spread of unemployment in America's cities.

Quick Instruction

Analyze Images Project the image of the unemployed men. Ask students to analyze the image and tell what the details in the picture tell them about the unemployment situation at the time. *(The presence of police keeping guard suggests that there might be problems or violence. Some of the men seem to be pushing forward in desperation. The search for employment was a desperate attempt for many to survive.)* Emphasize that the Great Depression had a deep and lasting impact on the lives of the people who lived through it, and that for many, their lives were never the same again.

Express Problems Clearly How did the depression impact many Americans who were able to retain their jobs in spite of the economic difficulties? *(Many had their wages or hours cut, resulting in paychecks that were 10, 20, sometimes 30 percent less than their pre-depression checks.)*

Summarize Challenge students to describe and analyze the effects of widespread unemployment on the U.S. economy and society in the 1930s. *(Widespread unemployment hurt millions of Americans. Many went hungry and lost their homes. These homeless, often entire families, lived on the streets or in make-shift temporary communities. The increasing unemployment continued the cycle of low consumer consumption, which led to more unemployment and drag on the economy.)*

ELL Use the ELL activity described in the ELL chart.

Further Instruction

Go through the Interactive Reading Notepad questions with the class. Use them as a springboard to discuss the effects of homelessness on families.

Hypothesize Do you think the depression changed people's goals and expectations of financial success? Why or why not? *(Yes. For many Americans who prospered during the 1920s, their dreams of continued success and prosperity were destroyed by poverty and homelessness caused by the depression.)*

Compare Herbert Hoover was viewed as symbol of prosperity in the 1928 presidential election. Yet, by the 1930s, how might millions of Americans have viewed Hoover? *(Many probably thought Hoover was responsible for the depression, or at least contributed to it. The makeshift shantytowns of tents and shacks built on public land or vacant lots were called Hoovervilles. By the early 1930s, Hoover had become a symbol of poverty and homelessness for many Americans.)*

DIGITAL TEXT 2

Rural America Struggles with Poverty

INTERACTIVE GALLERY

Effects of The Dust Bowl

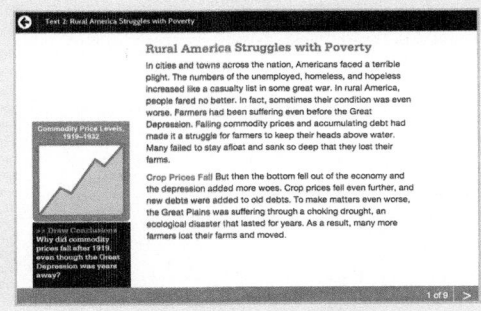

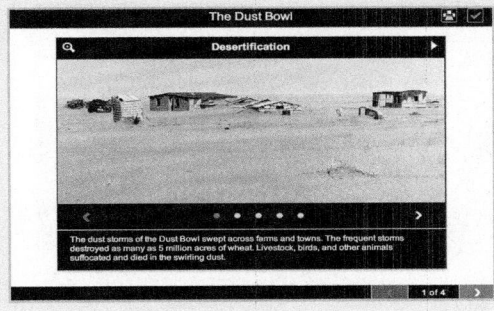

Objectives 2: Analyze the effects of the Great Depression on farmers; 3: Analyze the impact of human and geographical factors that created the Dust Bowl.

Quick Instruction

Interactive Gallery: Effects of The Dust Bowl Project the interactive gallery and click through the images. Discuss the combination of factors that caused the Dust Bowl. Emphasize the impact of physical geographic factors such as the persistent drought conditions and human geographic factors, such as more aggressive farming techniques that in turn exacerbated the conditions that led to the Dust Bowl. Also, discuss the role population growth and distribution played in the region.

Draw Conclusions Based on the information in the images and text, what was the most devastating impact of the Dust Bowl on Americans? *(The greatest impact of the Dust Bowl was the great numbers of farmers who lost their farms or livelihoods and left the region during the 1930s; however, the area did eventually recover.)*

Express Problems Clearly What human geographic factors contributed to conditions that brought about the Dust Bowl? *(More and more farmers moved onto the plains and plowed away much of the natural grasses that in the past had prevented the topsoil from blowing away during periods of drought. New tractor-pulled disk plows pulverized the soil, making it more vulnerable to wind erosion.)*

🎓 ACTIVE CLASSROOM

Project the map of the Dust Bowl on the board. Using the A Closer Look strategy, ask students to pose and answer questions about the geographic patterns and distributions shown on the map.

D Differentiate: **Challenge** Challenge students to research government actions that were put in place to stop land and soil deterioration caused by overgrazing and to protect and manage water supplies. Have students share their findings.

Further Instruction

Go through the Interactive Reading Notepad questions with the class. Broaden the discussion by asking students to describe how crop prices became the main problem of farmers during the depression. *(Falling commodity prices made it a struggle for farmers to earn enough money to continue farming. They could not pay their debts, purchase more seed, repair equipment, and buy what their families needed to survive.)*

Identify Central Issues Describe the relationship between environmental change affecting farmers living on the Great Plains during the 1930s and migration patterns. *(Several environmental changes affected farmers living on the Great Plains. One was a bad drought that lasted for years. As a result, many farmers lost their farms and moved. The Dust Bowl conditions on the Great Plains made farming almost impossible. Consequently, many more farmers had to abandon farming or migrate to wherever they could find work.)*

Draw Conclusions How did the Dust Bowl shift the balance between large farm operations and small, family-owned farms? *(Large farming operations were in a much better position to survive the agriculture crisis during the depression and Dust Bowl. They had enough resources and money to continue farming. In addition, they often bought repossessed land at rock-bottom prices and expanded their holdings into even larger commercial farms.)*

Analyze Maps Project the map of the Dust Bowl region showing patterns of migration. What role did the Dust Bowl and farming problems play in changing demographic patterns within the United States? *(The collapse of agriculture and the Dust Bowl forced millions of Americans to move from rural areas to urban areas of the country. Rural states lost population while states with large cities gained population.)*

Americans Suffer

DIGITAL TEXT 3

Hard Times Hit Most Americans

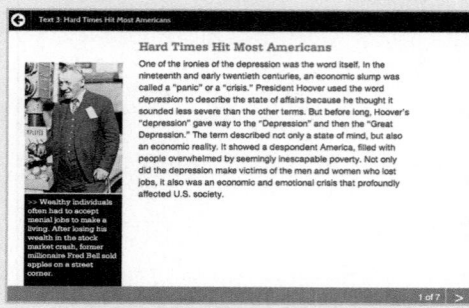

INTERACTIVE GALLERY

Life During the Great Depression

Objective 4: Describe how the Great Depression affected family life and the lives of African Americans and Mexican Americans.

Quick Instruction

Interactive Gallery: Life During the Great Depression Project the interactive gallery and click through the images. Remind students that the depression affected most Americans on a personal level. People responded to their problems in their own way.

Analyze Images What were some of the positive ways in which people responded to the depression? (*Many Americans volunteered to help others as relief workers. Americans sought out entertainment to take their minds off their problems.*) What were some of the negative responses? (*Some Americans rioted in the streets, demonstrated against their former employers, and turned to violence.*)

Analyze Effects Ask students to analyze the effects of the deportation and repatriation of people of Mexican, European, and other heritages on the U.S. economy and society during the Great Depression. (*The effects were significant because these people, many of them American citizens, had been valuable members and workers in society. The loss of hundreds of thousands of people had a negative effect on the economy. These people had made lives in the United States and had made valuable contributions to American culture and in communities. By deporting them, America lost future contributions and hurt existing communities, in addition to violating the rights of those who were citizens.*)

◤◢ ACTIVE CLASSROOM

Direct students to have a "Conversation with Fred Bell." Tell students to imagine that they are having a conversation with Bell as he is selling apples from his street apple cart. Direct each student to write down a question he or she would like to ask, then how Bell would respond, and then what the student would say in response.

ELL Use the ELL activity described in the ELL chart.

Further Instruction

Summarize How did the depression take a toll on women, children and minorities in America? (*Women often had to take on jobs to support their families as well as looking after children. Children suffered from hunger and the lack of other necessities. African Americans and Mexican Americans were often the first workers fired and the last to get hired. They faced additional discrimination when looking for employment.*)

Synthesize Information Why did some men find their role in the family diminished during the depression? (*Unemployed men could no longer support their families. Wives often became the sole moneymaker in many families.*) What were some of the ways these men reacted? (*Many labored tirelessly to find a new job, while others sank into shame and despair. Some even deserted their families.*)

SYNTHESIZE

DIGITAL ACTIVITY

Your Life During the Depression

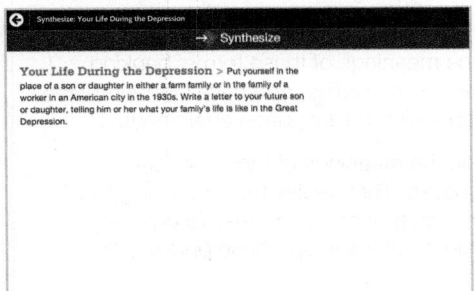

Discuss Before students begin their letters, lead the class in a brief review of how the Great Depression affected urban and rural Americans. Encourage students to think about the personal stories of the industrial workers or farmers they read about and to think about how their lives were greatly changed because of the economic hardships they endured.

DEMONSTRATE

LESSON QUIZ

Lesson Quiz and Class Discussion Board

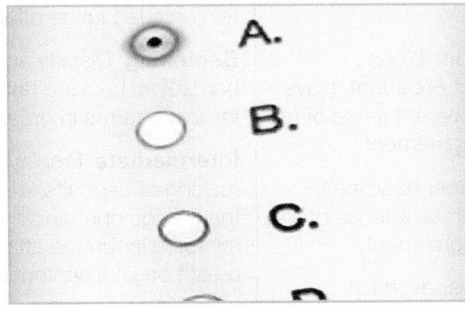

Assign the online Lesson Quiz for this lesson if you haven't already done so. Students will be offered automatic remediation or enrichment based on their score.

Pose these questions to the class on the Discussion Board:

In *Americans Suffer*, you read about how the Great Depression and the Dust Bowl, two momentous events, caused large numbers of Americans to lose their jobs and homes.

Make Predictions What effect will the thousands of Okies moving to new communities and regions have on the residents of those places?

Identify Patterns What, if any, economic or environmental conditions like those that happened during the Great Depression or Dust Bowl era have resurfaced since the 1930s?

Topic Inquiry
Have students continue their investigations for the Topic Inquiry.

Two Presidents Respond

Supporting English Language Learners

Use with Digital Text 3, **Americans Turn to Roosevelt.**

Writing
Review the meanings of *subject* and *verb* in order to prepare students to edit writing for standard grammar and usage, including subject-verb agreement.

Beginning Display these mock newspaper headlines from 1932: Americans _____ Voting Today; Roosevelt _____ the Next President. Have students complete each with *is* or *are*. Then review the present tense of *to be* and have students edit their writing for subject-verb agreement.

Intermediate Ask small groups to create mock newspaper headlines from 1932 using the words *is* and *are*. Then review the present tense of *to be* and have students edit their writing for subject-verb agreement.

Advanced Ask pairs of students to write a short victory speech for Roosevelt, in which they use each of the words *am*, *are*, and *is* at least twice. Then review the present tense of *to be* and have students edit their writing for subject-verb agreement.

Advanced High Ask students to write a short concession speech for Hoover, in which they use each of the words *am*, *are*, and *is* at least twice. Then review the present tense of *to be* and have students edit their writing for subject-verb agreement. Provide time for students to read their speech to a partner.

Use with Digital Text 4, **The New Deal Begins.**

Listening
Play a recording of the first paragraph (approximately 1-1/2 minutes) of Roosevelt's first fireside chat on the banking crisis in order to build and reinforce language attainment.

Beginning Display and review the meanings of these terms: banking, hardships, banking holiday. Replay the recording, and have students listen for these terms in order to build and reinforce language attainment.

Intermediate Display and explain the meanings of these phrases: making of deposits, drawing of checks. Then replay the first sentence of the fireside chat and have students listen for these terms. To build and reinforce language attainment, help students adapt these phrases to create original sentences.

Advanced Display a transcript of the fireside chat's first paragraph. Underline and discuss these terms: proclamations, couched, inconvenience. Then have students listen to the recording again in order to build and reinforce language attainment.

Advanced High Have students read a transcript of the fireside chat's first paragraph and identify unfamiliar words. Ask pairs of students to discuss the meanings of the words they have identified, using a dictionary as needed. Then replay the recording in order to build and reinforce language attainment.

◨ Differentiate Instruction

Use the Differentiated Instruction notes throughout the lesson plan to support the varied skill sets, levels of readiness, and interests in the mixed-ability classroom.

Challenge These notes include suggestions for expanding the activity for advanced students.

On-Level These notes include suggestions for modifying the activity to address different interests or learning styles.

Extra Support These notes include ideas for providing more scaffolding or reading spuport.

Special Needs These notes provide ideas for adapting instruction to support the needs of various special needs students.

◼ NOTES

PEARSON
realize™
www.PearsonRealize.com

Go online to access additional resources including:
Primary Sources • Biographies • Supreme Court cases •
21st Century Skill Tutorials • Maps • Graphic Organizers.

Objectives

Objective 1: Evaluate Hoover's approaches to resolving the Great Depression and how Americans reacted to them.

Objective 2: Contrast Hoover's approach to the economic crisis with Franklin D. Roosevelt's approach.

Objective 3: Describe the programs that were part of the first New Deal and their immediate effect on Americans' lives.

Objective 4: Identify the New Deal's opponents and their major criticisms.

LESSON 3 ORGANIZER		PACING: APPROX. 1 PERIOD, .5 BLOCKS		
	OBJECTIVES	**PACING**	**Online**	**Print**
Connect				
DIGITAL START UP ACTIVITY **What Are the Government's Duties?**		5 min.	●	
Investigate				
DIGITAL TEXT 1 **Hoover's Response Fails**	Objective 1	10 min.	●	●
DIGITAL TEXT 2 **Challenging Economic Times Lead to Protest**	Objective 2	10 min.	●	●
DIGITAL TEXT 3 **Americans Turn to Roosevelt**		10 min.	●	●
DIGITAL TEXT 4 **The New Deal Begins**	Objective 3	10 min.	●	●
INTERACTIVE TIMELINE **FDR's First One Hundred Days**		10 min.	●	
DIGITAL TEXT 5 **Critics of the New Deal**	Objective 4	10 min.	●	●
INTERACTIVE GALLERY **Enduring New Deal Programs**		10 min.	●	
Synthesize				
DIGITAL ACTIVITY **The Depression Challenges Ideas of Governmental Duties**		5 min.	●	
Demonstrate				
LESSON QUIZ **Lesson Quiz and Class Discussion Board**		10 min.	●	

Two Presidents Respond

■ CONNECT

DIGITAL START UP ACTIVITY
What Are the Government's Duties?

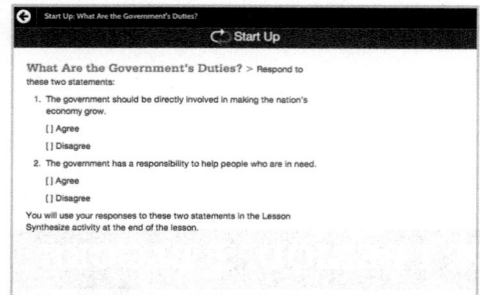

Project the Start Up Activity Ask students to make a list of the responsibilities of the federal government. Then have them write what they think the role of government in society should be. Have students share their ideas with a partner.

Discuss Take a moment to reflect on how the Great Depression affected Americans who were unable to help themselves. Do you agree with the statements? Remind students to hold onto their responses for future use.

Tell students that in this lesson they will be learning about how Presidents Hoover and Roosevelt responded to the problems the nation faced during the depression.

Aa Vocabulary Development: Use the Interactive Reading Notepad to preview the Key Terms and Academic Vocabulary in this lesson with students.

⇈ FLIP IT!
Assign the Flipped Video for this lesson.

■ STUDENT EDITION PRINT PAGES: 532–542

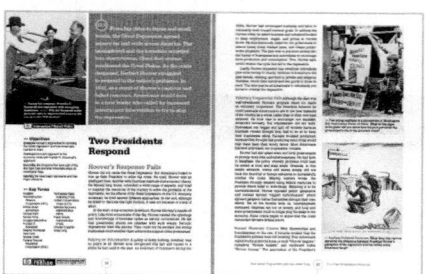

■ INVESTIGATE

DIGITAL TEXT 1
Hoover's Response Fails

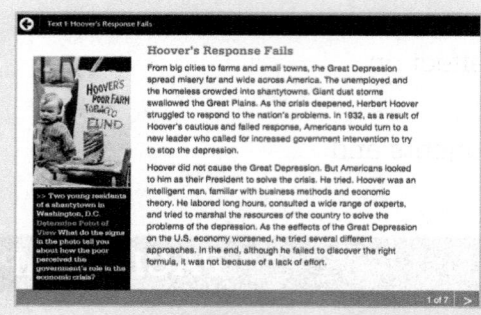

Objective 1: Evaluate Hoover's approaches to resolving the Great Depression and how Americans reacted to them.

Quick Instruction

Analyze Images Project the image of the shantytown children. Ask: What do the details in the photograph suggest about the effects of the Great Depression on the U.S. economy and society? *(The photo tells me that the depression has hit these kids hard, and that the weak economy has force many people to live in the shantytowns like this one.)* Explain that even though he tried several different approaches to end the depression, Hoover failed. Direct students' attention to the signs in the photograph. Point out that the association of the President's name with suffering and want indicated Americans' negative feelings about Hoover and his failed policies.

Determine Point of View How did Hoover's views on government influence his response to the depression? *(Hoover believed that the federal government should not get involved in what he considered to be a stage in the business cycle. Hoover resisted using federal resources to provide direct relief to individuals because he believed that such relief was unconstitutional. Rather, Hoover supported localism, the policy whereby problems could best be solved at local and state levels.)*

Draw Conclusions Why did Hoover turn from volunteerism and localism to more activist policies to fight the depression? *(His reliance on volunteerism and localism was not working so he had to change plans.)*

Further Instruction

Use the chart about trickle-down or supply-side economics to begin a discussion about trickle-down-economics. Make sure students understand the concept. *(Trickle-down economics is an economic theory that holds that financial benefits given to banks and large businesses will trickle down to smaller businesses, workers, and consumers.)*

Express Problems Clearly Why did the Reconstruction Finance Corporation (RFC) fail in its goals? *(Many bankers did not increase their loans to businesses, which was a primary purpose of the program. In addition, when some businesses did get loans, they did not use the money they received to hire more workers.)*

Infer What environmental benefit would the Hoover Dam have on the region? *(The dam might be able to aid in managing the water supplies for communities throughout the Southwest.)*

DIGITAL TEXT 2
Challenging Economic Times Lead to Protest

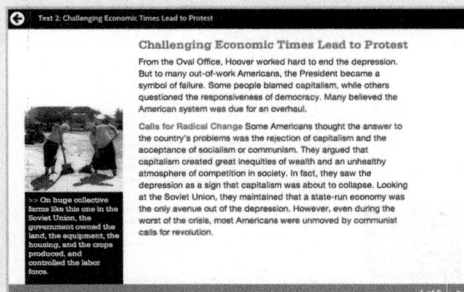

DIGITAL TEXT 3
Americans Turn to Roosevelt

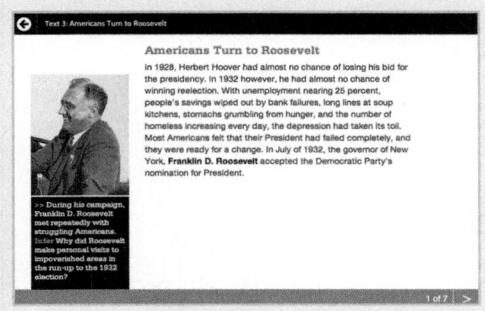

DIGITAL TEXT 4
The New Deal Begins

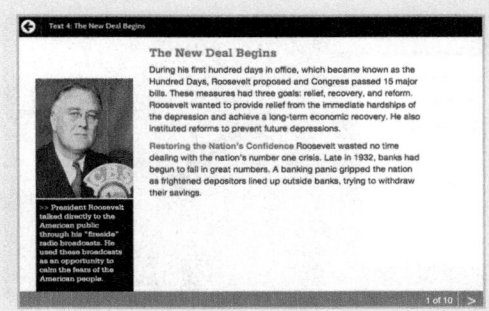

Objective 2: Contrast Hoover's approach to the economic crisis with Franklin D. Roosevelt's approach.

Quick Instruction
Project the photograph of members of the Bonus Army. Ensure understanding of the Bonus Army by reviewing why the group formed and what its goals were. Challenge students to discuss whether the Bonus Army was justified in its protest. Invite volunteers to share their ideas with the class. *(No. They had an agreement that they should have honored. Considering the economic crisis in the country at the time, their demands would have drained money from the government when it could have been used for other projects.)*

Summarize how Hoover and Franklin D. Roosevelt differed in their approaches to resolving the effects of the economic crisis. *(Hoover believed that depression relief should come from state and local governments and private agencies. Roosevelt believed that the depression required strong action and leadership by the federal government.)*

Distinguish Between Fact and Opinion How would you characterize General MacArthur's claims about the goals of the Bonus Army? *(MacArthur's claim that the Bonus Army marchers were a gang of revolutionaries bent on taking over the government sounds like an exaggeration.)*

ELL Use the ELL activity described in the ELL chart.

Further Instruction
Draw Conclusions How do you think Roosevelt's earlier jobs and life experiences prepared him to serve as President? *(Roosevelt was well-educated, confident, and had strong government experience. He had suffered political defeats and battled polio but did not let those setbacks break his spirit or his determination.)*

Express Ideas Clearly Some Americans argued that socialism, communism, or fascism were viable alternatives to American capitalism. In your opinion, why did most Americans reject this claim? *(Americans valued individual freedom and dreams of progress and opportunity that capitalism could produce. Most Americans had too much faith in the ability of the country to respond to and overcome great crisis that they couldn't fully abandon capitalism or democracy.)*

Support Ideas with Examples Did Roosevelt display qualities of effective leadership in the early stages of his presidency? Why or why not? *(Yes. He reached out to struggling Americans to show his concern. He brought in experts from across the political spectrum to help him plan the New Deal. He also recognized the value of his wife Eleanor as a representative of his administration and government in general to interact with the American public.)*

Objective 3: Describe the programs that were part of the first New Deal and their immediate affect on Americans' lives.

Quick Instruction
Interactive Timeline: FDR's First Hundred Days Project the interactive timeline and have students select the squares to explore the strategies and accomplishments of FDR's first hundred days.

Analyze Information How did the programs of the first 100 days benefit both the economy and the environment? *(Many of the new programs involved industrial recovery through business-government cooperation, agricultural recovery through loans and subsidies to farmers, and federal spending on construction projects to pump money into the economy. Programs such as the Civilian Conservation Corps, Tennessee Valley Authority, and Agricultural Adjustment Act involved protecting and managing natural resources in more efficient ways.)*

👥 ACTIVE CLASSROOM
Have students break into groups and use the Circle Write Strategy to address the prompt, "Why did FDR push for large federal government programs to fight the effects of the depression?" Have students write as much as they can for 1 minute and then switch with the person on their right. The next person tries to improve or elaborate the response where the other person left off. Continue to switch until the paper comes back to the first person. The group decides which is the best composition and shares that with the class.

Two Presidents Respond

INTERACTIVE TIMELINE
FDR's First One Hundred Days

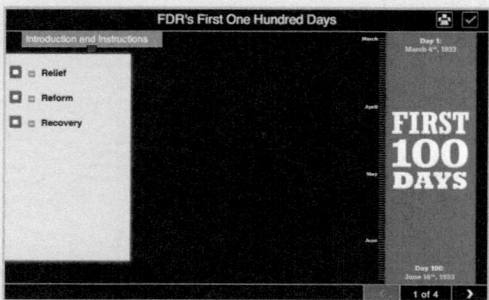

ELL Use the ELL activity described in the ELL chart.

Further Instruction

Ensure that students understand the three basic goals of the first round of programs in Roosevelt's New Deal *(Relief programs would provide relief from the immediate hardships of the depression; recovery programs would achieve a long-term economic recovery; reform programs would prevent future depressions.)* Help them to understand the effects of the New Deal governmental actions on individuals by asking the following questions.

Express Problems Clearly What were some of the unintended negative consequences of the Agricultural Adjustment Act (AAA)? *(Some farmers plowed under crops and killed off excess livestock just to stop overproduction. This drew concern because many Americans believed it was immoral to kill livestock or destroy crops while people went hungry. In addition, not all farmers qualified for the program. When food prices did go up, these farmers and millions of other depression-era poor struggled to buy food. The AAA also hurt tenant farmers, most of whom were African American. Large landowners took the land they were farming out of production resulting in the tenant farmers losing their jobs and homes.)*

Infer Why did New Deal programs place a greater emphasis on employing men than women? *(Men were especially hit hard by the unemployment wave that swept America during the depression because they made up the majority of the workforce. Men traditionally*

were the breadwinners in most families, so the New Deal programs sought to put to work the great number of out-of-work men.)

Analyze Consequences Why do you think that critics were so concerned about FDR cutting the connection between the gold standard and the paper dollar in 1933? *(Possible answer: They may have feared that cutting the connection would make the money worthless because it was no longer backed by anything with tangible value. Inflation would soar, making money worthless as had happened in Germany following World War I.)*

DIGITAL TEXT 5
Critics of the New Deal

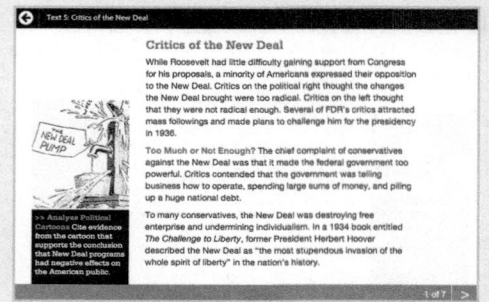

Objective 4: Identify the New Deal's opponents and their major criticisms.

Quick Instruction

Interactive Gallery: Enduring New Deal Programs Project the interactive gallery and click through the images. Discuss how many of the agencies and programs created during the New Deal were temporary measures designed to meet specific problems and needs arising from the Great Depression. Challenge students to name the large federal government programs with which they are familiar. Ask: Do any of the programs you know of trace their origins to FDR's New Deal?

Identify Central Issues Challenge students to describe how various New Deal agencies and programs, such as the Federal Deposit Insurance Corporation and the Securities and Exchange Commission, continue to affect the lives of U.S. citizens. *(The Federal Deposit Insurance Corporation provides federal government insurance for depositors in the event of a bank collapse. The Securities and Exchange Commission continues to regulate the stock market to make it a safer place for Americans' investments.)*

🎬 ACTIVE CLASSROOM

Have students Make Headlines for the enduring New Deal agencies and programs. Ask: If you were to write a headline for the each of the enduring New Deal programs that captured the most important aspect that should be remembered, what would that headline be? Allow students to use subheadings to communicate more information. Encourage them to present the enduring New Deal programs as part of the larger Great Depression era. Have students pass their headlines to a partner for them to review.

SYNTHESIZE

DEMONSTRATE

INTERACTIVE GALLERY
Enduring New Deal Programs

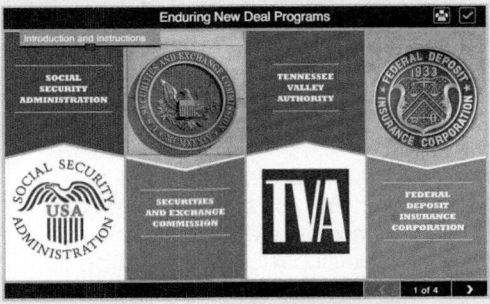

D **Differentiate: Challenge** Challenge students to research other New Deal programs to find out their effectiveness and to discover what happened to them. Have students use the information they gather to write a short essay tracing how these acts helped pull the country out of the depression.

Further Instruction

Compare Points of View Why did both the right and the left protest the New Deal? *(The chief complaint of conservatives against the New Deal was that it made the government too powerful. These people believed that the New Deal was destroying free enterprise and undermining individualism. Some critics on the left criticized the New Deal because they felt Roosevelt had deserted the Democratic Party's principles of a limited federal government. Others on the left thought the New Deal did not do enough to help those who were suffering and in need.)*

Evaluate Arguments Challenge students to compare and evaluate the New Deal policies and its opponents' approaches to resolving the economic effects of the Great Depression. *(The New Deal programs had some success in fighting the depression. The size and power of government increased significantly, but the effects of the depression were reduced. Hoover's plans, which relied on localism and supply-side economics, didn't seem to work. Francis Townsend's plan doesn't seem like it would do enough to help the majority of unemployed Americans, who were under the age of 60. Father Coughlin's plan to nationalize industry and Huey Long's plan to tax the wealthy and redistribute their wealth sound too radical and counter to the American principles of free enterprise and individual freedom and responsibility.)*

DIGITAL ACTIVITY
The Depression Challenges Ideas of Governmental Duties

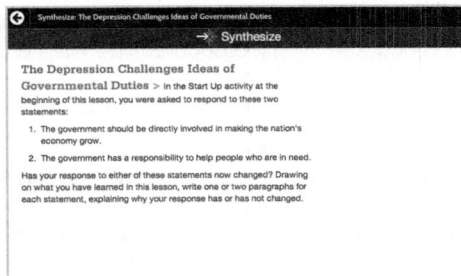

Have students review the lesson and discuss how the government responded to the Great Depression. Ask students to think about the following question. How did individual philosophies of the role of government shape the responses of presidents Hoover and Roosevelt?

Engage students in reviewing their responses from the Connect activity at the beginning of this lesson. Ask students if they would change any of their responses now the they have learned more about the Great Depression.

LESSON QUIZ
Lesson Quiz and Class Discussion Board

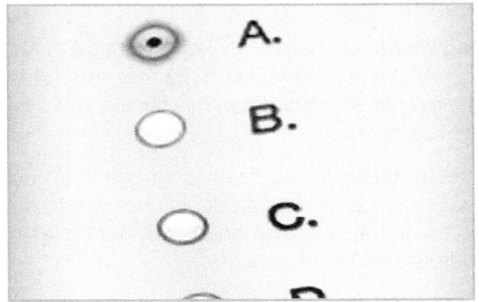

Assign the online Lesson Quiz for this lesson if you haven't already done so. Students will be offered automatic remediation or enrichment based on their score.

Pose these questions to the class on the Discussion Board:

In *Two Presidents Respond*, you read about "a contest between two philosophies of government" that played out during the great economic crisis during the depression. Hoover believed that depression relief should come from state and local governments and private agencies. Roosevelt believed that the depression required strong action and leadership by the federal government.

Make Generalizations How much did one's individual philosophy of the role of the federal government influence most Americans casting ballots in the 1932 presidential election?

Predict Consequences FDR's New Deal greatly expanded the power and reach of the federal government. How might these actions impact responses to future economic crisis?

Topic Inquiry
Have students continue their investigations for the Topic Inquiry.

The New Deal Expands

Supporting English Language Learners

Use with Digital Text 1, **Expanding New Deal Programs.**

Listening
Explain that as you speak, students should listen for the general meaning of what you say in order to understand the general meaning of spoken language.

Beginning Use basic spoken language to retell information about the Social Security Act found in the text. Help students understand the general meaning of your words on this familiar topic by asking: What topic did I just talk about?

Intermediate Use spoken language to tell about Social Security, both in 1935 and today. Help students understand the general meaning of your words on these familiar and unfamiliar topics by asking: What did I just compare and contrast?

Advanced Use spoken language to explain the Social Security and Medicare programs in this country. Ask students to identify the general meaning of what you said about these familiar and unfamiliar topics.

Advanced High Use spoken language to provide an overview of the various issues people face in retirement, as well as some government programs available to assist them. Ask pairs of students to discuss the general meaning of what you said about this mostly unfamiliar topic.

Use with Digital Text 2, **Labor Unions Thrive.**

Writing
Review the meaning of pronoun to prepare students to edit writing for standard grammar and usage related to pronoun agreement.

Beginning Have students write these sentences and fill in the blanks with pronouns: The Wagner Act was part of the New Deal. _____ let workers join unions. Unions helped workers. _____ fought for better hours and wages. Then display the subject pronouns and have students edit their writing.

Intermediate Display these sentences: The Wagner Act was part of the New Deal. Unions were formed to help workers. Ask students to copy each sentence and write a follow-up sentence using a subject pronoun. Then display the subject pronouns and have students edit their writing.

Advanced Ask pairs of students to write a paragraph using these subjects and their subject pronouns: United Mine Workers, workers, John L. Lewis. Then display the subject pronouns and have pairs edit their writing. Ask: Why is United Mine Workers singular and workers plural?

Advanced High Ask students to write a paragraph about the UAW strike using three subject pronouns and three object pronouns. Then display the subject and object pronouns and have students edit their writing. Ask: Which pronouns are the same in both the subject and object positions?

▣ Differentiate Instruction

Use the Differentiated Instruction notes throughout the lesson plan to support the varied skill sets, levels of readiness, and interests in the mixed-ability classroom.

Challenge These notes include suggestions for expanding the activity for advanced students.

On-Level These notes include suggestions for modifying the activity to address different interests or learning styles.

Extra Support These notes include ideas for providing more scaffolding or reading spuport.

Special Needs These notes provide ideas for adapting instruction to support the needs of various special needs students.

■ NOTES

PEARSON
realize™
www.PearsonRealize.com

Go online to access additional resources including:
Primary Sources • Biographies • Supreme Court cases •
21st Century Skill Tutorials • Maps • Graphic Organizers.

Objectives

Objective 1: Analyze ways that the New Deal promoted social and economic reform and its long-term effects.

Objective 2: Explain how New Deal legislation affected the growth of organized labor.

Objective 3: Evaluate the impact of Roosevelt's plan to increase the number of U.S. Supreme Court justices on the course of the New Deal.

LESSON 4 ORGANIZER		PACING: APPROX. 1 PERIOD, .5 BLOCKS		
			RESOURCES	
	OBJECTIVES	**PACING**	**Online**	**Print**
Connect				
DIGITAL START UP ACTIVITY **Was the New Deal Really Working?**		5 min.	●	
Investigate				
DIGITAL TEXT 1 **Expanding New Deal Programs**	Objective 1	10 min.	●	●
INTERACTIVE TIMELINE **Milestones in Social Security**		10 min.	●	
DIGITAL TEXT 2 **Labor Unions Thrive**	Objective 2	10 min.	●	●
DIGITAL TEXT 3 **Opposition to the New Deal**	Objective 3	10 min.	●	●
INTERACTIVE CHART **Left and Right Opposition to the New Deal**		10 min.	●	
Synthesize				
DIGITAL ACTIVITY **Effects of the New Deal Today**		5 min.	●	
Demonstrate				
DIGITAL QUIZ **Lesson Quiz and Class Discussion Board**		10 min.	●	

The New Deal Expands

■ CONNECT

DIGITAL START UP ACTIVITY
Was the New Deal Really Working?

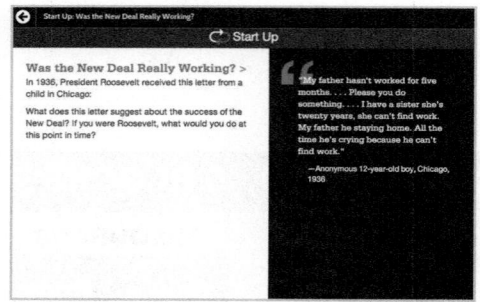

Project the Start Up Activity Ask students to read the letter as they enter and get settled. Then have them share their ideas with another student, either in class or through a chat or blog space.

Discuss What does this letter suggest about the success of the New Deal? *(The letter suggests that all the programs of the New Deal had not been successful in helping many Americans.)* If you were Roosevelt, what would you do? *(Create more programs to help more people.)*

Tell students that in this lesson they will be learning how Roosevelt did respond to the ongoing problems of the Great Depression.

Aa Vocabulary Development: Use the Interactive Reading Notepad to preview the Key Terms and Academic Vocabulary in this lesson with students.

🔁 FLIP IT!
Assign the Flipped Video for this lesson.

■ STUDENT EDITION PRINT PAGES: 543–549

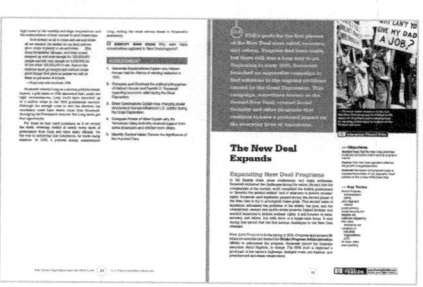

■ INVESTIGATE

DIGITAL TEXT 1
Expanding New Deal Programs

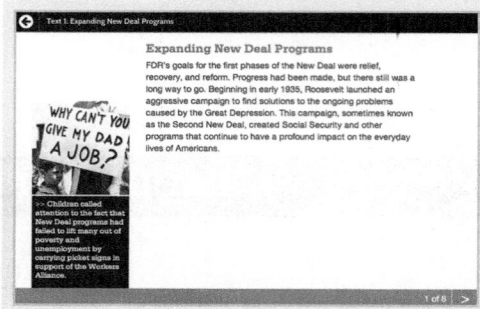

INTERACTIVE TIMELINE
Milestones in Social Security

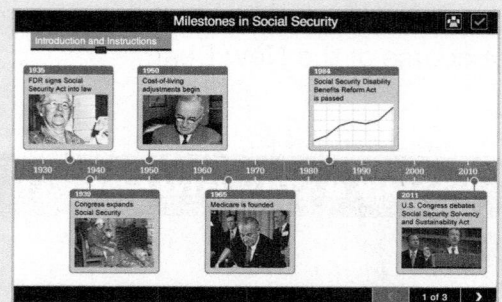

Objective 1: Analyze ways that the second New Deal promoted social and economic reform and its long-term effects

Quick Instruction
Interactive Timeline: Milestones in Social Security Project the timeline and select the events to reveal details about significant developments in the Social Security program. Review with students how Social Security is funded. *(The program is based on contributions that workers make into the system. While citizens are employed, they pay into Social Security; they receive benefits later when they retire. Workers and their employers pay into Social Security in the form of the Federal Insurance Contributions Act (FICA) payroll taxes that are withheld from most paychecks.)*

Summarize how the Social Security Administration has adapted to changing issues and continues to affect the lives of U.S. citizens. *(Social Security was expanded in 1939 to pay benefits to the survivors of deceased workers or retirees. In 1950, a revision added annual cost-of-living increases to monthly benefits to offset the effect of inflation on fixed Social Security incomes. The 1950 amendments also made farm workers, domestic workers, and self-employed persons eligible for Social Security. Medicare and Medicaid were created to provide a health insurance program for Americans age 65 and older needy persons of any age. In 1984 Congress expanded eligibility for Social Security disability benefits. Point out that the costs of programs such as these has increased over time and that the solvency of long-term entitlements such as Social Security continues to be debated in Congress.)*

Infer Why might members of Congress vote against the Social Security Solvency and Sustainability Act to reform the Social Security system? *(Social Security is a very popular program. Lawmakers were probably afraid that they would face a voter backlash if they supported changes to the current system that so many Americans like.)*

🗣 ACTIVE CLASSROOM
Have students use the Take a Stand Strategy to take a stand on the following issue: Evaluate if the government can afford to provide basic economic security to millions of Americans through Social Security. Have students take their place on a continuum line of 1–10 depending on how strongly they agree with the ability of the government to pay for Social Security. Have students create an opening statement defending their position.

ELL Use the ELL activity described in the ELL chart.

Further Instruction
Ask students to list the New Deal programs initiated in 1935 and after that are described in the reading. *(WPA, Social Security Act, REA; New Deal public-works water projects)*

Evaluate Arguments John Maynard Keynes argued that deficit spending was needed to end the depression. The government paid for projects with money it did not have. Do you agree with Keynes? Why or why not? *(Yes. The Great Depression created such severe economic problems that it was necessary for the government to help lower the unemployment*

DIGITAL TEXT 2

Labor Unions Thrive

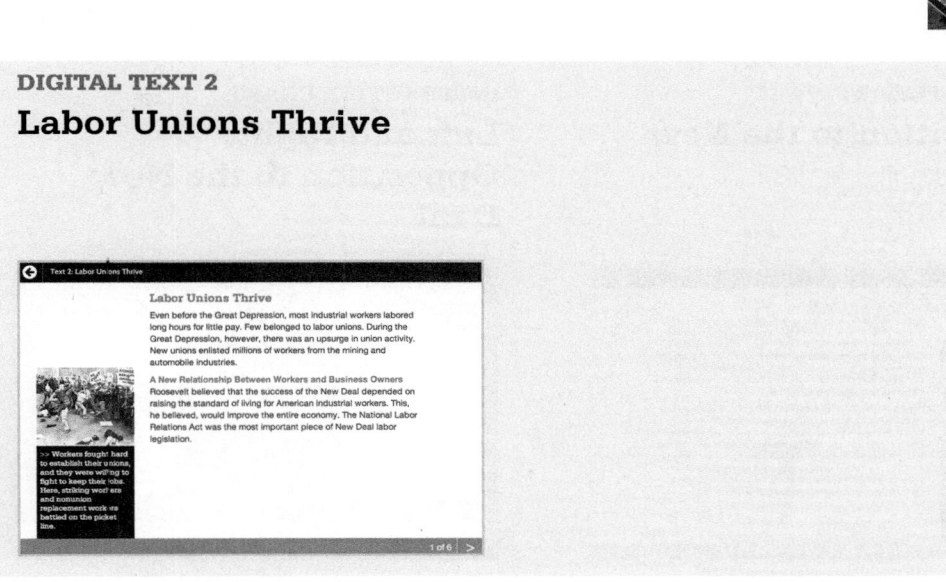

rate, which in turn would increase consumer spending and stimulate the economy. No. The government should not have gone into debt to pay for public works programs. many of which were considered wasteful and politically motivated. Increasing government debt would slow economic recovery.)

Identify Central Issues What were the most important reforms of the second phase of the New Deal? (Social Security was the most important reform because it affected so many Americans then and continues to this day. The Works Progress Administration has had lasting impact because of the infrastructure work accomplished.)

Draw Conclusions How did government actions like New Deal programs affect farming communities in America? (Congress established the Rural Electrification Administration (REA) to help utility companies bringing electricity to isolated rural areas for the first time. Price supports, or subsidies, for agriculture, helped farmers survive the tough times and eventually stabilized farm prices.)

Objective 2: Explain how New Deal legislation affected the growth of organized labor

Quick Instruction

Analyze Graphs Project the graph of labor union membership and have students identify any trends they see from 1920 to 1940. (Students should identify the 1920s as a decade of decreasing union membership and the 1930s as a decade of significant increases in union membership.)

Compare Why did American labor make greater progress during the 1930s than during the prosperous 1920s? (There was less incentive for workers to unionize during the prosperous 1920s. The economy was doing well and most Americans were employed and seeing economic gains. The depression changed all that and workers had to fight to save and protect jobs. New Deal legislation like the Wagner Act recognized the right of employees to join labor unions and gave workers the right to collective bargaining. The Fair Labor Standards Act of 1938 provided workers with additional rights, so all of these factors gave unions more power, which attracted more workers.)

Infer How do you think strikes affected union membership? (Successful strikes gave hope and more power to unions. When workers saw the gains being made by unions, they were more likely to become members.)

ELL Use the ELL activity described in the ELL chart.

Further Instruction

Go through the Interactive Reading Notepad questions with the class. Use them as a springboard to extend the discussion of unions by focusing on the minimum wage. Use the questions below to help students gain a better understand of the issues surrounding the minimum wage.

Draw Conclusions What political motives might FDR have had to support the Fair Labor Standards Act of 1938, which established a minimum wage? (Supporting the minimum wage would have bolstered FDR's political support among working Americans.)

Evaluate Arguments Describe the arguments of opponents of the minimum wage and evaluate their claims. (Opponents argue that producers will pass the wage increases on to consumers in the form of higher prices. While some students may agree, others may say that this is a short-term issue, and that if workers earn more money they will spend more money on purchases, which will help producers. Opponents also claim that employers will cut jobs to keep their labor costs the same. Again, some students may agree, but others may argue that if consumers are buying more products because they have more money, producers will have to increase production, which means hiring more workers to make more products.)

The New Deal Expands

DIGITAL TEXT 3
Opposition to the New Deal

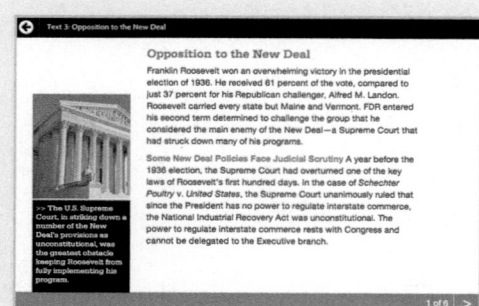

INTERACTIVE CHART
Left and Right Opposition to the New Deal

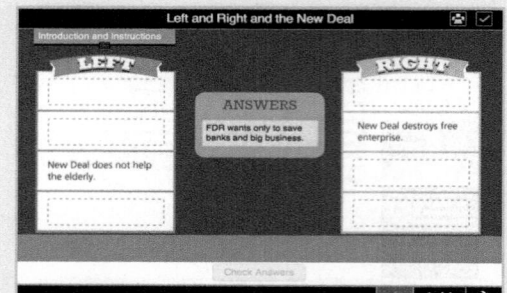

Objective 3: Evaluate the impact of Roosevelt's plan to increase the number of U.S. Supreme Court justices on the course of the New Deal.

Quick Instruction

Interactive Gallery: Left and Right Opposition to the New Deal Project the interactive chart and have students look at the information. Identify the important individuals whose opposition to New Deal programs created obstacles for FDR.

Evaluate Impact How did FDR's court-packing plan impact the relationship between the legislative, executive and judicial branches? *(The number of justices remained at nine; however, the court-packing plan weakened FDR politically. Public support for more New Deal programs diminished and Roosevelt was forced to work more with those in the legislative branch who opposed his policy proposals.)*

Summarize How did opponents of the New Deal in both parties differ in their critique of the federal programs? *(Opponents on the left based their arguments on the idea that they did not do enough to help people. Those on the right argued the New Deal was economically unsound and that it upset the balance of power between the federal government and localized governance.)*

📷 ACTIVE CLASSROOM

Have students use the Sticky Notes Strategy and take 3 minutes, to jot down their ideas about why opposition to the New Deal was so contentious. Then ask, "Did the New Deal try to do too much to ease the problems of the depression?" Have students post their stickies on a wall, then sort and discuss their responses as a group.

D Differentiate: **Challenge** Challenge students to research one of the figures who opposed the New Deal. Have students use the information they gather to write a short essay tracing how these opponents tried to gain support for their ideas.

Further Instruction

Be sure students understand FDR's court packing scheme and why he thought he was justified in proposing the idea.

Evaluate Arguments Do you think that FDR's court-packing plan was justified or did federal government policy changes under FDR raise constitutional issues? Explain your answer. *(FDR was clearly trying to "rig" the Court to prevent it from overturning New Deal programs. His court-packing plan seriously shook the concepts of separation of powers and checks and balances, which are crucial in maintaining a balance of power and trust in government. Political changes like these raised important constitutional issues.)*

■ SYNTHESIZE

■ DEMONSTRATE

DIGITAL ACTIVITY
Effects of the New Deal Today

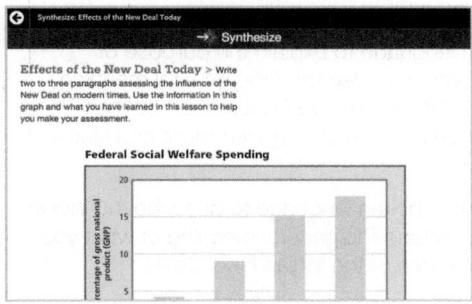

Ask students to take five minutes to write down some brief notes that describe how the New Deal tried to fight the effects of the Great Depression. Then have students use the information in the graph and what they have learned in this lesson to help to write two to three paragraphs assessing the influence of the New Deal on modern times.

Have students think about the following question: Have the enduring programs from the New Deal had a positive or negative effect on the nation? Have students use evidence from the text and their own experiences.

DIGITAL QUIZ
Lesson Quiz and Class Discussion Board

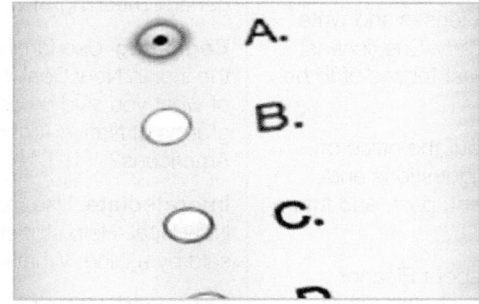

Assign the online Lesson Quiz for this lesson if you haven't already done so. Students will be offered automatic remediation or enrichment based on their score.

Pose these questions to the class on the Discussion Board:

In *The New Deal Expands*, you read about the Roosevelt administration's efforts to combat the Great Depression by adding new programs to help farmers and the elderly. These new programs, however, ran into significant opposition that led to conservative candidates picking up political power.

Predict Consequences Will labor unions hold on to their new-found power and influence in the coming decade? Why or why not?

Draw Conclusions What impact did Roosevelt's court-packing plan have on how the Supreme Court operates?

Topic Inquiry
Have students continue their investigations for the Topic Inquiry.

Effects of the New Deal

Supporting English Language Learners

Use with Digital Text 1, **Women Play Increasingly Significant Roles.**

Writing

Review the meaning of verb tense to prepare students to edit writing for standard grammar and usage of appropriate verb tenses.

Beginning Have students select the appropriate verb tenses and write these sentences: Eleanor Roosevelt (is/was) the First Lady. She (is/was) still remembered today. Then review the present and past tenses of *to be* and have students edit their writing.

Intermediate Ask students to suggest sentences about the office of First Lady that use *is*, *was*, and *will be*. Record their suggestions and have students write them down. Then review the present, past, and future tenses of *to be* and have students edit their writing.

Advanced Have pairs of students write a paragraph about Eleanor Roosevelt and her legacy, using verbs in the present, past, and future tenses. Ask pairs to exchange their paragraphs and edit one another's writing for appropriate use of these verb tenses.

Advanced High Ask students to write an installment for Eleanor Roosevelt's *My Day* column, using the present, past, future, and conditional verb tenses. Have students exchange their columns and edit one another's writing for appropriate use of these verb tenses.

Use with Digital Text 3, **New Deal Legislation for Native Americans.**

Listening

Explain that when someone speaks using a lot of unfamiliar language, students may miss many of the details. However, they can still grasp the general meaning of what was said.

Beginning Use familiar spoken language to explain the purpose of the Indian New Deal. Help students to understand the general meaning of what you said by asking: Was the Indian New Deal made between groups of Native Americans or between the U.S. government and Native Americans?

Intermediate Use mostly familiar spoken language to describe the Indian New Deal. Help students to understand the general meaning of what you said by asking: What was the purpose of the Indian New Deal?

Advanced Use a mix of familiar and unfamiliar spoken language to describe the Indian New Deal and its consequences. Help students to understand the general meaning of what you said by asking: How can you state the meaning of what I said in one sentence?

Advanced High Use a high degree of unfamiliar spoken language to describe the Indian New Deal and its consequences. Then have pairs of students discuss the general meaning of what you said.

▣ Differentiate Instruction

Use the Differentiated Instruction notes throughout the lesson plan to support the varied skill sets, levels of readiness, and interests in the mixed-ability classroom.

Challenge These notes include suggestions for expanding the activity for advanced students.

On-Level These notes include suggestions for modifying the activity to address different interests or learning styles.

Extra Support These notes include ideas for providing more scaffolding or reading spuport.

Special Needs These notes provide ideas for adapting instruction to support the needs of various special needs students.

■ NOTES

PEARSON realize™
www.PearsonRealize.com

Go online to access additional resources including:
Primary Sources • Biographies • Supreme Court cases •
21st Century Skill Tutorials • Maps • Graphic Organizers.

Objectives

Objective 1: Identify the social and political contributions of Eleanor Roosevelt, Frances Perkins, and other women involved in New Deal programs.

Objective 2: Explain how the New Deal expanded economic opportunities for racial and ethnic minorities.

Objective 3: Analyze how the New Deal changed the shape of American party politics and lessened ethnic and social divisions within American society.

Objective 4: Evaluate the effect of the New Deal on the historical role of the federal government and Franklin D. Roosevelt on the presidency.

LESSON 5 ORGANIZER		PACING: APPROX. 1 PERIOD, .5 BLOCKS		
	OBJECTIVES	PACING	Online	Print
Connect				
DIGITAL START UP ACTIVITY **Federal Programs and Public Infrastructure**		5 min.	●	
Investigate				
DIGITAL TEXT 1 **Women Play Increasingly Significant Political Roles**	Objective 1	10 min.	●	●
DIGITAL TEXT 2 **A Stronger Political Voice for African Americans**	Objective 2	10 min.	●	●
DIGITAL TEXT 3 **New Deal Legislation for Native Americans**		10 min.	●	●
DIGITAL TEXT 4 **A New Political Coalition Emerges**	Objective 3	10 min.	●	●
INTERACTIVE CHART **Roosevelt's Leadership**		10 min.	●	
DIGITAL TEXT 5 **New Deal Legislation Expands the Historical Role of Government**	Objective 4	10 min.	●	●
INTERACTIVE MAP **PWA & WPA Projects**		10 min.	●	
Synthesize				
DIGITAL ACTIVITY **Did Federal Programs Meet Their Goals?**		5 min.	●	
Demonstrate				
DIGITAL QUIZ **Lesson Quiz and Class Discussion Board**		10 min.	●	

Effects of the New Deal

■ CONNECT

DIGITAL START UP ACTIVITY
Federal Programs and Public Infrastructure

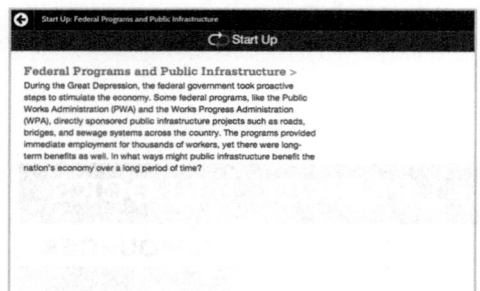

Project the Start Up Activity As students enter and get settled, ask them to consider this question: what makes a community, large city, or region a strong economic force? Encourage students to think about their own communities and others in the region to make comparisons and identify the reasons why one community might be experiencing a healthy economy while another isn't. Have them keep their ideas in mind as they answer the Start Up Activity question.

Tell students that in this lesson they will be learning how the New Deal expanded economic opportunities for minorities, changed American politics, and affected the role of the federal government and the executive branch in the lives of American citizens.

Aa Vocabulary Development: Use the Interactive Reading Notepad to preview the Key Terms and Academic Vocabulary in this lesson with students.

⇪ FLIP IT!
Assign the Flipped Video for this lesson.

■ STUDENT EDITION PRINT PAGES: 550–557

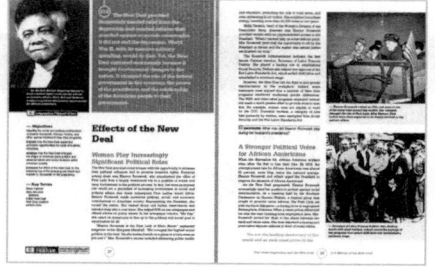

■ INVESTIGATE

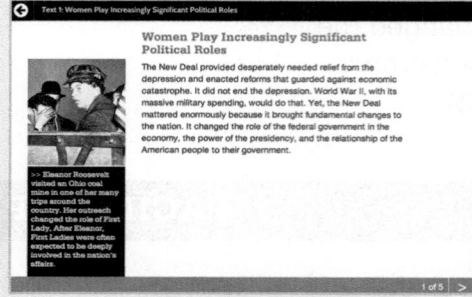

DIGITAL TEXT 1
Women Play Increasingly Significant Political Roles

Objective 1: Identify the social and political contributions of Eleanor Roosevelt, Frances Perkins, and other women involved in New Deal programs

Quick Instruction

Analyze Images Project the image of Eleanor Roosevelt. Ask students to describe what the photograph suggests about Eleanor Roosevelt. *(She's a woman of action, brave, curious about workers and how and where they work.)* Point out the Roosevelt transformed the office of First Lady from a largely ceremonial role to a position of action and involvement in the political process.

Identify Central Issues Challenge students to identify the political, social, and economic contributions of Eleanor Roosevelt to American society. *(Politically, Mrs. Roosevelt was deeply engaged in the President's politics, becoming his "eyes and ears." She traveled across the country promoting FDR's policies and New Deal programs that expanded and protected women's economic opportunities and political rights. She also worked tirelessly to promote social causes such improving public health and education, bringing the arts to rural areas, and addressing flood control.)*

ELL Use the ELL activity described in the ELL chart.

Further Instruction

Evaluate Impact Who was Frances Perkins and how did she help expand economic opportunities for women and others in American society? *(Frances Perkins was the first female Cabinet member, serving as*

FDR's Secretary of Labor. Perkins played a guiding role in establishing Social Security. She also helped win approval of the Fair Labor Standards Act, which ended child labor and established a minimum wage.)

Summarize What impact did the New Deal have on women? *(The New Deal provided some women with expanded political opportunities and gave them additional influence to promote women's rights.)*

DIGITAL TEXT 2

A Stronger Political Voice for African Americans

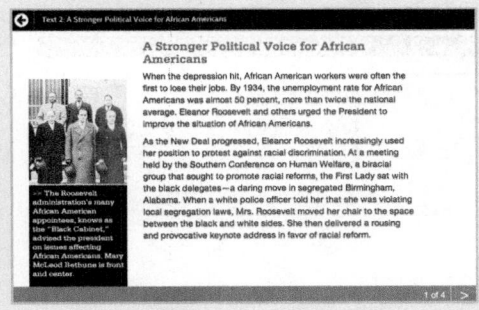

DIGITAL TEXT 3

New Deal Legislation for Native Americans

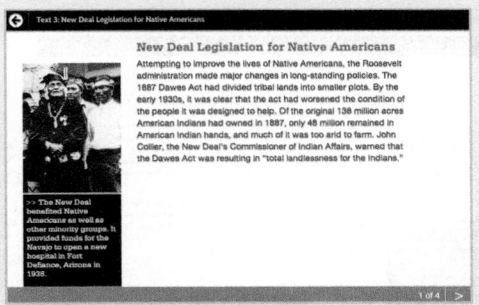

DIGITAL TEXT 4

A New Political Coalition Emerges

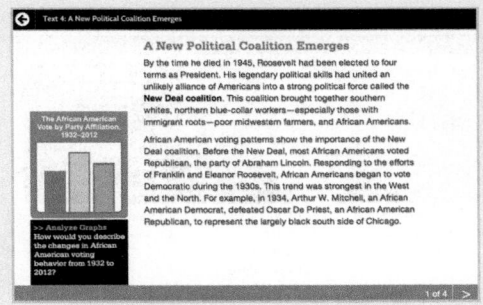

Objective 2: Explain how the New Deal expanded economic opportunities for racial and ethnic minorities

Quick Instruction

Analyze Images Project the image of Mary McLeod Bethune. Explain that Bethune was an African American who served as a special adviser on minority affairs to President Franklin D. Roosevelt. Point out that she was also an educator who founded what became Bethune Cookman College.

Identify Central Issues Challenge students to explain actions taken by Mary McLeod Bethune that helped expand economic opportunities and political rights for African Americans in American society. *(She was a powerful champion of racial equality. Serving on FDR's Black Cabinet, she promoted programs and causes that addressed issues that greatly affected African Americans.)*

Recognize Cause and Effect Why do you think African Americans suffered more extensive discrimination during the depression than during more prosperous times? *(The depression heightened discrimination against African Americans because almost all Americans were suffering. Fewer jobs and other life necessities created more competition among members of society.)*

ELL Use the ELL activity described in the ELL chart.

Further Instruction

Express Problems Clearly How did politics become an obstacle to advancing more economic and political rights for African Americans? *(President Roosevelt needed the support of southern Democrats in Congress to pass his legislation. Southern Democrats usually were against expanding civil rights for African Americans. Consequently, FDR decided not to pursue new civil rights laws.)*

Draw Conclusions In what ways did the New Deal alter U.S. policies toward Native Americans? *(The Indian New Deal program gave Indians economic assistance and greater control over their own affairs. New Deal policies also encouraged the practice of Indian religions, native languages, and traditional customs, a reversal of previous policies.)*

Objective 3: Analyze how the New Deal changed the shape of American party politics and lessened ethnic and social divisions within American society

Quick Instruction

Interactive Chart: Roosevelt's Leadership Project the chart. Invite volunteers to briefly summarize the situations associated with FDR's presidency. Discuss each situation ensuring student understanding. When students have completed the interactivity, invite them to share with the class.

⬛ ACTIVE CLASSROOM

Conduct a Take a Stand Activity. Ask students to take a stand on the following question: Was Franklin D. Roosevelt an effective leader during the depression? Ask students to divide into two groups based on their answer and move to separate areas of the classroom. Ask students to talk with each other to compare their reasons for answering yes or no. Ask a representative from each side to present and defend the group's point of view.

D Differentiate: **Extra Support** Some students may struggle with connecting the leadership qualities to the situations presented on the interactivity. For these students, it is maybe useful to review the situations again and focus on their significance and why they may have been controversial. Draw analogies using the leadership qualities as they might be displayed in more familiar contexts, such as at home, among friends, and at school.

Effects of the New Deal

INTERACTIVE CHART
Roosevelt's Leadership

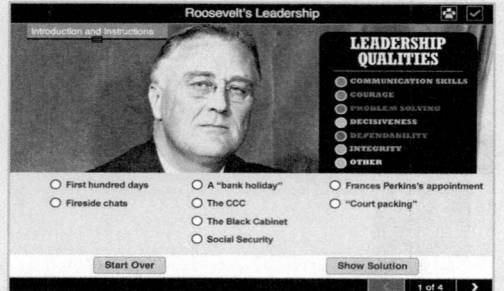

DIGITAL TEXT 5
New Deal Legislation Expands the Historical Role of Government

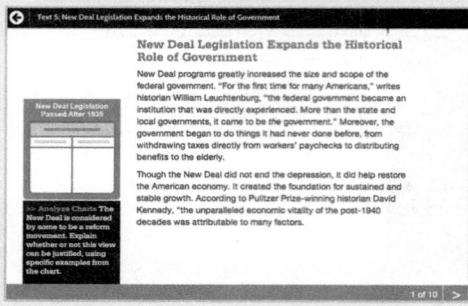

INTERACTIVE MAP
PWA & WPA Projects

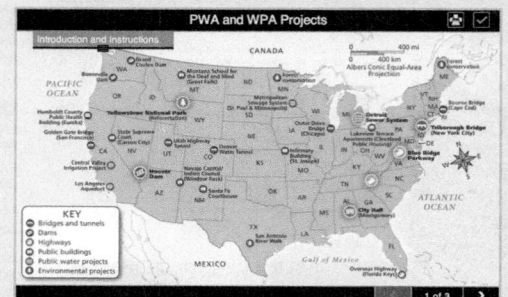

Further Instruction

Use the interactivity discussion and the Interactive Reading Notepad questions to extend the discussion of Roosevelt's leadership qualities and his influence in shifting the voting patterns of Americans. Ask students to explain FDR's influence on voting trends. *(FDR's political skills had united southern whites, northern blue-collar workers, poor mid-western farmers, and African Americans and made them strong Democratic supporters.)*

Draw Conclusions Did the New Deal policies have a positive or negative effect on ethnic and social divisions? Explain. *(Students may say that New Deal policies had a very positive effect on closing social and ethnic divisions. Immigrant communities, in particular, gained a greater sense of belonging to the mainstream. Programs such as the CCC and WPA allowed individuals of varied backgrounds to get to know one another, breaking down regional and ethnic prejudices.)*

Identify Cause and Effect What effect did the New Deal coalition have on the balance of power in Congress? *(Many people of varied backgrounds from different parts of the country came together to vote Democratic in federal elections. As a result, the House of Representatives generally remained under Democratic control for decades.)*

Objective 4: **Evaluate the effect of the New Deal on the historical role of the federal government and Franklin D. Roosevelt on the presidency.**

Quick Instruction

Interactive Map: PWA & WPA Projects Project the map and click through the hot spots on the map. After you have worked your way through the entire map, challenge students to use the question words (who, what, where, when, why, and how) to generate six separate questions about the costs and benefits of these large PWA and WPA projects and answer them.

Analyze Information Besides giving jobs to the unemployed, describe other ways that PWA and WPA projects might have helped local economies. *(Many of the projects would have benefited communities by improving their infrastructures. Sewer lines, highways and roads, and dams providing water and electricity would have made the communities more productive and attractive to businesses. Schools, hospitals, parks, and libraries contributed to improving the quality of life in these communities. Some of the environmental projects would have boosted tourism and attracted industries.)*

Explain Problems Clearly Challenge students to explain constitutional issues raised by federal government policy changes during times of significant events, including the Great Depression and World War II and why the constitution was amended after the war. *(Many Americans believed that New Deal powers gave too much power to the executive branch,*

offsetting the delicate balance between the different branches of government and between the federal and state governments as stated in the constitution. During the war, presidential power increased. After the war, the constitution was amended to prevent anyone from becoming President for more than two terms, as Roosevelt had done.)

📷 ACTIVE CLASSROOM

Conduct a Graffiti Concepts Activity. Ask students to reflect on the benefits of the WPA and PWA projects and create a visual image and/or phrase that represents each benefit. (Allow approximately 3–5 minutes.) Then ask students to post their "graffiti" on the board or on chart paper and ask students to look at all the various causes then discuss them as a group.

Further Instruction

Begin a discussion in which you guide students in evaluating the impact of New Deal legislation on the historical roles of state and federal government. Be sure students understand that the New Deal made the federal government much more important in Americans' lives. The New Deal introduced the idea that the federal government, not state or local government, was responsible for the welfare of all Americans.

Evaluate Arguments Should the powers of the federal government have been expanded to enact New Deal policies designed to resolve the economic effects of the Great Depression? Explain your answer. *(Answers will vary, but some students may say that in order to lessen the effects of the depression, the federal government had to step in a take on a greater*

SYNTHESIZE

DIGITAL ACTIVITY

Did Federal Programs Meet Their Goals?

DEMONSTRATE

DIGITAL QUIZ

Lesson Quiz and Class Discussion Board

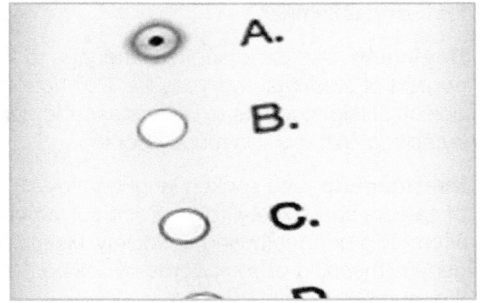

role to provide the resources for large projects. Other students may say New Deal policies inhibited economic growth and that welfare programs were best left to individual states to implement under the Tenth Amendment.)

Determine Relevance What does the creation ofNew Deal federal programs such as Social Securitysay about the changing priorities of the United States? How do programs such as Social Security continue to affect the lives of U.S. citizens today? Give examples to support your answer. (Priorities shifted to become more centered on citizens' well being, rather than on foreign policy or concern for large industries. So many New Deal programs were aimed at relieving the hardships that Americans were enduring. Many Americans today draw on Social Security as a means of income after retirement.)

Suggest that students create a table with three column headings: Government Programs, Intended Effects, and Actual Effects. Then have student partners review the lesson to complete the table by listing the depression-era government programs.

Discuss Before students answer the activity question, ask them to think about what might have happened if the government did nothing at all.

Assign the online Lesson Quiz for this lesson if you haven't already done so. Students will be offered automatic remediation or enrichment based on their score.

Pose these questions to the class on the Discussion Board:

In Effects of the New Deal, you read about efforts by the federal government to assist citizens who were in need. That assistance took many forms, and some of those programs, to one degree or another, are still with us today.

Summarize How did the New Deal change the social, economic, and political landscape of the United States for future generations?

Express Ideas Clearly Do you think that the costs of the enduring social safety net programs outweigh their benefits? Explain.

Evaluate Impact Was FDR's impact on the role of the presidency positive or negative? Explain your answer.

Topic Inquiry
Have students continue their investigations for the Topic Inquiry.

Culture During the Depression

Supporting English Language Learners

Use with Digital Text 2, **Increased Funding for the Arts.**

Listening
Project the WPA mural. Prompt students to understand the general meaning of spoken language ranging from situations in which contexts are familiar to unfamiliar.

Beginning Use basic spoken language to talk about the mural in the context of students' everyday life. Point out familiar places, people, and objects. Help students to understand the general meaning of your words by asking: What is this mural about?

Intermediate Use spoken language to talk about the mural in the context of careers and societal roles. Point out various people and how they are interacting or contributing to society. Help students to understand the general meaning of your words by asking: What are the people doing in the mural?

Advanced Use spoken language to talk about the mural in the context of story. Tell a story that is supported by the picture. Then help students to understand the general meaning of your words by asking: What was my story generally about?

Advanced High Use spoken language to talk about the mural in the context of art appreciation. Use vocabulary such as *light, shadow, perspective, subject, foreground,* and *background* to share your opinion of the picture. Help students to understand the general meaning of your words by asking: What do I generally think of this mural?

Use with Digital Text 3, **The Depression Era Reflected in Literature.**

Writing
Display this sentence from the text: The most famous novel of the 1930s was John Steinbeck's *The Grapes of Wrath.* Explain the use of the possessive case (apostrophe –s) as you prompt students to employ increasingly complex grammatical structures.

Beginning Display these sentences: Lillian Hellman's _____ featured strong roles for women. Richard _____ Native Son dealt with racial prejudice. Have students write the sentences and complete them in a way that uses the possessive case (apostrophe –s) correctly.

Intermediate Brainstorm a list of other words that could follow John Steinbeck's (i.e., other things he could possess). Then have students write a sentence that includes John Steinbeck's and a word from the list.

Advanced Ask pairs of students to write a paragraph about depression-era literature that uses the possessive case (apostrophe –s) correctly with the following: Wright's, writer's, Hellman's, play's. Have them share their paragraph with another pair of students.

Advanced High Ask students to write a paragraph about depression-era literature that uses the possessive case (apostrophe –s) at least three times. Have them read a partner's paragraph and explain each use of the possessive case that they encounter.

D Differentiate Instruction

Use the Differentiated Instruction notes throughout the lesson plan to support the varied skill sets, levels of readiness, and interests in the mixed-ability classroom.

Challenge These notes include suggestions for expanding the activity for advanced students.

On-Level These notes include suggestions for modifying the activity to address different interests or learning styles.

Extra Support These notes include ideas for providing more scaffolding or reading spuport.

Special Needs These notes provide ideas for adapting instruction to support the needs of various special needs students.

◼ NOTES

PEARSON
realize™
www.PearsonRealize.com

Go online to access additional resources including:
Primary Sources • Biographies • Supreme Court cases •
21st Century Skill Tutorials • Maps • Graphic Organizers.

Objectives

Objective 1: Trace the growth of radio and the movies in the 1930s and how both mediums reflected to the characteristics and issues of their.

Objective 2: Explain the relationship between the New Deal and the arts.

Objective 3: Describe the major themes of literature in the Depression era.

LESSON 6 ORGANIZER		PACING: APPROX. 1 PERIOD, .5 BLOCKS			
				RESOURCES	
		OBJECTIVES	PACING	Online	Print
Connect					
	DIGITAL START UP ACTIVITY **Art Reflects Its Times**		5 min.	●	
Investigate					
	DIGITAL TEXT 1 **A New Age in American Entertainment**	Objective 1	10 min.	●	●
	INTERACTIVE GALLERY **Entertainment in the Depression Era**		10 min.	●	
	DIGITAL TEXT 2 **Increased Funding for the Arts**	Objective 2	10 min.	●	●
	INTERACTIVE GALLERY **The New Deal and Culture**		10 min.	●	
	DIGITAL TEXT 3 **The Depression Era Reflected in Literature**	Objective 3	10 min.	●	●
Synthesize					
	DIGITAL ACTIVITY **Synthesize: Themes of Depression-Era Literature**		5 min.	●	
Demonstrate					
	DIGITAL QUIZ **Lesson Quiz and Class Discussion Board**		10 min.	●	

Culture During the Depression

■ CONNECT

DIGITAL START UP ACTIVITY
Art Reflects Its Times

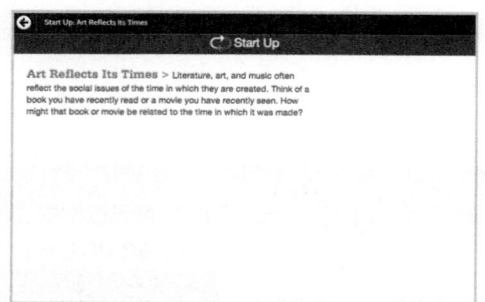

Project the Start Up Activity Ask students to think about and answer the question as they enter and get settled. Then have them share their responses with another student, either in class or through a chat or blog space.

Discuss Ask students to consider this question: Should art be a direct reflection of the realities of life or should it provide an escape?

Tell students that in this lesson they will be learning about the movies, music, and works of literature produced during the depression era and how they helped Americans cope with the effects of the Great Depression.

Aa Vocabulary Development: Use the Interactive Reading Notepad to preview the Key Terms and Academic Vocabulary in this lesson with students.

↷ FLIP IT!

Assign the Flipped Video for this lesson.

■ STUDENT EDITION PRINT PAGES: 558–562

■ INVESTIGATE

DIGITAL TEXT 1
A New Age in American Entertainment

INTERACTIVE GALLERY
Entertainment in the Depression Era

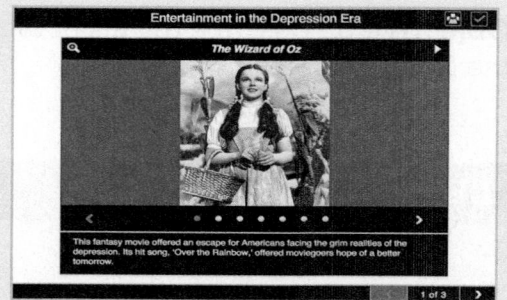

Objective 1: Trace the growth of radio and the movies in the 1930s and how both mediums related to their times.

Quick Instruction

Interactive Gallery: Entertainment in the Depression Era Project the interactive gallery and have students look through the images and listen to the recordings. Lead students in a discussion about how the arts reflected the effects of the great depression on U.S. society. Encourage students to explore and describe the positive and negative impacts of significant examples of cultural movements in the art, music, and literature of the 1930s. *(Student responses might touch on the way music and other forms of art brought people together to share experiences during difficult times. Latin, Folk, and ethnic music gained large followings during the 1930s and exposed many Americans to more diverse styles. Some music. literature, and art was critical of government and its leaders, causing concern for many.)*

Make Generalizations What values did the movies of the depression era reinforce for Americans? *(Many movies emphasized hope and a positive outlook. Determination and courage in the face of adversity were other values that movies stressed.)*

Compare How do the works of some African Americans presented in the interactivity differ from the other forms of entertainment? *(The African Americans described in the interactivity used entertainment to make statements on issues such as the social condition of African Americans in America.)*

📹 ACTIVE CLASSROOM

Have students break into groups and use the Circle Write Strategy to address the prompt, "Why were the movies and radio so important to Americans in the depression era?" Have students write as much as they can for 1 minute and then switch with the person on their right. The next person tries to improve or elaborate the response where the other person left off. Continue to switch until the paper comes back to the first person. The group decides which is the best composition and shares that with the class.

Further Instruction

Identify Cause and Effect How was the success of some New Deal programs reflected in the popularity of Hollywood movies? *(New Deal programs helped restore confidence in government and those who worked in government. Hollywood started to make movies in which government workers were the "good guys" rather than the villains.)*

Describe What other issues and characteristics about U.S. history during this era are reflected in various genres of film? *(People's desire to escape from the grim circumstances surrounding them was reflected in fantasy and animated movies like The Wizard of Oz and Snow White and the Seven Dwarves. Films directed by Frank Capra showed the common man fighting and winning against adversity in inspiring ways.)*

Infer Why did the movie and radio industries flourish during an era of such economic crisis? *(Most Americans were looking to escape the worries of the depression and the hardships they were facing.)*

DIGITAL TEXT 2
Increased Funding for the Arts

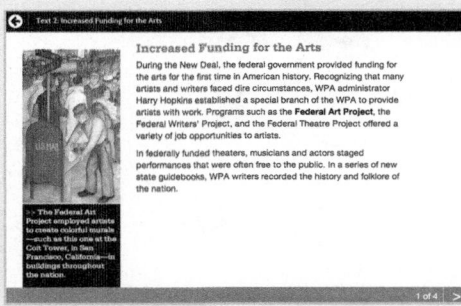

INTERACTIVE GALLERY
The New Deal and Culture

Objective 2: **Explain the relationship between the New Deal and the arts**

Quick Instruction

Interactive Gallery: The New Deal and Culture Project the gallery and click on the images to reveal information about the WPA cultural programs. Discuss each program described in the gallery. Point out that these programs marked the first time that the federal government provided funding for the arts.

Support Ideas with Examples Did the positive impacts of establishing WPA cultural programs such as the Federal Art Project, the Federal Writers' Project, and the Federal Theatre Project outweigh the negative impacts? Why or why not? *(Some students may say, yes; the programs gave Americans hope, entertainment, and new experiences they otherwise would never have had. Some programs served important historical purposes, like John Lomax's work recordings of American folk music. The WPA Federal Writers' Project preserved the stories of former enslaved people that otherwise would have been lost forever. The negative impacts would be in terms of money spent on non-essential projects and possible radical influences receiving government support.)*

▣▣ ACTIVE CLASSROOM

Have students Make Headlines for the WPA's arts projects. Ask: If you were to write a headline for the WPA's arts projects that captured the most important aspect that should be remembered, what would that headline be? Allow students to use subheadings to communicate more information. Encourage them to present the WPA's arts projects as part of the larger New Deal era. Have students pass their headlines to a partner for them to review.

D **Differentiate: Challenge** Challenge students to research WPA projects in their community or state and share their findings with class. Encourage students to include visual or audio examples to enhance their presentations.

ELL Use the ELL activity described in the ELL chart.

Further Instruction

Explain to students that federal funding for the arts remains a controversial issue today. Challenge students to discuss why it might be controversial. *(Student responses might include comments that government should have no role in promoting the arts or that many people do not want their tax dollars paying for artwork that portrays viewpoints that they disagree with or find offensive.)*

Identify Central Issues What radical values did some members of Congress fear might be promoted through the Federal Art; Writers', and Theatre programs? *(They feared that communist values would be spread.)* In your opinion, were these fears justified? Why or why not? *(Some students may say, no; most art from the era served entertainment, educational, or inspirational purposes.)*

Evaluate Impact How did federal support of the arts benefit both artists and the public? *(It provided jobs for unemployed artists and allowed them to continue to produce work. The public benefited from the entertainment and education the artists provided and communities benefited from public works of art.)*

Culture During the Depression

DIGITAL TEXT 3

The Depression Era Reflected in Literature

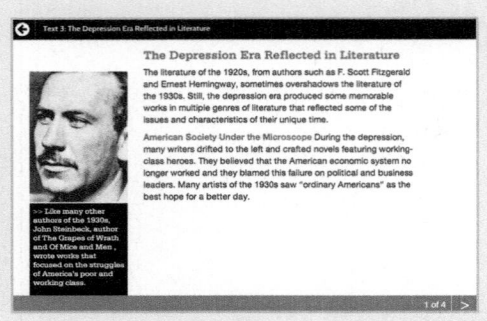

Objective 3: Describe the major themes of literature in the Depression era

Quick Instruction

Analyze Images Project the image of Superman. Invite volunteers to describe qualities that come to mind when they think of Superman/Clark Kent and why such characters would be very popular in the depression era. *(Strong, confident, brave, righteous. He was popular because he represented "good" and he always solved problems and Americans were looking for those things in their struggles during the depression.)*

Summarize Describe how issues of the depression era were reflected in influential novels of the time. *(Steinbeck's* The Grapes of Wrath *described the devastating effects of the Dust Bowl and the struggles of a family forced to leave their farm. Richard Wright's* Native Son *explored racial prejudice and discrimination against African Americans.)*

ELL Use the ELL activity described in the ELL chart.

Further Instruction

Infer How were women's gains of the New Deal era reflected in the literature and theater of the time? *(Women writers and playwrights had new and more opportunities to present their works that featured prominent women characters.)*

Compare How did the themes in the popular comic books differ from those of the notable novels of the era? *(In the comic books, good triumphs over evil, while many novels depicted the harsh realities of life during the depression.)*

DIGITAL ACTIVITY

Synthesize: Themes of Depression-Era Literature

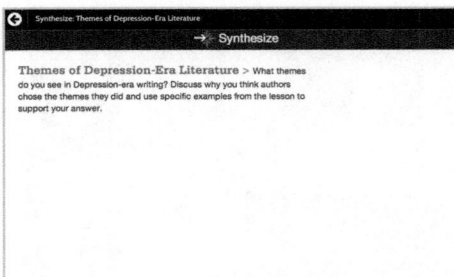

Ask students to recall their responses to the Start Up Activity at the beginning of the lesson. Then have them use the Think Pair Share Strategy to answer the questions in the Synthesize: Themes of Depression-Era Literature activity.

Have partners think about the following questions. Are works of literature that reflect important issues and characteristics of an era more powerful and effective than other forms of communication? How well does literature reflect the issues and characteristics in U.S. history compared to art, music, and film? Have pairs share their answers with the class.

DIGITAL QUIZ

Lesson Quiz and Class Discussion Board

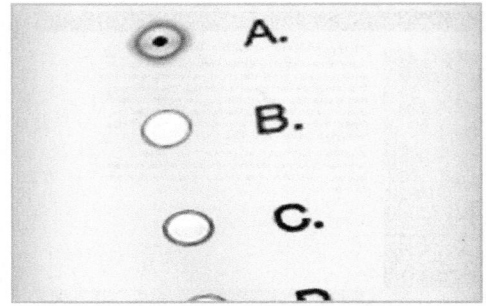

Assign the online Lesson Quiz for this lesson if you haven't already done so. Students will be offered automatic remediation or enrichment based on their score.

Pose these questions to the class on the Discussion Board:

In *Culture During the Depression*, you read about how radio, movies, literature, and music were often diversions that helped Americans momentarily escape their troubles during the depression. Some of the works from the time cheered people up and helped them cope. Other works reflected some of the difficulties people were experiencing.

Determine Point of View How did the work of New Deal era artists and writers contribute to our appreciation today of the New Deal?

Connect Do you think Hollywood movies give an accurate picture of contemporary American life? Should they? Explain.

Topic Inquiry

Have students continue their investigations for the Topic Inquiry.

PEARSON
realize™

www.PearsonRealize.com
Access your Digital Lesson

The Great Depression and the New Deal

SYNTHESIZE

DIGITAL ACTIVITY

The Great Depression and the New Deal

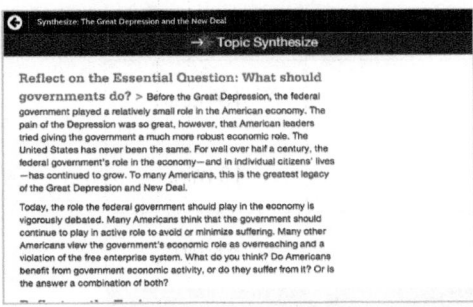

Ask students to reconsider the Essential Question for the Topic: What should governments do? Remind students that the federal government had a limited role in the economy of the United States prior to the Great Depression. Ask students to answer the following questions:

- What changed that prompted federal government to increase its role in the economy?

- Did government programs and policies have a positive or a negative impact on people during the Great Depression? Support your ideas with evidence.

Discuss students' responses as a class, or have them post their ideas on the Class Discussion Board.

Next, tell students to reflect on what they have learned. Instruct them to write down three questions that they thought about during the Topic. Share these examples to get them started:

- How might the Great Depression have affected Americans' attitudes about the country and the government?

- Do hard times bring out the best in people, or the worst?

- What would you do if you faced an economic depression?

Have students discuss their questions and write answers in pair or small groups. You may ask students to share their questions and answers on the Class Discussion Board.

Topic Inquiry
Have students complete Step 3 of the Topic Inquiry.

DEMONSTRATE

DIGITAL TOPIC REVIEW AND ASSESSMENT

The Great Depression and the New Deal

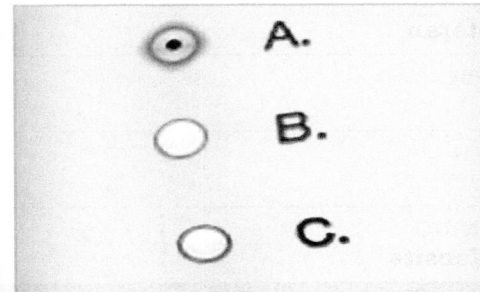

Students can prepare for the Topic Test by answering the questions in the Topic Review and Assessment online or the Assessment questions in the Print Student text. They can also prepare by reviewing their answers to the Interactive Reading Notepad questions or reviewing their notes in the Reading and Notetaking Study Guide.

DIGITAL TOPIC TEST

The Great Depression and the New Deal

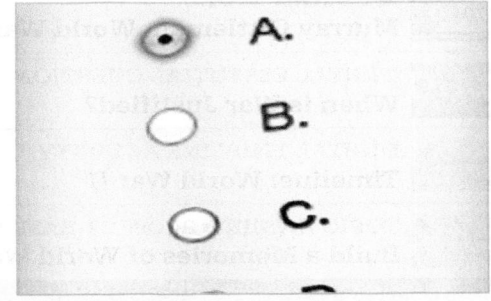

TOPIC TEST
Assign the Topic Test to assess students' understanding of topic content.

BENCHMARK TESTS
Assign these benchmark tests as you complete the relevant topics to monitor student progress toward mastering the course content and as preparation for the End-of-Course Test.

Benchmark Test 1: Topics 1–3

Benchmark Test 2: Topics 4–6

Benchmark Test 3: Topics 7–9

Benchmark Test 4: Topics 10–12

Benchmark Test 5: Topics 13–15

Benchmark Test 6: Topics 16–18

Benchmark Test 7: Topics 19–20

Topic 14

World War II

TOPIC 14 ORGANIZER	PACING: APPROX. 11 PERIODS, 5.5 BLOCKS	
		PACING
Connect		1 period
MY STORY VIDEO **Murray Gittleman, World War II Veteran**		10 min.
DIGITAL ESSENTIAL QUESTION ACTIVITY **When is War Justified?**		10 min.
DIGITAL TIMELINE ACTIVITY **Timeline: World War II**		10 min.
TOPIC INQUIRY: PROJECT-BASED LEARNING **Build a Memories of World War II Website**		20 min.
Investigate		4–8 periods
TOPIC INQUIRY: PROJECT-BASED LEARNING **Build a Memories of World War II Website**		Ongoing
LESSON 1 Rise of Aggressive Dictators		30–40 min.
LESSON 2 America Debates Involvement		30–40 min.
LESSON 3 America Enters World War II		30–40 min.
LESSON 4 A War on Two Fronts		30–40 min.
LESSON 5 The Home Front		30–40 min.
LESSON 6 The Allies Win World War II		30–40 min.
LESSON 7 The Holocaust		30–40 min.
LESSON 8 Impact of World War II		30–40 min.
Synthesize		1 period
DIGITAL ACTIVITY **Reflect on the Essential Question and Topic**		10 min.
TOPIC INQUIRY: PROJECT-BASED LEARNING **Build a Memories of World War II Website**		20 min.
Demonstrate		1–2 periods
DIGITAL TOPIC REVIEW AND ASSESSMENT **World War II**		10 min.
TOPIC INQUIRY: PROJECT-BASED LEARNING **Build a Memories of World War II Website**		20 min.

TOPIC INQUIRY: PROJECT-BASED LEARNING

Build a Memories of World War II Website

What was life really like for people who lived through World War II? In this Topic Inquiry, students will work in teams to research the lives of three Americans who experienced World War II. They will then build a website capturing the stories of these individuals. Learning about the impact of war on people will contribute to students' understanding of the Topic Essential Question: When Is War Justified?

STEP 1: CONNECT
Develop Questions and Plan the Investigation

Understand Your Assignment
Display the invitation, *Entry Event,* from the American Association of World War II Veterans. Call on students to read aloud the invitation. Give students a few minutes to underline key points, and then have students share their points.

Explain that students will work in teams to identify, research, and develop profiles of three Americans who participated in World War II. Share with students the criteria for the Americans that they select, and ask them to consider which Americans they want to research.

Suggestion: If you'd like to ensure that a variety of criteria are chosen, assign the experiences rather than letting the teams choose them. Otherwise, tell students to highlight or circle the three types of Americans whom they would like to research to discuss with their teams.

Prepare for Project Work
Project the rubric, and review the expectations for students' projects. Then, organize students into teams, and instruct teams to work together to review the tutorial, the contract, and the roles worksheet. Ask students to select a project manager to begin documenting their work in the project tracker.

Resources
- Project Launch
- Student Instructions
- Work in Teams Tutorial
- Project Tracker
- Project Contract
- Website Rubric
- Roles for a Website Project

⏻ PROFESSIONAL DEVELOPMENT

Project-Based Learning
Be sure to view the Project-Based Learning Professional Development resources in the online course.

STEP 2: INVESTIGATE
Apply Disciplinary Concepts and Tools

Identify Profile Subjects
Direct teams to discuss the three Americans they would like to research. Students may have specific people in mind. If not, advise them to select three types of criteria to find appropriate individuals. Tell students to consider people in their families or their communities who may have lived during the war, and guide them to useful websites, such as those listed in the Student Instructions.

Suggestion: If teams have difficulty agreeing on criteria or individuals, then offer them problem-solving strategies. For example, they can vote and go with the majority, or they can draw people or criteria out of a hat at random. They could also let one or two students each choose one of the people to research.

Research Your Profiles
To guide their research, teams will make a list of Need-to-Know Questions about the people they are profiling. Refer students to helpful resources within the core content of the topic to help answer their questions. For example, if they are researching a veteran who fought abroad in 1943, refer them to Lesson 4 readings and activities. Help students begin to fill out the Information Organizer.

Suggestion: If your class has limited access to the Internet, you could make several books available to students, such as *The Story of World War II* by Donald Miller and *Our Mother's War* by Emily Yellin.

Write and Edit Your Profiles
Direct teams to plan how to present their research, including what types of media to use in their profiles. Encourage them to consider what they find appealing in a website. Then, have students write their profiles and peer review one another's writing. Remind students to offer detailed, constructive criticism of one another's work.

Resources
- Student Instructions
- Need-to-Know Questions
- Project Tracker
- Information Organizer

Build a Memories of World War II Website *(continued)*

STEP 3: SYNTHESIZE
Evaluate Sources and Use Evidence to Formulate Conclusions

Build Your Website

Now, ask students to work together to build their websites. Begin by looking at a model website, and advise students to view the *Getting Started with WordPress Tutorial* before they begin planning. Project the *Plan Your Website* document to get students started. If students have trouble sharing the work of this part of the project, remind them to review the *Roles for a Website* document to see how they planned to divide the work. Remind students to track their progress in the *Project Tracker*, and review teams' websites as they work to keep students focused.

Suggestion: For a less technology-dependent end product, have students build dossiers or a museum exhibit with their profiles. To take the technology a step further, have students set up a mock blog and conduct discussions using their profiles as personas.

Write a Conclusion

Ask teams to review their websites and draw conclusions about what they have learned. To help teams start, direct each team member to write down his or her answer to a different question listed in the *Student Instructions*. Have students share their answers in their teams. Then, instruct teams to write a short summary in response to all four questions to include with their websites.

Suggestion: To ensure students discuss their responses, have each student in a team explain something that he or she does or does not agree with and why, in another student's answer.

Resources
- Plan Your Website
- Student Instructions
- Getting Started with WordPress Tutorial
- Project Tracker
- Roles for a Website

STEP 4: DEMONSTRATE
Communicate Conclusions and Take Informed Action

Present Your Website

Have students prepare their website presentations. Remind them to practice presenting and to review their website for mistakes. Watch the team presentations in class. To help teams structure their time, set up a clock in the back of the room, and alert them when they have only a few minutes left. Post links to students' website projects from the class blog.

Suggestion: If time allows, permit a short question-and-answer session at the end of each presentation.

Reflect on the Project

After students have finished their *Team Assessments,* help them review what they thought went well and what did not. Tell them to use what they have learned to write a note to themselves about how to be even more effective with future projects and presentations. Remind teams to complete their *Project Tracker*.

Suggestion: As an extension activity, challenges students to research people's experiences overseas during a recent conflict, such as in Afghanistan and Iraq. Tell students to make comparisons, where appropriate, with the World War II experiences they just chronicled.

Resources
- Website Rubric
- Project Tracker
- Team Assessment

INTRODUCTION

World War II

The Great Depression that struck the United States also affected the rest of the world. Many parts of Europe and Asia were still recovering from World War I. Economic hardship contributed to the rise of dictators in Europe and Asia. Soon, some of these dictators took aggressive action to gain more territory. As war broke out across the Atlantic and the Pacific Oceans, many Americans opposed becoming involved. Eventually, however, the United States did enter the war. How did this second world war change the United States and the world?

CONNECT

MY STORY VIDEO
Murray Gittleman, World War II Veteran

Project the My Story Video that introduces students to a World War II veteran who flew bomber missions over Europe.

Infer What do you think flying in a B-24 Bomber was like for men like Murray Gittleman? *(frightening, exhausting)*

Check Understanding What was Murray's job aboard the B-24? *(He was a radio operator; his job was to keep in touch with ground.)*

Identify Central Issues Why were men like Murray willing to risk their lives to fight in the war? *(They believed that stopping the advance of the Axis Powers was worth fighting for and that the only way to stop this advance was to go to war.)*

Evaluate Impact Why is it important to hear the personal stories of people who lived through World War II? *(Hearing the story of a real person helps you understand how much the people who fought in the war sacrificed and how strongly they believed in the importance of fighting for freedom.)*

DIGITAL ESSENTIAL QUESTION ACTIVITY
When Is War Justified?

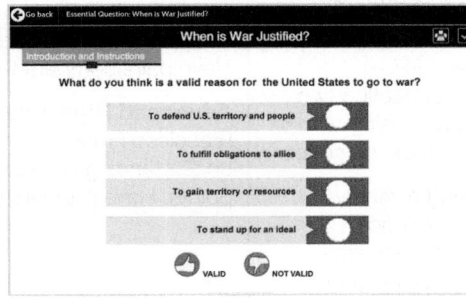

Ask students to think about the Essential Question for this topic: When Is War Justified? Point out that war takes a terrible human cost and also results in economic and environmental damage. People who fight in the war and those at home suffer. So, why do people fight? What circumstances might justify going to war?

If students have not already done so, ask them to respond to the poll and answer the question in the activity. Then, organize students into groups to discuss their ideas and complete the group activity.

Support a Point of View with Evidence Why did you rate this reason as most valid?

Identify Central Issues What types of ideals might a country be willing to fight for? *(human rights, democracy, freedom)*

Cause and Effect What resources might a country fight for? Why? *(water, soil, oil, coal, diamonds; to increase wealth, gain a source of energy to fuel factories, economy, feed people)*

DIGITAL TIMELINE ACTIVITY
World War II

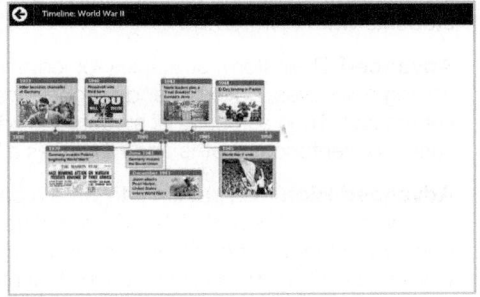

Display the timeline showing the major turning points in World War II. During this topic, students will learn about these events and many more. This timeline will provide a framework to better understand the context and chronology of the other events they study. It will also help them perceive how the war unfolded over a long period of time and series of actions.

D Differentiate: **Extra Support** Demonstrate to students how to read the timeline. How many years pass between the beginning of World War II and the United States entering the war? *(more than two)* Model how you found the answer by pointing out that the war began in 1939 and the United States entered the war in 1941.

D Differentiate: **On Level** Tell students to copy the timeline. As they move through the lesson, have them add other significant events to the timeline.

Analyze Timelines How many years was the United States at war during World War II? *(four years, 1941 through 1945)*

Topic Inquiry
Launch the Topic Inquiry with students after introducing the topic.

Rise of Aggressive Dictators

Supporting English Language Learners

Use with Digital Text 3, **Germany and Japan Change Leadership**.

Writing
Display this sentence: Hitler was a dictator. Discuss why a short sentence like this can have a powerful effect, as well as why adding detail to it can also be effective. Prompt students to write using a variety of grade-appropriate sentence lengths in increasingly accurate ways as more English is acquired.

Beginning Have students write using a variety of sentence lengths by adding to the above sentence in different ways: Hitler was a dictator in _____. Hitler was a dictator, and he _____. Hitler was a _____ dictator.

Intermediate Have students suggest at least five ways to alter the length of the above sentence, creating a new sentence anywhere from five words to more than ten. Record students' suggestions, and have students write them down.

Advanced Brainstorm strategies for lengthening sentences (e.g., adding adjectives, adverbs, and prepositional phrases; connecting two sentences). Then ask pairs of students to write a paragraph using a variety of sentence lengths and *Hitler was a dictator* as a topic sentence.

Advanced High Ask students to write a paragraph using a variety of sentence lengths and *Hitler was a dictator* as a topic sentence. Encourage them to include at least one sentence longer than twelve words. Ask: How did you decide which sentences would be longer or shorter? What is the rhythm of your paragraph?

Use with Digital Text 4, **Dictators Move to Gain Territory**.

Listening
Discuss strategies that students can use to identify and understand a speaker's main points, whether or not the topic is familiar.

Beginning Use spoken language to paraphrase the section titled *Dictators Support War in Spain*. Then help students understand the main points of this familiar topic by asking: In what country was the civil war? Who supported Franco and the Nationalists?

Intermediate Use spoken language to paraphrase and expand on the section titled *Dictators Support War in Spain*. Then ask students to show their understanding of this familiar topic by identifying three main points.

Advanced Use spoken language to describe the Spanish Civil War in some detail. Ask pairs of students to demonstrate their understanding of this mostly unfamiliar topic by discussing and listing your main points. Have pairs compare the lists they made.

Advanced High Use spoken language to talk about the life of General Francisco Franco in some detail. Ask students to demonstrate their understanding of this unfamiliar topic by creating a list of your main points. Have partners share and compare their lists.

D Differentiate Instruction

Use the Differentiated Instruction notes throughout the lesson plan to support the varied skill sets, levels of readiness, and interests in the mixed-ability classroom.

Challenge These notes include suggestions for expanding the activity for advanced students.

On-Level These notes include suggestions for modifying the activity to address different interests or learning styles.

Extra Support These notes include ideas for providing more scaffolding or reading spuport.

Special Needs These notes provide ideas for adapting instruction to support the needs of various special needs students.

■ NOTES

PEARSON
realize™
www.PearsonRealize.com

Go online to access additional resources including:
Primary Sources • Biographies • Supreme Court cases •
21st Century Skill Tutorials • Maps • Graphic Organizers.

Objectives

Objective 1: Explain the rise of dictatorships in the Soviet Union, Italy, Germany, and Japan in the 1930s.

Objective 2: Summarize acts of aggression by Italy, Germany, and Japan.

Objective 3: Analyze the responses of Britain, France, and the United States to the aggressive regimes.

LESSON 1 ORGANIZER		PACING: APPROX. 1 PERIOD, .5 BLOCKS			
				RESOURCES	
		OBJECTIVES	**PACING**	**Online**	**Print**
Connect					
	DIGITAL START UP ACTIVITY **Compare Life Under Different Governments**		5 min.	●	
Investigate					
	DIGITAL TEXT 1 **Peace Dissolves**	Objective 1	10 min.	●	●
	INTERACTIVE GALLERY **Characteristics of Totalitarianism**		10 min.	●	
	DIGITAL TEXT 2 **Strict Regimes in the Soviet Union and Italy**		10 min.	●	●
	DIGITAL TEXT 3 **Germany and Japan Change Leadership**		10 min.	●	●
	INTERACTIVE GALLERY **Life Under Nazi Rule**		10 min.	●	
	DIGITAL TEXT 4 **Dictators Move to Gain Territory**	Objective 2	10 min.	●	●
	INTERACTIVE MAP **Military Action, 1930–1939**		10 min.	●	
	DIGITAL TEXT 5 **Aggression Meets Appeasement**	Objective 3	10 min.	●	●
Synthesize					
	DIGITAL ACTIVITY **Understand the Chronology of Events**		5 min.	●	
Demonstrate					
	DIGITAL QUIZ **Lesson Quiz and Class Discussion Board**		10 min.	●	

Rise of Aggressive Dictators

▊ CONNECT

DIGITAL START UP ACTIVITY
Compare Life Under Different Governments

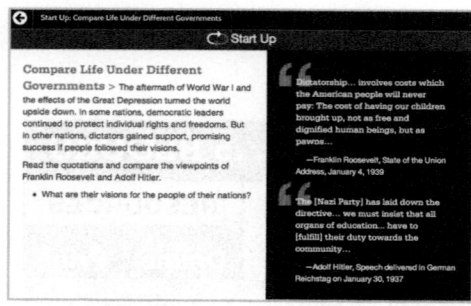

Project the Start Up Activity Ask students to answer the questions as they enter and get settled. Then have them share their ideas with another student, either in class or through a chat or blog space.

Tell students that in this lesson they will be learning about the reasons for U.S. involvement in World War II.

Aa Vocabulary Development: Use the Interactive Reading Notepad to preview the Key Terms and Academic Vocabulary in this lesson with students.

⚡ FLIP IT!

Assign the Flipped Video for this lesson.

▊ STUDENT EDITION PRINT
PAGES: 568–575

▊ INVESTIGATE

DIGITAL TEXT 1
Peace Dissolves

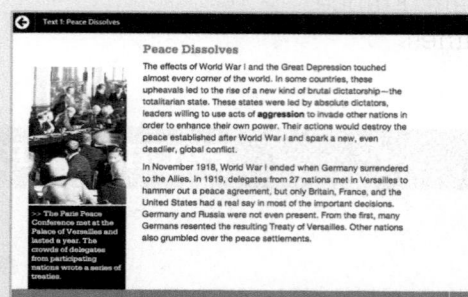

INTERACTIVE GALLERY
Characteristics of Totalitarianism

Objective 1: Explain the rise of dictatorships in the Soviet Union, Italy, Germany, and Japan in the 1930s.

Quick Instruction

Interactive Gallery: Characteristics of Totalitarianism Project the interactive gallery. What is a dictatorship? *(rule by a single person)* What is totalitarianism? *(a theory of government in which a single party or leader controls the economic, social, and cultural lives of its people)* Explain that a totalitarian controls all aspects of life, and that totalitarianism is more extreme than a simple dictatorship. Then click on the images to reveal the main characteristics of totalitarianism (cult of personality, lack of civil rights, militarism, propaganda, and youth indoctrination). Totalitarian regimes would arise in Italy and Germany as well as in the Soviet Union. Tell students that an Italian dictatorship, a German dictatorship, and a Japanese dictatorship would prove to be reasons for U.S. involvement in World War II.

Interactive Gallery: Life Under Nazi Rule Project the interactive gallery. Ask students to consider the mass psychology of support for Hitler. Have them suggest reasons why they think individuals often go along with the actions of the "crowd," even when they are not comfortable doing so. Why might average, good people support a leader who is dangerous? *(out of fear, desire to gain pride or economic status, desire for stability, and tradition of obedience to authority.)* Why do you think people supported a German dictatorship, an Italian dictatorship, and a Soviet dictatorship? *(The leaders were*

charismatic and offered a path out of the nation's crises.) Why do you think people were willing to give up their individuality? *(afraid to be different, fear of reprisal, desire to have someone else make decisions for them, and willing to trade individuality for security.)*

👥 ACTIVE CLASSROOM

Conduct a Write 1-Get 3 Activity with the class. Ask students: What are four key characteristics of totalitarianism? Have students take a piece of paper and fold it into quarters, write down one response in the first box, and then go around room asking to hear other responses. If you think a response is correct, write it in one of your boxes until you have three more responses on your page. Share responses with class. Ask: What is a fifth characteristic?

👥 ACTIVE CLASSROOM

Have students Make Headlines to capture the rise of dictatorships in the Soviet Union, Italy, Germany, and Japan in the 1930s. Divide the class into four groups— one for each country. Each group should write headlines that identify the causes and effects of the changes in government during the years leading up to World War II. Allow them to use subheadings if they would like. Have groups share their headlines with the other group. Arrange the headlines into a mock newspaper or web page.

ELL Use the ELL activity described in the ELL chart.

DIGITAL TEXT 2

Strict Regimes in the Soviet Union and Italy

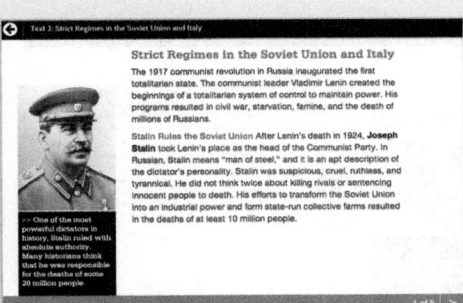

DIGITAL TEXT 3

Germany and Japan Change Leadership

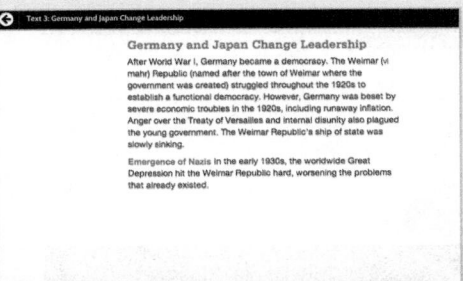

INTERACTIVE GALLERY

Life Under Nazi Rule

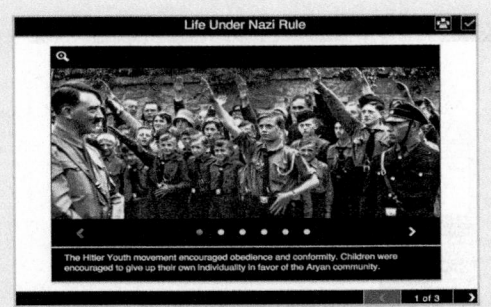

Further Instruction

Compare and Contrast Remind students that the communist revolution of 1917 caused great havoc in the Soviet Union, and Stalin used that disruption to establish his absolute power. The Italian economic crisis allowed Mussolini the opportunity to do the same. How did Stalin and Mussolini compare with one another? *(Both were dictators who outlawed opposition and tried to control the press; Stalin relied heavily on the use of terror and had greater control over his country than Mussolini had over his country.)* How did Stalin want to transform the Soviet Union? *(He wanted to create an industrial power and turn the economy into a communist system with state-run farms.)* What was the result of his economic policies? *(the deaths of more than 10 million people)*

Compare and Contrast Ask students what similarities did Germany and Japan have. *(Both had the desire for military conquest, strong racial pride, and a godlike leader.)* How were the roles of the leaders different? *(The Japanese emperor was separate from the military leadership. He was the constitutional monarch, but not seen as being involved in the everyday decisions or general military strategy.)* What effect might this difference have on how the country was ruled? *(Japan was not necessarily a totalitarian regime. In Japan, the emperor continued to have an influence on the Japanese people, separate from the military leaders. Although the Japanese valued obedience to the emperor, Japanese civilians were not subjected to the same level of terror and control as Germans were under Hitler.)*

Rise of Aggressive Dictators

DIGITAL TEXT 4
Dictators Move to Gain Territory

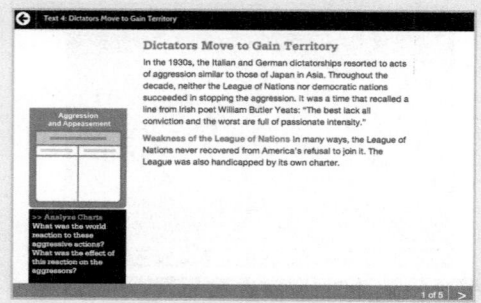

INTERACTIVE MAP
Military Action, 1930–1939

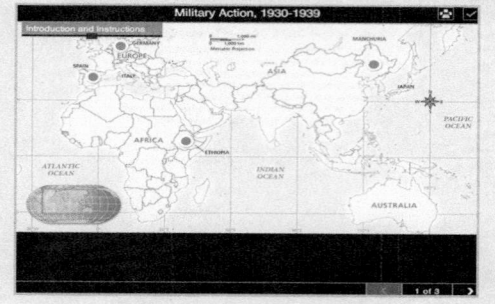

DIGITAL TEXT 5
Aggression Meets Appeasement

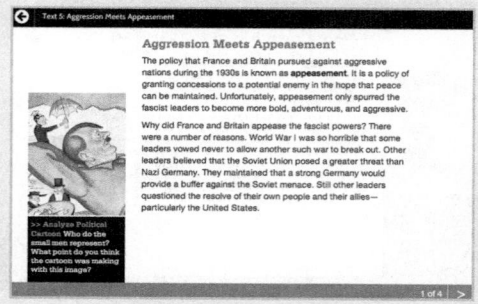

Objective 2: Summarize acts of aggression by Italy, Germany, and Japan.

Quick Instruction

Interactive Map: Military Action, 1930–1939 Project the interactive map and select the hotspots to read about the conflict in that area. Look at the change in the Japanese empire between 1930 and 1939. Ask: What impact did the U.S. policy of isolationism seem to have on Japan? *(Japan felt it would not be challenged by the United States and therefore could begin its territorial expansion.)* What acts of aggression did Japan take in those years? *(It invaded Manchuria and areas in China, including Hong Kong.)*

Summarize What choices by the Italian dictatorship and the German dictatorship may have encouraged subsequent U.S. involvement in World War II? *The Italian dictatorship invaded Ethiopia in 1935. This act increased U.S. concerns of further Italian aggression. The German dictatorship sent German troops into the Rhineland, a demilitarized part of Germany.*

🗣 ACTIVE CLASSROOM

Pair students. Have the first student give the second a verbal "tour" of the map—what does each hotspot show? Have the second student give the first an explanation of what it means.

ELL Use the ELL activity described in the ELL chart.

Further Instruction

Identify Central Ideas Review the term "civil war" with students. (a war between opposing groups within a country) Have them work in pairs to answer these questions. What was the Spanish Civil War? *(a conflict between Spain's democratic Republican government and Nationalist forces led by General Francisco Franco)* Why did other nations become involved in the conflict? *(Germany and Italy did not want a democratic government to be in power in Spain; the Soviet Union wanted the Republicans to stay in power.)*

Interpret Explain to students that many people of the Rhineland welcomed German soldiers. Ask: What is the reaction of the people? *(They are using the Nazi salute to welcome the soldiers.)* How might their reaction explain the world's silence about this act of aggression and the violation of Treaty of Versailles? *(Since the civilians were supportive of the troops coming into the area, there would be no reason to criticize or stop the action.)*

Objective 3: Analyze the responses of Britain, France, and the United States to the aggressive regimes.

Quick Instruction

Infer Tell students that Winston Churchill, then a member of the British Parliament, was critical of the Munich Pact. Project the table that shows the different steps of appeasement from the first screen of *Dictators Move to Gain Territory*. Ensure student understanding of appeasement (policy of granting concessions in order to keep peace) and how it relates to Sudetenland and the Munich Pact. (The Munich Pact sacrificed the Sudetenland to Hitler to preserve the peace.) Discuss the value of appeasement as an instrument of foreign policy with students. Do they think it can be successful?

D Differentiate: Extra Support Have students make a concept web to record the main ideas about the policies of Great Britain, France, and the United States toward aggressive nations. Tell them to label the center circle "Appeasement" and then have four sub-circles to record the main ideas. *(World War I was so horrible that some leaders vowed never to allow such a war to happen again; Some felt that the Soviet Union was a greater threat than Nazi Germany and that Germany would provide a buffer against communism; Some thought that their citizens would not have the resolve to stand up to the aggressors; Some were more concerned with their own economic issues than the actions of the aggressors.)*

SYNTHESIZE

DIGITAL ACTIVITY
Understand the Chronology of Events

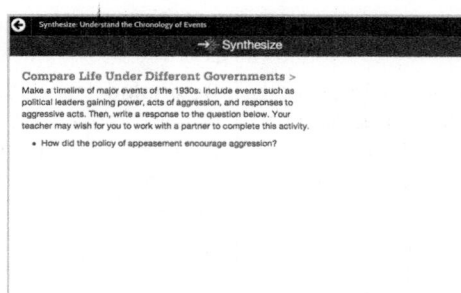

DEMONSTRATE

DIGITAL QUIZ
Lesson Quiz and Class Discussion Board

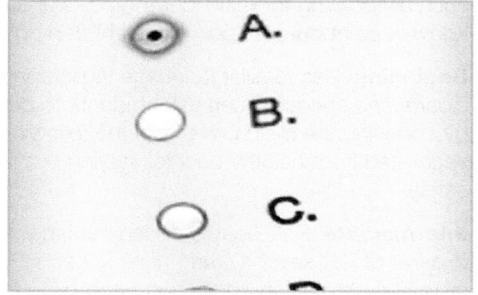

Further Instruction

Connect Point out that appeasement means to give in to some demands from an opponent in the hope that there will be no fight. This is usually done unwillingly. Ask student to think about a time when they have observed appeasement in action in daily life. Have student volunteers share their observations. Help students make the connections between their examples and the content they are reading.

Support Ideas with Evidence Although still following an isolationist policy, Roosevelt seemed to be preparing for possible world conflict. What steps did Roosevelt take to ensure the United States would have allies if needed? *(He expanded the Good Neighbor Policy with nations in Latin America. He improved relations with the Soviet Union.)*

The United States watched the events overseas with great concern. Project the timeline from the synthesize activity on the board to help students see the progressive rise of dictatorships and their acts of aggression.

Hypothesize What possible reactions could the United States have to the aggressive acts? *(take care to avoid involvement by staying neutral about all actions; build up its own military; make alliances in case a war began.)*

Assign the online Lesson Quiz for this lesson if you haven't already done so. Students will be offered automatic remediation or enrichment based on their score.

Pose these questions to the class on the Discussion Board:

In *The Rise of Aggressive Dictatorships*, you have read how different countries responded to economic and political crises. Some countries, such as the United States, tried new programs (e.g., the New Deal) and maintained a democratic form of government. In other countries, new leaders made more extreme changes.

Connect Have students consider people who are leaders in the United States today. What characteristics make this person an effective or ineffective leader? *(the leader's vision for the country, the solutions offered for problems, personality or charisma)*

Express Ideas Clearly Ask students to consider what makes the difference in whether a leader will use power in good or bad way. What safeguards does the United States have to prevent a president from becoming a dictator? *(Constitution and Bill of Rights, system of checks and balances, separation of powers)*

Topic Inquiry
Have students continue their investigation for the Topic Inquiry.

America Debates Involvement

Supporting English Language Learners

Use with Digital Text 1, **Roosevelt Criticizes Acts of War**.

Listening
Brainstorm and discuss strategies that can help students understand the main points of spoken language when some of the words are unfamiliar, such as listening for main ideas instead of details and using prior knowledge about the topic to establish a context.

Beginning Use familiar language to paraphrase the excerpt of Roosevelt's *Quarantine* speech. Then ask students to demonstrate their understanding by choosing the main point from the following: sick people should be separated from healthy people; staying out of war does not guarantee safety.

Intermediate Rely heavily on familiar language as you paraphrase the excerpt of Roosevelt's *Quarantine* speech. Pair students with similar language abilities and have them complete the following frame: Roosevelt compares war to _____ to show how it far and fast it can spread.

Advanced Blend familiar and unfamiliar language as you paraphrase the excerpt of Roosevelt's *Quarantine* speech. Then have pairs of students demonstrate their understanding by listing the main points of what you said. Ask pairs to share their lists with one another.

Advanced High Read the excerpt of Roosevelt's *Quarantine* speech without modifying any unfamiliar language. Then ask students to demonstrate their understanding by listing your main points. Have pairs compare and contrast the items on their lists.

Use with Digital Text 3, **American Reaction is Divided**.

Writing
Review the terms *subject* and *verb,* reminding students that these parts of speech are the basic building blocks of any sentence. From the sentence-verb pattern, many other sentence patterns can be formed. Explain that students will practice writing using a variety of sentence patterns.

Beginning Introduce the subject-verb-complement sentence pattern with this sentence: *Lindbergh was an isolationist*. Point out that the complement *isolationist* renames Lindbergh. Explain that a complement is either a noun—a word that names a person, place, or thing—or an adjective that describes. Have partners with similar language abilities write other SVC sentences using these frames: Americans were _____. Roosevelt was _____.

Intermediate Display and discuss examples of the subject-verb and subject-verb-object sentence patterns: *Americans debated. Americans debated policies.* Have groups with similar language abilities write sentences using the SV and SVO patterns using these subjects: *Roosevelt, Lindbergh, Allies.*

Advanced Display and discuss examples of the subject-verb-object and subject-verb-object-complement sentence patterns: *Americans reelected Roosevelt. Americans reelected Roosevelt President.* Ask partners with similar language abilities to write two sentences about the lesson using the SVO pattern and two using the SVOC pattern.

Advanced High Review the SVC, SVO, and SVOC sentence patterns. Ask partners to use a variety of sentence patterns to write a paragraph about the American debate about whether to join the war. Have pairs read each other's paragraphs and identify the sentence patterns used.

⊡ Differentiate Instruction

Use the Differentiated Instruction notes throughout the lesson plan to support the varied skill sets, levels of readiness, and interests in the mixed-ability classroom.

Challenge These notes include suggestions for expanding the activity for advanced students.

On-Level These notes include suggestions for modifying the activity to address different interests or learning styles.

Extra Support These notes include ideas for providing more scaffolding or reading spuport.

Special Needs These notes provide ideas for adapting instruction to support the needs of various special needs students.

▆ NOTES

PEARSON
realize™
www.PearsonRealize.com

Go online to access additional resources including:
Primary Sources • Biographies • Supreme Court cases • 21st Century Skill Tutorials • Maps • Graphic Organizers.

Objectives

Objective 1: Understand the course of the early years of World War II in Europe.

Objective 2: Describe Franklin Roosevelt's foreign policy in the mid-1930s and the great debate between interventionists and isolationists.

Objective 3: Explain how the United States became more involved in the conflict.

LESSON 2 ORGANIZER		PACING: APPROX. 1 PERIOD, .5 BLOCKS			
				RESOURCES	
		OBJECTIVES	PACING	Online	Print
Connect					
	DIGITAL START UP ACTIVITY **A Difficult Decision**		5 min.	●	
Investigate					
	DIGITAL TEXT 1 **Roosevelt Criticizes Acts of War**		10 min.	●	●
	DIGITAL TEXT 2 **War Breaks Out in Europe**		10 min.	●	●
	INTERACTIVE MAP **Axis Aggression in Europe 1936–1941**	Objective 1	10 min.	●	
	INTERACTIVE GALLERY **Battle of Britain**		10 min.	●	
	DIGITAL TEXT 3 **American Reaction Is Divided**	Objective 2	10 min.	●	●
	DIGITAL TEXT 4 **America Moves Closer Toward War**	Objective 3	10 min.	●	●
	INTERACTIVE GALLERY **Norman Rockwell's Four Freedoms**		10 min.	●	
Synthesize					
	DIGITAL ACTIVITY **Two Viewpoints**		5 min.	●	
Demonstrate					
	DIGITAL QUIZ **Lesson Quiz and Class Discussion Board**		10 min.	●	

America Debates Involvement

■ CONNECT

A Difficult Decision

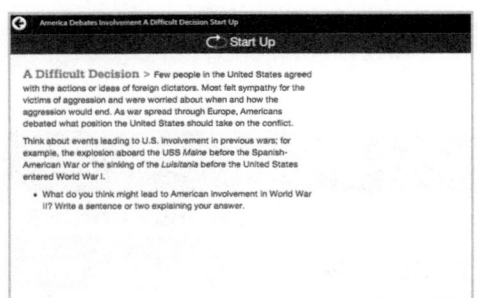

Project the Start Up Activity Ask students to consider U.S. participation in various wars over time. Then have them share their ideas with another student, either in class or through a chat or blog space.

Identify Central Issues Discuss wars the United States fought with foreign countries before 1941. What were the main issues? *(Revolutionary War–independence, create democracy; War of 1812 – independence, defend democracy; Spanish-American War – property attacked, sinking of the Maine; World War I – property attacked, sinking of Lusitania)*

Compare and Contrast How did these reasons compare to why the United States finally entered World War II? *(World War II dealt with the ideals of freedom, democracy, and retaliation against a wrong.)*

Aa **Vocabulary Development:** Use the Interactive Reading Notepad to preview the Key Terms and Academic Vocabulary in this Lesson with students.

⇅ FLIP IT!

Assign the Flipped Video for this lesson.

■ STUDENT EDITION PRINT PAGES: 576–584

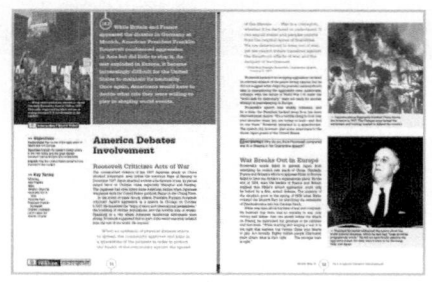

■ INVESTIGATE

Roosevelt Criticizes Acts of War

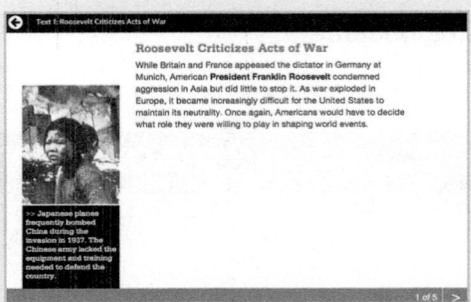

Objective 1: Understand the course of the early years of World War II in Europe.

Quick Instruction

Before the United States joined World War II in 1941, several turning points in the years that lead up to the war set the stage for U.S. involvement.

Interactive Map: Axis Aggression in Europe 1936–1941 Project the interactive map and click through the boxes to reveal the spread of Axis aggression. Have students look at the map of Axis Powers, 1939. Ask: Why would France and Britain sign a pledge promising to help Poland in the Spring of 1939? *(The Axis powers had partially surrounded Poland, and it seemed likely Poland would be Hitler's next target.)* Have students compare the map of Axis Powers, 1939, and the map of Axis Advances, 1941. Ask: What can you conclude about the pattern of the conflict? *(The Axis Powers, especially Germany, were having great success in the war.)*

Interactive Gallery: Battle of Britain Project the interactive gallery and click through the images. Discuss the impact of the blitz on civilians. Ask: Why might it be important to keep daily life as normal as possible in times of stress? *(It is important to be productive in order to maintain the fight against the enemy.)* Why do you think the evacuation from Dunkirk raised morale in Britain? *(It showed that the British troops could survive even in the face of seeming defeat. Civilians volunteered to pilot their boats in the rescue operation, making them all feel a part of effort to save the troops.)* Tell students the phrase "Dunkirk spirit" refers to the attitude of people pulling together and refusing to accept defeat.

War Breaks Out in Europe

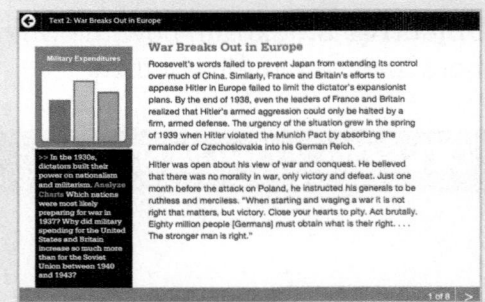

🔊 ACTIVE CLASSROOM

Pair students. Have students conduct an Audio Tour Activity of the hotspots on the map Axis Aggression in Europe 1936–1941. Challenge students to make an mp3 of the tour to share on the class blog.

🔊 ACTIVE CLASSROOM

Conduct a Circle Write Activity about how the images in the Interactive Gallery help students better understand The Battle of Britain. Have groups share their final response on a class blog, or have them read aloud and discuss as a whole class.

D Differentiate: Challenge Have students compare the military technology and strategy of World War I and World War II. For example, how does the blitzkrieg compare to the trench warfare? Why did France base its defense along the Maginot Line? Have them report their results to the class.

ELL Use the ELL activity described in the ELL chart.

Further Instruction

In the years that led up to U.S. involvement in World War II, the European theater underwent significant turning points in 1939, 1940, and 1941. Germany signed a Non-Aggression Pact with the Soviet Union in 1939, the same year Germany attacked Poland. Then in 1940, Germany broke its pact with the Soviet Union, won control of several other European nations including France, and began its Blitz on Britain.

INTERACTIVE MAP

Axis Aggression in Europe 1936–1941

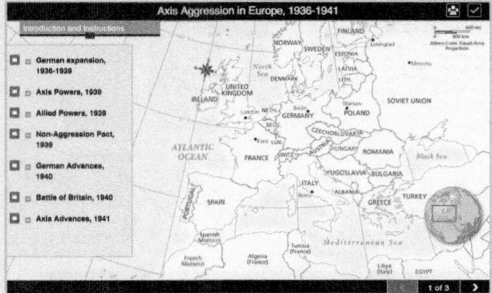

INTERACTIVE GALLERY

Battle of Britain

DIGITAL TEXT 3

American Reaction Is Divided

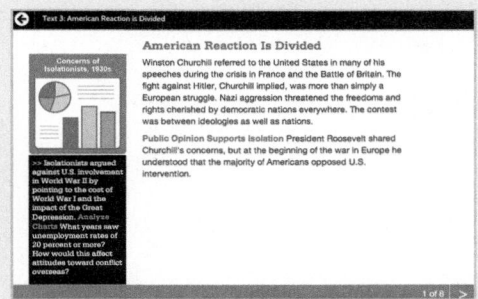

Interpret Explain to students how appeasing the dictators did not stop their aggression. War began in Europe with Germany's attack on Poland. Using the blitzkrieg, Germany soon dominated much of Europe. Have students reread Hitler's directive to his generals just before the attack on Poland. Have students analyze and interpret this social studies information. Discuss the impact this message would have on German troops.

Objective 2: **Describe Franklin Roosevelt's foreign policy in the mid-1930s and the great debate between interventionists and isolationists.**

Quick Instruction

Display the Concerns of Isolationists chart and review the information. Discuss with students the impact World War I had on the United States. Point out that over four million men were mobilized. What do you think the impact of the war was on them? On their families? How would this affect Americans' view of another possible war?

Infer How did President Roosevelt's leadership influence the United States's relationship with its allies? *(Roosevelt knew it was important to maintain good relationships with U.S. allies and showed empathy with their concerns. Even though the United States had yet to enter the war, FDR shared Churchill's concerns about Nazi Germany and took measures to support Britain. For example, he gave Britain 50 World War I-era battleships in exchange for eight British defense bases.)*

D **Differentiate: Extra Support** Have students read the quote from Lindbergh aloud. Have partners use appropriate skills, such as paraphrasing, to analyze and interpret social studies information. After partners have paraphrased, allow them time to discuss the reasons for Lindbergh's isolationism.

ELL Use the ELL activity described in the ELL chart.

America Debates Involvement

DIGITAL TEXT 4

America Moves Closer Toward War

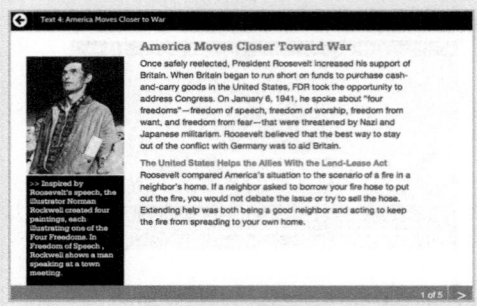

INTERACTIVE GALLERY

Norman Rockwell's Four Freedoms

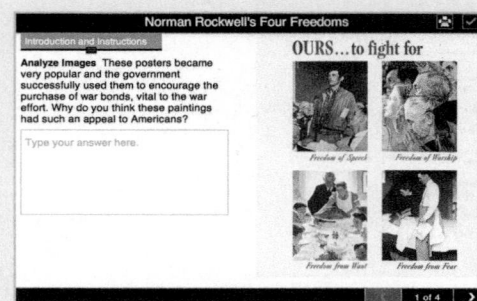

Further Instruction

Explain to students that, as the war spread in Europe, the United States needed to evaluate its stance about whether to enter the war. Isolationists and interventionists debated the best way to keep America safe.

Generate Explanations Remind students of Washington's Farewell Address, in which he warned America to beware of "entangling alliances" that would lead to overseas war. Point out how the position of Lindbergh and other isolationists was in keeping with Washington's. Ask: How might the geographic location of the United States affect Americans' attitude toward the war in Europe? *(The United States was separated by the Atlantic Ocean. It did not feel in imminent danger of attack. Washington also thought the ocean would protect the United States from European conflicts.)*

Objective 3: Explain how the United States became more involved in the conflict.

Quick Instruction

As the war escalated in Europe, Franklin D. Roosevelt exhibited bold international leadership when he bolstered U.S. support for the Allies, creating the Lend-Lease Act, which allowed for the United States to fund Britain in the war against Germany, and signed the Atlantic Charter, which deepened the U.S.-British alliance. His *Four Freedoms* speech rallied Americans to fight for freedom, and German attacks on U.S. ships furthered U.S. involvement in World War II.

Interactive Gallery: Norman Rockwell's Four Freedoms Project the Norman Rockwell's Four Freedoms, explaining that these images were inspired by Roosevelt's speech of the same title. Have students look at each image and respond to the following questions: How does it make you feel? Does it capture the freedom expressed in the title? Then have students analyze the Four Freedoms speech in Primary Sources; Four Freedoms.

📖 ACTIVE CLASSROOM

Divide students into groups and assign each group one image from Norman Rockwell's Four Freedoms. Have groups conduct the If Art Could Talk Activity. For each image, have students choose a central figure and explain what the person would likely say. Be sure students support their interpretations with evidence from the art.

Further Instruction

Point out that, by 1941, the Axis Powers dominated most of Europe and a large portion of Southeast Asia. The United States moved closer to involvement in the war. Challenge students to evaluate the international leadership of Franklin D. Roosevelt during World War II, including the U.S. relationship with its allies. Ask: What can you conclude about his leadership from the election of 1940? *(He was reelected to an unprecedented third term, so the people were satisfied with his leadership.)*

Support a Point of View with Evidence Roosevelt wanted to aid the Allies, but he realized the majority of Americans were unwilling to get involved. Cite examples from your reading showing how he moved the United States toward the support the Allies. (He gave the Quarantine Speech that prepared Americans for war to reach their doorsteps; He established the Neutrality Act of 1939—cash and carry favors Great Britain and gave Britain old battleships in exchange for British defense bases. He convinced Americans to become the "arsenal" for the Allies, creating the Lend-Lease Act to fund Britain. He signed the Atlantic Charter further allying the United States and Britain in a cause of freedom.)

Identify Cause and Effect How much did President Roosevelt consider American public opinion when deciding how to respond to the conflict in Europe? Why did he need to consider public opinion at all? *(He wanted to right the American economy before becoming involved in foreign affairs, and he felt he needed the support of the American people*

■ SYNTHESIZE

DIGITAL ACTIVITY
Two Viewpoints

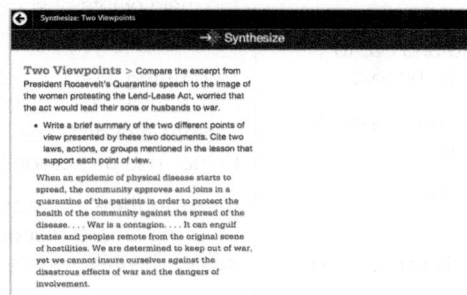

Recall with students that, for most of the 1930s, the United States struggled with its foreign policy. Should it stay completely isolated? Should it give aid and support to one side (the Allies)? Should it actively get involved?

Sequence Events Ask students to identify the steps, short of declaring war, that Roosevelt take to help Britain and the Soviet Union prior to the end of 1941. *(the Lend-Lease Act, exchanging older battleships for British defense bases)* How did Roosevelt try to reassure the isolationists? *(He said that his actions were taken to keep the United States out of the conflict. Giving support to the Allies would help defeat Germany, which would avoid the need to go to war.)*

Identify Challenge students to identify the peaceful actions the United States took to stop the spread of aggression. *(stop selling military goods to the aggressors, stop all trade with aggressors, public demonstrations against aggressive acts, stop citizens from traveling to or from aggressive nations, funding the Allies through the Lend-Lease Act, and donating ships to Britain)*

■ DEMONSTRATE

DIGITAL QUIZ
Lesson Quiz and Class Discussion Board

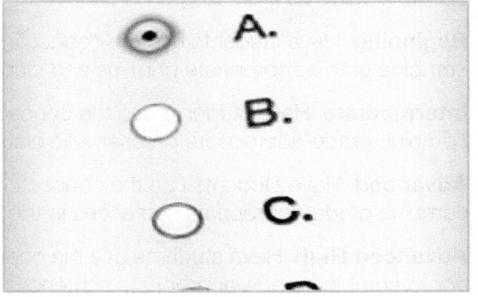

Assign the online Lesson Quiz for this lesson if you haven't already done so. Students will be offered automatic remediation or enrichment based on their score.

Pose these questions to the class on the Discussion Board:

In *America Debates Involvement*, you read about the spread of aggression in Europe and Asia and the debate about the role the United States should take in the conflicts. Gradually, the United States moved closer to involvement in the war.

Apply Concepts Think about the arguments of both the isolationists and interventionists. Evaluate the international leadership of Franklin D. Roosevelt, including the U.S. relationship with its allies. Do you think President Roosevelt could have done more to keep the United States neutral? Explain.

Support Ideas with Evidence Who would you think was the greater threat to the United States in 1939: Germany, Japan, or the Soviet Union? Support your answer with evidence from your reading.

Topic Inquiry
Have students continue their investigations for the Topic Inquiry.

---

before taking action because no American President can succeed in anything without popular support. Also, Roosevelt hoped to win the 1940 Presidential election and to get legislation he favored (such as Lend-Lease Act) passed.)

Make Predictions Roosevelt and Churchill signed the Atlantic Charter, envisioning a post-war world based on an international system of "general security." What do you think they meant? How would it be achieved? *(They hoped for a system that would allow nations to feel safe and resolve their differences peacefully. Nations would have to work together to ensure everyone's safety.)*

The United States Enters World War II

Supporting English Language Learners

Use with Digital Text 1, **Japan Attacks the United States**.

Writing
Prompt students to write using a variety of grade-appropriate connecting words to combine phrases, clauses, and sentences in increasingly accurate ways as more English is acquired.

Beginning Have students use the connecting words *and* and *but* to combine grade-appropriate phrases and clauses related to the text.

Intermediate Have students use the connecting words *and* and *but* to combine grade-appropriate phrases and clauses in the text.

Advanced Have students use the connecting words *or* and *so* to combine grade-appropriate sentences in the text.

Advanced High Have students use the connecting words *yet*, *for* and *nor* to combine grade-appropriate sentences in the text

Use with Digital Text 2, **Patriotism Inspires Rapid Mobilization**.

Listening
Read aloud, or ask a volunteer to read, the first paragraph under *Patriotism Inspires Rapid Mobilization*. Prompt students to understand the main points of spoken language and demonstrate their listening comprehension skills.

Beginning Discuss with students the meaning of *patriotism* and *mobilization*. Ask students to describe examples of patriotism and examples of mobilization. Have students complete the following sentence frame: This paragraph is about _____.

Intermediate Have students tell what the main idea of the paragraph is by giving an oral response. Have students complete the following sentence frame: Patriotism inspired rapid mobilization because _____.

Advanced Have students recount the main idea of the paragraph and explain how patriotism inspired rapid mobilization.

Advanced High Have students summarize the paragraph in their own words by describing how patriotism inspired rapid mobilization after the attack on Pearl Harbor.

D Differentiate Instruction

Use the Differentiated Instruction notes throughout the lesson plan to support the varied skill sets, levels of readiness, and interests in the mixed-ability classroom.

Challenge These notes include suggestions for expanding the activity for advanced students.

On-Level These notes include suggestions for modifying the activity to address different interests or learning styles.

Extra Support These notes include ideas for providing more scaffolding or reading spuport.

Special Needs These notes provide ideas for adapting instruction to support the needs of various special needs students.

NOTES

PEARSON
realize™
www.PearsonRealize.com

Go online to access additional resources including:
Primary Sources • Biographies • Supreme Court cases •
21st Century Skill Tutorials • Maps • Graphic Organizers.

Objectives

Objective 1: Explain why Japan decided to attack Pearl Harbor, and describe the attack itself.

Objective 2: Outline how the United States mobilized for war after the attack on Pearl Harbor.

Objective 3: Summarize the course of the war in the Pacific through the summer of 1942.

LESSON 3 ORGANIZER		PACING: APPROX. 1 PERIOD, .5 BLOCKS			
				RESOURCES	
		OBJECTIVES	**PACING**	**Online**	**Print**
Connect					
	DIGITAL START UP ACTIVITY **A Turning Point**		5 min.	●	
Investigate					
	DIGITAL TEXT 1 **Japan Attacks the United States**	Objective 1	10 min.	●	●
	INTERACTIVE MAP **Surprise Attack on Pearl Harbor**		10 min.	●	
	DIGITAL TEXT 2 **Patriotism Inspires Rapid Mobilization**	Objective 2	10 min.	●	●
	INTERACTIVE GALLERY **Americans Mobilize for War**		10 min.	●	
	DIGITAL TEXT 3 **The Early War in the Pacific**	Objective 3	10 min.	●	●
	INTERACTIVE MAP **Japanese Aggression, December 1941–June 1942**		10 min.	●	
Synthesize					
	DIGITAL ACTIVITY **Pearl Harbor Provokes the United States**		5 min.	●	
Demonstrate					
	DIGITAL QUIZ **Lesson Quiz and Class Discussion Board**		10 min.	●	

The United States Enters World War II

■ CONNECT

DIGITAL START UP ACTIVITY
A Turning Point

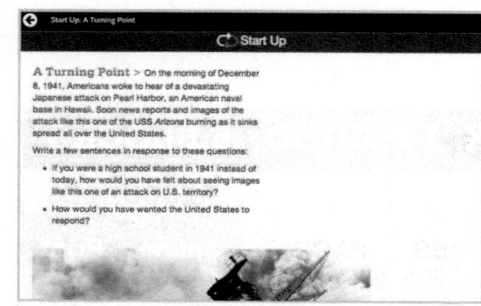

Project the Digital Start Up Activity Ask students to answer the questions as they enter and get settled. Then have them share their ideas with another student, either in class or through a chat or blog space.

Discuss If you were a high school student in 1941 instead of today, how would you have felt about an attack like this one on U.S. territory? *(shocked, horrified, angered)* How would you have wanted the United States to respond? *(by immediate retaliation, by censuring Japan in some way short of war)*

Tell students that in this lesson they will be learning how the United States did respond to the attack on Pearl Harbor.

⚡ FLIP IT!
Assign the Flipped Video for this lesson.

■ STUDENT EDITION PRINT
PAGES: 585–593

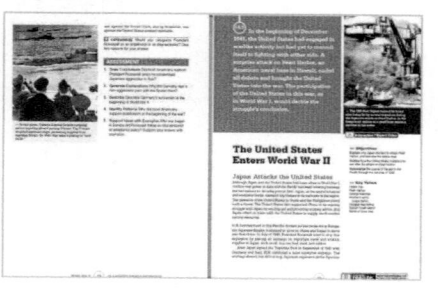

■ INVESTIGATE

DIGITAL TEXT 1
Japan Attacks the United States

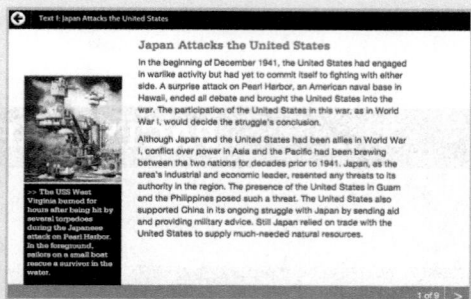

Objective 1: Explain why Japan decided to attack Pearl Harbor, and describe the attack itself.

Quick Instruction
Surprise Attack on Pearl Harbor: Interactive Map Project the interactive map and click through the hot spots. Introduce the map activity by telling students that by the beginning of December 1941, the United States had engaged in warlike activity but had yet to declare war. A surprise attack by the Japanese on an American naval base in Pearl Harbor, Hawaii, on December 7 was a turning point: it ended debate and brought the United States into the war.

🗣 ACTIVE CLASSROOM

Have students form an Opinion Line to answer the following question: Was the Japanese attack on Pearl Harbor successful or not from the point of view of the Japanese? Yes or no? *(Yes: It caused huge destruction to the Pacific fleet; it caught the United States off guard. No: The attack did not destroy enough of the American fleet; the attack united Americans in support of entering the war.)*

D Differentiate: **Extra Support** After asking the students to take a stand, allow students five minutes to think about the question individually. Tell them to write down their response (yes or no) and two reasons why they answered that way. Then continue with the group activity.

ELL Use the ELL activity described in the ELL chart.

INTERACTIVE MAP
Surprise Attack on Pearl Harbor

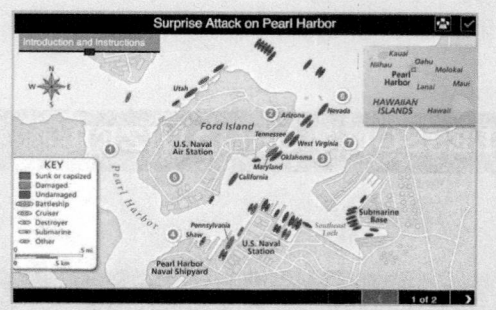

Further Instruction
Japan Attacks the United States: Interactive Reading Notepad Project and discuss the Close Reading Notepad questions, including the graphic organizer asking students to explain the causes and effects of Japan's attack on Pearl Harbor. Review the causes and effects with the class and fill in the graphic organizer on the whiteboard as you go.

Be sure students understand that the attack on Pearl Harbor was just one immediate reason for U.S. involvement in World War II. Discuss whether the United States would have become involved in the war if the attack on U.S. soil had not occurred. Pearl Harbor ended the debate between isolationists and interventionists. The United States became allied with Britain, France, and the Soviet Union.

Predict Consequences Ask students to predict what the international impact of U.S. participation in World War II will be. *(The United States will add considerable power to the Allied effort.)*

PEARSON **realize**™   www.PearsonRealize.com
Access your Digital Lesson

DIGITAL TEXT 2

Patriotism Inspires Rapid Mobilization

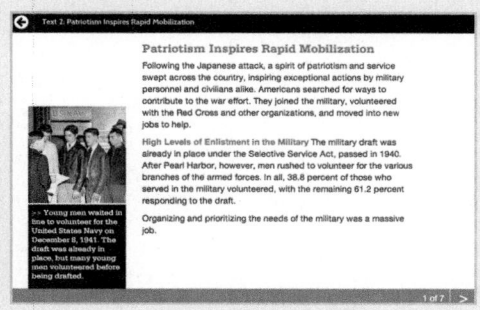

INTERACTIVE GALLERY

Americans Mobilize for War

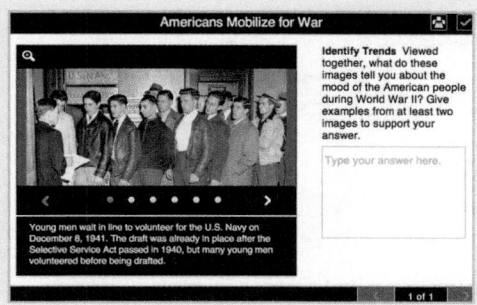

Objective 2: Outline how the United States mobilized for war after the attack on Pearl Harbor.

Quick Instruction
Americans of all races and ethnicities were motivated by patriotism to enlist in the military or help the war effort at home. The huge mobilization of both people and industry in the United States on the home front proved to be one of the Allies' main strengths during World War II.

Interactive Gallery: Americans Mobilize for War Project the slideshow. Look at each image individually and then the collection of images as a whole. How does the second image in the gallery, the Coast Guard poster, seek to inspire people to join the Coast Guard? *(It uses the exciting scene of a Coast Guard ship fighting off an attack to stimulate the patriotism of the viewers and dramatize the Coast Guard's need for good fighters.)*

Draw Inferences What was the domestic impact of U.S. participation in World War II in the early days of the war and how did this offer opportunities for women and minorities? *(Many Americans, including women and minorities, left their families and jobs to join the military. Many people, especially women and minorities, went to work in factories to produce war materials. Unemployment dropped and the Great Depression came to an end.)*

ACTIVE CLASSROOM
Ask the following question using the Sticky Note Strategy: Viewed together, what do these images tell you about the mood of the American people during World War II? *(The expressions of the people in most of the photos shows that the mood of the American people was determined and serious.)*

ELL Use the ELL activity described in the ELL chart.

Further Instruction
President Roosevelt recognized the importance of American production to the Allied effort in World War II. The "production miracle" that prepared the nation for war also turned the economy around. Ask students to find examples of Roosevelt's domestic leadership as the nation mobilized for war. *(FDR's rousing address asking Congress to declare war helped galvanize and unify the nation after the attack; FDR led the massive rapid-mobilization for the war effort.)*

Identify Cause and Effect How did the mobilization for war finally end the Great Depression? *(Massive spending stimulated the economy and put people to work churning out war materials.)* How did domestic industry's rapid mobilization for the war effort show the international leadership of President Roosevelt? *(President Roosevelt willingly addressed the concerns of U.S. European allies and ensured their military efforts were well-supplied.)*

Summarize George Marshall's military contributions during World War II. *(General Marshall served as the U.S. Army Chief of Staff. He not only directed military operations but also oversaw domestic production and distribution of military supplies.)*

Evaluate Data Ask students to summarize the data about military enlistment in *High Levels of Enlistment in the Military*. What do these high enlistment levels suggest about the mood of the country following the attack on Pearl Harbor? *(People were inspired by patriotism to serve their country.)*

The United States Enters World War II

DIGITAL TEXT 3

The Early War in the Pacific

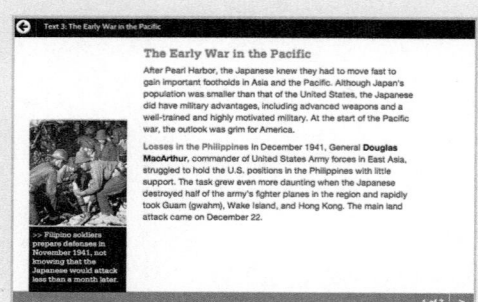

INTERACTIVE MAP

Japanese Aggression, December 1941–June 1942

Objective 3: Summarize the course of the war in the Pacific through the summer of 1942.

Quick Instruction

Remind students that American forces were trying to hold positions against the Japanese in the Pacific before new troops and supplies could reach them.

Interactive Map: Japanese Aggression, December 1941–June 1942 Step through the Japanese Aggression, December 1941–June 1942 interactive map with students. Point out that it shows how control of Southeast Asia and the Pacific region changed over several months in 1941 and 1942.

Express Problems Clearly Ask students to explain the events leading up to the Bataan Death March and analyze how it may have been avoided. *(The march followed months of fighting in the Philippines. The Japanese army could have treated the prisoners according to the rules of the Geneva Convention, which would have avoided the large death toll.)*

🗣 ACTIVE CLASSROOM

Have students use the Ranking Strategy to go through the events in the Pacific shown in the activity and rank which ones had the greatest impact on the course of the war.

Draw Conclusions American leaders knew that Doolittle's Raid would not have much of a military impact on Japan. Why do you think they ordered the raid anyway? *(They wanted to strike back symbolically at Japan to boost the morale of Americans.)*

D **Differentiate: Challenge/Gifted** Ask students to do additional research on the Bataan Death March and present their findings.

Further Instruction

During the Japanese advances in East Asia, General Douglas MacArthur tried to hold U.S. positions. When he left to command the Southwest Pacific, other groups bravely contributed to the fight against Japan.

Draw Inferences Ask students to evaluate the military contributions of General Douglas MacArthur during this time. *(MacArthur did the best he could under the circumstances, but the surrender of the Philippines was a low point in his career. He vowed to return to the Philippines.)*

Evaluate Impact Who were the Flying Tigers? How did their exceptional actions show patriotism and give hope to Americans during the early days of the war in the Pacific? *(The Flying Tigers were volunteers who achieved success against the Japanese at a time when the Americans otherwise seemed to be losing the war in the Pacific.)*

■ SYNTHESIZE

DIGITAL ACTIVITY

Pearl Harbor Provokes the United States

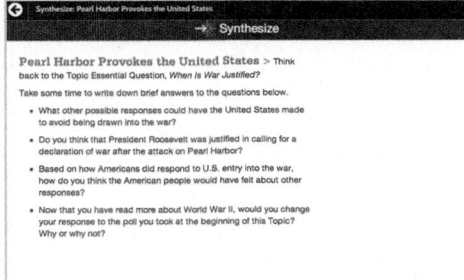

■ DEMONSTRATE

DIGITAL QUIZ

Lesson Quiz and Class Discussion Board

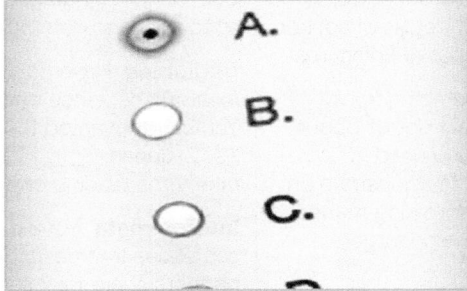

Ask students to recall the Topic Essential Question, *When Is War Justified?* Have them use the Think-Pair-Share strategy to answer the questions in the Pearl Harbor Provokes the United States activity. Ask them to take five minutes to write down some brief answers to the questions below and then share their answers with a talking partner.

Have partners think about the following question: Do you think Roosevelt was justified in calling for a declaration of war after the attack on Pearl Harbor? Have pairs share their answers with the class.

Discuss Ask students to think about the Essential Question activity they did at the beginning of this topic. Ask if they would change any of their responses now that they have learned more about World War II.

Assign the online Lesson Quiz for this lesson if you haven't already done so. Students will be offered automatic remediation or enrichment based on their score.

Pose these questions to the class on the Discussion Board:

In *The United States Enters World War II*, you read about the productive capacity of the United States: the country's ability to quickly build thousands of ships, airplanes, tanks, armaments, and munitions in factories across the country. Productive capacity includes having material resources, money, technical know-how, and human labor.

Predict Consequences Do you think the productive capacity of the United States will give the Allies an advantage over their enemies during the course of the war?

Draw Inferences What differences affect the productive capacities of the enemies? Hint: Think about where the war will be fought.

Topic Inquiry
Have students continue their investigations for the Topic Inquiry.

A War on Two Fronts

Supporting English Language Learners

Use with Digital Text 3, **Axis Powers on the Defensive**.

Listening
Explain that speakers usually present a main idea and then share important details to support that idea. Discuss how activating prior knowledge, identifying the main idea, and listening for transitional words and phrases can help students understand the important details of spoken language ranging from situations in which topics are familiar to unfamiliar.

Beginning Explain the familiar topic of the practice of bombing from airplanes during war. In your explanation, include important details about the strategies of saturation bombing and strategic bombing used in World War II. Have partners with similar language abilities demonstrate an understanding of important details orally completing the following frames: _____ bombing targets everyone in a country. _____ bombing targets military and government buildings.

Intermediate Summarize the section titled Allied Bombers Attack Germany. Have partners with similar language abilities demonstrate understanding of important details by completing the following sentence frames: The goal of the saturation bombing of Germany was to _____. The goal of the strategic bombing of Germany was to _____.

Advanced Discuss the somewhat unfamiliar topic of the Tuskegee Airmen. Include information not found in the text. Then have pairs of students collaborate to write a list of three important details you mentioned. Have pairs of students compare their lists.

Advanced High Use spoken language to talk about the mostly unfamiliar topic of African Americans in the military during World War II. Use the text as a starting point, but primarily discuss information not included in the text. Have students record the important details you mentioned and then compare lists with one another.

Use with Digital Text 4, **Turning Points in the Pacific**.

Writing
Explain to students that when they narrate, or write a story, they should order events in sequence and include specific details to make it interesting. Use the following activities to challenge students to narrate with increasing specificity and detail in order to fulfill content area writing needs.

Beginning Have partners work together to copy and complete the following sentence frames in order to tell the story of the Battle of Midway: Yamamoto wanted to _____. But the U.S. Navy knew _____. On June 4, 1942, Japan _____. That same day, the United States _____. Invite pairs to take turns reading one another's completed writing.

Intermediate Have partners narrate the Battle of Midway by writing three sentences that describe the beginning, middle, and end of the battle. Have partners share their sentences with other pairs.

Advanced Ask pairs of students to write a narrative of the Battle of Midway. Once their narration is complete, encourage them to reread it and revise each sentence to add specific details.

Advanced High Have students visualize the Battle of Midway as a movie. Ask: How would a movie add specific detail? How would a movie create more drama? Have students use this exercise to help them write a narration of the Battle of Midway using specific details about the events.

▷ Differentiate Instruction

Use the Differentiated Instruction notes throughout the lesson plan to support the varied skill sets, levels of readiness, and interests in the mixed-ability classroom.

Challenge These notes include suggestions for expanding the activity for advanced students.

On-Level These notes include suggestions for modifying the activity to address different interests or learning styles.

Extra Support These notes include ideas for providing more scaffolding or reading spuport.

Special Needs These notes provide ideas for adapting instruction to support the needs of various special needs students.

■ NOTES

PEARSON
realize™
www.PearsonRealize.com

Go online to access additional resources including:
Primary Sources • Biographies • Supreme Court cases •
21st Century Skill Tutorials • Maps • Graphic Organizers.

Objectives

Objective 1: Analyze the reasons for and impact of the Allies' "Europe First" strategy.

Objective 2: Explain why the battles of Stalingrad and Midway were major turning points in the war.

Objective 3: Discuss how the Allies put increasing pressure on the Axis in North Africa and Europe.

LESSON 4 ORGANIZER			PACING: APPROX. 1 PERIOD, .5 BLOCKS		
		OBJECTIVES	PACING	**RESOURCES** Online	Print
Connect					
	DIGITAL START UP ACTIVITY **Flying in the Army Air Forces**		5 min.	●	
Investigate					
	DIGITAL TEXT 1 **Allied Strategy**	Objective 1	10 min.	●	●
	DIGITAL TEXT 2 **The European Front**		10 min.	●	●
	INTERACTIVE GALLERY **War in the North Atlantic**	Objective 2	10 min.	●	
	DIGITAL TEXT 4 **Turning Points in the Pacific**		10 min.	●	●
	DIGITAL TEXT 3 **Axis Powers on the Defensive**		10 min.	●	●
	INTERACTIVE GALLERY **War in North Africa**	Objective 3	10 min.	●	
	3-D MODEL **The B-24 Liberator**		10 min.	●	
Synthesize					
	DIGITAL ACTIVITY **Turning the Tide**		5 min.	●	
Demonstrate					
	DIGITAL QUIZ **Lesson Quiz and Class Discussion Board**		10 min.	●	

A War on Two Fronts

■ CONNECT

DIGITAL START UP ACTIVITY
Flying in the Army Air Forces

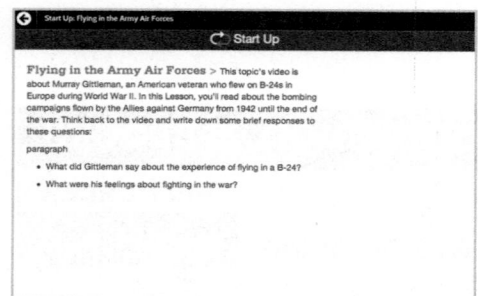

Project the Start Up Activity Then, tell students that in this lesson, they'll learn about bombing campaigns flown by the Allies against Germany during the war. Replay the Topic video "Murray Gittleman, World War II Veteran." Then have a class discussion about how firsthand accounts can enhance the meaning of the war for students.

Discuss What did Gittleman say about flying in a B-24? *(He remembered it was so cold his oxygen mask would freeze on his chest.)* What were his feelings about fighting in the war? *(He "wasn't happy about" getting drafted but knew he had to do his part.)* What crew position did Gittleman have on the B-24? *(He was the radio operator and used Morse code to communicate with the ground.)*

Aa Vocabulary Development: Use the Interactive Reading Notepad to preview the Key Terms and Academic Vocabulary in this lesson with students.

⇗ FLIP IT!
Assign the Flipped Video for this lesson.

■ STUDENT EDITION PRINT PAGES: 594–600

■ INVESTIGATE

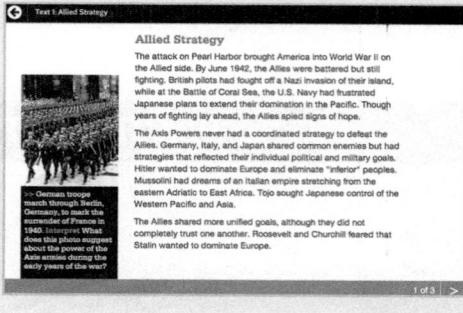

DIGITAL TEXT 1
Allied Strategy

Objective 1: Analyze the reasons for and impact of the Allies' "Europe First" strategy.

Quick Instruction
World War II was waged between two major alliances: the Axis Powers and the Allied Powers. Of the Axis Powers, only Germany had the resources to fight the war on multiple fronts. As a result, the Allied Powers agreed on a "Europe First" strategy in order to address the largest threat to democracy.

Analyze Information Project the War Goals chart. Explain to students that despite their differences, the three Allied leaders—Roosevelt, Churchill, and Stalin—were able to agree on a strategy to defeat the Axis. Discuss as a class how having a common goal bolstered the Allied Powers as they fought the Axis nations. *(Having a common goal united the forces and their progress, so everyone fought for the same gain. They were not distracted by their individual agendas.)*

Further Instruction
As an international leader during World War II, Franklin D. Roosevelt understood the importance of uniting with Churchill and even Stalin, who under normal circumstances would be considered an opponent.

Evaluate How would you evaluate Roosevelt's international leadership during World War II, especially his handling of the United States' relationship with the other major Allies? Consider Roosevelt's meetings with Churchill before the United States entered the war, as well his handling of Stalin. *(Roosevelt was empathetic to Churchill's needs in Europe. Although Roosevelt*

and Stalin were ideological opposites, Roosevelt pragmatically worked with the Soviet leader to address common interests.)

Identify Main Ideas Ask students to identify the major differences in ideology separating the major Allies. Why do you think they were able to set aside these differences to create a unified strategy? *(The United States and Britain were democratic, capitalist nations, while the Soviet Union was a totalitarian communist dictatorship. The Axis presented an immediate threat that all three Allied nations had to defeat in order to survive.)*

Predict Consequences How might the different strategies of the Axis and Allied powers affect the course of the war? *(the Allies shared a common goal and developed a unified strategy for achieving that goal. This might give them an advantage over the Axis Powers, who were distracted by their individual agendas.)*

DIGITAL TEXT 2
The European Front

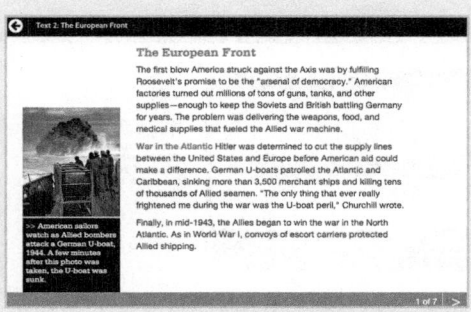

INTERACTIVE GALLERY
War in the North Atlantic

DIGITAL TEXT 4
Turning Points in the Pacific

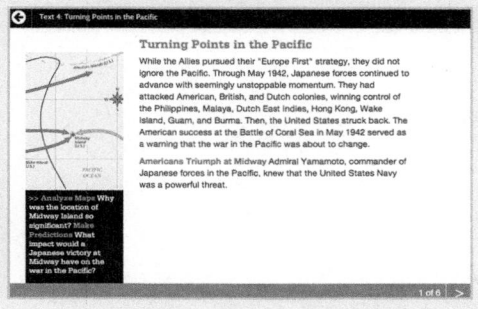

Objective 2: Explain why the battles of Stalingrad and Midway were major turning points in the war.

Quick Instruction

Tell students that "Europe First" was a sound, sensible military strategy for the Allies. Even so, the Allies were challenged with fighting World War II on multiple fronts, including the Soviet Union, the North Atlantic, North Africa, and the Pacific. The military leadership of Dwight D. Eisenhower and George Patton would prove indispensable as the Allies took control of North Africa. Around the globe, U.S. participation in World War II had begun in the Pacific, and Americans were eager to avenge the bombing of Pearl Harbor. The 1942 Battle of Midway marked a turning point in the war in the Pacific. Under the command of Admiral Chester Nimitz, the U.S. Navy defeated Japan and crippled its ability to fight future naval battles.

Interactive Gallery: War in the North Atlantic Project the "War in the North Atlantic" Interactive Gallery and click through the visuals with students. Ask: What does the image of sailors watching an explosion in the water suggest about the dangers of transporting supplies across the Atlantic? *(It was difficult to defend Allied supply ships from German U-boats, which could approach ships with little warning.)* What do these images suggest about the role of the convoy system in the war in the North Atlantic? *(Large numbers of Allied ships were needed to carry supplies across the Atlantic to Britain. It was safer for ships to travel together in large convoys for protection from the dangers of German U-boats.)*

🖵 ACTIVE CLASSROOM

Conduct two Circle Write Activities about major military events of World War II: one about the Battle of Stalingrad and one about the Battle of Midway. For each, have students write as much as they can for one minute then switch with the person on their right. The next person tries to improve or elaborate the response where the other person left off. Continue to switch until the paper comes back to the first person. The group then decides which is the best composition (or response) and shares that with the larger group. When students have finished, point out that the U.S. victory during the Battle of Midway marked the beginning of the U.S. military advancement through the Pacific islands.

D Differentiate: **Challenge** Organize the class into small groups. Have half of the groups conduct research about life on an Allied supply ship during the war and the other half conduct research about life on a German U-boat. Have each group write a letter or a series of journal entries that a person on their ship or U-boat might have written during the war. Writings should include details about living conditions, daily tasks, and battles.

ELL Use the ELL activity described in the ELL chart.

Further Instruction

Summarize Challenge students to summarize the military contributions of Dwight Eisenhower and George Patton toward the Allies' "Europe First" strategy in

1942 and 1943. *(Eisenhower commanded the U.S. invasion of North Africa, while Patton's forces and the British forced German and Italian troops to surrender in Tunisia.)* What contributions did Omar Bradley make in North Africa and Italy? *(Serving under Patton, Bradley commanded American troops to victory in Tunisia and led forces in the invasion of Sicily.)*

A War on Two Fronts

DIGITAL TEXT 3

Axis Powers on the Defensive

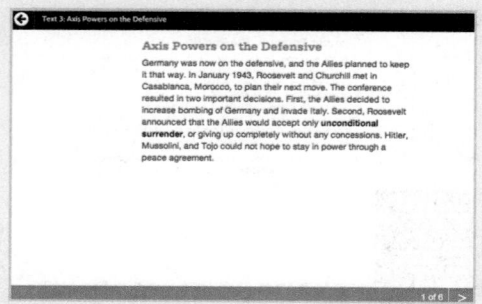

INTERACTIVE GALLERY

War in North Africa

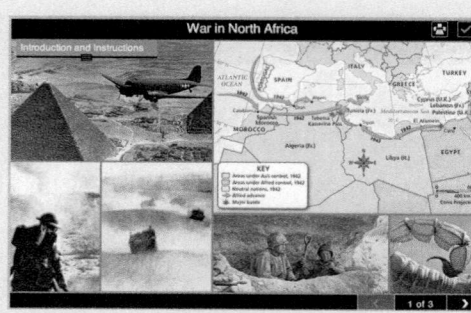

3-D MODEL

The B-24 Liberator

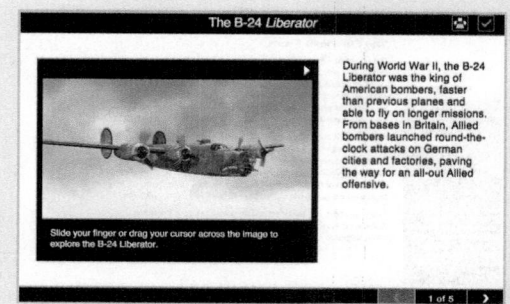

Objective 3: **Discuss how the Allies put increasing pressure on the Axis in North Africa and Europe.**

Quick Instruction

After winning control of North Africa, Roosevelt solidified his international leadership during World War II by announcing that the Allies would accept nothing but unconditional surrender. The Allies continued to fight on multiple fronts, attacking Italy and beginning the saturation bombing of Germany. The B-24 Liberator was a state-of-the-art bomber that advanced the Allied cause. However, this huge plane needed the protection of fighter planes. The Tuskegee Airmen provided this protection for many bombers during the course of the war. This group of African American military pilots showed incredible bravery and exceptional ability in their service.

Interactive Gallery: War in North Africa Project the interactive gallery. Explain that the North African front was considered part of the Allied "Europe First" strategy, since in North Africa, Allied troops directly confronted German and Italian forces, and North Africa was a stepping stone to an invasion of Italy on the European mainland.

3-D Model: The B-24 Liberator Work through The B-24 Liberator Activity with students. Tell students that the B-24 Liberator was faster than previous American bombers and able to carry a heavy load of bombs on long missions. How do you think this air war affected the outcome of World War II? How do you think it affected Europe in terms of lives lost and rebuilding after the war? *(The air war had an important impact on World War II in Europe, relieving pressure on the Soviet*

Union, harming Germany's ability to make war, and making it possible for an all-out Allied offensive in France. The bombing likely killed many people and made the postwar rebuilding process more challenging.)*

🗣 ACTIVE CLASSROOM

Conduct a Conversations with History Activity. Direct students to have a mock Conversations with one of the people in the visuals or text covered in this lesson. Each student should write down a question he or she would like to ask, the answer that person would give, and what the student would say in response.

🗣 ACTIVE CLASSROOM

Conduct a Thumbs Up When Ready Activity. Ask students to think about this statement: "True or false: By the end of 1943, the Allies were poised for final victory in World War II." Ask students to put their thumbs up to indicate that they have finished their thinking. When all have responded, ask them to share their thoughts in pairs or in small groups.

ELL Use the ELL activity described in the ELL chart.

Further Instruction

Explain that the Allied victory in North Africa provided the first stepping stone for American and British troops to invade the European mainland. As a result, Italy became the first Axis Power to fall to the Allies. Meanwhile, Allied bombers pounded targets in Germany, but a full-scale assault on Western Europe would have to wait.

Draw Conclusions Have students identify the actions the Allies took as a result of the conference in Casablanca? *(They invaded Italy and increased bombing of Germany)* Which of these actions had a greater impact on the course of the war? *(The bombing of Germany had a greater impact. It harmed Germany's capacity to make war and relieved pressure on the Soviets. The Allied advance in Italy was slow and had relatively little impact on Germany.)*

Support a Point of View with Evidence Challenge students to describe the effects of geography on the war in North Africa. How did fighting in North Africa differ from fighting in Europe and in the Pacific? Tell students to support their answers with evidence from the images and text in the lesson. *(The deserts and mountains of North Africa posed special challenges to soldiers, who had to deal with sandstorms, poisonous animals, and warfare on open desert and rugged hills. Fighting in North Africa was similar in some ways to sea warfare in the North Atlantic and the Pacific, with mobile fighting units and aircraft traveling over large areas in search of the enemy.)*

Summarize Invite students to explain how American patriotism inspired exceptional actions by military personnel, including the bravery and contributions of the Tuskegee Airmen. *(American men and women were inspired by patriotism to sacrifice during the war. They sacrificed their time, their energy, their families, their fortunes, and their lives in countless acts of exceptional bravery and endurance. The Tuskegee Airmen did so as they protected American bombers in the strategic bombing of Germany. The bombing paved the way for the Allied invasion of Europe and the success of the "Europe First" strategy.)*

SYNTHESIZE

DIGITAL ACTIVITY
Turning the Tide

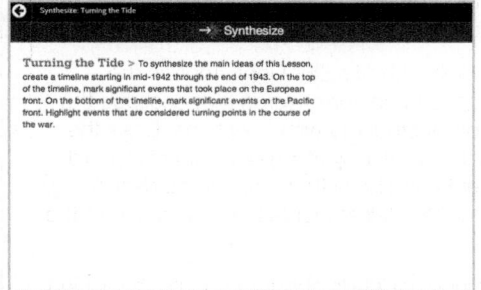

By the end of 1943, the story for the Allies was quite different than it had been at the beginning of 1942. To put together the main ideas of this lesson, have students create a timeline starting in mid-1942 and continuing through the end of 1943. On the top of the timeline, they should mark significant events that took place on the European front. On the bottom of the timeline, they should mark significant events on the Pacific front. Highlight events that are considered turning points in the course of the war.

Sequence Events Ask: Which event was the key turning point on the European front? Which was the turning point on the Pacific front? *(Stalingrad on the European front; Midway on the Pacific front.)*

Draw Conclusions Ask student if they think that the Allied leaders knew in 1943 they had passed key turning points on both fronts. *(The idea of a turning point is applied by historians after the fact. Most likely, Allied leaders did not realize that they had passed key turning points, but they would have known that they had won decisive victories and followed up on the advantages they gained from those victories.)*

DEMONSTRATE

DIGITAL QUIZ
Lesson Quiz and Class Discussion Board

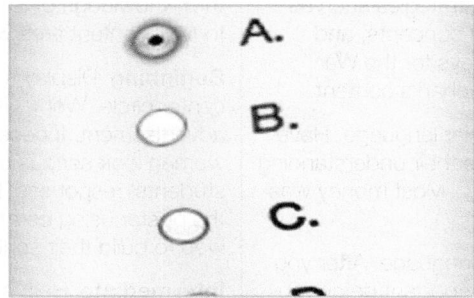

Assign the online Lesson Quiz for this lesson if you haven't already done so. Students will be offered automatic remediation or enrichment based on their score.

Pose these questions to the class on the Discussion Board:

In *A War on Two Fronts*, you read about the impact of the Allies' "Europe First" strategy and about major turning points in the war. American military leaders had an important impact during these crucial years of World War II.

Infer Why did President Franklin Roosevelt support a "Europe First" strategy even though it was Japan that had attacked the United States?

Interpret Evaluate the military contributions of these leaders during World War II: George Patton, Dwight Eisenhower, and Chester A. Nimitz.

Topic Inquiry
Have students continue their investigations for the Topic Inquiry.

The Home Front

Supporting English Language Learners

Use with Digital Text 1, **Patriotism on the Home Front**.

Listening
Explain to students that speakers often share a main idea and then support it with important details. To understand important details in both familiar and unfamiliar contexts, they can call on strategies such as activating prior knowledge, listening for key words and concepts, and identifying the main idea. Display the chart "America Pays for the War." Explain that you refer to the graphs as you explain the chart's content.

Beginning Explain the left half of the chart using familiar language. Have partners complete the following frames to demonstrate their understanding of important details: Spending was the highest in _____. Most money was spent on _____.

Intermediate Explain the three graphs using familiar language. After you finish with each graph, ask partners to each state an important detail you shared. After you finish speaking, ask partners to identify three important details about the topic in general.

Advanced Use familiar and unfamiliar language to explain the chart's information. Ask pairs of students to sketch each graph and caption it with important details you gave about it. Have pairs share their work with one another.

Advanced High Use familiar and unfamiliar language to explain the chart's information. Ask students to individually list the most important details you mentioned.

Use with Digital Text 3, **Increased Opportunities in Employment**.

Writing
Display the image of the poster of the woman using a drill, and discuss the meaning of the slogan "It's Our Fight Too!" Explain that students will use their knowledge of English to describe with increasing specificity and detail to fulfill content area writing needs.

Beginning Display a concept web with "It's Our Fight, Too!" in the center circle. Work with students to brainstorm words that describe the advertisement. If necessary, prompt students with questions: Does the woman look serious or silly? Is the woman working or playing? Record students' responses. Pair students and have them take turns describing the poster using complete sentences. Tell students to use ideas from the web to build their sentences.

Intermediate Help students pinpoint details about the poster by asking the following questions: What color are the woman's eyes? What is her facial expression? Where is she looking? Pair students and have them write three sentences about the poster. Allow time for partners to share their work with other pairs.

Advanced Ask pairs of students to write a paragraph describing the woman and what she is doing, using as much specificity and detail as possible. Have pairs share their writing and compare the details they included.

Advanced High Ask students to write two paragraphs describing the details in the poster and explaining their effect. Encourage them to include as much specificity and detail as possible.

◗ Differentiate Instruction

Use the Differentiated Instruction notes throughout the lesson plan to support the varied skill sets, levels of readiness, and interests in the mixed-ability classroom.

Challenge These notes include suggestions for expanding the activity for advanced students.

On-Level These notes include suggestions for modifying the activity to address different interests or learning styles.

Extra Support These notes include ideas for providing more scaffolding or reading spuport.

Special Needs These notes provide ideas for adapting instruction to support the needs of various special needs students.

◼ NOTES

PEARSON
realize™
www.PearsonRealize.com

Go online to access additional resources including:
Primary Sources • Biographies • Supreme Court cases •
21st Century Skill Tutorials • Maps • Graphic Organizers.

Objectives

Objective 1: Examine how the need to support the war effort changed American lives.

Objective 2: Analyze the effects of the war on civil liberties for Japanese Americans and others.

Objective 3: Explain how World War II increased opportunities for women and minorities.

Objective 4: Describe how World War II caused migration within the United States and the effects of that migration.

LESSON 5 ORGANIZER	PACING: APPROX. 1 PERIOD, .5 BLOCKS			
			RESOURCES	
	OBJECTIVES	PACING	Online	Print
Connect				
DIGITAL START UP ACTIVITY **A New Home Front**		5 min.	●	
Investigate				
DIGITAL TEXT 1 **Patriotism on the Home Front**	Objective 1	10 min.	●	●
DIGITAL TEXT 2 **Japanese Internment During World War II**	Objective 2	10 min.	●	●
INTERACTIVE GALLERY **The Experience of Japanese Internment**		10 min.	●	
DIGITAL TEXT 3 **Increased Opportunities in Employment**	Objective 3	10 min.	●	●
INTERACTIVE GALLERY **African Americans and World War II**		10 min.	●	
DIGITAL TEXT 4 **Migration During World War II**	Objective 4	10 min.	●	●
Synthesize				
DIGITAL ACTIVITY **Working for Victory on the World War II Home Front**		5 min.	●	
Demonstrate				
DIGITAL QUIZ **Lesson Quiz and Class Discussion Board**		10 min.	●	

The Home Front

CONNECT

DIGITAL START UP ACTIVITY
A New Home Front

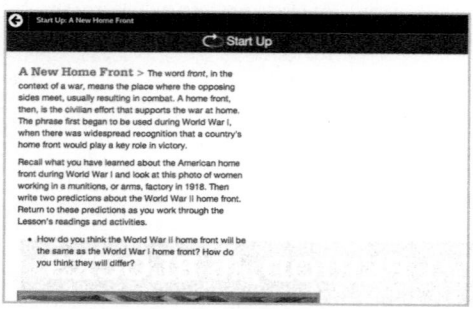

Have students read the prompt, look at the photograph, and then make predictions about how the World War II home front will compare to the World War I home front. Have students share their predictions with a partner, either in class or through a chat or blog space.

Discuss What similarities might the home fronts share? How might they differ? *(Similarities: Women will enter the workforce again; people producing war material will contribute. Differences: The World War II home front will be more technologically advanced. More people might be involved since the war was already larger in scope by 1942 than all of World War I.)*

Aa Vocabulary Development: Use the Interactive Reading Notepad to preview the Key Terms and Academic Vocabulary in this lesson with students.

📲 FLIP IT!
Assign the Flipped Video for this lesson.

STUDENT EDITION PRINT PAGES: 601–608

INVESTIGATE

DIGITAL TEXT 1
Patriotism on the Home Front

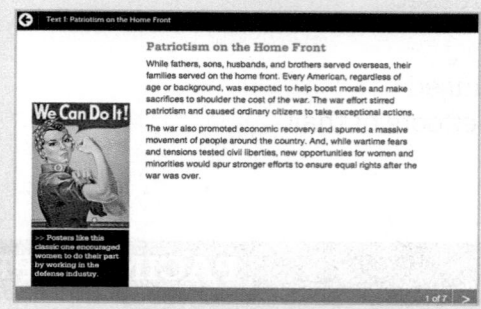

Objective 1: Examine how the need to support the war effort changed American lives.

Quick Instruction
Display the America Pays for War infographic to emphasize the gigantic costs of a world war. Explain that during World War II, nearly every American worked or made some sacrifice, including enduring rationing, to keep the fighting forces overseas safe, supplied, and ultimately, victorious. The economic effects of the war on the home front included increased opportunities for women and ethnic minorities. However, these opportunities led to obstacles in the form of prejudice and discrimination faced by women and ethnic minorities. Explain how American patriotism inspired exceptional actions by citizens, including volunteerism, the purchase of war bonds, and the growing of Victory Gardens.

Identify Central Issues Show the video about how people on the American home front received news during the war. Have students name one aspect of the home front discussed in the video.

ELL Use the ELL activity described in the ELL chart.

Further Instruction
Explain that keeping up morale with soldiers, as well as on the home front, was a major issue during World War II. The American government created the Office of War Information to work with the media to boost morale.

Make Generalizations Ask: How did the media help the Office of War Information function during the war? *(The Office of War Information tried to downplay domestic concerns while the media continued to frame the war as a struggle between dictators and democracy. Documentaries and other films were made that depicted the war in a heroic way. Celebrities filmed public service announcements promoting joining the service or buying bonds.)*

List What exceptional actions did patriotism on the home front inspire? *(volunteerism, coping with rationing, planting Victory Gardens, buying war bonds, taking new jobs or working overtime in factories, working to keep morale high.)*

Summarize Were these actions part of a citizens' duties or beyond them? *(While defending the nation is a duty of citizenship, many actions taken to aid the war effort during World War II went beyond the normal call of duty.)*

DIGITAL TEXT 2

Japanese Internment During World War II

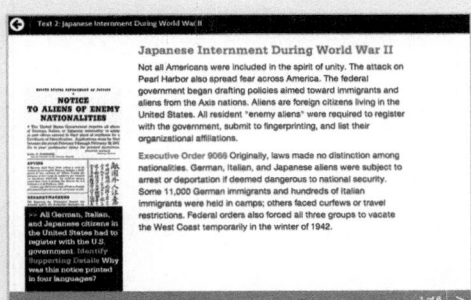

INTERACTIVE GALLERY

The Experience of Japanese Internment

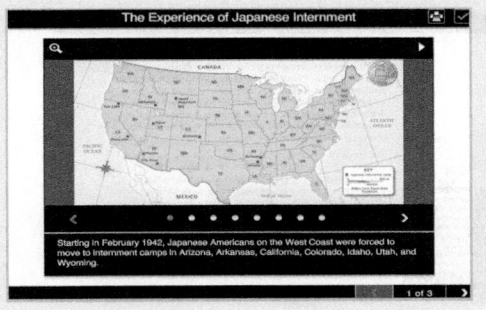

DIGITAL TEXT 3

Increased Opportunities in Employment

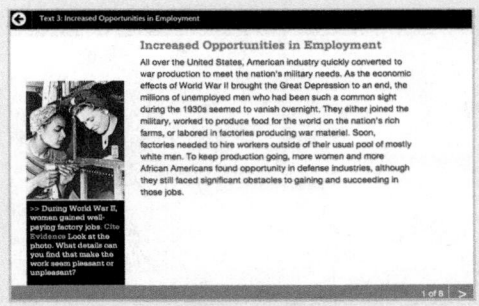

Objective 2: Analyze the effects of the war on civil liberties for Japanese Americans and others.

Quick Instruction

As World War II was waged in Europe, American immigrants of German, Italian, and Japanese descent suffered extreme prejudice and government sanctioned internment. Soon, Germans and Italians were released, but Japanese internment escalated with Executive Order 9066.

Interactive Gallery: The Experience of Japanese Internment Project the interactive gallery. Explain that one of the responses to the Japanese attack on Pearl Harbor was fear and distrust of Japanese, German, and Italian immigrants. Japanese Americans—both immigrants and those born in America—faced the harshest treatment and made up most of the population of the internment camps. Progress through the photos in the image gallery, inviting volunteers to read the captions. Make sure students understand that *Nisei* refers to someone born in the United States whose parents were immigrants from Japan. Discuss each image and caption.

▶ ACTIVE CLASSROOM

Conduct a Quick Write Activity. Ask students to write a diary entry from the perspective of a person who was interned at Manzanar or Tule Lake. Have them refer to scenes from the photos in the activity in their entries.

D Differentiate: **Challenge** Challenge students to research the internment of German Americans and Italian Americans. Although a major issue of World War II, the internment of these two groups has received much less attention than the internment of Japanese Americans, largely because of racial issues and the fact that far fewer German Americans and Italian Americans were interned. Have students create a digital presentation and present the information to the class.

Further Instruction

Review the information about the internment of Japanese Americans and Executive Order 9066. Then, show the Landmark Supreme Court Cases lesson *Korematsu v. United States*.

Identify Central Issues What constitutional issues were raised by the internment of Japanese Americans and Executive Order 9066? *(The internment policy threatened several constitutional principles: equal protection, freedom of speech, freedom of the press, right to privacy.)*

Generate Explanations Ask students why they think this kind of discrimination occurs. *(When people are threatened by a specific enemy that is out of reach, they might lash out at a person they believe represents that enemy so they feel some sort of control over what is happening.)* How might it be possible to avoid this type of reaction? *(More information about different groups of people and their beliefs might keep misunderstandings from developing; reminders during traumatic times about reacting in haste might also help.)*

Objective 3: Explain how World War II increased opportunities for women and minorities.

Quick Instruction

Remind students that as a result of World War II, the American economy on the home front finally reached full production, ending the Great Depression. Soon, labor shortages led to opportunities for women and African Americans to gain well-paying factory jobs for the first time. However, for both groups, the obstacles of sexism and racism accompanied the new employment opportunities.

Interactive Gallery: African Americans and World War II Project the African Americans During World War II Interactive Gallery and click on the six images and read the accompanying text. Discuss the information that is revealed. What was the Double Victory? *(victory over the Axis Powers abroad and discrimination at home)* How were opportunities and obstacles intertwined for African Americans during World War II? *(The opportunities were only available after overcoming obstacles, and the opportunities themselves included obstacles: for example, an opportunity for a job may include an obstacle of mistreatment of minorities.)*

The Home Front

INTERACTIVE GALLERY
African Americans and World War II

DIGITAL TEXT 4
Migration During World War II

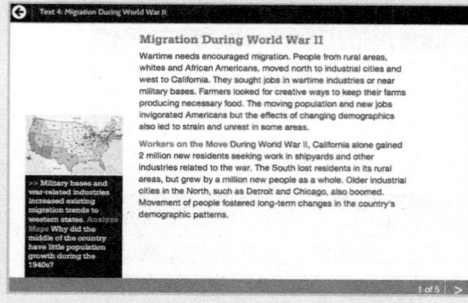

📷 ACTIVE CLASSROOM

Use the Quick Draw Strategy to have students reflect on the opportunities and obstacles African Americans encountered during World War II. Allow five minutes for students to create a visual image that represents those obstacles and opportunities. Ask students to share their drawings in pairs or small groups.

ELL Use the ELL activity described in the ELL chart.

Further Instruction

The wartime economy brought increased employment opportunities for women, including more job opportunities in better-paying positions. This led to a growing sentiment of independence, confidence, and satisfaction at contributing to the war effort. On the other hand, women faced obstacles, including lower pay for equal work and resentment from male workers.

Predict Consequences What do you predict will happen to the jobs filled by women and African Americans during World War II after the men in the service return home at the war's end? *(The jobs will go back to men returning from their stint in the armed forces.)*

Objective 4: Describe how World War II caused migration within the United States and the effects of that migration.

Quick Instruction

Tell students that during World War II, new job opportunities and other war-related factors caused millions of Americans to migrate within the United States. Most people moved from rural to urban environments to be near manufacturing facilities. The government also worked with Mexico to bring workers from Mexico north under the bracero program to work mainly on farms. Migration helped to fill labor needs. Unfortunately, migration had some negative effects, including tension between new and old residents that manifested in racism and riots.

Analyze Context Ask students to consider the culture and the mood of Americans as the war in Europe progressed. Tell them to keep in mind that Americans were experiencing rationing and shortages in goods, while worrying about their safety and the safety of those they loved who were fighting abroad. How do you think this context contributed to the effects of rural residents, African Americans, Mexicans, and women migrating to cities? *(People were already tense and feeling deprived and scared. At the time, women, African Americans, and other minorities did not have civil rights as they do today. The influx of minorities and women gave the frightened and tense urban residents a target for their negative feelings.)*

Further Instruction

Identify Cause and Effect Ask: What caused demographic patterns to change during World War II? *(New job opportunities in industry and near military bases were located in specific regions.)* Identify one effect of these changes. *(More people lived in cities; population shifted to northern cities and the south and west, particularly California; racial tensions grew in the community and in the workplace, leading to violence in some cases.)*

Predict Consequences What long-term effects would the U.S. government's decision to partner with Mexico have on labor trends in the coming years? *(The decision started a trend of migratory labor in the west that continued for decades.)*

Summarize What opportunities and obstacles existed for Mexicans and Mexican-Americans during World War II? *(The U.S. government initiated the Bracero program to encourage Mexicans to accept employment on American farms. However, racism still continued to challenge both Mexicans and Mexican-Americans.)*

SYNTHESIZE

DIGITAL ACTIVITY

Working for Victory on the World War II Home Front

Project the interactivity. Ask students to match each poster with its purpose. Connect all the posters with the idea that many Americans were contributing both directly and indirectly to the war effort.

Hypothesize Have students respond to the following questions: If you had been living on the home front during World War II, what do you think you would have done to contribute to the war effort? How would it have contributed to the war effort?

DEMONSTRATE

DIGITAL QUIZ

Lesson Quiz and Class Discussion Board

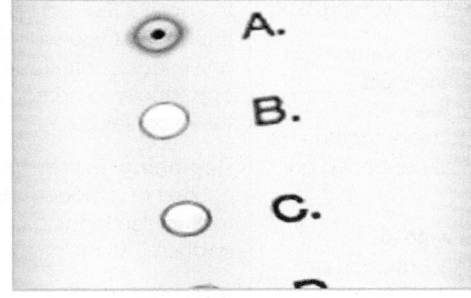

Assign the online Lesson Quiz for this lesson if you haven't already done so. Students will be offered automatic remediation or enrichment based on their score.

Pose these questions to the class on the Discussion Board:

In *The Home Front*, you read about constitutional issues raised by the internment of Japanese Americans during World War II. The Supreme Court upheld the practice of internment on the basis that "pressing public necessity may sometimes justify restrictions which curtail the civil rights of a single racial group." The Supreme Court shared the fear that people of Japanese ancestry would sympathize with Japan and endanger the security of the West Coast (where most Japanese Americans lived).

Evaluate Arguments Is it appropriate for the federal government to restrict the civil rights of U.S. citizens during times when the country is at war, such as during World War II? If so, what criteria should be used to determine when it is appropriate to restrict civil rights in the cause of national security?

Topic Inquiry
Have students continue their investigations for the Topic Inquiry.

The Allies Win World War II

Supporting English Language Learners

Use with Digital Text 2, **The Invasion of Normandy**.

Writing
Tell students that they will listen to your recap of the main events that set the stage for D-Day and those of D-Day itself. They will then have the opportunity to explain in specific detail the events of the day in writing.

Beginning Have students write down the following sentence frames: On June 6, 1944, the _____ landed on the beaches of Normandy. On _____ beaches, the Allies easily landed. At _____, the Germans were ready for the landing. Pair students with similar language abilities to work together to complete these sentences in order to explain in detail what happened on D-Day.

Intermediate Have students work with small groups to write an explanation of the plan that Eisenhower set up for the Allied invasion on D-Day. Tell students to include specific details about the trick the Allies used and their plans to land on the beaches.

Advanced Have students work with partners to write a brief paragraph that explains with specificity and detail what happened on D-Day. Remind students to include specific details, such as the date of the event, the names of the beaches, and the exact outcome. Allow students to review the text if needed.

Advanced High Have students work individually to write a brief paragraph that explains with specificity and detail what happened on D-Day. Remind students to include specific details, such as the date of the event, the names of the beaches, and the exact outcome. Allow students to review the text if needed.

Use with Digital Text 5, **The War Comes to an End**.

Listening
Discuss how an event can be interpreted and understood differently depending on when, how, or by whom it is considered. Then, summarize the events that led up to Truman's decision to drop the atomic bomb. Explain that you will share different interpretations of this event based on various contexts—both familiar and unfamiliar. Students will have the opportunity to demonstrate their understanding of important details in these contexts.

Beginning Explain Truman's decision to use the bomb in the familiar context of a modern American looking back. Have students demonstrate their understanding of important details by completing these frames with a partner: The main reason Truman dropped the bomb was _____.

Intermediate Explain Truman's decision to use the bomb in the context of a 1945 American news report. Divide students into groups and have them demonstrate their understanding by listing three important details they heard. Record groups' responses on a class list.

Advanced Explain the use of the atomic bomb by Truman in the context of an American student speaking in 1945. Have pairs of students discuss the important details of what you said.

Advanced High Explain the use of the atomic bomb by Truman in the unfamiliar context of a Japanese student speaking in 1945. Have pairs of students discuss the important details of what you said. Ask: How does the context change your understanding of the event?

▣ Differentiate Instruction

Use the Differentiated Instruction notes throughout the lesson plan to support the varied skill sets, levels of readiness, and interests in the mixed-ability classroom.

Challenge These notes include suggestions for expanding the activity for advanced students.

On-Level These notes include suggestions for modifying the activity to address different interests or learning styles.

Extra Support These notes include ideas for providing more scaffolding or reading spuport.

Special Needs These notes provide ideas for adapting instruction to support the needs of various special needs students.

◼ NOTES

PEARSON
realize™
www.PearsonRealize.com

Go online to access additional resources including:
Primary Sources • Biographies • Supreme Court cases •
21st Century Skill Tutorials • Maps • Graphic Organizers.

Objectives

Objective 1: Analyze the planning and impact of the invasion of Normandy.

Objective 2: Understand how the Allies achieved final victory in Europe.

Objective 3: Explore the reasons President Truman decided to use the atomic bomb against Japan.

LESSON 6 ORGANIZER		PACING: APPROX. 1 PERIOD, .5 BLOCKS			
		OBJECTIVES	PACING	RESOURCES Online	Print
Connect					
DIGITAL START UP ACTIVITY **June 6, 1944**			5 min.	●	
Investigate					
DIGITAL TEXT 1 **Planning Germany's Defeat**		Objective 1	10 min.	●	●
DIGITAL TEXT 2 **The Invasion of Normandy**		Objective 1	10 min.	●	●
INTERACTIVE GALLERY **D-Day**			10 min.	●	
DIGITAL TEXT 3 **Defeat of Germany**		Objective 2	10 min.	●	●
INTERACTIVE MAP **World War II in Europe, 1942–1945**			10 min.	●	
DIGITAL TEXT 4 **Americans Advance Toward Japan**			10 min.	●	●
INTERACTIVE MAP **World War II in the Pacific, 1942–1945**		Objective 3	10 min.	●	
DIGITAL TEXT 5 **The War Comes to an End**			10 min.	●	●
INTERACTIVE GALLERY **Hiroshima, Before and After**			10 min.	●	
Synthesize					
DIGITAL ACTIVITY **Final Turning Points**			5 min.	●	
Demonstrate					
DIGITAL QUIZ **Lesson Quiz and Class Discussion Board**			10 min.	●	

The Allies Win World War II

▮ CONNECT

DIGITAL START UP ACTIVITY
June 6, 1944

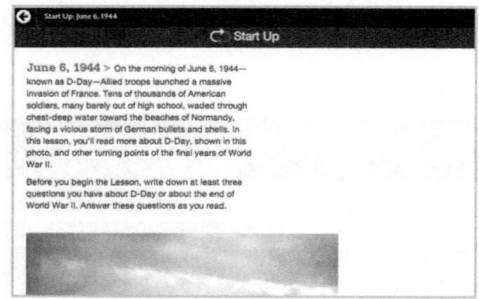

Project the Start Up Activity Ask students to study the image and write down their questions as they enter and get settled. List the questions on the board for the class to answer as you move through the lesson.

Discuss How do you think the Allied and Axis soldiers who fought on D-Day felt as they landed along the shores of Normandy? *(scared, anxious, determined, horrified)*

Tell students that in this lesson they will analyze major military events of World War II, including the invasion of Normandy and the U.S. military advancement through the Pacific islands. They will evaluate the contributions of significant leaders, including Omar Bradley, Dwight Eisenhower, and Douglas MacArthur, and explore the development and use of conventional and atomic weapons in the war.

Aa Vocabulary Development: Use the Interactive Reading Notepad to preview the Key Terms and Academic Vocabulary in this lesson with students.

⇅ FLIP IT!
Assign the Flipped Video for this lesson.

▮ STUDENT EDITION PRINT PAGES: 609–617

▮ INVESTIGATE

DIGITAL TEXT 1
Planning Germany's Defeat

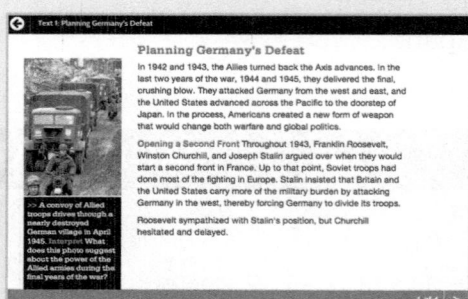

Objective 1: Analyze the planning and impact of the invasion of Normandy.

Quick Instruction
When the United States first entered the war, the Allies focused on fighting the European front in the North Atlantic and in North Africa. That left Stalin and the Soviet Union alone to fight Germany from the East. Stalin wanted Churchill and Roosevelt to open a western front of attack in France. This would add to the challenge of the war by introducing another front of combat. But multiple fronts would force Germany to divide its resources and possibly weaken its strength. Eventually, Roosevelt agreed that this was the best tactic and convinced Churchill. In this lesson, students will analyze the opening of that front in France—the invasion of Normandy, also known as "D-Day." They will also evaluate the military contributions of leaders such as George Marshall and Dwight Eisenhower.

Interactive Gallery: D-Day Project the gallery, and click through the icons. Call on students to read aloud the text. Based on the images, what two geographic advantages did German forces have during the invasion of Normandy? *(Germany held the high ground and had already built fortifications and mined the beaches.)* How did the Allies manage to overcome those advantages? Identify three non-geographic Allied advantages. *(numbers of soldiers, air support, and surprise)*

DIGITAL TEXT 2
The Invasion of Normandy

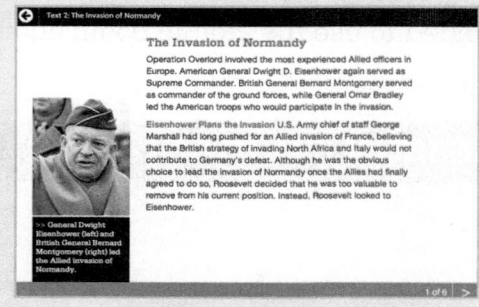

👥 ACTIVE CLASSROOM
Organize students into pairs. Have groups use the See-Think-Wonder Strategy to analyze the Interactive Gallery. Then, tell students to switch partners, and repeat the exercise. Call on volunteers to share their Wonder questions. List the questions on the board to revisit later.

ELL Use the ELL activity described in the ELL chart.

Further Instruction
Analyze Maps Project a map of Europe, preferably one from the topic. Highlight the eastern European front, where Soviet forces battled the Nazis, and the North African theater, where largely British Allied forces battled Axis forces, and the Italian front, where British and American troops fought the Axis. Point out that Hitler's armies occupied most of western Europe, including France and Belgium. Where were the Nazis not engaged in battle? *(western Europe)*

Make Predictions What would happen if the Axis powers suddenly had to confront the Allies on a western European front, too? *(Their troops, resources, and attention would be further divided.)*

Be sure that students understand that D-Day was a decisive turning point in the war in Europe. The Allies wanted to focus on stopping Hitler's armies and reclaiming Europe before turning more attention to the Pacific

INTERACTIVE GALLERY

D-Day

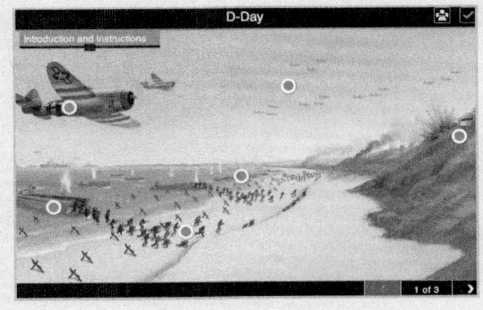

DIGITAL TEXT 3

Defeat of Germany

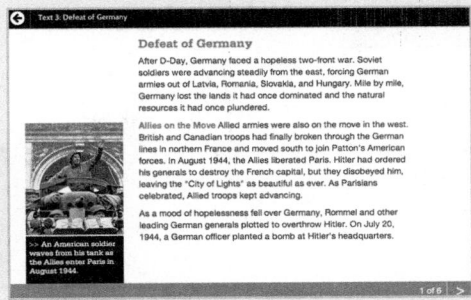

INTERACTIVE MAP

World War II in Europe, 1942–1945

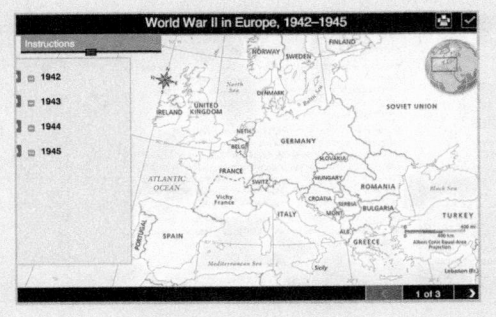

---

theater and Japan. The Nazis never recovered from the combined assaults from east, south, and west. In effect, they were forced to retreat to home ground until they were trapped.

Solve Problems What military contribution did General Eisenhower make to solve the problem of confronting the full might of Germany's western forces at Normandy? *(Eisenhower ordered a diversion to be created across the channel from Calais. Germany sent part of its forces to defend Calais, leaving Normandy less fortified.)*

Objective 2: Understand how the Allies achieved final victory in Europe.

Quick Instruction

Explain that this lesson examines how fighting the war on multiple fronts proved too much for the Nazis. Students will also learn about the contributions of American soldiers, including congressional Medal of Honor recipients.

Interactive Map: World War II in Europe, 1942–1945 Project the interactive map. Point out that Germany was engaged from three directions: east, south, and west. Allied forces from North Africa crossed the Mediterranean and stormed through Italy to merge with Allies on the western front. Where did the Allied forces from the eastern and western fronts meet? *(Berlin, Germany)* Why do you think Allied forces from North Africa crossed and came up through Italy? *(It was a short crossing and enabled Allied forces to defeat Italy's armies. Italy was still one of the Axis powers. Then, the Allies could meet up with the rest of their forces coming from France on the west and press on toward Germany.)*

⬛ ACTIVE CLASSROOM

Organize students into four to eight groups. Use the Closer Look Strategy by assigning each group one quadrant of the Interactive Map. Have groups describe what they observe and explain the significance of the information. Share group findings as a class.

Further Instruction

Transfer Information Have students transfer information from the Interactive Map to a timeline. Challenge partners to develop a sequence of events detailing the military advances that brought the Allies to Berlin. Direct students to add details to their timelines as they move through the Text. Display the completed timelines in the class or have students post them on a class blog.

Check Understanding Why did fighting the war on multiple fronts prove too much for Nazi forces? *(They had to divide their forces and resources, and they were forced to retreat, becoming boxed in by the combined Allied forces.)*

Determine Relevance Show students the chart of Selected Recipients of the Congressional Medal of Honor. Point out that Congressional Medal of Honor recipients include individuals of all races and genders. Ask students to discuss the importance of congressional Medal of Honor recipients during World War II. *(Medal of Honor recipients represent the valor, determination, and fortitude of U.S. soldiers. Their actions, as well as the actions of all soldiers, helped secure the Allied victory in World War II. They serve as a model and an inspiration to other members of the armed forces as well as to civilian citizens.)*

The Allies Win World War II

DIGITAL TEXT 4

Americans Advance Toward Japan

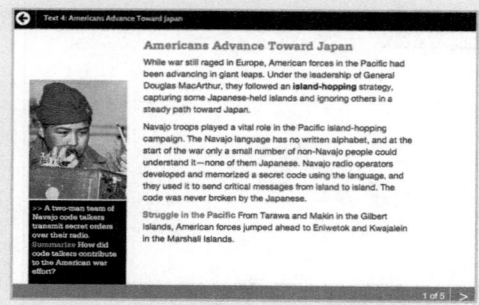

INTERACTIVE MAP

World War II in the Pacific, 1942–1945

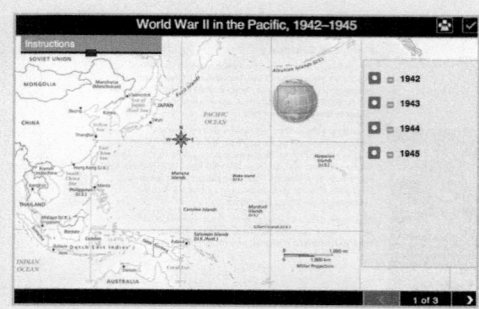

DIGITAL TEXT 5

The War Comes to an End

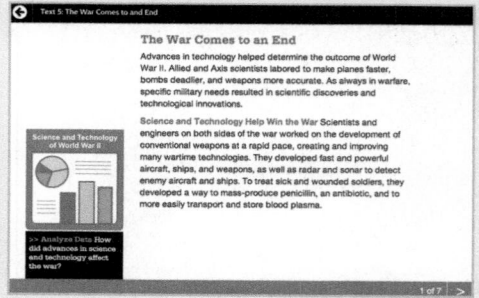

Objective 3: **Explore the reasons President Truman decided to use the atomic bomb against Japan.**

Quick Instruction

After Germany was defeated, the U.S. military turned its attention to advancement through the Pacific islands. The impact of technology on the war, including the development of conventional and atomic weapons, proved to be significant in Allied success. The Allies needed to win the war as quickly as possible in order to minimize loss of life. Scientific discoveries and technological innovation by scientists allowed them to do just that.

Interactive Map: World War II in the Pacific, 1942–1945 Project the Interactive Map, and call on students to identify key elements, such as shaded areas, arrows, and battles. Where were most of the battles in the Pacific fought? *(on small islands)*

Interactive Gallery: Hiroshima: Before and After Project the Interactive Gallery. Call on a student to read aloud the Introduction. Then, move the slider to show the impact of the atomic bomb. Why do you think the devastation caused by the atomic bomb persuaded Japan to surrender? *(The atomic weapon was unlike any weapon used before. It caused such immediate, widespread and total destruction that Japan must have feared that the entire nation would be destroyed. Japan could not hope to defend against such weaponry.)*

📹 ACTIVE CLASSROOM

Conduct a See-Think-Wonder Activity. Have students examine the interactive map and then respond to the following questions: What do you see? What does that make you think? What are you wondering about now that you've seen this? Share insights with the class.

📹 ACTIVE CLASSROOM

Instruct students to read aloud the statements from President Truman and the scientists. Conduct a poll in which students Take a Stand on whether Truman was right to authorize the use of the atomic weapons. Organize students into groups based on their responses, and ask each group to share their ideas with the class.

ELL Use the ELL activity described in the ELL chart.

Further Instruction

Explain How did the exceptional actions of the Navajo Code Talkers contribute to U.S. military advancements in the Pacific islands? *(The Navajo Code Talkers developed a code for communicating among U.S. forces scattered across the islands. The Japanese could not break the code, which enabled U.S. forces to communicate securely about their plans and strategies.)*

Draw Conclusions What strategy did General Douglas MacArthur employ for U.S. forces in the Pacific? Why do you think it worked? *(MacArthur employed an island-hopping strategy. U.S. forces moved from island to island. They captured and kept some to hold as bases, but kept moving toward Japan. I think this strategy worked because Americans did not get bogged down or stuck in any one place; however, they held onto enough islands to use as staging grounds for planes, resources, and other purposes. This enabled them to advance steadily toward Japan itself, with fall back and support closer than U.S. territories farther way.)*

Identify Central Issues How did atomic weapons end the war? Why did the issue of their use spur more debate than the use of conventional weapons? How did the decision to drop the bombs reflect Truman's leadership. *(The atomic bombs caused immediate destruction and loss of life, and Japan surrendered rather than face the threat of further atomic attacks. They were able not only to kill more people than other weapons on impact but also due to radiation exposure. Many people considered such power to be too dangerous, fearing that it would lead to the destruction of humanity itself. Truman understood the ethical issues, but he wanted to end the war quickly to save American lives.)*

SYNTHESIZE

■ DEMONSTRATE

INTERACTIVE GALLERY
Hiroshima, Before and After

DIGITAL ACTIVITY
Final Turning Points

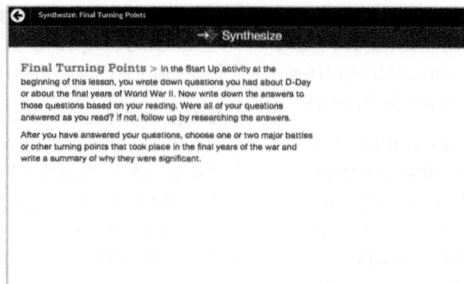

DIGITAL QUIZ
Lesson Quiz and Class Discussion Board

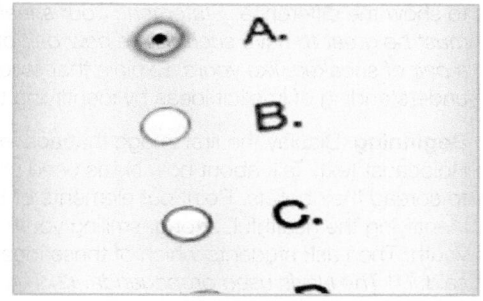

Tell students to review the questions that they wrote in the Start Up Activity. Have them answer the questions they can now that they have completed the lesson. If they cannot answer a question, challenge them to identify how they can find the answer. Encourage them to use approved resources to answer all of their questions. Invite volunteers to share their questions and answers or post the answers to class questions on a class blog.

Discuss What two turnings points in the final years of the war were most significant, and why? When students have finished discussing, direct them to complete the Synthesize activity by writing a summary about the significance of one of these events.

Assign the online Lesson Quiz for this lesson if you haven't already done so. Students will be offered automatic remediation or enrichment based on their score.

Pose these questions to the class on the Discussion Board:

In *The Allies Win World War II*, you learned how the Allies opened multiple fronts in Europe to defeat the Nazis and how the Americans won a decisive victory against Japan through the use of atomic weapons. You also learned not only about the exceptional contributions of individuals but also about the terrible cost of the war's conduct and end.

Make Predictions How do you think the war's end will affect the peace that follows? What would you expect to happen in the postwar period?

Make Decisions Did the United States have to use atomic weapons to win the war in the Pacific? Why or why not?

Topic Inquiry
Have students continue their investigations for the Topic Inquiry.

The Holocaust

Supporting English Language Learners

Use with Digital Text 1, **Roots of the Holocaust**.

Listening

Explain to students that implicit ideas are not directly stated. Instead, they are suggested or hinted at instead. Give students an everyday example to show the difference. *Statement: Your sneakers look so comfortable. It must be great to have such a nice new pair of shoes. Implicit idea: I want a pair of sneakers like yours.* Explain that students will demonstrate their understanding of implicit ideas by identifying them in spoken language.

Beginning Display the first image that accompanies the Roots of the Holocaust text. Talk about how Nazis used propaganda, or a campaign to spread their beliefs. Point out elements of the poster as you speak, identifying the healthful, strong, smiling youth that represented all Aryan youth. Then ask students which of these ideas was implicit in what you said: *(1) The Nazis used propaganda. (2) The Nazis knew how to use propaganda to influence people.*

Intermediate Explain Nazi propaganda using familiar and unfamiliar language. Have partners answer the following question to identify implicit ideas about Nazi propaganda: *How did the Nazis hope the comic books would affect children?*

Advanced Use somewhat complex language to explain how Jews sought refuge in various countries. Explain that the United States refused to help Jewish refugees on the *St. Louis.* Then ask pairs of students to discuss implicit ideas with this question: *What might this suggest about the United States?*

Advanced High Use a more complex spoken language to explain how Jews sought refuge in various countries. Then ask students to write an answer to this question: *What implicit ideas are related to some countries refusing to help Jewish refugees?* Provide time for partners to share their answers.

Use with Digital Text 2, **Hitler's "Final Solution"**.

Learning

Explain to students that they can use prior knowledge to understand meanings in English. Use the following activities to preview the reading **Hitler's "Final Solution"**. Ask students to write down the term *Final Solution,* and to think about where they have seen these words independently before.

Beginning Group students with similar language abilities. Display a T-chart with *Final* and *Solution* as column heads. Have each group copy the chart and record each of the following related ideas or terms in the correct column: *last, problem, answer, not able to be changed.* Help students understand that Hitler's "Final Solution" was to murder all the Jews, whom he considered a problem—an act that could not be undone.

Intermediate Display a T-chart with *Final* and *Solution* as column heads. Ask partners to use prior knowledge to think of words and phrases associated with each term, and record their responses in the appropriate column. Ask students to draw on their prior knowledge of the Nazis from earlier lessons to predict the meaning of Hitler's plan.

Advanced Call on student volunteers to define the words "final" and "solution." Then, have pairs of students discuss what they already know about Nazi treatment of Jews. Ask them to use knowledge from previous lessons as well as what they may have seen in movies and television shows about the Holocaust. Then ask pairs to volunteer their thoughts, and record their responses. Work as a class to develop the understanding that Hitler perceived Jews as a problem and genocide as the "Final Solution" to it.

Advanced High Ask students to write a prediction of what Hitler's "Final Solution" could be. Remind them to draw on what they have learned in previous lessons as well as what they may have seen in movies and television shows about the Holocaust. After student volunteers read aloud the text, ask them return to their predictions and discuss how their prior knowledge helped them understand what they read.

D Differentiate Instruction

Use the Differentiated Instruction notes throughout the lesson plan to support the varied skill sets, levels of readiness, and interests in the mixed-ability classroom.

Challenge These notes include suggestions for expanding the activity for advanced students.

On-Level These notes include suggestions for modifying the activity to address different interests or learning styles.

Extra Support These notes include ideas for providing more scaffolding or reading spuport.

Special Needs These notes provide ideas for adapting instruction to support the needs of various special needs students.

■ NOTES

PEARSON realize™
www.PearsonRealize.com

Go online to access additional resources including:
Primary Sources • Biographies • Supreme Court cases •
21st Century Skill Tutorials • Maps • Graphic Organizers.

Objectives

Objective 1: Trace the roots and progress of Hitler's campaign against the Jews.

Objective 2: Explain the goals of Hitler's "final solution" and the nature of Nazi death camps.

Objective 3: Examine how the United States responded to the Holocaust.

LESSON 7 ORGANIZER		OBJECTIVES	PACING	RESOURCES	
				Online	Print
Connect					
DIGITAL START UP ACTIVITY **Report from Buchenwald**			5 min.	●	
Investigate					
DIGITAL TEXT 1 **Roots of the Holocaust**		Objective 1	10 min.	●	●
DIGITAL TEXT 2 **Hitler's "Final Solution"**			10 min.	●	●
INTERACTIVE GALLERY **Inside a Nazi Concentration Camp**		Objective 2	10 min.	●	
INTERACTIVE CHART **Jewish Populations in Europe, 1933–1950**			10 min.	●	
DIGITAL TEXT 3 **Allied Response to the Holocaust**		Objective 3	10 min.	●	●
Synthesize					
DIGITAL ACTIVITY **Preventing Another Holocaust**			5 min.	●	
Demonstrate					
DIGITAL QUIZ **Lesson Quiz and Class Discussion Board**			10 min.	●	

PACING: APPROX. 1 PERIOD, .5 BLOCKS

Topic ⑭ Lesson 7

The Holocaust

■ CONNECT

DIGITAL START UP ACTIVITY
Report from Buchenwald

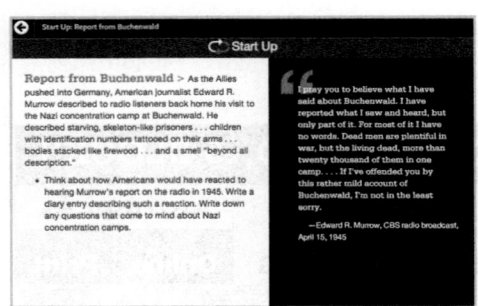

Project the Start Up Activity Tell students to read and respond to the activity as they get settled. Remind them to record questions they have about Nazi concentration camps. When students have completed the Start Up Activity, invite volunteers to share their responses. List questions on the whiteboard or the class blog to revisit as you move through the lesson.

Discuss If you were a high school student listening to Ed Murrow's report in 1945, how would it have made you feel? What might you have done in response to his report?

Tell students that in this lesson they will investigate and analyze the Holocaust and the liberation of the concentration camps.

Aa Vocabulary Development: Use the Interactive Reading Notepad to preview the Key Terms and Academic Vocabulary in this lesson with students.

> ### 🔁 FLIP IT!
> Assign the Flipped Video for this lesson.

■ STUDENT EDITION PRINT PAGES: 618–623

■ INVESTIGATE

DIGITAL TEXT 1
Roots of the Holocaust

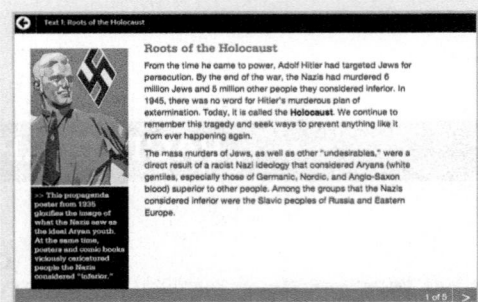

Objective 1: Trace the roots and progress of Hitler's campaign against the Jews.

Quick Instruction

Adolf Hitler rose to power in the 1930s by taking advantage of many Germans' anger regarding reparations from World War I and the subsequent economic challenges. Hitler was a powerful, persuasive speaker who rallied people to the Nazi cause. During this time, he also targeted Jewish people and others he saw as "undesirable" as responsible for the hardships in Germany. Again, he channeled German anger and fear to build a mighty political and military force. Hitler's attack on Jews was another way of spreading Nazi dominance across the continent and reshaping European life. Tell students that this lesson will analyze the events leading up to and culminating in the Holocaust.

Analyze Images Project the propaganda poster from 1935. Ask volunteers to describe what they see in the poster. What feelings do you think it was meant to instill in the German people? *(It was likely meant to convince Germans of their superiority, strength, and happiness as "ideal" Aryans.)* How might the Nazis have used posters such as this to garner support for policies that led to the Holocaust? *(By making the Aryan youth so attractive, it convinced others to join the Nazi party by implying that the same would be true of them.)*

D Differentiate: On Level Explain that *Holocaust* comes from a Greek word meaning "thing wholly burnt." In Hebrew, Jews referred to the events of the Holocaust as *Shoah,* meaning "catastrophe." The term *Holocaust* was coined in the 1950, to describe the Nazi genocide of the Jews and other peoples. Ask students to write a

short response to the following question: Why was *Holocaust* an apt name for these events? *(The Holocaust resulted in the deaths of millions of people and imprisonment of millions more. The Nazis destroyed property and nearly destroyed an entire group of people.)*

ELL Use the ELL activity described in the ELL chart.

Further Instruction

Interactive Reading Notepad Project the Interactive Reading Notepad questions, including the graphic organizer. Instruct students to answer the questions as they move through the texts. Have them review their responses and complete the graphic organizer in small groups.

Analyze Information Project "A Timeline of Discrimination." Be sure that students understand that Hitler's anti-Semitic policies evolved over a long period of time. How much time passed between the first anti-Semitics laws and the laws requiring Jews to wear yellow stars? *(eight years)* Remind students that all these events happened as Hitler pressed his military advantage across Europe, invading Czechoslovakia, Poland, Denmark, Norway, France, and other nations.

Analyze Context How did Hitler and the Nazis pursue policies against the Jews that would lead to the Holocaust? What historical, economic and cultural factors made the Holocaust possible? *(Hitler and the Nazis pursued their anti-Semitic policies over a long period of time. Their policies began as economic and then unfolded as social and political. They took advantage of economic hardships resulting from World War I, as well as cultural differences that made it easier to*

DIGITAL TEXT 2

Hitler's "Final Solution"

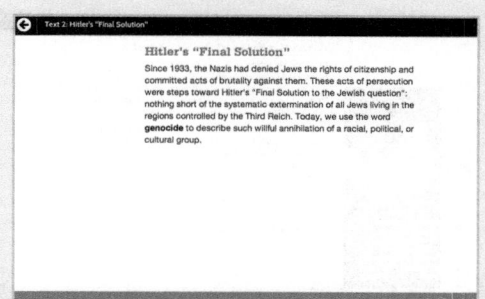

INTERACTIVE GALLERY

Inside a Nazi Concentration Camp

target specific groups, like the Jews. They also pursued their policies while building military power and pursuing political and military dominance in Europe. These factors worked together to enable Hitler and the Nazis to persecute the Jews with little interference, especially as most other nations were more concerned about containing German military might.)

Objective 2: Explore the goals of Hitler's "final solution" and the nature of Nazi death camps.

Quick Instruction

The Holocaust began as escalating anti-Semitic policies, including the forced relocation of Jews to concentration camps, and ended with the murder of about six million of Jews and five million others. These camps served as labor camps and prisons, meant to contain and exploit Jews and other people the Nazis deemed "undesirable." Tell students that in this lesson, they will analyze major issues of World War II, including Hitler's "Final Solution," or the Holocaust, and will examine the role of Allied liberators in documenting the genocide.

Note: The narrative and images in this lesson may prove difficult for some of your students. You may wish to prepare your students in advance for the upsetting nature of some of the content. Be especially sensitive to students who may belong to groups that were targeted by the Nazis. Do not single them out, but if any of them expresses a personal reaction, be prepared to discuss the issue in a forthright, supportive manner.

Interactive Gallery: Inside a Nazi Concentration Camp Prepare students by explaining that the images they will see are disturbing. Then, project the Interactive Gallery, and guide students through the slides. Prompt students to discuss how does each image represents the horror of the Holocaust and why it was significant that Allied forces captured these images during the liberation of the camps.

Interactive Chart: Jewish Populations in Europe 1933–1950 Project the Interactive Gallery, and guide students through the layers in the graph. Discuss the change in Jewish populations in Europe from the 1930s to 1950 and how that change relates to the Holocaust.

👥 ACTIVE CLASSROOM

Tell students to use the Sticky Note Strategy to respond to the images in the Interactive Gallery. Each student should select one image to analyze. Have students post and review their Sticky Notes.

ELL Use the ELL activity described in the ELL chart.

Further Instruction

Analyze Maps Project the map of concentration and death camps from the beginning of the Text. Point out the differences in locations, and call on students to answer the Analyze Maps question. Then, challenge students to preview the Text by finding and recording definitions for *concentration camp* and *death camp*. Post these words to the class Word Wall.

Determine Relevance Why does it matter that the Nazis erected concentration camps years before they launched the Final Solution and built death camps? *(People, including those in other nations, might have reacted more quickly had the Nazis started building death camps right away. The Nazis were able to build their power and work toward the Final Solution by first segregating Jews and other*

The Holocaust

INTERACTIVE CHART
Jewish Populations in Europe, 1933–1950

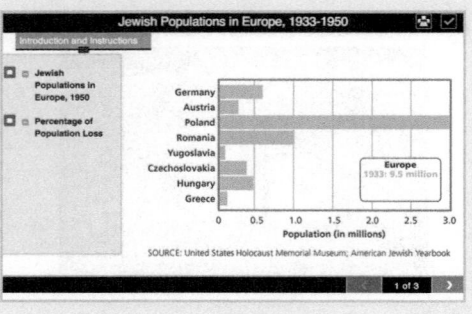

DIGITAL TEXT 3
Allied Response to the Holocaust

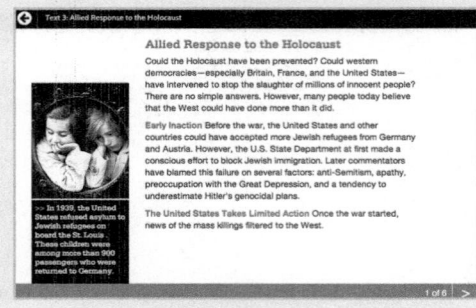

peoples in concentration camps, using them for labor, and confiscating their property and wealth.)

Infer Almost every war results in civilian casualties. What makes the Holocaust different from, for example, the bombing of London or the siege of Stalingrad? *(Civilian casualties are usually part of a larger military objective, such as the conquest of Britain or the Soviet Union. The Holocaust was a deliberate, well-planned attempt to wipe out a group of people. Hitler's campaign against the Jews began before World War II and did not help Hitler achieve his war objectives.)*

Objective 3: **Examine how the United States responded to the Holocaust.**

Quick Instruction
Explain that in this lesson, students will explore the response of the United States and other Allies to the Holocaust. They will take a closer look at the Allied liberation of the concentration and death camps. Finally, they will assess how the Holocaust impacted U.S. involvement in the Middle East, including the continued support for Israel.

Analyze Information Ask students to consider the issue of Jewish refugees. Why was there early inaction on this issue? *(anti-Semitism, apathy, preoccupation with the Great Depression, underestimating Hitler's genocidal plans.)* How was FDR's domestic and international leadership important in taking concrete steps to address this issue? *(He established the War Refugee Board, a government agency that worked with the Red Cross to save thousands of Eastern European Jews.)*

Analyze Information Why was the liberation of the concentration camps an important turning point in World War II? *(Only with the reports from the liberation of the concentration camps did Allied troops and Americans understand the scope of the Holocaust.)*

Further Instruction
Explain that Britain established rule over Palestine following World War I. Many Jews in Europe began emigrating to the land at that time. However, during and after World War II, immigration increased dramatically. Britain

tried to slow this immigration, which led to conflict among British and Jewish forces in Palestine. Meanwhile, calls for independent Jewish nation, Israel, increased. Tell students that they will learn about President Harry Truman's leadership in recognizing the new nation of Israel and U.S. involvement in the Middle East in supporting Israel.

Identify Cause and Effect Why do you think the revelation of the Holocaust led to increased U.S. support for Israel? *(Many Americans felt that Jews might be subject to future persecution if they did not have an independent homeland. Support for Israel might be seen as a way of preventing another Holocaust.)*

SYNTHESIZE

DIGITAL ACTIVITY
Preventing Another Holocaust

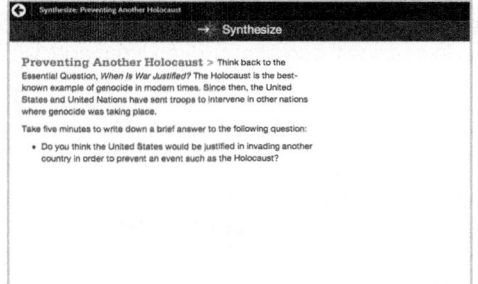

Ask students to recall the Topic Essential Question, "When Is War Justified?" Have them Quick Write in answer to the question in the Synthesize activity. Tell them to take five minutes to write down their ideas. Then, use the Take a Stand Strategy to organize students into groups based on their initial responses. Have students share their writings in their groups and decide on the best defense of their position to share with the class.

Challenge students to analyze the causes of the Holocaust. Have them list reasons that the Holocaust was able to happen as it did. Record students' ideas on the whiteboard.

Discuss Ask students whether another genocide such as the Holocaust could happen in the world today. Why or why not? *(Point out that other genocides have occurred in the Balkans, in Rwanda, and in Darfur in the recent decades, though the number of lives lost were fewer than in the Holocaust.)* What steps can be taken at the local, national, and international level to defend against, or prevent, future genocides?

DEMONSTRATE

DIGITAL QUIZ
Lesson Quiz and Class Discussion Board

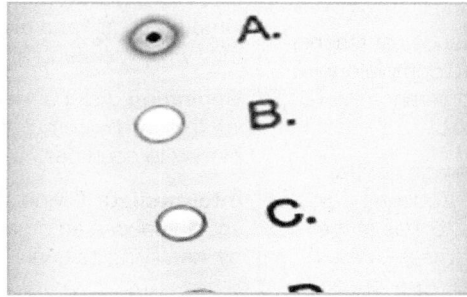

Assign the online Lesson Quiz for this lesson if you haven't already done so. Students will be offered automatic remediation or enrichment based on their score.

In *The Holocaust*, you read about events that led up to the Holocaust, the horrors of Holocaust, and the Allied liberation of Nazi concentration and death camps. You learned about the domestic and international leadership of President Franklin D. Roosevelt during this period and President Harry S. Truman's recognition and support of Israel.

Pose this question to the class on the Discussion Board:

Make Decisions Do you think it is important for students in the United States to learn about the events of the Holocaust? What about students in other parts of the world? Explain your reasoning.

Topic Inquiry
Have students continue their investigations for the Topic Inquiry.

Impact of World War II

Supporting English Language Learners

Use with Digital Text 1, **Planning the Postwar World**.

Learning
Reread or summarize the first paragraph of the section The Yalta Conference. Explain that students will use prior experiences to better understand the meaning of conference.

Beginning Ask students to think about their prior experiences at teacher-student conferences. Have students work with partners to complete this sentence frame: People _____ ideas and opinions at a conference. Have partners take turns reading their completed sentence aloud.

Intermediate Divide students into pairs with similar language abilities. Have students share their prior experiences with teacher-student conferences. Ask these questions to guide discussion: Who was at the conference? What did you talk about? What plan did you make? When pairs have answered these questions about their personal experiences, have them answer the same questions about the Yalta Conference.

Advanced Have pairs of students discuss their prior experiences participating in a teacher-student conference. Then have them complete a Venn diagram that compares and contrasts the events and participants in the teacher-student conference and the Yalta Conference.

Advanced High Have students think about their prior experiences participating in teacher-student conferences. Then have them write a sentence explaining how this experience helps them understand what happened at the Yalta Conference.

Use with Digital Text 3, **International Organizations and Treaties**.

Listening
Recall with students that after World War II, the world economy was in need of support and reorganization. Discuss with students why these changes were needed. Display the chart "International Economic Organizations," and explain its content. Tell students that as they progress they will understand information in increasingly complex spoken language.

Beginning Ask partners to demonstrate their understanding of information by completing this sentence frame: _____ and _____ lend money to countries.

Intermediate Divide students into groups of three. Each group member should choose an organization/agreement and demonstrate understanding by identifying its goal.

Advanced Explain the World Bank in greater detail than is found in the chart "International Economic Organizations." Ask pairs of students to demonstrate their understanding by listing as much information as they can remember from what you said.

Advanced High Explain the World Bank and IMF in greater detail. Then, ask pairs of students to demonstrate their understanding of what you said by comparing and contrasting information about the two organizations.

▣ Differentiate Instruction

Use the Differentiated Instruction notes throughout the lesson plan to support the varied skill sets, levels of readiness, and interests in the mixed-ability classroom.

Challenge These notes include suggestions for expanding the activity for advanced students.

On-Level These notes include suggestions for modifying the activity to address different interests or learning styles.

Extra Support These notes include ideas for providing more scaffolding or reading spuport.

Special Needs These notes provide ideas for adapting instruction to support the needs of various special needs students.

■ NOTES

PEARSON
realize™
www.PearsonRealize.com

Go online to access additional resources including:
Primary Sources • Biographies • Supreme Court cases •
21st Century Skill Tutorials • Maps • Graphic Organizers.

Objectives

Objective 1: Evaluate the goals that Allied leaders set for the postwar world.

Objective 2: Describe the steps that United States and other nations took toward international cooperation.

Objective 3: Explain the impact of World War II on the postwar United States.

LESSON 8 ORGANIZER		PACING: APPROX. 1 PERIOD, .5 BLOCKS		
	OBJECTIVES	PACING	**RESOURCES**	
			Online	Print
Connect				
DIGITAL START UP ACTIVITY **Plans for a Postwar World**		5 min.	●	
Investigate				
DIGITAL TEXT 1 **Planning the Postwar World**		10 min.	●	●
DIGITAL TEXT 2 **International Impact of the War**	Objective 1	10 min.	●	●
INTERACTIVE MAP **Europe in 1942 and 1950**		10 min.	●	
DIGITAL TEXT 3 **International Organizations and Treaties**	Objective 2	10 min.	●	●
INTERACTIVE GALLERY **The Nuremberg Trials: What Is a War Crime?**		10 min.	●	
DIGITAL TEXT 4 **The Domestic Impact of the War**	Objective 3	10 min.	●	●
INTERACTIVE GALLERY **World War II and the U.S. Economy**		10 min.	●	
Synthesize				
DIGITAL ACTIVITY **Postwar Plans Revisited**		5 min.	●	
Demonstrate				
DIGITAL QUIZ **Lesson Quiz and Class Discussion Board**		10 min.	●	

■ CONNECT

DIGITAL START UP ACTIVITY
Plans for a Postwar World

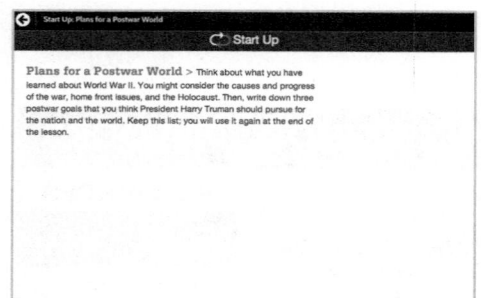

Project the Start Up Activity Tell students to complete the activity and make their lists as they enter and get settled.

Discuss Why did the United States enter World War II? *(to respond to the attack on Pearl Harbor and to stop Japanese and Nazi aggression)* What were U.S. leaders' concerns at the end of World War II? *(preventing Nazi Germany and Japan from conducting military invasions and inciting future wars.)*

Tell students they will evaluate the international leadership of President Harry Truman and explore various outcomes of the war in the United States and abroad.

Aa Vocabulary Development: Use the Interactive Reading Notepad to preview the Key Terms and Academic Vocabulary in this lesson with students.

↻ FLIP IT!

Assign the Flipped Video for this lesson.

■ STUDENT EDITION PRINT
PAGES: 624–630

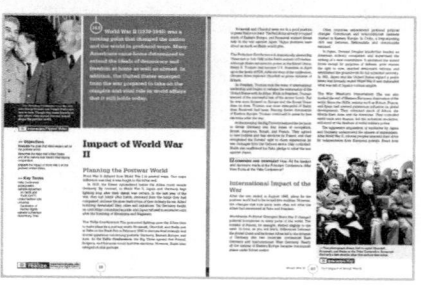

■ INVESTIGATE

DIGITAL TEXT 1
Planning the Postwar World

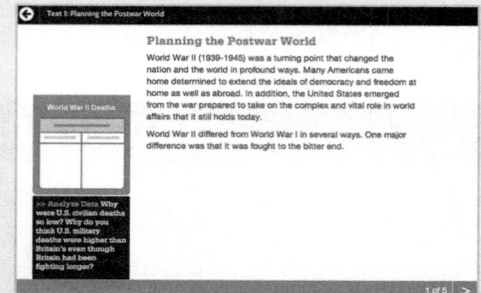

DIGITAL TEXT 2
International Impact of the War

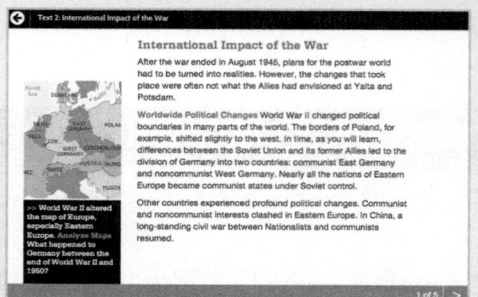

Objective 1: Evaluate the goals that Allied leaders set for the postwar world.

Quick Instruction
As World War II drew to an end, Germany and Japan refused to surrender despite definitive losses. The Allied Leaders, namely Stalin, Churchill, and Roosevelt, had the opportunity, as they drove the Germans out of occupied territory, to make plans for the postwar world. The first plans were made at the Yalta and Potsdam Conferences. Tell students that they will learn how the end of the conflict resulted in changes in political boundaries and how the Allies concluded the war through participation in international treaties. Remind them that World War II marked a turning point in international relations. No longer were Germany, France, and Britain among the great powers. Now only two "superpowers" remained—the United States and the Soviet Union.

Interactive Map: Europe in 1942 and 1950 Project the interactive map. Call on a student to read the introductory text. Then, demonstrate how to slide the screen from one map to the other. Answer the multiple choice questions as a class. Point out major changes in boundaries, including how Germany had been split into two countries.

Analyze Information Why was the end of World War II a turning point in international relations? *(After the war, the United States and the Soviet Union emerged as world superpowers. They dominated international relations, reshaping how nations around the world interacted and dealt with one another. Britain, France, and other European nations*

lost their empires and their global dominance. The Soviet Union and Soviet communism would come to dominate Eastern Europe. The conclusion of the war reworked the map of Europe, as well as of large parts of Africa and Asia.)

📹 ACTIVE CLASSROOM

Organize students into groups, and have them use the Plus/Minus/Interesting Strategy to evaluate the outcomes of the war's end. Then, call on groups to share their ideas. Record group PMIs in a class chart on the board.

ELL Use the ELL activity described in the ELL chart.

Further Instruction
Europe, including European Russia, suffered devastating losses of life, property, and productivity as a result of the war. So, too, did Japan. The United States lost many soldiers but came away from the war in a stronger position economically and politically than it had been in prior to the war. The country also had a new leader, President Harry Truman. He would have the opportunity to exercise international leadership as World War II came to an end and he developed relationships with various allies.

Analyze Charts To make the loss of life, and the differences between countries more real to students, ask them to review the chart about military and civilian deaths and pose and answer questions to one another about the geographical distributions and patterns shown

INTERACTIVE MAP

Europe in 1942 and 1950

DIGITAL TEXT 3

International Organizations and Treaties

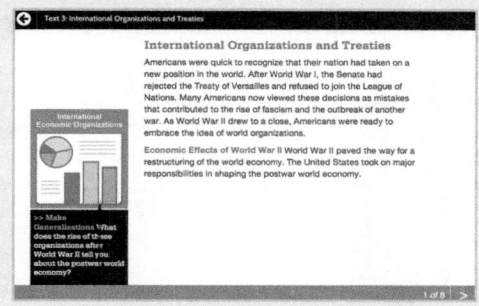

INTERACTIVE GALLERY

The Nuremberg Trials: What Is a War Crime?

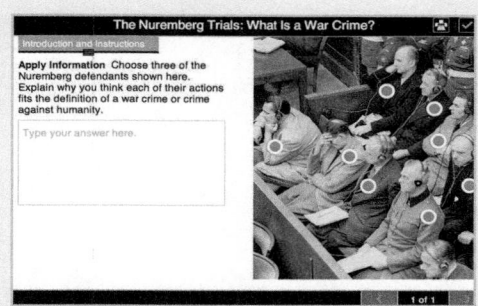

there among combatant countries and how those patterns might affect the postwar world. *(The Soviet Union suffered the most deaths, which Germany, China, and Japan coming next. The Soviet Union, as the victorious Ally who had lost the most people during the war, might feel like they were entitled to more of a say in the postwar negotiations)*

Cite Evidence President Truman showed effective international leadership at the Potsdam Conference and following the war. Do you agree or disagree with this statement? Evaluate Truman's leadership role, and cite evidence to support your position. Be sure to consider how Truman handled the U.S. relationship with its allies, especially the Soviet Union. *(Yes, I think Truman showed effective leadership. He led negotiations at Potsdam that resulted in zones of occupation in Germany and ensured Stalin would help fight Japan. No, I think Truman could have done more to ensure that the Soviet Union would not make Eastern Europe communist satellites.)*

Explain Why did so many political boundaries change as a result of World War II? *(The war weakened imperial powers like France and Britain, allowing many lands in Asia and Africa to break from colonial rule. In Europe, Germany had conquered many lands, but was now itself occupied. The Allies agreed to treaties that redrew many political boundaries there.)*

Objective 2: Describe the steps that United States and other nations took toward international cooperation.

Quick Instruction

The Allies had won the war, and the United States and the Soviet Union had emerged as superpowers. The scale and the costs of World War II were staggering. As a result, the United States played a key role in the development of global organizations and international trade policies following World War II. The Allies were determined to help prevent such global conflict from happening again. Tell students that this lesson examines the participation of the United States in international treaties and organizations, such as the United Nations.

Interactive Gallery: The Nuremberg Trials: What Is a War Crime? Project the interactive gallery. Click through the icons on the defendants. Announce each name and position as you go, and call on students to read aloud the charges and the sentences.

Categorize International treaties and global organizations serve a variety of purposes, including political, social or humanitarian, and economic. List organizations and treaties established after World War II, and describe the purpose of each. (Some may have more than one.) *(The IMF, the World Bank, and GATT each served an economic purpose. The IMF and the World Bank also served humanitarian purposes. The United Nations served mainly political and humanitarian purposes though its focus on peaceful cooperation also supported*

economic purposes such as global trade. The Nuremberg Trials served a mainly political purpose but also had social importance.)

ACTIVE CLASSROOM

Instruct students to use the Rank It Strategy to complete the Apply Information activity in the Interactive Gallery. Tell them to rank each defendant's crimes, in order of severity. Have them complete the activity individually and then share and discuss their responses in small groups. Call on each group to report on their three worst offenders, and to explain their reasoning.

ELL Use the ELL activity described in the ELL chart.

Further Instruction

Analyze Context What are the pros and cons of U.S. participation in international treaties? How might treaties undermine U.S. sovereignty? Why was the United States more inclined to participate in global organizations and international treaties following World War II than after World War I? *(One disadvantage of participation in international bodies is that they may undermine U.S. sovereignty by asking the U.S. government to obey international law. One advantage of participating in treaties and international organizations is the opportunity to shape global events in ways that work in the nation's favor. After World War I, the Senate had rejected the Treaty of Versailles and the League of Nations, which may have contributed to the rise of fascism and the outbreak of another war. The United States was in a much stronger position following*

Impact of World War II

The Domestic Impact of the War

World War II and the U.S. Economy

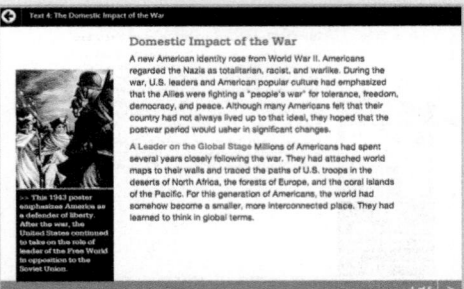

World War II and could play a leading role in shaping global organizations and international treaties.)

Summarize How did the U.S. support Israel after World War II? *(The United States supported international agreements, such as the Geneva Conventions, which was the legal basis for the Nuremberg Trials. The United States also participated in international organizations such as the United Nations, supporting the creation of Israel in 1947.)*

Draw Conclusions What contributions did Eleanor Roosevelt make to the postwar world? How might these contributions have political, social, and economic importance for American society? *(Eleanor Roosevelt, the former First Lady, served as the nation's first ambassador to the United Nations. She became chair of the Commission on Human Rights, and helped draft the Universal Declaration of Human Rights. She became an important international political figure, and the efforts of the UN helped promote global stability. More stability benefited American society through trade, which helped the U.S. economy. It also reinforced American pride and ideals.)*

Objective 3: **Explain the impact of World War II on the postwar United States.**

Quick Instruction

As a result of World War II, Americans began to see the world from a global perspective. They realized that the United States played an important role in the global community and was poised to take a leadership role. This was one of the many ways that World War II was a turning point for the United States. In addition, the war had ended the Great Depression and brought important economic advances to U.S. citizens. As a result of international trade policies and the U.S. free enterprise system, the economy of postwar America boomed.

Interactive Gallery: World War II and the U.S. Economy Project the Interactive Gallery. Click through the slideshow, and call on students to read the captions.

Connect How did U.S. participation in GATT support the nation's free enterprise system? *(GATT reduced tariffs to encourage global trade in which American businesses, grounded in a free enterprise system, could flourish.)*

🖳 ACTIVE CLASSROOM

Pause on the third image in the Interactive Gallery. Ask students to consider how life in the United States might have been different had this been an American city. Tell students to Quick Write how they think the United States and its citizens might have conducted themselves differently after World War II had there been large-scale destruction on U.S. soil. Share students' responses on the class blog.

D **Differentiate: Extra Support** Highlight key points on the unemployment graph, and demonstrate how students can follow the *x* and *y* axes to read the numbers. Connect the information in the graph to specific events such as the Great Depression and World War II.

Further Instruction

Synthesize Why was World War II a turning point for African Americans who hoped to win equality in civil rights? *(Many African Americans served and fought in the war and worked in the war industries to support the war effort, which many believed strengthened the case for equal civil rights. Also, Presidents Roosevelt and Truman had issued Executive Orders barring discrimination in military service and government industries.)*

Explain How did the expansion of presidential power during World War II raise a constitutional issue that would lead to future debate? *(The crisis of World War II resulted in Congress granting expanded powers to the executive branch under the War Powers Act. Both Presidents Roosevelt and Truman made use of these powers, issuing Executive Orders that exceeded the traditional roles of the President. Some worry that greater executive power threatens the separation of powers and checks and balances enshrined in the Constitution.)*

■ SYNTHESIZE

DIGITAL ACTIVITY

Postwar Plans Revisited

Begin by having students revisit the lists that made during the Start Up Activity. Tell students to identify items on their lists that match up with actions taken by President Truman following World War II. Call on students to share their matches and to explain why Truman likely made the choices that he did. What was the motivating reason or the goal behind this action?

Next, ask students to recall the Topic Essential Question: When is war justified? Invite students to recall the valid reasons they selected in the Essential Question activity at the start of the topic. Organize students into small groups to share those reasons and to discuss whether any of those reasons applied to U.S. conduct in World War II. Call on groups to share their ideas.

Discuss Was U.S. involvement in World War II justified? Use the Take a Stand strategy to organize the class into groups based on their responses. If most of the class answers one way, then you may still wish to organize students into smaller groups. Have groups discuss the reasons for their position. Then, instruct each group to select a spokesperson to share their reasons with the class or record them on the class blog.

■ DEMONSTRATE

DIGITAL QUIZ

Lesson Quiz and Class Discussion Board

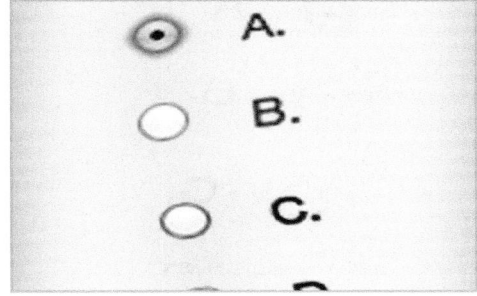

Assign the online Lesson Quiz for this lesson if you haven't already done so. Students will be offered automatic remediation or enrichment based on their score.

Pose these questions to the class on the Discussion Board:

In *Impact of World War II*, you learned that the United States emerged as a global superpower, with tremendous economic and political influence. With the other Allies, the nation defined the post-war boundaries of many countries. The United States also engaged in international treaty-making and helped shape global organizations like the United Nations that remain influential today.

Analyze Context What about the conditions of World War II and the conduct of the war made it possible for the United States and the Soviet Union to become superpowers?

Hypothesize Had President Truman not authorized the use of atomic weapons, or had scientists not invented atomic weapons, how do you think the war would have ended? In what ways do you think the postwar world would have been different?

Topic Inquiry

Have students continue their investigations for the Topic Inquiry.

World War II

■ SYNTHESIZE

DIGITAL ACTIVITY
Reflect on the Essential Question and Topic

First ask students to reconsider the Essential Question for the topic: When Is War Justified? Project the reasons that students considered at the start of the topic:

- to defend U.S. territory and people
- to fulfill obligations to allies
- to gain territory or resources
- to stand up for an idea

Ask students whether they would add any other ideas to the list. Call on volunteers to share their ideas. Then, tell students to consider whether their responses to the polls would change now.

Pose this question: *Do you think the United States was justified in entering World War II?* Challenge students to Quick Write a response, providing at least three reasons to support their positions. Then, direct students to share their responses in small groups or post their responses on the Class Discussion Board.

Next, ask students to reflect on the topic as a whole, and to jot down two or three questions that have arisen during the topic. Share these examples, if students need help getting started:

- How do the patriotic actions of people during World War II compare to peoples' patriotic expressions of support for the nation or armed forces today?
- What happens when the United States is attacked on its own soil?
- What motivates someone to enlist in the armed forces?
- What are the human costs of war?

Ask students to share their questions and answers on the Class Discussion Board.

Topic Inquiry
Have students complete Step 3 of the Topic Inquiry.

■ DEMONSTRATE

DIGITAL TOPIC REVIEW AND ASSESSMENT
World War II

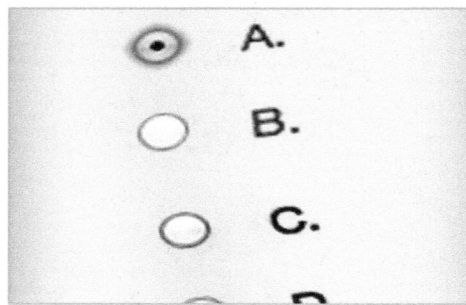

Students can prepare for the Topic Test by answering the questions in the Topic Review and Assessment online or the Assessment questions in the Print Student text. They can also prepare by reviewing their answers to the Interactive Reading Notepad questions or reviewing their notes in the Reading and Notetaking Study Guide.

DIGITAL TOPIC TEST
World War II

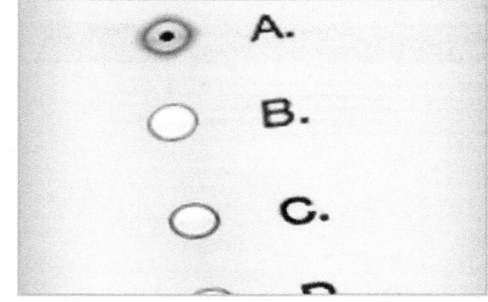

TOPIC TEST
Assign the Topic Test to assess students' understanding of topic content.

BENCHMARK TESTS
Assign these benchmark tests as you complete the relevant topics to monitor student progress toward mastering the course content and as preparation for the End-of-Course Test.

Benchmark Test 1: Topics 1–3
Benchmark Test 2: Topics 4–6
Benchmark Test 3: Topics 7–9
Benchmark Test 4: Topics 10–12
Benchmark Test 5: Topics 13–15
Benchmark Test 6: Topics 16–18
Benchmark Test 7: Topics 19–20

Postwar America

TOPIC 15 ORGANIZER	PACING: APPROX. 10 PERIODS, 5 BLOCKS	
		PACING
Connect		1 period
MY STORY VIDEO **Margaret Chase Smith, A Declaration of Conscience**		10 min.
DIGITAL ESSENTIAL QUESTION ACTIVITY **What is America's Role in the World?**		10 min.
DIGITAL OVERVIEW ACTIVITY **Duck and Cover Drills**		10 min.
TOPIC INQUIRY: DOCUMENT-BASED QUESTION **McCarthyism in the 1950s**		20 min.
Investigate		3–7 periods
TOPIC INQUIRY: DOCUMENT-BASED QUESTION **McCarthyism in the 1950s**		Ongoing
LESSON 1 The Beginning of the Cold War		30–40 min.
LESSON 2 The Korean War		30–40 min.
LESSON 3 The Cold War Intensifies		30–40 min.
LESSON 4 Cold War Fears at Home		30–40 min.
LESSON 5 Postwar Prosperity		30–40 min.
LESSON 6 Mass Culture in the 1950s		30–40 min.
LESSON 7 Social Issues of the 1950s		30–40 min.
Synthesize		1 period
DIGITAL ACTIVITY **Reflect on the Essential Question and Topic**		10 min.
TOPIC INQUIRY: DOCUMENT-BASED QUESTION **McCarthyism in the 1950s**		20 min.
Demonstrate		1–2 periods
DIGITAL TOPIC REVIEW AND ASSESSMENT **Postwar America**		10 min.
TOPIC INQUIRY: DOCUMENT-BASED QUESTION **McCarthyism in the 1950s**		20 min.

McCarthyism in the 1950s

In this Topic Inquiry, students use primary and secondary sources to investigate this question: Why did McCarthyism have such a powerful effect on American life in the 1950s? Learning how the fear of communism and the Soviet Union gripped the nation will contribute to students' understanding of the Topic Essential Question: What is America's Role in the World?

STEP 1: CONNECT
Develop Questions and Plan the Investigation

Watch the Video
Before directing students to watch the video, set the scene with a brief overview of America in the 1950s: The country's relationship with the communist Soviet Union had deteriorated rapidly since their alliance during World War II. A fear of communism gripped the people of the United States. They thought that a communist takeover from within the country was just as possible as a communist invasion by a foreign power.

Suggestion: You can pause the video at key points to ensure students understand who the individuals being interviewed are, and what role they played in the McCarthy drama.

Discuss
Lead students in the discussion questions:

- What was the Red Scare?
- What is "McCarthyism"?
- What did Murrow mean when he stated, "we must not confuse dissent with disloyalty?"

Suggestion: During the discussions, you might consider having students take notes of any ideas that are new to them so they can refresh their memory as they proceed.

Resources
- Video: *Murrow vs. McCarthy*

⏻ PROFESSIONAL DEVELOPMENT

Document-Based Question
Be sure to view the Document-Based Question Professional Development resources in the online course.

STEP 2: INVESTIGATE
Apply Disciplinary Concepts and Tools

Analyze the Documents
Direct students to review the six sources and to answer the questions that follow each one. While they should examine each source in detail, they should not lose sight of their main goal of answering the question, Why did McCarthyism have such a powerful effect on American life in the 1950s?

Suggestion: Have students note the date of Document F: An Excerpt From *The Crucible* (1953) and compare it to Document A: A Time Line Of The Early Years Of The Cold War, to provide context. Point out that Miller's satirical play was published just after all of the events on the time line took place.

Check Your Understanding
Consider pausing here to review students' answers before proceeding. Clarify any misunderstandings before students move on to the next step.

Suggestion: Consider pausing here to review students' answers before proceeding. Clarify any misunderstandings before students move on to the next step.

Resources
- Document A: A time line of the early years of the Cold War
- Document B: A political cartoon on the House Un-American Activities Committee
- Document C: A newspaper article about "subversive organizations"
- Document D: Excerpts from Senator Joseph McCarthy's speech at Wheeling, West Virginia
- Document E: The judge's statement upon sentencing the Rosenbergs for espionage
- Document F: An excerpt from *The Crucible*

STEP 3: SYNTHESIZE
Evaluate Sources and Use Evidence to Formulate Conclusions

Write Your Essay

Before students write their essays, review what is expected of them:

- Clearly state your view in a topic sentence.
- Use evidence from at least three documents. Clearly identify which documents you are using.
- Support your viewpoint with relevant facts.
- Consider and respond to at least one argument opposed to your own viewpoint.
- Use a logical organization, including an introduction and a conclusion. Include a strong topic sentence.
- Use correct spelling, grammar, and punctuation.
- Read and revise your essay before submitting it to your teacher.

Tell students to base their topic sentence on this question: Why did McCarthyism have such a powerful effect on American life in the 1950s?

Be sure that students use social studies terminology correctly and use standard grammar, spelling, sentence structure, and punctuation.

Suggestion: Remind students to take the time to prewrite before they begin writing. Prewriting includes the reviewing of the documents and outlining their writing projects.

STEP 4: DEMONSTRATE
Communicate Conclusions and Take Informed Action

Publish the Writing Projects

When students have completed their writing projects, hold a class discussion about the Topic Inquiry question. See if the class can reach a consensus on one or more reasons why. Record these reasons on the whiteboard.

Then, ask the class to turn these conclusions into informed action. Ask: What is the value in understanding why McCarthyism took hold? Challenge them to explain how they can take informed action to prevent anything like McCarthyism from happening again.

Suggestion: Extend the activity by having students conduct Internet research to locate examples of other people or events being compared to McCarthy and McCarthyism.

INTRODUCTION

Postwar America

The conclusion of World War II found the U.S. in a new relationship with an increasingly aggressive Soviet Union, leaving many Americans wondering what role the country should assume on the world stage. Cold War conflicts developed around the globe, and the fear of communism shaped domestic politics. However, the U.S. economy grew significantly in the 1950s and many Americans moved to suburbs outside of cities or even to warmer states in the southern and western regions of the country.

■ CONNECT

MY STORY VIDEO
Margaret Chase Smith, A Declaration of Conscience

Watch a video showing the courageous stand taken by Senator Smith during the McCarthy era.

Check Understanding Why did Senator Smith make the Declaration of Conscience speech? *(to speak out in favor of protecting Americans' basic civil liberties)*

Draw Conclusions Why did so few political leaders at the time speak out against Senator McCarthy? *(Many leaders no doubt feared political retribution if, during the 1950s Red Scare, they were accused of being soft on communism.)*

DIGITAL ESSENTIAL QUESTION ACTIVITY
What is America's Role in the World?

Read the Essential Question—What is America's role in the world?—aloud. Should the country play no role at all or should it be closely involved in other nations' affairs?

Distinguish What do you think America's role should be? As a beacon of freedom? As the spreader of democracy? As the world's policeman? *(Answers will vary. Some may say that the United States traditionally has served as a beacon of freedom, at times spreading democracy, although many argue that this violates other countries' right to self-determination. Functioning as the world's policeman is a hotly debated topic; on one hand, the United States has a mighty military, on the other, U.S. participation is not always welcomed and success is not guaranteed.)*

Interpret Do you think that, as victor in World War II, the United States implicitly accepted a certain role in the world? Explain. *(Answers will vary. Many students will think that with great power comes great responsibility to those who were U.S. allies in the war and to those former enemies whom the United States wanted to transform into allies.)*

DIGITAL OVERVIEW ACTIVITY
Postwar America

Display the image. Ask students if they know what the children in the photograph are doing. Explain that they are doing a drill, much like students do fire or tornado drills today. Only this drill is called "duck and cover," and it was practice for what to do in case the United States was attacked with atomic weapons by the Soviet Union.

D Differentiate: Extra Support Remind students that atomic weapons are so powerful that a single one can destroy an entire city. Two such bombs dropped by Americans on two Japanese cities forced Japan to surrender at the end of World War II.

Infer What can students infer from this? *(Reasonable inferences are that the Soviet Union had atomic weapons and the means to deliver them to the United States, that there was tension between the United States and the Soviet Union, and that U.S. officials thought the threat of a Soviet attack was legitimate and thus should be prepared for.)*

Topic Inquiry
Launch the Topic Inquiry with students after introducing the topic.

The Beginning of the Cold War

Supporting English Language Learners

Use with Digital Text 2, **Responding to the Soviet Challenge.**

Learning Strategies

Read aloud the section titled *The Truman Doctrine Opposes Soviet Aggression*, or invite volunteers to do so. After modeling how to read the section for students, invite students to read aloud while monitoring their oral-language production. Ask them to use self-corrective techniques as they complete the following tasks.

Beginning Have students complete this sentence and read it aloud: President Truman wanted to use money to help _____. Repeat their sentence, revising it for correct pronunciation, word choice, and grammar. Then ask students to self-correct as they repeat after you.

Intermediate Ask students to make a statement that defines the Truman Doctrine. Repeat their sentence verbatim, and invite students to identify and correct errors as needed. Then have them say their revised statement.

Advanced Record students as they read aloud President Truman's quotation about his foreign policy strategy (the first three paragraphs, until the first ellipsis). Play back the recordings. Encourage students to identify areas to improve and to practice rereading the quotation.

Advanced High Invite pairs of students to read President Truman's quote about his foreign policy and take turns summarizing it aloud. After each student's summary, have the partner offer suggestions for improving pronunciation, word choice, and grammar.

Use with Digital Text 4, **Soviet Aggression Drives Cold War.**

Listening

Read aloud the section titled *United States and Britain Respond with Berlin Airlift*, or invite volunteers to do so. Use the accompanying photograph to help explain the section's content as you give content and grade-level appropriate directions in order to encourage listening comprehension.

Beginning Ask students to locate words in the text, using spoken directions (e.g., Find the word *airlift*. Find a weather word.). Repeat the directions slowly if needed.

Intermediate Ask students to locate information in the text, using spoken directions (e.g., Locate a sentence that lists the supplies received. Read aloud a sentence that compares West Berlin and East Berlin.). Repeat the directions at regular speed if needed.

Advanced Give students spoken directions consisting of two steps in order (e.g., Reread the section, and write a definition of Berlin airlift.). Tell them to repeat the directions to themselves before beginning the task.

Advanced High Give students spoken directions consisting of two steps out of order (e.g., Write a new caption for the photograph, but first reread the section in order to find a detail to include.). Encourage students to restate or write out the directions before beginning the task.

▣ Differentiate Instruction

Use the Differentiated Instruction notes throughout the lesson plan to support the varied skill sets, levels of readiness, and interests in the mixed-ability classroom.

Challenge These notes include suggestions for expanding the activity for advanced students.

On-Level These notes include suggestions for modifying the activity to address different interests or learning styles.

Extra Support These notes include ideas for providing more scaffolding or reading spuport.

Special Needs These notes provide ideas for adapting instruction to support the needs of various special needs students.

■ NOTES

The Beginning of the Cold War

Objectives

Objective 1: Trace the reasons that the wartime alliance between the United States and the Soviet Union unraveled.

Objective 2: Explain how President Truman responded to Soviet aggression in Eastern Europe.

Objective 3: Describe the causes and results of Stalin's blockade of Berlin.

LESSON 1 ORGANIZER	PACING: APPROX. 1 PERIOD, .5 BLOCKS				
				RESOURCES	
		OBJECTIVES	PACING	Online	Print
Connect					
DIGITAL START UP ACTIVITY **Allies Become Rivals**			5 min.	●	
Investigate					
DIGITAL TEXT 1 **Background of the Cold War**		Objective 1	10 min.	●	●
DIGITAL TEXT 2 **Responding to the Soviet Challenge**			10 min.	●	●
DIGITAL TEXT 3 **The United States Contains Soviet Expansion**		Objective 2	10 min.	●	●
INTERACTIVE TIMELINE **U.S. Response to Soviet Aggression**			10 min.	●	
DIGITAL TEXT 4 **Soviet Aggression Drives Cold War**		Objective 3	10 min.	●	●
INTERACTIVE GALLERY **The Berlin Airlift Saves a City**			10 min.	●	
Synthesize					
DIGITAL ACTIVITY **Responding to Soviet Aggression**			5 min.	●	
Demonstrate					
DIGITAL QUIZ **Lesson Quiz and Class Discussion Board**			10 min.	●	

PEARSON •••
realize™
www.PearsonRealize.com

Go online to access additional resources including:
Primary Sources • Biographies • Supreme Court cases •
21st Century Skill Tutorials • Maps • Graphic Organizers.

■ CONNECT

DIGITAL START UP ACTIVITY
Allies Become Rivals

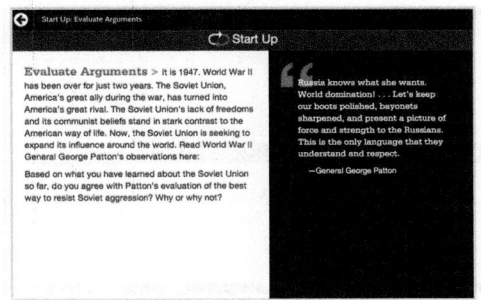

Project the Start Up Activity As students enter and get settled, ask them to think about how the United States and the Soviet Union went from allies in World War II to the opposite—rivals—in the Cold War.

Discuss Invite a volunteer to read General George Patton's statement aloud. Based on what you have learned about the Soviet Union so far, do you agree with Patton's evaluation of the best way to resist Soviet aggression? Why or why not? *(Those who agree with Patton might allude to Soviet aggression into Eastern Europe. Those who disagree might allude to the fact that the United States and the Soviet Union were recent allies.)*

Aa **Vocabulary Development:** Use the Interactive Reading Notepad to preview the Key Terms and Academic Vocabulary in this lesson with students.

↳ FLIP IT!
Assign the Flipped Video for this lesson.

■ STUDENT EDITION PRINT PAGES: 636–641

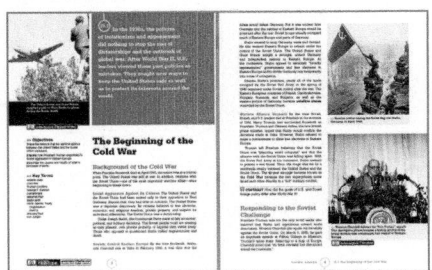

■ INVESTIGATE

DIGITAL TEXT 1
Background of the Cold War

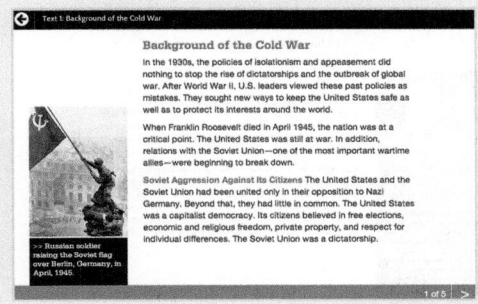

Objective 1: **Trace the reasons that the wartime alliance between the United States and the Soviet Union unraveled.**

Quick Instruction
Summarize Invite a student to identify the main idea of the map. *(Soviet control of Eastern Europe)* Ask students what major Soviet aggressions took place at the end of and immediately after World War II that led to the unraveling of the U.S.-Soviet alliance, and that made American officials fearful of Soviet expansionism. *(Soviet control of Eastern Europe after the war, despite Soviet dictator Joseph Stalin's promise at Yalta to establish "broadly representative" governments and free elections there.)*

Discuss Harry Truman's leadership and the U.S. relationship with its allies as World War II was coming to a conclusion. Although Truman had recently become President following Roosevelt's death, negotiations between the Allied powers continued as planned through the summer of 1945. Note that Truman expected Stalin to stand by the promises he made at Yalta during the Potsdam Conference.

D **Differentiate: Extra Support** Students may get confused as they encounter synonymous terminology associated with the Cold War. Help them understand that the following are roughly synonymous: The United States and its allies, Western nations, the West, the Western bloc, NATO, the free world. The following are also roughly synonymous: The Soviet Union and its allies, The Eastern bloc, the Warsaw Pact, communist countries.

Further Instruction
Go through the Interactive Reading Notepad questions and discuss the answers with the class.

Project the interactive graphic organizer. Emphasize that these underlying differences between the United States and the Soviet Union contributed to the existence and severity of the Cold War. Point out also, though, that something like the Cold War might have developed even if the two countries had not been ideological opponents, due to the fact that they were both powerful countries seeking leadership roles in the world, and so natural rivals.

Compare and Contrast the United States and the Soviet Union in the late 1940s. As you read *Background of the Cold War*, use the graphic organizer below to take notes about each country's form of government, political beliefs about human rights, and ideas about the governance of Germany and Eastern Europe. *(Form of Government: United States—capitalist democracy; Soviet Union—communist dictatorship. Political Beliefs: United States—free elections, economic freedom including right to own private property, freedom of religion; Soviet Union—no free elections, no economic freedom or right to own private property, no freedom of religion. Ideas about the Governance of Germany and Eastern Europe: United States—wanted a strong, united Germany, wanted nations in Eastern European to be independently governed; Soviet Union—wanted a weak, divided Germany and control of East Germany; wanted Eastern European nations to become Soviet satellite states.)*

The Beginning of the Cold War

DIGITAL TEXT 2

Responding to the Soviet Challenge

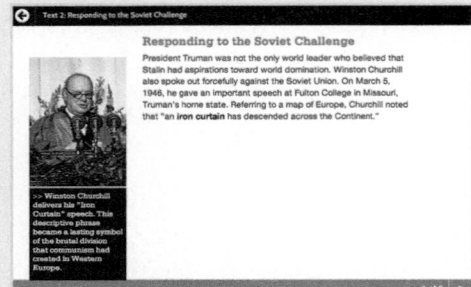

DIGITAL TEXT 3

The United States Contains Soviet Expansion

INTERACTIVE TIMELINE

U.S. Response to Soviet Aggression

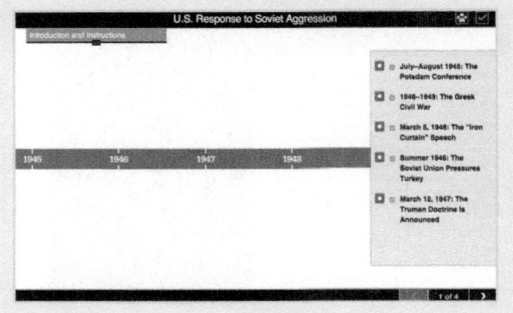

Objective 2: **Explain how President Truman responded to Soviet aggression in Eastern Europe.**

Quick Instruction

Interactive Timeline: U.S. Response to Soviet Aggression Project the timeline and select the squares to reveal details about the events. Point out that each event was quite significant on its own, and that there were several events in a short period of time. Thus, both the frequency and intensity of Soviet aggression was alarming to U.S. officials.

Express Ideas Clearly What was the Truman Doctrine and how did it relate to Soviet aggression? *(The Truman Doctrine was President Harry Truman's promise to aid nations struggling against communist movements in order to contain communism and Soviet aggression.)* How did the Marshall Plan help Europeans resist Soviet aggression? *(By helping the devastated nations of Europe recover economically, the Marshall Plan helped protect free Europe from the threat of communism.)*

▶️ ACTIVE CLASSROOM

Direct students to have a "Conversation with President Truman." Tell students to imagine that they are having a conversation with Truman as he is developing what will become known as the Truman Doctrine. Direct each student to write down a question he or she would like to ask, then how Truman would respond, and then what the student would say in response. Suggest that students reflect on Truman's international leadership as they formulate their questions.

ELL Use the ELL activity described in the ELL chart.

Further Instruction

Go through the Interactive Reading Notepad questions and discuss the answers with the class.

Tell students that a doctrine is a principle of government policy. Explain how a doctrine is the idea behind specific actions.

Generate Explanations How was the Marshall Plan an example of the Truman Doctrine in action? *(The good relationships that the aid provided under the plan worked against the expansion of communism.)*

DIGITAL TEXT 4

Soviet Aggression Drives Cold War

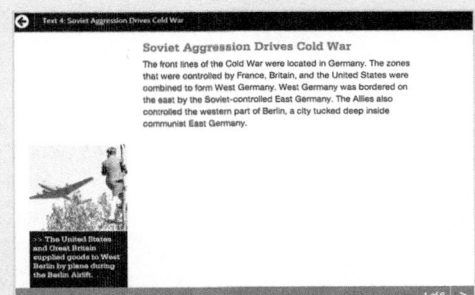

INTERACTIVE GALLERY

The Berlin Airlift Saves a City

Objective 3: Describe the causes and results of Stalin's blockade of Berlin.

Quick Instruction

Interactive Gallery: The Berlin Airlift Saves a City Project the Interactive Gallery on the whiteboard. Select the images to reveal important facts about this historic action. Challenge students to explain what the airlift was and then explain why the Berlin Airlift is sometimes called "America's first Cold War victory." *(The Berlin Airlift was the 1948–1949 airlift of food, fuel, medical supplies, and other needed goods in response to Soviet aggression in Berlin. The United States succeeded in keeping West Berlin free from Soviet control.)*

📷 ACTIVE CLASSROOM

Have students Make Headlines for the Berlin Airlift. Ask: If you were to write a headline for the Berlin Airlift that captured the most important aspect that should be remembered, what would that headline be? Allow students to use subheadings to communicate more information. Encourage them to present the Berlin Airlift as part of the larger Cold War. Have students pass their headlines to a partner for them to review.

ELL Use the ELL activity described in the ELL chart.

Further Instruction

Go through the Interactive Reading Notepad questions and discuss the answers with the class.

Identify Central Issues Identify two major U.S. responses to Soviet aggression after World War II. *(The Berlin Airlift and the establishment of the North Atlantic Treaty Organization (NATO).*

Interpret Why should the Berlin Airlift be considered a victory for the United States in the Cold War? *(Because the Airlift succeeded in keeping West Berlin free from communist control.)*

Identify Cause and Effect How did the Soviet Union respond to West Germany joining the North Atlantic Treaty Organization (NATO)? *(The Soviet Union and its satellite states formed a rival military alliance, the Warsaw Pact.)*

The Beginning of the Cold War

■ SYNTHESIZE

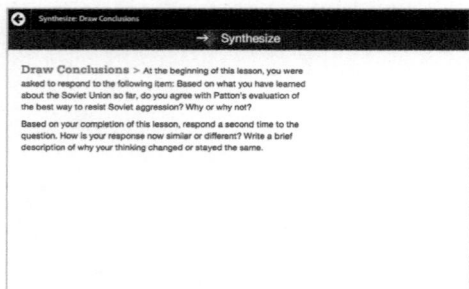

DIGITAL ACTIVITY
Responding to Soviet Aggression

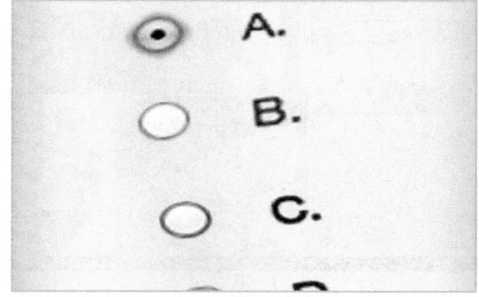

Discuss Before students begin their descriptions, lead the class in a brief review of Soviet aggression and U.S. responses to that aggression in the years immediately after World War II. Ask if they think any of these acts would have surprised General Patton.

■ DEMONSTRATE

DIGITAL QUIZ
Lesson Quiz and Class Discussion Board

Assign the online Lesson Quiz for this lesson if you haven't already done so. Students will be offered automatic remediation or enrichment based on their score.

Pose these questions to the class on the Discussion Board:

Interpret Pilots who flew the Berlin Airlift flights were highly dedicated, often working to the point of exhaustion. Many even fell asleep while flying. What do you think motivated them?

Predict Consequences NATO was formed in 1949. In 1955, West Germany became a member of NATO. In response, the Soviet Union and its satellite states formed a rival military alliance, called the Warsaw Pact. How might this development affect the course of the Cold War?

Topic Inquiry
Have students continue their investigations for the Topic Inquiry.

The Korean War

Supporting English Language Learners

Use with Digital Text 2, **U.S. Involvement in Korea.**

Learning
Read aloud the section titled *Reasons for U.S. Involvement*, or invite volunteers to do so. Summarize the main idea of the section and encourage students to employ self-corrective techniques as they monitor their written language production.

Beginning Say a basic key word from the text, and have students write down what they hear. Then display the word, and invite students to correct their work.

Intermediate Pose a question about the text, such as: Did Truman ask Congress for a formal declaration of war? Have students write down their response as a complete sentence and then check it against the text for spelling and content.

Advanced Ask pairs of students to write a paragraph describing the decisions made by President Truman regarding Korea. Encourage students to discuss aspects of the writing process as they work, such as spelling, word choice, and grammar.

Advanced High Ask students to write a paragraph describing the decisions made by President Truman regarding Korea. Tell students to revise their paragraph once, and then to submit it to a partner for feedback.

Use with Digital Text 3, **Outcomes of the Korean War.**

Listening
Read aloud the text, or invite volunteers to do so. Explain the terms *short-term outcome* and *long-term outcome*. Allow students to take notes as they listen. Then have students retell or summarize the information that they have heard. In order for students to demonstrate listening comprehension, commensurate with their grade-level needs set them the following tasks.

Beginning Briefly state outcomes of the Korean War. After each outcome, ask students to say whether it is a "short-term outcome" or a "long-term outcome."

Intermediate Read aloud a short list of the Korean War's short-term outcomes. Ask students to retell the list's content in their own words. Repeat using a list of the war's long-term outcomes.

Advanced Read aloud the second paragraph of the section titled Long-Term Outcomes of the Korean War. Ask students to summarize the paragraph. Reread the paragraph if needed.

Advanced High Read aloud the section titled Long-Term Outcomes of the Korean War. Encourage students to take notes as they listen to you read. Then ask them to use the notes to retell the section's content in their own words.

▶ Differentiate Instruction

Use the Differentiated Instruction notes throughout the lesson plan to support the varied skill sets, levels of readiness, and interests in the mixed-ability classroom.

Challenge These notes include suggestions for expanding the activity for advanced students.

On-Level These notes include suggestions for modifying the activity to address different interests or learning styles.

Extra Support These notes include ideas for providing more scaffolding or reading spuport.

Special Needs These notes provide ideas for adapting instruction to support the needs of various special needs students.

■ NOTES

The Korean War

Objectives

Objective 1: Explain how Mao Zedong and the communists gained power in China.

Objective 2: Describe the causes and the reasons for U.S. involvement in the Korean War.

Objective 3: Identify the long-term effects and outcomes of the Korean War.

LESSON 2 ORGANIZER		PACING: APPROX. 1 PERIOD, .5 BLOCKS			
				RESOURCES	
		OBJECTIVES	PACING	Online	Print
Connect					
DIGITAL START UP ACTIVITY **Mapping the Korean War**			5 min.	●	
Investigate					
DIGITAL TEXT 1 **China Turns Communist**		Objective 1	10 min.	●	●
DIGITAL TEXT 2 **U.S. Involvement in Korea**		Objective 2	10 min.	●	●
INTERACTIVE MAP **Phases of the Korean War**			10 min.	●	
DIGITAL TEXT 3 **Outcomes of the Korean War**		Objective 3	10 min.	●	●
Synthesize					
DIGITAL ACTIVITY **The Hot War in Korea**			5 min.	●	
Demonstrate					
DIGITAL QUIZ **Lesson Quiz and Class Discussion Board**			10 min.	●	

PEARSON
realize™
www.PearsonRealize.com

Go online to access additional resources including:
Primary Sources • Biographies • Supreme Court cases •
21st Century Skill Tutorials • Maps • Graphic Organizers.

CONNECT

DIGITAL START UP ACTIVITY
Mapping the Korean War

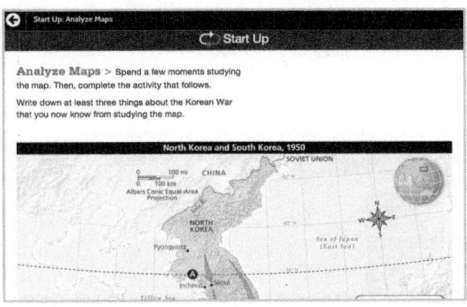

Project the Start Up Activity As students enter, draw their attention to the map. Encourage them to take a few minutes to digest the information the map provides before they write down three things about the Korean War.

Discuss When they have completed their lists, consider working together as a group to reach a consensus master list of all that can be gleaned from the map. *(Possible list items: North Korea invaded South Korea in June 1950; The United States and South Korea halted their retreat near Pusan in July 1950; North Korea's invasion was a success; South Korea and the United States were allies.)*

Aa Vocabulary Development: Use the Interactive Reading Notepad to preview the Key Terms and Academic Vocabulary in this lesson with students.

⇅ FLIP IT!
Assign the Flipped Video for this lesson.

■ STUDENT EDITION PRINT
PAGES: 642–646

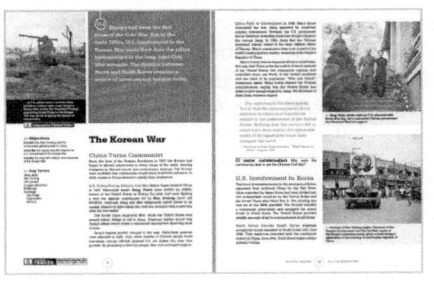

INVESTIGATE

DIGITAL TEXT 1
China Turns Communist

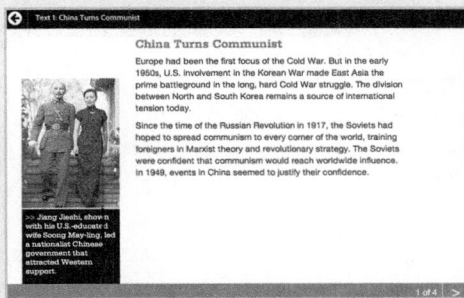

Objective 1: Explain how Mao Zedong and the communists gained power in China.

Quick Instruction
Analyze Images Invite students to identify the person in the portraits. *(Mao Zedong)* Ask: Why would people be celebrating with these portraits in 1949? *(They were celebrating the victory of communist forces under Mao Zedong in the Chinese civil war.)* Ensure students understand that this victory resulted in China turning communist. How do students think many people in the United States felt about this? *(Shocked, concerned, and certain that communism was on the march)*

Further Instruction
Go through the Interactive Reading Notepad questions and discuss the answers with the class.

Project the Interactive Graphic Organizer. After students complete "China Turns Communist," use the problem-solution graphic organizer to note problems and the steps that President Truman took to solve them. *(Problem—Communists threaten takeover of China. Solution—The United States sends several billion dollars in aid to Jiang Jieshi. Problem—Communist forces led by Mao Zedong dominate civil war in China. Solution—The United States refuses to support the corrupt Jiang Jieshi by sending troops to support his forces.)*

Identify Central Issues In the 1940s, what did the question "Who lost China?" mean? *(China was "lost" to communism through Mao's victory in the Chinese civil war. It was a loss for Americans in the Cold War against communism, and Americans asked the question in order to find a more effective way of containing communism.)*

Identify Cause and Effect What was the reason for the lack of U.S. military support for Jiang Jieshi as he opposed communism in China? *(Jiang Jieshi was corrupt, having already used U.S. aid dollars for enrichment instead of helping the people or fighting communism.)* What outcome resulted due to the lack of U.S. involvement? *(Communists gained control of China)*

The Korean War

DIGITAL TEXT 2
U.S. Involvement in Korea

INTERACTIVE MAP
Phases of the Korean War

DIGITAL TEXT 3
Outcomes of the Korean War

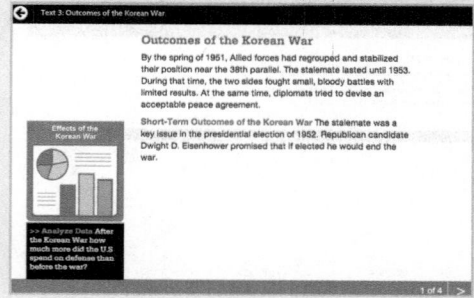

Objective 2: Describe the causes and the reasons for U.S. involvement in the Korean War.

Quick Instruction

Interactive Map: Phases of the Korean War Project the map and select the squares one at a time to reveal the phases of the Korean War. Point out that the war was very much a back-and-forth affair, with North Korea (the aggressor) having early success, U.N. (primarily U.S.) forces pushing back and invading at Inchon, and then North Korea again successful owing to Chinese participation. Ask: After all the bitter fighting and enormous loss of life, the North-South border remained about where it had been before the war. Tell students that the war ended in stalemate, but ask students who might be considered a victor in the war, and why. *(The South Korean and UN (primarily U.S.) troops; they succeeded in preventing a communist takeover of South Korea.)*

📷 ACTIVE CLASSROOM

Play a game of Connect Two about the Korean War. List the following terms on the board: North Korea, South Korea, United Nations, China, United States, 38th Parallel, Inchon, General MacArthur, President Truman, Yarlu River, Containment Policy. Direct students to copy the terms down on notecards or small slips of paper, one term to a card or piece of paper. Review the list of terms with students. Ask students to "connect two," or choose two terms they think belong together, and state the reason for their connection. Encourage students to connect these terms to reasons for U.S. involvement in the Korean War. Challenge students to connect as many pairs of terms as possible. Conduct this activity before, during, and/or after student reading.

ELL Use the ELL activity described in the ELL chart.

Further Instruction

Go through the Interactive Reading Notepad questions and discuss the answers with the class.

Project the Interactive Graphic Organizer on the whiteboard. After students complete *U.S. Involvement in Korea*, use the problem-solution graphic organizer to note problems and the steps that President Truman took to solve them. *(Problem—Soviet-backed North Korean forces attack across the 38th parallel in Korea, overtaking the South Korean capital city of Seoul. Solution—Supported by a UN resolution, Truman increases U.S. involvement in the Korean War as part of the containment policy. Problem—In late 1950, a large force of Chinese soldiers attack South Korean and U.S. positions in North Korea, forcing back UN troops. Solution—Truman decides to fight a limited war, without making a commitment to send large numbers of troops or use nuclear weapons.)*

Identify Patterns Explain the relationship of U.S. involvement in the Korean War to the containment policy. *(The containment policy meant holding the line against communist expansion. The Korean War is a textbook example of containing the spread of communism; the Korean War kept it contained in North Korea.)*

Objective 3: Identify the long-term effects and outcomes of the Korean War.

Quick Instruction

Analyze Graphs Project the graphs showing the effects of the Korean War. Invite a volunteer to describe what they depict. *(joint military exercises between U.S. and South Korean forces)* and what it represents *(the U.S.-South Korean alliance)*. Tell students that this alliance is one of the main long-term outcomes of the Korean War. What are the other long-term outcomes of U.S. involvement in the Korean War? *(Precedent of president committing U.S. troops to battle without a congressional declaration of war, support of the idea that the fall of one nation to communism would lead to others in the region falling to communism (which came to be called the Domino Theory), increased military spending, creation of the Southeast Asia Treaty Organization (SEATO))*

📷 ACTIVE CLASSROOM

Use the Ranking Strategy to help students assess the importance of each outcome. Place students in small groups and ask them to rank immediate and long-term outcomes of the Korean War separately. Each group should then provide justification for the highest ranked immediate and long-term outcome, and share both with the class.

■ **SYNTHESIZE**

■ **DEMONSTRATE**

DIGITAL ACTIVITY
The Hot War in Korea

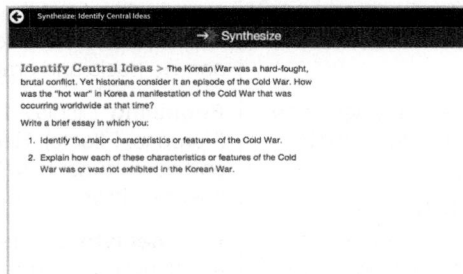

DIGITAL QUIZ
Lesson Quiz and Class Discussion Board

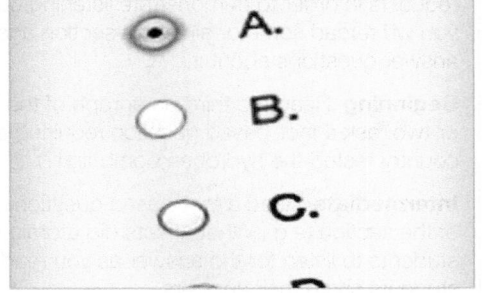

D **Differentiate: Challenge** Invite interested students to learn more about the Demilitarized Zone (DMZ) between North and South Korea. Students can share what they learn on a poster or a Web page with the class.

ELL Use the ELL activity described in the ELL chart.

Further Instruction
Go through the Interactive Reading Notepad questions and discuss the answers with the class.

Express Ideas Clearly Which of the long-term outcomes for U.S. involvement in the Korean War do you think is most important? Why? *(Answers will vary, but should include the U.S.-South Korean alliance, the precedent of a president committing U.S. troops without congressional declaration of war, increased support for the Domino Theory, and increased military spending have all proved to be significant factors in American domestic and foreign policy for more than half a century.)* word

Discuss Before students begin their essays, lead a brief discussion to ensure student understanding of the fundamentals of the Cold War, including the U.S. containment policy. Then remind them that the Korean peninsula was divided into a communist North and a non-communist South.

Assign the online Lesson Quiz for this lesson if you haven't already done so. Students will be offered automatic remediation or enrichment based on their score.

Pose these questions to the class on the Discussion Board:

Identify Central Ideas Think about the question "Who lost China?" What did it mean? Why was it important? What do you think the proper answer was?

Predict Consequences One of the long-term consequences of the Korean War was that it "seemed to support the growing belief among policymakers that the fall of one nation to communism could have a ripple effect throughout the region." This came to be called the Domino Theory. How might belief in the Domino Theory affect the reasons and outcomes for U.S. involvement in foreign countries in the future?

Topic Inquiry
Have students continue their investigations for the Topic Inquiry.

The Cold War Intensifies

Supporting English Language Learners

Use with Digital Text 1, **The Arms Race Intensifies Tensions.**

Listening
Read aloud the section titled *The Arms Race Speeds Up*, then have students respond to content and grade-level specific questions and requests in order to demonstrate listening comprehension. Explain that you will reread some or all of this section again so that students can answer questions about it.

Beginning Read the third paragraph of the section. After every sentence or two, ask a fact-based question requiring a brief response (e.g., Which country tested the hydrogen bomb first?).

Intermediate Read a fact-based question about the third paragraph of the section (e.g., What effects did atomic testing have?). Then ask students to listen for the answer as you read aloud the paragraph. Have students share their answers.

Advanced Read the third paragraph of the section. Then ask students fact-based questions to be answered using complete sentences (e.g., What effects did atomic testing have?).

Advanced High Read the third paragraph of the section. Ask students to share their opinions about atomic testing. Have them include information from the paragraph to support their opinions.

Use with Digital Text 3, **International Cold War Conflicts.**

Learning
Read aloud the sections titled *The Eisenhower Doctrine* and *The Space Race Increases Tensions*, or invite students to do so. Draw attention to the paragraphs about the CIA and NASA as students use strategic learning techniques such as concept mapping or comparing and contrasting to acquire basic and grade-level vocabulary.

Beginning Display a chart with two columns (CIA, NASA) and two rows (Purpose, Effects). Reread the paragraphs about the CIA and NASA, and have students help you complete the chart. Ask: What did the two agencies have in common?

Intermediate Create the blank chart from the beginning level, but with an additional row (Long-term Effects). Have students refer to the text to help you complete the chart. Ask: Which agency do you think was more helpful to the people of the United States? Why?

Advanced Create the blank chart from the intermediate level. Ask pairs of students to complete a copy of the chart. Ask: How are the agencies alike? How are they different?

Advanced High Create the blank chart from the intermediate level, and ask students to copy and complete it independently. Then have them use the chart to write a paragraph comparing and contrasting the CIA and NASA.

◨ Differentiate Instruction

Use the Differentiated Instruction notes throughout the lesson plan to support the varied skill sets, levels of readiness, and interests in the mixed-ability classroom.

Challenge These notes include suggestions for expanding the activity for advanced students.

On-Level These notes include suggestions for modifying the activity to address different interests or learning styles.

Extra Support These notes include ideas for providing more scaffolding or reading spuport.

Special Needs These notes provide ideas for adapting instruction to support the needs of various special needs students.

◼ NOTES

PEARSON
realize™
www.PearsonRealize.com

Go online to access additional resources including:
Primary Sources • Biographies • Supreme Court cases • 21st Century Skill Tutorials • Maps • Graphic Organizers.

Objectives

Objective 1: Describe how Cold War tensions were intensified by the arms race between the United States and the Soviet Union.

Objective 2: Explain how Eisenhower's response to communism differed from that of Truman.

Objective 3: Analyze the impact on the United States of significant international Cold War conflicts.

Objective 4: Describe how Cold War tensions were intensified by the space race.

LESSON 3 ORGANIZER		PACING: APPROX. 1 PERIOD, .5 BLOCKS			
				RESOURCES	
		OBJECTIVES	**PACING**	**Online**	**Print**
Connect					
DIGITAL START UP ACTIVITY **Cold War Policies**			5 min.	●	
Investigate					
DIGITAL TEXT 1 **The Arms Race Intensifies Tensions**		Objective 1	10 min.	●	●
INTERACTIVE CHART **Experience the Cold War**			10 min.	●	
DIGITAL TEXT 2 **Eisenhower's Response to Soviet Aggression**		Objective 2	10 min.	●	●
INTERACTIVE GALLERY **Cold War Technological Advances**			10 min.	●	
DIGITAL TEXT 3 **International Cold War Conflicts**		Objectives 3, 4	10 min.	●	●
INTERACTIVE MAP **Global Cold War, 1946–1956**			10 min.	●	
Synthesize					
DIGITAL ACTIVITY **The Cold War Heats Up**			5 min.	●	
Demonstrate					
DIGITAL QUIZ **Lesson Quiz and Class Discussion Board**			10 min.	●	

The Cold War Intensifies

■ CONNECT

DIGITAL START UP ACTIVITY
Cold War Policies

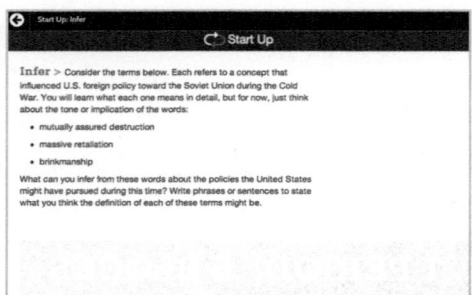

Project the Start Up Activity As students enter and get settled, draw their attention to the activity. Allow students to work in pairs as they consider the terms *mutually assured destruction*, *massive retaliation*, and *brinkmanship*.

Discuss Point out that mutually assured destruction makes an interesting acronym (MAD), and that they should consider this as they complete the writing activity to answer this question: What can you infer from these words about the policies that U.S. leaders might have discussed during this time?

Aa **Vocabulary Development:** Use the Interactive Reading Notepad to preview the Key Terms and Academic Vocabulary in this lesson with students.

ⓝ FLIP IT!
Assign the Flipped Video for this lesson.

■ STUDENT EDITION PRINT
PAGES: 647–652

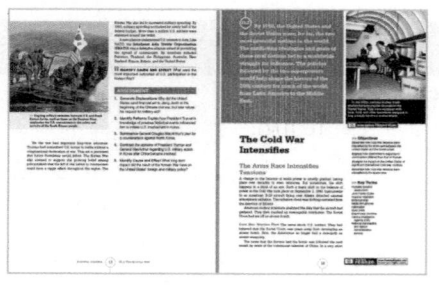

■ INVESTIGATE

DIGITAL TEXT 1
The Arms Race Intensifies Tensions

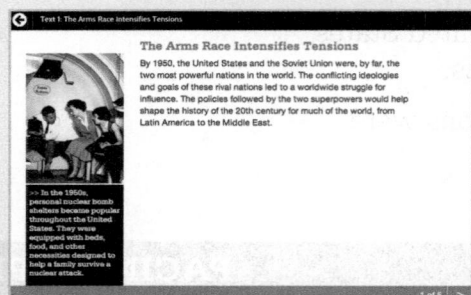

Objective 1: Describe how Cold War tensions were intensified by the arms race between the United States and the Soviet Union.

Quick Instruction
Interactive Chart: Experience the Cold War Project the interactive chart. Select the white icons to reveal important aspects life in the United States during the height of Cold War. Emphasize to students that the fear of utter annihilation was real. Cold War tensions were intensified by an arms race fueled by military technological innovation. People felt that the world might be destroyed at any moment. Explain that, in fact, the United States and the Soviet Union came extremely close to a nuclear war more than once. Yet people continued to lead their day-to-day lives. Ask students how they can account for this behavior. (*Answers will vary. Ordinary people had little influence over world events and thus lived as best they could.*)

🎭 ACTIVE CLASSROOM
Project the interactive chart and have students use it as a base to play an Act It Out game. Tell students to bring the figures in the chart to life by stating what each must be thinking and feeling at the moment, and telling what happened just before and after the image of each figure was made. Before they act, remind students of the Cold War tensions and fear that permeated the country.

ELL Use the ELL activity described in the ELL chart.

INTERACTIVE CHART
Experience the Cold War

Further Instruction
Go through the Interactive Reading Notepad questions and discuss the answers with the class.

Project the Interactive Graphic Organizer on the whiteboard. As students progress in this lesson, use the chart to take notes about the Cold War tensions between the United States and the Soviet Union. In the first column, note causes, or reasons for the continuing Cold War and arms race. In the second column, note effects, or outcomes of each cause. (*Cause—Mao Zedong and the Communist Party assume control of China. Effect—The United States and Soviet Union begin to stockpile nuclear weapons.*)

Interpret Why was the arms race between the United States and the Soviet Union during the Cold War called a "race"? *Each country was trying to get ahead of the other in number and quality of weapons.*)

Identify Central Issues How did the arms race lead to the concept of "mutually assured destruction"? (*Both the United States and the Soviet Union both had immensely powerful atomic and then hydrogen bombs. The way to deter the enemy from attacking was to have enough firepower to ensure the attacker's destruction.*)

DIGITAL TEXT 2

Eisenhower's Response to Soviet Aggression

INTERACTIVE GALLERY

Cold War Technological Advances

Objective 2: Explain how Eisenhower's response to communism differed from that of Truman.

Quick Instruction

Interactive Gallery: Cold War Technological Advances Project the gallery on the whiteboard and select the images to reveal the captions. Explain that the specific needs of the Cold War made technological innovation in the military and scientific discoveries necessary. Ask students what specific needs would have prompted such innovation. *(the need to counter the Soviet threat with the ability to strike the USSR with improved missiles and nuclear weapons)* Challenge students to explain how technology formed the basis of President Eisenhower's response to Soviet aggression, and how that differed from President Truman's. *(Truman increased military spending to compete with the Soviets. Eisenhower opposed spending vast sums on conventional forces but chose to invest in nuclear technology.)*

ACTIVE CLASSROOM

Break students into groups for a quick Circle Write activity. Provide this as a writing prompt: Explain how Eisenhower's response to Soviet aggression differed from that of Truman. Have students write as much as they can for one minute then switch with the person on their right. The next person tries to improve or elaborate the response where the other person left off. Continue to switch until the paper comes back to the first person. The group then decides which is the best composition (or response) and shares that with the larger group.

Further Instruction

Project the Interactive Graphic Organizer on the whiteboard. As students progress in this lesson, use the chart to take notes about the Cold War tensions between the United States and the Soviet Union, noting the reasons for the arms race and the outcomes of each reason. *(Cause—Dwight D. Eisenhower becomes president. Effect—Convinced that any war with the Soviets would be nuclear rather than conventional, the U.S. downgrades conventional military forces and stockpiles nuclear weapons. The Soviet Union also stockpiles nuclear weapons. Cause—Stalin dies and Khrushchev becomes premier. Effect—Relations between the United States and Soviet Union improve slightly.)*

Analyze Information President Eisenhower's secretary of state, John Foster Dulles, believed containment could prevent the possibility of one country after another falling under communist rule. What is this idea known as? *(the Domino Theory)*

Predict Consequences How might belief in the Domino Theory influence the reasons and outcomes for U.S. involvement in foreign countries? *(U.S. officials may think they need to get involved in foreign countries to prevent communism from spreading any further.)*

The Cold War Intensifies

DIGITAL TEXT 3
International Cold War Conflicts

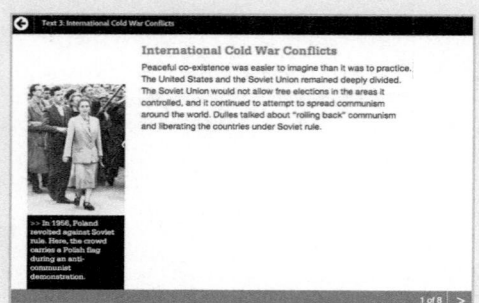

INTERACTIVE MAP
Global Cold War, 1946–1956

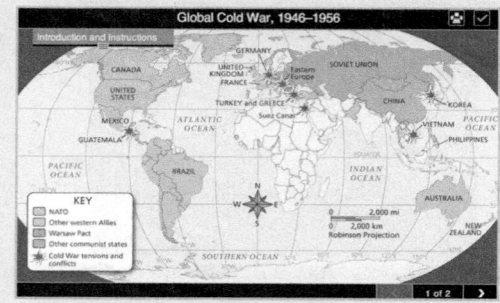

Objectives 3: **Analyze the impact of significant international Cold War conflicts on the United States; 4:** **Describe how Cold War tensions were intensified by the space race.**

Quick Instruction

Interactive Map: Global Cold War, 1946–1956 Project the map on the whiteboard. Indicate each of the events. For each, ask the following questions: Who was involved? What happened? What impact did it have on the United States? Then click on the starburst icon to confirm student understanding.

📺 ACTIVE CLASSROOM

Have students make headlines for the space race. Ask: If you were to write a headline about the space race that captured what should be remembered, what would that headline be? Allow students to use subheadings to communicate more information. Ensure the class uses all of the following words in their headlines: Space race, Soviet Union, United States, Sputnik, Laika, National Defense Education Act, and National Aeronautics and Space Administration (NASA). Have students review each others' headlines.

D Differentiate: **Challenge** Invite an interested student to learn more about Sputnik I and America's first satellite, *Explorer I*, and share what they learn with the class through a verbal or online presentation.

ELL Use the ELL activity described in the ELL chart.

Further Instruction

Go through the Interactive Reading Notepad questions and discuss the answers with the class.

Project the Interactive Graphic Organizer on the whiteboard. As students progress in this lesson, use the chart to take notes about the Cold War tensions between the United States and the Soviet Union. In the first column, note causes, or reasons, for the continuing Cold War, arms race, and space race. In the second column, note effects, or outcomes of each cause. *(Cause—The Soviets launch Sputnik. Effect—The United States forms NASA, and the space race begins.)*

Compare and Contrast How were the 1956 events in Poland and Hungary similar? How were they different? *(They were both uprisings against Soviet rule. The Soviet leaders allowed them in Poland since the Polish government did not attempt to leave the Warsaw Pact. In Hungary, however, Soviet leaders crushed the uprising.)*

Predict Consequences Besides the National Defense Education Act and creating the National Aeronautics and Space Administration (NASA), how do you think the United States might respond to the launching of the Soviet satellite Sputnik I? *(by achieving the necessary technological innovation to launch its own satellite and participating in a space race with the Soviet Union)*

SYNTHESIZE

DIGITAL ACTIVITY
The Cold War Heats Up

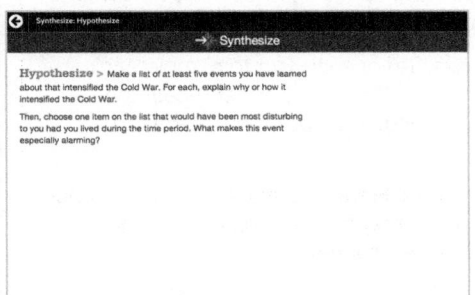

Discuss Before students begin their lists, lead a brief discussion about the intensity of the Cold War over time. Explain that the tension between the Western and Eastern bloc was continuous, but that it varied in intensity over time. Many of the events they have read about were crises that served to heighten tensions.

DEMONSTRATE

DIGITAL QUIZ
Lesson Quiz and Class Discussion Board

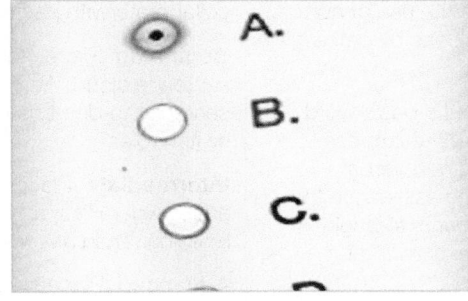

Assign the online Lesson Quiz for this lesson if you haven't already done so. Students will be offered automatic remediation or enrichment based on their score.

Pose these questions to the class on the Discussion Board:

Infer The United States spent huge sums of money on defense during the Cold War. Describe what you think the economic impact of defense spending on education priorities was.

Predict Consequences Think about how space technology developed during the Space Race might have improved the quality of life.

Topic Inquiry
Have students continue their investigations for the Topic Inquiry.

Cold War Fears at Home

Supporting English Language Learners

Use with Digital Text 1, **Cold War Tensions Rise at Home.**

Learning Strategies

Read aloud the section titled *The House Un-American Activities Committee*, or invite volunteers to do so. Explain the HUAC while prompting students to utilize learning strategies such as the use of non-verbal cues, synonyms, and circumlocution, conveying ideas by defining or describing when exact English words are not known.

Beginning Reread the section's last paragraph. Point out a basic word (e.g., powerful), and help students think of alternative ways to express it (using synonyms or circumlocution) or to show it (using non-verbal cues). Then have students work with a partner, requesting assistance to understand the meaning of other words. Encourage students to begin requests with "Can you help me...." "Would you please explain..." and so on.

Intermediate Reread the section's last paragraph. Ask students to restate one of the sentences in their own words. Encourage them to use non-verbal cues, synonyms, and circumlocution, as well as to ask for help from a more advanced English speaker if necessary.

Advanced Ask pairs of students to reread the section's first paragraph and to discuss its content in their own words. Encourage them to use non-verbal cues, synonyms, and circumlocution, as well as to ask each other for help if necessary.

Advanced High Ask students to explain the boldface terms included in the section of text. Explain that they cannot use any part of the term in their explanation. Instead, encourage them to practice using synonyms and circumlocution.

Use with Digital Text 2, **Domestic Spy Cases Increase Fears.**

Listening

Read aloud the text, or invite volunteers to do so. Point out the images of the spies and rad the corresponding captions. Encourage students to collaborate with peers as they complete the following activities.

Beginning Place students in pairs. Tell one student to complete this sentence aloud: Alger Hiss was _____. Have the partner repeat the sentence to demonstrate good listening. Then ask the students to switch roles.

Intermediate Place students in pairs. Have one student say a sentence about Alger Hiss, and have the partner repeat it to demonstrate good listening. Then ask the students to switch roles.

Advanced Place students in pairs. Have one student use at least two sentences to describe the Alger Hiss case, while the partner restates the description in his or her own words. Then ask the students to switch roles and describe the Rosenbergs.

Advanced High Have pairs of students discuss this question: If not for the Verona Papers, would you have thought that Hiss and the Rosenbergs were innocent? Tell students that each of their statements must connect to what their partner has just said.

▣ Differentiate Instruction

Use the Differentiated Instruction notes throughout the lesson plan to support the varied skill sets, levels of readiness, and interests in the mixed-ability classroom.

Challenge These notes include suggestions for expanding the activity for advanced students.

On-Level These notes include suggestions for modifying the activity to address different interests or learning styles.

Extra Support These notes include ideas for providing more scaffolding or reading spuport.

Special Needs These notes provide ideas for adapting instruction to support the needs of various special needs students.

■ NOTES

PEARSON
realize™
www.PearsonRealize.com

Go online to access additional resources including:
Primary Sources • Biographies • Supreme Court cases •
21st Century Skill Tutorials • Maps • Graphic Organizers.

Objectives

Objective 1: Describe the efforts of President Truman and the House Un-American Activities Committee to fight communism at home.

Objective 2: Explain how domestic spy cases intensified fears of communist influence in the U.S. government.

Objective 3: Analyze the rise and fall of Senator Joseph McCarthy and the methods of McCarthyism.

LESSON 4 ORGANIZER — PACING: APPROX. 1 PERIOD, .5 BLOCKS

		OBJECTIVES	PACING	Online	Print
Connect					
DIGITAL START UP ACTIVITY **Cold War in the Homeland**			5 min.	●	
Investigate					
DIGITAL TEXT 1 **Cold War Tensions Rise at Home**		Objective 1	10 min.	●	●
INTERACTIVE GALLERY **Red Scare Culture**			10 min.	●	
DIGITAL TEXT 2 **Domestic Spy Cases Increase Fears**		Objective 2	10 min.	●	●
DIGITAL TEXT 3 **McCarthyism**		Objective 3	10 min.	●	●
INTERACTIVE TIMELINE **Red Scare and the Government**			10 min.	●	
Synthesize					
DIGITAL ACTIVITY **Fears of Communism**			5 min.	●	
Demonstrate					
DIGITAL QUIZ **Lesson Quiz and Class Discussion Board**			10 min.	●	

Cold War Fears at Home

CONNECT

DIGITAL START UP ACTIVITY
Cold War in the Homeland

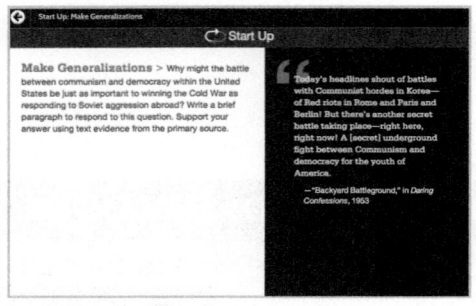

Project the Start Up Activity As students enter, draw their attention to the activity. Point out that "hordes" is a derogatory term for large groups of people moving together like swarms or herds. You may also need to remind students that the term *Red* means communist.

Discuss Prompt student discussion by reminding them that the Cold War was also a war of propaganda that was waged within the country as well as outside its borders. Why was this domestic battle also important? *(Possible answers should respond to the idea the perception of winning or losing the battle against encroaching communism was important.)*

Aa **Vocabulary Development:** Use the Interactive Reading Notepad to preview the Key Terms and Academic Vocabulary in this lesson with students.

⇅ FLIP IT!
Assign the Flipped Video for this lesson.

■ STUDENT EDITION PRINT PAGES: 653–658

INVESTIGATE

DIGITAL TEXT 1
Cold War Tensions Rise at Home

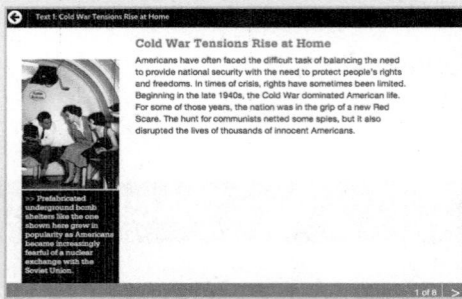

INTERACTIVE GALLERY
Red Scare Culture

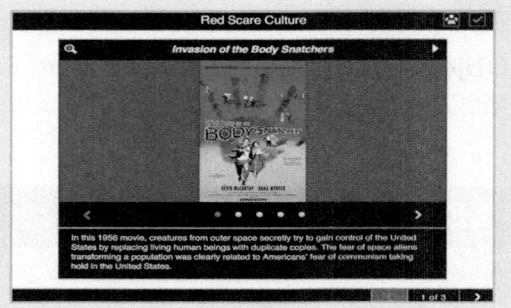

Objective 1: Describe the efforts of President Truman and the House Un-American Activities Committee to fight communism at home.

Quick Instruction
Interactive Gallery: Red Scare Culture
Project the interactive gallery. Before you review the images with students, tell them that characteristics and issues in U.S. history are reflected in various genres of literature and film. Have them describe identify the issue reflected in the gallery (fear of communism) and describe its characteristics (wide spread fear permeated culture; this fear was justified but inspired panic). Then review each image with the students. Point out that all of them reflect a fear of communism, while one of them (Dr. Strangelove) satirizes that fear.

Summarize Point out that, while being reflected in literature and film, the fear of communism was also reflected in government activities. Ask: How did President Truman and the House Un-American Activities Committee fight communism at home? *(Truman created a Federal Employee Loyalty Program in March 1947 that permitted the FBI and other government security agencies to screen federal employees for signs of disloyalty. The House of Representatives' House Un-American Activities Committee conducted several hearings on communist activities in the United States.)*

■★ ACTIVE CLASSROOM
Conduct a Take a Stand Activity. Ask students if the American fear of the United States falling to communism was a legitimate concern or an overreaction. Ask students to divide into two groups based on their answer and move to separate areas of the classroom. Ask students to talk with each other to compare their reasons for their position.

D **Differentiate: Extra Support** Some students may struggle with the concept of national mood, zeitgeist, and cultural change. For these students, it is useful to draw an analogy with a much smaller group of people, such as spectators at a sports event—and discuss how quickly shifts in mood among individuals can spread to others.

ELL Use the ELL activity described in the ELL chart.

Further Instruction
Go through the Interactive Reading Notepad questions and discuss the answers with the class.

Make Generalizations What adjectives would you use to describe the Red Scare in the United States in the 1950s? Why would you choose each one? *(Adjectives will vary but should be explained. Possible answers include: overstated, exaggerated, panicked)*

DIGITAL TEXT 2

Domestic Spy Cases Increase Fears

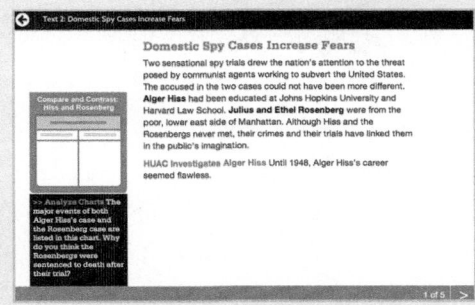

Objective 2: Explain how domestic spy cases intensified fears of communist influence in the U.S. government.

Quick Instruction

Analyze Images Project the image of Ethel Rosenberg. Point out that it is from a newspaper, and that the headline "On Way to Chair" refers to the electric chair. Invite students to summarize the Rosenberg case. *(Klaus Fuchs was charged with sending atomic secrets to the Soviet Union. The investigation against Fuchs led to the arrest of Ethel and Julius Rosenberg in 1950. The Rosenbergs claimed that they were being persecuted for being Jewish and for holding unpopular beliefs. They plead innocent but were found guilty and executed.)*

Summarize How have the Venona Paper saffected our understanding of this case? *(Decades afterwards, the Rosenberg's guilt was confirmed by the Venona Papers, which were secret Soviet messages that the United States had intercepted in the 1940s.)*

ELL Use the ELL activity described in the ELL chart.

Further Instruction

Go through the Interactive Reading Notepad questions and discuss the answers with the class.

Project the Venn diagram to note similarities and differences between the espionage cases of Alger Hiss and the Rosenbergs. Consider both the facts and the impact of the two spy cases. *(Alger Hiss—powerful government official; accused of stealing government documents; many believed he was innocent; sent to prison. The Rosenbergs—poor Jewish immigrants; accused of helping Soviets with the atomic bomb; executed. Both: Later documents proved some communist connections; contributed to anti-communist paranoia.)*

Interpret President Truman's Attorney General, J. Howard McGrath, warned that communists "are everywhere—in factories, offices, butcher stores, on street corners, and private businesses. And each carries in himself the death of our society." Why would statements like this have intensified tensions in the United States? *(They would have helped spread fear, mistrust, and suspicion of others.)*

Identify Patterns How did the Alger Hiss and Rosenberg cases heighten Cold War tensions in the United States? *(These two cases of communist spying seemed to prove the communists were, in fact, infiltrating the United States, and so it made other accusations of communist activity more credible, heightening the fear.)*

DIGITAL TEXT 3

McCarthyism

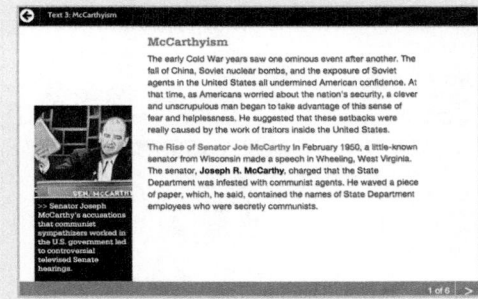

Objective 3: Analyze the rise and fall of Senator Joseph McCarthy and the methods of McCarthyism.

Quick Instruction

Interactive Timeline: Red Scare and the Government Project the timeline on the whiteboard. Ask students how many years the timeline covers. *(about seven)* Point out that each year in the seven-year timeline, except one, is marked by an event. Point out how frequently news of the communist threat was broadcast to the American public.

Identify Central Issues How would these Cold War tensions help Joseph McCarthy gain fame and power? *(People were prepared to believe tales of communist activities since so many had already taken place.)* How did McCarthyism, in turn, intensify Cold War tensions? *(McCarthy's statements and accusations made people in the United States believe that communists working within the country were about to overthrow the government.)*

▶ ACTIVE CLASSROOM

Have students cartoon it by creating a quick copy of the image of Joseph McCarthy from this lesson on a piece of paper and turn it into a political cartoon. Suggest they use a speech bubble to capture the essence of McCarthyism in a fictional statement by McCarthy.

Cold War Fears at Home

SYNTHESIZE

DEMONSTRATE

INTERACTIVE TIMELINE
Red Scare and the Government

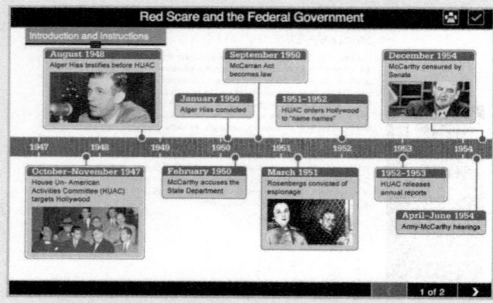

DIGITAL ACTIVITY
Fears of Communism

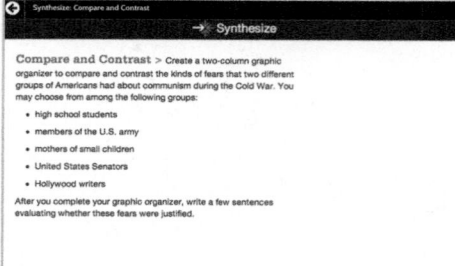

DIGITAL QUIZ
Lesson Quiz and Class Discussion Board

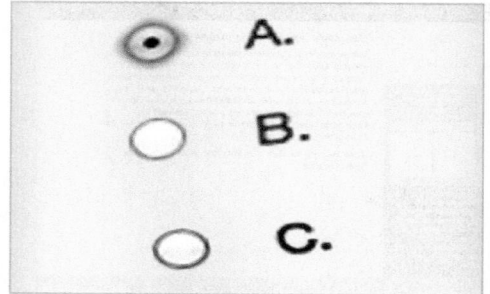

Further Instruction

Go through the Interactive Reading Notepad questions and discuss the answers with the class.

Infer McCarthy claimed to have "a list of 205" communists who worked at the State Department. He later claimed he had meant that there were "205 bad security risks." Then, he claimed that 57 employees were communists. Over the next months, the numbers on his list changed. McCarthy never did produce the list of communists. What can you infer from this? *(That he was lying)* Why do you think many Americans at the time failed to make this inference? *(Because they were gripped by the fear of communism, McCarthy was in a position of authority and power, and there were, in fact, some communists operating in the United States.)*

Discuss Before students begin their activity, lead a brief discussion about how Cold War fears and Cold War tensions were intensified by each of the following:

- the House Un-American Activities Committee (HUAC)
- films and literature
- McCarthyism
- Soviet Aggression

Assign the online Lesson Quiz for this lesson if you haven't already done so. Students will be offered automatic remediation or enrichment based on their score.

Pose these questions to the class on the Discussion Board:

Generate Explanations Why do you think so many people believed Joseph McCarthy's accusations?

Identify How were Cold War fears and tensions reflected in various genres of film and literature?

Topic Inquiry

Have students continue their investigations for the Topic Inquiry.

Postwar Prosperity

PEARSON
realize™

www.PearsonRealize.com
Access your Digital Lesson

Supporting English Language Learners

Use with Digital Text 1, **Causes and Effects of Prosperity in the 1950s.**

Listening
Invite volunteers to read aloud the section titled *Impact of the GI Bill*. As they read, model taking notes for students, then prompt the students to take notes commensurate with their content and grade-level needs.

Beginning Provide students with this sentence: The GI Bill helped with: _____, _____, and housing. Then read the following sentence at least twice while students take notes to complete their sentences: The GI Bill of Rights helped veterans with work, college, and housing after the war.

Intermediate Read the following sentence, and ask students to write down key information as you do so: The GI Bill of Rights of 1944 helped veterans with work, college, and housing after the war. Have students compare the notes they took.

Advanced Provide students with a partially-completed bullet-point outline of the section's second paragraph. Then read aloud the paragraph while students complete the outline. Reread the paragraph if necessary.

Advanced High Read aloud the section's second paragraph while students take notes. Have students discuss the task and share the notes they took. Then reread the paragraph and allow students to revise or add to their notes.

Use with Digital Text 5, **Eisenhower Leads a Thriving Nation.**

Learning
Read aloud the text, or invite volunteers to do so. Have students practice reading and pronouncing the name *Dwight Eisenhower*. Prompt students to use and reuse his name in context to build concept and language attainment.

Beginning Display this sentence: Eisenhower was popular because he was _____. Have students complete it with a descriptive word or phrase from the text and say the entire sentence aloud.

Intermediate Display a list of words from the text that describe Eisenhower's personality and leadership, intermingled with words that do not describe him. Invite students to choose a word that describes Eisenhower and use it in a statement about him.

Advanced Ask: Why do you think Eisenhower was a popular and effective leader? Encourage students to answer the question aloud using descriptive words and phrases from the text.

Advanced High Have pairs of students list qualities of Eisenhower's personality and leadership and discuss whether these qualities are always considered favorable in a president.

▶ Differentiate Instruction

Use the Differentiated Instruction notes throughout the lesson plan to support the varied skill sets, levels of readiness, and interests in the mixed-ability classroom.

Challenge These notes include suggestions for expanding the activity for advanced students.

On-Level These notes include suggestions for modifying the activity to address different interests or learning styles.

Extra Support These notes include ideas for providing more scaffolding or reading spuport.

Special Needs These notes provide ideas for adapting instruction to support the needs of various special needs students.

■ NOTES

Postwar Prosperity

Objectives

Objective 1: Describe how the Unites States made the transformation to a booming peacetime economy.

Objective 2: Discuss the growth of the Sunbelt and the effects of migration.

Objective 3: Describe changes in the U.S. economy in the postwar period.

Objective 4: Discuss the accomplishments and leadership qualities of Presidents Harry Truman and Dwight Eisenhower.

LESSON 5 ORGANIZER		PACING: APPROX. 1 PERIOD, .5 BLOCKS			
				RESOURCES	
		OBJECTIVES	PACING	Online	Print
Connect					
DIGITAL START UP ACTIVITY **The G.I. Bill of Rights**			5 min.	●	
Investigate					
DIGITAL TEXT 1 **Causes and Effects of Prosperity in the 1950s**		Objective 1	10 min.	●	●
DIGITAL TEXT 2 **Americans Migrate to the Sunbelt**		Objective 2	10 min.	●	●
DIGITAL TEXT 3 **Innovations and Economic Development**		Objective 3	10 min.	●	●
INTERACTIVE GALLERY **Postwar Entrepreneurs**			10 min.	●	
DIGITAL TEXT 4 **Truman's Postwar Leadership**			10 min.	●	●
DIGITAL TEXT 5 **Eisenhower Leads a Thriving Nation**		Objectives 3, 4	10 min.	●	●
INTERACTIVE GRAPH **1950s Prosperity Sparks Growth**			10 min.	●	
Synthesize					
DIGITAL ACTIVITY **Post-War Economic Conditions**			5 min.	●	
Demonstrate					
DIGITAL QUIZ **Lesson Quiz and Class Discussion Board**			10 min.	●	

PEARSON **realize**™
www.PearsonRealize.com

Go online to access additional resources including:
Primary Sources • Biographies • Supreme Court cases •
21st Century Skill Tutorials • Maps • Graphic Organizers.

CONNECT

DIGITAL START UP ACTIVITY
The G.I. Bill of Rights

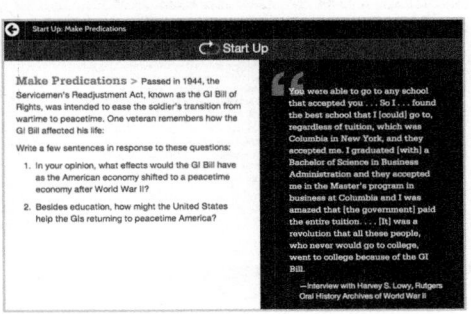

Project the Start Up Activity Ask students to answer the questions as they enter and get settled. Then have them share their ideas with another student, either in class or through a chat or blog space.

Discuss Besides the GI Bill, how might the United States help the military service members returning to peacetime America in a way that would lead to more economic growth and prosperity? *(Low-interest loans to returning service members; Job fairs or other employment networking systems would help service members find good jobs; Low-rent housing; transportation or relocation money)*

Aa Vocabulary Development: Use the Interactive Reading Notepad to preview the Key Terms and Academic Vocabulary in the lesson with students.

⇅ FLIP IT!
Assign the Flipped Video for this lesson.

■ STUDENT EDITION PRINT
PAGES: 659–666

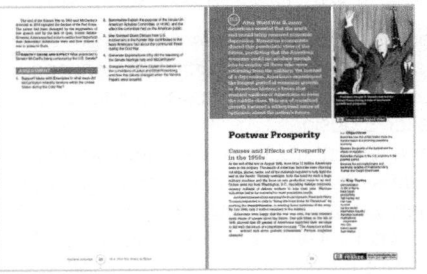

■ INVESTIGATE

DIGITAL TEXT 1
Causes and Effects of Prosperity in the 1950s

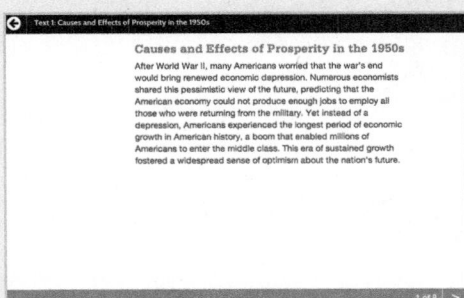

Objective 1: Describe how the United States made the transformation to a booming peacetime economy.

Quick Instruction
Point out to students that at the end of World War II in August 1945, more than 12 million Americans were in the military. Millions more were working in factories helping to make ships, planes, tanks, and all the materials required to help fight the war. Remind students that virtually overnight, both the need for such a huge military machine and the focus on war production came to an end.

Generate Explanations Ask students to speculate about the connection between rising consumer spending and rising birth rates. Guide them to understand the correlation between the two. Ask: What specific industries would have benefited from the increase in birth rates? *(the housing and retail industries)*

Ask students to identify and explain government and private sector actions that helped boost the U.S. economy. *(The government created the GI Bill to help millions of returning soldiers get college educations, which increased productivity and wages. The free market system provided private businesses and agricultural industries to develop and use new technology—often developed during the war—to create new products and increase productivity and consumer spending.)*

Synthesize Information How did the lifting of wartime restrictions lead to economic growth? *(Lifting the restrictions led to more consumer purchases. Demand increased*

dramatically and businesses had to hire more workers to make their goods. This created a cycle in which people bought new goods, leading businesses to hire more workers, who in turn bought more goods.)

ELL Use the ELL activity described in the ELL chart.

Further Instruction
Go through the Interactive Reading Notepad questions and discuss the answers with the class. World War II helped open many economic and employment opportunities for women and minorities. The effort to win the war also helped end the Great Depression. Many servicemen returning from the war resumed their former jobs, often pushing women out of the workforce. A population boom soon swept the country as returning servicemen married and started families with their wives.

Identify Cause and Effect What connection did the baby boom have on the postwar economy? *(The baby boom increased demand for products, such as homes, clothing, food, and services. People spent more money, which forced companies to increase production by hiring more workers. All this led to more spending that fueled economic growth.)*

Make Predictions Ask students to predict how the postwar economic growth in the late 1940s will affect American lives in the 1950s. *(Americans will be much wealthier in the 1950s than they had been previously and will use their money to continue a long and prosperous economic era.)*

Postwar Prosperity

DIGITAL TEXT 2
Americans Migrate to the Sunbelt

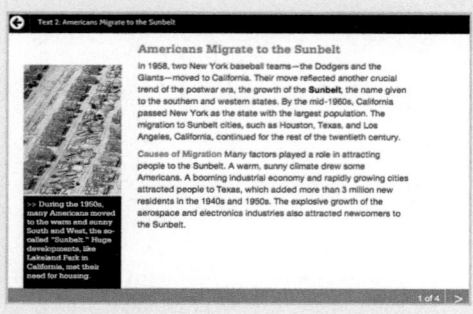

DIGITAL TEXT 3
Innovations and Economic Development

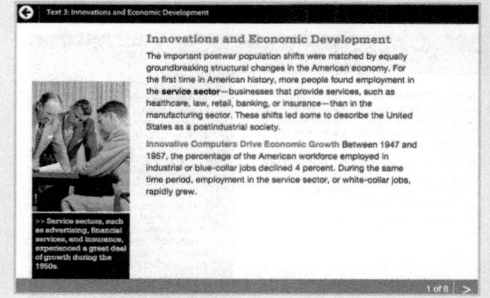

Objective 2: Discuss the growth of the Sunbelt and the effects of migration.

Quick Instruction
Project the map that shows the migration to the Sunbelt on the whiteboard. Introduce the map activity by asking students to identify the states that saw population increases in the 1940 and 1950s.

Summarize What motivated so many people in the United States to migrate to the Sunbelt? *(Many people were attracted to the warm, sunny climates in the Sunbelt. Growing industrial economies in Sunbelt regions attracted people as well.)*

Point out that the shift to the suburbs and the Sunbelt had huge effects on U.S. society. Be sure students understand that as people in the United States moved, their political power went with them. Areas that saw population increases gained political representation. Those areas that saw population declines lost political power.

Generate Explanations What possible implications might this gain in political power have for the Sunbelt? *(The economic and political interests of those in the Sunbelt will become more influential because of the increased political power.)*

Further Instruction
Discuss the Interactive Reading Notepad questions. Mention that urban and suburban growth created environmental concerns. Discuss the geographical features and environmental issues in many of the regions in the Sunbelt, such as Southern California, Texas, and Arizona.

Synthesize Information What were the negative effects of large migrations of people to regions that did not have the abundant resources or adequate infrastructure? *(In some regions of the Sunbelt, water and fertile land for agriculture were scarce. Sudden increases in populations strained these resources. Inadequate infrastructure caused crowding and congestion and inefficient transportation systems.)*

Predict Consequences Ask students to predict the impact of migration to the Sunbelt on American society. *(As the population shifts, more regions of the United States will become more important, economically and politically.)*

Objective 3: Describe changes in the U.S. economy in the postwar period.

Quick Instruction
The postwar U.S. economy underwent a groundbreaking structural change. More people in the United States were working in the service sector. Many worked in information industries, included those who built or operated the first computers. Such technological innovations contributed to the economic boom. Point out that entrepreneurs often were at the forefront in developing new products and management innovations that enhanced productivity. During this time, millions of small business entrepreneurs achieved the American dream.

Interactive Gallery: Postwar Entrepreneurs Project the slide show and discuss each image and caption.

Contrast In what ways did the management innovations of the McDonald brothers and Estée Lauder differ? *(The McDonalds brothers streamlined the production process to make their foods so they could sell more product at lower prices. Lauder focused her products in higher-priced stores and personalized the shopping experience for her customers.)*

Generate Explanations How might the changing demographics from Americans moving to the Sunbelt have benefited Sam Walton's business and his influenced his management decisions? *(Walton started his business in the South and focused on rural areas, places that were seeing increases in population. Many Americans were moving away from large urban areas, so Walton's*

INTERACTIVE GALLERY
Postwar Entrepreneurs

Postwar Entrepreneurs

Richard and Maurice McDonald

The McDonald brothers revolutionized the restaurant industry. By streamlining production and precooking food, the brothers made huge quantities of food at low prices.

1 of 4

decision to build Wal-Mart stores in those areas was good business.)

📷 ACTIVE CLASSROOM
Ask students to think about the roles of the McDonald brothers, Sam Walton, and Estee Lauder in shaping the postwar American economy. Use the Ranking Strategy to have students rank which of their achievements had the greatest impact on boosting and changing the economy.

Further Instruction
Discuss the changes in labor demographics in postwar America, including the increase in working women and the decline of Americans working in agriculture. Ask students to identify causes and effects of these changes. *(Many households required women to work to help pay bills and remain in the middle class. Farming technological innovations made it possible for fewer farmers to produce even more products.)*

Draw Conclusions What was the impact of technological innovations, such as the computer, on business and labor? *(Technology and computers made workers and companies more efficient and productive, resulting in greater profits. However, many of the jobs once done by people was often taken over by computers or automated machines. This resulted in many people losing jobs.)*

DIGITAL TEXT 4
Truman's Postwar Leadership

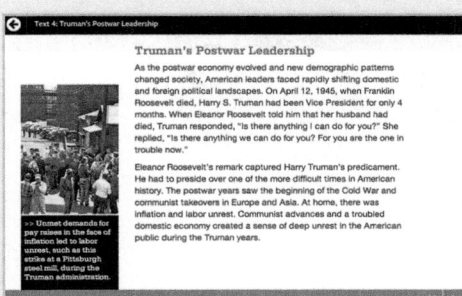

Text 4: Truman's Postwar Leadership

Truman's Postwar Leadership

As the postwar economy evolved and new demographic patterns changed society, American leaders faced rapidly shifting domestic and foreign political landscapes. On April 12, 1945, when Franklin Roosevelt died, Harry S. Truman had been Vice President for only 4 months. When Eleanor Roosevelt told him that her husband had died, Truman responded, "Is there anything I can do for you?" She replied, "Is there anything we can do for you? For you are the one in trouble now."

Eleanor Roosevelt's remark captured Harry Truman's predicament. He had to preside over one of the more difficult times in American history. The postwar years saw the beginning of the Cold War and communist takeovers in Europe and Asia. At home, there was inflation and labor unrest. Communist advances and a troubled domestic economy created a sense of deep unrest in the American public during the Truman years.

>> Unmet demands for pay raises in the face of inflation led to labor unrest, such as this strike at a Pittsburgh steel mill, during the Truman administration.

1 of 6

Objectives 3: Describe changes in the U.S. economy in the postwar period; 4: Discuss the accomplishments and leadership qualities of Presidents Harry Truman and Dwight Eisenhower.

Quick Instruction
President Harry Truman was in office as the postwar economy evolved and new demographic patterns changed society. Truman presided over an economy that was wrestling with inflation and labor unrest. The postwar economic expansion continued under Dwight D. Eisenhower. His presidency was one of the most prosperous in the twentieth century.

Interactive Graph: 1950s Prosperity Sparks Growth Project the interactivity on the whiteboard and move the slider over the charts that describe increasing consumerism.

Evaluate Data What does the economic data suggest about the effects of prosperity on businesses? *(Americans were spending a lot of money on a variety of products, which greatly benefited businesses in many industries.)*

DIGITAL TEXT 5
Eisenhower Leads a Thriving Nation

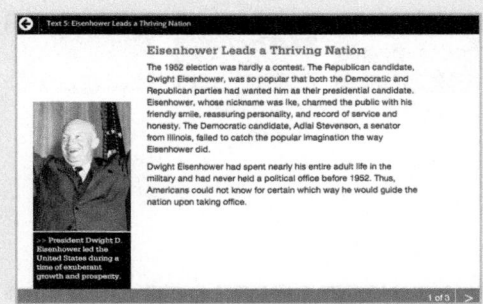

Text 5: Eisenhower Leads a Thriving Nation

Eisenhower Leads a Thriving Nation

The 1952 election was hardly a contest. The Republican candidate, Dwight Eisenhower, was so popular that both the Democratic and Republican parties had wanted him as their presidential candidate. Eisenhower, whose nickname was Ike, charmed the public with his friendly smile, reassuring personality, and record of service and honesty. The Democratic candidate, Adlai Stevenson, a senator from Illinois, failed to catch the popular imagination the way Eisenhower did.

Dwight Eisenhower had spent nearly his entire adult life in the military and had never held a political office before 1952. Thus, Americans could not know for certain which way he would guide the nation upon taking office.

>> President Dwight D. Eisenhower led the United States during a time of exuberant growth and prosperity.

1 of 3

📷 ACTIVE CLASSROOM
Use the Make Headlines strategy by asking students to write a newspaper headline that reflects the effects of consumerism in the 1950s. Ask: If you were to write a headline that captures the economic climate of the 1950s, what would that headline be? Pass your headline to a partner for them to review. You and your partner can keep the headlines or pass them back to revise.

D Differentiate: Challenge Ask students to do additional research on other products that reflect growing consumerism in the 1950s. Suggest that they use the dates in the interactivity charts as a guide. Have students present their findings.

ELL Use the ELL activity described in the ELL chart.

Postwar Prosperity

   **SYNTHESIZE**  **DEMONSTRATE**

INTERACTIVE GRAPH
1950s Prosperity Sparks Growth

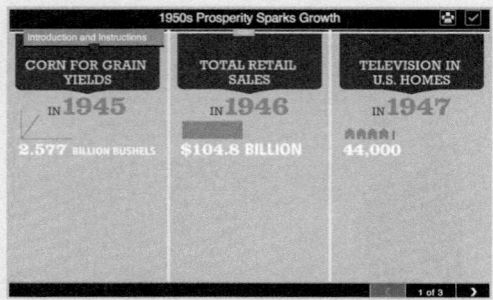

DIGITAL ACTIVITY
Post-War Economic Conditions

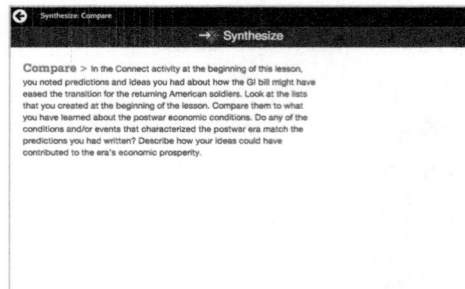

DIGITAL QUIZ
Lesson Quiz and Class Discussion Board

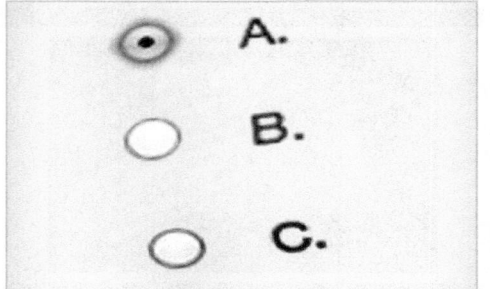

Further Instruction
Go through the Interactive Reading Notepad questions and discuss the answers with the class.

Presidents Truman and Eisenhower dealt with a variety of economic and foreign policy issues in their terms. To keep the American economy humming and to thwart the expansion of communism, they took different actions and showed contrasting leadership qualities.

Support Ideas with Examples Ask students to find examples of effective leadership qualities displayed by Presidents Truman and Eisenhower. *(Truman fought for what he believed in, such as civil rights legislation and health insurance. Eisenhower was a calm leader who struck a balance between liberal and conservative positions. Eisenhower saw the need to increase government presence in building the Interstate Highway system and in science education.)*

Predict Consequences Ask students to predict what the economic and foreign policy impact of Truman's inability to achieve victory in the Korean War will be. *(The United States will have to increase defense spending to fight the expansion of communist countries. This will probably lead to new technologies that will eventually help the economy in the long run. However, it might cause more conflicts with U.S. enemies.)*

Have partners think about the following question: How should a country repay its service men and women once they return from serving their countries? Have pairs share their answers with the class.

Ask students to think about and review their responses to the Lesson Start Up activity questions.

Discuss Do any of the conditions and/or events that characterized the postwar era match the predictions you had written? Describe how your ideas could have contributed to the era's economic prosperity.

Assign the online Lesson Quiz for this lesson if you haven't already done so. Students will be offered automatic remediation or enrichment based on their score.

Pose this question to the class on the Discussion Board:

In *Postwar Prosperity*, you read about how the United States transitioned from a wartime to a peacetime economy and how the actions taken by the government and private sector created a changing yet robust economy. By enacting the GI Bill of Rights, which provided financial assistance for returning veterans to go to college, build homes, and start businesses, the government helped energize an economy that had been straddled first by depression and then wartime restrictions. In addition, the free enterprise system allowed entrepreneurs the ability to develop innovative products and services that led to increased consumerism.

Make Predictions How long will the U.S. economy continue to grow and what factors might affect it? *(Because many countries are still recovering from the effects of World War II, the U.S. economy will continue to grow for another decade or two. Conflicts with communist countries could halt economic progress, and inflation and labor unrest could further impede growth.)*

Topic Inquiry
Have students continue their investigations for the Topic Inquiry.

Topic 15 Lesson 6

Mass Culture in the 1950s

Supporting English Language Learners

Use with Digital Text 2, **Increased Consumption and Consumerism.**

Speaking
Read aloud the section titled *Technological Innovations Drive New Conveniences* while students follow along. Read slowly enough that students can look at each word as you read it. Then prompt students to practice producing sounds of newly acquired vocabulary such as long and short vowels in order to pronounce English words in an increasingly comprehensible manner.

Beginning Review the long *i* and short *i* sounds. Then display the words enterprise and improved from the text. Mark the i's with a macron or a breve, and practice pronouncing the words together.

Intermediate Review the long *i* and short *i* sounds. Then display separate lists of long *i* and short *i* words from the text. Have students practice reading the words.

Advanced Display a scrambled list of long *i* and short *i* words from the text. Have students write the words on index cards, sort them according to their *i* sound, and read them aloud. Then have them shuffle the cards and practice reading the words.

Advanced High Ask pairs of students to identify the long *i* and short *i* words in the text and read them aloud. Then have them take turns reading the text, paying particular attention to their pronunciation of long *i* and short *i* words.

Use with Digital Text 3, **Families and Communities in the Fifties.**

Learning
Read aloud the section titled *Specific Needs Lead to Medical Innovations*, or invite volunteers to do so. Prompt students to internalize new basic language by using and reusing it in meaningful ways to build concept and language attainment. Explain that many of the medical terms in this section occur frequently in other contexts.

Beginning Display the words *medicine*, *vaccine*, and *disease*. Also display these sentences: _____ improved in the 1950s. Dr. Salk made a _____ to stop the spread of a _____. Have students copy the sentences, using the three words to complete them.

Intermediate Help students to identify three unfamiliar words related to medicine from the text. Together, look up their definitions and create sentences using them. Have students copy the sentences.

Advanced Display a list of five terms related to medicine from the text (e.g., disease, antibiotics, bacteria, diet, life expectancy). Ask students to look up unfamiliar words in a dictionary, and to write a sentence using each of the words.

Advanced High Display a list of five terms related to medicine from the text (e.g., disease, antibiotics, bacteria, diet, life expectancy). Ask students to use the five terms to write an original, well-structured paragraph about 1950s medicine.

▶ Differentiate Instruction

Use the Differentiated Instruction notes throughout the lesson plan to support the varied skill sets, levels of readiness, and interests in the mixed-ability classroom.

Challenge These notes include suggestions for expanding the activity for advanced students.

On-Level These notes include suggestions for modifying the activity to address different interests or learning styles.

Extra Support These notes include ideas for providing more scaffolding or reading spuport.

Special Needs These notes provide ideas for adapting instruction to support the needs of various special needs students.

◼ NOTES

Mass Culture in the 1950s

Objectives

Objective 1: Examine the rise of the suburbs and the growth of the interstate highway system.

Objective 2: Explain the causes and effects of prosperity in the 1950s on consumers.

Objective 3: Discuss postwar changes in family life.

Objective 4: Describe changes in education in the postwar period.

Objective 5: Describe the rise of new forms of mass culture.

LESSON 6 ORGANIZER		PACING: APPROX. 1 PERIOD, .5 BLOCKS			
				RESOURCES	
		OBJECTIVES	PACING	Online	Print
Connect					
DIGITAL START UP ACTIVITY **Mass Migration**			5 min.	●	
Investigate					
DIGITAL TEXT 1 **Suburban Migration**		Objective 1	10 min.	●	●
BEFORE AND AFTER **Suburban Sprawl: 1950s to the Present**			10 min.	●	
DIGITAL TEXT 2 **Increased Consumption and Consumerism**		Objective 2	10 min.	●	●
DIGITAL TEXT 3 **Families and Communities in the Fifties**		Objective 3	10 min.	●	●
INTERACTIVE GALLERY **Medical Advances of the Postwar Era**			10 min.	●	
DIGITAL TEXT 4 **Educational Opportunities and Priorities**		Objective 4	10 min.	●	●
DIGITAL TEXT 5 **Television Shapes American Culture**		Objective 5	10 min.	●	●
Synthesize					
DIGITAL ACTIVITY **Results of Mass Migration**			5 min.	●	
Demonstrate					
DIGITAL QUIZ **Lesson Quiz and Class Discussion Board**			10 min.	●	

PEARSON

realize™

www.PearsonRealize.com

Go online to access additional resources including:
Primary Sources • Biographies • Supreme Court cases •
21st Century Skill Tutorials • Maps • Graphic Organizers.

■ CONNECT

DIGITAL START UP ACTIVITY
Mass Migration

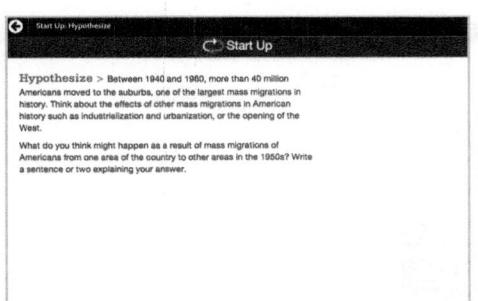

Project the Start Up Activity Ask students
to answer the questions as they enter and get
settled. Then have them share their ideas with
another student, either in class or through a
chat or blog space.

Discuss What do you think might happen as
a result of mass migrations of Americans from
one area of the country to other areas in the
1950s?

Tell students that in this lesson they will explore
how a unique postwar U.S. culture developed
as new suburban communities spread, and
advances in technology, science, medicine
and the free enterprise systems raised the
quality of life.

Aa Vocabulary Development: Use the
Interactive Reading Notepad to preview the
Key Terms and Academic Vocabulary in the
lesson with students.

⭘ FLIP IT!

Assign the Flipped Video for this lesson.

■ STUDENT EDITION PRINT
PAGES: 667–673

■ INVESTIGATE

DIGITAL TEXT 1
Suburban Migration

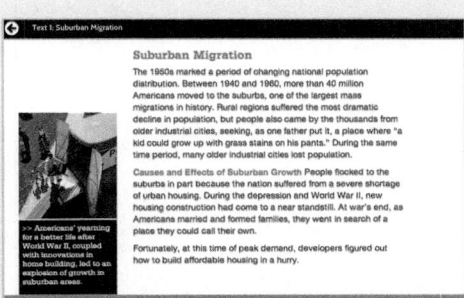

BEFORE AND AFTER
Suburban Sprawl: 1950s
to the Present

Objective 1: **Examine the rise of
the suburbs and the growth of the
interstate highway system.**

Quick Instruction

**Before and After: Suburban Sprawl: 1950s
to the Present** Point out that people from
the United States were not just moving from
region to region in the postwar era. Remind
students that between 1940 and 1960, more
than 40 million Americans moved from urban
centers to the suburbs, one of the largest
mass migrations in history.

Project the interactive activity on the
whiteboard and move the slider to reveal the
before and after photos of Las Vegas. Discuss
the effects of changing patterns of population
distribution on the physical environment.
Mention that transportation innovations such
as safer automobiles and highways affected
many Americans' standards of living. Ask
students to identify other scientific discoveries
and technological innovations that affected
Americans who moved to the suburbs or
new communities like Las Vegas. *(affordable
housing with improved appliances, shopping
centers, drive-in movie theaters)*

Generate Explanations How did the
migration to new communities and suburbs
affect U.S. society? *(The move to the suburbs
resulted in more dependence on cars.
Suburbs became self-contained communities,
which often left urban areas struggling with the
loss of people and businesses.)*

🖳 ACTIVE CLASSROOM

Project an image of Las Vegas and use
a whiteboard tool to divide it into four
numbered quadrants. Have students count
off 1 to 4. Then have them look closely
at the part of the image in their quadrant.
Have them tell you what they see and what
they learned as a result of their focus on
this part of the image. Collect insights for
each quadrant.

Further Instruction

Project and discuss the Interactive Reading
Notepad questions, including the graphic
organizer. Review students' notes as a
class and fill in the graphic organizer on the
whiteboard as you go. Point out that families
were not the only people interested in moving
to the suburbs. The free enterprise system
provided entrepreneurs with the necessary
tools to develop innovative products and
services for thousands of new communities
throughout the country. Discuss examples of
entrepreneurs having a great impact on these
new communities.

Analyze Information Do you think life in
the suburbs became the "new" model for the
American dream? Explain. *(Yes. The suburbs
offered Americans the possibility of owning a
home, land, and enjoying a new way of life.)*

Mass Culture in the 1950s

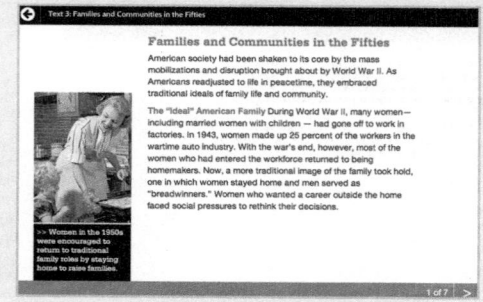

DIGITAL TEXT 2

Increased Consumption and Consumerism

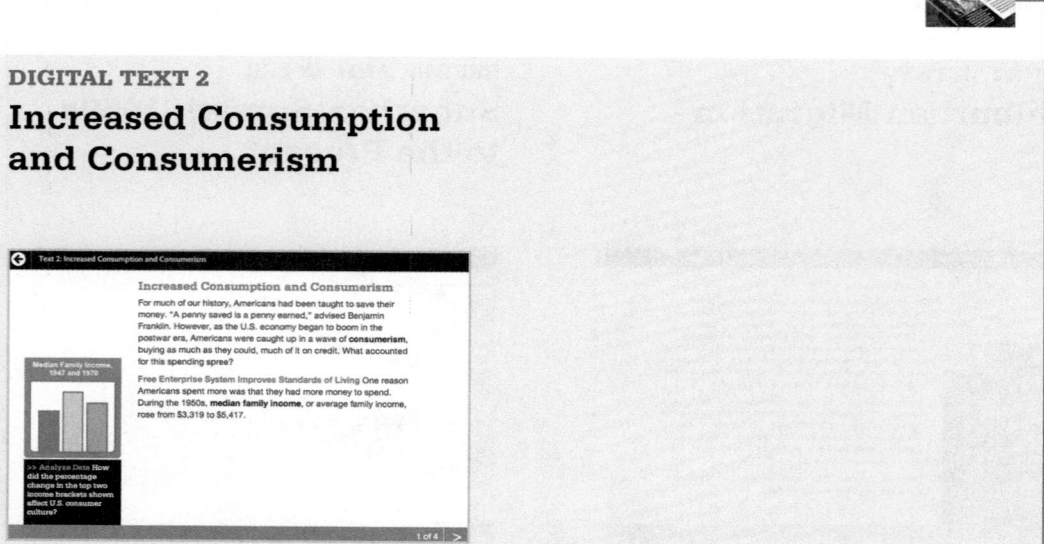

Text 2: Increased Consumption and Consumerism

Increased Consumption and Consumerism

For much of our history, Americans had been taught to save their money. "A penny saved is a penny earned," advised Benjamin Franklin. However, as the U.S. economy began to boom in the postwar era, Americans were caught up in a wave of **consumerism**, buying as much as they could, much of it on credit. What accounted for this spending spree?

Free Enterprise System Improves Standards of Living One reason Americans spent more was that they had more money to spend. During the 1950s, **median family income**, or average family income, rose from $3,319 to $5,417.

>> **Analyze Data** How did this percentage change in the top two income brackets shown affect U.S. consumer culture?

Median Family Income, 1947 and 1970

1 of 4 >

Objective 2: Explain the causes and effects of prosperity in the 1950s on consumers.

Quick Instruction

Project the income bracket chart on the whiteboard and discuss the data. Point out that as the U.S. economy began to boom in the postwar era, Americans were caught up in a wave of consumerism and increased consumption. People bought as much as they could, even if they didn't have the money on hand. New forms of financial tools, such as credit cards, helped them pay for new products and services.

Draw Conclusions How might credit cards both help and harm many Americans? *(People could buy new products that would give them more free time and make them more productive. However, credit cards can often lead people into too much debt that they cannot pay off.)*

ELL Use the ELL activity described in the ELL chart.

Further Instruction

Review and discuss the Interactive Reading Notepad questions. Given opportunity in the American free enterprise system, businesses and entrepreneurs rushed to develop technological and purchasing innovations that improved the standard of living.

Categorize Home appliances topped the list of the goods that Americans bought. Ask students to find examples of innovative products that transformed life for many Americans. *(washing machines and dryers, televisions, refrigerators)*

Synthesize Information How did the U.S. economy and American families benefit from the application of scientific discoveries and technological innovations? *(Innovative products made Americans more productive and gave them more free time, which led many to spend more money on entertainment and other things. The increased spending helped businesses and that led to a stronger economy and higher standards of living for many Americans.)*

DIGITAL TEXT 3

Families and Communities in the Fifties

Text 3: Families and Communities in the Fifties

Families and Communities in the Fifties

American society had been shaken to its core by the mass mobilizations and disruption brought about by World War II. As Americans readjusted to life in peacetime, they embraced traditional ideals of family life and community.

The "Ideal" American Family During World War II, many women—including married women with children — had gone off to work in factories. In 1943, women made up 25 percent of the workers in the wartime auto industry. With the war's end, however, most of the women who had entered the workforce returned to being homemakers. Now, a more traditional image of the family took hold, one in which women stayed home and men served as "breadwinners." Women who wanted a career outside the home faced social pressures to rethink their decisions.

>> Women in the 1950s were encouraged to return to traditional family roles by staying home to raise families.

1 of 7 >

Objective 3: Discuss postwar changes in family life.

Quick Instruction

During the 1950s, social scientists described the nuclear family, or a household consisting of a mother and father and their children, as the backbone of American society. Family life revolved around children. Parents were eager to provide the best possible environments in which to rear their children, including all the best medical treatments and preventative measures.

Interactive Gallery: Medical Advances of the Postwar Era Project the interactive gallery and discuss each image and caption. Explain how specific needs resulted in scientific discoveries and technological innovations in medicine.

Generate Explanations How did specific needs result in scientific discoveries and technological innovations in medicine? *(Diseases and illnesses such as polio and the flu were major problems for Americans and other people around the world. The need to find cures or vaccines drove innovators to find solutions.)*

🖳 ACTIVE CLASSROOM

List the medical innovations on stickies on the wall. Break students into small groups. Ask each group to choose the sticky with what they think is the most significant medical innovation of the postwar era. Ask the group to discuss among themselves why they think it is most significant. Ask one person from each group to stand and explain why.

INTERACTIVE GALLERY
Medical Advances of the Postwar Era

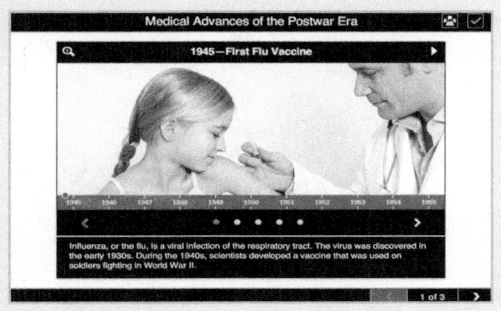

D Differentiate: **Extra Support** Point out that students are consumers when they buy products or purchase services. Have students list three examples of companies or businesses that market their goods and services to teenagers.

ELL Use the ELL activity described in the ELL chart.

Further Instruction
Discuss the ways in which children and teenagers' lives were different during the baby boom of the 1950s. Ask students to find examples. *(Parents spent more time and money on their kids. Teenagers and young adults became significant consumers, helping to fuel economic growth.)*

Be sure that students understand that the emphasis on the nuclear family in the 1950s was strengthened by a religious revival that stressed traditional ideals of family life and community. The increasing number of children during the baby boom also played a significant role in reinforcing social ideals of family.

Apply Concepts What impact did religious leaders like Billy Graham have on 1950s U.S. society? *(Billy Graham and others helped religion become more popular. New churches were built, which often helped unite communities. Religious ideas and mottos, such as "In God We Trust" and "under God," became popular as a way to differentiate American society from communist societies, which were officially atheist.)*

DIGITAL TEXT 4
Educational Opportunities and Priorities

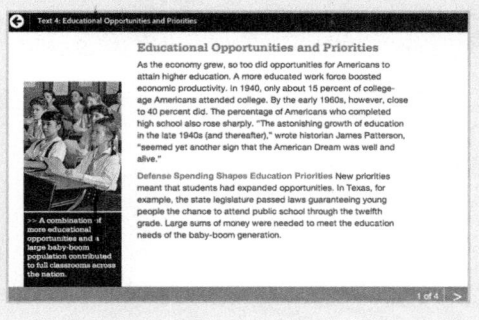

Objective 4: Describe changes in education in the postwar period.

Quick Instruction
Direct students' attention to the photo of the classroom. Point out that more Americans were attaining higher levels of education than ever before. New priorities and a booming economy meant that students had expanded opportunities. Discuss the impact of defense priorities on education and the great drive for innovative technology and services in all aspects of American society.

Infer What was the economic impact of defense spending on education priorities in the postwar era? *(To keep pace with the Soviet Union in space and weapon technology, defense spending influenced the shift in education to science subjects.)*

Further Instruction
Go through the Interactive Reading Notepad questions and discuss the answers with the class. Point out that as the U.S. economy grew in the postwar era, so too did opportunities for Americans to attain higher education. A more educated work force boosted economic productivity, so many people tried to create a movement to make education more accessible and equal for all Americans, including minorities.

Ask students to identify examples of actions taken to make education more accessible to more Americans. *(California Master Plan; new or expanded state college and university systems; challenges to segregated school systems)*

Predict Consequences Ask students to predict what the effects of desegregation decisions, such as *Brown* v. *Board of Education* will be. *(The Brown v. Board of Education decision will help many African Americans attain more equal educational opportunities.)*

DIGITAL TEXT 5
Television Shapes American Culture

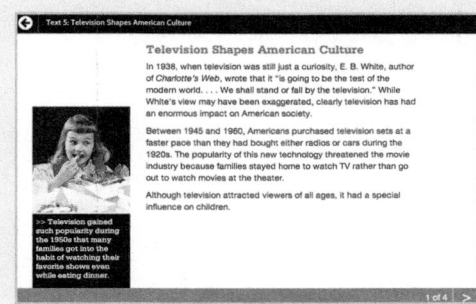

Objective 5: Describe the rise of new forms of mass culture.

Quick Instruction
Point out that one of the effects of the postwar prosperity was the emergence of television as a powerful form of communication. Between 1945 and 1960, Americans purchased television sets at a faster pace than they had bought either radios or cars during the 1920s. Direct students' attention to the photo of the family in the sitcom. Television programs promoted an idealized version of the nuclear family in the 1950s. Remind students that new forms of mass communication, such as nationally broadcast television programs, helped erode distinct regional and ethnic cultural identities. Television also promoted a global diffusion of American culture as shows produced in the United States became increasingly popular overseas.

Identify Central Issues Why was television a better medium than radio to encourage increased consumption? *(Television provided viewers with visual images of products and services, making it much more effective as a means of advertising and selling products.)*

Summarize How did television contribute to the development of a national postwar culture in the United States? *(Americans in every region of the country watched the same shows and bought the same goods they saw advertised.)*

Further Instruction
Identify Central Issues Why was television such an influential media in political campaigns? *(Along with its power in expanding consumerism, television allowed*

Mass Culture in the 1950s

SYNTHESIZE

DIGITAL ACTIVITY
Results of Mass Migration

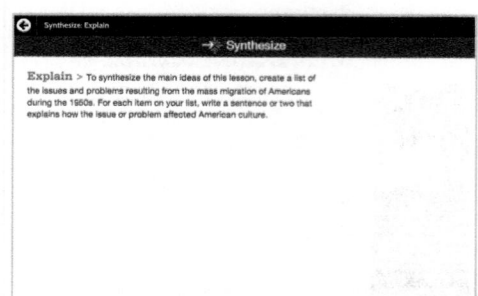

DEMONSTRATE

DIGITAL QUIZ
Lesson Quiz and Class Discussion Board

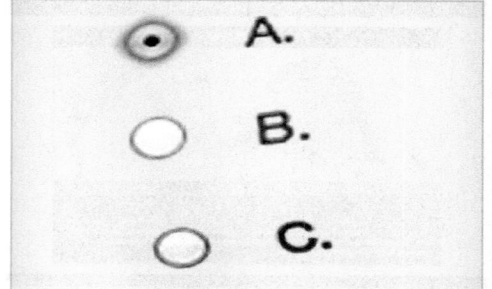

Americans to see the candidates and observe their behavior. Voters are more likely to support candidates who are attractive and appear confident, so television played an increasingly important role in determining elections.)

Have partners use the Think Pair Share strategy to discuss the prompt. Ask them to take five minutes to create their lists individually, before sharing them with the class.

Discuss Discuss several of the most listed issues and problems and engage students in describing how each issue or problem affected American culture.

Assign the online Lesson Quiz for this lesson if you haven't already done so. Students will be offered automatic remediation or enrichment based on their score.

Pose these questions to the class on the Discussion Board:

In *Mass Culture of the 1950s*, you read about significant forces that had great impact on American society in the postwar era. As more Americans throughout the country bought televisions and watched the same shows and bought the same goods, a uniquely American mass culture developed that reflected life in the postwar era.

Apply Concepts Is the development of an American mass culture good for the country if it erodes distinct regional and ethnic cultures? *(Yes. An American mass culture is good because it gives the country an identity that all American citizens can embrace and it helps unite different groups of people.)*

Topic Inquiry
Have students continue their investigations for the Topic Inquiry.

PEARSON realize™
www.PearsonRealize.com
Access your Digital Lesson

Social Issues of the 1950s

Supporting English Language Learners

Use with Digital Text 1, **Critics and Rebels Emerge.**

Learning
Read aloud the section titled *The Impact of the Beat Generation on American Society*, or invite volunteers to do so. Prompt students to internalize new academic language by using and reusing it in meaningful ways to build concept and language attainment. Also, point out the corresponding photograph and caption so students can better understand the term *beatnik*.

Beginning Display the second sentence of the section, and underline the words *conform to*. Define *conform to* as "follow" or "accept." Then have them complete and say this sentence: Beatniks did not conform to _____.

Intermediate Display the second sentence of the section, and underline the words *conform to*. Ask students to suggest synonyms for *conform to*. Then have them use *conform to* in an original spoken sentence.

Advanced Display the words *conform*, *conformity*, and *nonconformity*, and point them out in the text. Compare and contrast their meanings and usage. Then have students make statements about 1950s U.S. society using the words.

Advanced High Display the words *conform*, *conformity*, and *nonconformity*, and point them out in the text. Compare and contrast their meanings and usage. Ask pairs of students to integrate the words into a discussion of 1950s U.S. society.

Use with Digital Text 2, **Poverty in the Cities and Rural Areas.**

Speaking
Read aloud the first three paragraphs of the section titled *Effects of Migration on Cities*, or invite volunteers to do so. Explain that post-World War II U.S. cities are being described in these paragraphs. Prompt students to expand and internalize their vocabulary with high-frequency English words necessary for identifying and describing objects and by learning routine language needed for classroom communication.

Beginning Demonstrate the use of from and to by describing the movement of objects. Then display these sentences: After the war, white families moved _____ cities _____ the suburbs. Minorities moved _____ cities _____ rural areas. Have students complete them and say them aloud.

Intermediate Display the phrases *as well* and *as well as*. Discuss their meanings and usage, and ask students to say a sentence about post-World War II cities using each of the phrases.

Advanced Display the words *during*, *because*, and *however*. Have students locate them in the text. Discuss their purpose and where they can occur in sentences. Then have students say a sentence about post-World War II cities using each of the words.

Advanced High Ask students to give a brief talk about post-World War II cities. Explain that they must use each of the following words or phrases in their talk: *such as*, *as well as*, *in turn*, *because*, *however*.

▣ Differentiate Instruction

Use the Differentiated Instruction notes throughout the lesson plan to support the varied skill sets, levels of readiness, and interests in the mixed-ability classroom.

Challenge These notes include suggestions for expanding the activity for advanced students.

On-Level These notes include suggestions for modifying the activity to address different interests or learning styles.

Extra Support These notes include ideas for providing more scaffolding or reading spuport.

Special Needs These notes provide ideas for adapting instruction to support the needs of various special needs students.

■ NOTES

Social Issues of the 1950s

Objectives

Objective 1: Summarize the arguments made by critics who rejected the culture of the fifties.

Objective 2: Describe the causes and effects of urban and rural poverty.

Objective 3: Explain the problems that many minority groups faced in the postwar era.

LESSON 7 ORGANIZER		PACING: APPROX. 1 PERIOD, .5 BLOCKS			
		OBJECTIVES	PACING	RESOURCES	
				Online	Print
Connect					
	DIGITAL START UP ACTIVITY **Urban African Americans**		5 min.	●	
Investigate					
	DIGITAL TEXT 1 **Critics and Rebels Emerge**	Objective 1	10 min.	●	●
	INTERACTIVE GALLERY **The Spread of Rock-and-Roll**		10 min.	●	
	DIGITAL TEXT 2 **Poverty in the Cities and Rural Areas**	Objective 2	10 min.	●	●
	DIGITAL TEXT 3 **Struggles of Minorities**	Objective 3	10 min.	●	●
	INTERACTIVE MAP **Demographic Trends of the 1950s**		10 min.	●	
Synthesize					
	DIGITAL ACTIVITY **Minority Challenges**		5 min.	●	
Demonstrate					
	DIGITAL QUIZ **Lesson Quiz and Class Discussion Board**		10 min.	●	

PEARSON
realize™
www.PearsonRealize.com

Go online to access additional resources including:
Primary Sources • Biographies • Supreme Court cases •
21st Century Skill Tutorials • Maps • Graphic Organizers.

■ CONNECT

DIGITAL START UP ACTIVITY
Urban African Americans

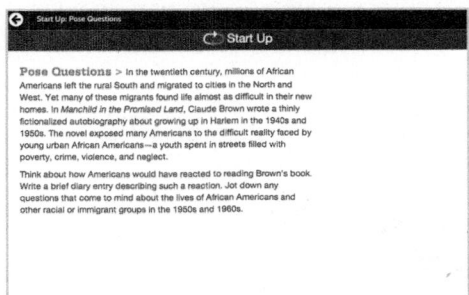

Project the Start Up Activity Ask students to answer the questions as they enter and get settled. Then have them share their ideas with another student, either in class or through a chat or blog space. Explicitly connect the passage to the effects of the rural-to-urban migration.

Invite a volunteer to read Claude Brown's passage aloud. Think about how people in the United States would have reacted to reading Brown's book. Invite students to share their diary entries and questions with the class.

Tell students that in this lesson they will explore how changing demographic patterns, migration, and new movements in the arts helped shape American culture in the 1950s.

Aa Vocabulary Development: Use the Interactive Reading Notepad to preview the Key Terms and Academic Vocabulary in the lesson with students.

⇅ FLIP IT!
Assign the Flipped Video for this lesson.

■ STUDENT EDITION PRINT PAGES: 674–679

■ INVESTIGATE

DIGITAL TEXT 1
Critics and Rebels Emerge

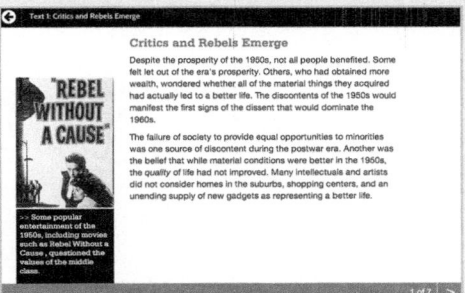

Objective 1: Summarize the arguments made by critics who rejected the culture of the fifties.

Quick Instruction
Interactive Gallery: The Spread of Rock-and-Roll Project the slide show. Select the images to reveal important facts about some of the first influential performers of the rock-and-roll era. Explain that rock-and-roll was a significant cultural movement and a symbol of the emerging youth culture and the growing power of youth on mainstream culture. Point out that the rapidity with which rock-and-roll spread around the world reveals the global influence of American culture. Ask students to identify some of the positive and negative cultural effects of rock-and-roll music on U.S. society. *Rock-and-roll music helped boost the economy in the 1950s because so many young Americans were buying rock-and-roll records or watching their favorite performers on television. However, it had a negative impact in that it created a divide between young Americans and older generations that didn't embrace the new music.*

Generate Explanations In what way does the emergence of rock-n-roll spotlight how people of various races helped shaped U.S. culture in the 1950s? *(Rock-and-roll originated in the rhythm and blues traditions of African Americans. White disc jockeys and performers embraced the music and helped make it popular.)*

INTERACTIVE GALLERY
The Spread of Rock-and-Roll

👥 ACTIVE CLASSROOM
Direct students to have a "Conversation with a Rock-and-Roll Opponent." Tell students to imagine that they are having a conversation with someone who believes that rock-and-roll is harmful to American society. Direct each student to write down a question he or she would like to ask, then how the opponent would respond, and finally what the student would say in response.

D Differentiate: Challenge Ask students to do additional research on one of the performers highlighted in the interactive activity or choose another early rock-and-roll performer to research. Encourage students to enhance their reports with audio samples of their performers.

ELL Use the ELL activity described in the ELL chart.

Further Instruction
Project and discuss the Interactive Reading Notepad questions, including the graphic organizer. Review students' notes as a class and fill in the graphic organizer on the whiteboard as you go. Ask students to find examples of other critics of mainstream U.S. society who voiced their opinions in the 1950s. *(Intellectuals—sociologists, novelists, feminists; the Beats; Hollywood directors and actors.)*

Make Generalizations What were the positive and negative impacts of significant Beat generation literature? *(The Beat writers provided a new view of U.S. culture, often using colorful or creative language and techniques. Like rock-and-roll, the Beats often angered or frightened Americans who did not understand or agree with their views.)*

Social Issues of the 1950s

DIGITAL TEXT 2

Poverty in the Cities and Rural Areas

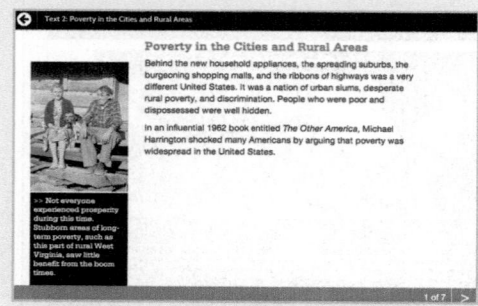

DIGITAL TEXT 3

Struggles of Minorities

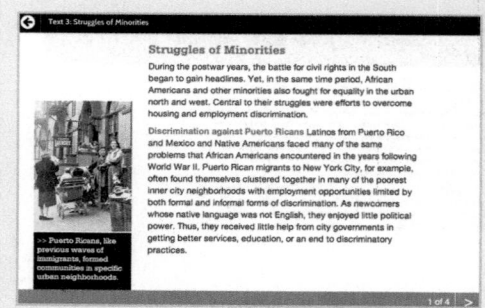

Objective 2: Describe the causes and effects of urban and rural poverty.

Quick Instruction

Analyze Data Project the graph depicting poverty and affluence and give students some time to look at the data. This graph shows how poverty levels changed from 1955–2005. Writer Michael Harrington wrote that despite growing U.S. affluence, poverty plagued African Americans in the inner cities, rural whites in areas such as Appalachia, and Hispanics in migrant farm labor camps and urban barrios.

Interpret What made the claims of Michael Harrington startling to many Americans? *(When Harrington made the claims, the poverty level in the United States had been declining.)*

Compare and Contrast What were the causes and effects of the changing demographics resulting from migration in the postwar era and how did it affect poverty levels? *(African Americans and other nonwhite minorities moved in great numbers from rural areas to cities looking for better economic opportunities. At the same time, middle-class white families moved to the suburbs from urban areas. Cities suffered because they lost tax revenue and could no longer provide adequate public services. Rural farmers faced economic challenges because corporations and large farm owners were taking over. These factors forced many minorities and small farmers in rural areas deeper into poverty.)*

ELL Use the ELL activity described in the ELL chart.

Further Instruction

Go through the Interactive Reading Notepad questions and discuss the answers with the class.

Summarize How would you describe the effects on U.S. society, and in particular large inner-city areas, of mass migration of people from rural areas? *(The effects were extremely negative in many cases. So many people moved into the inner cities that it created great problems. For example, many people could not find adequate housing. This led to people living in unhealthy places. City services were stretched to the limit, which made the problem even worse. Life in extremely difficult circumstances often leads to crime and other social problems.)*

Synthesize Information During the 1950s, many middle-class Americans were unaware of poverty. Why was this the case? *(Perhaps the media didn't report on issues like poverty as much as on other issues. Consequently, many Americans did not realize the extent of the problem.)*

Objective 3: Explain the problems that many minority groups faced in the postwar era.

Quick Instruction

Interactive Map: Demographic Trends of the 1950s Project the interactive map. Encourage students to make generalizations about the regions in the country that experienced population increases and declines. Emphasize to students that the country was experiencing significant population shifts because of economic and cultural factors. Point out that U.S. minority groups, as well as newly arrived immigrants from Mexico, Puerto Rico, and Asia, struggled to overcome various forms of discrimination.

ACTIVE CLASSROOM

Project the images from the interactive map hot spots and have students use one photograph to play an Act It Out game. Ask students to bring the subjects in the photos to life by stating what each must be thinking and feeling at the moment, and telling what each person hopes to achieve in their new homes.

Hypothesize Why would African Americans or immigrants move to regions of the U.S. where they faced various forms of discrimination? *(The economic opportunities in the new regions far outweighed the problems they faced in their former homes.)*

■ SYNTHESIZE

■ DEMONSTRATE

INTERACTIVE MAP
Demographic Trends of the 1950s

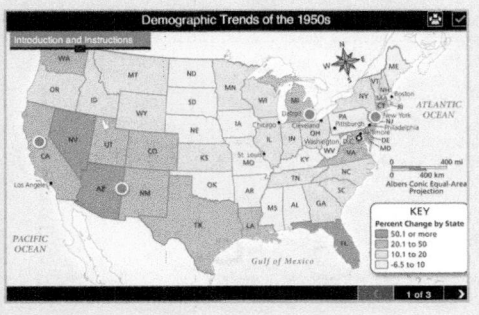

DIGITAL ACTIVITY
Minority Challenges

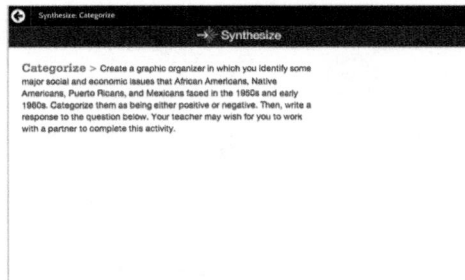

DIGITAL QUIZ
Lesson Quiz and Class Discussion Board

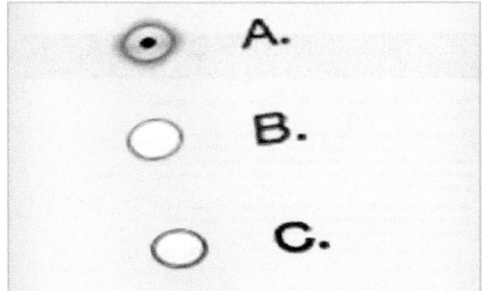

Further Instruction

Go through the Interactive Reading Notepad questions and discuss the answers with the class.

Point out that when groups of people or cultures are assimilated into a larger society, the assimilated people often lose aspects of their culture. Discuss the benefits and costs of assimilation.

Summarize Many Americans and government leaders promoted an Americanization movement, an idea that encouraged immigrants and other minority groups to be assimilated into U.S. culture. Point out that in 1953, the federal government enacted the termination policy, a major change in the rules governing Native Americans. Ask students to identify the key policies of the termination policy. *(The law sought to end tribal government and to relocate Native Americans to the nation's cities. It also terminated federal responsibility for the health and welfare of Native Americans.)*

Apply Concepts Explain how the various racial groups you learned about have shaped U.S. culture. *(As mentioned earlier, African Americans have made significant contributions to music, language, and the arts. Puerto Ricans and Mexican Americans have contributed much to American English, as well culinary and artistic contributions. Asian Americans have contributed a great entrepreneurial drive to American society, and have added to the American arts and food scenes.)*

Before students begin their graphic organizers, lead a brief discussion about the struggles that immigrants have faced throughout American history. Encourage students to compare and contrast the struggles of African Americans, Native Americans, and other minority groups in the 1950 to earlier groups of people.

Discuss Have the issues and struggles minorities faced in the 1950s that you identified been solved today? Explain. *(Many of the issues, such as housing and employment discrimination have not been solved. Many low-income urban areas struggle with crowding issues and high levels of crime.)*

Assign the online Lesson Quiz for this lesson if you haven't already done so. Students will be offered automatic remediation or enrichment based on their score.

Pose these questions to the class on the Discussion Board:

In *Social Issues of the 1950s*, you read about how rebels and critics emerged to challenge postwar values, and how U.S. society and culture was also rapidly changing due to migration and greater contact among various racial groups.

Evaluate Arguments Were the 1950s critics of U.S. consumption and consumerism making valid arguments?

Predict Consequences How will rock-and-roll shape the attitudes of the baby boom generation?

Topic Inquiry

Have students continue their investigations for the Topic Inquiry.

Postwar America

SYNTHESIZE

DIGITAL ACTIVITY
Reflect on the Essential Question and Topic

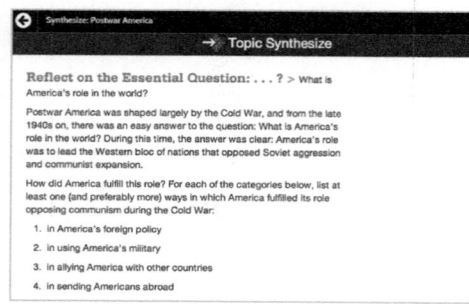

Direct students to reflect on the Essential Question for the Topic: What is America's role in the world? Remind students of the possible roles they considered at the beginning of the Topic:

- as a beacon of freedom
- as a haven for refugees
- as the world's policeman
- as the spreader of democracy
- as an international peacemaker

Challenge students to identify which of these roles, or perhaps others, they think America played during postwar years. Discuss their answers as a class or ask students to post their answers on the Class Discussion Board.

Next, ask students to reflect on the Topic as a whole and jot down 1-3 questions they've thought about during the Topic. Share these examples if students need help getting started:

- How did the United States hope to "win" the Cold War?
- Could anything like McCarthyism happen again?
- Did the Cold War change what Americans thought their role in the world should be?

Topic Inquiry
Have students complete Step 3 of the Topic Inquiry.

DEMONSTRATE

DIGITAL TOPIC REVIEW AND ASSESSMENT
Postwar America

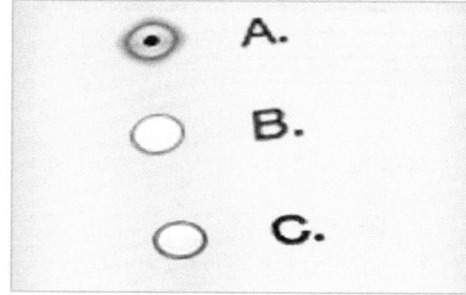

Students can prepare for the Topic Test by answering the questions in the Topic Review and Assessment online or the Assessment questions in the Print Student text. They can also prepare by reviewing their answers to the Interactive Reading Notepad questions or reviewing their notes in the Reading and Notetaking Study Guide.

DIGITAL TOPIC TEST
Postwar America

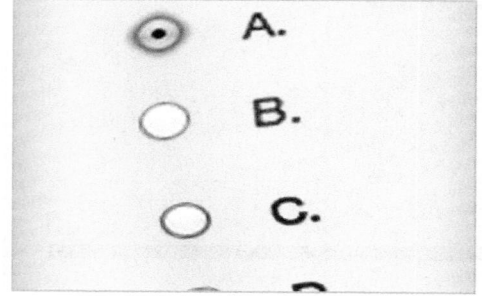

TOPIC TEST
Assign the Topic Test to assess students' understanding of topic content.

BENCHMARK TESTS
Assign these benchmark tests as you complete the relevant topics to monitor student progress toward mastering the course content and as preparation for the End-of-Course Test.

Benchmark Test 1: Topics 1–3
Benchmark Test 2: Topics 4–6
Benchmark Test 3: Topics 7–9
Benchmark Test 4: Topics 10–12
Benchmark Test 5: Topics 13–15
Benchmark Test 6: Topics 16–18
Benchmark Test 7: Topics 19–20

PEARSON
realize.™

www.PearsonRealize.com
Access your Digital Lesson

Civil Rights and Reform in the 1960s

TOPIC 16 ORGANIZER	PACING: APPROX. 8 PERIODS, 4 BLOCKS
	PACING
Connect	1 period
MY STORY VIDEO **Minnijean Brown-Trickey**	10 min.
DIGITAL ESSENTIAL QUESTION ACTIVITY **How Can We Ensure Equality for All?**	10 min.
DIGITAL OVERVIEW ACTIVITY **Civil Rights and Reform in the 1960s**	10 min.
TOPIC INQUIRY: PROJECT-BASED LEARNING **Create an Interactive Time Line on Civil Rights**	20 min.
Investigate	2–5 periods
TOPIC INQUIRY: PROJECT-BASED LEARNING **Create an Interactive Time Line on Civil Rights**	Ongoing
LESSON 1 The Civil Rights Movement Strengthens	30–40 min.
LESSON 2 The Movement Achieves Gains	30–40 min.
LESSON 3 Successes and Setbacks	30–40 min.
LESSON 4 Kennedy's Reforms	30–40 min.
LESSON 5 Reform Under Johnson	30–40 min.
Synthesize	1 period
DIGITAL ACTIVITY **Reflect on the Essential Question and Topic**	10 min.
TOPIC INQUIRY: PROJECT-BASED LEARNING **Create an Interactive Time Line on Civil Rights**	20 min.
Demonstrate	1–2 periods
DIGITAL TOPIC REVIEW AND ASSESSMENT **Civil Rights and Reform in the 1960s**	10 min.
TOPIC INQUIRY: PROJECT-BASED LEARNING **Create an Interactive Time Line on Civil Rights**	20 min.

 TOPIC INQUIRY: PROJECT-BASED LEARNING

Create an Interactive Time Line on Civil Rights

In this Topic Inquiry, students conduct research and use what they discover to create a timeline about key events and changes in the lives of African Americans since the 1960s. Knowing more about the events that affected the lives of African Americans during and after the civil rights movement will deepen their understanding of the Topic Essential Question: How can we ensure equality for all?

STEP 1: CONNECT
Develop Questions and Plan the Investigation

Launch the Project and Generate Questions
Direct students to the fictional letter from the Civil Rights Semi-centennial Committee. After they have read it, review the project instructions with them. Emphasize that their time line needs to show, not just events, but change over time. The change should be indicated in the lives of African Americans in general and in the personal lives of people who participated in events of the Civil Rights Movement. Point out the bulleted lists of the number and kind of entries to include and the number and kind of artifacts to include in the timeline.

Suggestion: Have students develop project checklists from these bulleted lists to help ensure the timeline is completed correctly.

Plan the Investigation
Guide students as they break down the Guiding Question: How have the lives of African Americans changed since the 1960s? Point out that this process of breaking down a question into smaller ones will be useful for them as they complete this project, but is a skill that will help them throughout their academic and professional careers.

Suggestion: Remind students that the Guiding Question is there to guide them; all of their work should be closely related to answering it. Also, remind them to keep their finished product, the timeline, in mind as they work. Consider telling them about the folk song "Keep Your Eyes on the Prize" that was an anthem of the Civil Rights Movement.

Resources
- Project Launch
- Student Instructions
- Project Contract
- Rubric for a Timeline of African Americans

STEP 2: INVESTIGATE
Apply Disciplinary Concepts and Tools

Research Major Civil Rights Movement Events (before or during the 1960s)
Point out that, in this step, students will focus on the early part of their timeline, before or during the 1960s. Encourage students to review any Skills Tutorials they might need to. Remind them to use the Project Tracker and complete the Information Organizer as they proceed. Then direct students to the bulleted list of the types of information they are searching for. Lead brief discussion about researching for each one. What are some good researching tips for this type of information? Encourage students to pool their knowledge.

Suggestion: Tell students to cross reference the types of information identified in the bulleted list with the required numbers of each type specified in Step 1.

Research Major Developments Affecting African Americans (after the 1960s)
Point out that, in this step, students will focus on the later part of their timeline, after the 1960s. Remind students to use the Project Tracker and the Information Organizer and to use smart research techniques.

Review Your Timeline Choices
Point out the two requirements student timeline must meet: answering the guiding question and including the required items.

Suggestion: Have students review the *Rubric for a Timeline of African Americans* to ensure they are on the correct course.

Resources
- Student Instructions
- Skills Tutorials
- Project Tracker
- Information Organizer
- Rubric for a Timeline of African Americans

⏻ PROFESSIONAL DEVELOPMENT

Project-Based Learning
Be sure to view the Project-Based Learning Professional Development resources in the online course.

STEP 3: SYNTHESIZE
Evaluate Sources and Use
Evidence to Formulate Conclusions

Select Your Timeline Authoring Tool
All of the timeline authoring tools will work well for this project. Work with students to find the one they are most comfortable using.

Create and Publish Your Timeline
Explain to students that they should think of authoring their timeline as a similar process to writing a paper. Point out how the five steps listed are similar to the steps they would take before turning in an essay.

Suggestion: Encourage students to announce the publication of their timeline through a blog post, email, or other appropriate venue. Some of the time line authoring tools include sharing options.

Resources
• Skills Tutorials

STEP 4: DEMONSTRATE
Communicate Conclusions
and Take Informed Action

Present Your Timeline of the African American Experience since the 1960s
Encourage students to outline the presentation with an introduction, major points, and conclusions. Tell them to be prepared to answer questions about the events on the timeline and the civil rights movement in general.

Suggestion: You may skip the presentation step order to save time.

Reflect on the Project
Have students complete the self assessment. Hold a brief class discussion on what students think about the civil rights movement. What was one interesting thing each student learned? What feelings were elicited in students?

Suggestion: Extend the activity by having individual students make separate timelines for individuals or events on their Timeline of Change.

Resources
• Self-Assessment

Civil Rights and Reform in the 1960s

If the 1950s were marked by growing tensions abroad, the 1960s were marked by growing tensions at home. The civil rights movement had grown during the 1950s, but it surged forward during the 1960s. The movement resulted in significant changes in law in the United States at the local, state, and national level. Gigantic new government programs reformed American life in significant ways. How was life in the United States much different at the end of the 1960s? What did various groups of Americans do to make it so different?

■ CONNECT

MY STORY VIDEO

Minnijean Brown-Trickey

Minnijean Brown-Trickey, A Sojourn to the Past Watch a video about the lessons Minnijean Brown-Trickey teaches to students today about a historical event in which she participated.

Check Understanding What was Minnijean Brown-Trickey's brush with history? *(She was one of the "Little Rock Nine," the nine black students who desegregated Little Rock's schools in 1957.)*

Identify Patterns What was the importance of Brown-Trickey's actions in 1957? *(She and her fellow students provided inspiration for many of the participants in the civil rights movement in the decade that followed. She continues to teach lessons about the civil rights movement today.)*

⟲ FLIP IT!

Assign the My Story video.

DIGITAL ESSENTIAL QUESTION ACTIVITY

How Can We Ensure Equality for All?

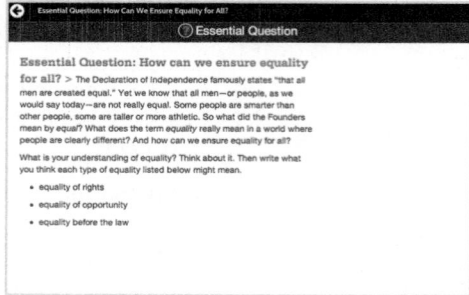

Invite a student to read the Essential Question— How can we ensure equality for all?—aloud. Focus their attention on the word *equality*, emphasizing that equality does not mean sameness, but something else.

Distinguish Ask students, if equality does not mean sameness, what does it mean? What might *equality of rights* mean? Equality of opportunity? Equality before the law? *(Students should understand that civil rights are the rights of citizens, and that an ideal in the United States is the legal equality of all citizens. Thus all citizens should have the same rights, opportunities, and treatment before the law.)*

Interpret Explain that equality of its citizenry is an American ideal, but it has not always been a reality. Ask students why they think this has been the case. *(Imperfect governmental institutions, distrust of people of different nationalities, religions, ethnicities, and races, and wealth inequality have all played a role.)*

DIGITAL OVERVIEW ACTIVITY

Civil Rights and Reform in the 1960s

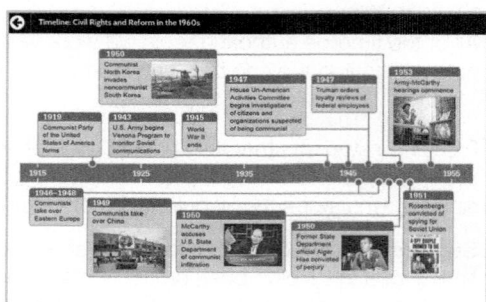

Display the timeline showing key events of the civil rights movement. Review each entry with students to gauge their knowledge about the event it represents. Invite interferences and speculation for any events that are unfamiliar. Point out that most of the entries concern civil rights for African Americans.

D Differentiate: Extra Support Remind students that segregation means "separation." In this context, it means separate facilities for African Americans. Desegregation is the policy and process of ending segregation. The desegregation of Central High in Little Rock meant the admission of African Americans into a formerly all white school.

Infer What can students infer from this? *(That progress in the civil rights movement meant progress for those who suffered discimination.)*

Topic Inquiry

Launch the Topic Inquiry with students after introducing the topic.

The Civil Rights Movement Strengthens

Supporting English Language Learners

Use with Digital Text 1, **Segregation Limits Equality.**

Learning Strategies
Read aloud the section titled *Discrimination Throughout the Country*, or invite volunteers to do so. Encourage students to internalize new academic language by using and reusing it in meaningful ways in writing activities that build concept and language attainment.

Beginning Display the word *widespread*, and define it by breaking it into the words *wide* and *spread*. Have students replace a phrase in this sentence with *widespread* and copy the new sentence: Discrimination in the United States was found in many places.

Intermediate Display the first sentence of the second paragraph. Have students define *widespread* using context clues and by breaking the word into smaller parts. Then write two sentences about segregation together, using *widespread* as an attributive adjective and as a predicate adjective.

Advanced Display the second sentence of the section and ask students to define *explicit* using prior knowledge and context clues. Then have pairs of students write three sentences about different aspects of segregation, using the word *explicit*.

Advanced High Display the second sentence of the section and ask students to define *explicit*. Then ask students to define its antonym *implicit*. Have students write two sentences using each word and then discuss and correct them with a partner.

Use with Digital Text 3, **Conflict between Federal and State Power.**

Speaking
Read aloud the section titled *Soldiers Arrive at a High School in Little Rock*, or invite volunteers to do so. Students will retell a simplified story of the first year of integration at Little Rock High School using pictures to help expand and internalize initial English vocabulary.

Beginning Display this sentence: When black students tried to enter the school, some white people _____. Have students think of a word or phrase to complete it, and then say the sentence aloud. Then have students work in pairs, using the photograph to retell the story.

Intermediate Ask students to say two sentences that chronologically describe events during the school's first year of integration. Then have them work in pairs, with one student describing the events surrounding the first photograph and the other student describing events pictured in the second photograph.

Advanced Have students as a group use the photographs in the text to retell the events of the school's first year of integration. Ask questions that guide the focus and pacing of the narrative. Remind them that referring to the text and accompanying photographs will help them add details and emotion.

Advanced High Ask pairs of students to use the photographs to retell the school's integration story. Tell them to take turns speaking sentences about the events, and work in pairs to discuss what the two photographs reveal about the story.

▶ Differentiate Instruction

Use the Differentiated Instruction notes throughout the lesson plan to support the varied skill sets, levels of readiness, and interests in the mixed-ability classroom.

Challenge These notes include suggestions for expanding the activity for advanced students.

On-Level These notes include suggestions for modifying the activity to address different interests or learning styles.

Extra Support These notes include ideas for providing more scaffolding or reading spuport.

Special Needs These notes provide ideas for adapting instruction to support the needs of various special needs students.

■ NOTES

The Civil Rights Movement Strengthens

Objectives

Objective 1: Describe efforts to end segregation in the 1940s and 1950s.

Objective 2: Explain the importance of the landmark case of Brown v. Board of Education.

Objective 3: Describe the controversy over school desegregation in Little Rock, Arkansas.

Objective 4: Discuss the Montgomery bus boycott and its impact.

LESSON 1 ORGANIZER		PACING: APPROX. 1 PERIOD, .5 BLOCKS			
				RESOURCES	
		OBJECTIVES	PACING	Online	Print
Connect					
DIGITAL START UP ACTIVITY **Educational Justice**			5 min.	●	
Investigate					
DIGITAL TEXT 1 **Segregation Limits Equality**		Objective 1	10 min.	●	●
INTERACTIVE GALLERY **Separate but Equal?**			10 min.	●	
DIGITAL TEXT 2 **A Landmark Supreme Court Decision**		Objective 2	10 min.	●	●
DIGITAL TEXT 3 **Conflict between Federal and State Power**		Objective 3	10 min.	●	●
INTERACTIVE GALLERY **Fighting for Justice**			10 min.	●	
DIGITAL TEXT 4 **The Montgomery Bus Boycott**		Objective 4	10 min.	●	●
INTERACTIVE GALLERY **Nonviolent Protest Through History**			10 min.	●	
Synthesize					
DIGITAL ACTIVITY **Integration and America's Schools**			5 min.	●	
Demonstrate					
LESSON QUIZ **Lesson Quiz and Class Discussion Board**			10 min.	●	

PEARSON realize.™
www.PearsonRealize.com

Go online to access additional resources including:
Primary Sources • Biographies • Supreme Court cases •
21st Century Skill Tutorials • Maps • Graphic Organizers.

■ CONNECT

■ INVESTIGATE

DIGITAL START UP ACTIVITY
Educational Justice

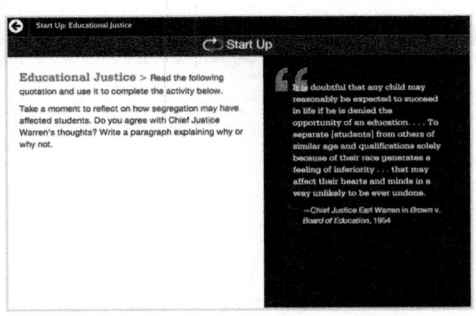

Project the Start Up Activity Ask students to read the quote as they enter and get settled. Then have them write a paragraph reflecting on the quote. Have students share their ideas with a partner, either in class or through a chat or blog space.

Discuss Take a moment to reflect on how segregation may have affected students. Do you agree with Chief Justice Warren's thoughts? *(Answers should show their thinking about Warren's quote.)*

Tell students that in this lesson they will be learning about the development of the civil rights movement in the 20th century, including the effects of landmark U.S. Supreme Court decisions and the contributions of significant individuals to civil rights.

Aa Vocabulary Development: Use the Interactive Reading Notepad to preview the Key Terms and Academic Vocabulary in the lesson with students.

⇗ FLIP IT!
Assign the Flipped Video for this lesson.

■ STUDENT EDITION PRINT PAGES: 684–690

DIGITAL TEXT 1
Segregation Limits Equality

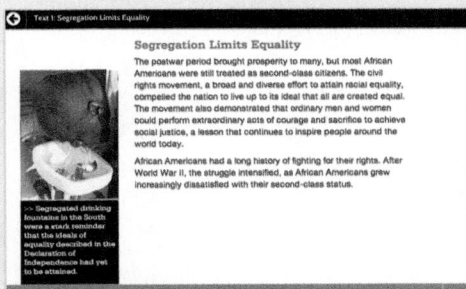

Objective 1: Describe efforts to end segregation in the 1940s and 1950s.

Quick Instruction
Review the definitions of de jure and de facto segregation. Explain that the effect of the U.S. Supreme Court decision *Plessy* v. *Ferguson* (1896) was to make segregation legal. Segregation was also a part of life even when it wasn't written into law.

Interactive Gallery: Separate but Equal? Project the interactive gallery and click through the hotspots. Discuss the examples of segregation with students.

Analyze Images What does the image of segregated water fountains tell you about de facto segregation? *(Answers: it was widespread; it affected every facet of life; it was part of social custom, even if it wasn't written into law)*

👥 ACTIVE CLASSROOM
Have students break into groups and use the Circle Write Strategy to address the prompt, *Why did the United States need a civil rights movement to develop in the 20th century?* Have students write as much as they can for 1 minute and then switch with the person on their right. The next person tries to improve or elaborate the response where the other person left off. Continue to switch until the paper comes back to the first person. The group decides which is the best composition and shares that with the class.

INTERACTIVE GALLERY
Separate but Equal?

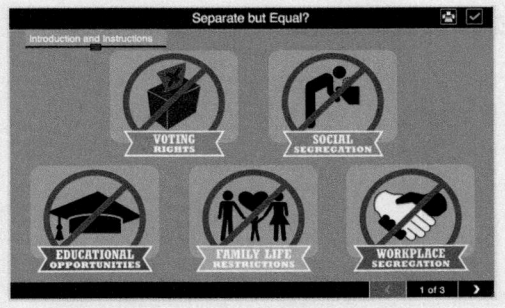

ELL Use the ELL activity described in the ELL chart.

Further Instruction
Go through the Interactive Reading Notepad questions and discuss the answers with the class. Be sure students can trace the historical development of the civil rights movement beginning in the 1940s and 1950s. Assign the primary source *Hind Swaraj* (Gandhi).

Generate Explanations Describe the role of the Congress of Racial Equality and explain how it promoted civil rights. *(It was formed to end discrimination and improve race relations. It organized non-violent protests.)*

Draw Conclusions Describe President Truman's actions to address minority rights in the United States, including desegregation of the armed forces. In light of Truman's efforts, evaluate the impact of relationships between the legislative and executive branches of government in advancing civil rights. *(Truman appointed a Committee on Civil Rights, but Congress did not support its recommendations. Truman then desegregated the military using his executive power. This suggests the legislative and executive branches did not agree on civil rights. Both had powers to block and advance initiatives.)*

Identify Central Issues Why did many African Americans begin nonviolent protests? *(Influenced by the teachings of Henry David Thoreau and Mohandas Gandhi, they organized nonviolent protests to confront the injustices of segregation.)*

The Civil Rights Movement Strengthens

DIGITAL TEXT 2

A Landmark Supreme Court Decision

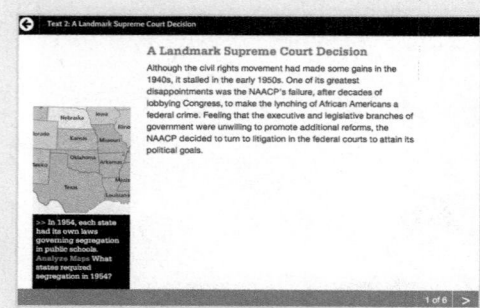

DIGITAL TEXT 3

Conflict between Federal and State Power

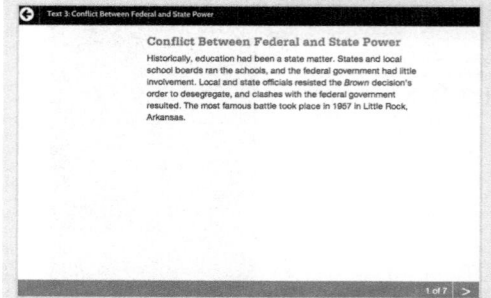

Objective 2: Explain the importance of the landmark case of *Brown* v. *Board of Education*.

Quick Instruction

Project the image of Thurgood Marshall. Discuss Marshall's contributions to the civil rights movement as an African American lawyer who argued the landmark case *Brown* v. *Board of Education* and became the first African American to serve on the Supreme Court.

Identify Patterns Why was litigation used as a method for achieving equality and expanding the right to participate in the democratic process? *(The legislative and executive branches were not promoting reforms.)*

D **Differentiate: Extra Support** Explain that litigation is another word for lawsuit, or the process of taking legal action. In the 1950s, attorneys took legal action to end segregation. Have students give an example of a court case that advanced civil rights.

Further Instruction

Go through the Interactive Reading Notepad questions and discuss the answers with the class.

Discuss the role of litigation in the historical development of the civil rights movement in the 20th century. Be sure students understand the effects of landmark U.S. Supreme Court cases, especially *Brown* v. *Board of Education*. To extend the lesson, assign the landmark Supreme Court cases *Sweatt* v. *Painter*, *Brown* v. *Board of Education*, and *Hernandez* v. *Texas*, as well as Government Basics: Basic Concepts and the Judicial Branch.

Compare Describe the roles played by litigation in the landmark cases *Brown* v. *Board of Education*, *Hernandez* v. *Texas*, and *Sweatt* v. *Painter* in protecting the rights of the minority during the civil rights movement.

Draw Conclusions How did the Congressional bloc of southern Democrats try to maintain the status quo after the Brown ruling? *(They endorsed the "Southern Manifesto," pledging to oppose the ruling in an effort to maintain segregation.)*

Identify Central Issues How did *Hernandez* v. *Texas* affect racial groups besides African Americans? *(It ended discriminatory practices against Mexican Americans.)*

Objective 3: Describe the controversy over school desegregation in Little Rock, Arkansas.

Quick Instruction

Interactive Gallery: Fighting for Justice Project the interactive gallery on the whiteboard and click through the images. Discuss the violence African Americans faced throughout the historical development of the civil rights movement of the 20th century and the efforts of leaders such as President Truman to protect them.

Hypothesize Why do you think many African Americans who faced violence as a result of the civil rights movement turned to nonviolent means of protesting? *(They hoped nonviolent protesting would prove an effective tool for political change; they thought nonviolent protesting would make people more sympathetic to their cause, especially in contrast to the violence of those discriminating against them.)*

⬛ ACTIVE CLASSROOM

Group students and have them use the PMI Strategy to make a 3-column organizer with the headings Plus/Minus/Interesting. Have groups use the organizer to record responses to the following three questions:

- What are the positive effects of using litigation to protect the rights of the minority during the civil rights movement?
- What are the negative effects of using litigation to expand civil rights?
- What is interesting about this strategy?

INTERACTIVE GALLERY
Fighting for Justice

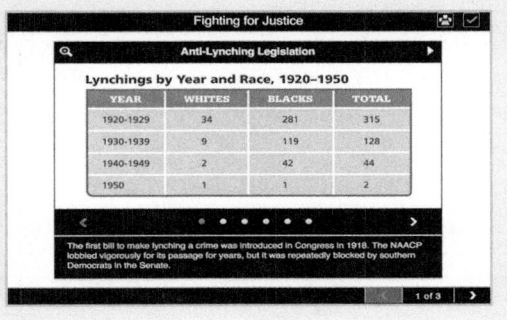

DIGITAL TEXT 4
The Montgomery Bus Boycott

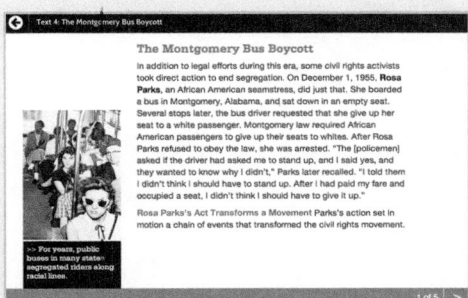

INTERACTIVE GALLERY
Nonviolent Protest Through History

ELL Use the ELL activity described in the ELL chart.

Further Instruction
Go through the Interactive Reading Notepad questions with the class. Be sure students understand the difficulties faced in implementing the Brown decision and desegregating schools.

Identify Cause and Effect Describe how governor Orval Faubus's efforts to maintain the status quo prompted Eisenhower to take action in Arkansas. *(Because Faubus would not desegregate schools, Eisenhower sent troops to Little Rock to protect the students and enforce the Court's decision.)*

Compare and Contrast Ask students to consider the actions taken by the president and Congress to address minority rights, including the Civil Rights Act of 1957. What were the benefits and drawbacks to this Act as a means of achieving equality of political rights? *(Benefits—it established a civil rights commission with the power to investigate civil rights violations; it gave the Attorney General power to bring lawsuits against civil rights violations and protect voting rights. Drawbacks—it was more symbolic than substantive.)*

Identify Central Issues How did political organizations that promoted civil rights influence presidential actions and congressional votes to address minority rights? *(They organized nonviolent protests and lobbied Congress.)*

Objective 4: Discuss the Montgomery bus boycott and its impact.

Quick Instruction
Interactive Gallery: Nonviolent Protest Through History Project the interactive gallery on the whiteboard and have students look at the images. Identify the important individuals whose nonviolent philosophies contributed to the development of the civil rights movement in the 20th century.

Evaluate Arguments Review the quotes by the Quaker Declaration of Pacifism, Thoreau, Gandhi, and Mandela. How did these examples contribute to the tactics of nonviolent protesting often used during the civil rights movement? *(They show a history of using nonviolent protesting to end injustice and bring about social change.)*

🗣 ACTIVE CLASSROOM

Have students use the Take a Stand Strategy to take a stand on the following issue: Evaluate how effective nonviolent protesting was in expanding the right to participate in the democratic process. Have students take their place on a continuum line of 1-10 depending on how strongly they agree with the efficacy of nonviolent protesting. Have students create an opening statement that defends their position.

Further Instruction
Go through the Interactive Reading Notepad questions with the class. Be sure students understand the issues surrounding the Montgomery bus boycott and can identify the role of Rosa Parks in supporting the civil rights movement.

Summarize Describe the role of the MIA in promoting civil rights. *(It organized the bus boycott against segregation.)*

Draw Conclusions Why do you think the Montgomery bus boycott used both nonviolent protesting and litigation as methods of expanding civil rights? *(Nonviolent protesting drew public attention to the injustices of segregation, putting social and economic pressure on the city. Debating the issue in a court of law provided legal strategy for changing segregation laws.)*

Identify Cause and Effect What personal qualities enabled Martin Luther King, Jr. to become a significant leader who facilitated the modern civil rights movement? *(He was an "inspirational" speaker who moved audiences to follow his lead.)*

Topic (16) Lesson 1

The Civil Rights Movement Strengthens

■ SYNTHESIZE

DIGITAL ACTIVITY
Integration and America's Schools

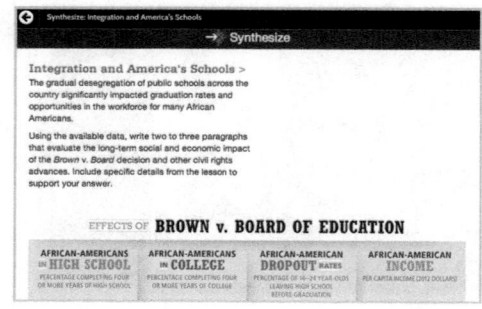

Have students use the data from the table to write 2 to 3 paragraphs evaluating the impact of the *Brown* v. *Board* decision, using details for support. Have students discuss their conclusions with a partner, explaining their reasoning.

Discuss Prompt students to think about the following question: What role did the judicial branch of government play in protecting the rights of the minority? Have students give specific examples from the text to support their answer.

■ DEMONSTRATE

DIGITAL QUIZ
Lesson Quiz and Class Discussion Board

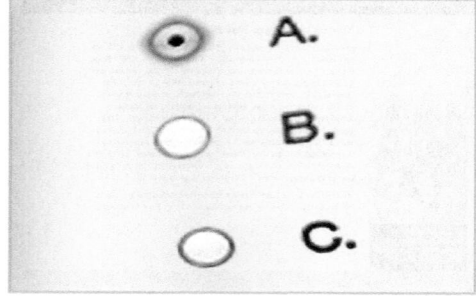

Assign the online Lesson Quiz for this lesson if you haven't already done so. Students will be offered automatic remediation or enrichment based on their score.

Pose these questions to the class on the Discussion Board:

In *The Civil Rights Movement Strengthens*, you read about changes and events in the United States that resulted from the civil rights movement.

Summarize What changes in the United States occurred in the early years of the civil rights movement? *(landmark Supreme Court cases challenged segregation and expanded civil rights; schools were desegregated by law, if not in practice; the Civil Rights Act of 1957 passed; significant political organizations formed in support of civil rights; segregation on Montgomery city buses was ruled unconstitutional)*

Identify Patterns What methods did significant leaders who supported the civil rights movement use to bring about these changes? *(nonviolent protesting, including sit-ins and boycotts; litigation; political lobbying)*

Topic Inquiry
Have students continue their investigations for the Topic Inquiry.

The Movement Achieves Gains

Supporting English Language Learners

Use with Digital Text 4, **Thousands Descend on the Nation's Capital.**

Speaking
Introduce the text by reviewing with students what they already know about Martin Luther King, Jr. As students speak, write important nouns and verbs for students to use when communicating with classmates. Point out that the following activities will help students expand and remember the kind of routine language needed for classroom communication.

Beginning Display this question: How do you say this word? Practice saying it with students. Have students break into small groups and take turns reading sentences from the text. When they encounter a difficult word, have them use the question to ask for help. Encourage students to create a list of words that are new to them.

Intermediate Display these questions: May I read next? How do you say this word? What does _____ mean? Discuss when it would be appropriate to ask them. Have students break into small groups compiling lists of unfamiliar vocabulary words. Students should take turns creating sentences with the vocabulary words from their lists.

Advanced Have students work in groups to discuss some of the situations described in the text. Students can expand their vocabulary by reading certain sentences and discussing the meaning of difficult words.

Advanced High Have students break into small groups to read paragraphs of the text. Have other students write down the most important words. Then encourage students to use the vocabulary words to guide them as they retell the stories described in the text.

Use with Digital Text 5, **A Significant Congressional Vote Addresses Minority Rights.**

Learning Strategies
Read aloud the text, or invite volunteers to do so. Encourage students to use language that is already accessible to them in order to learn new language in the process. Remind students that one way to do this is to use familiar words to help determine the meanings of unfamiliar words.

Beginning Display the second paragraph, and highlight the word *assumed*. Help students figure out the meaning of this word from its context. Ask: The sentence before it says that President Kennedy was assassinated or killed. What would the Vice President have to do if the President was killed?

Intermediate Display the second paragraph, and highlight the words *assassinated* and *assumed*. Ask students to use context clues to determine the meanings of these words.

Advanced Ask students what someone is doing if they oppose something. Then display the first sentence of the fourth paragraph. Ask: Given what you know about the word oppose, what do you think opposition means? How are the words similar and different? Have students work in pairs to use these words in sentences.

Advanced High Display the first two sentences of the third paragraph, and highlight the word *undistinguished*. Ask: How can you use familiar words, such as however and surprised, to help you guess the meaning of undistinguished? Have students examine the new word's context in order to define it.

▣ Differentiate Instruction

Use the Differentiated Instruction notes throughout the lesson plan to support the varied skill sets, levels of readiness, and interests in the mixed-ability classroom.

Challenge These notes include suggestions for expanding the activity for advanced students.

On-Level These notes include suggestions for modifying the activity to address different interests or learning styles.

Extra Support These notes include ideas for providing more scaffolding or reading spuport.

Special Needs These notes provide ideas for adapting instruction to support the needs of various special needs students.

■ NOTES

The Movement Achieves Gains

Objectives

Objective 1: Describe the sit-ins, freedom ride, and the actions of James Meredith in the early 1960s.

Objective 2: Explain how the protests at Birmingham and the March on Washington were linked to the Civil Rights Act of 1964.

Objective 3: Describe how the Civil Rights Act of 1964 addressed minority rights in the United States.

LESSON 2 ORGANIZER		PACING: APPROX. 1 PERIOD, .5 BLOCKS			
				RESOURCES	
		OBJECTIVES	PACING	Online	Print
Connect					
	DIGITAL START UP ACTIVITY **Is Nonviolence Effective?**		5 min.	●	
Investigate					
	DIGITAL TEXT 1 **Student Activists Promote Civil Rights**		10 min.	●	●
	INTERACTIVE GALLERY **Nonviolent Strategies in the Civil Rights Movement**	Objective 1	10 min.	●	
	DIGITAL TEXT 2 **Freedom Rides Begin Throughout the South**		10 min.	●	●
	INTERACTIVE TIMELINE **Riding for Freedom**		10 min.	●	
	DIGITAL TEXT 3 **Public Institutions Open Doors to Minorities**	Objectives 1, 2	10 min.	●	●
	DIGITAL TEXT 4 **Thousands Descend on the Nation's Capital**	Objective 2	10 min.	●	●
	DIGITAL TEXT 5 **A Significant Congressional Vote Addresses Minority Rights**	Objective 3	10 min.	●	●
Synthesize					
	DIGITAL ACTIVITY **Thoreau's Lasting Influence**		5 min.	●	
Demonstrate					
	DIGITAL QUIZ **Lesson Quiz and Class Discussion Board**		10 min.	●	

PEARSON realize™
www.PearsonRealize.com

Go online to access additional resources including:
Primary Sources • Biographies • Supreme Court cases •
21st Century Skill Tutorials • Maps • Graphic Organizers.

CONNECT

DIGITAL START UP ACTIVITY
Is Nonviolence Effective?

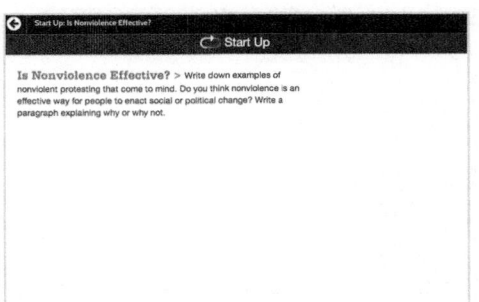

Project the Start Up Activity Ask students to make a list of examples of nonviolent protesting activities as they enter and get settled. Then have them write a paragraph explaining why they do or do not think nonviolence is an effective method for expanding rights. Have students share their ideas with a partner, either in class or through a chat or blog space.

Discuss Do you think nonviolence is an effective way for people to enact social or political change? Why or why not? (*Answers should demonstrate student reasoning.*)

Tell students that in this lesson they will be learning about actions taken by people to expand economic opportunities and political rights during the civil rights movement.

Aa Vocabulary Development: Use the Interactive Reading Notepad to preview the Key Terms and Academic Vocabulary in this lesson with students.

⇅ FLIP IT!
Assign the Flipped Video for this lesson.

STUDENT EDITION PRINT PAGES: 691–697

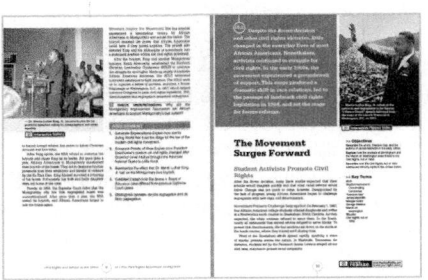

INVESTIGATE

DIGITAL TEXT 1
Student Activists Promote Civil Rights

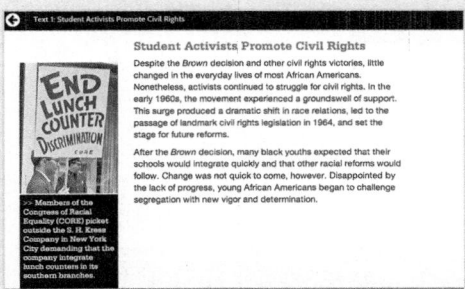

INTERACTIVE GALLERY
Nonviolent Strategies in the Civil Rights Movement

Objective 1: Describe the sit-ins, freedom rides, and the actions of James Meredith in the early 1960s.

Quick Instruction
Interactive Gallery: Nonviolent Strategies in the Civil Rights Movement Project the interactive gallery and discuss the images of nonviolent protest with students.

Analyze Images Based on the photo of the lunch counter protest, how did nonviolent protesting bring about changes in the United States? (*It challenged discrimination in businesses and public places.*)

🎞 ACTIVE CLASSROOM
Have students use the Sticky Notes Strategy and take three minutes to jot down their ideas about how nonviolent protesting expanded rights and opportunities for racial minorities in American society. Then ask, "Why is nonviolent protesting an important method for promoting civil rights?" Have students post their stickies on a wall, then sort and discuss their responses as a group.

Further Instruction
Go through the Interactive Reading Notepad questions and discuss the answers with the class. Begin filling out the graphic organizer on events that led to the passage of the Civil Rights Act of 1964.

Support Ideas with Evidence What evidence from the text supports the idea that political organizations played a significant role

in the civil rights movement? (*Organizations like SNCC and the NAACP helped develop a grass roots movement that promoted racial equality through nonviolent protest.*)

The Movement Achieves Gains

DIGITAL TEXT 2

Freedom Rides Begin Throughout the South

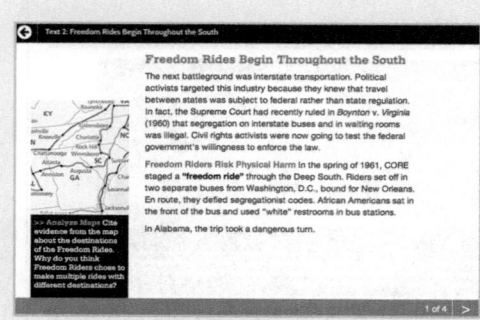

INTERACTIVE TIMELINE

Riding for Freedom

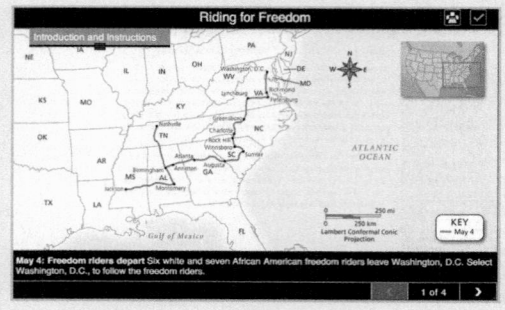

DIGITAL TEXT 3

Public Institutions Open Doors to Minorities

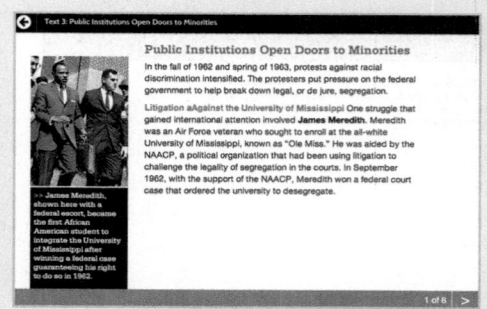

Objective 1: Describe the sit-ins, freedom rides, and the actions of James Meredith in the early 1960s.

Quick Instruction

Interactive Timeline: Riding for Freedom
Project the timeline. Look at each image individually and the collection of images as a whole. Prompt students to identify the connection between the non-violent protesting inherent in the Freedom Rides and expanding the right to participate in the political process.

🗂 ACTIVE CLASSROOM

Ask students to use the Sticky Notes Strategy to comment on each of the images in the Interactive Timeline. Viewed together, how do these images portray different perspectives on the actions taken by different people to expand political rights for racial minorities?

Further Instruction

Go through the Interactive Reading Notepad questions and discuss the answers with the class.

Draw Conclusions Describe presidential actions to address minority rights. What do President Kennedy's actions on civil rights suggest about the relationship between the executive and judicial branches of government? *(Kennedy helped release King from prison, but allowed freedom riders to be jailed in exchange for the desegregation of interstate transportation. This suggests the executive and judicial branches were sometimes at odds. They compromised over what changes each branch would enact.)*

Objectives 1: Describe the sit-ins, freedom rides, and the actions of James Meredith in the early 1960s; **2:** Explain how the protests at Birmingham and the March on Washington were linked to the Civil Rights Act of 1964.

Quick Instruction

Remind students that many public institutions such as schools were segregated. The decision of individuals like James Meredith to enroll at the University of Mississippi gradually opened doors to higher education for others, and subsequently increased the social and economic opportunities available to minorities.

Determine Point of View What were George Wallace's views on maintaining the status quo of segregation in Alabama schools? How do you know? What role did Wallace play in maintaining the status quo? *(Wallace wanted to maintain the status quo, which was segregation in schools. This is clear from his pledge to maintain "segregation forever" and prevent African American students from registering. He tried to keep the University of Alabama segregated but backed down when President Kennedy called in the Alabama National Guard to enforce integration.)*

Further Instruction

Go through the Interactive Reading Notepad questions and discuss the answers with the class. Begin filling out the graphic organizer on events that led to the passage of the Civil Rights Act of 1964. Assign the primary source *Letter from a Birmingham Jail* (Martin Luther King, Jr.).

DIGITAL TEXT 4

Thousands Descend on the Nation's Capital

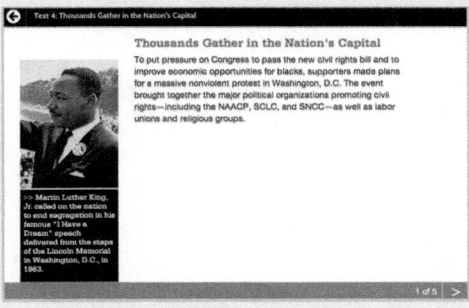

Text 4: Thousands Gather in the Nation's Capital

Thousands Gather in the Nation's Capital
To put pressure on Congress to pass the new civil rights bill and to improve economic opportunities for blacks, supporters made plans for a massive nonviolent protest in Washington, D.C. The event brought together the major political organizations promoting civil rights—including the NAACP, SCLC, and SNCC—as well as labor unions and religious groups.

>> Martin Luther King, Jr. called on the nation to end segregation in his famous "I Have a Dream" speech delivered from the steps of the Lincoln Memorial in Washington, D.C., in 1963.

1 of 5 >

Cite Evidence Cite evidence that Martin Luther King, Jr.'s *Letter from a Birmingham Jail* made an impact on the civil rights movement by giving activists a sense of urgency. *(King urged people not to wait to achieve civil rights by showing how discrimination would hurt their children— "as you seek to explain to your six-year-old daughter.")*

Objective 2: Explain how the protests at Birmingham and the March on Washington were linked to the Civil Rights Act of 1964.

Quick Instruction

Project the image of the March on Washington on the whiteboard. Explain that the march was a nonviolent protest organized to pressure Congress to pass a civil rights bill. Discuss the roles of the significant leaders and political organizations supporting the march, including Martin Luther King, Jr.

Draw Conclusions How was the March on Washington an important moment in the historical development of the civil rights movement in the 20th century? *(It increased awareness, built momentum for civil rights legislation, and became an important symbol of the movement.)*

ELL Use the ELL activity described in the ELL chart.

Further Instruction

Go through the Interactive Reading Notepad questions and discuss the answers with the class. Continue filling out the graphic organizer on events that led to the passage of the Civil Rights Act of 1964. To extend the lesson, assign the primary source *I Have a Dream* (Martin Luther King, Jr.).

Be sure students understand the significant role of Martin Luther King, Jr. in leading the civil rights movement.

Evaluate Arguments Do you agree with SNCC that the use of nonviolent protesting was too slow a method for expanding rights?

Explain your reasoning. *(No, because African Americans were still successful in gaining rights and overturning discriminatory policies using nonviolent practices.)*

Summarize What vision did Martin Luther King, Jr.'s *I Have a Dream* speech put forth? What impact do you think this speech had on audiences? *(The speech described a colorblind society in which everyone was free and equal. It probably moved audiences and made them want to bring about such a world.)*

The Movement Achieves Gains

DIGITAL TEXT 5

A Significant Congressional Vote Addresses Minority Rights

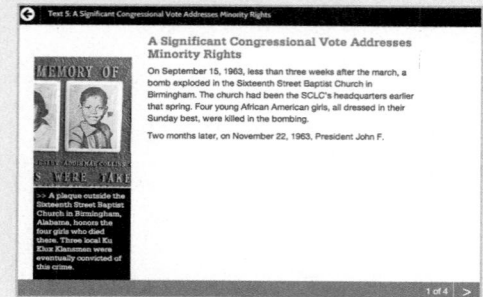

Objective 3: Describe how the Civil Rights Act of 1964 addressed minority rights in the United States.

Quick Instruction

Project the image of the plaque outside the Sixteenth Street Baptist Church. Explain that although violence followed the March on Washington, further changes and events resulted from the civil rights movement when Johnson assumed the presidency.

Draw Conclusions What does the Civil Rights Act of 1964 suggest about the development of the civil rights movement in the 20th century? *(The civil rights movement was gaining momentum and expanding, compelling the legislature to implement new protections.)*

D Differentiate: **Challenge** Challenge students to research other Civil Rights Acts of the 19th and 20th centuries. Have students use the information they gather to write a short essay tracing how these acts expanded political rights and economic opportunities for minorities in the United States.

ELL Use the ELL activity described in the ELL chart.

Further Instruction

Go through the Interactive Reading Notepad questions and discuss the answers with the class. Have students complete the graphic organizer on the events that led to the passage of the Civil Rights Act of 1964. To extend the lesson, assign Government Basics: How to Participate in Politics.

Cite Evidence Provide evidence that the Congressional bloc of southern Democrats sought to maintain the status quo following Johnson's assumption of the presidency. What does this evidence suggest about the relationship between the legislative and executive branches of government regarding the passage of the Civil Rights Act of 1964? *(Southern Democrats attempted to block passage of the act with a filibuster that lasted more than 80 days; the Senate tried to prevent the act even though it was supported by the executive branch and the House, leading to the conclusion that the legislative branch would not always support the agenda of the executive branch.)*

Summarize How did the Civil Rights Act of 1964 expand political rights and economic opportunities for racial minorities in American society? *(It banned segregation in public accommodations; gave the federal government power to make school boards desegregate schools; let the Justice Department prosecute civil rights violations; outlawed discrimination in employment on account of race; established the EEOC.)*

SYNTHESIZE

DIGITAL ACTIVITY
Thoreau's Lasting Influence

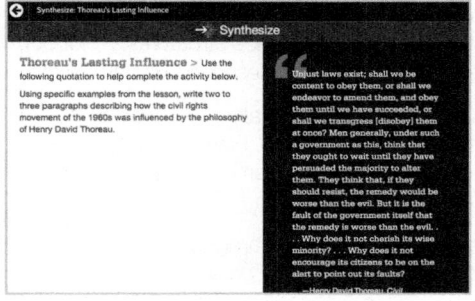

Have students discuss the quote and then review the lesson, taking notes on specific examples to support their claims. Have students share their paragraphs with the class and discuss the examples used.

Discuss Have students think about the following question: How did a philosophy of nonviolence shape the civil rights movement? Ask students to share their evaluation of the changes and events that resulted from the use of nonviolent protesting in the civil rights movement.

DEMONSTRATE

DIGITAL QUIZ
Lesson Quiz and Class Discussion Board

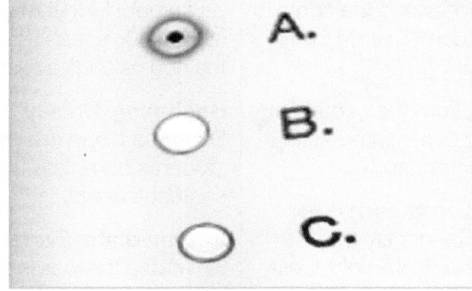

Assign the online Lesson Quiz for this lesson if you haven't already done so. Students will be offered automatic remediation or enrichment based on their score.

Pose these questions to the class on the Discussion Board:

In *The Movement Surges Forward*, you continued to trace the historical development of the civil rights movement in the 20th century, reading about the actions taken to expand civil rights and the impact of Martin Luther King, Jr.'s writings.

Identify Cause and Effect Describe a strategy used by a political organization that promoted civil rights during this time and explain its causes and effects. *(Strategy: CORE organized a freedom ride through the South. Causes:* Boynton v. Virginia *made segregation on interstate buses illegal; CORE wanted to test whether the government would enforce the law. Effects: violence broke out in Birmingham; the Federal Transport Commission mandated desegregation on interstate buses.)*

Contrast the writings of Martin Luther King, Jr. such as his "Letter from Birmingham Jail" and "I Have a Dream" speech, with the efforts of those who sought to maintain the status quo, such as George Wallace and the Congressional bloc of southern Democrats. Why do you think King's writings had such an impact on the civil rights movement?

Topic Inquiry
Have students continue their investigations for the Topic Inquiry.

Topic 16 Lesson 3

Successes and Setbacks

Supporting English Language Learners

Use with Digital Text 1, **Increasing Participation in the Political Process.**

Learning Strategies

Read aloud the section titled *Martin Luther King, Jr., Leads the March on Selma*, or invite volunteers to do so. Ensure students understand the context of the Sheyann Webb quotation as you prompt them to demonstrate their ability to distinguish between formal and informal English.

Beginning Display these two sentences (the first being from the quotation): It was like a nightmare. It was a harrowing and traumatic experience. Ask pairs of students to identify each sentence as formal or informal.

Intermediate Ask pairs of students to read the quotation to each other using appropriate emotion and tone of voice. Tell them to identify the quotation as formal or informal, and to locate specific words and phrases that support their opinion.

Advanced Ask students to read the quotation to themselves and to determine whether it uses formal or informal English. Then have them list specific words or phrases that support their opinion. Provide time for students to compare lists.

Advanced High Have students draw a continuum with the words *informal* and *formal* on either end. Remind them that language often falls between these two extremes. Have students reread the quotation, mark the continuum at the quotation's degree of formality, and justify their opinion to a partner.

Use with Digital Text 5, **Results of the Civil Rights Movement.**

Speaking

Read aloud the section titled *Controversies over Busing and Affirmative Action*, or invite volunteers to do so. Display the last sentence of the first paragraph. Model reading that sentence aloud in order to encourage students to speak accurately using a variety of sentence structures. Point out the non-restrictive relative clause, and explain that it describes Richard Nixon.

Beginning Display this sentence: Thurgood Marshall, _____ was a Supreme Court justice, supported affirmative action. Have pairs of students complete the sentence with the correct word (who) and say the sentence aloud.

Intermediate Display the last sentence of the first paragraph. Ask students to replace the words *succeeded Lyndon Johnson as president* with new information about Nixon, and then to say the revised sentence aloud.

Advanced Ask students to describe the structure of the last sentence of the first paragraph. Then have pairs of students formulate and say an original sentence about affirmative action that includes a relative clause (that begins with *which*).

Advanced High Ask students to describe the structure of the last sentence of the first paragraph. Then have them say original sentences about Richard Nixon, Thurgood Marshall, and affirmative action (with each sentence having a relative clause that begins with *who* or *which*).

◻ Differentiate Instruction

Use the Differentiated Instruction notes throughout the lesson plan to support the varied skill sets, levels of readiness, and interests in the mixed-ability classroom.

Challenge These notes include suggestions for expanding the activity for advanced students.

On-Level These notes include suggestions for modifying the activity to address different interests or learning styles.

Extra Support These notes include ideas for providing more scaffolding or reading spuport.

Special Needs These notes provide ideas for adapting instruction to support the needs of various special needs students.

■ NOTES

PEARSON realize.
www.PearsonRealize.com

Go online to access additional resources including:
Primary Sources • Biographies • Supreme Court cases •
21st Century Skill Tutorials • Maps • Graphic Organizers.

Objectives

Objective 1: Explain the significance of Freedom Summer, the march on Selma, and why violence erupted in some American cities in the 1960s.

Objective 2: Compare and contrast the goals and approaches taken by African American leaders to expand political rights and economic opportunities.

Objective 3: Describe the social and economic situation of African Americans by 1975.

LESSON 3 ORGANIZER		PACING: APPROX. 1 PERIOD, .5 BLOCKS			
				RESOURCES	
		OBJECTIVES	PACING	Online	Print
Connect					
	DIGITAL START UP ACTIVITY **Is Voting Necessary?**		5 min.	●	
Investigate					
	DIGITAL TEXT 1 **Increasing Participation in the Political Process**	Objective 1	10 min.	●	●
	DIGITAL TEXT 2 **Violence Troubles Civil Rights Efforts**	Objective 1	10 min.	●	●
	INTERACTIVE MAP **Violent Conflicts During the Civil Rights Era**		10 min.	●	
	DIGITAL TEXT 3 **New Civil Rights Groups**	Objective 2	10 min.	●	●
	DIGITAL TEXT 4 **King Expands His Dream**		10 min.	●	●
	DIGITAL TEXT 5 **Results of the Civil Rights Movement**	Objective 3	10 min.	●	●
	INTERACTIVE CHART **Opposing Views on Affirmative Action**		10 min.	●	
Synthesize					
	DIGITAL ACTIVITY **Voting Rights for All**		5 min.	●	
Demonstrate					
	DIGITAL QUIZ **Lesson Quiz and Class Discussion Board**		10 min.	●	

Successes and Setbacks

■ CONNECT

DIGITAL START UP ACTIVITY
Is Voting Necessary?

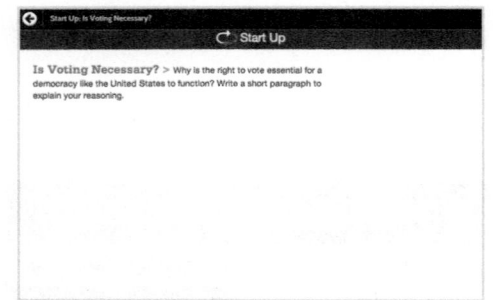

Project the Start Up Activity Ask students to answer the questions as they enter and get settled. Then have them share their ideas with another student, either in class or through a chat or blog space.

Discuss Why is the right to vote essential for a democracy like the United States?

Tell students that in this lesson they will be learning about the actions taken by people to expand the political rights, including the right to vote, of racial minorities in the 1960s.

Aa Vocabulary Development: Use the Interactive Reading Notepad to preview the Key Terms and Academic Vocabulary in the lesson with students.

🔃 FLIP IT!
Assign the Flipped Video for this lesson.

■ STUDENT EDITION PRINT PAGES: 698–706

■ INVESTIGATE

DIGITAL TEXT 1
Increasing Participation in the Political Process

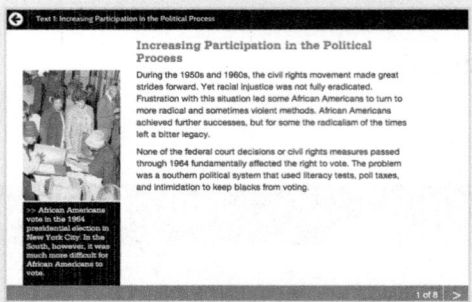

Objective 1: Explain the significance of Freedom Summer, the march on Selma, and why violence erupted in some American cities in the 1960s.

Quick Instruction
Analyze Images Project the image of Mr. Luther King, Jr., marching at Selma. Point out that the photo was taken in 1965 during one of the significant civil rights marches of the 1960s. Invite students to evaluate changes in the United States that resulted from the civil rights movement, including increased participation of minorities in the political process. What actions of President Johnson, Congress, civil rights activists, and political organizations that promoted civil rights addressed minority rights? *(SNCC organized voter education projects in Mississippi. In 1964 the group organized the Freedom Summer campaign. About 1,000 volunteers helped register African Americans to vote. Early in 1965, Martin Luther King, Jr., and SCLC organized a major campaign in Selma, Alabama, to pressure the federal government to enact voting rights legislation. Pressured by protesters, the NAACP, President Johnson, and Congress passed the Voting Rights Act of 1965.)*

Draw Conclusions Why did many civil rights supporters think that the only way to expand the right to participate in the democratic process was to amend the U.S. Constitution? *(Historically, regulation of voting rights had been left to the states. Individual states could create laws that restricted or made it very difficult for minorities to vote, and citizens is*

those states would have no way to fight the discrimination. A constitutional amendment would make these state laws illegal.)

Interpret Ask students to evaluate the importance of the Twenty-fourth Amendment to the Constitution as a means of achieving equality of political rights. *(The amendment banned the poll tax, eliminating one measure that had been used to keep poor African Americans from voting.)*

ELL Use the ELL activity described in the ELL chart.

Further Instruction
Discuss the various means used to achieve equality of political rights. Ask students to describe these methods. Make sure students understand how constitutional amendments helped, how protesting and other actions of individuals and political organizations forced changes, how lobbying by individuals and groups worked, and that litigation resulted in rulings favorable to expanding the right to participate in the democratic process.

Support Ideas with Examples Evaluate the various means used to achieve equality of political rights. In your opinion, which method was the most successful and why? *(The constitutional amendments were the most effective because they outlawed practices in states that denied political rights. Other means could still be thwarted by state or local lawmakers or ignored by Congress.)*

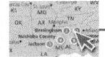

DIGITAL TEXT 2

Violence Troubles Civil Rights Efforts

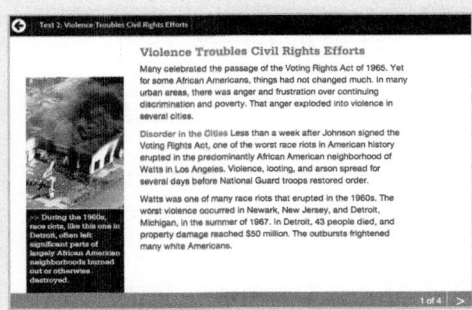

INTERACTIVE MAP

Violent Conflicts During the Civil Rights Era

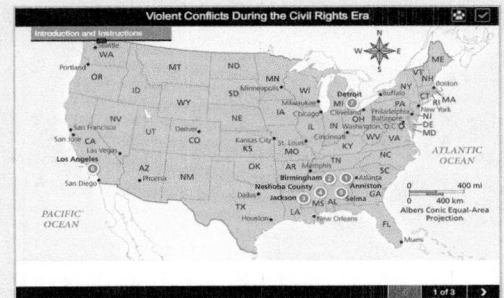

DIGITAL TEXT 3

New Civil Rights Groups

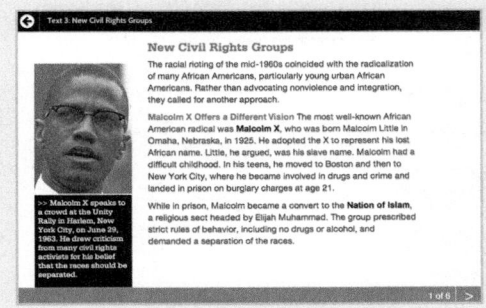

Objective 1: Explain the significance of Freedom Summer, the march on Selma, and why violence erupted in some American cities in the 1960s.

Quick Instruction

Interactive Map: Violent Conflicts During the Civil Rights Era Project the interactive map. Click on each hotspot individually and then review the collection of images and information as a whole. Set the conflicts in the interactive map within the larger context of the historical development of the civil rights movement in the twentieth century.

Identify Cause and Effect What factors contributed to the outbreak of riots in the 1960s? *(Violent conflicts in the South were mostly the result of backlash from those who opposed expanded rights for minorities. The riots outside the South were started because of the perceived persistence of discrimination against African Americans and the lack of any strategies to remedy the problems.)*

📺 ACTIVE CLASSROOM

Direct students to have a "Conversation with a Freedom Rider." Tell students to imagine that they are having a conversation with a Freedom Rider. Direct each student to write down a question he or she would like to ask one of the Freedom Riders and then write how the Freedom Rider would respond. Encourage students to write several questions to form a conversation.

Further Instruction

Predict Consequences What effects do you think the violence would have on the civil rights movement's goal of achieving equality of political rights? *(Possible answer: The violent outbreaks may bring added attention to the fight for civil rights, leading to more and quicker action to try to expand rights for all Americans.)*

Objective 2: Compare and contrast the goals and approaches taken by African American leaders to expand political rights and economic opportunities.

Quick Instruction

Analyze Images Project the image of Malcolm X. Ask: In your opinion, what were the positive and negative aspects of Malcolm X's views on race relations? *(Malcolm X preached a message of self-reliance and black pride, which were positive. However, his call for black nationalism and the separation of races only made race relations worse.)* Ask students to name some of the African American social and political organizations that promoted civil rights. *(Nation of Islam, Black Panthers, SNCC, CORE, SCLC.)*

Compare and Contrast How did the approach taken by the Black Panthers differ from the approach taken by Martin Luther King, Jr.? *(The Black Panthers often used radical methods to achieve their goals, including the threat of violence. They questioned the concept of racial integration. In contrast, Martin Luther King, Jr., disagreed with the call for "black power" and continued his nonviolent protests to defeat economic and political injustice.)*

Further Instruction

To extend the teaching of this objective, engage students in a discussion of the actions taken by the new civil rights groups that emerged in the 1960s. Students should be able to list voter registration drives, nonviolent marches by Martin Luther King, Jr., and other nonviolent groups. Students might mention

Successes and Setbacks

DIGITAL TEXT 4
King Expands His Dream

King Expands His Dream

Martin Luther King understood the anger and frustration of many urban African Americans whose lives had changed little despite the civil rights reforms of the 1960s. However, he disagreed with the call for "black power" and sought a nonviolent alternative to combat economic injustice.

After spending about a year in Chicago's slums to protest conditions there, King made plans for a massive "Poor People's Campaign." The campaign's goal was to broaden civil rights' goals to address economic inequality in America.

King's Assassination: A Turning Point As part of this effort, King journeyed to Memphis, Tennessee, in early April 1968. There, he offered his assistance to sanitation workers who were striking for better wages and working conditions.

On April 3, King addressed his followers. He referred to threats that had been made against his life. "Like anybody, I would like to live a long life," King declared. "But I'm not concerned about that now.

>> Poor People's Campaign members march through Atlanta on May 10, 1968, to promote economic justice. Draw Conclusions How did the goal of this march differ from previous civil rights demonstrations?

1 of 4   >

DIGITAL TEXT 5
Results of the Civil Rights Movement

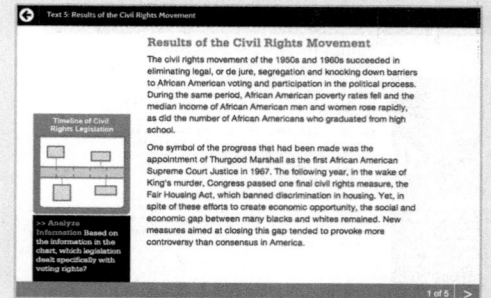

Results of the Civil Rights Movement

The civil rights movement of the 1950s and 1960s succeeded in eliminating legal, or de jure, segregation and knocking down barriers to African American voting and participation in the political process. During the same period, African American poverty rates fell and the median income of African American men and women rose rapidly, as did the number of African Americans who graduated from high school.

Timeline of Civil Rights Legislation

One symbol of the progress that had been made was the appointment of Thurgood Marshall as the first African American Supreme Court Justice in 1967. The following year, in the wake of King's murder, Congress passed one final civil rights measure, the Fair Housing Act, which banned discrimination in housing. Yet, in spite of these efforts to create economic opportunity, the social and economic gap between many blacks and whites remained. New measures aimed at closing this gap tended to provoke more controversy than consensus in America.

>> Analyze Information Based on the information in the chart, which legislation dealt specifically with voting rights?

1 of 5   >

the Black Panthers' armed patrols of city neighborhoods, armed protests in government buildings, and violent confrontations with police. Make sure students understand the significance of the year 1968 in the ongoing civil rights battle (Assassinations of Martin Luther King, Jr., and Bobby Kennedy.)

Infer Ask students to describe the role of Lester Maddox in maintaining the status quo of racial inequality. What does the story of Lester Maddox tell you about the success of the civil rights movement in the 1960s? *(Lester Maddox closed the restaurant he owned rather than comply with 1964 Civil Rights Act that banned discrimination against African Americans. Maddox then ran for and was elected governor of Georgia. After King's assassination, Governor Maddox would not even allow the civil rights leader's body to lie in state in the Georgia state capitol building. Although Dr. King's and others' efforts had increased minority participation in the political process and encouraged racial integration, there were many white Americans who wanted to maintain the status quo. In short, there was still a great deal of hostility to the aims of the civil rights movement.)*

Interpret Point out that after Stokely Carmichael gave his "black power" speech, Huey Newton and Bobby Seale formed the Black Panther Party in Oakland, California. The Black Panthers became the symbol of young militant African Americans. Ask students to explain what Carmichael meant by the phrase "Black Power". *(Carmichael believed that African Americans should collectively use their economic and political muscle, or "Black Power," to gain equality.)*

Draw Conclusions In your opinion, which actions were most effective in achieving equality of political rights? *(The nonviolent protests of Martin Luther King, Jr., were more effective. Although nonviolent protests did not always bring immediate results, peaceful demonstrations and beliefs were much more effective in winning support for the cause.)*

Objective 3: Describe the social and economic situation of African Americans by 1975.

Quick Instruction
Introduce the interactive activity by explaining that in spite of efforts to create economic opportunity, the social and economic gap between minorities and whites remained. New measures aimed at closing this gap were often very controversial.

Interactive Chart: Opposing Views on Affirmative Action Project the interactive chart and invite students to discuss the two passages.

Identify Central Issues According to its supporters, how does affirmative action expand the economic opportunities of racial minorities? *(Affirmative action should improve the educational opportunities of racial minorities. This will lead to higher paying and more stable employment. Businesses following affirmative action programs will hire more minorities even without advanced education, and state and local governments will protect expanded opportunities to minorities.)*

Identify Central Issues Ask students to analyze the unintended consequences of affirmative action raised by Shelby Steele. *(Steele argues that affirmative action indirectly encourages blacks to exploit the injustices of the past as a source of power and privilege. He thinks that affirmative action sends the message that success can be bought by invoking the past rather than by earning it through hard work.)*

INTERACTIVE CHART

Opposing Views on Affirmative Action

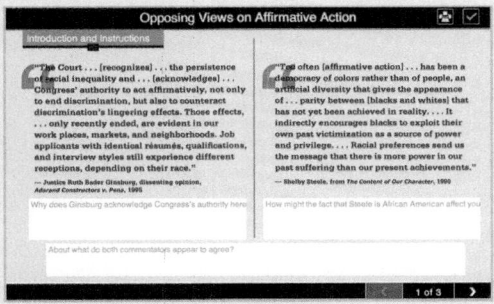

ACTIVE CLASSROOM

Conduct a Take a Stand Activity:

- Ask students to take a stand on the following question: Is affirmative action an effective method to create economic opportunities for citizens?
- Ask students to divide into two groups based on their answer and move to separate areas of the classroom.
- Ask students to talk with each other to compare their reasons for their position.
- Ask a representative from each group to present and defend the group's point of view.

D Differentiate: **Extra Support** After asking the students to take a stand, allow students five minutes to think about the question individually. Tell them to write down their response (Yes or No) and two reasons why they answered that way. Then continue with the group activity.

ELL Use the ELL activity described in the ELL chart.

Further Instruction

Extend the discussion by asking students to think about and discuss ways in which the political rights of racial and ethnic minorities were expanded. Ask students to identify actions that led to these expansions and those responsible for carrying them out. *(Congress has strengthened the Voting Rights Act 1965 over the years and passed the Fair Housing Act.)*

Discuss the effects of *White* v. *Regester*, in which the Supreme Court ruled that legislative reapportionment of congressional districts in Texas was unconstitutional because it discriminated against racial and ethnic groups.

Draw Conclusions In your opinion, was the Supreme Court correct in weakening the Voting Rights Act of 1965 by releasing nine states from federal supervision? Explain. *(Possible answer: The decision was correct. The states showed that events and changes brought about by the civil rights movement had increased minority participation in the political process enough that supervision wasn't necessary. Possible answer: The decision was incorrect. The Voting Rights Act was working as intended.)*

Successes and Setbacks

■ SYNTHESIZE

DIGITAL ACTIVITY
Voting Rights for All

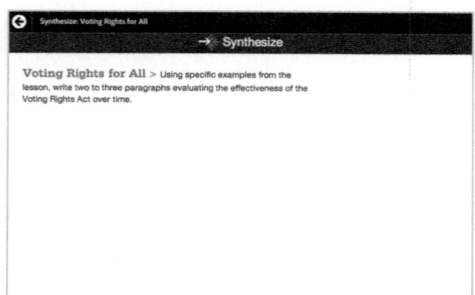

Discuss Before students begin their activity, lead a brief discussion about what it means to vote and what implications there are for casting votes.

Invite students to share their paragraphs with the class as a whole.

■ DEMONSTRATE

DIGITAL QUIZ
Lesson Quiz and Class Discussion Board

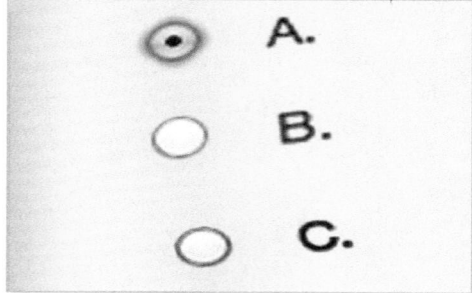

Assign the online Lesson Quiz for this lesson if you haven't already done so. Students will be offered automatic remediation or enrichment based on their score.

Pose these questions to the class on the Discussion Board:

In *Civil Rights and Reform in the 1960s*, you read about the actions of individuals and groups of people who supported expanding the political participation of minorities. Dr. Martin Luther King, Jr., and his followers charted a course of nonviolence. Others, such as Malcolm X and the Black Panthers rejected the tactic of nonviolent protests and even questioned integration.

Draw Inferences What challenges did the conflict between the tactics of Martin Luther King, Jr., and the Black Panthers create for the civil rights movement?

Identify Central Ideas Does Robert Kennedy's request to honor Dr. King's memory by replacing anger and desire for revenge "with an effort to understand with compassion and love" reflect Dr. King's message? Why or why not?

Topic Inquiry
Have students continue their investigations for the Topic Inquiry.

PEARSON
realize™

www.PearsonRealize.com
Access your Digital Lesson

Kennedy's Reforms

Supporting English Language Learners

Use with Digital Text 1, **A Torch is Passed to a New Generation.**

Learning Strategies

Read aloud the section titled *Television Influences Voter Opinion*, or invite volunteers to do so. Briefly explain the nature of a presidential debate (or show a video clip of one) and prompt students to use formal and informal English commensurate with grade-level learning expectations.

Beginning Display two greetings that a candidate could use in a debate: *Good evening, my fellow Americans* and *Hey there, folks!* Have students identify each as informal or formal English, and ask them which would be more appropriate.

Intermediate Ask students to choose a level of formality for the headline of a news article about a presidential debate. Then have them write one or more appropriate headlines for the 1960 Nixon-Kennedy debate.

Advanced Have pairs of students mark a continuum (with the words *informal* and *formal* at either end) to show what type of English should be used in a presidential debate, when talking about it with friends, and when reporting it on the news. Ask them to explain their decisions.

Advanced High Have students mark a continuum (with the words *informal* and *formal* at either end) to show what type of English should be used in a presidential debate, when talking about it with friends, and when reporting it on the news. Then have pairs of students demonstrate each situation.

Use with Digital Text 3, **Domestic Priorities.**

Speaking

Read aloud the section titled *First to the Moon*, or invite volunteers to do so. Point out how sentence length varies throughout the section as you prompt students to speak using a variety of sentence lengths.

Beginning Review the term *space race*. Then display this sentence frame: The space race was _____. Have students complete the sentence with a word or phrase and say it aloud.

Intermediate Display the last sentence of the third paragraph. Read it aloud and have students repeat after you. Then remove the words *Kennedy's bold dream*. Have students replace it with an original word or phrase and say the sentence aloud.

Advanced Display the first sentence of the fourth paragraph both in its original form and without its two prepositional phrases. Discuss what the prepositional phrases add to the sentence. Then have pairs of students practice making statements about the space race that include prepositional phrases.

Advanced High Display the second sentence of the section. Discuss its structure, including the use of dependent and independent clauses. Ask students to write a similarly structured sentence about the space race that begins with the word *although*.

▶ Differentiate Instruction

Use the Differentiated Instruction notes throughout the lesson plan to support the varied skill sets, levels of readiness, and interests in the mixed-ability classroom.

Challenge These notes include suggestions for expanding the activity for advanced students.

On-Level These notes include suggestions for modifying the activity to address different interests or learning styles.

Extra Support These notes include ideas for providing more scaffolding or reading spuport.

Special Needs These notes provide ideas for adapting instruction to support the needs of various special needs students.

▮ NOTES

Kennedy's Reforms

Objectives

Objective 1: Discuss the election of 1960.

Objective 2: Evaluate Kennedy's domestic policies.

Objective 3: Assess the impact of Kennedy's assassination.

LESSON 4 ORGANIZER		PACING: APPROX. 1 PERIOD, .5 BLOCKS			
				RESOURCES	
		OBJECTIVES	**PACING**	**Online**	**Print**
Connect					
DIGITAL START UP ACTIVITY **Far Out Inventions**			5 min.	●	
Investigate					
DIGITAL TEXT 1 **The Torch is Passed to a New Generation**		Objective 1	10 min.	●	●
INTERACTIVE GALLERY **The Election of 1960**			10 min.	●	
DIGITAL TEXT 2 **A President's Unique Charisma**		Objective 2	10 min.	●	●
DIGITAL TEXT 3 **Domestic Priorities**			10 min.	●	●
DIGITAL TEXT 4 **Kennedy is Assassinated**		Objective 3	10 min.	●	●
Synthesize					
DIGITAL ACTIVITY **Answering the Call**			5 min.	●	
Demonstrate					
DIGITAL QUIZ **Lesson Quiz and Discussion Board**			10 min.	●	

PEARSON
realize™
www.PearsonRealize.com

Go online to access additional resources including:
Primary Sources • Biographies • Supreme Court cases •
21st Century Skill Tutorials • Maps • Graphic Organizers.

▶ CONNECT

DIGITAL START UP ACTIVITY
Far Out Inventions

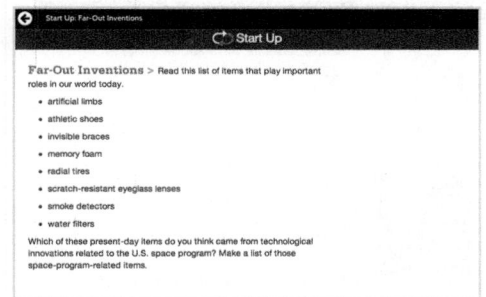

Project the Start Up Activity Ask students to answer the questions as they enter and get settled. Then have them share their ideas about how space exploration improves the quality of life with another student, either in class or through a chat or blog space.

Discuss Review the list of items on the activity before students create their lists. After students have made their lists, have them share the lists with the class.

Tell students that in this lesson they will be learning about the Kennedy administration and how technological innovation in the U.S. space program improved the quality of life for many Americans.

Aa Vocabulary Development: Use the Interactive Reading Notepad to preview the Key Terms and Academic Vocabulary in the lesson with students.

⇅ FLIP IT!
Assign the Flipped Video for this lesson.

▶ STUDENT EDITION PRINT
PAGES: 707–712

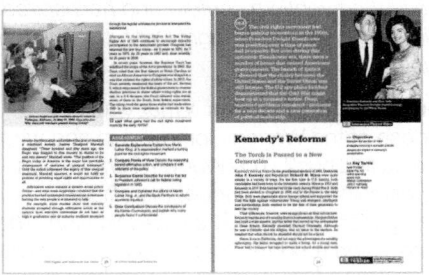

▶ INVESTIGATE

DIGITAL TEXT 1
The Torch is Passed to a New Generation

Objective 1: Describe the election of 1960.

Quick Instruction
Interactive Gallery: The Election of 1960 Introduce activity by telling students that the election of 1960 was significant in several ways: It saw the largest voter turnout yet in the nation's history, it was the closest election in nearly 100 years; and the Kennedy-Nixon debates marked the first televised presidential campaign. Project the interactive gallery and click through the hot spots.

🖳 ACTIVE CLASSROOM
Have students Make Headlines for the first presidential debate between Kennedy and Nixon. Ask: If you were to write a headline about the results of the debate in Chicago, what would it be? Allow students to use subheadings to communicate more information. Have students share to review each other's headlines.

ELL Use the ELL activity described in the ELL chart.

Further Instruction
Explicitly connect the presidential election of 1960 and President Kennedy's commitment to the civil rights movement with the larger historical development of the civil rights movement in the 20th century.

Identify Central Issues How did civil rights issues enter the 1960 presidential election? *(Civil rights leader Martin Luther King, Jr., was arrested before the election. Kennedy reached out to King and worked to get him released.*

INTERACTIVE GALLERY
The Election of 1960

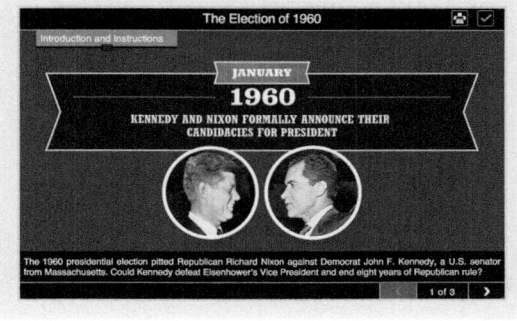

By doing this, Kennedy gained the support of many African Americans and showed a strong commitment to the civil rights movement.)

Infer How did television change political campaigns and presidential elections? *(Television coverage focussed more attention on candidates' appearance, than on their political policies. Many people think that Kennedy "won" the first debate because he looked younger and more energetic than Nixon, not necessarily because he had better ideas.)*

Kennedy's Reforms

DIGITAL TEXT 2

A President's Unique Charisma

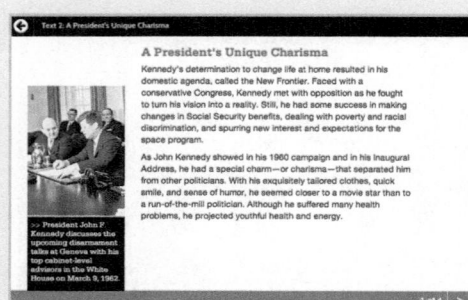

DIGITAL TEXT 3

Domestic Priorities

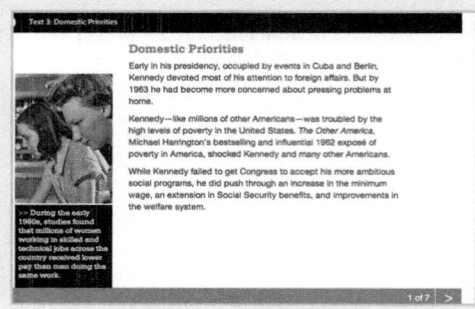

DIGITAL TEXT 4

Kennedy is Assassinated

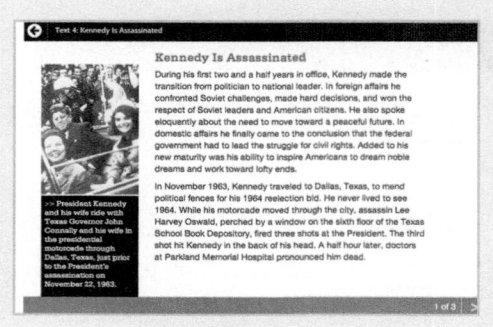

Objective 2: Evaluate Kennedy's domestic policies.

Quick Instruction

Project the Interactive Graphic Organizer from the Interactive Reading Notepad. Use the information students have recorded to begin a discussion about Kennedy's administration. Ask: Based on the information you recorded about John F. Kennedy, what type of people would you expect him to bring into his administration? *(Kennedy would bring in people similar to him—wealthy, Ivy-league graduates with similar backgrounds. I think he'd probably bring in younger-than-normal politicians or experts.)*

Be sure that students understand the significance of 1969: this was the year Neil Armstrong became the first person to walk on the moon, making it a pivotal year in the space race.

Summarize Point out that although Kennedy was heavily occupied by foreign policy issues during the first few years of his administration, he did tackle domestic issues, such as expanding the rights of women and African Americans. What actions did the Kennedy administration take to protect and expand the rights of women and minorities? What role did he play in the historical development of the civil rights movement in the 20th century? *(President's Commission on the Status of Women, Equal Pay Act of 1963, introduced stronger civil rights legislation, including voting-rights legislation, also supported more federal money for school desegregation)*

D Differentiate: Challenge Ask students to research other technologies developed by the space program that have uses in everyday

life. Have them present their findings and explain how the products that emerged from space exploration improved the quality of life.

ELL Use the ELL activity described in the ELL chart.

Further Instruction

To extend the teaching of this objective, engage students in a brief review of the way in which the Cold War and international competition led to space exploration. *(The Cold War build-up in military and technology between the United States and the Soviet Union pushed both countries to spend large sums of money to gain advantages. The space race and space exploration was a result of this.)*

Infer Although initially a competition with the Soviet Union for control of space, the space race had a profound impact on the everyday lives of Americans. Discuss specific examples of how space exploration improved the quality of life of many Americans. *(Technology used in the space program was used to create new products in non-space applications. New materials for eye glasses helped Americans see better. More-versatile power tools, newer and convenient foods for adults and infants, and materials like memory foam all improved how people lived their lives.)*

Identify Central Issues What was the effect of Apollo 11's successful flight to the moon and back? *(The United States gained dominance over the Soviet Union in the space race.)*

Identify Central Issues What challenges did Kennedy face in moving forward with his civil rights legislation? *(Kennedy did not have strong support in Congress, especially from conservative Democrats from the South, who did not support more civil rights laws.)*

Objective 3: Assess the impact of the Kennedy assassination.

Quick Instruction

Analyze Images Project the image of JFK in the motorcade. Ask students to summarize the events of November 22, 1963. *(President Kennedy, in Dallas on a political visit to build support for the presidential election in 1964, was assassinated by Lee Harvey Oswald during a motorcade parade through the city.)*

Make Predictions Without Kennedy's charisma and ability to inspire, what do you think will happen to the New Frontier programs and the space program? *(Because Vice President Lyndon Johnson became President, the New Frontier and space programs will move forward without Kennedy.)*

Further Instruction

Extend the discussion by explaining that 250,000 Americans paid their respects as Kennedy's body lay in state in the Capitol Rotunda. Millions more watched the television coverage of the funeral on November 25.

Hypothesize In your opinion, why did the Kennedy assassination affect Americans so deeply? *(Kennedy represented a new America for many citizens. He was the first president born in the twentieth century and he inspired millions with visions of a greater future for the country.)*

Identify Central Issues What was the purpose of the Warren Commission and what were its findings? *(The Warren Commission was established to conduct the official investigation of Kennedy's assassination. The Commission reported that Lee Harvey Oswald acted alone.)*

PEARSON

realize™

www.PearsonRealize.com
Access your Digital Lesson

■ SYNTHESIZE

DIGITAL ACTIVITY
Answering the Call

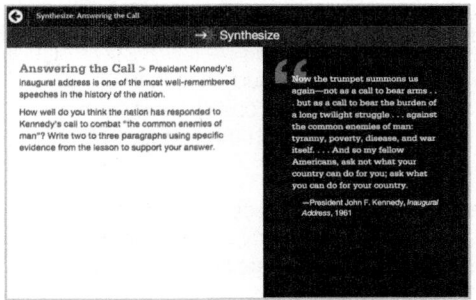

Identify Main Ideas After students write their paragraphs, ask students to provide additional examples not drawn from the lesson that show how well the nation has answered Kennedy's call.

■ DEMONSTRATE

DIGITAL QUIZ
Lesson Quiz and Discussion Board

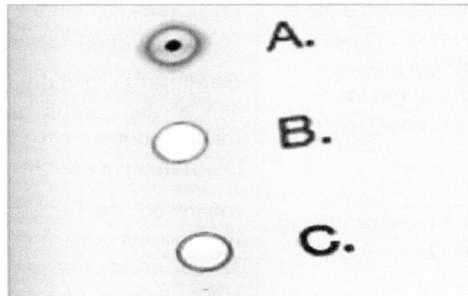

Assign the online Lesson Quiz for this lesson if you haven't already done so. Students will be offered automatic remediation or enrichment based on their score.

Pose these questions to the class on the Discussion Board:

In *Kennedy's Reforms*, you read about President John F. Kennedy's vision for the future of the nation. Kennedy stated, "We stand today on the edge of a new frontier—the frontier of the 1960s—the frontier of unknown opportunities and perils —a frontier of unfulfilled hopes and threats."

Interpret What world events and issues influenced President Kennedy to refer to the 1960s as being a "frontier"?

Cite Evidence How effective would you rate President Kennedy's domestic programs? Use specific examples from the text to support your answer.

Topic Inquiry
Have students continue their investigations for the Topic Inquiry.

Reform Under Johnson

Supporting English Language Learners

Use with Digital Text 2, **Creating the Great Society.**

Speaking
Read aloud the section titled *Increasing Access to Healthcare*, or invite volunteers to do so. Then review the end punctuation marks and how these marks can identify some of the different sentence types: declarative, interrogative, exclamatory, and imperative. Model how English speakers use intonation by voicing the contrast between a declarative statement and the rising sound of a question. Then have students complete the following tasks by using a variety of sentence types with increasing accuracy and ease as they speak.

Beginning Display these sentence frames: Is Medicare _____? Does Medicare _____? Ask students to select a frame, think of a word or phrase to complete it, and say the question aloud (it is okay if they already know the answer).

Intermediate Ask students a variety of questions about Medicare and Medicaid. Have them respond using declarative or exclamatory sentences.

Advanced Have pairs of students ask each other questions about Medicare and Medicaid whose answers can be found in, or inferred from, the text. Encourage students to try to respond using both declarative and exclamatory sentences.

Advanced High Ask students to give a short talk about Medicare and Medicaid that uses each sentence type (declarative, interrogative, exclamatory, imperative). Suggest that they conclude with an imperative sentence directed toward government or citizens about these programs' solvency.

Use with Digital Text 3, **The Impact of the Warren Court.**

Learning Strategies
Read aloud the text, or invite volunteers to do so. Point out the many names of court cases presented in the text (e.g., *Baker* v. *Carr* (1962)) to encourage students to look for patterns in language commensurate with grade-level learning expectations.

Beginning Point out the pattern used for citing a court case (names, v., italics, year, parentheses). Then display several court case names from the text, but with missing parts. Have students search the text for the information needed to complete them.

Intermediate Discuss the pattern used for citing a court case (including that the first party mentioned is suing the second party). Then display several court case names from the text, but with at least one error each. Have students use the text to correct them.

Advanced Discuss the pattern used for citing a court case. Then orally summarize a court case from the text, and have students create a citation for it. Ask: If strangers read the citation, what could they automatically know about the case? What would they not know?

Advanced High Discuss the pattern used for citing a court case. Then have pairs of students create a scenario and citation for an imaginary court case. Invite students to share their cases.

▶ Differentiate Instruction

Use the Differentiated Instruction notes throughout the lesson plan to support the varied skill sets, levels of readiness, and interests in the mixed-ability classroom.

Challenge These notes include suggestions for expanding the activity for advanced students.

On-Level These notes include suggestions for modifying the activity to address different interests or learning styles.

Extra Support These notes include ideas for providing more scaffolding or reading spuport.

Special Needs These notes provide ideas for adapting instruction to support the needs of various special needs students.

■ NOTES

PEARSON

realize.
www.PearsonRealize.com

Go online to access additional resources including:
Primary Sources • Biographies • Supreme Court cases •
21st Century Skill Tutorials • Maps • Graphic Organizers.

Objectives

Objective 1: Evaluate Johnson's policies up to his victory in the 1964 presidential election.

Objective 2: Analyze Johnson's goals and actions as seen in his Great Society programs.

Objective 3: Assess the achievements of the Great Society in creating economic opportunities for citizens.

Objective 4: Analyze the effects of U.S. Supreme Court decisions.

LESSON 5 ORGANIZER		OBJECTIVES	PACING	RESOURCES	
				Online	Print
Connect					
DIGITAL START UP ACTIVITY **The Land of the Free?**			5 min.	●	
Investigate					
DIGITAL TEXT 1 **Johnson's Path to the Presidency**		Objective 1	10 min.	●	●
DIGITAL TEXT 2 **Creating the Great Society**		Objectives 2, 3	10 min.	●	●
BEFORE AND AFTER **Johnson's Great Society**			10 min.	●	
DIGITAL TEXT 3 **The Impact of the Warren Court**		Objective 4	10 min.	●	●
INTERACTIVE GALLERY **The Warren Court**			10 min.	●	
Synthesize					
DIGITAL ACTIVITY **Did Johnson Succeed?**			5 min.	●	
Demonstrate					
DIGITAL QUIZ **Lesson Quiz and Class Discussion Board**			10 min.	●	

PACING: APPROX. 1 PERIOD, .5 BLOCKS

Reform Under Johnson

■ CONNECT

DIGITAL START UP ACTIVITY
The Land of the Free?

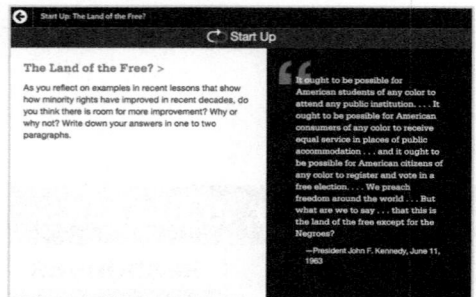

Project the Start Up Activity As students enter and get settled, direct their attention to the quote from President Kennedy. Ensure students understand that *public accommodation* includes private entities such as hotels, restaurants, and retail stores. Also ensure that students understand that *Negroes* was a commonly accepted term for African Americans when Kennedy spoke. Place Kennedy's speech within the larger context of the historical development of the civil rights movement in the twentieth century.

Tell students that in this lesson they will be learning about the Johnson administration, Great Society programs and the impact of the Warren Court.

Aa Vocabulary Development: Use the Interactive Reading Notepad to preview the Key Terms and Academic Vocabulary in this lesson with students.

⇅ FLIP IT!
Assign the Flipped Video for this lesson.

■ STUDENT EDITION PRINT
PAGES: 713–719

■ INVESTIGATE

DIGITAL TEXT 1
Johnson's Path to the Presidency

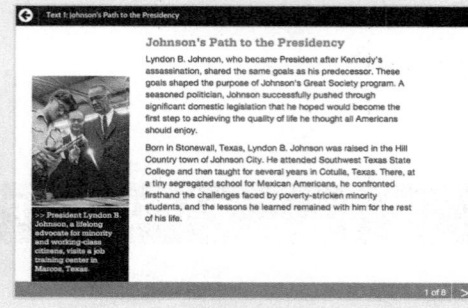

Objective 1: Evaluate Johnson's policies up to his victory in the 1964 presidential election.

Quick Instruction
Summarize Project the image of Johnson being sworn in as president. Challenge students to summarize Johnson's signature achievements as he completed this first term in office. Ask: What actions did Johnson take to expand economic opportunities, including those for ethnic and racial minorities, in American society? *(Major actions include the 1964 the Civil Rights Act, the War on Poverty, the Economic Opportunity Act, Job Corps, VISTA, Head Start)*

D Differentiate: Extra Support Clarify for students that President Johnson did not single-handedly create the programs for which he is credited, but rather used his political ability to get the programs passed by Congress.

Further Instruction
Go through the Interactive Reading Notepad questions and discuss the answers with the class.

Make Predictions Your reading referred to Johnson's idea that America should be a "Great Society." What do you think this means? *(Answers might allude to including increased participation of minorities in the political process and creating economic opportunities for citizens, especially ethnic minorities and women.)*

Compare and Contrast Johnson became President upon the death of President Kennedy. In 1964, he ran to be elected as President in his own right. Johnson, a Democrat, ran against a Republican, Barry Goldwater. How did the views of these significant political and social leaders differ? *(Generally, Johnson was a liberal who believed that the government could best regulate the economy and promote social justice, in contrast to Goldwater, a conservative who believed that social and economic issues, such as racism and poverty, should not be addressed by the federal government.)*

DIGITAL TEXT 2

Creating the Great Society

BEFORE AND AFTER

Johnson's Great Society

DIGITAL TEXT 3

The Impact of the Warren Court

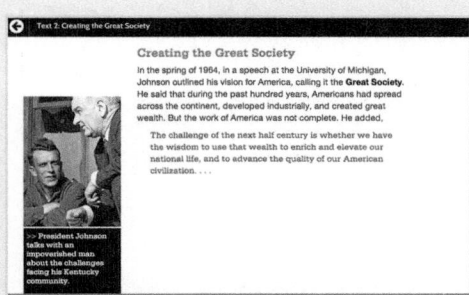

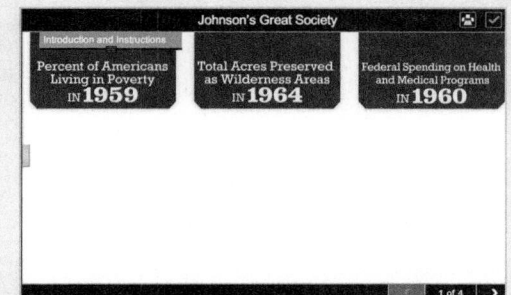

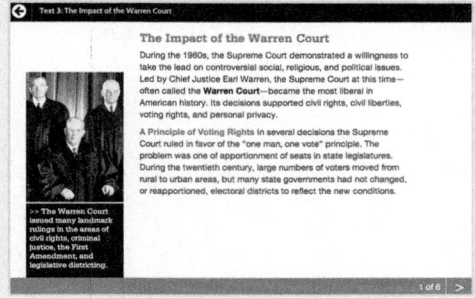

Objectives 2: Analyze Johnson's goals and actions as seen in his Great Society programs; 3: Assess the achievements of the Great Society in creating economic opportunities for citizens.

Quick Instruction

Before and After: Johnson's Great Society
Read Johnson's statement to the class. What effect might Johnson's upbringing have had on his policies as President? *(He knew about poverty first hand, and was determined that fewer Americans would suffer from it.)* What was the Great Society? *(Johnson's domestic program; the collective name for a variety of federal programs aimed at eliminating poverty and racial injustice.)*

Analyze Information Discuss the before and after statistics for poverty, wilderness areas, graduation rates, and federal spending on health and medical programs such as Medicare with students. How does the graph illustrate the Great Society's involvement in providing healthcare for elderly and poor Americans? *(It shows an increase in federal spending and so a corresponding increase in government involvement.)*

📷 ACTIVE CLASSROOM

Direct students to have a "Conversation with President Johnson." Tell students to imagine that they are having a conversation with Johnson as he is developing what will become known as the Great Society. Direct each student to write down a question he or she would like to ask, then how Johnson would respond, and then what the student would say in response.

ELL Use the ELL activity described in the ELL chart.

Further Instruction

Go through the Interactive Reading Notepad questions and discuss the answers with the class.

Identify Cause and Effect Challenge students to analyze the causes and effects of changing demographic patterns resulting from legal immigration to the United States. Ask: What Great Society program caused immigration patterns to change after 1965? *(Immigration and Nationality Act of 1965)* What effect did it have? *(It ended an immigration system that favored Western European immigrants and opened the door to millions of people from Latin America, Central America, the Caribbean, and Asia.)* How has this affected the population of the United States? *(There is a greater diversity of racial and ethnic minorities.)*

Objective 4: Analyze the effects of U.S. Supreme Court decisions.

Quick Instruction

Remind students that periods of American legal history, are typically named after the Chief Justice who presided over Supreme Court decisions of that particular time period. For example, the Warren Court lasted from 1953 to 1969, when Chief Justice Earl Warren presided.

Interactive Gallery: The Warren Court Project the interactive gallery. Review each of the cases with students Ask students how they would rule in each case and why they made that decision. *(Answers will vary but should be supported.)* Then click on the case to reveal how the Warren Court decided. For each decision, ask students whether they consider the decision to be liberal or conservative. How would they evaluate the constitutional change in each case in terms of strict construction versus judicial interpretation? *(They are considered examples of judicial interpretation.)*

Reform Under Johnson

INTERACTIVE GALLERY
The Warren Court

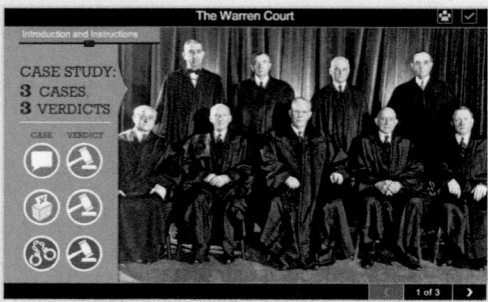

📖 ACTIVE CLASSROOM

Have students Take a Stand.

- Ask students to take a stand on the following issue: Which is the better way to interpret cases before the Supreme Court: strict construction or judicial interpretation?

- Ask students to divide into two groups based on their answer and move to separate areas of the classroom.

- Ask students to talk with each other to compare their reasons for their answers.

- Ask a representative from each side to present and defend the group's point of view.

Consider conducting similar activities for specific court cases.

ELL Use the ELL activity described in the ELL chart.

Further Instruction

Go through the Interactive Reading Notepad questions and discuss the answers with the class.

Identify Central Issues Name each of the major Warren Court cases mentioned in the lesson and have students respond with the essential outcome of the case. *(Reynolds v. Sims ("one man, one vote"); Tinker v. Des Moines School District ("symbolic" speech); Mapp v. Ohio (illegally obtained evidence excluded from trial); Gideon v. Wainwright (right to a lawyer even if cannot pay for one); Escobedo v. Illinois (lawyer before questioning); Miranda v. Arizona (informed of rights); Engel v. Vitale (no school prayer); Abington v. Schempp (no Bible reading in public schools)*

Make Generalizations What generalizations do you think would be fair to make about the Warren Court? *(Answers should center on the fact that it was liberal and favored judicial interpretation over strict constructionism.)*

Identify Central Issues How did the judicial interpretation of the Warren Court impact the relationships among the legislative, executive, and judicial branches of government? *It verified the checks and balances between the three branches in that the judicial branch can decide if laws passed by the legislative are legal.*

▌ SYNTHESIZE

DIGITAL ACTIVITY
Did Johnson Succeed?

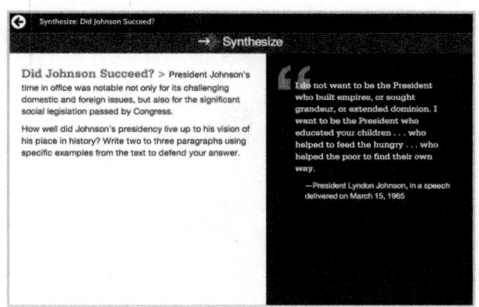

Identify Main Ideas Before students write their brief essays, hold a quick round table in which students each identify a Great Society program. For each, have the group identify it as one that was intended to "educate," "feed," or "help the poor."

▌ DEMONSTRATE

DIGITAL QUIZ
Lesson Quiz and Class Discussion Board

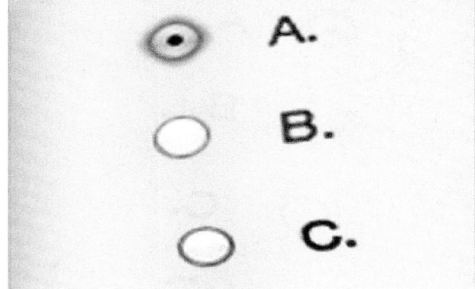

Assign the online Lesson Quiz for this lesson if you haven't already done so. Students will be offered automatic remediation or enrichment based on their score.

Pose these questions to the class on the Discussion Board:

Express Ideas Clearly On balance, was the Great Society's increased role of government good or bad for the country? Explain.

Identify Central Issues Describe the effects of immigration after the Immigration and Nationality Act of 1965 on American society.

Topic Inquiry
Have students continue their investigations for the Topic Inquiry.

Civil Rights and Reform in the 1960s

SYNTHESIZE

DIGITAL ACTIVITY

Reflect on the Essential Question and Topic

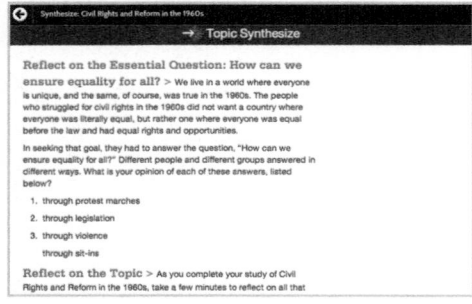

Direct students to reflect on the Essential Question for the Topic: How can we ensure equality for all? Remind students that the equality referred to is equality of rights, in economic opportunities, and before the law. Point out the methods that were used during the civil rights movement to work toward equality.

- through protest marches
- through legislation
- through violence
- through litigation

Challenge students to identify which of these methods were most effective, and why. Discuss their answers as a class or ask students to post their thoughts on the Class Discussion Board.

Next, ask students to reflect on the Topic as a whole and jot down 1-3 questions they've thought about during the Topic. Share these examples if students need help getting started:

- What were the major accomplishments of the civil rights movement?
- How do Great Society programs still affect American life today?
- How equal are the citizens of the United States today?

Topic Inquiry

Have students complete Step 3 of the Topic Inquiry.

DEMONSTRATE

DIGITAL TOPIC REVIEW AND ASSESSMENT

Civil Rights and Reform in the 1960s

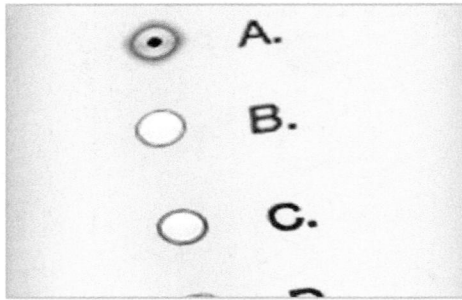

Students can prepare for the Topic Test by answering the questions in the Topic Review and Assessment online or the Assessment questions in the Print Student text. They can also prepare by reviewing their answers to the Interactive Reading Notepad questions or reviewing their notes in the Reading and Notetaking Study Guide.

DIGITAL TOPIC TEST

Civil Rights and Reform in the 1960s

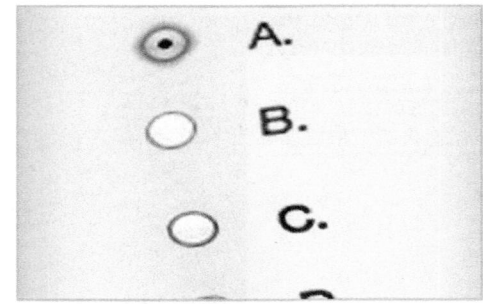

TOPIC TEST

Assign the Topic Test to assess students' understanding of topic content.

BENCHMARK TESTS

Assign these benchmark tests as you complete the relevant topics to monitor student progress toward mastering the course content and as preparation for the End-of-Course Test.

Benchmark Test 1: Topics 1–3

Benchmark Test 2: Topics 4–6

Benchmark Test 3: Topics 7–9

Benchmark Test 4: Topics 10–12

Benchmark Test 5: Topics 13–15

Benchmark Test 6: Topics 16–18

Benchmark Test 7: Topics 19–20

The Vietnam War Era

TOPIC 17 ORGANIZER	PACING: APPROX. 7 PERIODS, 3.5 BLOCKS	
		PACING
Connect		1 period
MY STORY VIDEO **Edie Meeks, Vietnam War Nurse**		10 min.
DIGITAL ESSENTIAL QUESTION ACTIVITY **What is America's role in the world?**		10 min.
DIGITAL IMAGE ACTIVITY **Napalm Attack on Vietnamese Village**		10 min.
TOPIC INQUIRY: DOCUMENT-BASED QUESTION **Reasons Behind the Antiwar Movement**		20 min.
Investigate		2–4 periods
TOPIC INQUIRY: DOCUMENT-BASED QUESTION **Reasons Behind the Antiwar Movement**		Ongoing
LESSON 1 The Cold War and Vietnam		30–40 min.
LESSON 2 America's Role Escalates		30–40 min.
LESSON 3 The Antiwar Movement		30–40 min.
LESSON 4 The War's End and Effects		30–40 min.
Synthesize		1 period
DIGITAL ACTIVITY **Reflect on the Essential Question and Topic**		10 min.
TOPIC INQUIRY: DOCUMENT-BASED QUESTION **Reasons Behind the Antiwar Movement**		20 min.
Demonstrate		1–2 periods
DIGITAL TOPIC REVIEW AND ASSESSMENT **The Vietnam War Era**		10 min.
TOPIC INQUIRY: DOCUMENT-BASED QUESTION **Reasons Behind the Antiwar Movement**		20 min.

TOPIC INQUIRY: DOCUMENT-BASED QUESTION

Reasons Behind the Antiwar Movement

In this Topic Inquiry, students will use a variety of primary and secondary sources to analyze and answer this historical question: Why did an antiwar movement develop in response to the Vietnam War? Learning how the American public helped shape U.S. foreign policy will enhance students' understanding of the Topic Essential Question: What is America's Role in the World?

STEP 1: CONNECT
Develop Questions and Plan the Investigation

Watch the Video

Before directing students to watch the video, set the scene with a brief overview of the status of the Vietnam War at the end of 1966. In February 1965, President Johnson escalated the U.S. role in the Vietnam War, first by authorizing air bombings and then by committing more ground troops. American strategy during this stage of the war yielded limited results and American casualties rose. By 1967, the war had devolved into a stalemate. In addition, most of the troops sent to Vietnam after 1965 were no longer volunteers who had enlisted in the army. Instead, they were draftees, young men drafted into military service. The perceived unfairness of the draft, lack of progress toward victory in Vietnam, and moral outrage over events in Vietnam created the foundation for an antiwar movement to emerge.

Suggestion: You can pause the video at key points to ensure students understand who the key individuals and groups of protesters are, and what role they played in the antiwar movement.

Discuss

Lead students in the discussion questions:

- What types of people participated in the antiwar movement?
- What did members of the antiwar movement do to express their disagreement with the war?
- Why might people so strongly oppose a war?

Suggestion: During the discussions, you might consider having students take notes of any ideas that are new to them so they can refresh their memory as they proceed.

Resources
- Video: Newsreel: Antiwar March, 1967

STEP 2: INVESTIGATE
Apply Disciplinary Concepts and Tools

Analyze the Documents

Direct students to review the six documents and to answer the questions that follow each one. While they should examine each source in detail, they should not lose sight of their main goal of answering the question, why did an antiwar movement develop in response to the Vietnam War?

Suggestion: Have students note and discuss the information about the authors and speakers of the documents and their points of view. Encourage students to consider the background experiences of the authors/speakers to evaluate the validity and relevance of the sources, particularly those of M.S. Aroni and Martin Luther King, Jr. Point out that students should think about language, possible bias in oral or print sources, and the historical context in which the source is set when evaluating the validity and usefulness of a source.

Check Your Understanding

Ensure students answer the multiple choice and short answer questions that accompany each document.

Resources
- Document A: Table of federal spending and revenue
- Document B: Excerpt from an antiwar speech by Martin Luther King, Jr.
- Document C: Audio clip of antiwar speech given by political activist M.S. Aroni
- Document D: Newspaper article about the release of the "Pentagon Papers"
- Document E: Web article about draft resistance during the Vietnam War

⏻ PROFESSIONAL DEVELOPMENT

Document-Based Question
Be sure to view the Document-Based Question Professional Development resources in the online course.

STEP 3: SYNTHESIZE
Evaluate Sources and Use Evidence to Formulate Conclusions

Write Your Essay

Before students write their essays, review what is expected of them:

- Clearly state your view in a topic sentence.

- Use evidence from at least three documents. Clearly identify which documents you are using.

- Support your viewpoint with relevant facts.

- Consider and respond to at least one argument opposed to your own viewpoint.

- Use a logical organization, including an introduction and a conclusion. Include a strong topic sentence.

- Use correct spelling, grammar, and punctuation.

- Read and revise your essay before submitting it to your teacher.

Consider distributing or reviewing the Rubric for DBQ Essay resource to better guide students in their writing.

Suggestion: Remind students to take the time to prewrite before they begin writing. Prewriting includes the reviewing of the documents an outlining their writing projects. As students move into the writing phase, emphasize the use of correct social studies terminology to explain historical concepts.

STEP 4: DEMONSTRATE
Communicate Conclusions and Take Informed Action

Publish the Writing Projects

When students have completed their writing projects, hold a class discussion about the question, Why did an antiwar movement develop in response to the Vietnam War? See if the class can reach a consensus on one or more reasons why. Record these reasons on the whiteboard.

Then, ask the class to turn these conclusions into informed action. Ask: what is the value of understanding why people become involved in antiwar movements? Challenge them to describe the positive and negative effects of antiwar movements and explain the role of public protests in a democracy like the United States.

Suggestion: Extend the activity by having students conduct library and Internet research to locate examples of other more recent antiwar movements.

The Vietnam War Era

The Cold War policy of containment and the domino theory led the United States to become increasingly involved in events in Vietnam. American officials were concerned that if Vietnam fell to communism, the entire region might be at risk. Most Americans supported the initial intervention in Vietnam. After several years, however, mounting casualties, rising debt, and lack of progress soon turned public opinion and undermined support. How did the war change the United States and the world?

▮ CONNECT

MY STORY VIDEO

Edie Meeks, Vietnam War Nurse

Watch a video about a nurse's experiences during the Vietnam War.

Check Understanding What was Edie Meeks' job in Vietnam? *(She was an intensive care nurse in field hospitals.)*

Evaluate Sources In what ways does Edie Meeks' story help us learn more about the Vietnam War? *(Her account helps us understand the common goal of doctors and nurses to trying to save the lives of soldiers who had been wounded in battle. The constant challenges she faced speak to the brutality of combat in Vietnam.)*

DIGITAL ESSENTIAL QUESTION ACTIVITY

What is America's role in the world?

Ask students to think about the Essential Question for this Topic: What is America's role in the world? Begin a discussion with students about how the United States interacts with other nations.

If students have not already done so, ask them to read the Essential Question Activity. Before students answer the question, encourage them to ask questions to clarify concepts.

Identify Central Issues What can the way the United States interacts with other nations reveal about America's role in the world? *(Military interactions can tell me that the United States has forces all over the world and is often called upon to resolve conflicts. Our economic interactions with other countries reveal that the United States is very influential in the world economy.)*

Predict Consequences With your answer to the question in mind, predict how the Vietnam War will affect the U.S. role as a superpower.

DIGITAL IMAGE ACTIVITY

Napalm Attack on Vietnamese Village

Display the image of a U.S. napalm attack on a Vietnamese village. In this Topic students will learn about the tactics, strategies, and weapons used in the Vietnam war and much more. This photo captures the destruction the war brought and shints at the clarity and detail with which the world's media will cover the conflict.

Analyze Photographs What does the photograph tell you about Vietnamese terrain on which the war was fought? *(The area in the photo looks flat and not too hilly. I see palm trees in the village so it must be a tropical region, which can mean it was hot and possible rainy.)*

Make Predictions What will the war's impact be on the physical geography of Vietnam? *(The war will devastate Vietnam's countryside, based on this picture.)*

Topic Inquiry

Launch the Topic Inquiry with students after introducing the Topic.

PEARSON
realize™

www.PearsonRealize.com
Access your Digital Lesson

The Cold War and Vietnam

Supporting English Language Learners

Use with Digital Text 3, **The Causes and Outcomes of the Berlin Crisis.**

Speaking
Read aloud the text, or invite volunteers to do so. In the first paragraph, draw attention to the sentences "Kennedy refused. He did not want to ... (etc.)" Point out that the second sentence shows why Kennedy refused. Elicit the connecting word that could be used to tie these two sentences into one sentence (because). Write other connecting words such as "so, yet, although" and tell students that they will be using these words in the following tasks.

Beginning Have students use two simple sentences explaining what they did and why they did it. Then have them combine the sentences using the word *because*.

Intermediate Provide the sentence "Khrushchev demanded that the United States end its military presence in West Berlin and explain how this sentence could be combined with the sentence" Kennedy refused by use of the word *however*. Have students work in pairs to create more sentences using the word *however*.

Advanced Explain the purpose of connecting words in creating complex sentences and have students create a list of such words. As a group, use these connecting words in original spoken sentences about Khrushchev and Kennedy.

Advanced High Ask students to think of connecting words or phrases (however, even so, nevertheless) and to use them in original sentences about Khrushchev and Kennedy. Have students share their sentences aloud, while listeners spell the connectors based on their sounds.

Use with Digital Text 5, **The United States Responds to Communism in Vietnam.**

Listening, Speaking
Explain to students that they will be learning new questions and expressions often heard in classroom instruction and interaction that they can use after listening for information. Prompt students to ask for information using vocabulary in both academic and social contexts.

Beginning Say: Could you speak more slowly? Could you repeat that? Have students listen and repeat after you. Explain when to use these questions. Then read aloud the text, encouraging students to ask questions as needed.

Intermediate Display these question starters: Where is _____? What is _____? Who is _____? Discuss when students have heard each in the classroom. Then read aloud the text, encouraging students to ask questions beginning with these words as needed.

Advanced Display these question starters: What was the result of _____? What were the consequences of _____? Discuss when they might be heard in a classroom. Then read aloud the text, encouraging students to ask questions beginning with these words as needed.

Advanced High Display these question starters: Is the author implying that _____? Does the author mean that _____? Discuss when they might be heard in a classroom. Then have pairs of students read aloud the text and ask each other content-based questions beginning with these words and expressions.

▣ Differentiate Instruction

Use the Differentiated Instruction notes throughout the lesson plan to support the varied skill sets, levels of readiness, and interests in the mixed-ability classroom.

Challenge These notes include suggestions for expanding the activity for advanced students.

On-Level These notes include suggestions for modifying the activity to address different interests or learning styles.

Extra Support These notes include ideas for providing more scaffolding or reading spuport.

Special Needs These notes provide ideas for adapting instruction to support the needs of various special needs students.

■ NOTES

The Cold War and Vietnam

Objectives

Objective 1: Explain the steps Kennedy took to change American foreign policy.

Objective 2: Analyze the causes and effects of the Bay of Pigs invasion and the Cuban Missile Crisis.

Objective 3: Assess the outcome of the Berlin Crisis and other foreign-policy events of the 1960s.

Objective 4: Describe the reasons that the United States helped the French fight the Vietnamese.

Objective 5: Identify ways in which the United States opposed communism in Southeast Asia.

Objective 6: Analyze how the United States increased its involvement in Vietnam.

LESSON 1 ORGANIZER	PACING: APPROX. 1 PERIOD, .5 BLOCKS			
			RESOURCES	
	OBJECTIVES	PACING	Online	Print
Connect				
DIGITAL START UP ACTIVITY **Hope for Independence**		5 min.	●	
Investigate				
DIGITAL TEXT 1 **Kennedy Strives to Win the Cold War**	Objective 1	10 min.	●	●
DIGITAL TEXT 2 **Kennedy Responds to Communism in Cuba**	Objective 2	10 min.	●	●
INTERACTIVE TIMELINE **Confronting Cuba**		10 min.	●	
DIGITAL TEXT 3 **The Causes and Outcomes of the Berlin Crisis**	Objective 3	10 min.	●	●
DIGITAL TEXT 4 **Reasons for U.S. Involvement in Indochina**	Objective 4	10 min.	●	●
DIGITAL TEXT 5 **America Responds to Communism in Vietnam**	Objectives 5, 6	10 min.	●	●
INTERACTIVE GALLERY **America Enters Vietnam**		10 min.	●	
Synthesize				
DIGITAL ACTIVITY **Fighting Communism**		5 min.	●	
Demonstrate				
LESSON QUIZ **Lesson Quiz and Class Discussion Board**		10 min.	●	

PEARSON
realize™
www.PearsonRealize.com

Go online to access additional resources including:
Primary Sources • Biographies • Supreme Court cases •
21st Century Skill Tutorials • Maps • Graphic Organizers.

CONNECT

DIGITAL START UP ACTIVITY
Hope for Independence

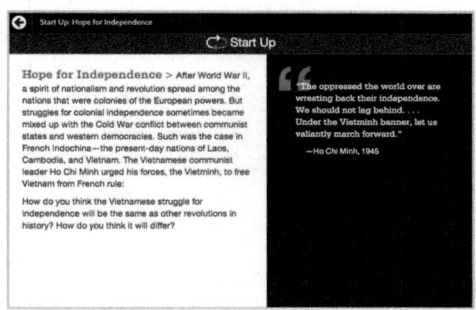

Project the Start Up Activity Ask students to read and think about the quote from Ho Chi Minh. Encourage students to share their ideas with a partner.

Discuss How do you think the Vietnamese struggle for independence will resemble other revolutions in history? How do you think it will differ? *(The Vietnamese conflict may involve many more countries than other revolutions. New weapon technology may cost more in terms of people's lives and property.)*

Tell students that in this lesson they will learn how Ho Chi Minh organized a struggle against the French and then the United States.

Aa Vocabulary Development Use the Interactive Reading Notepad to preview the Key Terms and Academic Vocabulary in this lesson with students.

↻ FLIP IT!

Assign the Flipped Video for this lesson.

■ STUDENT EDITION PRINT
PAGES: 724–732

INVESTIGATE

DIGITAL TEXT 1
Kennedy Strives to Win the Cold War

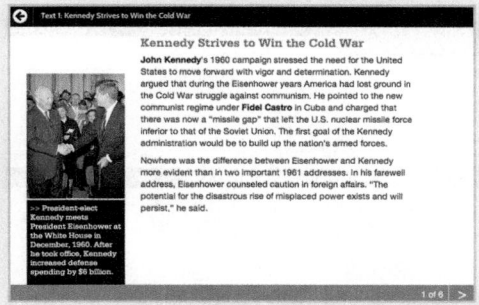

Objective 1: Explain the steps Kennedy took to change U.S. Foreign policy.

Quick Instruction

Summarize Project the image of Kennedy and Eisenhower. Invite a volunteer to summarize President Eisenhower's policy to contain the spread of communism. (Eisenhower's defense policy was built around the concept of "massive retaliation." The Eisenhower administration emphasized the construction of nuclear weapons.) Ask: What foreign policy issues did Kennedy face as he assumed the Presidency? *(Kennedy faced the Cold War struggle against communism. Cuba now had a new communist regime led by Fidel Castro. Kennedy argued that the U.S. nuclear missile force was inferior to that of the Soviet Union.)*

Infer Ask students to explain reasons for Kennedy's promotion of U.S. involvement in foreign countries. *(Kennedy believed that programs that economically and politically strengthened the nations of the Third World would contain or limit the spread of communism.)*

Further Instruction

Be sure students understand the concept of the "Third World," (The developing nations in Africa, Asia, and Latin America that did not align themselves with the United States or the Soviet Union.) Ask students to identify programs that the Kennedy administration created to foster better relations with the Third World. *(Peace Corps, Alliance for Progress)*

Identify Central Issues What measures did President Kennedy begin to fight the spread of communism and deter Soviet aggression? *(Kennedy increased military spending by 6 billion dollars. He wanted a defense policy that prepared the United States to fight any type of conflict. Kennedy's idea was that he wanted the United States prepared to fight both conventional wars and conflicts against guerrilla forces, including better prepared Army Special Forces, such as the Green Berets.)*

The Cold War and Vietnam

DIGITAL TEXT 2

Kennedy Responds to Communism in Cuba

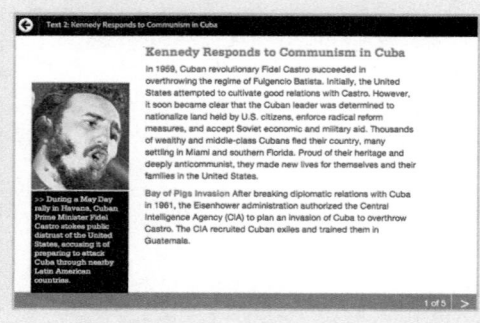

INTERACTIVE TIMELINE

Confronting Cuba

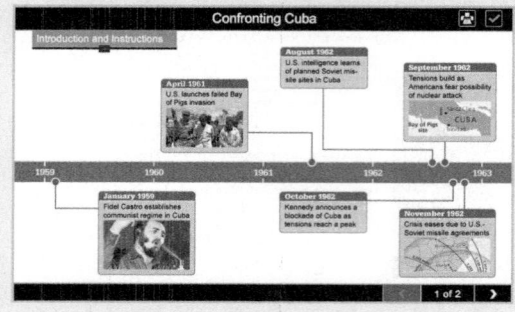

DIGITAL TEXT 3

The Causes and Outcomes of the Berlin Crisis

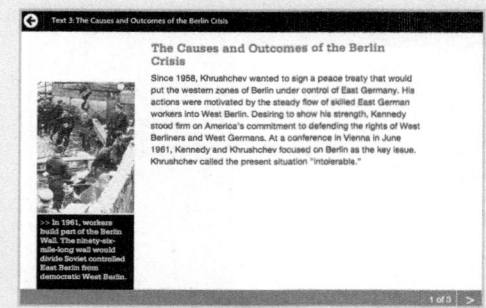

Objective 2: **Analyze the causes and effects of the Bay of Pigs invasion and the Cuban Missile Crisis.**

Quick Instruction

Interactive Timeline: Confronting Cuba Project the timeline and select the events to learn more about how this conflict evolved, escalated, and the outcome of U.S. involvement. For each event, ask students how it might have affected average Americans of the time. Then challenge students to predicting what the consequences of the crisis might be.

Draw Conclusions How would you describe John F. Kennedy's role in the Cuban Missile Crisis and the U.S. response to Soviet aggression after World War II? *(Kennedy showed great strength, courage, and leadership by not backing down. Although Kennedy compromised and agreed to remove U.S. missiles from Turkey, he was able to avert a possible nuclear conflict.)*

🎥 ACTIVE CLASSROOM

Have students Make Headlines for each event described on the interactive timeline. Ask: If you were to write a headline for each event that captured the most important aspect that should be remembered, what would that headline be? Emphasize to students that their headlines should express the significance of each event, how it will affect the escalating Cold War, and so on. Allow them to use subheadings if they like. Have students pass their headlines to a partner for them to review.

Further Instruction

Determine Points of View How did the Cuban missile crisis affect public opinion about President Kennedy and Soviet leader Khrushchev? *(The public viewed Kennedy as a mature and thoughtful leader, one who remained calm in a difficult situation. Khrushchev, on the other hand, was viewed by Americans as dangerous and reckless.)*

Draw Conclusions How did the Cuban Missile Crisis affect U.S. relations with Cuba and the Soviet Union? *(The crisis prompted the countries to embrace détente—a relaxing of tension between rivals. A telephone system called the hot line improved communication between the leaders of the two countries. More important, in 1963, the United States, Great Britain, and the Soviet Union signed the first nuclear-weapons agreement.)*

Objective 3: **Assess the outcome of the Berlin Crisis and other foreign-policy events of the 1960s.**

Quick Instruction

Identify Central Issues Project the image of the Berlin Wall on the whiteboard. Be sure students understand why the wall was a symbol of Soviet aggression by asking volunteers to identify the reasons Khrushchev had the wall built. *(Many highly skilled East German workers were leaving East Berlin to live in West Berlin. Khrushchev wanted the United States to recognize the formal division of Germany.)* Challenge students to describe how the wall might have affected the citizens of Berlin. *(The wall basically cut Berlin in half, stopping all movement to and from the two sections of the city. Many people probably lost jobs and were not allowed to visit family and friends who lived on the other side.)*

ELL Use the ELL activity described in the ELL chart.

Further Instruction

Express Problems Clearly How did the issues surrounding the status of East and West Germany contribute to Cold War tensions between the United States and the Soviet Union? *(Both the United States and the Soviet Union refused to compromise on the issue of a divided Germany. Kennedy wanted to increase military spending, and he sent more soldiers to West Berlin. Khrushchev ordered the construction of a wall between East and West Berlin. The wall became the greatest symbol of the tensions between the communist East and the democratic West.)*

DIGITAL TEXT 4

Reasons for U.S. Involvement in Indochina

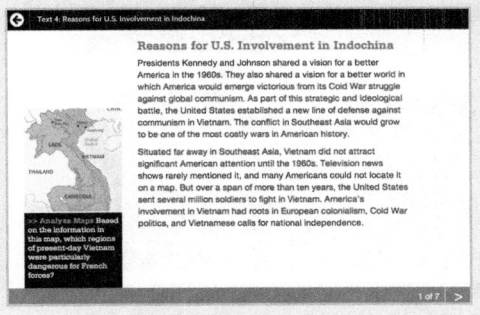

Text 4: Reasons for U.S. Involvement in Indochina

Reasons for U.S. Involvement in Indochina

Presidents Kennedy and Johnson shared a vision for a better America in the 1960s. They also shared a vision for a better world in which America would emerge victorious from its Cold War struggle against global communism. As part of this strategic and ideological battle, the United States established a new line of defense against communism in Vietnam. The conflict in Southeast Asia would grow to be one of the most costly wars in American history.

Situated far away in Southeast Asia, Vietnam did not attract significant American attention until the 1960s. Television news shows rarely mentioned it, and many Americans could not locate it on a map. But over a span of more than ten years, the United States sent several million soldiers to fight in Vietnam. America's involvement in Vietnam had roots in European colonialism, Cold War politics, and Vietnamese calls for national independence.

>> Analyze Maps Based on the information in this map, which regions of present-day Vietnam were particularly dangerous for French forces?

1 of 7

Predict Consequences
Ask students to predict what the outcome of U.S. involvement in Berlin will be. *(Tensions created by the wall and rising mistrust between the Soviet Union and the United States will escalate the Cold War.)*

Objective 4: Describe the reasons that the United States helped the French fight the Vietnamese.

Quick Instruction

Summarize Direct students' attention to the map of French Indochina. If possible, use a classroom world map to locate Indochina as well. Ask a student to explain who Ho Chi Minh was. *(the leader of the communist Vietnamese called the Vietminh)* Ask students to identify the areas of present day Vietnam in which Vietminh forces were active during the French occupation. *(mostly coastal and rural areas)*

Hypothesize Ask students to speculate why the Vietminh had support in these regions. *(French businesses acquired large rice and rubber plantations in the countryside and controlled the mineral wealth of the country, often at the expense of poorer country folk. Wealthier Vietnamese who benefited from western culture and technology lived in the larger cities that were under French control.)*

Determine Relevance How did the communist victory in the Chinese civil war affect U.S. involvement in foreign countries like Vietnam? *(Vietnam was a neighbor of China. And since many American leaders believed in the Domino Theory, they were worried about a eventual communist takeover of Vietnam. Also, they were concerned that China would now supply aid to the communists in Vietnam.)*

ELL Use the ELL activity described in the ELL chart.

Further Instruction

In order for students to understand the reasons for U.S. involvement in Vietnam, ask a volunteer to read the statement President Eisenhower gave to a journalist about the fight in Vietnam. Be sure students understand Eisenhower's argument that stopping the communists in Vietnam was important to the protection of the entire region. Ask students to summarize Eisenhower's "domino theory" analogy. *(The domino theory was the idea that if Vietnam fell to communism, its closest neighbors would follow, falling just like a row of dominoes.)*

Express Problems Clearly Ask students to explain the reasons and outcomes for U.S. involvement in foreign countries such as Vietnam and how this involvement was related to the Domino Theory. *(By providing money first and then combat troops to fight the Vietnam War, the United States became involved in Vietnam to try to stop the communists from taking control of the country. American leaders believed that if Vietnam fell to the communists, Japan, the Philippines, and Australia might fall to communist governments as well, which was the idea of the Domino Theory.)*

The Cold War and Vietnam

DIGITAL TEXT 5

America Responds to Communism in Vietnam

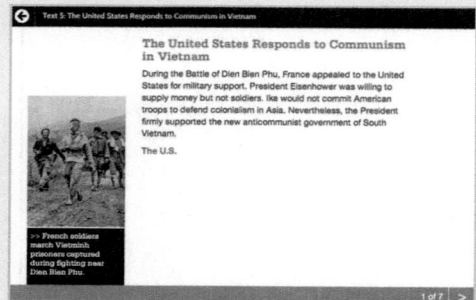

INTERACTIVE GALLERY

America Enters Vietnam

Objectives 5: Identify ways in which the United States opposed communism In Southeast Asia; 6: Analyze how the United States increased its involvement in Vietnam.

Quick Instruction

Interactive Gallery: America Enters Vietnam Project the gallery. Clicking on each image will identify the major issues and key factors that led the United States into war in Vietnam. Explain that upon assuming the Presidency, President Johnson was careful in not escalating the situation in Vietnam. Johnson was, however, determined to prevent South Vietnam from becoming communist. Ask students what they know or think they know about each image in the gallery, followed by a brief discussion.

Analyze Images What does the fifth image in the gallery tell you about opposition to Diem in South Vietnam? *(The image reveals how intensely some Vietnamese people opposed Diem's policies. A person willing to set himself on fire to protest against a government can project a powerful statement that inspires others to rebel.)*

Draw Conclusions Ask students to describe the impact of the Gulf of Tonkin Resolution on the relationship between the legislative and executive branches of government. *(By passing the resolution, Congress gave up its Constitutional war powers to the executive branch, giving the President considerable power to act militarily without having to get approval from Congress.)*

📷 ACTIVE CLASSROOM

Play a game of Connect Two about issues leading the U.S. into the Vietnam War. List the following terms on the board: North Vietnam, South Vietnam, The Geneva Accords, the French army, Ngo Dinh Diem, Vietnamese Buddhists, 17th Parallel, President Eisenhower, President Johnson, Gulf of Tonkin Resolution, Dien Bien Phu, U.S. Congress. Direct students copy the terms down on notecards or small slips of paper, one term to a card or piece of paper. Review the list of terms with students. Ask students to "connect two" or choose two terms they think belong together, and state the reason for their connection. Challenge students to connect as many pairs of terms as possible. Conduct this activity before, during, and/or after student reading.

Further Instruction

Summarize Ngo Dinh Diem faced considerable challenges governing South Vietnam from the outset. Invite students to summarize the challenges Diem faced. (Diem lacked popular support among the Vietnamese people. The National Liberation Front (NLF), had committed itself to undermining his government. Diem was Catholic in a Buddhist nation, and he signed anti-Buddhist legislation.)

Identify Central Issues What goals motivated President Kennedy's policy decisions regarding Vietnam? *(Kennedy's goal was to fight and contain communism in a more aggressive manner. The Kennedy administration finally realized that Diem had to be removed from power.)*

Predict Consequences Ask students to predict what the impact of the Gulf of Tonkin Resolution will be on American involvement in Vietnam. *(Johnson will use his new power to send more American combat troops to Vietnam. This will lead to more fighting and a full-scale war.)*

■ SYNTHESIZE

DIGITAL ACTIVITY

Fighting Communism

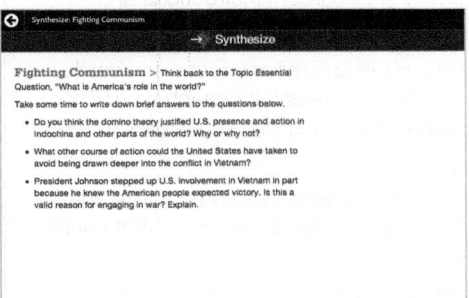

Ask students to recall the Topic Essential Question, "What is America's role in the world?" Have them use the Think Pair Share strategy to answer the questions in the Fighting Communism activity. Ask them to take five minutes to write down some brief answers to the questions below, then discuss their answers with a partner.

Have partners think about the following question. *Do you think the United States was justified in intervening in the political issues of Indochina and eventually Vietnam?* Have pairs share their answers with the class.

■ DEMONSTRATE

LESSON QUIZ

Lesson Quiz and Class Discussion Board

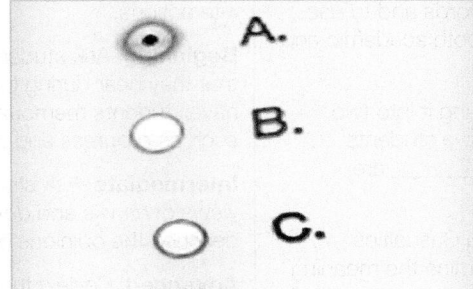

Assign the online Lesson Quiz for this lesson if you haven't already done so. Students will be offered automatic remediation or enrichment based on their score.

Pose these questions to the class on the Discussion Board:

In *The Cold War and Vietnam*, you read about the actions the United States took to stop the spread of communism in Southeast Asia. The Cold War policy of containment led the United States to become increasingly involved in Vietnam.

Express Ideas Clearly Compare the involvement of Presidents Truman, Eisenhower, Kennedy, and Johnson in Indochina and Vietnam.

Make Predictions Do you think the American people will be as supportive of their government during the Vietnam conflict as they had been in previous wars? Explain.

Topic Inquiry
Have students continue their investigations for the Topic Inquiry.

America's Role Escalates

Supporting English Language Learners

Use with Digital Text 1, **Escalation of Forces in Vietnam.**

Speaking
Read aloud the text, or invite volunteers to do so. Point out that students can often guess at the meaning of an unfamiliar word by hunting for context clues. Encourage students to remember new words and to use grade-level content area vocabulary when speaking in both academic and social contexts.

Beginning Display the word *airstrike*. Show how breaking it into two smaller words helps with understanding its meaning. Have students complete and say this sentence: In an _____, _____ are dropped on enemies.

Intermediate Draw attention to the heading "American Casualties Escalate" and have students use context clues to determine the meaning of the verb *escalate*. Ask: What two things escalated in the Vietnam War? What other things can escalate? Have students use a form of the word *escalate* when speaking their answers.

Advanced Reread the text's first paragraph, and point out the word *quagmire*. Ask students to use context clues to define it. Have pairs of students use this word as they discuss why the Vietnam War was considered a quagmire for the United States.

Advanced High Display this sentence: There were escalations of forces and casualties in the Vietnam War. Ask students to prepare and give a short talk that expands on this sentence, draws from details in the text, and includes forms of the words *escalations*, *forces*, and *casualties*.

Use with Digital Text 3, **Doubt Grows on the Home Front.**

Listening
Read aloud the text, or invite volunteers to do so. Prompt students to identify basic vocabulary heard during classroom instructions and interactions.

Beginning Ask students to create a list of unfamiliar vocabulary words that they hear during instruction. Explain the meaning of each word and have students memorize the key vocabulary by applying gestures to terms such as *progress* and *victory*.

Intermediate Ask students to listen as you compare and contrast the views of *hawks* and *doves*. Ask students to write down words that might describe the opinions of each group.

Advanced Review the meaning of the word *viewpoint*. Then have students discuss the viewpoints of *hawks* and *doves* with a partner. Each students should make a note of any unfamiliar words that they hear during the discussion and investigate the word's meaning.

Advanced High Have students take turns reading paragraphs from the text. Ask (What were the *pros* and *cons* of Johnson's war policy? Have students identify and define unfamiliar words. Then have them use the words as they give a brief talk that answers the question.

◧ Differentiate Instruction

Use the Differentiated Instruction notes throughout the lesson plan to support the varied skill sets, levels of readiness, and interests in the mixed-ability classroom.

Challenge These notes include suggestions for expanding the activity for advanced students.

On-Level These notes include suggestions for modifying the activity to address different interests or learning styles.

Extra Support These notes include ideas for providing more scaffolding or reading spuport.

Special Needs These notes provide ideas for adapting instruction to support the needs of various special needs students.

■ NOTES

PEARSON
realize.™
www.PearsonRealize.com

Go online to access additional resources including:
Primary Sources • Biographies • Supreme Court cases •
21st Century Skill Tutorials • Maps • Graphic Organizers.

Objectives

Objective 1: Analyze the major issues and events that caused President Johnson to increase American troop strength in Vietnam.

Objective 2: Assess the nature of the war in Vietnam and the difficulties faced by each side.

Objective 3: Evaluate the effects of low morale on American troops and on the home front.

LESSON 2 ORGANIZER		PACING: APPROX. 1 PERIOD, .5 BLOCKS			
				RESOURCES	
		OBJECTIVES	**PACING**	**Online**	**Print**
Connect					
DIGITAL START UP ACTIVITY **A Difficult War**			5 min.	●	
Investigate					
DIGITAL TEXT 1 **Escalation of Forces in Vietnam**		Objective 1	10 min.	●	●
DIGITAL TEXT 2 **Patriotism, Heroism, and Sinking Morale**		Objective 2	10 min.	●	●
INTERACTIVE CHART **Challenges of Escalation**			10 min.	●	
DIGITAL TEXT 3 **Doubt Grows on the Home Front**		Objective 3	10 min.	●	●
Synthesize					
DIGITAL ACTIVITY **Winning the War**			5 min.	●	
Demonstrate					
DIGITAL QUIZ **Lesson Quiz and Class Discussion Board**			10 min.	●	

America's Role Escalates

■ CONNECT

DIGITAL START UP ACTIVITY
A Difficult War

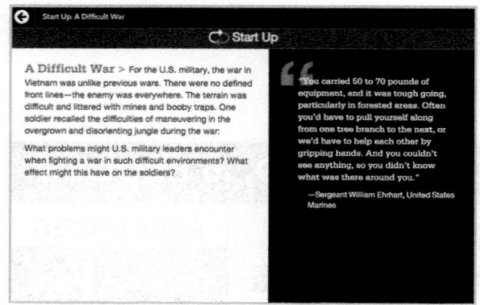

Project the Start Up Activity As students enter and get settled, ask them to think about what they've learned about the conditions American soldiers endured in previous wars. Invite a volunteer to read Sergeant William Ehrhart's statement aloud.

Discuss What problems might U.S. military leaders encounter fighting in difficult environments? What effect might this have on the soldiers? (*U.S. military leaders will have very little information about the Vietnamese forces. The terrain provides adverse conditions for the U.S. troops, whose high-tech weapons and firepower will not be as effective. This will have a negative effect on U.S. soldiers, like high casualties and low morale.*)

Aa Vocabulary Development: Use the Interactive Reading Notepad to preview the Key Terms and Academic Vocabulary in this lesson with students.

⏭ FLIP IT!
Assign the Flipped Video for this lesson.

■ STUDENT EDITION PRINT
PAGES: 733–738

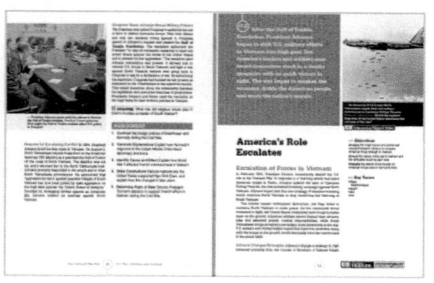

■ INVESTIGATE

DIGITAL TEXT 1
Escalation of Forces in Vietnam

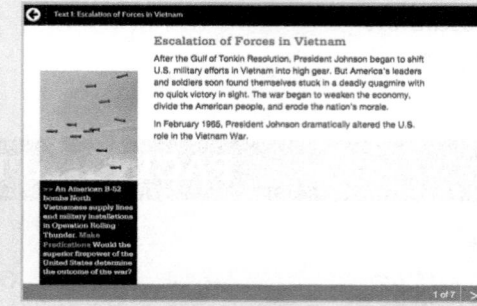

Objective 1: Analyze the major issues and events that caused President Johnson to increase American troop strength in Vietnam.

Quick Instruction

Summarize Direct students attention to the image of the B-52 bomber. Use it as a springboard for a class discussion about why President Johnson advocated an escalation of forces. Ask: Why did Johnson order the start of Operation Rolling Thunder? (*In response to a Vietcong attack that killed American troops at Pleiku.*) Review the strategic goals of Operation Rolling Thunder, a major event in the Vietnam War. (to convince North Vietnam to stop reinforcing the Vietcong in South Vietnam) and then invite students to describe the success of the operation. (The great amount of bombs dropped during Operation Rolling Thunder caused considerable destruction, but North Vietnam still did not want to make peace.)

Evaluate Arguments What was the reasoning behind the perceived need to "Americanize" the war effort? (*Secretary of Defense Robert McNamara and General Westmorland believed that the United States needed to increase its military presence in Vietnam and do more of the fighting in order to win the war.*)

Summarize how the U.S. military adopted strategies to employ in the unique fighting situation in Vietnam? (*To fight an elusive enemy, American pilots dropped napalm and sprayed Agent Orange. These unconventional weapons covered large areas in flames and killed plant life to eliminate hiding locations and disrupt the enemy's food supply.*)

ELL Use the ELL activity described in the ELL chart.

Further Instruction

Compare How were the Vietcong combat tactics different from those of American troops? (Vietcong forces were usually lightly armed and supplied compared to U.S. forces. Vietcong wanted to fight small engagements. They employed guerrilla tactics, hiding in tunnels during the day and coming out at night to ambush American patrols. They also set booby traps that proved devastating to American troops.)

Draw Conclusions Why did the fighting in Vietnam turn into a stalemate by the mid-1960s? (*Even with the increase in troops in Vietnam, The United States could not swing the tide of the war or win the support of the Vietnamese people. The guerrilla warfare was costing more and more American lives and a lot more money. A U.S. goal was to win the "hearts and minds" of the Vietnamese, but the U.S.-backed government was corrupt and had little support outside of the major cities.*)

DIGITAL TEXT 2
Patriotism, Heroism, and Sinking Morale

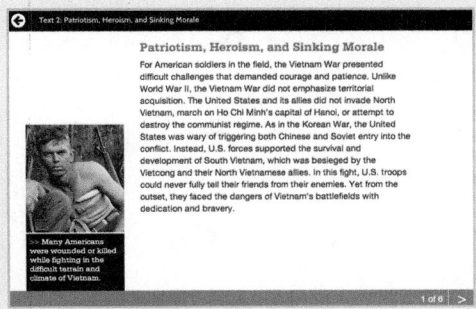

INTERACTIVE CHART
Challenges of Escalation

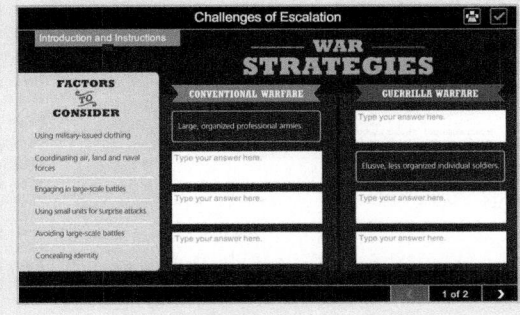

DIGITAL TEXT 3
Doubt Grows on the Home Front

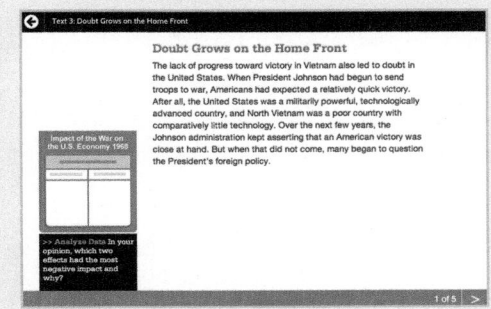

Objective 2: Assess the nature of the war in Vietnam and the difficulties faced by both sides.

Quick Instruction
Remind students that the United States entered the Vietnam War with one of the most powerful and technologically sophisticated armies in the world. Lacking the firepower of the U.S. forces, the Vietcong had to rely on different tactics. Developing flexible counter-tactics to battle the Vietcong was one of the major issues of the Vietnam War.

Challenges of Escalation: Interactive Chart
Project the chart and provide appropriate time for students to categorize the warfare tactics.

Support a Point of View with Evidence
Based on the information in the activity and from your reading, which side—the Vietcong or the United States—was in a better position to win the war? *(Students may say that the Vietcong had the advantage. The guerrilla tactics used by the Vietcong were very effective in eliminating the American advantage in firepower. The United States would not be able to sustain a long-term war at the level needed to defeat the Vietcong.)*

ACTIVE CLASSROOM
Use the Ranking Strategy to have students go through the guerilla warfare tactics listed in the activity, and rank which ones had the greatest impact on fighting the American forces in Vietnam.

Differentiate: Challenge/Gifted Ask students to do research on some of the key battles in the Vietnam War and briefly describe the tactics used by both sides. Invite students to share their findings.

Further Instruction
Invite students to make a list of words to describe American servicemen and women that they learned about when studying previous wars. *(Brave, resourceful, victorious, committed)* Point out that the men and women who served in Vietnam did so with the same intensity and dedication that U.S. forces had shown in earlier wars, such as World Wars I and II.)

Evaluate Impact How would you describe the role of the common American soldier and nurse during the Vietnam War? *(American soldiers fought courageously and successfully in very difficult conditions and against a difficult enemy. Nurses provided needed medical care and had to care for dying and wounded soldiers every day.)* How did their actions reflect patriotism and honor? *(Many soldiers and nurses volunteered to serve in the military because their country needed them. Many fought and worked for the principles of freedom and to protect villagers in Vietnam from communism.)*

Infer Why might drafted soldiers be more likely to question the reasons for the Vietnam War and the causes for which they were supposed to fight? *(Drafted soldiers did not volunteer for military service, and many did not want to serve in Vietnam. Many drafted soldiers did not share the same level of dedication to a war they did not understand or support.)*

Objective 3: Evaluate the effects of low morale on American troops and on the home front.

Quick Instruction
Point out that one response to the war became a major issue of the Vietnam War—the emerging antiwar movement in the United States.

Express Problems Clearly What factors led to the growing doubt on the home front? *(Many Americans were upset and concerned that U.S. forces were not making progress toward victory in Vietnam. Americans had expected a relatively quick victory based on President Johnson's views. The longer the war dragged on, the more people began to question the President's foreign policy.)*

Remind students that the troop build up in Vietnam required massive financial commitment from the government. The economics of the war was becoming a concern for many Americans as well.

Identify Cause and Effect Ask students to describe the impact of defense spending for the Vietnam War on the American economy and business cycle and on education priorities. *(The costs of fighting a war on the other side of the world along with President Johnson's Great Society plan strained government finances. Although massive government spending lowered the unemployment rate, it also led to rising prices and inflation. The combination of heavy government spending, rising prices, and inflation forced Johnson to raise taxes. This strained government plans to improve education, among other things.)*

America's Role Escalates

 SYNTHESIZE

DEMONSTRATE

DIGITAL ACTIVITY
Winning the War

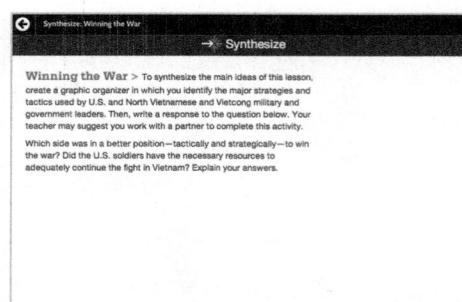

DIGITAL QUIZ
Lesson Quiz and Class Discussion Board

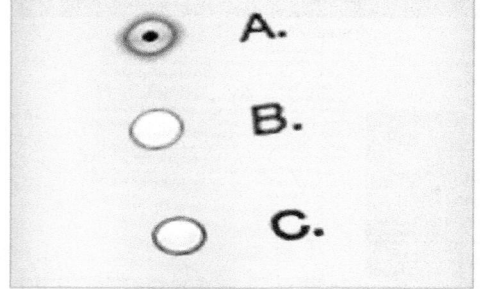

 ELL Use the ELL activity described in the ELL chart.

Further Instruction

Contrast How did the disagreement between hawks and doves reflect different views about war and world politics? *(Hawks supported the concept of containment of communism and the domino theory. Hawks were willing to accept the war casualties and the price of war if it meant a victory in the Cold War. Doves, on the other hand, questioned the war on moral and strategic grounds. Many doves were pacifists who condemned warfare out of principle. Doves viewed the Vietnam War as a localized civil war, not a vital Cold War battleground.)*

Make Predictions Ask students to predict the impact the antiwar movement will have on the U.S. war effort in Vietnam. *(The antiwar movement will have a significant impact on the war effort. More young people and potential soldiers will become more vocal in opposition to the war, causing problems. Also, more government officials will push back against Johnson's war plans.)*

Discuss Before students begin their graphic organizers, lead the class in a brief review of major strategies and tactics used by U.S. and North Vietnamese and Vietcong military and government leaders. Explain that tactics refers to short-term decisions about the organization, movement, and actions of troops during combat. Strategy refers to a plan of action or policy designed to achieve a major or overall aim.

Assign the online Lesson Quiz for this lesson if you haven't already done so. Students will be offered automatic remediation or enrichment based on their score.

Pose these questions to the class on the Discussion Board:

In *America's Role Escalates*, you read about the challenges American military forces faced in the unconventional war in Vietnam. The U.S. military was forced to adapt new tactics to fight the guerrilla tactics of the Vietcong and North Vietnamese forces.

Generate Explanations What factors make a fighting force effective and difficult to defeat?

Make Predictions Will U.S. military leaders adjust and implement new tactics and strategies in Vietnam that lead to greater success before the American public completely drops its support for the war?

Topic Inquiry
Have students continue their investigations for the Topic Inquiry.

The Antiwar Movement

Supporting English Language Learners

Use with Digital Text 1, **Antiwar Sentiment Grows.**

Speaking
Read aloud the text up to the section titled *The Twenty-sixth Amendment*, or invite volunteers to do so. Encourage students to express opinions from communicating single words to participating in extended discussions on grade-appropriate topics, such as the antiwar movement.

Beginning Display the words *Selective Service System*. Have students repeat the words after you and explain the meaning of each word. Have students express their opinion with this sentence: I do (not) think the Selective Service System is a good idea because _____.

Intermediate Display the words *Selective Service System* and explain that this was the formal name for the draft. Then have students explain whether they think the SSS was a good idea and why.

Advanced Display these words from the text: antiwar, draftees, deferments, rallies. Then have pairs of students use all the words as they share their opinions about antiwar sentiment.

Advanced High Display these words from the text: antiwar, draftees, deferments, rallies. Then have them prepare and give a talk on their opinion about antiwar sentiment that uses all four words.

Use with Digital Text 2, **The Tet Offensive.**

Listening, Speaking
Read aloud the section titled *Widespread Attacks*, or invite volunteers to do so. Direct students' attention to academic vocabulary—words they will need to understand and discuss the content—and encourage them to use this kind of grade-level content vocabulary when they discuss the issues being studied.

Beginning Read the section's last two sentences, and point out the word *demonstrated*. Explain that it means "showed." Then have students complete and say this sentence: The Tet Offensive demonstrated that _____.

Intermediate Read the section's last two sentences, and point out the word *demonstrated*. Ask students to come up with a definition or synonym of it. Then have them use the word to say an original sentence about the Tet Offensive.

Advanced Read the last sentence of the section's first paragraph, and ask students to define the word *coordinated*. Have students use the word to say an original sentence about the Tet Offensive. Then ask: What else in U.S. history has been coordinated?

Advanced High Read the last sentence of the section's first paragraph, and ask students to define the word *coordinated*. Have pairs of students use the word in a discussion about the Tet Offensive and other aspects of the Vietnam War.

Ⓓ Differentiate Instruction

Use the Differentiated Instruction notes throughout the lesson plan to support the varied skill sets, levels of readiness, and interests in the mixed-ability classroom.

Challenge These notes include suggestions for expanding the activity for advanced students.

On-Level These notes include suggestions for modifying the activity to address different interests or learning styles.

Extra Support These notes include ideas for providing more scaffolding or reading spuport.

Special Needs These notes provide ideas for adapting instruction to support the needs of various special needs students.

■ NOTES

The Antiwar Movement

Objectives

Objective 1: Describe the divisions within American society over the Vietnam War.

Objective 2: Analyze the Tet Offensive and the American reaction to it.

Objective 3: Summarize the factors that influenced the outcome of the 1968 presidential election.

LESSON 3 ORGANIZER		PACING: APPROX. 1 PERIOD, .5 BLOCKS			
		OBJECTIVES	PACING	**RESOURCES**	
				Online	Print
Connect					
DIGITAL START UP ACTIVITY **From Support to Division**			5 min.	●	
Investigate					
DIGITAL TEXT 1 **Antiwar Sentiment Grows**		Objective 1	10 min.	●	●
INTERACTIVE CHART **Doves and Hawks**			10 min.	●	
DIGITAL TEXT 2 **The Tet Offensive**		Objective 2	10 min.	●	●
INTERACTIVE GALLERY **The Living Room War**			10 min.	●	
DIGITAL TEXT 3 **The 1968 Presidential Race**		Objective 3	10 min.	●	●
INTERACTIVE TIMELINE **1968: The Whole World is Watching**			10 min.	●	
Synthesize					
DIGITAL ACTIVITY **Many Reasons**			5 min.	●	
Demonstrate					
DIGITAL QUIZ **Lesson Quiz and Class Discussion Board**			10 min.	●	

PEARSON realize™
www.PearsonRealize.com

Go online to access additional resources including:
Primary Sources • Biographies • Supreme Court cases •
21st Century Skill Tutorials • Maps • Graphic Organizers.

CONNECT

DIGITAL START UP ACTIVITY
From Support to Division

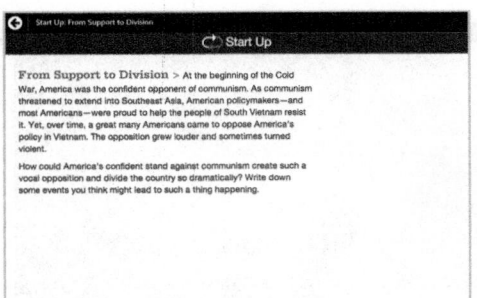

Project the Start Up Activity As students enter and get settled, ask them to think about how Americans voice their disagreements with government policies. Focus their attention on the question, "What rights and responsibilities do Americans have when they disagree with the war policies of their government?"

Discuss How could America's confident stand against communism create such a vocal opposition and divide the country so dramatically?

Tell students that in this lesson they will be learning how many Americans created an antiwar movement in the United States as the Vietnam War dragged on with no end or victory in sight.

Aa Vocabulary Development Use the Interactive Reading Notepad to preview the Key Terms and Academic Vocabulary in this lesson with students.

🔃 FLIP IT!
Assign the Flipped Video for this lesson.

■ STUDENT EDITION PRINT PAGES: 739–745

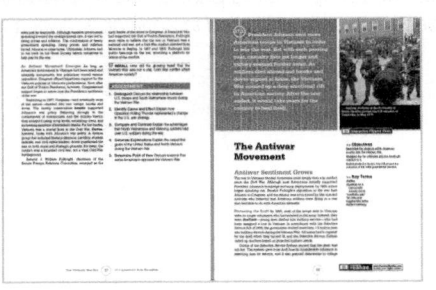

INVESTIGATE

DIGITAL TEXT 1
Antiwar Sentiment Grows

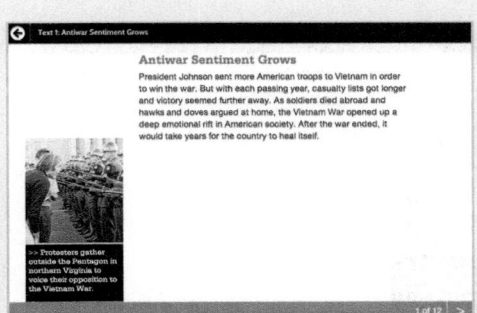

Objective 1: Describe the divisions within American society over the Vietnam War.

Quick Instruction
Interactive Chart: Doves and Hawks
Project the chart that shows common beliefs of doves and hawks. Review the beliefs with students and then ask them to complete the drag and drop activity. When students have finished, discuss their answers. Ask: What are two ways that the pro-war and antiwar movements were alike?

Make Generalizations What generalizations can you make about doves and hawks? *(Hawks are often more conservative politically while doves are generally more liberal. Hawks view support for the military in all cases a patriotic duty. Doves view military actions on a moral basis and do not always support the government's motives.)*

Apply Concepts Can you identify instances in recent years in which U.S. foreign policy has been influenced by debates between pro- and antiwar movements? Explain. *(Yes. With the conflicts in Afghanistan, Iraq, Syria, and Libya, hawks supported more American intervention, while doves stressed caution and opposed American military involvement.)*

ELL Use the ELL activity described in the ELL chart.

INTERACTIVE CHART
Doves and Hawks

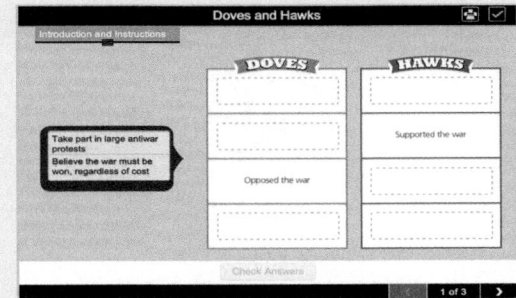

👥 ACTIVE CLASSROOM
Ask students to take a stand on the following question: Were the doves justified in protesting against the Vietnam War? Yes or No? Ask students to divide into two groups based on their answer and move to separate areas of the classroom. Ask a representative from each side to present and defend the group's point of view. Encourage students to talk with each other to compare their reasons for answering yes or no.

Further Instruction
Point out to students that the antiwar movement included many Americans who protested against the draft. Ask students to identify key issues that many Americans had with the draft. *(Critics of the draft thought that it was unfair because working-class or poor men were most often drafted to serve in Vietnam. Others argued that the number of African Americans drafted was disproportionately high.)*

Reference the Landmark Case *Tinker* v. *Des Moines* for students to better place the antiwar movement in context and understand it from the perspective of a middle school protest that led to a Supreme Court decision over freedom of speech.

Summarize how the fight to ratify the Twenty-sixth Amendment was a response to the Vietnam War. After students have answered, point out that the draft issue was one of the historical reasons that the constitution has been amended. Discuss how amendments to the constition are one way of

The Antiwar Movement

DIGITAL TEXT 2
The Tet Offensive

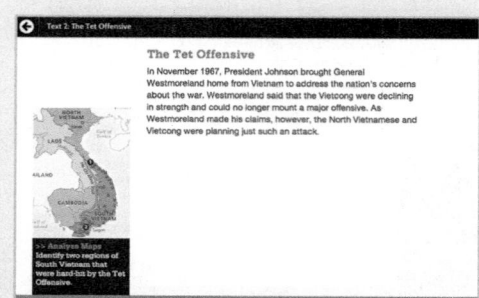

INTERACTIVE GALLERY
The Living Room War

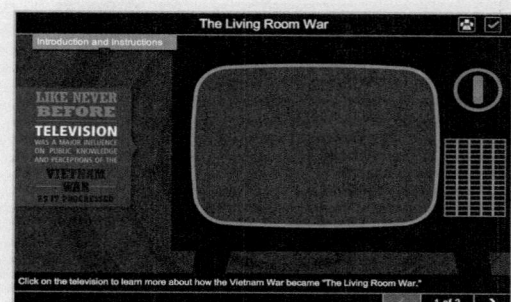

achieving equality of political rights. (American men 18 to 20 years old believed that it was wrong that they were eligible for the draft and service in Vietnam but not yet old enough to vote for the political leaders who were determining foreign policy.)

Draw Conclusions What role did the media play in creating the credibility gap?' *(The media repeated optimistic statements made by government and military leaders. However, news reports from Vietnam contradicted those optimistic statements. The media helped create the American public's growing distrust of the statements made by the government.)*

Objective 2: Analyze the Tet Offensive and the American reaction to it.

Quick Instruction

The Living Room War: Interactive Gallery
Project the gallery on the whiteboard and select the images to reveal the captions. Discuss each image with students and review the war support figures in the pie chart. Remind students that in the 1960s most Americans relied on TV news reports to get news of the war. The war in Vietnam became the first "living-room war."

Analyze Images How might the fifth image in the gallery, the photo from My Lai, demonstrate the role of the media on Americans' responses to the Vietnam war? *(An image like this would have had a powerful effect on Americans, forcing them to question what was really happening in Vietnam and swaying public opinion.)*

Analyze Information How was the Tet Offensive, a major event of the Vietnam War, both a victory and a defeat for the United States? *(The United States won a tactical victory on the ground in Vietnam by preventing the Vietcong and North Vietnamese Army from achieving their objectives. It was a strategic defeat in that it demonstrated that the communists had not lost the will or the ability to fight on. It also was demoralizing for many Americans who saw victory in the war slipping further away.)*

ACTIVE CLASSROOM

Break students into groups for a quick Circle Write Activity. Provide this as a writing prompt: Explain how television contributed to the decline in support for the Vietnam War. Have students write as much as they can for 1 minute then switch with the person on their right. The next person tries to improve or elaborate the response where the other person left off. Continue to switch until the paper comes back to the first person. The group then decides which is the best composition (or response) and shares that with the larger group.

ELL Use the ELL activity described in the ELL chart.

Further Instruction

Review key details about the Tet Offensive, such as dates, origin of the name, goals of the Vietcong and North Vietnamese, and key battles.

Draw Conclusions What were significant outcomes of the Tet Offensive? *(Following the Tet Offensive, an objective review of the military and political situation in Vietnam resulted in the shift of U.S. policy from one that pursued victory to one that pursued a negotiated peace. Many Americans also became more engaged in antiwar activities.)*

Identify Central Issues How did the Tet Offensive and the inability of U.S. forces to show clear signs of progress in Vietnam affect the political position of President Johnson? *(Lack of progress in the war was undermining his presidency. The Tet Offensive forced Johnson to change the strategic U.S. goals in Vietnam. Johnson's weakening opened the door for several influential Democrats to challenge Johnson for the upcoming elections, with Johnson eventually deciding not to seek reelection.)*

DIGITAL TEXT 3
The 1968 Presidential Race

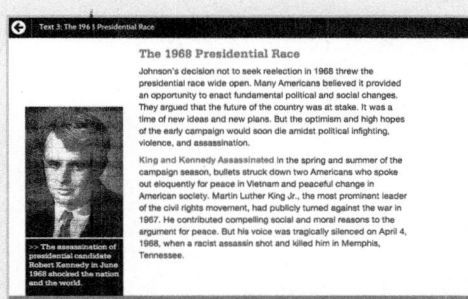

INTERACTIVE TIMELINE
1968: The Whole World is Watching

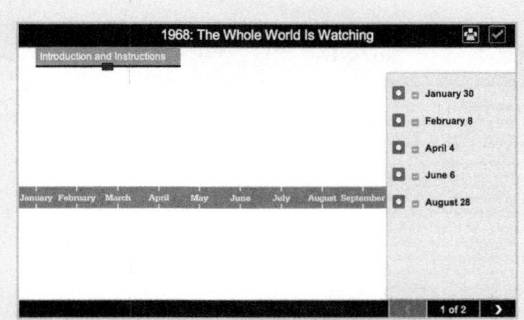

Objective 3: Summarize the factors that influenced the outcome of the 1968 presidential election.

Quick Instruction

Interactive Timeline: 1968: The Whole World is Watching Project the timeline on the whiteboard and select the squares to reveal details about the events. Point out of each event was quite significant on its own, but taken as a whole they cast a dark shadow over the entire year. Invite students to summarize the three important events that made 1968 such a violent year in the Untied States. *(Two influential American leaders were assassinated in 1968, Martin Luther King, Jr., and Robert Kennedy. The third event was the violent protests that marked the Democratic convention in Chicago in August.)*

👥 ACTIVE CLASSROOM

Engage students in creating a piece of "wallpaper" by first reviewing the information in the interactive timeline activity. Have each student design a wallpaper that encapsulates the events of 1968. Students can then take a gallery walk and note what others have written/illustrated. Encourage students to jot down ideas as they occur.

D **Differentiate: Extra Support** After asking the students to review the information in the interactive timeline activity, engage students in a question/answer session to clarify any issues they might have about key aspects of the events. Then continue with the group activity.

Further Instruction

During the 1968 presidential campaign, Richard Nixon promised to unite the fractured country and restore law and order. This appealed to many Americans who feared their country was spinning out of control. Nixon called these supporters the Silent Majority. Explain that the emergence of the silent majority was a response to the Vietnam War. Many in the Silent Majority were patriotic veterans of World War II and the Korean War, middle class blue-collar workers, conservative young Americans, and many others.

Draw Conclusions What were the chief weaknesses of the Democrats in the 1968 election? *(Democrats were divided on a number of key issues. They were tarnished by the troubles at the convention in Chicago. George Wallace, once a Southern Democrat, threatened to take votes away from the Democrat nominee.)* How did these weaknesses aid the election of Richard Nixon? *(These weaknesses severely divided the Democrats, allowing Nixon to win.)*

Hypothesize What might have happened if Wallace had renounced his candidacy and rejoined the Democratic ranks? *(There is a good chance the Humphrey might have been able to pick enough Wallace supporters to defeat Nixon.)*

Be sure students understand the political consequences of the 1968 election. Nixon's southern strategy pulled conservative Democrats away from their traditional support of the Democratic Party. Governor Wallace, who supported the war effort also pulled votes away from the Democrats. The election marked the end of the Democratic "Solid South" and signaled significant changes in the nation's political landscape.

The Antiwar Movement

▌SYNTHESIZE

DIGITAL ACTIVITY
Many Reasons

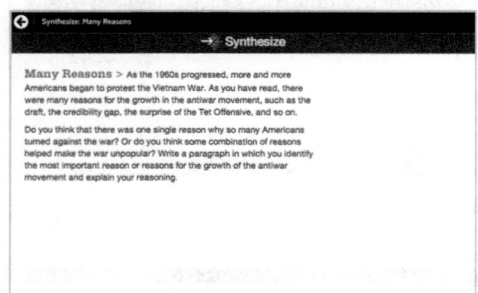

Discuss Before students begin their paragraphs, briefly review the reasons many Americans lost support for the Vietnam War. Read the essay assignment question "Do you think that there was one single reason why so many Americans turned against the war? Or do you think some combination of reasons helped make the war unpopular?" Encourage students to look for connections between reasons.

Ask students to recall the Topic Essential Question, *What is America's role in the world?* Have them use the Think Pair Share Strategy to think about and discuss the following question. What do the antiwar protests during the Vietnam War tell you about how Americans viewed their country's role in the world?

▌DEMONSTRATE

DIGITAL QUIZ
Lesson Quiz and Class Discussion Board

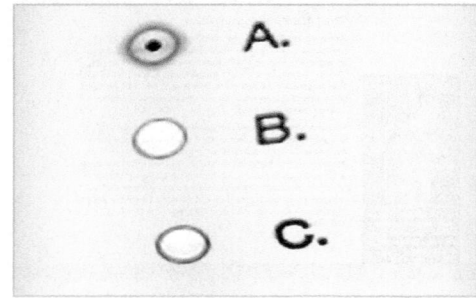

Assign the online Lesson Quiz for this lesson if you haven't already done so. Students will be offered automatic remediation or enrichment based on their score.

Pose these questions to the class on the Discussion Board:

In *The Antiwar Movement*, you read about how a deep divide opened between Americans who supported the war (hawks) and those who opposed it (doves). With each passing year, the casualty lists got longer and victory seemed further away. This vanishing prospect of victory forced American leaders to reevaluate and shift the strategic goals in Vietnam.

Predict Consequences What impact do you think America's antiwar movement will have on the war effort and the military's ability to win?

Draw Inferences How important is public support for a country to successfully fight a war?

Topic Inquiry
Have students continue their investigations for the Topic Inquiry.

The War's End and Effects

Supporting English Language Learners

Use with Digital Text 3, **The Vietnam War Ends.**

Listening
Read aloud the text, or invite volunteers to do so. Prompt students to learn new language structures such as prepositional phrases during classroom instruction and interactions. Explain that prepositional phrases often begin a sentence to convey a sense of time.

Beginning Display and read the first sentence of the text's second paragraph. Underline the phrase *In October 1972.* Ask: When was a peace settlement reached?

Intermediate Display and read the first sentence of the text's second paragraph. Ask: When was a peace settlement reached? Have students underline the phrase containing the answer and then locate similar phrases in the text.

Advanced Display these phrases: *in October 1972, in the spring of 1975, by the end of April.* Have pairs of students locate them in the text. Ask: What is the purpose of these phrases? When might you hear similar phrases in the classroom?

Advanced High Ask partners to locate prepositional phrases in the text that show time. Have them discuss their purpose and take turns using similar phrases to talk about classroom events.

Use with Digital Text 2, **Effects of the Vietnam War.**

Listening, Speaking
Read aloud the section titled *The Impact on U.S. Domestic and Foreign Policies*, or invite volunteers to do so. Monitor understanding of spoken language as students share information and express ideas on a variety of grade-appropriate academic topics.

Beginning Make a statement about the War Powers Act. Have students ask you to repeat or clarify it if necessary. Then have students share their thoughts using this sentence frame: The War Powers Act was passed because _____.

Intermediate Arrange students in a circle. Make a statement about the War Powers Act. Then have the first student ask you to repeat or clarify it if necessary and state his or her own thought. Repeat this process for the second student and around the entire circle.

Advanced Arrange students in a circle. Make a statement about the War Powers Act. Have the first student directly respond to your statement before adding his or her own thought. Then have the second student respond to the first student and add his or her thought. Repeat for the entire circle.

Advanced High Have pairs of students discuss the War Powers Act. After each student speaks, the partner must either respond to the previous comment or ask a question about it, as well as add his or her own comment.

ⅅ Differentiate Instruction

Use the Differentiated Instruction notes throughout the lesson plan to support the varied skill sets, levels of readiness, and interests in the mixed-ability classroom.

Challenge These notes include suggestions for expanding the activity for advanced students.

On-Level These notes include suggestions for modifying the activity to address different interests or learning styles.

Extra Support These notes include ideas for providing more scaffolding or reading spuport.

Special Needs These notes provide ideas for adapting instruction to support the needs of various special needs students.

■ NOTES

The War's End and Effects

Objectives

Objective 1: Assess Nixon's new approach to the war, and explain why protests continued.

Objective 2: Explain what led to the Paris Peace Accords and why South Vietnam eventually fell to the communists.

Objective 3: Evaluate the impact of the Vietnam War on the United States.

LESSON 4 ORGANIZER		PACING: APPROX. 1 PERIOD, .5 BLOCKS			
				RESOURCES	
		OBJECTIVES	**PACING**	**Online**	**Print**
Connect					
DIGITAL START UP ACTIVITY **A Great Dilemma**			5 min.	●	
Investigate					
DIGITAL TEXT 1 **Attempts to Withdraw from Vietnam**		Objective 1	10 min.	●	●
DIGITAL TEXT 2 **Events Intensify the Antiwar Movement**			10 min.	●	●
DIGITAL TEXT 3 **The Vietnam War Ends**		Objective 2	10 min.	●	●
INTERACTIVE TIMELINE **Final Years of the Vietnam War**			10 min.	●	
DIGITAL TEXT 4 **Effects of the Vietnam War**		Objectives 3	10 min.	●	●
INTERACTIVE GALLERY **Postwar Experiences of Vietnam Veterans**			10 min.	●	
Synthesize					
DIGITAL ACTIVITY **The Legacy of Vietnam**			5 min.	●	
Demonstrate					
LESSON QUIZ **Lesson Quiz and Class Discussion Board**			10 min.	●	

PEARSON
realize™
www.PearsonRealize.com

Go online to access additional resources including:
Primary Sources • Biographies • Supreme Court cases •
21st Century Skill Tutorials • Maps • Graphic Organizers.

CONNECT

DIGITAL START UP ACTIVITY
A Great Dilemma

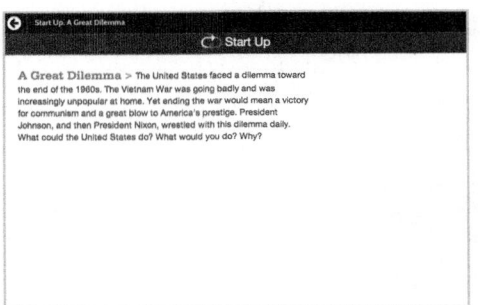

Project the Start Up Activity As students enter and get settled, draw their attention to the activity. Have partners Think-Pair-Share the information in the activity.

Discuss Engage students in discussing possible resolutions to the conflict in Vietnam that would allow the U.S. to achieve its strategic goals.

Tell students that in this lesson they will be learning how the United States ended its struggle to contain communism in Vietnam.

Aa Vocabulary Development Use the Interactive Reading Notepad to preview the Key Terms and Academic Vocabulary in this lesson with students.

⚑ FLIP IT!

Assign the Flipped Video for this lesson.

■ STUDENT EDITION PRINT
PAGES: 746–753

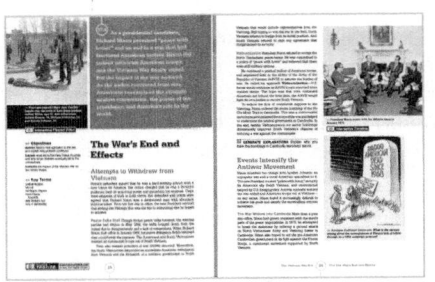

■ INVESTIGATE

DIGITAL TEXT 1
Attempts to Withdraw from Vietnam

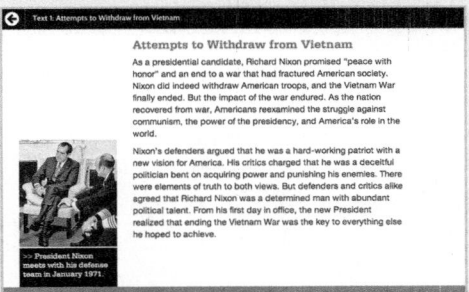

DIGITAL TEXT 2
Events Intensify the Antiwar Movement

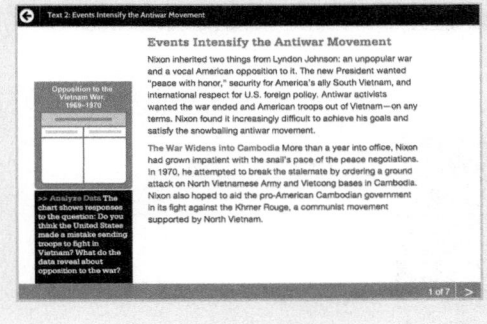

Objective 1: **Assess Nixon's new approach to the war, and explain why protests continued.**

Quick Instruction

Analyze Images Project the image of Nixon on the whiteboard. Explain that President Nixon realized that ending the Vietnam War was the key to everything else he hoped to achieve as President. Invite volunteers to explain Nixon's position on the Vietnam War when he took office in January 1969. *(Nixon wanted to end the war but he wanted "peace with honor," security for America's ally South Vietnam, and international respect for U.S. foreign policy.)*

Analyze Information How did Nixon redirect the peace process when he became President? *(Nixon developed a plan called Vietnamization, a major issue and event of the Vietnam War. Vietnamization involved ARVN troops taking over more combat duties as U.S. forces withdrew to secure South Vietnam)* Did his plan have the desired result? *(No. the ARVN forces were not successful.)*

Categorize In his efforts to end the Vietnam War, Nixon followed some policies that seemed to lessen U.S. involvement and some that seemed to increase U.S. involvement. Ask students to find examples of each type of policy. *(Nixon reduced the number of American combat troops in Vietnam and passed on more combat responsibilities to the ARVN. However, Nixon ordered the secret bombing of the Ho Chi Minh Trail in Cambodia. He also ordered a ground attack on North Vietnamese Army and Vietcong bases in Cambodia.).*

The attacks on bases in Cambodia was a controversial move because it widened the scope of the war and helped to undermine the neutral government in Cambodia.

Further Instruction

As the fighting continued in Vietnam, public response to the war intensified, and the American home front became its own physical and emotional battlefield. Some of Nixon's new Vietnam policies provoked sharp criticism and protests. Pivotal events in 1970 and in 1971 increased the antiwar movement's pressure on Nixon to pull U.S. troops out of Vietnam.

Identify Cause and Effect How did the invasion of Cambodia lead to the shootings at Kent State and the confrontation at Jackson State University? *(The invasion sparked angry protests on many college campuses, including Kent State, four days after Nixon told the country of the invasion. The confrontation and deaths at Jackson State University were in response to the killings at Kent State.)*

Draw Conclusions How did coverage of the My Lai Massacre and the release of The Pentagon Papers reflect an ongoing credibility gap? *(Both events revealed ongoing withholding of information by military or government officials, leading to more mistrust and less confidence by the American public.)*

The War's End and Effects

DIGITAL TEXT 3
The Vietnam War Ends

INTERACTIVE TIMELINE
Final Years of the Vietnam War

DIGITAL TEXT 4
Effects of the Vietnam War

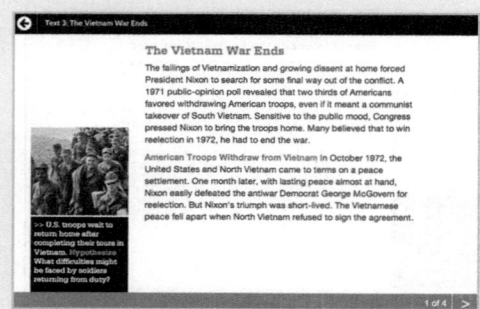

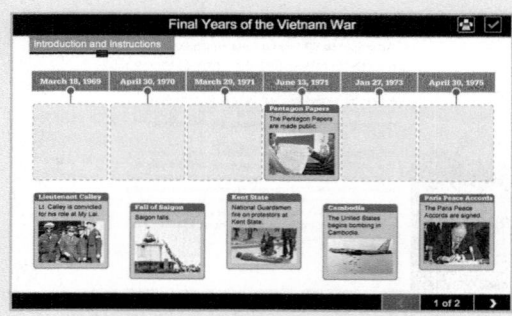

Objective 2: Explain what led to the Paris Peace Accords and why South Vietnam eventually fell to the communists.

Quick Instruction
Interactive Timeline: Final Years of the Vietnam War Project the timeline and have students complete the activity. Then select the squares to reveal details about the events.

📖 ACTIVE CLASSROOM
Have students Make Headlines for the final years of the Vietnam War. Ask: If you were to write a headline for the end of the Vietnam War that captured the most important aspect that should be remembered, what would that headline be? Allow students to use subheadings to communicate more information. Encourage students to present the end of the Vietnam War as part of America's role in the world. Have students pass their headlines to a partner for them to review.

Further Instruction
A 1971 public opinion poll revealed that two thirds of Americans favored withdrawing American troops, even if it meant a communist takeover of South Vietnam. With his reelection chances on the line, many Americans pushed President Nixon to finally find a way out of Vietnam.

Summarize What did the signing parties agree to in the Paris Peace Accords? *(The parties agreed to a cease-fire and the withdrawal of U.S. troops from South Vietnam. POW's would be exchanged, but North Vietnamese troops would remain in South Vietnam. The Vietcong would be allowed to become a legitimate political party in South Vietnam, and South Vietnam's non-communist government would remain in power until a political settlement could be reached.)*

Compare Points of View How would you describe the fall of Saigon from an American perspective? *(Students might describe it as the end of a long, costly disaster.)* From the Vietnamese perspective? *(Students might describe it as the final event in the long civil war in the country. The fall of Saigon would have created intense feelings of triumph and pride for supporters of the communist forces and a great sense of fear and uncertainty for those who supported the South Vietnamese government.)*

Objective 3: Evaluate the impact of the Vietnam War on the United States.

Quick Instruction
Interactive Gallery: Postwar Experiences of Vietnam Veterans Project the gallery and select the images to reveal the captions. Discuss the sacrifices of the servicemen and women who served in the Vietnam War and the importance of congressional Medal of Honor recipients, including individuals of all races and genders such as Roy Benavidez.

Summarize the key issues that returning Vietnam War vets faced. (Many veterans returned home with physical disabilities and health issues. Many others faced difficulties getting used to life at home. This was particularly true of POWs.)

📖 ACTIVE CLASSROOM
Have students imagine they are having a conversation with one of the people shown in the interactive gallery. Tell students to write down a question they'd like to ask, then what that person might say to them, and what they would say in response.

D Differentiate: Challenge Ask students to do additional research on Roy Benavidez that includes more details about the actions that earned him the Congressional Medal of Honor. Have students present their findings.

INTERACTIVE GALLERY
Postwar Experiences of Vietnam Veterans

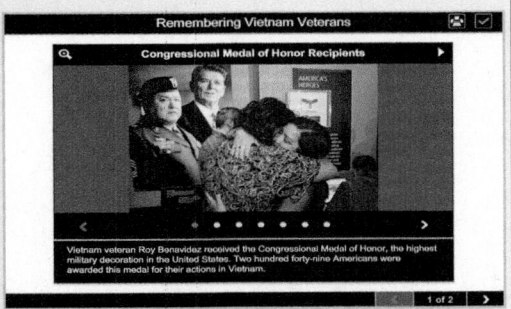

Remembering Vietnam Veterans

Congressional Medal of Honor Recipients

Vietnam veteran Roy Benavidez received the Congressional Medal of Honor, the highest military decoration in the United States. Two hundred forty-nine Americans were awarded this medal for their actions in Vietnam.

1 of 2

Further Instruction

Project and discuss the Close Reading Notepad questions, including the graphic organizer. Review and discuss key information and fill in the graphic organizer on the whiteboard as you go.

Express Problems Clearly Initiate a discussion in which students explain constitutional issues raised by federal government policy changes during the Vietnam War. *(When Congress passed the Gulf of Tonkin Resolution in 1964, it handed its war powers described in the Constitution to the President. With this Resolution, President Johnson did not need Congressional approval to escalate American intervention in Vietnam. The Constitutional question of who ultimately is in charge of war powers remains an issue to this day.)*

Draw Conclusions Ask students to describe the impact of the War Powers Act on the relationship between the legislative and executive branches of government. *(The Act created a sense of mistrust between the two branches and tension because of the struggle for ultimate power over who really controls U.S. military action.)*

Summarize What economic impact did defense spending during the Vietnam War have on Great Society programs? *Defense spending accounted for a significant amount of the federal budget, and many Great Society programs related to education such as textbooks and school lunch programs had less money as a result.*

◼ SYNTHESIZE

DIGITAL ACTIVITY
The Legacy of Vietnam

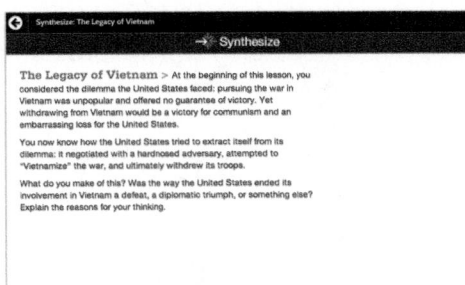

Synthesize: The Legacy of Vietnam

→ Synthesize

The Legacy of Vietnam > At the beginning of this lesson, you considered the dilemma the United States faced: pursuing the war in Vietnam was unpopular and offered no guarantee of victory. Yet withdrawing from Vietnam would be a victory for communism and an embarrassing loss for the United States.

You now know how the United States tried to extract itself from its dilemma: it negotiated with a hardnosed adversary, attempted to "Vietnamize" the war, and ultimately withdrew its troops.

What do you make of this? Was the way the United States ended its involvement in Vietnam a defeat, a diplomatic triumph, or something else? Explain the reasons for your thinking.

Remind students that at the beginning of this lesson, they considered the dilemma the United States faced: pursuing the war in Vietnam was unpopular and offered no guarantee of victory. Yet withdrawing from Vietnam would be a victory for communism and an embarrassing loss for the United States.

Review the costs and benefits of the Vietnam War with students. Discuss the terms of the Paris Peace Accords.

◼ DEMONSTRATE

LESSON QUIZ
Lesson Quiz and Class Discussion Board

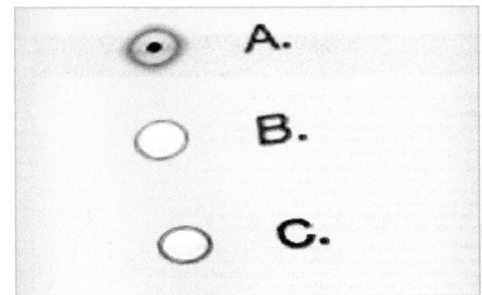

Assign the online Lesson Quiz for this lesson if you haven't already done so. Students will be offered automatic remediation or enrichment based on their score.

Pose these questions to the class on the Discussion Board:

In *The War's End and Effects*, you read about the U.S. exit from one of the most complicated conflicts in the country's history and how it changed American society.

Make Predictions How might the experiences in Vietnam influence American leaders when debating future intervention in a foreign conflicts?

Draw Inferences What lasting impact did the Vietnam War have on the American public's opinion of the government?

Topic Inquiry
Have students continue their investigations for the Topic Inquiry.

The Vietnam War Era

SYNTHESIZE

DIGITAL ACTIVITY
Reflect on the Essential Question and Topic

Direct students to reflect on the Essential Question for the Topic: What is America's role in the world? Remind students of the discussions and ideas they considered at the beginning of the Topic:

Challenge students to identify which of these roles, or perhaps others, they think America played during the Vietnam era. Discuss their answers as a class or ask students to post their answers on the Class Discussion Board.

Next ask students to reflect on the Topic as a whole and jot down 1–3 questions they've thought about during the Topic. Share these examples if students need help getting started:

- How did the war in Vietnam relate to the Cold War?

- Could anything on the scale of the Vietnam War protests and the antiwar movement happen again?

- Did the Vietnam War change what Americans thought their role in the world should be?

You may ask students to share their questions and answers on the Class Discussion Board.

Topic Inquiry
Have students complete Step 3 of the Topic Inquiry.

DEMONSTRATE

DIGITAL TOPIC REVIEW AND ASSESSMENT
The Vietnam War Era

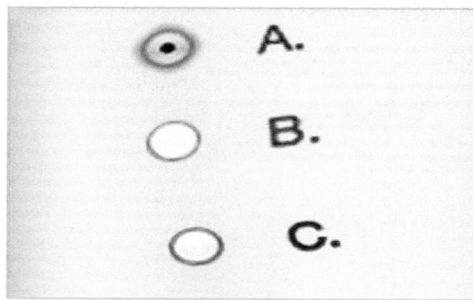

Students can prepare for the Topic Test by answering the questions in the Topic Review and Assessment online or the Assessment questions in the Print Student text. They can also prepare by reviewing their answers to the Interactive Reading Notepad questions or reviewing their notes in the Reading and Notetaking Study Guide.

DIGITAL TOPIC TEST
The Vietnam War Era

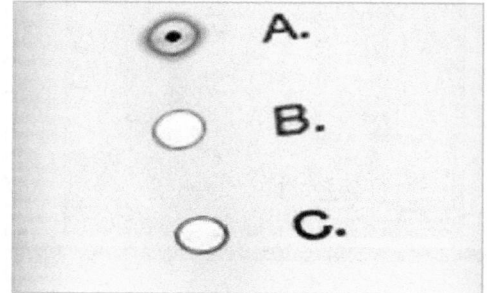

TOPIC TEST
Assign the Topic Test to assess students' understanding of topic content.

BENCHMARK TESTS
Assign these benchmark tests as you complete the relevant topics to monitor student progress toward mastering the course content and as preparation for the End-of-Course Test.

Benchmark Test 1: Topics 1–3
Benchmark Test 2: Topics 4–6
Benchmark Test 3: Topics 7–9
Benchmark Test 4: Topics 10–12
Benchmark Test 5: Topics 13–15
Benchmark Test 6: Topics 16–18
Benchmark Test 7: Topics 19–20

An Era of Change

TOPIC 18 ORGANIZER	PACING: APPROX. 9 PERIODS, 4.5 BLOCKS
	PACING
Connect	**1 period**
MY STORY VIDEO **Betty Friedan, The Feminine Mystique**	10 min.
DIGITAL ESSENTIAL QUESTION ACTIVITY **What are the challenges of diversity?**	10 min.
DIGITAL TIMELINE ACTIVITY **An Era of Change**	10 min.
TOPIC INQUIRY: DOCUMENT-BASED QUESTION **Leadership Qualities of Nixon, Ford, and Carter**	20 min.
Investigate	**3–6 periods**
TOPIC INQUIRY: DOCUMENT-BASED QUESTION **Leadership Qualities of Nixon, Ford, and Carter**	Ongoing
LESSON 1 The Counterculture of the 1960s	30–40 min.
LESSON 2 The Women's Rights Movement	30–40 min.
LESSON 3 Expanding the Push for Equality	30–40 min.
LESSON 4 The Environmental Movement	30–40 min.
LESSON 5 The Two Sides of the Nixon Presidency	30–40 min.
LESSON 6 Ford and Carter Struggle	30–40 min.
Synthesize	**1 period**
DIGITAL ACTIVITY **Reflect on the Essential Question and Topic**	10 min.
TOPIC INQUIRY: DOCUMENT-BASED QUESTION **Leadership Qualities of Nixon, Ford, and Carter**	20 min.
Demonstrate	**1–2 periods**
DIGITAL TOPIC REVIEW AND ASSESSMENT **An Era of Change**	10 min.
TOPIC INQUIRY: DOCUMENT-BASED QUESTION **Leadership Qualities of Nixon, Ford, and Carter**	20 min.

 TOPIC INQUIRY: DOCUMENT-BASED QUESTION

Leadership Qualities of Nixon, Ford, and Carter

In this Topic Inquiry, students examine evidence to analyze the leadership styles of Presidents Nixon, Ford, and Carter. In doing so, they infer how these Presidents were both affected by and affected a nation divided along ethic and political lines. This will lead students to a deeper understanding of the Topic Essential Question: What are the challenges of diversity?

STEP 1: CONNECT
Develop Questions and Plan the Investigation

Watch the Video

In this step, students prepare for the project by watching and discussing a famous video of President Nixon saying *I'm not a crook*. Before students watch the video, consider setting a historical context by inviting them to share what terms come to mind when they think of various decades. (The Roaring Twenties for the 1920s, The Great Depression for the 1930s, and so on.) Focus students on the 1970s. What terms do they associate with that decade? Explain that they will learn much more about it by studying the leadership qualities of the Presidents of the period. Remind them that President Richard M. Nixon served as President from 1968 to 1974. Share the video.

Suggestion: Ensure students understand the word and concept of *impeachment*: a process in which a legislative body charges a government official with serious misconduct.

Discuss

Use the questions as a basis for class or partner discussion. As the discussion winds down, explain that students will be working individually to analyze a set of documents. Each student will write his or her own essay based on their analysis of the documents. Consider sharing the Rubric at this point so students can begin considering how their essays will be evaluated.

Suggestion: Consider having an appropriate adult visit the classroom and share some of their relevant memories of the Nixon Administration in general and Watergate in particular.

Resources
• Student Instructions • Connect Video • Project Rubric

STEP 2: INVESTIGATE
Apply Disciplinary Concepts and Tools

Analyze the Documents

In this step, students begin their analysis, focusing on six documents of various types and answering multiple-choice and short answer questions about each one. Focus students on their ultimate goal: to write essays in which they consider the qualities of leadership and explain what effects the leadership styles of Presidents Nixon, Ford, and Carter had on the nation. Encourage them to keep their goal in mind as they analyze each document. They should strive to understand each document in general, but analyze each document keeping their essay topic in mind.

Suggestion: Preview the documents with students to ensure they understand what type of document each one is. Have them provide hypothetical examples of other documents of the same type.

Check Your Understanding

Encourage students to read the introduction to each document. Explain why reading an introduction is vital: it provides context for the document. Point out, too, how the questions are designed to help them focus on the purpose of their analysis: the quality and effects of the leadership styles of Presidents of the 1970s. To encourage proper analysis, suggest students write down the main idea of each document as it relates to their essay topic.

Suggestion: You might want to work through Document A, including the introduction and questions, as a class, modeling document analysis for the students.

Resources
• Student Instructions • Documents A-F

⏻ PROFESSIONAL DEVELOPMENT

Document-Based Question
Be sure to view the Document-Based Question Professional Development resources in the online course.

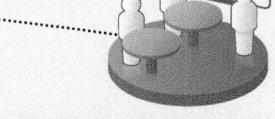

STEP 3: SYNTHESIZE
Evaluate Sources and
Use Evidence to Formulate Conclusions

Write Your Essay

Having completed their analysis of the documents, students are now prepared to begin writing their essays. Before students begin their essays, make sure they review the bulleted list of things that they should make sure to do. Tell them to use some form of the topic question—What effects did the leadership styles of Presidents Nixon, Ford, and Carter have on the nation?—as their topic sentences. Review the Rubric.

Suggestion: Remind students to take the time to use prewriting techniques before they begin writing their essays proper. Have students consider freewriting (jotting down all they know about the topic) and then making an outline to follow when writing the essay.

Resources
- Student Instructions
- Documents A-F
- Project Rubric

STEP 4: DEMONSTRATE
Communicate Conclusions
and Take Informed Action

Publish Your Essay

In this step, students share their essays with the class or others to demonstrate how they have considered multiple sources of evidence and points of view to form an educated and carefully reasoned opinion of the quality and effects of the leadership styles of Presidents Nixon, Ford, and Carter on the nation.

Suggestion: Have students share their conclusions with each other. Guide the class into a consensus of two or three main ideas about how the effects of the leadership styles of Presidents Nixon, Ford, and Carter affected the United Students during the Era of Change that was the 1970s.

Resources
- Project Rubric

An Era of Change

The America of the 1960s and 1970s was a different country than the America of the 1950s. Deep cultural shifts marked this period of great change. The counterculture of the 1960s posed a fundamental challenge to traditional values and customs, and the women's rights movement brought gender disparities to the forefront of the American consciousness. Even people's relationship with the nation's landscape and resources was brought into question, as the environmental movement emerged. The Nixon presidency, called a "long national nightmare" by his successor, Ford, was followed by the difficulties of the Carter administration.

▌CONNECT

MY STORY VIDEO

Betty Friedan, The Feminine Mystique

Watch a video showing the impact of Betty Friedan and her book, *The Feminine Mystique* on the Woman's Movement.

Check Understanding What was the feminine mystique that Friedan criticized? *(the idea that women could find fulfillment in life through traditional roles in the home)*

Compare and Contrast To what degree has the role of women in society changed since Friedan wrote her book? *(Students should cite evidence of the presence of women in all walks of life today, the availability of day care, advances made in reproductive rights, protections offered by legislation, etc. Some students may mention the continuing inequality in salaries and other impediments to social equality.)*

DIGITAL ESSENTIAL QUESTION ACTIVITY

What are the challenges of diversity?

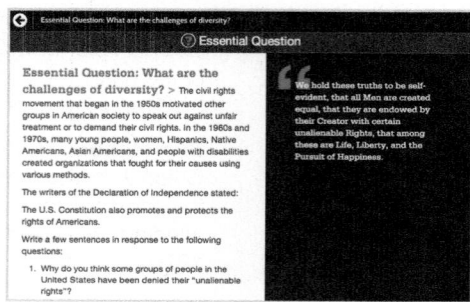

Ask students to think about the Essential Question for this Topic: What are the challenges of diversity? Ensure they understand the definition and concept of diversity. Ensure that they can provide examples of diversity in the United States.

Generate Explanations Through what means did women expand their political and economic rights? *(Political organizations pursued change through the courts with litigation and through Congress with lobbying and legislation, while individual women accompanied those efforts with non-violent protest.)*

DIGITAL TIMELINE ACTIVITY

An Era of Change

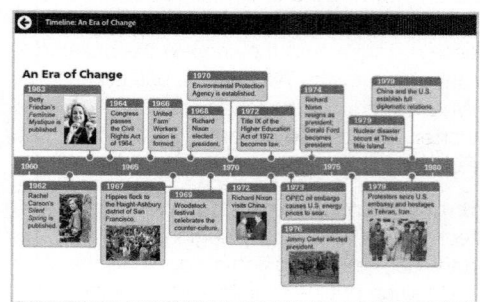

Point out that the Timeline covers a fairly long time—two decades—of the history of a large and diverse country. Acknowledge that trying to learn history can be overwhelming because of the number of events that have taken place over the centuries. Then point to the title of the Topic and the Timeline: An Era of Change. Tell students that historians label periods in history with titles like this to help organize and understand the relationship among events that took place during a particular stretch of time. Review several of the Timeline entries with students, challenging them to explain how each is related to the title concept of "An Era of Change."

Transfer Information Have students write paragraphs that summarize the Timeline. Provide them with the following topic sentence: "The 1960s and 1970s was an era of change in the United States." (Paragraphs will vary but should support the topic sentence with examples from the Timeline.)

Topic Inquiry

Launch the Topic Inquiry with students after introducing the Topic.

The Counterculture of the 1960s

Supporting English Language Learners

Use with Digital Text 1, **A Counterculture Emerges.**

Listening
Explain that when people speak, students can ask clarifying questions to better understand what was said.

Beginning Display and explain these questions: What do you mean? Could you say that another way? Use basic spoken language to describe some countercultural values of the 1960s hippie culture. Encourage students to seek clarification using the above questions as needed, both during and after your talk.

Intermediate Display these questions: What does _____ mean? What did you mean when you said _____ ? Model using each question frame. Then use spoken language to describe the 1960s counterculture. Encourage students to seek clarification using the above questions as needed, both during and after your talk.

Advanced Display and explain these questions: Can you explain further? Can you give an example? Can you be more specific? Have small groups discuss positive and negative aspects of the 1960s counterculture, using the above questions as needed to seek clarification from their peers.

Advanced High Ask pairs of students to discuss positive and negative aspects of the 1960s counterculture. Encourage them to seek clarification from each other as needed, and to record the ways in which they do so. Have students share their methods for seeking clarification.

Use with Digital Text 2, **The Counterculture Shapes a Generation.**

Speaking
In preparation for the activity, review the difference between analyzing a text and expressing feelings about it. Prompt students to express feelings ranging from single words and phrases to participation in extended discussions.

Beginning Ask: How would you feel if you were growing up in 1960s America? Brainstorm a list of single words and short phrases with students. Then have them complete and say this sentence: I would feel _____.

Intermediate Ask: How would you feel if you were growing up in 1960s America, and why? Have students answer the question and provide a supporting reason. If needed, use this sentence frame: I would feel _____ because _____.

Advanced Ask small groups to express feelings by answering the following questions in complete sentences: How do rock music, art, and literature make you feel? Do you think they would have made you feel different in 1960s America? Why or why not? Encourage students to respond to one another's statements, as well as to the questions.

Advanced High Ask pairs of students to participate in an extended discussion about all aspects of hippie culture. Encourage them to express their feelings in complete sentences and respond to each other's statements.

▶ Differentiate Instruction

Use the Differentiated Instruction notes throughout the lesson plan to support the varied skill sets, levels of readiness, and interests in the mixed-ability classroom.

Challenge These notes include suggestions for expanding the activity for advanced students.

On-Level These notes include suggestions for modifying the activity to address different interests or learning styles.

Extra Support These notes include ideas for providing more scaffolding or reading spuport.

Special Needs These notes provide ideas for adapting instruction to support the needs of various special needs students.

■ NOTES

The Counterculture of the 1960s

Objectives

Objective 1: Describe the rise of the counterculture.

Objective 2: List the major characteristics of the counterculture.

Objective 3: Evaluate the positive and negative impacts of the counterculture movement on American society.

LESSON 1 ORGANIZER		PACING: APPROX. 1 PERIOD, .5 BLOCKS			
				RESOURCES	
		OBJECTIVES	PACING	Online	Print
Connect					
DIGITAL START UP ACTIVITY **The Hippie Code**			5 min.	●	
Investigate					
DIGITAL TEXT 1 **A Counterculture Emerges**		Objective 1	10 min.	●	●
INTERACTIVE GALLERY **Generation Gap Issues**			10 min.	●	
DIGITAL TEXT 2 **The Counterculture Shapes a Generation**		Objectives 2, 3	10 min.	●	●
INTERACTIVE GALLERY **Culture of the Counterculture**			10 min.	●	
Synthesize					
DIGITAL ACTIVITY **The Hippie Code Revisited**			5 min.	●	
Demonstrate					
DIGITAL QUIZ **Lesson Quiz and Class Discussion Board**			10 min.	●	

PEARSON
realize.™
www.PearsonRealize.com

Go online to access additional resources including:
Primary Sources • Biographies • Supreme Court cases •
21st Century Skill Tutorials • Maps • Graphic Organizers.

CONNECT

DIGITAL START UP ACTIVITY
The Hippie Code

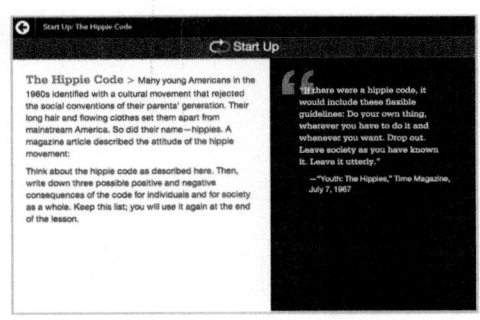

Project the Start Up Activity As students enter and get settled, ask them to think about the *codes of conduct* they follow in various situations—home, school, public areas and why they think the codes are important or not important. Then have them share their ideas with another student.

Discuss Invite a volunteer to read the quote from *Time* magazine aloud. Before students write their lists, ask them to share their initial reactions to the advice. (Shock, anger, agreement) Have students write down three possible positive and negative consequences of the code for individuals and for society as a whole. Remind students to keep their lists for later use.

Aa Vocabulary Development: Use the Interactive Reading Notepad to preview the Key Terms and Academic Vocabulary in this lesson with students.

⇗ FLIP IT!

Assign the Flipped Video for this lesson.

■ STUDENT EDITION PRINT PAGES: 758–761

INVESTIGATE

DIGITAL TEXT 1
A Counterculture Emerges

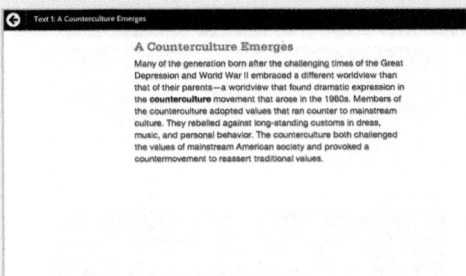

Objective 1: Describe the rise of the counterculture.

Quick Instruction

Interactive Gallery: Generation Gap Issues Project the gallery and click on each image to reveal more information about the generation gap. Point out that a lack of understanding and communication between older and younger generations has been a common feature of every era but became a significant societal issue during this time period. Challenge students to identify reasons why the generation gap appeared particularly wide in the United States in the 1960s. (On-going war in Vietnam; emergence of rock-n-roll; increased racial tensions)

🎭 ACTIVE CLASSROOM

Use the Ranking Strategy to have students go through the images shown in the activity, and rank which issues had the greatest impact on widening the generation gap.

ELL Use the ELL activity described in the ELL chart.

INTERACTIVE GALLERY
Generation Gap Issues

Further Instruction

Summarize the core ideals of the members of the counterculture. (Members of the counterculture valued youth, spontaneity, and freedom of expression. Counterculture members valued individuality.)

Determine Point of View What assumptions about mainstream culture were made by the counterculture? *(Like the Beat movement before it, the counterculture viewed mainstream culture as one dominated by materialism and one that emphasized and valued conformity rather than personal experience.)*

The Counterculture of the 1960s

DIGITAL TEXT 2

The Counterculture Shapes a Generation

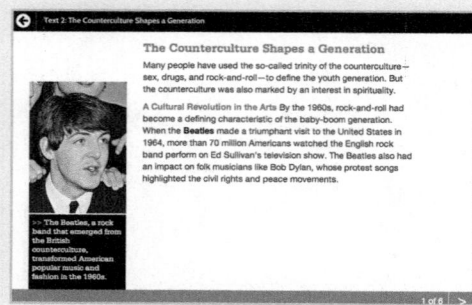

INTERACTIVE GALLERY

Culture of the Counterculture

Objectives 2: **List the major characteristics of the counterculture; 3: Evaluate the positive and negative impacts of the counterculture movement on American society.**

Quick Instruction

Interactive Gallery: Culture of the Counterculture Project the gallery. Click each image to display significant examples of cultural movements in art, music, and literature associated with the counterculture movement. Discuss how the issues of the day were reflected in the art of the time. As you guide students through the gallery, have them compare and contrast the aspects of the counterculture in the 1960s to similar aspects of life today.

Analyze Information Challenge students to describe the positive and negative impacts of significant examples of cultural movements in music, such as rock-n-roll and folk music. (Rock-n-roll provided entertainment for many young Americans and became a valuable creative outlet for them. Rock and folk also advanced noble causes such as civil rights, as well as having a significant positive economic impact. The lyrics of popular music, however, often contributed to harmful behavior, especially when it glorified violence and excessive drug use.) Direct students' attention to the art of the 1960s and discuss the positive and negative impact of cultural movements in art. Then ask if students are familiar with the literature of the time. Encourage a discussion of the positive and negative impacts of cultural movements in literature.

📖 ACTIVE CLASSROOM

Conduct a Graffiti Concepts Activity. Ask students to reflect on key elements of the counterculture of the 1960s and create a visual image and/or phrase that represents each element. (Allow approximately 3–5 minutes.) Then ask students to post their "graffiti" on the board or on chart paper and ask students to look at all the various causes then discuss them as a group.

D **Differentiate: Challenge/Gifted** Ask students to do additional research on one of the people or works of art displayed in the interactivity and present their findings.

ELL Use the ELL activity described in the ELL chart.

Further Instruction

Determine Relevance What impact did the music of the Beatles and Bob Dylan have on the counterculture? *(The Beatles brought rock-n-roll to a much larger audience and to a much more prominent place in American culture, especially among young Americans. The Beatles also influenced folk musicians like Bob Dylan. Dylan and other folk artists wrote and performed protest songs inspired by the civil rights and peace movements, key causes of the counterculture.)*

Identify Central Issues How did the counterculture's promotion of the "sexual revolution" reflect the widening generation gap? *(Polls showed that younger Americans had much more accepting views of nontraditional forms of sexual behavior than the older generations.)*

Evaluate What lasting impact did the counterculture have on the nation? *(Students may say that the counterculture influenced many aspects of American society, such as race relations, music and art, and fashion. In challenging traditional values and customs it also encouraged more open thinking.)*

SYNTHESIZE

DIGITAL ACTIVITY
The Hippie Code Revisited

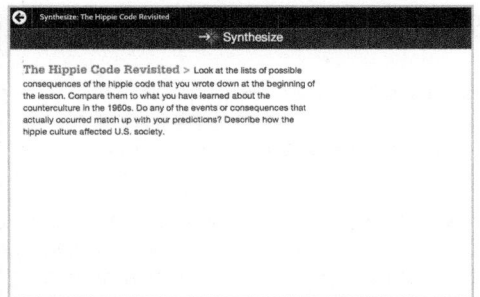

Have partners think about the following questions. Do you think it is possible for an individual to completely "drop out" of society? Why or why not? Is there value in challenging traditional cultural values? Why or why not? Have pairs share their answers with the class.

Discuss Ask students to think about the lists of possible consequences of the hippie code that they wrote down at the beginning of the lesson and to compare these lists to what they have learned about the counterculture in the 1960s. Ask if they would change any of their responses now that they have learned more about the counterculture.

DEMONSTRATE

DIGITAL QUIZ
Lesson Quiz and Class Discussion Board

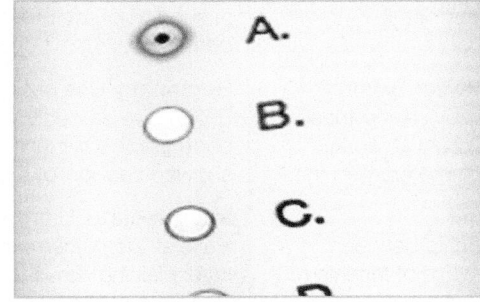

Assign the online Lesson Quiz for this lesson if you haven't already done so. Students will be offered automatic remediation or enrichment based on their score.

Pose these questions to the class on the Discussion Board:

In *The Counterculture of the 1960s*, you read about the emergence of a large counterculture in the United States created by millions of young Americans disenchanted with society. This counterculture changed modern music, art, and the ways in which we view other Americans who embrace different lifestyles.

Predict Consequences What kind of political movement might arise in reaction to the counterculture and what would be its aims?

Draw Conclusions In what ways was the counterculture movement a significant societal issue of this time period?

Topic Inquiry
Have students continue their investigations for the Topic Inquiry.

The Women's Rights Movement

Supporting English Language Learners

Use with Digital Text 1, **A New Feminist Movement Pushes for Equality.**

Speaking
Review with students that when we narrate events, we tell the story of what happened—and that the process is similar for fiction and nonfiction. Prompt students to narrate with increasing specificity and detail appropriate for grade-level activities.

Beginning Ask students to narrate the relationship between women and the workplace during the second wave of feminism by saying these sentences in their correct order: Women demanded equality at work. Women were often expected to be housewives. When more women got jobs, they faced discrimination.

Intermediate Ask students to narrate how the relationship between women and the workplace evolved during the second wave of feminism. Guide their narration with these questions: What did most women do in the 1950s? What was the 1960s workplace like for women? What did women start demanding?

Advanced Ask pairs of students to narrate how women's participation in the workforce evolved during the second wave of feminism. Encourage them to order the events in chronological order and describe them with some specificity and detail.

Advanced High Ask pairs of students to narrate the course of the second wave of feminism. Encourage them to shape their narration as a story with a beginning, a middle, an end, and specific details.

Use with Digital Text 2, **The Role of Women's Civil Rights Organizations.**

Listening
Use visual support to enhance and confirm understanding of increasingly complex and elaborated spoken language. Display the image of marchers in support of the ERA, and introduce related vocabulary (e.g. *march, sign, demand*).

Beginning Use basic spoken language to explain the purpose of the ERA. Have students enhance and confirm understanding by using the photograph's visual support to complete this sentence: Some women showed support of the ERA by _____.

Intermediate Use spoken language to explain the purpose of the ERA. Have students use visual support to enhance and confirm understanding by explaining how the photograph illustrates support for the amendment. Record and display students' responses.

Advanced Use somewhat complex and elaborated spoken language to explain the establishment of NOW and its focus on the ERA. Have pairs of students use visual support to enhance and confirm understanding by discussing the ways that NOW raised awareness and support for their goal.

Advanced High Use complex and elaborated spoken language to explain the establishment of NOW and its focus on the ERA. Have pairs of students enhance and confirm understanding by answering these questions: What does the photograph tell you about NOW's fight for the ERA? What questions do you still have?

▣ Differentiate Instruction

Use the Differentiated Instruction notes throughout the lesson plan to support the varied skill sets, levels of readiness, and interests in the mixed-ability classroom.

Challenge These notes include suggestions for expanding the activity for advanced students.

On-Level These notes include suggestions for modifying the activity to address different interests or learning styles.

Extra Support These notes include ideas for providing more scaffolding or reading spuport.

Special Needs These notes provide ideas for adapting instruction to support the needs of various special needs students.

■ NOTES

PEARSON
realize™
www.PearsonRealize.com

Go online to access additional resources including:
Primary Sources • Biographies • Supreme Court cases •
21st Century Skill Tutorials • Maps • Graphic Organizers.

Objectives

Objective 1: Analyze why a movement to expand women's political rights arose in the 1960s.

Objective 2: Identify the goals and methods that political organizations used to promote women's rights.

Objective 3: Assess the impact of the women's movement on American society.

LESSON 2 ORGANIZER		PACING: APPROX. 1 PERIOD, .5 BLOCKS		
			RESOURCES	
	OBJECTIVES	**PACING**	**Online**	**Print**
Connect				
DIGITAL START UP ACTIVITY **Challenging a Stereotype**		5 min.	●	
Investigate				
DIGITAL TEXT 1 **A New Feminist Movement Pushes for Equality**	Objective 1	10 min.	●	●
DIGITAL TEXT 2 **The Role of Women's Civil Rights Organizations**	Objective 2	10 min.	●	●
INTERACTIVE TIMELINE **The Fight for the Equal Rights Amendment**		10 min.	●	
DIGITAL TEXT 3 **The Impact of the Women's Movement**	Objective 3	10 min.	●	●
INTERACTIVE GRAPH **Women in the Workforce**		10 min.	●	
Synthesize				
DIGITAL ACTIVITY **Equality Under the Law?**		5 min.	●	
Demonstrate				
DIGITAL QUIZ **Lesson Quiz and Class Discussion Board**		10 min.	●	

The Women's Rights Movement

■ CONNECT

DIGITAL START UP ACTIVITY
Challenging a Stereotype

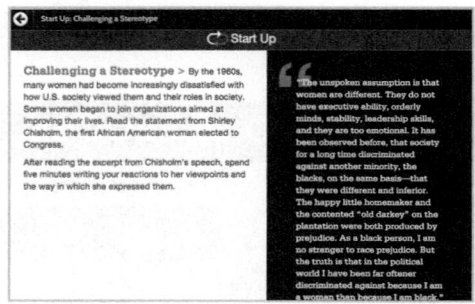

Project the Start Up Activity Ask students to read the quote as they enter and get settled. Then have them write a paragraph reflecting on the quote. Have students share their ideas with a partner, either in class or through a chat or blog space.

Discuss Take a moment to reflect on how gender discrimination may have affected women in the past and how opportunities for women have evolved over time.

Tell students that in this lesson they will be learning how women like Shirley Chisholm and many others challenged the traditional roles of women in the home and in the workforce, changing American society.

Aa **Vocabulary Development:** Use the Interactive Reading Notepad to preview the Key Terms and Academic Vocabulary in this lesson with students.

⇅ FLIP IT!
Assign the Flipped Video for this lesson.

■ STUDENT EDITION PRINT PAGES: 762–767

■ INVESTIGATE

DIGITAL TEXT 1
A New Feminist Movement Pushes for Equality

Objective 1: Analyze why a movement to expand women's political rights arose in the 1960s.

Quick Instruction

Analyze Images Direct students attention to the image of the women's rights protest. Use it as a springboard for a class discussion about one of the significant societal issues of this time period: the challenges that women have faced getting equal rights in America. (Denied voting rights until the 1920s; continued unequal pay for doing the same job.) Point out that the women's movement in the 1960s and 1970s fundamentally changed American life.

Summarize What role did Betty Friedan play in supporting the women's rights movement? (*Friedan's book,* The Feminine Mystique, *articulated what many women were feeling about their roles at home and their status in the workplace. She shifted public opinion and galvanized the supporters of women's rights.*)

Determine Point of View What beliefs led women to support the women's movement? (*Many believed that society judged and discriminated against them as a group. Women also believed that the housewife stereotype was inaccurate and that life should offer women many more opportunities.*)

ELL Use the ELL activity described in the ELL chart.

Further Instruction

Summarize how women faced discrimination in the workplace. (*It was very difficult for women to advance or keep their jobs, regardless of qualifications or quality of their performance. Women who became pregnant could lose their jobs or get demotions. Pregnant women were often denied leave or forced to take unpaid leave.*)

Infer Why did so much time elapse between the first and second waves of feminism? (*Significant events like the Great Depression and World War II overshadowed the women's movement. Many Americans' views on gender issues had changed, especially after World War II, when people wanted to return to simpler and more traditional times and gender roles.*)

Hypothesize What effect might Sandra Day O'Connor's experiences as a recent law school graduate have had on her career later in life? (*O'Connor was probably motivated to work harder because of the difficulty of finding employment. The discriminatory practices she had to faced might have pushed her to end them through her work.*)

DIGITAL TEXT 2
The Role of Women's Civil Rights Organizations

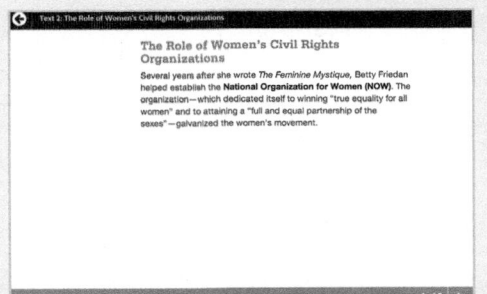

INTERACTIVE TIMELINE
The Fight for the Equal Rights Amendment

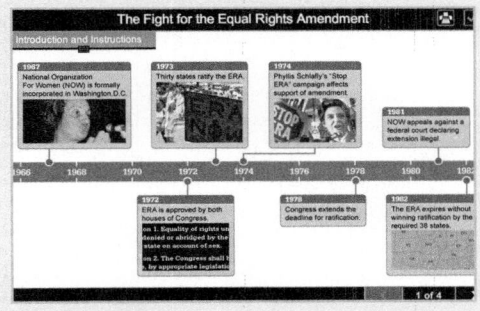

DIGITAL TEXT 3
The Impact of the Women's Movement

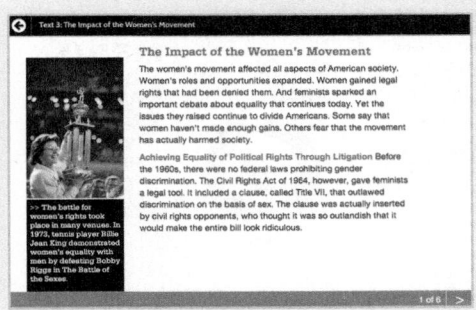

Objective 2: Identify the goals and methods that political organizations used to promote women's rights.

Quick Instruction
Interactive Timeline: The Fight for the Equal Rights Amendment Display the timeline showing key events in the fight for the Equal Rights Amendment. Review each entry with students to gauge their knowledge about the event, person, or group it describes and to help them better understand the actions taken by people to expand political and civil rights for women in American society. Invite interferences and speculation for any events that are unfamiliar.

Evaluate Impact Who is Phyllis Schlafly and what role did she play in the debate over the ERA and in the conservative resurgence of the 1980s? *(Schlafly is a conservative political activist who rejected women's liberation and worked hard to defeat the ERA. Her argument resonated with many conservatives who helped usher in the conservative resurgence in the early 1980s.)*

▶ ACTIVE CLASSROOM
Conduct a Take a Stand Activity on the following question: Should the Equal Rights Amendment be ratified? Ask students to divide into two groups based on their answer and move to separate areas of the classroom. Ask students to talk with each other to compare their reasons for answering yes or no. Ask a representative from each side to present and defend the group's point of view.

ELL Use the ELL activity described in the ELL chart.

Further Instruction
Be sure that students understand the various methods of expanding the right to participate in the democratic process, including lobbying and nonviolent protesting. Ask students to describe the goals of these actions. *(Women's rights advocates who engaged in lobbying wanted political reforms and the government to enforce existing legislation that banned discrimination. Protesters wanted to show how society trapped women into adopting restrictive roles.)*

Summarize What successes and failures did the women's movement experience during the fight for the ERA? *(The women's movement was successful in getting Congress to pass the ERA. It was also successful in winning key legal battles dealing with the ERA deadline. However, shadowing these successes were significant failures, such as losing momentum when a conservative wave swept the country in the early 1980s, which included the Republican Party dropping support for the ERA in its official platform. The biggest failure is obviously not getting enough states to ratify the ERA before the deadline expired in 1982.)*

Objective 3: Assess the impact of the women's movement on American society.

Quick Instruction
Interactive Graph: Women in the Workforce Project the chart. Move the slider to track the progress women have made in the American workforce between 1970 and 2012. Ask: in general, how might you characterize the changes brought about by women in the workforce? *(Generally, women have made progress in several areas. More women than ever are in the workforce. Women are making more money than they were in the past. Some professions have seen significant increases in the number of women in those fields.)*

Express Problems Clearly Ask students to identify and describe the unintended consequences of actions meant to create economic opportunity for citizens such as Title IX. *(Title IX helped popularize women's college athletics. However, increased competition for coaching positions has reduced the number of women head coaches.)*

Determine Relevance How did the Civil Rights Act of 1964 expand women's right to participate in the democratic process? *(The Civil Rights Act of 1964 outlawed discrimination on the basis of sex. The act provided a basis for women to challenge discrimination using litigation.)*

The Women's Rights Movement

INTERACTIVE GRAPH
Women in the Workforce

🖳 ACTIVE CLASSROOM

Break students into groups for a quick Circle Write Activity. Provide this as a writing prompt: What progress have women made in the workforce since 1970? Have students write as much as they can for 1 minute and then switch with the person on their right. The next person tries to improve or elaborate the response where the other person left off. Continue to switch until the paper comes back to the first person. The group then decides which is the best composition (or response) and shares that with the larger group.

D Differentiate: **Extra Support** Explain that median annual earnings is the amount which divides the income distribution into two equal groups, half of which have earnings above that amount, and half of which have earnings below that amount.

Further Instruction

Discuss the different perspectives of the landmark case *Roe* v. *Wade* with students.

Summarize How did the government and private sector expand economic opportunities for women in American society? *(Many people worked to establish the Commission on the Status of Women to examine workplace discrimination. Others helped create the Equal Employment Opportunity Commission (EEOC) to enforce the federal prohibition on job discrimination. The Equal Credit Opportunity Act made it illegal to deny credit to a woman just because of her gender. Many people also promoted increased educational opportunities for women, which greatly affects economic opportunities.)*

Draw Conclusions What might account for the dramatic increase in the number of women in the legal profession? *(More women than ever attended college and then law school. The chance for women to earn higher levels of education opened the door to women to careers that were dominated by men.)*

PEARSON
realize™

www.PearsonRealize.com
Access your Digital Lesson

■ SYNTHESIZE

DIGITAL ACTIVITY
Equality Under the Law?

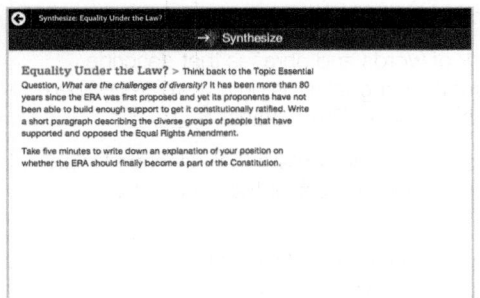

Before students begin their paragraphs, have them use the Think Pair Share Strategy to review the individuals and groups involved in the Equal Rights Amendment issue. Have pairs share their thoughts with the class.

Discuss Ask students to think about the following question: Should the ERA finally become a part of the Constitution? Ask students to share information that may persuade them one way or another on the issue.

■ DEMONSTRATE

DIGITAL QUIZ
Lesson Quiz and Class Discussion Board

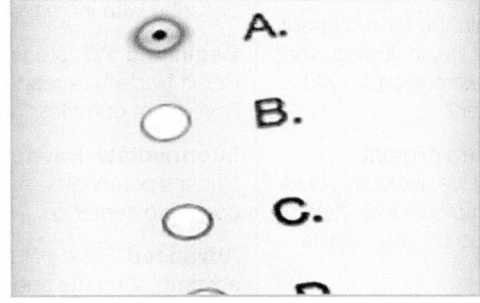

Assign the online Lesson Quiz for this lesson if you haven't already done so. Students will be offered automatic remediation or enrichment based on their score.

Pose these questions to the class on the Discussion Board:

In *The Women's Rights Movement*, The Women's Rights Movement you read about how many American joined organizations that worked to protect and expand their rights as citizens and improve their role in society. Women and organizations brought about changes through litigation, lobbying, and education.

Draw Conclusions What has been the most effective methods of expanding the right to participate in the democratic process and expanding economic opportunities for women?

Make Predictions Will the Equal Rights Amendment be presented again?

Topic Inquiry
Have students continue their investigations for the Topic Inquiry.

Expanding the Push for Equality

Supporting English Language Learners

Use with Digital Text 2, **Latino Organizations Fight for Rights.**

Listening
Discuss why it might be easier to talk with someone in person rather than over the phone. Point out that visual cues, or contextual support, can enhance and confirm understanding of spoken language.

Beginning Rely heavily on contextual support to explain the term migrant farmworker (e.g., act out a migrant farmworker's way of life, including work and travel, and use other physical gestures and facial expressions). Ask: What adjectives describe the life of a migrant farmworker?

Intermediate Use contextual support to explain the term migrant farmworker (e.g., act out a migrant farmworker's way of life, including work and travel, and use other physical gestures and facial expressions). Ask students to give a definition of migrant farmworker based on your words and actions.

Advanced Use contextual support, such as physical gestures and facial expressions, to explain the life of a migrant farmworker and the work of Chavez and Huerta. Ask students how the contextual support enhances their understanding of the farmworkers' trials and the activists' passion.

Advanced High Have pairs of students discuss the lives of migrant farmworkers and the work of Chavez and Huerta. Encourage them to accompany their words with appropriate contextual support, such as gestures and facial expressions.

Use with Digital Text 4, **Activists Win Rights for Consumers and the Disabled.**

Speaking
Discuss how describing a person or thing in detail can make it more understandable and more interesting for a listener. Prompt students to describe with increasing specificity and detail.

Beginning Ask students to think of words and phrases that describe Ralph Nader's personality. Record their suggestions on a word web. Then have them complete and say this sentence: Ralph Nader is _____.

Intermediate Have students think of specific details that describe Ralph Nader's personality. Ask them to use one or more of these details in a complete sentence.

Advanced Have pairs of students name each of Ralph Nader's accomplishments and say a descriptive sentence about it. After each student says his or her sentence, challenge the partner try to add even more specificity and detail to it.

Advanced High Have pairs of students describe Ralph Nader and his accomplishments. Encourage students to ask their partners questions that draw out further specificity and detail.

▣ Differentiate Instruction

Use the Differentiated Instruction notes throughout the lesson plan to support the varied skill sets, levels of readiness, and interests in the mixed-ability classroom.

Challenge These notes include suggestions for expanding the activity for advanced students.

On-Level These notes include suggestions for modifying the activity to address different interests or learning styles.

Extra Support These notes include ideas for providing more scaffolding or reading spuport.

Special Needs These notes provide ideas for adapting instruction to support the needs of various special needs students.

■ NOTES

PEARSON
realize™
www.PearsonRealize.com

Go online to access additional resources including:
Primary Sources • Biographies • Supreme Court cases •
21st Century Skill Tutorials • Maps • Graphic Organizers.

Objectives

Objective 1: Analyze the causes of the growth of the Latino population after World War II.

Objective 2: Evaluate significant leaders and the methods they used to achieve equality in political rights for Latinos.

Objective 3: Evaluate the means by which Native Americans sought to expand their rights.

Objective 4: Describe the expansion of rights for consumers and the disabled.

LESSON 3 ORGANIZER		PACING: APPROX. 1 PERIOD, .5 BLOCKS			
				RESOURCES	
		OBJECTIVES	PACING	Online	Print
Connect					
DIGITAL START UP ACTIVITY **Continuing the Fight for Rights**			5 min.	●	
Investigate					
DIGITAL TEXT 1 **Latino Immigration Surges**		Objective 1	10 min.	●	●
DIGITAL TEXT 2 **Latino Organizations Fight for Rights**		Objective 2	10 min.	●	●
INTERACTIVE GALLERY **Case Study—UFW Grape Boycott**			10 min.	●	
DIGITAL TEXT 3 **Native Americans and Asian Americans Battle Discrimination**		Objective 3	10 min.	●	●
INTERACTIVE GALLERY **The Fight for American Indian Rights**			10 min.	●	
DIGITAL TEXT 4 **Activists Win Rights for Consumers and the Disabled**		Objective 4	10 min.	●	●
Synthesize					
DIGITAL ACTIVITY **Identify the Social Issues Affecting Various Minorities**			5 min.	●	
Demonstrate					
DIGITAL QUIZ **Lesson Quiz and Class Discussion Board**			10 min.	●	

Expanding the Push for Equality

■ CONNECT

DIGITAL START UP ACTIVITY
Continuing the Fight for Rights

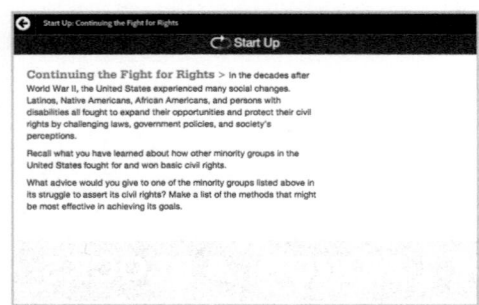

Project the Start Up Activity Ask students to make a list of what they have learned about how other minority groups in the United States fought for and won basic civil rights. Have students share their ideas with a partner, either in class or through a chat or blog space.

Discuss Ask students what advice they would give to minority groups in its struggle to assert its civil rights. List methods that might be most effective in achieving its goals. (Government lobbying, nonviolent demonstrations; violent protests; consumer boycotts)

Tell students that in this lesson they will be learning about the expanding civil rights movement in the 20th century, including movements organized by Latino Americans, Native Americans, Asian Americans, citizens with disabilities, and consumers.

Aa Vocabulary Development: Use the Interactive Reading Notepad to preview the Key Terms and Academic Vocabulary in this lesson with students.

🔃 FLIP IT!
Assign the Flipped Video for this lesson.

■ STUDENT EDITION PRINT
PAGES: 768–773

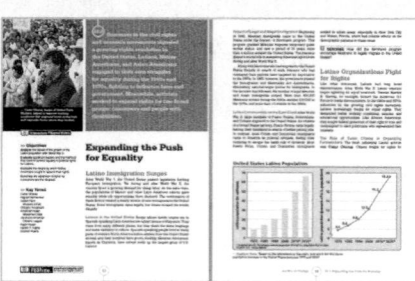

■ INVESTIGATE

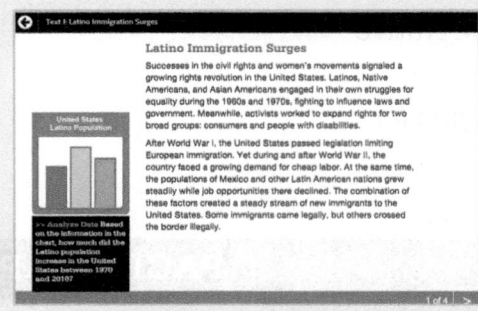

DIGITAL TEXT 1
Latino Immigration Surges

Objective 1: Analyze the causes of the growth of the Latino population after World War II.

Quick Instruction

Analyze Graphs Project the graph. Ensure understanding of the graph itself by reviewing the title, the bars, and the term *projected growth*. Ask: What is the main idea of this graph? (The significant increase in Latino immigration to the United States between 1970 and 2020.) Use the graph as a springboard to discuss what students know about the causes and effects of immigration.

Draw Inferences How did the government make immigration for Latinos easier in the 1960s? *(The government passed the Immigration and Nationality Act Amendments, eliminating national-origin quotas for immigrants.)*

Draw Conclusions How did the Bracero Program contribute to changing demographic patterns resulting from illegal immigration to the United States? *(More than 4 million Mexicans entered the United States under the bracero, or farmhand, program. Many stayed illegally in the United States once their temporary guest worker status expired, which contributed the increase in Latinos living in the country.)*

Further Instruction

Summarize The causes and effects of changing demographic patterns resulting from legal and illegal Latino immigration to the United States. (Most Latinos left their homelands in search of better-paying jobs and greater economic opportunities. Some left as political refugees, fleeing their countries to escape the harsh rule of dictators. Communities of Latino immigrants grew in East Coast cities and regions of the West and Southwest, changing the makeup of the population.)

Contrast What made legal immigration easier for Puerto Ricans wishing to move to the United States? *(Puerto Rico was a U.S. territory, so Puerto Ricans could move to the United States legally with fewer obstacles.)*

Infer What impact did Latino immigration to communities on the East Coast have on cities as a whole? *(The Latino immigration would have brought more diversity to East Coast cities. Cultural elements like language, food, and music would have changed because of the large number of Latino immigrants.)*

DIGITAL TEXT 2
Latino Organizations Fight for Rights

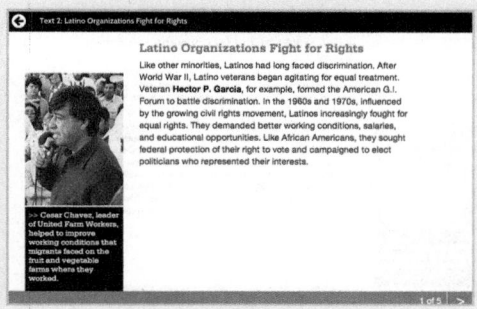

INTERACTIVE GALLERY
Case Study—UFW Grape Boycott

Objective 2: Evaluate significant leaders and the methods they used to achieve equality in political rights for Latinos.

Quick Instruction
Interactive Gallery: Case Study—UFW Grape Boycott Project the gallery on the whiteboard and select the images to reveal the captions. Discuss each step in the table grape boycott. Ask students to summarize Cesar Chavez's role and his actions to help expand economic opportunities for farmworkers. *(Chavez was the leader and key organizer of the grape boycott that helped win better working conditions and pay for migrant farm laborers.)*

Draw Conclusions In your opinion, what strategy was most important in winning recognition from the grape growers? Explain. *(Reaching out to consumers was the key. The largest impact possible on the growers was lack of sales. When Americans throughout the country refused to buy grapes, the economic impact on the growers was devastating to their businesses.)*

◼ ACTIVE CLASSROOM

Have students Make Headlines for the United Farmworkers' Grape Boycott. Ask: If you were to write a headline about events during the grape boycott that captured the most important aspect that should be remembered, what would that headline be? Allow students to use subheadings to communicate more information. Have students share review each others' headlines.

D Differentiate: Challenge Invite interested students to learn more about Cesar Chavez and his actions during the grape boycott and share what they learn with the class through a verbal or online presentation.

ELL Use the ELL activity described in the ELL chart.

Further Instruction
Ensure that students understand that many organizations and individuals created a broader Mexican American social and political effort that was known as the Chicano movement. Challenge students to identify key movements within the Latino community and to identify the roles of significant leaders, such as Dolores Huerta. *(Students should show understanding of the roles of political organizations that promoted civil rights, including ones from Chicano civil rights movements, such as Hector Garcia and the American GI Forum, Dolores Huerta and her political, social, and economic contributions to American society, José Angel Gutierrez and the political party La Raza Unida.)*

Introduce students to the significance of the landmark cases *Mendez* v. *Westminster* and *Delgado* v. *Bastrop I.S.D.*, both of which took steps toward reducing segregation of minorities in public school systems.

Support Ideas with Evidence What evidence would you use to support the idea that the Chicano Mural Movement was a significant cultural movement in art? *(The Chicano Mural Movement encouraged the creation of large murals which celebrated Latino culture and prompted increased*

---

awareness of Latino history and culture. It was part of the larger Chicano Movement, which sought increased political and economic opportunity for Latinos.)

Identify Central Issues Why was it particularly important to Latino activists to gain political and civil rights? *(They realized that by gaining political power they could exert more influence to pass legislation that protected or expanded civil, economic, and educational rights of Latinos.)*

Expanding the Push for Equality

DIGITAL TEXT 3

Native Americans and Asian Americans Battle Discrimination

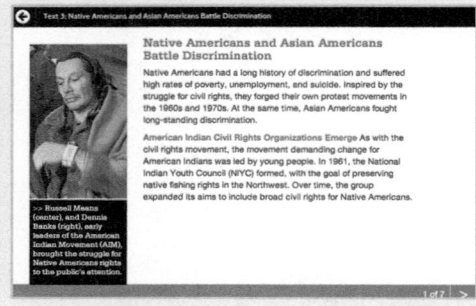

INTERACTIVE GALLERY

The Fight for American Indian Rights

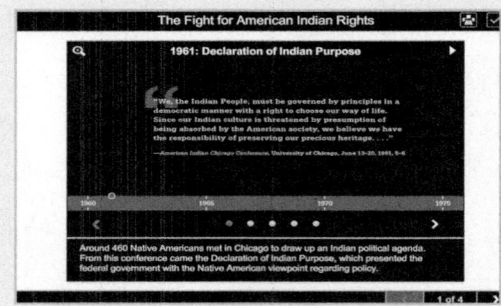

DIGITAL TEXT 4

Activists Win Rights for Consumers and the Disabled

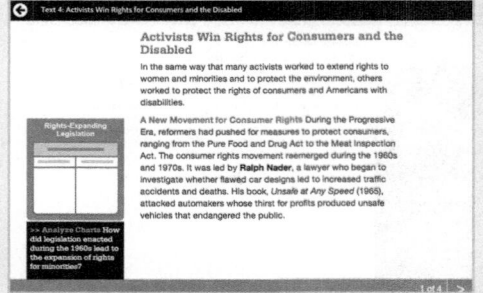

Objective 3: Evaluate the means by which Native Americans sought to expand their rights.

Quick Instruction

Interactive Gallery: The Fight for American Indian Rights Project the gallery and click through the images to reveal information about the roles of political organizations that promoted civil rights, including ones from American Indian civil rights movements.

Analyze Images What does the image of President Nixon meeting with Native Americans in traditional tribal dress in tell you about the role of culture in the Native American's struggle for civil rights? *(Culture and history were important elements of the Native American experience. The Native American chiefs' tribal dress clearly demonstrated the importance of their cultural past to their identities today.)*

📷 ACTIVE CLASSROOM

Have students break into groups and use the Circle Write Strategy to address the prompt "Was it necessary for Native American civil rights organizations to use militant tactics?" Have students write as much as they can for one minute and then switch with the person on their right. The next person tries to improve or elaborate the response where the other person left off. Continue to switch until the paper comes back to the first person. The group decides which is the best composition and shares that with the class.

Further Instruction

Be sure students show understanding of the roles of political organizations that promoted civil rights, including ones from other civil rights movements and how Native American groups were related to the others.

Generate Explanations Describe how litigation such as the landmark case of *Delgado* v. *Bastrop I.S.D.* helped pave the way for Native American legal challenges to discrimination. (Cases such as Delgado v. Bastrop I.S.D. *and* Mendez v. Westminster *outlawed segregation based on ethnicity, giving Native Americans legal grounds to challenge discriminatory practices.)*

Identify Central Issues What had been the main cause of the Japanese American Citizens League? *(This group had worked for decades to receive government compensation for property lost by Japanese Americans interned in camps during World War II.)*

Objective 4: Describe the expansion of rights for consumers and the disabled.

Quick Instruction

Project the image of the Special Olympics on the whiteboard. Explain that Marshall was an African American lawyer who argued the landmark case *Brown* v. *Board of Education* and became the first African American to serve on the Supreme Court. Why was litigation used as a method for achieving equality and expanding the right to participate in the democratic process? *(The legislative and executive branches were not promoting reforms.)* Ask students to name other methods of expanding the right to participate in the democratic process. (lobbying and non-violent protesting) Ask students how Congress can help achieve equality of political rights. (by passing congressional acts)

Predict Consequences Do you think rights for people with disabilities would have been achieved earlier if FDR had openly shown his disability? Explain. *(Yes. FDR's refusal to show his disability only hid the issue from the American people. Had he been more open about it, he would have shown the American people that people with disabilities could function as influential members of society.)*

Determine Relevance How did returning soldiers from World War II and the Korean War contribute to the fight for civil rights for people with disabilities? *(Many veterans of these wars were disabled during their times of service. As they moved back into American society they took part in this activism.)*

PEARSON realize ™
www.PearsonRealize.com
Access your Digital Lesson

■ SYNTHESIZE

DIGITAL ACTIVITY

Identify the Social Issues Affecting Various Minorities

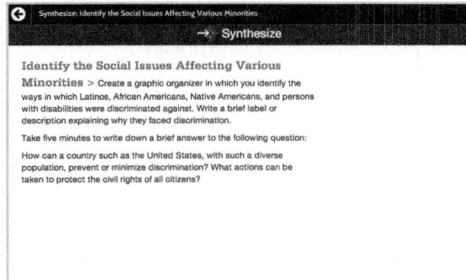

Have students use information from the readings to create a graphic organizer in which they identify the ways in which Latinos, African Americans, Native Americans, and persons with disabilities were discriminated against. Have students discuss their conclusions with a partner, explaining their reasoning.

Have students think about the following question: How can a country such as the United States, with such a diverse population, prevent or minimize discrimination? What actions can be taken to protect the civil rights of all citizens? Have students give examples from the text.

■ DEMONSTRATE

DIGITAL QUIZ

Lesson Quiz and Class Discussion Board

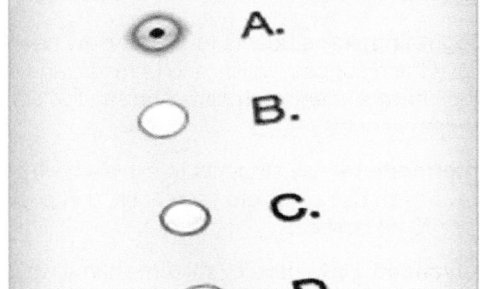

Assign the online Lesson Quiz for this lesson if you haven't already done so. Students will be offered automatic remediation or enrichment based on their score.

Pose these questions to the class on the Discussion Board:

In *Expanding the Push for Equality*, you continued your exploration of the historical development of the civil rights movement in the 20th century, reading about the actions taken by diverse minority groups.

Identify Cause and Effect Protest was often used to expand the right to participate in the democratic process. Describe a protest used by a political organization that promoted expanded civil rights during the 1960s and 1970s and explain its causes and effects. *(The United Farmworkers used a boycott strategy. First, activists identified the problem; Then organizers generated awareness; Organizers gather support from others who refused to buy grapes; The boycott forced businesses or producers to respond to economic pressure. Effects: In the end, the grape growers signed historic contracts with the Chavez-led workers in 1969 that led to better working conditions.)*

Contrast The methods to expand civil rights used by Latinos with the efforts of those in the American Indian Movement. Why did the American Indian Movement face a backlash from its efforts? *(The United Farmworkers relied on nonviolent methods, while AIM often used violent tactics that upset many Americans.)*

Topic Inquiry

Have students continue their investigations for the Topic Inquiry.

ELL Use the ELL activity described in the ELL chart.

Further Instruction

Review with students how reformers had pushed for measures to protect consumers during the Progressive Era. (Upton Sinclair's book The Jungle, *the Pure Food and Drug Act, Meat Inspection Act)*

Draw Conclusions How did technology spur a new consumer rights movement during the 1960s and 1970s? *(New automobile designs and technology led Ralph Nader to investigate whether flawed car designs led to increased traffic accidents and deaths.)*

Identify Central Issues How did the groups that promoted consumer protections influence government legislation? *(They conducted scientific research and lobbied Congress.)*

The Environmental Movement

Supporting English Language Learners

Use with Digital Text 1, Environmental Activists Sound the Alarm.

Speaking

Tell students that when they explain something, they clarify it by giving details about it. Prompt students to explain with increasing specificity and detail.

Beginning Ask students to explain how people harm the environment. Have them suggest words and phrases, and record them on a list. Then have students complete and say this sentence: People harm the environment by _____.

Intermediate Ask students to explain how people harm the environment. Have them use complete sentences, and encourage them to be as specific as possible.

Advanced Have pairs of students name ways that people harm the environment and explain specifically how or why they are harmful. To structure and record their discussion, encourage pairs to record the actions and explanatory details in a two-column chart.

Advanced High Have pairs of students take turns explaining these boldface words from the text: *Rachel Carson, toxic waste, Earth Day, EPA*. Encourage them to include as much specificity and detail as possible, using both information from the text and any background knowledge they have.

Use with Digital Text 2, Impact of Environmental Regulations.

Listening

Explain that before speaking about a topic from the text, you will be providing students linguistic support by pre-teaching new or difficult vocabulary in order to enhance and confirm student understanding.

Beginning Pre-teach basic key vocabulary that you will use to speak about the incident at Love Canal. Have students confirm their understanding of spoken language by answering this question: What were companies dumping in the ground at Love Canal?

Intermediate Pre-teach key vocabulary that you will use to speak about the incident at Love Canal. Have students confirm their understanding of spoken language by answering this question: Why were residents of Love Canal getting sick?

Advanced Pre-teach key vocabulary that you will use to speak about the meltdown at Three Mile Island and the reaction to it. Have small groups enhance and confirm their understanding of spoken language by discussing how they would react if such an event happened near their home.

Advanced High Pre-teach key vocabulary that you will use to compare and contrast Love Canal and Three Mile Island. Have pairs of students enhance and confirm their understanding of spoken language by using the pre-taught vocabulary to retell what you said.

▶ Differentiate Instruction

Use the Differentiated Instruction notes throughout the lesson plan to support the varied skill sets, levels of readiness, and interests in the mixed-ability classroom.

Challenge These notes include suggestions for expanding the activity for advanced students.

On-Level These notes include suggestions for modifying the activity to address different interests or learning styles.

Extra Support These notes include ideas for providing more scaffolding or reading spuport.

Special Needs These notes provide ideas for adapting instruction to support the needs of various special needs students.

■ NOTES

PEARSON
realize™
www.PearsonRealize.com

Go online to access additional resources including:
Primary Sources • Biographies • Supreme Court cases •
21st Century Skill Tutorials • Maps • Graphic Organizers.

Objectives

Objective 1: Assess the causes and effects of the environmental movement.

Objective 2: Analyze why environmental protection became a controversial issue.

LESSON 4 ORGANIZER		OBJECTIVES	PACING	RESOURCES	
PACING: APPROX. 1 PERIOD, .5 BLOCKS				Online	Print
Connect					
DIGITAL START UP ACTIVITY **An Environmental Wake-up Call**			5 min.	●	
Investigate					
DIGITAL TEXT 1 **Environmental Activists Sound the Alarm**		Objective 1	10 min.	●	●
INTERACTIVE CHART **Environmental Protection Versus Economic Development**			10 min.	●	
DIGITAL TEXT 2 **Impact of Environmental Regulations**		Objective 2	10 min.	●	●
INTERACTIVE MAP **Superfund Sites**			10 min.	●	
Synthesize					
DIGITAL ACTIVITY **Addressing Environmental Concerns**			5 min.	●	
Demonstrate					
DIGITAL QUIZ **Lesson Quiz and Class Discussion Board**			10 min.	●	

The Environmental Movement

■ CONNECT

DIGITAL START UP ACTIVITY
An Environmental Wake-up Call

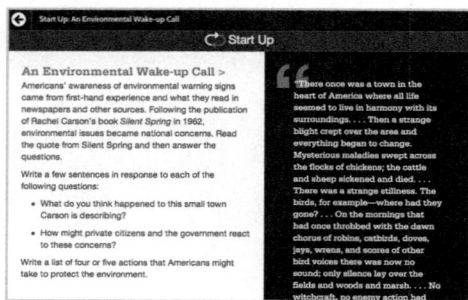

Project the Start Up Activity Ask students to read the quote as they enter and get settled. Then have them write a paragraph reflecting on the quote. Have students share their ideas with a partner, either in class or through a chat or blog space.

Discuss Take a moment to reflect on how the mysterious environmental maladies that Carson describes may have alarmed the residents of the community. What do you think the community residents would have done next?

Tell students that in this lesson they will be learning about the emergence of an environmental movement in which private citizens and the government assumed roles in managing the environment.

Aa Vocabulary Development: Use the Interactive Reading Notepad to preview the Key Terms and Academic Vocabulary in this lesson with students.

⇅ FLIP IT!
Assign the Flipped Video for this lesson.

■ STUDENT EDITION PRINT PAGES: 774–777

■ INVESTIGATE

DIGITAL TEXT 1
Environmental Activists Sound the Alarm

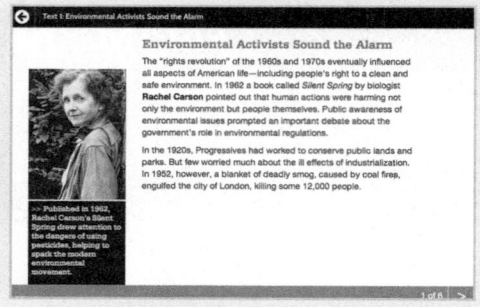

INTERACTIVE CHART
Environmental Protection Versus Economic Development

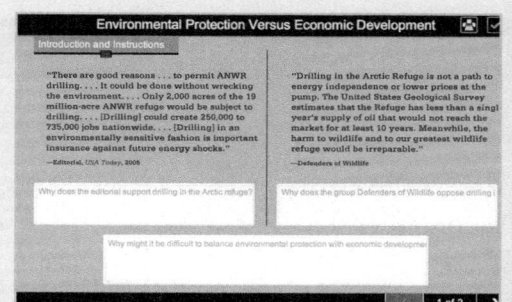

Objective 1: **Assess the causes and effects of the environmental movement.**

Quick Instruction
Interactive Chart: Environmental Protection Versus Economic Development Project the interactive chart and have student volunteers read the quotes. Challenge students to identify what they think are the key issues involved in drilling in Alaska's Arctic National Wildlife Refuge. (The key issue is whether it is possible to drill for oil safely in an area that is environmentally sensitive.)

Summarize Challenge students to identify the roles of governmental entities and private citizens in managing the environment. *(Private citizens belonged to environmental groups like the Sierra Club and the Wilderness Society that worked to protect environmentally sensitive areas. Millions of private citizens also took part in Earth Day activities in support of environmental issues. The federal government created the Environmental Protection Agency (EPA) to protect the "entire ecological chain." The government also passed legislation like the Endangered Species Act, the Clean Air Act, and the Clean Water Act to protect endangered plants and animals and to limit pollution in the air and water.)*

Evaluate Arguments What are the overriding concerns of the two arguments presented? *(The chief concern expressed in the USA Today editorial is the beneficial economic impact drilling might have. In this argument, jobs and energy security are the most important considerations. The Defenders of Wildlife argument is based on concern for the*

environment. It argues that harm to wildlife and the refuge due to drilling would be irreparable.)

💬 ACTIVE CLASSROOM

Have students use the Take a Stand Strategy to take a stand on the following issue: Should private citizens or the government play a more significant role in managing the environment? Ask students to divide into two groups based on their answer and move to separate areas of the classroom. Engage students in talking with each other to compare their reasons for their answers. Ask a representative from each side to present and defend the group's point of view.

D Differentiate: **Extra Support** After asking the students to take a stand, allow students five minutes to think about the question individually. Tell them to write down their response (Yes or No) and two reasons why they answered that way. Then continue with the group activity.

Further Instruction
Go through the Interactive Reading Notepad questions with the class. Be sure students understand the significant events that led to the emergence of the environmental movement. (London's Great Smog in 1952, publication of Silent Spring; Cuyahoga River fire)

Evaluate Impact Who was Rachel Carson and what role did she play in the environmental movement? *(Rachel Carson was an American biologist who wrote the book Silent Spring. In the book, Carson described how pesticides were harming birds*

DIGITAL TEXT 2

Impact of Environmental Regulations

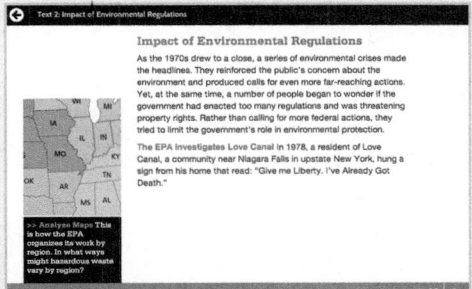

INTERACTIVE MAP

Superfund Sites

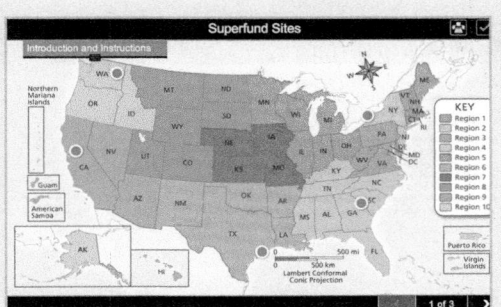

and other animals. She argued that human activity drastically altered the environment and that humans had a responsibility to protect it. Her work inspired widespread environmental activism among Americans.)

Interpret In what way does the *USA Today* editorial reflect concern over the impact of energy on the American way of life? *(The editorial urges drilling as a way to protect the nation against future energy shocks.)*

Objective 2: Analyze why environmental protection became a controversial issue.

Quick Instruction

Interactive Map: Superfund Sites Project the map and click through the hot spots on the map. Introduce the map activity by telling students that Congress established Superfund, a program financed by taxes on oil and certain chemicals, to clean up sites that had extreme environmental pollution.

Evaluate Arguments Some argue that private citizens would do a better job in managing the environment than the government because the owners had an interest in preserving the profitability of their land. Do you agree with this argument? Why or why not? *(Yes, I agree with the statement because private citizens who rely on their property to earn a living must do what's in the best interest to protect their land. They are more familiar with it and can probably act quicker to fix problems.)*

Draw Conclusions What does establishment of the Superfund program suggest about how the government viewed its role in protecting the environment? *(In some circumstances, the government believed that it needed to step in and stop pollution either because private businesses couldn't or wouldn't clean up the pollution on their own.)*

📰 ACTIVE CLASSROOM

Have students Make Headlines for each Superfund site depicted in the Interactive Map. Ask: If you were to write a headline for each site that captured the most important aspect that should be remembered, what would that headline be? Emphasize to students that their headlines should not just describe the pollution at the site, but also capture how it affected individuals and communities. Allow them to use subheadings if they would like. Have students pass their headlines to a partner for them to review.

Further Instruction

Point out that many Americans had concerns with far-reaching government environmental regulations. Many believed then and now that these regulations threaten personal property rights. Challenge students to discuss how government actions impact individuals, industries, communities and their respective Fifth Amendment property rights. To extend the lesson, assign *Geography Core Concepts: People's Impact on the Environment.*

Identify Point of View What basic assumptions about the environment did opponents to environmental regulation have? *(Many people thought that the environment provided valuable economic interests that the regulations obstructed.)*

The Environmental Movement

■ SYNTHESIZE

■ DEMONSTRATE

DIGITAL ACTIVITY
Addressing Environmental Concerns

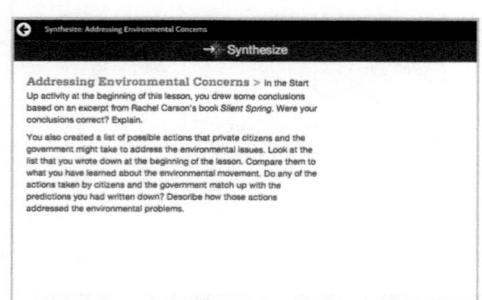

DIGITAL QUIZ
Lesson Quiz and Class Discussion Board

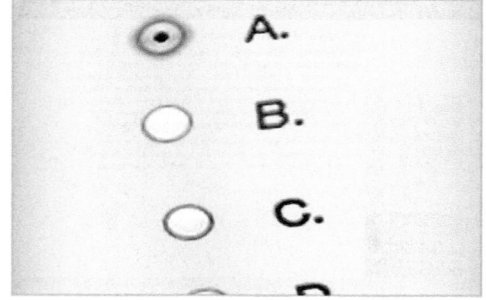

Discuss Before beginning the activity, lead the class in a brief review of how private citizens and government actions worked to manage the environment. Encourage students to use examples from the lesson. Then have students review their lists of possible actions that private citizens and the government might take to address the environmental issues that they created at the beginning of the lesson. Ask students to discuss how any of the actions taken by citizens and the government match up with the predictions they had written down.

Assign the online Lesson Quiz for this lesson if you haven't already done so. Students will be offered automatic remediation or enrichment based on their score.

Pose these questions to the class on the Discussion Board:

In *The Environmental Movement*, you read about how private citizens and the government worked to manage the environment.

Interpret Americans who became involved in the environmental movement were often very dedicated. What do you think motivated them?

Predict Consequences What impact will the environmental movement have on how the United States manages its public lands and natural resources?

The Two Sides of the Nixon Presidency

Supporting English Language Learners

Use with Digital Text 2, **Opening Relations with China.**

Speaking
Review the meaning of formal language and when it might be used. Explain that students will be adapting spoken language appropriately for a formal purpose.

Beginning Ask students to imagine meeting a Chinese leader to promote peace between nations. Have students choose the more formal greeting and say it aloud: (a) Thank you for your invitation to visit this beautiful nation. (b) Thanks! I'm thrilled to be here.

Intermediate Have students imagine meeting a Chinese leader to promote peace between nations. Ask them to share what they would say upon arriving in China and speaking with this person for the first time.

Advanced Have students imagine meeting a Chinese leader to promote peace between nations. Ask them to share what they would say upon arriving in China and speaking with this person for the first time. Then ask: How would your language change if it were informal instead?

Advanced High Have students imagine being part of meeting between American and Chinese leaders who wanted to promote peace between their nations. Ask pairs of students to play the roles of these leaders during their first meeting, using appropriate formal language.

Use with Digital Text 6, **The Watergate Scandal Brings Nixon Down.**

Listening
Locate a video or audio recording of President Nixon's resignation speech (it is available online). To prepare students for the activity, review the reason for Nixon's resignation. Prompt students to listen to and derive meaning from a variety of media to build and reinforce concept attainment.

Beginning Play the beginning of Nixon's resignation speech. To build and reinforce concept attainment, pause after every one or two sentences in order to restate a key point or answer students' questions.

Intermediate Play the beginning of Nixon's resignation speech. Bring up key points in the speech, and encourage students to ask questions about it, in order to build and reinforce concept attainment. Then play the recording again so students can derive further meaning from it.

Advanced Play Nixon's resignation speech. Then ask small groups to build and reinforce concept attainment by identifying the main points of the speech. Consider providing a transcript of the speech to help students recall the content.

Advanced High Play Nixon's resignation speech. Then ask pairs of students to build and reinforce concept attainment by discussing these questions: What main points did Nixon make? How did the speech add to your understanding of Nixon's presidency and the Watergate scandal?

▣ Differentiate Instruction

Use the Differentiated Instruction notes throughout the lesson plan to support the varied skill sets, levels of readiness, and interests in the mixed-ability classroom.

Challenge These notes include suggestions for expanding the activity for advanced students.

On-Level These notes include suggestions for modifying the activity to address different interests or learning styles.

Extra Support These notes include ideas for providing more scaffolding or reading spuport.

Special Needs These notes provide ideas for adapting instruction to support the needs of various special needs students.

■ NOTES

The Two Sides of the Nixon Presidency

Objectives

Objective 1: Describe Richard Nixon's leadership in foreign policy.

Objective 2: Define Nixon's foreign policy toward China and the Soviet Union.

Objective 3: Describe Richard Nixon's attitude toward "big" government.

Objective 4: Analyze Nixon's southern strategy.

Objective 5: Describe the effects of the Watergate political scandal.

LESSON 5 ORGANIZER		PACING: APPROX. 1 PERIOD, .5 BLOCKS		
	OBJECTIVES	**PACING**	**Online**	**Print**
Connect				
DIGITAL START UP ACTIVITY **To Impeach or Not?**		5 min.	●	
Investigate				
DIGITAL TEXT 1 **Nixon's New Approach to Foreign Policy**	Objective 1	10 min.	●	●
DIGITAL TEXT 2 **Opening Relations With China**		10 min.	●	●
DIGITAL TEXT 3 **Nixon's Policy of Détente**	Objective 2	10 min.	●	●
INTERACTIVE MAP **Nixon's Foreign Policy**		10 min.	●	
DIGITAL TEXT 4 **Nixon's Domestic Policy**	Objective 3	10 min.	●	●
DIGITAL TEXT 5 **Nixon's "Southern Strategy"**	Objective 4	10 min.	●	●
DIGITAL TEXT 6 **The Watergate Scandal Brings Nixon Down**		10 min.	●	●
INTERACTIVE CHART **Key Events of the Watergate Scandal**	Objective 5	10 min.	●	
Synthesize				
DIGITAL ACTIVITY **The Presidency at Stake**		5 min.	●	
Demonstrate				
DIGITAL QUIZ **Lesson Quiz and Class Discussion Board**		10 min.	●	

PEARSON
realize™
www.PearsonRealize.com

Go online to access additional resources including:
Primary Sources • Biographies • Supreme Court cases •
21st Century Skill Tutorials • Maps • Graphic Organizers.

■ CONNECT

DIGITAL START UP ACTIVITY
To Impeach or Not?

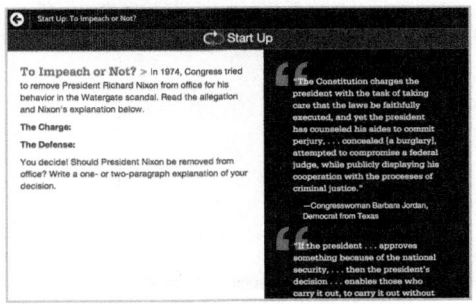

Project the Start Up Activity As students
enter and get settled, direct their attention
to the quotes from the Watergate scandal.
Ensure students understand that "perjury"
means lying under oath. Encourage students
to spend a minute prewriting—organizing their
thoughts, jotting down a rough outline—before
they begin writing their paragraphs. Have
students share their ideas with a partner.

Tell students that in this lesson they will
be learning about the presidential terms
of Richard Nixon, and how the Watergate
scandal rocked his presidency and the nation's
trust in its government and leaders.

Aa **Vocabulary Development:** Use the
Interactive Reading Notepad to preview the
Key Terms and Academic Vocabulary in this
lesson with students.

↕ FLIP IT!
Assign the Flipped Video for this lesson.

■ STUDENT EDITION PRINT
PAGES: 778–788

■ INVESTIGATE

DIGITAL TEXT 1
Nixon's New Approach to Foreign Policy

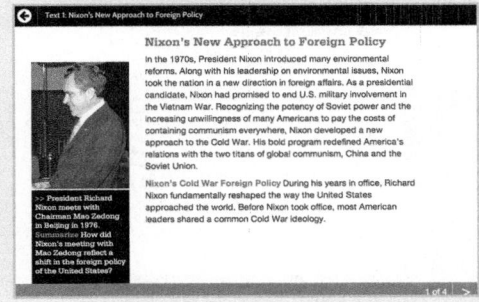

Objective 1: Describe Richard Nixon's leadership in foreign policy.

Quick Instruction

Analyze Images Project the image of
President Nixon and Mao Zedong. Use the
image as a springboard to begin a discussion
on the tensions that existed between the
United States and the communist countries at
the time. Challenge students to identify some
of the key reasons that created these tensions.
(The key issue was the most American and
communist leaders shared a common Cold
War ideology. They stressed that a basic
conflict existed between democratic, capitalist
countries and totalitarian, communist ones.
The alliances that formed between countries
on this issue also heightened tensions.)

Draw Conclusions Ask students to analyze
information by drawing conclusions. Ask: Did
Richard Nixon position the United States to
reduce tensions during the Cold War? Why
or why not *(Yes. Nixon's new approach to
dealing with the communist countries was
more flexible and pragmatic and avoided
focusing on the ideological absolutes that
caused tensions. Nixon was more open to
trying different strategies, including more talks
and possible economic cooperation. These
new approaches lessened tensions between
rival countries.)*

Further Instruction

Go through the Interactive Reading Notepad
questions and use them to extend the
discussion of Nixon's foreign policies shifts.
Be sure students understand the concept of
realpolitik: (political goals should be defined by
concrete national interests instead of abstract
ideologies).

Contrast How did Nixon and Kissinger's view
of communism differ from that of previous
Presidents and American foreign policy
leaders? *(Unlike previous American leaders,
Nixon and Kissinger believed that there was
no united worldwide communist movement.
Nixon and Kissinger also saw China and
the Soviet Union—America's ideological
enemies— as potential trading partners.)*

The Two Sides of the Nixon Presidency

DIGITAL TEXT 2
Opening Relations With China

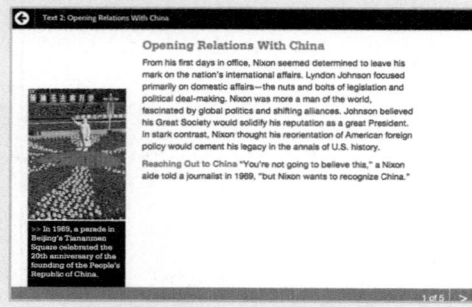

DIGITAL TEXT 3
Nixon's Policy of Détente

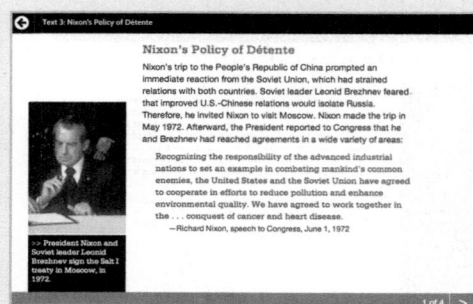

INTERACTIVE MAP
Nixon's Foreign Policy

Objective 2: Define Nixon's foreign policy toward China and the Soviet Union.

Quick Instruction

Interactive Map: Nixon's Foreign Policy Project the interactive map and have students click on the red hotspots to learn more about Nixon's policies and actions in various parts of they world. How did Nixon's actions in response the political turmoil in Chile reflect previous presidents' view of communism? *(Nixon's aiding anticommunist groups in Chile is similar to what happened in Vietnam. Nixon's actions seemed to be motivated by the "domino theory." If communism gained a foothold in South America then other countries might also succumb.)*

Summarize Describe Richard M. Nixon's leadership in the normalization of relations with China. *(Nixon showed great courage in breaking with the long-held policy of not recognizing communist China. He also showed keen foresight and political intelligence in seeing China as a possible partner in various ways.)*

🗣 ACTIVE CLASSROOM

Have students break into groups and use the Circle Write Strategy to address the prompt, "Why was normalizing relations with China a smart political decision?" Have students write as much as they can for one minute and then pass their response to the person on their right. Students then try to to improve or elaborate the response where the other person left off. Continue to pass papers until each paper returns to its original author. The group decides which is the best composition and shares that with the class.

ELL Use the ELL activity described in the ELL chart.

Further Instruction

Discuss the events that precipitated the thawing of relations between the Soviet Union and the United States. *(Nixon's trip to the People's Republic of China concerned Soviet leader Leonid Brezhnev. The Soviet Union had strained relations with both China and the United States. Brezhnev feared that improved U.S.-Chinese relations would isolate the Soviets.).* Be sure students understand the concept of détente and Nixon's leadership in adopting the policy. *(Nixon promoted the concept of détente—a flexible diplomacy—to ease tensions between the United States, Soviet Union, and People's Republic of China.)*

Draw Conclusion Why did Nixon and Kissinger believe détente was a beneficial foreign policy? *(Détente allowed the United States to adopt more flexible policies with the Soviet Union and China. Opening deeper relationships with these countries eased the mistrust between them. It also offered economic benefits.)*

Determine Relevance What was the significance of the SALT I treaty? *(In the short-term, SALT I froze the deployment of intercontinental ballistic missiles (ICBMs) and placed limits on antiballistic missiles (ABMs). The long-term significance was that it reduced tensions between the Soviet Union and the United States.)*

DIGITAL TEXT 4

Nixon's Domestic Policy

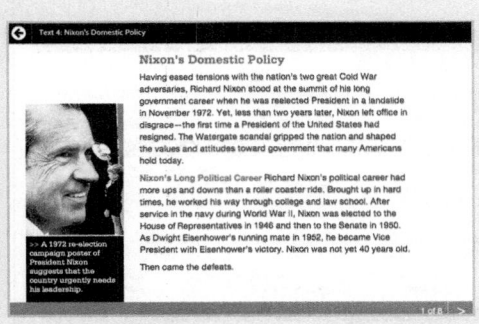

Nixon's Domestic Policy

Having eased tensions with the nation's two great Cold War adversaries, Richard Nixon stood at the summit of his long government career when he was reelected President in a landslide in November 1972. Yet, less than two years later, Nixon left office in disgrace—the first time a President of the United States had resigned. The Watergate scandal gripped the nation and shaped the values and attitudes toward government that many Americans hold today.

Nixon's Long Political Career Richard Nixon's political career had more ups and downs than a roller coaster ride. Brought up in hard times, he worked his way through college and law school. After service in the navy during World War II, Nixon was elected to the House of Representatives in 1946 and then to the Senate in 1950. As Dwight Eisenhower's running mate in 1952, he became Vice President with Eisenhower's victory. Nixon was not yet 40 years old.

Then came the defeats.

>> A 1972 re-election campaign poster of President Nixon suggests that the country urgently needs his leadership.

DIGITAL TEXT 5

Nixon's "Southern Strategy"

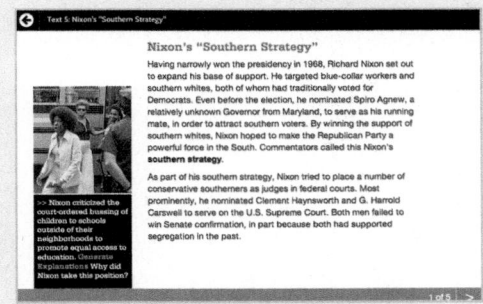

Nixon's "Southern Strategy"

Having narrowly won the presidency in 1968, Richard Nixon set out to expand his base of support. He targeted blue-collar workers and southern whites, both of whom had traditionally voted for Democrats. Even before the election, he nominated Spiro Agnew, a relatively unknown Governor from Maryland, to serve as his running mate, in order to attract southern voters. By winning the support of southern whites, Nixon hoped to make the Republican Party a powerful force in the South. Commentators called this Nixon's **southern strategy.**

As part of his southern strategy, Nixon tried to place a number of conservative southerners as judges in federal courts. Most prominently, he nominated Clement Haynsworth and G. Harrold Carswell to serve on the U.S. Supreme Court. Both men failed to win Senate confirmation, in part because both had supported segregation in the past.

>> Nixon criticized the court-ordered bussing of children to schools outside of their neighborhoods to promote equal access to education. Generate Explanations Why did Nixon take this position?

Objective 3: Describe Richard Nixon's attitude toward "big" government.

Quick Instruction

Review the term *stagflation* with students and discuss the causes of the stagflation that gripped the United States during the Nixon Presidency. (Stagflation is when a country is experiencing a stagnating economy along with inflationary pressures. The stagflation in the 1970s was caused by expanding federal budget deficits and rising foreign competition, which cost thousands of Americans their jobs. The nation's financial troubles were also tied to the economic impact of defense spending during the Vietnam War.)

Analyze Images Project the image of the Nixon 1972 presidential campaign poster. Invite students to suggest reasons why Nixon and his supporters used the phrase "Now more than ever." *(They believed that Nixon could build on the successes he had with foreign policy to tackle domestic issues that were emerging.)*

Identify Central Issues Challenge students to describe the dynamic relationship between U.S. international trade policies and the U.S. free enterprise system such as the Organization of Petroleum Exporting Countries (OPEC) oil embargo. *(The United States relied on importing nearly one-third of its energy, including oil that was regulated by OPEC. When OPEC's Arab members placed an oil embargo on Israel's allies, including the United States, oil prices skyrocketed 400 percent in a single year. These policies ran counter to the U.S. free enterprise system because prices*

and the supply of oil were heavily regulated by governments rather than by market demands.)

D Differentiate: Extra Support Explain that inflation is an economic term that means rising prices. During inflationary periods, the value of your money decreases and it takes more money to buy things.

Further Instruction

Under Nixon, aid to long-term entitlement programs like Medicare increased. Discuss the solvency of such programs with students.

Support a Point of View with Evidence Why might some people argue that Nixon's goal of reducing the power of the federal government large government was undermined by the actions his administration took? *(The Nixon administration created new government agencies to deal with domestic issues, like the Occupational Safety and Health Administration, the Drug Enforcement Administration, and the Environmental Protection Agency.)*

Summarize the goal of President Nixon's "new federalism." (Nixon wanted to reverse the flow of power and resources from Washington back to the states and communities. Nixon proposed that the federal government give the states the money to fund social programs. The states then controlled the operations of these programs.)

Summarize How did Nixon respond to the economic problems he faced as President? *(To fight the stagflation, Nixon ended the convertibility between dollars and gold, meaning that dollars were no longer tied to gold prices. Nixon also placed a 90-day freeze on all wages and prices.)*

Objective 4: Analyze Nixon's southern strategy.

Quick Instruction

Analyze Maps Project the image of the 1972 Election Results Map. Explain that Nixon barely won the presidency in 1968. He realized that he needed to expand his base of support. During his first term, Nixon targeted blue-collar workers and southern whites, both of whom had traditionally voted for Democrats. Invite volunteers to describe what was significant about the presidential election of 1972? *(Nixon won in a landslide, capturing almost every state.)* Point out that Nixon became the first Republican presidential candidate to sweep the entire South.

Formulate Questions Ask students to think about how the government and the private sector have attempted to create economic opportunities for citizens through policies such as affirmative action. Challenge students to think of arguments for and against affirmative action. (Some students may say that affirmative action policies are form of discrimination based race or gender, while others may say that groups facing discrimination need support.)

Further Instruction

Go through the Interactive Reading Notepad questions with the class and use them to extend the discussion of Nixon's civil rights policies. Be sure students understand affirmative action. (Policies that give special consideration to women and minorities in the fields of education and employment, in order to make up for past discrimination.)

The Two Sides of the Nixon Presidency

DIGITAL TEXT 6

The Watergate Scandal Brings Nixon Down

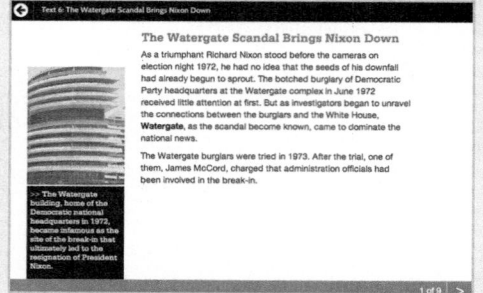

INTERACTIVE CHART

Key Events of the Watergate Scandal

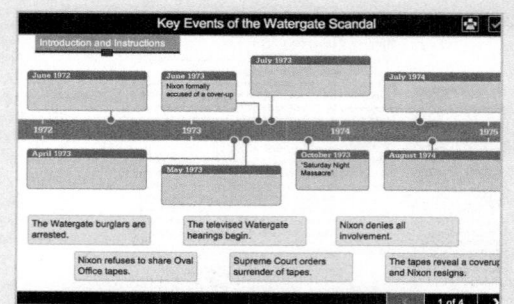

Draw Conclusions In your opinion, why did Nixon call for a moratorium, or freeze, on court-ordered busing as part of his "southern strategy"? *(The greatest opposition to busing students and desegregation was in the South. By appealing to the interests of many Southern whites on this issue, Nixon gained support in Southern states.)*

Determine Point of View In what ways did Nixon appear to send mixed messages about civil rights? *(Nixon criticized the court-ordered busing of children to schools outside of their neighborhoods to promote equal access to education. He also tried to place a number of conservative southerners who had supported segregation in the past as judges on federal courts. Yet the Nixon administration also initiated affirmative action policies like the Philadelphia Plan, a program that promoted the hiring of minorities.)*

Objective 5: Describe the effects of the Watergate political scandal.

Quick Instruction

Interactive Chart: Key Events of the Watergate Scandal Project the interactive chart and have students look through the events and place the events in their appropriate location on the timeline. What does Nixon's refusal to turn over the White House tapes tell you about his view of the presidency? *(Nixon believed that the President is more powerful than Congress and has the right to keep some information private.)*

Analyze Information Ask students to describe the effects of the Watergate political scandal on the views of U.S. citizens concerning trust in the federal government and its leaders. *(Nixon's involvement in the Watergate scandal damaged the reputation of the presidency and shook the public's confidence in government. Polls revealed the percentage of Americans who believed in the truth of government statements plummeted from 80 percent to 33 percent.)*

📖 ACTIVE CLASSROOM

Direct students to have a "Conversation with President Nixon." Tell students to imagine that they are having a conversation with Nixon as the Watergate Hearings are proceeding. Direct each student to write down a question he or she would like to ask, then how Nixon would respond, and then what the student would say in response.

Further Instruction

Extend the lesson by assigning the landmark Supreme Court case *United States v. Nixon.* Review the concept of executive privilege. (The principle that the president has the right to keep certain information confidential) and ask students to describe instances in which executive privilege might be justified. (In situations that involve national security and when lives are at risk if the information is made public.)

Generate Explanations Do you think the numerous reforms Congress enacted after Watergate helped restore the public's confidence and faith in government and prevented abuses of power in the future? Explain. *(Americans are still skeptical of the government leaders. Calls for term limits is evidence of a general mistrust of officials who serve for long periods of time in government.)*

Draw Conclusions How did the Watergate scandal reveal the strength of American democracy? *(The scandal showed the system of checks and balances works when put to the test and that no person, not even the President, is above the law.)*

SYNTHESIZE

DIGITAL ACTIVITY
The Presidency at Stake

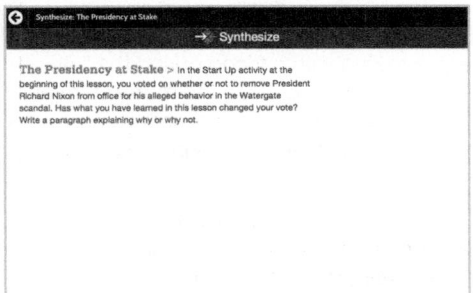

Engage students in reviewing their paragraphs from the activity at the beginning of this lesson, in which they explain their decision about removing President Richard Nixon from office for his alleged behavior in the Watergate scandal. Before students write their brief essays, hold a quick round table in which students review the details of the Watergate scandal.

Discuss Ask students if they would change their responses based on what they have learned in this lesson. Invite volunteers to share their answers and reasons with the class.

DEMONSTRATE

LESSON QUIZ
Lesson Quiz and Class Discussion Board

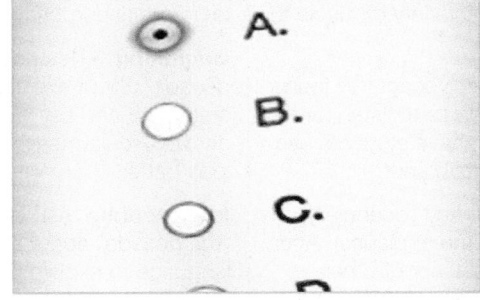

Assign the online Lesson Quiz for this lesson if you haven't already done so. Students will be offered automatic remediation or enrichment based on their score.

Pose these questions to the class on the Discussion Board:

In *The Two Sides of the Nixon Presidency*, you learned about Nixon the hard-line "Cold Warrior," a career-long opponent of communism who relaxed the nation's inflexible stance toward communism and applied a more pragmatic approach to foreign policy. You also read about his downfall—a result of his involvement in the Watergate scandal.

Predict Consequences Do you think Nixon's foreign policy breakthroughs will eventually lead to the United States to win the Cold War?

Draw Inferences Should Presidents be held to higher professional and legal standards than ordinary citizens? Why or why not?

Topic Inquiry
Have students continue their investigations for the Topic Inquiry.

Ford and Carter Struggle

Supporting English Language Learners

Use with Digital Text 5, **Success and Setback in the Middle East.**

Listening
Locate a video or audio recording of President Carter's remarks on the Camp David summit to use during the activity (it is available online). Prompt students to listen to and derive meaning from a variety of media to build and reinforce language attainment.

Beginning To build language attainment, pre-teach key vocabulary found in the opening sentences of Carter's remarks. Ask students to listen for the words as you play that segment of the recording. Then have students use the words in simple sentences to reinforce language attainment.

Intermediate To build language attainment, pre-teach key vocabulary found in the first two minutes of Carter's remarks (until the applause). After playing that segment of the recording, have students ask about other unfamiliar words. To reinforce language attainment, have students use the words in sentences related to the remarks.

Advanced To build language attainment, pre-teach key vocabulary found in Carter's remarks. After playing the recording, invite students to ask about additional words. Then have small groups use the vocabulary in a discussion about the remarks in order to reinforce language attainment.

Advanced High Play the recording of Carter's remarks, and prompt students to ask about the meanings of unfamiliar words. Answer students' questions in order to build language attainment. Then replay the recording to reinforce language attainment.

Use with Digital Text 6, **Unease Over Changing Values.**

Speaking
Review the meaning of informal language and when it might be used. Explain that students will be adapting spoken language appropriately for an informal purpose.

Beginning Ask students to imagine talking with a friend during the "me decade" about exercising more. Have students choose the more informal statement and say it aloud: (a) If I engage in more physical activity, my cardiovascular health will improve. (b) I'm going to start running so I can look better.

Intermediate Ask students to imagine talking with a friend during the "me decade" about self-improvement. Have them use informal spoken language to explain what activity they want to start and why.

Advanced Ask pairs of students to pretend they are friends talking about self-improvement during the "me decade." Have them use informal spoken language to talk about activities they have tried or want to try, such as meditation, eating healthy, and different types of exercise.

Advanced High Have students prepare a sales pitch for one of the "me decade" self-improvement activities mentioned in the text, using informal spoken language to sell their "product." Then place students in pairs, and have partners try out their sales pitches on each other.

▶ Differentiate Instruction

Use the Differentiated Instruction notes throughout the lesson plan to support the varied skill sets, levels of readiness, and interests in the mixed-ability classroom.

Challenge These notes include suggestions for expanding the activity for advanced students.

On-Level These notes include suggestions for modifying the activity to address different interests or learning styles.

Extra Support These notes include ideas for providing more scaffolding or reading spuport.

Special Needs These notes provide ideas for adapting instruction to support the needs of various special needs students.

■ NOTES

PEARSON **realize**.™
www.PearsonRealize.com

Go online to access additional resources including:
Primary Sources • Biographies • Supreme Court cases •
21st Century Skill Tutorials • Maps • Graphic Organizers.

Objectives

Objective 1: Evaluate the presidency of Gerald Ford.

Objective 2: Evaluate Ford's foreign policies.

Objective 3: Assess the domestic policies of Jimmy Carter.

Objective 4: Discuss changing U.S. foreign policy in the developing world.

Objective 5: Analyze how American society changed in the 1970s.

LESSON 6 ORGANIZER		PACING: APPROX. 1 PERIOD, .5 BLOCKS			
		OBJECTIVES	**PACING**	**RESOURCES**	
				Online	**Print**
Connect					
DIGITAL START UP ACTIVITY **President Ford's Risky Decision**			5 min.	●	
Investigate					
DIGITAL TEXT 1 **Ford Governs Through Difficult Times**		Objective 1	10 min.	●	●
DIGITAL TEXT 2 **Ford Continues Nixon's Foreign Policies**		Objective 2	10 min.	●	●
DIGITAL TEXT 3 **A New President Faces Challenges**		Objective 3	10 min.	●	●
DIGITAL TEXT 4 **Foreign Policy Changes Under Carter**			10 min.	●	●
DIGITAL TEXT 5 **Success and Setback in the Middle East**		Objective 4	10 min.	●	●
INTERACTIVE TIMELINE **Iran Hostage Crisis**			10 min.	●	
DIGITAL TEXT 6 **Unease Over Changing Values**		Objective 5	10 min.	●	●
INTERACTIVE CHART **The Supreme Court and Social Issues of the 1970s**			10 min.	●	
Synthesize					
DIGITAL ACTIVITY **Crisis of Confidence**			5 min.	●	
Demonstrate					
DIGITAL QUIZ **Lesson Quiz and Class Discussion Board**			10 min.	●	

Ford and Carter Struggle

CONNECT

DIGITAL START UP ACTIVITY

President Ford's Risky Decision

Project the Start Up Activity Ask students to think about the reasons Richard Nixon resigned from the office of the President and what might be the best way for the country to move beyond the Watergate scandal. Have students share their ideas with a partner.

Discuss Before students beginning writing their paragraphs in response to the question, "Should President Ford have pardoned former President Nixon for any crimes he might have committed while President?" have them think about the role of the President and how that contributes to Americans' view of government.

Tell students that in this lesson they will be learning about how Presidents Ford and Carter tried to move the nation beyond the Watergate scandal during the 1970s.

Aa Vocabulary Development: Use the Interactive Reading Notepad to preview the Key Terms and Academic Vocabulary in this lesson with students.

⇅ FLIP IT!

Assign the Flipped Video for this lesson.

■ STUDENT EDITION PRINT PAGES: 789–798

INVESTIGATE

DIGITAL TEXT 1

Ford Governs Through Difficult Times

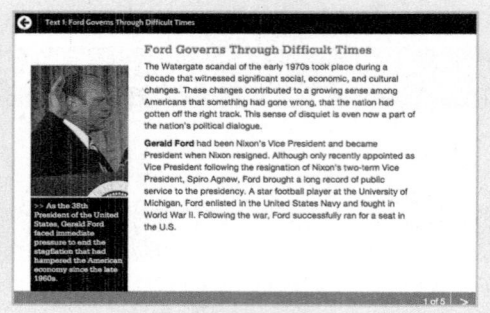

Objective 1: Evaluate the presidency of Gerald Ford.

Quick Instruction

Analyze Images Project the image of the group of people protesting the Nixon pardon. Invite volunteers to explain why Ford pardoned Nixon and how the public reacted. (Ford believed that giving Nixon a pardon would help to restore confidence in government and perhaps put the scandal to rest. Many Americans, however, had the opposite reaction. Many questioned Ford's integrity, implying that he had made a secret deal with Nixon to get the Vice President position. The pardon seemed to heighten the public's mistrust of government.)

Summarize the problems Ford faced as he assumed the presidency. (Ford had to deal with the fallout from the Watergate scandal. The scandal had helped cause the public to lose faith in government. Also, the United States was still struggling with severe economic problems.)

Further Instruction

Go through the Interactive Reading Notepad questions and use them to extend the discussion of the economic problems facing the United States at the time. Be sure students have an understanding of stagflation and inflation.

Draw Conclusions What aspect of Ford's WIN program might have led to its failure? (Students may say that the program was mostly voluntary.)

DIGITAL TEXT 2

Ford Continues Nixon's Foreign Policies

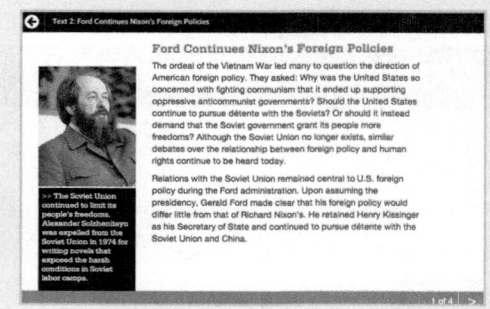

Objective 2: Evaluate Ford's Foreign Policies.

Quick Instruction

Analyze Images Project the image of Alexander Solzhenitsyn. Explain that he was a Russian writer who had spent eight years in Soviet prisons and labor camps for writing a letter in which he criticized Soviet leader Joseph Stalin. Solzhenitsyn's writing, which often described the harsh conditions in Soviet labor camps, earned him the Nobel Prize in Literature in 1970. He was expelled from the Soviet Union in 1974.

Express Problems Clearly What concerns did some Americans voice about U.S. participation in international treaties, such as Ford's continuation of detente and working on an arms treaty with the Soviet Union? (Some thought that Soviet violations of human rights should be forcefully addressed by Ford before reaching arms agreements.)

Generate Explanations What role should human rights play in American foreign policy? (Some students may say that human rights should be one of the chief concerns of U.S. foreign policy because our country has long been a supporter of protecting rights both at home and abroad.)

DIGITAL TEXT 3

A New President Faces Challenges

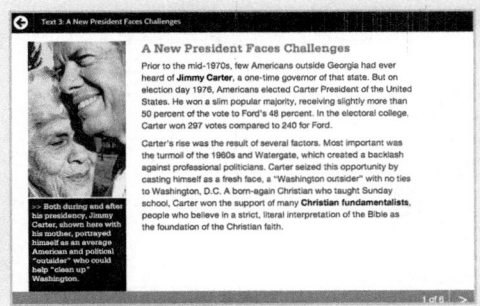

Text 3: A New President Faces Challenges

A New President Faces Challenges

Prior to the mid-1970s, few Americans outside Georgia had ever heard of **Jimmy Carter**, a one-time governor of that state. But on election day 1976, Americans elected Carter President of the United States. He won a slim popular majority, receiving slightly more than 50 percent of the vote to Ford's 48 percent. In the electoral college, Carter won 297 votes compared to 240 for Ford.

Carter's rise was the result of several factors. Most important was the turmoil of the 1960s and Watergate, which created a backlash against professional politicians. Carter seized this opportunity by casting himself as a fresh face, a "Washington outsider" with no ties to Washington, D.C. A born-again Christian who taught Sunday school, Carter won the support of many **Christian fundamentalists**, people who believe in a strict, literal interpretation of the Bible as the foundation of the Christian faith.

>> Both during and after his presidency, Jimmy Carter, shown here with his mother, portrayed himself as an average American and political "outsider" who could help "clean up" Washington.

1 of 6   >

Further Instruction

Briefly review the causes of the Vietnam War and the causes of U.S. involvement. Students should understand how the conflict divided Vietnam into two countries, the communist North and noncommunist South. Point out that North Vietnam took control of South Vietnam during Gerald Ford's presidency and established one nation under communist rule. Challenge students to describe how the fall of South Vietnam might affect the citizens of South Vietnam. *(Vietnamese who had supported the noncommunist South Vietnam government were probably afraid of what might happen to them. They were probably looking for ways to leave.)*

Hypothesize Why might American leaders have refused to intervene to when the communist Khmer Rouge government of Cambodia began a genocidal slaughter of civilians? *(The Vietnam War was still fresh in many American leaders' minds and they were probably concerned that getting involved in Cambodia would lead to another unpopular conflict in Southeast Asia.)*

Objective 3: Assess the domestic policies of Jimmy Carter.

Quick Instruction

Analyze Images Project the image of Jimmy Carter on the whiteboard. Explain that Carter took advantage of the public's unfavorable opinions of Washington and politicians and presented himself as a "Washington outsider" with no ties to Washington, D.C. Carter was a born-again Christian who taught Sunday school and sought to portray himself as an ordinary man—a "citizens' President." Ask: How might this photo of the President have contrasted with more formal images of previous Presidents? *(The photograph humanizes the Presidency.)*

Identify Central Issues Challenge students to identify and discuss the goals of the Community Reinvestment Act of 1977 in the private and public sectors. How did this act create economic opportunity for citizens? *(The Act's goal was to enable many low-to moderate-income Americans, especially ethnic minorities, to become homeowners for the first time. Banks were required to make loans in the same neighborhoods where they took deposits, which meant many citizens had the economic opportunity of home ownership.)* What was one possible unintended consequence of this attempt to create economic opportunity for citizens? *(the Community Reinvetment Act may have contributed to the mortgage crisis that triggered the Great Recession of 2007 to 2011.)*

Draw Conclusions What was the impact of Carter granting amnesty to Americans who had evaded the draft during the Vietnam War? *(Many Americans criticized the President for forgiving those who had refused to fight.)*

Further Instruction

Like Ford, Carter had to deal with a severe economic problems during his presidency. Ask students to identify the economic issues that plagued the United States during Carter's term. *(The two main issues were an energy crisis and severe inflation.)*

Summarize What impact did the energy crisis have on the American way of life during Carter's presidency? *The energy crisis had a negative impact on many Americans' standard of living. Gasoline prices increased and fuel shortages were difficult on businesses.*

Express Problems Clearly How did Jimmy Carter's inexperience hurt his presidency? *(Carter was an outsider and did not have close ties with the Democratic leadership in Congress. Carter submitted numerous bills to Congress, but few of them passed without major changes by his own party. He also surrounded himself with aides whose experience in Washington was limited.)*

Support a Point of View with Evidence How would you describe Jimmy Carter's response to the ongoing economic problems the country faced? *(Carter's response was not as successful as was necessary.)* What evidence supports your view? *(His response to the oil crisis was severely weakened because the final bill that passed Congress had few of his ideas in it and gas prices, inflation, and unemployment all increased.)*

Ford and Carter Struggle

DIGITAL TEXT 4

Foreign Policy Changes Under Carter

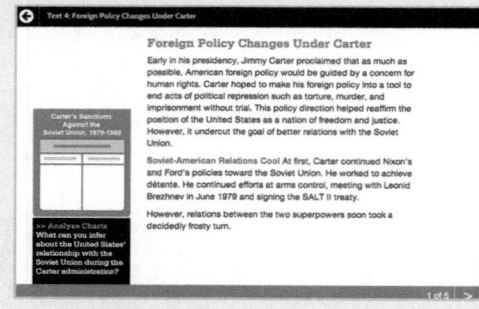

DIGITAL TEXT 5

Success and Setback in the Middle East

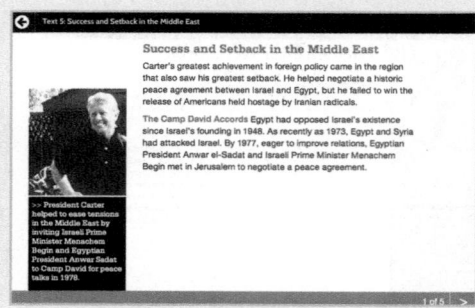

INTERACTIVE TIMELINE

Iran Hostage Crisis

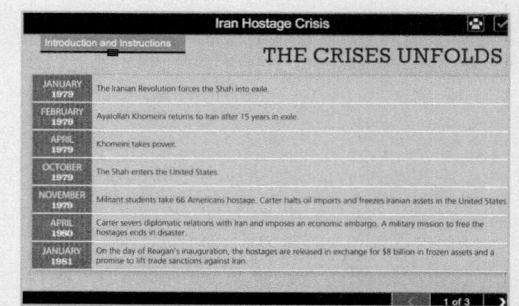

Objective 4: Discuss changing U.S. foreign policy in the developing world.

Quick Instruction

Interactive Timeline: Iran Hostage Crisis Project the interactive timeline and have students look through the images and information that describe U.S. involvement in the Middle East and the Iran Hostage Crisis. Ask students to explain the events leading up to the Iran Hostage Crisis and analyze how it may have been avoided. (The crisis followed months of growing anti-American sentiments in Iran. Some students may say that Carter could have held to his initial decision to not allow the Shah to come to the United States for medical treatment.)

Draw Inferences What did Carter's inability to secure the release of the hostages in Iran symbolize to many Americans? (For many Americans, it symbolized the growing weakness of America in world affairs.)

📷 ACTIVE CLASSROOM

Project the interactive timeline and have students use the images as a base to play an Act It Out game. Tell students to bring the figures in the images to life by stating what each must be thinking and feeling at the moment, and telling what happened just before and after the moment the image of each figure was made.

ELL Use the ELL activity described in the ELL chart.

Further Instruction

Go through the Interactive Reading Notepad questions and use them as a springboard to extend the discussion of changing U.S. foreign policy in the developing world. Ensure students' understanding of U.S. involvement in the Middle East and its support of Israel.

Draw Conclusions What role did the Camp David Accords play in the U.S. involvement in the Middle East? (The Camp David Accords helped to facilitate peace agreements between Egypt and Israel. As a result of the Camp David Accords, Egypt became the first Arab state to formally recognize Israel as a country.)

Identify Central Issues Identify and describe two regions in the world in which Carter's policies had a major impact. (Carter's policies had great impact in the Middle East and in Latin America. Carter's emphasis on expanding human rights through foreign policy led him to change the U.S. relationship with Latin American dictators. Carter continued U.S. support for Israel and led to the Camp David Accords and the easing of tension between Israel and Arab states in the region.)

DIGITAL TEXT 6

Unease Over Changing Values

INTERACTIVE CHART

The Supreme Court and Social Issues of the 1970s

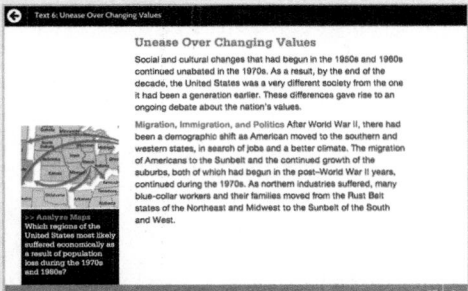

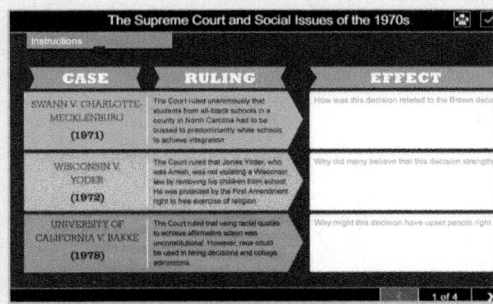

Objective 5: Analyze how American Society changed in the 1970s.

Quick Instruction

Remind students that demographic patterns began to change. Migration from within the United States from the Rust Belt to the Sun Belt continued. This was caused by the attraction of jobs and a warm climate. Demographic patterns also changed due to legal and illegal immigration to the United States. There were many reasons for this demographic shift over time. For example, many immigrants entered the country legally through work programs, while others crossed the border illegally. What were some effects of these changes? *(Immigrants came looking for work and a better life. As the population some immigrant groups grew, politicians began courting their vote.)*

Interactive Chart: The Supreme Court and Social Issues of the 1970s Project the chart to introduce students to some significant societal issues of this time period. Invite a volunteer to remind the class of why Supreme Court rulings are so important. *(The Supreme Court is the highest court in the land; its decisions cannot be appealed and have lasting effects on a great number of Americans.)* Discuss each case, and the general motivations of those who were involved. Ask students whether they agree with each decision, and why.

Evaluate Impact Ask students to evaluate the impact of groups such as the Moral Majority on American politics in the 1980s and how this was tied to societal issues of this time period. *(In response to societal changes such as the spread of countercultural values, groups like the Moral Majority helped create a conservative*

resurgence. Religious conservatives began forming alliances with other conservatives that led to them becoming a new political majority.)

🎦 ACTIVE CLASSROOM

Conduct a Circle Write Activity. Break into groups and provide the objective as a writing prompt: "Explain how the government and private citizens used litigation to expand rights." Have students write as much as they can for 1 minute then switch with the person on their right. The next person tries to improve or elaborate the response where the other person left off. Continue to switch until the paper comes back to the first person. The group then decides which is the best composition (or response) and shares that with the larger group.

D Differentiate: Type Ask students to do additional research on one of the cases presented in the interactivity and present their findings.

ELL Use the ELL activity described in the ELL chart.

Further Instruction

Begin a discussion on the causes and effects of the changing demographic patterns resulting from migration within the United States. Focus on Americans moving from the Rust Belt to the Sun Belt. Ensure students understand that many industries in the North were struggling. Many blue-collar workers and their families moved from the Rust Belt states of the Northeast and Midwest to the Sunbelt of the South and West for more employment and economic opportunities.

Infer Why might Americans who associated themselves with the Moral Majority have been pleased with the decision in *Wisconsin* v. *Yoder*? *Members of the Moral Majority were increasingly concerned with what they saw as a lack of religious freedom in the United States. The decision in* Wisconsin v. Yoder *upheld the constitutional principle of free exercise of religion.*

Analyze Information Based on the readings, how did changing demographics shift political power in the 1970s? *(The shift of population to the Sunbelt increased the likelihood of electing Presidents from the Sunbelt. The larger populations also shifted congressional power because House representation is based on power. Sunbelt states gained seats and Rust Belt states lost seats in the House.)*

Ford and Carter Struggle

■ SYNTHESIZE

DIGITAL ACTIVITY
Crisis of Confidence

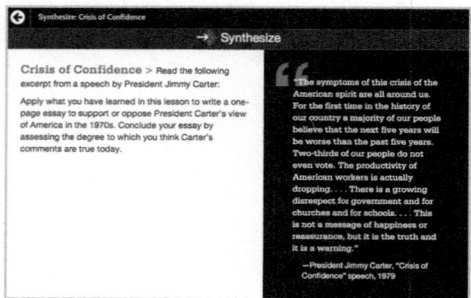

Have students discuss the quote and then review the lesson, taking notes on specific information to support their views. Have students share their paragraphs with the class and discuss the evidence used.

Have students think about the following question. What is the state of the "American Spirit" today?

■ DEMONSTRATE

LESSON QUIZ
Lesson Quiz and Class Discussion Board

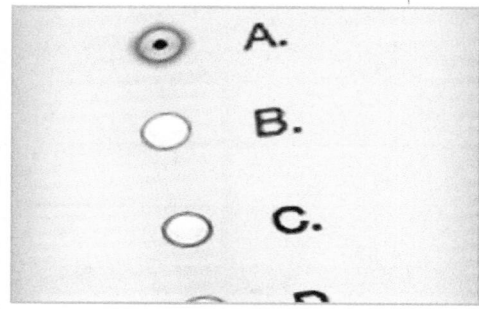

Assign the online Lesson Quiz for this lesson if you haven't already done so. Students will be offered automatic remediation or enrichment based on their score.

Pose these questions to the class on the Discussion Board:

In *Ford and Carter Struggle*, you read about a period in American history during which citizens developed negative opinions of their government and leaders. Economic crisis, shifting values, and an increasingly unstable developing world all contributed to this decade of unease.

Predict Consequences How do you think continued American support for Israel will affect U.S. foreign relations in the Middle East? Will the Camp David Accords achieve lasting peace?

Identify Cause and Effect How did the counterculture movement of the 1960s influence the changing values and styles of the "Me Decade" of the 1970s?

Topic Inquiry
Have students continue their investigations for the Topic Inquiry.

An Era of Change

SYNTHESIZE

DIGITAL ACTIVITY
Reflect on the Essential Question and Topic

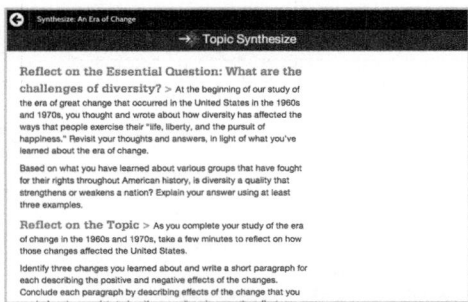

First ask students to reconsider the Essential Question for the Topic: What are the challenges of diversity? Remind students of that they considered this question in relation to various American groups seeking their "inalienable rights," including "life, liberty, and the pursuit of happiness."

Ask students "Do you think diversity is a quality that strengthens or weakens a nation?"Ask them to give at least two reasons to support their position. Discuss their answers as a class or ask students to post their answers on the Class Discussion Board.

Next ask students to reflect on the Topic as a whole and jot down 1-3 questions they've thought about during the Topic. Share these examples if students need help getting started:

- How do political and social divisions in the United States today compare to those of the 1960s and 1970s?
- Why did so many Americans feel such a sense of unease in the 1970s?
- How might the office of the President have been changed by the Nixon, Ford, and Carter administrations?

You may ask students to share their questions and answers on the Class Discussion Board.

Topic Inquiry
Have students complete Step 3 of the Topic Inquiry.

DEMONSTRATE

DIGITAL TOPIC REVIEW AND ASSESSMENT
An Era of Change

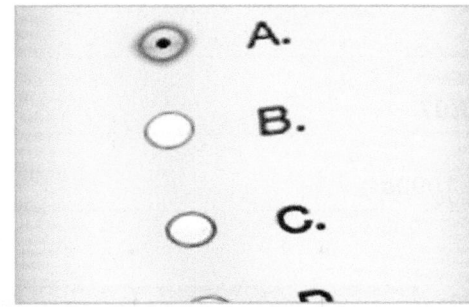

Students can prepare for the Topic Test by answering the questions in the Topic Review and Assessment online or the Assessment questions in the Print Student text. They can also prepare by reviewing their answers to the Interactive Reading Notepad questions or reviewing their notes in the Reading and Notetaking Study Guide.

DIGITAL TOPIC TEST
An Era of Change

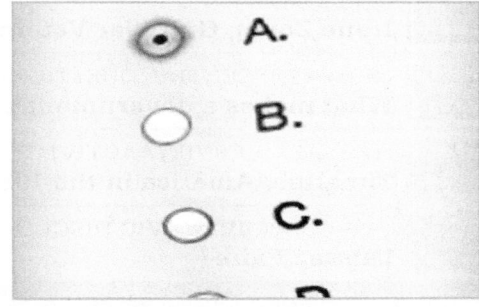

TOPIC TEST
Assign the Topic Test to assess students' understanding of topic content.

BENCHMARK TESTS
Assign these benchmark tests as you complete the relevant topics to monitor student progress toward mastering the course content and as preparation for the End-of-Course Test.

Benchmark Test 1: Topics 1–3

Benchmark Test 2: Topics 4–6

Benchmark Test 3: Topics 7–9

Benchmark Test 4: Topics 10–12

Benchmark Test 5: Topics 13–15

Benchmark Test 6: Topics 16–18

Benchmark Test 7: Topics 19–20

America in the 1980s and 1990s

TOPIC 19 ORGANIZER	PACING: APPROX. 8 PERIODS, 4 BLOCKS
	PACING
Connect	1 period
MY STORY VIDEO **Irene Zoppi, Gulf War Veteran**	10 min.
DIGITAL ESSENTIAL QUESTION ACTIVITY **What makes a government successful?**	10 min.
DIGITAL OVERVIEW ACTIVITY **Timeline: America in the 1980s and 1990s**	10 min.
TOPIC INQUIRY: CIVIC DISCUSSION **Laissez Faire?**	20 min.
Investigate	2–5 periods
TOPIC INQUIRY: CIVIC DISCUSSION **Laissez Faire?**	Ongoing
LESSON 1 The Conservative Movement Surges	30–40 min.
LESSON 2 The Reagan Era	30–40 min.
LESSON 3 The Cold War Ends	30–40 min.
LESSON 4 A New Era in Foreign Policy	30–40 min.
LESSON 5 Clinton and the 1990s	30–40 min.
Synthesize	1 period
DIGITAL ACTIVITY **Reflect on the Essential Question and Topic**	10 min.
TOPIC INQUIRY: CIVIC DISCUSSION **Laissez Faire?**	20 min.
Demonstrate	1–2 periods
DIGITAL TOPIC REVIEW AND ASSESSMENT **America in the 1980s and 1990s**	10 min.
TOPIC INQUIRY: CIVIC DISCUSSION **Laissez Faire?**	20 min.

TOPIC INQUIRY: CIVIC DISCUSSION

Laissez Faire?

In this Topic Inquiry, students work in teams to examine different perspectives on this issue by analyzing several sources, arguing both sides of a Yes/No question, then developing and discussing their own point of view on the question: **Would laissez faire be the best economic policy for the United States?**

STEP 1: CONNECT
Develop Questions and Plan the Investigation

Launch the Civic Discussion
Divide the class into groups of four students. Students can access the materials they'll need in the online course or you can distribute copies to each student. Read the main question and introduction with the students.

Have students complete Step 1 by reading the Discussion Launch and filling in Step 1 of the Information Organizer. The Discussion Launch provides YES and NO arguments on the main question. Students should extract and paraphrase the arguments from the reading in Step 1 of their Information Organizers.

Next, students share within their groups the arguments and evidence they found to support the YES and NO positions. The group needs to agree on the major YES and NO points and each student should note those points in their Information Organizer.

Resources
- Student Instructions
- Discussion Launch
- Information Organizer

⏻ PROFESSIONAL DEVELOPMENT

Civic Discussion
Be sure to view the Civic Discussion Professional Development resources in the online course.

STEP 2: INVESTIGATE
Apply Disciplinary Concepts and Tools

Examine Sources and Perspectives
Students will examine sources with the goal of extracting information and perspectives on the main question. They analyze each source and describe the author's perspective on the main question and key evidence the author provides to support that viewpoint in Information Organizer Step 2.

Ask students to keep in mind:

- **Author/Creator:** Who created the source? An individual? Group? Government agency?
- **Audience:** For whom was the source created?
- **Date/Place:** Is there any information that reveals where and when the source was created?
- **Purpose:** Why was the source created? Discuss with students the importance of this question in identifying bias.
- **Relevance:** How does the source support one argument or another?

Suggestion: Reading the source documents and filling in Step 2 of the Information Organizer could be assigned as homework.

Resources
- Student Instructions
- Source documents
- Information Organizer

Laissez Faire? *(continued)*

STEP 3: SYNTHESIZE
Use Evidence to Formulate Conclusions

Formulate Compelling Arguments with Evidence

Now students will apply perspectives and evidence they extracted from the sources to think more deeply about the main question by first arguing one side of the issue, then the other. In this way students become more prepared to formulate an evidence-based conclusion on their own.

Within each student group, assign half of the students to take the position of YES on the main question and the others to take the position of NO. Students will work with their partners to identify the strongest arguments and evidence to support their assigned YES or NO position.

Present Yes/No Positions

Within each group, those assigned the YES position share arguments and evidence first. As the YES students speak, those assigned NO should listen carefully, take notes to fill in the rest of the Compelling Arguments Chart (Step 3 in Information Organizer) and ask clarifying questions.

When the YES side is finished, students assigned the NO position present while those assigned YES should listen, take notes, and ask clarifying questions. Examples of clarifyin questions are:

- I think you just said [x]. Am I understanding you correctly?
- Can you tell me more about [x]?
- Can you repeat [x]? I am not sure I understand, yet.

Suggestion: You may want to set a 5 minute time limit for each side to present. Provide a two-minute warning so that students make their most compelling arguments within the time frame.

Switch Sides

The students will switch sides to argue the opposite point of view. To prepare to present the other position, partners who first argued YES will use the notes they took during the NO side's presentation, plus add any additional arguments and evidence from the reading and sources. The same for students who first argued the NO position.

STEP 4: DEMONSTRATE
Communicate Conclusions and Take Informed Action

Individual Points of View

Now the students will have the opportunity to discuss the main question from their own points of view. To help students prepare for this discussion, have them reflect on the YES/NO discussions they have participated in thus far and fill in Step 4 of their Information Organizers.

After all of the students have shared their points of view, each group should list points of agreement, filling the last portion of Step 4 on their Information Organizers.

Reflect on the Discussion

Ask students to reflect on the civic discussion thinking about:

- The value of having to argue both the YES and NO positions.
- If their individual views changed over the course of the discussion and why.
- What they learned from participating in the discussion.

Resources

- Student Instructions
- Information Organizer

 PEARSON realize™

www.PearsonRealize.com
Access your Digital Lesson

INTRODUCTION

America in the 1980s and 1990s

After several decades during which progressive and liberal ideas dominated America politics, conservatism made a comeback in the 1980s. In the 1980s, voters elected Republican President Ronald Reagan whose foreign policies contributed to the collapse of the Soviet Union. The United States emerged from the Cold War as the world's sole superpower, but the country encountered obstacles as it tried to find its place in the "new world order." The 1990s brought prosperity as new technologies helped drive a decade of robust economic growth and change in many aspects of American life.

CONNECT

MY STORY VIDEO
Irene Zoppi, Gulf War Veteran

Watch a video about a military officer's experiences in the Gulf War.

Determine Point of View What was the Gulf War? *(The first war after the cold war, the Gulf War was the response of the United States and its allies to Iraq's invasion of neighboring Kuwait.)*

Determine Point of View What, according to Irene Zoppi, were the benefits to serving in the military? *(Irene Zoppi left Puerto Rico to join the military. She gained proficiency in English, and during her years of service was able to learn leadership skills, discipline, and a better understanding of people. She was able to serve while marrying and raising a family.)*

DIGITAL ESSENTIAL QUESTION ACTIVITY
What makes a government successful?

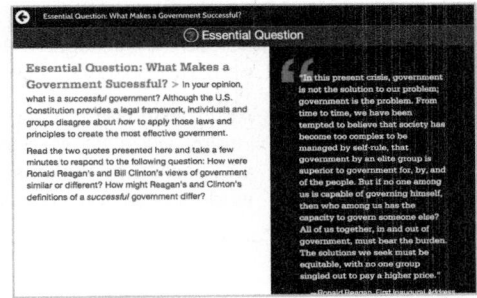

Ask students to think about the Essential Question for this topic: What makes a government successful? Determining the role, powers, and limits of the federal government has been a struggle throughout American history. What factors and forces influence Americans' relationship with the federal government? Have partners work together to list responsibilities and achievements that a government must accomplish to be considered "successful."

If students have not already done so, ask them to read the quotes and answer the questions. Then review student responses as a class.

Determine Point of View What responsibilities does a citizen have according to Ronald Reagan? *(Each citizen must be involved in the governing of the country by first being accountable for his or her own actions before asking government to rule.)*

Identify Central Issues Why does Clinton suggest a special role for America's younger generations? *(Clinton appears to be saying that the younger generations are still filled with idealism and are still young in spirit.)*

DIGITAL OVERVIEW ACTIVITY
Timeline: America in the 1980s and 1990s

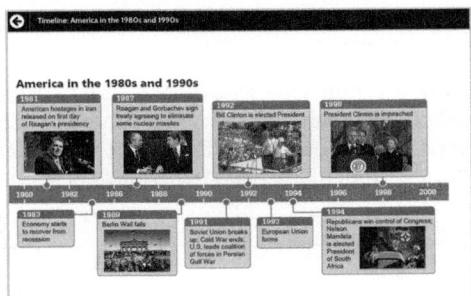

Display the timeline showing the major events in the 1980s and 1990s. During this topic students will learn about all of these events and many more. This timeline will provide a framework for students to organize the events of these decades.

Infer What can students infer from the events in the timeline? *(The 1980s and 1990s were decades of great political upheaval in the United States and around the world.)*

Topic Inquiry
Launch the Topic Inquiry with students after introducing the topic.

The Conservative Movement Surges

Supporting English Language Learners

Use with Digital Text 1, **Liberals and Conservatives Diverge.**

Listening
Review the definitions of *liberal* and *conservative* as well as the U.S. political parties associated with these terms. Then, describe liberalism's ideals and goals in the 1970s. Ensure students understand the general meaning of your spoken language as you ask them to complete the following activities.

Beginning Pair students with similar language abilities. Have students copy and complete the following sentence frame with a word from the parentheses: *Liberals believed the federal government should help needy people ____. (more, less)*

Intermediate Ask students to write a complete sentence in response to the following question: Did liberals believe that federal government should be more or less involved in people's lives?

Advanced Orally contrast liberalism's and conservatism's ideas and goals in the 1970s. Ask students to demonstrate understanding of your general meaning of this familiar topic by writing a sentence in response to this question: What was the main difference between liberalism and conservatism?

Advanced High Use spoken language to expand on the economic ideas of Milton Friedman. Ask pairs of students to demonstrate understanding of your general meaning of this mostly unfamiliar topic by discussing this question: What made Friedman's ideas conservative?

Use with Digital Text 3, **A Conservative Wins the White House.**

Speaking
Play part of Ronald Reagan's 1964 speech *A Time for Choosing* in order to present information using an audio/visual medium (the video can be found online). Repeat the main ideas of the segment of Reagan's speech you played. Students will respond orally to information presented in this visual media to build and reinforce concept attainment.

Beginning Explain that Ronald Reagan was a well-known actor before he joined politics. Display the following words and read them aloud: *nervous, prepared, well-spoken*. Ask students to choose the words that describe Ronald Reagan in this video. Have students take turns as they respond orally to the visual media.

Intermediate Remind students that Ronald Reagan was speaking in support of the Republican candidate Barry Goldwater. Ask small groups of students to respond orally to the visual media by identifying information in the speech that shows how Reagan feels about Republican ideas.

Advanced Recall concepts from the text dealing with conservatism's ideas. Then ask pairs of students to respond orally to this question: Why do you think Reagan's *A Time for Choosing* speech won the admiration of many conservatives?

Advanced High Ask pairs of students to act out the parts of an interviewer in 1964 asking Reagan about his life, conservative beliefs, and political aspirations, and Reagan answering the questions. Then have students switch roles and repeat the activity.

▣ Differentiate Instruction

Use the Differentiated Instruction notes throughout the lesson plan to support the varied skill sets, levels of readiness, and interests in the mixed-ability classroom.

Challenge These notes include suggestions for expanding the activity for advanced students.

On-Level These notes include suggestions for modifying the activity to address different interests or learning styles.

Extra Support These notes include ideas for providing more scaffolding or reading spuport.

Special Needs These notes provide ideas for adapting instruction to support the needs of various special needs students.

■ NOTES

PEARSON
realize™
www.PearsonRealize.com

Go online to access additional resources including:
Primary Sources • Biographies • Supreme Court cases •
21st Century Skill Tutorials • Maps • Graphic Organizers.

Objectives

Objective 1: Describe the differences between liberal and conservative viewpoints.

Objective 2: Analyze the causes behind the conservative resurgence in the early 1980s.

Objective 3: Explain why Ronald Reagan won the presidency in 1980.

LESSON 1 ORGANIZER		PACING: APPROX. 1 PERIOD, .5 BLOCKS		
				RESOURCES
	OBJECTIVES	**PACING**	**Online**	**Print**
Connect				
DIGITAL START UP ACTIVITY **The Conservative Movement Surges**		5 min.	●	
Investigate				
DIGITAL TEXT 1 **Liberals and Conservatives Diverge**	Objective 1	10 min.	●	●
DIGITAL TEXT 2 **The Increasing Popularity of the New Right**	Objective 2	10 min.	●	●
INTERACTIVE CHART **Two Views—Liberal and Conservative**		10 min.	●	
DIGITAL TEXT 3 **A Conservative Wins the White House**	Objective 3	10 min.	●	●
INTERACTIVE TIMELINE **Presidential Elections, 1964–1980**		10 min.	●	
Synthesize				
DIGITAL ACTIVITY **The Conservative Movement Surges**		5 min.	●	
Demonstrate				
DIGITAL QUIZ **Lesson Quiz and Class Discussion Board**		10 min.	●	

The Conservative Movement Surges

CONNECT

DIGITAL START UP ACTIVITY
The Conservative Movement Surges

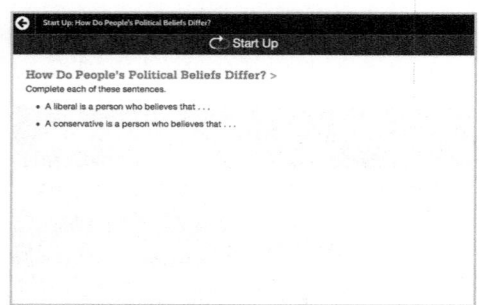

Project the Start Up Activity Ask students to complete the sentences, then share with a partner or in small groups.

Advise students that the meanings of *conservative* and *liberal* have changed over time. Explain that *conservative* comes from a Latin word meaning "to preserve, or keep intact," and that *liberal* comes from a Latin word meaning "generous" and "free."

Discuss What is the difference between what liberals and conservatives expect from their government? *(Conservatives expect government to be limited, while liberals support a more robust government role.)* How might these political labels be misapplied today? *(Not all conservatives or liberals share the same ideas about domestic and foreign policy, economics, and social standards.)*

Aa Vocabulary Development: Use the Interactive Reading Notepad to preview the Key Terms and Academic Vocabulary in this lesson with students.

⬆ FLIP IT!
Assign the Flipped Video for this lesson.

◼ STUDENT EDITION PRINT PAGES: 804–809

INVESTIGATE

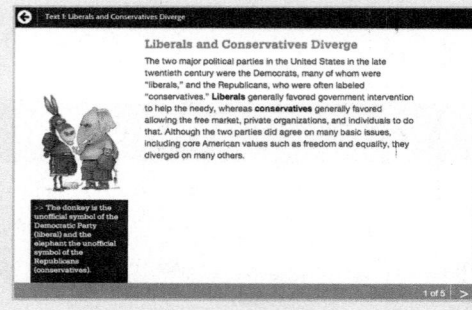

DIGITAL TEXT 1
Liberals and Conservatives Diverge

Objective 1: Describe the differences between liberal and conservative viewpoints.

Quick Instruction
In the 1980s, the United States was still immersed in the Cold War. The nation had only recently come out of Vietnam and had just gotten through the oil crisis and the record inflation of the late 1970s. International attention was held by the Iranian hostage crisis. Domestically, the nation was facing a clash of cultures, as some struggled to hold onto traditional values while others fought to expand freedoms for women, African Americans, Native Americans, and other groups. In this climate, political ideologies began to polarize. The Republican party became one key organization for a conservative resurgence.

Display the *Liberal Viewpoint* and *Conservative Viewpoint* charts. Encourage students to record the information in their notebooks, either as T-charts or as Venn diagrams.

Distinguish Contrast the viewpoints of liberals and conservatives. What are major points on which they differ? *(Conservatives favor a smaller central government with less oversight and power. Liberals promote more social programs to help the poor, elderly, and disadvantaged. Conservatives also want to reduce taxes and reduce regulation of industry. Liberals support more laws to protect rights of minorities and women.)*

Ⅾ Differentiate: **Extra Support**
Demonstrate how to make a T-chart in which to record details about liberals and conservatives. Have students work in pairs as they move through the Core Reading. Instruct them to

record specific viewpoints, policies, and details for each point of view. Then, compile a class T-chart using students' notes. Highlight or draw attention to significant points on which liberals and conservatives diverge.

ELL Use the ELL activity described in the ELL chart.

Further Instruction
Ask students to share their definitions of *conservative* and *liberal* from the Start Up Activity. Then, invite volunteers look up and read aloud the general definition of the terms in the dictionary. Draw a T-chart on the board, and call on students to write their ideas about these groups beneath each heading. Revisit their ideas as you move through and discuss the Core Reading.

Be sure to emphasize that *conservative* and *liberal* are generalizations. Explain that political ideologies like *conservative* and *liberal* exist on a continuum. People can be more or less conservative and more or less liberal about a variety of issues, ranging from foreign policy to taxes to welfare programs to gun ownership. Explain that people that hover between the two ideologies are often considered *moderates*.

Connect Tell students to consider the political continuum and the Core Reading. What makes the viewpoints of the conservative resurgence of the 1980s conservative? That is, how did they tend toward preserving tradition? *(Students may say that the United States, when founded, provided for less government regulation of business and industry, fewer social programs, and lower taxes. This changed over time. Conservatives wanted to return to what they consider more traditional ideas of small government, low taxes, and less oversight and regulation.)*

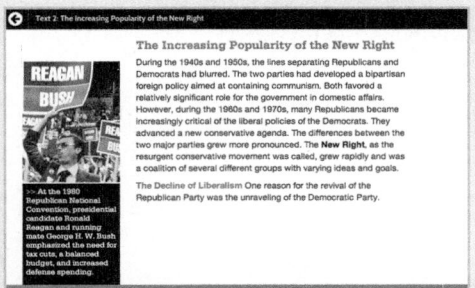

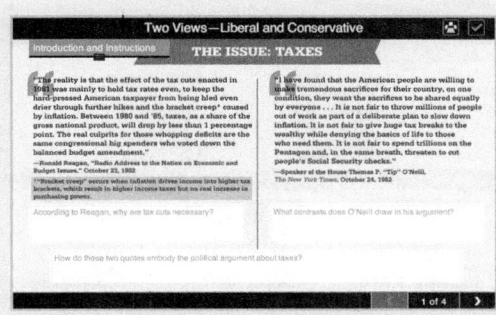

DIGITAL TEXT 2
The Increasing Popularity of the New Right

INTERACTIVE CHART
Two Views—Liberal and Conservative

Objective 2: Analyze the causes behind the conservative resurgence in the early 1980s.

Quick Instruction

During the mid-20th century, federal spending on social programs increased. Social Security had been established through New Deal legislation. Medicare and Medicaid had been launched through President Johnson's Great Society. Through union efforts, government had taken a more active role in business regulation. The size, cost, and role of federal government in American society had grown. In the 1980s, key individuals, such as Phyllis Schlafly, and key organizations, such as the Moral Majority, called attention to these dynamics and tried to change them.

Interactive Chart: Two Views—Liberal and Conservative Project the interactive chart. Call on students to read aloud the quotes. Organize students into small groups to answer the questions. Then, call on a student from each group to record their answers on the class projection of the graphic organizer.

Explain Describe the efforts of the Moral Majority, key organization of the conservative resurgence in the 1980s. Explain how this organization's focus on social issues affected national politics. *(The Moral Majority represented a a conservative religious resurgence. It worked to fulfill religious goals in government. The Moral Majority opposed abortion, gay rights, the Equal Rights Amendment for women, and restrictions on religious teaching in schools. The Moral Majority focused on specific issues that motivate people to turn out and vote in local, state, and national elections.)*

📷 ACTIVE CLASSROOM

Ask students to select one of the issues presented in the interactive chart. Then, instruct them to complete a Quick Write in which they summarize the points of view of the individuals and identify whose point of view they share and explain why.

Further Instruction

Display the following terms: *New Right, Moral Majority, Reverend Jerry Falwell,* and *sagebrush rebels.* Identify each as a key organization, group, or individual from the conservative resurgence. As students come to these terms in the Core Reading, have them write definitions to add to the class Word Wall.

Be sure that students understand the various contributing factors to the conservative resurgence in the United States. For example, the United States confronted significant societal issues in the 1960s, 1970s and 1980s, including the civil rights movement, the women's rights movement, the Vietnam War, an oil crisis, and economic hardship through recession and stagflation. Instruct students to list significant societal issues and other causes of the conservative resurgence in a concept web in their notebooks. Review these causes as a class.

Check Understanding What caused changing demographic patterns within the United States and what effect did these changing demographic patterns have on the rise of conservatism? *(Changing demographic patterns were caused by migration from urban to suburban regions, which had the effect of diluting the Democratic base and shifting support to Republicans. As*

economic hardship drove more people from the Rust Belt to the Sunbelt, Republican political power grew.)

Summarize What unintended political consequences did liberal programs such as the Great Society and affirmative action have? *(Liberal programs like the Great Society and affirmative action, though meant to help people, caused a backlash that encouraged a shift to conservatism. Social programs proved costly, and taxes went up, encouraging support of conservative promises to lower taxes and reduce government spending. Although Great Society programs did a lot of good, they did not "cure" poverty and inequality.)*

The Conservative Movement Surges

DIGITAL TEXT 3

A Conservative Wins the White House

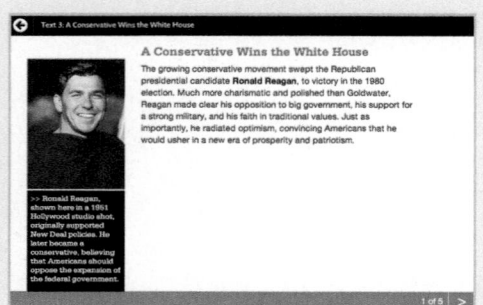

INTERACTIVE TIMELINE

Presidential Elections, 1964–1980

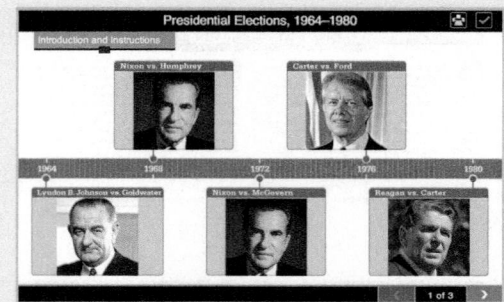

Objective 3: **Explain why Ronald Reagan won the presidency in 1980.**

Quick Instruction

Remind students that several different factors converged to produce the conservative resurgence. What the movement really needed was a political leader that could rally the many faces of the New Right to win the White House and push policy through Congress. The conservative resurgence found its leader in Ronald Reagan.

Interactive Timeline: Presidential Elections, 1964–1980 Project the interactive timeline. Identify each president and the president's political party. Remind students that up until the 1980s, the political divide between Republicans and Democrats was not as sharp as it is today.

Analyze Timelines Which presidential elections were dominated by the significant societal issue of the Vietnam War? *(The 1968 election of Nixon over Humphrey and the 1972 victory of Nixon over McGovern featured the Vietnam War as a key issue.)*

📖 ACTIVE CLASSROOM

Organize students into small groups to study the interactive timeline. Instruct them to use the Circle Write Strategy to respond to the following question: What do these maps suggest about shifting political trends in the United States?

ELL Use the ELL activity described in the ELL chart.

Further Instruction

Call attention to standout data on the interactive timeline. For example, in the 1964 map, five of the six states that did not go for President Johnson were in the South. Remind students that the South had been solidly Democratic since the Civil War. This changed with the civil rights movement.

Interpret How do Reagan's words reflect a conservative point of view? *(Reagan alludes to the American Revolution and to the capacity for self-government, a founding principle of the nation. He is appealing to tradition, and encouraging people to support conservative efforts to preserve tradition through small government.)*

Describe What made Ronald Reagan a key individual of the conservative resurgence? *(Ronald Reagan was a talented speaker and communicator with a likeable, optimistic presence. He became a key leader on conservatism while campaigning for Barry Goldwater. His speeches energized and caught the attention of conservatives. Reagan used his popularity and his powers of persuasion to win the California governorship and then the presidency. Reagan's efforts helped unite the New Right to take the White House and the Senate and to usher in a new era of conservative governance.)*

SYNTHESIZE

DIGITAL ACTIVITY

The Conservative Movement Surges

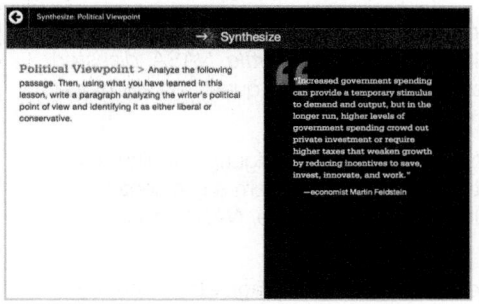

Call on one student to read aloud the quote. Ask students to discuss the following question in small groups: Is this statement conservative or liberal in its ideas? To help students identify the conservative tone of the statement, highlight such key phrases as "crowd out private investment" and "require higher taxes."

Discuss Challenge students to Take a Stand and determine whether they agree or disagree with the political statement. Split the room into groups according to their responses, and instruct groups to discuss their rationales. Then, have each group appoint a spokesperson to present the group's position and reasoning.

DEMONSTRATE

DIGITAL QUIZ

Lesson Quiz and Class Discussion Board

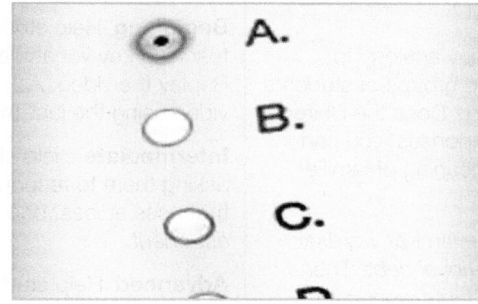

Assign the online Lesson Quiz for this lesson if you haven't already done so. Students will be offered automatic remediation or enrichment based on their score.

Pose these questions to the class on the Discussion Board:

In *The Conservative Movement Surges*, you learned about societal issues and demographic changes that contributed to the rise of conservatism in the 1980s. You also examined the roles of key organizations and individuals in the conservative resurgence.

Predict Consequences Ronald Reagan and the New Right took the White House and the Senate in 1980. What conservative policies do you think they would pursue in the coming term? How would these policies affect society, economics, and international relations?

Synthesize Conservatism surged by rallying around key issues to garner support and drive a backlash against liberal policies. Around what key issues do you think liberals would begin to rally to try to win back voters?

Topic Inquiry
Have students continue their investigations for their Topic Inquiry.

The Reagan Era

Supporting English Language Learners

Use with Digital Text 1, **A New Direction for the American Economy.**

Listening
Review strategies, from the basics of listening for cognates and word order to drawing on background knowledge and listening for the main idea, that students can use to understand a speaker's general meaning even when some of the language is unfamiliar.

Beginning Use basic familiar language and an everyday analogy to explain the term *national debt.* Pose these questions to groups of students with similar ability levels: Is a national debt good or bad? Does the United States carry a national debt? As groups share their responses, you can determine whether students understand the general meaning of familiar spoken language.

Intermediate Use familiar language and one or two unfamiliar words to compare and contrast the terms *budget deficit* and *national debt.* Then display a T-chart labeled with the two terms. Have students work with partners to demonstrate understanding of your general meaning by adding information to the chart.

Advanced Use mostly familiar language to define *budget deficit* and explain the Gramm Rudman-Hollings Act. Ask pairs of students to discuss the general meaning of what you said with this question: What was the effect of the Gramm Rudman-Hollings Act on U.S. budget deficits?

Advanced High Use a mix of familiar and unfamiliar language to define *budget deficit* and *national debt* and explain their relationship. Ask pairs of students to discuss the general meaning of what you said with this question: How does a budget deficit affect the national debt?

Use with Digital Text 3, **Culture, Challenge, and Change.**

Speaking
Show students a video of a news report of the Challenger disaster. Explain that students will be expected to respond orally to information presented in the visual media in order to build and reinforce language attainment.

Beginning Help students build and reinforce language attainment by teaching key vocabulary used in the video *(e.g., shuttle, NASA, disaster).* Replay the video. Ask students to respond orally to questions about the video using the just-taught vocabulary.

Intermediate Help students build and reinforce language attainment by asking them to respond orally to the video. Have them say a sentence that uses at least one of the following words: *shuttle, NASA, disaster, astronaut.*

Advanced Help students build and reinforce language attainment by asking them to respond orally to the video. Have pairs of students discuss their reaction to it, using the following words in their discussion: *shuttle, NASA, disaster, crew, astronaut.*

Advanced High Help students build and reinforce language attainment by asking them to respond orally to the video. Have pairs of students act out a mock news report about the Challenger disaster. Encourage them to use the following words in their report: *shuttle, NASA, disaster, crew, astronaut.*

▣ Differentiate Instruction

Use the Differentiated Instruction notes throughout the lesson plan to support the varied skill sets, levels of readiness, and interests in the mixed-ability classroom.

Challenge These notes include suggestions for expanding the activity for advanced students.

On-Level These notes include suggestions for modifying the activity to address different interests or learning styles.

Extra Support These notes include ideas for providing more scaffolding or reading spuport.

Special Needs These notes provide ideas for adapting instruction to support the needs of various special needs students.

■ NOTES

PEARSON
realize™
www.PearsonRealize.com

Go online to access additional resources including:
Primary Sources • Biographies • Supreme Court cases •
21st Century Skill Tutorials • Maps • Graphic Organizers.

Objectives

Objective 1: Analyze Reagan's economic policies as President.

Objective 2: Examine Reagan's leadership and how he strengthened the conservative movement.

Objective 3: Evaluate the steps taken to address various issues in the 1980s and early 1990s.

LESSON 2 ORGANIZER		PACING: APPROX. 1 PERIOD, .5 BLOCKS			
		OBJECTIVES	PACING	**RESOURCES** Online	Print
Connect					
DIGITAL START UP ACTIVITY **The Reagan Budget**			5 min.	●	
Investigate					
DIGITAL TEXT 1 **A New Direction for the American Economy**		Objective 1	10 min.	●	●
DIGITAL TEXT 2 **Conservative Momentum Continues**		Objective 2	10 min.	●	●
INTERACTIVE CHART **Identifying Political Views**			10 min.	●	
DIGITAL TEXT 3 **Culture, Challenge, and Change**		Objective 3	10 min.	●	●
3-D MODEL **Space Shuttle Science**			10 min.	●	
Synthesize					
DIGITAL ACTIVITY **Reagan's Assessment**			5 min.	●	
Demonstrate					
DIGITAL QUIZ **Lesson Quiz and Class Discussion Board**			10 min.	●	

The Reagan Era

▌ CONNECT

DIGITAL START UP ACTIVITY

The Reagan Budget

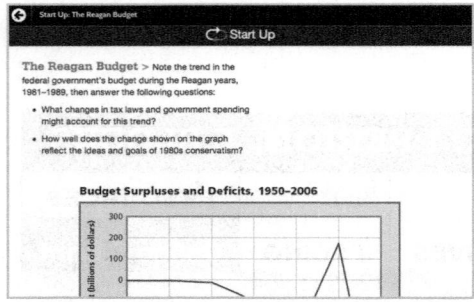

Project the Start Up Activity Ask students to answer the questions as they enter and get settled. Have them share and discuss their responses with partners. Allow them time to make adjustments to the responses as needed.

Discuss What does the chart show about tax revenues during the Reagan administration? *(They went down.)* What does the chart show about government spending during the Reagan administration? *(It decreased, too.)* Discuss the changes in tax laws and government spending that might account for this trend. *(Under the Reagan budget, Congress probably cut taxes and reduced spending by cutting programs.)*

Aa Vocabulary Development: Use the Interactive Reading Notepad to preview the Key Terms and Academic Vocabulary in this Lesson with students.

⚡FLIP IT!

Assign the Flipped Video for this lesson.

▌ STUDENT EDITION PRINT
PAGES: 810–817

▌ INVESTIGATE

DIGITAL TEXT 1

A New Direction for the American Economy

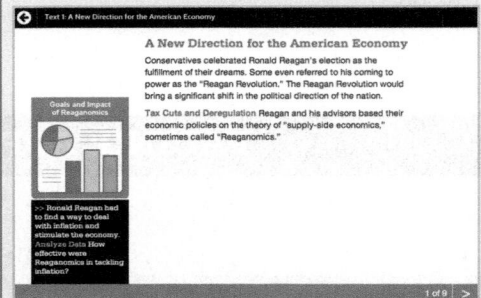

Objective 1: Analyze Reagan's economic policies as President.

Quick Instruction

Analyze Graphs Display the infographic. Challenge students to define *interest rates* and *inflation*. Help students understand the inverse relationship between interest rates—the costs of borrowing money—and inflation—the increase in prices of goods and services over time. Increasing inflation rates were making it more difficult for people to afford goods and services.

Integrate Information Point out that Reagan believed that private initiative could create economic opportunities for citizens. Ask students to think of an example of economic opportunity being created by the private sector. *(An organization called the Clearinghouse on Corporate Social Responsibility endorsed socially responsible investments. It's expansion to include life and health insurance trade associations was an unintended consequence of growth for an organization that had evolved from a committee of insurance company CEOs.)*

Analyze Data How could raising interest rates help decrease inflation? *(When demand for goods and services drops, producers lower prices to boost demand. By raising interest rates, the federal government would help lower demand in order to spur producers to lower prices, which would encourage increased consumer spending.)* Why would Reagan and other conservatives want to encourage consumer spending? *(to provide more income to private business and industry in order to invigorate the economy and increase employment)*

D Differentiate: Extra Support Help students understand interests rates through an example. A parent loans $100 to a child to spend on an outing with friends but charges an interest rate of 10 percent. What would the cost of borrowing $100 at an interest rate of 10 percent be? *($10)* How much money would the borrower, in this case the child, have to pay back? *($110)* If the interest rate increases, would the child be more or less likely to borrow money again? *(less likely because it would cost him more)*

ELL Use the ELL activity described in the ELL chart.

Further Instruction

Check Understanding Point out that an increase in legal and illegal immigration were caused by immigrants seeking employment and better living conditions. Discuss the effects that immigration would have had on demographic patterns.

Emphasize the domestic policies Reagan pursued and the ideas that drove Reaganomics by drawing a concept web on the board. Invite volunteers to add details from the Core Reading, such as deregulation of industry, supply-side economics, tax cuts, and more defense spending. Challenge students to identify potential positive and negative consequences of deregulation. *(encouraging business growth, which might stimulate the economy, induce innovation, and provide jobs. Negatives include potential industry and bank failures, fraud, and job losses if companies were to choose to shift jobs overseas.)* Ask students to consider the economic situation that caused the adoption of such conservative approaches to economics.

DIGITAL TEXT 2

Conservative Momentum Continues

INTERACTIVE CHART

Identifying Political Views

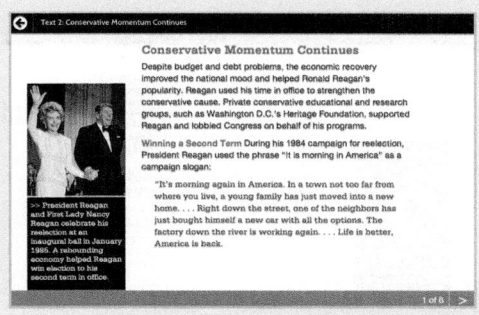

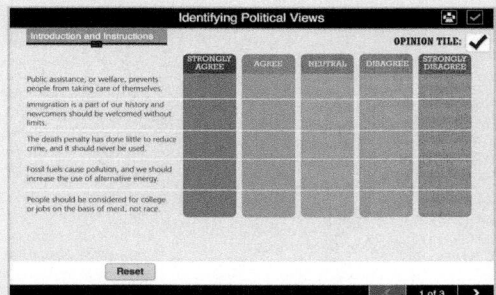

Explain How did litigation in the landmark case of *Edgewood I.S.D.* v. *Kirby* play a role in protecting the rights of the minority? *(In this case, a predominantly minority community sued the state of Texas over unequal funding for minority education. The case resulted in a new funding system that reallocated funds from more affluent districts to support education in districts with less funding, helping to promote more equal educational opportunities.)*

Synthesize How did Social Security contribute to economic challenges? How did Reagan's leadership respond to this societal issue, and why do you think he took that course of action? *(Social Security contributed to budget deficits because the number of retirees was increasing and the government was paying more in Social Security benefits. Reagan led the push to raise the retirement age for Social Security to reduce costs and signed the Social Security Reform Act in 1983. Reagan and conservatives supported reduced government spending, particularly on government programs, so this action was in line with conservative economic philosophy.)*

Objective 2: Examine Reagan's leadership and how he strengthened the conservative movement.

Quick Instruction

Explain that in this lesson, students will learn about the response to Reagan's leadership in domestic policies. They will also explore the contributions of key organizations of the conservative resurgence, such as the Heritage Foundation, and of significant political leaders such as Sandra Day O'Connor.

Interactive Chart: Identifying Political Views Project the interactive chart and guide students through its completion. Call on students to read aloud the quotations. Remind students that conservatism was not the only viewpoint in federal government or the nation during the 1980s. Liberals, largely under the Democratic Party, still served in local, state, and national office and provided a counter-voice to Reaganomics.

Identify Main Ideas Review the first set of quotes by Reagan and O'Neill. What is the most important concern to Reagan? What is the most important concern to O'Neill? *(Reagan is mainly concerned with keeping taxes low, or keeping income in the hands of citizens. O'Neill is mainly concerned with reducing disparity, or ensuring citizens have jobs, Social Security, and the basics of life.)*

⚞ ACTIVE CLASSROOM

Challenge students to interpret the quotations in the interactive chart through the Cartoon It Strategy. Have each student select one set of quotations from the activity. Tell them to illustrate the main point of disagreement in the quotations through a political cartoon. Remind them to depict both speakers, and advise students that their cartoons should focus on the quotes' main ideas. Point out that political cartoons should reveal a particular point of view, such as the cartoonist's opinion of the speakers and their ideas.

Further Instruction

Key to Reagan's conservative agenda was establishing a conservative Supreme Court, and he did so by appointing Antonin Scalia, Anthony Kennedy, and Sandra Day O'Connor. As the first female Justice, Sandra Day O'Connor became a significant political and social leader in the United States as she voted mostly with conservatives on the court.

Draw Conclusions Describe the contributions of the Heritage Foundation to the conservative resurgence. Do you think Reagan and Republicans would have been as successful in their campaigns without such key organizations? Why or why not? *(The Heritage Foundation promoted Reagan's domestic policies and lobbied Congress to pass Reagan's initiatives. Such organizations helped rally popular and Congressional support for Reaganomics and other conservative policies. Reagan and Republicans probably would have enjoyed some success without the Heritage Foundation, but perhaps not as much.)*

The Reagan Era

DIGITAL TEXT 3

Culture, Challenge, and Change

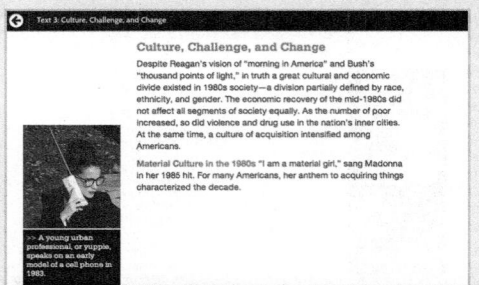

3-D MODEL

Space Shuttle Science

Describe What contributions did political leaders like Sandra Day O'Connor, Antonin Scalia, and Anthony Kennedy make to the conservative resurgence? *(As conservatives, they largely helped support conservative laws that came before the court for judicial review. This not only had an immediate impact, in terms of policy, but also set precedents for lawmakers and courts.)*

Compare and Contrast How did Reagan's leadership and Bush's leadership differ in domestic politics? *(Bush did not push to lower taxes further but did promise not to raise taxes. He did not pursue the same manner of budget cuts as Reagan. Also, he supported the ADA, a new law with social as well as economic significance.)*

Objective 3: Evaluate the steps taken to address various issues in the 1980s and early 1990s.

Quick Instruction

3-D Model: Space Shuttle Science Project the 3-D Model, and click through the hotspots with students. Call on students to read aloud the details about different parts of the space station. Prompt students to discuss how space technology improved the quality of life.

Make Generalizations What effect did the space program had on education and other aspects of culture? *(The space program bolstered American pride in its achievements. It also increased interest in science, technology, engineering, and math studies. Space exploration probably added a sense of excitement to the national culture and sparked thought about our place in the universe.)*

🖳 ACTIVE CLASSROOM

Provide the following stem: *The space program was/was not worth the cost to the nation because...* Have students Circle Write and share their responses. At the conclusion of this lesson, have students revisit their ideas. and conduct another Circle Write.

ELL Use the ELL activity described in the ELL chart.

Further Instruction

Have students brainstorm a list of key issues and developments that characterized the 1980s in the United States. Highlight key developments such as the inception of MTV in 1981, early forms of cordless and cellular phones, and the rise of the personal computer. Point out that the 1980s were also rife with significant societal issues, such as drug traffic, AIDS, and an attempted assassination of President Reagan. Explain that they will learn how key organizations, such as the National Rifle Association, reacted to this attempt.

Describe What role did the National Rifle Association play in the conservative resurgence of the 1980s? *(The NRA became the self-appointed defender of Americans' right to own and bear arms. As a conservative organization, it defended citizens' individual liberty with regards to weapons, specifically, firearms, which also benefited weapons makers and distributors.)*

Infer Explain how space technology impacted quality of life in the 1980s and beyond. Would American society have developed in the same way without the space program? *(Space technology inspired the innovation of many modern consumer goods, like cordless vacuum cleaners, firefighting gear, and improved tires. These goods improved the quality of life for many Americans. Without the space program, which inspired a focus on technology through education, research, and product development, society would not likely have developed the same way.)*

SYNTHESIZE

DIGITAL ACTIVITY
Reagan's Assessment

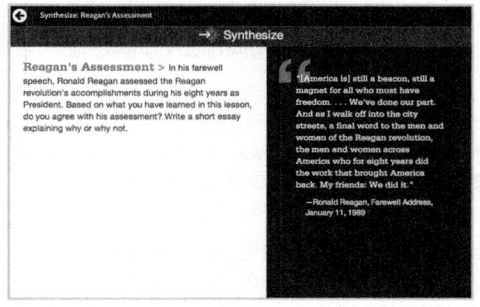

Analyze Primary Sources What is Reagan's overall assessment of his leadership? *(His assessment is generally positive.)* What evidence from the excerpt supports your position? *("We've done our part." "... did the work that brought America back. My friends: We did it."*

Support Ideas with Evidence Tell students to write a short essay in response to the following question: Based on what you have learned in this lesson, do you agree with Reagan's self-assessment? Why or why not? Encourage students to cite specific examples from the lesson to support their ideas.

DEMONSTRATE

DIGITAL QUIZ
Lesson Quiz and Class Discussion Board

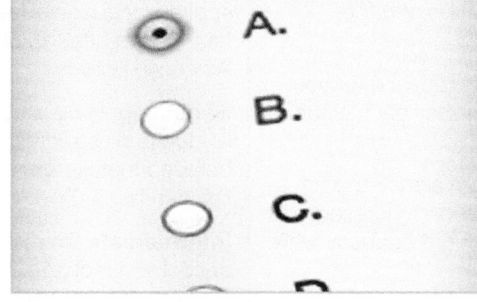

Assign the online Lesson Quiz for this lesson if you haven't already done so. Students will be offered automatic remediation or enrichment based on their score.

Pose these questions to the class on the Discussion Board:

Predict Consequences What lasting effect would the economic and social policies of the 1980s likely have on the United States in the coming decades?

Contrast How might the conservative and liberal assessments of the policies of the Reagan and Bush administrations differ?

Topic Inquiry
Have students continue their investigations for the Topic Inquiry.

The Cold War Ends

Supporting English Language Learners

Use with Digital Text 1, **Reagan Leads with "Peace Through Strength"**.

Reading

Display the word *though* and read it aloud. Point out that the letters *ough* work together to make a long *o* sound in this word. Explain that students will be learning about the relationship between these letters and the sounds they represent.

Beginning Say *though* aloud again, and have students repeat after you. Then display these words: *although, thorough, furlough*. Say each aloud as you point to it. Have students repeat after you.

Intermediate Display *through* next to *though*. Say them aloud, and have students repeat after you. Ask students to identify the sound represented by *ough* in each. Then have students pronounce each word correctly while using it in a sentence.

Advanced Display these words from the text: *through, sought*. Read each word aloud. Ask students to read them and identify the sound represented by *ough* in each. Ask partners to think of another word that shares each sound. Then, ask them to identify the letters that make up the sounds in their words.

Advanced High Display these words: *though, through, sought, tough, drought*. Ask partners to take turns reading them and identifying the sound represented by *ough* in each. Then, have students individually write a sentence related to the text using one of the words. Have partners read aloud each other's sentences.

Use with Digital Text 3, **U.S. Involvement in the Middle East and the Iran-Contra Affair.**

Listening

Point out the United States, Iran, and Nicaragua on a world map. Use the map as a visual aid to help students understand the general meaning of spoken language about international situations as you speak about the Iran-Contra affair. Explain the Iran-Contra affair in the familiar context of American politics.

Beginning Have students demonstrate their understanding of spoken language by selecting the general meaning of what you said: (1) Americans believed that Reagan should go to jail, or (2) Americans' opinion of Reagan fell.

Intermediate To make sure students understand the general meaning of spoken language in a familiar context, pose this question: How did Americans react toward Reagan when the scandal came out? Have students share their answers in small groups.

Advanced Explain the Iran-Contra affair in the less familiar context of foreign relations. Have students demonstrate their understanding of your general meaning by discussing this question with a small group: How did this scandal affect the way other countries viewed the United States?

Advanced High Explain the Iran-Contra affair in the less familiar context of foreign relations. Have pairs of students demonstrate their understanding of spoken language by discussing the general meaning of what you said.

▣ Differentiate Instruction

Use the Differentiated Instruction notes throughout the lesson plan to support the varied skill sets, levels of readiness, and interests in the mixed-ability classroom.

Challenge These notes include suggestions for expanding the activity for advanced students.

On-Level These notes include suggestions for modifying the activity to address different interests or learning styles.

Extra Support These notes include ideas for providing more scaffolding or reading spuport.

Special Needs These notes provide ideas for adapting instruction to support the needs of various special needs students.

■ NOTES

PEARSON
realize™
www.PearsonRealize.com

Go online to access additional resources including:
Primary Sources • Biographies • Supreme Court cases •
21st Century Skill Tutorials • Maps • Graphic Organizers.

Objectives

Objective 1: Analyze the ways that Ronald Reagan challenged communism and the Soviet Union.

Objective 2: Explain the end of the Cold War.

Objective 3: Describe other foreign policy challenges that faced the United States in the 1980s.

LESSON 3 ORGANIZER		PACING: APPROX. 1 PERIOD, .5 BLOCKS		
			RESOURCES	
	OBJECTIVES	PACING	Online	Print
Connect				
DIGITAL START UP ACTIVITY **A Strong Resistance to Communism**		5 min.	●	
Investigate				
DIGITAL TEXT 1 **Reagan Leads with "Peace Through Strength"**	Objective 1	10 min.	●	●
INTERACTIVE CHART **Reagan's Leadership**		10 min.	●	
DIGITAL TEXT 2 **Impact of the End of the Cold War**	Objective 2	10 min.	●	●
INTERACTIVE GALLERY **The Fall of Communism in Europe**		10 min.	●	
DIGITAL TEXT 3 **U.S. Involvement in the Middle East and the Iran-Contra Affair**	Objective 3	10 min.	●	●
Synthesize				
DIGITAL ACTIVITY **A Moral Conflict**		5 min.	●	
Demonstrate				
DIGITAL QUIZ **Lesson Quiz and Class Discussion Board**		10 min.	●	

The Cold War Ends

DIGITAL START UP ACTIVITY
A Strong Resistance to Communism

Project the Start Up Activity Ask students to read the quote as they enter and get settled. Then have them write a paragraph reflecting on the quote. Have students share their ideas with a partner, either in class or through a chat or blog space.

Discuss Reflect on how the relationship between the United States and the Soviet Union evolved from World War II to the 1980s. Do you agree with Reagan's statement that the Soviet Union was an "evil empire"? Why or why not?

Tell students that in this lesson they will learn about President Ronald Reagan's tough stance toward the Soviet Union and the accompanying military build-up.

Aa Vocabulary Development: Use the Interactive Reading Notepad to preview the Key Terms and Academic Vocabulary in this lesson with students.

⚑FLIP IT!

Assign the Flipped Video for this lesson.

■ **STUDENT EDITION PRINT PAGES: 818–823**

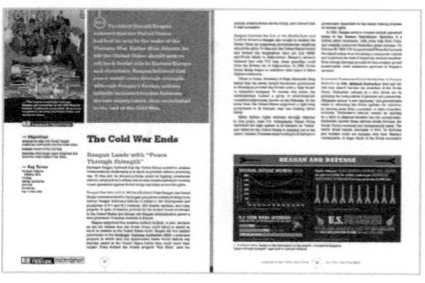

■ **INVESTIGATE**

DIGITAL TEXT 1
Reagan Leads with "Peace Through Strength"

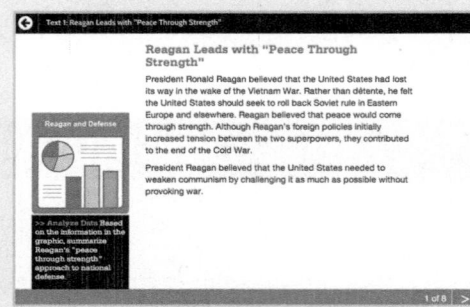

INTERACTIVE CHART
Reagan's Leadership

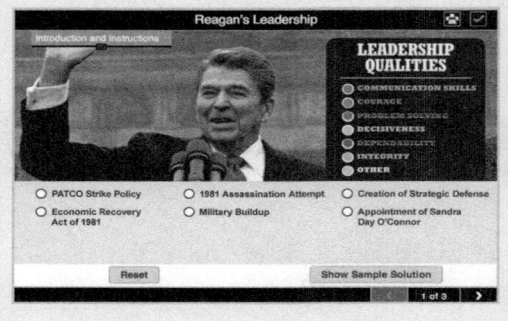

Objective 1: Analyze the ways that Ronald Reagan challenged communism and the Soviet Union.

Quick Instruction
Interactive Chart: Reagan's Leadership Project the interactive chart. Invite volunteers to briefly summarize the situations associated with Reagan's presidency. Discuss each situation to ensure student understanding. When students have completed the interactivity, invite them to share with the class.

Support a Point of View with Evidence Challenge students to describe and evaluate Ronald Reagan's leadership in international policies, especially his "peace through strength" policy. (*Reagan showed determination and resolve in consistently supporting the military buildup plan to fight communism. He also displayed foresight and decisiveness in supporting the untested Strategic Defense Initiative.*)

📷 ACTIVE CLASSROOM
Conduct a Take a Stand Activity. Ask students to take a stand on the following question: Was Ronald Reagan an effective leader? Ask students to divide into two groups based on their opinion and move to separate areas of the classroom. Ask students to talk with each other to compare their reasons for answering *yes* or *no*. Ask a representative from each side to present and defend the group's point of view.

ELL Use the ELL activity described in the ELL chart.

Further Instruction
Infer How did Reagan's foreign policy differ from that of Carter? (*Reagan, unlike Carter, focused American foreign policy on fighting communism. Carter was more interested in protecting and promoting human rights.*)

Summarize What were *glasnost* and *perestroika* ? (*Glasnost means "a new openness," and perestroika refers to reforming the Soviet system by moving away from a socialist, or state-controlled, economy. Glasnost and perestroika were reform policies that Gorbachev pursued.*) What effect did these reforms have on the Soviet Union? (*These reforms created an opening for a shift in relations between the Soviet Union and the United States.*)

Draw Conclusions Based on what you have read, what were the key factors in the thawing of relations between the United States and Soviet Union during Reagan's second term? (*The Soviet Union's economy was struggling to survive, and Gorbachev realized that his nation could not match the military buildup initiated by the Reagan administration. In addition, Gorbachev's policies and personality helped soften the Soviet Union's international image. Reagan responded to this change by moderating his own stance toward the Soviet Union.*)

DIGITAL TEXT 2
Impact of the End of the Cold War

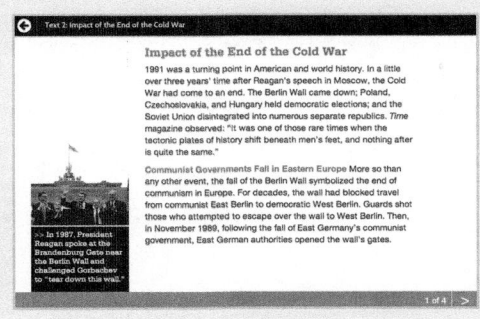

INTERACTIVE GALLERY
The Fall of Communism in Europe

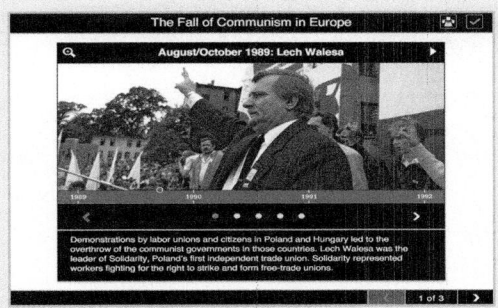

DIGITAL TEXT 3
U.S. Involvement in the Middle East and the Iran-Contra Affair

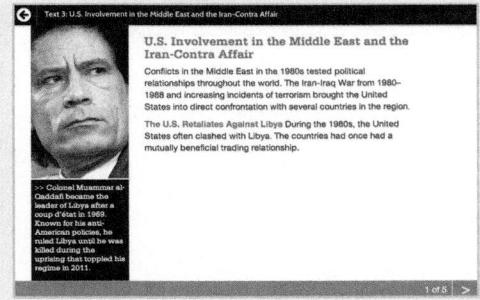

Objective 2: Explain the end of the Cold War.

Quick Instruction

Interactive Gallery: The Fall of Communism in Europe Project the interactive gallery and click through the images. What made the celebration on the Berlin Wall so poignant? *(The Berlin Wall had become a prominent symbol of communist power in Europe. Taking part in tearing down the wall provided people with the opportunity to "tear down" communism.)*

Identify Central Issues How did Reagan and U.S. involvement in world affairs influence Soviet policy in the mid-1980s, leading to the end of the Cold War in 1991? *(Reagan and the United States challenged the Soviet Union and other communist nations throughout the 1980s. Reagan's military buildup strained the Soviet economy as it tried to keep pace with the U.S. Soviet leaders were forced to make changes.)*

⬛ ACTIVE CLASSROOM

Have students Make Headlines for the fall of communism in Europe. Ask: If you were to write a headline that captured the most important aspect that should be remembered about the fall of communism in Europe, what would that headline be? Allow students to use subheadings to communicate more information. Encourage them to present the fall of communism in Europe as part of the larger Cold War. Have students pass their headlines to a partner for review.

D **Differentiate: Extra Support** Some students may have difficulty identifying important aspects of the fall of communism. Have these students take five minutes to discuss the task and gallery with a partner. Tell them to jot down notes and possible headline ideas. Then continue with the group activity, allowing student partners to continue to work together to create their headlines.

Further Instruction

Make Predictions What might be some of the unintended consequences of the fall of communism in Europe based on the information in the gallery? *(Some of the new smaller countries will still have deep economic struggles that could cause unrest. Yugoslavia, because of the ethnic issues between the people in the region, might experience more tensions and conflicts in the future.)*

Evaluate Impact Who was Boris Yeltsin? *(Boris Yeltsin led millions of Russians as they rallied in the streets of Moscow in support of Gorbachev.)* What role did he play in bringing out the collapse of the Soviet Union? *(The show of support from millions of Russians defeated the attempted coup in 1991.)*

Draw Conclusions How did the end of the Cold War affect U.S. relations with the new Russian states? *(The tension and rivalry between the U.S. and the Soviet Union was over. American leaders and new Russian leaders signed agreements to scale down and even eliminate certain types of nuclear weapons. In 1992, Bush and Yeltsin issued a joint statement pledging friendship and cooperation.)*

Objective 3: Describe other foreign policy challenges that faced the United States in the 1980s.

Quick Instruction

Analyze Images Project the image of the Marine HQ building in Beirut. Invite a volunteer to summarize the event. *(On October 23, 1983, a truck loaded with thousands of pounds of explosives smashed through barriers at the headquarters of the United States Marines in Beirut. The explosion killed 241 marines.)*

Summarize Ask students to describe why the Marines were in Lebanon. *(In 1982, Reagan sent a group of 800 United States Marines to Lebanon as part of an international force trying to bring peace to that nation, which was torn by civil war.)*

Synthesize Information Why did Reagan order an air raid on Libya? *(Reagan blamed Qaddafi and Libya for the 1986 terrorist attack on a Berlin nightclub.)*

ELL Use the ELL activity described in the ELL chart.

Further Instruction

Begin a discussion in which students describe U.S. involvement in the Middle East and the Iran-Contra Affair. *(The affair began in 1985 when the United States sold weapons to Iran in exchange for Iran's promise to pressure terrorist groups in Lebanon to release some American hostages. Then the Reagan administration used the money from the sale to fund the Contras, a group of Nicaraguan anticommunist counterrevolutionaries.)*

The Cold War Ends

SYNTHESIZE

DEMONSTRATE

DIGITAL ACTIVITY
A Moral Conflict

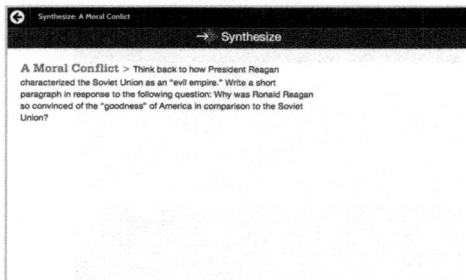

DIGITAL QUIZ
Lesson Quiz and Class Discussion Board

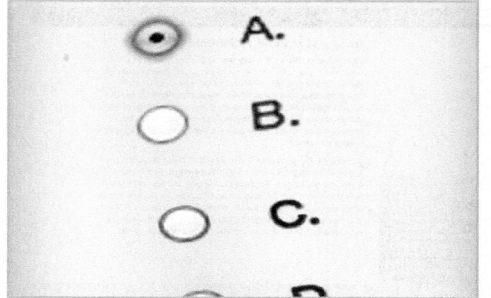

Identify Central Issues In the Iran-Contra affair, what actions of several members of Reagan's administration went against the policies of the federal government? *(The plan to sell weapons to Iran in exchange for Iran's promise to pressure terrorist groups contradicted the administration's policy of refusing to negotiate with terrorists. The administration's use of the money from the sale to fund the Contras in Nicaragua, was in direct violation of a ban issued in 1983 by Congress.)*

Discuss Lead a brief discussion to ensure student understanding of the fundamentals of why so many Americans thought the Soviet Union was an "evil empire." Then have partners work together to discuss the question on *A Moral Conflict* before writing their paragraphs.

Assign the online Lesson Quiz for this lesson if you haven't already done so. Students will be offered automatic remediation or enrichment based on their score.

Pose these questions to the class on the Discussion Board:

In *The Cold War Ends*, you read about President Reagan's plan to weaken communism by challenging it as much as possible without provoking war. His policies ranged from building new nuclear missile systems to funding covert operations against Soviet troops and allies around the globe.

Identify Central Issues Describe the impact of Ronald Reagan on American foreign policy in the 1980s.

Predict Consequences Although Reagan's military buildup helped to cause the collapse of the Soviet Union and communism in Europe, it also dramatically added to the federal debt. What will be the lingering effects of the added debt to the U.S. economy?

Topic Inquiry
Have students continue their investigations for the Topic Inquiry.

PEARSON realize™
www.PearsonRealize.com
Access your Digital Lesson

A New Era in Foreign Policy

Supporting English Language Learners

Use with Digital Text 1, **Bush Forges a New Role in the World.**

Reading
Explain that identifying familiar word parts can help with decoding, or sounding out, unfamiliar words.

Beginning Display these words from the text: *Union, United*. Sound out the words with students. Then have them apply their knowledge of these words to decode the word *unity*.

Intermediate Display these words from the text: *leading, leaders, leadership*. Help students identify the familiar word *lead* in each example and use that knowledge to decode all three words. Then have students decode these words from the text: *elected, elections*.

Advanced Display these words from the text: *unopposed, disintegrated*. Help students separate the affixes and root in these words and use that knowledge to decode the words. Then have pairs of students do the same with these words from the text: *illegal, pro-democracy, international*.

Advanced High Display these words from the text: *international, nations*. Have students identify the familiar root in these words, and discuss why that information can help with decoding the words but only in a limited way (i.e., the letter a sound changes). Ask students to identify a word related to *democracy* but with a slightly different pronunciation.

Use with Digital Text 3, **Clinton Wins the 1992 Election.**

Listening
Review the United States' situation in 1992, both at home and abroad. Then, describe the three principal candidates of the 1992 presidential election. Explain that knowing the context can help students understand the main points of spoken language.

Beginning Pair students with similar language abilities. Ask pairs to demonstrate their understanding of this familiar topic's main points by naming the three men who ran for President in 1992.

Intermediate Pair students with similar language abilities. Ask pairs to demonstrate their understanding of this familiar topic's main points by naming the three men who ran for President in 1992 and identifying the political party of each.

Advanced Divide students with similar language abilities into small groups. Have groups demonstrate their understanding of this familiar topic's main points by answering this question: What were two main issues discussed during the campaign?

Advanced High Explain Clinton's ideology of the "New Democrat." Have pairs of students demonstrate their understanding of this somewhat unfamiliar topic by explaining how this ideology led to Clinton's winning the election.

▣ Differentiate Instruction

Use the Differentiated Instruction notes throughout the lesson plan to support the varied skill sets, levels of readiness, and interests in the mixed-ability classroom.

Challenge These notes include suggestions for expanding the activity for advanced students.

On-Level These notes include suggestions for modifying the activity to address different interests or learning styles.

Extra Support These notes include ideas for providing more scaffolding or reading spuport.

Special Needs These notes provide ideas for adapting instruction to support the needs of various special needs students.

■ NOTES

A New Era in Foreign Policy

Objectives

Objective 1: Analyze why George H.W. Bush decided to use force in some foreign disputes and not in others.

Objective 2: Summarize the Persian Gulf War and its results.

Objective 3: Explain why Bill Clinton won the presidency in 1992.

Objective 4: Assess the foreign policy goals and actions of the Clinton administration.

Objective 5: Describe U.S. relations with various Middle Eastern countries and groups.

LESSON 4 ORGANIZER		PACING: APPROX. 1 PERIOD, .5 BLOCKS			
				RESOURCES	
		OBJECTIVES	PACING	Online	Print
Connect					
DIGITAL START UP ACTIVITY **A New World Order**			5 min.	●	
Investigate					
DIGITAL TEXT 1 **Bush Forges a New Role in the World**		Objective 1	10 min.	●	●
INTERACTIVE MAP **U.S. Foreign Affairs under George H.W. Bush**			10 min.	●	
DIGITAL TEXT 2 **The Persian Gulf War**		Objective 2	10 min.	●	●
INTERACTIVE GALLERY **The Persian Gulf War, 1991**			10 min.	●	
DIGITAL TEXT 3 **Clinton Wins the 1992 Election**		Objectives 3	10 min.	●	●
DIGITAL TEXT 4 **Clinton Intervenes with Mixed Success**		Objectives 4	10 min.	●	●
DIGITAL TEXT 5 **America and the Middle East in the 1990s**		Objectives 5	10 min.	●	●
Synthesize					
DIGITAL ACTIVITY **Key Events in American Foreign Policy**			5 min.	●	
Demonstrate					
LESSON QUIZ **Lesson Quiz and Class Discussion Board**			10 min.	●	

PEARSON
realize™
www.PearsonRealize.com

Go online to access additional resources including:
Primary Sources • Biographies • Supreme Court cases •
21st Century Skill Tutorials • Maps • Graphic Organizers.

■ CONNECT

DIGITAL START UP ACTIVITY
A New World Order

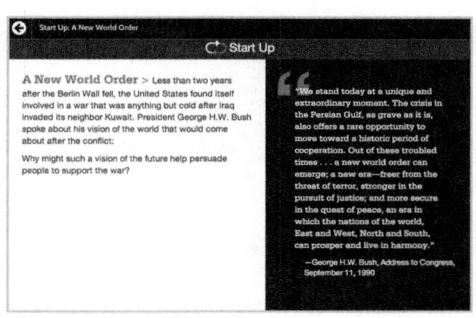

Project the Start Up Activity Ask students to read the quote as they enter and get settled. Then have them write a paragraph reflecting on the quote. Have students share their ideas with a partner, either in class or through a chat or blog space.

Discuss How did President Bush see this crisis as an opportunity? What arguments are used to make a case for and against involvement in regional conflicts? Did President Bush's hopes for the future come true?

Tell students that in this lesson they will be learning about U.S. involvement in the Persian Gulf War and how the nations and peoples of the world responded as President Bush and then President Clinton tried to build a "new world order."

Aa Vocabulary Development: Use the Interactive Reading Notepad to preview the Key Terms and Academic Vocabulary in this lesson with students.

⚡ FLIP IT!
Assign the Flipped Video for this lesson.

■ STUDENT EDITION PRINT
PAGES: 824–831

■ INVESTIGATE

DIGITAL TEXT 1
Bush Forges a New Role in the World

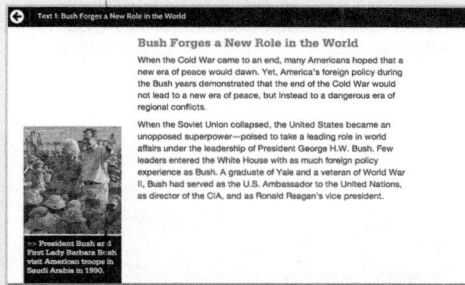

Objective 1: Analyze why George H.W. Bush decided to use force in some foreign disputes and not in others.

Quick Instruction
Interactive Map: U.S. Foreign Affairs under George H.W. Bush Project the interactive map and click through the hot spots on the map. Introduce the map activity by telling students many nations had for decades defined themselves by their relationship to the United States or the Soviet Union. The early 1990s would see the beginnings of what President Bush called "a new world order."

Identify Central Issues How did Bush's approach in Somalia differ from his approach in Panama? *(He sent military troops to both countries, but the mission in Somalia was for humanitarian purposes, as was not the case in Panama, where he sent more than 12,000 U.S. troops to arrest Panama's dictator Manuel Noriega.)*

🖼 ACTIVE CLASSROOM
Direct students to have a "Conversation with President Bush." Tell students to consider what they would like to have said to or asked Bush as he was developing what he believed to be a "new world order." Direct students to write down a question for Bush, the answer Bush would likely give based on the information students have gathered about him, and their response to his answer.

INTERACTIVE MAP
U.S. Foreign Affairs under George H.W. Bush

ELL Use the ELL activity described in the ELL chart.

Further Instruction
Go through the Interactive Reading Notepad questions and discuss the answers with the class. Be sure students understand the role of Nelson Mandela and the issues surrounding the anti-apartheid movement within South Africa and around the globe. Assign the Primary Source Document: Nelson Mandela, Glory, and Hope.

Identify Cause and Effect How did the United States react to the crisis in the Balkans? *(President Bush did not send troops but backed a UN plan to restore peace.)*

A New Era in Foreign Policy

DIGITAL TEXT 2

The Persian Gulf War

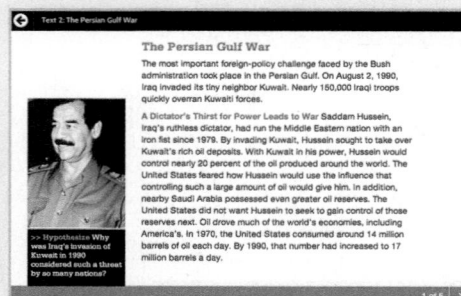

INTERACTIVE GALLERY

The Persian Gulf War, 1991

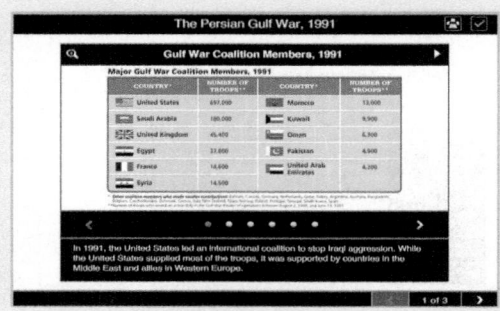

DIGITAL TEXT 3

Clinton Wins the 1992 Election

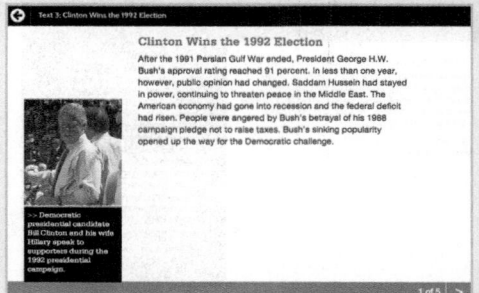

Objective 2: Summarize the Persian Gulf War and its results.

Quick Instruction

Interactive Gallery: The Persian Gulf War, 1991 Project the Interactive Gallery on the whiteboard and have students look at the table and the images. Identify the important individuals who led the coalition forces and the technological innovations involved in the war. Explain that in this lesson, students will learn about U.S. involvement in world affairs and the Middle East, including the Persian Gulf War.

Compare How was the Persian Gulf War conducted differently from the Vietnam War? *(During the Persian Gulf War, the United States organized a coalition of nations from around the world and generated great support. Both sides used technological advancements in weapons, such as long-range missiles, GPS guided weapons systems, and radar-eluding stealth bombers. In contrast to the way the Vietnam War was waged, the United States used most of its non-nuclear military capabilities in a quick, decisive strike against Iraqi forces.)*

📷 ACTIVE CLASSROOM

Have students form an Opinion Line to answer the following question: Was the Persian Gulf War successful from the point of view of the coalition countries? Explain. *(Yes: It forced Iraq to withdraw its troops from Kuwait and inflicted heavy casualties. No: The war did not result in the toppling of Saddam Hussein"s regime.)*

D Differentiate: Challenge Ask students to conduct additional research on new weapons technology used in the Persian Gulf War and present their findings.

Further Instruction

Be sure that students understand the impact of America's growing reliance on petroleum for energy. In essence, the need to maintain oil supplies led to U.S. involvement in the Persian Gulf War. Explain that the United States did not fight alone in this war. In fact, the U.S. not only participated in but also spearheaded the UN forces that led the attack against Iraq. Tell students that they will have the opportunity to evaluate the pros and cons of U.S. participation in international organizations, including the lasting impact of the U.S. involvement in the Persian Gulf War.

Draw Conclusion Why did the United States-led coalition decide not to invade Baghdad or try to oust Hussein after driving Iraq out of Kuwait? *(Bush chose to limit American actions to enforcing the U.N. resolution that Iraqi troops withdraw from Kuwait.)*

Express Problems Clearly What were some of the negative consequences of the victory in the Persian Gulf War. *(Saddam Hussein still ruled Iraq, Iraqis grew to resent the U.S. presence, and al-Qaeda was strengthened.)*

Objective 3: Explain why Bill Clinton won the presidency in 1992.

Quick Instruction

As Bush's popularity plummeted in response to an increasing deficit, a failing economy, and broken promises in the form of tax hikes, Bill Clinton attracted national attention and won the 1992 election as a "New Democrat," a centrist who enticed liberals, moderate Democrats, and even moderate Republicans to cast their ballot in his favor.

Analyze Images Project the image of the Clintons. Invite volunteers to describe the personal and professional differences between Bill Clinton and George H.W. Bush. *(Clinton was born in 1946 into a humble home and had worked his way through college and law school before being elected governor of Arkansas in 1978. Bush, on the other hand, grew up in a very wealthy family and attended Yale. Bush had much more experience than Clinton, serving in World War II, as the U.S. Ambassador to the United Nations, as director of the CIA, and as Ronald Reagan's Vice President.)*

Draw Conclusions How did Clinton use his stance as a moderate to attract voters? *(Clinton's centrist position attracted conservative and liberal Democrats, as well as moderate Republicans. His position as a moderate, practical Democrat had broad appeal for a wide range of voters.)*

ELL Use the ELL activity described in the ELL chart.

DIGITAL TEXT 4

Clinton Intervenes with Mixed Success

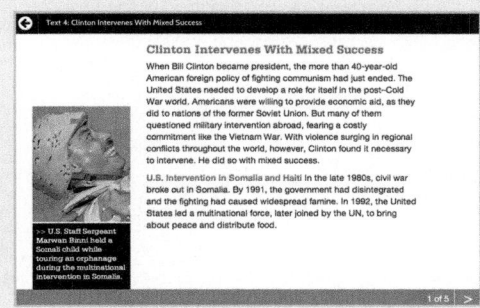

Text 4: Clinton Intervenes With Mixed Success

Clinton Intervenes With Mixed Success

When Bill Clinton became president, the more than 40-year-old American foreign policy of fighting communism had just ended. The United States needed to develop a role for itself in the post-Cold War world. Americans were willing to provide economic aid, as they did to nations of the former Soviet Union. But many of them questioned military intervention abroad, fearing a costly commitment like the Vietnam War. With violence surging in regional conflicts throughout the world, however, Clinton found it necessary to intervene. He did so with mixed success.

U.S. Intervention in Somalia and Haiti In the late 1980s, civil war broke out in Somalia. By 1991, the government had disintegrated and the fighting had caused widespread famine. In 1992, the United States led a multinational force, later joined by the UN, to bring about peace and distribute food.

>> U.S. Sergeant Marwan Bzzzi held a Somali child while touring as orphanage during the multinational intervention in Somalia.

1 of 5 >

Further Instruction

Go through the Interactive Reading Notepad questions and discuss the answers with the class. Be sure students understand how Clinton positioned himself ideologically in order to win over both Democrats and Republicans in the 1992 election. Point out that he distanced himself from the stereotype of "tax and spend" liberals and promoted himself as a "New Democrat" who supported strong national defense, tough stands on crime, free trade, welfare reform, and closer ties with corporations.

Draw Conclusions What does Clinton's victory in the 1992 election suggest about the priorities of the American electorate at the time? *(Voters' focus was shifting from foreign policy to domestic issues, like the struggling economy and growing inequality of wealth.)*

Generate Explanations What was the impact of Ross Perot's third party campaign for the presidency? *(Many believe that Perot attracted votes that would have gone to the established parties.)*

Objective 4: Assess the foreign policy goals and actions of the Clinton administration.

Quick Instruction

As a new President, Clinton was faced with the decision of whether to intervene in various global crises and conflicts. Under his direction, the United States participated in international organizations, such as the UN and NATO, to aid Somalians, and to end the Balkins Crisis. Ultimately, these interventions met with limited success.

Analyze Images Project the image of the US troops in Somalia. Briefly review the U.S. involvement in Somalia that began under President George H.W. Bush. (In the late 1980s, civil war broke out in Somalia. By 1991, the government had disintegrated and the fighting had caused widespread famine. In 1992, the United States led a multinational force, later joined by the UN, to bring about peace and distribute food.) Point out that Clinton pulled U.S. troops from Somalia when coalition forces, including the United States, suffered steep casualty rates.

Draw Conclusions What does Clinton's decision to pull U.S. troops from Somalia suggest about the willingness of Presidents to intervene in foreign crises? *(U.S. Presidents were becoming less willing to keep American soldiers in potentially long and complicated situations involving warring factions within foreign nations, even when there was a humanitarian mission involved.)*

Further Instruction

Briefly review what happened in the Balkans and specifically the former country of Yugoslavia. *(The collapse of communism broke up the country of Yugoslavia, leaving the country with no unifying forces. Soon, four of Yugoslavia's six major republics broke away and became independent nations, and long-suppressed ethnic and religious hostilities came boiling to the surface.)* Use the following questions to ensure understanding of U.S. involvement in the Balkans Crisis.

Compare How did Clinton's approach to the conflict in the former Yugoslavia differ from President Bush's approach? *(Although Bush eventually backed a modest UN plan to restore peace in Bosnia, he did so hesitantly because he feared that the tangled conflict could embroil the United States in another Vietnam. Clinton encouraged NATO to bomb Serbian strongholds. This was the first time the organization had gone into combat, and its use of force quickly brought about a cease-fire, though it did not solve all the problems.)*

Analyze Information What basic assumption about the U.S. role as sole superpower underlies American peacekeeping efforts of the 1990s? *(As the sole superpower, the U.S. was expected to lead peacekeeping missions and provide the bulk of soldiers and resources.)*

A New Era in Foreign Policy

DIGITAL TEXT 5

America and the Middle East in the 1990s

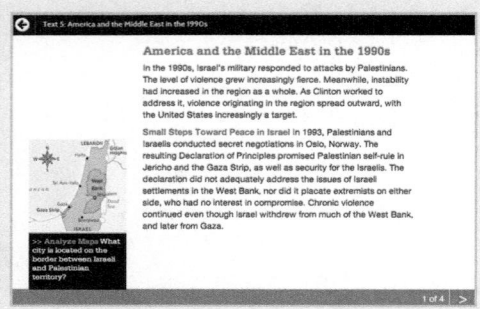

Objective 5: Describe U.S. relations with various Middle Eastern countries and groups.

Quick Instruction

In the 1990s, U.S. involvement in the Middle East included negotiations with Israel and Palestine. In general, the United States mostly supported Israel in its conflict with Palestine. Project the map of Israel and the Gaza Strip on the whiteboard. Explain that the modern-day nation of Israel was created by the United Nations in 1947, by dividing British-ruled Palestine into two states, one Jewish and the other Arab. Conflicts between Israelis and Palestinian Arabs have marked the region since, with implications for the entire Middle East.

Analyze Information Why has the United States become involved in the Middle East? *(The United States has become involved because of the strategic location of the Middle East, its support of the state of Israel, and to protect its interests in the vast supplies of oil in the region.)*

Generate Explanations How did Clinton seek peace in the Middle East? *(In 2000, Clinton invited Palestinian leader Yasir Arafat and Israeli prime minister Ehud Barak to Camp David to work on a peace agreement.)*

Further Instruction

Ask students to recall the bombing of the U.S. Marine headquarters in Beirut, Lebanon, in 1983. Be sure students understand the devastating effects of the bombing and the political shift it created provided a new tactic for terrorists to follow.

Infer Why did terrorist organizations turn to truck and car bombings? *(These types of attacks provided a powerful way for smaller, less-trained and equipped organizations to stand up against the powerful American military.)*

Make Generalizations Why did the United States become targets of terrorists in the Middle East? *(The continued American presence in the Middle East and in Islamic countries was resented by the terrorists.)*

Determine Relevance How helpful was the Declaration of Principles in resolving problems in the Middle East? *(The declaration was not that successful because it did not adequately address the issues of Israeli settlements in the West Bank, nor did it placate extremists on either side, who had no interest in compromise. Violence continued even after the declaration was signed.)* After students have answered this question, discuss the pros and cons of U.S participation in international organizations and treaties.

SYNTHESIZE

DIGITAL ACTIVITY

Key Events in American Foreign Policy

Discuss Before students begin their timelines, lead the class in a brief review of the role the U.S. played in world affairs during the Cold War. Encourage students to think about the changes in foreign policy as the U.S. became the sole superpower following the collapse of the Soviet Union.

DEMONSTRATE

LESSON QUIZ

Lesson Quiz and Class Discussion Board

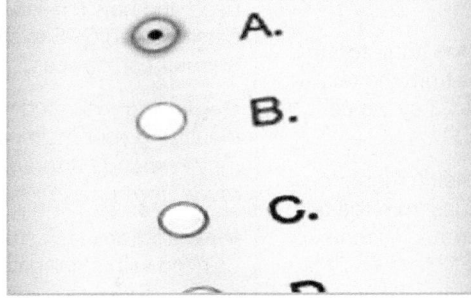

Assign the online Lesson Quiz for this lesson if you haven't already done so. Students will be offered automatic remediation or enrichment based on their score.

Pose these questions to the class on the Discussion Board:

In *A New Era in Foreign Policy*, you read about the emergence of the United States as the world's sole superpower following the breakup of the Soviet Union. America's foreign policy during the Bush and Clinton presidencies demonstrated that the end of the Cold War would not lead to a new era of peace, but instead to a dangerous era of regional conflicts.

Express Ideas Clearly Based on what you've learned about U.S. foreign policy in the 1980s and 1990s, do you think the United States should intervene in conflicts in the world? What problems can result from such a policy?

Predict Consequences Will the continued U.S. presence in the Middle East eventually lead to a breakthrough in a lasting peace between Israel and Palestinians and neighboring Arab nations? Explain.

Topic Inquiry

Have students continue their investigations for the Topic Inquiry.

Clinton and the 1990s

Supporting English Language Learners

Use with Digital Text 1, **Clinton Enacts New Domestic Policies.**

Reading

Review the definitions of *letter, word, sentence*, and *paragraph*, and ask volunteers to identify examples of each. Explain that when reading English, like many other languages, they will scan the words from left to right and top to bottom.

Beginning Demonstrate the directionality of English (left to right, top to bottom) by pointing to each word as you read a few lines from the text. Then ask students to recognize directionality of English as they locate the phrase that follows *Early in his presidency....*

Intermediate Demonstrate the directionality of English (left to right, top to bottom) by pointing to each word as you read a few lines from the text. Then have partners take turns reading the page, using strategies to keep from skipping or repeating lines.

Advanced Demonstrate how the directionality of English (left to right, top to bottom) also applies to the reading of titles and subheadings. Discuss why these text features should not be skipped over. Have partners take turns reading the text.

Advanced High Discuss why it can be helpful to preview titles and subheadings by themselves (following the rules of directionality, such as left to right and top to bottom). Have pairs of students read the text's title and subheadings and discuss what they might reveal about the text's content.

Use with Digital Text 4, **Digital Technology Changes American Life.**

Listening

Tell students that they will have a chance to practice identifying the main points of spoken language—both familiar and unfamiliar. Use familiar language to explain what a satellite is and does. Then explain how GPS is used and how it relies on satellite technology to work. Display images of satellites and GPS systems and ask volunteers to share what they know about these devices.

Beginning Ask students to demonstrate their understanding by identifying your main points about satellites from these choices: *satellites move around Earth; they send and receive information; they land on the moon; they give driving directions; they help cell phones work.*

Intermediate Ask students to demonstrate their understanding by working with small groups to state the main points you made. Have groups record their responses in a two-column chart (with headings *satellites* and *GPS*).

Advanced Ask pairs of students to demonstrate their understanding by recording your main points in a two-column chart (with headings *satellites* and *GPS*).

Advanced High Ask students to demonstrate their understanding by working individually to list your main points in complete sentences. When students finish writing, have them compare their lists with partners and make adjustments as needed.

▣ Differentiate Instruction

Use the Differentiated Instruction notes throughout the lesson plan to support the varied skill sets, levels of readiness, and interests in the mixed-ability classroom.

Challenge These notes include suggestions for expanding the activity for advanced students.

On-Level These notes include suggestions for modifying the activity to address different interests or learning styles.

Extra Support These notes include ideas for providing more scaffolding or reading spuport.

Special Needs These notes provide ideas for adapting instruction to support the needs of various special needs students.

■ NOTES

PEARSON
realize™
www.PearsonRealize.com

Go online to access additional resources including:
Primary Sources • Biographies • Supreme Court cases •
21st Century Skill Tutorials • Maps • Graphic Organizers.

Objectives

Objective 1: Assess the success of Clinton's domestic policies.

Objective 2: Describe the Contract With America and its impact.

Objective 3: Analyze the Clinton impeachment.

Objective 4: Evaluate the changes that new technological innovations brought to the economy and daily life in the 1990s.

LESSON 5 ORGANIZER		OBJECTIVES	PACING	RESOURCES	
PACING: APPROX. 1 PERIOD, .5 BLOCKS				Online	Print
Connect					
	DIGITAL START UP ACTIVITY **Becoming President**		5 min.	●	
Investigate					
	DIGITAL TEXT 1 **Clinton Enacts New Domestic Policies**	Objective 1	10 min.	●	●
	DIGITAL TEXT 2 **Republicans Lead a Conservative Resurgence**	Objective 2	10 min.	●	●
	INTERACTIVE GALLERY **The Gun Debate**		10 min.	●	
	DIGITAL TEXT 3 **Scandals, Impeachment, and Trial**	Objective 3	10 min.	●	●
	INTERACTIVE CHART **Checks and Balances in Action**		10 min.	●	
	DIGITAL TEXT 4 **Digital Technology Changes American Life**	Objective 4	10 min.	●	●
	INTERACTIVE ILLUSTRATION **Free Enterprise Spreads Technological Innovation**		10 min.	●	
Synthesize					
	DIGITAL ACTIVITY **The United States in the 1990s**		5 min.	●	
Demonstrate					
	LESSON QUIZ **Lesson Quiz and Class Discussion Board**		10 min.	●	

Clinton and the 1990s

■ CONNECT

DIGITAL START UP ACTIVITY
Becoming President

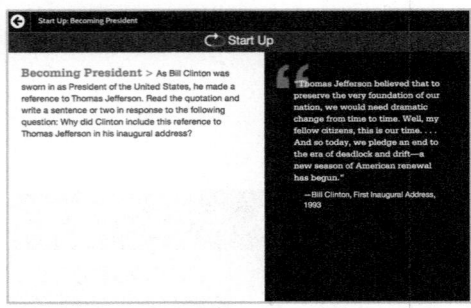

Project the Start Up Activity Engage students in thinking about the political, domestic, and foreign policy issues that Bill Clinton would have to face as he took the office of the president. Then have students share their ideas with a partner, either in class or through a chat or blog space.

Discuss Take a moment to reflect on Thomas Jefferson's ideas that Clinton invoked. Do you agree with Jefferson's premise? *(Responses should consider Jefferson's belief in dramatic change from time to time.)*

Tell students that in this lesson they will learn about President Clinton and a new kind of Democrat—more moderate while still pursuing goals such as healthcare reform. President Clinton would oversee America's longest peacetime economic expansion.

Aa Vocabulary Development: Use the Interactive Reading Notepad to preview the Key Terms and Academic Vocabulary in this lesson with students.

⇅ FLIP IT!
Assign the Flipped Video for this Lesson.

■ STUDENT EDITION PRINT PAGES: 832–838

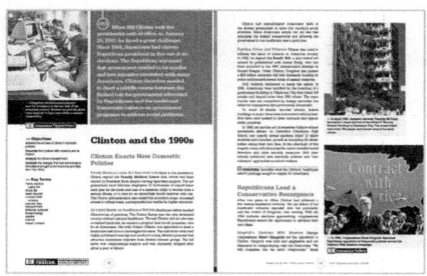

■ INVESTIGATE

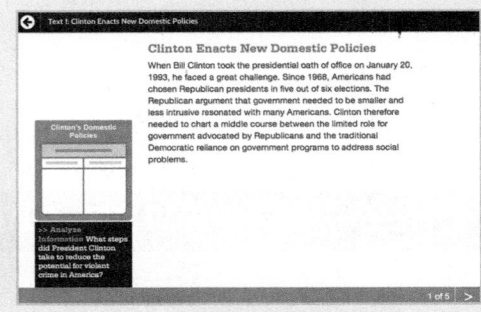

DIGITAL TEXT 1
Clinton Enacts New Domestic Policies

Objective 1: Assess the success of Clinton's domestic policies.

Quick Instruction
As President Clinton took office, he looked at several significant social and political issues that faced Americans, including high crime rates, incidents of extreme violence, and a need for healthcare reform. As First Lady, Hillary Clinton became a signficant political and social leader as she championed healthcare reform.

Analyze Charts Project the chart that shows significant domestic policies of the Clinton administration. Review the policies with students and them ask them to assess the success of each. Which Clinton policies related to family issues? *(Defense of Marriage Act, Family and Medical Leave Act, Health Insurance Portability and Accountability Act)* Which policies were aimed at addressing crime? *(Brady Bill, Violent Crime Control and Law Enforcement Act)*

Hypothesize Why might President George H.W. Bush have vetoed the Family and Medical Leave Act? *(The Act could be viewed as being potentially harmful to businesses, which were forced to provide medical leave for employees. As a conservative, Bush might have considered this an overreach on the part of the federal government.)*

ELL Use the ELL activity described in the ELL chart.

Further Instruction
Point out that providing healthcare for all Americans has been a significant social and political issue across the political spectrum since the Progressive Era. Presidents since have worked to provide adequate healthcare for Americans and to combat escalating costs.

Express Problems Clearly Why did Clinton's healthcare reform policies fail? *(Diverse interest groups criticized the plan and the bill never won congressional support. Clinton had miscalculated Americans' confidence in the federal government to solve the country's social problems. In addition, Clinton lacked large support from the American people, many of whom did not want to enlarge the federal bureaucracy and allow the government to run healthcare.)*

DIGITAL TEXT 2
Republicans Lead a Conservative Resurgence

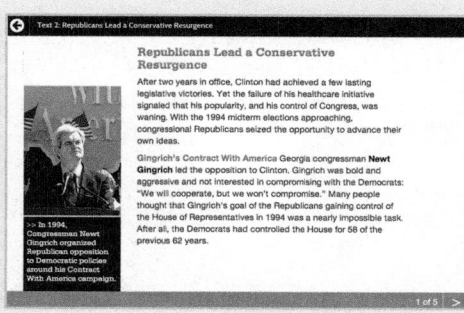

INTERACTIVE GALLERY
The Gun Debate

DIGITAL TEXT 3
Scandals, Impeachment, and Trial

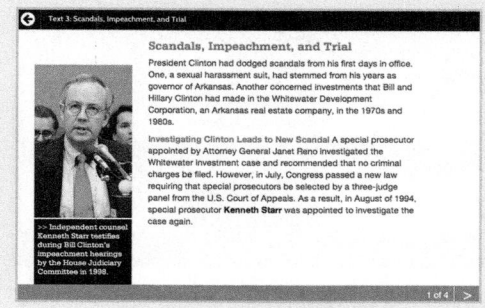

Objective 2: Describe the Contract with America and its impact.

Quick Instruction

As midterm elections approached, Newt Gingrich stepped up the Republican agenda and conservative resurgence with his Contract with America. As in the 1980s, the causes of this conservative resurgence were clear: many Americans wanted to see a reduction of the federal bureaucracy, large tax cuts, and welfare reform, among other things. As a result of his work, Republicans took control of the House for the first time in decades.

Interactive Gallery: The Gun Debate Project the interactive gallery and click through the images and information. Invite volunteers to identify significant political advocacy organizations and their leaders involved in the gun debate. *(Charlton Heston; the National Rifle Association; Wayne LaPierre of the NRA; James Brady and his anti-gun advocacy movement.)*

Analyze Information What does the timeline showing significant cases centering on the Second Amendment tell you about the gun debate in America? *(The debate has been an issue for a long time, and there are different interpretations of the Second Amendment.)*

👥 ACTIVE CLASSROOM

Have students break into groups and use the Circle Write Strategy to address the prompt, "Why does the Second Amendment draw such heated debate in the United States?" Have students write as much as they can for one minute and then switch with the person on their right. The next person tries to improve or elaborate the response where the other person left off. Continue to switch until the paper comes back to the first person. The group decides which is the best composition and shares that with the class.

Further Instruction

Challenge student volunteers to set the political scene in the run-up to the 1994 midterm elections. Be sure students identify and describe key organizations of the conservative resurgence of the 1990s, including the Contract with America and the influential leaders across the political spectrum, that played key roles, such as Newt Gingrich.

Identify Point of View On what domestic issues did Republicans focus to win the 1994 midterm elections? *(They called for congressional term limits, reduction of the federal bureaucracy, a balanced budget amendment to the Constitution, and large tax cuts, significant welfare reform, and tough anti-crime legislation.)*

Synthesize Information What factors led to Clinton winning reelection in 1996? *(As the 1996 election approached, the American economy was so strong that few Americans had a compelling reason to change leadership. In addition, Ross Perot ran as a third party candidate again and shifted votes away from Republican Robert Dole, helping Clinton.)*

Objective 3: Analyze the Clinton impeachment.

Quick Instruction

Political scandal plagued the Clinton presidency, from Whitewater to Clinton's impeachment. The effects of these scandals culminated in U.S. citizens' mistrust of the federal government and its leaders.

Interactive Chart: Checks and Balances in Action Project the Interactive chart and click through the hot spots. Work your way through each case so students get a sense of how the branches of government have the power to "check" the others.

👥 ACTIVE CLASSROOM

Have students use the Sticky Notes Strategy and take three minutes to jot down their ideas about how the process of checks and balances works. Then ask, "Why is checks and balances necessary?" Have students post their stickies on a wall. Sort and discuss their responses as a group.

D Differentiate: Extra Support Because the interactive chart contains a great deal of information, provide extra time and support for students having difficulty identifying the roles of each branch of government. Provide opportunities for these students to Think-Pair-Share with a partner.

Clinton and the 1990s

INTERACTIVE CHART	DIGITAL TEXT 4	INTERACTIVE ILLUSTRATION

Checks and Balances in Action

Digital Technology Changes American Life

Free Enterprise Spreads Technological Innovation

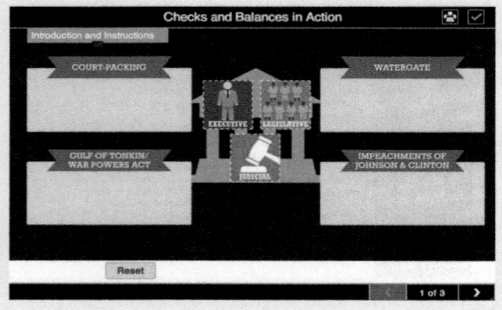

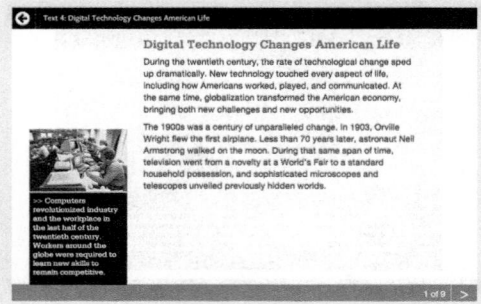

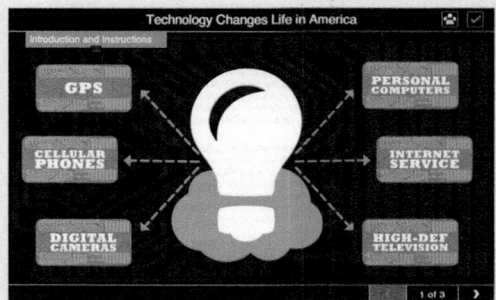

Further Instruction

Begin a discussion of the Clinton impeachment by asking students to summarize the key events.

Identify Central Issues How could Clinton be impeached but remain in office? *(The House of Representatives is the chamber that brings charges of impeachment against the President. The Senate is the chamber that tries the case. In the Clinton case, the Republican majority in House impeached Clinton, but the Senate acquitted him on both counts.)*

Generate Explanations Challenge students to describe the effects of Bill Clinton's impeachment on the views of U.S. citizens concerning trust in the federal government and its leaders. *(Most Americans condemned Clinton's actions but opposed impeachment. Like Nixon and the Watergate scandal, Americans lost trust in Clinton and other government leaders because of the scandal.)*

Objective 4: Evaluate the changes that new technological innovations brought to the economy and daily life in the 1990s.

Quick Instruction

The 1980s and 1990s hosted scientific discoveries and technological innovations that would fuel economic development of the United States and change daily life for Americans. Entrepreneurs such as Bill Gates, Ted Turner, and Robert Johnson cashed in on technological innovations to develop personal computers and use satellite technology to broadcast news and entertainment 24 hours a day via paid television.

Interactive Illustration: Free Enterprise Spreads Technological Innovation Project the interactive illustration and have students look through the images. Ask students to explain the effects of scientific discoveries and technological innovations such as satellite communications and computers on the economic development of the United States. (Student responses should include understanding that satellite communications and computers streamlined business operations, making them more efficient and profitable. The race to develop newer and better technology jump-started a race among companies and entrepreneurs, creating new industries and consumers.)

Identify Cause and Effect How has the computer sped up the pace of globalization? *(The computer and its related technology have made the sharing and accessing of information almost instantaneous. Companies and customers can communicate and work together from anywhere in the world using computer technology.)*

📷 ACTIVE CLASSROOM

Conduct a Graffiti Concepts Activity. Ask students to reflect on the technological innovations that came to prominence in the 1990s and create a visual image and/or phrase that represents each innovation. (Allow approximately 3–5 minutes.) Then ask students to post their "graffiti" on the board or on chart paper and ask students to look at all the various causes then discuss them as a group.

ELL Use the ELL activity described in the ELL chart.

Further Instruction

Review with students the development and resulting effects of key technological innovations, such as the computer, Internet, and global positioning products.

SYNTHESIZE

DIGITAL ACTIVITY
The United States in the 1990s

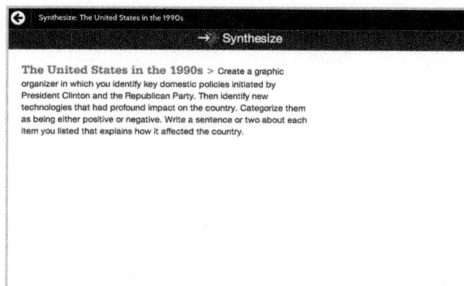

Synthesize Information Challenge students to explain how the development of the computer, Internet, and global positioning products was a result of government and the free enterprise system working together. *(These innovations were all developed initially through government research or funding. However, bringing the technologies to average citizens and further developing them was the result of companies and entrepreneurs working within the free enterprise system.)*

Summarize Ask students to explain how the free enterprise system applies technological innovation in the marketplace, such as inexpensive personal computers and global positioning products. *(The great demand for newer, faster, and more versatile digital devices—coupled with the potential fortunes awaiting those who successfully delivered them—motivated inventors and entrepreneurs. These inventors and entrepreneurs developed newer technologies and manufacturing systems that drove down costs, allowing even a great number of people to use these new technologies.)*

Discuss Before students begin their graphic organizers, ask them to recall the Topic Essential Question, "What makes a government successful?" Lead the class in a brief review of how the system of checks and balances contributes to a successful government. Remind students of Newt Gingrich's statement, "We will cooperate, but we won't compromise." Ask them to take five minutes to write some brief thoughts about the statement, as well as how Gingrich and the Republicans along with the Clinton administration helped create such booming economic times. Have students share their thoughts with the class.

DEMONSTRATE

LESSON QUIZ
Lesson Quiz and Class Discussion Board

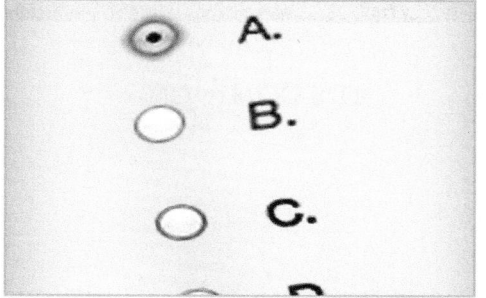

Assign the online Lesson Quiz for this lesson if you haven't already done so. Students will be offered automatic remediation or enrichment based on their score.

Pose these questions to the class on the Discussion Board:

In *Clinton and the 1990s*, you read about how President Clinton and the Congressional Republicans were able to work together to create the longest peacetime economic expansion in U.S. history. Fueled in part by the high-tech boom, the U.S. economy in the 1990s flourished.

Analyze Information Clinton charted a middle course between the limited role for government advocated by Republicans and the traditional Democratic reliance on government programs to address social problems. He presided over the federal government's first balanced budget since the late 1960s and held the largest budget surplus in U.S. history. In 1996, during his reelection campaign, Clinton announced, "The era of big government is over." Cite evidence supporting or refuting this statement.

Draw Inferences What makes the American free enterprise system so dynamic and productive? *(Free enterprise allows for competition in business and industry, which, in turn, leads to innovation. As competitors try to keep up, they provide different options for consumers, which results in the reduction of costs.)*

Topic Inquiry
Have students continue their investigations for the Topic Inquiry.

America in the 1980s and 1990s

PEARSON realize™
▶
www.PearsonRealize.com
Access your Digital Lesson

■ SYNTHESIZE

DIGITAL ACTIVITY

Reflect on the Essential Question and Topic

First ask students to reconsider the Essential Question for the topic: What makes a government successful? Remind students of the list of responsibilities and achievements they created at the beginning of the topic.

Ask students "Do you think the U.S. government was a success in the 1980s and 1990s?" Ask them to give at least three reasons to support their position. Discuss their answers as a class or ask students to post their answers on the Class Discussion Board.

Next ask students to reflect on the topic as a whole and jot down 1–3 questions they've thought about during the topic. Share these examples if students need help getting started:

- How do the values of conservatives and liberals differ?
- Is the United States the best equipped nation to be the world's sole superpower? Why or why not?
- What role do governments have, if any, in the free enterprise system?

You may ask students to share their questions and answers on the Class Discussion Board.

Topic Inquiry

Have students complete Step 3 of the Topic Inquiry.

■ DEMONSTRATE

DIGITAL TOPIC REVIEW AND ASSESSMENT

America in the 1980s and 1990s

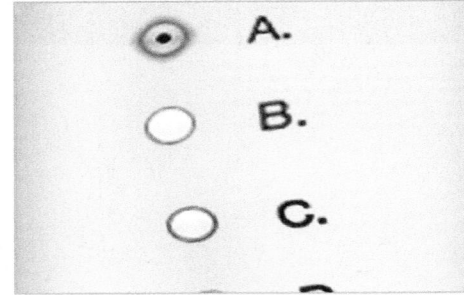

Students can prepare for the Topic Test by answering the questions in the Topic Review and Assessment online or the Assessment questions in the Print Student text. They can also prepare by reviewing their answers to the Interactive Reading Notepad questions or reviewing their notes in the Reading and Notetaking Study Guide.

DIGITAL TOPIC TEST

America in the 1980s and 1990s

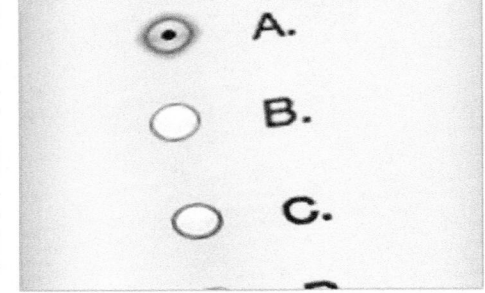

TOPIC TEST

Assign the Topic Test to assess students' understanding of topic content.

BENCHMARK TESTS

Assign these benchmark tests as you complete the relevant topics to monitor student progress toward mastering the course content and as preparation for the End-of-Course Test.

Benchmark Test 1: Topics 1–3

Benchmark Test 2: Topics 4–6

Benchmark Test 3: Topics 7–9

Benchmark Test 4: Topics 10–12

Benchmark Test 5: Topics 13–15

Benchmark Test 6: Topics 16–18

Benchmark Test 7: Topics 19–20

America in the Twenty-First Century

TOPIC 20 ORGANIZER	PACING: APPROX. 7 PERIODS, 3.5 BLOCKS
	PACING
Connect	1 period
MY STORY VIDEO **Leslie Bradshaw, Guiding Innovation**	10 min.
DIGITAL ESSENTIAL QUESTION ACTIVITY **What Are the Benefits and Costs of Technology?**	10 min.
DIGITAL TIMELINE ACTIVITY **America in the Twenty-First Century**	10 min.
TOPIC INQUIRY: PROJECT-BASED LEARNING **Create a U.S. History Course for New Citizens**	20 min.
Investigate	2–4 periods
TOPIC INQUIRY: PROJECT-BASED LEARNING **Create a U.S. History Course for New Citizens**	Ongoing
LESSON 1 America and the World Economy	30–40 min.
LESSON 2 The George W. Bush Presidency	30–40 min.
LESSON 3 The Barack Obama Presidency	30–40 min.
LESSON 4 Americans Look to the Future	30–40 min.
Synthesize	1 period
DIGITAL ACTIVITY **Reflect on the Essential Question and Topic**	10 min.
TOPIC INQUIRY: PROJECT-BASED LEARNING **Create a U.S. History Course for New Citizens**	20 min.
Demonstrate	1–2 periods
DIGITAL TOPIC REVIEW AND ASSESSMENT **America in the Twenty-First Century**	10 min.
TOPIC INQUIRY: PROJECT-BASED LEARNING **Create a U.S. History Course for New Citizens**	20 min.

TOPIC INQUIRY: PROJECT-BASED LEARNING

Create a U.S. History Course for New Citizens

In this Topic Inquiry, students work in teams to create a multimedia course for individuals wishing to become American citizens. Remind students that U.S. citizens are people from numerous places throughout the world who hold a common bond in standing for certain self-evident truths. These truths include the civic values that unite American society. Using technology to explore the values of American society and the ways new citizens can fulfill the duties and responsibilities of citizenship will contribute to students' understanding of America in the twenty-first century, including the Topic Essential Question: What are the benefits and costs of technology?

STEP 1: CONNECT
Develop Questions and Plan the Investigation

Launch the Project and Generate Questions
Have students read the *Project Launch* and underline key parts of the article. First, they will examine American values as described in Alexis de Tocqueville's 1830 book, *Democracy in America*. Second, they will create a timeline of five historical eras corresponding to five American values. Lastly, they will create and present a multimedia course for people wishing to become American citizens. The course will include their timeline of major historical eras, quotes on the values that defined each era, and an assessment on American values.

Suggestion: As you lead the class discussion on the *Project Launch*, have students explain the five values in their own terms: liberty, egalitarianism, individualism, populism, and laissez faire. Ask students to come up with an example of each value to show their understanding.

Plan the Investigation
Form students into teams. Have them read and sign the *Project Contract* and begin filling out the *Need-to-Know Questions*. Encourage them to answer the sample questions and then generate more of their own.

Suggestion: To help students break the Guiding Question into more manageable questions, have them consider the American values defined by de Tocqueville and then ask about role of the United States in the twenty-first century.

Resources
- Project Launch
- Student Instructions
- Need-to-Know Questions
- Project Contract

STEP 2: INVESTIGATE
Apply Disciplinary Concepts and Tools

Read and Select Quotes
Have students review the Skills Tutorial *Work in Teams* and begin using the *Project Tracker*. Then have students follow the link to *Democracy in America* and read about the American values de Tocqueville identifies.

Research Major Historical Eras of U.S. History
Students will match the quotes they found from *Democracy in America* to each major era. Students should use reliable online resources and school-library.

Suggestion: Encourage groups to look at a variety of sources and perspectives and then discuss how to divide the historical eras.

Create a Timeline of Five Eras of United States History
Students will use their research to create a multimedia timeline. Each era should have its own slide and include a visual or audio element, a description of the era, a quote by de Tocqueville, and text supporting the connection between the value and the era.

Write the Course Introduction and Assessment
Students will create a written introduction and a citizenship test.

Resources
- Work in Teams
- Project Tracker
- Information Organizer
- Search for Information on the Internet and Evaluate Websites
- 21st Century Skill Tutorials: Being an Informed Citizen
- 21st Century Skill Tutorials: Voting
- 21st Century Skill Tutorials: Political Participation

⏻ PROFESSIONAL DEVELOPMENT

Project-Based Learning
Be sure to view the Project-Based Learning Professional Development resources in the online course.

STEP 3: SYNTHESIZE
Evaluate Sources and Use Evidence to Formulate Conclusions

Create Your Multimedia Course

Now have students build their multimedia course using their timeline, introduction, and assessment. Following the assessment, students should also include one slide that summarizes their conclusions. Student groups should decide which multimedia presentation software to use and how to organize and present their information. If students are having trouble sharing the work of this part of the project, remind them to review the *Work in Teams* tutorial and look at their *Project Tracker* to make sure they are fulfilling their roles.

Suggestion: If students are having trouble organizing their course, have them create a mock-up of each slide modeling on paper how they want to present the information. Alternately, you may encourage students to explore the multimedia presentation software to discover new ways to organize their courses.

Formulate Your Conclusions

Student groups should write a short summary of what they have learned about the values that form the foundation of American citizenship. Have students use the questions to guide their thinking. Remind students that these questions should help them focus their multimedia course and show the importance of the values they detailed in the introduction, timeline, and assessment questions. Allow students to go back and make changes to the multimedia course if writing their summaries changes their thinking.

Suggestion: Before students write their summaries, have them present the multimedia course to one another and discuss their responses.

Resources
- Work in Teams
- Project Tracker

STEP 4: DEMONSTRATE
Communicate Conclusions and Take Informed Action

Present your Course

Have students prepare their multimedia presentations and then watch each group's presentation. Give students time to practice their presentations and make any improvements. Allow time at the end of the presentations to discuss the values and historical eras that each group identified, noting any differences or overlap among groups.

Reflect on the Project

After students have finished their Team Assessments, guide them to consider what went well and what did not so that they can be even more effective in the future.

Suggestion: As an extension of the activity, have students find a contemporary news story about a Congressional debate, a new law, a court ruling, or a social, economic, or political reform and write a paragraph about how it reflects the values they presented in their multimedia course.

America in the Twenty-First Century

America in the twenty-first century faces both challenges and opportunities. Changes in the economy have tied the country more closely to the rest of the world, bringing economic growth as well as competition. Technology accelerates these changes as innovations in computers, media, and the Internet impact every facet of American life. The terrorist attacks of September 11, 2001 inaugurated a new era of domestic and foreign policy, raising questions about security and civil rights.

CONNECT

MY STORY VIDEO

Leslie Bradshaw, Guiding Innovation

Watch a video that introduces students to entrepreneur Leslie Bradshaw and the company she started.

Check Understanding What three pillars does Leslie Bradshaw say help define her? *(The three pillars are to take risks, keep learning, and remember your past.)*

Draw Conclusions How do you think Leslie Bradshaw's heritage affected her ability to start her own company. *(Her ancestors, who were pioneers moving across the Oregon Trail, had been risk takers, and as a child she had learned the value of hard work from growing up on her parents' farm.)*

DIGITAL ESSENTIAL QUESTION ACTIVITY

What Are the Benefits and Costs of Technology?

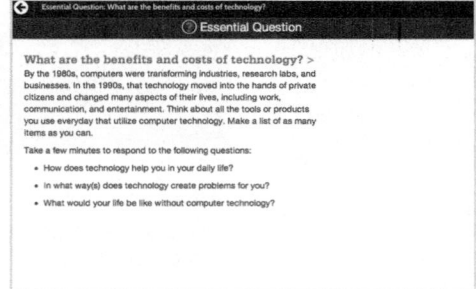

Ask students to think about the Essential Question for this topic: What are the benefits and costs of technology? Americans use technology every day, transforming how we work, learn, and communicate.

If students have not already done so, ask them to generate a list of ways they use technology and then answer the questions. Have students share their ideas with a partner.

Hypothesize How do you think that the Technological Revolution has changed American society in the contemporary era?

Make Predictions How do you think technological innovations will affect the American economy in the twenty-first century?

DIGITAL TIMELINE ACTIVITY

America in the Twenty-First Century

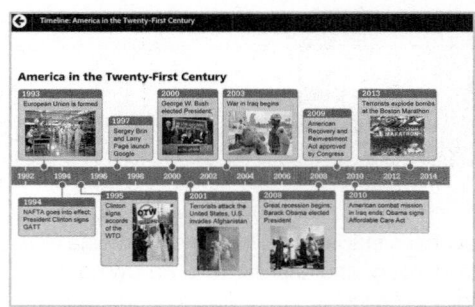

Display the timeline showing the major events of the late twentieth and early twenty-first centuries. During this topic students will learn about all of these events and many more, but this timeline will provide a framework into which they can place the events they learn about.

Identify Patterns What trends to you notice leading towards a more globalized world economy? *(the European Union, NAFTA, GATT, and WTO accords)*

Identify Cause and Effect How did the 2001 terrorist attacks shape American foreign policy in the twenty-first century? *(The attacks led America to go to war in Afghanistan and then Iraq.)*

Topic Inquiry

Launch the Topic Inquiry with students after introducing the topic.

America and the World Economy

PEARSON
realize™

www.PearsonRealize.com
Access your Digital Lesson

Supporting English Language Learners

Use with Digital Text 1, **Free Trade and Treaties.**

Reading

Explain that just as prepositions are basic sight vocabulary, certain phrases that include prepositions are also used routinely in written classroom materials.

Beginning Display the last sentence of the text, and point out the phrase *for example*. Explain its meaning in the context of classroom materials, and have students complete and read aloud these sentences: Clinton signed many free trade agreements. For example, _____.

Intermediate Display the first sentence of the fourth paragraph. Discuss the meaning of *in theory* in the context of classroom materials. Have students suggest sentences using the phrase. Record their suggestions, and read aloud the sentences together.

Advanced Display the last sentence of the third paragraph, and discuss the meaning of *depending on* in the context of classroom materials. Have pairs of students write two sentences beginning with the phrase. Ask pairs to take turns reading one another's sentences.

Advanced High Point out the two instances of went into effect toward the end of the section *The United States Joins NAFTA*. Ask students to use the phrase *to go into effect* in two written sentences: once in the past tense, and once in the future tense. Then have partners read each other's sentences.

Use with Digital Text 2, **Technological and Management Innovations in the American Economy.**

Listening

Prompt students to understand the main points of spoken language as you ask them to share the ways they use technology in their everyday lives. Discuss how their lives might be different without it.

Beginning Use basic spoken language to explain globalization in the familiar context of the average American consumer. Help students to demonstrate understanding of your main points by completing this sentence: Globalization is good for consumers because _____.

Intermediate Use spoken language to explain globalization in the somewhat familiar context of cultural heritage. Ask students to demonstrate understanding of your main points by naming ways that globalization has affected the uniqueness of cultures around the world.

Advanced Use spoken language to explain globalization in the somewhat unfamiliar context of the local business economy. Ask pairs of students to demonstrate understanding of your main points by discussing ways that local businesses are affected by globalization.

Advanced High Use spoken language to explain globalization in the somewhat unfamiliar context of Internet entrepreneurship. Ask students to write a paragraph that summarizes your main points. Provide time for partners to compare their work.

◘ Differentiate Instruction

Use the Differentiated Instruction notes throughout the lesson plan to support the varied skill sets, levels of readiness, and interests in the mixed-ability classroom.

Challenge These notes include suggestions for expanding the activity for advanced students.

On-Level These notes include suggestions for modifying the activity to address different interests or learning styles.

Extra Support These notes include ideas for providing more scaffolding or reading spuport.

Special Needs These notes provide ideas for adapting instruction to support the needs of various special needs students.

▮ NOTES

America and the World Economy

Objectives

Objective 1: Understand how the United States is affected by emerging economic issues such as changes in the global economy.

Objective 2: Explain how globalization and the rise of the service sector affects the American economy.

Objective 3: Understand the productivity enhancements resulting from management innovations.

Objective 4: Understand the global economic challenges facing the United States.

LESSON 1 ORGANIZER	PACING: APPROX. 1 PERIOD, .5 BLOCKS			
			RESOURCES	
	OBJECTIVES	PACING	Online	Print
Connect				
DIGITAL START UP ACTIVITY **Calling for a "Shared Future"**		5 min.	●	
Investigate				
DIGITAL TEXT 1 **Free Trade and Treaties**	Objective 1	10 min.	●	●
INTERACTIVE GALLERY **Evaluate the U.S. Role in the World Bank**		10 min.	●	
DIGITAL TEXT 2 **Technological and Management Innovations in the American Economy**	Objectives 2, 3	10 min.	●	●
DIGITAL TEXT 3 **The Role of the United States in the Future Economy**	Objective 4	10 min.	●	●
BEFORE AND AFTER **The U.S. Role in the Global Economy**		10 min.	●	
Synthesize				
DIGITAL ACTIVITY **Evaluating Globalization**		5 min.	●	
Demonstrate				
DIGITAL QUIZ **Lesson Quiz and Class Discussion Board**		10 min.	●	

PEARSON **realize**™
www.PearsonRealize.com

Go online to access additional resources including:
Primary Sources • Biographies • Supreme Court cases •
21st Century Skill Tutorials • Maps • Graphic Organizers.

■ CONNECT

Calling for a "Shared Future"

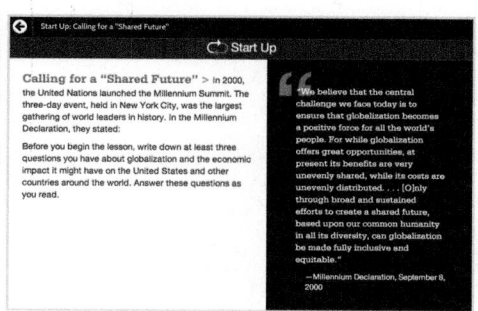

Project the Start Up Activity Ask students to read the quote from the Millennium Declaration and write down at least three questions they have about the economic impact of globalization. Have students share their questions with a partner, either in class or through a blog space.

Tell students that in this lesson they will be learning about how multinational corporations, government policies, and globalization have impacted the twenty-first century economy.

Aa Vocabulary Development: Use the Interactive Reading Notepad to preview the Key Terms and Academic Vocabulary in this lesson with students.

↥ FLIP IT!

Assign the Flipped Video for this lesson.

■ STUDENT EDITION PRINT PAGES: 844–849

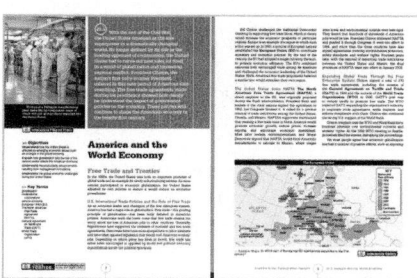

■ INVESTIGATE

Free Trade and Treaties

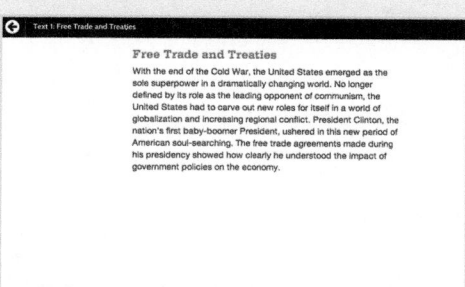

Evaluate the U.S. Role in the World Bank

Objective 1: Understand how the United States is affected by emerging economic issues such as changes in the global economy.

Quick Instruction

Interactive Gallery: Evaluate the U.S. Role in the World Bank Project the interactive gallery and click through the images. Discuss the pros and cons of U.S. participation in the World Bank.

Make Generalizations How do U.S. international trade policies promote free trade? *(eliminating trade restrictions, engaging in trade with other countries, creating trade blocs to stimulate growth)*

🔲 ACTIVE CLASSROOM

Group students to use the PMI Strategy to evaluate the pros and cons of U.S. participation in international organizations. Ask students to consider the possibility that global organizations are undermining U.S. sovereignty through the use of treaties. Give each group a 3-column organizer with the headings Plus/Minus/Interesting. Have students use the organizer to record responses to the following questions: 1. What are the positive effects of participating in international organizations? 2. What are the negative effects of this? 3. What is interesting about this?

ELL Use the ELL activity described in the ELL chart.

Further Instruction

Go through the Interactive Reading Notepad questions and discuss the answers with the class. To extend the lesson, assign Economics Basics: Trade and Economics Basics: Development.

Identify Central Issues Describe the dynamic relationship between the U.S. free enterprise system and NAFTA. How does NAFTA promote free trade? What are the potential drawbacks to this? *(NAFTA promotes free trade by removing restrictions among the United States, Canada, and Mexico in order to create a free trade zone. This reduces prices, encourages investment, and promotes exports and growth. Drawbacks include the fear that American manufacturers will move to Mexico, causing Americans to lose their jobs.)* How have social and political advocacy organizations affected the debate over NAFTA? *(These organizations, depending on their position on the political spectrum have argued both for and against joining NAFTA.)*

Summarize Describe the General Agreement of Tariffs and Trade. Why was this international trade policy implemented? *(Passed in 1994, GATT reduces tariffs in order to encourage free trade.)*

Support Ideas with Examples Give an example of a government policy enacted under Clinton designed to increase U.S. participation in international markets and explain its impact on the twenty-first century economy. *(Clinton pushed NAFTA through Congress, signed 270 free trade agreements, and supported the World Bank. These policies increased free trade and gave the United States a strong role in promoting economic globalization.)*

America and the World Economy

DIGITAL TEXT 2

Technological and Management Innovations in the American Economy

Text 2: Technological and Management Innovations in the American Economy

Technological and Management Innovations in the American Economy

Today, technological changes continue to have a dramatic effect on the American economy, raising the standard of living. New technology influences how and where people do their jobs. In this changing economy, one sector—the service industry—has grown rapidly. A lower percentage of Americans than ever before work on assembly lines or on farms. Instead, they provide services.

Objectives 2: Explain how globalization and the rise of the service sector affects the American economy; 3: Understand the productivity enhancements resulting from management innovations.

Quick Instruction

Define globalization as the process by which national economies, politics, cultures, and societies become integrated with those of other nations around the world. Project the chart on the whiteboard and discuss the effects of economic globalization on the U.S. economy.

Support Ideas with Examples Identify the impact of multinational corporations on the twenty-first century economy, including both positive and negative examples. *(Economies and nations are more integrated around the world. As a result, more goods and services are available to more people; prices are often lower; some nations have grown more developed; manufacturing jobs have moved from developed to less developed nations; economic problems in one region quickly spread.)*

Identify Cause and Effect How have computers affected economic development in the United States? *(Jobs have become more dependent on computers, and jobs that use computers have grown. Computers can be used to increase productivity in industries and efficiency in businesses that need to track and predict demand. Computers have also led America to expand its service sector by enabling workers to produce services in addition to—or instead of—manufactured goods.)Name some individuals whose technological innovations have had an impact on the twenty-first century economy. (Sergey Brin and Larry Page, who launched Google; Mark Zuckerberg who launched Facebook.)*

D Differentiate: Extra Support Have students identify the root word *global* in the word *globalization*. Ask them to come up with an example of how a national company might grow to become more global through its workers, products, location, markets, raw materials, or other factors.

ELL Use the ELL activity described in the ELL chart.

Further Instruction

Go through the Interactive Reading Notepad questions and discuss the answers with the class. To extend the lesson, assign Geography Basics: The Impact of Globalization.

Summarize Describe how applications of technological innovations in communication have affected the workplace. *(Work has changed, as people are connected by communication technologies such as computers and cell phones. Workers can telecommute and hold meetings with people from around the world.)*

Compare How have technological and management enhancements affected the productivity of labor? *(Jobs in the service industry vary widely. Many workers have had to learn new skills to compete. Computer-driven industrial robots perform assembly-line manufacturing tasks that used to be done by humans, and productivity has increased. On the other hand, entrepreneurs have had new opportunities to create successful businesses.)*

Summarize How have technological and management innovations such as just-in-time inventory management improved productivity? *(Technological innovations have allowed businesses to better anticipate demand for their products, which in turn helps them to reduce the costs of excess inventory.)*

DIGITAL TEXT 3

The Role of the United States in the Future Economy

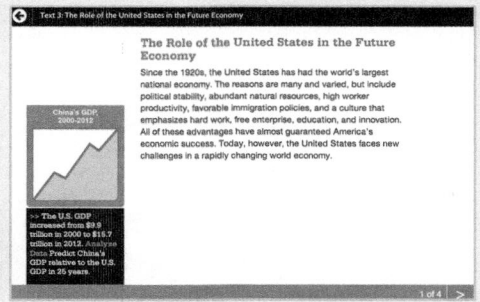

BEFORE AND AFTER

The U.S. Role in the Global Economy

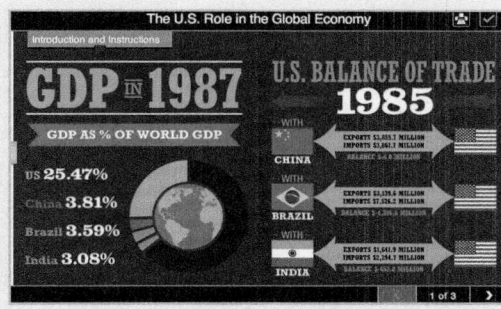

Objective 4: Understand the global economic challenges facing the United States.

Quick Instruction

Before and After: The U.S. Role in the Global Economy Project the before and after activity on the whiteboard and use the slider. Have students use the data to draw a conclusion about the impact of multinational corporations on the U.S. economy.

Identify Central Issues How have multinational corporations created economic benefits and challenges for the United States? (*Multinationals help the economy grow, but that growth creates competition among nations. Multinational corporations often increase jobs in other markets rather than in the United States When other countries experiencing economic growth increase exports to the United States, the United States experiences a trade deficit.*)

📷 ACTIVE CLASSROOM

Have students break into groups and use the Circle Write Strategy to respond to the following prompt: How has the role of the United States in the global economy changed since the early 1900s? What factors caused these changes, and what have been the effects? Have students write as much as they can for one minute and switch with the person on their right. The next person tries to improve or elaborate the response where the other person left off. Continue to switch until the paper comes back to the first person. The group then decides which is the best composition and shares that with the larger group.

Further Instruction

Go through the Interactive Reading Notepad questions and discuss the answers with the class. To extend the lesson, assign Economics Core Concepts: Challenges of a Global Economy.

Draw Conclusions In what ways have government policies in China impacted the twenty-first century economy? (*China's government has moved to promote a modified free market system, but it has different ideas than the United States over issues relating to patents, intellectual property, spying, and computer hacking. The country has become a major economic competitor of the United States, but the government has also signed trade agreements that help both economies grow.*)

Hypothesize How do you think the spread of American culture has impacted the economy around the world? (*American companies and multinationals spread American values including hard work, free enterprise, education, and innovation. These values likely encourage other nations such as China to open their markets and adopt similar business practices.*)

America and the World Economy

SYNTHESIZE

DIGITAL ACTIVITY

Evaluating Globalization

Have students review the questions they asked at the beginning of the lesson and use the material from the lesson or additional research to answer their questions. Then ask students to choose one or two examples of globalization and write their summaries.

Discuss Have students share their summaries and discuss the advantages and disadvantages to globalization. Ask students whether their perspective on globalization changes depending on whether they are thinking about an American worker in the service industry, an American manufacturer, a worker in another country, a factory owner, a corporate executive, or other individuals. Have students explain their reasoning.

DEMONSTRATE

DIGITAL QUIZ

Lesson Quiz and Class Discussion Board

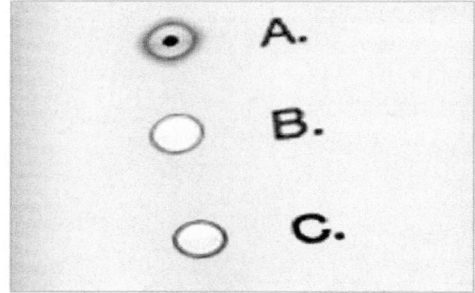

Assign the online Lesson Quiz for this lesson if you haven't already done so. Students will be offered automatic remediation or enrichment based on their score.

Pose these questions to the class on the Discussion Board:

Draw Conclusions How have innovations in technology and management enhanced productivity in the workplace? Do you think these changes are good for workers, businesses, and the economy? Explain your reasoning.

Compare and Contrast economic nationalism and globalization. What are the effects of creating a new global economy?

Topic Inquiry
Have students continue their investigations for the Topic Inquiry.

The George W. Bush Presidency

Supporting English Language Learners

Use with Digital Text 1, **Controversy in the 2000 Election.**

Reading
Prompt students to derive meaning of environmental print as you display the image depicting protesters of the 2000 election decision.

Beginning Read the sign that says, *This is America. Count every vote.* Have students derive meaning of environmental print by selecting the sign's correct interpretation: (1) You are located in America; (2) In America, every vote matters; or (3) Votes usually are not counted in other countries.

Intermediate Read the sign that says, *This is America. Count every vote.* Have students derive meaning of environmental print by restating the sign's message in their own words.

Advanced Read the sign that says, *Politics triumphs 5 to 4.* Have pairs of students derive meaning of environmental print by answering these questions: Did the protesters triumph? What do the protesters think of politics?

Advanced High Read the sign that says, *Politics triumphs 5 to 4.* Have students derive meaning of environmental print by writing answers to these questions: How did politics triumph? What does "politics" represent? Then ask pairs of students to share their answers and create an original protest sign.

Use with Digital Text 4, **Bush's Second Term.**

Listening
Prompt students to understand the important details of spoken language. Discuss the meaning of hurricane, as well as the tradition of naming hurricanes. Ask students to share their knowledge and experience of hurricanes.

Beginning Use basic spoken language to tell about Hurricane Katrina and its destruction along the Gulf Coast, particularly in New Orleans. Help students demonstrate understanding of this familiar topic by choosing from a list the important details you said.

Intermediate Use spoken language to tell about the government's response to Hurricane Katrina, including the role that FEMA played. Have students demonstrate understanding of this mostly familiar topic by recalling important details that you said. Record these items in a list.

Advanced Use spoken language to tell about the government's response to Hurricane Katrina, including the role that FEMA played. Have pairs of students demonstrate understanding of this mostly familiar topic by listing the important details you said. Then ask pairs to compare lists.

Advanced High Use spoken language to tell about the New Orleans geography and its hurricane risk factors. Have students demonstrate understanding of this unfamiliar topic by listing the important details you said. Ask students to compare lists with a partner.

▶ Differentiate Instruction

Use the Differentiated Instruction notes throughout the lesson plan to support the varied skill sets, levels of readiness, and interests in the mixed-ability classroom.

Challenge These notes include suggestions for expanding the activity for advanced students.

On-Level These notes include suggestions for modifying the activity to address different interests or learning styles.

Extra Support These notes include ideas for providing more scaffolding or reading spuport.

Special Needs These notes provide ideas for adapting instruction to support the needs of various special needs students.

■ NOTES

The George W. Bush Presidency

Objectives

Objective 1: Assess the outcome of the 2000 presidential election.

Objective 2: Explain the goals and achievements of George W. Bush's domestic policy.

Objective 3: Explain the significance of terrorist attacks on the United States and U.S. involvement in world affairs.

Objective 4: Summarize the important issues of Bush's second term.

Objective 5: Understand the causes and effects of the 2008 financial crisis and economic recession.

LESSON 2 ORGANIZER		PACING: APPROX. 1 PERIOD, .5 BLOCKS			
				RESOURCES	
		OBJECTIVES	**PACING**	**Online**	**Print**
Connect					
DIGITAL START UP ACTIVITY **A Two-Term President**			5 min.	●	
Investigate					
DIGITAL TEXT 1 **Controversy in the 2000 Election**		Objective 1	10 min.	●	●
DIGITAL TEXT 2 **The Bush Domestic Agenda**		Objective 2	10 min.	●	●
INTERACTIVE CHART **Long-Term Health of Entitlements**			10 min.	●	
DIGITAL TEXT 3 **The September 11, 2001 Attacks and the War on Terror**		Objective 3	10 min.	●	●
INTERACTIVE MAP **United States and the Middle East, 2001–2010**			10 min.	●	
DIGITAL TEXT 4 **Bush's Second Term**		Objective 4	10 min.	●	●
DIGITAL TEXT 5 **The Financial Crisis of 2008**		Objective 5	10 min.	●	●
Synthesize					
DIGITAL ACTIVITY **The George W. Bush Presidency**			5 min.	●	
Demonstrate					
DIGITAL QUIZ **Lesson Quiz and Class Discussion Board**			10 min.	●	

PEARSON realize™
www.PearsonRealize.com

Go online to access additional resources including:
Primary Sources • Biographies • Supreme Court cases •
21st Century Skill Tutorials • Maps • Graphic Organizers.

CONNECT

DIGITAL START UP ACTIVITY

A Two-Term President

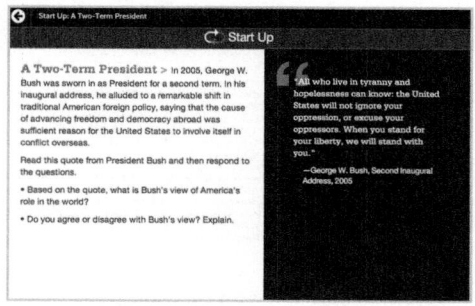

Project the Start Up Activity Ask students
to read the quote and answer the questions
as they enter and get settled. Have students
share their responses with a partner, either in
class or through a blog space.

Discuss Based on the quote, what is Bush's
view of America's role in the world? *(The
United States should support liberty and end
oppression around the world.)* Do you agree or
disagree with Bush's view? Explain.

Tell students that in this lesson they will be
learning about the significant events, policy
changes, and legislation of George W. Bush's
presidency.

Aa **Vocabulary Development:** Use the
Interactive Reading Notepad to preview the
Key Terms and Academic Vocabulary in this
lesson with students.

⇅ FLIP IT!

Assign the Flipped Video for this lesson.

■ STUDENT EDITION PRINT
PAGES: 850–857

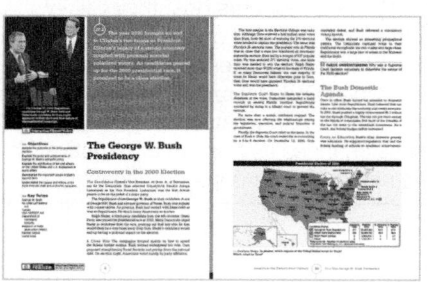

INVESTIGATE

DIGITAL TEXT 1

Controversy in the 2000 Election

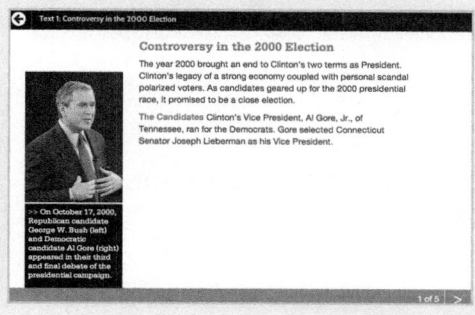

**Objective 1: Assess the outcome
of the 2000 presidential election.**

Quick Instruction

Project the map of the 2000 election results.
Have students use the map to explain why the
election was contested.

Generate Explanations Explain why
the judicial branch became involved in
the presidential election of 2000. *(Neither
candidate clearly won the Florida vote, leading
to an automatic statewide recount in Florida.
Because the recount was so close, Democrats
called for a hand recount in some counties.
Republicans sued to prevent the recount and
the case went to the Supreme Court, which
put a stop to the second recount.)*

ELL Use the ELL activity described in
the ELL chart.

Further Instruction

Go through the Interactive Reading Notepad
questions and discuss the answers with
the class. To extend the lesson, assign
Government Basics: Executive Branch.

Draw Conclusions What does the
presidential election of 2000 suggest about the
relationships among the legislative, executive,
and judicial branches of government? Explain
your reasoning. *(The election shows how
the system of checks and balances keeps
elections democratic. The legislature makes
laws that determine how votes should be
counted and elections run. The judicial branch
intervenes if questions arise over the fairness
of a recount.)*

Evaluate Arguments Do you think that Gore
was right to concede, even though he won the
popular vote? Why or why not? *(Students should
weigh the popular vote against the Electoral
College system to support their views.)*

The George W. Bush Presidency

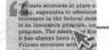

DIGITAL TEXT 2

The Bush Domestic Agenda

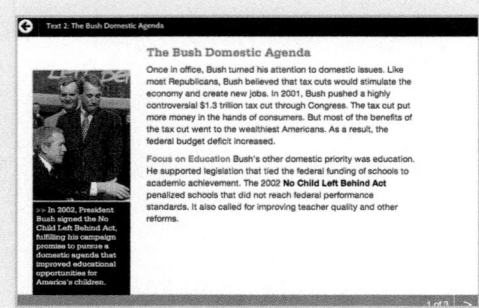

INTERACTIVE CHART

Long-Term Health of Entitlements

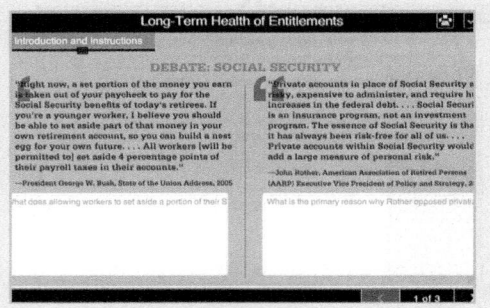

DIGITAL TEXT 3

The September 11, 2001 Attacks and the War on Terror

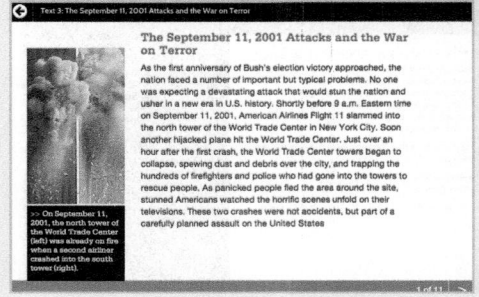

Objective 2: Explain the goals and achievements of George W. Bush's domestic policy.

Quick Instruction

Interactive Chart: Long-Term Health of Entitlements Project the interactive chart and have students read the quotes. Discuss the reasons the long-term health of entitlements has been called into question. Why does this issue matter to both seniors and working Americans?

Support Ideas with Evidence Draw a conclusion about how Bush's domestic policies impacted the nation's economy in the twenty-first century, citing evidence for support. *(Bush's policies had mixed effects; his tax cuts were intended to stimulate the economy but increased the federal deficit. Medicare was also expensive and he was not able to address the solvency of Social Security, a major cost to the government.)* Then ask students to give examples of how other individuals have had an impact on the twenty-first century economy.

ACTIVE CLASSROOM

Have students Take a Stand on the following question: Should Social Security be privatized? Ask students to divide into two groups based on their answer and move to separate areas of the classroom. Ask students to talk with each other to compare their reasons for answering yes or no. Ask a representative from each side to present and defend the group's point of view.

D Differentiate: Extra Support In business, solvency refers to the ability to meet a long-term financial obligations. Explain that in Social Security, workers pay a portion of their income to support retirees. If Social Security is not solvent, it cannot meet its long-term financial obligation to pay retired workers.

Further Instruction

Go through the Interactive Reading Notepad questions and discuss the answers with the class.

Hypothesize Discuss the solvency of long-term entitlement programs such as Social Security and Medicare. Why were these programs important to Bush's domestic agenda? Why is it difficult to make changes to the way these government programs are run? *(These programs account for a significant portion of the federal budget; the money available to them will run out as the population ages and cost of living adjustments increase. Bush wanted to make these programs more cost-effective and solvent in the long run. It is difficult to make changes for a number of reasons: those who paid into the system as workers do not want to receive fewer benefits when they retire, seniors dependent on these programs do not want to lose benefits, and Americans disagree about the best paths to reform.)*

Objective 3: Explain the significance of terrorist attack on the United States.

Quick Instruction

Interactive Map: United States and the Middle East, 2001–2010 Project the interactive map and click on the circles. Have students sequence the events of the War on Terror.

Draw Conclusions In what ways were the 2001 terrorist attacks on the World Trade Center and the Pentagon a turning point for the nation? *(The attacks caused a shift in U.S. foreign policy. Americans united to defend the nation. Government policies promoted security over civil liberties. The United States went to war in Afghanistan and Iraq and instituted a global War on Terror, in which the government exercised broad powers.)*

ACTIVE CLASSROOM

Have students use the Sticky Notes Strategy and spend three minutes answering the question: How has U.S. involvement in world affairs changed as a result of the global War on Terror and 9/11? Have students post their Sticky Notes on the board or on chart paper and look at the various responses. Discuss similarities and differences in the responses as a group. Ask whether students see these changes as positive or negative for the nation and for other countries.

INTERACTIVE MAP
United States and the Middle East, 2001–2010

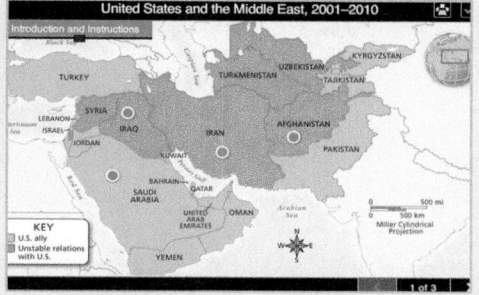

DIGITAL TEXT 4
Bush's Second Term

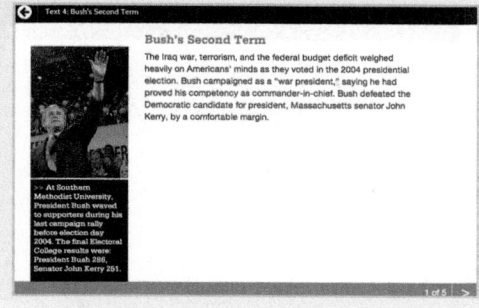

Further Instruction
Go through the Interactive Reading Notepad questions and discuss the answers with the class.

Summarize What constitutional issues have been raised by federal government policy changes following 9/11? *(how to maintain privacy and civil liberties in the face of surveillance and security measures; whether prisoners can be held without a writ of habeas corpus; whether the government can use military tribunals instead of civilian courts to try suspected terrorists)*

Identify Cause and Effect Why did the 9/11 attacks have such a negative effect on the nation's economy? *(Americans did not want to travel on planes, which hurt the airline industry. Due to uncertainty following the attacks, businesses and households decreased spending. People lost their jobs and the country's output was reduced. Wars and defense also cost the country money.)*

Evaluate Arguments Discuss the role of the USA Patriot Act of 2001 in the war on terror. Do you think that this kind of contemporary government legislation is fair? Why or why not? *(The Patriot Act gives law enforcement greater power to monitor suspected terrorists. Student responses should weigh the need for security after 9/11 against the importance of civil liberties.)*

Objective 4: Summarize the important issues of Bush's second term.

Quick Instruction
Project the image from Hurricane Katrina on the whiteboard and discuss the devastation it caused. Define a levee as an embankment built to prevent a body of water from overflowing. Damage from the hurricane intensified when the levees protecting the city broke.

Summarize How did physical geographic factors impact the levee failure in New Orleans after Hurricane Katrina? *(The city is low-lying and the levees could not withstand the rising waters.)*

Draw Conclusions Consider how human geography impacted the levee failure after Katrina. What human activities worsened the damage from the storm? *(The government was slow to respond; there were not adequate resources for those in need; people were not prepared for the levees to be breached.)*

ELL Use the ELL activity described in the ELL chart.

Further Instruction
Go through the Interactive Reading Notepad questions and discuss the answers with the class.

Infer Discuss Lionel Sosa's role in the 2004 election. How did Sosa increase voter turnout? *(He created an advertising campaign that encouraged Latinos to vote for Bush.)*

Evaluate Arguments Do you agree with Bush that the Kyoto Protocol undermines U.S. sovereignty? Would you say that this is an example of a global treaty undermining U.S. sovereignty? Explain your reasoning. *(Answers will vary but should weigh the importance of controlling global warming against the need to promote U.S. economic growth and independence. Some students may agree that this is an example of U.S. sovereignty being undermined by a global treaty.)*

The George W. Bush Presidency

 **SYNTHESIZE**

 DEMONSTRATE

DIGITAL TEXT 5
The Financial Crisis of 2008

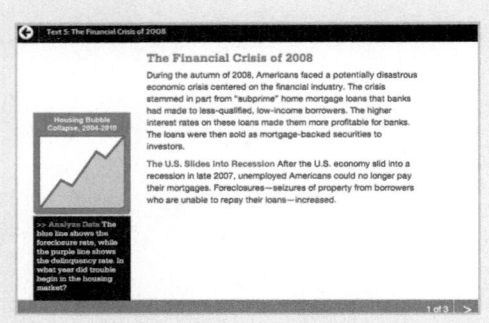

DIGITAL ACTIVITY
The George W. Bush Presidency

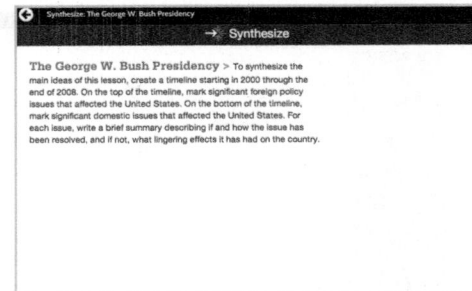

DIGITAL QUIZ
Lesson Quiz and Class Discussion Board

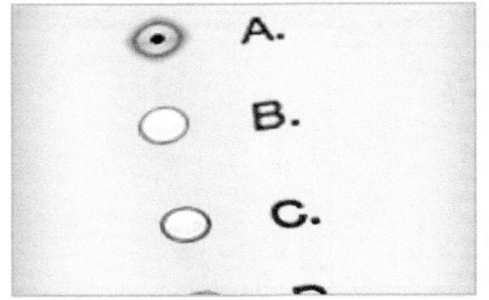

Objective 5: **Understand the causes and effects of the 2008 financial crisis and economic recession.**

Quick Instruction
Project the chart of housing prices on the whiteboard and ask what trends students observe. Discuss how a "housing bubble" contributed to an economic crisis in 2008.

Analyze Information What impact did Henry Paulson and Ben Bernanke have on the U.S. economy in the twenty-first century? Do you agree with the steps they took? Why or why not? *(Treasury secretary Paulson and Federal Reserve chair Bernanke bailed out the banks that had made risky loans and investments. Students should discuss whether the bailout prevented a worse financial collapse or was an unfair use of taxpayer dollars.)*

Further Instruction
Go through the Interactive Reading Notepad questions and discuss the answers with the class.

Generate Explanations Explain how the U.S. slid into a financial crisis in 2008. *(Banks made subprime home mortgage loans to less-qualified borrowers and then sold the loans to investors. As the economy slid into a recession and Americans lost their jobs, they couldn't pay back these mortgages. Foreclosures increased, housing prices fell, and investments lost their value.)*

Make a Prediction about the effects of the 2008 financial crisis. *(the economy may be slow to recover; there may be controversial steps taken to stimulate the economy; voters may elect candidates they see as unassociated with the economic downturn; there may be new financial reforms to banks and regulations over mortgages and lending practices)*

Have students create a timeline from 2000 through the end of 2008 and write a summary of each event or issue. Have students share their timelines with a partner and discuss the major events they wrote down.

Discuss Have students review their timelines and discuss how the terrorist attacks on the World Trade Center and the Pentagon, the global War on Terror, Hurricane Katrina, and the financial crisis of 2008 reshaped the nation during the George W. Bush presidency. Ask what foreign and domestic policy changes resulted during this time, and what the impact of these events may be going forward.

Assign the online Lesson Quiz for this lesson if you haven't already done so. Students will be offered automatic remediation or enrichment based on their score.

Pose these questions to the class on the Discussion Board:

Support a Point of View with Evidence Do you think the United States was right to go to war in Iraq as part of the global War on Terror? Why or why not?

Identify Central Issues What constitutional issues were raised as a result of 9/11? How do you think the federal government should balance the need for security with the civil liberties of Americans?

Topic Inquiry
Have students continue their investigations for the Topic Inquiry.

The Barack Obama Presidency

Supporting English Language Learners

Use with Digital Text 2, **President Obama Takes Action.**

Reading

Pre-teach the following topic-related vocabulary that is used routinely in written classroom materials: appointment, nomination, diversity, advocate.

Beginning As you read aloud the section titled *Obama's Appointments*, have students repeat after you. Then ask students to demonstrate comprehension of the pre-taught vocabulary by completing and reading aloud a fill-in-the-blank sentence for each word.

Intermediate Ask volunteers to read aloud the section titled *Obama's Appointments* while students follow along. Have students locate the pre-taught vocabulary. Then ask them to demonstrate comprehension of these words by using each in an original sentence about the section. Record and display students' sentences.

Advanced Ask pairs of students to read the section titled *Obama's Appointments* and locate uses of the pre-taught vocabulary. Then have pairs demonstrate comprehension of these words by using each in an original sentence about the section.

Advanced High Ask students to read the section titled *Obama's Appointments* and locate uses of the pre-taught vocabulary. Then have them demonstrate comprehension of these words by using them in a cohesive paragraph about the section. Provide time for partners to read each other's paragraphs.

Use with Digital Text 3, **Obama's Second Term.**

Listening

Use increasingly complex spoken language commensurate with students' level of English to describe Obama's second-term economic challenges.

Beginning Have students demonstrate understanding by identifying the important details from a list that also includes false statements. Then check students' understanding of implicit ideas: If these economic problems are a continuation, what does that say about the economy of Obama's first term?

Intermediate Have students demonstrate understanding of what you said by stating the important details. Then check students' understanding of implicit ideas: What does it mean that both the stock market and gas and home prices went up? Was everyone affected by the economy in the same way?

Advanced Have pairs of students demonstrate understanding of what you said by discussing the important details. Then have them demonstrate understanding of implicit ideas with this question: What does it say about the parties in Congress if they refused to pass a budget bill on time?

Advanced High Have students demonstrate understanding of what you said by listing the important details. Then have them demonstrate understanding of implicit ideas by writing a paragraph about Obama's ability to influence the many forces acting on the economy.

▣ Differentiate Instruction

Use the Differentiated Instruction notes throughout the lesson plan to support the varied skill sets, levels of readiness, and interests in the mixed-ability classroom.

Challenge These notes include suggestions for expanding the activity for advanced students.

On-Level These notes include suggestions for modifying the activity to address different interests or learning styles.

Extra Support These notes include ideas for providing more scaffolding or reading spuport.

Special Needs These notes provide ideas for adapting instruction to support the needs of various special needs students.

▮ NOTES

The Barack Obama Presidency

Objectives

Objective 1: Assess the outcome of the 2008 presidential election.

Objective 2: Explain the goals of Barack Obama's economic and healthcare policy.

Objective 3: Describe Barack Obama's involvement in world affairs.

Objective 4: Summarize Obama's Second Term.

LESSON 3 ORGANIZER		PACING: APPROX. 1 PERIOD, .5 BLOCKS			
		OBJECTIVES	PACING	RESOURCES	
				Online	Print
Connect					
DIGITAL START UP ACTIVITY **Barack Obama**			5 min.	●	
Investigate					
DIGITAL TEXT 1 **The 2008 Election**		Objective 1	10 min.	●	●
INTERACTIVE CHART **Presidential Election of 2008**			10 min.	●	
DIGITAL TEXT 2 **President Obama Takes Action**		Objectives 2, 3	10 min.	●	●
INTERACTIVE GALLERY **Fighting al Qaeda Worldwide**			10 min.	●	
DIGITAL TEXT 3 **Obama's Second Term**		Objective 4	10 min.	●	●
INTERACTIVE CHART **Checks and Balances Among Branches of Government**			10 min.	●	
Synthesize					
DIGITAL ACTIVITY **The Role of Government**			5 min.	●	
Demonstrate					
DIGITAL QUIZ **Lesson Quiz and Class Discussion Board**			10 min.	●	

Go online to access additional resources including:
Primary Sources • Biographies • Supreme Court cases • 21st Century Skill Tutorials • Maps • Graphic Organizers.

■ CONNECT

DIGITAL START UP ACTIVITY
Barack Obama

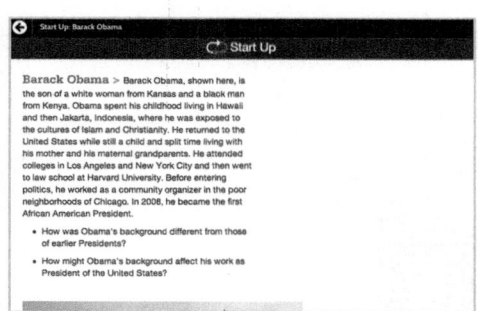

Project the Start Up Activity Ask students to read the bio on Obama and answer the questions as they enter and get settled. Have students share their responses with a partner, either in class or through a blog space.

Discuss How did Obama's background differ from earlier Presidents? *(He was African American and spent part of his childhood living abroad. He also worked as a community organizer.)* How might Obama's background affect his work as President of the United States? *(As an African American who has worked in poor neighborhoods, he might have a different perspective on race and poverty in America.)*

Aa Vocabulary Development: Use the Interactive Reading Notepad to preview the Key Terms and Academic Vocabulary in this lesson with students.

↑↓ FLIP IT!
Assign the Flipped Video for this lesson.

■ STUDENT EDITION PRINT PAGES: 858–863

■ INVESTIGATE

DIGITAL TEXT 1
The 2008 Election

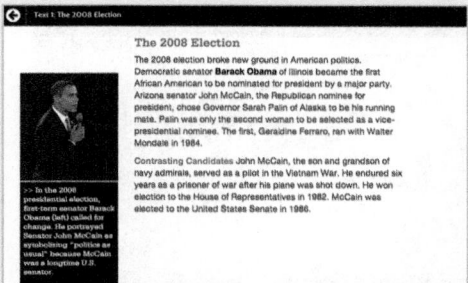

INTERACTIVE CHART
Presidential Election of 2008

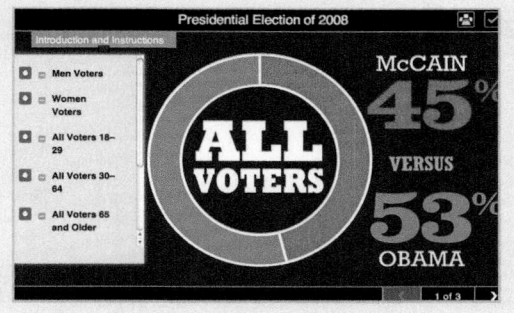

Objective 2: Assess the outcome of the 2008 presidential election.

Quick Instruction
Interactive Chart: Presidential Election of 2008 Project the interactive chart and click through the squares. Have students identify the patterns they observe.

Summarize Discuss the historical significance of the 2008 presidential election. Why was this an historic moment for the country? *(Obama was the first African American to be nominated for president by a major candidate and the first African American president; Sarah Palin was only the second woman to be a vice-presidential nominee.)*

■ ACTIVE CLASSROOM
Have students use the Sticky Notes Strategy and spend three minutes jotting down their ideas about how demographic changes in the country impacted the 2008 election and many continue to shape elections in the future. Have students post their Sticky Notes on the board or on chart paper and look at all the various responses. Discuss similarities and differences in the responses as a group.

Further Instruction
Go through the Interactive Reading Notepad questions and discuss the answers with the class. To extend the lesson, assign Biography: Barack Obama.

Paraphrase Paraphrase the quote from Obama's victory rally. What does his speech suggest about the democratic process? *(If people have doubts about the possibilities and opportunities available to all Americans, Obama's victory is a sign of what is possible for ordinary individuals in this country to achieve. This shows how citizens participate equally in the democratic process as voters and as nominees. Power is vested in the people to choose their representatives, allowing groups that have historically not been in power to hold elected office.)*

Infer Why do you think the presidential election of 2008 is understood as a turning point? Explain your reasoning. *(The election of an African American president will open new doors for other minorities; there will be a Democratic majority and policy shifts following the Bush presidency.)*

The Barack Obama Presidency

DIGITAL TEXT 2

President Obama Takes Action

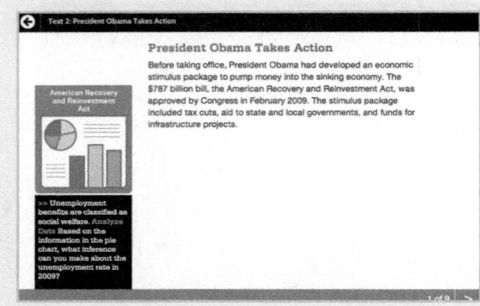

INTERACTIVE GALLERY

Fighting al Qaeda Worldwide

DIGITAL TEXT 3

Obama's Second Term

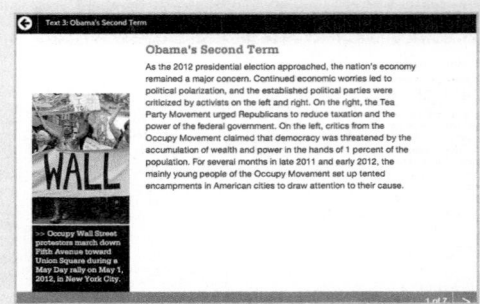

Objective 1: Understand the causes and effects of the 2008 financial crisis and economic recession.

Quick Instruction

Interactive Gallery: Fighting al Qaeda Worldwide Project the interactive gallery on the whiteboard and click through the images. Call on students to describe the U.S. involvement in world affairs and the global War on Terror during Obama's presidency.

Hypothesize Do you think Obama's foreign policy in Iraq and Afghanistan raises constitutional issues? Why or why not? *(constitutional issues: spying, surveillance, and intelligence gathering techniques; racial profiling; legality of actions taken against suspected and known terrorists, including assassination and detainment)*

📷 ACTIVE CLASSROOM

Have students select one of the reforms, policies, or changes enacted under Obama's leadership and use the Make Headlines Strategy to write a headline capturing the significance of the event. Have students share their headlines with a partner to review and then discuss the major events as a class.

ELL Use the ELL activity described in the ELL chart.

Further Instruction
Go through the Interactive Reading Notepad questions and discuss the answers with the

class. To extend the lesson, assign Geography Basics: The World's Richest Regions, Biography: Hillary Clinton, Biography: Sonia Sotomayor, Landmark Supreme Court Cases: *National Federation of Independent Business v. Sebelius*, Economics Basics: Money, and Economics Basics: Banking.

Summarize Explain contemporary government legislation such as the American Recovery and Reinvestment Act of 2009 and discuss how it impacted the public sector. *(It was a $787 billion stimulus package. By cutting taxes, providing aid to state and local governments, and funding infrastructure projects, it put money into the public sector to boost the economy after the financial crisis of 2008.)*

Compare Evaluate the contributions of Hillary Clinton and Sonia Sotomayor. How did their appointments shape American politics and society during Obama's presidency? *(Clinton — served as Secretary of State. Sotomayor — first Hispanic Supreme Court Justice and one of only a few women on the court. Both appointments brought diversity to the federal government.)*

Draw Conclusions Identify the ways Obama had an impact on the twenty-first century economy. Consider factors that are not directly related to finance but have an economic impact. *(He developed the American Recovery and Reinvestment Act; reformed healthcare; ended combat in Iraq; increased American military presence in Afghanistan; signed reform bill to increase federal oversight of financial institutions and increase consumer protections.)*

Objective 5: Summarize Obama's Second Term.

Quick Instruction
Interactive Chart: Contemporary Conflict Among Branches of Government Project the interactive chart on the whiteboard. Have students complete the graphic organizer.

Identify Cause and Effect Describe the U.S. involvement in world affairs during Obama's second term. How did this involvement impact the country at home and abroad? *(Obama pulled troops from Iraq but the country remained unstable; troops stayed in Afghanistan; America brokered an agreement with Iran to stop parts of its nuclear program. Continued engagement with the Middle East caused some to oppose involvement in civil war in Syria and led to a domestic terrorist attack at the Boston Marathon.)*

📷 ACTIVE CLASSROOM

Use the Walking Tour Strategy to post passages from the reading on individual pages around the room. Group students to tour the room to discuss each passage, then summarize the major issues of Obama's second term, how he resolved them, and what challenges remain.

D Differentiate: Extra Support Have students preview the lesson and identify any words or concepts they don't understand, such as "political polarization," "income inequality," "changing demographics," "unfavorable balance of trade," "consumer debt," "political concessions," and "sectarian violence."

INTERACTIVE CHART
Checks and Balances Among Branches of Government

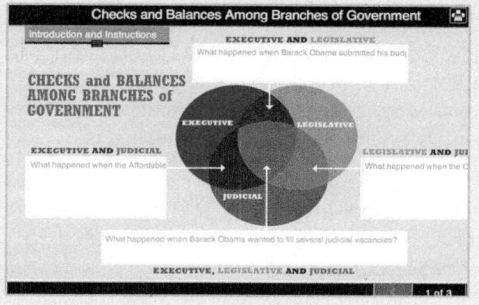

Group students to use context clues to define these and any other unfamiliar terms as they take the Walking Tour.

ELL Use the ELL activity described in the ELL chart.

Further Instruction
Go through the Interactive Reading Notepad questions and discuss the answers with the class.

Compare How did the presidential election of 2012 compare to that of 2008? What factors contributed to the similarities and differences? *(The election was much closer. The country was in an ongoing recession and military problems continued. Obama's health care reform and the war on terror were major issues. As in 2008, demographics played a major role. Obama appealed to minority voters and the young, suggesting Republicans had to reach these voters in order to win in the future.)*

Compare and Contrast the views of the Tea Party Movement and the Occupy Movement. What did each group think the president should do to impact the economy? Do you agree with either group, or neither? Explain your reasoning. *(Tea Party: reduce taxes, limit the power of the federal government over the economy. Occupy: address the division of wealth in the country; have the federal government play a greater role in the economy. Students should explain their view.)*

■ SYNTHESIZE

DIGITAL ACTIVITY
The Role of Government

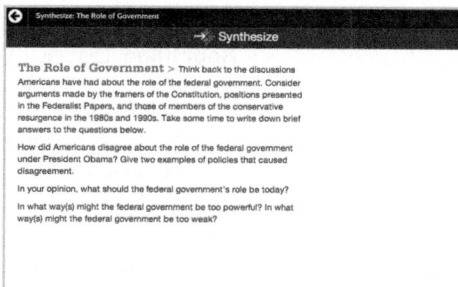

Have students review past arguments about the role of the federal government and then answer the questions. Have students share their responses with a partner and discuss any differences of opinion with the class.

Discuss Ask students to explain how they think Obama viewed the role of the federal government, citing examples of policies for support. Discuss how this differed from the views of George W. Bush and how they think this shift in policy impacted the nation in the early twenty-first century.

■ DEMONSTRATE

DIGITAL QUIZ
Lesson Quiz and Class Discussion Board

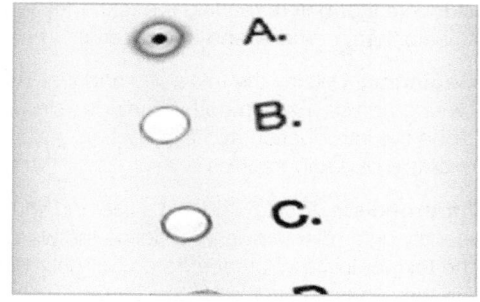

Assign the online Lesson Quiz for this lesson if you haven't already done so. Students will be offered automatic remediation or enrichment based on their score.

Pose these questions to the class on the Discussion Board:

Support Ideas with Examples What role did contemporary government legislation in the private and public sectors play in the financial crisis of 2008 and its aftermath? Assess the impact of this legislation, using examples for support.

Evaluate Arguments In what ways, if any, do you consider the 2008 election of Barack Obama to be a significant turning point in American history? In what ways, if any, do you disagree with that assessment? Cite specific examples, policies, and issues for support.

Topic Inquiry
Have students continue their investigations for the Topic Inquiry.

Americans Look to the Future

Supporting English Language Learners

Use with Digital Text 2, **American Demographics in Transition.**

Reading
Use prereading supports such as pretaught topic-related vocabulary and other activities to enhance comprehension of written text. Explain to students that before reading the text, they will learn some new vocabulary to help them comprehend the material.

Beginning Display the text's title and first subheading. Define *demographics*. Explain both headings using simpler vocabulary. Then read aloud the introduction and first section. Ask: How is the divorce rate an example of demographics?

Intermediate Display the text's title and first subheading. Ask students to identify unfamiliar words, and define the words for them. Then read aloud the text, or invite volunteers to do so. Ask: What are demographics? How are they changing in the United States?

Advanced Display the text's title and first subheading. As a group, look up unfamiliar words in the dictionary, and restate the headings using other words. Then have pairs of students read the text together.

Advanced High Display the text's title and first subheading. Have students independently look up unfamiliar words in the dictionary and read the text. Then ask them to summarize each section with a partner.

Use with Digital Text 3, **Energy and the Environment.**

Reading
Prompt students to comprehend English language structures used routinely in written classroom materials. Explain that a comparative adjective is a language structure that expresses a difference between nouns.

Beginning Display this sentence: Some people say that we need stronger environmental laws than before. Explain what the word *stronger* compares. Then ask students to demonstrate comprehension of comparative adjectives by completing this sentence with an *-er* word: Arctic ice is _____ than it used to be.

Intermediate Point out the words *stronger* and *higher*, and have students demonstrate comprehension of comparative adjectives by using these two words correctly in original sentences about the text.

Advanced Display the first two sentences of the last paragraph (beginning *As buildings become...*). Point out the words *healthier* and *safer*. Have pairs of students demonstrate comprehension of comparative adjectives by answering these questions: What should be healthier than what? What should be safer than what?

Advanced High Display the first two sentences of the last paragraph (beginning *As buildings become...*). Point out the words *more energy-efficient* and *healthier*, and explain the two ways to form a comparative adjective. Have pairs of students demonstrate their comprehension by finding two comparative adjectives in the second sentence and identifying what they compare.

▶ Differentiate Instruction

Use the Differentiated Instruction notes throughout the lesson plan to support the varied skill sets, levels of readiness, and interests in the mixed-ability classroom.

Challenge These notes include suggestions for expanding the activity for advanced students.

On-Level These notes include suggestions for modifying the activity to address different interests or learning styles.

Extra Support These notes include ideas for providing more scaffolding or reading spuport.

Special Needs These notes provide ideas for adapting instruction to support the needs of various special needs students.

■ NOTES

PEARSON
realize ™
www.PearsonRealize.com

Go online to access additional resources including:
Primary Sources • Biographies • Supreme Court cases •
21st Century Skill Tutorials • Maps • Graphic Organizers.

Objectives

Objective 1: Analyze the causes and effects of immigration on American society.

Objective 2: Summarize the causes and effects of changing demographics.

Objective 3: Discuss the environmental issues facing Americans.

Objective 4: Explain the effects of communications technology on the economy.

Objective 5: Understand the issues Americans face in the 21st century.

LESSON 4 ORGANIZER	PACING: APPROX. 1 PERIOD, .5 BLOCKS				
		OBJECTIVES	PACING	RESOURCES Online	RESOURCES Print
Connect					
DIGITAL START UP ACTIVITY **Achieving the American Dream**			5 min.	●	
Investigate					
DIGITAL TEXT 1 **Immigration Changes American Society**		Objective 1	10 min.	●	●
DIGITAL TEXT 2 **American Demographics in Transition**		Objective 2	10 min.	●	●
DIGITAL TEXT 3 **Energy and the Environment**		Objective 3	10 min.	●	●
INTERACTIVE GALLERY **Efforts to Manage the Environment**			10 min.	●	
DIGITAL TEXT 4 **Technology Transforms Life**		Objectives 4, 5	10 min.	●	●
3-D MODEL **The World Today**			10 min.	●	
Synthesize					
DIGITAL ACTIVITY **Living with Technology**			5 min.	●	
Demonstrate					
DIGITAL QUIZ **Lesson Quiz and Class Discussion Board**			10 min.	●	

Americans Look to the Future

■ CONNECT

DIGITAL START UP ACTIVITY
Achieving the American Dream

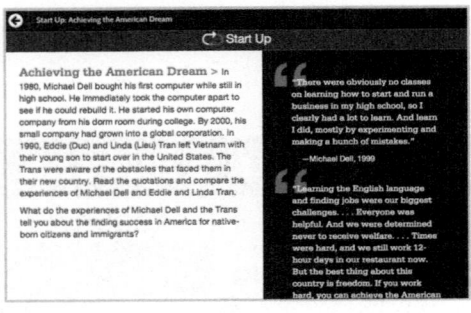

Project the Start Up Activity Ask students to read and compare the quotes and answer the question as they enter and get settled. Have students share their responses with a partner, either in class or through a blog space.

Discuss What do the experiences of Michael Dell and the Trans tell you about finding success in America for native-born citizens and immigrants? *(There are opportunities for both native-born citizens and immigrants to learn new skills, take risks, and develop businesses.)*

Tell students that in this lesson they will learn about changing demographic patterns and technological innovations in social and political life.

Aa Vocabulary Development: Use the Interactive Reading Notepad to preview the Key Terms and Academic Vocabulary in this lesson with students.

⚑ FLIP IT!

Assign the Flipped Video for this lesson.

■ STUDENT EDITION PRINT PAGES: 864–872

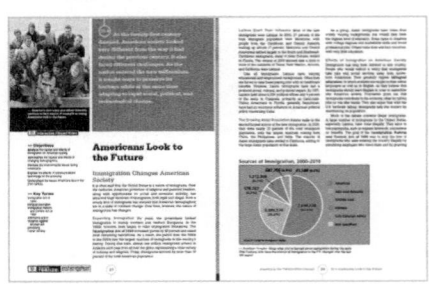

■ INVESTIGATE

DIGITAL TEXT 1
Immigration Changes American Society

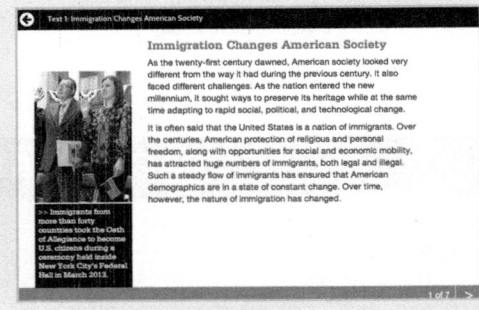

Objective 1: Analyze the causes and effects of immigration on American society.

Quick Instruction
Project the chart on the whiteboard and discuss the trends. Describe U.S. citizens as people from numerous places throughout the world who hold a common bond in standing for certain self-evident truths. Point out that America has long attracted immigrants who shape the country and stand up for its values.

Summarize How has immigration to the United States—both legal and illegal—caused demographic patterns to change? *(The population of immigrants has grown to make up more than 10 percent of the total population. Most new immigrants are Latinos or Asians.)*

D Differentiate: Extra Support Define demographics as sectors that show how populations change over time. Have students brainstorm demographics that can be used to understand populations, such as age, race, ethnicity, religion, gender, and income level.

Further Instruction
Go through the Interactive Reading Notepad questions and discuss the answers with the class. Assign Government Basics: What is Citizenship?, Government Basics: Responsibilities, and Culture Basics: What is Culture?.

Identify Cause and Effect Identify factors that caused both legal and illegal immigration to change American demographics. *(The Immigration Act of 1990 increased quotes and eased restrictions to increase legal immigration. The Immigration Reform and Control Act of 1986 tried to stem illegal immigration but mostly did not succeed. Many immigrants both legal and illegal came in search of work, often in low-paying jobs without benefits.)*

Generate Explanations Give an example of how immigrant groups have participated in the democratic process. Explain how this participation reflects our national ethos, our patriotism, and our civic responsibility. *(holding political office—in 2001, Latinos held about 5,000 political offices and especially influenced policies concerning Cuba. Voting, running for office, and shaping policy shows a love of country and reflects our civic responsibility to contribute to the nation.)*

Compare and Contrast Identify different points of view on the significant social and political issues resulting from legal and illegal immigration to the United States. *(Proponents: Immigrants contribute to the economy and help the United States maintain its population. Many bring marketable skills or do jobs that others do not want. Workers who may be illegal are still necessary to the economy. Opponents: Immigrants take jobs and social services from those born in the United States. They should not receive a bilingual education because they need to learn English and assimilate. Illegal immigrants should not be given jobs or paths to citizenship.)*

DIGITAL TEXT 2

American Demographics in Transition

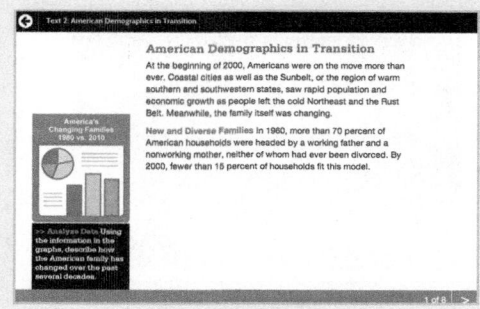

DIGITAL TEXT 3

Energy and the Environment

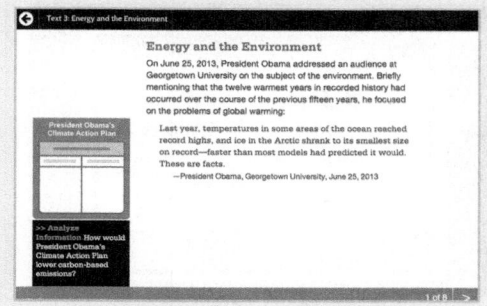

Objective 2: Summarize the causes and effects of changing demographics.

Quick Instruction

Project the statistics of changing family structures on the whiteboard. Ask students what they think caused the demographics of American families to shift so dramatically since the 1960s. What do they think are the effects of these changes?

Compare and Contrast Identify the role of President Johnson in creating economic opportunity for citizens by spearheading affirmative action. Identify contemporary views of the policy across the political spectrum, including concerns about the program's unintended consequences. *(Johnson introduced affirmative action to improve opportunities for women and minorities. Proponents say it helps correct generations of discrimination. Opponents say it discriminates against non-minorities. The Supreme Court has held that race can be one of several deciding factors in school admissions.)*

ELL Use the ELL activity described in the ELL chart.

Further Instruction

Go through the Interactive Reading Notepad questions and discuss the answers with the class. To extend the lesson, assign Culture Core Concepts: Cultural Diffusion and Change and Landmark Decisions of the Supreme Court: *Grutter* v. *Bollinger*.

Summarize Trace the historical development of civil rights in the twenty-first century for various groups. What roles have social advocacy organizations played in this development? *(Organizations such as the NAACP and NOW fought for civil rights for African Americans and women, for example by advocating for equal rights legislation. The National Gay and Lesbian Task Force, Lambda Legal, and other LGBT advocacy organizations lobbied for laws against anti-gay discrimination and same-sex marriage.)*

Identify Cause and Effect What factors have called into question the solvency of long-term entitlement programs such as Social Security and Medicare, and why? *(An aging population, declining birth rates, earlier retirements, and longer lifespans have strained social welfare programs for the elderly. As a result, there will not be enough money in the system to support retiring baby boomers and their health care needs.)*

Objective 3: Discuss the environmental issues facing Americans.

Quick Instruction

Interactive Gallery: Efforts to Manage the Environment Project the interactive gallery and click through the images. Discuss the different roles that citizens, businesses, and the government play in managing the environment. Also discuss the effects of populations growth and distribution on the physical environment.

Compare and Contrast Identify opposing viewpoints about global warming. *(Many people, including those in the Obama Administration, call for stronger federal environmental legislation to raise pollution standards and reduce carbon emissions. Some deny global warming or that it is caused by human activities and do not want environmental legislation restricting industrial activities.)*

📷 ACTIVE CLASSROOM

Have students use the Take a Stand Strategy to take a stand on the following issue: The United States should impose stronger legislation to protect the environment and address global warming. Have students move to opposite sides of the room and group up with others with like minded ideas. Have groups create a justification or opening statement defending their position to the class.

Americans Look to the Future

INTERACTIVE GALLERY

Efforts to Manage the Environment

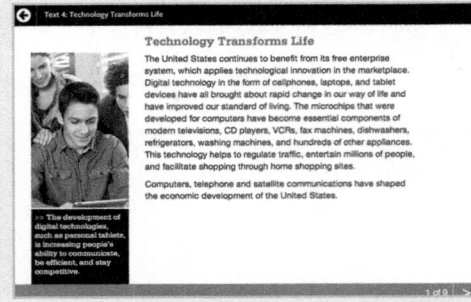

DIGITAL TEXT 4

Technology Transforms Life

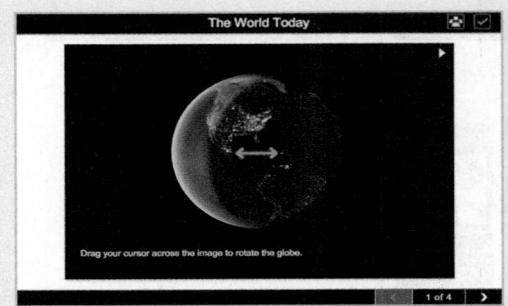

3-D MODEL

The World Today

Further Instruction

Go through the Interactive Reading Notepad questions and discuss the answers with the class.

Identify Patterns How have innovations in the petroleum industry effected the economy in the twenty-first century? *(Scientists and engineers are developing new ways to extract oil and locating new energy sources.)*

Compare Points of View Consider the views of environmental advocacy groups and those advocating for American industries and the economy. In what ways do these groups disagree? On what issues do you think they could find common ground? *(Environmental groups—legislation should protect the environment, reduce pollution, and guard against the risks and negative effects of oil and other industries. Industry—environmental legislation hurts the economy; drilling, fracking, and oil transportation reduce American dependency on foreign oil and boost the economy. Potential common ground: safety measures; a need for minimal environmental protection as well as for economic growth; options for companies to participate in caring for the environment.)*

Objective 4: Explain the effects of communications technology on the economy; 5: Understand the issues Americans face in the 21st century.

Quick Instruction

3-D Model: The World Today Project the 3-D model on the whiteboard and click through the images. Discuss what the models reveals about population distribution and technological innovations in the modern world.

Draw Conclusions How have various media contributed to the global diffusion of American culture through the entertainment industry? What do you think are the benefits and drawbacks of this phenomenon? *(Digital media spreads American culture through music, movies, television, and the Internet. Benefits—shared information; the spread of American freedoms and economic opportunities. Drawbacks—American entertainment can dominate over local cultures; it has provoked violent reactions against American influence.)*

Identify Cause and Effect How have technological innovations in computers and communication (including satellite communication) affected the economic development of the United States? *(Digital technologies improve standards of living, create new industries, and increase American economic competitiveness. Information technology connects people through the Internet and mobile devices, spreading American products, services, and values around the globe.)*

⬛ ACTIVE CLASSROOM

Select 10 or 12 words or phrases you think are important for students to know prior to reading, such as: technology, culture, marketplace, civic ideals, entrepreneurs, media, entertainment, standard of living, digital revolution, diversity, democracy. Have students use the Connect Two Strategy and choose two words from the list and explain why they belong together. During reading, have students look for evidence to support or refute their connections.

Further Instruction

Go through the Interactive Reading Notepad questions and discuss the answers with the class. To extend the lesson, assign Biography: Oprah Winfrey and Economics Basics: Entrepreneurs. Prompt students to discuss the impact of technological and management innovations such as just-in-time inventory management, computer management, and robotics on American businesses and the economy as a whole.

Summarize Identify the social and economic contributions of Oprah Winfrey to American society. *(Winfrey rose out of poverty to become an influential television host. She is a philanthropist, social leader and role model for how to overcome adversity to succeed.)*

Check Understanding Discuss the final paragraph of the book. Ask students to explain the meaning of "our national ethos." Point out that U.S. citizens are people or the descendents of people from numerous places

SYNTHESIZE

DIGITAL ACTIVITY
Living with Technology

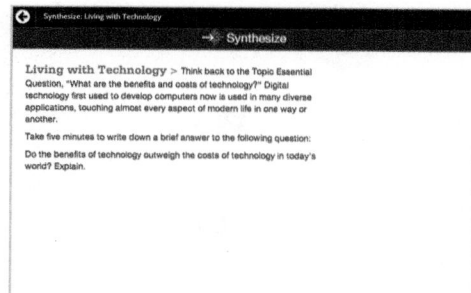

DEMONSTRATE

DIGITAL QUIZ
Lesson Quiz and Class Discussion Board

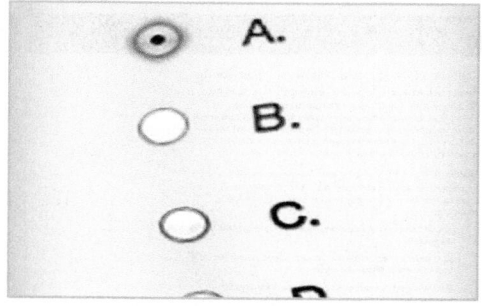

throughout the world who hold a common bond in standing for certain self-evident truths. Discuss the civic ideals that unite a country of such ethnic and religious diversity, and how these ideals can help us form a "more perfect union." Ask students why participation in the democratic process is a reflection of our patriotism and civic responsibility.

Cite Evidence of how the free enterprise system affects technological innovations. *(The United States continues to benefit from its free enterprise system, which applies technological innovation in the marketplace. The free enterprise system drives technological innovationand applies technological innovation in the marketplace, providing us with things such as cell phones, and personal computers. In medecine, specific needs result in scientific discoveries and innovations in medicine, such as vaccines. In this way, the application of scientific discoveries and technological innovations by the free enterprise system continues to improve the standard of living in the United States.)*

Have students review the Topic Essential Question and answer the question about the benefits and costs of technology. Have students share their responses with a partner and discuss their opinions with the class.

Discuss Ask students how technology from mobile devices to medical treatment has changed the way Americans live in the twenty-first century. Discuss the social, political, and economic impact of recent scientific discoveries and technological innovations, using examples for support.

Assign the online Lesson Quiz for this lesson if you haven't already done so. Students will be offered automatic remediation or enrichment based on their score.

Pose these questions to the class on the Discussion Board:

Support Ideas with Examples How does participation in the democratic process reflect our progress to build a "more perfect union"? Given an example from the lesson that explains how an immigrant group, social advocacy organization, entrepreneur, or social or political leader has served the nation through democratic participation.

Identify Patterns Identify two examples of changing demographic patterns in the United States in the twenty-first century and explain their causes and effects.

Topic Inquiry
Have students continue their investigations for the Topic Inquiry.

Topic 20

America in the Twenty-First Century

SYNTHESIZE

DIGITAL ACTIVITY
Reflect on the Essential Question and Topic

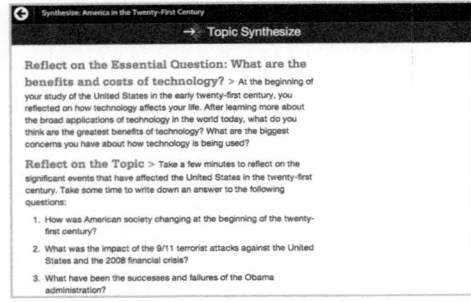

First ask students to reconsider the Essential Question for this topic: How should we handle conflict? Have students review the lists they made at the beginning of the topic and then write down or discuss with a partner the benefits and drawbacks of technology use today.

Ask students, "How has technology improved your lives? What questions or concerns do you have about how you use technology and its application in business, industry, or other fields?" Discuss their responses as a class or ask students to post their answers on the Class Discussion Board.

Next ask students to reflect on the topic as a whole and write down answers to the questions. Remind students to use specific examples from the text when considering the events that affected the United States.

Topic Inquiry
Have students complete Step 3 of the Topic Inquiry.

DEMONSTRATE

DIGITAL TOPIC REVIEW AND ASSESSMENT
America in the Twenty-First Century

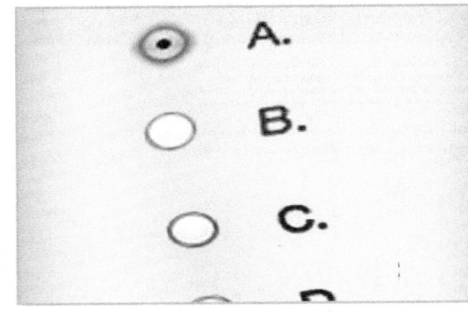

Students can prepare for the Topic Test by answering the questions in the Topic Review and Assessment online or the Assessment questions in the Print Student text. They can also prepare by reviewing their answers to the Interactive Reading Notepad questions or reviewing their notes in the Reading and Notetaking Study Guide.

DIGITAL TOPIC TEST
America in the Twenty-First Century

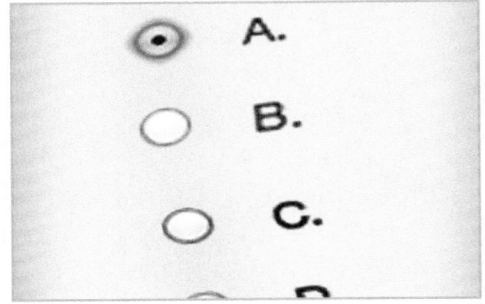

TOPIC TEST
Assign the Topic Test to assess students' understanding of topic content.

BENCHMARK TESTS
Assign these benchmark tests as you complete the relevant topics to monitor student progress toward mastering the course content and as preparation for the End-of-Course Test.

Benchmark Test 1: Topics 1–3
Benchmark Test 2: Topics 4–6
Benchmark Test 3: Topics 7–9
Benchmark Test 4: Topics 10–12
Benchmark Test 5: Topics 13–15
Benchmark Test 6: Topics 16–18
Benchmark Test 7: Topics 19–20

END-OF-COURSE TESTS
Assign End-Of-Course Test 1 or 2 to measure students' progress in mastering the course content.